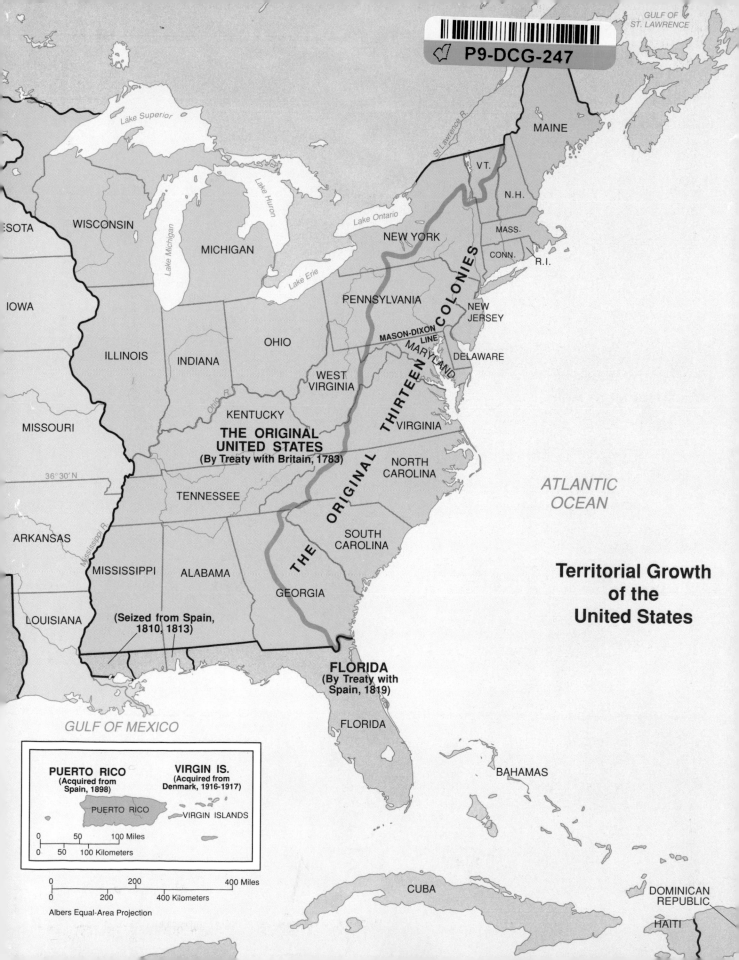

GULF OF ST. LAWRENCE

Lake Superior

MAINE

Lake Huron

Lake Michigan

WISCONSIN

MICHIGAN

ESOTA

Lake Ontario

VT.

N.H.

IOWA

Lake Erie

NEW YORK

MASS.

CONN.

R.I.

PENNSYLVANIA

NEW JERSEY

ILLINOIS

INDIANA

OHIO

MASON-DIXON LINE

MARYLAND

DELAWARE

WEST VIRGINIA

MISSOURI

KENTUCKY

THE ORIGINAL THIRTEEN COLONIES

VIRGINIA

THE ORIGINAL UNITED STATES
(By Treaty with Britain, 1783)

36°30′ N

NORTH CAROLINA

ATLANTIC OCEAN

TENNESSEE

Ohio R.

ARKANSAS

SOUTH CAROLINA

THE ORIGINAL

Mississippi R.

MISSISSIPPI

ALABAMA

GEORGIA

Territorial Growth
of the
United States

LOUISIANA

(Seized from Spain,
1810, 1813)

FLORIDA
(By Treaty with
Spain, 1819)

GULF OF MEXICO

FLORIDA

BAHAMAS

PUERTO RICO
(Acquired from
Spain, 1898)

VIRGIN IS.
(Acquired from
Denmark, 1916-1917)

PUERTO RICO

VIRGIN ISLANDS

0   50   100 Miles

0   50   100 Kilometers

0   200   400 Miles

0   200   400 Kilometers

Albers Equal-Area Projection

CUBA

DOMINICAN
REPUBLIC

HAITI

THE
American Pageant

THE
American Pageant

A History of the Republic

ELEVENTH EDITION

Thomas A. Bailey

David M. Kennedy
Stanford University

Lizabeth Cohen
Harvard University

HOUGHTON MIFFLIN COMPANY   BOSTON   NEW YORK

Senior Sponsoring Editor: Patricia A. Coryell
Basic Book Editor: Ann West
Senior Project Editor: Rosemary R. Jaffe
Senior Designer: Henry Rachlin
Senior Production/Design Coordinator: Jill Haber
Senior Manufacturing Coordinator: Marie Barnes

Cover Design: Henry Rachlin
Cover Image: George Luks, *Armistice Night,* detail. 1918, oil canvas, 37 x $68\frac{3}{4}$
inches. Collection of the Whitney Museum of American Art, Gift of an
anonymous donor. (Please see back cover for a reproduction of the complete
painting.)

Credits for photographs are found following the Index at the end of the book.

Library of Congress Catalog Card Number: 97-72501

Printed in the U.S.A.

ISBN: 0-669-39728-8

7   8   9-VH-02   01   00

ABOUT THE AUTHORS

Thomas A. Bailey, (1903–1983), taught history for nearly forty years at Stanford University, his alma mater. Long regarded as one of the nation's leading historians of American diplomacy, he was honored by his colleagues in 1968 with election to the presidencies of both the Organization of American Historians and the Society for Historians of American Foreign Relations. He was the author, editor, or co-editor of some twenty books, but the work in which he took most pride was *The American Pageant* through which, he liked to say, he had taught American history to several million students.

David M. Kennedy is the Donald J. McLachlan Professor of History at Stanford University. Born and raised in Seattle, he received his undergraduate education at Stanford and did his graduate training at Yale in American Studies, combining the fields of history, economics, and literature. His

book, *Birth Control in America: The Career of Margaret Sanger* (1970) was honored with both the Bancroft Prize and the John Gilmary Shea Prize. His study of World War I, *Over Here: The First World War and American Society* (1980) was a Pulitzer Prize finalist. He is currently finishing a volume in the *Oxford History of the United States* series, covering the Great Depression and World War II. At Stanford he teaches courses in American social, political, and diplomatic history, American literature, and the history of American political thought. He is the recipient of several teaching awards, including the Dean's Award for Distinguished Teaching. He has been a visiting professor at the University of Florence, Italy, and in 1995–1996 served as the Harmsworth Professor of American History at Oxford University. He has also served on the Advisory Board for the PBS television series, *The American Experience,* and as a consultant to documentary films, including *The Great*

War and *Cadillac Desert.* From 1990 to 1995 he chaired the Test Development Committee for the Advanced Placement United States History examination. In 1996 he was elected to membership in the American Academy of Arts and Sciences. Married and the father of three children, in his leisure time he enjoys hiking, bicycling, river-rafting, and fly-fishing.

Lizabeth Cohen has recently joined the history department at Harvard University. Previously, she taught at New York University (1992–1997) and Carnegie Mellon University (1986–1992). Born and raised in the New York metropolitan area, she earned her A.B. from Princeton University and

her M.A. and Ph.D. from the University of California at Berkeley. Her book, *Making a New Deal: Industrial Workers in Chicago, 1919–1939* (1990) won the Bancroft Prize in American History and the Philip Taft Labor History Award, and was a finalist for the Pulitzer Prize. Her article, "Encountering Mass Culture at the Grassroots: The Experience of Chicago Workers in the 1920s," (1989) was awarded the Constance Roarke Prize of the American Studies Association. Currently, she is writing a book about how an economy, landscape, and culture built around mass consumption have shaped politics and social life in post–World War II America. At Harvard, she teaches courses in twentieth-century America, material and popular culture, and gender and working-class history. Before attending graduate school, she taught history at the secondary level and worked in history and art museums. She continues to write about and develop public history programs for general audiences. She is married to an historian of modern France, with whom she has two daughters. For leisure, she enjoys swimming and bicycling with her family, and reading fiction.

CONTENTS

Population, Percentage Change, and Racial Composition for the United States, 1790–1990 • Population Density and Distribution, 1790–1990 • Changing Characteristics of the U.S. Population • Changing Lifestyles in the Twentieth Century • Characteristics of the U.S. Labor Force • Leading Economic Sectors • Per Capita Disposable Personal Income in Constant (1987) Dollars, 1940–1994 • Comparative Tax Burdens • Value of Imports and Exports by Selected Place of Origin and Destination • The U.S. Balance of Trade, 1900–1994 • Tariff Levies on Dutiable Imports, 1821–1994 • Gross Domestic Product in Current and Constant 1995 Dollars • Presidential Elections • Presidents and Vice Presidents • Admission of States • Estimates of Total Costs and Number of Battle Deaths of Major U.S. Wars

MAPS

Charts and Tables

PREFACE

This eleventh edition of *The American Pageant* introduces a new co-author, Professor Lizabeth Cohen of Harvard University. Together, we have undertaken one of the most thorough revisions of the book since it was first published in 1956. Yet for all the innovations in this edition, it also contains much that is familiar. In particular, we have carefully preserved those elements that have long distinguished the *Pageant* from other American history textbooks and made it both appealing and useful to countless students: clarity, concreteness, a consistent chronological narrative, strong emphasis on major themes, avoidance of clutter, access to a variety of interpretive perspectives, and a colorful writing style leavened, as appropriate, with wit.

To a remarkable degree, our scholarly interests as well as our professional careers mirror one another's. David Kennedy is primarily a political and economic historian who was raised in the West, trained in the East (at Yale), and returned to the West to teach at Stanford. Lizabeth Cohen is primarily a social and cultural historian who was raised in the East, trained in the West (at the University of California at Berkeley), and returned to the East to teach first at Carnegie-Mellon University, then at New York University, and now at Harvard. She has also taught at the middle-school level and has had extensive experience working in historical museums—a background that gives her a practiced teacher's sensitive touch and a keen eye for illustrative material to enhance the teaching purposes of the text. Her book, *Making a New Deal: Industrial Workers in Chicago, 1919–1939*, a Bancroft Prize winner and Pulitzer Prize finalist, combines the approaches of both social and political history. In undertaking the revisions for this edition, she has been especially concerned with integrating the rich recent scholarship in social history into the *Pageant's* core political narrative. The two of us share a commitment to telling the story of the American past as vividly and clearly as possible,

without sacrificing a sense of the often sobering seriousness of history, and of its sometimes challenging complexity.

Changes in the Eleventh Edition

To help students come to grips with the complexity of the past, we have divided the book into six sections, organized around sets of major issues that shaped successive stages of American history. Each section begins with an essay that establishes the basic thematic contours of the group of chapters that follow. The essay on "Founding a New Society," for example, introduces the chapters dealing with the settlement and colonial periods. It emphasizes the themes of racial, ethnic, religious, and regional diversity in Britain's North American colonies, and the slow emergence of an "American" national identity, culminating in the Revolution of 1776. To take another example, the essay on "Making Modern America" opens the discussion of the post–World War II years. It highlights the role of that war both in propelling the phenomenal wave of postwar prosperity at home and setting the stage for the Cold War that dominated both the domestic and international scenes for nearly half a century after World War II's conclusion.

The six introductory essays, new in this edition, provide frameworks within which students can better understand the *Pageant's* detailed examinations of the major phases of American history. The essays are intended to guide readers into unfamiliar material, to serve as reference points with which to make sense of the material as they work through it, and as tools for reviewing their understanding of the larger structures and deeper dynamics of history that are often obscured by a preoccupation with discrete facts. The essays reflect our conviction that historical study should strive for synthesis and informed interpretation. Students should not merely seek to memorize mountains of data, but to identify patterns in the often baffling welter of factual detail, and to appreciate complex chains of cause and consequence. Students will learn more effectively, we believe, if they take from these introductory essays a sense of the contexts in which particular historical facts fit, and in which their relative historical significance can be judged.

We have also substantially revised the "Varying Viewpoints" essays. They offer overviews of the scholarly debates that have surrounded major historical issues, and they encourage students to think critically about the ways in which historians disagree. Rather than appearing briefly at the end of each chapter, as in previous editions, the Varying Viewpoints essays have been consolidated into much more substantial discussions of twenty-two major controversies in American history and are found only at the conclusions of relevant chapters.

This edition also contains five new "Makers of America" essays, on the Loyalists during the Revolution, the pioneers of the old Northwest, the Oneida Community, the Knights of Labor, and the suburbanites of the post–World War II era. Along with the twenty-two existing "Makers" essays, these additions help constitute a comprehensive mosaic of the diverse peoples and groups that have composed our strikingly pluralistic society.

Readers will find other new features in this edition of the *Pageant* as well: enriched discussion at many points of the contributions of women; expanded treatment of working-class life; extensive analysis of the concept of republicanism; a thoroughly updated account of Reconstruction; substantial attention to African-American and Native American history; careful integration of social, political, and cultural themes in the post–World War II period; and many fresh voices in the numerous box-quotes. We have also compressed and reorganized the material concerning the period from 1800 to 1824, formerly Chapters 11, 12 and 13. That material is now broken up into two chapters that cover the Jefferson and Madison presidencies, 1800 to 1812 (Chapter 11) and the War of 1812 through the Monroe Doctrine, 1812–1824 (Chapter 12). In addition, the Eleventh Edition features an exciting new design, many revised maps and charts, and several entirely new maps and photographs. Completely updated bibliographies at the conclusion of every chapter and a revised Appendix, with abundant statistical data on many aspects of the American historical experience, complete the text package.

Goals of *The American Pageant*

Like its predecessors, this edition of *The American Pageant* tries to cultivate in its readers the capacity for balanced judgment and informed understanding about American society by holding up to the present the mirror and measuring rod that is the past. The book's goal is not to teach the art of prophecy but the much subtler and more difficult arts of seeing things in context, of understanding the roots and direction and pace of change, and of distinguishing what is truly new under the sun from what is not. The study of history, it has been rightly said, does not make one smart for the next time, but wise forever.

We hope that the *Pageant* will help to develop those intellectual assets in its readers, and that those who use the book will take from it both a fresh appreciation of what has gone before and a seasoned perspective on what is to come. And we hope, too, that readers will take as much pleasure in reading *The American Pageant* as we have had in writing it.

Supplements Available with *The American Pageant,* Eleventh Edition

A complete supplementary program accompanies the eleventh edition of *The American Pageant*. The supplements comprise the following items.

FOR STUDENTS:

- **The American Spirit, Ninth Edition, Volumes I and II** (primary-source readers)

- **Complete Guidebook** (study guide without answers to exercises)

- **Guidebook, Volumes I and II** (study guides with answers to exercises)

- **Computerized Guidebook**

- **Getting the Most out of Your U.S. History Course: The History Student's Vade Mecum,** Second Edition

- **Rand McNally Atlas of American History**

- **Regional Document Sets:** For the South; Texas and the Southwest; and California and the West

- **Surveying the Land: Skills and Exercises in U.S. Historical Geography, Volumes I and II**

- **The American Pageant Interactive Edition** (comprises the complete text of the book, illustrations from the book and other sources, an extensive collection of maps, some of which are animated to show change over time, multimedia chapter overviews, historical video and audio; tables of numeric data, and an extensive array of documents, as well as self-tests, a glossary, chronologies, and a notebook)

FOR INSTRUCTORS:

- **Instructor's Resource Guide**

- **Quizbook** (test item file)

- **Computerized Testing** for Macintosh, IBM, and Apple computers

- **The Houghton Mifflin U.S. History Transparency Set, Volumes I and II**

- **Videodisk** (*An American Portfolio,* provides thousands of still images of historic events, personages, and artifacts with twenty-seven minutes of full-motion historic video footage and numerous animated maps showing change over time)

@history

The most exciting addition to our ancillary lineup is *@history: an interactive American history source.* This multimedia teaching/learning package combines a variety of material—primary sources (text and graphic), videos, audio, and links to Web sites—with activities that can be used to analyze, interpret, and discuss primary sources; to enhance collaborative learning; and to create multimedia presentations. *@history* provides instructors with an interactive multimedia tool that can improve the analytical skills of students and introduce them to historical sources.

Acknowledgments

Many people have contributed to this revision of *The American Pageant.* Foremost among them are the countless students and teachers who have written unsolicited letters of comment or inquiry. We have learned from every one of them, and encourage all readers to offer us suggestions for improving future editions. Several colleagues have also given us the benefit of their assistance, including:

Terry Alford, *Northern Virginia Community College*
Ricardo Almarez, *Allan Hancock College*
John Belohlavek, *University of South Florida, Tampa*
Leslie Berlin, *Stanford University*
Max Brandon, *Polk Community College*
Donald Burdick, *Harford Community College*
Paul Cunningham, *Cottonsville Community College*
Michelle Forman, *Middlebury Union High School*
Scott Garrett, *Paducah Community College*
Joe Hapak, *Moraine Valley Community College*
Gary L. Huey, *Ferris State University*
Horace P. Jones, *Northeast Louisiana University*
David Kammerance, *Florence-Darlington Technical College*
Judy Kane, *Choctawhatchee High School*
Jerold Kellman, *Oakton Community College*
Steve Kramer, *The Hockaday School*
Michael Lerner, *New York University*
Glenn M. Linden, *Southern Methodist University*
Louise Maxwell, *New York University*
William Mendelsohn, *Clayton High School*
Stephen Mihm, *New York University*
Virginia Mulrooney, *West Los Angeles College*
David P. Smith, *Highland Park High School, Dallas*
William Tobin, *St. Patrick's College, Ireland*
Jane Wu, *College of Du Page*

Our warm thanks to each of them.

David M. Kennedy

Lizabeth Cohen

Sail, sail thy best, ship of Democracy,
Of value is thy freight, 'tis not the Present only,
The Past is also stored in thee,
Thou holdest not the venture of thyself alone, not of
   the Western continent alone,
Earth's résumé entire floats on thy keel, O ship, is
   steadied by thy spars,
With thee Time voyages in trust, the antecedent
   nations sink or swim with thee,
With all their ancient struggles, martyrs, heroes, epics,
   wars, thou bear'st the other continents,
Theirs, theirs as much as thine, the destination-port
   triumphant....

Walt Whitman
Thou Mother with Thy Equal Brood, 1872

THE
American Pageant

PART ONE

Founding the New Nation

The European explorers who followed Christopher Columbus to North America in the sixteenth century had no notion of founding a new nation. Neither did the first European settlers who peopled the thirteen English colonies on the eastern shores of the continent in the seventeenth and eighteenth centuries. These original colonists may have fled poverty or religious persecution in the Old World, but they continued to view themselves as Europeans, and as subjects of the English king. They regarded America as but the western rim of a transatlantic European world.

Yet life in the New World made the colonists different from their European cousins, and eventually, during the American Revolution, the Americans came to embrace a vision of their country as an independent nation. How did this epochal transformation come about? How did the colonists overcome the conflicts that divided them,

unite against Britain, and declare themselves at great cost to be an "American" people?

They had much in common to begin with. Most were English-speaking. Most came determined to create an agricultural society modeled on English customs. Conditions in the New World deepened their common bonds. Most learned to live lives unfettered by the tyrannies of royal authority, official religion, and social hierarchies that they had left behind. They grew to cherish ideals that became synonymous with American life—reverence for individual liberty, self-government, religious tolerance, and economic opportunity. They also commonly displayed a willingness to subjugate outsiders—first Indians, who were nearly annihilated through war and disease, and then Africans, who were brought in chains to serve as slave labor, especially on the tobacco, rice, and indigo plantations of the southern colonies.

Algonquin Indians Fishing
English watercolorist John White accompanied the first English expedition to Roanoke Island (later part of Virginia) in 1585. His paintings faithfully recorded the Indian way of life that was now imperiled by the arrival of the Europeans.

But if the settlement experience gave people a common stock of values, both good and bad, it also divided them. The thirteen colonies were quite different from one another. Puritans carved tight, pious, and relatively democratic communities of small family farms out of rocky-soiled New England. Theirs was a homogeneous world in comparison to most of the southern colonies, where large landholders, mostly Anglicans, built plantations along the coast from which they lorded over a labor force of black slaves and looked down upon the poor white farmers who settled the backcountry. Different still were the middle colonies stretching from New York to Delaware. There diversity reigned. Well-to-do merchants put their stamp on New York City, as Quakers did on Philadelphia, while out in the countryside sprawling estates were interspersed with modest homesteads. Within individual colonies, conflicts festered over economic interests, ethnic rivalries, and religious practices. All those clashes made it difficult for colonists to imagine that they were a single people with a common destiny, much less that they ought to break free from Britain.

The American colonists in fact had little reason to complain about Britain. Each of the thirteen colonies enjoyed a good deal of self-rule. Many colonists profited from trade within the British Empire. But by the 1760s this stable arrangement began to crumble, a victim of the imperial rivalry between France and Britain. Their struggle for supremacy in North America began in the late seventeenth century and finally dragged in the colonists during the French and Indian War from 1756 to 1763. That war in one sense strengthened ties with Britain, since colonial militias fought triumphantly alongside the British army against their mutual French and Indian enemies. But by driving the French from the North American continent, the British made themselves less indispensable to the American colonies. More important still, after 1763 a financially overstretched British government made the fateful choice of imposing taxes on colonies that had been accustomed to answering mainly to their own colonial assemblies. By the 1770s issues of taxation, self-rule, and trade restrictions brought the crisis of imperial authority to a head. Although as late as 1775 most people in the colonies clung to the hope of some kind of accommodation short of outright independence, royal intransigence soon thrust the colonists into a war of independence that neither antagonist could have anticipated just a few years before.

Eight years of revolutionary war did more than anything in the colonial past to bring Americans together as a nation. Comradeship in arms and the struggle to shape a national government forced Americans to subdue their differences as best they could. But the spirit of national unity was hardly universal. One in five colonists sided with the British as "Loyalists," and a generation would pass before the wounds of this first American "civil war" fully healed. Yet in the end, Americans won the Revolution, with no small measure of help from the French, because in every colony people shared a belief that they were fighting for the "unalienable rights" of "life, liberty, and the pursuit of happiness," in the words of Thomas Jefferson's magnificent Declaration of Independence. Almost two hundred years of living a new life had prepared Americans to found a new nation.

Philadelphia, Corner of Second and High Streets
Delegates to the Constitutional Convention in 1787 gathered in Philadelphia, the largest city in North America, a vivid symbol of the rise of American society from its precarious beginnings at Jamestown and Plymouth nearly two centuries earlier.

1

New World Beginnings

33,000 B.C.–A.D. 1769

*I have come to believe that this is a mighty
continent which was hitherto unknown. . . .
Your Highnesses have an Other World here.*

Planetary Perspectives

Several billion years ago that whirling speck of dust
known as the earth, fifth in size among the planets,
came into being.

About six thousand years ago—only a minute
ago in geological time—recorded history of the
Western world began. Certain peoples of the Middle
East, developing a primitive culture, gradually
emerged from the haze of the past.

Five hundred years ago—only a few seconds in
the past, figuratively speaking—European explorers
stumbled on the American continents. This dramatic
accident forever altered the future of both the Old
World and the New, and of Africa and Asia as well.

The two American continents eventually
brought forth a score of sovereign republics. By far
the most influential of this brood—the United
States—was born a pygmy and grew to be a giant. It
was destined to leave a deep imprint upon the rest

of the world as a result of its refreshingly liberal
ideals, its revolutionary democratic experiment,
and its boundless opportunities for the common
folk of foreign lands. Its enormous economic output
ultimately made it a decisive weight in the world
balance of power. Its achievements in science, technology, and the arts shaped people's lives in every
corner of the planet.

The American Republic, which is still relatively
young when compared with the Old World, was
from the outset uniquely favored. It started from
scratch on a vast and virgin continent, whose native
peoples were so few and so scattered that they were
easily—sometimes brutally—shouldered aside. This
rare opportunity for a great social and political

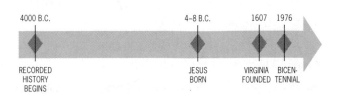

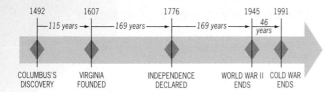

1492	1607	1776	1945	1991
←—115 years—→	←———169 years———→	←———169 years———→	46 years	
COLUMBUS'S DISCOVERY	VIRGINIA FOUNDED	INDEPENDENCE DECLARED	WORLD WAR II ENDS	COLD WAR ENDS

experiment may never come again, for no other huge, fertile, and relatively uninhabited areas are left in the temperate zones of the increasingly crowded earth.

Despite its remarkable development, the United States will one day reach its peak, like Greece and Rome. Its glory will eventually fade, as did theirs. But whatever uncertainties the future may hold, the past at least is secure and richly repays examination.

The Shaping of North America

Planet earth took on its present form slowly. Some 225 million years ago a single supercontinent contained all the world's dry land. Then enormous chunks of terrain began to drift away from this colossal continent, opening the Atlantic and Indian oceans, narrowing the Pacific Ocean, and forming the great landmasses of Eurasia, Africa, Australia, Antarctica, and the Americas. The existence of a sin-gle original continent has been proved in part by the discovery of nearly identical species of fish that swim today in the long-separated freshwater lakes of the various continents.

Continued shifting and folding of the earth's crust thrust up mountain ranges. The Appalachians were probably formed even before continental separation, perhaps 350 million years ago. The majestic ranges of western North America—the Rockies, the Sierra Nevada, the Cascades, and the Coast Range—arose much more recently, geologically speaking, some 135 million to 25 million years ago. They are truly "American" mountains, born after the continent took on its own separate geological identity.

By about 10 million years ago, nature had sculpted the basic geological shape of North America (see the map on the inside back cover). The continent was anchored in its northeastern corner by the massive Canadian Shield—a zone undergirded by ancient rock, probably the first part of what became the North American landmass to have emerged above sea level. A narrow eastern coastal plain, or "tidewater" region, creased by many river valleys, sloped gently upward to the timeworn ridges of the Appalachians. Those ancient mountains slanted away on their western side into the huge midcontinental basin that rolled downward to the Mississippi Valley bottom and then rose relentlessly to the towering peaks of the Rockies. From the

The Final Shore The Pacific Coast near Monterey, California.

5

Rocky Mountain crest—the "roof of America"—the land fell off jaggedly into the intermountain Great Basin, bounded by the Rockies in the east and the Sierra and Cascade ranges on the west. The valleys of the Sacramento and San Joaquin Rivers and the Willamette–Puget Sound trough seamed the interiors of present-day California, Oregon, and Washington. The land at last met the foaming Pacific, where the Coast ranges rose steeply from the sea.

Nature laid a chill hand over much of this terrain in the Great Ice Age, beginning about 2 million years ago. Two-mile-thick ice sheets crept from the polar regions to blanket parts of Europe, Asia, and the Americas. In North America the great glaciers carpeted most of present-day Canada and the United States as far southward as a line stretching from Pennsylvania through the Ohio country and the Dakotas to the Pacific Northwest.

When the glaciers finally retreated about 10,000 years ago, they left the North American landscape transformed, and much as we know it today. The weight of the gargantuan ice mantle had depressed the level of the Canadian Shield. The grinding and flushing action of the moving and melting ice had scoured away the shield's topsoil, pitting its rocky surface with thousands of shallow depressions into which the melting glaciers flowed to form lakes. The same glacial action scooped out and filled the Great Lakes. They originally drained southward through the Mississippi River system to the Gulf of Mexico. When the melting ice unblocked the Gulf of St. Lawrence, the lake water sought the St. Lawrence River outlet to the Atlantic Ocean, lowering the Great Lakes' level and leaving the Missouri-Mississippi-Ohio system to drain the enormous midcontinental basin between the Appalachians and the Rockies. Similarly, in the west, water from the melting glaciers filled sprawling Lake Bonneville, covering much of present-day Utah, Nevada, and Idaho. It drained to the Pacific Ocean through the Snake and Columbia River systems until diminishing rainfall from the ebbing icecap lowered the water level, cutting off access to the Snake River outlet. Deprived of both inflow and drainage, the giant lake became a gradually shrinking inland sea. It grew increasingly saline, slowly evaporated, and left an arid, mineral-rich desert. Only Great Salt Lake remained as a relic of Bonneville's former vastness. Today Lake Bonneville's ancient beaches are visible on mountainsides up to 1,000 feet above the dry floor of the Great Basin.

The First Discoverers of America

The Great Ice Age shaped more than the geological history of North America. It also accounted for the origins of the continent's human history. Some 35,000 years ago, much of the water in the world-ocean was congealed into massive icepack glaciers, lowering the level of the sea. As the sea level dropped, it exposed a land bridge connecting Eurasia with North America in the area of the present-day Bering Sea between Siberia and Alaska. Across that bridge, probably following migrating herds of game, ventured small bands of nomadic Asian hunters—the first "discoverers" of America and the ancestors of the Native Americans. They continued to trek across the Eurasian-American isthmus for some 250 centuries, slowly peopling the American continents.

As the Ice Age ended and the glaciers melted, the sea level rose again, inundating the land bridge about 10,000 years ago. Nature thus barred the door to further immigration for many thousands of years, leaving this part of the human family marooned for millennia on the now-isolated American continents.

Time did not stand still for these original Americans. The same climatic warming that melted the ice and drowned the bridge to Eurasia gradually opened ice-free valleys through which vanguard bands groped their way southward and eastward across the Americas. Roaming slowly through this awesome wilderness, they eventually reached the far tip of South America, some 15,000 miles from Siberia. By the time Europeans arrived in America in 1492, perhaps 72 million people inhabited the two American continents.* Over the centuries they split into countless tribes, evolved more than two thousand separate languages, and developed many diverse religions, cultures, and ways of life.

Incas in Peru, Mayans in Central America, and Aztecs in Mexico shaped stunningly sophisticated civilizations. Their advanced agricultural practices, based primarily on the cultivation of maize, which is Indian corn, fed large populations, perhaps as many as 21 million in Mexico alone. Although without large draft animals such as horses and oxen, and

---

*Much controversy surrounds estimates of the pre-Columbian Native American population. The figures here are from William M. Denevan, ed., *The Native Population of the Americas in 1472* (Madison: University of Wisconsin Press, 1976).

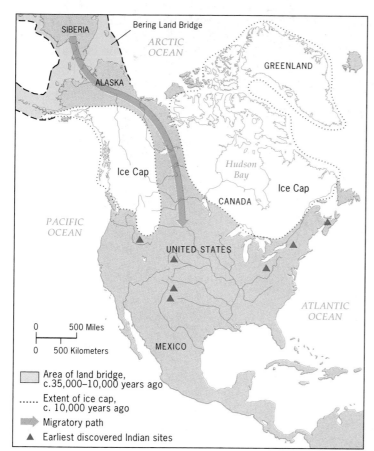

Area of land bridge,
c.35,000–10,000 years ago

Extent of ice cap,
c. 10,000 years ago

Migratory path

▲ Earliest discovered Indian sites

The First Discoverers of America

For some 25,000 years, people crossed the Bering land bridge from Eurasia to North America. Gradually, they dispersed southward down ice-free valleys, populating both the American continents.

Incan Culture

This mortar and corncob-shaped pestle from the Incan stronghold in present-day Peru vividly illustrate the importance of corn in Incan life.

lacking even the simple technology of the wheel, these peoples built elaborate cities and carried on far-flung commerce. Talented mathematicians, they made strikingly accurate astronomical observations. The Aztecs also routinely sought the favor of their gods by offering human sacrifices, cutting the hearts out of the chests of living victims, who were often captives conquered in battle. By some accounts more than five thousand people were ritually slaughtered to celebrate the crowning of one Aztec chieftain.

The Earliest Americans

Agriculture, especially corn growing, accounted for the size and sophistication of the Native American civilizations in Mexico and South America. About 5000 B.C. hunter-gatherers in highland Mexico developed a wild grass into the staple crop of corn, which became their staff of life and the foundation of the complex, large-scale, centralized Aztec and Incan nation-states that eventually emerged. Cultivation of corn spread across the Americas from the Mexican heartland. Everywhere it was planted, corn began to transform nomadic hunting bands into settled agricultural villagers, but this process went forward slowly and unevenly.

Corn planting reached the present-day American Southwest by about 1200 B.C. and powerfully molded Pueblo culture. The Pueblo peoples in the Rio Grande Valley constructed intricate irrigation systems to water their cornfields. They were dwelling in villages of multistoried, terraced buildings when Spanish explorers made contact with them in the sixteenth century. (*Pueblo* means "village" in Spanish.)

Corn cultivation reached other parts of North America considerably later. The timing of its arrival in different localities explains much about the relative rates of development of different Native

American peoples. Throughout the continent to the north and east of the land of the Pueblos, social life was less elaborately developed—indeed "societies" in the modern sense of the word scarcely existed. No dense concentrations of population or complex nation-states comparable to the Aztec empire existed in North America outside of Mexico at the time of the Europeans' arrival—one of the reasons for the relative ease with which the European colonizers subdued the native North Americans.

North American Indian Tribes at the Time of European Colonization   This map illustrates the great diversity of the Indian population — and suggests the inappropriateness of identifying all the Native American peoples with the single label *Indian*. The more than two hundred tribes were deeply divided by geography, language, and customs.

The Mound Builders of the Ohio River Valley and the Mississippian culture of the lower Midwest did sustain some large settlements after the incorporation of corn planting into their way of life during the first millennium A.D. The Mississippian settlement at Cahokia, near present-day East St. Louis, Illinois, was home to perhaps 40,000 people in about A.D. 1100. But mysteriously, around the year 1300, both the Mound Builder and Mississippian cultures had fallen into decline.

The cultivation of maize, as well as of high-yielding strains of beans and squash, reached the southeastern Atlantic seaboard region of North America about A.D. 1000. These plants made possible "three-sister" farming, with beans growing on the trellis of the cornstalks and squash covering the planting mounds to retain moisture in the soil. The rich diet provided by this environmentally clever farming technique produced some of the highest population densities on the continent, among them the Creek, Choctaw, and Cherokee peoples.

The Iroquois in the northeastern woodlands, inspired by a legendary leader named Hiawatha, in the sixteenth century created perhaps the closest North American approximation to the great nation-states of Mexico and Peru. The Iroquois Confederacy developed the political and organizational skills to sustain a robust military alliance that menaced its neighbors, Native American and European alike, for well over a century (see "Makers of America: The Iroquois," pp. 38–39).

But for the most part, the native peoples of North America were living in small, scattered, and impermanent settlements on the eve of the Europeans' arrival. Loosely defined tribes would periodically gather into encampments along a riverbank at fish-spawning time and then disperse in tiny bands of two or three families for the winter's hunting. In more settled agricultural groups, women tended the crops while men hunted, fished, gathered fuel, and cleared fields for planting. This pattern of life frequently conferred substantial authority on women, and many North American native peoples, including the Iroquois, developed matrilinear cultures, in which power and possessions passed down the female side of the family line.

Unlike the Europeans, who would soon arrive with the presumption that humans had dominion over the earth and with the technologies to alter the very face of the land, the Native Americans had neither the desire nor the means to manipulate nature aggressively. They revered the physical world and endowed nature with spiritual properties. Yet they did sometimes ignite massive forest fires, deliberately torching thousands of acres of trees to create better hunting habitats, especially for deer. This practice accounted for the open, parklike appearance of the eastern woodlands that so amazed early European explorers.

But in a broad sense, the land did not feel the hand of the Native Americans heavy upon it, partly because they were so few in number. They were so

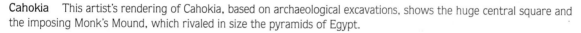

Cahokia   This artist's rendering of Cahokia, based on archaeological excavations, shows the huge central square and the imposing Monk's Mound, which rivaled in size the pyramids of Egypt.

The New World as Paradise
This sixteenth-century engraving by the Flemish artist Theodore de Bry illustrates the Indian method of hunting by setting fires to drive wild game into bow range.

thinly spread across the continent that vast areas were virtually untouched by a human presence. In the fateful year 1492, probably no more than 4 million Native Americans padded through the whispering, primeval forests and paddled across the sparkling, virgin waters of North America. They were blissfully unaware that the historic isolation of the Americas was about to end forever, as the land and the native peoples alike felt the full shock of the European "discovery."

Indirect Discoverers of the New World

Europeans, for their part, were equally unaware of the existence of the Americas. Blond-bearded Norse seafarers from Scandinavia had chanced upon the northeastern shoulder of North America about A.D. 1000. They landed at a place, probably in Newfoundland, that abounded in wild grapes, which led them to name the spot Vinland. But no strong nation-state, yearning to expand, supported these venturesome voyagers. Their flimsy settlements consequently were soon abandoned, and their discovery was forgotten, except in Scandinavian saga and song.

For several centuries thereafter, other restless Europeans, with the growing power of ambitious nation-states behind them, sought contact with a wider world, whether for conquest or trade. They thus set in motion the chain of events that led to a drive toward Asia, the penetration of Africa, and the completely accidental discovery of the New World.

Christian crusaders must rank high among America's indirect discoverers. Clad in shining armor, tens of thousands of these European warriors tried from the eleventh to the fourteenth century to wrest the Holy Land from Muslim control. Foiled in their military assaults, the crusaders nevertheless acquired a taste for the exotic delights of Asia. Goods that had been virtually unknown in Europe now were craved—silk for clothing, drugs for aching flesh, perfumes for unbathed bodies, colorful draperies for gloomy castles, and spices—especially sugar, a rare luxury in Europe before the crusades—for preserving and flavoring food. Europe's developing sweet tooth would have momentous implications for world history.

The luxuries of the East were prohibitively expensive in Europe. They had to be transported enormous distances from the Spice Islands (Indonesia), China, and India, in creaking ships and on swaying camelback. The journey led across the

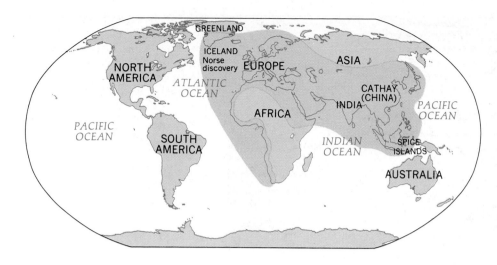

The World Known to Europe, 1492

Indian Ocean, the Persian Gulf, and the Red Sea or along the tortuous caravan routes of Asia or the Arabian peninsula, ending at the ports of the eastern Mediterranean. Muslim middlemen exacted a heavy toll en route. By the time the strange-smelling goods reached Italian merchants at Venice and Genoa, they were so costly that purchasers and profits alike were narrowly limited. European consumers and distributors were naturally eager to find a less expensive route to the riches of Asia or to develop alternate sources of supply.

Europeans Enter Africa

European appetites were further whetted when footloose Marco Polo, an Italian adventurer, returned to Europe in 1295 and began telling tales of his nearly twenty-year sojourn in China. Though he may in fact never have seen China (legend to the contrary, the hard evidence is sketchy), he must be regarded as an indirect discoverer of the New World, for his book, with its descriptions of rose-tinted pearls and golden pagodas, stimulated European desires for a cheaper route to the treasures of the East.

These accumulating pressures brought a breakthrough for European expansion in the fifteenth century. Before the middle of that century, European sailors refused to sail southward along the coast of West Africa because they could not beat their way home against the prevailing northerly winds and south-flowing currents. About 1450, Portuguese mariners overcame those obstacles. Not only had they developed the caravel, a ship that

could sail more closely into the wind, but they had discovered that they could return to Europe by sailing northwesterly from the African coast toward the Azores, where the prevailing westward breezes would carry them home.

The new world of sub-Saharan Africa now came within the grasp of questing Europeans. The northern shore of Africa, as part of the Mediterranean world, had been known to Europe since antiquity.

Wooden Antelope Headdress from Mali, Africa
The empire of Mali flourished in the fourteenth century under Emperor Mansu Musa. Laden with slaves and gold, he made a pilgrimage to Mecca in 1324. This display reflected Mali's status as one of the medieval world's chief suppliers of gold.

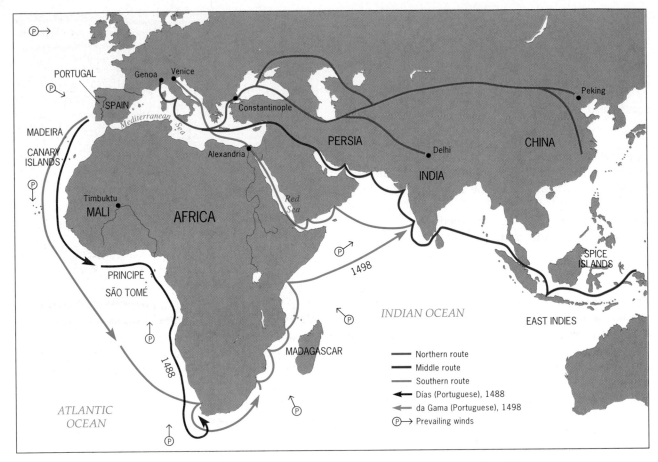

Trade Routes with the East   Goods on the early routes were passed through so many hands along the way that their ultimate source remained mysterious to Europeans.

But because sea travel down the African coast had been virtually impossible, Africa south of the forbidding Sahara Desert barrier had remained remote and mysterious. African gold, perhaps two-thirds of Europe's supply, crossed the Sahara on camelback, and shadowy tales may have reached Europe about the flourishing West African kingdom of Mali in the Niger River Valley, with its impressive Islamic university at Timbuktu. But Europeans had no direct access to sub-Saharan Africa until the Portuguese navigators began to creep down the West African coast in the middle of the fifteenth century.

The Portuguese promptly set up trading posts along the African shore for the purchase of gold—and slaves. Arab flesh-merchants and Africans themselves had traded slaves for centuries before the Europeans arrived. They routinely charged higher prices for slaves from distant sources, who could not easily flee to their native villages nor be easily rescued by their kin. Slave brokers also delib-

erately separated persons from the same tribes and mixed unlike people together to frustrate organized resistance. Thus from its earliest days, even before Europeans arrived in Africa, slavery by its very nature fostered the extinction of regional African cultures and tribal identities.

The Portuguese adopted these Arab and African practices. They built up their own systematic traffic in slaves to work the sugar plantations that Portugal, and later Spain, established on the African coastal islands of Madeira, the Canaries, São Tomé, and Principe. The Portuguese appetite for slaves was enormous and dwarfed the modest scale of the pre-European traffic. Slave trading became a big business. Some forty thousand Africans were carried away to the Atlantic sugar islands in the last half of the fifteenth century. Millions more were to be wrenched from their home continent after the discovery of the Americas. In these fifteenth-century Portuguese adventures in Africa were to be found the origins of the modern plantation system, based on large-scale commercial agriculture and the wholesale exploitation of slave labor. This kind of plantation economy would shape the destiny of much of the New World.

The seafaring Portuguese pushed still farther southward in search of the water route to Asia. Edging cautiously down the African coast, Bartholomeu Días rounded the southernmost tip of the "Dark Continent" in 1488. Ten years later Vasco da Gama finally reached India (hence the name "Indies," given by Europeans to all the mysterious lands of the Orient), and returned home with a small but tantalizing cargo of jewels and spices.

Meanwhile, the kingdom of Spain became united—an event pregnant with destiny—in the late fifteenth century. This new unity resulted primarily from the marriage of two sovereigns, Ferdinand of Aragon and Isabella of Castile, and from the brutal expulsion of the "infidel" Muslim Moors from Spain after centuries of Christian-Islamic warfare. Glorying in their sudden strength, the Spaniards were eager to outstrip their Portuguese rivals in the race to tap the wealth of the Indies. To the south and east, Portugal controlled the African coast and thus controlled the gateway to the round-Africa water route to India. Of necessity, therefore, Spain looked westward.

Columbus Comes upon a New World

The stage was now set for a cataclysmic shift in the course of history—the history not only of Europe but of all the world. Europeans clamored for more and cheaper products from the lands beyond the Mediterranean. Africa had been established as a source of cheap slave labor for plantation agriculture. The Portuguese voyages had demonstrated the feasibility of long-range ocean navigation. In Spain a modern national state was taking shape, with the unity, wealth, and power to shoulder the formidable tasks of discovery, conquest, and colonization. The dawn of the Renaissance in the fourteenth century nurtured an ambitious spirit of optimism and adventure. Printing presses, introduced about 1450, facilitated the spread of scientific knowledge. The mariner's compass, possibly borrowed from the Arabs, eliminated some of the uncertainties of sea travel. Meanwhile, across the ocean, the vast and virginal New World innocently awaited its European discoverers.

Christopher Columbus (1451–1506), by Ridolfo di Domenico Ghirlandaio   No portrait from life exists of Columbus, so all likenesses of him, including this one, are somewhat fanciful.

Onto this stage stepped Christopher Columbus. This skilled Italian seafarer persuaded the Spanish monarchs to outfit him with three tiny but seaworthy ships, manned by a motley crew. Daringly, he unfurled the sails of his cockleshell craft and headed westward. His superstitious sailors, fearful of venturing into the oceanic unknown, grew increasingly mutinous. After six weeks at sea, failure loomed until, on October 12, 1492, the crew sighted an island in the Bahamas. A new world thus swam within the vision of Europeans.

Columbus's sensational achievement obscures the fact that he was one of the most successful failures in history. Seeking a new water route to the fabled Indies, he in fact had bumped into an enormous land barrier blocking the ocean pathway. For decades thereafter explorers strove to get through it or around it. The truth gradually dawned that sprawling new continents had been discovered. Yet Columbus was at first so certain that he had skirted the rim of the "Indies" that he called the native peoples Indians, a gross geographical misnomer that somehow stuck.

Columbus's discovery would eventually convulse four continents—Europe, Africa, and the two Americas. Thanks to his epochal voyage, an interdependent global economic system emerged on a scale undreamed-of before he set sail. Its workings touched every shore washed by the Atlantic Ocean. Europe provided the markets, the capital, and the technology; Africa furnished the labor; and the New World offered its raw materials, especially its precious metals and its soil for the cultivation of sugar cane. For Europeans as well as for Africans and Native Americans, the world after 1492 would never be the same, for better or worse.

When Worlds Collide

Two ecosystems—the fragile, naturally evolved networks of relations among organisms in a stable environment—commingled and clashed when Columbus waded ashore. The reverberations from that historic encounter echoed for centuries after 1492. The flora and fauna of the Old and New Worlds had been separated for thousands of years. European explorers marveled at the strange sights that greeted them, including exotic beasts such as iguanas and "snakes with castanets" (rattlesnakes). Native New World plants such as tobacco, maize, beans, tomatoes, and especially the lowly potato eventually revolutionized the international economy as well as the European diet, feeding the rapid population growth of the Old World. These foodstuffs were among the most important Indian gifts to the Europeans and to the rest of the world. Perhaps three-fifths of the crops cultivated around the globe today originated in the Americas. Ironically, the introduction into Africa of New World foodstuffs like maize, manioc, and sweet potatoes may have fed an African population boom that numerically, though not morally, more than offset the losses inflicted by the slave trade.

In exchange the Europeans introduced Old World crops and animals to the Americas. Columbus returned to the Caribbean island of Hispaniola (present-day Haiti and the Dominican Republic) in 1493 with seventeen ships that unloaded twelve hundred men and a virtual Noah's Ark of cattle, swine, and horses. The horses soon reached the North American mainland through Mexico and in less than two centuries had spread as far as Canada. North American Indian tribes like the Apaches,

Sioux, and Blackfoot swiftly adopted the horse, transforming their cultures into highly mobile, wide-ranging hunter societies that roamed the grassy Great Plains in pursuit of the shaggy buffalo. Columbus also brought seedlings of sugar cane, which thrived in the warm Caribbean climate. A "sugar revolution" consequently took place in the European diet, fueled by the forced migration of millions of Africans to work the canefields and sugar mills of the New World.

Unwittingly, the Europeans also brought other organisms in the dirt on their boots and the dust on their clothes, such as the seeds of Kentucky bluegrass, dandelions, and daisies. Most ominous of all, in their bodies they carried the germs that caused smallpox, yellow fever, and malaria. Indeed, Old World diseases would quickly devastate the Native Americans. During the Indians' millennia of isolation in the Americas, most of the Old World's killer maladies had disappeared from among them. But generations of freedom from those illnesses had also wiped out protective antibodies. Devoid of natural resistance to Old World sicknesses, Indians died in droves. Within fifty years of the Spanish arrival, the population of the Taino natives in Hispaniola dwindled from some 1 million people to about two hundred. Enslavement and armed aggression took their toll, but the deadliest killers were microbes, not muskets. The lethal germs spread among the

The Plant Exchange: New World and Old World Crops

Native American Plants Taken to Europe	Old World Plants Brought to America
American persimmon	apple
beans	beet
bell and hot pepper	cabbage
blueberry	carrot
cranberry	celery
maize (corn)	cucumber
manioc	eggplant
papaya	grapefruit
pineapple	lemon
pumpkin	peach
squash	plum
sweet potato	olive
tobacco	sugar cane
tomato	
white potato	
wild rice	

The Devastation of Disease
This engraving of a burial service records the horrendous impact of Old World diseases on the vulnerable Native Americans.

New World peoples with the speed and force of a hurricane, swiftly sweeping far ahead of the human invaders; most of those afflicted never laid eyes on a European. In the century after Columbus's landfall, nearly 90 percent of the Native Americans perished, a demographic catastrophe without parallel in human history. This depopulation was surely not intended by the Spanish; but it was nevertheless so severe that entire cultures and ancient ways of life were extinguished forever. Baffled, enraged, and vengeful, Indian slaves sometimes kneaded tainted blood into their masters' bread, to little effect. Perhaps it was poetic justice that the Indians unintentionally did take a kind of revenge by infecting the early explorers with syphilis, injecting that lethal sexually transmitted disease for the first time into Europe.

The Spanish *Conquistadores*

Gradually, Europeans realized that the American continents held rich prizes, especially the gold and silver of the advanced Indian civilizations in Mexico and Peru. Spain secured its claim to Columbus's discovery in the Treaty of Tordesillas (1494), dividing with Portugal the "heathen lands" of the New World. The lion's share went to Spain, but Portugal received compensating territory in Africa and Asia, as well as title to lands that one day would be Brazil.

Spain became the dominant exploring and colonizing power in the 1500s. In the service of God, as well as in search of gold and glory, Spanish *conquistadores* (conquerors) fanned out across the Caribbean and eventually onto the mainland of the American continents (see "Makers of America: The Spanish *Conquistadores*," pp. 16–17). On Spain's long roster of notable deeds, two spectacular exploits must be headlined. Vasco Nuñez Balboa, hailed as the discoverer of the Pacific Ocean, waded

> *Bartolomé de Las Casas (1474–1566), a reform-minded Dominican friar, wrote* The Destruction of the Indies *in 1542 to chronicle the awful fate of the Native Americans and to protest Spanish policies in the New World. He was especially horrified at the catastrophic effects of disease on the native peoples.*
>
> "Who of those in future centuries will believe this? I myself who am writing this and saw it and know the most about it can hardly believe that such was possible."

MAKERS OF AMERICA

The Spanish *Conquistadores*

In 1492, the same year that Columbus sighted America, the great Moorish city of Granada, in Spain, fell after a ten-year siege. For five centuries the Christian kingdoms of Spain had been trying to drive the North African Muslim Moors ("the Dark Ones," in Spanish) off the Iberian peninsula, and with the fall of Granada they succeeded. But the lengthy "Reconquista" had left its mark on Spanish society. Centuries of military and religious confrontation nurtured an obsession with status and honor, bred religious zealotry and intolerance, and

created a large class of men who regarded manual labor and commerce contemptuously. With the Reconquista ended, some of these men turned their restless gaze to Spain's New World frontier.

At first, Spanish hopes for America focused on the Caribbean and on finding a sea route to Asia. Gradually, however, word filtered back of rich kingdoms on the mainland. Between 1519 and 1540, Spanish *conquistadores* swept across the Americas in two wide arcs of conquest—one driving from Cuba through Mexico into what is now the southwestern United States, the other starting from Panama and pushing south into Peru. Within half a century of Columbus's arrival in the Americas, the

Indians Bearing Gifts of Gold to Balboa, by Theodore de Bry A European rendering of the triumphant arrival of a *conquistador.*

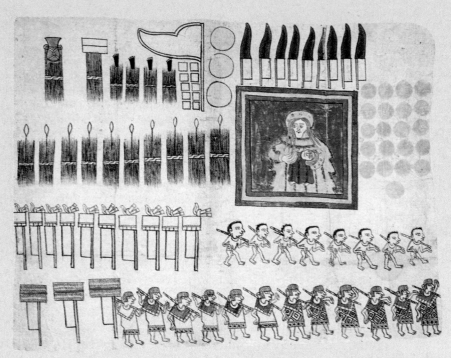

An Aztec View of the Conquest, 1531
Produced just a dozen years after Cortés's arrival in 1519, this drawing by an Aztec artist pictures the Indians rendering tribute to their conquerors. The inclusion of the banner showing Madonna and child also illustrates the early incorporation of Christian beliefs by the Indians.

conquistadores had extinguished the great Aztec and Incan empires and claimed for church and crown a territory that extended from Colorado to Argentina, including much of what is now the continental United States.

The military conquest of this vast region was achieved by just ten thousand men, organized in a series of private expeditions. Hernán Cortés, Francisco Pizarro, and other aspiring conquerors signed contracts with the Spanish monarch, raised money from investors, and then went about recruiting an army. Only a small minority of the *conquistadores*—leaders or followers—were nobles. About half were professional soldiers and sailors; the rest comprised peasants, artisans, and members of the middling classes. Most were in their twenties and early thirties, and all knew how to wield a sword.

Diverse motives spurred these motley adventurers. Some hoped to win royal titles and favors by bringing new peoples under the Spanish flag. Others sought to assure God's favor by spreading Christianity to the pagans. Some men hoped to escape dubious pasts, and others sought the kind of historical adventure experienced by heroes of classical antiquity. Nearly all shared a lust for gold. As one of Cortés's foot soldiers put it, "We came here to serve God and the king, and also to get rich."

Armed with horses and gunpowder and preceded by disease, the *conquistadores* quickly overpowered the Indians. But most never achieved their dreams of glory. Few received titles of nobility, and many of the rank and file remained permanently indebted to the absentee investors who paid for their equipment. Even when an expedition captured exceptionally rich booty, the spoils were unevenly divided: men from the commander's home region often received more, and men on horseback generally got two shares to the infantryman's one. The *conquistadores* lost still more power as the crown gradually tightened its control in the New World. By the 1530s in Mexico and the 1550s in Peru, colorless colonial administrators had replaced the freebooting *conquistadores*.

Nevertheless, the *conquistadores* achieved a kind of immortality. Because of a scarcity of Spanish women in the early days of the conquest, many *conquistadores* married Indian women. The soldiers who conquered Paraguay received three native women each, and Cortés's soldiers in Mexico—who were forbidden to consort with pagan women—quickly had their lovers baptized into the Catholic faith. Their offspring, the "new race" of *mestizos,* formed a cultural and biological bridge between Latin America's European and Indian races.

into the foaming waves off Panama in 1513 and boldly claimed for his king all the lands washed by that sea! Ferdinand Magellan started from Spain in 1519 with five tiny ships. After beating through the storm-lashed strait off the tip of South America that still bears his name, he was slain by the inhabitants of the Philippines. His one remaining vessel creaked home in 1522, completing the first circumnavigation of the globe.

Other ambitious Spaniards ventured into North America. In 1513 and 1521, Juan Ponce de León explored Florida, which he at first thought was an island. Seeking gold—and probably not the mythical "fountain of youth"—he instead met with death by an Indian arrow. In 1540–1542 Francisco Coronado, in quest of fabled golden cities that turned out to be adobe pueblos, wandered with a clanking cavalcade through Arizona and New Mexico, penetrating as far east as Kansas. En route his expedition discovered two awesome natural wonders: the Grand Canyon of the Colorado River and enormous herds of buffalo (bison). Hernando de Soto, with six hundred armor-plated men, undertook a fantastic gold-seeking expedition during 1539–1542. Floundering through marshes and pine barrens, from Florida westward, he discovered and crossed the majestic Mississippi River just north of its junction with the Arkansas River. After brutally mistreating the Indians with iron collars and fierce dogs, he at length died of fever and wounds. His troops secretly disposed of his remains at night in the Mississippi,

lest the Indians exhume and abuse their abuser's corpse.

Meanwhile in South America, the ironfisted conqueror Francisco Pizarro crushed the Incas of Peru in 1532 and added a huge hoard of booty to Spanish coffers. By 1600 Spain was swimming in New World silver, mostly from the fabulously rich mines at Potosí in present-day Bolivia, as well as from Mexico. This flood of precious metal touched off a price revolution in Europe that increased consumer costs by as much as 500 percent in the hundred years after the mid–sixteenth century. Some scholars see in this ballooning European money supply the fuel that fed the growth of the economic system known as capitalism. Certainly, New World bullion helped transform the world economy. It swelled the vaults of bankers from Spain to Italy, laying the foundations of the modern commercial banking system. It clinked in the purses of merchants in France and Holland, stimulating the spread of commerce and manufacturing. And it paid for much of the burgeoning international trade with Asia, whose sellers had little use for any European good except silver.

The islands of the Caribbean Sea—the West Indies as they came to be called, in yet another perpetuation of Columbus's geographic confusion—served as offshore bases for the staging of the Spanish invasion of the mainland Americas. Here supplies could be stored, and men and horses could be rested and acclimated, before proceeding to the

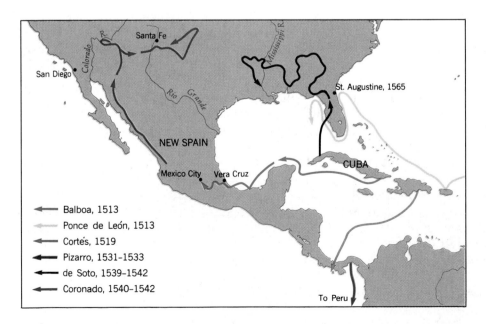

Legend:
- Balboa, 1513
- Ponce de León, 1513
- Cortés, 1519
- Pizarro, 1531–1533
- de Soto, 1539–1542
- Coronado, 1540–1542

Principal Early Spanish Explorations and Conquests Note that Coronado traversed northern Texas and Oklahoma. In present-day eastern Kansas he found, instead of the great golden city he sought, a drab encampment, probably of Witchita Indians.

conquest of the continents. The loosely organized and vulnerable native communities of the West Indies also provided laboratories for testing the techniques that would eventually subdue the advanced Indian civilizations of Mexico and Peru. The most important such technique was the institution known as the *encomienda*. It allowed the government to "commend," or give, Indians to certain colonists in return for the promise to try to Christianize them. In all but name, it was slavery. Spanish missionary Bartolomé de Las Casas, appalled by the *encomienda* system in Hispaniola, called it "a moral pestilence invented by Satan."

The Conquest of Mexico

In 1519 Hernán Cortés set sail from Cuba with sixteen fresh horses and several hundred men aboard eleven ships, bound for Mexico and for destiny. On the island of Cozumel off the Yucatan peninsula, he rescued a Spanish castaway who had been enslaved for several years by the Mayan-speaking Indians. A short distance farther on, he picked up the female Indian slave Malinche, who knew both Mayan and Nahuatl, the language of the powerful Aztec rulers of the great empire in the highlands of central Mexico. In addition to his superior firepower, Cortés now had the advantage, through these two interpreters, of understanding the speech of the native peoples whom he was about to encounter, including the Aztecs. Malinche eventually learned Spanish and was baptized with the Spanish name of Doña Marina.

Near present-day Vera Cruz, Cortés made his final landfall. Through his interpreters he learned of unrest within the Aztec empire among the peoples from whom the Aztecs demanded tribute. He also heard alluring tales of the gold and other wealth stored up in the legendary Aztec capital of Tenochtitlán. He lusted to tear open the coffers of the Aztec kingdom. To quell his mutinous troops, he boldly burned his ships, cutting off any hope of retreat. Gathering a force of some twenty thousand Indian allies, he marched on Tenochtitlán and toward one of history's most dramatic and fateful encounters.

As Cortés proceeded, the Aztec chieftain Montezuma sent ambassadors bearing fabulous gifts to welcome the approaching Spaniards. These only whetted the *conquistador*'s appetite. "We Spanish suffer from a strange disease of the heart," Cortés allegedly informed the emissaries, "for which the only known remedy is gold." The ambassadors reported this comment to Montezuma, along with the astonishing fact that the newcomers rode on the backs of "deer" (horses). The superstitious Montezuma also believed that Cortés was the god Quetzalcoatl, whose return from the eastern sea was predicted in Aztec legends. Expectant yet apprehensive, Montezuma allowed the *conquistadores* to approach his capital unopposed.

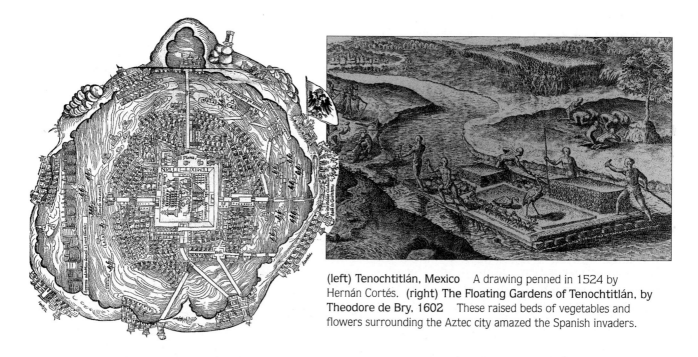

(left) Tenochtitlán, Mexico   A drawing penned in 1524 by Hernán Cortés. (right) The Floating Gardens of Tenochtitlán, by Theodore de Bry, 1602   These raised beds of vegetables and flowers surrounding the Aztec city amazed the Spanish invaders.

Cortés and Malinche, c. 1540 (detail)
Though done by an Indian artist, this drawing identifies Malinche by her Christian name, "Marina." She eventually married one of Cortés's soldiers, with whom she traveled to Spain and was received at the Spanish court.

As the Spaniards entered the Valley of Mexico, the sight of the Aztec capital of Tenochtitlán amazed them. With three hundred thousand inhabitants spread over ten square miles, it rivaled in size and pomp any city in contemporary Europe. The Aztec metropolis rose from an island in the center of a lake, surrounded by floating gardens of extraordinary beauty. It was connected to the mainland by a series of causeways and supplied with fresh water by an artfully designed aqueduct.

Montezuma treated Cortés hospitably at first, but soon the Spaniards' hunger for gold and power exhausted their welcome. "They thirsted mightily for gold; they stuffed themselves with it; they starved for it; they lusted for it like pigs," said one Aztec. On the *noche triste* (sad night) of June 30, 1520, the Aztecs attacked, driving the Spanish down the causeways from Tenochtitlán in a frantic, bloody retreat. Cortés then laid siege to the city, and it capitulated on August 13, 1521. That same year a smallpox epidemic burned through the Valley of Mexico. The combination of conquest and disease took a grisly toll. The Aztec empire gave way to three centuries of Spanish rule. The temples of Tenochtitlán were destroyed to make way for the Christian cathedrals of Mexico City, built on the site of the ruined Indian capital. And the native population of Mexico, winnowed mercilessly by the invader's dis-

eases, shrank from more than 20 million to 2 million people in less than a century.

Yet the invader brought more than conquest and death. He brought his crops and his animals, his language and his laws, his customs and his religion, all of which proved adaptable to the peoples of Mexico. He intermarried with the surviving Indians, creating a distinctive culture of *mestizos*, people of mixed Indian and European heritage. To this day Mexican civilization remains a unique blend of the Old World and the New, producing both ambivalence and pride among people of Mexican heritage. Cortés's translator Malinche, for example, has given her name to the Mexican language in the word *malinchista*, or "traitor." But Mexicans also celebrate Columbus Day as the *Dia de la Raza*—the birthday of a wholly new race of people.

The Spread of Spanish America

Spain's colonial empire grew swiftly and impressively. Within about half a century of Columbus's landfall, hundreds of Spanish cities and towns flourished in the Americas, especially in the great silver-producing centers of Peru and Mexico. Some 160,000 Spaniards, mostly men, had subjugated millions of Indians. Majestic cathedrals dotted the land, printing presses turned out books, and scholars studied at distinguished universities including those at Mexico City and Lima, Peru, both founded in 1551, eighty-five years before Harvard, the first college established in the English colonies.

But how secure were these imperial possessions? Other powers were already sniffing around the edges of the Spanish domain, eager to bite off their share of the promised wealth of the new lands. The upstart English sent Giovanni Caboto (known in English as John Cabot) to explore the northeastern coast of North America in 1497 and 1498. The French king dispatched another Italian mariner, Giovanni da Verrazano, to probe the eastern seaboard in 1524. Ten years later the Frenchman Jacques Cartier journeyed hundreds of miles up the St. Lawrence River.

To secure the northern periphery of their New World domain against such encroachments and to convert more Indian souls to Christianity, the Spanish began to fortify and settle their North American borderlands. In a move to block French ambitions

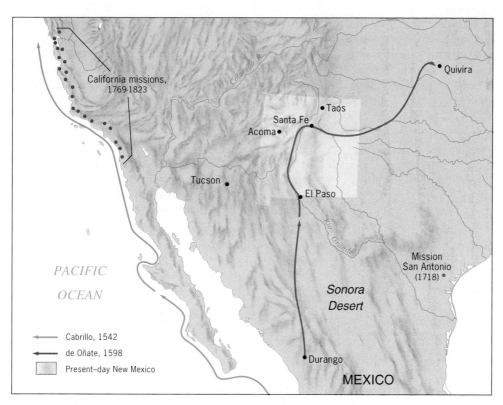

Spain's North American Frontier, 1542–1823

and to protect the sea lanes to the Caribbean, the Spanish erected a fortress at St. Augustine, Florida, in 1565, thus founding the oldest continually inhabited European settlement in the future United States.

In Mexico the tales of Coronado's expedition of the 1540s to the upper Rio Grande and Colorado River regions continued to beckon the *conquistadores'* interest northward. A dust-begrimed expeditionary column, with eighty-three rumbling wagons and hundreds of grumbling men, traversed the bare Sonora Desert from Mexico into the Rio Grande Valley in 1598. Led by Don Juan de Oñate, the Spaniards cruelly abused the Pueblo peoples they encountered. In the battle of Acoma in 1599, the Spanish severed one foot of each survivor. They proclaimed the area to be the province of New Mexico in 1609 and founded its capital at Santa Fe the following year.

The Spanish settlers in New Mexico found a few furs and precious little gold, but they did discover a wealth of souls to be harvested for the Christian religion. The Roman Catholic mission became the central institution in colonial New Mexico until the missionaries' efforts to suppress native religious customs provoked an Indian uprising called Popé's Rebellion in 1680. The Pueblo rebels destroyed every Catholic church in the province and killed a score of priests and hundreds of Spanish settlers. In a reversal of Cortés's treatment of the Aztec temples more than a century earlier, the Indians rebuilt a *kiva*, or ceremonial religious chamber, on the ruins of the Spanish plaza at Santa Fe. It took nearly half a century for the Spanish fully to reclaim New Mexico from the insurrectionary Indians.

Meanwhile, as a further hedge against the ever-threatening French, who had sent an expedition under Robert de La Salle down the Mississippi River in the 1680s, the Spanish began around 1716 to establish settlements in Texas. Some refugees from the Pueblo uprising trickled into Texas, and a few missions were established there, including the one at San Antonio later known as the Alamo. But for at least another century, the Spanish presence remained weak in this distant northeastern outpost of Spain's Mexican empire.

To the west, in California, no serious foreign threat loomed, and Spain directed its attention there only belatedly. Juan Rodriguez Cabrillo had explored the California coast in 1542, but he failed to find San Francisco Bay or anything else of much interest. For some two centuries thereafter, California slumbered undisturbed by European intruders. Then in 1769 Spanish missionaries led by Father Junipero Serra founded at San Diego the first of a chain of twenty-one missions that wound up the coast as far as Sonoma, north of San Francisco Bay. Father Serra's brown-robed Franciscan friars toiled with zealous devotion to Christianize the three hundred thousand native Californians. They gathered the seminomadic Indians into fortified missions and taught them horticulture and basic crafts. These "mission Indians" did adopt Christianity, but they also lost contact with their native cultures and often lost their lives as well, as the white man's diseases doomed these biologically vulnerable peoples.

The misdeeds of the Spanish in the New World obscured their substantial achievements and helped give birth to the "Black Legend." This false concept held that the conquerors merely tortured and butchered the Indians ("killing for Christ"), stole their gold, infected them with smallpox, and left little but misery behind. The Spanish invaders did indeed kill, enslave, and infect countless natives, but they also erected a colossal empire, sprawling from California and Florida to Tierra del Fuego. They grafted their culture, laws, religion, and language onto a wide array of native societies, laying the foundations for a score of Spanish-speaking nations.

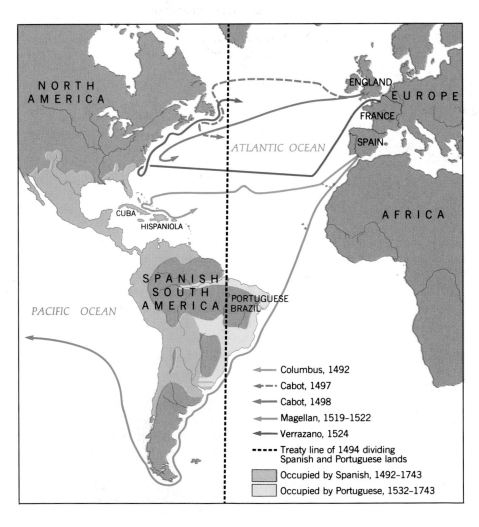

Principal Voyages of Discovery Spain, Portugal, France, and England reaped the greatest advantages from the New World, but much of the earliest exploration was done by Italians, notably Christopher Columbus of Genoa. John Cabot, another native of Genoa (his original name was Giovanni Caboto), sailed for England's King Henry VII. Giovanni da Verrazano was a Florentine employed by France.

Columbus, 1492
Cabot, 1497
Cabot, 1498
Magellan, 1519–1522
Verrazano, 1524
Treaty line of 1494 dividing Spanish and Portuguese lands
Occupied by Spanish, 1492–1743
Occupied by Portuguese, 1532–1743

Clearly, the Spaniards, who had more than a century's head start over the English, were genuine empire builders and cultural innovators in the New World. As compared with their Anglo-Saxon rivals, their colonial establishment was larger and richer, and it endured more than a quarter of a century longer. And in the last analysis, the Spanish paid the Native Americans the high compliment of fusing with them through marriage and incorporating indigenous culture into their own, rather than shunning and eventually isolating the Indians as their English adversaries would do.

Chronology

c. 33,000-8000 B.C.	First humans cross into Americas from Asia
c. 5000 B.C.	Corn is developed as a staple crop in highland Mexico
c. 4000 B.C.	First civilized societies develop in the Middle East
c. 1200 B.C.	Corn planting reaches present-day American Southwest
c. A.D. 1000	Norse voyagers discover and briefly settle in northeastern North America Corn cultivation reaches Midwest and southeastern Atlantic seaboard
c. A.D. 1100	Height of Mississippian settlement at Cahokia
c. A.D. 1100-1300	Christian crusades arouse European interest in the East
1295	Marco Polo returns to Europe
late 1400s	Spain becomes united
1488	Díaz rounds southern tip of Africa
1492	Columbus lands in the Bahamas
1494	Treaty of Tordesillas between Spain and Portugal
1498	da Gama reaches India Cabot explores northeastern coast of North America for England
1513	Balboa claims all lands touched by the Pacific Ocean for Spain
1513, 1521	Ponce de León explores Florida
1519-1521	Cortés conquers Mexico for Spain
1522	Magellan's vessel completes circumnavigation of the world
1524	Verrazano explores eastern seaboard of North America for France
1532	Pizarro crushes Incas
1534	Cartier journeys up the St. Lawrence River
1539-1542	de Soto explores the Southeast and discovers the Mississippi River
1540-1542	Coronado explores present-day Southwest
1542	Cabrillo explores California coast for Spain
1565	Spanish build fortress at St. Augustine
late 1500s	Iroquois Confederacy founded, according to Iroquois legend
c. 1598-1609	Spanish under Oñate conquer Pueblo peoples of Rio Grande Valley
1609	Spanish found New Mexico
1680	Popé's rebellion in New Mexico
1680s	French expedition down Mississippi River under La Salle
1769	Serra founds first California mission, at San Diego

SUGGESTED READINGS

PRIMARY SOURCE DOCUMENTS

Hernán Cortés's *Letters from Mexico** have been translated into English by A. R. Pagden (1971). Bartolomé de Las Casas, *Thirty Very Judicial Propositions** (1552), and Juan Ginés de Sepúlveda, *The Second Democrates** (1547), reflect the Spanish *conquistadores'* efforts to understand the native peoples of the New World. See also Las Casas's *The Destruction of the Indies* (1542). *The Broken Spears: The Aztec Account of the Conquest of Mexico,** edited by Miguel León-Portilla (1962), is an anthology of texts compiled from indigenous sources. Olaudah Equiano, *Equiano's Travels** (1789), is a fascinating account by an African in the New World in the eighteenth century.

SECONDARY SOURCES

Brian M. Fagan reviews the sketchy evidence concerning the earliest humans to arrive in the Americas in *The Great Journey: The Peopling of Ancient America* (1987). For more on the pre-Columbian history of the Americas, see Norman Hammond, *Ancient Maya Civilization* (1982); Brian M. Fagan, *Kingdoms of Gold, Kingdoms of Jade: The Americas Before Columbus* (1991); and Stuart J. Fiedel, *Prehistory of the Americas* (1992). Immanuel Wallerstein, *The Modern World System: Capitalist Agriculture and the Origins of the European World in the Sixteenth Century* (1974), provides a theoretical overview of the international economic background to European colonization. Early African history is sketched in J. D. Fage, *A History of West Africa* (1969). Philip D. Curtin discusses *The Atlantic Slave Trade* (1969). See also John Thornton, *Africa and Africans in the Making of the Atlantic World, 1400–1680* (1992). Samuel E. Morison has written several masterful accounts of the discoveries; among the best are *Admiral of the Ocean Sea* (2 vols.,

1942; condensed as *Christopher Columbus, Mariner,* 1956), *The European Discovery of America: The Northern Voyages, A.D. 500–1600* (1971), and *The European Discovery of America: The Southern Voyages, A.D. 1492–1616* (1974). A fascinating brief synthesis of early European contact with the Americas is J. H. Elliott, *The Old World and the New, 1492–1650* (1970). Alfred Crosby discusses *The Columbian Exchange: Biological and Cultural Consequences of 1492* (1972). See also Alfred W. Crosby, Jr., *Ecological Imperialism: The Biological Expansion of Europe, 900–1900* (1986). A marvelously illustrated volume portraying the impact of America on the European imagination is Hugh Honour, *The New Golden Land* (1975). See also Kirkpatrick Sale, *The Conquest of Paradise: Christopher Columbus and the Columbian Legacy* (1990), Stephen Greenblatt, *Marvelous Possessions: The Wonder of the New World* (1991), and Herman J. Viola and Carolyn Margolis, *Seeds of Change: Five Hundred Years Since Columbus* (1991). D. W. Meinig presents a geographical overview of immigration in *The Shaping of America: A Geographical Perspective on 500 Years of History. Atlantic America, 1492–1800* (1986). Patricia Seed compares different forms of European conquest in *Ceremonies of Possession* (1995). Various aspects of the Spanish and Portuguese conquests of America are described in James Lockhart and Stuart B. Schwartz, *Early Latin America* (1983); Charles Gibson, *Spain in America* (1966); and L. McAlister, *Spain and Portugal in the New World, 1492–1700* (1984). William H. Prescott, *History of the Conquest of Mexico* (1843) and *History of the Conquest of Peru* (1847), are two of the greatest narrative histories of the nineteenth century. Nathan Wachtel presents the Indians' view of the Spanish conquest in *The Vision of the Vanquished* (1977). The spread of Spanish America northward is traced in Edward H. Spicer, *Cycles of Conquest: The Impact of Spain, Mexico and the United States on the Indians of the Southwest, 1533–1960* (1962); Elizabeth A. H. John, *Storms Brewed in Other Men's Worlds: The Confrontation of Indians, Spanish, and French in the Southwest, 1540–1795* (1975); Ramon A. Gutierrez, *When Jesus Came, the Corn Mothers Went Away* (1991); and David J. Weber's masterful synthesis, *The Spanish Frontier in North America* (1992).

---

*An asterisk indicates that the document, or an excerpt from it, can be found in Thomas A. Bailey and David M. Kennedy, eds., *The American Spirit: United States History as Seen by Contemporaries,* 9th ed. (Boston: Houghton Mifflin, 1998).

2

The Planting of English America
1500–1733

. . . For I shall yet to see it [Virginia] an Inglishe nation.

SIR WALTER RALEIGH, 1602

England's Imperial Stirrings

As the seventeenth century dawned, scarcely a century after Columbus's momentous landfall, the human face of much of the New World had already been profoundly transformed. Native American peoples had been nearly extinguished, mostly from disease. From Tierra del Fuego in the south to Hudson's Bay in the north, only about 10 percent of the Indian population of 1492 survived. Several hundred thousand African slaves toiled on Caribbean and Brazilian sugar plantations. From Florida and New Mexico southward, most of the southern half of the New World lay firmly within the grip of imperial Spain.

But *North* America in 1600 remained largely unexplored and effectively unclaimed by Europeans. As if to herald the coming century of colonization and conflict in the northern continent, three European powers planted three primitive outposts in three distant corners of the continent within three years of one another: the Spanish at Santa Fe in 1610, the French at Quebec in 1608, and, most consequentially for the future United States, the English at Jamestown, Virginia, in 1607.

Feeble indeed were England's efforts in the 1500s to compete with the sprawling Spanish Empire. As Spain's ally in the first half of the century, England took little interest in establishing its own overseas colonies. Religious conflict, moreover, disrupted England in midcentury, after King Henry VIII broke with the Roman Catholic church in the 1530s, launching the English Protestant Reformation. Catholics battled Protestants for decades, and the religious balance of power seesawed. But after the Protestant Elizabeth ascended to the English throne in 1558, Protestantism became dominant in England, and rivalry with Catholic Spain intensified.

Ireland, which nominally had been under English rule since the twelfth century, became an early scene of that rivalry. The Catholic Irish sought help from Catholic Spain to throw off the yoke of the new Protestant English queen. But Spanish aid never amounted to much; in the 1570s and 1580s, Elizabeth's troops crushed the Irish uprising with terrible ferocity, inflicting unspeakable atrocities upon the native Irish people. The English crown confiscated Catholic Irish lands and "planted" them with new Protestant landlords from Scotland and England. This policy also planted the seeds of the centuries-old religious conflicts that persist in Ireland to the present day. Many English soldiers developed in Ireland a sneering contempt for the "savage" natives, an attitude that they brought with them to the New World.

Elizabeth Energizes England

Encouraged by the ambitious Queen Elizabeth, hardy English buccaneers now swarmed out upon the shipping lanes. They sought to promote the twin goals of Protestantism and plunder by seizing Spanish treasure ships and raiding Spanish settlements, even though England and Spain were technically at peace. The most famous of these semipiratical "sea dogs" was the courtly Francis Drake. He plundered his way around the planet, returning in 1580 with his ship heavily ballasted with Spanish booty. The venture netted profits of about 4,600 percent to his financial backers, among whom, in secret, was Queen Elizabeth. Defying Spanish protest, she brazenly knighted Drake on the deck of his barnacled ship.

The bleak coast of Newfoundland was the scene of the first English attempt at colonization. This effort collapsed when its promoter, Sir Humphrey Gilbert, lost his life at sea in 1583. Gilbert's ill-starred dream inspired his gallant half brother Sir Walter Raleigh to try again in warmer climes. Raleigh organized a group of settlers who landed in 1585 on North Carolina's Roanoke Island, off the coast of Virginia—a vaguely defined region named by the "Virgin Queen" Elizabeth in honor of herself. With Raleigh busy at home, the hapless Roanoke colony mysteriously vanished, swallowed up by the wilderness.

These pathetic English failures at colonization contrasted embarrassingly with the glories of the Spanish Empire, whose profits were fabulously enriching Spain. Philip II of Spain, self-anointed foe of the Protestant Reformation, used part of his

Sir Walter Raleigh (c. 1552–1618)
Here he is shown "drinking tobacco," as smoking was first called. He is credited with introducing both tobacco and the potato into England. A dashing courtier, he launched important colonizing failures in the New World. After seducing (and marrying) one of Queen Elizabeth's maids of honor, he fell out of favor and was ultimately beheaded for treason.

imperial gains to amass an "Invincible Armada" of ships for an invasion of England. The showdown came in 1588, when the lumbering Spanish flotilla, 130 strong, hove into the English Channel. The English sea dogs fought back. Using craft that were swifter, more maneuverable, and more ably manned, they inflicted heavy damage on the cumbersome, overladen Spanish ships. Then a devastating storm arose (the "Protestant wind"), scattering the crippled Spanish fleet.

The rout of the Spanish Armada marked the beginning of the end of Spanish imperial dreams, though Spain's New World empire would not fully collapse for three more centuries. Within a few decades, the Spanish Netherlands (Holland) would secure their independence, and much of the Spanish Caribbean would slip from Spain's grasp. Bloated by Peruvian and Mexican silver and cockily convinced of its own invincibility, Spain had overreached itself, sowing the seeds of its own decline.

England's victory over the Spanish Armada also marked a red-letter day in American history. It dampened Spain's fighting spirit and helped ensure England's naval dominance in the North Atlantic. It

exhilarating atmosphere, with Shakespeare, at its forefront, making occasional poetical references to England's American colonies. The English were seized with restlessness, with thirst for adventure, and with curiosity about the unknown. Everywhere there blossomed a new spirit of self-confidence, of vibrant patriotism, and of boundless faith in the future of the English nation. When England and Spain finally signed a treaty of peace in 1604, the English people were poised to plunge headlong into the planting of their own colonial empire in the New World.

England on the Eve of Empire

England's scepter'd isle, as Shakespeare called it, throbbed with social and economic change as the seventeenth century opened. Its population was mushrooming, from some 3 million people in 1550 to about 4 million in 1600. In the ever-green English countryside, landlords were "enclosing" croplands for sheep grazing, forcing many small farmers into precarious tenancy or off the land altogether. It was no accident that the woolen districts of eastern and western England—where Puritanism had taken

Elizabeth I (1533–1603), by Marcus Gheeraets the Younger, c. 1592   Although accused of being vain, fickle, prejudiced, and miserly, she proved to be an unusually successful ruler. She never married (hence, the "Virgin Queen"), although various royal matches were projected.

started England on its way to becoming master of the world oceans—a fact of enormous importance to the American people. Indeed England now had many of the characteristics that Spain displayed on the eve of its colonizing adventure a century earlier: a strong, unified national state under a popular monarch; a measure of religious unity after a protracted struggle between Protestants and Catholics; and a vibrant sense of nationalism and national destiny.

A wondrous flowering of the English national spirit bloomed in the wake of the Spanish Armada's defeat. A golden age of literature dawned in this

In the years immediately following the defeat of the Spanish Armada, the English writer Richard Hakluyt (1552?–1616) extravagantly exhorted his countrymen to cast off their "sluggish security" and undertake the colonization of the New World:

"There is under our noses the great and ample country of Virginia; the inland whereof is found of late to be so sweet and wholesome a climate, so rich and abundant in silver mines, a better and richer country than Mexico itself. If it shall please the Almighty to stir up Her Majesty's heart to continue with transporting one or two thousand of her people, she shall by God's assistance, in short space, increase her dominions, enrich her coffers, and reduce many pagans to the faith of Christ."

Main Sources of the Puritan "Great Migration" to New England, 1620–1650

strong root—supplied many of the earliest immigrants to America. When economic depression hit the woolen trade in the late 1500s, thousands of footloose farmers took to the roads. They drifted about England, chronically unemployed, often ending up as beggars and paupers in cities like Bristol and London.

This remarkably mobile population alarmed many contemporaries. They concluded that England was burdened with a "surplus population," though present-day London holds twice as many people as did all of England in 1600.

At the same time, laws of primogeniture decreed that only eldest sons were eligible to inherit landed estates. Landholders' ambitious younger sons, among them Gilbert, Raleigh, and Drake, were forced to seek their fortunes elsewhere. Bad luck plagued their early, lone-wolf enterprises. But by the early 1600s the joint-stock company, forerunner of the modern corporation, was perfected. It enabled a considerable number of investors, called "adventurers," to pool their capital.

Peace with a chastened Spain provided the opportunity for English colonization. Population growth provided the workers. Unemployment, as well as a thirst for adventure, for markets, and for religious freedom, provided the motives. Joint-stock companies provided the financial means. The stage was now set for a historic effort to establish an English beachhead in the still uncharted North American wilderness.

England Plants the Jamestown Seedling

In 1606, two years after peace with Spain, the hand of destiny beckoned toward Virginia. A joint-stock company, known as the Virginia Company of London, received a charter from King James I of England for a settlement in the New World. The main attraction was the promise of gold, combined with a strong desire to find a passage through America to the Indies. Like most joint-stock companies of the day, the Virginia Company was intended to endure for only a few years, after which its stockholders hoped to liquidate it for a profit. This arrangement put severe pressure on the luckless colonists, who were threatened with abandonment in the wilderness if they did not quickly strike it rich on the company's behalf. Few of the investors thought in terms of long-term colonization. Apparently no one even faintly suspected that the seeds of a mighty nation were being planted.

The charter of the Virginia Company is a significant document in American history. It guaranteed to the overseas settlers the same rights of Englishmen that they would have enjoyed if they had

King James I (1566–1625) had scant enthusiasm for the Virginia experiment, partly because of his hatred of tobacco smoking, which had been introduced into the Old World by the Spanish discoverers. In 1604 he published the pamphlet A Counterblast to Tobacco:

"A custom loathsome to the eye, hateful to the nose, harmful to the brain, dangerous to the lungs, and in the black stinking fume thereof, nearest resembling the horrible Stygian smoke of the pit [Hades] that is bottomless."

The Tudor Rulers of England*

Name, Reign	Relation to America
Henry VII, 1485–1509	Cabot voyages, 1497, 1498
Henry VIII, 1509–1547	English Reformation began
Edward VI, 1547–1553	Strong Protestant tendencies
"Bloody" Mary, 1553–1558	Catholic reaction
Elizabeth I, 1558–1603	Break with Roman Catholic Church final; Drake; Spanish Armada defeated

*See p. 52 for a continuation of the table.

stayed at home. This precious boon was gradually extended to the other English colonies and became a foundation stone of American liberties.

Setting sail in late 1606, the Virginia Company's three ships landed near the mouth of Chesapeake Bay, where Indians attacked them. Pushing on up the bay, the tiny band of colonists eventually chose a location on the wooded and malarial banks of the James River, named in honor of King James I. The site was easy to defend, but it was mosquito-infested and devastatingly unhealthful. There, on May 24, 1607, about a hundred English settlers, all of them men, disembarked. They called the place Jamestown.

The early years of Jamestown proved a nightmare for all concerned—except the buzzards. Forty would-be colonists perished during the initial voyage in 1606–1607. Another expedition in 1609 lost its leaders and many of its precious supplies in a shipwreck off Bermuda. Once ashore in Virginia, the settlers died by the dozens from disease, malnutrition, and starvation. Ironically, the woods rustled with game and the rivers flopped with fish, but the greenhorn settlers, many of them self-styled "gentlemen" unaccustomed to fending for themselves, wasted valuable time grubbing for nonexistent gold when they should have been gathering provisions.

Virginia was saved from utter collapse at the start largely by the leadership and resourcefulness of an intrepid young adventurer, Captain John Smith. Taking over in 1608, he whipped the gold-hungry colonists into line with the rule, "He who shall not work shall not eat." He had been kidnapped in December 1607 and subjected to a mock execution by the Indian chieftain Powhatan, whose daughter Pocahontas had "saved" Smith by dramatically interposing her head between his and the war clubs of his captors. The symbolism of this ritual was apparently intended to impress Smith with Powhatan's power and with the Indians' desire for peaceful relations with the Virginians. Pocahontas became an intermediary between the Indians and the settlers, helping to preserve a shaky peace and to provide needed foodstuffs.

Pocahontas (c. 1595–1617)
Taken to England by her husband, she was received as a princess. She died when preparing to return, and her infant son ultimately reached Virginia, where hundreds of his descendants have lived, including the second Mrs. Woodrow Wilson.

Ætatis suæ 21. A°. 1616.

Matoaka als Rebecka daughter to the mighty Prince Powhatan, Emperour of Attanoughkomouck als Virginia converted and baptized in the Christian faith, and Wife to the worth Mr. Tho: Rolff.

> *The authorities meted out harsh discipline in the young Virginia colony. One Jamestown settler who publicly criticized the governor was sentenced to*
>
> "be disarmed [and] have his arms broken and his tongue bored through with an awl [and] shall pass through a guard of 40 men and shall be butted [with muskets] by every one of them and at the head of the troop kicked down and footed out of the fort."

Still, the colonists died in droves, and living skeletons were driven to desperate acts. They were reduced to eating "dogges, Catts, Ratts, and Myce" and even to digging up corpses for food. One hungry man killed, salted, and ate his wife, for which misbehavior he was executed. Of the four hundred settlers who managed to make it to Virginia by 1609, only sixty survived the "starving time" winter of 1609–1610.

Diseased and despairing, the colonists dragged themselves aboard homeward-bound ships in the spring of 1610, only to be met at the mouth of the James River by a long-awaited relief party headed by a new governor, Lord De La Warr. He ordered the settlers back to Jamestown, imposed a harsh military regime on the colony, and soon undertook aggressive military action against the Indians.

Disease continued to reap a gruesome harvest among the Virginians. By 1625 Virginia contained only some twelve hundred hard-bitten survivors of the nearly 8,000 adventurers who had tried to start life anew in the ill-fated colony.

Cultural Clash in the Chesapeake

When the English landed in 1607, the chieftain Powhatan dominated the native peoples living in the James River area. He had asserted supremacy over a few dozen small tribes, loosely affiliated in what somewhat grandly came to be called Powhatan's Confederacy. The English colonists dubbed all the local Indians, somewhat inaccurately, the Powhatans. Powhatan at first may have considered the English potential allies in his struggle to extend his power still further over his Indian rivals, and he tried to be con-

A Carolina Indian Woman and Child, by John White The artist was a member of the Raleigh expedition of 1585. Notice that the Indian girl carries a European doll, illustrating the mingling of cultures that had already begun.

ciliatory. But relations between the Indians and the English remained tense, especially as the starving colonists took to raiding Indian food supplies.

The atmosphere grew even more strained after Lord De La Warr arrived in 1610. He carried orders from the Virginia Company that amounted to a declaration of war against the Indians in the Jamestown region. A veteran of the vicious campaigns against the Irish, De La Warr now introduced "Irish tactics" against the Indians. His troops raided Indian villages, burned houses, confiscated provisions, and torched cornfields. A peace settlement ended this First Anglo-Powhatan War in 1614, sealed by the marriage of Pocahontas to the colonist John Rolfe— the first known interracial union in Virginia.

A fragile respite followed, which endured eight years. But the Indians, pressed by the land-hungry whites and ravaged by European diseases, struck back in 1622. A series of Indian attacks left 347 settlers dead, including John Rolfe. In response the Virginia Company issued new orders calling for "a perpetual war without peace or truce," one that would prevent the Indians "from being any longer a people." Periodic punitive raids systematically reduced the native population and drove the survivors ever farther westward.

In the Second Anglo-Powhatan War in 1644, the Indians made one last effort to dislodge the Virginians. They were again defeated. The peace treaty of 1646 repudiated any hope of assimilating the native peoples into Virginian society or of peacefully coexisting with them. Instead it effectively banished the Chesapeake Indians from their ancestral lands and formally separated Indian from white areas of settlement—the origins of the later reservation system. By 1669 an official census revealed that only about two thousand Indians remained in Virginia, perhaps 10 percent of the population the original English settlers had found in 1607. By 1685 the English considered the Powhatan peoples extinct.

It had been the Powhatans' calamitous misfortune to fall victim to three Ds: disease, disorganization, and disposability. Like native peoples throughout the New World, they were extremely susceptible to European-borne maladies. Epidemics of smallpox and measles raced mercilessly through their villages. The Powhatans also—despite the apparent cohesiveness of "Powhatan's Confederacy"—lacked the unity with which to make effective opposition to the comparatively well-organized and militarily disciplined whites. Finally, unlike the Indians whom the Spaniards had encountered to the south, who could be put to work in the mines and had gold and silver to trade, the Powhatans served no economic function for the Virginia colonists. They provided no reliable labor source and, after the Virginians began growing their own food crops, had no valuable commodities to offer in commerce. The natives therefore could be disposed of without harm to the colonial economy. Indeed the Indian presence frustrated the colonists' desire for a local commodity the Europeans desperately wanted: land.

Virginia: Child of Tobacco

John Rolfe, the husband of Pocahontas, became father of the tobacco industry and an economic savior of the Virginia colony. By 1612 he had perfected methods of raising and curing the pungent weed, eliminating much of the bitter tang. Soon the European demand for tobacco was nearly insatiable. A tobacco rush swept over Virginia, as crops were planted in the streets of Jamestown and even between the numerous graves. So exclusively did the colonists concentrate on planting the yellow leaf that at first they had to import some of their foodstuffs. Colonists who had once hungered for food now hungered for land, ever more land on which to plant ever more tobacco. Relentlessly, they pressed the frontier of settlement up the river valleys to the west, abrasively edging against the Indians.

Virginia's prosperity was finally built on tobacco smoke. This "bewitching weed" played a vital role in putting the colony on firm economic foundations. But tobacco—King Nicotine—was something of a tyrant. It was ruinous to the soil when greedily planted in successive years, and it enchained the fortunes of Virginia to the fluctuating price of a single crop. Fatefully, tobacco also promoted the broad-acred plantation system and with it a brisk demand for fresh labor.

In 1619, the year before the Plymouth Pilgrims landed in New England, what was described as a Dutch warship appeared off Jamestown and sold

---

Benjamin Franklin (1706–1790) in a 1753 letter to Peter Collinson commented on the attractiveness of Indian life to Europeans:

"When an Indian child has been brought up among us, taught our language and habituated to our customs, yet if he goes to see his relations and make one Indian ramble with them, there is no persuading him ever to return. [But] when white persons of either sex have been taken prisoners by the Indians, and lived awhile among them, though ransomed by their friends, and treated with all imaginable tenderness to prevail with them to stay among the English, yet in a short time they become disgusted with our manner of life, and the care and pains that are necessary to support it, and take the first good opportunity of escaping again into the woods, from whence there is no reclaiming them."

some twenty Africans. The scanty record does not reveal whether they were purchased as lifelong slaves or as servants committed to limited years of servitude. However it transpired, this simple commercial transaction planted the seeds of the North American slave system. Yet blacks were too costly for most of the hard-pinched white colonists to acquire, and for decades few were brought to Virginia. In 1650 Virginia counted but three hundred blacks, although by the end of the century blacks, most of them enslaved, made up approximately 14 percent of the colony's population.

Representative self-government was also born in primitive Virginia, in the same cradle with slavery and in the same year—1619. The London Company authorized the settlers to summon an assembly,

Advertisement of a Voyage to America, 1609

known as the House of Burgesses. A momentous precedent was thus feebly established, for this assemblage was the first of many miniature parliaments to sprout from the soil of America.

As time passed, James I grew increasingly hostile to Virginia. He detested tobacco and he distrusted the representative House of Burgesses, which he branded a "seminary of sedition." In 1624 he revoked the charter of the bankrupt and beleaguered Virginia Company, thus making Virginia a royal colony directly under his control.

Maryland: Catholic Haven

Maryland—the second plantation colony but the fourth English colony to be planted—was founded in 1634 by Lord Baltimore, of a prominent English Catholic family. He embarked upon the venture partly to reap financial profits and partly to create a refuge for his fellow Catholics. Protestant England was still persecuting Roman Catholics; among numerous discriminations, a couple seeking wedlock could not be legally married by a Catholic priest.

Absentee proprietor Lord Baltimore hoped that the two hundred settlers who founded Maryland at St. Marys, on Chesapeake Bay, would be the vanguard of a vast new feudal domain. Huge estates were to be awarded to his largely Catholic relatives, and gracious manor houses, modeled on those of England's aristocracy, were intended to arise amidst the fertile forests. As in Virginia, colonists proved willing to come only if offered the opportunity to acquire land of their own. Soon they were dispersed around the Chesapeake region on modest farms,

The wife of a Virginia governor wrote to her sister in England in 1623 of her voyage:

"For our Shippe was so pestered with people and goods that we were so full of infection that after a while we saw little but throwing folkes over board: It pleased god to send me my helth till I came to shoare and 3 dayes after I fell sick but I thank god I am well recovered. Few else are left alive that came in that Shippe. . . ."

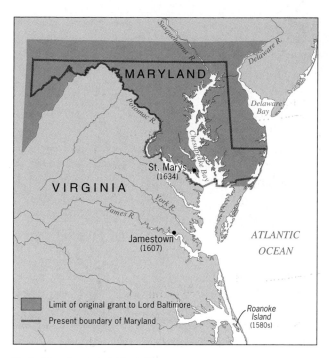

Early Maryland and Virginia

and the haughty land barons, mostly Catholic, were surrounded by resentful backcountry planters, mostly Protestant. Resentment flared into open rebellion near the end of the century, and the Baltimore family for a time lost its proprietary rights.

Despite these tensions Maryland prospered. Like Virginia, it blossomed forth in acres of tobacco. Also like Virginia, it depended for labor in its early years mainly on white indentured servants—penniless persons who bound themselves to work for a number of years to pay their passage. In both colonies it was only in the later years of the seventeenth century that black slaves began to be imported in large numbers.

Lord Baltimore, a canny soul, permitted unusual freedom of worship at the outset. He hoped that he would thus purchase toleration for his own fellow worshipers. But the heavy tide of Protestants threatened to submerge the Catholics and place severe restrictions on them, as in England. Faced with disaster, the Catholics of Maryland threw their support behind the famed Act of Toleration, which was passed in 1649 by the local representative assembly.

Maryland's new religious statute guaranteed toleration to all Christians. But, less liberally, it decreed the death penalty for those, like Jews and atheists, who denied the divinity of Jesus. The law thus sanctioned less toleration than had previously existed in the settlement, but it did extend a temporary cloak of protection to the uneasy Catholic minority. One result was that when the colonial era ended, Maryland probably sheltered more Roman Catholics than any other English-speaking colony in the New World.

The West Indies: Way Station to Mainland America

While the English were planting the first frail colonial shoots in the Chesapeake, they also were busily colonizing the West Indies. Spain, weakened by military overextension and distracted by its rebellious Dutch provinces, relaxed its grip on much of the Caribbean in the early 1600s. By mid–seventeenth century, England had secured its claim to several West Indian islands, including the large prize of Jamaica in 1655.

Sugar formed the foundation of the West Indian economy. What tobacco was to the Chesapeake, sugar cane was to the Caribbean—with one crucial difference. Tobacco was a poor man's crop. It could be planted easily, it produced commercially marketable leaves within a year, and it required only simple processing. Sugar cane, in contrast, was a rich man's crop. It had to be planted extensively to yield commercially viable quantities of sugar. Extensive planting, in turn, required extensive and arduous land clearing. And the cane stalks yielded their sugar only after an elaborate process of refining in a sugar mill. The need for land and for the labor to clear it and to run the mills made sugar cultivation a capital-intense business. Only wealthy growers with abundant capital to invest could succeed in sugar.

The sugar lords extended their dominion over the West Indies in the seventeenth century. To work their sprawling plantations, they imported enormous numbers of African slaves—more than a quarter of a million in the five decades after 1640. By about 1700, black slaves outnumbered white settlers in the English West Indies by nearly four to one, and the region's population has remained predominantly black ever since. West Indians thus take their place among the numerous children of the African diaspora—the vast scattering of African peoples throughout the New World in the three and a half centuries following Columbus's discovery.

To control this large and potentially restive population of slaves, English authorities devised formal

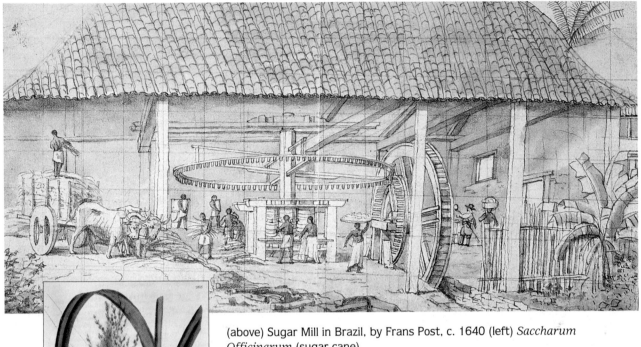

(above) Sugar Mill in Brazil, by Frans Post, c. 1640 (left) *Saccharum Officinarum* (sugar cane)

inspired statutes governing slavery throughout the mainland colonies. Carolina officially adopted a version of the Barbados slave code in 1696. Just as the West Indies had been a testing ground for the *encomienda* system that the Spanish had brought to Mexico and South America, so the Caribbean islands now served as a staging area for the slave system that would take root elsewhere in English North America.

"codes" that defined the slaves' legal status and masters' prerogatives. The notorious Barbados slave code of 1661 denied even the most fundamental rights to slaves and gave masters virtually complete control over their laborers, including the right to inflict vicious punishments for even slight infractions.

The profitable sugar-plantation system soon crowded out almost all other forms of Caribbean agriculture. The West Indies increasingly depended on the North American mainland for foodstuffs and other basic supplies. And smaller English farmers, squeezed out by the greedy sugar barons, began to migrate to the newly founded southern mainland colonies. A group of displaced English settlers from Barbados arrived in Carolina in 1670. They brought with them a few African slaves, as well as the model of the Barbados slave code, which eventually

African slaves destined for the West Indian sugar plantations were bound and branded on West African beaches and ferried out in canoes to the waiting slave ships. An English sailor described the scene:

"The Negroes are so wilful and loth to leave their own country, that have often leap'd out of the canoes, boat and ship, into the sea, and kept under water till they were drowned, to avoid being taken up and saved by our boats, which pursued them; they having a more dreadful apprehension of Barbadoes than we can have of hell."

> *The Barbados slave code (1661) declared,*
>
> "If any Negro or slave whatsoever shall offer any violence to any Christian by striking or the like, such Negro or slave shall for his or her first offence be severely whipped by the Constable. For his second offence of that nature he shall be severely whipped, his nose slit, and be burned in some part of his face with a hot iron. And being brutish slaves, [they] deserve not, for the baseness of their condition, to be tried by the legal trial of twelve men of their peers, as the subjects of England are. And it is further enacted and ordained that if any Negro or other slave under punishment by his master unfortunately shall suffer in life or member, which seldom happens, no person whatsoever shall be liable to any fine therefore."

Colonizing the Carolinas

Civil wars convulsed England in the 1640s. King Charles I had dismissed Parliament in 1629, and when he eventually recalled it in 1640, the members were mutinous. Finding their great champion in the Puritan-soldier Oliver Cromwell, they ultimately beheaded Charles in 1649, and Cromwell ruled England for nearly a decade. Finally, Charles II, son of the decapitated king, was restored to the throne in 1660.

Colonization had been interrupted during this period of bloody unrest. Now, in the so-called Restoration period, empire building resumed with even greater intensity—and royal involvement. Carolina, named for Charles II, was formally created in 1670, after the king granted to eight of his court favorites, the Lords Proprietors, an expanse of wilderness ribboning across the continent to the Pacific. These aristocratic founders hoped to grow foodstuffs to provision the sugar plantations in Barbados and to export non-English products like wine, silk, and olive oil.

Carolina prospered by developing close economic ties with the flourishing sugar islands of the English West Indies. In a broad sense, the mainland colony was but the most northerly of those outposts. Many original Carolina settlers in fact had emigrated from Barbados, bringing that island's slave system with them. They also established a vigorous slave trade in Carolina itself. Enlisting the aid of the coastal Savannah Indians, they forayed into the interior in search of captives. The Lords Proprietors in London protested against Indian slave trading in their colony, but to no avail. Manacled Indians soon were among the young colony's major exports. As many as ten thousand Indians were dispatched to lifelong labor in the West Indian canefields and sugar mills. Others were sent to New England. One Rhode Island town in 1730 counted more than two hundred Indian slaves from Carolina in its midst.

In 1707 the Savannah Indians decided to end their alliance with the Carolinians and to migrate to the backcountry of Maryland and Pennsylvania, where a new colony founded by Quakers under William Penn promised better relations between whites and Indians. But the Carolinians determined to "thin" the Savannahs before they could depart. A series of bloody raids all but annihilated the Indian tribes of coastal Carolina by 1710.

After much experimentation, rice emerged as the principal export crop in Carolina. Rice was then an exotic food in England; no rice seeds were sent out from London in the first supply ships to Carolina. But rice was grown in Africa, and the Carolinians were soon paying premium prices for West African slaves experienced in rice cultivation. The Africans' agricultural skill and their relative immunity to malaria (thanks to a genetic trait that also,

Early Carolina Coins
These copper halfpennies bore the image of an elephant, an unofficial symbol of the colony, and a prayer for the Lords Proprietors.

unfortunately, made them and their descendants susceptible to sickle-cell anemia) made them ideal laborers on the hot and swampy rice plantations. By 1710 they constituted a majority of Carolinians.

Moss-festooned Charles Town—also named for the king—rapidly became the busiest seaport in the South. Many high-spirited sons of English landed families, deprived of an inheritance, came to the Charleston area and gave it a rich aristocratic flavor. The village became a colorfully diverse community, to which French Protestant refugees and others were attracted by religious toleration.

Nearby, in Florida, the Catholic Spaniards abhorred the intrusion of these Protestant heretics. Carolina's frontier was often aflame. Spanish-incited Indians brandished their tomahawks, and armor-clad warriors of Spain frequently unsheathed their swords during the successive Anglo-Spanish wars. But by 1700 Carolina was too strong to be wiped out.

The Emergence of North Carolina

The wild northern expanse of the huge Carolina grant bordered on Virginia. From the older colony there drifted down a ragtag group of poverty-stricken outcasts and religious dissenters. Many of them had been repelled by the rarefied atmosphere of Virginia, dominated as it was by big-plantation gentry belonging to the Church of England. North Carolinians, as a result, have been called "the quintessence of Virginia's discontent." The newcomers,

The Thirteen Original Colonies

Name	Founded by	Year	Charter	Made Royal	1775 Status
1. Virginia	London Co.	1607	1606 1609 1612	1624	Royal (under the Crown)
Plymouth	Separatists	1620	None		(Merged with Mass., 1691)
Maine	F. Gorges	1623	1639		(Bought by Mass., 1677)
2. New Hampshire	John Mason and others	1623	1679	1679	Royal (absorbed by Mass., 1641–1679)
3. Massachusetts	Puritans	c. 1628	1629	1691	Royal
4. Maryland	Lord Baltimore	1634	1632	———	Proprietary (controlled by proprietor)
5. Connecticut	Mass. emigrants	1635	1662	———	Self-governing (under local control)
6. Rhode Island	R. Williams	1636	1644 1663	———	Self-governing
New Haven	Mass. emigrants	1638	None		(Merged with Conn., 1662)
7. N. Carolina	Virginians	1653	1663	1729	Royal (separated informally from S.C., 1691)
8. New York	Dutch	c. 1613			
	Duke of York	1664	1664	1685	Royal
9. New Jersey	Berkeley and Carteret	1664	None	1702	Royal
10. Carolina	Eight nobles	1670	1663	1729	Royal (separated formally from N.C., 1712)
11. Pennsylvania	William Penn	1681	1681	———	Proprietary
12. Delaware	Swedes	1638	None	———	Proprietary (merged with Pa., 1682; same governor, but separate assembly, granted 1703)
13. Georgia	Oglethorpe and others	1733	1732	1752	Royal

who frequently were "squatters" without legal right to the soil, raised their tobacco and other crops on small farms, with little need for slaves.

Distinctive traits developed rapidly in North Carolina. The poor but sturdy inhabitants, regarded as riffraff by their snobbish neighbors, earned a reputation for being irreligious and hospitable to pirates. Isolated from neighbors by raw wilderness and stormy Cape Hatteras, "graveyard of the Atlantic," the North Carolinians developed a strong spirit of resistance to authority. Their location between aristocratic Virginia and aristocratic South Carolina caused the area to be dubbed "a vale of humility between two mountains of conceit." Following much friction with governors, North Carolina was officially separated from South Carolina in 1712, and subsequently each segment became a royal colony.

North Carolina shares with tiny Rhode Island several distinctions. These two outposts were the most democratic, the most independent-minded, and the least aristocratic of the original thirteen English colonies.

Although northern Carolina, unlike the colony's southern reaches, did not at first import large numbers of African slaves, both regions shared in the ongoing tragedy of bloody relations between Indians and Europeans. Tuscarora Indians fell upon the fledgling settlement at Newbern in 1711. The North Carolinians, aided by their heavily armed brothers from the south, retaliated by crushing the Tuscaroras in battle, selling hundreds of them into slavery and leaving the survivors to wander northward to

Early Carolina and Georgia Settlements

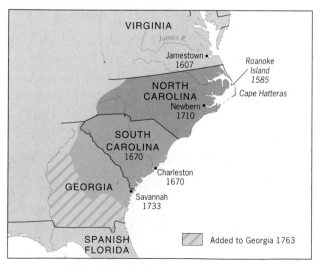

seek the protection of the Iroquois. The Tuscaroras eventually became the Sixth Nation of the Iroquois Confederacy. In another ferocious encounter four years later, the South Carolinians defeated and dispersed the Yamasee Indians.

With the conquest of the Yamasees, virtually all the coastal Indian tribes in the southern colonies had been utterly devastated by about 1720. Yet in the interior, in the hills and valleys of the Appalachian Mountains, the powerful Cherokees, Creeks, and Iroquois (see "Makers of America: The Iroquois," pp. 38–39) remained. Stronger and more numerous than their coastal cousins, they managed for half a century more to contain British settlement to the coastal plain east of the mountains.

Late-Coming Georgia: The Buffer Colony

Pine-forested Georgia, with the harbor of Savannah nourishing its chief settlement, was formally founded in 1733. It proved to be the last of the thirteen colonies to be planted—126 years after the first, Virginia, and 52 years after the twelfth, Pennsylvania. Chronologically Georgia belongs elsewhere, but geographically it may be grouped with its southern neighbors.

The English crown intended Georgia to serve chiefly as a buffer. It would protect the more valuable Carolinas against vengeful Spaniards from Florida and against the hostile French from Louisiana. Georgia indeed suffered much buffeting, especially when wars broke out between Spain and England in the European arena. As a vital link in imperial defense, the exposed colony received monetary subsidies from the British government at the outset—the only one of the "original thirteen" to enjoy this benefit in its founding stage.

Named in honor of King George II of England, Georgia was launched by a high-minded group of philanthropists. In addition to protecting their neighboring northern colonies and producing silk and wine, they were determined to carve out a haven for wretched souls imprisoned for debt. They were also determined, at least at first, to keep slavery out of Georgia. The ablest of the founders was the dynamic soldier-statesman James Oglethorpe, who became keenly interested in prison reform after one of his friends died in a debtor's jail. As an able military leader, Oglethorpe repelled Spanish attacks. As

MAKERS OF AMERICA

The Iroquois

Long before the crowned heads of Europe turned their eyes and their dreams of empire toward the New World, a great military power had emerged in the Mohawk Valley of what is now New York State. The Iroquois Confederacy, dubbed by whites the "League of the Iroquois," bound together five Indian nations—the Mohawks, the Oneidas, the Onondagas, the Cayugas, and the Senecas. According to Iroquois legend, it was founded in the late 1500s by two leaders, Deganawidah and Hiawatha. This proud and potent league vied initially with neighboring Indians for territorial supremacy, then with the French, English, and Dutch for control of the fur trade. Ultimately, infected by the white man's diseases, intoxicated by his whiskey, and intimidated by his muskets, the Iroquois struggled for their very survival as a people.

The building block of Iroquois society was the longhouse (see photo at right). This wooden structure deserved its descriptive name. Only twenty-five feet in breadth, the longhouse stretched from eight to two hundred feet in length. Each building contained three to five fireplaces around which gathered two nuclear families, consisting of parents and children. All families residing in the longhouse were related, their connections of blood running exclusively through the maternal line. A single long-

Iroquois Lands and European Trade Centers, c. 1590–1650

An Iroquois Canoe
In frail but artfully constructed craft like this, the Iroquois traversed the abundant waters of their Confederacy, and traded with their neighbors, Indians as well as whites.

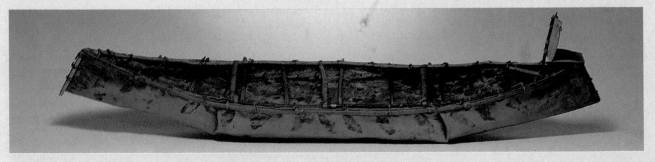

38

house might shelter a woman's family and those of her mother, sisters, and daughters—with the oldest woman being the honored matriarch. When a man married, he left his childhood hearth in the home of his mother to join the longhouse of his wife. Men dominated in Iroquois society, but they owed their positions of prominence to their mothers' families.

As if sharing one great longhouse, the five nations joined in the Iroquois Confederacy but kept their own separate fires. Although they celebrated together and shared a common policy toward outsiders, they remained essentially independent of one another. On the eastern flank of the league, the Mohawks, known as the Keepers of the Eastern Fire, specialized as middlemen with European traders, whereas the outlying Senecas, the Keepers of the Western Fire, became fur suppliers.

After banding together to end generations of warfare among themselves, the Five Nations vanquished their rivals, the neighboring Hurons, Eries, and Petuns. Some other tribes, such as the Tuscaroras, were peacefully absorbed into the Iroquois alliance system. But the arrival of gun-toting Europeans threatened this supremacy and enmeshed the Iroquois in a web of diplomatic maneuverings. Throughout the seventeenth and eighteenth centuries, they allied alternately with the English against the French and vice versa, for a time successfully working this perpetual rivalry to their own advantage. But when the American Revolution broke out, the confederacy could reach no consensus on which side to support. Each tribe was left to decide independently; most, though not all, sided with the British. The ultimate British defeat left the confederacy in tatters. Many Iroquois, especially the Mohawk, moved to new lands in British Canada; others were relegated to reservations in western New York.

Reservation life proved unbearable for a proud people accustomed to domination over a vast territory. Morale sank; brawling, feuding, and alcoholism became rampant. Out of this morass arose a prophet, an Iroquois called Handsome Lake. In 1799 angelic figures clothed in traditional Iroquois garb appeared to Handsome Lake in a vision and warned him that the moral decline of his people must end if they were to endure. He awoke from his vision to warn his tribespeople to mend their ways. His socially oriented gospel inspired many Iroquois to forsake alcohol, to affirm family values, and to revive old Iroquois customs. Handsome Lake died in 1815, but his teachings, in the form of the Longhouse religion, survive to this day.

The Longhouse (reconstruction)
Bent saplings and sheets of elm bark made for sturdy, weather-tight shelters.

an imperialist and a philanthropist, he saved "the Charity Colony" by his energetic leadership and by heavily mortgaging his own personal fortune.

The hamlet of Savannah, like Charleston, was a melting-pot community. German Lutherans and kilted Scots Highlanders, among others, added color to the pattern. All Christian worshipers except Catholics enjoyed religious toleration. Many missionaries armed with Bibles and hope arrived in Savannah to work among debtors and Indians. Prominent among them was young John Wesley, who later returned to England and founded the Methodist church.

Georgia grew with painful slowness and at the end of the colonial era was perhaps the least populous of the colonies. The development of a plantation economy was thwarted by an unhealthful climate, by early restrictions on black slavery, and by demoralizing Spanish attacks.

The Plantation Colonies

Certain distinctive features were shared by England's southern mainland colonies: Maryland, Virginia, North Carolina, South Carolina, and Georgia. Broad-acred, these outposts of empire were all in some degree devoted to exporting commercial agricultural products. Profitable staple crops were the rule, notably tobacco and rice, though to a lesser extent in small-farm North Carolina. Slavery was found in all the plantation colonies, though only after 1750 in reform-minded Georgia. Immense acreage in the hands of a favored few fostered a strong aristocratic atmosphere, except in North Carolina and to some extent in debtor-tinged Georgia. The wide scattering of plantations and farms, often along stately rivers, retarded the growth of cities and made the establishment of churches and schools both difficult and expensive. In 1671 the governor of Virginia thanked God that no free schools or printing presses existed in his colony.

All the plantation colonies permitted some religious toleration. The tax-supported Church of England became the dominant faith, though weakest of all in nonconformist North Carolina.

These colonies were in some degree expansionary. "Soil butchery" by excessive tobacco growing drove settlers westward, and the long, lazy rivers invited penetration of the continent—and continuing confrontation with Native Americans.

Chronology

1558	Elizabeth I becomes queen of England
c. 1565–1590	English crush Irish uprising
1577	Drake circumnavigates the globe
1585	Raleigh founds Roanoke colony
1588	England defeats Spanish Armada
1603	James I becomes king of England
1604	Spain and England sign peace treaty
1607	Virginia colony founded at Jamestown
1612	Rolfe perfects tobacco culture in Virginia
1614	First Anglo-Powhatan War ends
1619	First Africans arrive in Jamestown Virginia House of Burgesses established
1624	Virginia becomes royal colony
1634	Maryland colony founded
1640s	Large-scale slave-labor system established in English West Indies
1644	Second Anglo-Powhatan War
1649	Act of Toleration in Maryland Charles I beheaded; Cromwell rules England
1660	Charles II restored to England throne
1661	Barbados slave code adopted
1670	Carolina colony created
1711–1713	Tuscarora War in North Carolina
1712	North Carolina formally separates from South Carolina
1715–1716	Yamasee War in South Carolina
1733	Georgia colony founded

SUGGESTED READINGS

PRIMARY SOURCE DOCUMENTS

Richard Hakluyt, *Divers Voyages Touching the Discovery of America and the Islands Adjacent,** edited by J. W. Jones (1850), supplied the rationale for the establishment of English colonies in North America. John Smith, "Generall Historie of Virginia," in *Travels and Works of Captain John Smith,** edited by Edward Arber (1910), is an account by the amazing, vain man who steered Jamestown through its precarious first few years.

SECONDARY SOURCES

England's involvement in overseas settlement in the sixteenth century is described in David B. Quinn, *England and the Discovery of America, 1481–1620* (1974). In *The Elizabethans and the Irish* (1966), Quinn details the role of Ireland in the origins of Elizabethan colonization. The international economic background to colonization is sketched in Ralph Davis, *The Rise of the Atlantic Economies* (1973), and in Kenneth R. Andrews, *Trade, Plunder, and Settlement: Maritime Enterprise and the Genesis of the British Empire, 1480–1630* (1984). The immediate English backdrop is colorfully presented in Peter Laslett, *The World We Have Lost* (1965), and in Carl Bridenbaugh, *Vexed and Troubled Englishmen, 1590–1642* (1968). James Lang, *Conquest and Commerce: Spain and England in the Americas* (1975), is a comparative chronicle of colonial rivalries; Jack P. Greene, *Pursuits of Happiness: The Social Development of Early Modern British Colonies and the Formation of American Culture* (1988), compares the process of English colonization in different regions of North America and the Caribbean. Contact between Indian and European cultures is handled in Karen Ordahl Kupperman, *Settling with the Indians: The Meeting of English and Indian Cultures in America, 1580–1640* (1980); and James Axtell, *The Invasion Within: The Contest of Cultures in Colonial America* (1985). James Merrell, *The Indian's New World* (1989), describing the wrenching experiences of the Catawba Indians, is the best ethnohistorical account of a single tribe for the early period. See also Daniel K. Richter, *The Ordeal of the Longhouse: The Peoples of the Iroquois League in the Era of European Colonization* (1992), and Richard D. White, *The Middle Ground: Indians, Empires, and Republics in the Great Lakes Region, 1650–1815* (1991). The Chesapeake region has recently received much fresh attention, especially in Aubrey C. Land et al., *Law, Society, and Politics in Early Maryland* (1977); Paul G. E. Clemens, *The Atlantic Economy and Colonial Maryland's Eastern Shore* (1980); Lois Green Carr et al., eds., *Colonial Chesapeake Society* (1988); Lois Green Carr et al., *Robert Cole's World: Agriculture and Society in Early Maryland* (1991); and James Horn, *Adapting to a New World: English Society in the Seventeenth-Century Chesapeake* (1994). Richard Dunn, *Sugar and Slaves: The Rise of the Planter Class in the English West Indies, 1624–1713* (1972), describes South Carolina society's West Indian roots. The most comprehensive account of the various colonial economies is contained in John J. McCusker and Russell R. Menard, *The Economy of British North America, 1607–1789* (1985). The role of slavery in early colonial society is examined perceptively in Edmund S. Morgan, *American Slavery, American Freedom* (1975). See also Winthrop Jordan's monumental *White over Black* (1968) and Peter Wood's account of South Carolina, *Black Majority* (1974). Gary Nash analyzes relations among all three races in *Red, White, and Black: The Peoples of Early America* (1974), as do Daniel H. Usner, Jr., in *Indians, Settlers, and Slaves in a Frontier Exchange Economy: The Lower Mississippi Valley Before 1783* (1992), and Timothy Silver, in *A New Face on the Countryside: Indians, Colonists, and Slaves in South Atlantic Forests, 1500–1800* (1990).

---

*An asterisk indicates that the document, or an excerpt from it, can be found in Thomas A. Bailey and David M. Kennedy, eds., *The American Spirit: United States History as Seen by Contemporaries*, 9th ed. (Boston: Houghton Mifflin, 1998).

3

Settling the Northern Colonies

1619–1700

God hath sifted a Nation that he might send Choice Grain into this Wilderness.

The Protestant Reformation Produces Puritanism

Little did the German friar Martin Luther suspect, when he nailed his protests against Catholic doctrines to the door of Wittenberg's cathedral in 1517, that he was shaping the destiny of a yet unknown nation. Denouncing the authority of priests and popes, Luther declared that the Bible alone was the source of God's word. He ignited a fire of religious reform (the "Protestant Reformation") that licked its way across Europe for more than a century, dividing peoples, toppling sovereigns, and kindling the spiritual fervor of millions of men and women—some of whom helped to found America.

The reforming flame burned especially brightly in the bosom of John Calvin of Geneva. This somber and severe religious leader elaborated Martin Luther's ideas in ways that profoundly affected the thought and character of generations of Americans yet unborn. Calvinism became the dominant theological credo not only of the New England Puritans but of other American settlers as well, including the Scottish Presbyterians, French Huguenots, and communicants of the Dutch Reformed church.

Calvin spelled out his basic doctrine in a learned Latin tome of 1536, entitled *Institutes of the Christian Religion*. God, Calvin argued, was all-powerful and all-good. Humans, because of the corrupting effect of original sin, were weak and wicked. God was also all-knowing—and he knew who was going to heaven and who was going to hell. Since the first moment of creation, some souls—the *elect*—had been destined for eternal bliss and others for eternal torment. Good works could not save those whom "predestination" had marked for the infernal fires.

But neither could the elect count on their predetermined salvation and lead lives of wild, immoral abandon. For one thing, no one could be certain of his or her status in the heavenly ledger. Gnawing doubts about their eternal fate plagued Calvinists. They constantly sought, in themselves and others, signs of "conversion," or the receipt of God's free gift of saving grace. Conversion was thought to be an intense, identifiable personal experience in which God revealed to the elect their heavenly destiny. Thereafter they were expected to lead "sanctified" lives, demonstrating by their holy behavior that they were among the "visible saints."

These doctrines swept into England just as King Henry VIII was breaking his ties with the Roman Catholic church in the 1530s, making himself the head of the Church of England. Henry would have been content to retain Roman rituals and creeds, but his action powerfully stimulated some English religious reformers to undertake a total purification of English Christianity. Many of these "Puritans," as it happened, came from the commercially depressed woolen districts (see p. 28). Calvinism, with its message of stark but reassuring order in the divine plan, fed on this social unrest and provided spiritual comfort to the economically disadvantaged. As time went on, Puritans grew increasingly unhappy over the snail-like progress of the Protestant Reformation in England. They burned with pious zeal to see the Church of England wholly de-Catholicized.

All Puritans agreed that only "visible saints" should be admitted to church membership. But the Church of England enrolled all the king's subjects, which meant that the "saints" had to share pews and communion rails with the "damned." Appalled by this unholy fraternizing, a tiny group of extreme Puritans, known as Separatists, vowed to break away entirely from the Church of England.

King James I, a shrewd Scotsman, was head of both the state and the church in England from 1603 to 1625. He quickly perceived that if his subjects could defy him as their spiritual leader, they might one day defy him as their political leader (as in fact they would later defy and behead his son, Charles I). He therefore threatened to harass the more bothersome Separatists out of the land.

The Pilgrims End Their Pilgrimage at Plymouth

The most famous congregation of Separatists, fleeing royal wrath, departed for Holland in 1608. During the ensuing twelve years of toil and poverty, they were increasingly distressed by the "Dutchification" of their children. They longed to find a haven where they could live and die as English men and women—and as purified Protestants. America was the logical refuge, despite the early ordeals of Jamestown, and despite tales of New World cannibals roasting steaks from their white victims over open fires.

A group of the Separatists in Holland, after negotiating with the Virginia Company, at length secured rights to settle under its jurisdiction. But their crowded *Mayflower*, sixty-five days at sea, missed its destination and arrived off the rocky coast of New England in 1620, with a total of 102 persons. One had died en route—an unusually short casualty list—and one had been born and appropriately named Oceanus. Fewer than half of the entire party were Separatists. Prominent among the nonbelongers was a peppery and stocky soldier of fortune, Captain Myles Standish, dubbed by one of his critics "Captain Shrimp." He later rendered indispensable service as an Indian fighter and negotiator.

The Pilgrims did not make their initial landing at Plymouth Rock, as commonly supposed, but undertook a number of preliminary surveys. They finally chose for their site the shore of inhospitable Plymouth Bay. This area was outside the domain of the Virginia Company, and consequently the settlers became squatters. They were without legal right to the land and without specific authority to establish a government.

Before disembarking, the Pilgrim leaders drew up and signed the brief Mayflower Compact. Although setting an invaluable precedent for later written constitutions, this document was not a constitution at all. It was a simple agreement to form a crude government and to submit to the will of the majority under the regulations agreed upon. The compact was signed by forty-one adult males, eleven of them with the exalted rank of "mister," though not by the servants and two seamen. The pact was a promising step toward genuine self-government,

Plymouth Plantation
Carefully restored, the modest village at Plymouth looks today much as it did nearly four hundred years ago.

for soon the adult male settlers were assembling to make their own laws in open-discussion town meetings—a great laboratory of liberty.

The Pilgrims' first winter of 1620–1621 took a grisly toll. Only 44 out of the 102 survived. At one time only 7 were well enough to lay the dead in their frosty graves. Yet when the *Mayflower* sailed back to England in the spring, not a single one of the courageous band of Separatists left. As one of them wrote, "It is not with us as with other men, whom small things can discourage."

God made his children prosperous, so the Pilgrims believed. The next autumn, that of 1621, brought bountiful harvests and with them the first Thanksgiving Day in New England. In time the frail colony found sound economic legs in fur, fish, and lumber. The beaver and the Bible were the early mainstays: the one for the sustenance of the body, the other for the sustenance of the soul. Plymouth proved that the English could maintain themselves in this uninviting region.

The Pilgrims were extremely fortunate in their leaders. Prominent among them was the cultured William Bradford, a self-taught scholar who read Hebrew, Greek, Latin, French, and Dutch. He was chosen governor thirty times in the annual elections. Among his major worries was his fear that independent, non-Puritan settlers "on their particu-

lar" might corrupt his godly experiment in the wilderness. Bustling fishing villages and other settlements did sprout to the north of Plymouth, on the storm-lashed shores of Massachusetts Bay, where many people were as much interested in cod as God.

Quiet and quaint, the little colony of Plymouth was never important economically or numerically. Its population numbered only seven thousand by 1691, when, still charterless, it merged with its giant neighbor, the Massachusetts Bay Colony. But the tiny settlement of Pilgrims was big both morally and spiritually.

William Bradford (1590–1657) wrote in Of Plymouth Plantation,

"Thus out of small beginnings greater things have been produced by His hand that made all things of nothing, and gives being to all things that are; and, as one small candle may light a thousand, so the light here kindled hath shone unto many, yea in some sort to our whole nation."

The Bay Colony Bible Commonwealth

The Separatist Pilgrims were dedicated extremists—the purest Puritans. More moderate Puritans sought to reform the Church of England from within. Though resented by bishops and monarchs, they slowly gathered support, especially in Parliament. But when Charles I dismissed Parliament in 1629 and sanctioned the anti-Puritan persecutions of the reactionary Archbishop William Laud, many Puritans saw catastrophe in the making.

In 1629 an energetic group of non-Separatist Puritans, fearing for their faith and for England's future, secured a royal charter to form the Massachusetts Bay Company. They proposed to establish a sizable settlement in the infertile Massachusetts area, with Boston soon becoming its hub. Stealing a march on both king and church, the newcomers brought their charter with them. For many years they used it as a kind of constitution, out of easy reach of royal authority. They steadfastly denied that they wanted to separate from the Church of England, only from its impurities. But back in England, the highly orthodox Archbishop Laud snorted that the Bay Colony Puritans were "swine which rooted in God's vineyard."

The Massachusetts Bay enterprise was singularly blessed. The well-equipped expedition of 1630, with eleven vessels carrying nearly a thousand immigrants, started the colony off on a larger scale than any of the other English settlements. Continuing turmoil in England tossed up additional enriching waves of Puritans on the shores of Massachusetts in the following decade (see "Makers of America: The English," pp. 48–49). During the "Great Migration" of the 1630s, about seventy thousand refugees left England. But not all of them were Puritans, and only about eleven thousand came to Massachusetts. Many were attracted to the warm and fertile West Indies, especially the sugar-rich island of Barbados. More Puritans came to this Caribbean islet than to all of Massachusetts.

Many fairly prosperous, educated persons immigrated to the Bay Colony, including John Winthrop, a well-to-do pillar of English society, who became the colony's first governor. A successful attorney and manor lord in England, Winthrop eagerly accepted the offer to become governor of the Massachusetts Bay Colony, believing that he had

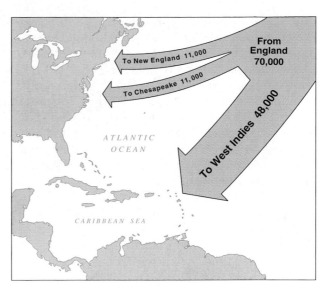

The Great English Migration, c. 1630–1642
Much of the early history of the United States was written by New Englanders, who were not disposed to emphasize the larger exodus of English migrants to the Caribbean islands. When the mainland colonials declared independence in 1776, they hoped that these island outposts would join them, but the existence of the British navy had a dissuading effect.

a "calling" from God to lead the new religious experiment. He served as governor or deputy governor for nineteen years. The resources and skills of talented settlers like Winthrop helped Massachusetts prosper, as fur trading, fishing, and shipbuilding blossomed into important industries, especially fish and ships. Massachusetts Bay Colony rapidly shot to the fore as both the biggest and the most influential of the New England outposts.

Massachusetts also benefited from a shared sense of purpose among most of the first settlers. "We shall be as a city upon a hill," a beacon to humanity, declared Governor Winthrop. The Puritan bay colonists believed that they had a covenant with God, an agreement to build a holy society that would be a model for humankind.

Building the Bay Colony

These common convictions deeply shaped the infant colony's life. Soon after arrival the franchise was extended to all "freemen"—adult males who belonged to the Puritan congregations, which in time came to be called collectively the Congregational church. Unchurched men remained voteless in provincial elections, as did women. On this basis about two-fifths of adult males enjoyed the franchise in provincial affairs, a far larger proportion than in contemporary England. Town governments, which conducted much important business, were even more inclusive. There all male property holders, and in some cases other residents as well, enjoyed the priceless boon of publicly discussing local issues, often with much heat, and of voting on them by a majority-rule show of hands.

Yet the provincial government, liberal by the standards of the time, was not a democracy. The able Governor Winthrop feared and distrusted the "commons" as the "meaner sort" and thought that democracy was the "meanest and worst" of all forms of government. "If the people be governors," asked one Puritan clergyman, "who shall be governed?" True, the freemen annually elected the governor and his assistants, as well as a representative assembly called the General Court. But only Puritans—the "visible saints" who alone were eligible for church membership—could be freemen. And according to the doctrine of the covenant, the whole purpose of government was to enforce God's laws—which applied to believers and nonbelievers alike. Moreover, nonbelievers as well as believers paid taxes for the government-supported church.

Religious leaders thus wielded enormous influence in the Massachusetts "Bible Commonwealth." They powerfully influenced admission to church membership, by conducting public interrogations of persons claiming to have experienced conversion. Prominent among the early clergy was fiery John Cotton. Educated at England's Cambridge University, a Puritan citadel, he emigrated to Massachusetts to avoid persecution for his criticism of the Church of England. In the Bay Colony he devoted his considerable learning to defending the government's duty to enforce religious rules. Profoundly pious, he sometimes preached and prayed up to six hours in a single day.

But the power of the preachers was not absolute. A congregation had the right to hire and fire its minister and to set his salary. Clergymen were also barred from holding formal political office. Puritans in England had suffered too much at the hands of a "political" Anglican clergy to permit in the New World another unholy union of religious and government power. In a limited way, the bay colonists thus endorsed the idea of the separation of church and state.

The Puritans were a worldly lot, despite—or even because of—their spiritual intensity. Like John Winthrop, they believed in the doctrine of a "calling" to do God's work on earth. They shared in what was later called the "Protestant ethic," which involved serious commitment to work and to engagement in worldly pursuits. Legend to the contrary, they also enjoyed simple pleasures: they ate plentifully, drank heartily, sang songs occasionally, and made love monogamously. Like other peoples of their time in both America and Europe, they passed laws aimed at making sure these pleasures stayed simple by repressing certain human instincts. In New Haven, for example, a young married couple was fined twenty shillings for the crime of kissing in public, and in later years Connecticut came to be dubbed "the Blue Law State." (It was so named for the blue paper on which the repressive laws—also known as "sumptuary laws"—were printed.)

Yet life was serious business, and hellfire was real—a hell where sinners shriveled and shrieked in vain for divine mercy. An immensely popular poem in New England, selling one copy for every twenty people, was clergyman Michael Wigglesworth's "Day of Doom" (1662). Especially horrifying were his descriptions of the fate of the damned:

> They cry, they roar for anguish sore,
>   and gnaw their tongues for horrour.
> But get away without delay,
>   Christ pitties not your cry:
> Depart to Hell, there may you yell,
>   and roar Eternally.

Trouble in the Bible Commonwealth

The Bay Colony enjoyed a high degree of social harmony, stemming from common beliefs, in its early years. But even in this tightly knit community, dissension soon appeared. Quakers, who flouted the authority of the Puritan clergy, were persecuted with fines, floggings, and banishment. In one extreme case, four Quakers who defied expulsion, one of them a woman, were hanged on the Boston Common.

A sharp challenge to Puritan orthodoxy came from Anne Hutchinson. She was an exceptionally

Anne Hutchinson, Dissenter
Mistress Hutchinson (1591–1643) held unorthodox views that challenged the authority of the clergy and the very integrity of the Puritan experiment in Massachusetts Bay Colony.

intelligent, strong-willed, and talkative woman, ultimately the mother of fourteen children. Swift and sharp in theological argument, she carried to logical extremes the Puritan doctrine of predestination. She claimed that a holy life was no sure sign of salvation and that the truly saved need not bother to obey the law of either God or man. This assertion, known as *antinomianism* (from the Greek, "against the law"), was high heresy.

Brought to trial in 1638, the quick-witted Hutchinson bamboozled her clerical inquisitors for days, until she eventually boasted that she had come by her beliefs through a direct revelation from God. This was even higher heresy. The Puritan magistrates had little choice but to banish her, lest she pollute the entire Puritan experiment. With her family, she set out on foot for Rhode Island, though pregnant. She finally moved to New York, where she and all but one of her household were killed by Indians. Back in the Bay Colony, the pious John Winthrop saw "God's hand" in her fate.

More threatening to the Puritan leaders was a personable and popular Salem minister, Roger Williams. Williams was a young man with radical ideas and an unrestrained tongue. An extreme Separatist, he hounded his fellow clergymen to make a clean break with the corrupt Church of England. He also challenged the legality of the Bay Colony's charter, which he condemned for expropriating the land from the Indians without fair compensation. As if all this were not enough, he went on to deny the authority of civil government to regulate religious behavior—a seditious blow at the Puritan idea of government's very purpose.

Their patience exhausted by 1635, the Bay Colony authorities found Williams guilty of disseminating "newe & dangerous opinions" and ordered him banished. He was permitted to remain several months longer because of illness, but he kept up his criticisms. The outraged magistrates, fearing that he might organize a rival colony of malcontents, made plans to exile him to England. But Williams foiled them.

The Rhode Island "Sewer"

Aided by friendly Indians, Roger Williams fled to the Rhode Island area in 1636, in the midst of a bitter winter. At Providence the courageous and far-visioned Williams built a Baptist church, probably the first in America. He established complete freedom of religion, even for Jews and Catholics. He demanded no oaths regarding religious beliefs, no compulsory attendance at worship, no taxes to support a state church. He even sheltered the abused Quakers, although disagreeing sharply with their views. Williams's endorsement of religious tolerance made Rhode Island more liberal than any of the other English settlements in the New World, and more advanced than most Old World communities as well.

Those outcasts who clustered about Roger Williams enjoyed additional blessings. They exercised simple manhood suffrage from the start, though this broad-minded practice was later narrowed by a property qualification. Opposed to special privilege of any sort, the doughty Rhode Islanders managed to achieve remarkable freedom of opportunity.

Other scattered settlements soon dotted Rhode Island. They consisted largely of malcontents and

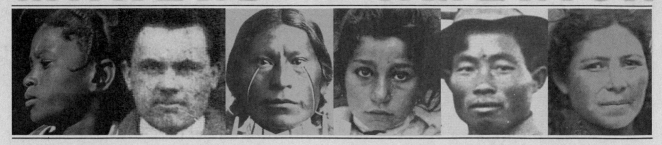

The English

During the late Middle Ages, the Black Death and other epidemics that ravaged England kept the island's population in check. But by 1500, increased resistance to such diseases allowed the population to soar; and a century later, the island nation was bursting at the seams. This population explosion, combined with economic depression and religious repression, sparked the first major European migration to England's New World colonies.

Some of those who voyaged to Virginia and Maryland in the seventeenth century were independent artisans or younger members of English gentry families. But roughly three-quarters of the English

Town Meetinghouse, Hingham, Massachusetts
Erected in 1681, it is still in use today.

migrants to the Chesapeake during this period came as servants, signed to "indentures" ranging from four to seven years. One English observer described such indentured servants as "idle, lazie, simple people," and another complained that many of those taking ship for the colonies "have been pursued by hue-and-cry for robberies, burglaries, or breaking prison."

In fact, most indentured servants were young men drawn from England's "middling classes." Some fled the disastrous slump in the cloth trade in the early seventeenth century. Many others had been forced off the land as the dawning national economy prompted landowners in southwestern England to convert from crop fields to pasture and to "enclose" the land for sheep grazing. Making their way from town to town in search of work, they eventually drifted into port cities such as Bristol and London. There they boarded ship for America, where they provided the labor necessary to cultivate the Chesapeake's staple crop, tobacco.

Some 40 percent of these immigrants of the mid–seventeenth century died before they finished their terms of indenture. (Because of the high death rate and the shortage of women, Chesapeake society was unable to reproduce itself naturally until the last quarter of the seventeenth century.) The survivors entered Chesapeake society with only their "freedom dues"—usually clothing, an axe and hoe, and a few barrels of corn.

Nevertheless, many of those who arrived early in the century eventually acquired land and moved into the mainstream of Chesapeake society. After 1660, however, opportunities for the "freemen" declined. In England the population spurt ended, and the great London fire of 1666 sparked a building boom that soaked up job seekers. As the supply of English indentured servants dried up in the late

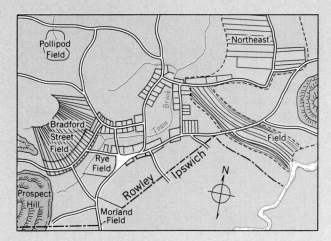

Land Use in Rowley, Massachusetts, c. 1650
The settlers of Rowley brought from their native Yorkshire the practice of granting families very small farming plots and reserving large common fields for use by the entire community, as this map clearly shows.

seventeenth century, southern planters looking for laborers turned increasingly to black slaves.

Whereas English immigration to the Chesapeake was spread over nearly a century, most English voyagers to New England arrived within a single decade. In the twelve years between 1629 and 1642, some eleven thousand Puritans swarmed to the Massachusetts Bay Colony. Fleeing a sustained economic depression and the cruel religious repression of Charles I, the Puritans came to plant a godly commonwealth in New England's rocky soil.

In contrast to the single indentured servants of the Chesapeake, the New England Puritans migrated in family groups, and in many cases whole communities were transplanted from England to America. Although they remained united by the common language and common Puritan faith they carried to New England, their English baggage was by no means uniform. As in England, most New England settlements were farming communities. But some New England towns re-created the specialized economies of particular localities in England. Marblehead, Massachusetts, for example, became a fishing village because most of its settlers had been fishermen in Old England. The townsfolk of Rowley, Massachusetts, brought from Yorkshire in northern England not only their town name, but also their distinctive way of life, revolving around textile manufacturing.

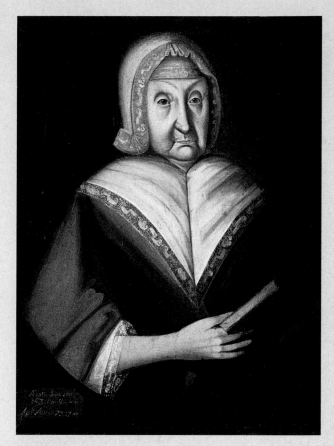

Mistress Anne Pollard
Born in England, Mistress Pollard arrived in Massachusetts as a child with John Winthrop's fleet in 1630. A tavern operator and the mother of 13 children, she was 100 years old when this portrait was painted in 1721. On her death 4 years later, she left 130 descendants, a dramatic example of the fecundity of the early New England colonists.

Political practices, too, reflected the towns' variegated English roots. In Ipswich, Massachusetts, settled by East Anglian Puritans, the ruling selectmen served long terms and ruled with an iron hand. By contrast, local politics in the town of Newbury were bitter and contentious, and officeholders were hard pressed to win reelection; the town's founders came from western England, a region with little tradition of local government. Although the Puritans' imperial masters in London eventually circumscribed such precious local autonomy, this diverse heritage of fiercely independent New England towns endured, reasserting itself during the American Revolution.

exiles, some of whom could not bear the stifling theological atmosphere of the Bay Colony. Many of these restless souls in "Rogues' Island," including Anne Hutchinson, had little in common with Roger Williams—except being unwelcome anywhere else. The Puritan clergy back in Boston sneered at Rhode Island as "that sewer" in which the "Lord's debris" had collected and rotted.

Planted by dissenters and exiles, Rhode Island became strongly individualistic and stubbornly independent. With good reason "Little Rhody" was later known as "the traditional home of the otherwise minded." Begun as a squatter colony in 1636 without legal standing, it finally established rights to the soil when it secured a charter from Parliament in 1644. A huge bronze statue of the "Independent Man" appropriately stands today on the dome of the statehouse in Providence.

New England Spreads Out

The smiling valley of the Connecticut River, one of the few highly fertile expanses of any size in all New England, had meanwhile attracted a sprinkling of Dutch and English settlers. Hartford was founded in 1635. The next year witnessed a spectacular beginning of the centuries-long westward movement across the continent. An energetic group of Boston Puritans, led by the Reverend Thomas Hooker, swarmed as a body into the Hartford area, with the ailing Mrs. Hooker carried on a horse litter.

Three years later, in 1639, the settlers of the new Connecticut River colony drafted in open meeting a trailblazing document known as the Fundamental Orders. It was in effect a modern constitution, which established a regime democratically controlled by the "substantial" citizens. Essential features of the Fundamental Orders were later borrowed by Connecticut for its colonial charter and ultimately for its state constitution.

Another flourishing Connecticut settlement began to spring up at New Haven in 1638. It was a prosperous community, founded by Puritans who contrived to set up an even closer church-government alliance than in Massachusetts. Although only squatters without a charter, the colonists dreamed of making New Haven a bustling seaport. But they fell into disfavor with Charles II as a result of having sheltered two of the judges who

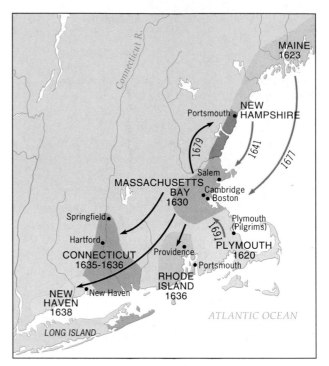

Seventeenth-Century New England Settlements
The Massachusetts Bay Colony was the hub of New England. All earlier colonies grew into it; all later colonies grew out of it.

had condemned his father, Charles I, to death. In 1662, to the acute distress of the New Havenites, the crown granted a charter to Connecticut that merged New Haven with the more democratic settlements in the Connecticut Valley.

Far to the north, enterprising fishermen and fur traders had been active on the coast of Maine for a dozen or so years before the founding of Plymouth. After disheartening attempts at colonization in 1623 by Sir Ferdinando Gorges, this land of lakes and forests was absorbed by Massachusetts Bay after a formal purchase in 1677 from the Gorges heirs. It remained a part of Massachusetts for nearly a century and a half before becoming a separate state.

Granite-ribbed New Hampshire also sprang from the fishing and trading activities along its narrow coast. It was absorbed in 1641 by the grasping Bay Colony, under a strained interpretation of the Massachusetts charter. The king, annoyed by this display of greed, arbitrarily separated New Hampshire from Massachusetts in 1679 and made it a royal colony.

Puritans versus Indians

The spread of English settlements inevitably led to clashes with the Indians, who were particularly weak in New England. Shortly before the Pilgrims had arrived at Plymouth in 1620, an epidemic, probably triggered by contact with English fishermen, had swept through the coastal tribes and killed more than three-quarters of the native people. Deserted Indian fields, ready for tillage, greeted the Plymouth settlers and scattered skulls and bones provided grim evidence of the impact of the disease.

In no position to resist the English incursion, the local Wampanoag Indians at first befriended the settlers. Cultural accommodation was facilitated by Squanto, a Wampanoag who had learned English from a ship's captain who had kidnapped him some years earlier. The Wampanoag chieftain Massasoit signed a treaty with the Plymouth Pilgrims in 1621 and helped them celebrate the first Thanksgiving after the autumn harvests that same year.

As more English settlers arrived and pushed inland into the Connecticut River valley, confrontations between Indians and whites ruptured these peaceful relations. Hostilities exploded in 1637 between the English settlers and the powerful Pequot tribe. Besieging a Pequot village on Connecticut's Mystic River, English militiamen and their Narragansett Indian allies set fire to the Indian wigwams and shot the fleeing survivors. The slaughter wrote a brutal finish to the Pequot War, virtually annihilated the Pequot tribe, and inaugurated four decades of uneasy peace between Puritans and Indians.

Lashed by critics in England, the Puritans made some feeble efforts at converting the remaining Indians to Christianity, although Puritan missionary zeal never equaled that of the Catholic Spanish and French. A mere handful of Indians were gathered into Puritan "praying towns" to make the acquaintance of the English God and to learn the ways of English culture.

The Indians' only hope for resisting English encroachment lay in intertribal unity—a pan-Indian alliance against the swiftly spreading English settlements. In 1675 Massasoit's son, Metacom, called King Philip by the English, forged such an alliance and mounted a series of coordinated assaults on English villages throughout New England. Frontier settlements were especially hard hit, and refugees fell back toward the relative safety of Boston. When the war ended in 1676, fifty-two Puritan towns had been attacked, and twelve destroyed entirely. Hundreds of colonists and many more Indians lay dead. Metacom's wife and son were sold into slavery; he himself was captured, beheaded, and drawn and quartered. His head was carried on a pike back to Plymouth, where it was mounted on grisly display for years.

King Philip's War slowed the westward march of English settlement in New England for several decades. But the war inflicted a lasting defeat on New England's Indians. Drastically reduced in numbers, dispirited, and disbanded, they never again seriously threatened the New England colonists.

Philip, King of Mount Hope
In 1675–1676 Philip was defeated in the last serious Indian challenge to white settlement in New England.

Seeds of Colonial Unity and Independence

A path-breaking experiment in union was launched in 1643, when four colonies banded together to form the New England Confederation. Old England was then deeply involved in civil wars, and hence the colonials were thrown upon their own resources. The primary purpose of the confederation was defense against foes or potential foes, notably the Indians, the French, and the Dutch. Purely intercolonial problems, such as runaway servants and criminals who had fled from one colony to another, also came within the jurisdiction of the confederation. Each member colony, regardless of size, wielded two votes—an arrangement highly displeasing to the most populous colony, Massachusetts Bay.

The confederation was essentially an exclusive Puritan club. It consisted of the two Massachusetts colonies (the Bay Colony and bantam-sized Plymouth) and the two Connecticut colonies (New Haven and the scattered valley settlements). The Puritan leaders blackballed Rhode Island as well as the Maine outposts. These places, it was charged, harbored too many heretical or otherwise undesirable characters. Shockingly, one of the Maine towns had made a tailor its mayor and had even sheltered an excommunicated minister of the gospel.

Weak though it was, the confederation was the first notable milestone on the long and rocky road toward colonial unity. The delegates took tottering but long-overdue steps toward acting together on matters of intercolonial importance. Rank-and-file colonists, for their part, received valuable experience in delegating their votes to properly chosen representatives.

Back in England the king had paid little attention to the American colonies during the early years of their planting. They were allowed, in effect, to become semiautonomous commonwealths. This era of benign neglect was prolonged when the crown, struggling to retain its power, became enmeshed during the 1640s in civil wars with the parliamentarians.

But when Charles II was restored to the English throne in 1660, the royalists and their Church of England allies were once more firmly in the saddle. Puritan hopes of eventually purifying the old English church withered. Worse, Charles II was determined to take an active, aggressive hand in the management of the colonies. His plans ran headlong against the habits that decades of relative independence had bred in the colonists.

Deepening colonial defiance was nowhere more glaringly revealed than in Massachusetts. One of the king's agents in Boston was mortified to find that royal orders had no more effect than old issues of the London *Gazette*. Punishment was soon forthcoming. As a slap at Massachusetts, Charles II gave rival Connecticut in 1662 a sea-to-sea charter grant, which legalized the squatter settlements. The very next year the outcasts in Rhode Island received a new charter, which gave kingly sanction to the most religiously tolerant government yet devised in America. A final and crushing blow fell on the stiff-necked Bay Colony in 1684, when its precious charter was revoked by the London authorities.

The Stuart Dynasty in England*

Name, Reign	Relation to America
James I, 1603–1625	Va., Plymouth founded; Separatists persecuted
Charles I, 1625–1649	Civil wars, 1642–1649; Mass., Md. founded
(Interregnum, 1649–1660)	Commonwealth; Protectorate (Oliver Cromwell)
Charles II, 1660–1685	The Restoration; Carolinas, Pa., N.Y. founded; Conn. chartered
James II, 1685–1688	Catholic trend; Glorious Revolution, 1688
William & Mary, 1689–1702 (Mary died 1694)	King William's War, 1689–1697

*See p. 29 for predecessors; p. 109 for successors.

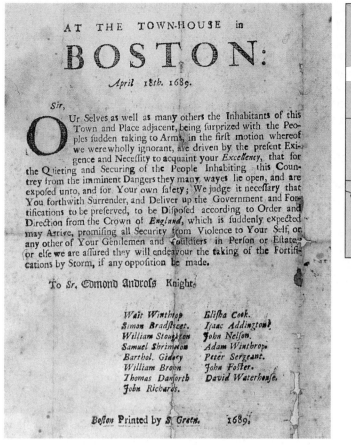

Sir Edmund Andros, 1637–1714; a Boston Broadside Urging Him to Surrender, 1689; and a Map Showing Andros's Dominion of New England   *After being expelled from New England, Andros eventually returned to the New World as governor of Virginia, 1692–1697.*

Andros Promotes the First American Revolution

Massachusetts suffered further humiliation in 1686, when the Dominion of New England was created by royal authority. Unlike the homegrown New England Confederation, it was imposed from London. Embracing at first all New England, it was expanded two years later to include New York and East and West Jersey. The dominion also aimed at bolstering colonial defense in the event of war with the Indians and hence, from the imperial viewpoint of Parliament, was a statesmanlike move.

More importantly, the Dominion of New England was designed to promote urgently needed efficiency in the administration of the English Navigation Laws. Those laws reflected the intensifying colonial rivalries of the seventeenth century. They sought to stitch England's overseas possessions more tightly to the motherland, by throttling American trade with countries not ruled by the English crown. Like colonial peoples everywhere, the Americans chafed at such confinements, and smuggling became an increasingly common and honorable occupation.

At the head of the new dominion stood autocratic Sir Edmund Andros, an able English military man, conscientious but tactless. Establishing headquarters in Puritanical Boston, he generated much hostility by his open affiliation with the despised Church of England. The colonials were also outraged by his noisy and Sabbath-profaning soldiers, who were accused of teaching the people "to drink, blaspheme, curse, and damn."

Andros was prompt to use the mailed fist. He ruthlessly curbed the cherished town meetings; laid heavy restrictions on the courts, the press, and the schools; and revoked all land titles. Dispensing with the popular assemblies, he taxed the people without the consent of their duly elected representatives. He also strove to enforce the unpopular Navigation Laws and suppress smuggling. Liberty-loving colonials, accustomed to unusual privileges during long decades of neglect, were goaded to the verge of revolt.

The people of old England, likewise resisting oppression, stole a march on the people of New England. In 1688–1689 they engineered the memorable Glorious (or Bloodless) Revolution. Dethroning the despotic and unpopular Catholic James II, they enthroned the Protestant rulers of the Netherlands, the Dutch-born William III and his English wife, Mary, daughter of James II.

When the news of the Glorious Revolution reached America, the ramshackle Dominion of New England collapsed like a house of cards. A Boston mob, catching the fever, rose against the existing regime. Sir Edmund Andros attempted to flee in woman's clothing but was betrayed by boots protruding beneath his dress. He was hastily shipped off to England.

Massachusetts, though rid of the despotic Andros, did not gain as much from the upheaval as it had hoped. In 1691 it was arbitrarily made a royal colony, with a new charter and a new royal governor. The permanent loss of the ancient charter was a staggering blow to the proud Puritans, who never fully recovered. Worst of all, the privilege of voting, once a monopoly of church members, was now to be enjoyed by all qualified male property holders.

England's Glorious Revolution reverberated throughout the colonies from New England to the Chesapeake. Inspired by the challenge to the Crown in old England, many colonists seized the occasion to strike against royal authority in America. Unrest rocked both New York and Maryland from 1689 to 1691, until newly appointed royal governors restored a semblance of order. Most importantly, the new monarchs relaxed the royal grip on colonial trade, inaugurating a period of "salutary neglect" when the much-resented Navigation Laws were only weakly enforced.

Yet residues remained of Charles II's effort to assert tighter administrative control over his empire. More English officials—judges, clerks, customs officials—now staffed the courts and strolled the wharves of English America. Many were incompetent, corrupt hacks who knew little and cared less about American affairs. Appointed by influential patrons in far-off England, by their very presence they blocked the rise of local leaders to positions of political power. Aggrieved Americans viewed them with mounting contempt and resentment as the eighteenth century wore on.

Old Netherlanders at New Netherland

Late in the sixteenth century, the oppressed people of the Netherlands unfurled the standard of rebellion against Catholic Spain. After bloody and protracted fighting, they finally succeeded, with the aid of Protestant England, in winning their independence.

The seventeenth century—the era of Rembrandt and other famous artists—was a golden age in Dutch history. This vigorous little lowland nation finally emerged as a major commercial and naval power and then ungratefully challenged the supremacy of its former benefactor, England. Three great Anglo-Dutch naval wars were fought in the

Early Settlements in the Middle Colonies, with Founding Dates

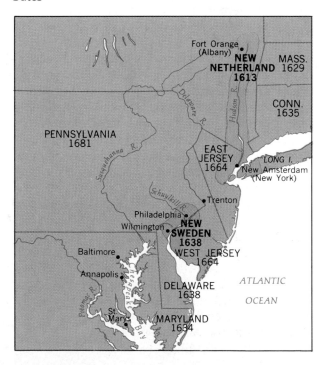

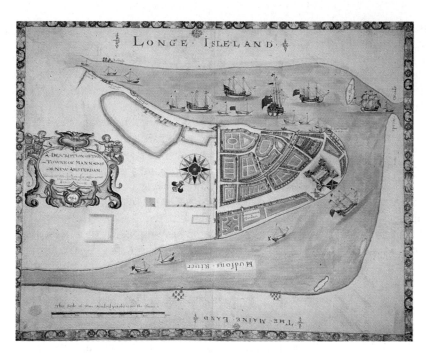

New York (then New Amsterdam), 1664
This drawing clearly shows the tip of
Manhattan Island protected by the wall
after which Wall Street was named.

seventeenth century, with as many as a hundred ships on each side. The sturdy Dutch dealt blows about as heavy as they received.

The Dutch Republic also became a leading colonial power, with by far its greatest activity in the East Indies. There it maintained an enormous and profitable empire for over three hundred years. The Dutch East India Company was virtually a state within a state and at one time supported an army of 10,000 men and a fleet of 190 ships, 40 of them men-of-war.

Seeking greater riches, this enterprising company employed an English explorer, Henry Hudson. Disregarding orders to sail northeast, he ventured into Delaware Bay and New York Bay in 1609 and then ascended the Hudson River, hoping that at last he had chanced upon the coveted shortcut through the continent. But, as the event proved, he merely filed a Dutch claim to a magnificently wooded and watered area.

Much less powerful than the mighty Dutch East India Company was the Dutch West India Company, which maintained profitable enterprises in the Caribbean. At times it was less interested in trading than in raiding and at one fell swoop in 1628 captured a fleet of Spanish treasure ships laden with loot worth $15 million. The company also established outposts in Africa and a thriving sugar industry in Brazil, which for several decades was its principal center of activity in the New World.

New Netherland, in the beautiful Hudson River area, was planted in 1623–1624 on a permanent basis. Established by the Dutch West India Company for its quick-profit fur trade, it was never more than a secondary interest of the founders. The company's most brilliant stroke was to buy Manhattan Island from the Indians (who did not actually "own" it) for virtually worthless trinkets—22,000 acres of what is now perhaps the most valuable real estate in the world for pennies per acre.

New Amsterdam—later New York City—was a company town. It was run by and for the Dutch company, in the interests of the stockholders. The investors had no enthusiasm for religious toleration, free speech, or democratic practices; and the governors appointed by the company as directors-general were usually harsh and despotic. Religious dissenters who opposed the official Dutch Reformed church were regarded with suspicion, and for a while Quakers were savagely abused. In response to repeated protests by the aggravated colonists, a local body with limited lawmaking power was finally established.

This picturesque Dutch colony took on a strongly aristocratic tinge and retained it for generations. Vast feudal estates fronting the Hudson River, known as patroonships, were granted to promoters who agreed to settle fifty people on them. One patroonship in the Albany area was slightly larger than the later state of Rhode Island.

Colorful little New Amsterdam attracted a cosmopolitan population, as is common in seaport towns. A French Jesuit missionary, visiting in the 1640s, noted that eighteen different languages were being spoken in the streets. New York's later babel of immigrant tongues was thus foreshadowed.

Friction with English and Swedish Neighbors

Vexations beset the Dutch company-colony from the beginning. The directors-general were largely incompetent. Company shareholders demanded their dividends, even at the expense of the colony's welfare. The Indians, infuriated by Dutch cruelties, retaliated with horrible massacres. As a defense measure, the hard-pressed settlers on Manhattan Island erected a stout wall, from which Wall Street derives its name.

New England was hostile to the growth of its Dutch neighbor, and the people of Connecticut finally ejected intruding Hollanders from their verdant valley. Three of the four member colonies of the New England Confederation were eager to wipe out New Netherland with military force. But Massachusetts, which would have had to provide most of the troops, vetoed the proposed foray.

The Swedes in turn trespassed on Dutch preserves, from 1638 to 1655, by planting the anemic colony of New Sweden on the Delaware River. This was the golden age of Sweden, during and following the Thirty Years' War of 1618–1648, in which its brilliant King Gustavus Adolphus had carried the torch for Protestantism. This outburst of energy in Sweden caused it to enter the costly colonial game in America, though on something of a shoestring.

Resenting the Swedish intrusion on the Delaware, the Dutch dispatched a small military expedition in 1655. It was led by the ablest of the directors-general, Peter Stuyvesant, who had lost a leg while soldiering in the West Indies and was dubbed "Father Wooden Leg" by the Indians. The main fort fell after a bloodless siege, whereupon Swedish rule came to an abrupt end. The colonists were absorbed by New Netherland.

New Sweden, never important, soon faded away, leaving behind in later Delaware a sprinkling of Swedish place names and Swedish log cabins (the first in America), as well as an admixture of Swedish blood.

Dutch Residues in New York

Lacking vitality, and representing only a secondary commercial interest of the Dutch, New Netherland lay under the menacing shadow of the vigorous English colonies to the north. In addition, it was honeycombed with New England immigrants.

New York Aristocrats
This prosperous family exemplified the comfortable lives and aristocratic pretensions of the "Hudson River lords" in colonial New York.

Peter Stuyvesant (1602–1682)
Despotic in government and intolerant in religion, he lived in a constant state of friction with the prominent residents of New Netherland. When protests arose, he replied that he derived his power from God and the company, not the people. He opposed popular suffrage on the grounds that "the thief" would vote "for the thief" and "the rogue for the rogue."

The conquered Dutch province tenaciously retained many of the illiberal features of earlier days. An autocratic spirit survived, and the aristocratic element gained strength when certain corrupt English governors granted immense acreage to their favorites. Influential landowning families—such as the Livingstons and the De Lanceys—wielded disproportionate power in the affairs of colonial New York. These monopolistic land policies, combined with the lordly atmosphere, discouraged many European immigrants from coming. The physical growth of New York was correspondingly retarded.

The Dutch peppered place names over the land, including Harlem (Haarlem), Brooklyn (Breuckelen), and Hell Gate (Hellegat). They likewise left their imprint on the gambrel-roofed architecture. As for social customs and folkways, no other foreign group of comparable size has made so colorful a contribution. Noteworthy were Easter eggs, Santa Claus, waffles, sauerkraut, bowling, sleighing, skating, and kolf (golf)—a dangerous game played with heavy clubs and forbidden in settled areas.

Penn's Holy Experiment in Pennsylvania

A remarkable group of dissenters, commonly known as Quakers, arose in England during the mid-1600s. Their name derived from the report that they "quaked" when under deep religious emotion. Officially they were known as the Religious Society of Friends.

Quakers were especially offensive to the authorities, both religious and civil. They refused to support the established Church of England with taxes. They built simple meetinghouses, congregated without a paid clergy, and "spoke up" themselves in meetings when moved. Believing that they were all children in the sight of God, they kept their broad-brimmed hats on in the presence of their "betters" and addressed others with simple "thee"s and "thou"s, rather than with conventional titles. They would take no oaths because Jesus had commanded, "Swear not at all." This peculiarity often embroiled them with government officials, for "test oaths" were still required to establish the fact that a person was not a Roman Catholic.

The Quakers, beyond a doubt, were a people of deep conviction. They abhorred strife and warfare and refused military service. As advocates of passive resistance, they would turn the other cheek and

Numbering about one-half of New Netherland's ten thousand souls in 1664, they might in time have seized control from within.

The days of the Dutch on the Hudson were numbered, for the English regarded them as intruders. In 1664, after the imperially ambitious Charles II had granted the area to his brother, the Duke of York, a strong English squadron appeared off the decrepit defenses of New Amsterdam. A fuming Peter Stuyvesant, short of all munitions except courage, was forced to surrender without firing a shot. New Amsterdam was thereupon renamed New York, in honor of the Duke of York. England won a splendid harbor, strategically located in the middle of the mainland colonies, and a stately Hudson River penetrating the interior. With the removal of this foreign wedge, the English banner now waved triumphantly over a solid stretch of territory from Maine to the Carolinas.

Yearly Meeting of the Quakers, London, 1696
William Penn (1647–1728), a prominent Quaker in both
America and England, sits to the right of the presiding officer.

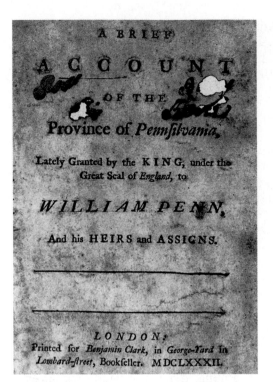

Selling the New Land   Accounts like this one
tried to induce settlers to come to Pennsylvania
with glowing descriptions of life in the new colony.

rebuild their meetinghouse on the site where their enemies had torn it down. Their courage and devotion to principle finally triumphed. Although at times they seemed stubborn and unreasonable, they were a simple, devoted, democratic people, contending in their own high-minded way for religious and civic freedom.

William Penn, a well-born and athletic young Englishman, was attracted to the Quaker faith in 1660, when only sixteen years old. His father, disapproving, administered a sound flogging. After various adventures in the army (the best portrait of the peaceful Quaker has him in armor), the youth firmly embraced the despised faith and suffered much persecution. The courts branded him a "saucy" and "impertinent" fellow. Several hundred of his less fortunate fellow Quakers died of cruel treatment, and thousands more were fined, flogged, or cast into dank prisons.

Penn's thoughts naturally turned to the New World, where a sprinkling of Quakers had already fled, notably to Rhode Island, North Carolina, and New Jersey. Eager to establish an asylum for his people, he also hoped to experiment with liberal ideas in government and at the same time make a profit. Finally, in 1681, he managed to secure from the king an immense grant of fertile land, in consideration of a monetary debt owed to his deceased father by the crown. The king called the area Pennsylvania ("Penn's Woodland") in honor of the sire. The modest son, fearing that critics would accuse him of naming it after himself, sought unsuccessfully to change the name.

Pennsylvania was by far the best advertised of all the colonies. Its founder—the "first American advertising man"—sent out paid agents and distributed countless pamphlets printed in English, Dutch, French, and German. Unlike the lures of many other American real estate promoters, then and later, Penn's inducements were generally truthful. He especially welcomed forward-looking spirits and substantial citizens, including industrious carpenters, masons, shoemakers, and other manual workers. His liberal land policy, which encouraged substantial holdings, was instrumental in attracting a heavy inflow of immigrants.

Quaker Pennsylvania and Its Neighbors

Penn formally launched his colony in 1681. His task was simplified by the presence of several thousand "squatters"—Dutch, Swedish, English, Welsh—who were already scattered along the banks of the Delaware River. Philadelphia, meaning "brotherly love" in Greek, was more carefully planned than most colonial cities and consequently enjoyed wide and attractive streets.

Penn farsightedly bought land from the Indians, including Chief Tammany, later patron saint of New York's political Tammany Hall. His treatment of the native peoples was so fair that the Quaker "broad brims" went among them unarmed and even employed them as babysitters. For a brief period, Pennsylvania seemed the promised land of amicable Indian-white relations. Some southern tribes even migrated to Pennsylvania, seeking the Quaker haven. But ironically, Quaker tolerance proved the undoing of Quaker Indian policy. As non-Quaker European immigrants flooded into the province, they undermined the Quakers' own benevolent policy toward the Indians. The feisty Scots-Irish were particularly unpersuaded by Quaker idealism.

Penn's new proprietary regime was unusually liberal and included a representative assembly elected by the landowners. No tax-supported state church drained coffers or demanded allegiance. Freedom of worship was guaranteed to all residents, although Penn, under pressure from London, was forced to deny Catholics and Jews the privilege of voting or holding office. The death penalty was imposed only for treason and murder, as compared with some two hundred capital crimes in England.

Among other noteworthy features, no provision was made by the peace-loving Quakers of Pennsylvania for a military defense. No restrictions were placed on immigration, and naturalization was made easy. The humane Quakers early developed a strong dislike of black slavery, and in the genial glow of Pennsylvania some progress was made toward social reform.

With its many liberal features, Pennsylvania attracted a rich mix of ethnic groups. They included numerous religious misfits who were repelled by the

Penn's Treaty, by Edward Hicks
The peace-loving Quaker founder of Pennsylvania made a serious effort to live in harmony with the Indians, as this treaty-signing scene illustrates. But the westward thrust of white settlement eventually caused friction between the two groups, as in other colonies.

harsh practices of neighboring colonies. This Quaker refuge boasted a surprisingly modern atmosphere in an unmodern age and to an unusual degree afforded economic opportunity, civil liberty, and religious freedom. Even so, "blue laws" prohibited "ungodly revelers," stage plays, playing cards, dice, games, and excessive hilarity.

Under such generally happy auspices, Penn's brainchild grew lustily. The Quakers were shrewd businesspeople, and in a short time the settlers were exporting grain and other foodstuffs. Within two years Philadelphia claimed three hundred houses and twenty-five hundred people. Within nineteen years—by 1700—the colony was surpassed in population and wealth only by long-established Virginia and Massachusetts.

William Penn, who altogether spent about four years in Pennsylvania, was never fully appreciated by his colonists. His governors, some of them incompetent and tactless, quarreled bitterly with the people, who were constantly demanding greater political control. Penn himself became too friendly with James II, the deposed Catholic king. Thrice arrested for treason, thrust for a time into a debtors' prison, and afflicted by a paralytic stroke, he died full of sorrows. His enduring monument was not only a noble experiment in government but also a new commonwealth. Based on civil and religious liberty, and dedicated to freedom of conscience and worship, it held aloft a hopeful torch in a world of semidarkness.

Small Quaker settlements flourished next door to Pennsylvania. New Jersey was started in 1664, when two noble proprietors received the area from the Duke of York. A substantial number of New Englanders, including many whose weary soil had petered out, flocked to the new colony. One of the proprietors sold West New Jersey in 1674 to a group of Quakers, who here set up a sanctuary even before

In a Boston lecture in 1869, Ralph Waldo Emerson (1803–1882) declared,

"The sect of the Quakers in their best representatives appear to me to have come nearer to the sublime history and genius of Christ than any other of the sects."

Pennsylvania was launched. East New Jersey was also acquired in later years by the Quakers, whose wings were clipped in 1702 when the crown combined the two Jerseys in a royal colony.

Swedish-tinged Delaware consisted of only three counties—two at high tide, the witticism goes—and was named after Lord De La Warr, the harsh military governor who had arrived in Virginia in 1610. Harboring some Quakers, and closely associated with Penn's prosperous colony, Delaware was granted its own assembly in 1703. But until the American Revolution it remained under the governor of Pennsylvania.

The Middle Way in the Middle Colonies

The middle colonies—New York, New Jersey, Delaware, and Pennsylvania—enjoyed certain features in common.

In general, the soil was fertile and the expanse of land was broad, unlike rock-bestrewn New England. Pennsylvania, New York, and New Jersey came to be known as the "bread colonies," by virtue of their heavy exports of grain.

Rivers also played a vital role. Broad, languid streams—notably the Susquehanna, the Delaware, and the Hudson—tapped the fur trade of the interior and beckoned adventuresome spirits into the backcountry. The rivers had few cascading waterfalls, unlike New England's, and hence presented little inducement to manufacturing with water-wheel power.

A surprising amount of industry nonetheless hummed in the middle colonies. Virginal forests abounded for lumbering and shipbuilding. The presence of deep river estuaries and landlocked harbors stimulated both commerce and the growth of seaports, such as New York and Philadelphia. Even Albany, more than a hundred miles up the Hudson, was a port of some consequence in colonial days.

The middle colonies were in many respects midway between New England and the southern plantation group. Except in aristocratic New York, the landholdings were generally intermediate in size—smaller than in the big-acreage South but larger than in small-farm New England. Local government lay somewhere between the personalized town meeting of New England and the diffused county government of the South. There were fewer industries in the middle colonies than in New England, more than in the South.

Yet the middle colonies, which in some ways were the most American part of America, could claim certain distinctions in their own right. Generally speaking, the population was more ethnically mixed than that of other settlements. The people were blessed with an unusual degree of religious toleration and democratic control. Earnest and devout Quakers, in particular, made a compassionate contribution to human freedom out of all proportion to their numbers. Desirable land was more easily acquired in the middle colonies than in New England or in the tidewater South. One result was that a considerable amount of economic and social democracy prevailed, though less so in aristocratic New York.

Modern-minded Benjamin Franklin, often regarded as *the* most representative American personality of his era, was a child of the middle colonies. Although it is true that Franklin was born a Yankee in puritanical Boston, he entered Philadelphia as a seventeen-year-old in 1720 with a loaf of bread under each arm and immediately found a congenial home in the urbane, open atmosphere of what was then North America's biggest city. One Pennsylvanian later boasted that Franklin "came to life at seventeen, in Philadelphia."

By the time Franklin arrived in the City of Brotherly Love, the American colonies were themselves "coming to life." Population was growing robustly. Transportation and communication were gradually improving. The British, for the most part, continued their hands-off policies, leaving the colonists to fashion their own local governments, run their own churches, and develop networks of intercolonial trade. As people and products criss-crossed the colonies with increasing frequency and in increasing volume, Americans began to realize that—far removed from Mother England—they were not merely surviving, but truly thriving.

Chronology

1517	Martin Luther begins Protestant Reformation
1536	John Calvin of Geneva publishes *Institutes of the Christian Religion*
1620	Pilgrims sail on the *Mayflower* to Plymouth Bay
1624	Dutch found New Netherland
1629	Charles I dismisses Parliament and persecutes Puritans
1630	Puritans found Massachusetts Bay Colony
1635–1636	Roger Williams convicted of heresy and founds Rhode Island colony
1635–1638	Connecticut and New Haven colonies founded
1637	Pequot War
1638	Anne Hutchinson banished from Massachusetts colony
1639	Connecticut's Fundamental Orders drafted
1642–1648	English Civil War
1643	New England Confederation formed
1655	New Netherland conquers New Sweden
1664	England seizes New Netherland from Dutch East and West Jersey colonies founded
1675–1676	King Philip's War
1681	William Penn founds Pennsylvania colony
1686	Royal authority creates Dominion of New England
1688–1689	Glorious Revolution overthrows Stuarts and Dominion of New England

Europeanizing America or Americanizing Europe?

The history of discovery and colonization raises perhaps the most fundamental question about all American history. Should it be understood as the extension of European civilization into the New World or as the gradual development of a uniquely "American" culture? An older school of thought tended to emphasize the Europeanization of America. Historians of that persuasion paid close attention to the situation in Europe, particularly England and Spain, in the fifteenth and sixteenth centuries. They also focused on the exportation of the values and institutions of the mother countries to the new lands in the western sea. Although some historians also examined the transforming effect of America on Europe, this approach, too, remained essentially Eurocentric.

More recently, historians have concentrated on the distinctiveness of America. The concern with European origins has evolved into a comparative treatment of European settlements in the New World. England, Spain, Holland, and France now attract more attention for the divergent kinds of societies they fostered in America than for the way they commonly pursued Old World ambitions in the New. The newest trend to emerge is a trans-Atlantic history that views European empires and their American colonies as part of a process of cultural cross-fertilization affecting not only the colonies but Europe as well.

This less Eurocentric approach has also changed the way historians explain the colonial development of America. Rather than telling the story of colonization as the imposition of European ways of life through "discovery" and "conquest," historians increasingly view the colonial period as one of "contact" between European and native populations. Works by Richard White, Alfred W. Crosby, William Cronon, and Karen Kupperman have enhanced understanding of the cultural conflicts and exchanges that occurred on the colonial frontier. Ramon Gutierrez's *When Jesus Came, the Corn Mothers Went Away* (1992) has expanded the colonial stage to include interactions between Spanish settlers and Native Americans in the colonial southwest that predated the settlement of New England.

The variety of American societies that emerged out of the interaction of European and Native Americans has also become better appreciated. Early histories by esteemed historians like Perry Miller exaggerated the extent to which the New England Puritan experience defined the essence of America. Not only did these historians overlook non-English experiences, they failed to recognize the diversity in motives, methods, and consequences that existed even within English colonization. The numbers alone tell an interesting story. By 1700 about 220,000 English colonists had emigrated to the Caribbean, about 120,000 to the southern mainland colonies, and only about 40,000 to the Middle Atlantic and New England colonies (although by the mid-eighteenth century, those headed for the latter destination would account for more than half the total). Studies such as Richard S. Dunn's *Sugar and Slaves* (1972) emphasize the importance of the Caribbean in early English colonization efforts and make clear that the desire for economic gain, more than the quest for religious freedom, fueled the migration to the Caribbean islands. Similarly, Edmund S. Morgan's *American Slavery, American Freedom* (1975) stresses the role of economic ambition in explaining the English peopling of the Chesapeake and the eventual importation of African slaves to that region. Studies by Bernard Bailyn and David Hackett Fisher demonstrate that there was scarcely a "typical" English migrant to the New World. English colonists migrated both singly and in families, and for economic, social, political, and religious reasons.

Recent studies have also paid more attention to the conflicts that emerged out of this diversity in settler populations and colonial societies. This perspective emphasizes the contests for economic and political supremacy within the colonies, such as the efforts of the Massachusetts Bay elite to ward off the challenges of religious "heretics" and the pressures that an increasingly restless lower class put on wealthy merchants and large landowners. Nowhere was internal conflict so prevalent as in the ethnically diverse middle colonies, where factional antagonisms became the defining feature of public life.

The picture of colonial America that is emerging from all this new scholarship is of a society unique—and diverse—from inception. No longer simply Europe transplanted, American colonial society by 1700 is now viewed as an outgrowth of many intertwining roots—of different European and African heritages, of varied encounters with native peoples and a wilderness environment, and of complicated mixtures of settler populations, each with its own distinctive set of ambitions.

SUGGESTED READINGS

PRIMARY SOURCE DOCUMENTS

John Winthrop, "A Model of Christian Charity" (1630), in *The American Primer*, edited by Daniel Boorstin, outlines the goals of the Puritan errand into the wilderness. Winthrop's "Speech on Liberty"* (1645), in his *History of New England* (1853), established the colony's fundamental political principles. William Bradford, *Of Plymouth Plantation,* * edited by Samuel E. Morison (1952), is a rich contemporary account.

SECONDARY SOURCES

New England has received more scholarly attention than any other colonial region. Harry Stout, *The New England Soul: Preaching and Culture in Colonial New England* (1986), is a recent comprehensive account. A brilliant and complex intellectual history is Perry Miller, *The New England Mind* (2 vols., 1939, 1953), a work that has long been a landmark for other scholars. Sacvan Bercovitch traces the heritage of the New England temperament in *The Puritan Origins of the American Self* (1975). Also see his *The American Jeremiad* (1978) More recent interpretations of Puritanism include Charles Hambrick-Stowe, *The Practice of Piety* (1982), and Andrew Delbanco, *The Puritan Ordeal* (1989). David Hall, *Worlds of Wonder, Days of Judgment: Popular Religious Belief in Early New*

England (1989), describes the relation between high Puritan doctrine and lay belief and practice. Jon Butler, *Awash in a Sea of Faith: Christianizing the American People* (1990), is comprehensive. John T. Ellis pays special attention to religious issues in *Catholics in Colonial America* (1965), as does Edmund S. Morgan in *Roger Williams: The Church and State* (1967). On other religious minorities, see Carla Gardina Pestana, *Quakers and Baptists in Colonial Massachusetts* (1991). For analyses of Puritan-Indian relations, see Francis Jennings, *The Invasion of America* (1975), and Neal Salisbury, *Manitou and Providence* (1982). For a fascinating account of some settlers' assimilation into Indian society, see John Demos, *The Unredeemed Captive: A Family Story from Early America* (1994). David S. Lovejoy discusses the impact of England's Glorious Revolution on the colonies in *The Glorious Revolution in America* (1975). Areas outside New England are dealt with in Gary Nash, *Quakers and Politics: Pennsylvania, 1681–1726* (1971); Patricia Bonomi, *A Factious People: Politics and Society in Colonial New York* (1971); Richard and Mary Dunn, eds., *The World of William Penn* (1986); Oliver A. Rink, *Holland on the Hudson: An Economic and Social History of Dutch New York* (1986); and Joyce D. Goodfriend, *Before the Melting Pot: Society and Culture in Colonial New York City, 1664–1730* (1992). The essays in Michael Zuckerman, ed., *Friends and Neighbors: Group Life in America's First Plural Society* (1982), argue that the middle colonies provide the best early model for America as a whole. Timothy H. Breen, *Puritans and Adventurers* (1980), draws contrasts between Virginia and New England.

---

*An asterisk indicates that the document, or an excerpt from it, can be found in Thomas A. Bailey and David M. Kennedy, eds. *The American Spirit: United States History as Seen by Contemporaries,* 9th ed. (Boston: Houghton Miffin, 1998).

4

American Life in the Seventeenth Century
1607–1692

Being thus passed the vast ocean, and a sea of troubles before in their preparation . . . , they had now no friends to wellcome them, nor inns to entertaine or refresh their weatherbeaten bodys, no houses or much less towns to repaire too, to seeke for succore.

WILLIAM BRADFORD, *OF PLYMOUTH PLANTATION*, C. 1630

The Unhealthy Chesapeake

Life in the American wilderness was nasty, brutish, and short for the earliest Chesapeake settlers. Malaria, dysentery, and typhoid took a cruel toll, cutting ten years off the life expectancy of newcomers from England. Half the people born in early Virginia and Maryland did not survive to celebrate their twentieth birthdays. Few of the remaining half lived to see their fiftieth — or even their fortieth, if they were women.

The disease-ravaged settlements of the Chesapeake grew only slowly in the seventeenth century, mostly through fresh immigration from England. The great majority of immigrants were single men in their late teens and early twenties, and most perished soon after arrival. Surviving males competed for the affections of the extremely scarce women, whom they outnumbered nearly six to one in 1650 and still outnumbered by three to two at the end of the century. Eligible women did not remain single for long.

Families were both few and fragile in this ferocious environment. Most men could not find mates. Most marriages were destroyed by the death of a partner within seven years. Scarcely any children reached adulthood under the care of two parents, and almost no one knew a grandparent. Weak family

64

ties were reflected in the many pregnancies among unmarried young girls. In one Maryland county, more than a third of all brides were already pregnant when they wed.

Yet despite these hardships, the Chesapeake colonies struggled on. The native-born inhabitants eventually acquired immunity to the killer diseases that had ravaged the original immigrants. The presence of more women allowed more families to form, and by the end of the seventeenth century the white population of the Chesapeake was growing on the basis of its own birthrate. As the eighteenth century opened, Virginia, with some fifty-nine thousand people, was the most populous colony. Maryland, with about thirty thousand, was the third largest (after Massachusetts).

The Tobacco Economy

Although unhealthy for human life, the Chesapeake was immensely hospitable to tobacco cultivation. Profit-hungry settlers often planted tobacco to sell before they planted corn to eat. (Cornfields were also feared as staging areas for Indian ambushes.) Seeking fresh fields to plant to tobacco, these new immigrants plunged ever farther up the river valleys, provoking Indian attacks.

Leaf-laden ships annually hauled some 1.5 million pounds (680,000 kilograms) of tobacco out of Chesapeake Bay by the 1630s and almost 40 million pounds (18 million kilograms) a year by the end of the century. This enormous production depressed prices, but colonial Chesapeake tobacco growers

> *An agent for the Virginia Company in London submitted the following description of the Virginia Colony in 1622:*
>
> "I found the plantations generally seated upon mere salt marshes full of infectious bogs and muddy creeks and lakes, and thereby subjected to all those inconveniences and diseases which are so commonly found in the most unsound and most unhealthy parts of England."

Early Tobacco Advertising
Crude woodcut labels like this were used to identify various "brands" of tobacco.

responded to falling prices in the familiar way of farmers: by planting still more acres to tobacco and bringing still more product to market.

More tobacco meant more labor, but where was it to come from? Families procreated too slowly to provide it by natural population increase. Indians died too quickly on contact with whites to be a reliable labor force. African slaves cost too much money. But England still had a "surplus" of displaced farmers, desperate for employment. Many of them, as "indentured servants," voluntarily mortgaged the sweat of their bodies for several years to Chesapeake masters. In exchange they received transatlantic passage and eventual "freedom dues," including a few barrels of corn, a suit of clothes—and perhaps a small parcel of land.

Both Virginia and Maryland employed the "headright" system to encourage the importation of servant workers. Under its terms, whoever paid the passage of a laborer received the right to acquire fifty acres of land. Masters—not the servants themselves—thus reaped the benefits of landownership from the headright system. Some masters, men who already had at least modest financial means, soon parlayed their investments in servants into huge fortunes in real estate. They became the great merchant-planters, lords of vast riverfront estates that came to dominate the agriculture and commerce of the southern colonies. Ravenous for both labor and land, Chesapeake planters brought some 100,000 indentured servants to the region by 1700. These "white slaves" represented more than three-quarters of all European immigrants to Virginia and Maryland in the seventeenth century.

Indentured servants led a hard but hopeful life in the early days of the Chesapeake settlements. They looked forward to becoming free and acquiring land of their own after completing their term of servitude. But as prime land became scarcer, masters became increasingly resistant to including land grants in "freedom dues." The servants' lot grew harsher as the seventeenth century wore on. Misbehaving servants, such as a housemaid who became pregnant or a laborer who killed a hog, might be punished with an extended term of service. Even after formal freedom was granted, penniless freed workers often had little choice but to hire themselves out for pitifully low wages to their former masters.

Frustrated Freemen and Bacon's Rebellion

An accumulating mass of footloose, impoverished freemen was drifting discontentedly about the Chesapeake region by the late seventeenth century. Mostly single young men, they were frustrated by their broken hopes of acquiring land, as well as by their gnawing failure to find single women to marry.

The swelling numbers of these wretched bachelors rattled the established planters. The Virginia assembly in 1670 disfranchised most of the landless knockabouts, accusing them of "having little interest in the country" and causing "tumults at the election to the disturbance of his majesty's peace." Virginia's Governor William Berkeley lamented his lot as ruler of this rabble: "How miserable that man is that governs a people where six parts of seven at least are poor, endebted, discontented, and armed."

Berkeley's misery soon increased. About a thousand Virginians broke out of control in 1676, led by a twenty-nine-year-old planter, Nathaniel Bacon. Many of the rebels were frontiersmen who had been forced into the untamed backcountry in search of arable land. They fiercely resented Berkeley's friendly policies toward the Indians, whose thriving fur trade the governor monopolized. When Berkeley refused to retaliate for a series of savage Indian attacks on frontier settlements, Bacon and his followers took matters into their own hands. They fell murderously upon the Indians, friendly and hostile alike, chased Berkeley from Jamestown, and put the torch to the capital. Chaos swept the raw colony, as frustrated freemen and resentful servants—described as "a rabble of the basest sort of people"—went on a rampage of plundering and pilfering.

As this civil war in Virginia ground on, Bacon suddenly died of disease, like so many of his fellow colonials. Berkeley thereupon crushed the uprising with brutal cruelty, hanging more than twenty rebels. Back in England Charles II complained, "That old fool has put to death more people in that naked country than I did here for the murder of my father."

The distant English king could scarcely imagine the depths of passion and fear that Bacon's Rebellion excited in Virginia. Bacon had ignited the smoldering unhappiness of landless former servants, and he had pitted the hard-scrabble backcountry frontiersmen against the haughty gentry of the tidewater plantations. The rebellion was now suppressed, but these tensions remained. Lordly planters, surrounded by a still-seething sea of malcontents, anxiously looked about for less troublesome laborers to toil in the restless tobacco kingdom. Their eyes soon lit on Africa.

Nathaniel Bacon assailed Virginia's Governor William Berkeley in 1676

"for having protected, favored, and emboldened the Indians against His Majesty's loyal subjects, never contriving, requiring, or appointing any due or proper means of satisfaction for their many invasions, robberies, and murders committed upon us."

For his part, Governor Berkeley declared:

"I have lived thirty-four years amongst you [Virginians], as uncorrupt and diligent as ever [a] Governor was, [while] Bacon is a man of two years amongst you, his person and qualities unknown to most of you, and to all men else, by any virtuous act that ever I heard of. . . . I will take counsel of wiser men than myself, but Mr. Bacon has none about him but the lowest of the people."

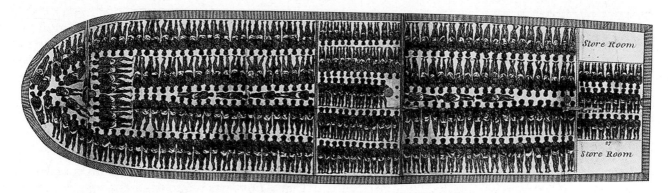

The "Middle Passage"   The "Middle Passage" referred to the transatlantic sea voyage that brought slaves to the New World—the long and hazardous "middle" segment of a journey that began with a forced march to the African coast and ended with a trek into the American interior.

Colonial Slavery

Perhaps 10 million Africans were carried in chains to the New World in the three centuries or so following Columbus's landing. Only about 400,000 of them ended up in North America, the great majority arriving after 1700. Most of the early human cargoes were hauled to Spanish and Portuguese South America or to the sugar-rich West Indies.

Africans had been brought to Jamestown as early as 1619, but as late as 1670 they numbered only about 2,000 in Virginia (out of a total population of some 35,000 persons) and about 7 percent of the 50,000 people in the southern plantation colonies as a whole. Hard-pinched white colonists, struggling to stay alive and to hack crude clearings out of the forests, could not afford to pay high prices for slaves who might die soon after arrival. White servants might die, too, but they were far less costly.

Drastic change came in the 1680s. Rising wages in England shrank the pool of penniless folk willing to gamble on a new life or an early death as indentured servants in America. At the same time, the large planters were growing increasingly fearful of the multitudes of potentially mutinous former servants in their midst. By the mid-1680s, for the first time, black slaves outnumbered white servants among the plantation colonies' new arrivals. In 1698 the Royal African Company lost its crown-granted monopoly on carrying slaves to the colonies.

Estimated Slave Imports to the New World, 1601–1810

	17th Century	18th Century	Total	Percent
Spanish America	292,500	578,600	871,100	11.7
Brazil	560,000	1,891,400	2,451,400	33
British Caribbean	263,700	1,401,000	1,664,700	22.5
Dutch Caribbean	40,000	460,000	500,000	6.7
French Caribbean	155,800	1,348,400	1,504,200	20.3
Danish Caribbean	4,000	24,000	28,000	.4
British North America and future United States	10,000	390,000	400,000	5.4
TOTAL			7,419,400	100

This table clearly shows the huge concentration of the slave system in the Caribbean and South America. British North America's southern colonies constituted the extreme northern periphery of this system.
[Source: Philip D. Curtin, *The Atlantic Slave Trade* (Madison: University of Wisconsin Press, 1969)]

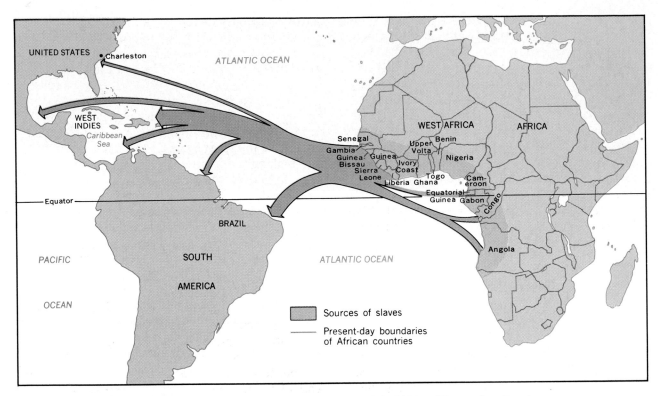

Main Sources of African Slaves, c. 1500–1800   The three centuries of the "African Diaspora" scattered blacks all over the New World, with about 400,000 coming to North America.

Enterprising Americans, especially Rhode Islanders, rushed to cash in on the lucrative slave trade, and the supply of slaves rose steeply. More than ten thousand Africans were pushed ashore in America in the decade after 1700, and tens of thousands more in the next half-century. Blacks accounted for nearly half the population of Virginia by 1750. In South Carolina they outnumbered whites two to one.

Most of the slaves who reached North America came from the west coast of Africa, especially the area stretching from present-day Senegal to Angola. They were originally captured by African coastal tribes, who traded them in crude markets on the shimmering tropical beaches to itinerant European—and American—flesh merchants. Usually branded and bound, the captives were herded aboard sweltering ships for the gruesome "middle passage," on which death rates ran as high as 20 percent. Terrified survivors were eventually shoved onto auction blocks in New World ports like Newport, Rhode Island, or Charleston, South Carolina, where a giant slave market traded in human misery for more than a century.

A few of the earliest African immigrants gained their freedom, and some even became slaveowners themselves. But as the number of Africans in their midst increased dramatically toward the end of the seventeenth century, white colonists reacted remorselessly to this supposed racial threat.

The Mennonites of Germantown, Pennsylvania, recorded the earliest known protest against slavery in America in 1688.

"There is a saying, that we should do to all men like as we will be done ourselves. . . . But to bring men hither, or to rob and sell them against their will, we stand against. . . . Pray, what thing in the world can be done worse towards us, than if men should rob or steal us away, and sell us for slaves to strange countries, separating husbands from their wives and children?"

Earlier in the century the legal difference between a slave and a servant was unclear. But now the law began to make sharp distinctions between the two—largely on the basis of race. Statutes appeared that formally decreed the iron conditions of slavery for blacks. These earliest "slave codes" made blacks *and their children* the property (or "chattels") for life of their white masters. Some colonies made it a crime to teach a slave to read or write. Not even conversion to Christianity could qualify a slave for freedom. Thus did the God-fearing whites put the fear of God into their hapless black laborers. Slavery might have begun in America for economic reasons, but by the end of the seventeenth century, it was clear that racial discrimination also powerfully molded the American slave system.

Africans in America

In the deepest South, slave life was especially severe. The climate was hostile to health, and the labor was life-draining. The widely scattered South Carolina rice and indigo plantations were lonely hells on earth where gangs of mostly male Africans toiled and perished. Only fresh imports could sustain the slave population under these loathsome conditions.

Blacks in the tobacco-growing Chesapeake region had a somewhat easier lot. Tobacco was a less physically demanding crop than those of the deeper South. Tobacco plantations were larger an one another than rice plantations. The proximity of these plantations permitted more frequent contact with friends and relatives. By about 1720 the proportion of females in the Chesapeake slave population had begun to rise, making family life possible. The captive black population of the Chesapeake area soon began to grow not only through new imports but also through its own fertility—making it one of the few slave societies in history to perpetuate itself by its own natural reproduction.

Native-born African-Americans contributed to the growth of a stable and distinctive slave culture, a mixture of African and American elements of speech, religion, and folkways (see "Makers of America: From African to African-American," pp. 70–71). On the sea islands off South Carolina's coast, blacks evolved a unique language, *Gullah* (probably a corruption of *Angola*, the African region from which many of them had come). It blended English with several African languages, including Yoruba, Ibo, and Hausa. Through it many African words have passed into American speech—such as *goober* (peanut), *gumbo* (okra), and *voodoo* (witchcraft). The ringshout, a West African religious dance performed by shuffling in a circle while answering a preacher's shouts, was brought to colonial America by slaves and eventually contributed to the development of jazz. The banjo and the bongo drum were other African contributions to American culture.

A Rice Plantation in the Colonial South
Rice cultivation, imported from Africa along with African slaves to work the swampy rice fields, made South Carolina the rice basket of the British Empire.

From African to African-American

Dragged in chains from West African shores, the first African-Americans struggled to preserve their diverse heritages from the ravages of slavery. Their children, the first generation of American-born slaves, melded these various African traditions—Guinean, Ibo, Yoruba, Angolan—into a distinctive African-American culture. Their achievement sustained them during the cruelties of enslavement and has endured to enrich American life to this day.

With the arrival of the first Africans in the seventeenth century, a cornucopia of African traditions poured into the New World: handicrafts and skills in numerous trades; a plethora of languages, musics, and cuisines; even rice-planting techniques that conquered the inhospitable soil of South Carolina. It was North America's rice paddies, tilled by experienced West Africans, that introduced rice into the English diet and furnished so many English tables with the sticky staple.

These first American slaves were mostly males. Upon arrival they were sent off to small isolated farms, where social contact with other Africans, especially women, was an unheard-of luxury. Yet their legal status was at first uncertain. A few slaves were able to buy their freedom in the seventeenth century. One, Anthony Johnson of Northampton County, Virginia, actually became a slaveholder himself.

But by the beginning of the eighteenth century, a settled slave society was emerging in the southern colonies. Laws tightened; slave traders stepped up their deliveries of human cargo; large plantations formed. Most significantly, a new generation of

(above) **Africans Destined for Slavery** The engraving from 1830 is an example of antislavery propaganda in the pre–Civil War era. It shows hapless Africans being brought ashore in America under the whips of slave traders and, ironically, under the figurative shadow of the national Capitol. (right) **A Royal African Company Account Log of Slaves Imported to the West Indies, 1698–1708** Note the rapid expansion of the slave trade as the eighteenth century opened.

An Account of the Number of Negroes delivered in to the Islands of Barbadoes, Jamaica, and Antego, from the Year 1698 to 1708, since the Trade was Opened, taken from the Accounts sent from the respective Governours of those Islands to the Lords Commissioners of Trade, whereby it appears the African Trade is encreas'd to four times more since its being laid Open, than it was under an Exclusive Company.

Between what Years deliver'd.	Nº. of Negroes delivered into Barbados.	Number delivered into Jamaica.	Number delivered into Antego.
Between the 8 April, 1698			
To April 1699	3436		
To April 1700	3080		
To 5 ditto 1701	4311		
To 10 ditto 1702	9213		
To 31 Mar. 1703	4461		
To 5 April 1704	1876?		
To 2d. ditto 1705	3319		
To 5 ditto 1706	1875		
To 12 May 1707	2720		
To 29 April 1708	1018		
Between 29 Sept. - - 1698 and 29 Decemb. 1698		1273	
Between 7 April - 1699 and 28 March 1700		5766	
From 28 Mar. to 3 Apr. 1701		6068	
3 Apr. 1701. to 20 dit. 1702		8505	
20 dit. 1702 to 12 dit. 1703		2258	
12 dit. 1703 to 18 dit. 1704		2711	
18 dit. 1704 to 24 dit. 1705		3421	
24 dit. 1705 to 27 dit. 1706		5462	
27 dit. 1706 to 22 dit. 1707		2122	
22 dit. 1707 to 26 dit. 1708		6623	
To June 1708		187	
1698			
June 1699			18
Between June - - 1700 and 24 April 1701			212
			364
Between 24 April - 1701 and 30 March 1702			2395
To April 1703			1670
To Nov. 1704			155
To 1705			269
To 1706			530
To 1707			114
	35409	44376	7123

Besides which there are 7 Separate Ships named in the foregoing List for Antego, but not the Number of Negroes, so we may well compute them at 1200 more, which arriv'd between 1699 and 1700.

UNITED STATES SLAVE TRADE. 1830.

(left) Yarrow Mamout, by Charles Willson Peale, 1819   When Peale painted this portrait, Mamout was over 100 years old. A devout Muslim brought to Maryland as a slave, he eventually bought his freedom and settled in Georgetown.
(right) The Emergence of an African-American Culture   In this scene from the mid-nineteenth century, African-Americans play musical instruments of European derivation, like the fiddle, as well as instruments of African origin, like the bones and banjo—a vivid illustration of the blending of the two cultures in the crucible of the New World.

American-born slaves joined their forebears at labor in the fields. By 1740 large groups of slaves lived together on sprawling plantations, the American-born outnumbered the African-born, and the importation of African slaves slowed.

Forging a common culture and finding a psychological weapon with which to resist their masters and preserve their dignity were daunting challenges for American-born slaves. Plantation life was beastly, an endless cycle of miserable toil in the field or foundry from sunup to sundown. Female slaves were forced to perform double duty. After a day's backbreaking work, women were expected to sit up for hours spinning, weaving, or sewing to clothe themselves and their families. Enslaved women also lived in constant fear of sexual exploitation by conscienceless masters.

Yet eventually a vibrant slave culture began to flower. And precisely because of the diversity of African peoples represented in America, the culture that emerged was a uniquely New World creation. It derived from no single African model and incorporated many Western elements, though often with significant modifications.

Slave religion illustrates this pattern. Cut off from their native African religions, most slaves became Christians, but fused elements of African and Western traditions and drew their own conclusions from Scripture. White Christians might point to Christ's teachings of humility and obedience to encourage slaves to "stay in their place"; but black Christians emphasized God's role in freeing the Hebrews from slavery and saw Jesus as the Messiah who would deliver them from bondage. They also often retained an African definition of heaven as a place where they would be reunited with their ancestors.

At their Sunday and evening-time prayer meetings, slaves also patched African remnants onto conventional Christian ritual. Black Methodists, for example, ingeniously evaded the traditional Methodist ban on dancing as sinful: three or four people would stand still in a ring, clapping hands and beating time with their feet (but never crossing their legs, thus not officially "dancing"), while others walked around the ring, singing in unison. This "ringshouting" derived from African practices; modern American dances, including the Charleston, in turn derived from this African-American hybrid.

Christian slaves also often used outwardly religious songs as encoded messages about escape or rebellion. "Good News, the Chariot's Comin" might sound like an innocent hymn about divine deliverance, but it could also announce the arrival of a guide to lead fugitives safely to the North. Similarly, "Wade in the Water" taught fleeing slaves one way of covering their trail. The "Negro spirituals" that took shape as a distinctive form of American music thus had their origins in *both* Christianity and slavery.

Indeed, much American music was born in the slave quarters from African importations. Jazz, with its meandering improvisations and complex syncopations and rhythms, constitutes the most famous example. But this rich cultural harvest came at the cost of generations of human agony.

Slaves also helped mightily to build the country with their labor. A few became skilled artisans—carpenters, bricklayers, and tanners. But chiefly they performed the sweaty toil of clearing swamps, grubbing out trees, and other menial tasks. Condemned to life under the lash, slaves naturally pined for freedom. A slave revolt erupted in New York City in 1712 that cost the lives of a dozen whites and caused the execution of twenty-one blacks, some of them burned at the stake over a slow fire. More than fifty resentful South Carolina blacks along the Stono River exploded in revolt in 1739 and tried to march to Spanish Florida, only to be stopped by the local militia. But in the end the slaves in the South proved to be a more manageable labor force than the white indentured servants they gradually replaced. No slave uprising in American history matched the scale of Bacon's Rebellion.

Southern Society

As slavery spread, the gaps in the South's social structure widened. The rough equality of poverty and disease of the early days was giving way to a defined hierarchy of wealth and status in the early eighteenth century. At the top of this southern social ladder perched a small but powerful covey of great planters. Owning gangs of slaves and vast domains of land, the planters ruled the region's economy and virtually monopolized political power. A clutch of extended clans—such as the Fitzhughs, the Lees, and the Washingtons—possessed among them horizonless tracts of Virginia real estate, and together they dominated the House of Burgesses. Just before the Revolutionary War, 70 percent of the leaders of the Virginia legislature came from families established in Virginia before 1690—the famed "first families of Virginia," or "FFVs."

Yet, legend to the contrary, these great seventeenth-century merchant planters were not silk-swathed cavaliers gallantly imitating the ways of English country gentlemen. They did eventually build stately riverfront manors, occasionally rode to the hounds, and some of them even cultivated the arts and accumulated distinguished libraries. But for the most part they were a hardworking, businesslike lot, laboring long hours over the problems of plantation management. Few problems were more vexatious than the unruly, often surly, servants. One Virginia governor had such difficulty keeping his servants sober that he struck a deal allowing them to get drunk the next day if they would only lay off the liquor long enough to look after his guests at a celebration of the queen's birthday in 1711.

Beneath the planters—far beneath them in wealth, prestige, and political power—were the small farmers, the largest social group. They tilled their modest plots and might own one or two slaves, but they lived a ragged, hand-to-mouth existence. Still lower on the social scale were the landless whites, most of them luckless former indentured servants. Under them were those persons still serving out the term of their indenture. Their numbers gradually diminished as black slaves increasingly replaced white indentured servants toward the end of the

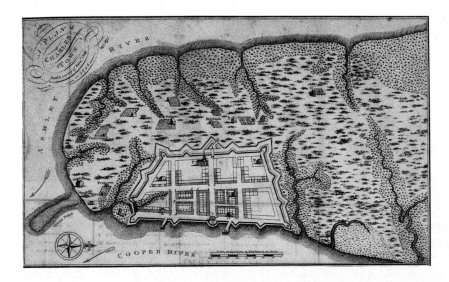

Plan of Early Charleston, South Carolina Founded in 1680, Charleston grew from these modest beginnings to become the largest city in the mostly rural southern colonies. It flourished as a seaport for the shipment to England of slave-grown Carolina rice.

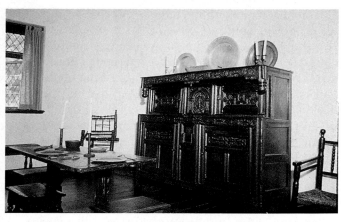

A Merchant Planter's Home and Its Dining Room
Simple by later standards, this house was home to the family of a substantial planter in the seventeenth century. It stands on land in the Virginia tidewater region first acquired by Adam Thoroughgood, who arrived in Virginia Colony as an indentured servant in 1621. By 1635, as a freeman, he had recruited 105 settlers to the colony and was rewarded, according to the practice of the headright system, with the title to some 5,250 acres along the Lynnhaven River. There his grandson erected this house in about 1680. It was continuously occupied by the Thoroughgood family for more than two centuries, until the 1920s.

seventeenth century. The oppressed black slaves, of course, remained enchained in society's basement.

Few cities sprouted in the colonial South, and consequently an urban professional class, including lawyers and financiers, was slow to emerge. Southern life revolved around the great plantations, distantly isolated from one another. Waterways provided the principal means of transportation. Roads were so wretched that in bad weather funeral parties could not reach church burial grounds—an obstacle that accounts for the development of family burial plots in the South, a practice unlike anything in old England or New England.

The New England Family

Nature smiled more benignly on pioneer New Englanders than on their disease-plagued fellow colonists to the south. Clean water and cool temperatures retarded the spread of killer microbes. In stark contrast to the fate of Chesapeake immigrants, settlers in seventeenth-century New England *added* ten years to their life spans by migrating from the Old World. One settler claimed that "a sip of New

England's air is better than a whole draft of old England's ale." The first generations of Puritan colonists enjoyed, on the average, about seventy years on this earth—not very different from the life expectancy of present-day Americans.

In further contrast with the Chesapeake, New Englanders tended to migrate not as single individuals but as families, and the family remained at the center of New England life. Almost from the outset, New England's population grew from natural reproductive increase. The people were remarkably fertile, even if the soil was not.

Early marriage encouraged the booming birthrate. Women typically wed by their early twenties and produced babies about every two years thereafter until menopause. Ceaseless childbearing drained the vitality of many pioneer women, as the weather-eroded colonial tombstones eloquently reveal. A number of the largest families were borne by several mothers, though claims about the frequency of death in childbirth have probably been exaggerated. But the dread of death in the birthing bed haunted many women, and it was small wonder that they came to fear pregnancy. A married woman could expect to experience up to ten pregnancies and rear as many as eight surviving children.

Massachusetts governor William Phips was one of twenty-seven children, all by the same mother. A New England woman might well have dependent children living in her household from the earliest days of her marriage up until the day of her death, and child raising became in essence her full-time occupation.

The longevity of the New Englanders contributed to family stability. Children grew up in nurturing environments where they were expected to learn habits of obedience, above all. They received guidance not only from their parents but from their grandparents as well. This novel intergenerational continuity has inspired the observation that New England "invented" grandparents. Family stability was reflected in low premarital pregnancy rates (again in contrast with the Chesapeake) and in the generally strong, tranquil social structure characteristic of colonial New England.

Still other contrasts came to differentiate the southern and New England ways of life. Oddly enough, the fragility of southern families advanced the economic security of southern women, especially of women's property rights. Because southern men frequently died young, leaving widows with small children to support, the southern colonies generally allowed married women to retain separate title to their property and gave widows the right to inherit their husband's estates. But in New England, Puritan lawmakers worried that recognizing women's

Mrs. Elizabeth Freake and Baby Mary
This portrait of a Boston mother and child in about 1674 suggests the strong family ties that characterized early New England society.

New England early acquired a reputation as a healthful environment. Urging his fellow Englishmen to emigrate to Massachusetts Bay Colony in 1630, the Reverend John White described New England (somewhat fancifully) as follows:

"No country yields a more propitious air for our temper than New England. . . . Many of our people that have found themselves always weak and sickly at home, have become strong and healthy there: perhaps by the dryness of the air and constant temper[ature] of it, which seldom varies from cold to heat, as it does with us. . . . Neither are the natives at any time troubled with pain of teeth, soreness of eyes, or ache in their limbs."

separate property rights would undercut the unity of married persons by acknowledging conflicting interests between husband and wife. New England women usually gave up their property rights, therefore, when they married. Yet in contrast to old England, the laws of New England made secure provision for the property rights of widows—and even extended important protections to women within marriage.

"A true wife accounts subjection her honor," one Massachusetts Puritan leader declared, expressing a sentiment then common in Europe as well as America. But in the New World, a rudimentary conception of women's rights as individuals was beginning to appear in the seventeenth century. Women still could not vote, and the popular attitude persisted that they were morally weaker than men—a belief rooted in the biblical tale of Eve's treachery in the Garden of Eden. But a husband's power over his wife was not absolute. The New England authorities could and did intervene to restrain abusive spouses. One man was punished for kicking his wife off a stool; another was disciplined for drawing an "uncivil" portrait of his mate in the snow. Women also had some spheres of autonomy. Midwifery—assisting with childbirths—was a virtual female monopoly, and midwives often fostered networks of women bonded by the common travails of motherhood. One Boston midwife alone delivered over 3,000 babies.

Above all, the laws of Puritan New England sought to defend the integrity of marriages. Divorce was exceedingly rare, and the authorities commonly ordered separated couples to reunite. Outright abandonment was among the very few permissible grounds for divorce. Adultery was another. Convicted adulterers—especially if they were women—were whipped in public, and forced foreverafter to wear the capital letter "A" cut out in cloth and sewed on their outer garment—the basis for Nathaniel Hawthorne's famous 1850 tale, *The Scarlet Letter*.

Life in the New England Towns

Sturdy New Englanders evolved a tightly knit society, the basis of which was small villages and farms. This development was natural in a people anchored by geography and hemmed in by the Indians, the French, and the Dutch. Puritanism likewise made for unity of purpose—and for concern about the moral health of the whole community. It was no accident that the nineteenth-century crusade for abolishing black slavery—with Massachusetts agitators at the forefront—sprang in some degree from the New England conscience, with its Puritan roots.

In the Chesapeake region, the expansion of settlement was somewhat random and was usually undertaken by lone-wolf planters on their own initiative; but New England society grew in a more orderly fashion. New towns were legally chartered by the colonial authorities, and the distribution of land was entrusted to the steady hands of soberminded town fathers, or "proprietors." After receiving a grant of land from the colonial legislature, the proprietors moved themselves and their families to the designated place and laid out their town. It usually consisted of a meetinghouse, which served as both the place of worship and the town hall, surrounded by houses. Also marked out was a village green, where the militia could drill. Each family received several parcels of land, including a woodlot for fuel, a tract suitable for growing crops, and another for pasturing animals.

Towns of more than fifty families were required to provide elementary education, and a majority of the adults knew how to read and write. As early as

Graveyard Art These New England colonists evidently died in the prime of life. Carving likenesses on grave markers was a common way of commemorating the dead.

Now the Child being entred in his Letters and Spelling, let him learn these and such like Sentences by Heart, whereby he will be both instructed in his Duty, and encouraged in his Learning.

The Dutiful Child's Promises,

I Will fear GOD, and honour the KING.
  I will honour my Father & Mother.
I will Obey my Superiours.
I will Submit to my Elders.
I will Love my Friends.
I will hate no Man.
I will forgive my Enemies, and pray to God for them.
I will as much as in me lies keep all God's Holy Commandments.

The New England Primer
Religious instruction loomed large in the early New England schools. This widely used schoolbook taught lessons of social duty and Christian faith, as well as reading and writing.

The Massachusetts School Law of 1647 stated:

"It being one chief project of the old deluder, Satan, to keep men from the knowledge of the Scriptures, as in former times by keeping them in an unknown tongue, it is therefore ordered that every township in this jurisdiction, after the Lord has increased them [in] number to fifty householders, shall then forthwith appoint one within their town to teach all such children as shall resort to him to write and read, whose wages shall be paid either by the parents or masters of such children, or by the inhabitants in general."

1636, just eight years after the colony's founding, the Massachusetts Puritans established Harvard College, today the oldest corporation in America, to train local boys for the ministry. Only in 1693, eighty-six years after staking out Jamestown, did the Virginians establish their first college, William and Mary.

Puritans ran their own churches, and democracy in Congregational church government led logically to democracy in political government. The town meeting, in which the adult males met together and each man voted, was a showcase and a classroom for democracy. New England villagers from the outset gathered regularly in their meetinghouses to elect their officials, appoint schoolmasters, and discuss such mundane matters as road repairs. The town meeting, observed Thomas Jefferson, was "the best school of political liberty the world ever saw."

The Half-Way Covenant and the Salem Witch Trials

Yet worries plagued the God-fearing pioneers of these tidy New England settlements. The pressure of a growing population was gradually dispersing the Puritans onto outlying farms, far from the control of church and neighbors. And although the core of Puritan belief still burned brightly, the passage of time was dampening the first generation's flaming religious zeal. About the middle of the seventeenth century a new form of sermon began to be heard from Puritan pulpits—the "jeremiad." Taking their cue from the doom-saying Old Testament prophet Jeremiah, earnest preachers scolded parishioners for their waning piety. Especially alarming was the apparent decline in conversions—testimonials by individuals that they had received God's grace and therefore deserved to be admitted to the church as members of the elect. Troubled ministers in 1662 announced a new formula for church membership, the "Half-Way Covenant." It offered partial membership rights to people not yet converted.

The Half-Way Covenant dramatized the difficulty of maintaining at fever pitch the religious devotion of the founding generation. Jeremiads continued to thunder from the pulpits, but as time went on, the doors of the Puritan churches swung fully open to all comers, whether converted or not.

Larger-scale witchcraft persecutions were then common in Europe, and several outbreaks had already flared forth in the colonies. But the reign of horror in Salem grew not only from the superstitions of the age but also from the unsettled social and religious conditions of the rapidly evolving Massachusetts village. Most of the accused witches were associated with Salem's prosperous merchant elite; their accusers came largely from the ranks of the poorer families in Salem's agricultural hinterland. The episode thus reflected the widening social stratification of New England, as well as the anxieties of many religious traditionalists that the Puritan heritage was being eclipsed by Yankee commercialism. The witchcraft hysteria eventually ended in 1693 when the governor, alarmed by an accusation against his own wife and supported by the more responsible members of the clergy, prohibited any further trials and pardoned those already convicted. Twenty years later a penitent Massachusetts legislature annulled the "convictions" of the "witches" and made reparations to their heirs. The Salem witchcraft delusion marked an all-time high in American experience of popular passions run wild. "Witch hunting" passed into the American vocabulary as a metaphor for the often dangerously irrational urge to find a scapegoat for social resentments.

The New England Way of Life

Oddly enough, the story of New England was largely written by rocks. The heavily glaciated soil was strewn with countless stones, many of which were forced to the surface after a winter freeze. In a sense the Puritans did not possess the soil; it possessed them by shaping their character. Scratching a living from the protesting earth was an early American success story. Back-bending toil put a premium on industry and penny-pinching frugality, for which New Englanders became famous. Traditionally sharp Yankee traders, some of them palming off wooden nutmegs, made their mark. Connecticut came in time to be called good-humoredly "the Nutmeg State." Cynics exaggerated when they said that the three stages of progress in New England were "to get on, to get honor, to get honest."

The grudging land also left colonial New England less ethnically mixed than its southern neighbors.

The Wonders of the Invisible World:

Being an Account of the

TRYALS

OF

Several Witches,

Lately Excuted in

NEW-ENGLAND:

And of several remarkable Curiosities therein Occurring.

Together with,

I. Observations upon the Nature, the Number, and the Operations of the Devils.

II. A short Narrative of a late outrage committed by a knot of Witches in Swede-Land, very much resembling, and so far explaining, that under which New-England has laboured.

III. Some Councels directing a due Improvement of the Terrible things lately done by the unusual and amazing Range of Evil-Spirits in New-England.

IV. A brief Discourse upon those Temptations which are the more ordinary Devices of Satan.

By COTTON MATHER.

Published by the Special Command of his EXCELLENCY the Governeur of the Province of the Massachusetts-Bay in New-England.

Printed first, at Boston in New-England; and Reprinted at London, for John Dunton, at the Raven in the Poultry. 1693.

Salem Witchcraft Hysteria
In this notorious tract of 1693, the Puritan minister Cotton Mather defended the death-sentence verdicts of several trials for witchcraft.

This widening of church membership gradually erased the distinction between the "elect" and other members of society. In effect, strict religious purity was sacrificed somewhat to the cause of wider religious participation. Interestingly, from about this time onward women were in the majority in the Puritan congregations.

Women also played a prominent role in one of New England's most frightening religious episodes. A group of adolescent girls in Salem, Massachusetts, claimed to have been bewitched by certain older women. A hysterical "witch hunt" ensued, leading to the legal lynching in 1692 of twenty individuals, nineteen of whom were hanged and one of whom was pressed to death. Two dogs were also hanged.

European immigrants were not attracted in great numbers to a site where the soil was so stony—and the sermons so sulfurous.

Climate likewise molded New England, where the summers were often uncomfortably hot and the winters cruelly cold. Many early immigrants complained of the region's extremes of weather. Yet the soil and climate of New England eventually encouraged a diversified agriculture and industry. Staple products like tobacco did not flourish, as in the South. Black slavery, although attempted, could not exist profitably on small farms, especially where the surest crop was stones. No broad, fertile expanses comparable to those in the tidewater South beckoned people inland. The mountains ran fairly close to the shore, and the rivers were generally short and rapid.

And just as the land shaped New Englanders, so they shaped the land. The Native Americans had left an early imprint on the New England earth. They traditionally beat trails through the woods as they migrated seasonally for hunting and fishing. They periodically burned the woodlands to restore leafy first-growth forests that would sustain the deer population. The Indians recognized the right to *use* the land, but the concept of exclusive, individual *ownership* of the land was alien to them.

The English settlers had a different philosophy. They condemned the Indians for "wasting" the earth by underutilizing its bounty and used this logic to justify their own expropriation of the land from the native inhabitants. Consistent with this outlook, the Europeans felt a virtual duty to "improve" the land by clearing woodlands for pasturage and tillage, building roads and fences, and laying out permanent settlements.

Some of the greatest changes resulted from the introduction of livestock. The English brought pigs, horses, sheep, and cattle from Europe to the settlements. Because the growing herds needed ever more pastureland, the colonists were continually clearing forests. The animals' voracious appetites and heavy hooves compacted the soil, speeding erosion and flooding. In some cases the combined effect of these developments actually may have changed local climates and made some areas even more susceptible to extremes of heat and cold.

Repelled by the rocks, the hardy New Englanders turned instinctively to their fine natural harbors. Hacking timber from their dense forests, they became experts in shipbuilding and commerce.

They also ceaselessly exploited the self-perpetuating codfish lode off the coast of Newfoundland—the fishy "gold mines of New England," which have yielded more wealth than all the treasure chests of the Aztecs. During colonial days the wayfarer seldom got far from the sound of the ax and hammer, or the swift rush of the ship down the ways to the sea, or the smell of rotting fish. As a reminder of the importance of fishing, a handsome replica of the "sacred cod" is proudly displayed to this day in the Massachusetts State House in Boston.

The combination of Calvinism, soil, and climate in New England made for energy, purposefulness, sternness, stubbornness, self-reliance, and resourcefulness. Righteous New Englanders prided themselves on being God's chosen people. They long boasted that Boston was "the hub of the universe"—at least in spirit. A famous jingle of later days ran

> *I come from the city of Boston*
> *The home of the bean and the cod*
> *Where the Cabots speak only to Lowells*
> *And the Lowells speak only to God.*

New England has had an incalculable impact on the rest of the nation. Ousted by their sterile soil, thousands of New Englanders scattered from Ohio to Oregon and even Hawaii. They sprinkled the land with new communities modeled on the orderly New England town, with its central green and tidy schoolhouse, and its simple town-meeting democracy. "Yankee ingenuity," originally fostered by the flinty fields and comfortless climate of New England, came to be claimed by all Americans as a proud national trait. And the fabled "New England conscience," born of the steadfast Puritan heritage, left a legacy of high idealism in the national character and inspired many later reformers.

The Early Settlers' Days and Ways

The cycles of the seasons and the sun set the schedules of all the earliest American colonists, men as well as women, blacks as well as whites. The overwhelming majority of colonists were farmers. They planted in the spring, tended their crops in the summer, harvested in the fall, and prepared in the winter to begin the cycle anew. They usually rose at dawn and went to bed at dusk. Chores might be performed after nightfall only if they were "worth the

Life and Death in Colonial America, by Prudence Punderson
Note the artist's initials, "P.P.", on the coffin. This embroidery suggests the stoic resolve of a colonial woman, calmly depicting the inevitable progression of her own life from the cradle to the grave.

candle," a phrase that has persisted in American speech.

Women, slave or free, on southern plantations or northern farms, wove, cooked, cleaned, and cared for children. Men cleared land; fenced, planted, and cropped it; cut firewood; and butchered livestock as needed. Children helped with all these tasks, while picking up such schooling as they could.

Life was humble but comfortable by contemporary standards. Compared to most seventeenth-century Europeans, Americans lived in affluent abundance. Land was relatively cheap, though somewhat less available in the planter-dominated South than elsewhere. In the northern and middle colonies, an acre of virgin soil cost about what American carpenters could earn in one day as wages, which were roughly three times those of their English counterparts.

"Dukes don't emigrate," the saying goes, for if people enjoy wealth and security, they are not likely to risk exposing their lives in the wilderness. Similarly, the very poorest members of a society may not possess even the modest means needed to pull up stakes and seek a fresh start in life. Accordingly, most white migrants to early colonial America came neither from the aristocracy nor from the dregs of European society—with the partial exception of the impoverished indentured servants.

Crude frontier life did not in any case permit the flagrant display of class distinctions, and seventeenth-century society in all the colonies had a certain simple sameness to it, especially in the more egalitarian New England and middle colonies. Yet many settlers, who considered themselves to be of the "better sort," tried to re-create on a modified scale the social structure they had known in the Old World. To some extent they succeeded, though yeasty democratic forces frustrated their full triumph. Resentment against upper-class pretensions helped to spark outbursts like Bacon's Rebellion of 1676 in Virginia and the uprising of Maryland's Protestants toward the end of the seventeenth century. In New York, animosity between lordly landholders and aspiring merchants fueled Leisler's Rebellion, an ill-starred and bloody insurgency that rocked New York City from 1689 to 1691.

For their part, would-be American blue bloods resented the pretensions of the "meaner sort" and passed laws to try to keep them in their place. Massachusetts in 1651 prohibited poorer folk from "wearing gold or silver lace," and in eighteenth-century Virginia a tailor was fined and jailed for arranging to race his horse—"a sport only for gentlemen." But these efforts to reproduce the finely stratified societies of Europe proved feeble in the early American wilderness, where equality and democracy found fertile soil—at least for white people.

Chronology

1619	First Africans arrive in Virginia	**1689–1691**	Leisler's Rebellion in New York
1636	Harvard College founded	**1692**	Salem witch trials in Massachusetts
1662	Half-Way Covenant for Congregational church membership established	**1693**	College of William and Mary founded
1670	Virginia assembly disfranchises landless freeman	**1698**	Royal African Company slave trade monopoly ended
1676	Bacon's Rebellion in Virginia	**1712**	New York City slave revolt
1680s	Mass expansion of slavery in colonies	**1739**	South Carolina slave revolt

SUGGESTED READINGS

PRIMARY SOURCE DOCUMENTS

Adolph B. Benson, ed., *The America of 1750; Petar Kalm's Travels in North America** (1937), records the observations of a visiting Swedish naturalist with a keen eye for the behavior of humans. The first slave laws of Virginia are collected in Warren M. Billings, ed., *The Old Dominion in the Seventeenth Century** (1975), as are firsthand accounts of Bacon's Rebellion. See also George L. Burr, ed., *Narratives of the Witchcraft Cases, 1648–1706** (1914).

SECONDARY SOURCES

On life and labor in the Chesapeake, consult Thad W. Tate and David L. Ammerman, eds., *The Chesapeake in the Seventeenth Century* (1979); and Edmund S. Morgan, *American Slavery, American Freedom* (1975), which concentrates on race and class relations. Further probing economic conflicts and their role in the introduction of slavery is Timothy H. Breen and Stephen Innes, *Myne Owne Ground: Race and Freedom on Virginia's Eastern Shore, 1640–1676* (1980). Gloria Main chronicles *The Tobacco Colony: Life in Early Maryland, 1650–1719* (1982). Darrett B. Rutman and Anita H. Rutman examine Virginia in *A Place in Time: Middlesex County, Virginia 1650–1750* (1984). Daniel Blake Smith looks *Inside the*

Great House: Planter Family Life in Eighteenth-Century Chesapeake Society (1980). Kenneth A. Lockridge analyzes the life of one of Virginia's most celebrated residents in *The Diary and Life of William Byrd II of Virginia, 1674–1744* (1987). Winthrop Jordan's magnificent *White over Black: American Attitudes toward the Negro, 1550–1812* (1968) discusses the evolution of racial attitudes. Life in New England's towns and homes is scrutinized in John Demos, *A Little Commonwealth: Family Life in Plymouth Colony* (1970); Philip Greven, *Four Generations: Population, Land, and Family in Colonial Andover, Massachusetts* (1970); Kenneth Lockridge, *New England Town: Dedham* (1970); Christine Heyrman, *Commerce and Culture: The Maritime Communities of Colonial Massachusetts, 1690–1750* (1984); and Daniel Vickers, *Farmers and Fishermen: Two Centuries of Work in Essex County, Massachusetts, 1630–1850* (1994). For a less idealized portrait of early New England, see John F. Martin, *Profits in the Wilderness: Entrepreneurship and the Founding of New England Towns in the Seventeenth Century* (1991), and Stephen Innes, *Creating the Commonwealth: The Economic Culture of Puritan New England* (1995). For more on the place of women in seventeenth-century society, see Lyle Koehler, *A Search for Power: The "Weaker Sex" in Seventeenth-Century New England* (1980); Laurel T. Ulrich, *Good Wives: Image and Reality in the Lives of Women in Northern New England, 1650–1750* (1982); Marylynn Salmon, *Women and the Law of Property in Early America* (1986); Mary Beth Norton, *Founding Mothers & Fathers* (1996); Cornelia Hughes Dayton, *Women Before the Bar: Gender, Law, and Society in Connecticut, 1639–1789* (1995); and Philip

---

*An asterisk indicates that the document, or an excerpt from it, can be found in Thomas A. Bailey and David M. Kennedy, eds., The American Spirit: United States History as Seen by Contemporaries, 9th ed. (Boston: Houghton Mifflin, 1998).

Greven, *The Protestant Temperament* (1977), which analyzes child-rearing practices. Edmund S. Morgan describes the crisis that beset the original Puritans when their children displayed a lesser degree of religiosity in *Visible Saints* (1963). David Grayson Allen emphasizes the persistence of English customs in *In English Ways: The Movement of Societies and the Transferral of English Local Law and Custom to Massachusetts Bay in the Seventeenth Century* (1981). See also David Cressy, *Coming Over: Migration and Communication Between England and New England in the Seventeenth Century* (1987), and David Hackett Fischer, *Albion's Seed: Four British Folkways in America* (1989). Witchcraft is the subject of Paul Boyer's and Stephen Nissenbaum's *Salem Possessed* (1974), John Demos's massive *Entertaining Satan* (1982), and Carol F. Karlsen's *The Devil in the Shape of a Woman: Witchcraft in Colonial New England* (1987). See also Richard Godbeer, *The Devil's Dominion: Magic and Religion in Early New England* (1992). A sweeping survey that emphasizes the diversity of cultures already present in seventeenth-century America is E. Brooks Holifield, *Era of Persuasion: American Thought and Culture, 1521–1680* (1989). The relationship of Indians and New England whites to their environment is the subject of William Cronon's intriguing *Changes in the Land* (1983). David Konig, *Law and Society in Puritan Massachusetts: Essex County, 1629–1692* (1979), considers the role of law in mitigating social tensions.

5

Colonial Society on
the Eve of Revolution
1700–1775

*Driven from every other corner of the earth,
freedom of thought and the right of private
judgment in matters of conscience direct their
course to this happy country as their last asylum.*

SAMUEL ADAMS, 1776

Conquest by the Cradle

The common term *thirteen original colonies* is misleading. Britain ruled thirty-two colonies in North America by 1775, including Canada, the Floridas, and the various islands of the Caribbean. But only thirteen of them unfurled the standard of revolt. A few of the nonrebels, such as Canada and Jamaica, were larger, wealthier, or more populous than some of the thirteen. And even among the revolting thirteen, dramatic differences in economic organization, social structure, and ways of life were evident.

All the eventually rebellious colonies did have one outstanding feature in common: their populations were growing by leaps and bounds. In 1700

they contained fewer than 300,000 souls, about 20,000 of whom were black. By 1775, 2.5 million people inhabited the thirteen colonies, of whom about half a million were black. White immigrants made up nearly 400,000 of the increased number, and black "forced immigrants" accounted for almost as many again. But most of the spurt stemmed from the remarkable natural fertility of all Americans, white and black. To the amazement and dismay of Europeans, the colonists were doubling their numbers every twenty-five years. Unfriendly Dr. Samuel Johnson, back in England, growled that the Americans were multiplying like their own rattlesnakes. They were also a youthful people, whose average age in 1775 was about sixteen.

This population boom had political consequences. In 1700 there were twenty English subjects for each American colonist. By 1775 the English advantage in numbers had fallen to three to one—setting the stage for a momentous shift in the balance of power between the colonies and England.

The bulk of the population was cooped up east of the Alleghenies, although by 1775 a vanguard of pioneers had trickled into the stump-studded clearings of Tennessee and Kentucky. The most populous colonies in 1775 were Virginia, Massachusetts, Pennsylvania, North Carolina, and Maryland—in that order. Only four communities could properly be called cities: Philadelphia, including suburbs, was first with about 34,000 residents, trailed by New York, Boston, and Charleston. About 90 percent of the people lived in rural areas.

A Mingling of the Races

Colonial America was a melting pot and had been from the outset. The population, although basically English in stock and language, was picturesquely mottled with numerous foreign groups.

Heavy-accented Germans constituted about 6 percent of the total population, or 150,000, by 1775. Fleeing religious persecution, economic oppression, and the ravages of war, they had flocked to America in the early 1700s and had settled chiefly in Pennsylvania. They belonged to several different Protestant sects—primarily Lutheran—and thus further enhanced the religious diversity of the colony. Known popularly but erroneously as the Pennsylvania Dutch (a corruption of the German word *Deutsch*, for "German"), they totaled about one-third of the colony's population. In Philadelphia the street signs were painted in both German and English.

These German newcomers moved into the backcountry of Pennsylvania, where their splendid stone barns gave—and still give—mute evidence of industry and prosperity. Not having been brought up English, they had no deep-rooted loyalty to the British crown, and they clung tenaciously to their German language and customs.

The Scots-Irish (see "Makers of America: The Scots-Irish," pp. 86–87), who in 1775 numbered about 175,000, or 7 percent of the population, were an important non-English group, although they spoke English. They were not Irish at all, but turbulent Scots Lowlanders. Over many decades, though, they had

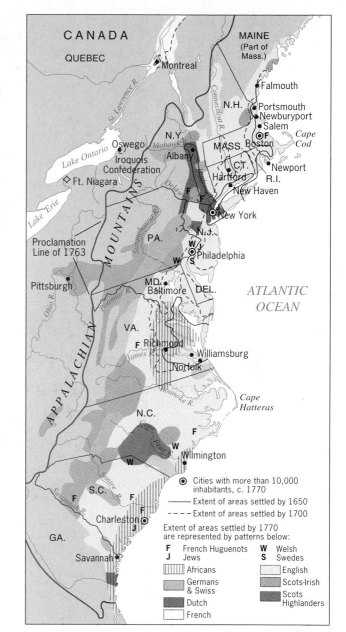

Immigrant Groups in 1775
America was already a nation of diverse nationalities in the colonial period. This map shows the great variety of immigrant groups, especially in Pennsylvania and New York. It also illustrates the tendency of later arrivals, particularly the Scots-Irish, to push into the backcountry.

been transplanted to Northern Ireland, where they had not prospered. The Irish Catholics already there, hating Scottish Presbyterianism, resented the intruders and still do. The economic life of the Scots-Irish was severely hampered, especially when the English

Estimated Population Elements, 1790*
(Based on Family Names)

Ethnic group	Number	Percentage
European		
English and Welsh	2,605,699	66.3%
Scottish (including		
Scots-Irish)	221,562	5.6
German	176,407	4.5
Dutch	78,959	2.0
Irish	61,534	1.6
French	17,619	0.4
All other whites	10,664	0.3
African	757,181	19.3
GRAND TOTAL	3,929,625	

*Rossiter, *A Century of Population Growth (1909).* "African," of course, embraces several different peoples, whose precise numbers are not reliably known.

government placed burdensome restrictions on their production of linens and woolens.

Early in the 1700s, tens of thousands of embittered Scots-Irish finally abandoned Ireland and came to America, chiefly to tolerant and deep-soiled Pennsylvania. Finding the best acres already taken by Germans and Quakers, they pushed out onto the frontier. There many of them illegally but defiantly squatted on the unoccupied lands and quarreled with both Indian and white owners. When the westward-flowing Scots-Irish tide lapped up against the Allegheny barrier, it was deflected southward into the backcountry of Maryland, down

The young Frenchman Michel Guillaume Jean de Crèvecoeur (1735–1813) wrote about 1770 of the diverse population:

"They are a mixture of English, Scotch, Irish, French, Dutch, Germans, and Swedes. From this promiscuous breed, that race now called Americans have arisen. . . . I could point out to you a family whose grandfather was an Englishman, whose wife was Dutch, whose son married a French woman, and whose present four sons have now four wives of different nations."

Virginia's Shenandoah Valley, and into the western Carolinas. Already experienced colonizers and agitators in Ireland, the Scots-Irish proved to be superb frontiersmen, though their readiness to visit violence on the Indians repeatedly inflamed the western districts. By the mid–eighteenth century, a chain of Scots-Irish settlements lay scattered along the "great wagon road," which hugged the eastern Appalachian foothills from Pennsylvania to Georgia.

It was said, somewhat unfairly, that the Scots-Irish kept the Sabbath—and all else they could lay their hands on. Pugnacious, lawless, and individualistic, they brought with them the Scottish secrets of whiskey distilling and dotted the Appalachian hills and hollows with their stills. They cherished no love for the British government that had uprooted them and still lorded over them—or for any other government, it seemed. They led the armed march of the Paxton Boys on Philadelphia in 1764, protesting the Quaker oligarchy's lenient policy toward the Indians, and a few years later spearheaded the Regulator movement in North Carolina, a small but nasty insurrection against eastern domination of the colony's affairs. Many of these hotheads—including the young Andrew Jackson—eventually joined the embattled American revolutionists. All told, about a dozen future presidents were of Scots-Irish descent.

Approximately 5 percent of the multicolored colonial population consisted of other European groups. These embraced French Huguenots, Welsh, Dutch, Swedes, Jews, Irish, Swiss, and Scots Highlanders—as distinguished from the Scots-Irish. Except for the Scots Highlanders, such hodgepodge elements felt little loyalty to the British crown. By far the largest single non-English group was African, accounting for nearly 20 percent of the colonial population in 1775 and heavily concentrated in the South.

The population of the thirteen colonies, though mainly Anglo-Saxon, was perhaps the most mixed to be found anywhere in the world. The South, holding about 90 percent of the slaves, already displayed its historic black-and-white racial composition. New England, mostly staked out by the original Puritan migrants, showed the least ethnic diversity. The middle colonies, especially Pennsylvania, received the bulk of later white immigrants and boasted an astonishing variety of peoples. Outside of New England, about one-half the population was non-English in 1775. Of the fifty-six signers of the Declaration of Independence in 1776, eighteen were non-English, and eight had not been born in the colonies.

A South Carolina Advertisement for Slaves in the 1760s
Note the reference to these slaves' origin in West Africa's "Rice Coast," a reminder of South Carolina's reliance on African skill and labor for rice cultivation. Note, too, that half the slaves are said to have survived smallpox and thus acquired immunity from further infection—and that care has been taken to insulate the others from a smallpox epidemic apparently then raging in Charleston.

As these various immigrant groups mingled and intermarried, they laid the foundations for a new multicultural American national identity unlike anything known in Europe. The French settler Michel-Guillaume de Crèvecoeur saw in America in the 1770s a "strange mixture of blood, which you will find in no other country," and he posed his classic question, "What then is the American, this new man?" Nor were white colonists alone in creating new societies out of diverse ethnic groups. The African slave trade long had mixed peoples from many different tribal backgrounds, giving birth to an African-*American* community far more variegated in its cultural origins than anything to be found in Africa itself. Similarly, the decimation and forced migration of Indian tribes scrambled Native American peoples together in wholly new ways. The Catawba nation of the southern piedmont region, for example, was formed from the splintered remnants of several different tribes.

The Structure of Colonial Society

In contrast with contemporary Europe, eighteenth-century America was a shining land of equality and opportunity—with the notorious exception of slavery. No titled nobility dominated society from on high, and no pauperized underclass threatened it from below. Most white Americans, and even some free blacks, were small farmers. Clad in buckskin breeches, they owned modest holdings and tilled them with their own hands and horses. The cities contained a small class of skilled artisans, with their well-greased leather aprons, as well as a few shopkeepers and tradespeople, and a handful of unskilled casual laborers. The most remarkable feature of the social ladder was the rags-to-riches ease with which an ambitious colonial, even a former indentured servant, might rise from a lower rung to a higher one, a rare step in old England.

Yet in contrast with seventeenth-century America, colonial society on the eve of the Revolution was beginning to show signs of stratification and barriers to mobility that raised worries about the "Europeanization" of America. The gods of war contributed to these developments. The armed conflicts of the 1690s and early 1700s had enriched a number of merchant princes in the New England and middle colonies. They laid the foundations of their fortunes with profits made as military suppliers. Roosting regally atop the social ladder, these elites now feathered their nests more finely. They sported imported clothing and dined at tables laid

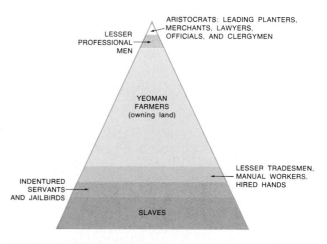

The Colonial Social Pyramid, 1775 (an approximation)

The Scots-Irish

As the British Empire spread its dominion across the seas in the seventeenth and eighteenth centuries, great masses of people poured forth to populate its ever-widening realms. Their migration unfolded in stages. They journeyed from farms to towns, from towns to great cities like London and Bristol, and eventually from the seaports to Ireland, the Caribbean, and North America. Among these intrepid wanderers, few were more restless than the Scots-Irish, the settlers of the first American West. Never feeling at home in the British Empire, these perennial outsiders always headed for its most distant outposts. They migrated first from their native Scottish lowlands to Northern Ireland and then on to the New World. And even in North America, the Scots-Irish remained on the periphery, ever distancing themselves from the reach of the English crown and the Anglican church.

Poverty weighed heavily on the Scottish lowlands in the 1600s; one observer winced at the sight of the Scots, with "their hovels most miserable, made of poles, wattled and covered with thin sods," their bodies shrunken yet swollen with hunger. But Scotland had long been an unyielding land, and it was not simply nature's stinginess that drove the lowlanders to the ports. The spread of commercial farming forced many Scots from the land and subjected others to merciless rent increases at the hands of the landowning *lairds* (lords)—a practice called rack-renting. Adding insult to injury, the British authorities persecuted the Presbyterian Scots, squeezing taxes from their barren purses to support the hated Anglican church.

Not surprisingly, then, some 200,000 Scots immigrated to neighboring Ireland in the 1600s. So great was the exodus that Protestant Scots eventually outnumbered Catholic natives in the several northern Irish counties that compose the province of Ulster. Still, Ireland offered only slender and temporary relief to many Scots. Although the north was prosperous compared with the rest of that unhappy nation, making a living was still devilishly hard in Ireland. Soon the Scots discovered that their migration had not freed them from their ancient woes. Their Irish landlords, with British connivance, racked rents just as ferociously as their Scottish *lairds* had done. Under such punishing pressures, waves of these already once-transplanted Scots, now called Scots-Irish, fled yet again across the sea throughout the 1700s. This time their destination was America.

Most debarked in Pennsylvania, seeking the religious tolerance and abundant land of William Penn's commonwealth. But these unquiet people

This Scottish Presbyterian church, built in 1794, still stands in Alexandria, Virginia.

Encouragement given for People to remove and settle in the Province of New-York in America.

THe Honourable *George Clarke*, Esq; Lieut. Governour and Commander in chief of the Province of *New-York*, Hath upon the Petition of Mr *Lauchline Campbell* from *Isla, North-Britain*, promised to grant him Thirty thousand Acres of Land at the *Wood-Creek*, free of all Charges, excepting the *Survey* and the King's *Quit-Rent*, which is about one Shilling and Nine Pence Farthing *Sterling* for each hundred Acres. *And also*, To grant to thirty Families already landed here Lands in proportion to each Family, from five hundred Acres unto one Hundred and Fifty only paying the *Survey* and the King's *Quit-Rent*. And all *Protestants* that incline to come and settle in this Colony may have Lands granted them from the Crown for three Pounds *Sterling* per hundred Acres and paying the yearly Quit-Rent.

Dated in New-York this 4th Day of December, 1738.   GEORGE CLARKE.

Printed by *William Bradford*, Printer to the King's most Excellent Majesty for the Province of *New-York*, 1738.

This British advertisement of 1738 urged Scots-Irish Protestants to settle in colonial New York.

Georgia Governor James Oglethorpe, in Scottish attire, visits Scottish settlers at New Inverness, Georgia.

did not stay put for long. They fanned out from Philadelphia into the farmlands of western Pennsylvania. Blocked temporarily by the Allegheny Mountains, these early pioneers then trickled south along the backbone of the Appalachian range, slowly filling the backcountry of Virginia, the Carolinas, and Georgia. There they built farms and towns, and these rickety settlements bore the marks of Scots-Irish restlessness. Whereas their German neighbors typically erected sturdy homes and cleared their fields meticulously, the Scots-Irish satisfied themselves with floorless, flimsy log cabins; they chopped down trees, planted crops between the stumps, exhausted the soil fast, and . . . moved on.

Almost every Scots-Irish community, however isolated or impermanent, maintained a Presbyterian church. Religion was the bond that yoked these otherwise fiercely independent folk. In backcountry towns, churches were erected before law courts, and clerics were pounding their pulpits before civil authorities had the chance to raise their gavels. In many such cases the local religious court, known as the Session, passed judgment on crimes like burglary and trespassing as well as on moral and theological questions. But the Scots-Irish, despite their intense faith, were no theocrats, no advocates of religious rule. Their bitter struggles with the Anglican church made them stubborn opponents of established churches in the United States, just as their seething resentment against the king of England ensured that the Scots-Irish would be well represented among the Patriots in the American Revolution.

with English china and gleaming silverware. Prominent individuals came to be seated in churches and schools according to their social rank.

The plague of war also created a class of widows and orphans, who became dependent for their survival on charity. Both Philadelphia and New York built almshouses in the 1730s to care for the destitute. Yet the numbers of poor people remained tiny compared to the numbers in England, where about a third of the population lived in impoverished squalor.

In the New England countryside the descendents of the original settlers faced more limited prospects than had their pioneering forebears. As the supply of unclaimed soil dwindled and families grew, existing landholdings were subdivided and the average size of farms shrank drastically. Younger sons were increasingly forced to hire out as wage laborers—or, eventually, to seek virgin tracts of land beyond the Appalachians.

In the South the power of the great planters continued to be bolstered by their disproportionate ownership of slaves. The riches created by the growing slave population in the eighteenth century were not distributed evenly among the whites. Wealth was concentrated in the hands of the largest slaveowners, widening the gap between the prosperous gentry and the "poor whites," who were more and more likely to become tenant farmers.

In all the colonies the ranks of the lower classes were further swelled by the continuing stream of indentured servants, many of whom ultimately achieved prosperity and prestige. Two became signers of the Declaration of Independence.

Far less fortunate than the voluntary indentured servants were the paupers and convicts involuntarily shipped to America. Altogether, about fifty thousand "jayle birds" were dumped on the colonies by the London authorities. This riffraff crowd—including robbers, rapists, and murderers—was generally sullen and undesirable, and not bubbling over with goodwill for the king's government. But many convicts were the unfortunate victims of circumstances and of a viciously unfair English penal code that included about two hundred capital crimes. Some of the deportees, in fact, came to be highly respectable citizens.

Least fortunate of all, of course, were the black slaves. They enjoyed no equality with whites and dared not even dream of ascending, or even approaching, the ladder of opportunity. Oppressed and downtrodden, the slaves were America's closest approximation to Europe's volatile lower classes,

and fears of black rebellion plagued the white colonists. Some colonial legislatures, notably South Carolina's in 1760, sensed the dangers present in a heavy concentration of resentful slaves and attempted to restrict or halt their importation. But the British authorities, seeking to preserve the supply of cheap labor for the colonies, especially the West Indies sugar plantations, repeatedly vetoed all efforts to stem the trans-Atlantic traffic in slaves. Many North American colonials condemned these vetoes as morally callous, although New England slave traders benefited handsomely from the British policy. The cruel complexity of the slavery issue was further revealed when Thomas Jefferson, himself a slaveholder, assailed the British vetoes in an early draft of the Declaration of Independence, but was forced to withdraw the proposed clause by a torrent of protest from southern slavemasters.

Clerics, Physicians, and Jurists

Most honored of the professions was the Christian ministry. In 1775 the clergy wielded less influence than in the early days of Massachusetts, when piety had burned more warmly. But they still occupied a position of high prestige.

Most physicians, on the other hand, were poorly trained and not highly esteemed. Not until 1765 was the first medical school established, although European centers attracted some students. Aspiring young doctors served for a while as apprentices to older practitioners and were then turned loose on their "victims." Bleeding was a favorite and frequently fatal remedy; when the physician was not available, a barber was often summoned.

On doctors and medicine, Poor Richard's Almanack *by Benjamin Franklin (1706–1790) offered some homely advice:*

"God heals and the doctor takes the fee."

"He's the best physician that knows the worthlessness of most medicines."

"Don't go to the doctor with every distemper, nor to the lawyer with every quarrel, nor to the pot for every thirst."

Plagues were a constant nightmare. Especially dreaded was smallpox, which afflicted one out of five persons, including the heavily pock-marked George Washington. A crude form of inoculation was introduced in 1721, despite the objections of many physicians and some of the clergy, who opposed tampering with the will of God. Powdered dried toad was a favorite prescription for smallpox. Diphtheria was also a deadly killer, especially of young people. One epidemic in the 1730s took the lives of thousands. This grim reminder of their mortality may have helped to prepare many colonists in their hearts and minds for the religious revival that was soon to sweep them up.

At first the law profession was not favorably regarded. In this pioneering society, which required much honest manual labor, the parties to a dispute often presented their own cases in court. Lawyers were commonly regarded as noisy windbags or troublemaking rogues; an early Connecticut law classed them with drunkards and brothel keepers. When future president John Adams was a young law student, the father of his wife-to-be frowned upon him as a suitor.

By about 1750, seaboard society had passed the pioneering stage, and trained attorneys were generally recognized as useful. Able to defend colonial rights against the crown on legal grounds, lawyers like the eloquent James Otis and the flaming Patrick Henry took the lead in the agitation that led to revolt. Other lawyer-orators played hardly less important roles in forging new constitutions and in serving in representative bodies.

Workaday America

Agriculture was the leading industry, involving about 90 percent of the people. Tobacco continued to be the staple crop in Maryland and Virginia. The fertile middle ("bread") colonies produced large quantities of grain, and by 1759 New York alone was exporting eighty thousand barrels of flour a year. Seemingly the farmer had only to tickle the soil with a hoe and it would laugh with a harvest. Overall, Americans probably enjoyed a higher standard of living than the masses of any country in history up to that time.

Fishing (including whaling), though ranking far below agriculture, was rewarding. Pursued in all the American colonies, this harvesting of the sea

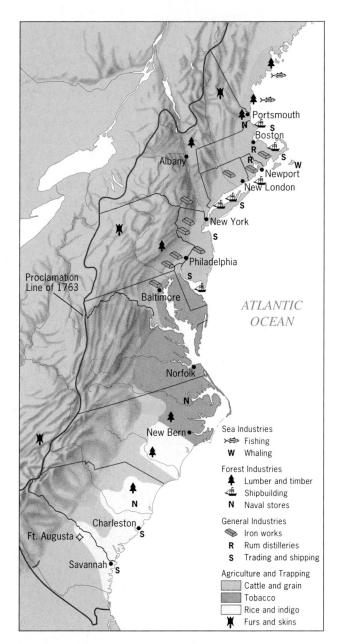

The Colonial Economy   By the eighteenth century, the various colonial regions had distinct economic identities. The northern colonies grew grain and raised cattle, harvested timber and fish, and built ships. The Chesapeake colonies and North Carolina were still heavily dependent on tobacco, whereas the southernmost colonies grew mostly rice and indigo. Cotton, so important to the southern economy in the nineteenth century, had not yet emerged as a major crop.

was a major industry in New England, which exported smelly shiploads of dried cod to the Catholic countries of Europe. The fishing fleet also stimulated shipbuilding and served as a nursery for the seamen who manned the navy and merchant marine.

A bustling commerce, both coastwise and overseas, enriched all the colonies, especially the New England group, New York, and Pennsylvania. Commercial ventures and land speculation, in the absence of later get-rich-quick schemes, were the surest avenues to speedy wealth. Yankee seamen were famous in many climes not only as skilled mariners but as tightfisted traders. They provisioned the Caribbean sugar islands with food and forest products. They hauled Spanish and Portuguese gold, wine, and oranges to London, to be exchanged for industrial goods, which were then sold for a juicy profit in America.

The so-called triangular trade was infamously profitable, though small in relation to total colonial commerce. A skipper, for example, would leave a New England port with a cargo of rum and sail to the Gold Coast of Africa. Bartering the fiery liquor with African chiefs for captured African slaves, he would proceed to the West Indies with his sobbing and suffocating cargo sardined below deck. There he would exchange the survivors for molasses, which he would then carry to New England, where it would be distilled into rum. He would then repeat the trip, making a handsome profit on each leg of the triangle.

Manufacturing in the colonies was of only secondary importance, although there was a surprising variety of small enterprises. As a rule, workers could get ahead faster in soil-rich America by tilling the land. Huge quantities of "kill devil" rum were distilled in Rhode Island and Massachusetts; and even some of the "elect of the Lord" developed an overfondness for it. Handsome beaver hats were manufactured in quantity, despite British restrictions. Smoking iron forges, including Pennsylvania's Valley Forge, likewise dotted the land and in fact were more numerous in 1775, though generally smaller, than those of England. In addition, household manufacturing, including spinning and weaving by women, added up to an impressive output. As in all pioneering countries, strong-backed laborers and

Sea Captains Carousing in Surinam, by John Greenwood, 1757–1758
This playful portrayal of Yankee sea captains in Dutch Guiana is a reminder of the distant trade connections established by American shippers in the colonial era. The lively alehouse merriment also confirms that not all seamen were sober-sided Puritans. The man pouring his drink over the seated figure in the center may be Stephen Hopkins, a signer of the Declaration of Independence. The artist, John Greenwood, has cleverly painted himself into the scene—or out of it as the figure taking his leave at the upper right.

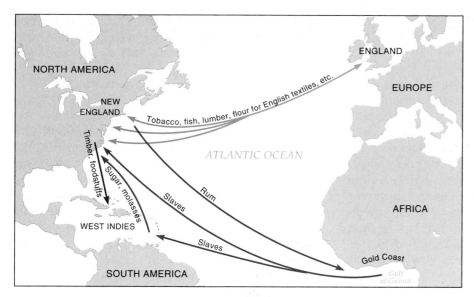

Colonial Trade Patterns, c. 1770
Future president John Adams noted about this time that "the commerce of the West Indies is a part of the American system of commerce. They can neither do without us, nor we without them. The Creator has placed us upon the globe in such a situation that we have occasion for each other."

skilled craftspeople were scarce and highly prized. In early Virginia a carpenter who had committed a murder was freed because his woodworking skills were needed.

Lumbering was perhaps the most important single manufacturing activity. Countless cartloads of virgin timber were consumed by shipbuilders, at first chiefly in New England and then elsewhere in the colonies. By 1770 about four hundred vessels of assorted sizes were splashing down the ways each year, and about one-third of the British merchant marine was American-built.

Colonial naval stores—such as tar, pitch, rosin, and turpentine—were highly valued, for Britain was anxious to gain and retain a mastery of the seas. London offered generous bounties to stimulate production of these items; otherwise Britain would have had to turn to the uncertain and possibly hostile Baltic areas. Towering trees, ideal as masts for His Majesty's navy, were marked with the king's broad arrow for future use. The luckless colonial who was caught cutting down this reserved timber was subject to a fine. Even though there were countless unreserved trees and the blazed ones were being saved for the common defense, this shackle on free enterprise engendered considerable bitterness.

Americans held an important flank of a thriving, many-sided Atlantic economy by the dawn of the eighteenth century. Yet strains appeared in this complex network as early as the 1730s. Fast-breeding Americans demanded more and more English products—yet the slow-growing English population early reached the saturation point for absorbing imports from America. This trade imbalance raised a question: how could the colonists sell the goods to make the money to buy what they wanted in England? The answer was obvious: by seeking foreign (non-English) markets.

By the eve of the Revolution the bulk of Chesapeake tobacco was filling pipes in France and in other Continental countries, though it passed through the hands of British re-exporters, who took a slice of the profits for themselves. More important was the trade with the West Indies, especially the French islands. West Indian purchases of North American timber and foodstuffs provided the crucial cash for the colonists to continue to make their own purchases in England. But in 1733, bowing to pressure from influential *British* West Indian planters, Parliament passed the Molasses Act, aimed at squelching North American trade with the *French* West Indies. If successful, this scheme would have struck a crippling blow to American international trade and to the colonists' standard of living. American merchants responded to the Act by bribing and smuggling their way around the law. Thus was foreshadowed the impending imperial crisis, when headstrong Americans would revolt rather than submit to the dictates of a far-off Parliament, apparently bent on destroying their very livelihood.

Horsepower and Sailpower

All sprawling and sparsely populated pioneer communities are cursed with oppressive problems of transportation. America, with a scarcity of both money and workers, was no exception.

Not until the 1700s did roads connect even the major cities, and these dirt thoroughfares were treacherously deficient. A wayfarer could have rumbled along more rapidly over the Roman highways in the days of Julius Caesar, nearly two thousand years earlier. It took young Benjamin Franklin nine long, rain-drenched days in 1720 to journey from Boston to Philadelphia, traveling by sailing sloop, rowboat, and foot. News of the Declaration of Independence in 1776 reached Charleston from Philadelphia twenty-nine days after the Fourth of July.

Roads were often clouds of dust in the summer and quagmires of mud in the winter. Stagecoach travelers braved such additional dangers as tree-strewn roads, rickety bridges, carriage overturns, and runaway horses. A traveler venturesome enough to journey from Philadelphia to New York, for example, would not think it amiss to make a will and pray with the family before departing.

Where man-made roads were wretched, heavy reliance was placed on God-grooved waterways. Population tended to cluster along the banks of navigable rivers. There was also much coastwise traffic, and although it was slow and undependable, it was relatively cheap and pleasant.

Taverns sprang up along the main routes of travel, as well as in the cities. Their attractions customarily included such amusements as bowling alleys, pool tables, bars, and gambling equipment. Before a cheerful, roaring log fire all social classes would mingle, including the village loafers and drunks. The tavern was yet another cradle of democracy.

Gossips also gathered at the taverns, which were clearinghouses of information, misinformation, and rumor—frequently stimulated by alcoholic refreshment and impassioned political talk. A successful politician, like the wire-pulling Samuel Adams, was often a man who had a large alehouse fraternity in places like Boston's Green Dragon Tavern. Taverns were important in crystallizing public opinion and proved to be hotbeds of agitation as the Revolutionary movement gathered momentum.

An intercolonial postal system was established by the mid-1700s, although private couriers remained. Some mail was handled on credit. Service was slow and infrequent, and secrecy was problematic. Mail carriers, serving long routes, would sometimes pass the time by reading the letters entrusted to their care.

A Colonial Tavern
Alehouses like this not only provided food, drink, shelter, and entertainment for colonial Americans, but were also raucous arenas for exchanging and debating political ideas.

Dominant Denominations

Two "established," or tax-supported, churches were conspicuous in 1775: the Anglican and the Congregational. A considerable segment of the population, surprisingly enough, did not worship in any church. And in those colonies that maintained an "established" religion, only a minority of the people belonged to it.

The Church of England, whose members were commonly called Anglicans, became the official faith in Georgia, North and South Carolina, Virginia, Maryland, and a part of New York. Established also

Estimated Religious Census, 1775

Name	Number	Chief Locale
Congregationalists	575,000	New England
Anglicans	500,000	N.Y., South
Presbyterians	410,000	Frontier
German churches (incl. Lutheran)	200,000	Pa.
Dutch Reformed	75,000	N.Y., N.J.
Quakers	40,000	Pa., N.J., Del.
Baptists	25,000	R.I., Pa., N.J., Del.
Roman Catholics	25,000	Md., Pa.
Methodists	5,000	Scattered
Jews	2,000	N.Y., R.I.
EST. TOTAL MEMBERSHIP	1,857,000	
EST. TOTAL POPULATON	2,493,000	
PERCENTAGE CHURCH MEMBERS	74%	

in England, it served in America as a major prop of kingly authority. British officials naturally made vigorous attempts to impose it on additional colonies, but they ran into a stone wall of opposition.

In America the Anglican church fell distressingly short of its promise. Secure and self-satisfied, like its parent in England, it clung to a faith that was less fierce and more worldly than the religion of Puritanical New England. Sermons were shorter; hell was less scorching; and amusements, like Virginia fox hunting, were less scorned. So dismal was the reputation of the Anglican clergy in seventeenth-century Virginia that the College of William and Mary was founded in 1693 to train a better class of clerics.

The influential Congregational church, which had grown out of the Puritan church, was formally established in all the New England colonies, except independent-minded Rhode Island. At first Massachusetts taxed all residents to support Congregationalism but later relented and exempted members of other well-known denominations. Presbyterianism, though closely associated with Congregationalism, was never made official in any colonies.

Ministers of the gospel, turning from the Bible to this sinful world, increasingly grappled with burning political issues. As the early rumblings of revolution against the British crown could be heard,

sedition flowed freely from pulpits. Presbyterianism, Congregationalism, and rebellion became a neo-trinity. Many leading Anglican clergymen, aware of which side their tax-provided bread was buttered on, naturally supported their king.

Anglicans in the New World were seriously handicapped by not having a resident bishop, whose presence would be convenient for the ordination of young ministers. American students of Anglican theology had to travel to England to be ordained. On the eve of the Revolution there was serious talk of creating an American bishopric, but the scheme was violently opposed by many non-Anglicans, who feared a tightening of the royal reins. This controversy poured holy oil on the smoldering fires of rebellion.

Religious toleration had indeed made enormous strides in America, at least when compared with its halting steps abroad. Roman Catholics were still generally discriminated against, as in England, even in office holding. But there were fewer Catholics in America, and hence the anti-papist laws were less severe and less strictly enforced. In general, people could worship—or not worship—as they pleased.

Established (Tax-Supported) Churches in the Colonies, 1775*

Colonies	Churches	Year Disestablished
Mass. (incl. Me.)	Congregational	1833
Connecticut	Congregational	1818
New Hampshire	Congregational	1819
New York	Anglican (in N.Y. City and three neighboring counties)	1777
Maryland	Anglican	1777
Virginia	Anglican	1786
North Carolina	Anglican	1776
South Carolina	Anglican	1778
Georgia	Anglican	1777
Rhode Island	None	
New Jersey	None	
Delaware	None	
Pennsylvania	None	

*Note the persistence of the Congregational establishment in New England.

Franklin's Poor Richard's Almanack *contained such thoughts on religion as*

"A good example is the best sermon."

"Many have quarreled about religion that never practiced it."

"Serving God is doing good to man, but praying is thought an easier service, and therefore more generally chosen."

"How many observe Christ's birthday; how few his precepts! O! 'tis easier to keep holidays than commandments."

The Great Awakening

In all the colonial churches, religion was less fervid in the early eighteenth century than it had been a century earlier, when the colonies were first planted. The Puritan churches in particular sagged under the weight of two burdens: their elaborate theological doctrines and their compromising efforts to liberalize membership requirements. Churchgoers increasingly complained about the "dead dogs" who droned out tedious, overerudite sermons from Puritan pulpits. Some ministers, on the other hand, worried that many of their parishioners had gone soft and that their souls were no longer kindled by the hellfire of orthodox Calvinism. Liberal ideas began to challenge the old-time religion. Some worshipers now proclaimed that human beings were not necessarily predestined to damnation and might save themselves by good works. Even more threatening to the Calvinist doctrine of predestination were the doctrines of the Arminians, followers of the Dutch theologian Jacobus Arminius, who preached that individual free will, not divine decree, determined a person's eternal fate. Pressured by these "heresies," a few churches grudgingly conceded that spiritual conversion was not necessary for church membership. Together, these twin trends toward clerical intellectualism and lay liberalism were sapping the spiritual vitality from many denominations.

The stage was thus set for a rousing religious revival. Known as the Great Awakening, it exploded in the 1730s and 1740s and swept through the colonies like a fire through prairie grass. The Awakening was first ignited in Northampton, Massachusetts, by a tall, delicate, and intellectual pastor, Jonathan Edwards. Perhaps the deepest theological mind ever nurtured in America, Edwards proclaimed with burning righteousness the folly of believing in salvation through good works and affirmed the need for complete dependence on God's grace. Warming to his subject, he painted in lurid detail the landscape of hell and the eternal torments of the damned. "Sinners in the Hands of an Angry God" was the title of one of his most famous sermons. He believed that hell was "paved with the skulls of unbaptized children."

Edwards's preaching style was learned and closely reasoned, but his stark doctrines sparked a warmly sympathetic reaction among his parishioners in 1734. Four years later the itinerant English parson George Whitefield loosed a different style of evangelical preaching on America and touched off a conflagration of religious ardor that revolutionized the spiritual life of the colonies. A former alehouse

George Whitefield Preaching
Americans of both genders and all races and regions were spellbound by Whitefield's emotive oratory.

attendant, Whitefield was an orator of rare gifts. His magnificent voice boomed sonorously over thousands of enthralled listeners in an open field. One of England's greatest actors of the day commented enviously that Whitefield could make audiences weep merely by pronouncing the word *Mesopotamia* and that he would "give a hundred guineas if I could only say 'O!' like Mr. Whitefield."

Triumphally touring the colonies, Whitefield trumpeted his message of human helplessness and divine omnipotence. His eloquence reduced Jonathan Edwards to tears and even caused the skeptical and thrifty Benjamin Franklin to empty his pockets into the collection plate. During these roaring revival meetings, countless sinners professed conversion, and hundreds of the "saved" groaned, shrieked, or rolled in the snow from religious excitation. Whitefield soon inspired American imitators. Taking up his electrifying new style of preaching, they heaped abuse on sinners and shook enormous audiences with emotional appeals. One preacher cackled hideously in the face of hapless wrongdoers. Another, naked to the waist, leaped frantically about in the light of flickering torches.

Orthodox clergymen, known as "old lights," were deeply skeptical of the emotionalism and the theatrical antics of the revivalists. "New light" ministers, on the other hand, defended the Awakening for its role in revitalizing American religion. Congregationalists and Presbyterians split over this issue, and many of the believers in religious conversion went over to the Baptists and other sects more prepared to make room for emotion in religion. The Awakening left many lasting effects. Its emphasis on direct, emotive spirituality seriously undermined the older clergy, whose authority had derived from their education and erudition. The schisms it set off in many denominations greatly increased the numbers and the competitiveness of American churches. It encouraged a fresh wave of missionary work among the Indians and even among black slaves, many of whom also attended the mass open-air revivals. It led to the founding of "new light" centers of higher learning such as Princeton, Brown, Rutgers, and Dartmouth. Perhaps most significant, the Great Awakening was the first spontaneous mass movement of the American people. It tended to break down sectional boundaries as well as denominational lines and contributed to the growing sense that Americans had of themselves as a single people, united by a common history and shared experiences.

Schools and Colleges

A time-honored English idea regarded education as a blessing reserved for the aristocratic few, not for the unwashed many. Education should be for leadership, not citizenship, and primarily for males. Only slowly and painfully did the colonials break the chains of these ancient restrictions.

Puritan New England, largely for religious reasons, was more zealously interested in education than any other section. Dominated by the Congregational church, it stressed the need for Bible reading by the individual worshiper. The primary goal of the clergy was to make good Christians rather than good citizens. A more secular approach was evident late in the eighteenth century, when some children were warned in the following verse:

Jonathan Edwards (1703–1758) preached hellfire, notably in one famous sermon:

"The God that holds you over the pit of hell, much as one holds a spider or some loathsome insect over the fire, abhors you, and is dreadfully provoked. His wrath toward you burns like fire; he looks upon you as worthy of nothing else but to be cast into the fire."

John Adams (c. 1736–1826) the future second president, wrote to his wife:

"The education of our children is never out of my mind. . . . I must study politics and war that my sons may have the liberty to study mathematics and philosophy. My sons ought to study mathematics and philosophy, geography, natural history, naval architecture, navigation, commerce, and agriculture, in order to give their children a right to study painting, poetry, music, architecture, statuary, tapestry, and porcelain."

Colonial Colleges

Name	Original Name (If Different)	Location	Opened or Founded	Denomination
1. Harvard		Cambridge, Mass.	1636	Congregational
2. William and Mary		Williamsburg, Va.	1693	Anglican
3. Yale		New Haven, Conn.	1701	Congregational
4. Princeton	College of New Jersey	Princeton, N.J.	1746	Presbyterian
5. Pennsylvania	The Academy	Philadelphia, Pa.	1751	Nonsectarian
6. Columbia	King's College	New York, N.Y.	1754	Anglican
7. Brown	Rhode Island College	Providence, R.I.	1764	Baptist
8. Rutgers	Queen's College	New Brunswick, N.J.	1766	Dutch Reformed
9. Dartmouth (begun as an Indian missionary school)		Hanover, N.H.	1769	Congregational

He who ne'er learns his A.B.C.
Forever will a blockhead be.
But he who learns his letters fair
Shall have a coach to take the air.

Education, principally for boys, flourished almost from the outset in New England. This densely populated region boasted an impressive number of graduates from the English universities, especially Cambridge, the intellectual center of England's Puritanism. New Englanders, at a relatively early date, established primary and secondary schools, which varied widely in the quality of instruction and in the length of time that their doors remained open each year. Back-straining farm labor drained much of a youth's time and energy.

Fairly adequate primary and secondary schools were also hammering knowledge into the heads of reluctant "scholars" in the middle colonies and in the South. Some of these institutions were tax-supported; others were privately operated. The South, with its white and black population diffused over wide areas, was severely handicapped by logistics in attempting to establish an effective school system. Wealthy families leaned heavily on private tutors.

The general atmosphere in the colonial schools and colleges continued grim and gloomy. Most of the emphasis was placed on religion and on the classical languages, Latin and Greek. The focus was not on experiment and reason, but on doctrine and dogma. The age was one of orthodoxy, and independence of thinking was discouraged. Discipline was quite severe, with many a mischievous child being "birched" with a switch cut from a birch tree. Sometimes punishment was inflicted by indentured-servant teachers, who could themselves be whipped for their failures as workers and who therefore were not inclined to spare the rod.

College education was regarded—at least at first in New England—as more important than instruction in the ABCs. Churches would wither if a new crop of ministers was not trained to lead the spiritual flocks. Many well-to-do families, especially in the South, sent their boys abroad to English institutions.

Harvard College   An eighteenth-century needlepoint.

For purposes of convenience and economy, nine local colleges were established during the colonial era. Student enrollments were small, numbering about 200 boys at the most; and at one time a few lads as young as eleven were admitted to Harvard. Instruction was poor by present-day standards. The curriculum was still heavily loaded with theology and the "dead" languages, although by 1750 there was a distinct trend toward "live" languages and other modern subjects. A significant contribution was made by Benjamin Franklin, who played a major role in launching what became the University of Pennsylvania, the first American college free from denominational control.

Culture in the Backwoods

The dawn-to-dusk toil of pioneer life left little vitality or aptitude for artistic effort. Americans were too busy chopping down trees to sit around painting landscapes, especially when a hostile Indian might burst from a nearby bush. There was no strong esthetic tradition; many of the clergy, in fact, regarded art as an invention of the Devil.

As the colonists gradually acquired some wealth and leisure time, their surplus energy went into religious and political leadership, not art. The materialistic atmosphere was not favorable to artistic endeavor. One famous painter, John Trumbull of Connecticut (1756–1843), was discouraged in his youth by his father with the chilling remark, "Connecticut is not Athens." Charles Willson Peale (1741–1827), best known for his portraits of George Washington, ran a museum, stuffed birds, and practiced dentistry. Gifted Benjamin West (1738–1820) and precocious John Singleton Copley (1738–1815) succeeded in their ambition to become famous painters, but they had to go to England to complete their training. Only abroad could they find subjects who had the leisure to sit for their portraits and the money to pay handsomely for them. Copley was regarded as a Loyalist during the Revolutionary War, and West, a close friend of George III and official court painter, was buried in London's St. Paul's Cathedral.

Architecture was largely imported from the Old World and modified to meet the peculiar climatic and religious conditions of the New World. Even the lowly log cabin was apparently borrowed from

Colonial Craftsmanship
In the "Pennsylvania Dutch" country, parents gave daughters painted wooden chests to hold their precious dowry linens at marriage. The horsemen, unicorns, and flower patterns on this dower chest confirm its origins in Berks County, Pennsylvania.

Sweden. The red-bricked Georgian style, so common in the pre-Revolutionary decades, was introduced about 1720 and is best exemplified by the beauty of now-restored Williamsburg, Virginia.

Colonial literature, like art, was generally undistinguished, and for much the same reasons. One noteworthy exception was the precocious poet Phillis Wheatley (c. 1753–1784), a slave girl brought to Boston at age eight and never formally educated. Taken to England when twenty years of age, she published a book of verse and subsequently wrote other polished poems that revealed the influence of Alexander Pope. Her verse compares favorably with the best of the poetry-poor colonial period, but the remarkable fact is that she could overcome her severely disadvantaged background and write any poetry at all.

Versatile Benjamin Franklin, often called "the first civilized American," also shone as a literary light. Although his autobiography is now a classic, he was best known to his contemporaries for *Poor Richard's Almanack*, which he edited from 1732 to 1758. This famous publication, containing many pithy sayings culled from the thinkers of the ages, emphasized such homespun virtues as thrift, industry, morality, and common sense. Examples are "What maintains one vice would bring up two children"; "Plough deep while sluggards sleep"; "Honesty is the best policy"; and "Fish and visitors stink in three days." *Poor Richard's* was well known in Europe and was more widely read in America than

"The Magnetic Dispensary," c. 1790
This British engraving made sport of the faddish preoccupations of Philadelphians with electricity.
Following Franklin's experiments, static electricity, generated here by the machine on the right,
was employed for "medicinal" purposes as well as for tingling entertainments.

anything except the Bible. As a teacher of both old and young, Franklin had an incalculable influence in shaping the American character.

Science, rising above the shackles of superstition, was making some progress, though lagging behind the Old World. A few botanists, mathematicians, and astronomers had won some repute, but Benjamin Franklin was perhaps the only first-rank scientist produced in the American colonies. Franklin's spectacular but dangerous experiments, including the famous kite-flying episode proving that lightning was a form of electricity, won him numerous honors in Europe. But his mind also had a practical turn, and among his numerous inventions were bifocal spectacles and the highly efficient Franklin stove. His lightning rod, not surprisingly, was condemned by some stodgy clergymen who felt it was "presuming on God" by attempting to control the "artillery of the heavens."

Pioneer Presses

Stump-grubbing Americans were generally too poor to buy quantities of books and too busy to read them. A South Carolina merchant in 1744 advertised the arrival of a shipment of "printed books, Pictures, Maps, and Pickles." A few private libraries of fair size could be found, especially among the clergy. The Byrd family of Virginia enjoyed perhaps the largest collection in the colonies, consisting of about four thousand volumes. Bustling Benjamin Franklin established in Philadelphia the first privately supported circulating library in America; and by 1776 there were about fifty public libraries and collections supported by subscription.

Hand-operated printing presses cranked out pamphlets, leaflets, and journals. On the eve of the

Revolution there were about forty colonial newspapers, chiefly weeklies that consisted of a single large sheet folded once. Columns ran heavily to dull essays, frequently signed with such pseudonyms as *Cicero, Philosophicus,* and *Pro Bono Publico* ("For the Public Good"). The "news" often lagged many weeks behind the event, especially in the case of overseas happenings, in which the colonials were deeply interested. Newspapers proved to be a powerful agency for airing colonial grievances and rallying opposition to British control.

A celebrated legal case, in 1734–1735, involved John Peter Zenger, a newspaper printer. Significantly, the case arose in New York, reflecting the tumultuous give-and-take of politics in the middle colonies, where so many different ethnic groups jostled against one another. Zenger's newspaper had assailed the corrupt royal governor. Charged with seditious libel, the accused was hauled into court, where he was defended by a former indentured servant, now a distinguished Philadelphia lawyer, Andrew Hamilton. Zenger argued that he had printed the truth, but the bewigged royal chief justice instructed the jury not to consider the truth or falsity of Zenger's statements; the mere fact of printing, irrespective of the truth, was enough to convict. Hamilton countered that "the very liberty of both exposing and opposing arbitrary power" was at stake. Swayed by his eloquence, the jurors defied the bewigged judges and daringly returned a verdict of not guilty. Cheers burst from the spectators.

The Zenger decision was a banner achievement for freedom of the press and for the health of democracy. It pointed the way to the kind of open public discussion required by the diverse society that colonial New York already was and that all America was to become. Although contrary to existing law and not immediately accepted by other judges and juries, in time it helped establish the doctrine that true statements about public officials could not be prosecuted as libel. Newspapers were thus eventually free to print responsible criticisms of powerful officials, though full freedom of the press was unknown during the pre-Revolutionary era.

The Great Game of Politics

American colonials may have been backward in natural or physical science, but they were making noteworthy contributions to political science.

The thirteen colonial governments took a variety of forms. By 1775, eight of the colonies had royal governors, who were appointed by the king. Three—Maryland, Pennsylvania, and Delaware—were under proprietors who themselves chose the governors. And two—Connecticut and Rhode Island—elected their own governors under self-governing charters.

Practically every colony utilized a two-house legislative body. The upper house, or council, was normally appointed by the crown in the royal colonies and by the proprietor in the proprietary colonies. It was chosen by the voters in the self-governing colonies. The lower house, as the popular branch, was elected by the people—or rather by those who owned enough property to qualify as voters. In several of the colonies, the backcountry elements were seriously underrepresented, and they hated the ruling colonial clique perhaps more than they did kingly authority. Legislatures, in which the people enjoyed direct representation, voted such taxes as they chose for the necessary expenses of colonial government. Self-taxation through representation was a precious privilege that Americans had come to cherish above most others.

Governors appointed by the king were generally able men, sometimes outstanding figures. Some, unfortunately, were incompetent or corrupt—broken-down politicians badly in need of jobs. The worst of the group was impoverished Lord Cornbury, first cousin of Queen Anne, who was made governor of New York and New Jersey in 1702. He proved to be a drunkard, a spendthrift, a grafter, an

Andrew Hamilton (c. 1676–1741) concluded his eloquent plea in the Zenger case with these words:

"The question before the court and you, gentlemen of the jury, is not of small nor private concern. It is not the cause of a poor printer, nor of New York alone, which you are now trying. No! It may, in its consequence, affect every freeman that lives under a British government on the main [land] of America. It is the best cause. It is the cause of liberty."

> *Junius, the pseudonym for a critic (or critics)
> of the British government from 1768 to 1772,
> published a pointed barb in criticizing one
> new appointee:*
>
> "It was not Virginia that wanted a governor
> but a court favorite that wanted a salary."

embezzler, a religious bigot, and a vain fool, especially when he appeared in public dressed like a woman. Even the best appointees had trouble with the colonial legislatures, basically because the royal governor embodied a bothersome transatlantic authority some 3,000 miles (4,800 kilometers) away.

The colonial assemblies found various ways to assert their authority and independence. Some of them employed the trick of withholding the governor's salary unless he yielded to their wishes. He was normally in need of money—otherwise he would not have come to this godforsaken country—so the power of the purse usually forced him to terms. But one governor of North Carolina died with his salary eleven years in arrears.

The London government, in leaving the colonial governor to the tender mercies of the legislature, was guilty of poor administration. In the interests of simple efficiency, the British authorities should have arranged to pay him from independent sources. As events turned out, control over the purse by the colonial legislatures led to prolonged bickering, which proved to be one of the persistent irritants that generated a spirit of revolt.*

Administration at the local level was also varied. County government remained the rule in the plantation South; town-meeting government predominated in New England; and a modification of the two developed in the middle colonies. In the town meeting, with its open discussion and open voting, direct democracy functioned at its best. In this unrivaled cradle of self-government, Americans learned to cherish their privileges and exercise their duties as citizens of the New World commonwealths.

---

*Parliament finally arranged for separate payment of the governors through the Townshend taxes of 1767, but by then the colonials were in such an ugly mood over taxation that this innovation only added fresh fuel to the flames.

Yet the ballot was by no means a birthright. Religious or property qualifications for voting, with even stiffer qualifications for office holding, existed in all the colonies in 1775. The privileged upper classes, fearful of democratic excesses, were unwilling to grant the ballot to every "biped of the forest." Perhaps half of the adult white males were thus disfranchised. But because of the ease of acquiring land and thus satisfying property requirements, the right to vote was not beyond the reach of most industrious and enterprising colonials. Yet somewhat surprisingly, eligible voters often did not exercise this precious privilege. They frequently acquiesced in the leadership of their "betters," who ran colonial affairs—though always reserving the right to vote misbehaving rascals out of office.

By 1775 America was not yet a true democracy—socially, economically, or politically. But it was far more democratic than England and the European Continent. Colonial institutions were giving freer rein to the democratic ideals of tolerance, educational advantages, equality of economic opportunity, freedom of speech, freedom of the press, freedom of assembly, and representative government. And these democratic seeds, planted in rich soil, were to bring forth a lush harvest in later years.

Colonial Folkways

Everyday life in the colonies may now seem glamorous, especially as reflected in antique shops. But judged by modern standards, it was drab and tedious. For most people the labor was heavy and constant—from "can see" to "can't see."

Food was plentiful, though the diet could be coarse and monotonous. Americans probably ate more bountifully, especially of meat, than any people in the Old World. Lazy or sickly was the person whose stomach was empty.

Basic comforts now taken for granted were lacking. Churches were not heated at all, except for charcoal foot-warmers that the women carried. During the frigid New England winters, the preaching of hellfire may not have seemed altogether unattractive. Drafty homes were poorly heated, chiefly by inefficient fireplaces. There was no running water in the houses, no plumbing, and probably not a single bathtub in all colonial America. Candles and whale-oil lamps provided faint and flickering illumination. Garbage disposal was primitive. Long-snouted hogs customarily ranged the streets to consume refuse, while buzzards, protected by law, flapped greedily over tidbits of waste.

Amusement was eagerly pursued where time and custom permitted. The militia assembled periodically for "musters," which consisted of several days of drilling, liberally interspersed with merry-making and flirting. On the frontier, pleasure was often combined with work at house-raisings, quilting bees, husking bees, and apple parings. Funerals and weddings everywhere afforded opportunities for social gatherings, which customarily involved the swilling of much strong liquor.

Winter sports were common in the North, whereas in the South card playing, horse racing, cockfighting, and fox hunting were favorite pastimes. George Washington, not surprisingly, was a superb rider. In the nonpuritanical South, dancing was the rage—jigs, square dances, the Virginia reel—and the agile Washington could swing his fair partner with the best of them.

Other diversions beckoned. Lotteries were universally approved, even by the clergy, and were used to raise money for churches and colleges, including Harvard. Stage plays became popular in the South but were frowned upon in Quaker and Puritan colonies and in some places forbidden by law. Many of the New England clergy saw playacting as time-consuming and immoral; they preferred religious lectures, from which their flocks derived much spiritual satisfaction.

Holidays were everywhere celebrated in the American colonies, but Christmas was frowned upon in New England as an offensive reminder of "Popery." "Yuletide is fooltide" was a common Puritan sneer. Thanksgiving Day came to be a truly American festival, for it combined thanks to God with an opportunity for jollification, gorging, and guzzling.

By the mid–eighteenth century Britain's several North American colonies, despite their differences, revealed some striking similarities. All were basically English in language and customs, and Protestant in religion, while the widespread presence of other peoples and faiths compelled every colony to cede at least some degree of ethnic and religious toleration. Compared with contemporary Europe, they all afforded to enterprising individuals unusual opportunities for social mobility. They all possessed some measure of self-government, though by no means complete democracy. Communication and transportation among the colonies were improving. British North America by 1775 looked like a patchwork quilt—each part slightly different, but stitched together by common origins, common ways of life, and by common beliefs in toleration, economic development, and, above all, self-rule. Fatefully, all the colonies were also separated from the seat of imperial authority by a vast ocean moat some 3,000 miles (4,800 kilometers) wide. These simple facts of shared history, culture, and geography set the stage for the colonists' struggle to unite as an independent people.

Chronology

1693	College of William and Mary founded
1701	Yale College founded
1721	Smallpox inoculation introduced
1732	First edition of Franklin's *Poor Richard's Almanack*
1734	Jonathan Edwards begins Great Awakening
1734-1735	Zenger free-press trial in New York
1738	George Whitefield spreads Great Awakening
1746	Princeton College founded
1760	Britain vetoes South Carolina anti–slave trade measures
1764	Paxton Boys march on Philadelphia / Brown College founded
1766	Rutgers College founded
1768-1771	Regulator protests
1769	Dartmouth College founded

Colonial America: Communities of Conflict or Consensus?

The earliest historians of colonial society portrayed close-knit, homogeneous, and hierarchical communities. Richard Bushman's *From Puritan to Yankee* (1967) challenged that traditional view when he described colonial New England as an expanding, opening society. In this view the colonists gradually lost the religious discipline and social structure of the founding generations, as they poured out onto the frontier or sailed the seas in search of fortune and adventure. Rhys Isaac viewed the Great Awakening in the South as similar evidence of erosion in the social constraints and deference that once held colonial society together. Unbridled religious enthusiasm, North and South, directed by itinerant preachers, encouraged the sort of quest for personal autonomy that eventually led Americans to demand national independence.

Other scholars have focused on the negative aspects of this alleged breakdown in the traditional order, particularly on the rise of new social inequalities. Social historians like Kenneth Lockridge have argued that the decline of cohesive communities, population pressure on the land, and continued dominance of church and parental authority gave rise to a landless class, forced to till tenant plots in the countryside or find work as manual laborers in the cities. Gary Nash, in *The Urban Crucible* (1979), likewise traced the rise of a competitive, individualistic social order in colonial cities, marking the end of the patronage and paternalism that had once bound communities together. Increasingly, Nash contended, class antagonisms split communities. The wealthy abandoned their traditional obligations toward the poor for more selfish capitalistic social relations that favored their class peers. The consequent politicization of the laboring classes helped motivate their participation in the American Revolution.

Some scholars have disputed that "declension" undermined colonial communities. Christine Heyrman, in particular, has argued in *Commerce and Culture* (1984) that the decline of traditional mores has been overstated; religious beliefs and commercial activities coexisted throughout the late seventeenth and early eighteenth centuries. Similarly, Jack Greene has recently suggested that the obsession with the decline of deference has obscured the fact that colonies outside of New England, like Virginia and Maryland, actually experienced a consolidation of religious and social authority throughout the seventeenth and eighteenth centuries, becoming more hierarchical and paternalistic.

Like Greene, many historians have focused on sectional differences between the colonies, and the peculiar nature of social equality and inequality in each. Much of the impetus for this inquiry stems from an issue that has long perplexed students of early America: the simultaneous evolution of a rigid racial caste system alongside democratic political institutions. Decades ago, when most historians came from Yankee stock, they resolved the apparent paradox by locating the seeds of democracy in New England. The aggressive independence of the people, best expressed by the boisterous town meetings, spawned the American obsession with freedom. On the other hand, this view holds, the slave societies of the South were hierarchical, aristocratic communities under the sway of a few powerful planters.

More recently, some historians have attacked this simple dichotomy, noting many undemocratic features in colonial New England and arguing that while the South may have been the site of tremendous inequality, it also produced most of the founding fathers. Washington, Jefferson, and Madison—the architects of American government with its foundation in liberty—all hailed from slaveholding Virginia. In fact, nowhere were republican principles stronger than in Virginia. Some scholars, notably Edmund S. Morgan in *American Slavery, American Freedom* (1975), consider the willingness of wealthy planters to concede the equality and freedom of all white males a device to ensure racial solidarity and to mute class conflict. In this view the concurrent emergence of slavery and democracy was no paradox. White racial solidarity muffled animosity between rich and poor and fostered the devotion to equality among whites that became a hallmark of American democracy.

Few historians still argue that the colonies offered boundless opportunities for inhabitants, white or black. But scholars disagree vigorously over what kinds of inequalities and social tensions most shaped eighteenth-century society and contributed to the revolutionary agitation that eventually consumed—and transformed—colonial America. Even so, whether one accepts Morgan's argument that "Americans bought their independence with slave labor," or those interpretations that point to rising social conflict between whites as the salient characteristic of colonial society on the eve of the Revolution, the once-common assumption that America was a world of equality and consensus no longer reigns undisputed. Yet because one's life chances were still unquestionably better in America than Europe, immigrants continued to pour in, imbued with high expectations about America as a land of opportunity.

SUGGESTED READINGS

PRIMARY SOURCE DOCUMENTS

Noting the ethnic diversity of colonial American society, Michel Guillaume Jean de Crèvecoeur, *Letters from an American Farmer** (1904), and Benjamin Franklin, "Observations on the Increase of Mankind,"* in Jared Sparks, ed., *The Works of Benjamin Franklin* (1840), respectively celebrate and express unease at that diversity. Franklin's entertaining *Autobiography** (1868) is an indispensable guide to the values and preoccupations of his time. It includes an account of George Whitefield's visit to Philadelphia during the Great Awakening.

SECONDARY SOURCES

Social history is painted with broad strokes in James Henretta, *The Evolution of American Society, 1700–1815* (1973), and Daniel Boorstin, *The Americans: The Colonial Experience* (1958). Richard Hofstadter takes a suggestive snapshot view in *America at 1750* (1971). Population trends are detailed in Robert V. Wells, *The*

Population of the British Colonies in America before 1776 (1975). Black "immigrants" are studied in Philip D. Curtin, *The African Slave Trade: A Census* (1969); indentured servants, in David W. Galenson, *White Servitude in Colonial America* (1981); and Sharon V. Salinger, *"To Serve Well and Faithfully": Labor and Indentured Servants in Pennsylvania, 1682–1800* (1987); convicts, in A. Roger Ekirch, *Bound for America: The Transportation of British Convicts to the Colonies, 1718–1775* (1987); British immigrants, in Bernard Bailyn, *The Peopling of British North America* (1986); Scottish immigrants, in Alan L. Karras, *Sojourners in the Sun: Scottish Migrants in Jamaica and the Chesapeake, 1740–1800* (1992); and colonial immigration in general, in Ida Altman and James Horn, eds., *"To Make America": European Emigration in the Early Modern Period* (1991). James Kettner describes *The Development of American Citizenship, 1608–1870* (1978). Large-scale economic patterns are traced in John J. McCusker and Russell R. Menard, *The Economy of British America, 1607–1789* (1991), and in Alice H. Jones, *The Wealth of a Nation to Be: The American Colonies on the Eve of the Revolution* (1980). Relations between blacks and whites are documented in Mechal Sobel, *The World They Made Together: Black and White Values in Eighteenth-Century Virginia* (1987), and William D. Piersen, *Black Yankees: The Development of an Afro-American Subculture in Eighteenth-Century New*

---

*An asterisk indicates that the document, or an excerpt from it, can be found in Thomas A. Bailey and David M. Kennedy, eds., *The American Spirit: United States History as Seen by Contemporaries,* 9th ed. (Boston: Houghton Mifflin, 1998).

England (1988). The toiling classes are probed in Gerald W. Mullin, *Flight and Rebellion: Slave Resistance in Eighteenth-Century Virginia* (1972); Gary B. Nash, *The Urban Crucible: Social Change, Political Consciousness and the Origins of the American Revolution* (1979); Allen Kulikoff, *Tobacco and Slaves: The Development of Southern Cultures in the Chesapeake, 1680–1800* (1986); Rhys Isaac, *The Transformation of Virginia, 1740–1790* (1982); and Marcus Rediker, *Between the Devil and the Deep Blue Sea: Merchant Seamen, Pirates, and the Anglo-American Maritime World, 1700–1750* (1987). Nash and Isaac link social conflict to the Great Awakening, as does Richard L. Bushman, *From Puritan to Yankee: Character and Social Order in Connecticut, 1690–1765* (1967). Patricia Bonomi also emphasizes religious conflict as a promoter of Revolutionary ideology in *Under the Cope of Heaven: Religion, Society, and Politics in Colonial America* (1986), as do the essayists in Ronald Hoffman and Peter J. Albert, eds., *Religion in a Revolutionary Age* (1994). Religious revivalism is chronicled in Edwin S. Gaustad, *The Great Awakening in New England* (1957); David S. Lovejoy, *Religious Enthusiasm in the New World: Heresy to Revolution* (1985); and Susan Juster, *Disorderly Women: Sexual Politics & Evangelicalism in Revolutionary New England* (1994). Cultural history is imaginatively presented in Howard M. Jones, *O Strange New World: American Culture in the Formative Years* (1964). Comprehensive is Henry May, *The Enlightenment in America* (1976). The sometimes heroic dedication to education is portrayed by Lawrence Cremin, *American Education: The Colonial Experience, 1607–1783* (1970); and the general social implications of the early educational system are studied in James Axtell, *School upon a Hill* (1974). Colonial politics are interpreted in a most suggestive way in Bernard Bailyn, *The Origins of American Politics* (1965). More fine-grained local studies are Charles S. Sydnor, *Gentlemen Freeholders* (1952); Richard L. Bushman, *King and People in Provincial Massachusetts* (1985); Robert Zemsky, *Merchants, Farmers and River Gods: An Essay on Eighteenth-Century American Politics* (1971); Jackson Turner Main, *Society and Economy in Colonial Connecticut* (1985); Patricia Bonomi, *A Factious People: Politics and Society in Colonial New York* (1971); James T. Lemon, *The Best Poor Man's Country* (1972), which deals with Pennsylvania; and Daniel Blake Smith, *Inside the Great House: Planter Family Life in Eighteenth-Century Chesapeake Society* (1980). Timothy Breen examines the ways in which the increasing indebtedness of the Virginia planters changed their behavior in *Tobacco Culture: The Mentality of the Great Tidewater Planters on the Eve of Revolution* (1985).

6

The Duel for North America
1608–1763

A torch lighted in the forests of America set all Europe in conflagration.

VOLTAIRE, C. 1756

France Finds a Foothold in Canada

Like England and Holland, France was a latecomer in the scramble for New World real estate, and for basically the same reasons. It was convulsed during the 1500s by foreign wars and domestic strife, including the frightful clashes between the Roman Catholics and the Protestant Huguenots. On St. Bartholomew's Day, 1572, over ten thousand Huguenots—men, women, and children—were butchered in cold blood.

A new era dawned in 1598 when the Edict of Nantes, issued by the crown, granted limited toleration to French Protestants. Religious wars ceased, and in the new century France blossomed into the mightiest and most feared nation in Europe, led by a series of brilliant ministers and by the vainglorious

King Louis XIV. Enthroned as a five-year-old boy, he reigned for no less than seventy-two years (1643–1715), surrounded by a glittering court and fluttering mistresses. Fatefully for North America, Louis XIV also took a deep interest in overseas colonies.

Success finally rewarded the exertions of France in the New World, after rocky beginnings. In 1608, the year after Jamestown, the permanent beginnings of a vast empire were established at Quebec, a granite sentinel commanding the St. Lawrence River. The leading figure was Samuel de Champlain, an intrepid soldier and explorer whose energy and leadership fairly earned him the title "Father of New France."

Champlain entered into friendly relations—a fateful friendship—with the nearby Huron Indian tribes. At their request, he joined them in battle against their foes, the federated Iroquois tribes of the upper New York area. Two volleys from the "lightning sticks" of the whites routed the terrified Iroquois, who left behind three dead and one wounded. France, to its sorrow, thus earned the lasting enmity of the Iroquois tribes. They thereafter hampered French penetration of the Ohio Valley, ravaged French settlements, and served as allies of the British in the prolonged struggle for supremacy on the continent.

The government of New France (Canada) finally fell under the direct control of the king, after various commercial companies had faltered or failed. This royal regime was almost completely autocratic. The people elected no representative assemblies; nor did they enjoy the right to trial by jury, as in the English colonies.

Population in Catholic New France grew at a listless pace. As late as 1750 only sixty thousand or so whites inhabited New France. Landowning French peasants, unlike the dispossessed English tenant farmers who embarked for the British colonies, had little economic motive to move. Protestant Huguenots, who might have had a religious motive to migrate, were denied a refuge in this raw colony. The French government, in any case, favored its Caribbean island colonies, rich in sugar and rum, over the snow-cloaked wilderness of Canada.

New France Fans Out

New France did contain one valuable resource: the beaver. European fashion-setters valued beaver-pelt hats for their warmth and opulent appearance. To adorn the heads of Europeans, French fur-trappers ranged over the woods and waterways of North America in pursuit of beaver. These colorful *coureurs de bois* ("runners of the woods") were also runners of risks—two-fisted drinkers, free spenders, free livers and lovers. They littered the land with scores of place names, including Baton Rouge (red stick), Terre Haute (high land), Des Moines (some monks), and Grand Teton (big breast).

Singing, paddle-swinging French *voyageurs* also recruited Indians into the fur business. The Indian fur flotilla arriving in Montreal in 1693 numbered

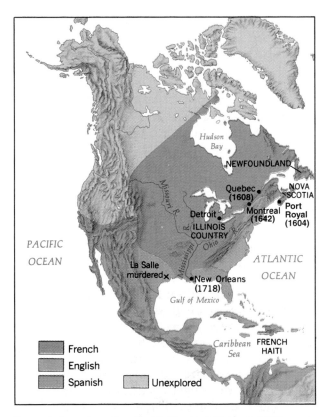

France's American Empire at Greatest Extent, 1700

Quebec Scene, by Jean-Baptiste-Louis Franquelin, c. 1699 (detail)   The metal cooking pot and the Indians' clothing and blankets show the Native Americans' growing reliance on European trade goods.

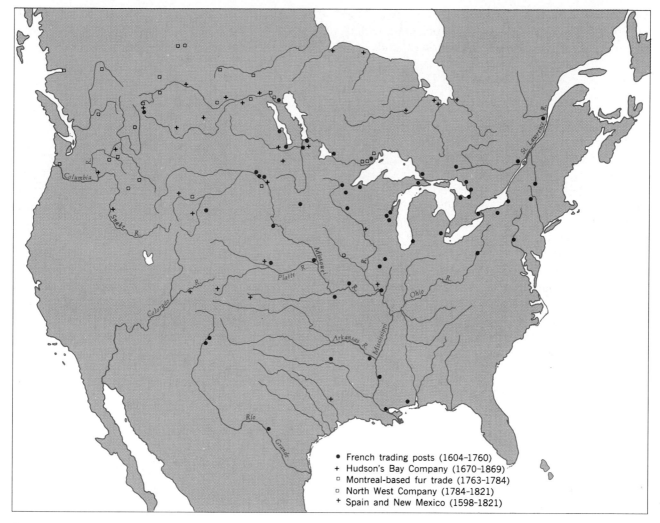

- ● French trading posts (1604–1760)
- + Hudson's Bay Company (1670–1869)
- ▫ Montreal-based fur trade (1763–1784)
- ▫ North West Company (1784–1821)
- + Spain and New Mexico (1598–1821)

Fur-Trading Posts   To serve the needs of European fashion, fur-traders pursued the beaver for more than two centuries over the entire continent of North America. They brought many Indians for the first time into contact with white culture.

four hundred canoes. But the fur trade had some disastrous drawbacks. Indians were decimated by the white man's diseases and debauched by his alcohol—"firewater"—often adulterated with pepper. Slaughtering beaver by the boatload violated many Indians' religious beliefs and sadly demonstrated the shattering effect that contact with Europeans wreaked on traditional Indian ways of life.

Pursuing the sharp-toothed beaver ever deeper into the heart of the continent, the French trappers and their Indian partners hiked, rode, snowshoed, sailed, and paddled amazing distances. They trekked in a huge arc across the Great Lakes, into present-day Saskatchewan and Manitoba, along the valleys of the Platte, the Arkansas, and the Missouri,

west to the Rockies, and south to the border of Spanish Texas (see map above). In the process they extinguished the beaver population in many areas, inflicting incalculable ecological damage.

French Catholic missionaries, notably the Jesuits, labored zealously to save the Indians for Christ and from the fur-trappers. Some of the Jesuit missionaries, their efforts scorned, suffered unspeakable tortures at the hands of the Indians. But though they made few permanent converts, the Jesuits played a vital role as explorers and geographers.

Other explorers sought neither souls nor fur, but empire. To thwart English settlers pushing into the Ohio Valley, Antoine Cadillac founded Detroit, "the City of Straits," in 1701. To check Spanish penetration

Chief of the Taensa Indians Receiving La Salle, March 20, 1682, by George Catlin, 1847–1848 (detail)
Driven by the dream of a vast North American empire for France, La Salle spent years exploring the Great
Lakes region and the valleys of the Illinois and Mississippi Rivers. This scene of his encounter with an
Indian chieftain is imaginatively re-created by the nineteenth-century artist George Catlin.

into the region of the Gulf of Mexico, ambitious Robert de La Salle floated down the Mississippi in 1682 to the point where it mingles with the gulf. He named the great interior basin "Louisiana," in honor of his sovereign, Louis XIV. Dreaming of empire, he returned to the gulf three years later with a colonizing expedition of four ships. But he failed to find the Mississippi delta, landed in Spanish Texas, and in 1687 was murdered by his mutinous men.

Undismayed, French officials persisted in their efforts to block Spain on the Gulf of Mexico. They planted several fortified posts in what is now Mississippi and Louisiana, the most important of which was New Orleans (1718). Commanding the mouth of the Mississippi River, this strategic semitropical outpost also tapped the fur trade of the huge interior valley. The fertile Illinois country—where the French established forts and trading posts at Kaskaskia, Cahokia, and Vincennes—became the garden of France's North American empire. Surprising amounts of grain were floated down the Mississippi for transshipment to the West Indies and to Europe.

The Clash of Empires

As the seventeenth century neared its sunset, a titanic struggle was shaping up for European mastery of the North American continent. The contest involved three Old World nations, England, France, and Spain, and it unavoidably disrupted Native American peoples as well. From 1688 to 1763, four bitter wars convulsed Europe. All four of these conflicts were world wars. They amounted to a death struggle for domination in Europe as well as in the New World and were fought on the waters and on the soil of two hemispheres. Counting these first four clashes, there have been nine world wars since 1688. The American people, whether as British subjects or as American citizens, proved unable to stay out of a single one of them. Isolation from the broils of Europe was all too often a hope rather than a reality.

The first two wars, known in America as King William's War and Queen Anne's War, pitted British colonials against the French *coureurs de bois* and their Indian allies. Neither France nor England at this stage considered America worth the commitment of regular troops, so a kind of primitive guerrilla warfare prevailed. French-inspired Indians ravaged with torch and tomahawk the British colonial frontiers, visiting especially horrible violence on the villages of Schenectady, New York, and Deerfield, Massachusetts (see map, p. 111). Spain, eventually allied with France, probed from its Florida base at outlying South Carolina settlements. For their part the English colonials failed miserably in attempts to capture Quebec and Montreal but did temporarily seize the stronghold of Port Royal in Acadia (present-day Nova Scotia).

Peace terms, signed at Utrecht in 1713, revealed how badly France and its Spanish ally had been beaten. England was rewarded with French-populated Acadia (which the English renamed Nova Scotia, or New Scotland) and the wintry wastes of Newfoundland and Hudson Bay. These immense tracts pinched the St. Lawrence settlements of France, foreshadowing their ultimate doom. A generation of peace ensued, during which Britain provided its American colonies with decades of "salutary neglect"—fertile soil for the roots of independence.

By the treaty of 1713 the British also won limited trading rights in Spanish America, but these later involved much friction over smuggling. Ill feeling flared up when the English Captain Jenkins, encountering Spanish revenue authorities, had one ear sliced off by a sword. The Spanish commander reportedly sneered, "Carry this home to the King, your master, whom, if he were present, I would serve in like fashion." The victim, with a tale of woe on his tongue and a shriveled ear in his hand, aroused furious resentment when he returned home to England.

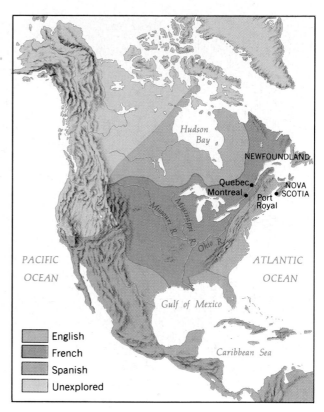

British Territory After Two Wars, 1713

English
French
Spanish
Unexplored

The War of Jenkins's Ear, curiously but aptly named, broke out in 1739 between the English and the Spaniards. It was confined to the Caribbean Sea and to the much-buffeted buffer colony of Georgia, where philanthropist-soldier James Oglethorpe fought his Spanish foe to a standstill.

This small-scale scuffle with Spain in America soon merged with the large-scale War of Austrian Succession in Europe, and came to be called King

Later English Monarchs*

Name, Reign	Relation to America
William III, 1689–1702	Collapse of Dominion of New England; King William's War
Anne, 1702–1714	Queen Anne's War, 1702–1713
George I, 1714–1727	Navigation Laws laxly enforced ("salutary neglect")
George II, 1727–1760	Ga. founded; King George's War; French and Indian War
George III, 1760–1820	American Revolution, 1775–1783

*See pp. 29, 52 for earlier ones.

New Englanders Capture Louisbourg, 1745   When the final peace settlement returned this fortress to France, the American colonials felt betrayed by their British masters.

George's War in America. Once again, France allied itself with Spain. And once again, a rustic force of New Englanders invaded New France. With help from a British fleet and with a great deal of good luck, the raw and sometimes drunken recruits captured the reputedly impregnable French fortress of Louisbourg, which was on Cape Breton Island and commanded the approaches to the St. Lawrence River (see map, p. 111).

When the peace treaty of 1748 handed Louisbourg back to their French foe, the victorious New Englanders were outraged. The glory of their arms—never terribly lustrous in any event—seemed tarnished by the wiles of Old World diplomats. Worse, Louisbourg was still a cocked pistol pointed at the heart of the American continent. France, powerful and unappeased, still clung to its vast holdings in North America.

The Nine World Wars

Dates	In Europe	In America
1688–1697	War of the League of Augsburg	King William's War, 1689–1697
1701–1713	War of Spanish Succession	Queen Anne's War, 1702–1713
1740–1748	War of Austrian Succession	King George's War, 1744–1748
1756–1763	Seven Years' War	French and Indian War, 1754–1763
1778–1783	War of the American Revolution	American Revolution, 1775–1783
1793–1802	Wars of the French Revolution	Undeclared French War, 1798–1800
1803–1815	Napoleonic Wars	War of 1812, 1812–1814
1914–1918	World War I	World War I, 1917–1918
1939–1945	World War II	World War II, 1941–1945

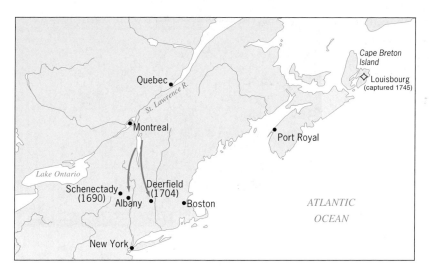

Scenes of the French Wars The arrows indicate French-Indian attacks. Schenectady was burned to the ground in the raid of 1690. At Deerfield, site of one of the New England frontier's bloodiest confrontations, invaders killed fifty inhabitants and sent over a hundred others fleeing for their lives into the winter wilderness. The Indian attackers also took over one hundred Deerfield residents captive, including the child Titus King. He later wrote: "Captivity is an awful school for children, when we see how quick they will fall in with the Indian ways. Nothing seems to be more taking [appealing]. In six months' time they forsake father and mother, forget their own land, refuse to speak their own tongue, and seemingly be wholly swallowed up with the Indians."

George Washington Inaugurates War with France

As the dogfight intensified in the New World, the Ohio Valley became the chief bone of contention between the French and British. The Ohio country was the critical area into which the westward-pushing English would inevitably penetrate. It was the key to the continent that the French had to retain, particularly if they were going to link their Canadian holdings with those of the lower Mississippi Valley. By the mid-1700s the English colonials, painfully aware of these basic truths, were no longer so reluctant to bear the burdens of empire. Alarmed by French land-grabbing and cutthroat fur-trade competition in the Ohio Valley, they were determined to fight for their economic security and for the supremacy of their way of life in North America.

Rivalry for the lush lands of the upper Ohio Valley brought tensions to the snapping point. In 1749 a group of English colonial speculators, chiefly influential Virginians, including the Washington family, had secured shaky legal "rights" to some 500,000 acres in this region. In the same disputed wilderness, the French were in the process of erecting a chain of forts commanding the strategic Ohio River. Especially formidable was Fort Duquesne at the pivotal point where the Monongahela and Allegheny Rivers join to form the Ohio—the later site of Pittsburgh.

In 1754 the governor of Virginia ushered George Washington, a twenty-one-year-old surveyor and fellow Virginian, onto the stage of history. To secure the Virginians' claims, Washington was sent to the Ohio country as a lieutenant colonel in command of about 150 Virginia militiamen. Encountering a small detachment of French troops in the forest about forty miles from Fort Duquesne, the Virginians fired the first shots of the globe-girdling new war. The French leader was killed, and his men retreated. An

The Ohio Country, 1753–1754

exultant Washington wrote, "I heard the bullets whistle, and believe me, there is something charming in the sound." It soon lost its charm.

The French promptly returned with reinforcements, which surrounded Washington in his hastily constructed breastworks, Fort Necessity. After a ten-hour siege he was forced to surrender his entire command in July 1754—ironically the fourth of July. But he was permitted to march his men away with the full honors of war.

With the shooting already started and in danger of spreading, the British authorities in Nova Scotia took vigorous action. Understandably fearing a stab in the back from the French Acadians, whom England had acquired in 1713, the British brutally uprooted some four thousand of them in 1755. These unhappy French deportees were scattered as far south as Louisiana, where the descendants of the French-speaking Acadians are now called "Cajuns" and number nearly a million.

Global War and Colonial Disunity

The first three Anglo-French colonial wars had all started in Europe, but the tables were now reversed. The fourth struggle, known as the French and Indian War, began in America. Touched off by George Washington in the wilds of the Ohio Valley in 1754, it rocked along on an undeclared basis for two years and then widened into the most far-flung conflict the world had yet seen—the Seven Years' War. It was fought not only in America but in Europe, in the West Indies, in the Philippines, in Africa, and on the ocean. The Seven Years' War was a seven-seas war.

In Europe the principal adversaries were England and Prussia on one side, arrayed against France, Spain, Austria, and Russia on the other. The bloodiest theater was in Germany, where Frederick the Great deservedly won the title of "Great" by repelling French, Austrian, and Russian armies, often with the opposing forces outnumbering his own three to one. The London government, unable to send him effective troop reinforcements, liberally subsidized him with gold. Luckily for the English colonials, the French wasted so much strength in this European bloodbath that they were unable to throw an adequate force into the New World. "America was conquered in Germany," declared Britain's great statesman William Pitt.

Famous Cartoon by Benjamin Franklin
Delaware and Georgia were omitted.

In previous colonial clashes, the Americans had revealed an astonishing lack of unity. Colonists who were nearest the shooting had responded much more generously with volunteers and money than those enjoying the safety of remoteness. Even the Indians had laughed at the inability of the colonials to pull together. Now, with musketballs already splitting the air in Ohio, the crisis demanded concerted action.

In 1754 the British government summoned an intercolonial congress to Albany, New York, near the Iroquois Indian country. Travel-weary delegates from only seven of the thirteen colonies showed up. The immediate purpose was to keep the scalping knives of the Iroquois tribes loyal to the British in the spreading war. The chiefs were harangued at length and then presented with thirty wagonloads of gifts, including guns.

The longer-range purpose at Albany was to achieve greater colonial unity and thus bolster the common defense against France. A month before the congress assembled, ingenious Benjamin Franklin published in his *Pennsylvania Gazette* the most famous cartoon of the colonial era. Showing the separate colonies as parts of a disjointed snake, it broadcast the slogan "Join, or Die."

Franklin himself, a wise and witty counselor, was the leading spirit of the Albany Congress. His outstanding contribution was a well-devised scheme for colonial home rule. The Albany delegates unanimously adopted the plan, but the individual colonies spurned it, as did the London regime. To the colonials, it did not seem to give enough independence; to the British officials, it seemed to give too much. The disappointing result confirmed one of Franklin's sage observations: all people agreed on the need for union, but their "weak noddles" were "perfectly distracted" when they attempted to agree on details.

Braddock's Blundering and Its Aftermath

The opening clashes of the French and Indian War went badly for the English colonials. Haughty and bullheaded General Braddock, a sixty-year-old officer experienced in European warfare, was sent to Virginia with a strong detachment of British regulars. After foraging scanty supplies from the reluctant colonists, he set out in 1755 with some two thousand men to capture Fort Duquesne. A considerable part of his force consisted of ill-disciplined colonial militiamen ("buckskins"), whose behind-the-tree methods of fighting Indians won "Bulldog" Braddock's professional contempt.

Braddock's expedition, dragging heavy artillery, moved slowly. Axmen laboriously hacked a path through the dense forest, thus opening a road that was later to be an important artery to the West. A few miles from Fort Duquesne, Braddock encountered a much smaller French and Indian army. At first the enemy force was repulsed, but it quickly melted into the thickets and poured a murderous fire into the ranks of the redcoats. In the ensuing debate, George Washington, an energetic and fearless aide to Braddock, had two horses shot from under him and four bullet holes in his coat, and Braddock himself was mortally wounded. The entire British force was routed after appalling losses.

Inflamed by this easy victory, the Indians took to a wider warpath. The whole frontier from Pennsylvania to North Carolina, left virtually naked by Braddock's bloody defeat, felt their fury. Scalping forays occurred within eighty miles of Philadelphia, and in desperation the local authorities offered bounties for Indian scalps: $50 for a woman's and $130 for a brave's. George Washington, with only three hundred men, tried desperately to defend the scorched frontier.

The British launched a full-scale invasion of Canada in 1756, now that the undeclared war in America had at last merged into a world conflict.

But they unwisely tried to attack a number of exposed wilderness posts simultaneously, instead of throwing all their strength at Quebec and Montreal. If these strongholds had fallen, all the outposts to the west would have withered for lack of riverborne supplies. But the British ignored such sound strategy, and defeat after defeat tarnished their arms, both in America and in Europe.

Pitt's Palms of Victory

In the hour of crisis Britain brought forth, as it repeatedly has, a superlative leader—William Pitt. A tall and imposing figure, whose flashing eyes were set in a hawklike face, he was popularly known as the "Great Commoner." Pitt drew much of his strength from the common people, who admired him so greatly that on occasion they kissed his

William Pitt (1708–1778) He opposed the king's stubborn policies against the colonies but never favored complete independence. Fort Duquesne, falling to Britain in the French and Indian War, was renamed Pittsburgh in his honor.

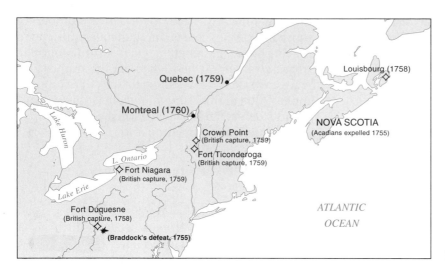

Events of 1755–1760

horses. A splendid orator endowed with a majestic voice, he believed passionately in his cause, in his country, and in himself.

In 1757 Pitt became a foremost leader in the London government. Throwing himself headlong into his task, he soon earned the title "Organizer of Victory." He wisely decided to soft-pedal assaults on the French West Indies, which had been bleeding away much British strength, and to concentrate on the vitals of Canada—the Quebec-Montreal area. He also picked young and energetic leaders, thus bypassing incompetent and cautious old generals.

Pitt first dispatched a powerful expedition in 1758 against Louisbourg. The frowning fortress, though it had been greatly strengthened, fell after a blistering siege. Wild rejoicing swept England, for this was the first significant British victory of the entire war.

Quebec was next on Pitt's list. For this crucial expedition he chose the thirty-two-year-old James Wolfe, who had been an officer since the age of fourteen. Though slight and sickly, Wolfe combined a mixture of dash with painstaking attention to detail. The British attackers were making woeful progress when Wolfe, in a daring night move, sent a detachment up a poorly guarded part of the rocky eminence protecting Quebec. This vanguard scaled the cliff, pulling itself upward by the bushes and showing the way for the others. In the morning the two armies faced each other on the Plains of Abraham on the outskirts of Quebec, the British under Wolfe and the French under the Marquis de Montcalm.

Both commanders fell fatally wounded, but the French were defeated and the city surrendered (see "Makers of America: The French," pp. 116–117).

The battle of Quebec in 1759 ranks as one of the most significant engagements in British and American history. When Montreal fell in 1760, the French flag waved in Canada for the last time. By the peace settlement at Paris (1763), French power was thrown completely off the continent of North America, leaving behind a fertile French population that is to this day a strong minority in Canada. This bitter pill was sweetened somewhat when the French were allowed to retain several small but valuable sugar islands in the West Indies, and two never-to-be-fortified islets in the Gulf of St. Lawrence for fishing stations. A final blow came when the French, to compensate their luckless Spanish ally for its losses, ceded to Spain all trans-Mississippi Louisiana, plus the outlet of New Orleans. Spain, for its part, turned Florida over to England in return for Cuba, where Havana had fallen to British arms.

Great Britain thus emerged as the dominant power in North America, while taking its place as the leading naval power of the world.

Restless Colonials

England's colonials, baptized by fire, emerged with increased confidence in their military strength. They had borne the brunt of battle at first; they had

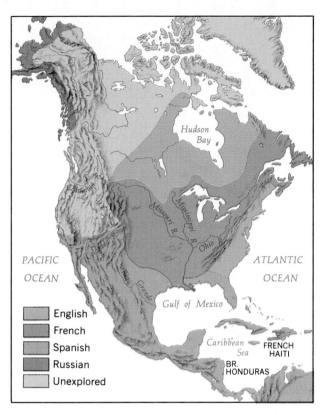

North America Before 1754

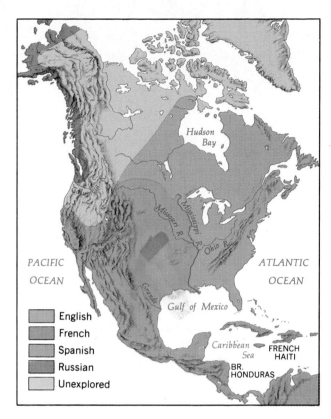

North America After 1763 (after French losses)

fought bravely beside the crack British regulars; and they had gained valuable experience, officers and men alike. In the closing days of the conflict some twenty thousand American recruits were under arms.

The French and Indian War, while bolstering colonial self-esteem, simultaneously shattered the myth of British invincibility. On Braddock's bloody field the "buckskin" militia had seen the demoralized regulars huddling helplessly together or fleeing their unseen enemy.

Ominously, friction had developed during the war between arrogant English officers and the raw colonial "boors." Displaying the contempt of the professional soldier for amateurs, the British refused to recognize any American militia commission above the rank of captain—a demotion humiliating to "Colonel" George Washington. They also showed the usual condescension of snobs from the civilized Old Country toward the "scum" who had confessed failure by fleeing to the "outhouses of civilization." General Wolfe referred to the colonial

militia, with exaggeration, as "in general the dirtiest, most contemptible, cowardly dogs that you can conceive." Energetic and hardworking American settlers, in contrast, believed themselves to be the cutting edge of British civilization. They felt that they deserved credit rather than contempt for risking their lives to secure a New World empire.

British officials were further distressed by the reluctance of the colonials to support the common cause wholeheartedly. American shippers, using fraudulent papers, developed a golden traffic with the enemy ports of the Spanish and French West Indies. This treasonable trade in foodstuffs actually kept some of the hostile islands from starving at the very time when the British navy was trying to subdue them. In the final year of the war, the British authorities, forced to resort to drastic measures, forbade the export of all supplies from New England and the middle colonies.

Other colonials, self-centered and alienated by distance from the war, refused to provide troops and money for the conflict. They demanded the rights

The French

At the height of his reign in the late seventeenth century, Louis XIV, France's "Sun King," turned his covetous eyes westward to the New World. He envisioned there a bountiful New France, settled by civilizing French pioneers, in the maritime provinces of Acadia and the icy expanses of Quebec. But his dreams flickered out like candles before the British juggernaut in the eighteenth century, and his former New World subjects had to suffer foreign governance in the aftermath of the French defeats in 1713

and 1763. Over the course of two centuries, many chafed under the British yoke and eventually found their way to the United States.

The first French to leave Canada were the Acadians, the settlers of the seaboard region that now comprises Nova Scotia, New Brunswick, Prince Edward Island, and part of Maine. In 1713 the French crown ceded this territory to the British, who demanded that the Acadians either swear allegiance to Britain or withdraw to French territory. At first doing neither, they managed to escape reprisals until *Le Grand Derangement* ("the Great Displacement") in 1755, when the British expelled them from

(above) Acadian Architecture   This architectural style was transplanted by the uprooted Acadians to the Cajun bayous of Louisiana.   (right) Franco-American Mill Workers in New England, c. 1910

Modern-Day Quebec
A bit of the old world in the new.

the region at bayonet point. The Acadians fled far south to the French colony of Louisiana, where they settled among the sleepy bayous, planted sugar cane and sweet potatoes, practiced Roman Catholicism, and spoke the French dialect that came to be called Cajun (a corruption of the English word *Acadian.*) The Cajun settlements were tiny and secluded, many of them accessible only by small boat.

For generations these insular people were scarcely influenced by developments outside their tight-knit communities. Louisiana passed through Spanish, French, and American hands, but the Cajuns kept to themselves. Cajun women sometimes married German, English, or Spanish men—today one finds such names as Schneider and Lopez in the bayous—but the outsiders were always absorbed completely into the large Cajun families. Not until the twentieth century did Cajun parents surrender their children to public schools and submit to a state law restricting French speech. Only in the 1930s, with a bridge-building spree engineered by Governor Huey Long, was the isolation of these bayou communities broken.

In 1763, as the French settlers of Quebec fell under British rule, a second group of French people began to leave Canada. By 1840 what had been an irregular southward trickle of Quebecois swelled to a steady stream, depositing most of the migrating French-Canadians in New England. These nineteenth-century emigrants were not goaded by

bayonets but driven away by the lean harvests yielded by Quebec's short growing season and scarcity of arable land. They frequently recrossed the border to visit their old homes, availing themselves of the train routes opened in the 1840s between Quebec and Boston. Most hoped someday to return to Canada for good.

They emigrated mostly to work in New England's lumberyards and textile mills, gradually establishing permanent settlements in the northern woods. Like the Acadians, these later migrants from Quebec stubbornly preserved their Roman Catholicism. And both groups shared a passionate love of their French language, believing it to be the cement that bound them, their religion, and their culture together. As one French-Canadian explained, "Let us worship in peace and in our own tongue. All else may disappear but this must remain our badge." Yet today, almost all Cajuns and New England French-Canadians speak English.

North of the border, in the land that these immigrants left behind, Louis XIV's dream of implanting a French civilization in the New World lingers on in the Canadian province of Quebec. Centuries have passed since the British won the great eighteenth-century duel for North America, but the French language still adorns the road signs of Quebec and rings out in its classrooms, courts, and markets, eloquently testifying to the continued vitality of French culture in North America.

The Reverend Andrew Burnaby, an observant Church of England clergyman who visited the colonies in the closing months of the French and Indian War, scoffed at any possibility of unification (1760):

". . . for fire and water are not more heterogeneous than the different colonies in North America. Nothing can exceed the jealousy and emulation which they possess in regard to each other. . . . in short . . . were they left to themselves there would soon be a civil war from one end of the continent to the other, while the Indians and Negros would . . . impatiently watch the opportunity of exterminating them all together."

and privileges of Englishmen, without the duties and responsibilities of Englishmen. Not until Pitt had offered to reimburse the colonies for a substantial part of their expenditures—some £900,000—did they move with some enthusiasm. If the Americans had to be bribed to defend themselves against a relentless and savage foe, would they ever unite to strike the mother country?

The curse of intercolonial disunity, present from early days, had continued throughout the recent hostilities. It had been caused mainly by enormous distances; by geographical barriers like rivers; by conflicting religions, from Catholic to Quaker; by varied nationalities, from German to Irish; by differing types of colonial governments; by many boundary disputes; and by the resentment of the crude backcountry settlers against the aristocratic bigwigs.

Yet unity received some encouragement during the French and Indian War. When soldiers and statesmen from widely separated colonies met around common campfires and council tables, they were often agreeably surprised by what they found. Despite deep-seated jealousy and suspicion, they discovered that they were all fellow Americans who generally spoke the same language and shared common ideals. Barriers of disunity began to melt, although a long and rugged road lay ahead before a nation could emerge.

Americans: A People of Destiny

The removal of the French menace in Canada profoundly affected American attitudes. While the French hawk had been hovering in the North and West, the colonial chicks had been forced to cling close to the wings of the mother hen. Now that the hawk was killed, they could range far afield with a new spirit of independence.

The French, humiliated by the British and saddened by the fate of Canada, consoled themselves with one wishful thought. Perhaps the loss of their American empire would one day result in Britain's loss of its American empire. In a sense the history of the United States began with the fall of Quebec and Montreal; the infant republic was cradled on the Plains of Abraham.

The Spanish and Indian menaces were also now substantially reduced. Spain was eliminated from Florida, although entrenched in Louisiana and New Orleans, and was still securely in possession of much of western North America, including the vast territory from present-day Texas to California. As for the Indians, the Treaty of Paris that ended the French and Indian War dealt a harsh blow to the Iroquois, Creeks, and other interior tribes. The Spanish removal from Florida and the French removal from Canada deprived the Indians of their most powerful diplomatic weapon—the ability to play off the rival European powers against one another. In the future, the Indians would have to negotiate exclusively with the British.

Sensing the newly precarious position of the Indian peoples, the Ottawa chief Pontiac in 1763 led several tribes that had been allied with the French in a brief but violent campaign to drive the British out of the Ohio Valley. Catching the British napping, the Indians wiped out all but three British posts west of the Appalachians, killing some two thousand colonists in the backcountry of Pennsylvania, Maryland, and Virginia. The whites swiftly and cruelly retaliated. One British commander ordered blankets infected with smallpox to be distributed among the Indians. Such tactics crushed the uprising and temporarily pacified the frontier. But the episode helped to convince the British of the need to stabilize Indian-white relations and, in the meantime, to keep troops stationed in the colonies.

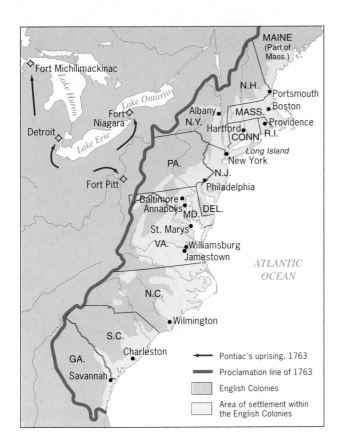

Settled Areas at End of French and Indian War, 1763
This map, showing the colonies thirteen years before the Declaration of Independence, helps to explain why the British would be unable to conquer their offspring. The colonials were spreading rapidly into the backcountry, where the powerful British navy could not flush them out. During the Revolutionary War, the British at one time or another captured the leading colonial cities—Boston, New York, Philadelphia, and Charleston; but the more remote interior remained a sanctuary for rebels.

Land-hungry American colonials were now free to burst over the dam of the Appalachian Mountains and flood out over the grassy western lands. A tiny rivulet of pioneers like Daniel Boone had already trickled into Tennessee and Kentucky; other courageous settlers made their preparations for the long, dangerous trek over the mountains.

Then, out of a clear sky, the London government issued its Proclamation of 1763. It flatly prohibited settlement in the area beyond the Appalachians, pending further adjustments. The truth is that this hastily drawn document was not designed to oppress the colonials at all, but to work out the Indian problem fairly and prevent another bloody eruption like Pontiac's uprising.

But countless Americans, especially land speculators, were dismayed and angered. Was not the land beyond the mountains their birthright? Had they not, in addition, purchased it with their blood in the recent war? In complete defiance of the proclamation, they clogged the westward trails. In 1765 an estimated one thousand wagons rolled through the town of Salisbury, North Carolina, on their way "up west." This wholesale flouting of royal authority boded ill for the longevity of British rule in America.

The French and Indian War also caused the colonials to develop a new vision of their destiny. With the path cleared for the conquest of a continent, with their birthrate high and their energy boundless, they sensed that they were a potent people on the march. And they were in no mood to be restrained.

Lordly Britons, whose suddenly swollen empire had tended to produce swollen heads, were in no mood for back talk. Puffed up over their recent victories, they were already annoyed with their unruly colonials. The stage was set for a violent family quarrel.

Chronology

1598	Edict of Nantes
1608	Champlain colonizes Quebec for France
1643	Louis XIV becomes king of France
1682	La Salle explores Mississippi River to the Gulf of Mexico
1689-1697	King William's War (War of the League of Augsburg)
1702-1713	Queen Anne's War (War of Spanish Succession)
1718	French found New Orleans
1739	War of Jenkin's Ear
1744-1748	King George's War (War of Austrian Succession)
1754	Washington battles French on frontier Albany Congress
1754-1763	French and Indian War (Seven Years' War)
1755	Braddock's defeat
1757	Pitt emerges as leader of British government
1759	Battle of Quebec
1763	Peace of Paris Pontiac's uprising Proclamation of 1763

SUGGESTED READINGS

PRIMARY SOURCE DOCUMENTS

"The Albany Plan of the Union" was the first great statement of colonial unity; "The Proclamation of 1763" forbade settlement west of the Appalachians. Both are collected in Henry Steele Commager, *Documents of American History.*

SECONDARY SOURCES

The workings of the British mercantile system are detailed in George L. Beer, *The Commercial Policy of England Toward the American Colonies* (1893); Charles M. Andrews's vast *Colonial Period of American History* (4 vols., 1935–1938); and in Lawrence H. Gipson's still more ambitious *British Empire before the American Revolution* (15 vols., 1936–1970). Further efforts to analyze the colonial empire are James Henretta, *"Salutary Neglect": Colonial Administration under the Duke of Newcastle* (1972), and Michael Kammen's especially interesting *Empire and Interest* (1970). More recent works on the British Empire include John Brewer, *The Sinews of Power: War, Money and the English State, 1688–1783* (1989); and Alison G. Olson, *Making the Empire Work: London and American Interest Groups, 1690–1790* (1992). The empire as seen through British eyes is captured in Paul David Nelson, *William Tryon and the Course of Empire: A Life in British Imperial Service* (1990). The French colonial effort is described in George M. Wrong, *The Rise and Fall of New France* (2 vols., 1928). Calvin Martin, *Keepers of the Game* (1978), offers a provocative interpretation of the fur trade and its impact on Indian societies. Other works on the role of Indians in larger imperial struggles include Richard Aquila, *The Iroquois Restoration: Iroquois Diplomacy on the Colonial Frontier, 1701–1754* (1983); Francis Jennings, *Empire of Fortune: Crowns, Colonies and Tribes in the Seven Years War in America* (1988); Gregory Evans Dowd, *A Spirited Resistance: The North American Indian Struggle for Unity, 1745–1815* (1992); and Richard White, *The Middle Ground: Indians, Empires, and Republics in the Great Lakes Region, 1650–1815* (1991). The Anglo-French struggle is recounted in Howard H. Peckham, *The Colonial Wars, 1689–1762* (1964). Alan Rogers, *Empire and Liberty: American Resistance to the British Authority, 1755–1763* (1974), investigates American participation in the Seven Years' War, as does Douglas E. Leach in *Roots of Conflict: British Armed Forces and Colonial Americans, 1677–1763* (1986). Fred Anderson focuses on colonial soldiers in *A People's Army: Massachusetts Soldiers and Society in the Seven Years' War* (1984). Classic accounts are Francis Parkman's several volumes, condensed, without serious loss of flavor, in *The Battle for North America*, edited by John Tebbel (1948), and *The Parkman Reader*, edited by Samuel E. Morison (1955). An impressive biography is Douglas S. Freeman, *Young Washington* (2 vols., 1948), a subject treated in less detail in James T. Flexner, *George Washington: The Forge of Experience* (1965).

7

The Road to Revolution

1763–1775

The Revolution was effected before the war commenced. The Revolution was in the minds and hearts of the people.

JOHN ADAMS, 1818

The Deep Roots of Revolution

In a broad sense, the American Revolution was not the same thing as the American War of Independence. The war itself lasted only eight years. But the Revolution lasted over a century and a half and began when the first permanent English settlers set foot on the new continent. Insurrection of thought usually precedes insurrection of deed. Over the years such a ferment had occurred in the thinking of the colonists that the Revolution was partially completed in their minds before the musketballs began to fly. America was a revolutionary force from the day of its discovery.

Pulling up stakes in the Old World was itself a revolutionary act of sorts; in a sense, to emigrate was to rebel. And the rebels who emigrated to America put a lot of distance between themselves and their former overlords. Boston was some 3,000 miles (4,800 kilometers) from London. Crossing those miles in a sailing ship took six to eight weeks, often much longer. Ships were frequently turned into virtual floating coffins by food shortages or disease; in one extreme case, 350 of 400 passengers and crew perished. Cannibalism was not unknown, and starving passengers fought over the bodies of vermin. As a sailors' song ran,

> *We ate the mice, we ate the rats,*
> *And through the hold we ran like cats.*

The perilous crossing left many emotional scars. Survivors who staggered ashore were, as a result, both physically and spiritually separated from the Old World. They knew that the long arm of the

121

London government could only weakly touch them across the broad ocean moat. Distance weakens authority; great distance weakens authority greatly.

The American environment itself further nurtured feelings of independence. Back in England some villagers lived in the shadow of graveyards that contained the bones of their ancestors for a thousand years past. Born into such changeless surroundings, many humble folk never questioned their lowly social status. But in the New World they were not subdued by the scowl of their superiors. In the dense American forests all was strange, fresh, different—here was a world that was theirs to make anew.

However different the migrants' reasons for leaving the Old World, in the New World they eventually came to share a common belief: that the authorities in Britain were fundamentally different from themselves and therefore fundamentally unfit to tell them what to do. Unintimidated by the "Mother of Parliaments" in London, they set up thirteen parliaments of their own, and came to regard them as every bit equal to the great assembly at Whitehall—possibly even superior to it. With the passage of time many of the colonists began to think of themselves not as transplanted Britons, but as "Americans." Over the century and half of the colonial era, a new people was born.

The Mercantile Theory

Britain's empire was acquired in a "fit of absent-mindedness," an old saying goes, and there is much truth in the jest. Not one of the original thirteen colonies, except Georgia, was formally planted by the British government. The actual founding was done haphazardly by trading companies, religious groups, land speculators, and others. Ignoring the high-minded and far-visioned aspirations of pioneering Puritans, Quakers, and other colonizers, authorities in London scarcely dreamed that a new nation was being born.

The British authorities nevertheless eventually embraced a theory that justified their control of the colonies. That theory was called mercantilism. Mercantilist ideas shaped the policies of all the major nations of Europe from the sixteenth to the eighteenth centuries. Mercantilists believed that wealth was power, and that a country's economic wealth (and hence its military and political power) could be measured by the amount of gold or silver in its trea-

> *Adam Smith (1723–1790), the Scottish "Father of Modern Economics," frontally attacked mercantilism in 1776:*
>
> "To prohibit a great people, however, from making all that they can of every part of their own produce, or from employing their stock and industry in the way that they judge most advantageous to themselves, is a manifest violation of the most sacred rights of mankind."

sury. In order to amass gold or silver, a country needed to export more than it imported. A nation that possessed colonies thus had a distinct advantage, since the colonies could both supply raw materials to the mother country (thereby reducing the need for foreign imports) and provide a guaranteed market for exports.

All the leading European nations relied on strong central governments to enforce these mercantilist doctrines. They all regarded their colonies as existing first and foremost to help the mother country achieve its mercantilist goals. Britain looked upon the American colonists more or less as tenants. They were expected to furnish products needed in England, buy British goods in return, and not to bother their heads with dangerous dreams of economic independence or, even worse, self-government.

Specifically, the Americans were expected to ensure Britain's naval supremacy by furnishing ships, ships' stores, sailors, and trade. In addition, they were to provide a profitable market for English manufactured goods, and were discouraged from buying the goods of other countries. Finally, they were to keep gold and silver money within the empire by growing products like tobacco and sugar that England would otherwise have to purchase from foreigners.

Mercantilist Trammels on Trade

Parliament passed numerous measures to enforce the mercantile system. Most famous were the Navigation Laws. The first of these, enacted in 1650, was aimed at rival Dutch shippers who were elbowing

The Female Combatants, 1776
Britain is symbolized as a lady of fashion, her rebellious daughter, America, as an Indian princess. Their shields of Obedience and Liberty seem mutually exclusive standards.

their way into the American carrying trade. The Navigation Laws restricted commerce to and from the colonies to English vessels. Such regulation not only kept money within the empire but bolstered the British—and colonial—merchant marine, which in turn was an indispensable auxiliary to the Royal Navy.

An alert Parliament from time to time enacted additional laws that were favorable to England. European goods consigned to America had to be landed first in England, where customs duties could be collected and where the British middleman would get his cut of the profit. Still other curbs required certain "enumerated" products, notably tobacco, to be shipped to England and not to a foreign market, even though prices in Europe might be higher.

In the interests of the empire, settlers were even restricted in what they might produce at home. They were forbidden to manufacture for export certain products, such as woolen cloth and beaver hats, because the colonies were supposed to complement and not compete with English industry.

Americans also felt the pinch in the area of currency. No banks existed in the colonies, and the money problem on the eve of the Revolution was acute. Industrious colonials were now busily buying more goods from England than they were selling there, so the difference had to be made up in hard cash. Every year gold and silver money, much of it in Spanish coins from the West Indies, was drained out of the colonies. The colonials simply did not have enough left for the convenience of everyday purchases. Barter became necessary, and even butter, nails, pitch, and feathers were used for purposes of exchange.

Currency problems came to a boil when dire need finally forced many of the colonies to issue paper money, which unfortunately depreciated. British merchants and creditors, understandably worried, squawked so loudly that Parliament was compelled to act. It restrained the colonial legislatures from printing paper currency and from passing lax bankruptcy laws—practices that might result in defrauding British merchants. The Americans, who felt that their welfare was again being sacrificed, reacted angrily. Another burning grievance was thus heaped upon the pile of combustibles already smoldering.

London officialdom naturally kept a watchful eye on the legislation passed by the colonial assemblies. If such laws conflicted with British regulations or policy, they might be summarily declared null and void by the Privy Council (the king's advisers).

This "royal veto" was in fact used rather sparingly—469 times in connection with 8,563 laws. But the colonists nevertheless fiercely resented it. They felt aggrieved when, in the interests of England, they were forbidden to make reforms that they deemed desirable, such as curbing the degrading trade in African slaves.

As the Boston Gazette *declared in 1765,*

"A colonist cannot make a button, a horseshoe, nor a hobnail, but some snooty ironmonger or respectable buttonmaker of Britain shall bawl and squall that his honor's worship is most egregiously maltreated, injured, cheated, and robbed by the rascally American republicans."

The Merits of Mercantilism

Americans have long assumed that the British mercantile system was thoroughly selfish and deliberately oppressive, if not downright malicious. The truth is that until 1763 the Navigation Laws imposed no intolerable burden, mainly because they were laxly enforced through a policy of "salutary neglect." Ingenious colonial merchants early learned to disregard or evade restrictions that they found vexatious. In fact, some of the early American fortunes were amassed by wholesale smuggling. Wealthy and vain John Hancock of Massachusetts came to be known as the "King of Smugglers," though his illicit activity was greatly exaggerated.

Americans also reaped direct benefits from the mercantile system. London paid liberal bounties or price supports to those colonials who produced

Paul Revere, by John Singleton Copley, c. 1768
This painting of the famed silversmith-horseman challenged convention—but reflected the new democratic spirit of the age—by portraying an artisan in working clothes. Note how Copley has depicted the serene confidence of the master craftsman and Revere's quiet pride in his work.

ships' parts and ships' stores, even though English competitors complained heatedly. When independence came the bounties dried up, and many American producers were forced to the wall.

Virginia tobacco planters, in particular, enjoyed valuable privileges. Although forbidden to ship their pungent yellow leaf to any place other than England, the planters were guaranteed a monopoly of the British market. Tobacco growing was also outlawed in England and Ireland, even though the plant had already been raised in England with some success.

American colonials additionally fared well in other fields. They enjoyed the undiluted rights of Englishmen, as well as unusual opportunities for self-government. They were not compelled to tax themselves to support a professional army and navy for protection against the French, Dutch, Spaniards, Indians, and pirates. Although the colonists went to some expense in "training" militias, they enjoyed the shield of a strong army of British redcoats and the mightiest navy in the world—without a penny of cost. After independence the American people would themselves be required to pay the costs of maintaining a tiny army and navy, both of which afforded paltry protection.

In manufacturing and trade, the New World settlers had little cause to complain. They were denied the privilege of fabricating specified articles for export, notably fur hats, but this regulation caused no serious hardships, because it was loosely enforced and because other pursuits were usually more profitable. Americans were forced to deal with British middlemen, but they would have done so anyhow, owing to a common language, standard pounds and shillings, liberal credit arrangements, and familiar business methods.

"Prosperity trickles down" is a common saying; and it is true that the Americans enjoyed a generous share of Britain's profits under the time-honored mercantile system. The average American was probably better off economically than the average English person at home. If the colonies existed for the benefit of England, it was hardly less true that England existed for the benefit of the colonies. The well-meaning officials in London were working for the welfare of the empire as a whole, and they gave overall unity to its policies. A wise owner does not disembowel or starve the goose that lays the golden eggs. Mistakes were made by the British authorities, but they were not, until revolt had erupted, mistakes of malice.

Mercantilism had sufficient merit to be widely adopted and long perpetuated. All other colonial nations of that age, including Spain and France, embraced mercantilistic principles completely and enforced them ironhandedly. Elements of mercantilism have endured to the present day, even in the United States. Manufacturers, workers, and farmers seek to ensure their prosperity through protective tariffs, and the government tries to enhance national security by prohibiting the export of high-technology products with possible military applications.

The Menace of Mercantilism

But even when painted in its rosiest colors, the mercantile system burdened the colonials with annoying liabilities. And when Britain began to enforce its mercantilist policies more vigorously after 1763, the fuse that eventually ignited the American Revolution was lit.

Mercantilism stifled economic initiative because Americans were not at liberty to buy, sell, ship, or manufacture under conditions that they found most profitable. The southern colonies, as "pets," were generally favored over the northern ones, chiefly because they grew non-English products like tobacco, sugar, and rice. Revolution was one seed that sprouted vigorously from the stony soil of New England, for the proud descendants of the Puritans greatly resented being treated like unwanted relatives.

One-crop Virginians, despite London's preference for the southern colonies, also nursed rankling grievances. Forced to sell their tobacco in England, they were at the mercy of British merchants, who often gouged them. Many of the fashionable Virginia planters were plunged into debt by the falling price of tobacco and were forced to buy their necessities in England by mortgaging future crops. Some debts, becoming hereditary, were bequeathed from one generation to the next.

Impoverished Virginia thus joined restless Massachusetts in agitating for revolt against England. Unfriendly critics sneered that the Virginians' cry, "Liberty or Death," might better have been "Liberty or Debt." Although this charge was unfair in many cases, countless Virginians welcomed the opportunity to end their economic bondage to the mother country.

English statesman Edmund Burke (1729–1797) warned in 1775,

"Young man, there is America—which at this day serves for little more than to amuse you with stories of savage men and uncouth manners; yet shall, before you taste of death, show itself equal to the whole of that commerce which now attracts the envy of the world."

Finally—and of supreme importance—mercantilism was debasing to the Americans. Many felt that the colonies were being used, or milked, as cows are milked. The colonies were to be kept in a state of perpetual economic adolescence and never allowed to come of age. As Benjamin Franklin wrote in 1775,

We have an old mother that peevish is
*   grown;*
She snubs us like children that scarce walk
*   alone;*
She forgets we're grown up and have sense
*   of our own.*

Revolution broke out, as Theodore Roosevelt later remarked, because England failed to recognize an emerging nation when it saw one.

The Stamp Tax Uproar

The costly Seven Years' War, which ended in 1763, forced Britain to redefine its relationship with its North American colonies. The ensuing revolution in British colonial policy precipitated the American Revolution.

Victory-flushed Britain emerged from the conflict possessing one of the biggest empires in the world—and also, less happily, the biggest debt. It amounted to £140 million, about half of which had been incurred in defending the American colonies. British officials wisely had no intention of asking the colonials to help pay off this crushing burden. But London did feel that the Americans should be asked to defray one-third the cost of maintaining a garrison of some ten thousand redcoats in America, ostensibly for the colonies' own protection.

A Royal Stamp   The motto in French is translated "Shame to him who evil thinks." Under the Stamp Act, a stamp like this one, certifying payment of tax, was required on all legal and commercial documents.

Prime Minister George Grenville, an honest and able financier not noted for tact, moved vigorously. Dedicated to efficiency, he aroused the resentment of the colonials in 1763 by ordering the British navy to begin strictly enforcing the Navigation Laws. He also secured from Parliament the so-called Sugar Act of 1764, the first law ever passed by that body for raising tax revenue in the colonies for the crown. Among various provisions, it increased the duty on foreign sugar imported from the West Indies. After bitter protests from the colonials, the duties were lowered substantially, and the agitation died down. But resentment was kept burning by the Quartering Act of 1765. This measure required certain colonies to provide food and quarters for British troops.

Then in the same year, 1765, Grenville imposed the most odious measure of all: a stamp tax, to raise revenues to support the new military force. The Stamp Act mandated the use of stamped paper or the affixing of stamps, certifying payment of tax. Stamps were required on bills of sale for about fifty trade items as well as on certain types of commercial and legal documents, including playing cards, pamphlets, newspapers, diplomas, bills of lading, and marriage licenses.

Grenville regarded all these measures as reasonable and just. He was simply asking the Americans to pay a fair share of the costs for their own defense, through taxes that were already familiar in England.

In fact, Englishmen for two generations had endured a stamp tax far heavier than that passed for the colonies.

Yet the Americans were angrily aroused at what they regarded as Grenville's fiscal aggression. The new laws pinched their pocketbooks, and, even more ominously, menaced the local liberties they had come to assume as a matter of right. Thus some colonial assemblies defiantly refused to comply with the Quartering Act or voted only a fraction of the supplies that it called for.

Worse still, Grenville's noxious legislation seemed to jeopardize the basic rights of the colonists as Englishmen. Both the Sugar Act and the Stamp Act provided for trying offenders in the hated admiralty courts, where juries were not allowed. The burden of proof was on the defendants, who were assumed to be guilty unless they could prove themselves innocent. Trial by jury and the precept of "innocent until proved guilty" were ancient privileges that the English people everywhere, including the American colonials, held most dear.

And why was a British army needed at all in the colonies, now that the French were expelled from the continent and Pontiac's warriors crushed? Could its real purpose be to whip rebellious colonials into line? Many Americans began to sniff the strong scent of a conspiracy to strip them of their historic liberties. They lashed back violently, and the Stamp Act became the target that drew their most ferocious fire.

Angry throats raised the cry, "No taxation without representation." There was some irony in the

The famous circular letter from the Massachusetts House of Representatives (1768) stated,

". . . considering the utter impracticability of their ever being fully and equally represented in Parliament, and the great expense that must unavoidably attend even a partial representation there, this House think that a taxation of their constituents, even without their consent, grievous as it is, would be preferable to any representation that could be admitted for them there."

slogan, because the seaports and tidewater towns that were most wrathful against the Stamp Act had long denied full representation to their own back-country pioneers. But now the aggravated colonials took the high ground of principle. They vividly recollected the theories of popular government developed during England's own Puritan revolution a century earlier. American firebrands hurled these doctrines back at their English masters, who were stunned at the keenness of the colonials' historical memory.

The Americans made a distinction between "legislation" and "taxation." They conceded the right of Parliament to legislate about matters that affected the entire empire, including the regulation of trade. But they steadfastly denied the right of Parliament, in which no Americans were seated, to impose taxes on Americans. Only their own elected colonial legislatures, the Americans insisted, could legally tax them. Taxes levied by the distant English Parliament amounted to robbery, a piratical assault on the sacred rights of property.

Grenville dismissed these American protests as hairsplitting absurdities. The power of Parliament was supreme and undivided, he asserted, and in any case the Americans *were* represented in Parliament. Elaborating the theory of "virtual representation," Grenville claimed that every member of Parliament represented all British subjects, even those Americans in Boston or Charleston who had never voted for a member of the London Parliament.

The Americans scoffed at the notion of virtual representation. And truthfully, they did not really want direct representation in Parliament, which might have seemed like a sensible compromise. If they had obtained it, any gouty member of the House of Commons could have proposed an oppressive tax bill for the colonies, and the American representatives, few in numbers, would have stood bereft of a principle with which to resist.

Thus the principle of no taxation without representation was supremely important, and the colonials clung to it with tenacious consistency. When the English replied that the sovereign power of government could not be divided between "legislative" authority in London and "taxing" authority in the colonies, they forced the Americans to deny the authority of Parliament altogether and to begin to consider their own political independence. This chain of logic eventually led, link by link, to revolutionary consequences.

Protesting the Stamp Act, 1765
Angry colonists burn the hated tax stamps in a bonfire.

Parliament Forced to Repeal the Stamp Act

Colonial outcries against the hated stamp tax took various forms. The most conspicuous assemblage was the Stamp Act Congress of 1765, which brought together in New York City twenty-seven distinguished delegates from nine colonies. After dignified debate the members drew up a statement of their rights and grievances and beseeched the king and Parliament to repeal the repugnant legislation.

The Stamp Act Congress, which was largely ignored in England, made little splash at the time in America. Its ripples, however, began to erode sectional suspicions, for it brought together around the same table leaders from the different and rival colonies. It was one more halting but significant step toward intercolonial unity.

More effective than the congress was the widespread adoption of nonimportation agreements against British goods. Woolen garments of homespun became fashionable, and the eating of lamb chops was discouraged so that the wool-bearing sheep would be allowed to mature. Nonimportation agreements were in fact a promising stride toward union; they spontaneously united the American people for the first time in common action.

Mobilizing in support of nonimportation gave ordinary American men and women new opportunities to participate in colonial protests. Many people who had previously stood on the sidelines now signed petitions swearing to uphold the terms of the consumer boycotts. Groups of women assembled in public to hold spinning bees and make homespun cloth as a replacement for shunned British textiles. Such public defiance helped spread revolutionary fervor throughout American colonial society.

Sometimes violence accompanied colonial protests. Groups of ardent spirits, known as Sons of Liberty and Daughters of Liberty, took the law into their own hands. Crying "Liberty, Property, and No Stamps," they enforced the nonimportation agreements against violators, often with a generous coat of tar and feathers. Patriotic mobs ransacked the houses of unpopular officials, confiscated their money, and hanged effigies of stamp agents on liberty poles.

Shaken by colonial commotion, the machinery for collecting the tax broke down. On that dismal day in 1765 when the new act was to go into effect, the stamp agents had all been forced to resign, and there was no one to sell the stamps. While flags flapped at half-mast, the law was openly and flagrantly defied—or rather, nullified.

England was hard hit. America then bought about one-quarter of all British exports, and about one-half of British shipping was devoted to the American trade. Merchants, manufacturers, and shippers suffered from the colonial nonimportation agreements, and hundreds of laborers were thrown out of work. Loud demands converged on Parliament for repeal of the Stamp Act. But many of the members could not understand why 7.5 million Britons had to pay heavy taxes to protect the colonies, whereas some 2 million colonials refused to pay for only one-third of the cost of their own defense.

After a stormy debate, and as a matter of expediency and not of right, Parliament in 1766 reluctantly repealed the Stamp Act. At the same time, and by an overwhelming vote, it saved face by passing the Declaratory Act. This futile measure proclaimed that Parliament had the right "to bind" the colonies "in all cases whatsoever." An abstract assertion of

Public Punishment (detail)
Boston customs official, John Malcolm, paraded after being tarred and feathered, January 25, 1774.

this right was but a feeble victory for England's authority, for the unruly colonials had proved that the London government could be forced to yield to boycotts and mob action.

America forthwith burst into an uproar of rejoicing. Grateful residents of New York erected a leaden statue to King George III—a tribute that was later melted into thousands of bullets to be fired at his own troops.

The Townshend Tea Tax and the Boston "Massacre"

Control of the British ministry was now seized by the gifted but erratic "Champagne Charley" Townshend, a man who could deliver brilliant speeches in Parliament even while drunk. Rashly promising to pluck feathers from the colonial goose with a minimum of squawking, he persuaded Parliament in 1767 to pass the Townshend Acts. The most important of these new regulations was a light import duty on glass, white lead, paper, paint, and tea. Townshend, seizing on a dubious distinction between internal and external taxes, made this tax, unlike the Stamp Act, an indirect customs duty payable at American ports. But to the increasingly restless colonials, this was a phantom distinction. For them the real difficulty remained taxes—in any form—without representation.

Flushed with their recent victory over the stamp tax, the colonists were in a rebellious mood. The impost on tea was especially irksome, for an estimated

Redcoats Landing in Boston

1 million people drank the refreshing brew twice a day, and even tipplers used it when alcohol was not available.

The new Townshend revenues, worse yet, would be used to pay the salaries of the royal governors and judges in America. From the standpoint of efficient administration by London, this was a reform long overdue. But the ultrasuspicious Americans, who had beaten the royal governors into line by controlling the purse, regarded Townshend's tax as another attempt to enchain them. Their worst fears took on greater reality when the London government, after passing the Townshend taxes, suspended the legislature of New York in 1767 for failure to comply with the Quartering Act.

Nonimportation agreements, previously potent, were quickly revived against the Townshend Acts. But they proved less effective than those devised against the Stamp Act. The colonials, again enjoying prosperity, took the new tax less seriously than might have been expected, largely because it was light and indirect. They found, moreover, that they could secure smuggled tea at a cheap price, and

---

Giving new meaning to the proverbial tempest in a teapot, a group of 126 Boston women signed an agreement, or "subscription list," which announced,

"We the Daughters of those Patriots who have and now do appear for the public interest . . . do with Pleasure engage with them in denying ourselves the drinking of Foreign Tea, in hopes to frustrate a Plan that tends to deprive the whole Community of . . . all that is valuable in Life."

The BLOODY MASSACRE perpetrated in King—Street ...on March 5th...by a party of the 29th Regt

The Boston Massacre, by Paul Revere, 1770   This widely reprinted engraving was both art and propaganda. The so-called Boston Massacre further inflamed the colonials against the British, especially after the conviction spread that the Americans had been wholly unoffending. Paul Revere, the artist, wrote, "Unhappy Boston! see thy sons deplore/Thy hallowed walks besmear'd with guiltless gore." Massacre Day was observed in Boston as a patriotic holiday until 1776, when the more glorious Fourth of July eclipsed it.

consequently smugglers increased their activities, especially in Massachusetts.

British officials, faced with a breakdown of law and order, landed two regiments of troops in Boston in 1768. Many of the soldiers were drunken and profane characters. Liberty-loving colonials, resenting the presence of the red-coated "ruffians," taunted the "bloody backs" unmercifully.

A clash was inevitable. On the evening of March 5, 1770, a crowd of some sixty townspeople set upon a squad of about ten Redcoats one of whom was hit by a club and another of whom was knocked down. Acting apparently without orders but under extreme provocation, the troops opened fire and killed or wounded eleven "innocent" citizens. One of the first to die was Crispus Attucks, described by contemporaries as a powerfully built runaway "mulatto" and as a leader of the mob. Both sides were in some degree to blame, and in the subsequent trial (in which future president John Adams served as defense attorney for the soldiers) only two of the redcoats were found guilty of manslaughter. The soldiers were released after being branded on the hand.

The Seditious Committees of Correspondence

By 1770 King George III, then only thirty-two years old, was strenuously attempting to restore the declining power of the British monarchy. He was a good man in his private morals, but he proved to be a bad ruler. Earnest, industrious, stubborn, and lustful for power, he surrounded himself with cooperative "yes men," notably his corpulent prime minister, Lord North.

The ill-timed Townshend Acts had failed to produce revenue, though they did produce near-rebellion. Net proceeds from the tax in one year were £295, and during that time the annual military costs to Britain in the colonies had mounted to £170,000. Nonimportation agreements, though feebly enforced, were pinching British manufacturers. The government of Lord North, bowing to various pressures, finally persuaded Parliament to repeal the Townshend revenue duties. But the three-pence toll on tea, the tax the colonists found most offen-

Samuel Adams (1722–1803)
A second cousin of John Adams, he contributed a potent pen and tongue to the American Revolution as a political agitator and organizer of rebellion. He was the leading spirit in hosting the Boston Tea Party. A failure in the brewing business, he was sent by Massachusetts to the First Continental Congress of 1774. He signed the Declaration of Independence and served in Congress until 1781.

Portrait Traditionally Said That of Abigail Adams, artist unknown
The wife of Revolutionary leader and future president John Adams, she was a prominent Patriot in her own right. She was also among the first Americans to see, however faintly, the implications of Revolutionary ideas for changing the status of women.

sive, was retained to keep alive the principle of parliamentary taxation.

Flames of discontent in America continued to be fanned by numerous incidents, including the redoubled efforts of the British officials to enforce the Navigation Laws. Resistance was further kindled by a master propagandist and engineer of rebellion, Samuel Adams of Boston, a cousin of John Adams. Unimpressive in appearance (his hands trembled), he lived and breathed only for politics. His friends had to buy him a presentable suit of clothes when he left Massachusetts on intercolonial business. Zealous, tenacious, and courageous, he was ultrasensitive to infractions of colonial rights. Cherishing a deep faith in the common people, he appealed effectively to what was called his "trained mob."

Skillful also as a pamphleteer, he soon became known as the "Penman of the Revolution."

Samuel Adams's signal contribution was to organize in Massachusetts the local committees of correspondence. After he had formed the first one in Boston during 1772, some eighty towns in the colony speedily set up similar organizations. Their chief function was to spread propaganda and information by interchanging letters and thus keep alive opposition to British policy. One critic referred to the committees as "the foulest, subtlest, and most venomous serpent ever issued from the egg of sedition." No more effective device for stimulating resistance could have been contrived.

Intercolonial committees of correspondence were the next logical step. Virginia led the way in

Peter Oliver (1713–1791), the chief justice of Massachusetts, penned a Loyalist account of the Revolution after the outbreak of hostilities. Recalling the popular protests of the early 1770s, he wrote that

"[The colonial] upper & lower House consisted of Men generally devoted to the Interest of the Faction. The Foundations of Government were subverted; & every Loyalist was obliged to submit to be swept away by the Torrent . . . . Some indeed dared to say that their Souls were their own; but no one could call his Body his own; for that was at the Mercy of the Mob, who like the Inquisition Coach, would call a Man out of his Bed, & he must step in whether he liked the Conveyance or not."

1773 by creating such a body as a standing committee of the House of Burgesses. Within a short time, every colony had established a central committee through which it could exchange ideas and information with other colonies. These intercolonial groups, which were supremely significant in stimulating and disseminating sentiment in favor of united action, evolved directly into the first American congresses.

Tea Parties at Boston and Elsewhere

Thus far—that is, by 1773—nothing had happened to make rebellion inevitable. Nonimportation was weakening. Increasing numbers of colonials were reluctantly paying the tea tax, because the legal tea was now cheaper than the smuggled tea, even cheaper than tea in England.

A new ogre entered the picture in 1773. The powerful British East India Company, overburdened with 17 million pounds of unsold tea, was facing bankruptcy. If it collapsed, the London government would lose heavily in tax revenue. The ministry therefore decided to assist the company by awarding it a complete monopoly of the American tea business. The giant corporation would now be able to sell the coveted leaves more cheaply than ever before, even with the three-pence tax tacked on. But many American tea drinkers, rather than rejoicing at the lower prices, cried foul. They saw this British move as a shabby attempt to trick the Americans, with the bait of cheaper tea, into swallowing the principle of the detested tax. For the determined Americans, principle was far more important than price.

If the British officials insisted on the letter of the law, violence would be inevitable. Fatefully, the British colonial authorities decided to enforce the

The Boston Tea Party, December 16, 1773 Crying "Boston harbor a tea-pot this night," Sons of Liberty disguised as Indians hurled chests of tea into the sea to protest the tax on tea, and to make sure that its cheap price did not prove an "invincible temptation" to the people.

law literally, and once more the colonials rose in their wrath. Not a single one of the several thousand chests of tea shipped by the East India Company reached the hands of the consignees. At Annapolis, the Marylanders burned both the cargo and the vessel, while proclaiming "Liberty and Independence or death in pursuit of it." At Boston, which was host to the most famous tea party of all, a band of white townsfolk, disguised as Indians, boarded the three tea ships on December 16, 1773. They smashed open 342 chests and dumped the "cursed weed" into Boston harbor, while a silent crowd watched approvingly from the wharves as salty tea was brewed for the fish.

Reactions varied. Extremists in America were elated. Conservatives complained that the destruction of private property was going too far. The British at home were outraged; even friends of America hung their heads. Punishment and coercion were the only possible responses of the London authorities, as long as the mercantilist philosophy prevailed and the colonials refused to accept responsibility. The granting of some kind of home rule to the Americans might have prevented rebellion, but not many Britons of that age were blessed with such magnanimous vision. Edmund Burke, the great conservative political theorist and a friend of America in Parliament, stoically declared, "To tax and to please, no more than to love and be wise, is not given to men."

Parliament Passes the "Intolerable Acts"

An irate Parliament responded speedily to the Boston Tea Party with measures that brewed a revolution. By huge majorities in 1774 it passed a series of "Repressive Acts," which were designed to chastise Boston in particular, Massachusetts in general. They were branded in America as "the massacre of American Liberty."

Most drastic of all was the Boston Port Act. It closed the tea-stained harbor until damages were paid and order could be assured. By other "Intolerable Acts"—as they were called in America—many of the chartered rights of colonial Massachusetts were swept away. Restrictions were likewise placed on the precious town meetings. Contrary to previous practice, enforcing officials who killed colonials in the line of duty could now be sent to England for trial. There, suspicious Americans assumed, they would be likely to get off scot-free.

By a fateful coincidence, the "Intolerable Acts" were accompanied in 1774 by the Quebec Act. Passed at the same time, it was erroneously regarded in English-speaking America as one of the "repressive" measures. Actually, the Quebec Act was a good law in bad company. For many years the British government had debated how it should administer the sixty thousand or so conquered

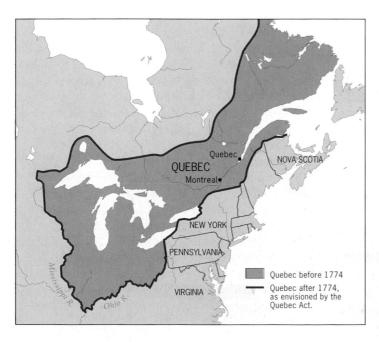

Quebec Before and After 1774
Young Alexander Hamilton voiced the fears of many colonists when he warned that the Quebec Act of 1774 would introduce "priestly tyranny" into Canada, making that country another Spain or Portugal. "Does not your blood run cold," he asked, "to think that an English Parliament should pass an act for the establishment of arbitrary power and Popery in such a country?"

French subjects in Canada, and it had finally framed this farsighted and statesmanlike measure. The French were guaranteed their Catholic religion. They were also permitted to retain many of their old customs and institutions, which did not include a representative assembly or trial by jury in civil cases. In addition, the old boundaries of the Province of Quebec were now extended southward all the way to the Ohio River.

The Quebec Act, from the viewpoint of the French Canadians, was a shrewd and conciliatory measure. If England had only shown as much foresight in dealing with its English-speaking colonies, it might not have lost them.

But from the viewpoint of the American colonials as a whole, the Quebec Act was especially noxious. All the other "repressive" laws slapped directly at Massachusetts, but this one had a much wider range. It seemed to set a dangerous precedent in America against jury trials and popular assemblies. It alarmed land speculators, who were distressed to see the huge trans-Allegheny area snatched from their grasp. It aroused anti-Catholics, who were shocked by the extension of Roman Catholic jurisdiction southward into a huge region that had once been earmarked for Protestantism—a region about as large as the thirteen original colonies. One angry Protestant cried that there ought to be a "jubilee in hell" over this enormous gain for "popery."

The Continental Congress and Bloodshed

American dissenters, chafing over the Quebec Act, responded sympathetically to the plight of Massachusetts. It had put itself in the wrong by the violent destruction of the tea cargoes; now England had put itself in the wrong by brutal punishment that seemed far too cruel for the crime. Flags were flown at half-mast throughout the colonies on the day that the Boston Port Act went into effect, and sister colonies rallied to send food to the stricken city. Rice was shipped even from faraway South Carolina.

Most memorable of the responses to the "Intolerable Acts" was the summoning of a Continental Congress in 1774. It was to meet in Philadelphia to consider ways of redressing colonial grievances. Twelve of the thirteen colonies, with Georgia alone

missing, sent fifty-five distinguished men, among them Samuel Adams, John Adams, George Washington, and Patrick Henry. Intercolonial frictions were partially melted away by social activity after working hours; in fifty-four days George Washington dined at his own lodgings only nine times.

The First Continental Congress deliberated for seven weeks, from September 5 to October 26, 1774. It was not a legislative but a consultative body—a convention rather than a congress. John Adams played a stellar role. Eloquently swaying his colleagues to a revolutionary course, he helped defeat by the narrowest of margins a proposal by the moderates for a species of American home rule under British direction. After prolonged argument the Congress drew up several dignified papers. These included a ringing Declaration of Rights, as well as solemn appeals to other British American colonies, to the king, and to the British people.

The most significant action of the Congress was the creation of The Association. Unlike previous nonimportation agreements, this one called for a *complete* boycott of British goods: nonimportation, nonexportation, and nonconsumption. A document known as The Association, by providing for concerted action, was the closest approach to a written constitution that the colonies as a unit had yet devised. But still there was no genuine drive toward independence—merely an effort to bring about a repeal of the offensive legislation and a return to the happy days before parliamentary taxation. If colonial grievances were redressed, well and good; if not, the Congress was to meet again in May 1775.

But the deadly drift toward war continued. The petitions of the Continental Congress were rejected, after considerable debate, by strong majorities in Parliament. In America chickens squawked and tar kettles bubbled as violators of The Association were tarred and feathered. Muskets were being collected, men were openly drilling, and a clash seemed imminent.

In April 1775 the British commander in Boston sent a detachment of troops to nearby Lexington and Concord. They were to seize stores of colonial gunpowder and also to bag the "rebel" ringleaders, Samuel Adams and John Hancock. At Lexington the colonial "Minute Men" refused to disperse rapidly enough, and shots were fired that killed eight Americans and wounded several more. The affair was more the "Lexington Massacre" than a battle. The redcoats pushed on to Concord, whence they were

A View of the Town of Concord, artist unknown, c. 1775   Redcoats here drill on the Concord Green, near where colonial militiamen soon would repel their advance on stores of rebel gunpower.

forced to retreat by the rough and ready Americans, whom Emerson immortalized:

> *By the rude bridge that arched the flood,*
> *Their flag to April's breeze unfurled,*
> *Here once the embattled farmers stood,*
> *And fired the shot heard round the world.**

The bewildered British, fighting off murderous fire from militiamen crouched behind thick stone walls, finally regained the sanctuary of Boston. Licking their wounds, they could count about three hundred casualties, including some seventy killed. England now had a war on its hands.

Imperial Strength and Weakness

Aroused Americans had brashly rebelled against a mighty empire. The population odds were about three to one against the rebels—some 7.5 million Britons to 2.5 million colonials. The odds in monetary wealth and naval power were overwhelmingly in favor of England.

Britain then boasted a professional army of some fifty thousand men, as compared with the numerous but wretchedly trained American militia. George III, in addition, had the treasury to hire foreign soldiers, and some thirty thousand Germans— so-called Hessians—were ultimately employed. The British enrolled about fifty thousand American Loyalists and enlisted the services of many Indians, who though unreliable fair-weather fighters, inflamed long stretches of the frontier. One British officer boasted that the war would offer no problems that could not be solved by an "experienced sheep herder."

Yet England was weaker than it seemed at first glance. Oppressed Ireland was a smoking volcano, and British troops had to be detached to watch it. France, bitter from its recent defeat, was awaiting an opportunity to stab Britain in the back. The London government was confused and inept. There was no William Pitt, "Organizer of Victory," only the stubborn George III and his pliant Lord North.

Many earnest and God-fearing Britons had no desire whatever to kill their American cousins. William Pitt withdrew a son from the army rather than see him thrust his sword into fellow Anglo-Saxons struggling for liberty. The English Whig factions, opposed to Lord North's Tory wing, openly

---

*Ralph Waldo Emerson, "Concord Hymn."

> *Privately (1776) General George Washington (1732–1799) expressed his distrust of militia:*
>
> "To place any dependence upon militia is assuredly resting on a broken staff. . . . The sudden change in their manner of living . . . brings on sickness in many, impatience in all, and such an unconquerable desire of returning to their respective homes that it not only produces shameful and scandalous desertions among themselves, but infuses the like spirit in others. . . . If I was called upon to declare upon oath whether the militia have been most serviceable or hurtful upon the whole, I should subscribe to the latter."

cheered American victories—at least at the outset. Aside from trying to embarrass the Tories politically, many Whigs believed that the battle for English freedom was being fought in America. If George III triumphed, his rule at home might become tyrannical. This outspoken sympathy in England, though plainly a minority voice, greatly encouraged the Americans. If they continued their resistance long enough, the Whigs might come into power and deal generously with them.

Britain's army in America had to operate under endless difficulties. The generals were second-rate; the soldiers, though on the whole capable, were brutally treated. There was one extreme case of eight hundred lashes on the bare back for striking an officer. Provisions were often scarce, rancid, and wormy. On one occasion a supply of biscuits, captured some fifteen years earlier from the French, was softened by dropping cannonballs on them.

Other handicaps loomed. The redcoats had to conquer the Americans; a draw would be a victory for the colonials. Britain was operating some 3,000 miles (4,800 kilometers) from its home base, and distance added greatly to the delays and uncertainties arising from storms and other mishaps. Military orders were issued in London that, when received months later, would not fit the changing situation.

America's geographical expanse was enormous: roughly 1,000 by 600 miles (1,600 by 970 kilometers). The united colonies had no urban nerve center, like France's Paris, whose capture would cripple the country as a whole. British armies took every city of any size, yet like a boxer punching a feather pillow, they made little more than a dent in the entire country. The Americans wisely traded space for time. Benjamin Franklin calculated that during the prolonged campaign in which the redcoats captured Bunker Hill and killed some 150 Patriots, about 60,000 American babies were born.

American Pluses and Minuses

The revolutionists were blessed with outstanding leadership. George Washington was a giant among men; Benjamin Franklin was a master among diplomats. Open foreign aid, theoretically possible from the start, eventually came from France. Numerous European officers, many of them unemployed and impoverished, volunteered their swords for pay. In a class by himself was a wealthy young French nobleman, the Marquis de Lafayette. Fleeing from boredom, loving glory and ultimately liberty, at age nineteen the "French gamecock" was made a major general in the colonial army. His commission was largely a recognition of his family influence and political connections, but the services of this teenage general in securing further aid from France were invaluable.

Other conditions aided the Americans. They were fighting defensively, with the odds, all things considered, favoring the defender. In agriculture, the colonies were mainly self-sustaining, like a kind of Robinson Crusoe's island. Colonial "buckskins," moreover, were a tough, self-reliant people. As marksmen, they far outshone the British, who often pointed rather than aimed their muskets. A competent American rifleman could hit a man's head at 200 yards (183 meters).

In addition, the Americans enjoyed the moral advantage that came from belief in a just cause. The historical odds were not impossible. Other peoples had triumphed in the face of greater obstacles: the Greeks against Persians, the Swiss against Austrians, the Dutch against Spaniards.

Yet the American rebels were badly organized for war. From the earliest days they had been almost fatally lacking in unity, and the new nation lurched forward uncertainly like an uncoordinated centipede. Even the Continental Congress, which directed the conflict, was hardly more than a debat-

Gilbert du Motier, Marquis de Lafayette (1757–1834), by Joseph Boze, 1790   This youthful French officer gave to America not only military services but some $200,000 of his private funds. He returned to France after the American Revolution to play a conspicuous role in the French Revolution.

> *General Washington's disgust with his countrymen is reflected in a diary entry for 1776:*
>
> "Chimney corner patriots abound; venality, corruption, prostitution of office for selfish ends, abuse of trust, perversion of funds from a national to a private use, and speculations upon the necessities of the times pervade all interests."

ing society, and it grew feebler as the struggle dragged on. "Their Congress now is quite disjoint'd," gibed an English satirist, "Since Gibbits (gallows) [are] for them appointed." Disorganized colonials fought almost the entire war before adopting a written constitution—the Articles of Confederation—in 1781.

Jealousy everywhere raised its hideous head. Individual states, proudly regarding themselves as sovereign, resented the attempts of Congress to exercise its flimsy powers. Sectional jealousy boiled up over the appointment of military leaders; some distrustful New Englanders almost preferred British officers to Americans from other sections.

Economic difficulties were nearly insuperable. Metallic money had already been heavily drained away. A cautious Continental Congress, unwilling to raise anew the explosive issue of taxation, was forced to print "Continental" paper money in great amounts. As this currency poured from the presses, it depreciated until the expression "not worth a Continental" became current. One barber contemptuously papered his shop with the near-worthless dollars. The confusion proliferated when the individual states were compelled to issue depreciated paper money of their own.

Inflation of the currency inevitably skyrocketed prices. Families of the soldiers at the fighting front were hard hit, and hundreds of anxious husbands and fathers deserted. Debtors easily acquired handfuls of the quasi-worthless money and gleefully paid their debts "without mercy"—sometimes with the bayonets of the authorities to back them up.

A Thin Line of Heroes

Basic military supplies in the colonies were dangerously scanty, especially firearms and gunpowder. Benjamin Franklin seriously proposed going back to the bow and arrow. Even where food was accumulated, wagons to haul it were sparse. At Valley Forge, in the winter of 1777–1778, the shivering American soldiers were without bread for three successive days. In one southern campaign, some men fainted for lack of food.

Manufactured goods were generally in short supply in agricultural America, and clothing and shoes were appallingly scarce. The path of the patriot fighting men was often marked by bloody snow. At frigid Valley Forge, during one anxious period, twenty-eight hundred men were barefooted or nearly naked. Woolens were desperately needed against the wintry blasts; and in general the only real uniform of the colonial army was uniform raggedness. During a grand parade at Valley Forge, some of the officers appeared wrapped in woolen bed covers. One Rhode Island unit was known as the "Ragged, Lousy, Naked Regiment."

American militiamen were numerous but also highly unreliable. Able-bodied American males—perhaps several hundred thousand of them—had received rudimentary training, and many of these recruits served for short terms in the rebel armies. But poorly trained plowboys, though better shots, could not stand up in the open field against professional British troops advancing with bare bayonets. Many of these undisciplined warriors would, in the words of Washington, "fly from their own shadows."

A few thousand regulars—perhaps seven or eight thousand at the war's end—were finally whipped into shape by stern drillmasters. Notable among them was an organizational genius, the salty German Baron von Steuben. He spoke no English when he reached America, but he soon taught his men that bayonets were not for broiling beefsteaks over open fires. As they gained experience, these soldiers of the Continental line more than held their own against crack British troops.

Blacks also fought and died for the American cause. Although many states initially barred them

---

Enslaved blacks hoped that the Revolutionary crisis would make it possible for them to secure their own liberty. On the eve of the war in South Carolina, merchant Josiah Smith, Jr., noted such a rumor among the slaves:

"[Freedom] is their common Talk throughout the Province, and has occasioned impertinent behavior in many of them, insomuch that our Provincial Congress now sitting hath voted the immediate raising of Two Thousand Men Horse and food, to keep those mistaken creatures in awe."

Despite such repressive measures, slave uprisings continued to plague the southern colonies through 1775 and 1776.

---

from militia service, by war's end more than five thousand blacks had enlisted in the American armed forces. The largest contingents came from the northern states with substantial numbers of free blacks.

Blacks fought at Trenton, Brandywine, Saratoga, and other important battles. Some, including Prince Whipple (later immortalized in Emanuel Leutze's famous painting "Washington Crossing the Deleware"), became military heroes. Others served as cooks, guides, spies, drivers, and roadbuilders.

African-Americans also served on the British side. In November 1775 Lord Dunmore, royal governor of Virginia, issued a proclamation promising freedom for any enslaved black in Virginia who joined the British army. News of Dunmore's decree traveled swiftly. Virginia and Maryland tightened slave patrols, but within one month three hundred slaves had joined what came to be called "Lord Dunmore's Ethiopian Regiment." In time, thousands of blacks fled plantations for British promises of emancipation. When one of James Madison's slaves was caught trying to escape to the British lines, Madison refused to punish him for "coveting that liberty" that white Americans proclaimed the "right & worthy pursuit of every human being." At war's end, the British kept their word, to some at least, and evacuated as many as fourteen thousand "Black Loyalists" to Nova Scotia, Jamaica, and England.

Morale in the Revolutionary army was badly undermined by American profiteers. Putting profits before patriotism, they sold to the British because the invader could pay in gold. Speculators forced prices sky-high; and some Bostonians made profits of 50 percent to 200 percent on army garb while the American army was freezing at Valley Forge. Washington never had as many as twenty thousand effective troops in one place at one time, despite bounties of land and other inducements. Yet if the rebels had thrown themselves into the struggle with Revolutionary zeal, they could easily have raised many times that number.

The brutal truth is that only a select minority of the American colonials attached themselves to the cause of independence with a spirit of selfless devotion. These were the dedicated souls who bore the burden of battle and the risks of defeat; these were the freedom-loving patriots who deserved the gratitude and esteem of generations yet unborn. Seldom have so few done so much for so many.

Chronology

1650	First Navigation Laws to control colonial commerce
1696	Board of Trade assumes goverance of colonies
1763	French and Indian War (Seven Years' War) ends
1764	Sugar Act
1765	Quartering Act Stamp Act Stamp Act Congress
1766	Declaratory Act
1767	Townshend Acts passed New York legislature suspended by Parliament
1768	British troops occupy Boston
1770	Boston Massacre All Townshend Acts except tea tax repealed
1772	Committees of correspondence formed
1773	British East India Company granted tea monopoly Boston Tea Party
1774	"Intolerable Acts" Quebec Act First Continental Congress The Association boycotts British goods
1775	Battle of Lexington and Concord

Whose Revolution?

Historians once assumed that the Revolution was just another chapter in the unfolding story of human liberty—an important way station on a divinely ordained pathway toward moral perfection in human affairs. This approach, often labeled the "Whig view of history," was best expressed in George Bancroft's ten-volume *History of the United States of America,* published between the 1830s and 1870s.

By the end of the nineteenth century, a group of historians known as the "imperial school" challenged Bancroft, arguing that the Revolution was best understood not as the fulfillment of national destiny, but as a constitutional conflict within the British Empire. For historians like George Beer, Charles Andrews, and Lawrence Gipson, the Revolution was the product of a collision between two different views of empire. While the Americans were moving steadily toward more self-government, old England increasingly tightened its grip, threatening a stranglehold that eventually led to wrenching revolution.

By the early twentieth century, these approaches were challenged by the so-called progressive historians, who argued that neither divine destiny nor constitutional quibbles had much to do with the Revolution. Rather, the Revolution stemmed from deep-seated class tensions within American society that, once released by revolt, produced a truly transformed social order. Living themselves in a reform age when entrenched economic interests cowered under heavy attack, progressive historians like Carl Becker insisted that the Revolution was not just about "home rule" within the British Empire, but also about "who should rule at home" in America, the upper or lower classes. J. Franklin Jameson took Becker's analysis one step further in his influential *The American Revolution Considered as a Social Movement* (1926). He claimed that the Revolution not only grew out of intense struggles between social groups, but also inspired many ordinary Americans to seek greater economic and political power, fundamentally democratizing society in its wake.

In the 1950s, the progressive historians fell out of favor as the political climate became more conservative. Interpretations of the American Revolution as a class struggle did not play well in a country obsessed with the spread of communism, and in its place arose the so-called consensus view. Historians such as Robert Brown and Daniel Boorstin argued that class conflict did not exist in the Revolutionary era, and that colonists of all ranks shared a commitment to certain fundamental political principles of self-government. The unifying power of ideas was now back in fashion almost a hundred years after Bancroft.

Since the 1950s, two broad interpretations have contended with each other and perpetuated the controversy over whether political ideals or economic and social realities were most responsible for the Revolution. The first, articulated most prominently by Bernard Bailyn, emphasized inherent ideological and psychological factors. Focusing on the power of ideas to foment revolution, Bailyn argued that the colonists, incited by their reading of seventeenth-century and early-eighteenth-century English political theorists, grew extraordinarily (perhaps even exaggeratedly) suspicious of any attempts to tighten the imperial reins on the colonies. When confronted with new taxes and commercial regulations, these hyper-sensitive colonists screamed "conspiracy against liberty" and "corrupt ministerial plot." In time, they took up armed insurrection in defense of their intellectual commitment to liberty.

A second school of historians, writing during the 1960s and 1970s and inspired by the social movements of that turbulent era, has revived the progressive interpretation of the Revolution. Gary Nash, in *An Urban Crucible* (1979), and Edward Countryman, in *A People in Revolution* (1981), pointed to the increasing social and economic divisions among Americans in both the urban seaports and the isolated countryside in the years leading up to the Revolution. Attacks by laborers on political elites and expressions of resentment toward wealth were taken as evidence of a society that was breeding revolutionary change from within, quite aside from British provocations. While the concerns of the progressive historians echo in these socioeconomic interpretations of the Revolution, the neoprogressives have been more careful not to reduce the issues simplistically to the one-ring arena of economic self-interest. Instead, they argue that the varying material circumstances of American participants led them to hold distinctive versions of republicanism, giving the Revolution a less unified and more complex ideological underpinning than the idealistic historians had previously suggested. The dialogue between proponents of "ideas" and "interests" is gradually leading to a more nuanced meeting of the two views.

SUGGESTED READINGS

PRIMARY SOURCE DOCUMENTS

Adam Smith, *An Inquiry into the Nature and Causes of the Wealth of Nations** (1776), is a penetrating analysis of British mercantilism. An intriguing Loyalist account of the Revolution, since reprinted, is Peter Oliver, *Origin & Progress of the American Rebellion* (1781). Patrick Henry,

"Speech Before the Virginia House of Burgesses Against the Stamp Act"* (1765), was an influential statement of colonial opposition to British policy, as was John Dickinson's response to the Townshend Acts, *Letters from a Farmer in Pennsylvania* (1768). Revolutionary writings may also be found in Bernard Bailyn, ed., *Pamphlets of the American Revolution, 1750–1776* (1965). For contemporary accounts of the beginning of hostilities, see Peter Force, ed., *American Archives*, Fourth Series, Vol. 2* (1839). For visual sources from the period, consult the edition compiled by Donald H. Cresswell, *The American Revolution in Drawings and Prints* (1975).

---

*An asterisk indicates that the document, or an excerpt from it, can be found in Thomas A. Bailey and David M. Kennedy, eds., *The American Spirit: United States History as Seen by Contemporaries,* 9th ed. (Boston: Houghton Mifflin, 1998).

SECONDARY SOURCES

The Revolution is interpreted as a divinely ordained event in George Bancroft's *History of the United States of America* (1852). Edmund S. Morgan, *The Birth of the Republic, 1763–1789* (1959), is among the best brief accounts of the Revolutionary era. It stresses the happy coincidence of the revolutionaries' principles and their interests, as do Daniel Boorstin, *The Genius of American Politics* (1953), and Robert E. Brown, *Middle-Class Democracy and the Revolution in Massachusetts, 1691–1780* (1955). Lawrence Gipson, *The Coming of the Revolution, 1763–1775* (1954), summarizes his fifteen-volume masterwork (cited in Chapter 6). A more recent effort at a general synthesis is Robert Middlekauff, *The Glorious Cause: The American Revolution, 1763–1789* (1982). Robert R. Palmer, *The Age of the Democratic Revolution: A Political History of Europe and America, 1760–1800* (2 vols., 1959, 1964), masterfully places American events in the larger context of Western history. Two enlightening collections of essays are Jack P. Greene, ed., *The Reinterpretation of the American Revolution, 1763–1789* (1968), and Alfred F. Young, ed., *The American Revolution* (1976), which generally represents a "new left" revisionist view, a perspective also found in Edward A. Countryman, *The American Revolution* (1987), and in Alfred F. Young, ed., *Beyond the American Revolution* (1993). An interesting effort to blend British and American perspectives is Ian R. Christie and Benjamin W. Labaree, *Empire or Independence, 1760–1776* (1976). The sources of American dissatisfaction with the British imperial system can be traced in Carl Ubbelohde, *The American Colonies in the British Empire, 1607–1763* (1968); and Thomas C. Barrow, *Trade and Empire: The British Customs Service in Colonial America* (1967). Oliver M. Dickerson, *The Navigation Acts and the American Revolution* (1951), concludes that the navigation system did not put undue burdens on the colonies. Bernhard Knollenberg examines the effects of the British tightening of the imperial system in the 1760s in *Origin of the American Revolution, 1759–1766* (1960), as does Michael Kammen in *Empire and Interest* (1970). John Shy imaginatively explores an important aspect of the imperial system's effect on America in *Toward Lexington: The Role of the British Army in the Coming of the American Revolution* (1965). A perceptive short account of the American reaction to British initiatives is Edmund S. Morgan and Helen M. Morgan, *The Stamp Act Crisis* (1953). Benjamin W. Labaree discusses another instance of American reaction in *The Boston Tea Party* (1964). Pauline Maier focuses on the crucial role of the "mob" in *From Resistance to Revolution: Colonial Radicals and the Development of American Opposition to Britain, 1765–1776* (1972). The British side is told in Peter D. G. Thomas, *British Politics and the Stamp Act Crisis* (1975); *The Townshend Duties Crisis* (1987); and *Tea Party to Independence* (1991). Bernard Bailyn's seminal *Ideological Origins of the American Revolution* (1967) stresses the importance of ideas in pushing the Revolution forward, as well as the colonists' fears of a conspiracy against their liberties. John Philip Reid, on the other hand, emphasizes legal ideas in *Constitutional History of the American Revolution: The Authority of Rights* (1987), as does Jerrilyn Greene Marston in *King and Congress: The Transfer of Political Legitimacy, 1774–1776* (1987). Useful local studies of American resistance are Richard D. Brown, *Revolutionary Politics in Massachusetts* (1970); Richard Ryerson, *The Revolution Is Now Begun: The Radical Committees of Philadelphia, 1765–1776* (1978); and David Hackett Fischer, *Paul Revere's Ride* (1994). On the meaning of the Revolution for African-Americans, see Sylvia R. Frey, *Water from the Rock: Black Resistance in a Revolutionary Age* (1991). Helpful biographies of key Revolutionary figures include Richard Beeman, *Patrick Henry* (1974); Merrill D. Peterson, *Thomas Jefferson and the New Nation* (1970); Dumas Malone, *Jefferson and His Time* (5 vols., 1948–1974); and Pauline Maier, *The Old Revolutionaries: Political Lives in the Age of Samuel Adams* (1980). Imaginative cultural history is found in Robert A. Gross, *The Minutemen and Their World* (1976). Edward A. Countryman emphasizes class conflict in *A People in Revolution: The American Revolution and Political Society in New York, 1760–1790* (1981). A psychological approach to the problem of the Revolutionary generation's assault on established authority is taken in Kenneth S. Lynn, *A Divided People* (1977), and Jay Fliegelman, *Prodigals and Pilgrims: The American Revolution Against Patriarchal Authority, 1750–1800* (1982).

8

America Secedes from the Empire

1775–1783

These are the times that try men's souls. The summer soldier and the sunshine patriot will, in this crisis, shrink from the service of their country; but he that stands it now, *deserves the love and thanks of man and woman.*

THOMAS PAINE, DECEMBER 1776

Congress Drafts George Washington

Bloodshed at Lexington and Concord, in April of 1775, was a clarion call to arms. About twenty thousand musket-bearing "Minute Men" swarmed around Boston, there to coop up the outnumbered British.

The Second Continental Congress met in Philadelphia the next month, on May 10, 1775; and this time the full slate of thirteen colonies was represented. The conservative element in Congress was still strong, despite the shooting in Massachusetts. There was no real sentiment for independence—

merely a desire to continue fighting in the hope that the king and Parliament would consent to a redress of grievances. Congress hopefully drafted new appeals to the British people and king—appeals that were spurned. Anticipating a possible rebuff, the delegates also adopted measures to raise money and to create an army and a navy.

Perhaps the most important single action of the Congress was to select George Washington, one of its members already in officer's uniform, to head the hastily improvised army besieging Boston. This choice was made with considerable misgivings. The tall, powerfully built, dignified Virginia planter, then forty-three, had never risen above the rank of a colonel in the militia. His largest command had numbered only twelve hundred men, and that had been some twenty years earlier. Falling short of true military genius, Washington would actually lose more pitched battles than he won.

But the distinguished Virginian was gifted with outstanding powers of leadership and immense strength of character. He radiated patience, courage, self-discipline, and a sense of justice. He was a great moral force rather than a great military mind—a symbol and a rallying point. People instinctively trusted him; they sensed that when he put himself at the head of a cause, he was prepared, if necessary, to go down with the ship. He insisted on serving without pay, though he kept a careful expense account amounting to more than $100,000. Later he sternly reprimanded his steward at Mount Vernon for providing the enemy, under duress, with supplies. He would have preferred instead to see the enemy put the torch to his mansion.

The Continental Congress, though dimly perceiving Washington's qualities of leadership, chose more wisely than it knew. His selection, in truth, was largely political. Americans in other sections, already jealous, were beginning to distrust the large New England army being collected around Boston. Prudence suggested a commander from Virginia, the largest and most populous of the colonies. As a man of wealth, both by inheritance and by marriage, Washington could not be accused of being a fortune seeker. As an aristocrat, he could be counted on by his peers to check "the excesses of the masses."

Bunker Hill and Hessian Hirelings

The clash of arms continued on a strangely contradictory basis. On the one hand, the Americans were emphatically affirming their loyalty to the king and earnestly voicing their desire to patch up difficulties. On the other hand, they were raising armies and shooting down His Majesty's soldiers. This curious war of inconsistency was fought for fourteen long months—from April 1775 to July 1776—before the fateful plunge into independence was taken.

Gradually the tempo of warfare increased. In May 1775 a tiny American force, under Ethan Allen and Benedict Arnold, surprised and captured the British garrisons at Ticonderoga and Crown Point, on the scenic lakes of upper New York. A priceless store of gunpowder and artillery for the siege of

Washington at Verplanck's Point, New York, 1782, Reviewing the French Troops After the Victory at Yorktown, by John Trumbull, 1790 This noted American artist accentuated Washington's already imposing height (6 feet, 2 inches; 1.88 meters) by showing him towering over his horse. Washington so appreciated this portrait of himself that he hung it in the dining room of his home at Mount Vernon, Virginia.

Boston was thus secured. In June 1775 the colonials seized a hill, now known as Bunker Hill (actually Breed's Hill), from which they menaced the enemy in Boston. The British, instead of cutting off the retreat of their foes by flanking them, blundered bloodily when they launched a frontal attack with three thousand men. Sharpshooting Americans, numbering fifteen hundred and strongly entrenched, mowed down the advancing Redcoats with frightful slaughter. But the colonials' scanty store of gunpowder finally gave out, and they were

Battle of Bunker Hill, June 17, 1795
This British engraving conveys the vulnerability of the British regulars to attacks by the American militiamen. Although a defeat for the colonists, the battle quickly proved a moral victory for the patriots. Outnumbered and outgunned, they held their own against the British and suffered many fewer casualties.

forced to abandon the hill in disorder. With two more such victories, remarked the French foreign minister, the British would have no army left in America.

Even at this late date, in July 1775, the Continental Congress adopted the "Olive Branch Petition," professing American loyalty to the crown and begging the king to prevent further hostilities. But following Bunker Hill, King George III slammed the door on all hope of reconciliation. In August 1775 he formally proclaimed the colonies rebellion; the skirmishes were now out and out treason, a hanging crime. The next month he widened the chasm when he sealed arrangements for hiring thousands of German troops to help crush his rebellious subjects. Six German princes involved in the transaction needed the money (one reputedly had seventy-four children); George III needed the men. Because most of these soldiers-for-hire came from the German principality of Hesse, the Americans called all the European mercenaries Hessians.

News of the Hessian deal shocked the colonials. The quarrel, they felt, was within the family. Why bring in outside mercenaries, especially foreigners who had an exaggerated reputation for butchery?

Hessian hirelings proved to be good soldiers in a mechanical sense, but many of them were more interested in booty than in duty. For good reason they were dubbed "Hessian flies." Seduced by American promises of land, hundreds of them finally deserted and remained in America to become respected citizens.

The Abortive Conquest of Canada

The unsheathed sword continued to take its toll. In October 1775, on the eve of a cruel winter, the British burned Falmouth (Portland), Maine. In that same autumn the rebels daringly undertook a two-pronged invasion of Canada. American leaders believed, erroneously, that the conquered French were explosively restive under the British yoke. A successful assault on Canada would add a fourteenth colony, while depriving Britain of a valuable base for striking at the colonies in revolt. But this large-scale attack, involving some two thousand American troops, contradicted the claim of the colonials that they were merely fighting defensively for a redress of grievances. Invasion northward was undisguised offensive warfare.

This bold stroke for Canada narrowly missed success. One invading column under the Irish-born General Richard Montgomery, formerly of the British army, pushed up the Lake Champlain route and captured Montreal. He was joined at Quebec by the bedraggled army of General Benedict Arnold, whose men had been reduced to eating dogs and shoe leather during their grueling march through the Maine woods. An assault on Quebec, launched on the last day of 1775, was beaten off. The able Montgomery was killed; the dashing Arnold was wounded in one leg. Scattered remnants under his command retreated up the St. Lawrence River, reversing the way Montgomery had come. French-Canadian leaders, who had been generously treated by the British in the Quebec Act of 1774, showed no real desire to welcome the plundering anti-Catholic invaders.

Bitter fighting continued in the colonies, though the Americans still disclaimed all desire for independence. In January 1776 the British set fire to the Virginia town of Norfolk. In March they were finally forced to evacuate Boston, taking with them the leading friends of the king. (Evacuation Day is still celebrated annually in Boston.) In the South the rebellious colonials won two victories in 1776—one in February against some fifteen hundred Loyalists at Moore's Creek Bridge, in North Carolina, and the other in June against an invading British fleet at Charleston Harbor.

Thomas Paine Preaches Common Sense

Why did Americans continue to deny any intention of independence? Loyalty to the empire was deeply ingrained; colonial unity was poor; and open rebellion was dangerous, especially against a formidable Britain. Irish rebels of that day were customarily hanged, drawn, and quartered. American rebels might have fared no better. As late as January 1776—five months before independence was declared—the king's health was being toasted by the officers of Washington's mess near Boston. "God save the king" had not yet been replaced by "God save the Congress."

Gradually the Americans were shocked into an awareness of their inconsistency. Their eyes were jolted open by harsh British acts like the burning of Falmouth and Norfolk, and especially by the hiring of the Hessians.

Then in 1776 came the publication of *Common Sense*, one of the most influential pamphlets ever written. Its author was the radical Thomas Paine, once an impoverished corset-maker's apprentice,

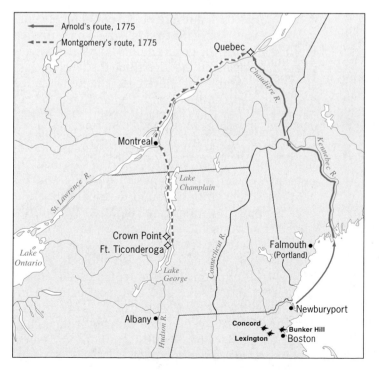

Revolution in the North, 1775–1776
Benedict Arnold's troops were described as "pretty young men" when they sailed from Massachusetts. They were considerably less pretty on their arrival in Quebec, after eight weeks of struggling through wet and frigid forests, often without food. "No one can imagine," one of them wrote, "the sweetness of a roasted shot-pouch [ammunition bag] to the famished appetite."

Thomas Paine, Engraving from a Portrait by Charles Willson Peale

In Common Sense, *Thomas Paine (1737–1809) argued for the superiority of a republic over a monarchy:*

"The nearer any government approaches to a republic the less business there is for a king. It is somewhat difficult to find a proper name for the government of England. Sir William Meredith calls it a republic; but in its present state it is unworthy of the name, because the corrupt influence of the crown, by having all the places in its disposal, hath so effectively swallowed up the power, and eaten out the virtue of the house of commons (the republican part of the constitution) that the government of England is nearly as monarchical as that of France or Spain."

who had come over from England a year earlier. His tract became a whirlwind best-seller and within a few months reached the astonishing total of 120,000 copies.

Paine flatly branded the shilly-shallying of the colonials as contrary to "common sense." Why not throw off the cloak of inconsistency? Nowhere in the physical universe did the smaller heavenly body control the larger one. Then why should the tiny island of England control the vast continent of America? As for the king, whom the Americans professed to revere, he was nothing but "the Royal Brute of Great Britain."

Paine and the Idea of "Republicanism"

Paine's passionate protest was as compelling as it was eloquent and radical—even doubly radical. It called not simply for independence, but for the creation of a new kind of political society, a democratic *republic,* where power flowed from the people themselves, not from a corrupt and despotic monarch. In language laced with biblical imagery familiar to common folk, he argued that all government officials—governors, senators, and judges, not just representatives in a house of commons—should derive their authority from popular consent.

Paine was hardly the first person to champion a republican form of government. Political philosophers had advanced the idea since the days of classical Greece and Rome. Revived in the Renaissance and in seventeenth-century England, republican ideals had uneasily survived within the British "mixed government," with its delicate balance of king, nobility, and commons. Republicanism particularly appealed to British politicians critical of excessive power in the hands of the king and his advisers. Their writings found a responsive audience among the American colonists, who interpreted the vengeful royal acts of the previous decade as part of a monarchical conspiracy to strip them of their liberties as English subjects. Paine's radical prescription for the colonies—to reject monarchy and empire and embrace an independent republic—fell on receptive ears.

The colonists' experience with governance had prepared them well for Paine's summons to create a republic. Many settlers, particularly New Englanders, had practiced a kind of republicanism in their democratic town meetings and annual elections, while the popularly elected committees of correspondence during 1774 and 1775 had demonstrated the feasibility of republican government. The absence of a hereditary aristocracy and the relative equality of condition enjoyed by landowning farmers meshed well with the republican repudiation of a fixed hierarchy of power.

Most Americans considered citizen "virtue" fundamental to any successful republican government. Because political power no longer rested with the central, all-powerful authority of the king, individuals in a republic needed to sacrifice their personal self-interest to the public good. The rights of "the people" mattered more than the private rights of any one person. Paine inspired his contemporaries to view America as fertile ground for the cultivation of such civic virtue.

Yet not all patriots agreed with Paine's ultrademocratic approach to republicanism. Some favored a republic ruled by a "natural aristocracy" of talent. Republicanism for them meant an end to hereditary aristocracy, but not an end to all social hierarchy. These more conservative republicans feared that the fervor for liberty would overwhelm the stability of the social order. They watched with trepidation as the "lower orders" of society—poorer farmers, tenants, and laboring classes in towns and cities—seemed to embrace a kind of runaway republicanism that amounted to radical "leveling." The contest to define the nature of American republicanism would noisily continue for the next hundred years.

George III (1738–1820), Studio of Alan Ramsay, c. 1767 America's last king, he was a good man, unlike some of his scandal-tainted brothers and sons, but a bad king. Doggedly determined to regain arbitrary power for the crown, he antagonized and then lost the thirteen American colonies. During much of his sixty-year reign, he seemed to be insane, but recently medical science has found that he was suffering from a rare metabolic and hereditary disease called porphyria.

Jefferson's "Explanation" of Independence

Members of the Philadelphia Congress, instructed by their respective colonies, gradually edged toward a clean break. On June 7, 1776, fiery Richard Henry Lee of Virginia moved that "These United Colonies are, and of right ought to be, free and independent states. . . ." After considerable debate, the motion was adopted nearly a month later, on July 2, 1776.

The passing of Lee's resolution was the formal "declaration" of independence by the American colonies, and technically this was all that was needed to cut the British tie. John Adams wrote confidently that ever thereafter July 2 would be celebrated annually with fireworks. But something more was required. An epochal rupture of this kind called for some formal explanation to "a candid world." An inspirational appeal was also needed to enlist other English colonies in the Americas, to invite assistance from foreign nations, and to rally resistance at home.

Shortly after Lee made his memorable motion on June 7, Congress appointed a committee to prepare an appropriate statement. The task of drafting it fell to Thomas Jefferson, a tall, freckled, sandy-haired Virginia lawyer of thirty-three. Despite his youth, he was already recognized as a brilliant writer, and he measured up splendidly to the awesome

The American signers of the Declaration of Independence had reason to fear for their necks. In 1802, twenty-six years later, George III (1738–1820) approved this death sentence for seven Irish rebels:

". . . [You] are to be hanged by the neck, but not until you are dead; for while you are still living your bodies are to be taken down, your bowels torn out and burned before your faces, your heads then cut off, and your bodies divided each into four quarters, and your heads and quarters to be then at the King's disposal; and may the Almighty God have mercy on your souls."

assignment. After some debate and amendment, the Declaration of Independence was formally approved by the Congress on July 4, 1776. It might better have been called "the Explanation of Independence" or, as one contemporary described it, "Mr. Jefferson's advertisement of Mr. Lee's resolution."

Jefferson's pronouncement, couched in a lofty style, was magnificent. He gave his appeal universality by invoking the "natural rights" of humankind—not just British rights. He argued persuasively that because the king had flouted these rights, the colonials were justified in cutting their connection. He then set forth a long list of the presumably tyrannous misdeeds of George III. The overdrawn bill of indictment included imposing taxes without consent, dispensing with trial by jury, abolishing valued laws, establishing a military dictatorship, maintaining standing armies in peacetime, cutting off trade, burning towns, hiring mercenaries, and inciting hostility among the Indians.*

Jefferson's withering blast was admittedly one-sided. But he was in effect the prosecuting attorney, and he took certain liberties with historical truth. He was not writing history; he was making it through what has been called "the world's greatest editorial." He owned many slaves, and his affirmation that "all men are created equal" was to haunt him and his fellow citizens for generations.

---

*For an annotated text of the Declaration of Independence, see the Appendix.

The formal declaration of independence cleared the air as a thundershower does on a muggy day. Foreign aid could be solicited with greater hope of success. Those patriots who defied the king were now rebels, not loving subjects shooting their way into reconciliation. They must all hang together, Franklin is said to have grimly remarked, or they would all hang separately. Or, in the eloquent language of the great declaration, "We mutually pledge to each other our lives, our fortunes and our sacred honor."

Jefferson's defiant Declaration of Independence had a universal impact unmatched by any other American document. This "shout heard round the world" has been a source of inspiration to countless revolutionary movements against arbitrary authority. Lafayette hung a copy on a wall in his home, leaving beside it room for a future French Declaration of the Rights of Man—a declaration that was officially born thirteen years later.

Patriots and Loyalists

The War of Independence, strictly speaking, was a war within a war. Colonials loyal to the king (Loyalists) fought the American rebels (Patriots), while the rebels also fought the British redcoats (see "Makers of America: The Loyalists," pp. 150–151). Loyalists were derisively called "Tories," after the dominant political factions in England, whereas Patriots were called "Whigs," after the opposition factions in England. A popular definition of a Tory among the Patriots betrayed bitterness: "A Tory is a thing whose head is in England, and its body in America, and its neck ought to be stretched."

Like many revolutions, the American Revolution was a minority movement. Many colonists were apathetic or neutral, including the Byrds of Virginia, who sat on the fence. The opposing forces contended not only against each other but also for the allegiance and support of the civilian population. In this struggle for the hearts and minds of the people, the British proved fatally inept, and the Patriot militias played a crucial role. The British military proved able to control only those areas where it could maintain a massive military presence. Elsewhere, as soon as the redcoats had marched on, the rebel militiamen appeared and took up the task of "political education"—sometimes by coercive means. Often lacking bayonets but always loaded with political zeal, the ragtag militia units proved remarkably effective agents of Revolutionary ideas. They convinced many colonists, even those indifferent to independence, that the British army was an unreliable friend and that they had better throw in their lot with the Patriot cause. They also mercilessly harassed small British detachments and occupation forces. One British officer ruefully observed that "the Americans would be less dangerous if they had a regular army."

Loyalists, numbering perhaps 20 percent of the American people, remained true to their king. Families often split over the issue of independence: Benjamin Franklin supported the Patriot side, whereas his handsome illegitimate son, William Franklin (the last royal governor of New Jersey), upheld the Loyalist cause.

The Loyalists were tragic figures. For generations the English in the New World had been taught fidelity to the crown. Loyalty is ordinarily regarded as a major virtue—loyalty to one's family, one's friends, one's country. If the king had triumphed, as he seemed likely to do, the Loyalists would have been acclaimed patriots, and defeated rebels like Washington would have been disgraced, severely punished, and probably forgotten.

Conservative Americans generally remained loyal—the people of education and wealth, of culture and caution. These moderate souls were satisfied with their lot and believed that any violent change would only be for the worse. Loyalists were also more numerous among the older generation.

Young people make revolutions, and from the outset energetic, purposeful, and militant young people surged forward—figures like the sleeplessly scheming Samuel Adams and the impassioned Patrick Henry. His flaming outcry before the Virginia Assembly—"Give me liberty or give me death!"—still quickens patriotic pulses.

Loyalists also included the king's officers and other beneficiaries of the crown—people who knew which side their daily bread came from. The same was generally true of the Anglican clergy and a large portion of their congregations, all of whom had long been taught submission to the king.

Usually the Loyalists were most numerous where the Anglican church was strongest. A notable exception was Virginia, where the debt-burdened Anglican aristocrats flocked into the rebel camp. The king's followers were well entrenched in aristocratic New York City and Charleston, and also in Quaker Pennsylvania and New Jersey, where General Washington felt that he was fighting in "the enemy's country." While his men were starving at Valley Forge, nearby Pennsylvania farmers were selling their produce to the British for the king's gold.

Loyalists were least numerous in New England, where self-government was especially strong and mercantilism was especially weak. Rebels were the most numerous where Presbyterianism and Congregationalism flourished, notably in New England. Invading British armies vented their contempt and anger by using Yankee churches for pigsties.

New York Patriots Pull Down the Statue of King George III Erected after the repeal of the Stamp Act in 1766, this statue was melted down by the revolutionaries into bullets to be used against the king's troops.

The Loyalists

In late 1776 Catherine Van Cortlandt wrote to her husband, a New Jersey merchant fighting in a Loyalist brigade, about the Patriot troops who had quartered themselves in her house. "They were the most disorderly of species," she complained, "and their officers were from the dregs of the people."

Like the Van Cortlandts, many Loyalists thought of themselves as the "better sort of people." They viewed their adversaries as "lawless mobs" and "brutes." Conservative, wealthy, and well-educated, Loyalists of this breed thought a break with Britain would invite anarchy. Loyalism made sense to them, too, for practical reasons. Viewing colonial militias as no match for His Majesty's army, Loyalist pamphleteer Daniel Leonard warned his Patriot enemies in 1775 that "Nothing short of a miracle could gain you one battle."

But Loyalism was hardly confined to the well-to-do. It also appealed to many people of modest means who identified strongly with England or who had reason to fear a Patriot victory. Thousands of British veterans of the Seven Years' War, for example, had settled in the colonies after 1763. Many of them took up farming on 200-acre land grants in New York. They were loath to turn their backs on the crown. So, too, were recent immigrants from non-English regions of the British Isles, especially from Scotland and Ireland, who had settled in Georgia or the backcountry of North and South Carolina. Many of these newcomers, resenting the plantation elite who ran these colonies, filled the ranks of such Tory brigades as the Volunteers of Ireland and the North Carolina Highlanders, organized by the British army to galvanize Loyalist support.

Other ethnic minorities found their own reasons to support the British. Some members of Dutch, German, and French religious sects believed that religious tolerance would be greater under the British than under Americans, whose prejudices they had already encountered. Above all, thousands of African-Americans joined Loyalist ranks in the hope that service to the British might offer an escape from bondage. British officials encouraged that belief. Throughout the war and in every colony some African-Americans fled to British lines, where they served as soldiers, servants, laborers, and spies. Many of them joined black regiments that special-

Miniatures of Catherine and Philip Van Cortland   Forced to abandon her New Jersey home to Washington's army for a hospital, Catherine fled with her nine children to New York, Nova Scotia, the Madeira Islands, and finally England, where she and her husband settled permanently. Catherine was said to have eventually given birth to as many as twenty-four children.

Loyalists Through British Eyes   This British cartoon depicts the Loyalists as doubly victimized—by Americans caricatured as "savage" Indians and by the British Prime Minister, the Earl of Shelburne, for offering little protection to England's defenders.

ized in making small sorties against Patriot militia. In Monmouth, New Jersey, the black Loyalist Colonel Tye and his band of raiders became legendary for capturing Patriots and their supplies.

As the war drew to an end in 1783, the fate of black Loyalists varied enormously. Many thousands who came to Loyalism as fugitive slaves managed to find a way to freedom, most notably the large group who won British passage from the port of New York to Nova Scotia. Other African-American Loyalists suffered betrayal. British general Lord Cornwallis abandoned over four thousand former slaves in Virginia, and many black Loyalists who boarded ships from British-controlled ports expecting to embark for freedom instead found themselves sold back into slavery in the West Indies.

White Loyalists faced no threat of enslavement but they did suffer punishments beyond mere disgrace: arrest, exile, confiscation of property, and loss of legal rights. Faced with such retribution, some 80,000 Loyalists fled abroad, mostly to England and the maritime provinces of Canada. Some settled contentedly as exiles, but many, especially those who went to England where they had difficulty becoming accepted, lived diminished and lonely lives—"cut off," as loyalist Thomas Danforth put it, "from every hope of importance in life . . . [and] in a station much inferior to that of a menial servant."

But most Loyalists remained in America, where they faced the special burdens of re-establishing themselves in a society that viewed them as traitors. Some succeeded remarkably despite the odds, such as Hugh Gaine, a printer in New York City who eventually reopened a business and even won contracts from the new government. Ironically, this former Loyalists soldier published the new national army regulations authored by the Revolutionary hero, Baron von Steuben. Like many former Loyalists, Gaine re-integrated himself into public life by siding with the Federalist call for a strong central government and powerful executive. When New York ratified the Constitution in 1788, Gaine rode the float at the head of the city's celebration parade. He had, like many other former Loyalists, become an American.

The Loyalist Exodus

Before the Declaration of Independence in 1776, persecution of the Loyalists was relatively mild. Yet they were subjected to some brutality, including tarring and feathering and riding astride fence rails.

After the Declaration of Independence, which sharply separated Loyalists from Patriots, harsher methods prevailed. The rebels naturally desired a united front. Putting loyalty to the colonies first, they regarded their opponents, not themselves, as traitors. Loyalists were roughly handled; hundreds were imprisoned; and a few noncombatants were hanged. But there was no wholesale reign of terror comparable to that which later bloodied both France and Russia during their revolutions. For one thing, the colonials reflected Anglo-Saxon regard for order; for another, the leading Loyalists were prudent enough to flee to the British lines.

About eighty thousand loyal supporters of George III were driven out or fled, but several hundred thousand or so of the mild Loyalists were permitted to stay. The estates of many of the fugitives were confiscated and sold—a relatively painless way to help finance the war. Confiscation often worked great hardship, as, for example, when two aristocratic women were forced to live in their former chicken house for leaning Toryward.

Some fifty thousand Loyalist volunteers at one time or another bore arms for the British. They also helped the king's cause by serving as spies, by inciting the Indians, and by keeping Patriot soldiers at home to protect their families. Ardent Loyalists had their hearts in their cause, and a major blunder of the haughty British was not to make full use of them in the fighting.

General Washington at Bay

With Boston evacuated in March 1776, the British concentrated on New York as a base of operations. Here was a splendid seaport, centrally located, where the king could count on cooperation from the numerous Loyalists. An awe-inspiring British fleet appeared off New York in July 1776. It consisted of some five hundred ships and 35,000 men—the largest armed force to be seen in America until the Civil War. General Washington, dangerously out-numbered, could muster only 18,000 ill-trained troops with which to meet the crack army of the invader.

Disaster befell the Americans in the summer and fall of 1776. Outgeneraled and outmaneuvered, they were routed at the Battle of Long Island, where panic seized the raw recruits. By the narrowest of margins, and thanks to a favoring wind and fog, Washington escaped to Manhattan Island. Retreating northward, he crossed the Hudson River to New Jersey and finally reached the Delaware River with the British close at his heels. Tauntingly, enemy buglers sounded the fox-hunting call, so familiar to Virginians of Washington's day. The Patriot cause was at low ebb when the rebel remnants fled across the river, after collecting all available boats to forestall pursuit.

The wonder is that Washington's adversary, General William Howe, did not speedily crush the demoralized American forces. But he was no military genius, and he well remembered the horrible slaughter at Bunker Hill, where he had commanded. The country was rough, supplies were slow in coming, and as a professional soldier Howe did not relish the rigors of winter campaigning. He evidently found more agreeable the bedtime company of his mistress, the wife of one of his subordinates—a scandal with which American satirists had a good deal of ribald fun.

Washington, who was now almost counted out, stealthily recrossed the ice-clogged Delaware River. At Trenton, on December 26, 1776, he surprised and captured a thousand Hessians who were sleeping off the effects of their Christmas celebration. A week later, leaving his campfires burning as a ruse, he slipped away and inflicted a sharp defeat on a smaller British detachment at Princeton. This brilliant New Jersey campaign, crowned by these two lifesaving victories, revealed "Old Fox" Washington at his military best.

Burgoyne's Blundering Invasion

London officials adopted an intricate scheme for capturing the vital Hudson River Valley in 1777. If successful, the British would sever New England from the rest of the states and paralyze the American cause. The main invading force, under an actor-playwright-soldier, General ("Gentleman Johnny") Burgoyne, would push down the Lake Champlain

Washington Crossing the Delaware, by Emanuel Gottlieb Leutze, 1851
On Christmas Day, 1776, George Washington set out from Pennsylvania with 2,400 men to surprise the British forces, chiefly Hessians, in their quarters across the river in New Jersey. The subsequent British defeat proved to be a turning point in the Revolution, as it checked the British advance toward Philadelphia and restored American morale. Seventy-five years later, Leutze, a German-born American painter, mythologized the heroic campaign in this painting.

route from Canada. General Howe's troops in New York, if needed, could advance up the Hudson River to meet Burgoyne near Albany. A third and much smaller British force, commanded by Colonel Barry St. Leger, would come in from the west by way of Lake Ontario and the Mohawk Valley.

British planners did not reckon with General Benedict Arnold. After his repulse at Quebec in 1775, he had retreated slowly along the St. Lawrence River back to the Lake Champlain area, by heroic efforts keeping an army in the field. The British had pursued his tattered force to Lake Champlain in 1776. But they could not move farther south until they had won control of the lake, which, in the absence of roads, was indispensable for carrying their supplies.

Where the British stopped to construct a sizeable fleet, tireless Arnold assembled and fitted out every floatable vessel. His tiny flotilla was finally destroyed after desperate fighting, but time, if not the battle, had been won. Winter was descending and the British were forced to retire to Canada. General Burgoyne had to start anew from this base the following year. If Arnold had not contributed his daring and skill, the British invaders of 1776 almost certainly would have recaptured Fort Ticonderoga. If Burgoyne had started from this springboard in 1777, instead of from Montreal, he almost certainly would have succeeded in his venture. (At last the apparently futile American invasion of Canada in 1775 was beginning to pay rich dividends.)

General Burgoyne began his fateful invasion with seven thousand regular troops. He was encumbered by a heavy baggage train and a considerable number of women, many of whom were wives of his officers. Progress was painfully slow, for sweaty

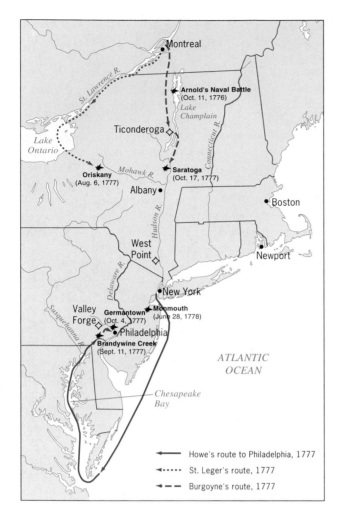

New York–Pennsylvania Theater, 1777–1778
Distinguished members of the Continental Congress fled from Philadelphia in near-panic as the British army approached. Thomas Paine reported that at three o'clock in the morning the streets were "as full of Men, Women, and Children as on a Market Day." John Adams had anticipated that "I shall run away, I suppose, with the rest," since "we are too brittle ware, you know, to stand the dashing of balls and bombs." Adams got his chance to decamp with the others into the interior of Pennsylvania and tried to put the best face on things. "This tour," he commented, "has given me an opportunity of seeing many parts of this country which I never saw before."

Revolutionary Standard of the Light-Horse of the City of Philadelphia, by John Folwell and James Claypoole, 1775
Silk flags like this were used to identify military units. In an exercise known as "trooping the colors," such flags were regularly paraded before the troops so that soldiers could recognize their own units in the confusion of battle.

axmen had to chop a path through the forest, while American militiamen began to gather like hornets on Burgoyne's flanks.

General Howe, meanwhile, was causing astonished eyebrows to rise. At a time when it seemed obvious that he should be starting up the Hudson River from New York to join his slowly advancing colleague, he deliberately embarked with the main British army for an attack on Philadelphia, the rebel capital. As scholars now know, he wanted to force a general engagement with Washington's army, destroy it, and leave the path wide open for Burgoyne's thrust. Howe apparently assumed that he had ample time to assist Burgoyne directly, should he be needed.

General Washington, keeping a wary eye on the British in New York, hastily transferred his army to the vicinity of Philadelphia. There, late in 1777, he was defeated in two pitched battles, at Brandywine Creek and Germantown. Pleasure-loving General Howe then settled down comfortably in the lively capital, leaving Burgoyne to flounder through the wilds of upper New York. Benjamin Franklin, recently sent to Paris as an envoy, truthfully jested that Howe had not captured Philadelphia but that Philadelphia had captured Howe. Washington finally retired to winter quarters at Valley Forge, a strong, hilly position some twenty miles northwest of Philadelphia, and there his frostbitten and hungry men were short of about everything except misery. This rabble was nevertheless whipped into a professional army by the recently arrived Prussian

> *Many in the Continental army became increasingly bitter with the lack of civilian support. As one Joseph Plumb Martin wrote about soldiering,*
>
> "[We] kept upon our parade in groups, venting our spleen at our country and government, then at our officers, and then at ourselves for our imbecility in staying there and starving in detail for an ungrateful people who did not care what became of us, so they could enjoy themselves while we were keeping a cruel enemy from them."

drillmaster, the profane but patient Baron von Steuben.

Burgoyne meanwhile had begun to bog down north of Albany, while a host of American militiamen, scenting the kill, swarmed about him. In a series of sharp engagements, in which General Arnold was again shot in the leg at Quebec, the British army was trapped. Meanwhile the Americans had driven back St. Leger's force at Oriskany. Unable to advance or retreat, Burgoyne was forced to surrender his entire command at Saratoga, on October 17, 1777, to the American General Horatio Gates.

Saratoga ranks high among the decisive battles of both American and world history. The victory immensely revived the faltering colonial cause. Even more important, it made possible the urgently needed foreign aid from France, which in turn helped ensure American independence.

Strange French Bedfellows

France, thirsting for revenge against Britain, was eager to inflame the quarrel that had broken out in America. The New World colonies were by far Britain's most valuable overseas possessions. If they could be wrestled from Britain, it presumably would cease to be a front-rank power. France might then regain its former position and prestige, the loss of which in the recent Seven Years' War rankled deeply.

America's cause rapidly became something of a fad in France. The bored aristocracy, which had developed some interest in the writings of liberal French thinkers like Rousseau, was rather intrigued by the ideal of American liberty. Hard-headed French officials, on the other hand, were not prompted by a love for America but by a realistic concern for the interests of France. Any marriage with America would be strictly one of convenience.

After the shooting at Lexington in April 1775, French agents undertook to blow on the embers. They secretly provided the Americans with life-saving amounts of gunpowder and other munitions, chiefly through a sham company rigged up for that purpose. About 90 percent of all the gunpowder used by the Americans in the first two and a half years of the war came from French arsenals.

Secrecy enshrouded all these French schemes. Open aid to the American rebels might provoke England into a declaration of war; and France, still weakened by its recent defeat, was not ready to fight. It feared that the American rebellion might fade out, for the colonies were proclaiming their desire to patch up differences. But the Declaration of Independence in 1776 showed that the Americans really meant business; and the smashing victory at Saratoga seemed to indicate that the Revolutionists had an excellent chance of winning their freedom.

After the humiliation at Saratoga in 1777, the British Parliament belatedly passed a measure that in effect offered the Americans home rule within the empire. This was essentially all that the colonials had ever asked for—except independence. If the French were going to break up the British Empire, they would have to bestir themselves. Wily and bespectacled old Benjamin Franklin, whose simple fur cap and witty sayings had captivated the French public, played skillfully on France's fears of reconciliation.

The French king, Louis XVI, was reluctant to intervene. Although somewhat stupid, he was alert enough to see grave dangers in aiding the Americans openly and incurring war with Britain. But his ministers at length won him over. They argued that hostilities were inevitable, sooner or later, to undo the victor's peace of 1763. If England should regain its colonies, it might join with them to seize the sugar-rich French West Indies and thus secure compensation for the cost of the recent rebellion. The French had better fight while they could have an American ally, rather than wait and fight both Britain and its reunited colonies.

After concluding the alliance, France sent a
minister to America, to the delight of one
Patriot journalist:

"Who would have thought that the American
colonies, imperfectly known in Europe a few
years ago and claimed by every pettifogging
lawyer in the House of Commons, every
cobbler in the beer-houses of London, as a
part of their property, should to-day receive
an ambassador from the most powerful
monarchy in Europe."

So France, in 1778, offered the Americans a
treaty of alliance. Their treaty promised everything
that Britain was offering—plus independence. Both
allies bound themselves to wage war until the
United States had won its freedom and until both
agreed to terms with the common foe.

This was the first entangling military alliance in
the experience of the Republic and one that later
caused prolonged trouble. The American people,
with ingrained isolationist tendencies, accepted the
French entanglement with distaste. They were
painfully aware that it bound them to a hereditary
foe that was also a Roman Catholic power. But when
one's house is on fire, one does not inquire too
closely into the background of those who carry the
water buckets.

The Colonial War Becomes a World War

England and France thus came to blows in 1778,
and the shot fired at Lexington rapidly widened into
a global conflagration. Spain entered the fray
against Britain in 1779, as did Holland. Combined
Spanish and French fleets outnumbered those of
England, and on two occasions the British Isles
seemed to be at the mercy of hostile warships.

The weak maritime neutrals of Europe, who had
suffered from Britain's dominance over the seas,
now began to demand more respect for their rights.
In 1780 the imperious Catherine the Great of Russia
took the lead in organizing the Armed Neutrality,
which she later sneeringly called the "Armed Nul-
lity." It lined up almost all the remaining European
neutrals in an attitude of passive hostility toward
England. The war was now being fought not only in
Europe and North America, but also in South America, the Caribbean, and Asia.

To say that America, with some French aid,
defeated England is like saying, "Daddy and I killed
the bear." To England, struggling for its very life, the
scuffle in the New World became secondary. The
Americans deserve credit for having kept the war
going until 1778, with secret French aid. But they
did not achieve their independence until the conflict erupted into a multipower world war that was
too big for Britain to handle. From 1778 to 1783,
France provided the rebels with large sums of

Britain Against the World

Britain and Allies	Enemy or Unfriendly Powers	
Great Britain Some Loyalists and Indians 30,000 hired Hessians (*Total population on Britain's side: c. 8 million*)	Belligerents (*Total population: c. 39.5 million*)	United States, 1775–1783 France, 1778–1783 Spain, 1779–1783 Holland, 1779–1783
		Ireland (restive)
	Members of the Armed Neutrality (with dates of joining)	Russia, 1780 Denmark-Norway, 1780 Sweden, 1780 Holy Roman Empire, 1781 Prussia, 1782 Portugal, 1782 Two Sicilies, 1783 (after peace signed)

money, immense amounts of equipment, about one-half of America's regular armed forces, and practically all of the new nation's naval strength.

France's entrance into the conflict forced the British to change their basic strategy in America. Hitherto they could count on blockading the colonial coast and commanding the seas. Now the French had powerful fleets in American waters, chiefly to protect their own valuable West Indian Islands, but in a position to jeopardize Britain's blockade and lines of supply. The British therefore decided to evacuate Philadelphia and concentrate their strength in New York City.

In June 1778 the withdrawing redcoats were attacked by General Washington at Monmouth, New Jersey, on a blisteringly hot day. Scores of men collapsed or died from sunstroke. But the battle was indecisive, and the British escaped to New York, although about one-third of their Hessians deserted. Henceforth, except for the Yorktown interlude of 1781, Washington remained in the New York area hemming in the British.

Blow and Counterblow

In the summer of 1780 a powerful French army of six thousand regular troops, commanded by the Comte de Rochambeau, arrived in Newport, Rhode Island. The Americans were somewhat suspicious of their former enemies; in fact, several ugly flare-ups, involving minor bloodshed, had already occurred between the new allies. But French gold and goodwill melted hard hearts. Dancing parties were arranged with the prim Puritan maidens; and one French officer related, doubtless with exaggeration, "The simple innocence of the Garden of Eden prevailed." No real military advantage came immediately from this French reinforcement, although preparations were made for a Franco-American attack on New York.

Improving American morale was staggered later in 1780, when General Benedict Arnold turned traitor. A leader of undoubted dash and brilliance, he was ambitious, greedy, unscrupulous, and suffering from a well-grounded but petulant feeling that his valuable services were not fully appreciated. He plotted with the British to sell out the key stronghold of West Point, which commanded the Hudson River, for £6,300 and an officer's commission. By the sheerest accident the plot was detected in

the nick of time, and Arnold fled to the British. "Whom can we trust now?" cried General Washington in anguish.

The British meanwhile had devised a plan to roll up the colonies, beginning with the South, where the Loyalists were numerous. The colony of Georgia was ruthlessly overrun in 1778–1779; Charleston, South Carolina, fell in 1780. The surrender of the city to the British involved the capture of five thousand men and four hundred cannon and was a heavier loss to the Americans, in relation to existing strength, than that of Burgoyne was to the British.

Warfare now intensified in the Carolinas, where Patriots bitterly fought their Loyalist neighbors. It was not uncommon for prisoners on both sides to be butchered in cold blood after they had thrown down their arms. The tide turned later in 1780 and early in 1781, when American riflemen wiped out a British detachment at King's Mountain and then defeated a smaller force at Cowpens. In the Carolina campaign of 1781, General Nathanael Greene, a Quaker-reared tactician, distinguished himself by his strategy of delay. Standing and then retreating, he exhausted his foe, General Charles Cornwallis, in vain pursuit. By losing battles but winning campaigns, the "Fighting Quaker" finally succeeded in clearing most of Georgia and South Carolina of British troops.

War in the South, 1780–1781

Joseph Brant, by Gilbert Stuart, 1786
Siding with the British, this Mohawk chief led Indian frontier raids so ferocious that he was dubbed "monster Brant." When he later met King George III, he declined to kiss the king's hand, but asked instead to kiss the hand of the queen.

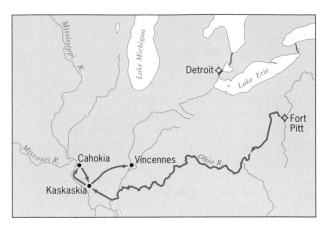

George Rogers Clark's Campaign, 1778–1779

The Land Frontier and the Sea Frontier

The West was ablaze during much of the war. Indian allies of George III, hoping to protect their land, were busy with torch and tomahawk; they were egged on by British agents branded as "hair buyers" because they allegedly paid bounties for American scalps. Fateful 1777 was known as "the bloody year" on the frontier. Although two nations of the Iroquois Confederacy, the Oneidas and the Tuscaroras, sided with the Americans, the Senecas and many other members of the powerful Six Nations of the Iroquois joined the British. They were urged on by Mohawk chief Joseph Brant, a convert to Anglicanism who believed, not without reason, that a victorious Britain would restrain American expansion into the West. Brant and the British ravaged large areas of backcountry Pennsylvania and New York until checked by an American force in 1779. In 1784 the pro-British Iroquois were forced to sign the Treaty of Fort Stanwix, the first treaty between the United States and an Indian nation. Under its terms the Indians ceded most of their land.

Yet even in wartime, the human tide of westward-moving pioneers did not halt its flow. Eloquent testimony is provided by place names in Kentucky, such as Lexington (named after the battle) and Louisville (named after America's new ally, Louis XVI).

In the wild Illinois country the British were especially vulnerable to attack, for they held only scattered posts that they had captured from the French. An audacious frontiersman, George Rogers Clark, conceived the idea of seizing these forts by surprise. In 1778–1779 he floated down the Ohio river with about 175 men and captured in quick succession the forts Kaskaskia, Cahokia, and Vincennes. Clark's admirers have argued, without positive proof, that his success forced the British to cede the region north of the Ohio River to the United States at the peace table in Paris.

America's infant navy had meanwhile been laying the foundations of a brilliant tradition. The naval establishment consisted of only a handful of nondescript ships, commanded by daring officers, the most famous of whom was a hard-fighting young Scotsman, John Paul Jones. As events turned out, this tiny naval force never made a real dent in Britain's thunderous fleets. Its chief contribution was in destroying British merchant shipping and thus carrying the war into the waters around the British Isles.

More numerous and damaging than ships of the regular American navy were swift privateers. These craft were privately owned armed ships—legalized pirates in a sense—specifically authorized by Congress to prey on enemy shipping. Altogether over a thousand American privateers, responding to the call of patriotism and profit, sallied forth with about seventy thousand men ("sailors of fortune"). They captured some six hundred British prizes, while British warships captured about as many American merchantmen and privateers.

Privateering was not an unalloyed asset. It had the unfortunate effect of diverting manpower from the main war effort and involving Americans, including Benedict Arnold, in speculation and graft. But the privateers brought in urgently needed gold, harassed the enemy, and raised American morale by providing victories at a time when victories were few. British shipping was so badly riddled by privateers and by the regular American navy that insurance rates skyrocketed. Merchant ships were compelled to sail in convoy, and British shippers and manufacturers brought increasing pressure on Parliament to end the war on honorable terms.

Yorktown and the Final Curtain

One of the darkest periods of the war was 1780–1781, before the last decisive victory. Inflation of the currency continued at full gallop. The government, virtually bankrupt, declared that it would repay many of its debts only at the rate of 2.5 cents on the dollar. Despair prevailed; the sense of unity withered; and mutinous sentiments infected the army.

Meanwhile, the British General Cornwallis was blundering into a trap. After futile operations in Virginia, he had fallen back to Chesapeake Bay at Yorktown to await seaborne supplies and reinforcements. He assumed Britain would continue to control the sea. But these few fateful weeks happened to be one of the brief periods during the war when British naval superiority slipped away.

The French were now prepared to cooperate energetically in a brilliant stroke. Admiral de Grasse, operating with a powerful fleet in the West Indies, advised the Americans that he was free to join with them in an assault on Cornwallis at Yorktown. Quick to seize this opportunity, General Washington made a swift march of more than 300 miles (483 kilometers) to the Chesapeake from the New York area. Accompanied by Rochambeau's French army, Washington beset the British by land, while de Grasse blockaded them by sea after beating off the British fleet. Completely cornered, Cornwallis surrendered his entire force of seven thousand men, on October 19, 1781, as his band appropriately played "The World Turn'd Upside Down." The triumph was no less French than American: the French provided essentially all the seapower and about half of the regular troops in the besieging army of some sixteen thousand men.

Stunned by news of the disaster, Prime Minister Lord North cried, "Oh God! It's all over! It's all over!" But it was not. George III stubbornly planned to continue the struggle, for England was far from being crushed. It still had 54,000 troops in North America, including 32,000 in the United States. Washington returned with his army to New York, there to continue keeping a vigilant eye on the British force of ten thousand men.

Fighting actually continued for more than a year after Yorktown, with Patriot-Loyalist warfare in the South especially savage. "No quarter for Tories" was the common battle cry. One of Washington's most valuable contributions was to keep the languishing cause alive, the army in the field, and the states together during these critical months. Otherwise a satisfactory peace treaty might never have been signed.

Baron von Steuben (1730–1794), a Prussian general who helped train the Continental army, found the Americans to be very different from other soldiers he had known. As von Steuben explained to a fellow European,

"The genius of this nation is not in the least to be compared with that of the Prussians, Austrians, or French. You say to your soldier, 'Do this' and he doeth it; but I am obliged to say, 'This is the reason why you ought to do that,' and then he does it."

Peace at Paris

After Yorktown, despite George III's obstinate eagerness to continue fighting, many Britons were weary of war and increasingly ready to come to terms. They had suffered heavy reverses in India and in the West Indies. The island of Minorca in the Mediterranean had fallen; the Rock of Gibraltar was tottering. Lord North's ministry collapsed in March 1782, temporarily ending the personal rule of George III. A Whig ministry, rather favorable to the Americans, replaced the Tory regime of Lord North.

Three American peace negotiators had meanwhile gathered at Paris: the aging but astute Benjamin Franklin; the flinty John Adams, vigilant for New England interests; and the impulsive John Jay of New York, deeply suspicious of Old World intrigue. The three envoys had explicit instructions from Congress to make no separate peace and to consult with their French allies at all stages of the negotiations. But the American representatives chafed under this directive. They well knew that it had been written by a subservient Congress, with the French Foreign Office indirectly guiding the pen.

France was in a painful position. It had induced Spain to enter the war on its side, in part by promising to deliver British-held Gibraltar. Yet the towering rock was defying frantic joint assaults by French and Spanish troops. Spain also coveted the immense trans-Allegheny area, on which restless American pioneers were already settling.

France, ever eager to smash Britain's empire, desired an independent United States, but one independent in the abstract, not in action. It therefore schemed to keep the new republic cooped up east of the Allegheny Mountains. A weak America—like a horse sturdy enough to plow but not vigorous enough to kick—would be easier to manage in promoting French interests and policy. France was paying a heavy price in men and treasure to win America's independence, and it wanted to get its money's worth.

But John Jay was unwilling to play France's game. Suspiciously alert, he perceived that the French could not satisfy the conflicting ambitions of both Americans and Spaniards. He saw signs—or thought he did—indicating that the Paris Foreign Office was about to betray America's trans-Allegheny interests to satisfy those of Spain. He

Benjamin Franklin (1706–1790), by Charles Willson Peale, 1789   He left school at age ten, and became a wealthy businessman, a journalist, an inventor, a scientist, a legislator, and preeminently a statesman-diplomat. He was sent to France in 1776 as the American envoy at age seventy, and he remained there until 1785, negotiating the alliance with the French and helping to negotiate the treaty of peace. His fame had preceded him, and when he discarded his wig for the fur cap of a simple "American argiculturist," he took French society by storm. French aristocratic women, with whom he was a great favorite, honored him by adopting the high *coiffure à la Franklin* in imitation of his cap.

Blundering George III, a poor loser, wrote this of America:

"Knavery seems to be so much the striking feature of its inhabitants that it may not in the end be an evil that they become aliens to this Kingdom."

therefore secretly made separate overtures to London, contrary to his instructions from Congress. The hard-pressed British, eager to entice one of their enemies from the alliance, speedily came to terms with the Americans. A preliminary treaty of peace was signed in 1782; the final peace, the next year.

By the Treaty of Paris of 1783, the British formally recognized the independence of the United States. In addition, they granted generous boundaries, stretching majestically to the Mississippi on the west, to the Great Lakes on the north, and to Spanish Florida on the south. (Spain had recently captured Florida from Britain.) The Yankees, though now divorced from the empire, were to retain a share in the priceless fisheries of Newfoundland. The Canadians, of course, were profoundly displeased.

The Americans, on their part, had to yield important concessions. Loyalists were not to be further persecuted, and Congress was to *recommend* to the state legislatures that confiscated Loyalist property be restored. As for the debts long owed to British creditors, the states vowed to put no lawful obstacles in the way of their collection. Unhappily for future harmony, the assurances regarding both Loyalists and debts were not carried out in the manner hoped for by London.

A New Nation Legitimized

Britain's terms were liberal almost beyond belief. The enormous trans-Allegheny area was thrown in as a virtual gift, for George Rogers Clark had captured only a small segment of it. Why the generosity? Had the United States beaten England to its knees?

The key to the riddle may be found in the Old World. At the time the peace terms were drafted, England was trying to seduce America from its French alliance, so it made the terms as alluring as possible. The shaky Whig ministry, hanging on by its fingernails for only a few months, was more friendly to the Americans than were the Tories. It was determined, by a policy of liberality, to salve recent wounds, reopen old trade channels, and prevent future wars over the coveted trans-Allegheny region. This far-visioned policy was regrettably not followed by the successors of the Whigs.

In spirit, the Americans made a separate peace—contrary to the French alliance. In fact, they did not. The Paris Foreign Office formally approved the terms of peace, though disturbed by the lone-wolf course of its American ally. France was

The Reconciliation Between Britannia and Her Daughter America (detail)
America (represented by an Indian) is invited to buss (kiss) her mother.

immensely relieved by the prospect of bringing the costly conflict to an end and of freeing itself from its embarrassing promises to the Spanish crown.

America alone gained from the world-girdling war. The British, though soon to stage a comeback, were battered and beaten. The French savored sweet revenge but plunged headlong down the slippery slope to bankruptcy and revolution. In truth, fortune smiled benignly on the Americans. Snatching their independence from the furnace of world conflict, they began their national career with a splendid territorial birthright and a priceless heritage of freedom. Seldom, if ever, have any people been so favored.

Chronology

1775 Battles of Lexington and Concord
Second Continental Congress
Americans capture British garrisons at
    Ticonderoga and Crown Point
Battle of Bunker Hill
King George III formally proclaims
    colonies in rebellion
Failed invasion of Canada
	1778-
	1779 Clark's victories in the West

	1781 Battle of King's Mountain Battle of Cowpens Greene leads Carolina campaign French and Americans force Cornwallis to surrender at Yorktown
1776 Paine's *Common Sense* Declaration of Independence Battle of Trenton	**1782** North's ministry collapses in Britain
	1783 Treaty of Paris
1777 Battle of Brandywine Battle of Germantown Battle of Saratoga	**1784** Treaty of Fort Stanwix
1778 Formation of French-American alliance Battle of Monmouth	

SUGGESTED READINGS

PRIMARY SOURCE DOCUMENTS

Thomas Paine's fiery *Common Sense** (1776) is the manifesto of the Revolution. "The Declaration of Independence"* (1776) is one of the foundations of American political theory. For eyewitness accounts of the war, see John C. Dann, *The Revolution Remembered* (1980). See also the "Treaty of Peace with Great Britain" (1783), in Henry Steele Commager, *Documents of American History*.

---

*An asterisk indicates that the document, or an excerpt from it, can be found in Thomas A. Bailey and David M. Kennedy, eds., *The American Spirit: United States History as Seen by Contemporaries*, 9th ed. (Boston: Houghton Mifflin, 1998).

SECONDARY SOURCES

The war is sketched in Don Higgenbotham's excellent military history, *The War of American Independence: Military Attitudes, Policies and Practice, 1763–1789* (1971). On the implications of the Revolutionary conflict, see John Shy, *A People Numerous and Armed: Reflections on the Military Struggle for American Independence* (1976); E. Wayne Carp, *To Starve the Army at Pleasure: Continental Army Administration and American Political Culture, 1775–1783* (1984); Charles Royster, *A Revolutionary People at War: The Continental Army and the American Character* (1980); and Ronald Hoffman et al., eds., *An Uncivil War: The Southern Backcountry During the American Revolution* (1985). The conflict is considered in its European setting in Piers Mackesy, *The War for America, 1775–1783* (1964). Carl Becker's classic *The Declaration of Independence* (1922) is masterful; on the same subject, see also Garry Wills, *Inventing America: Jefferson's Declaration of Independence* (1980). The role of the Loyalists is treated in Robert M. Calhoon, *The Loyalists in Revolutionary America* (1973); Mary Beth Norton, *The British-Americans: The Loyalist Exiles in England* (1972); John E. Ferling, *The Loyalist Mind: Joseph Galloway and the American Revolution* (1977); Sheila L. Skemp, *William Franklin: A Man in the Middle* (1990); Janice Potter-MacKinnon, *While the Women Only Wept: Loyalist Refugee Women* (1993); and Bernard Bailyn's unusually sensitive biography of the governor of colonial Massachusetts, *The Ordeal of Thomas Hutchinson* (1974). A general treatment of an often neglected subject is Benjamin Quarles, *The Negro in the American Revolution* (1961); Ronald Hoffman and Ira Berlin, eds., *Slavery and Freedom in the Age of the American Revolution* (1983); and Sylvia R. Frey, *Water from the Rock: Black Resistance in a Revolutionary Age* (1991). See also Duncan J. MacLeod, *Slavery, Race and the American Revolution* (1974), and David B. Davis, *The Problem of Slavery in the Age of Revolution, 1770–1823* (1975), an able, gracefully written book. International implications are developed in James H. Hutson, *John Adams and the Diplomacy of the American Revolution* (1980), and Jonathan R. Dull, *A Diplomatic History of the American Revolution* (1985). Attention to the social history of the Revolution has been largely inspired by John F. Jameson's seminal *The American Revolution Considered as a Social Movement* (1926). Jackson T. Main, *The Social Structure of Revolutionary America* (1969), takes the exploration further along the same lines, with conclusions somewhat at variance with Jameson's. Local studies of this issue include Edward A. Countryman, *A People in Revolution: The American Revolution and Political Society in New York, 1760–1790* (1981); Gary Nash, *The Urban Crucible: Social Change, Political Consciousness and the Origins of the American Revolution* (1979); Steven Rosswurm, *Arms, Country, and Class: The Philadelphia Militia and the 'Lower Sort' during the American Revolution* (1987); and Billy G. Smith, *The "Lower Sort": Philadelphia's Laboring People, 1750–1800* (1990). For information on the role of the Indian in the Revolution, see Barbara Graymont, *The Iroquois in the American Revolution* (1972); Isabel T. Kelsay, *Joseph Brant, 1743–1807: Man of Two Worlds* (1984); and Colin G. Calloway, *The American Revolution in Indian Country* (1995). Thomas Doerflinger describes economic change during the Revolution in *A Vigorous Spirit of Enterprise: Merchants and Economic Development in Revolutionary Philadelphia* (1986). Interesting biographies are Samuel E. Morison's swashbuckling *John Paul Jones* (1959); Eric Foner, *Tom Paine and Revolutionary America* (1976); James T. Flexner, *George Washington in the American Revolution, 1775–1783* (1968); and Charles Royster, *Light Horse Harry Lee and the Legacy of the American Revolution* (1981). British troubles are laid bare in William B. Willcox, *Portrait of a General: Sir Henry Clinton in the War of Independence* (1964). Women are the subject of Linda K. Kerber, *Women of the Republic: Intellect and Ideology in Revolutionary America* (1980); Mary Beth Norton, *Liberty's Daughters: The Revolutionary Experience of American Women* (1980); and Joy Day Buel and Richard Buel, Jr., *The Way of Duty: A Woman and Her Family in Revolutionary America* (1984). A fascinating account of a woman's life in rural Maine may be found in Laurel Thatcher Ulrich, *A Midwife's Tale: The Life of Martha Ballard, Based on Her Diary, 1785–1812* (1990). Michael Kammen brilliantly evokes the ways that the Revolution has been enshrined in the national memory in *A Season of Youth: The American Revolution and the Historical Imagination* (1978).

PART TWO

Building the New Nation

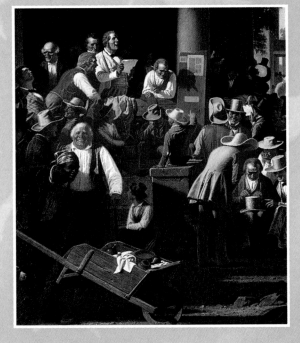

By 1783 Americans had won their freedom. Now they had to build their country. To be sure, they were blessed with a vast and fertile land, and they inherited from their colonial experience a proud legacy of self-rule. But history provided scant precedent for erecting a democracy on a national scale. No law of nature guaranteed that the thirteen rebellious colonies would stay glued together as a single nation, nor that they would preserve, not to mention expand, their democratic way of life. New institutions had to be created, new habits of thought cultivated. Who could predict whether the American experiment in government by the people would succeed?

The ramshackle national government cobbled together under the Articles of Confederation during the Revolutionary War soon proved woefully inadequate to the task of nation-building. In less than ten years after the Revolutionary War's conclusion, the Articles were replaced by a new Constitution, but even its adoption did not end the debate over just what form American democracy should take. Would the president, or the congress, or the courts be the dominant branch of government? What should be the proper division of authority between the federal government and the states? How could the rights of individuals be protected against a potentially powerful government? What economic policies would best serve the infant republic? How should the nation defend itself against foreign foes? What principles should guide foreign policy? Was America a

The Verdict of the People (detail)
This election-day crowd exudes the exuberant spirit of the era of Andrew Jackson, when the advent of universal white male suffrage made the United States the modern world's first mass participatory democracy. Yet the black man with the wheelbarrow, literally pushing his way into the painting, is a pointed reminder that the curse of slavery still blighted this happy scene.

nation at all, or was it merely a geographic expression, destined to splinter into several bitterly quarreling sections, as had happened to so many other would-be countries?

After a shaky start under George Washington and John Adams in the 1790s, buffeted by foreign troubles and domestic crises, the new Republic passed a major test when power was peacefully transferred from the conservative Federalists to the more liberal Jeffersonians in the election of 1800. A confident President Jefferson proceeded boldly to expand the national territory with the landmark Louisiana Purchase in 1803. But before long Jefferson, and then his successor, James Madison, were embroiled in what eventually proved to be a fruitless effort to spare the United States from the ravages of the war then raging in Europe.

America was dangerously divided during the War of 1812, and suffered a humiliating defeat. But a new sense of national unity and purpose was unleashed in the land thereafter. President Monroe, presiding over this "Era of Good Feelings," proclaimed in the Monroe Doctrine of 1823 that both of the American continents were off-limits to further European intervention. The foundations of a continental-scale economy were laid, as a "transportation revolution" stitched the country together with canals and railroads and turnpikes. Settlers flooded over those new arteries into the burgeoning West, often brusquely shouldering aside the native peoples. Immigrants, especially from Ireland and Germany, flocked to American shores. The combination of new lands and new labor fed the growth of a market economy, including the commercialization of agri-

culture and the beginnings of the factory system of production. Old ways of life withered as the market economy drew women as well as men, children as well as adults, blacks as well as whites, into its embrace. Ominously, the slave system grew robustly as cotton production, mostly for sale on European markets, exploded into the booming southwest.

Meanwhile, the United States in the era of Andrew Jackson gave the world an impressive lesson in political science. Between roughly 1820 and 1840 Americans virtually invented mass democracy, creating huge political parties and enormously expanding political participation by enfranchising nearly all adult white males. Nor was the spirit of innovation confined to the political realm. A wave of reform and cultural vitality swept through many sectors of American society. Utopian experiments proliferated. Religious revivals and even new religions, like Mormonism, flourished. A national literature blossomed. Crusades were launched for temperance, prison reform, women's rights, and the abolition of slavery.

By the second quarter of the nineteenth century, the outlines of a distinctive American national character had begun to emerge. Americans were a diverse, restless people, tramping steadily westward, eagerly forging their own nascent industrial revolution, proudly exercising their democratic political rights, impatient with the old, in love with the new, testily asserting their superiority over all other peoples—and increasingly divided, in heart, in conscience, and in politics, over the single greatest blight on their record of nation-making and democracy-building: slavery.

Women Weavers at Work (detail)
These simple cotton looms heralded the dawn of the industrial revolution, which transformed the lives of Americans even more radically than the events of 1776.

9

The Confederation and the Constitution

1776–1790

This example of changing the constitution by assembling the wise men of the state, instead of assembling armies, will be worth as much to the world as the former examples we have given it.

THOMAS JEFFERSON

A Revolution of Sentiments

The American Revolution was not a revolution in the sense of a radical or total change. It did not suddenly and violently overturn the entire political and social framework, as later occurred in the French and Russian revolutions. What happened was accelerated evolution rather than outright revolution. During the conflict itself, people went on working and praying, marrying and playing. Most of them were not seriously disturbed by the actual fighting, and many of the more isolated communities scarcely knew that a war was on.

Yet some striking changes were ushered in, affecting social customs, political institutions, and ideas about society, government, and even gender roles. The exodus of some eighty thousand substantial Loyalists robbed the new ship of state of conservative ballast. This weakening of the aristocratic upper crust, with all its culture and elegance, paved the way for new, Patriot elites to emerge. It also cleared the field for the "leveling" ideas of unbridled democracy to sweep across the land.

Equality was everywhere the watchword. When a group of Continental Army officers in 1783 formed an exclusive military order, the Society of the Cincinnati, they were roundly denounced for their lordly pretensions. Most states reduced (but usually did not eliminate altogether) property-holding requirements for voting. Social democracy was further stimulated by the growth of trade organizations for artisans and laborers. Citizens in several states, flushed with republican fervor, also sawed off the remaining shackles of medieval inheritance laws, such as primogeniture, which awarded all of a father's property to the eldest son.

A protracted fight for separation of church and state resulted in notable gains. Although the well-entrenched Congregational church continued to be legally established in some New England states, the Anglican church, tainted by association with the British crown, was humbled. De-Anglicized, it re-formed as the Protestant Episcopal church and was everywhere disestablished. The struggle for divorce between religion and government proved to be bitterest in Virginia. It was prolonged to 1786, when free-thinking Thomas Jefferson and his co-reformers, including the Baptists, won a complete victory with the passage of the Virginia Statute for Religious Freedom. (See the table of established churches, p. 93.)

The egalitarian sentiments unleashed by the war likewise challenged the institution of slavery. Philadelphia Quakers in 1775 founded the world's first antislavery society. Hostilities hampered the noxious trade in "black ivory," and the Continental Congress in 1774 called for the complete abolition of the slave trade, a summons to which most of the states responded positively. Several northern states went further and either abolished slavery outright or provided for the gradual emancipation of blacks.

These laws codified the Declaration's ringing concept that "all men are created equal," though laws against interracial marriage sprang up at the same time. Even in slave-burdened Virginia, a few idealistic masters freed their human chattels. In this still sadly incomplete revolution of sentiments, symbolized and inspired by the Declaration of Independence, were to be found the first frail sprouts of the later abolitionist movement.

But why in this dawning democratic age did abolition not go further and cleanly blot the evil of slavery from the fresh face of the new nation? The sorry truth is that the fledgling idealism of the Founding Fathers was sacrificed to political expediency. A fight over the slavery issue would have fractured the fragile national unity that was so desperately needed. Nearly a century later, the same issue did wreck the Union—temporarily.

Likewise incomplete was the extension of the doctrine of equality to women. Some women did serve (disguised as men) in the military, and New Jersey's new constitution in 1776 even for a time enabled women to vote. But though Abigail Adams teased her husband John in 1776 that "the ladies" were determined "to foment a rebellion" of their own if they were not given political rights, most of

Elizabeth "Mumbet" Freeman (c. 1744–1829), by Susan Anne Livingston Ridley Sedgwick, 1811   In 1781, having overheard revolutionary-era talk about the "rights of man," Mumbet sued her Massachusetts master for her freedom from slavery. She won her suit and lived the rest of her life as a paid domestic servant in the home of the lawyer who had pleaded her case.

The impact of the American Revolution was worldwide. About 1783 a British ship stopped at some islands off the East African coast, where the natives were revolting against their Arab masters. When asked why they were fighting they replied,

"America is free. Could not we be?"

The Copley Family, by John Singleton Copley, c. 1776–1777
The composition and use of light in this family portrait illustrate the importance of the mother in the era's ideal vision of the family. Mrs. Copley is here the visual center of the painting; the light falls predominantly on her, and she sits at the focus of activity in the family group. The artist thus powerfully expressed the sentiment of the age about "republican motherhood"— a sentiment that reverenced the role of women as homemakers and especially as mothers, responsible for the cultivation of good republican values in young citizens.

the women in the Revolutionary era were still doing traditional women's work.

Yet women did not go untouched by Revolutionary ideals. Central to republican ideology was the concept of "civic virtue"—the notion that democracy depended on the unselfish commitment of each citizen to the public good. And who could better cultivate the habits of a virtuous citizenry than mothers, to whom society entrusted the moral education of the young? Indeed, the selfless devotion of a mother to her family was often cited as the very model of proper republican behavior. The idea of "republican motherhood" thus took root, elevating women to a newly prestigious role as the special keepers of the nation's conscience. Whereas previously women's lives within the home were considered irrelevant to the masculine world of politics, now republican mothers bore crucial responsibility for the survival of the nation.

The Revolution enhanced the expectations and power of women as wives and mothers. As one "matrimonial republican" wrote in 1792,

"I object to the word 'obey' in the marriage-service because it is a general word, without limitations or definition. . . . The obedience between man and wife, I conceive, is, or ought to be mutual. . . . Marriage ought never to be considered a contract between a superior and an inferior, but a reciprocal union of interest, an implied partnership of interests, where all differences are accommodated by conference; and where the decision admits of no retrospect."

Constitution Making in the States

The Continental Congress in 1776 called upon the colonies to draft new constitutions. In effect, the Continental Congress was actually asking the colonies to summon themselves into being as new states. The sovereignty of these new states, according to the theory of republicanism, would rest on the authority of the people. For a time the manufacture of governments was even more pressing than the manufacture of gunpowder. Although the states of Connecticut and Rhode Island merely retouched their colonial charters to reflect the new vigors of republican thinking, constitution writers elsewhere worked tirelessly to capture on black-inked parchment the democratic spirit of the age.

Massachusetts contributed one especially noteworthy innovation when it called a special convention to draft its constitution and then submitted the final draft directly to the people for ratification. Once adopted in 1780, the Massachusetts constitution could be changed only by another specially called constitutional convention. This procedure was later imitated in the drafting and ratification of the federal Constitution.

The newly penned state constitutions had many features in common. Their similarity, as it turned out, made easier the drafting of a workable federal charter when the time was ripe. As *written* documents the state constitutions were intended to represent a *fundamental* law, superior to the transient whims of ordinary legislation. Most of these documents included bills of rights, specifically guaranteeing long-prized liberties against later legislative encroachment. Most of them required the annual election of legislators, who were thus forced to stay in touch with the mood of the people. All of them deliberately created weak executive and judicial branches, at least by present-day standards. A generation of quarreling with His Majesty's officials had implanted a deep distrust of despotic governors and arbitrary judges.

In all the new state governments, the legislatures, as presumably the most democratic branch of government, were given sweeping powers. But as Thomas Jefferson warned, "173 despots [in a legislature] would surely be as oppressive as one." Many Americans soon came to agree with him.

The democratic character of the new state legislatures was vividly reflected by the presence of many members from the recently enfranchised poorer western districts. Their influence was powerfully felt in their several successful movements to relocate state capitals from the haughty eastern seaports into the less pretentious interior. In the Revolutionary era, the capitals of New Hampshire, New York, Virginia, North Carolina, South Carolina, and Georgia were all moved westward. These geographical shifts portended political shifts that deeply discomfited many more conservative Americans.

Economic Crosscurrents

Economic changes begotten by the war were likewise noteworthy, but not overwhelming. States seized control of former crown lands, and although rich speculators had their day, many of the large Loyalist holdings were confiscated and eventually cut up into small farms. Roger Morris's huge estate in New York, for example, was sliced into 250 parcels —thus accelerating the spread of economic democracy. The frightful excesses of the French Revolution were avoided, partly because cheap land was easily available. People do not chop off heads so readily when they can chop down trees. It is highly significant that in the United States, economic democracy, broadly speaking, preceded political democracy.

A sharp stimulus was given to manufacturing by the prewar nonimportation agreements and later by the war itself. Goods that had formerly been imported from England were mostly cut off, and the ingenious Yankees were forced to make their own. Ten years after the Revolution, the busy Brandywine Creek, south of Philadelphia, was turning the waterwheels of numerous mills along an eight-mile (thirteen-kilometer) stretch. Yet America remained overwhelmingly a nation of soil-tillers.

Economically speaking, independence had drawbacks. Much of the coveted commerce of England was still reserved for the loyal parts of the empire; and now that the Americans were outsiders, they were forced to find new customers. Fisheries were disrupted, and bounties for ships' stores had abruptly ended. In some respects the hated British Navigation Laws were more disagreeable after independence than before.

New commercial outlets, fortunately, compensated partially for the loss of old ones. Americans could now trade freely with foreign nations, subject to local restrictions—a boon they had not enjoyed in the days of mercantilism. Enterprising Yankee shippers ventured boldly—and profitably—into the Baltic and China seas. In 1784 the *Empress of China*, carrying a valuable weed (ginseng) that was highly prized by Chinese herb doctors as a cure for impotence, led the way into the East Asian markets.

Yet the general economic picture was far from rosy. War had spawned demoralizing extravagance,

Western Merchants Negotiating the Purchase of Tea, artist unknown, c. 1790–1800
Yankee merchants and shippers figured prominently in the booming trade with China in the late eighteenth century. Among the American entrepreneurs who prospered in the China trade was Warren Delano, ancestor of President Franklin Delano Roosevelt.

speculation, and profiteering, with profits for some as indecently high as 300 percent. Runaway inflation had been ruinous to many citizens, and Congress had failed in its feeble attempts to curb economic laws by fixing prices. The average citizen was probably worse off financially at the end of the shooting than at the start.

The whole economic and social atmosphere was unhealthy. A newly rich class of profiteers was noisily conspicuous, whereas many once-wealthy people were left destitute. The controversy leading to the Revolutionary War had bred a keen distaste for taxes; and the wholesale seizure of Loyalist estates had encouraged disrespect for private property and for the majesty of the law generally. John Adams had been shocked when gleefully told by a horse-jockey neighbor that the courts of justice were all closed—a plight that proved to be only temporary.

A Shaky Start Toward Union

What would the Americans do with the independence they had so dearly won? London had dumped the responsibility of creating and operating a new central government squarely into their laps.

Prospects for erecting a lasting regime were far from bright. It is always difficult to set up a new government, doubly difficult to set up a new type of government. The picture was further clouded in America by leaders preaching "natural rights" and looking suspiciously at all persons clothed with authority. America was more a name than a nation, and unity ran little deeper than the color on the map.

Disruptive forces stalked the land. The departure of the conservative Tory element left the political system inclined toward experimentation and innovation. Patriots had fought the war with a high degree of disunity, but they had at least concurred on allegiance to a common cause. Now even that was gone. It would have been almost a miracle if any government fashioned in all this confusion had long endured.

Hard times, the bane of all regimes, set in shortly after the war and hit bottom in 1786. As if other troubles were not enough, British manufacturers, with dammed-up surpluses, began flooding the American market with cut-rate goods. War-baby American industries, in particular, suffered industrial colic from such ruthless competition. One Philadelphia newspaper in 1783 urged readers to don home-stitched garments of homespun cloth:

Of foreign gewgaws let's be free,
And wear the webs of liberty.

Yet hopeful signs could be discerned. The thirteen sovereign states were basically alike in governmental structure and functioned under similar constitutions. Americans enjoyed a rich political inheritance, derived partly from England and partly from their own homegrown devices for self-government. Finally, they were blessed with political leaders of a high order in men like George Washington, James Madison, John Adams, Thomas Jefferson, and Alexander Hamilton.

Creating a Confederation

The Second Continental Congress of Revolutionary days was little more than a conference of ambassadors from the thirteen states. It was totally without constitutional authority and in general did only what it dared to do, though it asserted some control over military affairs and foreign policy. In nearly all respects the thirteen states were sovereign, for they coined money, raised armies and navies, and erected tariff barriers. The legislature of Virginia even ratified separately the treaty of alliance of 1778 with France.

Shortly before declaring independence in 1776, the Congress appointed a committee to draft a written constitution for the new nation. The finished product was the Articles of Confederation. Adopted by Congress in 1777, it was translated into French

after the Battle of Saratoga so as to convince France that America had a genuine government in the making. In due course this new constitution was sent out to the states for their approval. But final action was delayed for four years, until 1781, less than eight months before the victory at Yorktown.

The chief apple of discord was western lands. Six of the jealous states, including Pennsylvania and Maryland, had no holdings beyond the Allegheny Mountains. Seven, notably New York and Virginia, were favored with enormous acreage, in most cases on the basis of earlier sea-to-sea charter grants. The six land-hungry states argued that the more fortunate states would not have retained possession of this splendid prize if all the other states had not fought for it also. A major complaint was that the land-blessed states could sell their trans-Allegheny tracts and thus pay off pensions and other debts incurred in the common cause. States without such holdings would have to tax themselves heavily to defray these obligations. Why not turn the whole western area over to the central government?

Unanimous approval of the Articles of Confederation by the thirteen states was required, and land-starved Maryland stubbornly held out until March 1, 1781. Maryland at length gave in when New York surrendered its western claims and Virginia seemed about to do so. To sweeten the pill, Congress pledged itself to dispose of these vast areas for the "common benefit." It further agreed to carve from the new public domain not colonies but a number of "republican" states, which in time would be admitted to the Union on terms of complete equality with all the others. This extraordinary commitment faithfully reflected the anticolonial spirit of the Revolution, and the pledge was later fully redeemed in the famed Northwest Ordinance of 1787.

Fertile public lands thus transferred to the central government proved to be an invaluable bond of union. The states that had thrown their heritage into the common pot had to remain in the Union if they were to reap their share of the advantages from the land sales. An army of westward-moving pioneers purchased their farms from the federal government, directly or indirectly, and they learned to look to the national capital, rather than to the state capitals—with a consequent weakening of local influence. Finally, a uniform national land policy was made possible.

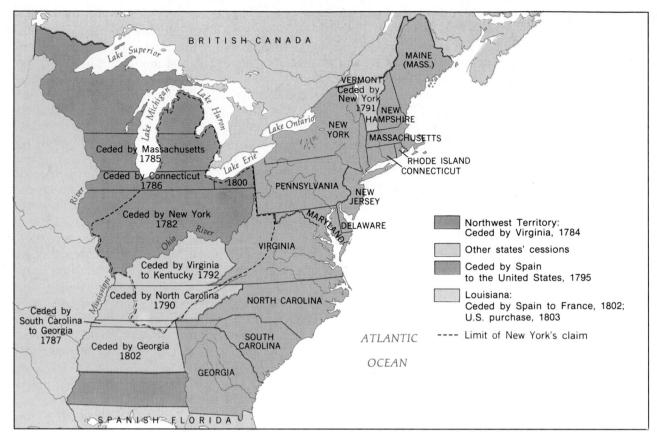

Western Land Cessions to the United States, 1782–1802

The Articles of Confederation: America's First Constitution

The Articles of Confederation—some have said "Articles of Confusion"—provided for a loose confederation or "firm league of friendship." Thirteen independent states were thus linked together for joint action in dealing with common problems, such as foreign affairs. A clumsy Congress was to be the chief agency of government. There was no executive branch—George III had left a bad taste—and the vital judicial arm was left almost exclusively to the states, which remained sovereign.

Congress, though dominant, was securely hobbled. Each state had a single vote, so that some 68,000 Rhode Islanders had the same voice as more than ten times that many Virginians. All bills dealing with specified subjects of importance required at least a two-thirds vote; any amendment of the Articles themselves required a unanimous vote. Unanimity was almost impossible, and this meant that the amending process, perhaps fortunately, was unworkable. If it had been workable, the Republic might have struggled along with a patched-up Articles of Confederation rather than replace it with an effective Constitution.

The shackled Congress was weak—and was purposely designed to be weak. Suspicious states, having just won control over taxation and commerce from Britain, had no desire to yield their newly acquired privileges to an American parliament—even one of their own making.

Two handicaps of the Congress were crippling. It had no power to regulate commerce, and this loophole left the states free to establish conflictingly different laws regarding tariffs and navigation. Nor could the Congress enforce its tax-collection program. It established a tax quota for each of the states and then asked them please to contribute their share on a voluntary basis. The central authority—a "government by supplication"—was lucky if in any year it received one-fourth of its requests.

The feeble national government in Philadelphia could advise and advocate and appeal. But in dealing with the independent states, it could not command or coerce or control. It could not act directly upon the individual citizens of a sovereign state; it could not even protect itself against gross indignities. In 1783 a dangerous threat came from a group of mutinous Pennsylvania soldiers who demanded back pay. After Congress had appealed in vain to the state for protection, the members were forced to move in disgrace to Princeton College in New Jersey. The new Congress, with all its paper powers, was even less effective than the old Continental Congress, which wielded no constitutional powers at all.

Yet the Articles of Confederation, weak though they were, proved to be a landmark in government. They were for those days a model of what a loose *con*federation ought to be. Thomas Jefferson enthusiastically hailed the new structure as the best one "existing or that ever did exist." To compare it with the European governments, he thought, was like comparing "heaven and hell." But although the Confederation was praiseworthy as confederations went, the troubled times demanded not a loosely woven *con*federation but a tightly knit federation. This involved the yielding by the states of their sovereignty to a completely recast federal government, which in turn would leave them free to control their local affairs.

In spite of their defects, the Articles of Confederation were a significant stepping-stone toward the present Constitution. They clearly outlined the general powers that were to be exercised by the central government, such as making treaties and establishing a postal service. As the first written constitution of the Republic, the Articles kept alive the flickering ideal of union and held the states together—until such time as they were ripe for the establishment of a strong constitution by peaceful, evolutionary methods. Even so, the anemic Articles represented to the states an alarming surrender of their power. Without this intermediary jump, they probably would never have consented to the breathtaking leap from the old boycott Association of 1774 to the Constitution of the United States.

Statehouse in 1778, from a drawing by Charles Willson Peale, by William L. Breton, c. 1830   Originally built in the 1730s as a meeting place for the Pennsylvania colonial assembly, this building witnessed much history: here Washington was given command of the Continental Army, the Declaration of Independence was signed, and the Constitution was hammered out. The building began to be called "Independence Hall" in the 1820s.

Landmarks in Land Laws

Handcuffed though the Congress of the Confederation was, it succeeded in passing supremely far-sighted pieces of legislation. These related to an immense part of the public domain recently acquired from the states and commonly known as the Old Northwest. This area of land lay northwest of the Ohio River, east of the Mississippi River, and south of the Great Lakes.

The first of these red-letter laws was the Land Ordinance of 1785. It provided that the acreage of the Old Northwest should be sold and that the proceeds should be used to help pay off the national debt. The vast area was to be surveyed before sale and settlement, thus forestalling endless confusion and lawsuits. It was to be divided into townships six miles square, each of which in turn was to be split into thirty-six sections of one square mile each. The sixteenth section of each township was set aside to be sold for the benefit of the public schools—a priceless gift to education in the Northwest. The orderly settlement of the Northwest Territory, where the land was methodically surveyed and titles duly recorded, contrasted sharply with the chaos south of the Ohio River, where uncertain ownership was the norm and fraud was rampant.

Even more noteworthy was the Northwest Ordinance of 1787, which related to the governing of the Old Northwest. This law came to grips with the problem of how a nation should deal with its colonial peoples—the same problem that had bedeviled the king and Parliament in London. The solution provided by the Northwest Ordinance was a judicious compromise: temporary tutelage, then permanent equality. First, there would be two evolutionary territorial stages, during which the area would be subordinate to the federal government. Then, when a territory could boast sixty thousand inhabitants, it might be admitted by Congress as a state, with all the privileges of the thirteen charter members. (This is precisely what the Continental Congress had promised the states when they surrendered their lands in 1781.) The ordinance also forbade slavery in the Old Northwest—a pathbreaking gain for freedom.

The wisdom of Congress in handling this explosive problem deserves warm praise. If it had attempted to chain the new territories in permanent subordination, a second American Revolution almost certainly would have erupted in later years, fought this time by the West against the East. Congress thus neatly solved the seemingly insoluble problem of empire. The scheme worked so well that its basic principles were ultimately carried over from the Old Northwest to other frontier areas.

The World's Ugly Duckling

Foreign relations, especially with London, continued troubled during these anxious years of the Confederation. England resented the stab in the back from its rebellious offspring and for eight years refused to send a minister to America's "backwoods" capital. England suggested, with barbed irony, that if it sent one, it would have to send thirteen.

Britain flatly declined to make a commercial treaty or to repeal its ancient Navigation Laws. Lord Sheffield, whose ungenerous views prevailed, argued persuasively in a widely sold pamphlet that England would win back America's trade anyhow. Commerce, he insisted, would naturally follow old channels. So why go to the Americans hat in hand? The British also officially shut off their profitable West Indian trade from the United States, though the Yankees, with their time-tested skill in smuggling, illegally partook nonetheless.

Scheming British agents were also active along the far-flung northern frontier. They intrigued with the disgruntled Allen brothers of Vermont and sought to annex that troubled area to Britain. Along

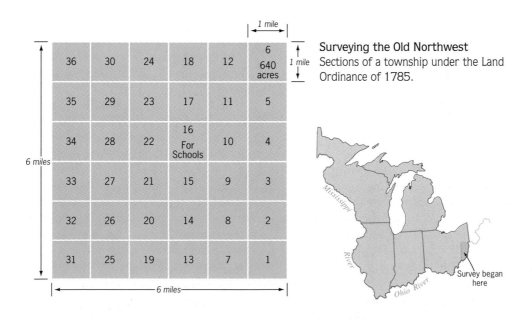

Surveying the Old Northwest
Sections of a township under the Land Ordinance of 1785.

the northern border the redcoats continued to hold a chain of trading posts on U.S. soil, and there they maintained their profitable fur trade with the Indians. One plausible excuse for remaining was the failure of the American states to honor the treaty of peace in regard to debts and Loyalists. But the main purpose of Britain in hanging on was probably to curry favor with the Indians and keep their tomahawks lined up on the side of the king as a barrier against future American attacks on Canada.

All these grievances against England were maddening to patriotic Americans. Some citizens demanded, with more heat than wisdom, that the United States force the British into line by imposing restrictions on their imports to America. But Congress could not control commerce, and the states refused to adopt a uniform tariff policy. Some "easy states" deliberately lowered their tariffs in order to attract an unfair share of trade.

Spain, though recently an enemy of England, was openly unfriendly to the new Republic. It controlled the mouth of the all-important Mississippi, down which the pioneers of Tennessee and Kentucky were forced to float their produce. In 1784 Spain closed the river to American commerce, threatening the West with strangulation. Spain likewise claimed a large area north of the Gulf of Mexico, including Florida, granted to the United States by the British in 1783. At Natchez, on disputed soil, it held an important fort. It also schemed with the neighboring Indians, grievously antagonized by the rapacious land policies of Georgia and North Carolina, to hem in the Americans east of the Alleghenies. Spain and England together, radiating their influence out among resentful Indian tribes, prevented America from exercising effective control over about half of its total territory.

Even France, America's comrade-in-arms, cooled off now that it had humbled Britain. The French demanded the repayment of money loaned during the war and restricted trade with their bustling West Indies and other ports.

Pirates of the North African states, including the arrogant Dey of Algiers, were ravaging America's Mediterranean commerce and enslaving Yankee sailors. The British purchased protection for their own subjects, and as colonials the Americans had enjoyed this shield. But as an independent nation, the United States was too weak to fight and too poor to bribe. A few Yankee shippers engaged in the Mediterranean trade with forged British protection papers, but not all were so bold or so lucky.

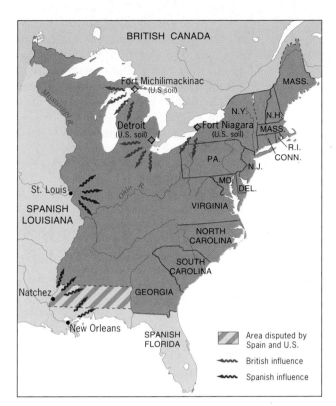

Main Centers of Spanish and British Influence After 1783
This map shows graphically that the United States in 1783 achieved complete independence in name only, particularly in the area west of the Appalachian Mountains. Not until twenty years had passed did the new Republic, with the purchase of Louisiana from France in 1803, eliminate foreign influence from the area east of the Mississippi River.

John Jay, secretary for foreign affairs, derived some hollow satisfaction from these insults. He hoped they would at least humiliate the American people into framing a new government at home that would be strong enough to command respect abroad.

The Horrid Specter of Anarchy

Economic storm clouds continued to loom in the mid-1780s. The requisition system of raising money was breaking down; some of the states refused to pay anything, while complaining bitterly about the tyranny of "King Congress." Interest on the public debt was piling up at home, and the nation's credit was evaporating abroad.

Individual states were getting out of hand. Quarrels over boundaries generated numerous minor pitched battles. Some of the states were levying duties on goods from their neighbors; New York, for example, taxed firewood from Connecticut and cabbages from New Jersey. A number of the states were again starting to grind out depreciated paper currency, and a few of them had passed laws sanctioning the semiworthless "rag money." As a contemporary rhymester put it,

Bankrupts their creditors with rage pursue;
No stop, no mercy from the debtor crew.

An alarming uprising, known as Shays's Rebellion, flared up in western Massachusetts in 1786. Impoverished backcountry farmers, many of them Revolutionary War veterans, were losing their farms through mortgage foreclosures and tax delinquencies. Led by Captain Daniel Shays, a veteran of the Revolution, these desperate debtors demanded cheap paper money, lighter taxes, and a suspension of property takeovers. Hundreds of angry agitators, again seizing their muskets, attempted to enforce their demands.

Massachusetts authorities responded with drastic action. Supported partly by contributions from wealthy citizens, they raised a small army. Several skirmishes occurred—at Springfield three Shaysites were killed, and one was wounded—and the movement collapsed. Daniel Shays, who believed that he was fighting anew against tyranny, was condemned to death but was later pardoned.

Social tensions reached a fever pitch during Shays's Rebellion in 1787. In an interview with a local Massachusetts paper, instigator Daniel Shays (1747–1825) explained how the debt-ridden farmers hoped to free themselves from the demands of a merchant-dominated government. The rebels would seize arms and

"march directly to Boston, plunder it, and then . . . destroy the nest of devils, who by their influence, make the Court enact what they please, burn it and lay the town of Boston in ashes."

Shays's followers were crushed—but the nightmarish memory lingered on. The outbursts of these and other distressed debtors struck fear in the hearts of the propertied class, who began to suspect that the Revolution had created a monster of "mobocracy." "Good God!" burst out George Washington, who felt that only a Tory or a Briton could have predicted such disorders. Unbridled republicanism, it seemed to many of the elite, had fed an insatiable appetite for liberty that was fast becoming license. Civic virtue was no longer sufficient to rein in self-interest and greed. It had become "undeniably evident," one skeptic sorrowfully lamented, "that some malignant disorder has seized upon our body politic." If republicanism was too shaky a ground upon which to construct a new nation, a stronger central government would provide the needed foundation. A few panicky citizens even talked of importing a European monarch to carry on where George III had failed.

How critical were conditions under the Confederation? Conservatives, anxious to safeguard their wealth and position, naturally exaggerated the seriousness of the nation's plight. They were eager to persuade their fellow citizens to scrap the Articles of Confederation, under which the states were sovereign, in favor of a muscular central government, in which the federal authority would predominate. But the poorer states' rights people, who favored at most a simple amending of the Articles, pooh-poohed the talk of anarchy. Many of them were debtors who feared that a powerful federal government would force them to pay their creditors.

Yet friends and critics of the Confederation agreed that it needed some strengthening. Popular toasts were "Cement to the Union" and "A hoop to the barrel." The chief differences arose over how this goal should be attained and how a maximum degree of states' rights could be reconciled with a strong central government. America probably could have muddled through somehow with amended Articles of Confederation. But the adoption of a completely new constitution certainly spared the Republic much costly indecision, uncertainty, and turmoil.

The nationwide picture was actually brightening before the Constitution was drafted. Nearly half the states had not issued semiworthless paper currency; and some of the monetary black sheep showed signs of returning to the sound-money fold. Congressional control of commerce was in sight, specifically by means of an amendment to the Articles of Confederation. Prosperity was beginning to emerge from the fog of depression. By 1789 overseas shipping had largely regained its place in the commercial world. If conditions had been as grim in 1787 as painted by foes of the Articles of Confederation, the move for a new constitution would hardly have encountered such heated opposition.

A Convention of "Demigods"

Control of commerce, more than any other problem, touched off the chain reaction that led to a constitutional convention. Interstate squabbling over this issue had become so alarming by 1786 that Virginia, taking the lead, issued a call for a convention at Annapolis, Maryland. Nine states appointed delegates, but only five were finally represented. With so laughable a showing, nothing could be done about the ticklish question of commerce. A charismatic New Yorker, thirty-one-year-old Alexander Hamilton, brilliantly saved the convention from complete failure by engineering the adoption of his report. It called upon Congress to summon a convention to meet in Philadelphia the next year, not to deal with commerce alone but to bolster the entire fabric of the Articles of Confederation.

Congress, though slowly and certainly dying in New York City, was reluctant to take a step that might hasten its day of reckoning. But after six of the states had seized the bit in their teeth and appointed delegates anyhow, Congress belatedly issued the call for a convention "*for the sole and express purpose of revising*" the Articles of Confederation.

Every state chose representatives, except for independent-minded Rhode Island (still "Rogues' Island"), a stronghold of paper-moneyites. These leaders were all appointed by the state legislatures, whose members had been elected by voters who could qualify as property holders. This double distillation inevitably brought together a select group of propertied men—though it is a grotesque distortion to claim that they shaped the Constitution primarily to protect their personal financial interests. When one of them did suggest restricting federal office to major property owners, he was promptly denounced for the unwisdom of "interweaving into a republican constitution a veneration for wealth."

Alexander Hamilton (1755–1804) clearly revealed his preference for an aristocratic government in his Philadelphia speech (1787):

"All communities divide themselves into the few and the many. The first are the rich and wellborn, the other the mass of the people. . . . The people are turbulent and changing; they seldom judge or determine right. Give therefore to the first class a distinct, permanent share in the government. They will check the unsteadiness of the second, and as they cannot receive any advantage by change, they therefore will ever maintain good government."

A quorum of the fifty-five emissaries from twelve states finally convened at Philadelphia on May 25, 1787, in the imposing red-brick statehouse. The smallness of the assemblage facilitated intimate acquaintance and hence compromise. Sessions were held in complete secrecy, with armed sentinels posted at the doors. Delegates knew that they would generate heated differences, and they did not want to advertise their own dissensions or put the ammunition of harmful arguments into the mouths of the opposition.

The caliber of the participants was extraordinarily high—"demigods," Jefferson called them. The crisis was such as to induce the ablest men to drop their personal pursuits and come to the aid of their country. Most of the members were lawyers, and most of them fortunately were old hands at constitution making in their own states.

George Washington, towering austere and aloof among the "demigods," was unanimously elected chairman. His enormous prestige, as "the Sword of the Revolution," served to quiet overheated tempers. Benjamin Franklin, then eighty-one, added the urbanity of an elder statesman, though he was inclined to be indiscreetly talkative in his declining years. James Madison, then thirty-six and a profound student of government, made contributions so notable that he has been dubbed "the Father of the Constitution." Alexander Hamilton, then only thirty-two, was present as an advocate of a super-powerful central government. His five-hour speech in behalf of his plan, though the most eloquent of the convention, left only one delegate convinced—himself.

Most of the fiery Revolutionary leaders of 1776 were absent. Thomas Jefferson, John Adams, and Thomas Paine were in Europe; Samuel Adams and John Hancock were not elected by Massachusetts. Patrick Henry, ardent champion of states' rights, was chosen as a delegate from Virginia but declined to serve, declaring that he "smelled a rat." It was perhaps well that these architects of revolution were absent. The time had come to yield the stage to leaders interested in fashioning solid political systems.

Patriots in Philadelphia

The fifty-five delegates were a conservative, well-to-do body: lawyers, merchants, shippers, land speculators, and moneylenders. Not a single spokesperson was present from the poorer debtor groups. They were young (the average age was about forty-two) but experienced statesmen. Above all, they were nationalists, more interested in preserving and strengthening the young Republic than in further stirring the roiling cauldron of popular democracy.

The delegates hoped to crystallize the last evaporating pools of revolutionary idealism into a stable political structure that would endure. They strongly desired a firm, dignified, and respected government. They believed in republicanism but sought to protect the American democratic experiment from its weaknesses abroad and excesses at home. In a broad sense the piratical Dey of Algiers, who drove the delegates to their work, was a Founding Father.

Thomas Jefferson (1743–1826), despite his high regard for the leaders at the Philadelphia convention, still was not unduly concerned about Shaysite rebellions. He wrote (November 1787),

"What country before ever existed a century and a half without a rebellion? . . . The tree of liberty must be refreshed from time to time with the blood of patriots and tyrants. It is its natural manure."

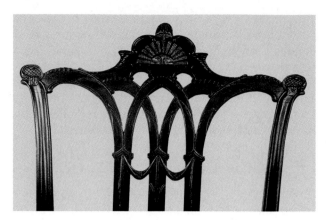

Rising Sun Symbol at the Top of Washington's Chair
This brass sun adorned the chair in which George Washington sat during the Constitutional Convention. Pondering the symbol, Benjamin Franklin observed that "I have the happiness to know it is a rising and not a setting sun."

They aimed to clothe the central authority with genuine power, especially in controlling tariffs, so that the United States could wrest satisfactory commercial treaties from foreign nations. The shortsighted hostility of the British mercantilists spurred the constitution framers to their task, and in this sense the illiberal Lord Sheffield was also a Founding Father.

Other motives hovered in the Philadelphia hall. Delegates were determined to preserve the union, forestall anarchy, and ensure security of life and property against dangerous uprisings by the "mobocracy." Above all, they sought to curb the unrestrained democracy rampant in the various states. "We have, probably, had too good an opinion of human nature in forming our confederation," Washington concluded. The specter of the recent outburst in Massachusetts was especially alarming, and in this sense Daniel Shays was yet another Founding Father. Grinding necessity extorted the Constitution from a reluctant nation. Fear occupied the fifty-sixth chair.

Hammering Out a Bundle of Compromises

Some of the travel-stained delegates, when they first reached Philadelphia, decided upon a daring step. They would completely *scrap* the old Articles of Confederation, despite explicit instructions from Congress to *revise*. Technically, these bolder spirits were determined to overthrow the existing government of the United States by peaceful means. The sovereign states were in danger of losing their sovereignty.

A scheme proposed by populous Virginia, and known as "the large-state plan," was first pushed forward as the framework of the Constitution. Its essence was that representation in both houses of a bicameral Congress should be based on population—an arrangement that would naturally give the larger states an advantage.

Tiny New Jersey, suspicious of brawny Virginia, countered with "the small-state plan." This provided for equal representation in a unicameral Congress by states, regardless of size and population, as under the existing Articles of Confederation. The weaker states feared that under the Virginia scheme the stronger states would band together and lord it over the rest. Angry debate, heightened by a stifling heat wave, led to deadlock. The danger loomed that the convention would unravel in complete failure. Even skeptical old Benjamin Franklin seriously proposed that the daily sessions be opened with prayer by a local clergyman.

After bitter and prolonged debate, the "Great Compromise" of the convention was hammered out and agreed upon. A cooling of tempers came coincidentally with a cooling of the temperature. The larger states were conceded representation by population in the House of Representatives (Art. I, Sec. II, para. 3; see Appendix at the end of this book), and the smaller states were appeased by equal representation in the Senate (see Art. I, Sec. III, para. 1). Each state, no matter how poor or small, would have two senators. The big states, which would have to bear the major burden of taxation, obviously yielded more. As a sop to them, the delegates agreed that

Gouverneur Morris (1752–1816), by James Sharples, 1810 A delegate from Pennsylvania to the Constitutional Convention of 1787, he spoke more frequently than any other member and served as principal draftsman of that superbly written document. A wealthy and rock-ribbed conservative, he had joined the Revolutionary movement with reluctance and to the end feared the "riotous mob."

every tax bill or revenue measure must originate in the House, where population counted more heavily (see Art. I, Sec. VII, para. 1). This critical compromise broke the log jam, and from then on success seemed within reach.

In a significant reversal of the arrangement most state constitutions had embodied, the new Constitution provided for a strong, independent executive in the presidency. The framers were here partly inspired by the example of Massachusetts, where a vigorous, popularly elected governor had suppressed Shays's Rebellion. The president was to be military commander in chief and to have wide powers of appointment to domestic offices—including judgeships. The president was also to have veto power over legislation.

The Constitution as drafted was a bundle of compromises; they stand out in every section. A vital compromise was the method of electing the

Jefferson was never a friend of strong government (except when himself president), and he viewed with suspicion the substitute that was proposed for the Articles of Confederation:

"Indeed, I think all the good of this new Constitution might have been couched in three or four new articles, to be added to the good, old, and venerable fabric."

Evolution of Federal Union

Years	Attempts at Union	Participants	
1643–1684	New England Confederation	4	colonies
1686–1689	Dominion of New England	7	colonies
1754	Albany Congress	7	colonies
1765	Stamp Act Congress	9	colonies
1772–1776	Committees of Correspondence	13	colonies
1774	First Continental Congress (adopts The Association)	12	colonies
1775–1781	Second Continental Congress	13	colonies
1781–1789	Articles of Confederation	13	states
1789–1790	Federal Constitution	13	states

president indirectly by the Electoral College, rather than by direct means (see Art. II, Sec. I, para. 2). One Virginia delegate insisted that to leave the choice to the people was like asking a blind person to choose colors.

Sectional jealousy also intruded. Should the voteless slave of the southern states count as a person in apportioning direct taxes and in according representation in the House of Representatives? The South, not wishing to be deprived of influence, answered "yes." The North replied "no," arguing that the North might as logically demand additional representation based on its horses. As a compromise between total representation and none at all, it was decided that a slave might count as three-fifths of a person. Hence the memorable, if somewhat illogical, "three-fifths compromise" (see Art. I, Sec. II, para. 3).

Most of the states wanted to shut off the African slave trade. But South Carolina and Georgia, requiring slave labor in their rice paddies and malarial swamps,

raised vehement protests. By way of compromise the convention stipulated that the slave trade might continue until the end of 1807, at which time Congress could turn off the spigot (see Art. I, Sec. IX, para. 1). It did so as soon as the prescribed interval had elapsed. Meanwhile, all the new state constitutions except Georgia's forbade overseas slave trade.

Safeguards for Conservatism

Heated clashes among the delegates have been overplayed. The area of agreement was actually large; otherwise the convention would have speedily disbanded. Economically, the members of the Constitutional Convention generally saw eye to eye; they demanded sound money and the protection of private property. Politically, they were in basic agreement; they favored a stronger government, with three branches and with checks and balances among them—what critics branded a "triple-headed monster." Finally, the convention was virtually unanimous in believing that manhood-suffrage democracy—government by "democratick babblers" —was something to be feared and fought.

Daniel Shays, the prime bogeyman, still frightened the conservative-minded delegates. They deliberately erected safeguards against the excesses of the "mob," and they made these barriers as strong as they dared. The awesome federal judges were to be appointed for life. The powerful president was to be elected *indirectly* by the Electoral College; the lordly senators were to be chosen *indirectly* by state legislatures (see Art I, Sec. III, para. 1). Only in the

One of the Philadelphia delegates recorded in his journal a brief episode involving Benjamin Franklin (1725–1802), who was asked by a woman when the convention ended,

"Well, Doctor, what have we got, a republic or a monarchy?"

The elder statesman answered,

"A republic, if you can keep it."

case of one-half of one of the three great branches—the House of Representatives—were qualified (propertied) citizens permitted to choose their officials by *direct* vote (see Art. I, Sec. II, para. 1).

Yet the new charter also contained democratic elements. Above all, it stood foursquare on the two great principles of republicanism: that the only legitimate government was one based on the consent of the governed, and that the powers of government should be limited—in this case specifically limited by a written constitution. The virtue of the people, not the authority of the state, was to be the ultimate guarantor of liberty, justice, and order. "We the people," the preamble began, in a ringing affirmation of these republican doctrines.

At the end of seventeen muggy weeks—May 25 to September 17, 1787—only forty-two of the original fifty-five members remained to sign the Constitution. Three of the forty-two, refusing to do so, returned to their states to resist ratification. The remainder, adjourning to the City Tavern, appropriately celebrated the toastworthy occasion. They little suspected that one day an Eighteenth Amendment would be added forbidding the manufacture and sale of alcoholic beverages.

No members of the convention were completely happy about the result. They were too near their work—and too weary. Whatever their personal desires, they finally had to compromise and adopt what was acceptable to the entire body, and what presumably would be acceptable to the entire country.

The Clash of Federalists and Antifederalists

The Framing Fathers early foresaw that nationwide acceptance of the Constitution would not be easy to obtain. A formidable barrier was unanimous ratification by all thirteen states, as required for amendment by the still-standing Articles of Confederation. But since absent Rhode Island was certain to veto the Constitution, the delegates boldly adopted a different scheme. They stipulated that when nine states had registered their approval through specially elected conventions, the Constitution would become the supreme law of the land in those states ratifying (see Art. VII).

This was extraordinary, even revolutionary. It was in effect an appeal over the heads of the Congress that had called the convention, and over the heads of the legislatures that had chosen its members, to the people—or those of the people who could vote. In this way the framers could claim greater popular sanction for their handiwork. Congress reluctantly submitted the document to the states on this basis, without recommendation of any kind.

The American people were somewhat shocked, so well had the secrets of the convention been concealed. The public had expected the old Articles of Confederation to be patched up; now it was handed a frightening new document in which, many thought, the precious jewel of state sovereignty was swallowed

Strengthening the Central Government

Under Articles of Confederation	Under Federal Constitution
A loose confederation of states	A firm union of people
1 vote in Congress for each state	2 votes in Senate for each state; representation by population in House (see Art. I, Secs. II, III)
$\frac{2}{3}$ vote (9 states) in Congress for all important measures	Simple majority vote in Congress, subject to presidential veto (see Art. I, Sec. VII, para. 2)
Laws executed by committees of Congress	Laws executed by powerful president (see Art. II, Secs. II, III)
No congressional power over commerce	Congress to regulate both foreign and interstate commerce (see Art. I, Sec. VIII, para. 3)
No congressional power to levy taxes	Extensive power in Congress to levy taxes (see Art. I, Sec. VIII, para. 1)
No federal courts	Federal courts, capped by Supreme Court (see Art. III)
Unanimity of states for amendment	Amendment less difficult (see Art. V)
No authority to act directly upon individuals and no power to coerce states	Ample power to enforce laws by coercion of individuals and to some extent of states

up. One of the hottest debates of American history forthwith erupted. The antifederalists, who opposed the stronger federal government, were arrayed against the federalists, who obviously favored it.

A motley crowd gathered in the antifederalist camp. It consisted primarily, though not exclusively, of the states' rights devotees, the backcountry dwellers, the one-horse farmers, the work-soiled artisans, the ill-educated and illiterate—in general, the poorer classes. They were joined by paper-moneyites and debtors, many of whom feared that a potent central government would force them to pay off their debts—and at full value. Large numbers of antifederalists suspected that the conniving upper crust were pulling off a sinister plot against the lowly common folk.

Silver-buckled federalists were more respectable; they generally embraced the cultured and propertied groups. Most of them lived in the settled areas along the seaboard, not in the raw backcountry. They were in outlook rather closely akin to the conservative Loyalist group of Revolutionary days. In fact, many of the remaining former Loyalists vigorously supported the Constitution; without them it might not have been ratified.

Antifederalists, their worst fears aroused, voiced vehement objections to the "gilded trap" known as the Constitution. They cried with much truth that it had been drawn up by the aristocratic elements and hence was antidemocratic. They likewise charged that the sovereignty of the states was being submerged and that the freedoms of the individual were jeopardized by the absence of a bill of rights. They decried the dropping of annual elections for congressional representatives, the erecting of a federal stronghold ten miles square (later the District of Columbia), the creation of a standing army, the omission of any reference to God, and the highly questionable procedure of ratifying with only two-thirds of the states. A Philadelphia newspaper added that Benjamin Franklin was "a fool from age" and George Washington "a fool from nature."

The Great Debate in the States

Special elections, some apathetic but others hotly contested, were held in the various states for members of the ratifying conventions. The candidates—federalist or antifederalist—were elected on the basis of their pledges for or against the Constitution.

With the ink barely dry on the parchment, four small states quickly accepted the Constitution, for they had come off much better than they expected. Pennsylvania, number two on the list of ratifiers, was the first large state to act, but not until high-handed irregularities had been employed by the federalist legislature in calling a convention. These included the forcible seating of two antifederalist members, their clothes torn and their faces red with rage, in order to complete a quorum.

Massachusetts, the second most populous state, provided an acid test. If the Constitution had

Ratification of the Constitution

State	Date	Vote in Convention	Rank in Population	1790 Population
1. Delaware	Dec. 7, 1787	Unanimous	13	59,096
2. Pennsylvania	Dec. 12, 1787	46 to 23	3	433,611
3. New Jersey	Dec. 18, 1787	Unanimous	9	184,139
4. Georgia	Jan. 2, 1788	Unanimous	11	82,548
5. Connecticut	Jan. 9, 1788	128 to 40	8	237,655
6. Massachusetts (incl. Maine)	Feb. 7, 1788	187 to 168	2	475,199
7. Maryland	Apr. 28, 1788	63 to 11	6	319,728
8. South Carolina	May 23, 1788	149 to 73	7	249,073
9. New Hampshire	June 21, 1788	57 to 46	10	141,899
10. Virginia	June 26, 1788	89 to 79	1	747,610
11. New York	July 26, 1788	30 to 27	5	340,241
12. North Carolina	Nov. 21, 1789	195 to 77	4	395,005
13. Rhode Island	May 29, 1790	34 to 32	12	69,112

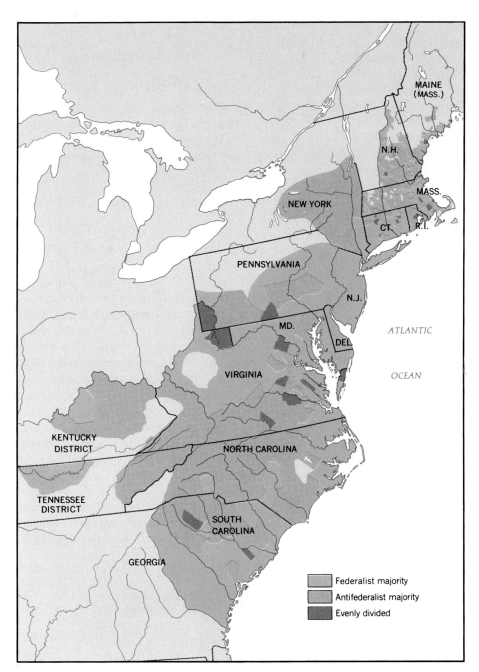

The Struggle over Ratification
This mottled map shows that federalist support tended to cluster around the coastal areas, which had enjoyed profitable commerce with the outside world, including the export of grain and tobacco. Impoverished frontiersmen, suspicious of a powerful new central government under the Constitution, were generally antifederalists.

Legend:
- Federalist majority
- Antifederalist majority
- Evenly divided

failed in Massachusetts, the entire movement might easily have bogged down. The Boston ratifying convention at first contained an antifederalist majority. It included grudging Shaysites and the suspicious Samuel Adams, that aging "Engineer of Revolution" who now distrusted change. The assembly buzzed with dismaying talk of summoning another constitutional convention, as though the nation had not already shot its bolt. Clearly the choice was not between this Constitution and a better one, but between this Constitution and the creaking Articles of Confederation. The absence of a bill of rights alarmed the antifederalists. But the federalists gave them solemn assurances that the first Congress would add such a safeguard by amendment, and ratification was then secured in Massachusetts by the rather narrow margin of 187 to 168.

Three more states fell into line. The last of these was New Hampshire, whose convention at first had contained a strong antifederalist majority. The federalists cleverly arranged a prompt adjournment and then won over enough waverers to secure ratification. Nine states—all but Virginia, New York, North Carolina, and Rhode Island—had now taken shelter under the "new federal roof," and the document was officially adopted on June 21, 1788. Francis Hopkinson exulted in his song "The New Roof":

> Huzza! my brave boys, our work is complete;
> The world shall admire Columbia's fair seat.

But such rejoicing was premature so long as the four dissenters, conspicuously New York and Virginia, dug in their heels.

The Four Laggard States

Proud Virginia, the biggest and most populous state, provided fierce antifederalist opposition. There the college-bred federalist orators, for once, encountered worthy antagonists, including the fiery Patrick Henry. He professed to see in the fearsome document the death warrant of liberty. George Washington, James Madison, and John Marshall, on the federalist side, lent influential support. With New Hampshire about to ratify, the new Union was going to be formed anyhow, and Virginia could not very well continue comfortably as an independent state.

> *Richard Henry Lee (1732–1794), a prominent antifederalist, attacked the proposed constitution in 1788:*
>
> "'Tis really astonishing that the same people, who have just emerged from a long and cruel war in defense of liberty, should now agree to fix an elective despotism upon themselves and their posterity."

After exciting debate in the state convention, ratification carried, 89 to 79.

New York, which also experienced an uphill struggle, was the only state that permitted a manhood-suffrage vote for the members of the ratifying convention. The result was a heavy antifederalist majority. Alexander Hamilton at heart favored a much stronger central government than that under debate, but he contributed his sparkling personality and persuasive eloquence to whipping up support for federalism as framed. He also joined John Jay and James Madison in penning a masterly series of articles for the New York newspapers. Though designed as propaganda, these essays remain the most penetrating commentary ever written on the Constitution and are still widely sold in book form as *The Federalist*. Probably the most famous of these is Madison's *Federalist* No. 10, which brilliantly refuted the conventional wisdom of the day that it

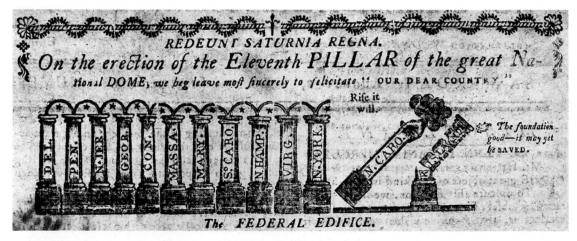

A Triumphant Cartoon   It appeared in the *Massachusetts Centinel* on August 2, 1788. Note the two laggards, especially the sorry condition of Rhode Island.

was impossible to extend a republican form of government over a large territory.

New York finally yielded. Realizing that the state could not prosper apart from the Union, the convention ratified the document by the close count of 30 to 27. At the same time, it approved thirty-two proposed amendments and—vain hope—issued a call for yet another convention to modify the Constitution.

Last-ditch dissent developed in only two states. A hostile convention met in North Carolina, then adjourned without taking a vote. Rhode Island did not even summon a ratifying convention. The two most ruggedly individualist centers of the colonial era—homes of the "otherwise minded"—thus ran true to form. They were to change their course, albeit unwillingly, only after the new government had been in operation for some months.

The race for ratification, despite much apathy, was close and quite bitter in some localities. No lives were lost, but riotous disturbances broke out in New York and Pennsylvania, involving bruises and bloodshed. There was much behind-the-scenes pressure on delegates who had promised their constituents to vote against the Constitution. The last four states ratified, not because they wanted to but because they had to. They could not safely exist outside the fold.

A Conservative Triumph

The minority had triumphed—twice. A militant minority of American radicals had engineered the military Revolution that cast off the unwritten British constitution. A militant minority of conservatives—now embracing many of the earlier radicals—had engineered the peaceful revolution that overthrew the inadequate constitution known as the Articles of Confederation. Eleven states, in effect, had seceded from the Confederation, leaving the two still in, actually out in the cold.

A majority had not spoken. Only about one-fourth of the adult white males in the country, chiefly the propertied people, had voted for delegates to the ratifying conventions. Careful estimates indicate that if the new Constitution had been submitted to a manhood-suffrage vote, as in New York, it would have encountered much more opposition, probably defeat.

Conservatism was victorious. Safeguards had been erected against mob-rule excesses, and the

The First Coin Authorized by Congress, 1787   The Fugio cent was minted by a private company and remained in circulation until the 1850s. The word *Fugio* "I fly" and the sundial show that time flies; "Mind Your Business" urges diligence.

democratic gains of the Revolution were conserved in the face of possible anarchy. Radicals like Patrick Henry, who had ousted British rule, had in turn been upended by American conservatives. The result was a kind of peaceful counterrevolution. It restored the economic and political stability of colonial years and set the drifting ship of state on a more promising course.

Yet if the architects of the Constitution were conservative, it is worth emphasizing that they conserved the principle of democratic government through a redefinition of popular sovereignty. Unlike the antifederalists, who believed that the sovereignty of the people resided in a single branch of government—the legislature—the federalists contended that every branch—executive, judiciary,

Referring to the belief that self-government is better than good government, Fisher Ames (1758–1808) of Massachusetts, a federalist member of the new Congress, is quoted as having said,

"A monarchy is like a merchantman [merchant ship]. You get on board and ride the wind and tide in safety and elation but, by and by, you strike a reef and go down. But democracy is like a raft. You never sink, but, damn it, your feet are always in the water."

and legislature—effectively represented the people. By ingeniously embedding the doctrine of self-rule in a self-limiting system of checks and balances among these branches, the Constitution reconciled the potentially conflicting principles of liberty and order. It represented a marvelous achievement, one that elevated the ideals of the Revolution even while setting boundaries to them. One of the distinctive—and enduring—paradoxes of American history was thus revealed: in the United States, conservatives and radicals alike have championed the heritage of democratic revolution.

Chronology

1774 First Continental Congress calls for abolition of slave trade

1775 Philadelphia Quakers found world's first antislavery society

1776 New Jersey constitution temporarily gives women the vote

1777 Articles of Confederation adopted by Second Continental Congress

1780 Massachusetts adopts first constitution drafted in convention and ratified by popular vote

1781 Articles of Confederation put into effect

1783 Military officers form Society of the Cincinnati

1785 Land Ordinance of 1785

1786 Virginia Statute for Religious Freedom
Shays's Rebellion
Meeting of five states to discuss revision of the Articles of Confederation

1787 Northwest Ordinance
Constitutional Convention in Philadelphia

1788 Ratification by nine states guarantees a new government under the Constitution

The Constitution: Revolutionary or Counterrevolutionary?

Although the Constitution has endured over two centuries as the basis of American government, historians have differed sharply over how to interpret its origins and meaning. The so-called Nationalist School of historians, writing in the late nineteenth century, viewed the Constitution as the logical culmination of the Revolution, and more generally, as a crucial step in the God-given progress of Anglo-Saxon peoples. As described in John Fiske's *The Critical Period of American History* (1888), the young nation, buffeted by foreign threats and growing internal chaos, with only a weak central government to lean on, was saved by the adoption of a more rigorous Constitution, the ultimate fulfillment of republican ideals.

By the early twentieth century, however, the progressive historians had turned a more critical eye to the Constitution. Having observed the Supreme Court of their own day repeatedly overrule legislation designed to better social conditions for the masses, they began to view the original document as an instrument created by elite conservatives to wrest political power away from the common people. For historians like Carl Becker and Charles Beard, the Constitution was part of the revolutionary struggle between the lower classes (small farmers, debtors, and laborers) and the upper classes (merchants, financiers, and manufacturers).

Beard's *An Economic Interpretation of the Constitution of the United States* (1913) argued that the Articles of Confederation had protected debtors and small property owners and displeased wealthy elites heavily invested in trade, the public debt, and the promotion of manufacturing. Only a stronger, more centralized government could protect their extensive property interests. Reviewing the economic holdings of the Founding Fathers, Beard determined that most of those men were indeed deeply involved in investments that would increase in value under the Constitution. In effect, Beard argued, the Constitution represented a successful attempt by conservative elites to buttress their own economic supremacy at the expense of less fortunate Americans. He further contended that the Constitution was ratified by default, because the people most disadvantaged by the new government did not possess the property qualifications needed to vote—more evidence of the class conflict underlying the struggle between federalists and antifederalists.

Beard's economic interpretation of the Constitution held sway through the 1940s. Historians like Merrill Jensen elaborated Beard's analysis by arguing that the 1780s were not in fact mired in chaos but rather were hopeful times for many Americans. In the 1950s, however, this analysis fell victim to the attacks of the "consensus" historians, who sought explanations for the Constitution in factors other than class interest. Scholars such as Robert Brown and Forrest McDonald convincingly disputed Beard's evidence about delegates' property ownership and refuted his portrayal of the masses as propertyless and disfranchised. They argued that the Constitution derived from an emerging consensus that the country needed a stronger central government.

Scholars since the 1950s have searched for new ways to understand the origins of the Constitution. The most influential work has been Gordon Wood's *Creation of the American Republic* (1969). Wood reinterpreted the ratification controversy as a struggle to define the true essence of republicanism. Antifederalists so feared human inclination toward corruption that they shuddered at the prospect of putting powerful political weapons in the hands of a central government. They saw small governments susceptible to local control as the only safeguard against tyranny. The federalists, on the other hand, believed that a strong, balanced national government would rein in selfish human instincts and channel them toward the pursuit of the common good. Alarmed by the indulgences of the state governments, the federalists, James Madison in particular (especially in *Federalist* No. 10), developed the novel ideal of an "extensive republic," a polity that would achieve stability by virtue of its great size and diversity. This conception challenged the conventional wisdom that a republic could survive only if it extended over a small area with a homogeneous population. In this sense, Wood argued, the Constitution represented a bold experiment—the fulfillment, rather than the repudiation, of the most advanced ideas of the Revolutionary era—even though it emanated from traditional elites determined to curtail dangerous disruptions to the social order.

SUGGESTED READINGS

PRIMARY SOURCE DOCUMENTS

A comparison of the text of the Articles of Confederation (1781), in Henry Steele Commager, *Documents of American History*, with the Constitution* makes an

---

*An asterisk indicates that the document, or an excerpt from it, can be found in Thomas A. Bailey and David M. Kennedy, eds., *The American Spirit: United States History as Seen by Contemporaries,* 9th ed. (Boston: Houghton Mifflin, 1998).

intriguing study. See also Madison, Hamilton, and Jay's explanations of the Constitution in *The Federalist* papers, especially *Federalist* No. 10.* Additional primary sources may be found in Bernard Bailyn, ed., *The Debate on the Constitution: Federalist and Antifederalist Speechs, Articles, and Letters During the Struggle over Ratification* (1993). For visual sources from the period, consult the volume compiled by Donald H. Cresswell, *The American Revolution in Drawings and Prints* (1975).

SECONDARY SOURCES

John Fiske, in *The Critical Period of American History* (1888), portrayed America under the Articles of Confederation as a crisis-ridden country. His view has been sharply qualified by Merrill Jensen in *The New Nation* (1950). Jack N. Rakove's *The Beginnings of National Politics* (1979) offers a history of the Continental Congress that substantially revises Jensen's work. Especially learned is Gordon S. Wood's massive and brilliant study of the entire period, *The Creation of the American Republic, 1776–1787* (1969), and his equally compelling work, *The Radicalism of the American Revolution* (1991), which documents the egalitarianism that swept revolutionary society during and after the war. For a similar argument that relies on the material culture of the era, see Richard Bushman, *The Refinement of America: Persons, Houses, Cities* (1992). See also Richard B. Morris, *The Forging of the Union, 1781–1787* (1987). An influential transatlantic perspective on the roots of American republicanism is J. G. A. Pocock, *The Machiavellian Moment: Florentine Political Thought and the Atlantic Republican Tradition* (1975). Edmund S. Morgan also looks at both England and America in *Inventing the People: The Rise of Popular Sovereignty in England and America* (1988). On the state constitutions, see Jackson T. Main, *The Sovereign States, 1775–1783* (1973), and Willi P. Adams, *The First American Constitutions* (1980). Peter S. Onuf carefully examines the Northwest Ordinance in *Statehood and Union: A History of the Northwest Ordinance* (1987). On the Constitutional Convention, see Richard Bernstein's superb synthesis of current scholarship, *Are We to Be a Nation? The Making of the Constitution* (1987). Bernstein's work was one of a host of useful studies inspired by the bicentennial of the drafting of the Constitution. Others were Ruth Bloch, *Visionary Republic: Millennial Themes in American Thought, 1756–1800* (1986); Richard Beeman et al., eds., *Beyond Confederation: Origins of the Constitution and American National Identity* (1987); Leonard Levy, *Original Intent and the Framers' Constitution* (1988); and Jack N. Rakove: *Original Meanings: Politics and Ideas in the Making of the Constitution* (1996). For a more general interpretation of the Constitution's role in American society, see Michael G. Kammen, *A Machine That Would Go of Itself* (1986). Robert A. Rutland, *The Ordeal of the Constitution* (1966), describes the ratification struggle. Charles A. Beard shocked conservatives with *An Economic Interpretation of the Constitution of the United States* (1913). It is seriously weakened by two blistering attacks: Robert E. Brown, *Charles Beard and the Constitution* (1956), and Forrest McDonald, *We the People: The Economic Origins of the Constitution* (1958). See also McDonald's *E Pluribus Unum: The Formation of the American Republic, 1776–1790* (1965). Jackson T. Main, *The Anti-Federalists* (1961), partially rehabilitates Beard. Gary Nash's *Race and Revolution* (1990) offers a perceptive study of controversies over race and slavery in the making of the Constitution, as do the contributors to John P. Kaminski, ed., *A Necessary Evil? Slavery and the Debate Over the Constitution* (1995). David Szatmary is perceptive on *Shays's Rebellion* (1980) as are the contributors to Robert Gross, ed., *In Debt to Shays* (1993). On similar episodes of agrarian radicalism, see Alan Taylor, *Liberty Men and Great Proprietors: The Revolutionary Settlement on the Maine Frontier, 1760–1820* (1990). Charles R. Kesler has edited a collection of essays on *The Federalist* papers, *Saving the Revolution: The Federalist Papers and the American Founding* (1987). Also see Morton White, *Philosophy, The Federalist, and the Constitution* (1987). A concise summary of the original federalist-antifederalist debate is Herbert J. Storing, *What the Anti-Federalists Were For* (1981). Relevant biographical studies of merit are John C. Miller, *Alexander Hamilton: Portrait in Paradox* (1959); and Irving Brant, *James Madison* (6 vols., 1941–1961).

10

Slavery in constitution

Launching the New Ship of State
1789–1800

> *I shall only say that I hold with Montesquieu, that a government must be fitted to a nation, as much as a coat to the individual; and, consequently, that what may be good at Philadelphia may be bad at Paris, and ridiculous at Petersburg [Russia].*

ALEXANDER HAMILTON, 1799

A New Ship on an Uncertain Sea

When the Constitution was launched in 1789, the Republic was continuing to grow at an amazing rate. Population was still doubling about every twenty-five years, and the first official census of 1790 recorded almost 4 million people. Cities had blossomed proportionately: Philadelphia numbered 42,000; New York, 33,000; Boston, 18,000; Charleston, 16,000; and Baltimore, 13,000.

America's population was still about 90 percent rural, despite the flourishing cities. All but 5 percent of the people lived east of the Appalachian moun-

tains. The trans-Appalachian overflow was concentrated chiefly in Kentucky, Tennessee, and Ohio, all of which were welcomed as states within fourteen years. (Vermont had preceded them, becoming the fourteenth state in 1791.) Foreign visitors to the new republic looked down their noses at the roughness and crudity resulting from ax-and-rifle pioneering life. Many observers wondered if the infant United States would ever grow to maturity.

The new ship of state did not spread its sails to the most favorable breezes. Within twelve troubled years the American people had risen up and thrown overboard both the British yoke and the Articles of Confederation. A decade of constitution smashing and law breaking was not the best training for

The French statesman Anne Robert Jacques Turgot (1727–1781) had high expectations for a united America:

"This people is the hope of the human race. . . . The Americans should be an example of political, religious, commercial and industrial liberty. . . . But to obtain these ends for us, America . . . must not become . . . a mass of divided powers, contending for territory and trade."

Washington Honored
This idealized portrait symbolized the reverential awe in which Americans held "the father of the country."

government making. Americans had come to regard a central authority, replacing that of George III, as a necessary evil—something to be distrusted, watched, and curbed.

People of the western waters—in the stump-studded clearings of Kentucky, Tennessee, and Ohio—were restive and dubiously loyal. The mouth of the Mississippi, their life-giving outlet, lay in the hands of unfriendly Spaniards. Slippery Spanish and British agents, jingling gold, moved freely among the settlers and held out seductive promises of independence.

Finances of the infant government were likewise precarious. The revenue had declined to a trickle, whereas the public debt, with interest heavily in arrears, was mountainous. Worthless paper money, both state and national, was as plentiful as metallic money was scarce.

The Americans, moreover, were brashly trying to erect a republic on an immense scale, something that no other people had attempted and that traditional political theory held to be impossible. The eyes of a skeptical world were on the upstart United States, and the bejeweled monarchs of Europe in particular feared that the new republic would provide a dangerous example for their own long-oppressed subjects.

Washington's Profederalist Regime

General Washington, the esteemed war hero, was unanimously drafted as president by the Electoral College in 1789—the only presidential nominee ever to be honored by unanimity. His presence was imposing: 6 feet 2 inches, 175 pounds (1.88 meters, 79.5 kilograms), broad and sloping shoulders, strongly pointed chin, and pockmarks (from smallpox) on nose and cheeks. Much preferring the quiet of Mount Vernon to the turmoil of politics, he was perhaps the only president who did not in some way angle for this exalted office. Balanced rather than brilliant, he commanded his followers by strength of character rather than by the arts of the politician.

Washington's long journey from Mount Vernon to New York City, the temporary capital, was a triumphal procession. He was greeted by roaring cannon, pealing bells, flower-carpeted roads, and singing and shouting citizens. With appropriate ceremony, he solemnly and somewhat nervously took the oath of office on April 30, 1789, on a crowded balcony overlooking Wall Street, which some have regarded as a bad omen.

Washington soon put his stamp on the new government, especially by establishing the cabinet. The Constitution does not mention a cabinet; it merely provides that the president "may require" written opinions of the heads of the executive-branch departments (see Art. II, Sec. II, para. 1). But this system proved so cumbersome, and involved so much homework, that cabinet meetings gradually evolved in the Washington administration.

At first only three full-fledged department heads served under the president: Secretary of State Thomas Jefferson, Secretary of the Treasury Alexander Hamilton, and Secretary of War Henry Knox.

The Bill of Rights

Drawing up a bill of rights headed the list of imperatives facing the new government. Many antifederalists had sharply criticized the Constitution drafted at Philadelphia for its failure to provide guarantees of individual rights such as freedom of religion and trial by jury. Many states had ratified the federal Constitution on the understanding that it would soon be amended to include such guarantees.

Amendments to the Constitution could be proposed in either of two ways—by a new constitutional convention requested by two-thirds of the states or by a two-thirds vote of both houses of Congress. Fearing that a new convention might unravel the narrow federalist victory in the ratification struggle, James Madison determined to draft the amendments himself. He then guided them through Congress, where his intellectual and political skills were quickly making him the leading figure.   *manipulative power*

Adopted by the necessary number of states in 1791, the first ten amendments to the Constitution, popularly known as the Bill of Rights, safeguard some of the most precious of American principles. Among these are protections for freedom of religion, speech, and the press; the right to bear arms and to be tried by a jury; and the right to assemble and petition the government for redress of grievances. The Bill of Rights also prohibits cruel and unusual punishments, and arbitrary government seizure of private property.

To guard against the danger that enumerating such rights might lead to the conclusion that they

Evolution of the Cabinet

Position	Date Established	Comments
Secretary of state	1789	
Secretary of treasury	1789	
Secretary of war	1789	Loses cabinet status, 1947
Attorney general	1789	Not head of Justice Dept. until 1870
Secretary of navy	1798	Loses cabinet status, 1947
Postmaster general	1829	Loses cabinet status, 1970
Secretary of interior	1849	
Secretary of agriculture	1889	
Secretary of commerce and labor	1903	Office divided in 1913
Secretary of commerce	1913	
Secretary of labor	1913	
Secretary of defense	1947	Subordinate to this secretary, without cabinet rank, are secretaries of army, navy, and air force.
Secretary of health, education, and welfare	1953	Office divided in 1979
Secretary of housing and urban development	1965	
Secretary of transportation	1966	
Secretary of energy	1977	
Secretary of health and human services	1979	
Secretary of education	1979	
Secretary of veterans' affairs	1989	

were the only ones protected, Madison inserted the crucial Ninth Amendment. It declares that specifying certain rights "shall not be construed to deny or disparage others retained by the people." In a gesture of reassurance to the states' righters, he included the equally significant Tenth Amendment, which reserves all rights not explicitly delegated or prohibited by the federal Constitution "to the States respectively, or to the people." By preserving a strong central government while specifying protections for minority and individual liberties, Madison's amendments partially swung the federalist pendulum back in an antifederalist direction. (See Amendments I–X, in the Appendix.)

The first Congress also nailed other newly sawed government planks into place. It created effective federal courts under the Judiciary Act of 1789. The act organized the Supreme Court, with a chief justice and five associates, as well as federal district and circuit courts, and established the office of attorney general. New Yorker John Jay, Madison's collaborator on *The Federalist* papers and one of the young Republic's most seasoned diplomats, became the first chief justice of the United States.

Confidence in the Constitution

This late-eighteenth-century printer's cut caught the spirit of optimism and hope that prevailed in the infant Republic.

Hamilton Revives the Corpse of Public Credit

The key figure in the new government was smooth-faced Treasury Secretary Alexander Hamilton, a thirty-four-year-old native of the British West Indies. Hamilton's genius was unquestioned, but critics claimed he loved his adopted country more than he loved his countrymen. Doubts about his character and his loyalty to the republican experiment always swirled about his head. Hamilton regarded himself as a kind of prime minister in Washington's cabinet and on occasion thrust his hands into the affairs of other departments, including that of his archrival, Thomas Jefferson, who served as secretary of state.

A financial wizard, Hamilton set out immediately to correct the economic vexations that had crippled the Articles of Confederation. His plan was to shape the fiscal policies of the administration in such a way as to favor the wealthier groups. They, in turn, would gratefully lend the government monetary and moral support. The new federal regime would thrive, the propertied classes would fatten, and prosperity would trickle down to the masses.

The youthful financier's first objective was to bolster the national credit. Without public confidence in the government, Hamilton could not secure the funds with which to float his risky schemes. He therefore boldly urged Congress to "fund" the entire national debt "at par" and to assume completely the debts incurred by the states during the recent war.

"Funding at par" meant that the federal government would pay off its debts at face value, plus accumulated interest—a then-enormous total of more than $54 million. So many people believed the

> *One of the most eloquent tributes to Hamilton's apparent miracle working came from Daniel Webster (1782–1852) in the Senate (1831):*
>
> "He smote the rock of the national resources, and abundant streams of revenue gushed forth. He touched the dead corpse of public credit, and it sprung upon its feet."

infant Treasury incapable of meeting those obligations that government bonds had depreciated to ten or fifteen cents on the dollar. Yet speculators held fistfuls of them, and when Congress passed Hamilton's measure in 1790, they grabbed for more. Some of them galloped into rural areas ahead of the news, buying for a song the depreciated paper holdings of farmers, war veterans, and widows.

Hamilton was willing, even eager, to have the new government shoulder additional obligations. While pushing the funding scheme, he urged Congress to assume the debts of the states, totaling some $21.5 million.

The secretary made a convincing case for "assumption." The state debts could be regarded as a proper national obligation, for they had been incurred in the war for independence. But foremost in Hamilton's thinking was the belief that assumption would chain the states more tightly to the "federal chariot." Thus the secretary's maneuver would shift the attachment of wealthy creditors from the states to the federal government. The support of the rich for the national administration was a crucial link in Hamilton's political strategy of strengthening the central government.

States burdened with heavy debts, like Massachusetts, were delighted by Hamilton's proposal. States with small debts, like Virginia, were less charmed. The stage was set for some old-fashioned horse trading. Virginia did not want the state debts assumed, but it did want the forthcoming federal district*—now the District of Columbia—to be located on the Potomac River. It would thus gain in commerce and prestige. Hamilton persuaded a reluctant Jefferson, who had recently come home from France, to line up enough votes in Congress for assumption. In return, Virginia would have the federal district on the Potomac. The bargain was carried through in 1790.

Customs Duties and Excise Taxes

The new ship of state thus set sail dangerously overloaded. The national debt had swelled to $75 million owing to Hamilton's insistence on honoring the outstanding federal and state obligations alike. Anyone less determined to establish such a healthy public

---

*Authorized by the Constitution, Art. I, Sec. VIII, para. 17.

Alexander Hamilton (1755–1804), by James Sharples, c. 1796   He was one of the youngest and most brilliant of the Founding Fathers, who might have become president but for his ultraconservatism, a scandalous adultery, and a duelist's bullet.

credit could have sidestepped $13 million in back interest and could have avoided the state debts entirely.

But Hamilton, "Father of the National Debt," was not greatly worried. His objectives were as much political as economic. He believed that within limits, a national debt was a "national blessing"—a kind of union adhesive. The more creditors to whom the government owed money, the more people there would be with a personal stake in the success of his ambitious enterprise. His unique contribution was to make a debt—ordinarily a liability—an asset for vitalizing the financial system as well as the government itself.

Where was the money to come from to pay interest on this huge debt and run the government? Hamilton's first answer was customs duties, derived from a tariff. Tariff revenues, in turn, depended on a vigorous foreign trade, another crucial link in Hamilton's overall economic strategy for the new Republic.

The first tariff law, imposing a low tariff of about 8 percent on the value of dutiable imports, was

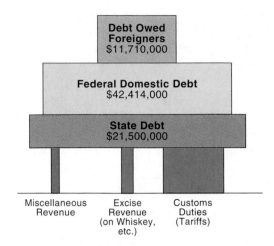

Hamilton's Financial Structure Supported by Revenues

speedily passed by the first Congress in 1789, even before Hamilton was sworn in. Revenue was by far the main goal, but the measure was also designed to erect a low protective wall around infant industries, which bawled noisily for more shelter than they received. Hamilton had the vision to see that the Industrial Revolution would soon reach America, and he argued strongly in favor of more protection for the well-to-do manufacturing groups—another vital element in his economic program. But Congress was still dominated by the agricultural and commercial interests, and it voted only two slight increases in the tariff during Washington's presidency.

Hamilton, with characteristic vigor, sought additional internal revenue and in 1791 secured from Congress an excise tax on a few domestic items, notably whiskey. The new levy of seven cents a gallon was borne chiefly by the distillers who lived in the backcountry, where the wretched roads forced the farmer to reduce (and liquify) bulky bushels of grain to horseback proportions. Whiskey flowed so freely on the frontier in the form of distilled liquor that it was used for money.

Hamilton Battles Jefferson for a Bank

As the capstone for his financial system, Hamilton proposed a Bank of the United States. An enthusiastic admirer of most things English, he took as his model the Bank of England. Specifically, he pro-

posed a powerful private institution, of which the government would be the major stockholder and in which the federal Treasury would deposit its surplus monies. The central government not only would have a convenient strongbox, but federal funds would stimulate business by remaining in circulation. The bank would also print urgently needed paper money and thus provide a sound and stable national currency, badly needed since the days when the Continental dollar was "not worth a Continental." The proposed bank would indeed be useful. But was it constitutional?

Jefferson, whose written opinion on this question Washington requested, argued vehemently against the bank. There was, he insisted, no specific authorization in the Constitution for such a financial octopus. He was convinced that all powers not specifically granted to the central government were reserved to the states, as provided in the about-to-be-ratified Bill of Rights (see Amendment X). He therefore concluded that the states, not Congress, had the power to charter banks. Believing that the Constitution should be interpreted "literally" or "strictly," Jefferson and his states' rights disciples zealously embraced the theory of "strict construction."

Hamilton, also at Washington's request, prepared a brilliantly reasoned reply to Jefferson's arguments. Hamilton in general believed that what the Constitution did not forbid it permitted; Jefferson, in contrast, generally believed that what it did not permit it forbade. Hamilton boldly invoked the clause of the Constitution that stipulates that Congress may pass any laws "necessary and proper" to carry out the powers vested in the various government agencies (see Art. I, Sec. VIII, para. 18). The government was explicitly empowered to collect taxes and regulate trade. In carrying out these basic functions, Hamilton argued, a national bank would be not only "proper" but "necessary." By inference or implication—that is, by virtue of "implied powers"—Congress would be fully justified in establishing the Bank of the United States. In short, Hamilton contended for a "loose" or "broad" interpretation of the Constitution. He and his federalist followers thus evolved the theory of "loose construction" by invoking the "elastic clause" of the Constitution—a precedent for enormous federal powers.

Hamilton's financial views prevailed. His eloquent and realistic arguments were accepted by Washington, who reluctantly signed the bank measure into law. This explosive issue had been debated with much heat in Congress, where the old North-South cleavage still lurked ominously. The most enthusiastic support for the bank naturally came from the commercial and financial centers of the North, whereas the strongest opposition arose from the agricultural South.

The Bank of the United States, as created by Congress in 1791, was chartered for twenty years. Located in Philadelphia, it was to have a capital of $10 million, one-fifth of it owned by the federal government. Stock was thrown open to public sale. To the agreeable surprise of Hamilton, a milling crowd oversubscribed in less than two hours, pushing aside many would-be purchasers.

Mutinous Moonshiners in Pennsylvania

The Whiskey Rebellion, which flared up in southwestern Pennsylvania in 1794, sharply challenged the new national government. Hamilton's high excise tax bore harshly on these homespun pioneer folk. They regarded it not as a tax on a frivolous luxury but as a burden on an economic necessity and a medium of exchange. Even preachers of the gospel were paid in "Old Monongahela rye." Rye and corn crops distilled into alcohol were more cheaply transported to Eastern markets than bales of grain. Defiant distillers finally erected whiskey poles, similar to the liberty poles of anti–stamp tax days in 1765, and raised the cry "Liberty and No Excise." Boldly tarring and feathering revenue officers, they brought collections to a halt.

President Washington, once a revolutionist, was alarmed by what he called these "self-created societies." With the hearty encouragement of Hamilton, he summoned the militia of several states. Anxious moments followed the call, for there was much doubt as to whether men in other states would muster to crush a rebellion in a sister state. Despite some opposition, an army of about thirteen thousand rallied to the colors, and two widely separated columns marched briskly forth in a gorgeous, leaf-tinted Indian summer, until knee-deep mud slowed their progress.

When the troops reached the hills of western Pennsylvania, they found no insurrection. The "Whiskey Boys" were overawed, dispersed, or cap-

Attorney Hugh Henry Brackenridge (1748–1816) mediated between the Whiskey Rebels and the town of Pittsburgh. He later wrote of the hated excise tax:

"I saw the operation to be unequal in this country. . . . It is true that the excise paid by the country would be that only on spirits consumed in it. But even in the case of exports, the excise must be advanced in the first instance by the distiller and this would prevent effectually all the poorer part from carrying on the business. I . . . would have preferred a direct tax with a view to reach unsettled lands which all around us have been purchased by speculating men."

tured. Washington, with an eye to healing old sores, pardoned the two small-fry convicted culprits.

The Whiskey Rebellion was minuscule—some three rebels were killed—but its consequences were mighty. George Washington's government, now substantially strengthened, commanded a new respect. Yet the numerous foes of the federalists condemned the administration for its brutal display of force—for having used a sledgehammer to crush a gnat.

The Emergence of Political Parties

Almost overnight, Hamilton's fiscal feats had established the government's sound credit rating. The Treasury could now borrow needed funds in the Netherlands on favorable terms.

But Hamilton's financial successes—funding, assumption, the excise tax, the bank, the suppression of the Whiskey Rebellion—created some political liabilities. All these schemes encroached sharply upon states' rights. Many Americans, dubious about the new Constitution in the first place, might never have approved it if they had foreseen how the states were going to be overshadowed by the federal colossus. Now, out of resentment against Hamilton's revenue-raising and centralizing policies, an organized opposition began to build. What once was a personal feud between Hamilton and Jefferson

Evolution of Major Parties*

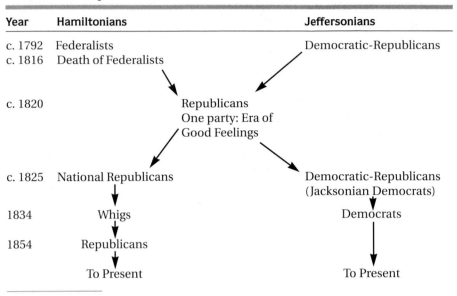

Year	Hamiltonians	Jeffersonians
c. 1792	Federalists	Democratic-Republicans
c. 1816	Death of Federalists	
c. 1820		Republicans One party: Era of Good Feelings
c. 1825	National Republicans	Democratic-Republicans (Jacksonian Democrats)
1834	Whigs	Democrats
1854	Republicans	
	To Present	To Present

*See Appendix (Presidential Elections) for third parties.

developed into a full-blown and frequently bitter political rivalry.

National political parties, in the modern sense, were unknown in America when George Washington took his inaugural oath. There had been Whigs and Tories, federalists and antifederalists, but these groups were factions rather than parties. They had sprung into existence over hotly contested special issues; they had faded away when their cause had triumphed or fizzled.

The Founders at Philadelphia had not envisioned the existence of permanent political parties. Organized opposition to the government—especially a democratic government based on popular consent—seemed tainted with disloyalty. Opposition to the government affronted the spirit of national unity that the glorious cause of the Revolution had inspired. The notion of a formal party apparatus was thus a novelty in the 1790s, and when Jefferson and Madison first organized their opposition to the Hamiltonian program, they confined their activities to Congress and did not anticipate creating a long-lived and popular party. But as their antagonism to Hamilton stiffened, and as the amazingly boisterous and widely read newspapers of the day spread their political message, and Hamilton's, among the people, primitive semblances of political parties began to emerge.

Republicanism Triumphant
Artists often used classical motifs to celebrate the triumph in America of republicanism—a form of government they traced back to ancient Greece and Rome.

The two-party system has existed in the United States since that time (see table at left). Ironically, in light of early suspicions about the very legitimacy of parties, their competition for power has actually proved to be among the indispensable ingredients of a sound democracy. The party out of power—"the loyal opposition"—traditionally plays the invaluable role of the balance wheel on the machinery of government, ensuring that politics never drifts too far out of kilter with the wishes of the people.

The Impact of the French Revolution

When Washington's first administration ended, early in 1793, Hamilton's domestic policies had already stimulated the formation of two political camps—Jeffersonian Democratic-Republicans and Hamiltonian Federalists. As Washington's second term began, foreign-policy issues brought the differences between them to a fever pitch.

Only a few weeks after Washington's inauguration in 1789, the curtain had risen on the first act of the French Revolution. Twenty-six years were to pass before the seething continent of Europe collapsed into a peace of exhaustion. Few non-American events have left a deeper scar on American political and social life. In a sense the French Revolution was misnamed: it was a *world* revolution that touched all civilized peoples.

In its early stages the upheaval was surprisingly peaceful, involving as it did a successful attempt to impose constitutional shackles on Louis XVI. The American people, loving liberty and deploring despotism, cheered. They were flattered to think that the outburst in France was but the second

English political observer William Cobbett (1763–1835) wrote of the frenzied reaction in America to the death of Louis XVI:

"Never was the memory of a man so cruelly insulted as that of this mild and humane monarch. He was guillotined in effigy, in the capital of the Union [Philadelphia], twenty or thirty times every day, during one whole winter and part of the summer. Men, women and children flocked to the tragical exhibition, and not a single paragraph appeared in the papers to shame them from it."

chapter of their own glorious Revolution, as to some extent it was. Only a few ultraconservative Federalists—fearing change, reform, and "leveling" principles—were from the outset dubious or outspokenly hostile to the "despicable mobocracy." The more ardent Jeffersonians were overjoyed.

The French Revolution entered a more ominous phase in 1792, when France declared war on hostile Austria. Powerful ideals and powerful armies alike were on the march. Late in that year the electrifying news reached America that French citizen armies had hurled back the invading foreigners and that France had proclaimed itself a republic. Americans enthusiastically sang "The Marseillaise" and other rousing French Revolutionary songs and they renamed thoroughfares with democratic flare. King Street in New York, for example, became Liberty Street, and in Boston, Royal Exchange Alley became Equality Lane.

The Contrast
Adaptation of an English cartoon that makes the former colonies' struggle for independence look virtuous compared to the French Revolution.

But centuries of pent-up poison could not be purged without baleful results. The guillotine was set up, the king was beheaded in 1793, the Church was attacked, and the head-rolling Reign of Terror was begun. Back in America, God-fearing Federalist aristocrats nervously fingered their tender white necks and eyed the Jeffersonian masses apprehensively. Lukewarm Federalist approval of the early Revolution turned, almost overnight, to heated opposition to "blood-drinking cannibals."

Sober-minded Jeffersonians regretted the bloodshed. But they felt, with Jefferson, that one could not expect to be carried from "despotism to liberty in a feather bed" and that a few thousand aristocratic heads were a cheap price to pay for human freedom.

Such gloating was shortsighted, for dire peril loomed ahead. The earlier battles of the French Revolution had not hurt America directly, but now Britain was sucked into the contagious conflict. The conflagration speedily spread to the New World, where it vividly affected the expanding young American Republic. Thus was repeated the familiar story of every major European war, beginning with 1689, that involved a watery duel for control of the Atlantic Ocean. (See the table on p. 110.)

Washington's Neutrality Proclamation

Ominously, the Franco-American alliance of 1778 was still on the books. By its own terms it was to last "forever." It bound the United States to help the French defend their West Indies against future foes; and the booming British fleets were certain to attack these strategic islands.

Many Jeffersonian Democratic-Republicans favored honoring the alliance. Aflame with the liberal ideals of the French Revolution, red-blooded Jeffersonians were eager to enter the conflict against Britain, the recent foe, at the side of France, the recent friend. America owed France its freedom, they argued, and now was the time to pay the debt of gratitude.

But President Washington, levelheaded as usual, was not swayed by the clamor of the crowd. Backed by Hamilton, he perceived that war had to be avoided at all costs. Washington was coolly playing for enormous stakes. The nation in 1793 was militarily weak, economically wobbly, and politically disunited. But solid foundations were being laid, and American cradles were continuing to rock a bumper crop of babies. Washington wisely reasoned that if America could avoid the broils of Europe for a generation or so, it would then be populous enough and powerful enough to assert its maritime rights with strength and success. Otherwise, it might invite catastrophe. The strategy of delay—of playing for time while the birthrate fought America's battles—was a cardinal policy of the Founding Fathers. Hamilton and Jefferson, often poles apart on other issues, were in agreement here.

Accordingly, Washington boldly issued his Neutrality Proclamation in 1793, shortly after the outbreak of war between Britain and France. This epochal document not only proclaimed the government's official neutrality in the widening conflict but sternly warned American citizens to be impartial toward both armed camps. As America's first formal declaration of aloofness from Old World quarrels, Washington's Neutrality Proclamation proved to be a major prop of the spreading isolationist tradition. It also proved to be enormously controversial. The pro-French Jeffersonians were enraged by the Neutrality Proclamation, especially by Washington's method of announcing it unilaterally, without consulting Congress. The pro-British Federalists were heartened.

Debate soon intensified. An impetuous, thirty-year-old representative of the French Republic, Citizen Edmond Genêt, had landed at Charleston, South Carolina. With unrestrained zeal he undertook to fit out privateers and otherwise take advantage of the existing Franco-American alliance. The giddy-headed envoy—all sail and no anchor—was soon swept away by his enthusiastic reception by the Jeffersonian Republicans. He foolishly came to believe that the Neutrality Proclamation did not reflect the true wishes of the American people, and he consequently embarked upon unneutral activity not authorized by the French alliance—including the recruitment of armies to invade Spanish Florida and Louisiana, as well as British Canada. Even Madison and Jefferson were soon disillusioned by his conduct. After he had threatened to appeal over the head of "Old Washington" to the sovereign voters, the president demanded Genêt's withdrawal and the Frenchman was replaced by a less impulsive emissary.

Washington's Neutrality Proclamation clearly illustrates the truism that self-interest is the basic cement of alliances. In 1778 both France and America stood to gain; in 1793 only France. Technically, the Americans did not flout their obligation because France never officially called upon them to honor it. American neutrality in fact favored France. The French West Indian Islands urgently needed Yankee foodstuffs. If the Americans had entered the war at France's side, the British fleets would have blockaded the American coast and cut off those essential supplies. America was thus much more useful to France as a reliable neutral provider than as a blockaded partner in arms.

Embroilments with Britain

President Washington's far-visioned policy of neutrality was sorely tried by the British. For ten long years they had been retaining the chain of northern frontier posts on U.S. soil, all in defiance of the peace treaty of 1783. The London government was reluctant to abandon the lucrative fur trade in the Great Lakes region and also hoped to build up an Indian buffer state to contain the ambitious Americans. British agents openly sold firearms and firewater to the Indians, who continued to attack pioneers invading their lands. When General "Mad Anthony" Wayne crushed the northwest Indians at the Battle of Fallen Timbers on August 20, 1794, the fleeing foe left on the field British-made arms, as well as the corpses of a few British-Canadians. In

American Posts Held by the British After 1783

the Treaty of Greenville in 1795, the Indians, finally abandoned by their red-coated friends, ceded their claims to a vast virgin tract in the Ohio country.

On the sea frontier, the British were eager to starve out the French West Indies and naturally expected the United States to defend them under the Franco-American alliance. Hard-boiled commanders of the Royal Navy, ignoring America's rights as a neutral, struck savagely. They seized about three hundred American merchant ships in the West Indies, impressed scores of seamen into service on English vessels, and threw hundreds of others into foul dungeons.

These actions incensed patriotic Americans. A mighty outcry arose, chiefly from Jeffersonians, that America should once again fight George III in defense of its liberties. At the very least, it should cut off all supplies to its oppressor through a nationwide embargo. But the Federalists stoutly resisted all demands for drastic action. War with Britain would be a lethal blow at the heart of the Hamiltonian financial system.

Jay's Treaty and Washington's Farewell

President Washington, in a last desperate gamble to avert war, decided to send Chief Justice John Jay to London in 1794. The Jeffersonians were acutely unhappy over the choice, partly because they feared that so notorious a Federalist and Anglophile would sell out his country. Arriving in London, Jay gave the Jeffersonians further cause for alarm when, at the presentation ceremony, he routinely kissed the queen's hand.

Unhappily, Jay entered the negotiations with weak cards, which were further sabotaged by Hamilton. The latter, fearful of war with England, secretly supplied the British with the details of America's bargaining strategy. Not surprisingly, Jay won few concessions. The British did promise to evacuate the chain of posts on U.S. soil—a pledge that inspired little confidence, since it had been made before in Paris (to the same John Jay!) in 1783. In addition, Britain consented to pay damages for the recent seizures of American ships. But the British stopped short of pledging anything about *future* maritime seizures and impressments or about supplying arms to Indians. And they forced

Thomas Paine (1737–1809), then in France and resenting George Washington's anti-French policies, addressed the president in an open letter (1796) that reveals his bitterness:

"And as to you, sir, treacherous in private friendship (for so you have been to me, and that in the day of danger) and a hypocrite in public life, the world will be puzzled to decide, whether you are an apostate or an imposter; whether you have abandoned good principles, or whether you ever had any."

Jay to give ground by binding the United States to pay the debts still owed to British merchants on pre-Revolutionary accounts.

When the Jeffersonians learned of Jay's concessions, their rage was fearful to behold. The treaty seemed like an abject surrender to Britain, as well as a betrayal of the Jeffersonian South. Southern planters would have to pay the major share of the pre-Revolutionary debts, while rich Federalist shippers were collecting damages for recent British seizures. Jeffersonian mobs hanged, burned, and guillotined in effigy that "damn'd archtraitor, Sir John Jay." His unpopular pact, more than any other issue, vitalized the newborn Democratic-Republican party of Thomas Jefferson. Even George Washington's huge popularity was compromised by the controversy over the treaty.

Jay's Treaty had other unforeseen consequences. Fearing that the treaty foreshadowed an Anglo-American alliance, Spain moved hastily to strike a deal with the United States. Pinckney's Treaty of 1795 with Spain granted the Americans virtually everything they demanded, including free navigation of the Mississippi and the large disputed territory north of Florida. (See the map on p. 175.)

Exhausted after the diplomatic and partisan battles of his second term, President Washington decided to retire. His choice contributed powerfully to establishing a two-term tradition for American presidents.* In his Farewell Address to the nation in 1796 (never delivered orally but printed in the news-

---

*Not broken until 1940 by Franklin D. Roosevelt and made a part of the Constitution in 1951 by the Twenty-second Amendment.

papers), Washington strongly advised the avoidance of "permanent alliances" like the still-vexatious French Treaty of 1778. Contrary to general misunderstanding, Washington did not oppose all alliances, but favored only "temporary alliances" for "extraordinary emergencies." This was admirable advice for a weak and divided nation in 1796. But what is sound counsel for a young stripling may not apply later to a mature and muscular giant.

Washington's contributions as president were enormous, even though the sparkling Hamilton at times seemed to outshine him. The central government, its fiscal feet now under it, was solidly established. The West was expanding. The merchant marine was plowing the seas. Above all, Washington had kept the nation out of both overseas entanglements and foreign wars. The experimental stage had passed, and the presidential chair could now be turned over to a less impressive figure. But republics are notoriously ungrateful. When Washington left office in 1797, he was showered with the brickbats of partisan abuse, quite in contrast with the bouquets that had greeted his arrival.

"Bonny Johnny" Adams Becomes President

Who should succeed the exalted "Father of His Country"? Alexander Hamilton was the best-known member of the Federalist party, now that Washington had bowed out. But his financial policies, some of which had fattened the speculators, had made him so unpopular that he could not hope to be elected president. The Federalists were forced to turn to Washington's vice president, the experienced but ungracious John Adams, a rugged chip off old Plymouth Rock. The Democratic-Republicans naturally rallied behind their master organizer and leader, Thomas Jefferson.

Political passions ran feverishly high in the presidential campaign of 1796. The lofty presence of Washington had hitherto imposed some restraints; now the lid was off. Cultured Federalists like Fisher Ames referred to the Jeffersonians as "fire-eating salamanders, poison-sucking toads." Federalists and Democrat-Republicans even drank their ale in separate taverns. The issues of the campaign, as it turned out, focused heavily on personalities. But the Jeffersonians again assailed the too-forceful

John Adams, by John Singleton Copley, 1783
When he entered Harvard College in 1751, Adams intended to prepare for the ministry, but four absorbing years of study excited him about other intellectual and career possibilities. "I was a mighty metaphysician, at least I thought myself such." Adams also tried his hand at being a mighty scientist, doctor, and orator. Upon graduation, he became a schoolmaster, but soon decided to take up the law.

Thomas Jefferson (1743–1826) wrote privately of John Adams in 1787:

"He is vain, irritable, and a bad calculator of the force and probable effect of the motives which govern men. This is all the ill which can possibly be said of him. He is as disinterested as the Being who made him."

ablest statesmen of his day, Adams at sixty-two was a stuffy figure. Sharp-featured, bald, relatively short (5 feet 7 inches; 1.7 meters), and thickset ("His Rotundity"), he impressed observers as a man of stern principles who did his duty with stubborn devotion. Although learned and upright, he was a tactless and prickly intellectual aristocrat, with no appeal to the masses and with no desire to cultivate any. Many citizens regarded him with "respectful irritation."

The crusty New Englander suffered from other handicaps. He had stepped into Washington's shoes, which no successor could hope to fill. In addition, Adams was hated by Hamilton, who had resigned from the Treasury in 1795 and who now headed the war faction of the Federalist party, known as the "High Federalists." The famed financier even secretly plotted with certain members of the cabinet against the president, who had a conspiracy rather than a cabinet on his hands. Adams regarded Hamilton as "the most ruthless, impatient, artful, indefatigable and unprincipled intriguer in the United States, if not in the world." Most ominous of all, Adams inherited a violent quarrel with France—a quarrel whose gunpowder lacked only a spark.

crushing of the Whiskey Rebellion and, above all, the negotiation of Jay's hated treaty.

John Adams, with most of his support in New England, squeezed through by the narrow margin of 71 votes to 68 in the Electoral College. Jefferson, as runner-up, became vice president.* One of the

---

*The possibility of such an inharmonious two-party combination in the future was removed by the Twelfth Amendment to the Constitution in 1804. (See text in the Appendix.)

Unofficial Fighting with France

The French were infuriated by Jay's Treaty. They condemned it as the initial step toward an alliance with England, their perpetual foe. They further assailed the pact as a flagrant violation of the Franco-American Treaty of 1778. French warships, in retaliation, began to seize defenseless American

merchant vessels, altogether about three hundred by mid-1797. Adding insult to outrage, the Paris regime haughtily refused to receive America's newly appointed envoy and even threatened him with arrest.

President Adams kept his head, temporarily, even though the nation was mightily aroused. True to Washington's policy of steering clear of war at all costs, he tried again to reach an agreement with the French and appointed a diplomatic commission of three men, including John Marshall, the future chief justice.

Adams's envoys, reaching Paris in 1797, hoped to meet Talleyrand, the crafty French foreign minister. They were secretly approached by three go-betweens, later referred to as X, Y, and Z in the published dispatches. The French spokesmen, among other concessions, demanded an unneutral loan of 32 million florins, plus what amounted to a bribe of $250,000, for the privilege of merely talking with Talleyrand.

These terms were intolerable. The American trio knew that bribes were standard diplomatic devices in Europe, but they gagged at paying a quarter of a million dollars for mere talk, without any assurances of a settlement. Negotiations quickly broke down, and John Marshall, on reaching New York in 1798, was hailed as a conquering hero for his steadfastness.

War hysteria swept through the United States, catching up even President Adams. The slogan of the hour became "Millions for defense, but not one cent for tribute." The Federalists were delighted at this unexpected turn of affairs, whereas all except the most rabid Jeffersonians hung their heads in shame over the misbehavior of their French friends.

War preparations in the United States were pushed along at a feverish pace, despite considerable Jeffersonian opposition in Congress. The Navy Department was created; the three-ship navy was expanded; the United States Marine Corps was established. A new army of ten thousand men was authorized (but was never fully raised).

Bloodshed was confined to the sea, and principally to the West Indies. In two-and-one-half years of undeclared hostilities (1798–1800), American privateers and men-of-war of the new navy captured over eighty armed vessels flying the French colors, though several hundred Yankee merchant ships were lost to the enemy. Evidently only a slight push would plunge both nations into a full-dress war.

The XYZ Affair   When President Adams's envoys to Paris were asked to pay a huge bribe as the price of doing diplomatic business, humiliated Americans rose up in wrath against France. Here an innocent young America is being plundered by Frenchmen as John Bull looks on in amusement from across the English Channel.

Preparation for War to Defend Commerce
The building of the frigate *Philadelphia*. In 1803 this frigate ran onto the rocks near Tripoli harbor, and about three hundred officers and men were imprisoned by the Tripolitans. The ship was refloated for service against the Americans, but Stephen Decatur led a party of men that set it afire.

Adams Puts Patriotism Above Party

Embattled France, its hands full in Europe, wanted no war. An outwitted Talleyrand realized that to fight the United States would merely add one more foe to his enemy roster. The British, who were lending the Americans cannon and other war supplies, were actually driven closer to their wayward cousins than they were to be again for many years. Talleyrand therefore let it be known, through roundabout channels, that if the Americans would send a new minister, he would be received with proper respect.

This French furor brought to Adams a degree of personal acclaim that he had never known before—and was never to know again. He doubtless perceived that a full-fledged war, crowned by the conquest of the Floridas and Louisiana, would bring new plaudits to the Federalist party—and perhaps a second term to himself. But the heady wine of popularity did not sway his final judgment. He, like other Founding Fathers, realized full well that war must be avoided while the country was relatively weak.

Adams unexpectedly exploded a bombshell when, early in 1799, he submitted to the Senate the name of a new minister to France. Hamilton and his war-hawk faction were enraged. But public opinion—Jeffersonian and reasonable Federalist alike—was favorable to one last try for peace.

America's envoys (now three) found the political skies brightening when they reached Paris early in 1800. The ambitious "Little Corporal," the Corsican Napoleon Bonaparte, had recently seized dictatorial power. He was eager to free his hands of the American squabble so that he might continue to redraw the map of Europe and perhaps create a New World empire in Louisiana. The afflictions and ambitions of the Old World were again working to America's advantage.

After a great deal of haggling, a memorable treaty known as the Convention of 1800 was signed

The firmness of President John Adams (1735–1826) was revealed in his message to Congress (June 1798):

"I will never send another minister to France without assurances that he will be received, respected, and honored as the representative of a great, free, powerful, and independent nation."

in Paris. France agreed to annul the twenty-two-year-old marriage of (in)convenience, but as a kind of alimony the United States agreed to pay the damage claims of American shippers. So ended the nation's only peacetime military alliance for a century and a half. Its troubled history does much to explain the traditional antipathy of the American people to foreign entanglements.

John Adams, flinty to the end, deserves immense credit for his belated push for peace, even though he was moved in part by jealousy of Hamilton. Adams not only avoided the hazards of war, but also unwittingly smoothed the path for the peaceful purchase of Louisiana three years later. He should indeed rank high among the forgotten purchasers of this vast domain. If America had drifted into a full-blown war with France in 1800, Napoleon would not have sold Louisiana to Jefferson on any terms in 1803.

President Adams, the bubble of his popularity pricked by peace, was aware of his signal contribution to the nation. He later suggested as the epitaph for his tombstone (not used), "Here lies John Adams, who took upon himself the responsibility of peace with France in the year 1800."

The Federalist Witch Hunt

Exulting Federalists had meanwhile capitalized on the anti-French frenzy to drive through Congress in 1798 a sheaf of laws designed to muffle or minimize their Jeffersonian foes.

The first of these oppressive laws was aimed at supposedly pro-Jeffersonian "aliens." Most European immigrants, lacking wealth, were scorned by the aristocratic Federalist party. But they were welcomed as voters by the less prosperous and more democratic Jeffersonians. The Federalist Congress, hoping to discourage the "dregs" of Europe, erected a disheartening barrier. They raised the residence requirements for aliens who desired to become citizens from a tolerable five years to an intolerable fourteen. This drastic new law violated the traditional American policy of open-door hospitality and speedy assimilation.

Two additional Alien Laws struck heavily at undesirable immigrants. The president was empowered to deport dangerous foreigners in time of

peace and to deport or imprison them in time of hostilities. Though defensible as a war measure—and an officially declared war with France seemed imminent—this was an arbitrary grant of power contrary to American tradition and to the spirit of the Constitution, even though the stringent Alien Laws were never enforced.

The "lockjaw" Sedition Act, the last measure of the Federalist clampdown, was a direct slap at two priceless freedoms guaranteed in the Constitution by the Bill of Rights—freedom of speech and freedom of the press (First Amendment). This law provided that anyone who impeded the policies of the government or falsely defamed its officials, including the president, would be liable to a heavy fine and imprisonment. Severe though the measure was, the Federalists believed that it was justified. The verbal violence of the day was unrestrained, and foul-penned editors, some of them exiled aliens, vilified Adams's anti-French policy in vicious terms.

Many outspoken Jeffersonian editors were indicted under the Sedition Act, and ten were brought to trial. All of them were convicted, often by packed juries swayed by prejudiced Federalist judges. Some of the victims were harmless partisans, who should have been spared the notoriety of martyrdom. Among them was Congressman

In 1800 James Callender (1758–1803) published a pamphlet that assailed the president in strong language. For blasts like the following tirade, Callender was prosecuted under the Sedition Act, fined $250, and sentenced to prison for nine months.

"The reign of Mr. Adams has, hitherto, been one continued tempest of *malignant* passions. As president, he has never opened his lips, or lifted his pen, without threatening and scolding. The grand object of his administration has been to exasperate the rage of contending parties, to calumniate and destroy every man who differs from his opinions. . . . Every person holding an office must either quit it, or think and vote exactly with Mr. Adams."

Congressional Pugilists
Satirical representation of Matthew Lyon's fight in Congress with the Federalist representative Roger Griswold.

Matthew Lyon (the "Spitting Lion"), who had earlier gained fame by spitting in the face of a Federalist. He was sentenced to four months in jail for writing of President Adams's "unbounded thirst for ridiculous pomp, foolish adulation, and selfish avarice." Another culprit was lucky to get off with a fine of $100 after he had expressed the wish that the wad of a cannon fired in honor of Adams had landed in the seat of the president's breeches.

The Sedition Act was in direct conflict with the Constitution. But the Supreme Court, dominated by Federalists, was of no mind to declare this Federalist law unconstitutional. (The Federalists intentionally wrote the law to expire in 1801, so that it could not be used against them if they lost the next election.) This attempt by the Federalists to crush free speech and silence the opposition party, high-handed as it was, undoubtedly made many converts for the Jeffersonians.

Yet the Alien and Sedition Acts, despite pained outcries from the Jeffersonians they muzzled, commanded widespread popular support. Anti-French hysteria played directly into the hands of witch-hunting conservatives. In the congressional elections of 1798–1799, the Federalists, riding a wave of popularity, scored the most sweeping victory of their entire history.

The Virginia (Madison) and Kentucky (Jefferson) Resolutions

Resentful Jeffersonians naturally refused to take the Alien and Sedition Laws lying down. Jefferson himself feared that if the Federalists managed to choke free speech and free press, they would then wipe out other precious constitutional guarantees. His own fledgling political party might even be stamped out of existence. If this had happened, the country might have slid into a dangerous one-party dictatorship.

Fearing prosecution for sedition, Jefferson secretly penned a series of resolutions, which the Kentucky legislature approved in 1798 and 1799. His friend and fellow Virginian James Madison drafted a similar but less extreme statement, which was adopted by the legislature of Virginia in 1798.

Both Jefferson and Madison stressed the compact theory—a theory popular among English political philosophers in the seventeenth and eighteenth centuries. As applied to America by the Jeffersonians, this concept meant that the thirteen sovereign states, in creating the federal government, had entered into a "compact," or contract, regarding its jurisdiction. The national government was consequently the agent or creation of the states. Since water can rise no higher than its source, the individual states were the final judges of whether their agent had broken the "compact" by overstepping the authority originally granted. Invoking this logic, Jefferson's Kentucky resolutions concluded that the federal regime *had* exceeded its constitutional powers and that with regard to the Alien and Sedition Acts "nullification"—a refusal to accept them—was the "rightful remedy."

No other state legislatures, despite Jefferson's hopes, fell into line. Some of them flatly refused to endorse the Virginia and Kentucky resolutions. Others, chiefly in Federalist states, added ringing condemnations. Many Federalists argued that the people, not the states, had made the original compact, and that it was up to the Supreme Court—not the states—to nullify unconstitutional legislation passed by Congress. This practice, though not specifically authorized by the Constitution, was finally adopted by the Supreme Court in 1803 (see p. 216).

The Virginia and Kentucky resolutions were a brilliant formulation of the extreme states' rights view regarding the Union. They were later used by southerners to support nullification—and ultimately secession. Yet neither Jefferson nor Madison, as Founding Fathers of the Union, had any intention of breaking it up: they were groping for ways to preserve it. Their resolutions were basically campaign documents designed to crystallize opposition to the Federalist party and to unseat it in the upcoming presidential election of 1800. The only real nullification that Jefferson had in view was the nullification of Federalist abuses.

Federalists versus Democratic-Republicans

As the presidential contest of 1800 approached, the differences between Federalists and Democratic-Republicans were sharply etched (see table below). As might be expected, most federalists of the pre-Constitution period (1787–1789) became Federalists in the 1790s. Largely welded by Hamilton into an effective group by 1793, they openly advocated rule by the "best people." "Those who own the country," remarked Federalist John Jay, "ought to govern it." With their intellectual arrogance and Tory tastes, Hamiltonians distrusted full-blown democracy as the fountain of all mischiefs and feared the "swayability" of the untutored common folk.

Hamiltonian Federalists also advocated a strong central government with the power to crush democratic excesses like Shays's Rebellion, protect the lives and estates of the wealthy, and subordinate the sovereignty-loving states. They believed that government should support private enterprise, not interfere with it. This attitude came naturally to the merchants, manufacturers, and shippers along the Atlantic seaboard, who made up the majority of

The Two Political Parties, 1793–1800

Federalist Features	Democratic-Republican (Jeffersonian) Features
Rule by the "best people"	Rule by the informed masses
Hostility to extension of democracy	Friendliness toward extension of democracy
A powerful central government at the expense of states' rights	A weak central government so as to conserve states' rights
Loose interpretation of Constitution	Strict interpretation of Constitution
Government to foster business; concentration of wealth in interests of capitalistic enterprise	No special favors for business; agriculture preferred
A protective tariff	No special favors for manufacturers
Pro-British (conservative Tory tradition)	Pro-French (radical Revolutionary tradition)
National debt a blessing, if properly funded	National debt a bane; rigid economy
An expanding bureaucracy	Reduction of federal officeholders
A powerful central bank	Encouragement to state banks
Restrictions on free speech and press	Relatively free speech and press
Concentration in seacoast area	Concentration in South and Southwest; in agricultural areas and backcountry
A strong navy to protect shippers	A minimal navy for coastal defense

Federalist support. Farther inland, few Hamiltonians dwelled.

Federalists were also pro-British in foreign affairs. Some of them still harbored mildly Loyalist sentiments from Revolutionary days. All of them recognized that foreign trade, especially with England, was a key cog in Hamilton's fiscal machinery.

Leading the anti-Federalists, who came eventually to be known as Democratic-Republicans or sometimes simply Republicans, was Thomas Jefferson. Lanky and relaxed in appearance, lacking personal aggressiveness, weak-voiced, and unable to deliver a rabble-rousing speech, he became a master political organizer through his ability to lead people rather than drive them. His strongest appeal was to the middle class and to the underprivileged—the "dirt" farmers, the laborers, the artisans, and the small shopkeepers.

Liberal-thinking Jefferson, with his aristocratic head set on a farmer's frame, was a bundle of inconsistencies. By one set of tests he should have been a Federalist, for he was a Virginia aristocrat and slaveowner who lived in an imposing hilltop mansion at Monticello. A so-called traitor to his upper class, Jefferson cherished uncommon sympathy for the common people, especially the downtrodden, the oppressed, and the persecuted. As he wrote in 1800, "I have sworn upon the altar of God eternal hostility against every form of tyranny over the mind of man."

Jeffersonian Republicans demanded a weak central regime. They believed that the best government was the one that governed least. The bulk of the power, Jefferson argued, should be retained by the states. There the people, in intimate contact with local affairs, could keep a more vigilant eye on their public servants. Otherwise, a dictatorship might develop. Central authority—a kind of necessary evil—was to be kept at a minimum through a strict interpretation of the Constitution. The national debt, which he saw as a curse illegitimately bequeathed to later generations, was to be paid off.

Jeffersonian Republicans, themselves primarily agrarians, insisted that there should be no special privileges for special classes, particularly manufacturers. Agriculture, to Jefferson, was the favored branch of the economy. He regarded farming as essentially ennobling; it kept people away from wicked cities, out in the sunshine and close to the sod—and God. Most of his followers naturally came from the agricultural South and Southwest.

Above all, Jefferson advocated the rule of the people. But he did not propose thrusting the ballot into the hands of *every* adult white male. He favored government *for* the people, but not by *all* the people—only by those men who were literate enough to inform themselves and wear the mantle of American citizenship worthily. Universal education would have to precede universal suffrage. The ignorant, he argued, were incapable of self-government. But he had profound faith in the reasonableness and teachableness of the masses and in their collective wisdom when taught.

Landlessness among American citizens threatened popular democracy as much as illiteracy, in Jefferson's eyes. He feared that propertyless dependents would be political pawns in the hands of their landowning superiors. How could the emergence of

Thomas Jefferson at Natural Bridge, by Caleb Boyle, c. 1801   A great statesman, he wrote his own epitaph: "Here was buried Thomas Jefferson, Author of the Declaration of Independence, of the Statute of Virginia for Religious Freedom, and Father of the University of Virginia."

Thomas Jefferson's vision of a republican America was peopled with virtuous farmers, not factory hands. As early as 1784, he wrote,

"While we have land to labor then, let us never wish to see our citizens occupied at a work-bench, or twirling a distaff. . . . For the general operations of manufacture, let our workshops remain in Europe. . . . The mobs of great cities add just so much to the support of pure government, as sores do to the strength of the human body."

speech the misdeeds of tyranny could not be exposed. Jefferson even dared to say that given the choice of "a government without newspapers" and "newspapers without a government," he would opt for the latter. Yet no other American leader, except perhaps Abraham Lincoln, ever suffered more foul abuse from editorial pens; Jefferson might well have prayed for freedom *from* the Federalist press.

Jeffersonian Republicans, unlike the Federalist "British boot-lickers," were basically pro-French. They earnestly believed that it was to America's advantage to support the liberal ideals of the French Revolution, rather than applaud the reaction of the English Tories.

So as the young Republic's first full decade of nationhood came to a close, the Founders' hopes seemed already imperiled. Conflicts over domestic politics and foreign policy undermined the unity of the Revolutionary era and called into question the very viability of the American experiment in democracy. As the presidential election of 1800 approached, the danger loomed that the fragile and battered American ship of state, like many another before it and after it, would founder on the rocks of controversy. The shores of history are littered with the wreckage of nascent nations torn asunder before they could grow to a stable maturity. Why should the United States expect to enjoy a happier fate?

a landless class of voters be avoided? The answer, in part, was by slavery. A system of black slave labor in the South insured that white yeoman farmers could remain independent landowners. Without slavery, poor whites would have to provide the cheap labor so necessary for the cultivation of tobacco and rice, and their low wages would preclude their ever owning property.

Yet for his time, Jefferson's confidence that white, free men could become responsible and knowledgeable citizens was open-minded. He championed their freedom of speech, for without free

Chronology

1789	Constitution formally put into effect Judiciary Act of 1789 Washington elected president French Revolution begins		**1794**	Whiskey Rebellion Battle of Fallen Timbers Jay's Treaty with Britain
1790	First official census		**1795**	Treaty of Greenville: Indians cede Ohio Pinckney's Treaty with Spain
1791	Bill of Rights adopted Vermont becomes fourteenth state Bank of the United States created Excise tax passed		**1796**	Washington's Farewell Address
			1797	Adams becomes president XYZ Affair
1792	Washington reelected president		**1798**	Alien and Sedition Acts
1792-1793	Federalist and Democratic-Republican parties formed		**1798-1799**	Kentucky and Virginia resolutions
1793	Louis XVI beheaded; radical phase of French Revolution France declares war on Britain and Spain Washington's Neutrality Proclamation Citizen Genêt affair		**1798-1800**	Undeclared war with France
			1800	Convention of 1800: peace with France

SUGGESTED READINGS

PRIMARY SOURCE DOCUMENTS

"The Report on Manufactures" (in Daniel Boorstin, ed., *American Primer*), the last of Alexander Hamilton's messages to Congress, presented the case for the development of American industry. Thomas Jefferson expounded his views in *Notes on the State of Virginia* (1784). For further study of the Hamiltonian-Jeffersonian debate, see Henry Cabot Lodge, ed., *The Works of Alexander Hamilton** (1904), and Paul L. Ford, ed., *The Writings of Thomas Jefferson** (1985). Important salvos in the battle between national power and state sovereignty, and between Federalists and Jeffersonians, were the Virginia and Kentucky resolutions* (1798) and the reply of Rhode Island* (1799). Washington's Farewell Address* (1796) established the foundation for American attitudes about party politics and foreign policy. See also Benjamin Franklin Bache's stinging editorial on Washington's retirement, Philadelphia *Aurora** (1797).

SECONDARY SOURCES

Perceptive introductions are provided by Marcus Cunliffe's succinct *The Nation Takes Shape, 1789–1837* (1959) and Stanley Elkins and Eric McKitrick's comprehensive work, *The Age of Federalism: The Early American Republic, 1788–1800* (1993). On administration, consult Leonard D. White, *The Federalists* (1948); on finance, Curtis P. Nettles, *The Emergence of a National Economy, 1775–1815* (1962). On the Bill of Rights, see Bernard Schwartz, *The Great Rights of Mankind: A History of the American Bill of Rights* (1991), and Patrick L. Conley and John P. Kaminski, eds., *The Bill of Rights and the States: The Colonial and Revolutionary Origins of American Liberties* (1992). On the use of party politics, see Richard Hofstadter's thoughtful *The Idea of a Party System* (1969); Richard Buel, Jr., *Securing the Revolution: Ideology in American Politics, 1789–1815* (1972); John Zvesper, *Political Philosophy and Rhetoric: A Study of the Origins of American Party Politics* (1977); John F.

Hoadley, *Origins of American Political Parties, 1789–1803* (1986); and Lance Banning, ed., *After the Constitution: Party Conflict in the New Republic* (1989). Among the newer interpretations of that subject, stressing the ideology of republicanism, are Drew McCoy, *The Elusive Republic: Political Economy in Jeffersonian America* (1980), and Lance Banning, *The Jeffersonian Persuasion* (1978). Charles G. Steffens examines the political beliefs of workers in *The Mechanics of Baltimore: Workers and Politics in the Age of Revolution, 1763–1812* (1984), as do Michael Merrill and Sean Wilentz in *The Key of Liberty: The Life and Democratic Writings of William Manning, "A Laborer," 1747–1814* (1992). For a trenchant analysis of Jeffersonianism, see Joyce Appleby, *Capitalism and a New Social Order: The Republican Vision* (1984), whose analysis emphasizes the role of liberalism in American political thought, a point earlier made by Louis Hartz in *The Liberal Tradition in America* (1955). Also illuminating is Gerald Stourzh, *Alexander Hamilton and the Idea of Republican Government* (1970). See also Gordon S. Wood, *The Radicalism of the American Revolution* (1991). Thomas P. Slaughter focuses on *The Whiskey Rebellion: Frontier Epilogue to the American Revolution* (1986). A comprehensive biography is James T. Flexner, *George Washington and the New Nation, 1783–1793* (1969). Consult also Forrest McDonald, *The Presidency of George Washington* (1974), and Garry Wills, *Cincinnatus: George Washington and the Enlightenment* (1984). Of special interest is Richard H. Kohn, *Eagle and Sword: The Federalists and the Creation of the Military Establishment in America, 1783–1802* (1975). On aspects of foreign policy, see Alexander De Conde, *Entangling Alliance* (1958); Gilbert Lycan, *Alexander Hamilton and American Foreign Policy* (1970); Jerald Combs, *The Jay Treaty* (1970); Lawrence S. Kaplan, *Colonies into Nation: American Diplomacy, 1763–1801* (1972); and Daniel G. Lang, *Foreign Policy in the Early Republic: The Law of Nations and the Balance of Power* (1985). For the view from across the Atlantic, see Charles R. Ritcheson, *Aftermath of Revolution: British Policy Toward the United States, 1783–1795* (1969). On Adams, consult Page Smith, *John Adams* (2 vols.) (1962), and Stephen G. Kurtz, *The Presidency of John Adams* (1957). James M. Smith, *Freedom's Fetters* (1956), treats the Alien and Sedition Acts, as does Leonard Levy, *Legacy of Suppression* (1960).

---

*An asterisk indicates that the document, or an excerpt from it, can be found in Thomas A. Bailey and David M. Kennedy, eds., *The American Spirit: United States History as Seen by Contemporaries*, 9th ed. (Boston: Houghton Mifflin, 1998).

11

The Triumphs and Travails of Jeffersonian Democracy

1800–1812

*Timid men . . . prefer the calm of despotism
to the boisterous sea of liberty.*

<small>THOMAS JEFFERSON, 1796</small>

Federalist and Republican Mudslingers

In the critical presidential contest of 1800, Adams and Jefferson were again the standard-bearers of their respective parties. The Federalists labored under heavy handicaps. Their Alien and Sedition Acts had aroused a host of enemies, although most of these critics were dyed-in-the-wool Jeffersonians anyhow. The Hamiltonian wing of the Federalist party, robbed of its glorious war with France, split openly with President Adams. Hamilton, a victim of arrogance, was so indiscreet as to attack the president in a privately printed pamphlet. Jeffersonians soon got hold of the pamphlet and gleefully published it.

The most damaging blow to the Federalists was the refusal of Adams to give them a rousing fight with France. Their feverish war preparations had

swelled the public debt and had required disagreeable new taxes, including a stamp tax. After all these unpopular measures, the war scare had petered out, and the country was left with an all-dressed-up-but-no-place-to-go feeling. The military preparations now seemed not only unnecessary but extravagant, as seamen for the "new navy" were called "John Adams's Jackasses." Adams himself was known, somewhat ironically, as "the Father of the American Navy."

Thrown on the defensive, the Federalists concentrated their fire on Jefferson himself, who became the victim of one of America's earliest "whispering campaigns." He was accused of having robbed a widow and her children of a trust fund and of having fathered numerous mulatto children by his own slave women. As a liberal in religion, Jefferson had earlier incurred the wrath of the orthodox clergy, largely through his successful struggle to separate church and state in his native Virginia.

The Reverend Timothy Dwight (1752–(1817), president of Yale College, predicted that in the event of Jefferson's election,

"The Bible would be cast into a bonfire, our holy worship changed into a dance of [French] Jacobin phrensy, our wives and daughters dishonored, and our sons converted into the disciples of Voltaire and the dragoons of Marat."

Jefferson won by a majority of 73 electoral votes to 65. In defeat, the colorless and presumably unpopular Adams polled more electoral strength than he had gained four years earlier—except for New York. The Empire State fell into the Jeffersonian basket, and with it the election, largely because Aaron Burr, a master wire-puller, turned New York to Jefferson by the narrowest of margins. The Virginian polled the bulk of his strength in the South and West, particularly in those states where universal white manhood suffrage had been adopted.

Jeffersonian joy was dampened by an unexpected deadlock. Through a technicality Jefferson, the presidential candidate, and Burr, his vice-presidential running mate, received the same number of electoral votes for the presidency. Under the Constitution the tie could be broken only by the

Although Jefferson did believe in God, preachers throughout New England, stronghold of Federalism and Congregationalism, thundered against his alleged atheism. Old ladies of Federalist families, fearing Jefferson's election, even buried their Bibles or hung them in wells.

The Providential Detection
(Federalist Propaganda)
The American eagle snatches the Constitution from Jefferson, who is about to burn it (together with the works of Voltaire, Paine, and others) on the altar to French Revolutionary despotism.

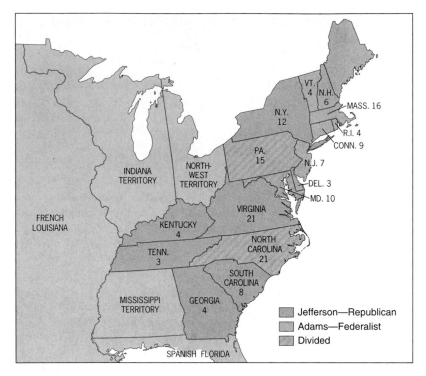

**Presidential Election of 1800
(with electoral vote by state)**
New York was the key state in this election, and Aaron Burr helped swing it away from the Federalists with tactics that anticipated the political "machines" of a later day. Federalists complained that Burr "travels every night from one meeting of Republicans to another, haranguing . . . them to the most zealous exertions. [He] can stoop so low as to visit every low tavern that may happen to be crowded with his dear fellow citizens." But Burr proved that the price was worth it. "We have beat you," Burr told kid-gloved Federalists after the election, "by superior *Management.*"

House of Representatives (see Art. II, Sec. I, para. 2). This body was controlled for several more months by the lame-duck Federalists, who preferred Burr to the hated Jefferson.* Voting in the House moved slowly to a climax, as exhausted representatives snored in their seats. The agonizing deadlock was broken at last when a few Federalists, despairing of electing Burr and hoping for moderation from Jefferson, refrained from voting. The election then went to the rightful candidate.

Jefferson later claimed that the election of 1800 was a "revolution" comparable to that of 1776. But it was no revolution in the sense of a massive popular upheaval or an upending of the political system. In truth, Jefferson had narrowly squeaked through to victory. A switch of some 250 votes in New York would have thrown the election to Adams. What *was* revolutionary was the peaceful and orderly transfer of power on the basis of an election whose results all parties accepted. This was a remarkable—indeed

even "revolutionary"—achievement for a raw young nation, especially after all the partisan bitterness that had agitated the country during Adams's presidency. It was particularly remarkable in that age; comparable successions would not take place in Britain for another generation. After a decade of division and doubt, Americans could take justifiable pride in the vigor of their experiment in democracy.

The Federalist Finale

John Adams, as fate would have it, was the last Federalist president of the United States. His party sank slowly into the mire of political oblivion and ultimately disappeared completely in the days of Andrew Jackson.

Whatever their shortcomings, the Federalists boasted a high concentration of brains, talent, and ability. Their political and financial leaders had built enduring foundations for the new government. Their diplomats, with a strong helping hand from Europe's distresses, had signed advantageous treaties with England, Spain, and France. Their statesmen had kept the peace during a crucial period when peace had to be kept.

---

*A "lame duck" has been humorously defined as a politician whose political goose has been cooked at the recent elections. The possibility of another such tie was removed by the Twelfth Amendment in 1804 (for text, see the Appendix). Before then, each elector had two votes, with the second-place finisher becoming vice president.

Mrs. Benjamin Tallmadge and Son Henry Floyd and Daughter Maria Jones; Colonel Benjamin Tallmadge and Son William Tallmadge, by Ralph Earl, 1790   The Tallmadges were among the leading citizens of Litchfield, a Federalist stronghold in the heavily Federalist state of Connecticut. Colonel Benjamin Tallmadge served with distinction in the Revolutionary War, became a wealthy merchant and banker, and represented his state in Congress from 1801 to 1817. Mary Floyd Tallmadge, like her husband, came from a prominent Long Island family. The opulence of the Tallmadges' clothing and surroundings in these paintings abundantly testify to the wealth, and the social pretensions, of the Federalist elite. Note the toy carriage near the feet of the Tallmadge daughter—a replica of the actual, and elegant, carriage owned by the Tallmadge family.

After all the turmoil of the American Revolution, a conservative party performed a valuable function in preserving democratic gains and fending off anarchy. The Federalists provided a welcome breathing spell, a chance for the nation to get its bearings. They served, in the words of historian Henry Adams, great-grandson of John Adams, as the "half-way house between the European past and the American future."

But by 1800 the Federalists, blessed with more talent than wisdom, were out of place. They were unable or unwilling to unbend and appeal to the common people. They could not adapt—so like the dinosaur they died.

Responsibility Breeds Moderation

"Long Tom" Jefferson was inaugurated president on March 4, 1801, in the swampy village of Washington, the crude new national capital. Tall (6 feet, 2.5 inches; 1.89 meters), with large hands and feet, red hair ("the Red Fox"), and prominent cheekbones and chin, he was an arresting figure. Believing that the customary pomp did not befit his democratic ideals, he spurned a horse-drawn coach and strode by foot to the Capitol from his boardinghouse.

Jefferson's inaugural address, beautifully phrased, was a classic statement of democratic principles. "The will of the majority is in all cases to prevail," Jefferson declared. But, he added, "that will to be rightful must be reasonable; the minority possess their equal rights, which equal law must protect, and to violate would be oppression." Seeking to allay Federalist fears of a bull-in-the-china-closet overturn, Jefferson blandly intoned, "We are all Republicans, we are all Federalists." As for foreign affairs, he pledged "honest friendship with all nations, entangling alliances with none."

With its rustic setting, Washington lent itself admirably to the simplicity and frugality of the Jeffersonian Republicans. In this respect it contrasted sharply with the elegant atmosphere of Federalist Philadelphia, the former temporary capital. Extending democratic principles to etiquette, Jefferson established the rule of pell-mell at official dinners—that is, seating without regard to rank. The resplendent British minister, who had enjoyed precedence among the pro-British Federalists, was insulted.

As a widower, Jefferson was shockingly unconventional. Having no wife to police his apparel, he would receive callers in sloppy attire—once in a dressing gown and heelless slippers. He started the precedent, unbroken until Woodrow Wilson's presidency 112 years later, of sending messages to Congress to be read by a clerk. Personal appearances, in the Federalist manner, suggested too strongly a monarchical speech from the throne. Besides, Jefferson was painfully conscious of his weak voice and unimpressive platform presence.

As if plagued by an evil spirit, Jefferson was forced to reverse many of the political principles he had so vigorously championed. There were in fact two Thomas Jeffersons. One was the scholarly private citizen, who philosophized in his study. The other was the harassed public official, who made the disturbing discovery that bookish theories worked out differently in the noisy arena of practical politics. The open-minded Virginian was therefore consistently inconsistent; it is easy to quote one Jefferson to refute the other.

The triumph of Thomas Jefferson's Democratic-Republicans and the eviction of the Federalists marked the first party overturn in American history. The vanquished naturally feared that the victors would grab all the spoils of office for themselves. But Jefferson, in keeping with his conciliatory inaugural address, showed unexpected moderation. To the dismay of his office-seeking friends, the new president dismissed few public servants for political

Jefferson in Casual Attire   As befitted a champion of the new democracy, Jefferson typically dressed casually, shunning the sartorial pretensions affected by many Federalists, such as the elegantly attired Talmadges shown on p. 213.

The toleration of Thomas Jefferson (1749–1826) was reflected in his inaugural address.

"If there be any among us who would wish to dissolve this Union or to change its republican form, let them stand undisturbed as monuments of the safety with which error of opinion may be tolerated where reason is left free to combat it."

Mad Tom in a Rage A Federalist cartoon shows "Mad Tom" Jefferson, assisted by brandy and the Devil, trying to pull down the federal edifice erected by Washington and Adams. In fact, Jefferson left most of the Federalist programs intact during his tenure as president.

President John F. Kennedy (1917–1963) once greeted a large group of Nobel Prize winners as "the most extraordinary collection of talent, of human knowledge, that has ever been gathered together at the White House, with the possible exception of when Thomas Jefferson dined alone."

Jeffersonian Restraint Helps to Further a "Revolution"

At the outset Jefferson was determined to undo the Federalist abuses begotten by the anti-French hysteria. The hated Alien and Sedition Acts had already expired. The incoming president speedily pardoned the "martyrs" who were serving sentences under the Sedition Act, and the government remitted many fines. Shortly after the Congress met, the Jeffersonians enacted the new naturalization law of 1802. This act reduced the unreasonable requirement of fourteen years of residence to the previous and more reasonable requirement of five years.

Jefferson actually kicked away only one substantial prop of the Hamiltonian system. He hated the excise tax, which bred bureaucrats and bore heavily on his farmer following, and he early persuaded Congress to repeal it. His devotion to principle thus cost the federal government about a million dollars a year in urgently needed revenue.

Swiss-born and French-accented Albert Gallatin, "Watchdog of the Treasury," proved to be as able a secretary of the treasury as Hamilton. Gallatin agreed with Jefferson that a national debt was a bane rather than a blessing and by strict economy succeeded in reducing it substantially while balancing the budget.

Except for excising the excise tax, the Jeffersonians left the Hamiltonian framework essentially intact. They did not tamper with the Federalist programs for funding the national debt at par and assuming the Revolutionary War debts of the states. They launched no attack on the Bank of the United States, nor did they repeal the mildly protective Federalist tariff. In later years they embraced Federalism

reasons. Patronage-hungry Jeffersonians watched the Federalist appointees grow old in office and grumbled that "few die, none resign."

Jefferson quickly proved an able politician. He was especially effective in the informal atmosphere of a dinner party. There he wooed congressional representatives while personally pouring imported wines and serving the tasty dishes of his French cook. In part, Jefferson had to rely on his personal charm because his party was so weak-jointed. Denied the power to dispense patronage, the Democratic-Republicans could not build a loyal political following. Opposition to the Federalists was the chief glue holding them together, and as the Federalists faded, so did Democratic-Republican unity. The era of well-developed, well-disciplined political parties still lay in the future.

to such a degree as to recharter a bigger bank and to boost the protective tariff to higher levels.

Paradoxically, Jefferson's moderation thus further cemented the gains of the "Revolution of 1800." That revolution had consisted above all in the peaceful replacement of one governing party by another. By shrewdly absorbing the major Federalist programs, Jefferson showed that a change of regime need not be disastrous for the defeated group. His restraint pointed the way toward the two-party system that was later to become a characteristic feature of American politics.

The "Dead Clutch" of the Judiciary

The "deathbed" Judiciary Act of 1801 was one of the last important laws passed by the expiring Federalist Congress. It created sixteen new federal judgeships and other judicial offices. President Adams remained at his desk until nine o'clock in the evening of his last day in office, supposedly signing the commissions of the Federalist "midnight judges." (Actually only three commissions were signed on his last day.)

This Federalist-sponsored Judiciary Act, though a long-overdue reform, aroused bitter resentment. "Packing" these lifetime posts with anti-Jeffersonian partisans was, in Republican eyes, a brazen attempt by the ousted party to entrench itself in one of the three powerful branches of government. Jeffersonians condemned the last-minute appointees in violent language, denouncing the trickery of the Federalists as open defiance of the people's will, expressed emphatically at the polls.

The newly elected Republican Congress bestirred itself to repeal the Judiciary Act of 1801 in the year after its passage. Jeffersonians thus swept sixteen benches from under the recently seated "midnight judges." Jeffersonians likewise had their knives sharpened for the scalp of Chief Justice John Marshall, whom Adams had appointed to the Supreme Court (as a fourth choice) in the dying days of his term. The strong-willed Marshall, with his rasping voice and steel-trap mind, was a cousin of Thomas Jefferson. Marshall's formal legal schooling had lasted only six weeks, but he dominated the Supreme Court with his powerful intellect and commanding personality. He shaped the American legal tradition more profoundly than any other single figure.

Marshall had served at Valley Forge during the Revolution. While suffering there from cold and hunger, he had been painfully impressed with the drawbacks of feeble central authority. The experience made him a lifelong Federalist, committed above all else to strengthening the power of the federal government. States'-rights Jeffersonians condemned the crafty judge's "twistifications," but Marshall pushed ahead inflexibly on his Federalist course. He served for about thirty days under a Federalist administration and thirty-four years under the administrations of Jefferson and subsequent presidents. The Federalist party died out, but Marshall lived on, handing down Federalist decisions serenely for many more years. For over three decades, the ghost of Alexander Hamilton spoke through the lanky, black-robed judge.

One of the "midnight judges" of 1801 presented John Marshall with a historic opportunity. He was obscure William Marbury, whom President Adams had named a justice of the peace for the District of Columbia. When Marbury learned that his commission was being shelved by the new secretary of state, James Madison, he sued for its delivery. Chief Justice Marshall knew that his Jeffersonian rivals, entrenched in the executive branch, would hardly spring forward to enforce a writ to deliver the commission to his fellow Federalist Marbury. He therefore dismissed Marbury's suit, avoiding a direct political showdown. But the wily Marshall snatched a victory from the jaws of this judicial defeat. In explaining his ruling, Marshall said that the part of the Judiciary Act of 1789 on which Marbury tried to base his appeal was unconstitutional. The act had attempted to assign to the Supreme Court powers that the Constitution had not foreseen.

In this self-denying opinion, Marshall greatly magnified the authority of the Court—and slapped at the Jeffersonians. Until the case of *Marbury* v. *Madison* (1803), controversy had clouded the question of who had the final authority to determine the meaning of the Constitution. Jefferson in the Kentucky resolutions (1798) had tried to allot that right to the individual states. But now his cousin on the Court had cleverly promoted the contrary principle of "judicial review"—the idea that the Supreme Court alone had the last word on the question of constitutionality. In this landmark case, Marshall inserted the keystone into the arch that supports

In his decision in Marbury v. Madison, *Chief Justice John Marshall (1755–1835) vigorously asserted his view that the Constitution embodied a "higher" law than ordinary legislation, and that the Court must interpret the Constitution:*

"The Constitution is either a superior paramount law, unchangeable by ordinary means, or it is on a level with ordinary legislative acts, and like other acts, is alterable when the legislature shall please to alter it.

"If the former part of the alternative be true, then a legislative act contrary to the constitution is now law; if the latter part be true, then written constitutions are absurd attempts, on the part of the people, to limit a power in its own nature illimitable. . . .

"It is emphatically the province and duty of the judicial department to say what the law is . . . .

"If, then, the courts are to regard the Constitution, and the Constitution is superior to any ordinary act of the legislature, the Constitution, and not such ordinary act, must govern the case to which they are both applicable."

the tremendous power of the Supreme Court in American life.*

Marshall's decision regarding Marbury spurred the Jeffersonians to seek revenge. Jefferson urged the impeachment of an arrogant and tart-tongued Supreme Court justice, Samuel Chase, who was so unpopular that Republicans named vicious dogs after him. Early in 1804 impeachment charges against Chase were voted by the House of Representatives, which then passed the question of guilt or innocence on to the Senate. The indictment by the House was based on "high crimes and misdemeanors," as specified in the Constitution.† Yet the

evidence was plain that the intemperate judge had not been guilty of "high crimes" but only of unrestrained partisanship and a big mouth. The Senate failed to muster enough votes to convict and remove Chase. The precedent thus established was fortunate. From that day to this, no really serious attempt has been made to reshape the Supreme Court by the impeachment weapon. Jefferson's ill-advised attempt at "judge breaking" was a reassuring victory for the independence of the judiciary and for the separation of powers among the three branches of the federal government.

The Pacifist Jefferson Turns Warrior

Jefferson distrusted large standing armies as standing invitations to dictatorship. Pinning his faith to the frail reed of an ill-trained militia, Jefferson reduced the military establishment to a mere police force of 2,500 officers and men. Navies, though also suspect, were less to be feared: they could not march inland and "endanger liberties." Still, the Republicans, primarily agrarians, saw little point in protecting a few Federalist shippers with a costly fleet. Accordingly, Jefferson shrank the navy to a peacetime footing.

But harsh realities forced a penny-pinching Jefferson to change his tune on navies and war. Pirates of the North African Barbary States had long made a national industry of blackmailing and plundering merchant ships that ventured into the Mediterranean. Preceding Federalist administrations, in fact, had been forced to buy protection. At the time of the French crisis of 1798, when Americans were shouting, "Millions for defense but not one cent for tribute," twenty-six barrels of blackmail dollars were being shipped to piratical Algiers.

At this price, war seemed cheaper than peace, and the showdown came in 1801. The pasha of Tripoli, dissatisfied with his share of protection money, informally declared war on the United States by cutting down the flagstaff of the American consulate. A gauntlet was thus thrown squarely into the face of Jefferson—the noninterventionist, the pacifist, the critic of a big-ship navy, and the political foe of Federalist shippers. He reluctantly rose to the challenge by dispatching the infant navy to the "shores of Tripoli," as related in the song of the U.S. Marine Corps. After four years of intermittent

---

*The next invalidation of a federal law by the Supreme Court came fifty-four years later, with the explosive Dred Scott decision (see p. 427).

†For impeachment, see Art. I, Sec. II, para. 5; Art. I, Sec. III, paras. 6, 7; Art. II, Sec. IV in the Appendix.

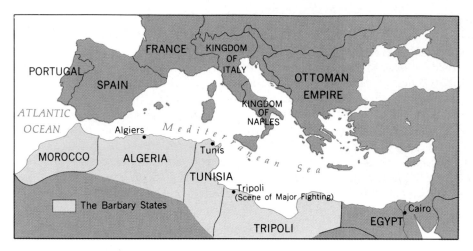

Four Barbary States of North Africa, c. 1805

fighting, marked by spine-tingling exploits, Jefferson succeeded in extorting a treaty of peace from Tripoli in 1805. It was secured at the bargain price of only $60,000—a sum representing ransom payments for captured Americans.

Small gunboats, which the navy had used with some success in the Tripolitan War, fascinated Jefferson. Pledged to tax reduction, he advocated a large number of little coastal craft—"Jeffs" or the "mosquito fleet," as they were contemptuously called. He believed these fast but frail vessels would prove valuable in guarding American shores, although not in defending Federalist merchantmen on the high seas.

About two hundred tiny gunboats were constructed, democratically in small shipyards where votes could be made for Jefferson. Often mounting only one unwieldy gun, they were sometimes more of a menace to the crew than to the prospective enemy. During a hurricane and tidal wave at Savannah, Georgia, one of them was deposited eight miles (12.9 kilometers) inland in a cornfield, to the derisive glee of the Federalists. They drank toasts to American gunboats as the best in the world—on land. Jefferson's pinch-penny economizing backfired badly when the War of 1812 broke out and the whole swarm of gunboats proved virtually stingless. The money could have been much more wisely invested in a few frigates of the *Constitution* class.

The Louisiana Godsend

A secret pact, fraught with peril for America, was signed in 1800. Napoleon Bonaparte induced the king of Spain to cede to France, for attractive considerations, the immense trans-Mississippi region of Louisiana, which included the New Orleans area.

Rumors of the transfer were partially confirmed in 1802, when the Spaniards at New Orleans withdrew the right of deposit guaranteed America by the treaty of 1795. Deposit (warehouse) privileges were vital to frontier farmers who floated their produce down the Mississippi to its mouth, there to await oceangoing vessels. A roar of anger rolled up the mighty river and into its tributary valleys. American pioneers talked wildly of descending upon New Orleans, rifles in hand. Had they done so, the nation probably would have been engulfed in war with both Spain and France.

Thomas Jefferson, both pacifist and anti-entanglement, was again on the griddle. Louisiana in the senile grip of Spain posed no real threat; America could seize the territory when the time was ripe. But Louisiana in the iron fist of Napoleon, the preeminent military genius of his age, foreshadowed a dark and blood-drenched future. The United States would probably have to fight to dislodge him; and because it alone was not strong enough to defeat his armies, it would have to seek allies, contrary to the deepening anti-alliance policy.

Hoping to quiet the clamor of the West, Jefferson moved decisively. Early in 1803 he sent James Monroe to Paris to join forces with the regular minister there, Robert R. Livingston. The two envoys were instructed to buy New Orleans and as much land to its east as they could get for a maximum of $10 million. If these proposals should fail and the situation became critical, negotiations were to be opened with England for an alliance. "The day that France takes possession of New Orleans," Jefferson wrote, "we must marry ourselves to the British fleet and nation." That remark dramatically demonstrated Jefferson's dilemma. Though a passionate hater of war and an enemy of entangling alliances, he was proposing to make an alliance with his old foe, England, against his old friend, France, in order to secure New Orleans.

At this critical juncture, Napoleon suddenly decided to sell all Louisiana and abandon his dream of a New World empire. Two developments prompted his change of mind. First, he had failed in his efforts to reconquer the sugar-rich island of Santo Domingo, for which Louisiana was to serve as a source of foodstuffs. Infuriated ex-slaves, ably led by the gifted Toussaint L'Ouverture, had put up a stubborn resistance that was ultimately broken. Then the island's second line of defense—mosquitoes carrying yellow fever—had swept away thousands of crack French troops. Santo Domingo could not be had, except perhaps at a staggering cost; hence there was no need for Louisiana's food supplies. "Damn sugar, damn coffee, damn colonies!" burst out Napoleon. Second, Bonaparte was about to end the twenty-month lull in his deadly conflict with Britain. Because the British controlled the seas, he feared that he might be forced to make them a

Toussaint L'Ouverture (c. 1743–1803)
A self-educated ex-slave and military genius, L'Ouverture was finally betrayed by the French, who imprisoned him in a chilly dungeon in France, where he coughed his life away. Indirectly, he did much to set up the sale of Louisiana to the United States.

Explaining the western outburst over the closing of the river, James Madison (1751–1836) wrote to Pinckney:

"The Mississippi is to them every thing. It is the Hudson, the Delaware, the Potomac, and all the navigable rivers of the Atlantic States, formed into one stream."

gift of Louisiana. Rather than drive America into the arms of England by attempting to hold the area, he decided to sell the huge wilderness to the Americans and pocket the money for his schemes nearer home. Napoleon hoped that the United States, strengthened by Louisiana, would one day be a military and naval power that would thwart the ambitions of the lordly British in the New World. The predicaments of France in Europe were again paving the way for America's diplomatic successes.

Events now unrolled dizzily. The American minister, Robert Livingston, pending the arrival of Monroe, was busily negotiating in Paris for a window on the Gulf of Mexico at New Orleans. Suddenly, out of a clear sky, the French foreign minister asked him how much he would give for all Louisiana. Scarcely able to believe his ears (he was partially deaf anyhow), Livingston nervously entered upon the negotiations. After about a week of haggling, while the fate of North America trembled in the balance, treaties were signed on April 30, 1803, ceding Louisiana to the United States for about $15 million.

When the news of the bargain reached America, Jefferson was startled. He had authorized his envoys to offer not more than $10 million for New Orleans, and as much to the *east* in the Floridas as they could get. Instead, they had signed three treaties that pledged $15 million for New Orleans, plus an immeasurable tract entirely to the *west*—an area that would more than double the size of the United States. They had bought a wilderness to get a city.

Once again the two Jeffersons wrestled with each other: the theorist and former strict constructionist versus the realist and public official. Where in his beloved Constitution was the president authorized to negotiate treaties incorporating a huge new expanse into the union—an expanse containing some fifty thousand Indian, white, and black inhabitants? There was no such clause.

Conscience-stricken, Jefferson privately proposed that a constitutional amendment be passed. But his friends pointed out in alarm that in the interval Napoleon, for whom thought was action, might suddenly withdraw the offer. So Jefferson shamefacedly submitted the treaties to the Senate, while admitting to his associates that the purchase was unconstitutional.

The senators were less finicky than Jefferson. Reflecting enthusiastic public support, they registered their prompt approval of the transaction.

In accepting the Louisiana Purchase, Jefferson thus compromised with conscience in a private letter:

"It is the case of a guardian, investing the money of his ward in purchasing an important adjacent territory; and saying to him when of age, I did this for your good; I pretend to no right to bind you; you may disavow me, and I must get out of the scrape as I can; I thought it my duty to risk myself for you."

Land-hungry Americans were not disposed to split constitutional hairs when confronted with perhaps the most magnificent real estate bargain in history—828,000 square miles (2,144,520 square kilometers) at about three cents an acre.

Louisiana in the Long View

Jefferson's bargain with Napoleon was epochal. Overnight he had avoided a possible rupture with France and the consequent entangling alliance with England. By scooping up Louisiana, America secured at one bloodless stroke the western half of the richest river valley in the world and further laid the foundations of a future major power. The ideal of a great agrarian republic, as envisioned by Jefferson, would have elbowroom in the vast "Valley of Democracy." At the same time, the transfer established a precedent that was to be followed repeatedly: the acquisition of foreign territory and peoples by purchase.

The extent of the vast new area was more fully unveiled by a series of explorations under the direction of Jefferson. In the spring of 1804, Jefferson sent his personal secretary, Meriwether Lewis, and a young army officer named William Clark to explore the northern part of the Louisiana Purchase. Aided by the Shoshoni woman Sacajawea, Lewis and Clark ascended the "Great Muddy" Missouri River from St. Louis, struggled through the Rockies, and descended the Columbia River to the Pacific coast.

Lewis and Clark's two-and-one-half-year expedition yielded a rich harvest of scientific observations, maps, knowledge of the Indians in the region, and hair-raising wilderness adventure stories. On the Great Plains they marveled at the "immense herds of buffalo, elk, deer, and antelope feeding in one common and boundless pasture." Lewis was lucky to come back alive. When he detached a group of just three other men to explore the Marias River in present-day western Montana, a band of teenage Blackfoot Indians, armed with crude muskets by British fur traders operating out of Canada, stole the horses of the small and vulnerable exploring party. Lewis foolishly pursued the horse thieves on foot. He shot one marauder through the belly, but the Indian returned the fire. "Being bareheaded," Lewis later wrote, "I felt the wind of his bullet very distinctly." After killing another Blackfoot and hanging

Meriwether Lewis He is portrayed in this painting as he looked on his return from the great expedition through the Louisiana Purchase and the West.

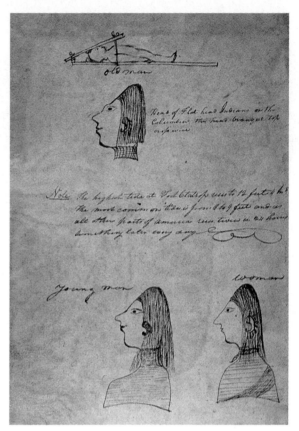

Flathead Indians, c. 1805
William Clark served as the artist and cartographer of the Lewis and Clark expedition. Here he has sketched the Flathead Indians of present-day Montana, showing the skull-molding practice from which they got their name.

one of the expedition's "peace and friendship" medals around the neck of the corpse as a warning to other Indians, Lewis and his terrified companions beat it out of the Marias country to rejoin their main party on the Missouri River.

The explorers also demonstrated the viability of an overland trail to the Pacific. Down the dusty track thousands of missionaries, fur traders, and pioneering settlers would wend their way in the ensuing decades, bolstering America's claim to the Oregon country. Other explorers also pushed into the uncharted West. Zebulon M. Pike trekked to the headwaters of the Mississippi River in 1805–1806. The next year Pike ventured into the Southern

portion of the Louisiana territory, where he sighted the Colorado peak that bears his name.

The Louisiana godsend also boosted national unity. Once-proud Federalists, now mere sectionalists, sank ever lower in public esteem as they were reduced to whining impotence. A few of their more extreme members attempted to plot with scheming Aaron Burr for the secession of New England and New York. But the intrigue failed, largely owing to the vigilance of Alexander Hamilton, who subsequently provoked Burr to a duel—with lethal results for Hamilton. The pistol with which Burr killed Hamilton in 1804 blew the brightest brain out of the Federalist party—and destroyed its one remaining hope of effective leadership.

Aaron Burr, turning his disunionist plottings to the trans-Mississippi West, was arrested in 1806 for

Gifts from the Great White Chief
Among the objectives of the Lewis and Clark expedition was to establish good relations with the Indians in the newly acquired Louisiana Purchase territory. The American explorers presented all chiefs with copies of these medals, showing President Jefferson and the hands of an Indian and a white man clasped in "peace and friendship" under a crossed "peace pipe" and hatchet. All chiefs also received an American flag and a military uniform jacket, hat, and feather.

treason. Tried the next year at Richmond, Virginia, he was freed after the presiding judge, Chief Justice Marshall, had infuriated the Jeffersonians by what seemed to be bias in favor of the accused. The government's case collapsed when two witnesses to the same overt act of treason could not be found, as required by the Constitution (see Art. III, Sec. III). Burr's schemes are still somewhat shrouded in mystery, but he apparently planned to separate the western part of the United States from the eastern and unite it with to-be-conquered Spanish territory west of the Louisiana Purchase. The very fact that so dashing a figure as Burr could muster only three-score followers was quite significant. It confirmed that the Louisiana Purchase was nurturing a deeper

sense of loyalty in the West to the federal government. People of the western waters were grateful to Washington for having safeguarded their interests, particularly in securing the mouth of the Mississippi. A new spirit of nationalism surged through the West.

America: A Nutcrackered Neutral

Jefferson was triumphantly reelected in 1804, with 162 electoral votes to only 14 votes for his Federalist opponent. But the laurels of Jefferson's first administration soon withered under the blasts of the new

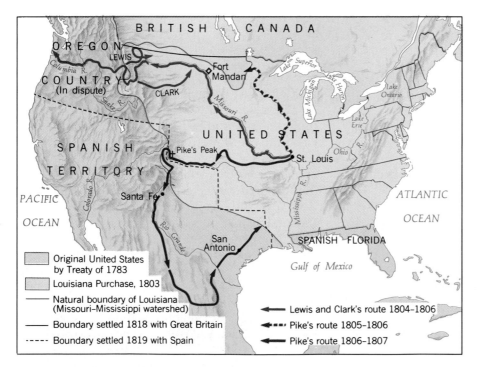

Exploring the Louisiana Purchase and the West
Seeking to avert friction with France by purchasing all of Louisiana, Jefferson bought trouble because of the vagueness of the boundaries. Among the disputants were Spain in the Floridas, Spain and Mexico in the Southwest, and Great Britain in Canada.

storm that broke in Europe. After unloading Louisiana in 1803, Napoleon deliberately provoked a renewal of his war with Britian—a conflict that crashed to an awesome close eleven long years later.

For two years a maritime United States—the number one neutral carrier since 1793—enjoyed juicy commercial pickings. But a setback came in 1805. At the Battle of Trafalgar, one-eyed Horatio Lord Nelson achieved immortality by smashing the combined French and Spanish fleets off the coast of Spain, thereby ensuring Britain's supremacy on the seas. At the Battle of Austerlitz in Austria—the Battle of the Three Emperors—Napoleon crushed the combined Austrian and Russian armies, thereby ensuring his mastery of the land. Like the tiger and the shark, France and Britain now reigned supreme in their chosen elements.

Unable to hurt each other directly, the two antagonists were forced to strike indirect blows. England ruled the waves and waived the rules. The London government, beginning in 1806, issued a series of Orders in Council. These edicts closed the ports under French continental control to foreign shipping, including American, unless the vessels first stopped at a British port. Napoleon struck back, ordering the seizure of all merchant ships, including American, that entered British ports.

Even more galling to American pride than the seizure of wooden ships was the seizure of flesh-and-blood American seamen. Impressment—the forcible enlistment of sailors—was a crude form of conscription that the British, among others, had employed for over four centuries. Clubs and stretchers (for men knocked unconscious) were standard equipment of press gangs from His Majesty's man-hungry ships. Some six thousand bona fide U.S. citizens were impressed by the "piratical man-stealers" of England from 1808 to 1811 alone. A number of these luckless souls died or were killed in His Majesty's service, leaving their kinfolk and friends bereaved and embittered.

Britain had its back to the wall, and its desperate plight colored its views. The British feared that they would lose the war if they gave up their ancient practice of conscription—and they would fight before forsaking impressment. England certainly would not abandon its brutal sailor-snatching at the behest of an upstart United States. Britons were making war; Americans were making money.

Intercourse or Impartial Dealings, 1809
A cartoon by "Peter Pencil" shows Jefferson being victimized by both England (left) and France (right).

> *Regarding the* Chesapeake *affair, the* Washington *Federalist reported,*
>
> "We have never, on any occasion, witnessed the spirit of the people excited to so great a degree of indignation, or such a thirst for revenge, as on hearing of the late unexampled outrage on the *Chesapeake*. All parties, ranks, and professions were unanimous in their detestation of the dastardly deed, and all cried aloud for vengeance."

Britain's determination was spectacularly highlighted in 1807. A royal frigate overhauled a U.S. frigate, the *Chesapeake*, about ten miles off the coast of Virginia. The British captain bluntly demanded the surrender of four alleged deserters. London had never claimed the right to seize sailors from a foreign warship, and the American commander, though totally unprepared to fight, refused the request. The British warship thereupon fired three devastating broadsides at close range, killing three Americans and wounding eighteen. Four deserters were dragged away, and the bloody hulk called the *Chesapeake* limped back to port.

Britain was clearly in the wrong, as the London Foreign Office admitted. But London's contrition availed little; a roar of national wrath went up from infuriated Americans. Jefferson, the peace lover, could easily have had war if he had wanted it.

Jefferson's Backfiring Embargo

National honor would not permit a slavish submission to British and French mistreatment. Yet a large-scale foreign war was contrary to the settled policy of the new Republic—and in addition it would be futile. The navy was weak, thanks largely to Jefferson's antinavalism; and the army was even weaker. A disastrous defeat would not improve America's plight.

The warring nations in Europe depended heavily upon the United States for raw materials and foodstuffs. In his eager search for an alternative to war, Jefferson seized upon this essential fact. He reasoned that if America voluntarily cut off its exports, the offending powers would be forced to bow, hat in hand, and agree to respect its rights.

Responding to the presidential lash, Congress hastily passed the Embargo Act late in 1807. This rigorous law forbade the export of all goods from the United States, whether in American or in foreign ships. It was a compromise between submission and shooting. Federalist New England could well have prayed for relief from its newly found Virginia friend, "Mad Tom" Jefferson. Forests of dead masts gradually filled once-bustling harbors; docks that had once rumbled were deserted (except for illegal trade); and soup kitchens cared for some of the hungry unemployed. Jeffersonian Republicans probably hurt the commerce of New England, which they avowedly were trying to protect, far more than Old England and France together were doing. Farmers of the South and West, the strongholds of Jefferson, suffered no less disastrously than New England. They were alarmed by the mounting piles of unexportable cotton, grain, and tobacco. Jefferson seemed to be waging war on his fellow citizens, rather than on the offending foreign powers.

An enormous illicit trade mushroomed in 1808, especially along the Canadian border, where bands of armed Americans on loaded rafts overawed or overpowered federal agents. Irate citizens cynically transposed the letters of "Embargo" to read "O Grab Me," "Go Bar 'Em," and "Mobrage," while heartily cursing the "Dambargo."

Jefferson nonetheless induced Congress to pass iron-toothed enforcing legislation. It was so inquisitorial and tyrannical as to cause some Americans to think more kindly of George III, whom Jefferson had berated in the Declaration of Independence. One indignant New Hampshirite denounced the president with this ditty:

> *Our ships all in motion,*
> *Once whiten'd the ocean;*
> *They sail'd and return'd with a Cargo;*
> *Now doom'd to decay*
> *They are fallen a prey,*
> *To Jefferson, worms, and EMBARGO.*

New England seethed with talk of secession; and Jefferson later admitted that he felt the foundations of government tremble under his feet.

An alarmed Congress, yielding to the storm of public anger, finally repealed the embargo, on March 1, 1809, three days before Jefferson's retirement. A half-loaf substitute was provided by the Non-Intercourse Act. This measure formally reopened trade with all the nations of the world, except the two most important, England and France. Though thus watered down, economic coercion continued to be the policy of the Jeffersonians from 1809 to 1812, when the nation finally plunged into war.

Why did the embargo, Jefferson's most daring act of statesmanship, collapse after fifteen dismal months? First of all, he underestimated the bulldog determination of the British, as others have, and overestimated their dependence on America's trade. Bumper grain crops blessed the British Isles during these years, and the revolutionary Latin American republics unexpectedly threw open their ports for compensating commerce.

The hated embargo was not continued long enough or tightly enough to achieve the desired results. But leaders must know the temper of their people, and Jefferson should have foreseen that such a self-crucifying weapon could not possibly command public support.

A crestfallen Jefferson himself admitted that the embargo was three times more costly than war. The irony is that with only a fraction of its cost to the country, he could have built a fairly strong navy. Such a fighting force would have won more respect for American rights on the high seas and might well have prevented the War of 1812.

A stoppage of exports hurt Federalist shipping but temporarily revived the Federalist party. Gain-

The Embargo (Ograbme)
As a snapping turtle, it halts overseas shipments.

ing new converts, its leaders hurled their nullification of the embargo into the teeth of the "Virginia lordlings" in Washington. In 1804, the discredited Federalists had polled only 14 electoral votes out of 176; in 1808, the embargo year, the figure rose to 47 out of 175.

Curiously enough, New England plucked a new prosperity from the ugly jaws of the embargo. With shipping tied up and imported goods scarce, the resourceful Yankees reopened old factories and erected new ones. The real foundations of modern

Launching of the Ship *Fame,* by George Ropes, Jr., 1802   Jefferson's embargo throttled thriving New England shipyards like this one, stirring bitter resentment.

A Federalist circular in Massachusetts against the embargo cried out,

"Let every man who holds the name of America dear to him, stretch forth his hands and put this accursed thing, this *Embargo* from him. Be resolute, act like sons of liberty, of God, and your country; nerve your arm with vengeance against the Despot [Jefferson] who would wrest the inestimable germ of your Independence from you—and you shall be *Conquerors*!!!"

America's industrial might were laid behind the protective wall of the embargo, followed by nonintercourse and the War of 1812. Jefferson, the avowed critic of factories, may have unwittingly done more for American manufacturing than Alexander Hamilton, industry's outspoken friend.

Jefferson's embargo, followed in mitigated form by nonintercourse, undeniably pinched England. Many British importers and manufacturers suffered severe losses, especially those dependent on American cotton. As thousands of factory workers were thrown out of jobs, agitation mounted for a repeal of the restrictions that had brought on the embargo. A petition to Parliament in 1812, from the city of Birmingham alone, bore twenty thousand names on a sheet of parchment 150 feet long. So strong was public pressure that two days before Congress declared war in June 1812, the British foreign secretary announced that the offensive Orders in Council would be immediately suspended. The supreme irony is that Jefferson's policy of economic coercion did prevail in the end, but America was not patient enough to reap the reward of its sacrifices.

Jefferson's Legacy

Thomas Jefferson retained much of his popularity, even though it was severely tarnished by the embargo. But because he feared setting a precedent for dictatorship, he spurned suggestions that he might run for a third term. Jefferson, rather than Washington, who had no serious constitutional qualms about continuing in office, was the true father of the two-term presidential tradition. After leaving the presidency at the age of sixty-five, Jefferson lived eighteen more years, glad to have escaped what he called the "splendid misery" of the presidential penitentiary. He strongly favored the nomination and election of a kindred spirit as his successor, his friend and fellow Virginian, the quiet, intellectual, and unassuming James Madison.

Thomas Jefferson and John Adams died on the same day—appropriately the Fourth of July, 1826. The last words of Adams, then ninety-one, were, "Thomas Jefferson still survives." He was wrong, for three hours earlier Jefferson had breathed his last breath. But Thomas Jefferson still survives in the democratic ideals and liberal principles of the great nation that he risked his all to found and that he served so long and faithfully.

Madison: Dupe of Napoleon

Scholarly James Madison took the presidential oath on March 4, 1809, as the awesome conflict in Europe was roaring to its climax. Madison was small of stature (5 feet, 4 inches; 1.62 meters), light of weight (about 100 pounds; 45 kilograms), bald of head, and weak of voice. Despite a distinguished career as a legislator, as president he fell tragically short of providing vigorous executive leadership. Crippled also by factions within his cabinet, he was unable to dominate his party, as Jefferson had once done.

Early in 1805 Jefferson privately foresaw the two-term Twenty-Second Amendment (1951).

"General Washington set the example of voluntary retirement after eight years. I shall follow it, and a few more precedents will oppose the obstacle of habit to anyone after a while who shall endeavor to extend his term. Perhaps it may beget a disposition to establish it by an amendment of the Constitution."

The Non-Intercourse Act of 1809—the limited substitute for the embargo aimed solely at Britain and France—would expire in about a year. Congress, desperately attempting to uphold American rights, adopted in 1810 a bargaining measure known as Macon's Bill No. 2. While permitting American trade with all the world, it dangled an attractive lure. If either England or France repealed its commercial restrictions, America would restore nonimportation against the nonrepealing nation. In short, the United States would bribe the belligerents into respecting its rights.

This opportunity was made to order for Napoleon, the master of deceit. He was eager to resume nonimportation against the British because it would serve as a partial blockade, which he would not have to raise a finger to enforce. Accordingly, he blandly announced, in August 1810, that his objectionable decrees had been repealed. Napoleon, prince of liars, had no intention whatever of repeal-

> *Insisted the editor of Niles's* Weekly Register *(June 27, 1812),*
>
> "The injuries received from France do not lessen the enormity of those heaped upon us by *England*. . . . In this 'straight betwixt two' we had an unquestionable right to select our enemy. We have given the preference to *Great Britain* . . . on account of her more flagrant wrongs."

ing his damaging decrees. But Madison, frantically seeking to wrest a recognition of American rights from England, accepted French bad faith as good faith. He formally announced, in November 1810, that France had complied with the terms of Macon's Bill No. 2 and that nonimportation would consequently be reestablished against Britain.

His decision was fateful. Once Madison had aligned his nation against England commercially, he found himself gravitating toward France politically—and edging toward the whirlpool of war. Events at sea as well as events on land soon tipped him into the maelstrom.

War Whoops Arouse the War Hawks

The complexion of the Twelfth Congress, which met late in 1811, differed markedly from that of its predecessor. Recent elections had swept away many of the older "submission men" and replaced them with young hotheads, chiefly from the South and West. The youthful newcomers—"the boys," Virginia congressman John Randolph sneeringly called them—were on fire for a new war with the old enemy. Not having had a conflict in their own generation, these war hawks were weary of hearing how their fathers had "whipped" the British single-handedly. They won control of the House of Representatives and elevated to the speakership the tall (6 feet, 2 inches; 1.88 meters), eloquent, and magnetic Henry Clay of Kentucky, the gallant "Harry of the West," then only thirty-four years old.

The war hawks wanted "Free Trade and Sailors' Rights," as well as free land. It may seem strange

President James Madison (1751–1836)
Although an eminent constitutionalist, legislator, and diplomatist, he was not a strong chief executive. He was the only president ever to go directly to the fighting front—a foolish gesture—but he quickly rode away as the British advanced on Washington in 1814.

Tecumseh (1768?–1813)   A Shawnee Indian born in the Ohio country, he was probably the most gifted organizer and leader of his people in U.S. history. A noted warrior, he fought the tribal custom of torturing prisoners and opposed the practice of permitting any one tribe to sell land that, he believed, belonged to all Indians.

that settlers beyond the mountains, many of whom had never seen a body of salt water larger than a salt lick, should want to fight for maritime rights. But the proud, nationalistic westerners were outraged by the manhandling of American sailors and by the British Orders in Council that dammed up their agricultural products from shipment to Europe. Westerners also joined many of their fellow citizens

> *In a speech at Vincennes, Indiana Territory, Tecumseh (1768?–1813) said,*
>
> "Sell a country! Why not sell the air, the clouds, and the great sea, as well as the earth? Did not the Great Spirit make them all for the use of his children?"

in believing that only a vigorous assertion of American rights could demonstrate the viability of American nationhood—and of democracy as a form of government. If America could not fight to protect itself, its experiment in republicanism would be discredited in the eyes of a scoffing world.

Western war hawks were especially eager to wipe out a dangerously renewed Indian threat to the pioneer settlers who were streaming steadily into the trans-Allegheny wilderness. As this white flood washed through the green forests, more and more Indians were pushed farther and farther toward the setting sun. Indian leaders particularly worried about white encroachment on the area known as Kentucky. Generations of Native Americans had observed a taboo against settling in the Kentucky region or even hunting extensively in it. Kentucky formed a buffer between the northern and southern tribes and served as a hunting reserve used only in times of scarcity. Now the Indians watched with mounting anxiety from the banks of the Ohio River as flatboat after flatboat of white settlers floated downstream, bound for Kentucky.

Two remarkable Shawnee brothers, Tecumseh and the Prophet, concluded that if this onrushing tide were ever to be stopped, that time had come. They began to weld together a far-flung confederacy of all the tribes east of the Mississippi. Theirs was a last, desperate attempt to realize the dream of a large-scale pan-Indian alliance against the whites that had repeatedly eluded their ancestors. They inspired a vibrant movement of Indian unity and cultural revitalization. They urged their followers to give up textile clothing in exchange for traditional buckskin garments. Their warriors foreswore firewater in order to be fit for the last-ditch battle with the "paleface" intruders. Tecumseh argued eloquently that Indians should not recognize whites' concept of "ownership" of the land. Rather, he urged, no Indian should cede control of land to whites unless all Indians agreed.

White frontierspeople and their war-hawk spokesmen in Congress were convinced that British "scalp buyers" in Canada were nourishing the Indians' growing strength. Seizing the initiative, American general William Henry Harrison advanced upon Tecumseh's headquarters at Tippecanoe in present-day Indiana on November 7, 1811. He forced the Indians from the village and burned it to the ground. Fighting alongside the British, Tecumseh was killed in 1813, at the Battle of the Thames. With him perished the dream of an Indian confederacy.

In the South, Andrew Jackson inflicted a similar, crushing defeat on the Creek Indians at the Battle of Horseshoe Bend (in present-day Alabama) on March 27, 1814. These victories effectively quashed Indian resistance to white expansion east of the Mississippi. The way now lay open for a surge of settlement into the Ohio country and the southwestern frontier.

Harrison's onslaught at Tippecanoe had broken the back of the Indian rebellion. It also made the blood course faster in the veins of the impetuous war hawks. People like Representative Felix Grundy of Tennessee, three of whose brothers had been killed in clashes with Indians, cried that there was only one way to remove the menace of the Indians: wipe out their Canadian base. Canada was a lush prize—so near, so desirable, and apparently so defenseless. "On to Canada, on to Canada" was the war hawks' ominous chant. Southern expansionists, less vocal, cast a covetous eye on Florida, then weakly held by Britain's ally Spain.

Militant war hawks, with scattered but essential support from other sections, finally engineered a declaration of war in June 1812. The vote in the

William Henry Harrison (1773–1841), Indian fighter and later president, called Tecumseh

"One of those uncommon geniuses who spring up occasionally to produce revolutions and overturn the established order of things. If it were not for the vicinity of the United States, he would perhaps be founder of an Empire that would rival in glory that of Mexico or Peru."

House was 79 to 49, in the Senate 19 to 13 (see table below). The close tally revealed a dangerous degree of national disunity. Representatives from the pro-British maritime and commercial centers, as well as from the middle Atlantic states, almost solidly opposed hostilities. Ironically, the West and Southwest, mostly landlocked, foisted upon the sea-fronting East a war for a free sea that the East vehemently resented.

War Vote in House of Representatives, 1812, Showing Western and Southwestern War Sentiment

States	Regions	For War	Against War
N.H.	Frontier New England	3	2
Vt.		3	1
Mass.	Maritime and Federalist New England; Mass (includes frontier Maine)	6	8
R.I.		0	2
Conn.		0	7
N.Y.	Commercial and Federalist middle states	3	11
N.J.		2	4
Del.		0	1
Pa.	Jeffersonian middle states	16	2
Md.		6	3
Va.	Jeffersonian southern states	14	5
N.C.		6	3
S.C.		8	0
Ga.		3	0
Ohio	The trans-Allegheny West—nest of war hawks	1	0
Ky.		5	0
Tenn.		3	0
		79	49

"Mr. Madison's War"

But why fight Britain rather than France, which had committed nearly as many maritime offenses? The traditional Republican attachment to France partly explains the choice of foe, as does the visibility of British impressments and the British arming of the Indians, who were smashing into pioneer cabins on the frontier.

The tempting prize of Canada also beckoned from the north. Americans fondly (but wrongly) believed that taking Canada would be absurdly simple, a "frontiersman's frolic." If this northern mirage had not been so inviting, the administration might well have waited a few more months and thereby learned of London's repeal of the Orders in Council, announced two days *before* Congress voted for war. Had there been an Atlantic cable, the war hawks probably could not have forced a declaration of hostilities through the Senate.

Seafaring New England damned the war for a free sea. The news of the declaration of war was greeted with muffled bells, flags at half-mast, and public fasting. Why the opposition? To New Englanders, impressment was an old and exaggerated wrong. New England shippers and manufacturers were still raking in money, and profits dull patriotism. Pro-British Federalists in the Northeast also sympathized with England and resented the Virginia dynasty's sympathy with Napoleon, whom they regarded as the "Corsican butcher" and the "anti-Christ of the age."

Federalists also condemned the War of 1812 because they opposed the acquisition of Canada, which would merely add more agrarian states from the wild Northwest. This, in turn, would increase the voting strength of the Jeffersonian Republicans. New England Federalists were determined, wrote one versifier,

> To rule the nation if they could,
> But see it damned if others should.

The bitterness of rule-or-ruin New Englanders against "Mr. Madison's War" led them to treason or near-treason. In a sense America had to fight two enemies simultaneously: Old England and New England. New England gold holders probably lent more dollars to the British exchequer than to the federal treasury. New England farmers sent huge quantities of supplies and foodstuffs to Canada, enabling British armies to invade New York. New England governors stubbornly refused to permit their militia to serve outside their own states.

Thus perilously divided, the barely United States, plunged into armed conflict against Britain, then the world's most powerful empire. No sober American could have much reasonable hope of victory.

The Present State of Our Country Partisan disunity over the War of 1812 threatens the nation's very existence. The prowar Jeffersonian at the left is attacking the pillar of federalism; the antiwar Federalist at the right is trying to pull down democracy. The spirit of Washington warns that the country's welfare depends upon all three pillars, including republicanism.

Chronology

1800	Jefferson defeats Adams for presidency		**1806**	Burr treason trial
1801	Judiciary Act of 1801		**1807**	*Chesapeake* affair Embargo Act
1801– **1805**	Naval war with Tripoli		**1808**	Madison elected president
1802	Revised naturalization law Judiciary Act of 1801 repealed		**1809**	Non-Intercourse Act replaces Embargo Act
1803	*Marbury* v. *Madison* Louisiana Purchase		**1810**	Macon's Bill No. 2 Napoleon announces (falsely) repeal of blockade decrees Madison reestablishes nonimportation against Britain
1804	Jefferson reelected president Impeachment of Justice Chase		**1811**	Battle of Tippecanoe
1804– **1806**	Lewis and Clark expedition		**1812**	United States declares war on Britain
1805	Peace treaty with Tripoli		**1813**	Battle of the Thames
1805– **1807**	Pike's explorations		**1814**	Battle of Horseshoe Bend

SUGGESTED READINGS

PRIMARY SOURCE DOCUMENTS

Thomas Jefferson's "First Inaugural Address" (1801), in Henry Steele Commager, *Documents of American History*, echoed the themes of Washington's Farewell Address and set the tone for his presidency. Reuben G. Thwaites, ed., *Original Journals of the Lewis and Clark Expedition** (1904), chronicles the explorers' adventures. For the political flavor of the age, see the debate over the Embargo Act* (1807); for Constitutional history, read the decision of John Marshall in *Marbury* v. *Madison** (1803). See James Madison, "War Message"* (1812), in James D. Richardson, ed., *Messages and Papers of the Presidents* (1896), Vol. I, pp. 500–504; and the protest of thirty-four Federalist congressmen, *Annals of Congress** 12 Cong., I sess., II cols. 2219–2221 (1812). John Marshall's decision in *McCulloch* v. *Maryland**, 4 Wheaton 316 (1819), is a leading statement of the era's surging nationalism. Timothy Dwight offers a participant's view of the opposition to the war in *The History of the Hartford Convention** (1833).

---

*An asterisk indicates that the document, or an excerpt from it, can be found in Thomas A. Bailey and David M. Kennedy, eds., *The American Spirit: United States History as Seen by Contemporaries,* 9th ed. (Boston: Houghton Mifflin, 1998).

SECONDARY SOURCES

A monument of American historical writing is Henry Adams, *History of the United States During the Administrations of Jefferson and Madison* (9 vols., 1889–1891), available in a one-volume abridgement edited by Ernest Samuels. Especially fascinating are Adams's prologue and epilogue on the United States in 1800 and 1817. A brief introduction is given in Marshall Smelser, *The Democratic Republic, 1801–1815* (1968). Problems with the judiciary can be traced in Albert J. Beveridge's still-respected *Life of John Marshall* (4 vols., 1919). A more recent and succinct analysis is Richard E. Ellis, *The Jeffersonian Crisis: Courts and Politics in the New Republic* (1971). For a broad understanding of legal developments in this period, see Lawrence Friedman, *A History of American Law* (1973); Morton J. Horwitz, *The Transformation of American Law, 1780–1860* (1977); Alfred H. Kelly, Winfred A. Harbison, and Herman Belz, *The American Constitution: Its Origins and Development* (6th ed., 1983). On the Supreme Court, see R. Kent Newmyer, *The Supreme Court under Marshall and Taney* (1986), and G. Edward White, *The Marshall Court and Cultural Change, 1815–1835* (1988). Politics are treated in a broad, imaginative context in James S. Young, *The Washington*

Community, 1800–1829 (1966), and more traditionally in Noble E. Cunningham's rebuttal, *The Process of Government under Jefferson* (1979). See also Robert M. Johnstone, Jr., *Jefferson and the Presidency* (1979), and the Joyce Appleby, Lance Banning, and Drew McCoy volumes cited in Chapter 10. Noble E. Cunningham, Jr., *In Pursuit of Reason: The Life of Thomas Jefferson* (1987), is a short biography. The standard scholarly biography is Merrill D. Peterson, *Thomas Jefferson and the New Nation* (1970). Peterson has also scrutinized *The Jefferson Image in the American Mind* (1960). Leonard D. White brings administrative history to life in *The Jeffersonians* (rev. ed., 1959). Forrest McDonald is highly critical of his subject in *The Presidency of Thomas Jefferson* (1976). Leonard Levy debunks Jefferson's liberalism in *Jefferson and Civil Liberties* (1963); Bernard W. Sheehan examines another important aspect of policy in *Seeds of Extinction: Jeffersonian Philanthropy and the American Indian* (1973). See also Reginald Horsman, *Expansion and American Indian Policy, 1783–1812* (1967), and Gregory Evans Dowd, *A Spirited Resistance: The North American Indian Struggle for Unity, 1745–1815* (1992). Donald

Jackson, *Thomas Jefferson and the Stony Mountain: Exploring the West from Monticello* (1981), captures Jefferson's fascination with the West. See, also Stephen E. Ambrose's spirited biography of Meriwether Lewis, *Undaunted Courage* (1996). A first-class study of the negotiator of the Louisiana Purchase is George Dangerfield, *Chancellor Robert R. Livingston of New York* (1960). An expansionist thesis is fully developed in Alexander De Conde, *This Affair of Louisiana* (1976). The embargo is treated in Burton Spivak, *Jefferson's English Crisis: Commerce, Embargo and the Republican Revolution* (1979). See also Doron S. Ben-Atar, *The Origins of Jeffersonian Commercial Policy and Diplomacy* (1993). Daniel Boorstin vividly evokes the intellectual climate of the age in *The Lost World of Thomas Jefferson* (1948). John C. Miller, *The Wolf by the Ears: Thomas Jefferson and Slavery* (1977), probes the third president's attitudes on an important question. Irving Brant looks at *James Madison, Secretary of State* (1953), and F. E. Ewing examines Jefferson's powerful treasury secretary in *America's Forgotten Statesman: Albert Gallatin* (1959)

12

The Second War for Independence and the Upsurge of Nationalism

1812–1824

*The American continents . . . are henceforth not to
be considered as subjects for future colonization
by any European powers.*

President James Monroe, December 2, 1823

On to Canada over Land and Lakes

The War of 1812, largely because of widespread disunity, ranks as one of America's worst-fought wars.
There was no burning national anger, as there had
been in 1807 following the *Chesapeake* outrage. The
supreme lesson of this conflict was the folly of leading a divided and apathetic people into war.

The regular army was scandalously inadequate,
for it was ill-trained, ill-disciplined, and widely scattered. It had to be supplemented by the even more
poorly trained militia, who were sometimes distinguished by their speed of foot in leaving the battlefield. Some of the ranking generals were semisenile

heirlooms from the Revolutionary War, rusting on
their laurels and lacking in vigor and vision.

The offensive strategy against Canada was especially poorly conceived. Had the Americans captured Montreal, the center of population and
transportation, everything to the west would have
died, just as the leaves of a tree wither when the
trunk is girdled. But instead of laying ax to the trunk,
the Americans frittered away their strength in the
three-pronged invasion of 1812. The trio of invading
forces that set out from Detroit, Niagara, and Lake
Champlain were all beaten back shortly after they
had crossed the Canadian border.

By contrast, the British and Canadians displayed energy from the outset. Early in the war they

233

The Three U.S. Invasions of 1812

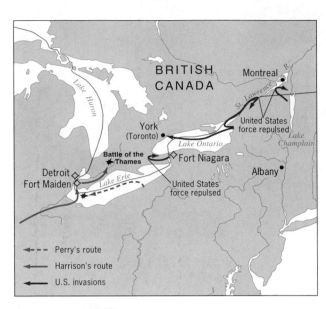

Campaigns of 1813

captured the American fort of Michilimackinac, which commanded the upper Great Lakes and the Indian-inhabited area to the south and west. Their brilliant defensive operations were led by the inspired British general Isaac Brock and assisted (in the American camp) by "General Mud" and "General Confusion."

When several American land invasions of Canada were again hurled back in 1813, Americans looked for success on water. Control of the Great Lakes was vital, and an energetic American naval officer, Oliver Hazard Perry, managed to build a fleet of green-timbered ships on the shores of Lake Erie, manned by even greener seamen. When he captured a British fleet in a furious engagement on Lake Erie, he reported to his superior, "We have met the enemy and they are ours." Perry's victory and his slogan infused new life into the drooping American cause. Forced to withdraw from Detroit and Fort Malden, the retreating redcoats were overtaken by General Harrison's army and beaten at the Battle of the Thames in October 1813.

Despite these successes, the Americans by late 1814, far from invading Canada, were grimly defending their own soil against the invading British. In Europe, the diversionary power of Napoleon was destroyed in mid-1814, and the dangerous despot was exiled to the Mediterranean isle of Elba. The United States, which had so brashly provoked war behind the protective skirts of Napoleon, was now left to face the music alone. As thousands of victorious veteran redcoats began to pour from the Continent into Canada, Europe's distresses, for once, failed the Americans.

Assembling some ten thousand crack troops, the British prepared in 1814 for a crushing blow into New York, along the familiar lake-river route. In the absence of roads, the invader was forced to bring supplies over the Lake Champlain waterway. A weaker American fleet, commanded by the thirty-year-old Thomas Macdonough, challenged the British. The ensuing battle was desperately fought near Plattsburgh, on September 11, 1814, on floating slaughterhouses. The American flagship at one point was in grave trouble. But Macdonough, unexpectedly turning his ship about with cables, confronted the enemy with a fresh broadside and snatched victory from the fangs of defeat.

The results of this heroic naval battle were momentous. The invading British army was forced to retreat. Macdonough thus saved at least upper New York from conquest, New England from further disaffection, and the Union from possible dissolution. He also profoundly affected the concurrent negotiations of the Anglo-American peace treaty in Europe.

Washington Burned and New Orleans Defended

A second formidable British force, numbering about four thousand, landed in the Chesapeake Bay area in August 1814. Advancing rapidly on Washington, it easily dispersed some six thousand panicky militia at Bladensburg ("the Bladensburg races"). The invaders then entered the capital and set fire to most of the public buildings, including the Capitol and the White House ("the Yankee Palace"). President Madison and his aides, chased into the surrounding hills like frightened rabbits, witnessed from afar the billowing smoke. The British fleet next appeared before Baltimore, a nest for privateers, but was beaten off by the doughty defenders at Fort McHenry, despite "bombs bursting in air." Francis Scott Key, a detained American anxiously watching the bombardment at Baltimore from a British ship, was inspired to write the words of "The Star-Spangled Banner." Set to the tune of a saucy English tavern refrain, the song quickly attained popularity.

A third British blow of 1814, aimed at New Orleans, menaced the entire Mississippi Valley. Gaunt and hawk-faced Andrew Jackson, fresh from crushing the southwest Indians at the Battle of Horseshoe Bend, was placed in command (see map, p. 251). His hodgepodge force consisted of seven thousand sailors, regulars, pirates, and Frenchmen, as well as militiamen from Louisiana, Kentucky, and Tennessee. Among the defenders were two Louisiana regiments of free black volunteers, numbering about four hundred men. The Americans threw up their entrenchment, and in the words of a popular song:

> *Behind it stood our little force—*
> *None wished it to be greater;*
> *For ev'ry man was half a horse,*
> *And half an alligator.*

The overconfident British, numbering some 8,000 battle-seasoned veterans, blundered badly. They made the mistake of launching a frontal assault, on January 8, 1815, on the entrenched American riflemen and cannoneers. The attackers suffered the most devastating defeat of the entire

The Fall of Washington, or Maddy in Full Flight   President Madison ("Maddy") was forced into humiliating withdrawal from the capital in 1814, when British forces put the torch to Washington, D.C.

Constitution and *Guerrière,* 1812   The *Guerrière* was heavily outweighed and outgunned, yet its British captain eagerly—and foolishly—sought combat. His ship was totally destroyed. Historian Henry Adams later concluded that this duel "raised the United States in one half hour to the rank of a first-class Power in the world." The buckler on the sword from the *U.S.S. Constitution* commemorates the famous battle. Today, the *U.S.S. Constitution,* berthed in Boston Harbor, remains the oldest actively commissioned ship in the U.S. Navy.

war, losing over 2,000, killed and wounded, in half an hour, as compared with some seventy for the Americans. This slaughter was as useless as it was horrible, for the treaty of peace had been signed at Ghent, in Europe, two weeks earlier. But Jackson became more than ever the hero of the West.

The "glorious news" from New Orleans reached Washington early in February 1815, and about two weeks later came the tidings of the treaty of peace. Naive citizens promptly concluded that the British, beaten to their knees by Jackson, had hastened to make terms.

Man for man and ship for ship, the American navy did much better than the army. American craft on the whole were more skillfully handled, had better gunners, and were manned by non–press-gang crews who were burning to avenge numerous indignities. The American frigates, notably the *Constitution* ("Old Ironsides"), had thicker sides, heavier firepower, and larger crews, of which one sailor in six was a free black.

Its wrath aroused, the Royal Navy had finally retaliated by throwing a ruinous naval blockade along America's coast and by landing raiding parties

A Wasp on a Frolic   U.S. sloops-of-war *Wasp* and *Hornet* sting John Bull's pride. The *Wasp* captured the *Frolic.*

almost at will. American economic life, including fishing, was crippled. Customs revenues were choked off, and near the end of the war the bankrupt Treasury was unable to meet its maturing obligations.

The Treaty of Ghent

Tsar Alexander I of Russia, hard-pressed by Napoleon's army and not wanting his British ally to fritter away its strength in America, proposed mediation between the clashing Anglo-Saxon cousins in 1812. The tsar's feeler eventually set in motion the machinery that brought five American peacemakers to the quaint Belgian city of Ghent in 1814. The bickering group was headed by early rising, puritanical John Quincy Adams, son of John Adams, who deplored the late-hour card playing of his high-living colleague Henry Clay.

Confident after their military successes, the British envoys made sweeping demands for a neutralized Indian buffer state in the Great Lakes region, control of the Great Lakes, and a substantial part of conquered Maine. The Americans flatly rejected these terms, and the talks appeared stalemated. But news of British reverses in upper New York and at Baltimore, and increasing war-weariness in Britain, made London more willing to compromise. Preoccupied with redrafting Napoleon's map of Europe at the Congress of Vienna and eyeing still-dangerous France, the British lion resigned

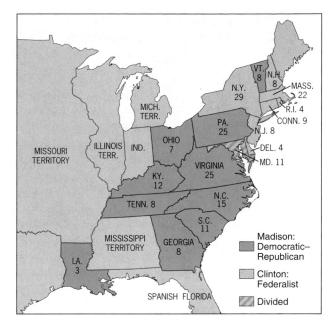

Presidential Election of 1812 (with electoral vote by state) The Federalists showed impressive strength in the North, and their presidential candidate, DeWitt Clinton, the future "father of the Erie Canal," almost won. If the 25 electoral votes of Pennsylvania had gone to the New Yorker, he would have won, 114 to 103.

Smarting from wounded pride on the sea, the London Times *(December 30, 1814) urged chastisement for Americans:*

"The people—naturally vain, boastful, and insolent—have been filled with an absolute contempt for our maritime power, and a furious eagerness to beat down our maritime pretensions. Those passions, which have been inflamed by success, could only have been cooled by what in vulgar and emphatic language has been termed "a sound flogging.""

itself to licking its wounds. Revenge against its upstart American offspring would be sweet—but expensive. Once again European distress brought American diplomatic success, for the War of 1812 came to its merciful end thanks to events in the Old World.

The Treaty of Ghent, signed on Christmas Eve in 1814, was essentially an armistice. Both sides simply agreed to stop fighting and to restore conquered territory. No mention was made of those grievances for which America had ostensibly fought: the Indian menace, search and seizure, Orders in Council, impressment, and confiscations. These discreet omissions have often been cited as further evidence of the insincerity of the war hawks. Rather, they are proof that the Americans had not managed to defeat the British. With neither side able to impose its will, the treaty negotiations—like the war itself—ended as a virtual draw. Relieved Americans boasted "Not One Inch of Territory Ceded or Lost"—a phrase that contrasted strangely with the "On to Canada" rallying cry of the war's outset.

Federalist Grievances and the Hartford Convention

Defiant New England remained a problem. It prospered during the conflict, owing largely to illicit trade with the enemy in Canada and to the absence of a British blockade until 1814. But the embittered opposition of the Federalists to the war continued unabated.

As the war dragged on, New England extremists became more vocal. A small minority of them proposed secession from the Union, or at least a separate peace with England. Ugly rumors were afloat about "Blue Light" Federalists—treacherous New Englanders who supposedly flashed lanterns on the shore so that blockading British cruisers would be alerted to the attempted escape of American ships.

The most spectacular manifestation of Federalist discontent was the ill-omened Hartford Convention. Late in 1814, when the capture of New Orleans seemed imminent, Massachusetts issued a call for a convention at Hartford, Connecticut. The states of Massachusetts, Connecticut, and Rhode Island dispatched full delegations; neighboring New Hampshire and Vermont sent partial representation. This group of prominent men, twenty-six in all, met in complete secrecy for about three weeks—December 15, 1814, to January 5, 1815—to discuss their grievances and to seek redress for their wrongs.

In truth, the Hartford Convention was actually less radical than the alarmists supposed. Though a minority of delegates gave vent to wild talk of secession, the convention's final report was quite moderate. It demanded, first, financial assistance from Washington to compensate for lost trade; and, second, constitutional amendments requiring a two-thirds vote in Congress before an embargo could be imposed, new states admitted, or war declared—except in case of invasion.

Three special envoys from Massachusetts carried these demands to the burned-out capital of Washington. The trio arrived just in time to be overwhelmed by the glorious news from New Orleans, followed by that from Ghent. Pursued by the sneers and jeers of the press, they sank away in disgrace and into obscurity.

The Hartford resolutions, as it turned out, were the death dirge of the Federalist party. In 1816, the next year, the Federalists nominated their last presidential candidate. He was handily trounced by James Monroe, yet another Virginian.

Unhappily, the stench of treason has clung to the Hartford Convention. The taint was not justified by its formal resolutions. Yet if the War of 1812 had not ended when it did, the convention might well have paved the way for treasonable courses.

Federalist doctrines of disunity, which long survived the party, blazed a fateful trail. Until 1815 there was far more talk of nullification and secession in New England than in any other section, including the South. The outright flouting of the Jeffersonian embargo and the later crippling of the war effort were the two most damaging acts of nullification in America prior to the events leading to the Civil War.

Three Wise Men of Gotham Went to Sea in a Bowl
This satirical anti-Federalist cartoon shows three Massachusetts men sailing precariously for Washington in a large chamber pot bearing Hartfordite demands. These "wise men" are trying to quiet their fears of sinking by exchanging off-color remarks.

The Second War for American Independence

The War of 1812 was a small war, involving about 6,000 Americans killed or wounded. It was but a footnote to the mighty European conflagration. In 1812, when Napoleon invaded Russia with about 500,000 men, Madison tried to invade Canada with about 5,000 men. But if the American conflict was globally unimportant, it had huge consequences for the United States.

The Republic had shown that it would resist, sword in hand, what it regarded as grievous wrongs. Other nations developed a new respect for America's fighting prowess. Naval officers like Perry and Macdonough were the most effective type of negotiators; the hot breath of their broadsides spoke the most eloquent diplomatic language. America's emissaries abroad were henceforth treated with less scorn. In a diplomatic sense, if not in a military sense, the conflict could be called the Second War for American Independence.

A new nation, moreover, was welded in the fiery furnace of armed conflict. Sectionalism, now identified with discredited New England Federalists, was dealt a black eye. The painful events of the war glaringly revealed, as perhaps nothing else could have done, the folly of sectional disunity. In a sense the most conspicuous casualty of the war was the Federalist party.

War heroes emerged, especially the two Indian-fighters, Andrew Jackson and William Henry Harrison. Both of them were to become president. Left in the lurch by their British friends at Ghent, the Indians were forced to make such terms as they could. They reluctantly consented, in a series of treaties, to relinquish vast areas of forested land north of the Ohio River.

Manufacturing prospered behind the fiery wooden wall of the British blockade. In an economic sense, as well as in a diplomatic sense, the War of 1812 may be regarded as the Second War for American Independence. The industries that were thus stimulated by the fighting rendered America less dependent on Europe's workshops.

Regrettably, the war revived and intensified bitterness toward England. The uglier incidents of the conflict, notably the burning of Washington, added fuel to a century of Britain hating and Britain baiting. Few Americans could have guessed in 1815 that it was to be the nation's last armed conflict with England.

Canadian patriotism and nationalism also received a powerful stimulus from the clash. Many Canadians felt betrayed by the Treaty of Ghent. They were especially aggrieved by the failure to secure an Indian buffer state or even mastery of the Great Lakes. Canadians fully expected the frustrated Yankees to return, and for a time the Americans and British engaged in a floating arms race on the Great

The War of 1812 won a new respect for America among many Britons. Michael Scott, a young lieutenant in the British navy, wrote,

"I don't like Americans; I never did, and never shall like them. . . . I have no wish to eat with them, drink with them, deal with, or consort with them in any way; but let me tell the whole truth, *nor* fight with them, were it not for the laurels to be acquired, by overcoming an enemy so brave, determined, and alert, and in every way so worthy of one's steel, as they have always proved."

Lakes. But in 1817 the Rush-Bagot agreement between Britain and the United States severely limited naval armament on the lakes. Better relations brought the last border fortifications down in the 1870s, with the happy result that the United States and Canada came to share the world's longest unfortified boundary—5,527 miles (8,899 kilometers) long.

After Napoleon's final defeat at Waterloo in 1815, Europe slumped into a peace of exhaustion. Deposed monarchs returned to battered thrones, as the Old World took the rutted road back to conservatism, illiberalism, and reaction. But the American people were largely unaffected by these European developments. Turning their backs on the Old World, they faced resolutely toward the untamed West—and toward the task of building their democracy.

Nascent Nationalism

The most impressive by-product of the War of 1812 was a heightened nationalism—the spirit of nation-consciousness or national oneness. America may not have fought the war as one nation, but it emerged as one nation.

The changed mood even manifested itself in the birth of a distinctively national literature. Washington Irving and James Fenimore Cooper attained international recognition in the 1820s, significantly as the nation's first writers of importance to use American scenes and themes. School textbooks,

View of the Capitol, by Charles Burton, 1824   This painting of the Capitol building, much smaller than it is today, reveals the rustic conditions of the early days in the nation's capital. A series of architects worked on the Capitol, following William Thornton's original design along neo-classical, or "Greek Revival" lines. After the British burned the building in 1814, Boston's Charles Bulfinch oversaw the reconstruction of the Capitol, finally completed in 1830.

often British in an earlier era, were now being written by Americans for Americans. In the world of magazines, the highly intellectual *North American Review* began publication in 1815—the year of the triumph at New Orleans. Even American painters increasingly celebrated their native landscapes on their canvases.

A fresh nationalistic spirit could be recognized in many other areas as well. The rising tide of nation-consciousness even touched finance. A revived Bank of the United States was voted by Congress in 1816. A more handsome national capital began to rise from the ashes of Washington. The army was expanded to ten thousand men. The navy further covered itself with glory in 1815 when it administered a thorough beating to the piratical plunderers of North Africa. Stephen Decatur, naval hero of the War of 1812 and of the Barbary Coast expeditions, pungently captured the country's nationalist mood in a famous toast made on his return from the Mediterranean campaigns: "Our country! In her intercourse with foreign nations may she always be in the right; but our country, right or wrong!"

"The American System"

Nationalism likewise manifested itself in manufacturing. Patriotic Americans took pride in the factories that had recently mushroomed forth, largely as a result of the self-imposed embargoes and the war.

When hostilities ended in 1815, British competitors undertook to recover lost ground. They began to dump the contents of their bulging warehouses on the United States, often cutting their prices below cost in an effort to strangle the American war-baby factories in the cradle. The infant industries bawled lustily for protection. To many red-blooded Americans it seemed as though the British, having failed to crush Yankee fighters on the battlefield, were now seeking to crush Yankee factories in the marketplace.

A nationalist Congress, out-Federalizing the old Federalists, responded by passing the path-breaking Tariff of 1816—the first tariff in American history instituted primarily for protection, not revenue. Its rates—roughly 20 to 25 percent on the value of dutiable imports—were not high enough to provide completely adequate safeguards, but the law was a bold beginning. A strongly protective trend was started that stimulated the appetites of the protected for more protection.

Nationalism was further highlighted by a grandiose plan of Henry Clay for developing a profitable home market. Still radiating the nationalism of war-hawk days, he threw himself behind an elaborate scheme known by 1824 as the American System. This system had three main parts. It began with a strong banking system, which would provide easy and abundant credit. Clay also advocated a protective tariff, behind which eastern manufacturing would flourish. Revenues gushing from the tariff would provide funds for the third component of the American system—a network of roads and canals, especially in the burgeoning Ohio Valley. Through these new arteries of transportation would flow foodstuffs and raw materials from the South and West to the North and East. In exchange, a stream of manufactured goods would flow in the return direction, knitting the country together economically and politically.

Persistent and eloquent demands by Henry Clay and others for better transportation struck a responsive chord with the public. The recent attempts to invade Canada had all failed partly because of oath-provoking roads—or no roads at all. People who have dug wagons out of hub-deep mud do not quickly forget their blisters and backaches. An outcry for better transportation, rising most noisily in the road-poor West, was one of the most striking aspects of the nationalism inspired by the War of 1812.

But attempts to secure federal funding for roads and canals stumbled on Republican constitutional scruples. Congress voted in 1817 to distribute $1.5 million to the states for internal improvements. But President Madison sternly vetoed this handout measure as unconstitutional. The individual states were thus forced to venture ahead with construction programs of their own, including the Erie Canal, triumphantly completed by New York in 1825. Jeffersonian Republicans, who had gulped down Hamiltonian loose constructionism on other important problems, choked on the idea of direct federal support of intrastate internal improvements. New England, in particular, strongly opposed federally constructed roads and canals, because such outlets would further drain away population and create competing states beyond the mountains.

Henry Clay (1777–1852), daguerreotype by Mathew Brady, 1849   A glamorous, eloquent, and ambitious member of the House and Senate for many years, Clay was thrice an unsuccessful candidate for the highest office in the land. "Sir," he declared in the Senate in 1850, "I would rather be right than be President." Right or wrong, he never made the grade, but his devotion to the Union was inspirational.

The So-Called Era of Good Feelings

James Monroe—6 feet (1.83 meters) tall, somewhat stooped, courtly, and mild-mannered—was nominated for the presidency in 1816 by the Republicans. They thus undertook to continue the so-called Virginia dynasty of Washington, Jefferson, and Madison. The fading Federalists ran a candidate for the last time in their checkered history, and he was crushed by 183 electoral votes to 34. The vanquished Federalist party was gasping its dying breaths, leaving the field to the triumphant Republicans and one-party rule.

In James Monroe, the man and the times auspiciously met. As the last president to wear an old-style cocked hat, he straddled two generations: the bygone age of the Founding Fathers and the emergent age of nationalism. Never brilliant, and perhaps

James Monroe (1758–1831), by Samuel F. B. Morse, 1819 Monroe fought in the Revolution (suffering a wound), served as minister to France, became copurchaser of Louisiana, and rose to the presidency in 1817. An excellent administrator, he presided over the Era of Good Feelings. His inaugural address declared, "National honor is national property of the highest value." His name is imperishably attached to the Monroe Doctrine and Monrovia, the capital city of Liberia in Africa. He had strongly backed the colonization there of ex-slaves. His wife and two daughters had expensive tastes, and like plantation owner Jefferson, he died deeply in debt.

Boston's Columbian Centinel *was not the only newspaper to regard President Monroe's early months as the Era of Good Feelings. The* Washington *National Intelligencer observed in July 1817,*

"Never before, perhaps, since the institution of civil government, did the same harmony, the same absence of party spirit, the same national feeling, pervade a community. The result is too consoling to dispute too nicely about the cause."

This happy phrase has been commonly used since then to describe the administrations of Monroe.

The Era of Good Feelings, unfortunately, was something of a misnomer. Considerable tranquility and prosperity did in fact smile upon the early years of Monroe, but the period was a troubled one. The acute issues of the tariff, the bank, internal improvements, and the sale of public lands were being hotly contested. Sectionalism was crystallizing, and the conflict over slavery was beginning to raise its hideous head.

The Panic of 1819 and the Curse of Hard Times

Much of the goodness went out of the good feelings in 1819, when a paralyzing economic panic descended. It brought deflation, depression, bankruptcies, bank failures, unemployment, soup kitchens, and overcrowded pesthouses known as debtors' prisons.

This was the first national financial panic since President Washington took office. Many factors contributed to the catastrophe of 1819, but looming large was overspeculation in frontier lands. The Bank of the United States, through its western branches, had become deeply involved in this popular type of outdoor gambling.

Financial paralysis from the panic, which lasted in some degree for several years, gave a rude setback to the nationalistic ardor. The West was especially hard hit. When the pinch came, the Bank of the United States forced the speculative ("wildcat")

not great, the serene Virginian with gray-blue eyes was in intellect and personal force the least distinguished of the first eight presidents. But the times called for sober administration, not dashing heroics. And Monroe was an experienced, levelheaded executive, with an ear-to-the-ground talent for interpreting popular rumblings.

Emerging nationalism was further cemented by a goodwill tour Monroe undertook early in 1817, ostensibly to inspect military defenses. He pushed northward deep into New England and then westward to Detroit, viewing en route the Niagara Falls. Even in Federalist New England, "the enemy's country," he received a heartwarming welcome; a Boston newspaper was so far carried away as to announce that an "Era of Good Feelings" had been ushered in.

western banks to the wall and foreclosed mortgages on countless farms. All this was technically legal but politically unwise. In the eyes of the western debtor, the nationalist Bank of the United States soon became a kind of financial devil.

The panic of 1819 also created backwashes in the political and social world. The poorer classes—the one-suspender men and their families—were severely strapped and in their troubles was sown the seedbed of Jacksonian democracy. Hard times also directed attention to the inhumanity of imprisoning debtors. In extreme cases, often overplayed, mothers were torn from their infants for owing a few dollars. Mounting agitation against imprisonment for debt bore fruit in remedial legislation in an increasing number of states.

Growing Pains of the West

Marvelous indeed had been the onward march of the West; nine frontier states had joined the original thirteen between 1791 and 1819. With an eye to preserving the North-South sectional balance, most of these commonwealths had been admitted alternately, free or slave. (See Admission of States in the Appendix.)

Why this explosive expansion? In part, it was simply a continuation of the generations-old westward movement, which had been going on since early colonial days. In addition, the siren song of cheap land—"the Ohio fever"—had a special appeal to European immigrants. Quaintly garbed newcomers from abroad were beginning to stream down the gangplanks in impressive numbers, especially after the war of boycotts and bullets. Land exhaustion in the older tobacco states, where the soil was "mined" rather than cultivated, likewise drove people westward. Glib speculators accepted small down payments, making it easier to buy new holdings.

The western boom was stimulated by additional developments. Acute economic distress during the embargo years turned many pinched faces toward the setting sun. The crushing of the Indians in the Northwest and South, by Generals Harrison and Jackson, pacified the frontier and opened up vast virgin tracts of land. The building of highways improved the land routes to the Ohio Valley. Noteworthy was the Cumberland Road, begun in 1811, which ran ultimately from western Maryland to Illinois. The use of the first steamboat on western waters, also in 1811, heralded a new era of upstream navigation.

But the West, despite the inflow of settlers, was still weak in population and influence. Not potent

Fairview Inn or Three Mile House on Old Frederick Road, by Thomas Coke Ruckle, c. 1829
This busy scene on the Frederick Road, leading westward from Baltimore, was typical as pioneers flooded into the newly secured West in the early 1800s.

enough politically to make its voice heard, it was forced to ally itself with other sections. Thus strengthened, it demanded cheap acreage and partially achieved its goal in the Land Act of 1820, which authorized a buyer to purchase 80 virgin acres at a minimum of $1.25 an acre in cash. The West also demanded cheap transportation and slowly got it, despite the constitutional qualms of the presidents and the hostility of easterners. Finally, the West demanded cheap money, issued by its own "wildcat" banks, and fought the powerful Bank of the United States to attain its goal (see "Makers of America: Settlers of the Old Northwest," pp. 246–247).

Slavery and the Sectional Balance

Sectional tensions, involving rivalry between the slave South and the free North over control of the virgin West, were stunningly revealed in 1819. In that year the territory of Missouri knocked on the doors of Congress for admission as a slave state. This fertile and well-watered area contained sufficient population to warrant statehood. But the House of Representatives stymied the plans of the Missourians by passing the incendiary Tallmadge amendment. It stipulated that no more slaves should be brought into Missouri and also provided for the gradual emancipation of children born to slave parents already there. A mounting roar of anger burst from slave-holding southerners. They were joined by many depression-cursed pioneers who favored unhampered expansion of the West and by many northerners, especially diehard Federalists, who were eager to use the issue to break the back of the "Virginia dynasty."

Southerners saw in the Tallmadge amendment, which they eventually managed to defeat in the Senate, an ominous threat to sectional balance. When the Constitution was adopted in 1788, the North and South were running neck and neck in wealth and population. But with every passing decade, the North was becoming wealthier and also more thickly settled—an advantage reflected in an increasing northern majority in the House of Representatives. Yet in the Senate, each state had two votes, regardless of size. With eleven states free and eleven slave, the southerners had maintained equality. They were therefore in a good position to thwart any northern effort to interfere with the expansion of slavery, and they did not want to lose this veto.

The future of the slave system caused southerners profound concern. Missouri was the first state entirely west of the Mississippi River to be carved out of the Louisiana Purchase, and the Missouri emancipation amendment might set a damaging precedent for all the rest of the area. Even more disquieting was another possibility. If Congress could abolish the "peculiar institution" in Missouri, might it not attempt to do likewise in the older states of the South? The wounds of the Constitutional Convention of 1787 were once more ripped open.

Burning moral questions also protruded, even though the main issue was political and economic balance. A small but growing group of antislavery agitators in the North seized the occasion to raise an outcry against the evils of slavery. They were determined that the plague of human bondage should not spread further into the virgin territories.

The Uneasy Missouri Compromise

Deadlock in Washington was at length broken in 1820 by the time-honored American solution of compromise—actually a bundle of three compromises. Courtly Henry Clay of Kentucky, gifted conciliator, played a leading role. Congress, despite abolitionist pleas, agreed to admit Missouri as a

Antislavery Propaganda in the 1820s
The abolitionist propaganda on the two purses reflects the prominent role of women in the antislavery movement.

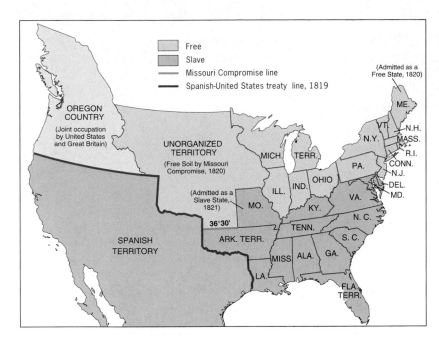

The Missouri Compromise and Slavery, 1820–1821   Note the 36° 30' line. In the 1780s Thomas Jefferson had written of slavery in America: "Indeed I tremble for my country when I reflect that God is just; that his justice cannot sleep forever; that . . . the Almighty has no attribute which can take side with us in such a contest." Now, at the time of the Missouri Compromise, Jefferson feared that his worst forebodings were coming to pass. "I considered it at once," he said of the Missouri question, "as the knell of the Union."

slave state. But at the same time, free-soil Maine, which until then had been a part of Massachusetts, was admitted as a separate state. The balance between North and South was thus kept at twelve states each and remained there for fifteen years. Although Missouri was permitted to retain slaves, all future bondage was prohibited in the remainder of the Louisiana Purchase north of the line of 36° 30'— the southern boundary of Missouri.

This horse-trading adjustment was politically evenhanded, though denounced by extremists on each side as a "dirty bargain." Both North and South yielded something; both gained something. The South won the prize of Missouri as an unrestricted slave state. The North won the concession that Congress could forbid slavery in the remaining territories. More gratifying to many northerners was the fact that the immense area north of 36° 30', except Missouri, was forever closed to the blight of slavery. Yet the restriction on future slavery in the territories was not unduly offensive to the slaveowners, partly because the northern prairie land did not seem suited to slave labor. Even so, a majority of southern congressmen voted against the compromise.

Neither North nor South was acutely displeased, although neither was completely happy. Fortunately, the Missouri Compromise lasted thirty-four years—a vital formative period in the life of the young Republic—and during that time it preserved the shaky compact of the states. Yet the embittered dispute over slavery heralded the future breakup of the Union. Ever after, the morality of the South's "peculiar institution" was an issue that could not be swept under the rug. The Missouri Compromise only ducked the question—it did not resolve it. Sooner or later, Thomas Jefferson predicted, it will "burst on us as a tornado."

While the debate over Missouri was raging, Thomas Jefferson (1743–1826) wrote to a correspondent,

"The Missouri question . . . is the most portentous one which ever yet threatened our Union. In the gloomiest moment of the revolutionary war I never had any apprehensions equal to what I feel from this source. . . . [The] question, like a firebell in the night, awakened and filled me with terror. . . . [With slavery] we have a wolf by the ears, and we can neither hold him nor safely let him go."

John Quincy Adams confided to his diary,

"I take it for granted that the present question is a mere preamble—a title-page to a great, tragic volume."

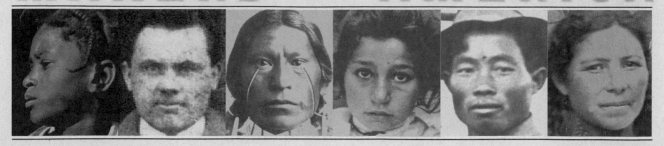

Settlers of the Old Northwest

The Old Northwest beckoned to settlers after the War of 1812. The withdrawal of the British protector weakened the Indians' grip on the territory. Then the transportation boom of the 1820s—steamboats on the Ohio, the National Highway stretching from Pennsylvania, the Erie Canal—opened broad arteries along which the westward movement flowed.

The first wave of newcomers came mainly from Kentucky, Tennessee, and the upland regions of Virginia and the Carolinas. Most migrants were rough-hewn white farmers who had been pushed from good land to bad by an expanding plantation economy. Like Joseph Cress of North Carolina, they were relieved to relinquish "them old red filds" where you "get nothing," in return for acres of new soil that "is as black and rich you wold want it." Some settlers acquired land for the first time. John Palmer, whose family left Kentucky for Illinois in 1831, recalled his father telling him "of land so cheap that we could all be landholders, where men were all *equal.*" Migrants from the South settled mainly in the southern portions of Ohio, Indiana, and Illinois.

As Palmer testified, the Old Northwest offered southern farmers an escape from the lowly social position they had endured as nonslaveholders in a slave society. Not that they objected to slavery or sympathized with blacks. Far from it: by enacting black codes in their new territories, they tried to prevent blacks from following them to paradise. They wanted their own democratic community, free of rich planters and African-Americans alike.

If southern "Butternuts," as these settlers were called, dominated settlement in the 1820s, the next decade brought Yankees from the Northeast. They were as land-starved as their southern counterparts. A growing population had gobbled up most of the good land east of the Appalachians. Yankee settlers came to the Old Northwest, especially to the north-

A Town Center, Marietta, Ohio
Forty-eight men from Massachusetts founded Marietta in 1788, making it the first settlement created under the provisions of the Ordinance of 1787. Within a decade, the town resembled the Yankee villages they had left behind.

ern parts of Ohio, Indiana, and Illinois, eager to make the region a profitable breadbasket for the Atlantic seaboard. Unlike Butternuts who wanted to quit forever the imposing framework of southern society, northerners hoped to recreate the world they had left behind.

Conflict soon emerged between Yankees and southerners. As self-sufficient farmers with little interest in producing for the market, the southerners viewed the northern newcomers as inhospitable, greedy, and excessively ambitious. "Yankee" became a term of reproach; a person who was cheated was said to have been "Yankeed." Northerners, in turn, viewed the southerners as uncivilized, a "coon dog and butcher knife tribe" with no interest in education, self-improvement, or agricultural innovation. Yankees, eager to tame both the land and its people, wanted to establish public schools and build roads, canals, and railroads—and they advocated taxes to fund such progress. Southerners opposed all these reforms, especially public schooling, which they regarded as an attempt to northernize their children.

Religion divided settlers as well. Northerners, typically Congregationalist and Presbyterian, wanted their ministers to be educated in seminaries. Southerners embraced the more revivalist Baptist and Methodist denominations. They preferred poor, humble preacher-farmers to professionally trained preachers whom they viewed as too distant from the Lord and the people. As the Baptist preacher Alexander Campbell put it, "The scheme of a learned priesthood . . . has long since proved itself to be a grand device to keep men in ignorance and bondage."

Not everyone, of course, fitted neatly into these molds. Abraham Lincoln, with roots in Kentucky, came to adopt views more akin to those of the Yankees than the southerners, whereas his New England-born archrival, Stephen Douglas, carefully cultivated the Butternut vote for the Illinois Democratic party.

As the population swelled and the region acquired its own character, the stark contrasts between northerners and southerners started to fade. By the 1850s northerners dominated numerically, and they succeeded in establishing public schools and fashioning internal improvements. Railroads and Great Lakes shipping tied the region ever more tightly to the northeast. Yankees and southerners sometimes allied as new kinds of cleavages emerged—between rich and poor, between city dwellers and farmers, and, once Irish and German immigrants started pouring into the region, between native Protestants and newcomer Catholics. Still, echoes of the clash between Yankees and Butternuts persisted. During the Civil War the southern counties of Ohio, Indiana, and Illinois, where southerners had first settled, harbored sympathizers with the South and served as a key area for Confederate military infiltration into the North. Decades later these same counties became a stronghold of the Ku Klux Klan. The Old Northwest may have become firmly anchored economically to the Northeast, but vestiges of its early dual personality persisted.

The Missouri Compromise and the concurrent panic of 1819 should have dimmed the political star of President Monroe. Certainly both unhappy events had a dampening effect on the Era of Good Feelings. But smooth-spoken James Monroe was so popular, and the Federalist opposition so weak, that in the presidential election of 1820 he received every electoral vote except one. Unanimity was an honor reserved for George Washington. Monroe, as it turned out, was the only president in American history to be reelected after a term in which a major financial panic began.

John Marshall and Judicial Nationalism

The upsurging nationalism of the post-Ghent years, despite the ominous setbacks concerning slavery, was further reflected and reinforced by the Supreme Court. The high tribunal continued to be dominated by the tall, thin, and aggressive Chief Justice John Marshall. One group of his decisions—perhaps the most famous—bolstered the power of the federal government at the expense of the states. A notable case in this category was *McCulloch* v. *Maryland* (1819). The suit involved an attempt by the state of Maryland to destroy a branch of the Bank of the United States by imposing a tax on its notes. John Marshall, speaking for the Court, declared the bank constitutional by invoking the Hamiltonian doctrine of implied powers (see p. 194). At the same time, he strengthened federal authority and slapped at state infringements when he denied the right of Maryland to tax the bank. With ringing emphasis, he affirmed "that the power to tax involves the power to destroy" and "that a power to create implies a power to preserve."

Marshall's ruling in this case gave the doctrine of "loose construction" its most famous formulation. The Constitution, he said, derived from the consent of the people and thus permitted the government to act for their benefit. He further argued that the Constitution was "intended to endure for ages to come and, consequently, to be adapted to the various crises of human affairs." Finally, he declared, "Let the end be legitimate, let it be within the scope of the Constitution, and all means which are appropriate, which are plainly adapted to that end, which are not prohibited, but consist with the letter and spirit of the Constitution, are constitutional."

John Marshall (1755–1835)   Born in a log cabin on the Virginia frontier, he attended law lectures for just a few weeks at the College of William and Mary—his only formal education.

Two years later (1821) the case of *Cohens* v. *Virginia* gave Marshall one of his greatest opportunities to defend the federal power. The Cohens, found guilty by the Virginia courts of illegally selling lottery tickets, appealed to the highest tribunal. Virginia "won," in the sense that the conviction of the Cohens was upheld. But in fact Virginia and all the individual states lost, because Marshall resoundingly asserted the right of the Supreme Court to review the decisions of the state supreme courts in all questions involving powers of the federal government. The states' rights proponents were aghast.

Hardly less significant was the celebrated "steamboat case," *Gibbons* v. *Ogden* (1824). The suit grew out of an attempt by the state of New York to grant to a private concern a monopoly of waterborne commerce between New York and New Jersey. Marshall sternly reminded the upstart state that the Constitution conferred on Congress alone the control of interstate commerce (see Art. I, Sec. VIII, para. 3). He thus struck with one hand another blow at states' rights, while upholding with the other the sovereign powers of the federal government. Interstate streams were thus cleared of this judicial snag; the departed spirit of Hamilton may well have applauded.

Judicial Dikes Against Democratic Excesses

Another sheaf of Marshall's decisions bolstered judicial barriers against democratic or demagogic attacks on property rights.

The notorious case of *Fletcher* v. *Peck* (1810) arose when a Georgia legislature, swayed by bribery, granted 35 million acres in the Yazoo River country (Mississippi) to private speculators. The next legislature, yielding to an angry public outcry, canceled the crooked transaction. But the Supreme Court, with Marshall presiding, decreed that the legislative grant was a contract (even though fraudulently secured) and that the Constitution forbids state laws "impairing" contracts (Art. I, Sec. X, para. 1). The decision was perhaps most noteworthy as further protecting property rights against popular pressures. It was also one of the earliest clear assertions of the right of the Supreme Court to invalidate state laws conflicting with the federal Constitution.

A similar principle was upheld in the case of *Dartmouth College* v. *Woodward* (1819), perhaps the best remembered of Marshall's decisions. The college had been granted a charter by King George III in 1769, but the democratic New Hampshire state legislature had seen fit to change it. Dartmouth appealed the case, employing as counsel its most distinguished alumnus, Daniel Webster ('01). The "Godlike Daniel" reportedly pulled out all the stops of his tear-inducing eloquence when he declaimed, "It is, sir, as I have said, a small college. And yet there are those who love it."

Marshall needed no dramatics in the *Dartmouth* case. He put the states firmly in their place when he ruled that the original charter must stand. It was a contract—and the Constitution protected contracts against state encroachments. The *Dartmouth* decision had the fortunate effect of safeguarding business enterprise from domination by the states' governments. But it had the unfortunate effect of creating a precedent that enabled chartered corporations, in later years, to escape the handcuffs of needed public control.

Daguerreotype of Daniel Webster (1782–1852), by Southworth and Hawes   Premier orator and statesman, he served many years in both houses of Congress and also as secretary of state. Often regarded as presidential timber, he was somewhat handicapped by an overfondness for good food and drink and was frequently in financial difficulties. His devotion to the Union was inflexible. "One country, one constitution, and one destiny," he declaimed in 1837.

If John Marshall was a Molding Father of the Constitution, Daniel Webster was an Expounding Father. Time and again he left his seat in the Senate, stepped downstairs to the Supreme Court chamber (then located in the Capitol building), and there expounded his Federalistic and nationalistic philosophy before the supreme bench. The eminent chief justice, so Webster reported, approvingly drank in the familiar arguments as a baby sucks in its mother's milk. The two men dovetailed strikingly

When Supreme Court Chief Justice John Marshall died, a New York newspaper rejoiced,

"The chief place in the supreme tribunal of the Union will no longer be filled by a man whose political doctrines led him always . . . to strengthen government at the expense of the people."

with each other. Webster's classic speeches in the Senate, challenging states' rights and nullification, were largely repetitious of the arguments that he had earlier presented before a sympathetic Supreme Court.

Marshall's decisions are felt even today. In this sense his nationalism was the most tenaciously enduring of the era. He buttressed the federal Union and helped to create a stable, nationally uniform environment for business. At the same time, Marshall checked the excesses of popularly elected state legislatures. In an age when white manhood suffrage was flowering and America was veering toward stronger popular control, Marshall almost single-handedly shaped the Constitution along conservative, centralizing lines that ran somewhat counter to the dominant spirit of the new country. Through him the conservative Hamiltonians partly triumphed from the tomb.

Sharing Oregon and Acquiring Florida

The robust nationalism of the years after the War of 1812 was likewise reflected in the shaping of foreign policy. To this end, the nationalistic President Monroe teamed with his nationalistic secretary of state, John Quincy Adams, the cold and scholarly son of the frosty and bookish ex-president. The younger Adams, a statesman of the first rank, happily rose above the ingrown Federalist sectionalism of his native New England and proved to be one of the great secretaries of state.

To its credit, the Monroe administration negotiated the much-underrated Treaty of 1818 with Britain. This pact permitted Americans to share the coveted Newfoundland fisheries with their Canadian cousins. This multisided agreement also fixed the vague northern limits of Louisiana along the forty-ninth parallel from the Lake of the Woods (Minnesota) to the Rocky Mountains (see the map below). The treaty further provided for a ten-year joint occupation of the untamed Oregon country, without a surrender of the rights or claims of either America or Britain.

To the south lay semitropical Spanish Florida, which many Americans believed geography and providence had destined to become part of the United States. Americans already claimed West Florida, where uninvited American settlers had torn down the hated Spanish flag in 1810. Congress ratified this grab in 1812, and during the War of 1812 against Spain's ally, Britain, a small American army seized the Mobile region. But the bulk of Florida remained, tauntingly, under Spanish rule.

When an epidemic of revolutions broke out in South America, notably in Argentina (1816), Venezuela (1817), and Chile (1818), Spain was forced to denude Florida of troops to fight the rebels. A chaotic situation rapidly developed in the swampy peninsula. Bands of Indians, runaway

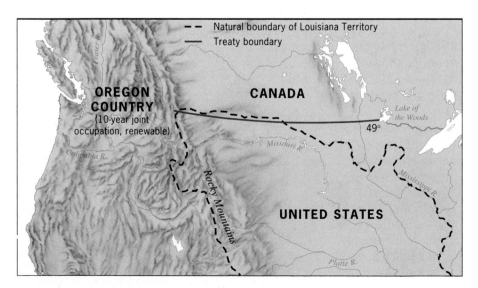

U.S.-British Boundary Settlement, 1818 Note that the United States gained considerable territory by securing a treaty boundary rather than the natural boundary of the Missouri River watershed. The line of 49° was extended westward to the Pacific Ocean under the Treaty of 1846 with Britain (see p. 390).

Andrew Jackson (1767–1845) by Thomas Sully, 1845
A self-taught and popularly elected major general of the militia, Andrew Jackson became a major general of the U.S. Army in 1814. He was noted for his stern discipline, iron will ("Old Hickory"), and good luck.

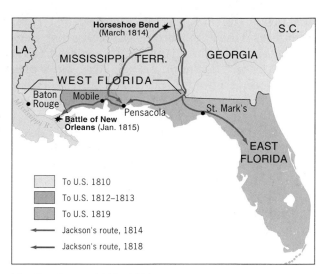

The Southeast, 1810–1819

slaves, and white outcasts poured across the border into American territory, burning and scalping, and then fled to safety behind the surveyor's line.

General Andrew Jackson, idol of the West and scourge of the Indians, reappeared in 1817. The Monroe administration formally commissioned Jackson to punish the Florida outlaws and, if necessary, to pursue them into Spanish territory. But he was to respect all posts under the Spanish flag.

Early in 1818 Jackson swept across the Florida border with all the fury of an avenging angel. He hanged two Indian chiefs without ceremony and, after hasty military trials, executed two British subjects for assisting the Indians. He also seized the two most important Spanish posts in the area, St. Marks and then Pensacola, where he deposed the Spanish governor, who was lucky enough to escape Jackson's jerking noose.

Jackson had clearly exceeded his instructions from Washington. Alarmed, President Monroe con-

sulted his cabinet. Its members were for disavowing or disciplining the overzealous Jackson—all except the lone wolf John Quincy Adams, who refused to howl with the pack. An ardent patriot and nationalist, the flinty New Englander took the offensive and demanded huge concessions from Spain.

In the mislabeled Florida Purchase Treaty of 1819, Spain ceded Florida, as well as shadowy Spanish claims to Oregon, in exchange for America's abandonment of equally murky claims to Texas, soon to become part of independent Mexico. The hitherto vague western boundary of Louisiana was made to run zigzag along the Rockies to the forty-second parallel and then to turn due west to the Pacific, dividing Oregon from Spanish holdings.

The Menace of Monarchy in America

After the Napoleonic nightmare, the rethroned autocrats of Europe banded together in a kind of monarchical protective association. Determined to restore the good old days, they undertook to stamp out the democratic tendencies that had sprouted from soil they considered richly manured by the ideals of the French Revolution. The world must be made safe *from* democracy.

The crowned despots acted promptly. With complete ruthlessness they smothered the embers of rebellion in Italy (1821) and in Spain (1823). According to the European rumor factory, they were also gazing across the Atlantic. Russia, Austria, Prussia, and France, acting in partnership, would presumably send powerful fleets and armies to the revolted colonies of Spanish America and there restore the autocratic Spanish king to his ancestral domains.

Many Americans were alarmed. Sympathetic to democratic revolutions everywhere, they had cheered when the Latin American republics rose from the ruins of monarchy. Americans feared that if the European powers intervened in the New World, the cause of republicanism would suffer irreparable harm. The physical security of the United States—the mother lode of democracy—would be endangered by the proximity of powerful and unfriendly forces.

The southward push of the Russian bear, from the chill region now known as Alaska, had already publicized the menace of monarchy to North America. In 1821 the tsar of Russia issued a decree extending Russian jurisdiction over 100 miles (161 kilometers) of the open sea down to the line of 51°, an area that embraced most of the coast of present-day British Columbia. The energetic Russians had already established trading posts almost as far south as the entrance to San Francisco Bay, and the fear prevailed in the United States that they were planning to cut the Republic off from California, its prospective window on the Pacific.

Great Britain, still Mistress of the Seas, was now beginning to play a lone-hand role on the complicated international stage. In particular, it recoiled from joining hands with the continental European powers in crushing the newly won liberties of the Spanish-Americans. These revolutionists had thrown open their monopoly-bound ports to outside trade, and British shippers, as well as Americans, had found the profits sweet.

Accordingly, in August 1823, George Canning, the haughty British foreign secretary, approached the American minister in London with a startling proposition. Would not the United States combine with Britain in a joint declaration, renouncing any interest in acquiring Latin American territory, and specifically warning the European despots to keep their harsh hands off the Latin American republics? The American minister, lacking instructions, referred this fateful scheme to his superiors in Washington.

Monroe and His Doctrine

The lone-wolf nationalist, Secretary Adams, was hardheaded enough to be wary of Britons bearing gifts. Why should the lordly British, with the mightiest navy afloat, need America as an ally—an America that had neither naval nor military strength? Such a union, argued Adams, was undignified—like a tiny American "cockboat" sailing "in the wake of the British man-of-war."

Adams, ever alert, thought that he detected the joker in the Canning proposal. The British feared that the aggressive Yankees would one day seize Spanish territory in the Americas—perhaps Cuba—which would jeopardize England's possessions in the Caribbean. If Canning could seduce the United States into joining with him in support of the territorial integrity of the New World, America's own hands would be morally tied.

A self-denying alliance with Britain would not only hamper American expansion, concluded Adams, but it was unnecessary. He suspected—correctly—that the European powers had not hatched any definite plans for invading the Americas. In any event the British navy would prevent the approach of hostile fleets because the South American markets had to be kept open at all costs for English merchants. It was presumably safe for Uncle Sam, behind the protective wooden petticoats of the British navy, to blow a defiant, nationalistic blast at all Europe. The distresses of the Old World set the stage once again for an American diplomatic coup.

The Monroe Doctrine was born late in 1823, when the nationalistic Adams won the nationalistic Monroe over to his way of thinking. The president, in his regular annual message to Congress on December 2, 1823, incorporated a stern warning to the European powers. Its two basic features were (1) noncolonization and (2) nonintervention.

Monroe first directed his verbal volley primarily at the lumbering Russian bear in the Northwest. He proclaimed, in effect, that the era of colonization in the Americas had ended and that henceforth the hunting season was permanently closed. What the great powers had they might keep, but neither they nor any other Old World governments could seize or otherwise acquire more.

At the same time, Monroe trumpeted a warning against foreign intervention. He was clearly con-

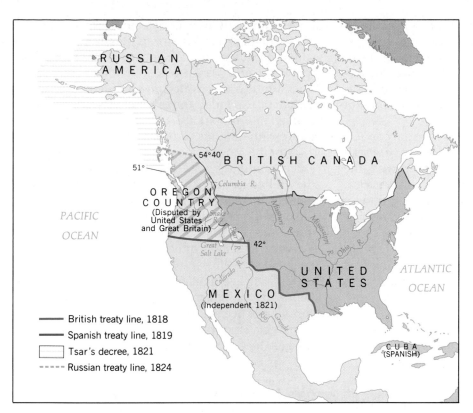

The West and Northwest, 1819–1824 The British Hudson's Bay Company moved to secure its claim to the Oregon country in 1824, when it sent a heavily armed expedition led by Peter Skene Ogden into the Snake River country. In May 1825, Ogden's party descended the Bear River "and found it discharged into a large Lake of 100 miles in length"—one of the first documented sightings by white explorers of Great Salt Lake. (The mountain man Jim Bridger is usually credited with being the first white man to see the lake.)

cerned with regions to the south, where fears were felt for the fledgling Spanish-American republics. Monroe bluntly directed the crowned heads of Europe to keep their hated monarchical systems out of this hemisphere. For its part the United States would not intervene in the war that the Greeks were then fighting against the Turks for their independence.

Monroe's Doctrine Appraised

The ermined monarchs of Europe were angered at Monroe's doctrine. Having resented the incendiary American experiment from the beginning, they were now deeply offended by Monroe's high-flown pronouncement—all the more so because of the gulf between America's loud pretensions and its soft military strength. But though offended by the upstart Yankees, the European powers found their hands tied, and their frustration increased their annoyance. Even if they had worked out plans for invading the Americas, they would have been helpless before the booming broadsides of the British navy.

Monroe's solemn warning, when issued, made little splash in the new-born republics to the south. Anyone could see that Uncle Sam was only secondarily concerned about his neighbors, because he was primarily concerned about defending himself against future invasion. Only a relatively few educated Latin Americans knew of the message, and they generally recognized that the British navy—not the paper pronouncement of James Monroe—stood between them and a hostile Europe.

In truth, Monroe's message did not have much contemporary significance. Americans applauded it and then forgot it. Not until 1845 did President Polk

Prince Metternich (1773–1859), the Austrian chancellor, wrote bitterly of the "dangerous" new manifesto with its

"unprovoked attacks . . . indecent declarations . . . evil doctrines and pernicious examples."

revive it, and not until midcentury did it become an important national dogma.

Even before Monroe's stiff message, the tsar had decided to retreat. This he formally did in the Russo-American Treaty of 1824, which fixed his southernmost limits at the line of 54° 40'—the present southern tip of the Alaska panhandle.

The Monroe Doctrine might more accurately have been called the Self-Defense Doctrine. President Monroe was concerned basically with the security of his own country—not of Latin America. The United States has never willingly permitted a powerful foreign nation to secure a foothold near its strategic Caribbean vitals. Yet in the absence of the British navy or other allies, the strength of the Monroe Doctrine has never been greater than America's power to eject the trespasser. The doctrine, as often noted, was just as big as the nation's armed forces—and no bigger.

The Monroe Doctrine has had a long career of ups and downs. It was never law—domestic or international. It was not, technically speaking, a pledge or an agreement. It was merely a simple, personalized statement of the policy of President Monroe. What one president says, another may unsay. And Monroe's successors have ignored, revived, distorted, or expanded the original version, chiefly by adding interpretations. Like ivy on a tree, it has grown with America's growth.

But the Monroe Doctrine in 1823 was largely an expression of the post-1812 nationalism energizing the United States. Although directed at a specific menace in 1823, and hence a kind of period piece, the doctrine proved to be the most famous of all the long-lived offspring of that nationalism. While giving voice to a spirit of patriotism, it simultaneously deepened the illusion of isolationism. Many Americans falsely concluded, then and later, that the Republic was in fact insulated from European dangers simply because it wanted to be and because, in a nationalistic outburst, Monroe had publicly warned the Old World powers to stay away.

Chronology

1810	*Fletcher* v. *Peck* ruling asserts right of the Supreme Court to invalidate state laws deemed unconstitutional
1812	United States declares war on Britain Madison reelected president
1812–1813	American invasions of Canada fail
1813	Battle of the Thames Battle of Lake Erie
1814	Battle of Plattsburgh British burn Washington Battle of Horseshoe Bend Treaty of Ghent signed
1814–1815	Hartford Convention
1815	Battle of New Orleans *North American Review* begins publication
1816	Second Bank of the United States founded Protectionist Tariff of 1816 Monroe elected president
1817	Madison vetoes Calhoun's Bonus Bill Rush-Bagot agreement limits naval armament on Great Lakes
1818	Treaty of 1818 with Britain Jackson invades Florida
1819	Panic of 1819 Spain cedes Florida to United States *McCulloch* v. *Maryland* case *Dartmouth College* v. *Woodward* case
1820	Missouri Compromise Missouri and Maine admitted to Union Land Act of 1820 Monroe reelected
1821	*Cohens* v. *Virginia* case
1823	Secretary Adams proposes Monroe Doctrine
1824	Russo-American Treaty of 1824 *Gibbons* v. *Ogden* case
1825	Erie Canal completed

SUGGESTED READINGS

PRIMARY SOURCE DOCUMENTS

Charles F. Adams, ed., *Memoirs of John Quincy Adams**
(1875), offers a behind-the-scenes portrait of the creation of the Monroe Doctrine. See also the text of Monroe's public statement in James D. Richardson, ed.,
*Messages and Papers of the Presidents** (1896), vol. II,
pp. 207 ff. "The Missouri Compromise" (1819–1820), in
Henry Steele Commager, *Documents of American History,* reveals the dangerous sectional animosities underlying such national pride.

SECONDARY SOURCES

An important work that sets the War of 1812 in a broad
context of early American history is J. C. A. Stagg, *Mr.
Madison's War: Politics, Diplomacy and Warfare in the
Early American Republic* (1983). Also see Steven Watts,
*The Republic Reborn: War and the Making of Liberal
America, 1790–1820* (1987) and Donald R. Hickey, *The
War of 1812: A Forgotten Conflict* (1989). On the causes of
the war, Julius W. Pratt, *Expansionists of 1812* (1925),
stresses western pressures; Bradford Perkins, *Prologue to
War: England and the United States, 1805–1812* (1961),
and Reginald Horsman, *The Causes of the War of 1812*
(1962), discuss free seas; Roger H. Brown, *The Republic
in Peril; 1812* (1964), emphasizes the need for saving the
republican form of government. On Indian affairs and
westward expansion, see Dorothy Jones, *License for
Empire: Colonialism by Treaty in Early America* (1982);
and the works of R. David Edmunds, *The Shawnee
Prophet* (1983) and *Tecumseh and the Quest for Indian
Leadership* (1984). The relevant volumes of Henry

Adams's nine-volume *History of the United States*
(1889–1891) still contain magnificent reading, both on
the war and on the peace. Federalist reaction to Republican foreign policy is vividly etched in David H. Fisher,
The Revolution of American Conservatism (1965), and
James M. Banner, *To the Hartford Convention: The Federalists and the Origins of Party Politics in Massachusetts*
(1970). Consult also James H. Broussard, *The Southern
Federalists, 1800–1816* (1979). Irving Brant reveals his
strong pro-Madison bias in *James Madison: Commander
in Chief, 1812–1836* (1961). More recent treatments of
Madison include Robert A. Rutland, *James Madison: The
Founding Father* (1987), Drew R. McCoy, *The Last of the
Fathers: James Madison and the Republican Legacy*
(1989), and Jack N. Rakove, *James Madison and the Creation of the American Republic* (1990). Other useful biographical studies are Bernard Mayo, *Henry Clay:
Spokesman of the New West* (1937), and Marquis James's
spirited *Andrew Jackson: The Border Captain* (1933). An
excellent introduction to nationalism is George Danger-
field, *The Awakening of American Nationalism,
1815–1828* (1965). See also Robert H. Wiebe's ambitious
*Opening of American Society: From the Adoption of the
Constitution to the Eve of Disunion* (1984). Arand Otto
Mayr and Robert C. Post, eds., detail *Yankee Enterprise:
The Rise of the American System of Manufactures* (1981).
Glover Moore, *The Missouri Controversy, 1819–1821*
(1953), and Charles S. Sydnor, *The Development of
Southern Sectionalism, 1819–1848* (1948), place the Mis-
souri Compromise in a broader context. On the Monroe
Doctrine, the best single volume is Dexter Perkins, *A His-
tory of the Monroe Doctrine* (1955). Ernest R. May has
somewhat unconvincingly tied the doctrine to domestic
politics, especially the impending election of 1824, in
The Making of the Monroe Doctrine (1975). See also
Harry Ammon, *James Monroe: The Quest for National
Identity* (1971). See also Samuel F. Bemis, *John Quincy
Adams and the Foundations of American Foreign Policy*
(1949).

---

*An asterisk indicates that the document, or an excerpt from it,
can be found in Thomas A. Bailey and David M. Kennedy, eds.,
*The American Spirit: United States History as Seen by Con-
temporaries,* 9th ed. (Boston: Houghton Mifflin, 1998).

13

The Rise of Jacksonian Democracy
1824–1830

In the full enjoyment of the gifts of Heaven and the fruits of superior industry, economy, and virtue, every man is equally entitled to protection by law; but when the laws undertake to add to those natural and just advantages artificial distinctions . . . and exclusive privileges . . . the humble members of society—the farmers, mechanics, and laborers . . . have a right to complain of the injustice of their government.

<small>ANDREW JACKSON, 1832</small>

Politics for the People

Democracy was something of a taint in the days of the lordly Federalists. Martha Washington, the first First Lady, was shocked after a presidential reception to find a greasy smear on the wallpaper—left there, she was sure, by an uninvited "filthy democrat."

But by the 1820s, if not before, aristocracy was becoming a taint, and democracy was becoming respectable. Politicians were now forced to unbend and curry favor with the voting masses. Lucky indeed was the aspiring office seeker who could boast of birth in a log cabin. In 1840 Daniel Webster publicly apologized for not being able to claim so humble a birthplace, though he quickly added that his brothers could. Hopelessly handicapped was the candidate who appeared to be too clean, too well dressed, too grammatical, too high-browishly intellectual. In the West, especially, the belief was spreading that a man was well qualified for high office if he was a superior militia commander or a victorious Indian fighter, like Andrew Jackson, or even an outstanding hunter, like Davy Crockett. The semiliterate Crockett was elected to Congress mainly on the basis of his prowess with a rifle. He once killed 105 bears in a season, and his Tennessee constituents began to talk of running him for the presidency. Yet colorful characters like Crockett were exceptions. Most high political offices continued to be filled by "leading citizens." But now these wealthy and prominent men had to forsake all social pretensions and cultivate the common touch if they hoped to win elections.

Jeffersonian democracy had proclaimed that the people should be governed as little as possible; Jacksonian democracy now added that whatever governing was to be done should be done directly by the people. The common man was at last moving to the center of the national political stage: the sturdy American who donned plain trousers rather than silver-buckled knee breeches, who sported a plain haircut and a coonskin cap rather than a powdered wig, and who wore no man's collar, often not even one of his own. Instead of the old divine right of kings, America was now bowing to the divine right of the people.

The New Democracy, so called, was based on universal white manhood suffrage rather than the old property qualifications. The frontier state of Vermont, admitted to the Union in 1791, was the first to place the ballot in the hands of all adult white males. This trend continued, notably in the West, where land was so easily obtained as to render almost meaningless the old property qualifications. Property tests for officeholding were also widely abolished, and even judges were now being popularly elected. The South trailed other regions in giving up property requirements, but it, too, eventually extended suffrage and the right to hold office to all white men.

Snobbish bigwigs, unhappy over the change, sneered at "coonskin congressmen" and at the newly enfranchised "bipeds of the forest." To them, the tyranny of King Numbers was no less offensive than that of King George. But these critics protested in vain. The masses marched unswervingly toward a fuller measure of control over the Republic's political affairs. If they made mistakes, they made them

Marketing the Crockett Legend David ("Davy") Crockett (1786–1836) was a semi-literate Tennessean who won fame as a rifleman, soldier, and three-time congressman. Rejected in politics, he left Tennessee to fight for Texas against Mexico and died at the Alamo. An accomplished story-teller and master of the frontier "tall tale," Crockett promoted his own image as a rough-hewn backwoods hero while alive. After his death, a small industry developed to advertise—and embellish—his legendary exploits.

themselves and were not the victims of aristocratic domination. If at times they stumbled, they stumbled forward. The New Democracy had arrived to stay.

Nourishing the New Democracy

What caused this lush flowering of political democracy? In part it was simply the logical outgrowth of the egalitarian ideas that had taken root in colonial days and been lavishly fertilized during the Revolutionary era. The new democracy was also nourished by the steady growth of the market economy, which led increasing numbers of people to understand how banks, tariffs, and internal improvements affected the quality of their lives. More immediately, the panic of 1819 and the Missouri Compromise of 1820 rank high on the list of the New Democracy's nutrients.

The economic downturn of Monroe's second term was blamed by many workers and farmers on banking irregularities and speculation. In particular, the panic nurtured burning resentment at the government-granted privileges of the banks. Farmers unable to pay their debts usually lost their farms; overextended bankers unable to fulfill their obligation to redeem their paper bank notes in coin simply suspended payment and escaped any further threat to their property. Holders of bank notes were left with worthless paper and might next find their own property under foreclosure, as the bank called in its debts. These kinds of practices reeked of favoritism and seemed to mock the democratic principles of equality and fair play. The desire to purge the land of this sort of "corruption" and restore the republican ideals of Jefferson's day invigorated the interest of many Americans in politics—

especially the followers of Andrew Jackson. They sought control of the government in order to tear the banks from its protective embrace, to substitute hard money for bank notes, and even to abolish the banks altogether. Opposed to the Jacksonians were those people who favored the current banking system and, more generally, who believed that the federal government had a legitimate role to play in promoting America's economic growth.

The Missouri Compromise likewise awakened many Americans, especially white southerners, to the importance of politics. The spectacle of organized northern resistance to admission of Missouri as a slave state aroused fears in the white South about further federal aggressions against states' rights—especially the right to perpetuate slavery. Controlling the federal government in order to prevent that result thus became a prime goal of white southerners, stimulating heightened involvement in politics.

Economic distress and the slavery issue together raised the political stakes in the 1820s, ushering in a whole new chapter in the history of American politics. The deference, apathy, and virtually nonexistent party organizations of the Era of Good Feelings gave way to the boisterous democracy,

Canvassing for a Vote, by George Caleb Bingham, 1852 This painting shows the "new politics" of the Jacksonian era. Politicians now had to take their message to the common man.

Election Day at the State House, by John Lewis Krimmel   Although politics was serious business in the Jacksonian era, it also provided the occasion for much socializing and merriment. This election-day crowd in Philadelphia appears to be in an especially festive mood.

frenzied vitality, and strong political parties of the Jacksonian era. Voter turnout rose dramatically; only about one-quarter of eligible voters cast a ballot in the presidential election of 1824, but that proportion doubled in 1828, and in the election of 1840 it reached 78 percent. A new style of politicking emerged, as candidates made increasing use of banners, badges, parades, barbecues, free drinks, and baby kissing in an effort to "get out the vote." The old suspicion of political parties as illegitimate disrupters of society's natural harmony was replaced by an acceptance of the sometimes wild contentiousness of political life. Vigorous political conflict even came to be celebrated as necessary for the health of democracy.

Everywhere the people flexed their political muscles. To an increasing degree, members of the Electoral College were being chosen directly by the people rather than by state legislatures. Presidential nominations by a congressional caucus, meeting secretly, took on a bad odor. This procedure was now condemned as furtive, elitist, and subversive of democracy. The delicate checks and balances among the three federal branches were thought to be weakened when the president was indirectly indebted to Congress for his exalted office.

New and more democratic methods of nominating presidential candidates were devised. In 1824 the voters, crying "The People Must Be Heard" and "Down with King Caucus," turned against the candidate (Crawford) who had been selected by the congressional clique. For a brief period, nominations were made by some of the state legislatures. But these did not seem democratic either, and in 1831 the first of the circuslike national nominating conventions was held (by the short-lived but significant Anti-Masonic party). Here the people appeared to exercise greater control, though their will was often thwarted by paunchy bosses in smoke-filled rooms.

The Adams-Clay "Corrupt" Bargaining

The woods were full of presidential timber in 1824. Four candidates towered above the others: Andrew Jackson of Tennessee, the tall, silver-maned, and hollow-cheeked "Old Hero" of New Orleans; Henry Clay of Kentucky, the gamy and gallant "Harry of the West"; William H. Crawford of Georgia, a giant of a man, able though ailing; and John Quincy Adams of Massachusetts, highly intelligent, experienced, and aloof.

All four rivals professed to be "Republicans." Well-organized parties had not yet emerged; their

Election of 1824

Candidates	Electoral Vote	Popular Vote	Popular Percentage
Jackson	99	153,544	42.16%
Adams	84	108,740	31.89
Crawford	41	46,618	12.95
Clay	37	47,136	12.99

identities were so fuzzy, in fact, that John C. Calhoun appeared as the vice-presidential candidate on both the Adams and the Jackson tickets.

The results of the noisy campaign were interesting but confusing. Jackson, the war hero, clearly had the strongest personal appeal, especially in the West. Foreshadowing the themes that would later shape the historical identity of his presidency, Jackson's campaign appealed for the salvation of republicanism from the forces of corruption and privilege in government, especially as embodied in "King Caucus." He polled almost as many popular votes as his next two rivals combined, but he failed to win a majority of the electoral vote (see table above). In such a deadlock the House of Representatives, as directed by the Twelfth Amendment (see the Appendix), must choose among the top three candidates. Clay was thus eliminated, yet he still presided over the very chamber that had to pick the winner. Since he enjoyed all the influence of a popular Speaker of the House, he was in a position to throw the election to the candidate of his choice.

Clay reached his fateful decision by a process of elimination. Crawford, recently felled by a paralytic stroke, was out of the picture. Clay hated the "military chieftain" Jackson, his archrival for the allegiance of the West. Jackson, in turn, bitterly resented Clay's public denunciation of his Florida foray in 1818. The only candidate left was the puritanical Adams, with whom Clay—a free-living gambler and duelist—had never established cordial personal relations. But the two men had much in common politically: both were fervid nationalists and advocates of the American System. Shortly before the final balloting in the House, Clay met privately with Adams and assured him of his support.

Decision day came early in 1825. The House of Representatives met amid tense excitement, with sick members being carried in on stretchers. On the first ballot, thanks largely to Clay's behind-the-scenes influence, Adams was elected president. A few days later, the victor announced that Henry Clay would be the new secretary of state.

The secretaryship of state was then the prize plum, even more so than today. Three of the four preceding secretaries had reached the presidency, and the high cabinet office was regarded as an almost certain runway to the White House. By allegedly dangling the secretaryship as a bribe before Clay, Adams, the second choice of the people, apparently defeated the first choice of the people, Andrew Jackson.

Masses of angered Jacksonians, most of them common folk, raised a roar of protest against the "corrupt bargain." The clamor continued for nearly four years. Jackson condemned Clay as the "Judas of the West," and John Randolph of Virginia publicly assailed the alliance between "the Puritan [Adams] and the black-leg [Clay]," who, he added "shines and stinks like rotten mackerel by moonlight." Clay,

---

Suspicions of a "corrupt bargain" have been strengthened by entries in the diary of John Quincy Adams (1767–1848). On January 1, 1825, after a public dinner, he wrote,

"He [Clay] told me [in a whisper] that he should be glad to have with me soon some confidential conversation upon public affairs. I said I should be happy to have it whenever it might suit his convenience."

The diary entry for January 9, reads in part,

"Mr. Clay came at six, and spent the evening with me in a long conversation explanatory of the past and prospective of the future."

Exactly a month later, with Clay's backing, Adams was elected.

outraged, challenged Randolph to a duel, though shaky nerves and poor marksmanship rendered the outcome bloodless.

No positive evidence has yet been unearthed to prove that Adams and Clay entered into a formal bargain, corrupt or otherwise. But appearances were so damning as to render denials unconvincing. Even if a bargain had been struck, it was not necessarily corrupt, for "deals" of a similar nature are the stock-in-trade of politicians. But this "bargain" differed from others in its apparent flouting of the popular will by both Adams and Clay. Both men erred, the one by offering the post in circumstances sure to arouse suspicion, the other by accepting it.

A Yankee Misfit in the White House

John Quincy Adams was a chip off the old family glacier. Short (5 feet, 7 inches; 1.7 meters), thickset, and billiard-bald, he was even more frigidly austere than his presidential father, John Adams. Shunning people, he often went for early morning swims, sometimes stark naked, in the then-pure Potomac River. Essentially a closeted thinker rather than a politician, he was irritable, sarcastic, and tactless. Yet few individuals have ever come to the presidency with a more brilliant record in statecraft, especially in foreign affairs. He ranks as one of the most successful secretaries of state, yet one of the least successful presidents.

A man of puritanical honor, Adams entered upon his four-year "sentence" in the White House smarting under charges of "bargain," "corruption," and "usurpation." Fewer than one- third of the voters had voted for him. As the first "minority president," he would have found it difficult to win popular support even under the most favorable conditions. He possessed almost none of the arts of the politician and scorned those who did. He had achieved high office by commanding respect rather than by courting popularity. In an earlier era, an aloof John Adams could win the votes of propertied men by sheer ability. But with the raw New Democracy in the driver's seat, his cold-fish son could hardly hope for success at the polls.

Political spoilsmen annoyed Adams. Whether through high-mindedness or political ineptitude, he resolutely declined to oust efficient officeholders in order to create vacancies for his supporters. During

President John Quincy Adams (1767–1848), daguerreotype by Phillip Haas, 1843   Adams wrote in his diary, in June 1819, nearly six years before becoming president, "I am a man of reserved, cold, austere, and forbidding manners: my political adversaries say, a gloomy misanthropist, and my personal enemies an unsocial savage.

his entire administration he removed only twelve public servants from the federal payroll. Such stubbornness caused countless Adams followers to throw up their hands in despair. If the president would not reward party workers with political plums, why should they labor to keep him in office?

Adams's nationalistic views involved him in further woes. The old Jeffersonian Republican party was breaking into fragments, most of which tended to coalesce around a common hatred of the Adams-Clay partnership. The flinty president refused to recognize that the popular tide was turning away from the post-Ghent nationalism toward states' rights and sectionalism. Confirmed nationalist that he was, Adams urged upon Congress in his first annual message the construction of roads and canals. He renewed George Washington's proposal for a national university and went so far as to advocate federal support for an astronomical observatory, similar to Europe's more than 130 "lighthouses of the skies."

The public reaction to some of these proposals was prompt and unfavorable. To many workaday Americans grubbing out stumps, astronomical observatories seemed like a scandalous waste of public funds. The South in particular bristled. If the federal government should take on such heavy financial burdens, it would have to continue the hated tariff duties. If it could meddle in local concerns like education and roads, it might even try to lay its hand on the "peculiar institution" of black slavery.

Adams's land policy likewise antagonized the westerners. They clamored for wide-open expansion and were angered by the president's well-meaning attempts to curb feverish speculation in the public domain. The fate of the Cherokee Indians, threatened with eviction from their holdings in Georgia, generated additional bitterness. White Georgians wanted the Cherokees out. Ruggedly honest Adams attempted to deal fairly with the friendless Indians. The Georgia governor, by threatening to resort to arms, successfully resisted the efforts of the Washington government to interpose federal authority on behalf of the Cherokees. Another fateful chapter was thus written in the nullification of the national will—and another nail was driven in Adams's political coffin.

The Tricky "Tariff of Abominations"

The touchy tariff issue became one of Adams's biggest headaches. Congress had increased the general tariff in 1824, from about 23 percent on dutiable goods to about 37 percent. But wool manufacturers, dissatisfied with their measure of protection, bleated for still-higher barriers.

Ardent Jacksonites, seeking to unhorse Adams, seized this opportunity to play politics with the Tariff of 1828. They rigged up a bill that was seemingly more concerned with manufacturing a president than with protecting manufacturers. A part of their scheme was to push the duties as high as about 45 percent on the value of certain manufactured items. At the same time, they would impose a heavy tariff on certain raw materials, notably wool. These materials were so urgently needed for manufacturing, especially in New England, that even this industrial

section would presumably vote against the entire measure. Adams, whose stronghold was New England, would thus be given another political black eye, and Jackson would receive a boost, especially in the middle states. There many voters were politically uncertain but protection-prone.

But the New Englanders spoiled this clever little game. Though disliking the proposed duties, they were anxious to continue the principle of protection. As a consequence, enough of them choked down the dishonest Tariff of 1828, as amended, to force its passage, and the Jacksonite ruse backfired. Daniel Webster, who had earlier fought the mild Tariff of 1816, and John C. Calhoun, who had sponsored it, had by this time completely reversed their positions. They and others now clearly saw that the future of New England lay in the factory, rather than on the waves, while the destiny of the South lay in the cotton fields.

Southerners, as heavy consumers of manufactured goods, were shocked by what they regarded as the outrageous rates of the Tariff of 1828. Hotheads promptly branded it the "Black Tariff" or the "Tariff of Abominations." Several southern states adopted formal protests; in South Carolina, flags were lowered to half-mast. "Let the *New* England beware how she imitates the *Old*," cried one eloquent South Carolinian who remembered 1776.

Why did the South, especially South Carolina, react so angrily against the tariff? Underlying the southern outcry were growing anxieties about possible federal interference with the institution of slavery. The congressional debate on the Missouri Compromise had kindled those anxieties, and they were further fanned by an ominous slave rebellion in Charleston in 1822, led by a free black, Denmark Vesey. The South Carolinians, still closely tied to the British West Indies, also knew full well how their slaveowning West Indian cousins were feeling the mounting pressure of British abolitionism on the London government. Abolitionism in America might similarly use the power of the government in Washington to suppress slavery in the South. If so, now was the time, and the tariff was the issue, for taking a strong stand on principle against all federal encroachments on states' rights.

Nearer the surface was the real economic distress of the Old South—the seaboard area first settled. It was now the least flourishing of all the sections. The bustling Northeast was experiencing a boom in manufacturing; the developing West was prospering from rising property values and a multi-

South Carolina Belle Sewing Palmetto Cockade
The "Tariff of Abominations" of 1828 drove many people in South Carolina—the "Palmetto State"—to flirt with secession. Anti-tariff protesters wore palmetto blossoms, real or sewn from fabric, to symbolize their defiance of the federal law.

plying population; and the energetic Southwest was expanding into virgin cotton lands. Overcropped acres of the Old South were petering out, and the price of cotton was falling sharply. John Randolph of Virginia grimly quipped that masters would soon cease to advertise for their fugitive slaves, and slaves would advertise for their fugitive masters. So the Old South was seeking a scapegoat, and the tariff proved to be a convenient and plausible one.

The Tariff Yoke in the South

Southerners believed, not illogically, that the "Yankee tariff" discriminated against them. They sold their cotton and other farm produce in a world market completely unprotected by tariffs and were forced to buy their manufactured goods in an American market heavily protected by tariffs.

The plight of the South may be illustrated by a hypothetical case. Suppose that in 1828 an English manufacturer sold shoes in South Carolina at $1.25 a pair, whereas a Massachusetts shoemaker, paying higher wages, would have to charge $1.50 for a pair of equal quality. South Carolinians would naturally buy the British footwear. But if a tariff of $0.50 a pair were levied on foreign shoes at the Charleston customshouse, the British shoes would cost $1.75 a pair. The Massachusetts shoemaker could now safely raise the price to anything less than $1.75—say, $1.74—and still undercut the British competitor by selling the cheapest shoes in South Carolina. South Carolinians would thus be forced to pay higher prices, while the profits of the Yankee manufacturer were commensurately fattened. This artificial inflation of prices has always been among the most objectionable features of high tariffs.

The South also objected to other consequences of towering tariffs. Higher prices generally lead to a reduced volume of purchases, in both directions. If Americans bought fewer English textiles, the British would in turn buy less southern cotton with which to make the textiles. Southerners thus would suffer both as consumers and as producers, as importers and exporters. Little wonder that southern leaders regarded the protective tariff as a foe of their economic development. On the other hand, many failed to appreciate that in the long run a prosperous manufacturing economy in the Northeast could itself contribute to their prosperity by consuming their cotton and other farm products.

South Carolinians took the lead in protesting against the "Tariff of Abominations." Their legislature went so far as to publish in 1828, though without formal endorsement, a pamphlet known as "The South Carolina Exposition." It had been secretly written by John C. Calhoun, one of the few topflight political theorists ever produced by America. (As vice president, he was forced to conceal his authorship.) "The Exposition" boldly denounced the recent tariff as unjust and unconstitutional. Going a stride beyond the Kentucky and Virginia resolutions of 1798, it bluntly and explicitly proposed that the states should nullify the tariff—that is, they should declare it null and void within their borders.

Calhoun found himself caught in an awkward straddle. Still a Unionist and a nationalist, he was also a southern sectionalist. He therefore desperately sought a formula that would protect the minority in the South from the "tyranny of the

John C. Calhoun (1782–1850), attributed to Charles Bird King, c. 1818–1825   Calhoun was a South Carolinian, educated at Yale. Beginning as a strong nationalist and Unionist, he reversed himself and became the ablest of the sectionalists and disunionists in defense of the South and slavery. As a foremost nullifier, he died trying to reconcile strong states' rights with a strong Union. In his last years he advocated a Siamese-twin presidency, probably unworkable, with one president for the North and one for the South. His former plantation home is now the site of Clemson University.

majority" in the North and West. Seizing upon nullification, he undertook by this explosive device to preserve the Union and prevent secession. Calhoun's aim was not to destroy the Union but to salvage it by quieting the fears of those forces that might one day destroy it.

Calhoun's "Exposition," at least immediately, was a false alarm. No other state joined South Carolina in its heated antitariff protest. But the disruptive theory of nullification was further publicized, and the even more dangerous doctrine of secession was foreshadowed. South Carolina was not then prepared to force the controversy to a showdown.

The election of Carolina-born Andrew Jackson to the presidency had occurred two weeks earlier, and the "Old Hero"—a fellow cotton planter and slave-owner—was expected to sympathize with the plight of the South.

Going "Whole Hog" for Jackson in 1828

The presidential campaign for Andrew Jackson had started early. It began on February 9, 1825, the day of John Quincy Adams's controversial election by the House, and continued noisily for nearly four years.

Even before the election of 1828, the temporarily united Republicans of the Era of Good Feelings had split into two camps. One was the National Republicans, with the ultranationalistic Adams as their standard-bearer. The other was the Democratic-Republicans, with the fiery Jackson heading their ticket. Rallying cries of the Jackson zealots were "Bargain and Corruption," "Huzza for Jackson," and "All Hail Old Hickory." Jacksonites planted hickory poles for their hickory-tough hero; "Adamsites" adopted the oak as the symbol of their oakenly independent candidate.

"Shall the people rule?" was the chief issue of 1828, at least to Jacksonians. They argued that the will of the voters had been thwarted in 1825 by the backstairs "bargain" of Adams and Clay. The only way to right the wrong was to seat Jackson, who would then bring about "reform" by sweeping out the "dishonest" Adams gang. "Jackson and Reform" was a widely mouthed slogan, and hickory brooms were brandished as tokens of a forthcoming "clean sweep." Seldom has the public mind been so successfully poisoned against an honest and honorable president.

One anti-Jackson newspaper declared,

"General Jackson's mother was a Common Prostitute, brought to this country by the British soldiers! She afterwards married a MULATTO man with whom she had several children, of which number GENERAL JACKSON is one."

Mudslinging reached a disgraceful level, partly as a result of the taste of the new mass electorate for bare-knuckle politics. Adams would not stoop to gutter tactics, but many of his backers were less squeamish. They described Jackson's mother as a prostitute; they printed black-bordered handbills, shaped like coffins, recounting his numerous duels and brawls and trumpeting his hanging of six mutinous militiamen. The "Old Hero" was also branded an adulterer. He had married an estimable woman, Rachel Robards, confident that her divorce had been granted. To the consternation of both, they discovered two years later that it had not been, and they made haste to correct the marital miscue.

Rachel Jackson was crushed by the vicious charges of bigamy and adultery. She lived to see her husband win the presidency, but she died—supposedly of a broken heart—before she could become First Lady. Jackson, devotedly attached to his wife, was convinced that his enemies' slander had killed her. He never forgave them.

Jackson men also hit below the belt. President Adams had purchased, with his own money and for his own use, a billiard table and a set of chessmen. In the mouths of rabid Jacksonites, these items became "gaming tables" and "gambling furniture" for the "presidential palace." Criticism was also unfairly directed at the large sums Adams had received over the years in federal salaries, well earned though they had been. He was even accused of having procured a servant girl for the lust of a Russian nobleman while minister to Russia—in short, of having served as a pimp.

The Jacksonian "Revolution of 1828"

General Jackson, victorious on the battlefields, was no less victorious at the ballot boxes. The popular tally was 647,286 votes for him to 508,064 for Adams, with an electoral count of 178 to 83. Support for Jackson came mainly from the West and South, and to a considerable extent from the sweat-stained laborers of the eastern seaboard. Generally speaking, the common people—though by no means all of them—voted for the Hero of New Orleans. Adams won the backing of his own New England, as well as the propertied "better elements" of the Northeast.

The election of 1828 has often been called the "Revolution of 1828." Actually, as in 1800, no upheaval or landslide swept out the incumbent. Adams, in fact, polled a respectable 44 percent of the popular vote. A considerable part of Jackson's support, moreover, was lined up by machine politicians, especially in New York and Pennsylvania, and not entirely among the leather-aproned artisans and other manual workers.

But the concept of a *political* revolution in 1828 is not completely far-fetched. The increased turnout of voters proved that the common people, especially in the universal-white-manhood-suffrage states, now had the vote and the will to use it for their ends. A discontented West, with its numerous rustics and debtors, generally voted for Jackson. The results show that the political center of gravity was continuing to shift away from the conservative eastern seaboard toward the emerging states across the mountains.

So in a broader sense the election *was* a "revolution," comparable to that of 1800. It was a peaceful revolution, achieved by ballots instead of bullets, by counting heads instead of crushing them. "Shall the people rule?" cried the Jacksonians. The answering

Rachel Jackson   A devoted wife who did not live to become First Lady, she had unwittingly, and hence innocently, involved herself and her husband in scandal.

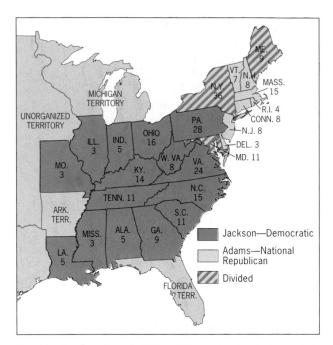

Presidential Election of 1828 (with electoral vote by state) Jackson swept the South and West, whereas Adams retained the old Federalist stronghold of the Northeast. Yet Jackson's inroads in the Northeast were decisive. He won twenty of New York's electoral votes, and all twenty-eight of Pennsylvania's. If those votes had gone the other way, Adams would have been victorious—by a margin of one vote.

roar seemed to reply, "The people *shall* rule!" In the struggle between the poorer masses and the entrenched classes, the homespun folk scored a resounding triumph, befuddling some members of the elite establishment. "I never saw anything like it," a puzzled Daniel Webster mused about Jackson's inaugural. "Persons have come five hundred miles to see General Jackson, and they really seem to think that the country is rescued from some dreadful danger."

America hitherto had been ruled by an elite of brains and wealth, whether aristocratic Federalist shippers or aristocratic Jeffersonian planters. Jackson's victory accelerated the transfer of national power from the countinghouse to the farmhouse, from the East to the West, and from the snobs to the mobs. If Jefferson had been the hero of the gentleman farmer, Jackson was the hero of the dirt farmer. The plowholders were now ready to take over the government —their government.

Adams, though president-reject, was still destined for a distinguish public career. Ever high-minded, he did not deem it beneath his dignity as an ex-president to accept election to the House of Representatives from Massachusetts. ("No person can be degraded by serving the people," he declared.) There he served with conspicuous success for seventeen fruitful years. Affectionately known as "Old Man Eloquent," he fought stalwartly for free government, free speech, free soil, and free people. A rough and savage debater, he finally was stricken on the floor of the House in 1848, at age eighty. His funeral was the greatest pageant of its kind that Washington had yet seen. Ironically, the popularity that had escaped him at the zenith of his power came to him in his sunset years.

The Advent of "Old Hickory" Jackson

Andrew Jackson cut a striking figure—tall (6 feet, 1 inch; 1.86 meters), gaunt, and with bushy iron-gray hair brushed high above a prominent forehead, craggy eyebrows, and blue eyes. His irritability and emaciated condition (140 pounds; 64 kilograms) probably had resulted in part from long-term bouts with dysentery, malaria, tuberculosis, and lead poisoning from two bullets that he carried in his body from near-fatal duels. His autobiography was largely written in his lined face.

To a considerable degree, Jackson personified the new West. He reflected its individualism, its jack-of-all-trades versatility, its opportunism, its energy, its directness, and its prejudices. He was a genuine folk hero—an uncommon common man. The backwoods preacher who cried that Jesus was "just another Andrew Jackson" reflected a sentiment that did not seem sacrilegious to some.

Jackson's upbringing was not of the best. Born in the Carolinas and early orphaned, "Mischievous Andy" grew up without parental restraints. As a youth he displayed much more interest in brawling and cockfighting than in his scanty opportunities for reading and spelling. Although he ultimately learned to express himself in writing with vigor and clarity, his grammar was always rough-hewn, and his spelling was often original, like that of many contemporaries. He sometimes misspelled a word two different ways in the same letter.

The youthful Carolinian had the foresight to emigrate "up West" to Tennessee, where a fighting man was more highly regarded than a writing man. There—through native intelligence, force of personality, and powers of leadership—he became a judge and a member of Congress. His passions were so profound that on occasion he would choke into silence when he tried to speak. He won his greatest fame as a commander of militia troops, who dubbed him "Old Hickory" in honor of his toughness. Afflicted with a violent temper, he early became involved in numerous duels, stabbings, and other bloody frays. But, rough and forthright as democracy itself, he made things move.

The first president from the West, the first nominated at a formal party convention (in 1832), and the first without a college education (except Washington), Jackson was unique. His university was adversity. He had risen from the masses, but he was not one of them, except insofar as he shared many of their prejudices. Essentially a frontier aristocrat, he owned many slaves, cultivated broad acres, and lived in one of the finest mansions in America—the Hermitage, near Nashville, Tennessee. More westerner than easterner, more country gentleman than common clay, more courtly than crude, he was hard to fit into a neat category:

> *He's none of your old New England stock,*
> *Or your gentry-proud Virginians,*
> *But a regular Western fighting-cock*
> *With Tennessee opinions.**

As befitted an authentic man of the people and hero of the one-suspender man, Jackson's political ideas had a stark simplicity. Like the antifederalists of an earlier day, he was suspicious of the federal government as a bastion of privilege, an institution dangerously remote from popular scrutiny. He was therefore determined to reduce it "to that simple machine which the Constitution created." That meant, among other things, hostility to the active federal economic role envisioned by Henry Clay's American System. Conversely, he and especially his followers were generally friendly toward the frothy

Jackson Sewing Box, 1828 Andrew Jackson was marketed as a military hero, an image that appealed to women and men alike, as illustrated by this sewing box.

democracy bubbling up in the states and looked with some favor on economic activism on the part of state governments. Yet Jackson was destined to disappoint some of his states' rights supporters in the South by his insistence on the sacredness of the Union and the ultimate supremacy of federal power over that of the states.

While president, Jackson proved to be a storm center. As a former military man, he demanded prompt and loyal support from his subordinates. If one was not for him, one was against him. Cherishing strong ideas as to his constitutional prerogatives, he ignored the Supreme Court on several

---

*"Andrew Jackson," from *A Book of Americans,* by Rosemary & Stephen Vincent Benét. Copyright 1933, by Rosemary & Stephen Vincent Benét. Copyright renewed ©, 1961, by Rosemary Carr Benét. Reprinted by permission of Brandt & Brandt Literary Agency, Inc.

In 1824 Thomas Jefferson (1743–1826) said of Jackson,

"When I was President of the Senate he was a Senator; and he could never speak on account of the rashness of his feelings. I have seen him attempt it repeatedly, and as often choke with rage. His passions are no doubt cooler now . . . but he is a dangerous man."

conspicuous occasions. He likewise defied or dominated Congress as few presidents have done. Jackson's six predecessors had wielded the veto a total of ten times; during his two terms he employed it twelve times, sometimes on grounds of personal distaste rather than constitutional principle. Jackson's modest use of the veto ax was perfectly legitimate, but his numerous enemies condemned him as "King Andrew the First."

Jackson's inauguration symbolized the newly won ascendancy of the masses. "Hickoryites" poured into Washington from far places, sleeping on hotel floors and in hallways. They were curious to see their hero take office and perhaps to pick up a well-paying office for themselves. Nobodies mingled with notables as the White House, for the first time, was thrown open to the multitude. A milling crowd of clerks, shopkeepers, hobnailed artisans, and grimy laborers surged in, wrecking the china and furniture, and threatening the "people's champion" with cracked ribs. Jackson was hastily spirited through a side door, and the White House miraculously emptied itself when the word was passed that huge bowls of well-spiked punch had been placed on the lawns. Such was "the inaugural brawl."

To conservatives, this orgy seemed like the end of the world. "King Mob" reigned triumphant as Jacksonian vulgarity replaced Jeffersonian simplicity. Faint-hearted traditionalists shuddered, drew their blinds, and recalled with trepidation the opening scenes of the French Revolution.

Jackson Nationalizes the Spoils System

Under Jackson the spoils system—that is, rewarding political supporters with public office—was introduced into the federal government on a large numerical scale. On a percentage basis, Jefferson, with reluctance and discrimination, had already made about as large a beginning. Jackson, with more ruthlessness, extended it to more people, while complaining about those "clamoring for a public tit from which to suck the treasury."

The basic idea was as old as politics. Its name came later from Senator William Marcy's classic remark in 1832, "To the victor belong the spoils of the enemy." The system had already secured a firm hold in New York and Pennsylvania, where well-

greased machines were operating. Professional politicians, by ladling out the "gravy" of office, had been able to make politics a full-time, full-course business rather than a sidedish. The emphasis was more on spoils than on responsibilities.

A housecleaning of some sort in Washington was clearly needed. No party overturn had occurred since the defeat of the Federalists in 1800, and even that had not produced wholesale evictions. During the ensuing twenty-eight years, festering evils had developed in the civil service. The old colonial-system ideal of holding office during good behavior had bred some incompetence and corruption, as well as considerable indifference and insolence ("uncivil servants"). A few officeholders, their commissions signed by President Washington, were lingering on into their eighties, drawing breath and salary but doing little else.

Jackson fully shared the view of the New Democracy that "every man is as good as his neighbor"— perhaps "equally better." As this was believed to be so, and as the routine of office was also thought to be simple enough for any upstanding American to learn quickly, why encourage the development of an aristocratic, bureaucratic, officeholding class? Experience, of course, had some value. But alertness and new blood had more—at least in the eyes of the Jacksonians.

The New Democracy also trumpeted the ideal of "rotation in office"— or "a turn about is fair play." Since experience was discounted and since officeholding provided valuable training for citizenship, let as many citizens as possible feed at the public trough for at least a short time. This was a polite way of saying, "Throw the rascals out and put our rascals in."

More Victors Than Spoils

Elected as a reformer, Jackson believed that the swiftest road to reform was to sweep out the Adams-Clay gang and bring in his own trusted henchmen. Furiously aroused against his foes, he agreed that the old Adams "barnacles" must "be scraped clean from the Ship of State."

The spoilsmen now had their inning. Office seekers hounded Jackson at every turn and even invaded his privacy: for every appointee there were seemingly ten disappointees. In view of such pressures, one may marvel that he removed so few incumbents rather than so many. During his eight years, only about one-fifth of the old civil servants were dismissed, leaving more than nine thousand out of the original eleven thousand. The "clean sweeps" were to come in later administrations.

Even so, a demoralizing practice was begun on a national scale. Insecurity replaced security and discouraged many able citizens from entering public service. Terrible hardships were worked on poor men with large families. One discharged employee cut his throat from ear to ear; another went raving mad. Fitness, merit, and the ideal of public service were subordinated, while offices were prostituted to political ends. The questions were not "What can he do for the country?" but "What has he done for the party?" or "Is he loyal to Jackson?"

Scandal inevitably accompanied the new system. Men who had openly bought their posts by campaign contributions were appointed to high office. Illiterates, incompetents, and plain crooks were given positions of public trust; scoundrels lusted for the spoils of office rather than the toils of office. Samuel Swartwout, despite ample warnings of his untrustworthiness, was awarded the lucrative post of collector of the customs of the port of New York. Nearly nine years later he "Swartwouted out" for England, leaving his accounts more than a million dollars short—the first person to steal a million from the Washington government.

Finally, the spoils system built up a potent, personalized political machine. Its delicate gears were lubricated by gifts from expectant party members and by percentage levies on the salaries of officeholders—a kind of political job insurance. The system at length secured such a tenacious hold that more than half a century passed before its grip could be even partially loosened.

> *One elderly postmaster, a Revolutionary War veteran, while personally appealing to Jackson not to evict him from office, removed his coat to display his war wounds. Jackson later exclaimed,*
>
> "By the eternal! I will not remove the old man. Do you know that he carries a pound of British lead in his body?"

Cabinet Crises and Nationalistic Setbacks

Jackson's cabinet was mediocre; its members were used primarily as executive clerks. The only person of noteworthy ability was the smooth-tongued and keen-witted secretary of state, Dutch-descended Martin Van Buren of New York, who shone as a gifted conciliator and wire-puller. A balding, sharp-featured man, he was affectionately addressed by Jackson as "Matty." But he was known to his enemies as the "Little Magician."

The official cabinet of six was privately supplemented by an extraofficial cabinet of about thirteen ever-shifting members. It grew out of Jackson's informal meetings with his advisers, some of whom were newspaper people who kept him in touch with the fickle winds of public opinion. The enemies of the president branded these shirt-sleeved cronies "the Kitchen Cabinet." Subsequent generations have retained the picture of an uncouth clique gathering around a kitchen table and spitting tobacco juice in the general direction of grimy spittoons. Actually, the group did not gather in the kitchen; it never even met officially; its overall influence has been grossly exaggerated; and it was not unconstitutional. Presidents are free to consult with such unofficial advisers as they desire.

The regular cabinet was wrecked in 1831, as a result of the "Eaton malaria." Secretary of War John H. Eaton had married the daughter of a Washington boardinghouse keeper, pretty Peggy O'Neale, whom the tongue of scandal had perhaps unfairly linked with the male boarders. She was consequently snubbed by the ladies of Jackson's official family, conspicuously by the blue-blooded wife of Vice President Calhoun. The president, whose own spouse had been victimized by scandalmongers, was chivalrously indignant in behalf of Peggy Eaton's chastity. With a zeal worthy of a better cause, he tried to force the social acceptance of the black-haired beauty. But the all-conquering general finally had to acknowledge defeat in the "Petticoat War" at the hands of the female phalanx.

The Eaton scandal played directly into the hands of Secretary Van Buren. As a fancy-free widower, he further curried favor with Jackson by paying marked attention to Peggy Eaton, whose physical charms helped to lighten this self-imposed

The Rats Leaving a Falling House, attributed to Edward W. Clay, 1831   This cartoonist satirized the defections from Jackson's cabinet in the wake of the Peggy Eaton affair. Martin Van Buren (second rat from the right) was later reinstated in the cabinet and eventually succeeded Jackson to the presidency.

task. Jackson turned increasingly against Calhoun, and finally broke with him completely. Followers of the South Carolinian were purged from the cabinet in 1831. Calhoun himself, resigning the vice presidency the next year, entered the Senate as a champion of South Carolina.

It would be absurd to say that Peggy Eaton caused the Civil War. But up to this time, Calhoun had publicly been a strong nationalist, despite his secret espousal of nullification in "The South Carolina Exposition" of 1828. As vice president, he thought himself in line for the presidency after Jackson had served one term. The open break with the incumbent, though foreshadowed earlier, blighted his hopes. He gradually abandoned his weakening nationalism and became an inflexible defender of southern sectionalism. Prescribing extreme medi-

cines for protecting the states and preserving the Union, the "Great Nullifier" contributed to the almost fatal illness of the Union.

Jackson himself, consistent with his Jeffersonian principles, dealt nationalism a body blow by his hostility to localized roads and canals. It is true that he signed a number of measures that appropriated federal funds for ambitious internal improvements. But his states' rights principles rebelled against spending money from the pinched Washington Treasury for roads built entirely within individual states and unconnected to an interstate network. He headlined his antagonism in 1830, when he flatly vetoed a bill for improving the Maysville Road, which lay completely within Henry Clay's Kentucky (but which was linked to an interstate artery). This setback slapped at the internal improvements aspect of the American System, so ardently championed by Clay, the "corrupt bargainer" whom Jackson never forgave. "Old Hickory's" veto was also a signal victory for eastern and southern states' rightism in its struggle with Jackson's own West.

The Webster-Hayne Forensic Duel

Sectional jealousies found a spectacular outlet in the Senate during 1829–1830. Hidebound New England, resenting the marvelous expansion of the West, was determined to call a halt. The lavish distribution of western acreage was draining off eastern population and, even worse, upsetting the political balance. Late in 1829, therefore, a New England senator introduced a resolution designed to curb the sale of public lands.

Sectional passions flared angrily in the Senate, as the western senators sprang furiously to the defense of their interests. The South, seeking sectional allies in its controversies with the Northeast, promptly sided with the West. Its most persuasive spokesman was Robert Y. Hayne, of South Carolina, one of the silver-tongued orators of his generation.

Hayne's rhetoric in the Senate was impressive. He roundly condemned the obvious disloyalty of New England during the War of 1812, as well as its selfish inconsistency on the protective tariff. Airing in detail the grievances of the South, he reserved his heavy fire for the "Tariff of Abominations" (1828). He then extolled Calhoun's dangerous doctrine of nullification as the only means of safeguarding the minority interests of his section. Hayne, like

Southern Sectionalism**   **271**

1839 Daniel Webster visited England,
where his distinguished bearing and
intellectual power made a great impression.
The Reverend Sydney Smith (1771–1845), a
merciless critic of America, reportedly
remarked,*

"Daniel Webster struck me much like a steam-engine in trousers . . . [He was also a] "living lie, because no man on earth could be so great as he looked."

Calhoun, did not advocate a breakup of the Union; rather, he was seeking to protect southern rights within the Union and under the Constitution. But his arguments were carefully stored up by nullifiers and secessionists for future use.

The "Godlike Daniel" Webster, spokesman for New England, now took the floor. Matchless orator and leader of the American bar, he awed audiences with his majestic presence. Webster had craglike brows, flashing eyes, a sonorous voice, a noble head, and a well-chested frame. His life up to this point, including his frequent appearances before Chief Justice Marshall, had been a preparation for this nine-day running debate with Hayne in January 1830.

After defending New England with vigor, if not complete candor, Webster, the ex-Federalist, passed on to the larger issue of Union. Insisting that the *people* and not the *states* had framed the Constitution (here he was on shaky historical ground*), he decried the insidious doctrine of nullification. Either the Supreme Court would judge the constitutionality of laws, or the Republic would be torn by revolution. If each of the twenty-four states were free to go its separate way in obeying or rejecting federal statutes, there would be no union but only a "rope of sand." Webster's concluding outburst, which brought tears to listeners' eyes, was a magnificent tribute to the Union, ending with those imperishable words, "Liberty and Union, now and forever, one and inseparable."

---

*The original preamble of the Constitution of 1787 had read, "We the people of the states of"—and then they were listed by name. But when it was objected that all the states might not ratify, the formula "We the people of the United States" was adopted. (For the text of the preamble, see the Appendix.)

Websterian Cement for the Union

Webster did not overpower Hayne with his thunderous oratory; Hayne did not defeat Webster with his seductive eloquence. There were no official judges. The polished southerner was sounder on historical and economic grounds; the impassioned New Englander was sounder on constitutional practicalities and common sense—on things as they were rather than as they had been. Each section was satisfied with its champion.

The impact of Webster's reply was spectacular. About forty thousand copies were printed in three months, and arguments for the Union were seared into the minds of countless northerners. Among them was young Abraham Lincoln, just turning twenty-one and moving from Indiana to the Illinois frontier. Webster's inspirational peroration was printed in the school readers and was memorized by tens of thousands of impressionable lads—the Boys in Blue who in 1861–1865 were willing to lay down their lives for the "inseparable" Union.

Webster, beyond a doubt, had a large hand in winning the Civil War. He probably did more than

---

Daniel Webster (1782–1852) challenged Robert Hayne in these words:

"The proposition that, in case of a supposed violation of the Constitution by Congress, the states have a constitutional right to interfere and annul the law of Congress is the proposition of the gentleman. I do not admit it. If the gentleman had intended no more than to assert the right of revolution for justifiable cause, he would have said only what all agree to. But I cannot conceive that there can be a middle course, between submission to the laws, when regularly pronounced constitutional, on the one hand, and open resistance, which is revolution or rebellion, on the other" (January 26, 1830).

Webster and Hayne thus clashed over the same question that had vexed Jefferson in the Kentucky resolutions and Marshall in Marbury v. Madison. *Where did final authority to interpret the Constitution lie?*

any other person to stir the oncoming generation of northerners to fight for the ideal of Union. His admirers have claimed that the nation was saved hardly less by the thunder of Webster's replies to Hayne on the Senate floor than by the thunder of General Grant's replies to General Lee on the battlefield.

Hot-tempered "Old Hickory" had meanwhile been keeping strangely silent on southern grievances. States' rights leaders, at a Jefferson Day banquet in 1830, schemed to smoke him out. Their strategy was to devise a series of toasts in honor of Jefferson, onetime foe of centralization, that would lean toward states' rights and nullification. The plotters assumed that the "Old Hero"—a fellow southerner—would be swept along by the tenor of the toasts and speak up in favor of states' rights.

Jackson, forewarned and inwardly fuming, had carefully prepared his response. At the proper moment he rose to his full height, fixed his eyes on Calhoun, and with dramatic intensity proclaimed,

"Our Union: It must be preserved!"

The southerners were dumbfounded; and Calhoun haltingly replied, in part,

"The union, next to our liberty, most dear!"

Some seventy other anticlimactic toasts followed this exchange, but in effect the party was over.

Jackson's military ire was aroused. As commander in chief, he would stand for no sass from the states or particularly from the despised Calhoun. But, as fate decreed, the showdown with defiant South Carolina was postponed for over two years.

Chronology

1822	Vesey slave rebellion in Charleston, South Carolina
1824	Lack of electoral majority for presidency throws election into the House of Representatives
1825	House elects John Quincy Adams president
1828	Tariff of 1828 ("Tariff of Abominations") Jackson elected president
1828	"The South Carolina Exposition" published
1830	Maysville Road veto Webster-Hayne debate
1831	Anti-Masonic party holds first national convention Eaton affair
1832	Calhoun resigns as vice president

SUGGESTED READINGS

PRIMARY SOURCE DOCUMENTS

Davy Crockett, *Exploits and Adventures in Texas** (1836), is a lively description of the democratic political order of Jacksonian America. C. W. Janson, *The Stranger in America, 1793–1806** (1807), exposes the seamier aspects of American egalitarianism. On the Tariff of Abominations and its implications, see the "Webster-Hayne Debate"* (1830). Webster's reply to Hayne is one of the greatest specimens of American political oratory.

---

*An asterisk indicates that the document, or an excerpt from it, can be found in Thomas A. Bailey and David M. Kennedy, eds., *The American Spirit: United States History as Seen by Contemporaries,* 9th ed. (Boston: Houghton Mifflin, 1998).

SECONDARY SOURCES

A still-living classic treatise on the Jacksonian period is Alexis de Tocqueville, *Democracy in America* (1835, 1840). Edward Pessen, *Jacksonian America: Society, Personality and Politics* (rev. ed., 1978) is a good general introduction that sharply disputes Tocqueville's findings. See also Frederick Jackson Turner, *The Frontier in American History* (1920), which casts Jackson as an exemplar of the democratic spirit of the frontier. Marvin Meyers, *The Jackson Persuasion* (1957), and John William Ward, *Andrew Jackson: Symbol for an Age* (1955), examine the broader cultural significance of Old Hickory and his supporters. Arthur M. Schlesinger, Jr., in his seminal *The Age of Jackson* (1945), stresses the support of eastern labor for Jackson, a view that has come under attack in

Lee Benson, *The Concept of Jacksonian Democracy: New York as a Test Case* (1961). Daniel Feller links political turmoil to land and labor disputes in *The Public Lands in Jacksonian Politics* (1984). For a general overview of political participation, see Chilton Williamson, *American Suffrage, from Property to Democracy* (1960). On the evolution of mass-based political parties, see Richard P. McCormick, *The Second American Party System* (1966), and two books by Ronald P. Formisano, *The Birth of Mass Political Parties: Michigan, 1827–1861* (1971) and *The Transformation of Political Culture: Massachusetts Parties, 1790s–1840s* (1983). See also Richard L. McCormick's general survey of party politics from Jackson into the twentieth century, *The Party Period and Public Policy: American Politics from the Age of Jackson to the Progressive Era* (1986). Three works that consider Jacksonian politics in the South are William J. Cooper, *The South and the Politics of Slavery, 1828–1856* (1978); J. Mills Thornton III, *Politics and Power in a Slave Society: Alabama, 1800–1860* (1978); and Harry L. Watson, *Jacksonian Politics and Community Conflict: The Emergence of the Second American Party System in Cumberland County, North Carolina* (1981), which discusses the opponents of Jackson. Samuel Flagg Bemis, *John Quincy Adams and the Union* (1956), is the second volume of a distinguished biography, as is Robert V. Remini, *Andrew Jackson and the Course of American Freedom, 1822–1832* (1981). Remini also has a fine biography of Clay, *Henry Clay: Statesman for the Union* (1991). A masterful analysis of the period's most celebrated statesmen is Merrill D. Peterson, *The Great Triumvirate: Webster, Clay and Calhoun* (1987). See also Sydney Nathans, *Daniel Webster and Jacksonian Democracy* (1973). The standard work on tariffs is Frank W. Taussig, *The Tariff History of the United States* (1931).

14

Jacksonian Democracy at Flood Tide

1830–1840

The vain threats of resistance by those who [in South Carolina] have raised the standard of rebellion shew their madness and folly. . . . In forty days, I can have within the limits of So. Carolina fifty thousand men. . . . The Union will be preserved.

ANDREW JACKSON, 1832

"Nullies" in South Carolina

The "abominable" Tariff of 1828 continued to rankle hot-blooded South Carolinians. They persisted in seeing it not only as economically punitive in the short run, but as a possible foothold for later federal interference with slavery in the southern states. In protest some South Carolinians took to wearing ill-fitting garments of homespun, untaxed by the hated Yankee tariff, while their slaves sported discarded broadcloth. The nullifiers—"nullies," they were called—tried strenuously to muster the necessary two-thirds vote for nullification in the South Carolina legislature. But they were blocked by a determined minority of Unionists, scorned as "submission men."

Back in Washington, Congress touched off the fuse by passing the new Tariff of 1832, which fell far short of meeting all southern demands. The measure did pare away the worst of the "abominations" of 1828, and it did lower the imposts to about the level of the moderate Tariff of 1824—roughly 35 percent, or a reduction of 10 percent. Yet the new law was still frankly protective, and to many southerners it had a disquieting air of permanence.

South Carolina was now nerved for drastic action. Nullifiers and Unionists clashed head-on in the state election of 1832. "Nullies," defiantly wearing palmetto ribbons on their hats, emerged with more than a two-thirds majority. The state legislature then called for a special convention. Several weeks later the delegates, meeting in Columbia, solemnly declared the existing tariff to be null and void within South Carolina. The hotheaded assemblage also called upon the state legislature to undertake any necessary military preparations. As a final act of defiance, the convention threatened to take South Carolina out of the Union if the Washington regime attempted to collect the customs duties by force.

President-General Jackson, his military instincts rasped, reacted violently. Hating Calhoun and pledged to uphold the Union, he privately threatened to hang the nullifiers. But fortunately for compromise, he was much less pugnacious in public. He dispatched modest naval and military reinforcements to the Palmetto State, while quietly preparing a sizable army. He also issued a ringing proclamation against nullification, to which the governor of South Carolina, ex-Senator Hayne, responded with a counterproclamation. If civil war were to be avoided, one side would have to surrender, or both would have to compromise.

Conciliatory Henry Clay of Kentucky, now in the Senate, stepped forward. An unforgiving foe of Jackson, he had no desire to see his old enemy win new laurels by crushing the Carolinians and returning with the scalp of Calhoun dangling from his belt. The gallant Kentuckian therefore threw his influence behind a compromise bill that would gradually reduce the Tariff of 1832 by about 10 percent over a period of eight years. By 1842 the rates would be at approximately the mildly protective level of 1816—that is, 20 percent to 25 percent on the value of dutiable goods.*

The compromise Tariff of 1833 finally squeezed through Congress. Debate was bitter, with most of the opposition naturally coming from protectionist New England and the middle states. Calhoun and the South favored the compromise, so it was evident that Jackson would not have to use firearms and rope. But at the same time, and partly as a face-saving device, Congress passed the Force Bill, known among Carolinians as the "Bloody Bill." It

authorized the president to use the army and navy, if necessary, to collect federal tariff duties.

Militant South Carolinians welcomed this opportunity to extricate themselves without loss of face from a dangerously tight corner. To the consternation of the Calhounites, no other southern states had sprung to their support, though Georgia and Virginia toyed with the idea. Moreover, an appreciable Unionist minority within South Carolina was gathering guns, organizing militia, and nailing Stars and Stripes to flagpoles. Faced with civil war within and invasion from without, the Columbia convention met again and repealed the ordinance of nullification. As a final but futile gesture of fist-shaking, it nullified the unnecessary Force Act and adjourned.

A Victory for Both Union and Nullification

Neither Jackson nor the "nullies" won a clear-cut triumph. Admirers of "Old Hickory" insisted that he had avoided an armed clash, induced the South Carolinians to repeal their ordinance of nullification, and preserved the Union. On the other hand, the danger of disunion seems to have been exaggerated.

South Carolina actually emerged with colors flying. Although confronted with overwhelming odds, it had forced a reduction of the tariff to as reasonable a level as it could have expected. It had not only saved face but it had surrendered no principle. Unrepentant and defiant, it felt that it had won; and the people of Charleston—the "Cradle of Secession"—gave a gala "victory ball" for the volunteer troops. Ominously, however, the South Carolinians had gradually abandoned nullification in favor of the more extreme remedy of secession.

Later generations, gazing back through the smoke of the Civil War, have condemned the "appeasement" of South Carolina in 1833 as sheer folly. Unbloodied and unbowed, it could have been voted the state most likely to secede. (In 1860 it was the first to go.) If Jackson had only strangled the serpent of secession in the nest, so the argument runs, there might have been no costly Civil War. During the crisis of 1832, medals were struck off in honor of Calhoun bearing the words, "First President of the Southern Confederacy."

*For the history of tariff rates, see the Appendix.

Yet force was the risky solution. The flare-up in South Carolina was no mere Whiskey Rebellion, and the nation was not yet ready to drink the cup of blood. Violence tends to beget violence. Armed invasion might have aroused other southern states and touched off a civil war, at a time when the Unionists were even worse prepared for fighting than in 1861. Force is a confession that statesmanship has failed. Reasonable compromise was in the American tradition, and in 1833 any other course seemed unwise.

The Bank as a Political Football

President Jackson did not hate all banks and all businesses, but he distrusted monopolistic banking and overbig business, as did his followers. A man of virulent dislikes, he came to share the prejudices of his own West against the "moneyed monster" known as the Bank of the United States (BUS). He might have tolerated a renewal of its charter in 1836, with adequate safeguards. But hated Henry Clay aroused his ire by throwing himself behind a premature move in the Senate to recharter the bank in 1832—four years early. "Gallant Harry" was the leading candidate of the National Republicans for the presidency, and with fateful blindness he looked upon the bank issue as a surefire winner.

Clay's scheme was to ram a recharter bill through Congress and then send it on to the White House. If Jackson signed it, he would alienate his worshipful western followers. If he vetoed it, as seemed certain, he would presumably lose the presidency in the forthcoming election by alienating the wealthy and influential groups in the East. Clay seems not to have fully realized that the "best people" were now only a minority and that they generally feared Jackson anyhow. The president growled privately, "The Bank . . . is trying to kill me, but I will kill it."

The recharter bill slid through Congress on greased skids, as planned, but was killed by a scorching veto from Jackson. The "Old Hero" assailed the plutocratic and monopolistic bank as unconstitutional. Of course, the Supreme Court had earlier declared it constitutional in the case of *McCulloch* v. *Maryland* (1819), but Jackson acted as though he regarded the executive branch as superior to the judicial branch. He had sworn to uphold the Constitution as he understood it, not as his foe John Marshall understood it.

Jackson's veto message went on to condemn the bank as not only antiwestern but anti-American. A substantial minority of its stockholders were foreigners, chiefly Britons, for whom Americans still harbored a war-born hate. Thus at one bold stroke, Jackson succeeded in mobilizing the prejudices of the West against the East. He was setting the log cabin against the business office, the apprehensive debtor against the steely-eyed creditor. More than that, the daringly divisive president was arousing the "native" American against the foreigner, the states' righter against the centralizer.

Jackson's veto message reverberated with constitutional consequences. It not only squashed the bank bill but vastly amplified the power of the presidency. All previous vetoes had rested almost exclusively on questions of constitutionality. But though Jackson invoked the Constitution in his bank-veto message, he essentially argued that he was vetoing

Symptoms of a Locked Jaw
An outraged and outmaneuvered Henry Clay vainly tries to "muzzle" Andrew Jackson after Jackson's stinging message vetoing the bill to recharter the Bank of the United States.

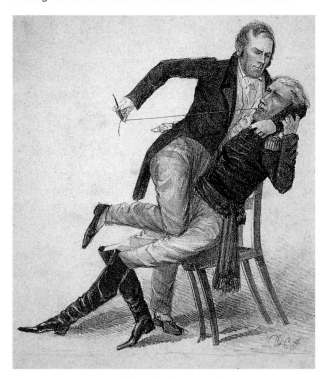

the bill because he personally found it harmful to the nation. In effect, he was claiming for the president alone a power equivalent to two-thirds of the votes in Congress. If the legislative and executive branches were partners in government, he implied, the president was unmistakably the senior partner.

The gods continued to misguide Henry Clay. Delighted with the financial fallacies of Jackson's message but blind to its political appeal, he arranged to have thousands of copies printed as a campaign document. The president's sweeping accusations may indeed have seemed demagogic to the moneyed people of the country, but they made perfect sense to the common people. The bank issue was now thrown into the noisy arena of the Clay-Jackson presidential canvass of 1832.

Brickbats and Bouquets for the Bank

What of Jackson's vigorous charges? The bank was undeniably antiwestern in its strong hostility to the wobbly "wildcat banks" that provided financial fuel—often volatile paper—for western expansion. It had foreclosed on many western farms and had thus drained "tribute" into eastern coffers. For that era it was a mammoth superbank—a "monster monopoly"—and hence out of touch with the sweaty New Democracy. It was undeniably plutocratic, run by an elite moneyed aristocracy, headed by the able but high-handed Nicholas Biddle (dubbed "Czar Nicholas I"). The bank was also in

Nicholas Biddle (1786–1844), by Henry Inman, 1839
A precociously brilliant linguist, writer, magazine editor, diplomat, legislator, and financier, he entered the University of Pennsylvania at age ten and completed the requirements for graduation at age thirteen. Drawn into high finance, he mastered the business and became president of the Bank of the United States.

Banker Nicholas Biddle (1786–1844) wrote to Henry Clay (August 1, 1832) expressing his satisfaction:

"I have always deplored making the Bank a party question, but since the President will have it so, he must pay the penalty of his own rashness. As to the veto message, I am delighted with it. It has all the fury of a chained panther biting the bars of his cage. It is really a manifesto of anarchy . . . and my hope is that it will contribute to relieve the country of the domination of these miserable [Jackson] people."

some degree autocratic and tyrannical, especially when it turned the screws on the weak "rag money" banks.

The charge that the bank was a "hydra of corruption" contained much truth. Biddle cleverly lent funds where they would make influential friends. In 1831 alone, a total of fifty-nine members of Congress borrowed sums from "Biddle's Bank" totaling about a third of a million dollars. Even a dog does not ordinarily bite the hand that feeds it. During one period Daniel Webster was a director of the bank, its chief paid counsel, its debtor in the sum of thousands of dollars, and a member of the Senate, where he eloquently battled for his employer's interests. Judicious loans by Biddle to newspaper editors likewise ensured a "good press" and led to the sneer, "Emperor Nick of the Bribery Bank." Whomever he could not corrupt, it was believed, he crushed.

Yet the bank had much to commend it. A financially sound organization, it imposed some restraint on fly-by-night banks—banks that often consisted of little more than a few chairs and a suitcase full of printed notes. It reduced bank failures and, at a time when the country was flooded with depreciated paper money, issued sound bank notes ("Old Nick's Money"). It promoted economic expansion by making credit and sound currency reasonably abundant. It was a safe depository for the funds of the Washington government, which it also served by transferring and disbursing money. But paradoxically, the bank's enormous economic power made it politically vulnerable.

The bank, in short, was a highly important and useful institution, but one whose very existence seemed to sin against the egalitarian credo of American democracy. Its officers were not only arrogant but were also not fully aware of their responsibilities to society in the management of what amounted to a public trust.

"Old Hickory" Wallops Clay in 1832

Clay, as a National Republican, and Jackson, as a Democrat, were the chief gladiators in the presidential contest of 1832. The gaunt old general, who had earlier favored one term for a president and rotation in office, was easily persuaded by his cronies not to rotate himself out of office. Presidential power is a heady brew—and can be habit-forming.

The ensuing campaign was colorful and noisy. The "Old Hero's" adherents again raised the hickory pole and bellowed, "Jackson Forever: Go the Whole Hog." Admirers of Clay shouted, "Freedom and Clay," while his detractors harped on his dueling, gambling, cockfighting, and fast living.

Novel features made the campaign of 1832 especially memorable. For the first time, a third party entered the field—the newborn Anti-Masonic party, which opposed the fearsome secrecy of the Masonic order. Energized by the mysterious disappearance and probable murder in 1826 of a New Yorker who was threatening to expose the secret rituals of the Masons, the Anti-Masonic party quickly became a potent political force in New York and spread its influence throughout the middle Atlantic and New England states. The Anti-Masons appealed to long-standing American suspicions of secret societies, which they condemned as citadels of privilege and monopoly—a note that harmonized with the democratic chorus of the Jacksonians. But since Jackson himself was a Mason, and publicly gloried in his membership, the Anti-Masonic party was also an anti-Jackson party. Moreover, the Anti-Masons attracted support from many evangelical Protestant groups seeking to use political power to effect moral and religious reforms, such as prohibiting mail deliveries on Sunday and otherwise keeping the Sabbath holy. This moral busybodiness was

Race over Uncle Sam's Course Clay, with his American System, is supposed to gain the White House as Jackson, with his veto club and Van Buren as running mate, falls on the bank issue in 1832. A falsely optimistic Whig cartoon.

anathema to the Jacksonians, who were generally opposed to all government meddling in social and economic life.

A further novelty of the presidential contest in 1832 was the calling of national nominating conventions (three of them) to name candidates. The Anti-Masons and a group of National Republicans added still another innovation when they adopted formal platforms, publicizing their positions on the issues.

Henry Clay and his overconfident National Republicans enjoyed impressive advantages. Ample funds flowed into their campaign chest, including $50,000 in "life insurance" from the BUS. Most of the newspaper editors, some of them "bought" with Biddle's bank loans, dipped their pens in acid when they wrote of Jackson. Oratorical artillery, including the incomparable Webster, was lined up on the side of Clay, as was true of the middle- and upper-income groups.

Yet Jackson won easily over the sparkling Kentuckian. The popular count stood at 687,502 to 530,189; the electoral count, 219 to 49. The Anti-Masons carried only Vermont. A Jacksonian wave swept over the West and South, surged into Pennsylvania and New York, and even washed into rock-ribbed New England.

Henry Clay, long bitten by the presidential bug, was crushed. Himself magnetically appealing, he had enlisted on his side the big money, the brilliant oratory, the "solid" citizenry, and the sound financial reasoning. But the peppery president, the idol of the masses, won because he had the votes. The poor easily outnumbered the rich—and in 1832, as in 1824 and 1828, the poor voted for "Old Andy" Jackson.

Badgering Biddle's Bank

A vindictive Jackson was not one to let the financial octopus die in peace. He was convinced that he now had a "mandate" from the voters, and he had good reason to fear that the slippery Biddle might try to manipulate the bank (as he did) so as to force its recharter. Jackson therefore decided to weaken the bank by "removing" federal deposits from its vaults. He proposed depositing no more funds with Biddle and gradually shrinking existing deposits by using them to defray the day-to-day expenses of the government. By slowly siphoning off the government's

funds, he would bleed the bank dry and ensure its demise when its charter expired in four years.

"Removing" the deposits involved nasty complications. Jackson, his dander up, was forced to reshuffle his cabinet before he could find a secretary of the treasury who would bend to his iron will. Surplus federal funds henceforth were placed in several dozen state institutions—the so-called pet banks or Jackson's pets. These new depositories were selected partly because of their pro-Jackson sympathies, but in general they were not nearly so weak as pictured by the president's enemies.

Biddle, for his part, was compelled to retrench after losing the federal deposits. But he called in loans with unnecessary severity and evidently for the purpose of forcing a reconsideration of the charter by Congress. A number of wobblier banks were driven to the wall by "Biddle's Panic," and the vengeful conduct of the dying "monster" seemed to justify the earlier accusations of its adversaries.

The teetering financial structure of the country received an additional shock in 1836, the year the bank breathed its last. "Wildcat" currency had become so unreliable, especially in the West, that Jackson authorized the Treasury to issue a Specie Circular—a decree that required all public lands to be purchased with "hard," or metallic, money. This drastic step was overdue, but coming at that time it gave the speculative bubble another sharp prick. The hard-money proviso brought hard feelings and hard times for the West.

Transplanting the Tribes

Wondrous indeed was the continued expansion of the American population. The unflagging fertility of the people, reinforced by immigration, brought the total figure to nearly 13 million by 1830, or more than three times that of 1790.* Most of the states east of the Mississippi had been admitted, leaving islands of Indians marooned on lands coveted by their white neighbors.

More than 125,000 Native Americans dwelled in the forests and prairies east of the Mississippi in the 1820s. Federal policy toward them varied. Beginning in the 1790s, the Washington government ostensibly recognized the tribes as separate nations and

---

*For population figures since 1790, see the Appendix.

agreed to acquire land from them only through formal treaties. In practice, however, the Indians were repeatedly coerced or tricked into ceding huge tracts of territory to whites.

Yet many white Americans also felt respect and admiration for the Indians and believed that the Native Americans could be assimilated into white society. Much energy therefore was devoted to "civilizing" and Christianizing the Indians. The Society for Propagating the Gospel Among Indians was founded in 1787, and many denominations sent missionaries into Indian villages. In 1793 Congress appropriated $20,000 for the promotion of literacy and agricultural and vocational instruction among the Indians.

Although many tribes violently resisted white encroachment, others followed the path of accommodation. The Cherokees of Georgia made especially remarkable efforts to learn the ways of the whites. They gradually abandoned their semi-nomadic life and adopted a system of settled agriculture and a notion of private property. Missionaries

opened schools among the Cherokees, and the Indian Sequoyah devised a Cherokee alphabet. In 1808 the Cherokee National Council legislated a written legal code, and in 1827 it adopted a written constitution that provided for executive, legislative, and judicial branches of government. Some Cherokees became prosperous cotton planters and even turned to slaveholding. Nearly 1,300 black slaves toiled for their Native American masters in the Cherokee nation in the 1820s. For these efforts, the Cherokees—along with the Creeks, Choctaws, Chickasaws, and Seminoles—were numbered by the whites among the "Five Civilized Tribes."

All this embrace of "civilization" apparently was not good enough for whites. In 1828 the Georgia legislature declared the Cherokee tribal council illegal and asserted its own jurisdiction over Indian affairs and Indian lands. The Cherokees appealed this move to the Supreme Court, which thrice upheld the rights of the Indians. But President Jackson, who clearly wanted to open Indian lands to white settlement, refused to recognize the Court's

The Removal of the Southern Tribes to the West

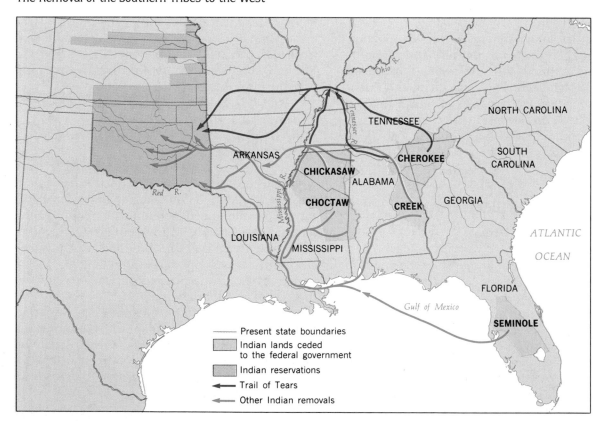

> *Henry Clay (1777–1852) expressed sentiments typical of his time when he said in the 1820s that*
>
> "[Indians are] essentially inferior to the Anglo-Saxon race . . . and their disappearance from the human family will be no great loss to the world."

> *In 1829, Andrew Jackson (1767–1845) reflected on the condition of the Indians, and on Indian-white relations:*
>
> "Our conduct toward these people is deeply interesting to our national character. . . . Our ancestors found them the uncontrolled possessors of these vast regions. By persuasion and force they have been made to retire from river to river and from mountain to mountain, until some of the tribes have become extinct and others have left but remnants to preserve for awhile their once terrible names. Surrounded by the whites with their arts of civilization, which by destroying the resources of the savage doom him to weakness and decay, the fate of the Mohegan, the Narragansett, and the Delaware is fast overtaking the Choctaw, the Cherokee, and the Creek. That this fate surely awaits them if they remain within the limits of the States does not admit of a doubt. Humanity and national honor demand that every effort should be made to avert such a calamity."

decisions. In a callous jibe at the Indians' defender, Jackson reportedly snapped, "John Marshall has made his decision; now let him enforce it."*

Yet Jackson, who had raised from infancy and then adopted an Indian boy, also harbored protective feelings toward the Native Americans. Their present condition, he told Congress in 1829, "contrasted sharply with what they once were, makes a most powerful appeal to our sympathies." Could not something be done, he implored, to preserve "this much injured race"? Jackson proposed a bodily removal of the remaining eastern tribes—chiefly Cherokees, Creeks, Choctaws, Chickasaws, and Seminoles—beyond the Mississippi. Emigration was supposed to be voluntary because it would be "cruel and unjust to compel the aborigines to abandon the graves of their fathers." Jackson evidently consoled himself with the belief that the Indians could preserve their native cultures in the wide-open West.

Jackson's policy sounded noble, but it led to the forced uprooting of more than 100,000 Indians. In 1830 Congress passed the Indian Removal Act, providing for the transplanting of all Indian tribes then resident east of the Mississippi. Ironically, the heaviest blows fell on the Five "Civilized" Tribes. In the ensuing decade, countless Indians died on the "Trail of Tears" to the newly established Indian Territory (present Oklahoma), where they were to be "permanently" free of white encroachments. The Bureau of Indian Affairs was established in 1836 to administer relations with America's original inhabitants. But as the land-hungry "palefaces" pushed west faster than anticipated, the government's guarantees went up in smoke. The "permanent" frontier lasted about fifteen years.

Suspicious of white intentions from the start, Sauk and Fox braves from Illinois and Wisconsin, ably led by Black Hawk, resisted eviction. They were bloodily crushed in 1832 by regular troops, including Lieutenant Jefferson Davis of Mississippi, and by volunteers, including Captain Abraham Lincoln of Illinois.

In Florida the Seminole Indians, joined by runaway black slaves, retreated to the swampy Everglades. For seven years (1835–1842) they waged a bitter guerrilla war that took the lives of some fifteen hundred soldiers and proved to be the costliest Indian conflict in American experience. The spirit of the Seminoles was at last broken in 1837, when the American field commander treacherously seized their half-breed leader, Osceola, under a flag of

---

*One hundred sixty years later, in 1992, the state of Georgia formally pardoned the two white missionaries, Samuel Austin Worcester and Elihu Butler, who had figured prominently in the decision Jackson condemned. They had been convicted of living on Cherokee lands without a license from the state of Georgia. They served sixteen months at hard labor on a chain gang and later accompanied the Cherokees on the "Trail of Tears" to Oklahoma.

The "Trail of Tears"   In the fall and winter of 1838–1839, the U.S. Army forcibly removed about 15,000 Cherokees, some of them in manacles, from their ancestral homelands in the southeastern United States and marched them to the "Indian Territory" of present-day Oklahoma. Freezing weather and inadequate food supplies led to unspeakable suffering. The escorting troops refused to slow the forced march so that the ill could recover, and some 4,000 Cherokees died on the 116-day journey.

Black Hawk and His Son Whirling Thunder, by John Wesley Jarvis, 1833   Chief Black Hawk and his son are here depicted in captivity. After their surrender in the Black Hawk War in 1832, they were put on public display throughout the United States.

truce. The war dragged on fitfully for five more years, but the Seminoles were doomed. Some fled deeper into the Everglades, where their descendants now live, but about four-fifths of them were moved to present Oklahoma, where about three thousand of the tribe survive.

The Lone Star of Texas Flickers

Americans, greedy for land, continued to covet the vast expanse of Texas, which the United States had abandoned to Spain when acquiring Florida in 1819. The Spanish authorities were desirous of populating this virtually unpeopled area, but before they could carry through their contemplated plans, the Mexicans won their independence. A new regime in Mexico City thereupon concluded arrangements in 1823 for granting a huge tract of land to Stephen Austin, with the understanding that he would bring into Texas three hundred American families. Immigrants were to be of the established Roman Catholic faith and upon settlement were to become properly Mexicanized.

These two stipulations were largely ignored. Hardy Texan pioneers remained Americans at heart, resenting the trammels imposed by a "foreign" government. They were especially annoyed by the presence of Mexican soldiers, many of whom were ragged ex-convicts.

Energetic and prolific, Texas-Americans numbered about thirty thousand by 1835 (see "Makers of America: Mexican or Texican?" pp. 284–285). Most of them were law-abiding, God-fearing people, but some of them had left the "states" only one or two jumps ahead of the sheriff. "G. T. T." (Gone to Texas) became current descriptive slang. Among the adventurers were Davy Crockett, the fabulous rifleman, and James Bowie, the presumed inventor of the murderous knife that bears his name. Bowie's blade was widely known in the Southwest as the "genuine Arkansas toothpick." A distinguished latecomer and leader was an ex-governor of Tennessee, Sam Houston. His life had been temporarily shattered in 1829 when his bride of a few weeks left him, and he took up transient residence with the Arkansas Indians, who dubbed him "Big Drunk." He subsequently took the pledge of temperance.

The pioneer individualists who came to Texas were not easy to push around. Friction rapidly increased between Mexicans and Texans over such issues as slavery, immigration, and local rights. Slavery was a particularly touchy issue. Mexico emancipated its slaves in 1830 and prohibited their further importation into Texas, as well as further colonization by troublesome Americans. The Texans refused to honor this decree. They kept their slaves in bondage, and new American settlers kept bringing more slaves into Texas. When Stephen Austin went to Mexico City in 1833 to negotiate these differences with the Mexican government, dictator Santa Anna clapped him in jail for eight months. The explosion finally came in 1835, when Santa Anna wiped out all local rights and started to raise an army to suppress the upstart Texans.

Early in 1836 the Texans declared their independence and unfurled their Lone Star flag—with Sam Houston as commander in chief. Santa Anna, at the head of about six thousand men, swept ferociously into Texas. Trapping a band of nearly two hundred pugnacious Texans at the Alamo in San Antonio, he wiped them out to a man after a thirteen-day siege. Their commander, Colonel W. B. Travis, had heroically declared, "I shall never surrender nor retreat. . . . Victory or Death." The victims included Jim Bowie, who was shot as he lay sick and crippled on his cot, and Davy Crockett, whose body was found riddled with bullets and surrounded by enemy corpses. But the Mexican losses were extremely heavy. A short time later a band of about four hundred surrounded and defeated American volunteers, having thrown down their arms at Goliad, were butchered as "pirates." All these operations further delayed the Mexican advance—and galvanized American opposition.

Texan war cries—"Remember the Alamo!" "Remember Goliad!" and "Death to Santa Anna!"—swept up into the United States. Scores of vengeful Americans seized their rifles and rushed to the aid of relatives, friends, and compatriots. But despite their efforts, the Lone Star was in grave danger of being dimmed forever as General Sam Houston's small army continued its thirty-seven-day eastward retreat.

But Houston proved equal to the occasion. A commanding figure of a man and a natural leader of the Texans, he lured the pursuers onward to San Jacinto, near the site of the city that now bears his

The Alamo as It Looks Today
When Moses Austin, father of famed Texas pioneer Stephen Austin, first saw this building on December 23, 1820, it was an abandoned mission, founded by Franciscan friars in 1718 as San Antonio de Valero. Renamed the Alamo, from the Spanish word for cottonwood tree, it was made into a fortress and became famous in 1836 when Santa Anna's armies wiped out its garrison of Americans.

Mexican or Texican?

Moses Austin, born a Connecticut Yankee in 1761, was determined to be Spanish—if that's what it took to acquire cheap land and freedom from pesky laws. In 1798 he tramped into untracked Missouri, still part of Spanish Louisiana, and pledged his allegiance to the king of Spain. He was not pleased when the Louisiana Purchase of 1803 restored him to American citizenship. In 1820, with his old Spanish passport in his saddlebag, he rode into Spanish Texas and asked for permission to establish a colony of three hundred families.

Austin's request posed a dilemma for the Texas governor. The Spanish authorities had repeatedly stamped out the bands of American horse thieves and squatters who periodically splashed across the Red and Sabine Rivers from the United States into Spanish territory. Yet the Spanish had lured only some three thousand of their own settlers into Texas during their three centuries of rule. If the land were ever to be wrestled from the Indians and "civilized," maybe Austin's plan could do it. Hoping that this band of the "right sort" of Americans might prevent the further encroachment of the buckskinned border ruffians, the governor reluctantly agreed to Austin's proposal.

Upon Moses Austin's death in 1821, the task of realizing his dream fell to his twenty-seven-year-old son, Stephen. "I bid an everlasting farewell to my native country," Stephen Austin said, and he crossed into Texas on July 15, 1821, "determined to fulfill rigidly all the duties and obligations of a Mexican citizen" (Mexico declared its independence from Spain early in 1821 and finalized its agreement with Austin in 1823). Soon he learned fluent Spanish and was signing his name as "Don Estévan F. Austin." In his new colony between the Brazos and Colorado

José Antonio Navarro (1795–1871)
A native of San Antonio, Navarro signed the Texas declaration of independence in 1836.

Rivers, he allowed "no drunkard, no gambler, no profane swearer, no idler"—and sternly enforced these rules. Not only did he banish several families as "undesirables," but he ordered the public flogging of unwanted interlopers.

Austin fell just three families short of recruiting the three hundred households that his father had contracted to bring to Texas. The original settlers were still dubbed "the Old Three Hundred," the Texas equivalent of New England's Mayflower Pilgrims or the "First Families of Virginia." Mostly Scots-Irish southerners from the trans-Appalachian frontier, the Old Three Hundred were cultured folk by frontier standards; all but four of them were literate. Other settlers followed, from Europe as well as America. Within ten years the "Anglos" (many of them French and German) outnumbered the Mexican residents, or *tejanos*, ten to one and soon evolved a distinctive "Texican" culture. The wide-ranging horse patrols organized to attack Indian camps became the Texas Rangers; Samuel Maverick, whose unbranded calves roamed the limitless prairies, left his surname as a label for rebellious loners who refuse to run with the herd; and Jared Groce, an Alabama planter whose caravan of fifty covered wagons and one hundred slaves arrived in 1822, etched the original image of the larger-than-life, big-time Texas operator.

The original Anglo-Texans brought with them the old Scots-Irish frontiersman's hostility to authority. When the Mexican government tried to impose its will on the Anglo-Texans in the 1830s, they protested. Like the American revolutionaries of the 1770s, who at first demanded only the rights of Englishmen, the Texans began by asking simply for Mexican recognition of their rights as guaranteed by the Mexican constitution of 1824. But bloodshed at the Alamo in 1836, like that at Lexington in 1775, transformed protest into rebellion.

Texas lay—and still lies—along the frontier where Hispanic and Anglo-American cultures met, mingled, and clashed. In part, the Texas Revolution was a contest between those two cultures. But it was also a contest about philosophies of government, pitting liberal frontier ideals of freedom against the conservative concept of centralized control. Stephen Austin sincerely tried to "Mexicanize" himself and his followers—until the Mexican government grew too arbitrary and authoritarian. And not all the Texan revolutionaries were "Anglos." Seven *tejanos* perished defending the Alamo. Among the fifty-nine signers of the Texas declaration of independence were several Hispanics, including the *tejanos* José Antonio Navarro and Francisco Ruiz. Lorenzo de Zavala, an ardent Mexican liberal who had long resisted the centralizing tendencies of Mexico's dominant political party, was designated vice president of the Texas Republic's interim government in 1836. Like the Austins, these *tejanos* and Mexicans had sought in Texas an escape from overbearing governmental authority. Their role in the revolution underscores the fact that the uprising was a struggle between defenders of local rights and the agents of central authority as much as it was a fight between Anglo and Mexican cultures.

West Side Main Plaza, San Antonio, Texas, (detail) by William G. M. Samuel, 1849   Even after annexation Texas retained strong Spanish-Mexican flavor, as the architecture and activities here illustrate.

name. The invaders numbered about thirteen hundred men; the Texans, about nine hundred. Suddenly, on April 21, 1836, Houston turned. Taking full advantage of the Mexican siesta hour, he wiped out the invading force and captured Santa Anna, who was found cowering in the tall grass near the battlefield. Confronted with thirsty bowie knives, the quaking dictator was speedily induced to sign two treaties. By their terms he agreed to withdraw Mexican troops and to recognize the Rio Grande as the extreme southwestern boundary of Texas. When released, he repudiated the whole agreement as illegal because it was extorted under duress.

Texas: An International Derelict

Mexico no doubt had a genuine grievance against the United States. The Texans, though courageous, could hardly have won their independence without unneutral help in men and supplies from their American cousins. The Washington government, as the Mexicans bitterly complained, had a solemn obligation under international law to enforce its leaky neutrality statutes. But American public opin-

Samuel ("Sam") Houston (1793–1863)   After a promising career in Tennessee as a soldier, lawyer, congressman, and governor, Houston became the chief leader and hero of the Texas rebels. Elected to the U.S. Senate and the governorship of Texas, he was forced into retirement when his love for the Union caused him to spurn the Confederacy in the Civil War.

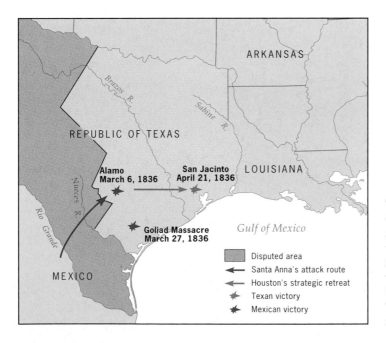

The Texas Revolution, 1835–1836
General Houston's strategy was to retreat and use defense in depth. His line of supply from the United States was shortened as Santa Anna's lengthened. The Mexicans were forced to bring up supplies by land because the Texas navy controlled the sea. This force consisted of only four small ships, but it was big enough to do the job.

ion, overwhelmingly favorable to the Texans, openly nullified the existing legislation. The federal authorities were powerless to act.

Jackson's heart was torn by the Texas issue. He disliked the Mexican overlords and admired the heroism of Sam Houston, his old comrade-in-arms against the Indians. But Jackson was in no hurry to recognize Texas formally as an independent republic. To do so would touch off the whole explosive issue of slavery, at a time when he was trying to engineer the election of his handpicked successor, Martin Van Buren. But after Van Buren had come safely under the wire, Jackson extended the right hand of recognition, on the day before he left office in 1837.

Many Texans wanted not just recognition of their independence, but outright union with the United States. What nation in its right mind, they reasoned, would refuse so lavish a dowry? The radiant Texan bride, officially petitioning for annexation in 1837, presented herself for marriage. But the expectant groom, Uncle Sam, was jerked back by the black hand of the slavery issue. Antislavery crusaders in the North were opposing annexation with increasing vehemence; they contended that the whole scheme was merely a conspiracy cooked up by the southern "slavocracy" to bring new slave pens into the Union.

At first glance a "slavery plot" charge seemed plausible. Most of the early settlers in Texas, as well as American volunteers during the revolution, had come from the states of the South and Southwest. But scholars have concluded that the settlement of Texas was merely the normal and inexorable march of the westward movement. Most of the immigrants came from the South and Southwest simply because these states were closer. The explanation was proximity rather than conspiracy. Yet the fact remained that many Texans were slaveholders, and admitting Texas to the Union inescapably meant enlarging American slavery.

Texas was left in a dangerous predicament. Fearing the return of the "villain," Santa Anna, it understandably went so far as to send feelers out to Britain and France for support. An ugly situation, threatening to introduce European great-power rivalry, and perhaps even European intervention, began to develop below the underbelly of the United States. It could not be allowed to go on indefinitely.

The Birth of the Whigs and the Election of 1836

New political parties were gelling as the 1830s lengthened. As early as 1828, the Democratic-Republicans of Jackson had unashamedly adopted the once-tainted name of "Democrats." Jackson's opponents, fuming at his ironfisted exercise of presidential power, condemned him as "King Andrew I" and began to coalesce as the Whigs—a name deliberately chosen to recollect eighteenth-century British and Revolutionary American opposition to the monarchy.

The Whig party contained so many diverse elements that it was mocked at first as "an organized incompatibility." Hatred of Jackson and his "executive usurpation" was its only apparent cement in its formative days. The Whigs first emerged as an identifiable group in the Senate, where Clay and Calhoun joined forces in 1834 to pass a motion censuring Jackson for his single-handed removal of federal deposits from the Bank of the United States. Thereafter, the Whigs rapidly evolved into a potent national political force by attracting other groups alienated by Jackson: supporters of Clay's American System; southern states' righters offended by Jackson's stand on nullification; the larger northern industrialists and merchants; and eventually many of the evangelical Protestants associated with the Anti-Masonic party.

As the presidential election of 1836 neared, the still-ramshackle organization of the Whigs showed in their inability to nominate a single presidential candidate. Their long-shot strategy was instead to run several prominent "favorite sons," who would so scatter the vote that no candidate would win a majority. The deadlock would then have to be broken by the House of Representatives, where the Whigs might have a chance. With Henry Clay rudely elbowed aside, the leading "favorite son" was heavy-jawed General William Henry Harrison of Ohio, hero of the Battle of Tippecanoe (see p. 228).

Martin Van Buren of New York, a smooth-as-silk politician, was Jackson's choice for "appointment" as his successor. The hollow-cheeked Jackson, now nearing seventy, was too old and ailing to consider a third term. But he was not loath to try to serve a third term through Van Buren, something of a "yes man." Leaving nothing to chance, Jackson carefully rigged the nominating convention and rammed his favorite down the throats of the delegates. Van Buren was supported by the Jacksonites without wild enthusiasm, even though he had promised "to tread generally" in the military-booted footsteps of his predecessor.

The finespun schemes of the Whigs availed nothing. Van Buren, the dapper "Little Van," squirmed into office by the close popular vote of 765,483 to 739,795, but by the comfortable margin of 170 votes to 124 in the Electoral College. Jackson could now step down.

In retrospect, the Jackson years were yeasty ones. It is true that they were marred by noise and bluster, as well as by bull-in-the-china-closet financial policies. Yet the rough-hewn general—through

President Martin Van Buren (1782–1862)   Ironically, Van Buren's agility as a politician has clouded his reputation as president. It was said of him that he rowed toward his objectives "with muffled oars." Yet he eventually took a strong stand against the expansion of slavery with his hopeless run for the presidency as the candidate of the Free Soil Party in 1848.

forthrightness, energy, and strength of character—left a lasting imprint on the presidency. To his credit, he bolstered the power of the executive branch; he signaled the political coming-of-age of the West; he led the common people into national politics; he united them into the powerful and long-lived Democratic party; and he proved that they could be trusted with the vote. Reasserting the prestige of the presidency, he amazed weak-kneed politicians by showing that the courageous course often wins the most votes.

The other side of the ledger is less satisfying. Jackson cannot escape blame for his encouragement of the spoils system and especially for the damage he inflicted on the nation's financial system. It is true that the BUS was a powerful and ultimately corrupting monopoly that needed curbing. But chopping off its head instead of clipping its wings deprived the nation of a sound central bank just as it was entering an era of rapid industrialization. Almost alone among the major industrial countries, the United States' banking "system" was composed of thousands of local banks, many of them woefully undercapitalized and poorly managed. The American banking industry was thus "democratized" in the sense that no bank held a monopoly on financial power and the banking field was open to all ambitious entrepreneurs, as befitted Jacksonian political philosophy. But Americans paid a stiff economic price for this wide-open system, as Jackson's "reforms" left a heartbreaking, century-long legacy of thousands of bank failures.

Big Woes for the "Little Magician"

Martin Van Buren, eighth president, was the first to be born under the American flag. Bland of face, bald of head, slender of figure, the adroit little New Yorker has been described as "a first-class second-rate man." An accomplished strategist and spoils-man—"the wizard of Albany"—he was also a statesman of wide experience in both legislative and administrative life. In intelligence, education, and training, he was above the average of the presidents since Jackson. The myth of his complete mediocrity sprouted from a series of misfortunes over which he had no control.

From the outset the new politician-president labored under severe handicaps. As a machine-made candidate, he incurred the resentment of many Democrats—those who objected to having a "bastard politician" smuggled into office beneath the tails of the old general's military coat. Jackson, the master showman, had been a dynamic type of executive whose administration had resounded with furious quarrels and cracked heads. Easygoing Martin Van Buren seemed to rattle about in the military boots of his testy predecessor. The people felt let down. Inheriting Andrew Jackson's mantle without his popularity, the polished New Yorker also inherited the ex-president's numerous and vengeful enemies.

Van Buren's four years overflowed with toil and trouble. A rebellion in Canada in 1837 stirred up ugly incidents along the northern frontier and threatened to trigger war with Britain. The president's attempt to play a neutral game led to the wail "Woe to Martin Van Buren!" The antislavery agitators in the North were in full cry. Among other grievances, they were condemning the prospective annexation of Texas.

Worst of all, Van Buren inherited the making of a searing depression from Jackson. Much of his energy had to be devoted to the purely negative task of battling the panic, and there were not enough rabbits in the "Little Magician's" tall silk hat. Hard times ordinarily blight the reputation of a president—and Van Buren was no exception.

Depression Doldrums and the Independent Treasury

The panic of 1837 was a symptom of the financial sickness of the times. Its basic cause was rampant speculation prompted by a mania of get-rich-quickism. Gamblers in western lands were doing a "land-office business" on borrowed capital, much of it in the shaky currency of "wildcat banks." The speculative craze spread to canals, roads, railroads, and slaves.

But speculation alone did not cause the crash. Jacksonian finance, including the "Bank War" and the Specie Circular, gave an additional jolt to an already teetering structure. Failures of wheat crops, ravaged by the Hessian fly, deepened the distress. Grain prices were forced so high that mobs in New York City, three weeks before Van Buren took the oath, stormed warehouses and broke open flour

Philip Hone (1780–1851), a New York businessman, described in his diary (May 10, 1837) a phase of the financial crisis:

"The savings-bank also sustained a most grievous run yesterday. They paid 375 depositors $81,000. The press was awful; the hour for closing the bank is six o'clock, but they did not get through the paying of those who were in at that time till nine o'clock. I was there with the other trustees and witnessed the madness of the people—women nearly pressed to death, and the stoutest men could scarcely sustain themselves; but they held on as with a death's grip upon the evidences of their claims, and, exhausted as they were with the pressure, they had strength to cry 'Pay! Pay!'"

barrels. The panic really began before Jackson left office, but its full fury burst about Van Buren's bewildered head.

Financial stringency abroad likewise endangered America's economic house of cards. Late in 1836, while Jackson was still president, the failure of two prominent British banks created tremors, and these in turn caused English investors to call in foreign loans. The resulting pinch in the United States, combined with other setbacks, heralded the beginning of the panic. Europe's economic distresses have often been America's distresses, for every major American financial panic has been affected by conditions overseas.

Hardship was acute and widespread. American banks collapsed by the hundreds, including some "pet banks," which carried down with them several millions in government funds. Commodity prices drooped, sales of public lands fell off, and customs revenues dried to a rivulet. Factories closed their doors, and unemployed workers milled in the streets.

The Whigs came forward with proposals for active government remedies for the economy's ills. They called for the expansion of bank credit, higher tariffs, and subsidies for internal improvements. But Van Buren, shackled by the Jacksonian philosophy of keeping the government's paws off the economy, spurned all such ideas.

The beleaguered Van Buren tried to apply vintage Jacksonian medicine to the ailing economy through his controversial "Divorce Bill." Convinced that some of the financial fever was fed by the injection of federal funds into private banks, he championed the principle of "divorcing" the government from banking altogether. By establishing a so-called independent treasury, the government could lock its surplus money in vaults in several of the larger cities. Government funds would thus be safe, but they would also be denied to the banking system as reserves, thereby shriveling available credit resources. Van Buren's desire for political purity triumphed over enlightened economics.

Van Buren's "divorce" scheme was never highly popular. It was supported only lukewarmly by his fellow Democrats, many of whom longed for the risky but lush days of the "pet banks." The new policy was condemned by the Whigs, primarily because it would squelch their hopes for a revived Bank of the United States. After a prolonged struggle, the Independent Treasury Bill passed Congress in 1840. Repealed the next year by the victorious Whigs, the scheme was reenacted by the triumphant Democrats in 1846 and then continued until merged with the Federal Reserve System in the next century.

"Tippecanoe" Versus "Little Van"

Martin Van Buren, though panic-plagued, was renominated by the Democrats in 1840, albeit without terrific enthusiasm. The party had no acceptable alternative to what the Whigs called "Martin Van Ruin."

The Whigs, hungering for the spoils of office, scented victory in the breeze. Pangs of the panic were still being felt; and voters blindly blamed their woes on the party in power. The Whigs turned again not to their ablest statesmen—Clay or Webster—but to their presumably ablest vote-getter: General Harrison, a coarse-featured military chieftain, with a long, thin face and medium build (5 feet, 8 inches; 1.72 meters).

The aging hero, nearly sixty-eight when the campaign ended, was a small-bore candidate. Despite an inflated reputation, he had been only moderately successful in civilian and military life, notably at the battles of Tippecanoe (1811) and the Thames (1813). "Old Tippecanoe" was then living

President William Henry Harrison (1773–1841), by Albert Gallatin Hoit, 1840   Harrison can claim several distinctions. At sixty-eight, he was the oldest man to be sworn in until Ronald Reagan's inauguration 140 years later; he delivered the longest inaugural address (two hours); dying shortly thereafter of pneumonia, he served the shortest term (thirty-one days); he obviously accomplished the least of any president; and he was responsible for the most progeny: 10 children, 48 grandchildren, 106 great-grandchildren. One of his grandchildren, Benjamin Harrison, became the twenty-third president of the United States.

quietly in a sixteen-room mansion, located on a three-thousand-acre farm near North Bend, Ohio. Harrison's views on current issues were only vaguely known. He was nominated primarily because he was issueless and enemyless—and a most unfortunate precedent was thus set. John Tyler of Virginia, an afterthought, was selected as his vice-presidential running mate.

The Whigs benefited from the economic distresses of Van Buren's term, and they were generally perceived as advocates of positive governmental steps to revive the economy. But officially, the Whigs played the political game with the cards close to their vests. They published no platform because

A BEAUTIFUL GOBLET OF
WHITE HOUSE CHAMPAGNE

AN UGLY MUG OF
LOG-CABIN HARD CIDER

Martin Van Buren Gags on Hard Cider
This 1840 "pull-card" showed Van Buren on the left as an aristocratic fop sipping champagne. When the right-hand card was pulled out, Van Buren's face soured as he discovered that his "champagne" was actually hard cider. The cartoonist clearly sympathized with Van Buren's opponent in the 1840 presidential election, William Henry Harrison, who waged the famous "log cabin and hard cider" campaign.

they feared making bothersome commitments and were unwilling to reveal the deep divisions within their own patchwork party. They hoped to sweep their hero into office with a frothy huzza-for-Harrison campaign.

A dull-witted Democratic editor played directly into Whig hands. Stupidly insulting the West, he lampooned Harrison as an impoverished old farmer who would be content with a pension, a log cabin, and a barrel of hard cider—the poor westerner's champagne. Whigs gleefully took up the challenge and, stressing the hard cider and log cabin theme, turned the campaign into a huge political revival meeting. Harrisonites portrayed their hero as the poor "Farmer of North Bend," who had been called from his plow and his log cabin to drive corrupt Jackson spoilsmen from the "presidential palace."

A nonexistent candidate rapidly began to take shape in the hands of Whig mythmakers. The real Harrison was not lowborn, but from one of the FFVs ("First Families of Virginia"). He was not poverty-stricken; he did not live in a one-room log cabin; he did not swill down gallons of hard cider (he evidently preferred whiskey); and he did not plow his fields with his own "huge paws."

Whig propagandists made merry with little "Matty" Van Buren, the "Flying Dutchman." Although reared in poverty, he was denounced as a supercilious aristocrat, who wore corsets and ate French food with golden teaspoons from golden plates. Jackson's rough-timbered Democratic party, deeply rooted in the West, was thus saddled with a simpering dandy from the aristocratic East. The aristocratic Whig party of Webster and Biddle, no less inconsistently, had come up with a backwoods nominee from the Democratic West—a reasonable facsimile of wrinkled old General Jackson. As a jeering Whig campaign song proclaimed,

Old Tip, he wears a homespun shirt,
He has no ruffled shirt, wirt, wirt.
But Matt, he has the golden plate,
and he's a little squirt, wirt, wirt.

The Log Cabins and Hard Cider of 1840

Eager Democrats, who had hurrahed Jackson into the White House, now discovered to their chagrin that this was a game two could play. Acres of Whig audiences and miles of Whig marchers shouted such slogans as "Harrison, Two Dollars a Day and Roast Beef" and "With Tip and Tyler We'll Bust Van's Biler [boiler]." Log cabins were dished up in every conceivable form. Bawling Whigs, stimulated by fortified cider, rolled huge inflated balls from village to village and state to state—balls that represented the snowballing majority for "Tip and Ty." They pushed, and sang

>   *Tippecanoe, and Tyler too.*
>   *And with them we'll beat little Van, Van,*
>   *Van,*
>   *Oh! Van is a used-up man.*

Claptrap was king, as the electoral debauch reached an unprecedented intellectual low. There was little sober discussion of solid issues. Democrats inquired earnestly about the bank, internal improvements, and the tariff. The replies were "log cabin," "hard cider," and "Harrison is a poor man." Van Burenites, kicking futilely, drowned in a wave of apple juice as America experienced its first mass-turnout election.

Harrison won by the surprisingly close margin of 1,274,624 popular votes to 1,127,781, but by the overwhelming electoral count of 234 to 60. The hard-ciderites had seemingly received a mandate to go to Washington, tear down the White House, and erect a log cabin.

Basically, the vote was a protest against hard times—a thunderous shout of "Out with the old and in with the new." But the blatant bunkum and silly slogans set an unfortunate example for future campaigns. Democracy calls for hard thinking, not hard cider; for dignity, not delirium. Yet an able, well-organized, and well-entrenched political party, committed to solid principles, was hooted out of office by an inane hoopla campaign.

The Democrats were baffled. They complained with much bitterness and no little truth that they had been shouted down, sung down, lied down, and drunk down. Yet though outsloganed, they had kept their ranks intact. Even in defeat they were a stronger party than the Whigs. Although temporarily submerged in hard cider, the Democrats would be heard from again.

The Two-Party System Emerges

The Jeffersonians of an earlier day had been so successful in absorbing the programs of their Federalist opponents that a full-blown two-party system had never truly emerged in the subsequent Era of Good Feelings. The idea had prevailed that parties of any sort smacked of conspiracy and "faction" and were injurious to the health of the body politic in a virtuous republic.

But the American political world changed dramatically in the era of the New Democracy. One of Andrew Jackson's most lasting legacies was the impetus he gave to the formation of a vigorous and durable two-party system, which had fully come of age by 1840.

Both parties, the Democrats as well as the Whigs, grew out of the rich soil of Jeffersonian republicanism, and each laid claim to different aspects of the republican inheritance. Jacksonians glorified the liberty of the individual and were

A Hard Road to Hoe!
Jackson urges Van Buren toward the White House over a road littered with log cabins and hard cider. Van Buren, handicapped also by his unpopular subtreasury policy, would evidently prefer the smoother road back to his Kinderhook home. Van Buren's campaign may have contributed the slang expression "O.K." to the language. A campaign cartoon of 1840.

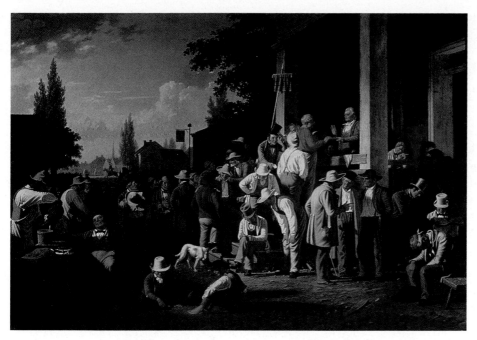

The County Election, by George Caleb Bingham, 1851–1852
The artist here gently satirizes the drinking and wheeler-dealing that sometimes marred the electoral process in the boisterous age of Jacksonian politics.

fiercely on guard against the inroads of "privilege" into government. Whigs trumpeted the natural harmony of society and the value of community, and were willing to use government to realize their objectives. Whigs also berated those leaders—and they considered Jackson to be one—whose appeals to self-interest fostered conflict among individuals, classes, or sections.

Democrats clung to states' rights and federal restraint in social and economic affairs as their basic doctrines. Whigs tended to favor a renewed national bank; protective tariffs; internal improvements; public schools; and increasingly, moral reforms such as the prohibition of liquor and eventually the abolition of slavery.

The two parties were thus separated by real differences of philosophy and policy. But they also had much in common. Both were mass-based, "catchall" parties that tried deliberately to mobilize as many voters as possible for their cause. Although it is true that Democrats tended to be more humble folk and Whigs more prosperous, both parties nevertheless commanded the loyalties of all kinds of Americans, from all social classes and in all sections. The social diversity of the two parties had important implications. It fostered horse-trading compromises *within* each party that prevented either from assuming extreme or radical positions. By the same token, the geographical diversity of the two parties retarded the emergence of purely sectional political parties—temporarily suppressing, through compromise, the ultimately uncompromisable issue of slavery. When the two-party system began to creak in the 1850s, the Union was mortally imperiled.

President Andrew Jackson (1767–1845) advised a supporter in 1835 on how to tell the difference between Democrats and "Whigs, nullies, and blue-light federalists." In doing so he neatly summarized the Jacksonian philosophy:

"The people ought to inquire [of political candidates]—are you opposed to a national bank; are you in favor of a strict construction of the Federal and State Constitutions; are you in favor of rotation in office; do you subscribe to the republican rule that the people are the sovereign power, the officers their agents, and that upon all national or general subjects, as well as local, they have a right to instruct their agents and representatives, and they are bound to obey or resign; in short, are they true Republicans agreeable to the true Jeffersonian creed?"

Chronology

1823   Mexico opens Texas to American settlers

1830   Indian Removal Act
Jackson vetoes bill to improve Maysville Road

1832   Jackson defeats Clay for presidency
"Bank War"—Jackson vetoes bill to
recharter Bank of the United States
Tariff of 1832
Black Hawk War

1832-
1833   South Carolina nullification crisis

1833   Compromise Tariff of 1833
Jackson removes federal deposits from
Bank of the United States

1835-   Southeastern Indians removed on
1839   "Trail of Tears"

1836   Bank of the United States expires
Specie Circular issued
Bureau of Indian Affairs established
Battle of the Alamo
Battle of San Jacinto
Texas wins independence from Mexico
Van Buren elected president

1837   Seminole Indians defeated and eventually
removed from Florida
United States recognizes republic of Texas
but refuses annexation
Panic of 1837

1840   Independent Treasury established
Harrison defeats Van Buren for presidency

What Was Jacksonian Democracy?

Aristocratic, eastern-born historians of the nineteenth century damned Jackson as a backwoods barbarian. They criticized Jacksonianism as democracy run riot—an irresponsible, ill-bred outburst that overturned the electoral system and wrecked the national financial structure.

In the late nineteenth and early twentieth centuries, however, another generation of historians came to the fore, many of whom grew up in the Midwest and rejected the elitist views of their predecessors. Frederick Jackson Turner and his disciples saw the western frontier as the fount of democratic virtue, and they hailed Jackson as a true hero sprung from the forests of the West to protect the will of the people against the monied interests, akin to the progressive reformers of their own day. In his famous 1893 essay, "The Significance of the Frontier in American History," Turner argued that the United States owed the survival of its democratic tradition to the rise of the West, not to its roots in the more conservative, aristocratic East.

When Arthur M. Schlesinger, Jr., published *The Age of Jackson* in 1945, however, the debate on Jacksonianism shifted dramatically. Although he shared the Turnerians' admiration for Jackson the democrat, Schlesinger cast the Jacksonian era not as a sectional conflict, but as a class conflict between poor farmers, laborers, and noncapitalists on the one hand, and the business community—epitomized by the Second Bank of the United States—on the other. In Schlesinger's eyes, the Jacksonians justifiably attacked the bank as an institution dangerously independent of democratic oversight. The political mobilization of the urban working classes in support of Jackson particularly attracted Schlesinger's interest.

Soon after Schlesinger's book appeared, the discussion again shifted ground and entirely new interpretations of Jacksonianism emerged. Richard Hofstadter argued in *The American Political Tradition and the Men Who Made It* (1948) that Jacksonian democracy was not a rejection of capitalism, as Schlesinger insisted, but rather the effort of aspiring entrepreneurs to secure laissez-faire policies that would serve their own interests against their entrenched, and monopolistic, eastern competitors. Marvin Meyers took a more psychological approach in his book *The Jacksonian Persuasion* (1957), suggesting that the Jacksonians suffered from a deep-seated insecurity about their status in society, which propelled them to attack imagined enemies like the national bank. Lee Benson contended in *The Concept of Jacksonian Democracy* (1961) that the political conflicts of the Jacksonian era did not correspond so much to class divisions as to different ethnic and religious splits within American society. Using new quantitative methods of analysis, Benson found no consistent demarcations—in class, occupation, or region—between the Jacksonians and their rivals. Local and cultural issues such as temperance and religion were far more influential in shaping political life than the national financial questions analyzed by previous historians.

In the 1980s, Sean Wilentz and other scholars began to resurrect some of Schlesinger's argument about the importance of class to Jacksonianism. In *Chants Democratic* (1984), Wilentz maintained that Jacksonian politics could not be properly understood without reference to the changing national economy. Artisans watched in horror as new manufacturing techniques put many of them out of business and replaced their craftsmanship with the unskilled hands of wage laborers. To these anxious small producers, America's infatuation with impersonal institutions and large-scale employers threatened the very existence of a republic founded on the principle that its citizens were virtuously self-sufficient. Thus, Jackson's attack on the Bank of the United States symbolized the antagonism these individuals felt toward the emergent capitalist economy and earned him their strong allegiance.

This interpretation is conspicuous in Charles Sellers's *The Market Revolution: Jacksonian America, 1815–1846* (1991), which raised a fascinating question: what was the relationship between American democracy and free-market capitalism? They are often assumed to be twins, born from the common parentage of freedom and opportunity, reared in the wide-open young republic, and mutually supporting each other ever since. But perhaps, Sellers suggested, they were really adversaries, with Jacksonians inventing mass democracy in order to hold capitalist expansion in check. Yet if this interpretation is correct, what explains the phenomenal growth of the capitalist economy in the years immediately following the triumphs of Jacksonianism? Further research and analysis are needed to sort out the varied commitments of the mix of Americans who spiritedly identified their own destinies with Jackson, as well as the intended and unintended consequences that resulted from their support.

SUGGESTED READINGS

PRIMARY SOURCE DOCUMENTS

An incisive commentary on Jacksonian politics is James Fenimore Cooper's *The American Democrat** (1838). On the Bank War, see Andrew Jackson, "Veto Message"* (July 10, 1832), in James D. Richardson, ed., *Messages and Papers of the Presidents* (1896), vol. II, pp. 576 ff, and Daniel Webster's "Speech on Jackson's Veto of the U.S. Bank Bill" (1832), in Richard Hofstadter, ed., *Great Issues in American History.*

SECONDARY SOURCES

A thorough introduction is the concluding volume of Robert V. Remini's biography, *Andrew Jackson and the Course of American Democracy, 1833–1845* (1984). On Van Buren see John Niven, *Martin Van Buren: The Romantic Age of American Politics* (1983). Incisive analysis can be found in Richard Hofstadter's essay on Jackson in *The American Political Tradition* (1948). See also Lawrence F. Kohl, *The Politics of Individualism: Parties and the American Character in the Jacksonian Era* (1989), and John Ashworth, *"Agrarians and Aristocrats": Party Political Ideology in the United States, 1837–1846* (1982). A superior monograph is William W. Freehling, *Prelude to Civil War: The Nullification Controversy in South Carolina* (1966). Also see Richard E. Ellis, *The Union at Risk: Jacksonian Democracy, States' Rights and the Nullification Crisis* (1987). On Calhoun, see Gerald

M. Capers, *John C. Calhoun, Opportunist* (1960), and John Niven, *John C. Calhoun and the Price of Union* (1988). Jacksonians are charged with ignorance and hypocrisy in Bray Hammond, *Banks and Politics in America from the Revolution to the Civil War* (1957). John McFaul looks at the broader picture in *The Politics of Jacksonian Finance* (1972), and Remini focuses on political questions in *Andrew Jackson and the Bank War* (1967). Jackson's Indian policies are scrutinized in Ronald N. Satz, *American Indian Policy in the Jacksonian Era* (1975), and Michael P. Rogin's heavily psychoanalytic *Fathers and Children: Andrew Jackson and the Subjugation of the American Indians* (1975). See also Michael D. Green, *The Politics of Indian Removal* (1982), and Anthony Wallace, *The Long, Bitter Trail: Andrew Jackson and the Indians* (1993). For studies of the so-called civilized tribes, see Charles Hudson, *The Southeastern Indians* (1976), and William G. McLaughlin, *Cherokee Renascence in the New Republic* (1986). Important political transformations are handled in the Ronald P. Formisano and Richard P. McCormick volumes cited in Chapter 13. See also the opening chapters of Michael F. Holt, *The Political Crisis of the 1850s* (1978), and Amy Bridges, *A City in the Republic: Antebellum New York and the Origins of Machine Politics* (1984). Daniel W. Howe provides a stimulating analysis of Jackson's opponents in *The Political Culture of the American Whigs* (1980). Also see Thomas Brown, *Politics and Statesmanship: Essays on the American Whig Party* (1985). Attempts to connect Jacksonian politics with the economic changes of the era include Harry L. Watson, *Liberty and Power* (1990), and Charles Sellers's monumental synthesis, *The Market Revolution* (1991). The color of the frothy presidential campaign of 1840 comes through in Robert G. Gunderson, *The Log-Cabin Campaign* (1957).

---

*An asterisk indicates that the document, or an excerpt from it, can be found in Thomas A. Bailey and David M. Kennedy, eds., *The American Spirit: United States History as Seen by Contemporaries,* 9th ed. (Boston: Houghton Mifflin, 1998).

15

Forging the National Economy
1790–1860

*The progress of invention is really a threat
[to monarchy]. Whenever I see a railroad I look
for a republic.*

RALPH WALDO EMERSON, 1866

The Westward Movement

The rise of Andrew Jackson, the first president from beyond the Appalachian Mountains, exemplified the inexorable westward march of the American people. The West, with its raw frontier, was the most typically American part of America. As Ralph Waldo Emerson wrote in 1844, "Europe stretches to the Alleghenies; America lies beyond."

The Republic was young, and so were the people —as late as 1850, half of Americans were under the age of thirty. They were also restless and energetic, seemingly always on the move, and always westward. One "tall tale" of the frontier described chickens that voluntarily crossed their legs every spring, waiting to be tied for the annual move west. By 1840 the "demographic center" of the American population map had

crossed the Alleghenies. By the eve of the Civil War, it had marched across the Ohio River.

Legend portrays an army of muscular axmen triumphantly carving civilization out of the western woods. But in reality, life was downright grim for most pioneer families. Poorly fed, ill clad, housed in hastily erected shanties (Abraham Lincoln's family lived for a year in a three-sided lean-to made of brush and sticks), they were perpetual victims of disease, depression, and premature death. Above all, unbearable loneliness haunted them, especially the women, who were often cut off from human contact, even their neighbors, for days or even weeks, while confined to the cramped orbit of a dark cabin in a secluded clearing. Breakdowns and even madness were all too frequently the "opportunities" that the frontier offered to pioneer women.

Frontier life could be tough and crude for men as well. No-holds-barred wrestling, which permitted

A Pioneer Homestead in Wisconsin, c. 1847   This frontier family had felled trees both to build their crude cabin and to provide fuel for cooking. After the remaining stumps had been burned, the cleared fields were ready for planting. Cooking outdoors (weather permitting) spared the rough shelter from smoke and odors.

such niceties as the biting off of noses and the gouging out of eyes, was a popular entertainment. Pioneering Americans, marooned by geography, were often ill informed, superstitious, provincial, and fiercely individualistic. Ralph Waldo Emerson's popular lecture-essay "Self-Reliance" struck a deeply responsive chord. Popular literature of the period abounded with portraits of unique, isolated figures like James Fenimore Cooper's heroic Natty Bumppo and Herman Melville's restless Captain Ahab—just as Jacksonian politics aimed to emancipate the lone-wolf, enterprising businessperson. Yet even in this heyday of "rugged individualism" there were important exceptions. Pioneers, in tasks clearly beyond their own individual resources, would call upon their neighbors for logrolling and barn raising and upon their governments for help in building internal improvements.

Shaping the Western Landscape

The westward movement also molded the physical environment. Pioneers in a hurry often exhausted the land in the tobacco regions and then pushed on, leaving behind barren and rain-gutted fields. In the Kentucky bottomlands, cane as high as fifteen feet posed a seemingly insurmountable barrier to the plow. But settlers soon discovered that when the cane was burned off, European bluegrass thrived in the charred canefields. "Kentucky bluegrass," as it was somewhat inaccurately called, made ideal pasture for livestock—and lured thousands more American homesteaders into Kentucky.

The American West felt the pressure of civilization in additional ways. By the 1820s American fur-trappers were setting their trap-lines all over the vast Rocky Mountain region. The fur-trapping empire was based on the "rendezvous" system. Each summer, traders ventured from St. Louis to a verdant Rocky Mountain valley, made camp, and waited for the trappers and Indians to arrive with beaver pelts to swap for manufactured goods from the East. This trade thrived for some two decades, until the hapless beavers had all but disappeared from the region. Trade in buffalo robes also flourished, leading eventually to the virtually total annihilation of the massive bison herds that once blanketed the western prairies. Still farther west, on the California coast, other traders bought up prodigious quantities of sea-otter pelts, driving the once-bountiful otters to the point of near extinction. Some historians have called this aggressive and often heedless exploitation of the West's natural bounty "ecological imperialism."

Yet Americans in this period also reverenced nature and admired its beauty. Indeed the spirit of nationalism fed the growing appreciation of the uniqueness of the American wilderness. Searching for the United States' distinctive characteristics in this nation-conscious age, many observers found the wild, unspoiled character of the land, especially in the West, to be among the young nation's defining attributes. Other countries might have impressive mountains or sparkling rivers, but none had the pristine, natural beauty of America, unspoiled by human hands and reminiscent of a time before the dawn of civilization. This attitude toward wilderness became in time a kind of national mystique, inspiring literature and painting, and eventually kindling a powerful conservation movement.

George Catlin, a painter and student of Native American life, was among the first Americans to advocate the preservation of nature as a deliberate national policy. In 1832 he observed Sioux Indians in South Dakota recklessly slaughtering buffalo in order to trade the animals' tongues for the white man's whiskey. Appalled at this spectacle and fearing for the preservation of Indians and buffalo alike, Catlin proposed the creation of a national park. His idea later bore fruit with the creation of a national park system, beginning with Yellowstone Park in 1872.

The March of the Millions

As the American people moved west, they also multiplied at an amazing rate. By midcentury the population was still doubling approximately every twenty-five years, as in fertile colonial days.

By 1860 the original thirteen states had more than doubled in number: thirty-three stars graced the American flag. The United States was the fourth most populous nation in the western world, exceeded only by three European countries—Russia, France, and Austria.

Urban growth continued explosively. In 1790 there had been only two American cities that could boast populations of 20,000 or more souls: Philadelphia and New York. By 1860 there were forty-three; and about three hundred other places claimed over 5,000 inhabitants apiece. New York was the metropolis; New Orleans, the "Queen of the South"; and Chicago, the swaggering lord of the Midwest, destined to be "hog butcher for the world."

Such overrapid urbanization unfortunately brought undesirable by-products. It intensified the problems of smelly slums, feeble street lighting, inadequate policing, impure water, foul sewage,

Fur-Traders Descending the Missouri, by George Caleb Bingham, 1844   Bingham, a Missourian, captured in this painting a moment of calm in the usually strenuous life of the rough-and-tumble fur-traders. The fragile dugout canoe on the ominously placid water, the tethered animal in the bow, and the recently shot duck evoke the pioneer's relentless battle with nature.

Year	White	Nonwhite	Percent Nonwhite	Total Population	
1790	3,172,000	757,000	19	3,929,000	
1800	4,306,000	1,002,000	19	5,308,000	
1810	5,862,000	1,378,000	19	7,240,000	
1820	7,867,000	1,772,000	18	9,639,000	
1830	10,537,000	2,329,000	18	12,866,000	
1840	14,196,000	2,874,000	17	17,070,000	
1850	19,553,000	3,639,000	16	23,192,000	
1860	26,922,000	4,521,000	14	31,443,000	

Population Increase, Including Slaves and Indians, 1790–1860
Increasing European immigration and the closing of the slave trade gradually "whitened" the population beginning in 1820. This trend continued into the early twentieth century.

ravenous rats, and improper garbage disposal. Hogs poked their scavenging snouts about many city streets as late as the 1840s. Boston in 1823 pioneered a sewage system; and New York in 1842 abandoned wells and cisterns for a piped-in water supply. The city thus unknowingly eliminated the breeding places of many disease-carrying mosquitoes.

A continuing high birthrate accounted for most of the increase in population, but by the 1840s the tides of immigration were adding hundreds of thousands more. Before this decade, immigrants had been flowing in at a rate of 60,000 a year; but sud-denly the influx was tripled in the 1840s and then quadrupled in the 1850s. During these two feverish decades, over a million and a half Irish, and nearly as many Germans, swarmed down the gangplanks. Why did they come?

The immigrants came partly because Europe seemed to be running out of room. The population of the Old World more than doubled in the nineteenth century, and Europe began to generate a seething pool of apparently "surplus" people. They were displaced and footloose in their homelands before they felt the tug of the American magnet. Indeed at least as many people moved about *within*

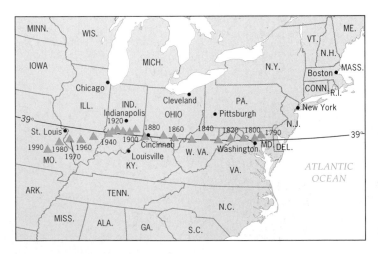

Westward Movement of Center of Population, 1790–1990 The triangles indicate the points at which a map of the United States weighted for the population of the country in a given year would balance. Note the remarkable equilibrium of the north-south pull from 1790 to about 1940; and the strong spurt west and south thereafter. The 1980 census revealed that the nation's center of population had at last moved west of the Mississippi River. The map also shows the slowing of the westward movement between 1890 and 1940—the period of heaviest immigration from Europe, which ended up mainly in East Coast cities.

Cincinnati in 1843
Famous as a processor of hogs, this "Queen City of the West" was a town of 2,540 people in 1800 and 161,044 in 1860, 45 percent of them foreign-born. Although tied to the South by downriver commerce on the Ohio and Mississippi Rivers, it remained loyal to the North during the Civil War.

Europe as crossed the Atlantic. America benefited from these people-churning changes but did not set them all in motion. Nor was the United States the sole beneficiary of the process: of the nearly 60 million people who abandoned Europe in the century after 1840, about 25 million went somewhere other than the United States.

Yet America still beckoned most strongly to the struggling masses of Europe, and the majority of migrants headed for the "land of freedom and opportunity." There was freedom from aristocratic caste and state church; there was abundant opportunity to secure broad acres and better one's condition. Much-read letters sent home by immigrants—"America letters"—often described in glowing terms the richer life: low taxes, no compulsory military service, and "three meat meals a day." The introduction of transoceanic steamships also meant that the immigrants could come speedily, in a matter of ten or twelve days instead of ten or twelve weeks. On board, they were still jammed into unsanitary quarters, thus suffering an appalling death rate from infectious diseases, but the nightmare was more endurable because it was shorter.

Irish and German Immigration by Decade, 1830–1900

Years	Irish	Germans
1831–1840	207,381	152,454
1841–1850	780,719	434,626
1851–1860	914,119	951,667
1861–1870	435,778	787,468
1871–1880	436,871	718,182
1881–1890	655,482	1,452,970
1891–1900	388,416	505,152
TOTAL	3,818,766	5,000,519

A German immigrant living in Cincinnati wrote to his relatives in Germany in 1847:

"A lot of people come over here who were well off in Germany but were enticed to leave their fatherland by boastful and imprudent letters from their friends or children and thought they could become rich in America. This deceives a lot of people, since what can they do here? If they stay in the city they can only earn their bread at hard and unaccustomed labor. If they want to live in the country and don't have enough money to buy a piece of land that is cleared and has a house then they have to settle in the wild bush and have to work very hard to clear the trees out of the way so they can sow and plant. But people who are healthy, strong, and hard-working do pretty well."

The Emerald Isle Moves West

Ireland, already groaning under the heavy hand of British overlords, was prostrated in the mid-1840s. A terrible rot attacked the potato crop, on which the people had become dangerously dependent, and about one-fourth of them were swept away by disease and hunger. Starved bodies were found dead by the roadsides with grass in their mouths. All told, about 2 million perished.

Tens of thousands of destitute souls, fleeing the Land of Famine for the Land of Plenty, flocked to America in the "Black Forties." Ireland's great export has been population; and the Irish take their place beside the Jews and the Africans as a dispersed people (see "Makers of America: The Irish," pp. 304–305).

These uprooted newcomers—too poor to move west and buy the necessary land, livestock, and equipment—swarmed into the larger seaboard cities. Noteworthy were Boston and particularly New York, which rapidly became the largest Irish city in the world. Before many decades had passed, more people of Hibernian blood lived in America than on the "ould sod" of Erin's Isle.

The luckless Irish immigrants received no red-carpet treatment. Forced to live in squalor, they were rudely crammed into the already-vile slums. They were scorned by the older American stock, especially "proper" Protestant Bostonians, who regarded the scruffy Catholic arrivals as a social menace. Barely literate "Biddies" (Bridgets) took jobs as kitchen maids. Broad-shouldered "Paddies" (Patricks) were pushed into pick-and-shovel drudgery on canals and railroads, where thousands left their bones as victims of disease and accidental explosions. It was said that an Irishman lay buried under every railroad tie. As wage-depressing competitors for jobs, the Irish were hated by native workers. "No Irish Need Apply" was a sign commonly posted at factory gates and was often abbreviated to NINA. The Irish, for similar reasons, fiercely resented the blacks, with whom they shared society's basement. Race riots between black and Irish dockworkers flared up in several port cities, and the Irish were generally cool to the abolitionist cause.

The friendless "Famine Irish" were forced to fend for themselves. The Ancient Order of Hibernians, a semisecret society founded in Ireland to fight rapacious landlords, served in America as a benevolent society, aiding the downtrodden. It also helped to spawn the "Molly Maguires," a shadowy Irish miners' union that rocked the Pennsylvania coal districts in the 1860s and 1870s.

The Irish tended to remain in low-skill occupations but gradually improved their lot, usually by acquiring modest amounts of property. The education of children was cut short as families struggled to save money to purchase a home. But for humble Irish peasants, cruelly cast out of their homeland, property ownership counted as a grand "success."

Politics quickly attracted these gregarious Gaelic newcomers. They soon began to gain control of powerful city machines, notably New York's Tammany Hall, and reaped the patronage rewards. Before long, beguilingly brogued Irishmen dominated police departments in many big cities, where they now drove the "Paddy wagons" that had once carted their brawling forebears to jail.

> *Margaret McCarthy, a recent arrival in America, captured much of the complexity of the immigrant experience in a letter she wrote from New York to her family in Ireland in 1850:*
>
> "This is a good place and a good country, but there is one thing that's ruining this place. The emigrants have not money enough to take them to the interior of the country, which obliges them to remain here in New York and the like places, which causes the less demand for labor and also the great reduction in wages. For this reason I would advise no one to come to America that would not have some money after landing here that would enable them to go west in case they would get no work to do here. But any man or woman without a family are fools that would not venture and come to this plentiful country where no man or woman ever hungered or ever will. I can assure you there are dangers upon dangers, but my friends, have courage and come all together courageously and bid adieu to that lovely place, the land of our birth."

An early–nineteenth-century French traveler recorded his impressions of America and Ireland:

"I have seen the Indian in his forests and the Negro in his chains, and thought, as I contemplated their pitiable condition, that I saw the very extreme of human wretchedness; but I did not then know the condition of unfortunate Ireland."

American politicians made haste to cultivate the Irish vote, especially in the politically potent state of New York. Irish hatred of the British lost nothing in the transatlantic transplanting. As the Irish-Americans increased in number—nearly 2 million arrived between 1830 and 1860—officials in Washington glimpsed political gold in those emerald green hills. Politicians often found it politically profitable to fire verbal volleys at London—a process vulgarly known as "twisting the British lion's tail."

The German Forty-Eighters

The influx of refugees from Germany between 1830 and 1860 was hardly less spectacular than that from Ireland. During these troubled years, over a million and a half Germans stepped onto American soil. (See "Makers of America: The Germans," pp. 308–309). The bulk of them were uprooted farmers, displaced by crop failures and other hardships. But a strong sprinkling were liberal political refugees. Saddened by the collapse of the democratic revolutions of 1848, they had decided to leave the autocratic fatherland and flee to America—the brightest hope of democracy.

Germany's loss was America's gain. Zealous German liberals like the lanky and public-spirited Carl Schurz, a relentless foe of slavery and public corruption, contributed richly to the elevation of American political life.

Many of the Germanic newcomers, unlike the Irish, possessed a modest amount of material goods. Most of them pushed out to the lush lands of the Middle West, notably Wisconsin, where they settled and established model farms. Like the Irish, they formed an influential body of voters whom American politicians shamelessly wooed. But the Germans were less potent politically because their strength was more widely scattered.

The hand of Germans in shaping American life was widely felt in still other ways. The Conestoga wagon, the Kentucky rifle, and the Christmas tree were all German contributions to American culture. Germans had fled from the militarism and wars of Europe and consequently came to be a bulwark of isolationist sentiment in the upper Mississippi Valley. Better educated on the whole than the stump-grubbing Americans, they warmly supported public schools, including their *Kindergarten* (children's garden). They likewise did much to stimulate art and music. As outspoken champions of freedom, they became relentless enemies of slavery during the fevered years before the Civil War.

Yet the Germans—often dubbed "damned Dutchmen"—were occasionally regarded with suspicion by their old-stock American neighbors. Seeking to preserve their language and culture, they sometimes settled in compact "colonies" and kept aloof from the surrounding community. Accustomed to the "Continental Sunday" and uncurbed by Puritan tradition, they made merry on the Sabbath and drank huge quantities of an amber beverage called *bier* (beer), which dates its real popularity in America to their coming. Their Old World drinking habits, like those of the Irish, spurred advocates of temperance in the use of alcohol to redouble their reform efforts.

Flare-Ups of Antiforeignism

The invasion by this so-called immigrant "rabble" in the 1840s and 1850s inflamed the prejudices of American "nativists." They feared that these foreign hordes would outbreed, outvote, and overwhelm the old "native" stock. Not only did the newcomers take jobs from "native" Americans, but the bulk of the displaced Irish were Roman Catholics, as were a substantial minority of the Germans. The Church of Rome was still widely regarded by many old-line Americans as a "foreign" church; convents were commonly referred to as "popish brothels."

The Irish

For a generation, from 1793 to 1815, war raged across Europe. Ruinous as it was on the continent, the fighting brought unprecedented prosperity to the long-suffering landsmen of Ireland, groaning since the twelfth century under the yoke of English rule. For as Europe's fields lay fallow, irrigated only by the blood of its farmers, Ireland fed the hungry armies that ravened for food as well as territory. Irish farmers planted every available acre, interspersing the lowly potato amongst their fields of grain. With prices for food products ever mounting, tenant farmers reaped a temporary respite from their perpetual struggle to remain on the land. Most landlords were satisfied by the prosperity and so relaxed their pressure on tenants; others, stymied by the absence of British police forces that had been stripped of manpower to fight in Europe, had little means to enforce eviction notices.

But the peace that brought solace to battle-scarred Europe changed all this. After 1815, war-inflated wheat prices plummeted by half. Hard-pressed landlords resolved to leave vast fields unplanted. Assisted now by a strengthened British constabulary, they vowed to sweep the pesky peasants from the retired acreage. Many of those forced to leave sought work in England; some went to America. Then in 1845 a blight that ravaged the potato crop sounded the final knell for the Irish peasantry. The resultant famine spread desolation throughout the island. In five years, more than a million people died. Another million sailed for America.

Irish Emigrants Preparing
to Leave from Cork, Ireland,
c. 1850

Saint Patrick's Day Parade in America, Union Square, c. 1870   This painting shows a Saint Patrick's Day parade in New York City. The religious festival was celebrated with greater fanfare in America than in Ireland itself, as Irish immigrants used it to boost their ethnic solidarity and assert their distinctive identity in their adopted country.

Of the emigrants, most were young and literate in English, the majority under thirty-five years old. Families typically pooled money to send strong young sons to the New World, where they would earn wages to pay the fares for those who waited at home. These "famine Irish" mostly remained in the port cities of the Northeast, abandoning the farmer's life for the dingy congestion of the urban metropolis.

The disembarking Irish were poorly prepared for urban life. They found progress up the economic ladder painfully slow. Their work as domestic servants or construction laborers was dull and arduous, and mortality rates were astoundingly high. Escape from the potato famine hardly guaranteed a long life to an Irish-American; a gray-bearded Irishman was a rare sight in nineteenth-century America. Most of the new arrivals toiled as day laborers. A fortunate few owned boardinghouses or saloons, where their dispirited countrymen sought solace in the bottle. For Irish-born women, opportunities were still scarcer; they worked mainly as domestic servants.

But it was their Roman Catholicism, more even than their penury or their perceived fondness for alcohol, that earned the Irish the distrust and resentment of their native-born, Protestant American neighbors. The cornerstone of social and reli-gious life for Irish immigrants was the parish. Worries about safeguarding their children's faith inspired the construction of parish schools, financed by the pennies of struggling working-class Irish parents.

If Ireland's green fields scarcely equipped her sons and daughters for the scrap and scramble of economic life in America's cities, life in the old country nevertheless had instilled in them an aptitude for politics. Irish-Catholic resistance against centuries of English-Anglican domination had instructed many old-country Irish in the ways of mass politics. That political experience readied them for the boss system of the political "machines" in America's northeastern cities. The boss's local representatives met each newcomer soon after landing in America. Asking only for votes, the machine supplied coal in wintertime, food, and help with the law. Irish voters soon became a bulwark of the Democratic party, reliably supporting the party of Jefferson and Jackson in cities like New York and Boston. As Irish-Americans like New York's "Honest John" Kelly themselves became bosses, white-collar jobs in government service opened up to the Irish. They became building inspectors, aldermen, and even policemen—an astonishing irony for a people driven from their homeland by the nightsticks and bayonets of the British police.

Roman Catholics were now on the move. Seeking to protect their children from Protestant indoctrination in the public schools, they began in the 1840s to construct an entirely separate Catholic educational system—an enormously expensive undertaking for a poor immigrant community, but one that revealed the strength of its religious commitment. They had formed a negligible minority during colonial days, and their numbers had increased gradually. But with the enormous influx of the Irish and Germans in the 1840s and 1850s, the Catholics became a powerful religious group. In 1840 they had ranked fifth, behind the Baptists, Methodists, Presbyterians, and Congregationalists. By 1850, with some 1.8 million communicants, they had bounded into first place—a position they have never lost.

Older-stock Americans were alarmed by these mounting figures. They professed to believe that in due time the "alien riffraff" would "establish" the Catholic church at the expense of Protestantism and would introduce "popish idols." The noisier American "nativists" rallied for political action. In 1849 they formed the Order of the Star-Spangled Banner, which soon developed into the formidable American, or "Know-Nothing," party—a name derived from its secretiveness. "Nativists" agitated for rigid restrictions on immigration and naturalization and for laws authorizing the deportation of alien paupers. They also promoted a lurid literature of

> *Strong antiforeignism was reflected in the platform of the American (Know-Nothing) party in 1856:*
>
> "Americans must rule America; and to this end, native-born citizens should be selected for all state, federal, or municipal offices of government employment, in preference to naturalized citizens."

exposure, much of it pure fiction. The authors, sometimes posing as escaped nuns, described the shocking sins they imagined the cloisters concealed, including the secret burial of babies. One of these sensational books—Maria Monk's *Awful Disclosures* (1836)—sold over 300,000 copies.

Even uglier was occasional mass violence. As early as 1834 a Catholic convent near Boston was burned by a howling mob, and in ensuing years a few scattered attacks fell upon Catholic schools and churches. The most frightful flare-up occurred during 1844 in Philadelphia, where the Irish Catholics fought back against the threats of the "nativists." The City of Brotherly Love did not quiet down until two Catholic churches had been burned and some thirteen citizens had been killed and fifty wounded in several days of fighting. These outbursts of intolerance, though infrequent and generally localized in the larger cities, remain an unfortunate blot on the record of America's treatment of minority groups.

Immigrants were undeniably making America a more pluralistic society—one of the most ethnically and racially varied in the history of the world—and perhaps it was small wonder that cultural clashes would occur. Why, in fact, were such episodes not even more frequent and more violent? Part of the answer lies in the robustness of the American economy. The vigorous growth of the economy in these years both attracted immigrants in the first place and ensured that, once arrived, they could claim their share of American wealth without jeopardizing the wealth of others. Their hands and brains, in fact, helped fuel economic expansion. Immigrants and the American economy, in short, needed one another. Without the newcomers a preponderantly agricultural United States might well have been condemned to watch in envy as the Industrial Revolution swept through nineteenth-century Europe.

Crooked Voting   A bitter "nativist" cartoon charging Irish and German immigrants with "stealing" elections.

The March of Mechanization

A group of gifted British inventors, beginning about 1750, perfected a series of machines for the mass production of textiles. This enslavement of steam multiplied the power of human muscles some ten thousandfold and ushered in the modern factory system—and with it, the so-called Industrial Revolution. It was accompanied by a no-less-spectacular transformation in agricultural production and in the methods of transportation and communication.

The factory system gradually spread from England —"the world's workshop"—to other lands. It took a generation or so to reach western Europe, and then the United States. Why was the youthful American Republic, destined to be an industrial giant, so slow to embrace the machine?

For one thing, virgin soil in America was cheap. Land-starved descendants of land-starved peasants were not going to coop themselves up in smelly factories when they might till their own acres in God's fresh air and sunlight. Labor was therefore generally scarce, and enough nimble hands to operate the machines were hard to find—until immigrants began to pour ashore in the 1840s. Money for capital investment, moreover, was not plentiful in pioneering America. Raw materials lay undeveloped, undiscovered, or unsuspected. The Republic was one day to become the world's leading coal producer, but much of the coal burned in colonial times was imported all the way from England.

Just as labor was scarce, so were consumers. The young country at first lacked a domestic market large enough to make factory-scale manufacturing profitable.

Long-established British factories, which provided cutthroat competition, posed another problem. Their superiority was attested by the fact that a few unscrupulous Yankee manufacturers, out to make a dishonest dollar, stamped their own products with faked English trademarks.

The British also enjoyed a monopoly of the textile machinery, whose secrets they were anxious to hide from foreign competitors. Parliament enacted laws, in harmony with the mercantilistic system, forbidding the export of the machines or the emigration of mechanics able to reproduce them.

Although a number of small manufacturing enterprises existed in the early Republic, the future industrial colossus was still snoring. Not until well past the middle of the nineteenth century did the value of the output of the factories exceed that of the farms.

Whitney Ends the Fiber Famine

Samuel Slater has been acclaimed the "Father of the Factory System" in America, and seldom can the paternity of a movement more properly be ascribed to one person. A skilled British mechanic of twenty-one, he was attracted by bounties being offered to English workers familiar with the textile machines.

America's First Textile Mill
This rude "factory," established by Samuel Slater in 1791 at Pawtucket, Rhode Island, drew its power from the falls of the Blackstone River. The mill at first produced only thread, which was then distributed to home weavers who turned it into cloth.

The Germans

Between 1820 and 1920, a sea of Germans lapped at America's shores and seeped into its very heartland. Their numbers surpassed those of any other immigrant group, even the prolific and often detested Irish. Yet this Germanic flood, unlike its Gaelic equivalent, stirred little panic in the hearts of native-born Americans because the Germans largely stayed to themselves, far from the madding crowds and nativist fears of northeastern cities. They prospered with astonishing ease, building towns in Wisconsin, agricultural colonies in Texas,

A German Homestead in Wisconsin
This settler's Germanic heritage is evident in the architecture of the log cabin. Traditional log cabins used log walls right up to the roofline, but the Germans closed their gables with vertical board siding.

and religious communities in Pennsylvania. They added a decidedly Germanic flavor to the heady brew of reform and community building that so animated antebellum America.

These "Germans" actually hailed from many different Old World lands, because there was no unified nation of Germany until 1871, when the ruthless and crafty Prussian Otto von Bismarck assembled the German state out of a mosaic of independent principalities, kingdoms, and duchies. Until that time, "Germans" came to America as Prussians, Bavarians, Hessians, Rhinelanders, Pomeranians, and Westphalians. They arrived at different times and for many different reasons. Some, particularly the so-called Forty-Eighters—the refugees from the abortive democratic revolution of 1848—hungered for the democracy they had failed to win in Germany. Others, particularly Jews, Pietists, and Anabaptist groups like the Amish and the Mennonites, coveted religious freedom. And they came not only to America. Like the Italians later, many Germans sought a new life in Brazil, Argentina, or Chile. But the largest number ventured into the United States.

Typical German immigrants arrived with fatter purses than their Irish counterparts. Small landowners or independent artisans in their native countries, they did not have to settle for bottom-rung industrial employment in the grimy factories of the Northeast and instead could afford to push on to the open spaces of the American West.

In Wisconsin these immigrants found a home away from home, a place with a climate, soil, and geography much like central Europe's. Milwaukee, a crude frontier town before the Germans' arrival, became the "German Athens." It boasted a German theater, German beer gardens, a German volunteer fire company, and a German-English academy. In

"Little Germany"
Cincinnati's "Over-the-Rhine" district in 1887.

described a visit to a German household where the settlers drank "coffee in tin cups upon Dresden saucers" and sat upon "barrels for seats, to hear a Beethoven symphony on the grand piano."

These Germanic colonizers of America's heartland also formed religious communities, none more distinctive or durable than the Amish settlements of Pennsylvania, Indiana, and Ohio. The Amish took their name from their founder and leader, the Swiss Anabaptist Jacob Amman. Like other Anabaptist groups, they shunned extravagance and reserved baptism for adults, repudiating the tradition of infant baptism practiced by most Europeans. For this they were persecuted, even imprisoned, in Europe. Seeking escape from their oppression, some five hundred Amish ventured to Pennsylvania in the 1700s, followed by three thousand in the years from 1815 to 1865.

In America they formed enduring religious communities—isolated enclaves where they could shield themselves from the corruption and the conveniences of the modern world. To this day the German-speaking Amish still travel in horse-drawn carriages and farm without heavy machinery. No electric lights brighten the darkness that nightly envelops their tidy farmhouses; no ringing telephones punctuate the reverent tranquility of their mealtime prayer; no ornaments relieve the austere simplicity of their black garments. The Amish remain a stalwart, traditional community in a rootless, turbulent society, a living testament to the religious ferment and social experiments of the antebellum era.

distant Texas, German settlements like New Braunfels and Friedrichsburg flourished. When the famous landscape architect and writer Frederick Law Olmsted stumbled upon these prairie outposts of Teutonic culture in 1857, he was shocked to be "welcomed by a figure in a blue flannel shirt and pendant beard, quoting Tacitus." These German colonies in the frontier Southwest mixed high European elegance with Texas ruggedness. Olmsted

Amish Country, near Lancaster, Pennsylvania
For more than two centuries, the Amish people have preserved their traditional way of life.

Eli Whitney (1765–1825)   Few men have been so pivotal in American history. His cotton gin revolutionized southern agriculture, ushering in the Cotton-and-Slave Kingdom of the early nineteenth century. His system of interchangeable parts revolutionized northern industry, giving the North economic and technological superiority in the Civil War that ultimately extinguished slavery.

grams) of seed was a full day's work for one slave, and this process was so expensive that cotton cloth was relatively rare.

Another mechanical genius, Massachusetts-born Eli Whitney, now made his mark. After graduating from Yale, he journeyed to Georgia to serve as a private tutor while preparing for the law. There he was told that the poverty of the South would be relieved if someone could only invent a workable device for separating the seed from the short-staple cotton fiber. Within ten days, in 1793, he built a crude machine called the cotton gin (short for en*gine*) that was fifty times more effective than the handpicking process.

Few machines have ever wrought so wondrous a change. The gin affected not only the history of America but that of the world. Almost overnight the raising of cotton became highly profitable, and the South was tied hand and foot to the throne of King Cotton. Human bondage had been dying out, but the insatiable demand for cotton reriveted the chains on the limbs of the downtrodden southern blacks.

After memorizing the plans for the machinery, he escaped in disguise to America, where he won the backing of Moses Brown, a Quaker capitalist in Rhode Island. Laboriously reconstructing the essential apparatus with the aid of a blacksmith and a carpenter, he put into operation in 1791 the first efficient American machinery for spinning cotton thread.

The ravenous mechanism was now ready, but where was the cotton fiber? Handpicking 1 pound (0.45 kilogram) of lint from 3 pounds (1.36 kilo-

Eli Whitney's Cotton Gin
Whitney's revolutionary little machine was artfully simple. Wire hooks on a rotating cylinder pulled the cotton fibers through slots too narrow to allow seeds to pass. A set of brushes then removed the fibers. Whitney's gin made possible the mass cultivation of upland or short-staple cotton, which was unprofitable to raise when its seeds had to be laboriously removed by hand. Before Whitney's invention, cotton growing had been largely confined to long-staple or Sea-Island cotton, which could only grow in hot, humid coastal areas. With the advent of the cotton gin, short-staple cotton cultivation spread across the southern interior—and so did slavery.

South and North both prospered. Slave-driving planters cleared more acres for cotton, pushing the Cotton Kingdom westward off the depleted tidewater plains, over the Piedmont, and onto the black loam bottomlands of Alabama and Mississippi. Humming gins poured out avalanches of snowy fiber for the spindles of the Yankee machines, though for decades to come the mills of England bought the lion's share of southern cotton. The American phase of the Industrial Revolution, which first blossomed in cotton textiles, was well on its way.

Factories at first flourished most actively in New England, though they branched out into the more populous areas of New York, New Jersey, and Pennsylvania. The South, increasingly wedded to the production of cotton, could boast of comparatively little manufacturing. Its capital was bound up in slaves; its local consumers for the most part were desperately poor.

New England was singularly favored as an industrial center for several reasons. Its narrow belt of stony soil discouraged farming and hence made manufacturing more attractive than elsewhere. A relatively dense population provided labor and accessible markets; shipping brought in capital; and snug seaports made easy the import of raw materials and the export of the finished products. Finally, the rapid rivers—notably the Merrimack in Massachusetts—provided abundant water power to turn the cogs of the machines. By 1860, more than 400 million pounds (182,000 metric tons) of southern cotton poured annually into the gaping maws of over a thousand mills, mostly in New England.

Marvels in Manufacturing

America's factories spread slowly until about 1807, when there began the fateful sequence of the embargo, nonintercourse, and the War of 1812. Stern necessity dictated the manufacture of substitutes for normal imports, while the stoppage of European commerce was temporarily ruinous to Yankee shipping. Both capital and labor were driven from the waves onto the factory floor, as New England, in the striking phrase of John Randolph, exchanged the trident for the distaff. Generous bounties were offered by local authorities for home-grown goods; "Buy American" and "Wear American" became popular slogans; and patriotism prompted the wearing of baggy homespun garments. President Madison donned some at his inauguration, where he was said to have been a walking argument for the better processing of native wool.

A Pioneer Woman Batting Cotton Making cotton "batts" from the raw fiber was the first step in making "homespun" cloth. Mechanical looms and sewing machines would soon make this traditional women's work obsolete.

One observer in 1836 published a newspaper account of conditions in some of the New England factories:

"The operatives work thirteen hours a day in the summer time, and from daylight to dark in the winter. At half past four in the morning the factory bell rings, and at five the girls must be in the mills. . . . So fatigued . . . are numbers of girls that they go to bed soon after receiving their evening meal, and endeavor by a comparatively long sleep to resuscitate their weakened frames for the toil of the coming day."

But the manufacturing boomlet broke abruptly with the peace of Ghent in 1815. British competitors unloaded their dammed-up surpluses at ruinously low prices, and American newspapers were so full of British advertisements for goods on credit that little space was left for news. In one Rhode Island district, all 150 mills were forced to close their doors, except the original Slater plant. Responding to pained outcries, Congress provided some relief when it passed the mildly protective Tariff of 1816—among the earliest political contests to control the shape of the economy.

As the factory system flourished, it embraced numerous other industries in addition to textiles. Prominent among them was the manufacturing of firearms, and here the wizardly Eli Whitney again appeared with an extraordinary contribution. Frustrated in his earlier efforts to monopolize the cotton gin, he turned to the mass production of muskets for the U.S. Army. Up to this time each part of a firearm had been hand-tooled, and if the trigger of one broke, the trigger of another might or might not fit. About 1798 Whitney seized upon the idea of having machines make each part, so that all the triggers, for example, would be as much alike as the successive imprints of a copperplate engraving. Journeying to Washington, he reportedly dismantled ten of his new muskets in the presence of skeptical officials, scrambled the parts together, and then quickly reassembled ten different muskets.

The principle of interchangeable parts was widely adopted by 1850, and it ultimately became the basis of modern mass-production, assembly-line methods. It gave to the North the vast industrial plant that ensured military preponderance over the South. The Yankee Eli Whitney, by perfecting the cotton gin, gave slavery a renewed lease on life and perhaps made inevitable the Civil War. The same Whitney, by popularizing the principle of interchangeable parts, caused factories to flourish in the North and contributed heavily to the winning of that war by the Union.

The sewing machine, invented by Elias Howe in 1846 and perfected by Isaac Singer, gave another strong boost to northern industrialization. The sewing machine became the foundation of the ready-made clothing industry, which took root about the time of the Civil War. It drove many a seamstress from the shelter of the private home to the factory where, like a human robot, she tended the clattering mechanisms.

Each momentous new invention seemed to stimulate still more imaginative inventions. For the decade ending in 1800 only 306 patents were registered in Washington; but the decade ending in 1860 saw the amazing total of 28,000. Yet in 1838 the clerk of the Patent Office had resigned in despair, complaining that all worthwhile inventions had been discovered.

Technical advances spurred equally important changes in the form and legal status of business organizations. The principle of limited liability aided the concentration of capital by permitting the individual investor, in cases of legal claims or bankruptcy, to risk no more than his own share of the corporation's stock. Fifteen Boston families formed one of the earliest investment capital companies, the Boston Associates. They eventually dominated the textile, railroad, insurance, and banking business of Massachusetts. Laws of "free incorporation," first passed in New York in 1848, meant that businessmen could create corporations without applying for individual charters from the legislature.

Samuel F. B. Morse's telegraph was among the inventions that tightened the sinews of an increasingly complex business world. A distinguished but poverty-stricken portrait painter, Morse finally secured from Congress, to the accompaniment of the usual jeers, an appropriation of $30,000 to support his experiment with "talking wires." In 1844 Morse strung a wire 40 miles (64 kilometers) from Washington to Baltimore, and tapped out the historic message, "What hath God wrought?" The

---

Said Abraham Lincoln (1809–1865) in a lecture in 1859,

"The patent system secured to the inventor for a limited time exclusive use of his invention, and thereby added the fuel of interest to the fire of genius in the discovery and production of new and useful things."

Ten years earlier Lincoln had received patent No. 6469 for a scheme to buoy steamboats over shoals. It was never practically applied, but he remains the only president ever to have secured a patent.

invention brought fame and fortune to Morse, as he put distantly separated people in almost instant communication with one another.

Workers and "Wage Slaves"

One ugly outgrowth of the factory system was an increasingly acute labor problem. Hitherto manufacturing had been done in the home, or in the small shop, where the master craftsman and his apprentice, rubbing elbows at the same bench, could maintain an intimate and friendly relationship. The industrial revolution submerged this personal association in the impersonal ownership of stuffy factories in "spindle cities." Around these, like tumors, the slumlike hovels of the "wage slaves" tended to cluster.

Clearly the early factory system did not shower its benefits evenly on all. While many owners waxed fat, workingpeople often wasted away at their workbenches. Hours were long, wages were low, and meals were skimpy and hastily gulped. Workers were forced to toil in unsanitary buildings that were poorly ventilated, lighted, and heated. They were forbidden by law to form labor unions to raise wages, for such cooperative activity was regarded as a criminal conspiracy. Not surprisingly, only twenty-four recorded strikes occurred before 1835.

Especially vulnerable to exploitation were child workers. In 1820, half the nation's industrial toilers were children under ten years of age. Victims of factory labor, many children were mentally blighted, emotionally starved, physically stunted, and even brutally whipped in special "whipping rooms." In Samuel Slater's mill of 1791, the first machine tenders were seven boys and two girls, all under twelve years of age.

By contrast, the lot of most adult wage workers improved markedly in the 1820s and 1830s. In the full flush of Jacksonian democracy, many of the states granted the laboring man the vote. Brandishing the ballot, he first strove to lighten his burden through workingmen's parties. Eventually, many workers gave their loyalty to the Democratic party of Andrew Jackson, whose attack on the Bank of the United States and against all forms of "privilege" reflected their anxieties about the emerging capitalist economy. In addition to such goals as the ten-

The Master Craftsman
Dignity and pride of workmanship are evident in this tidy wheelwright's shop. Small-scale, intimate workplaces like this were eventually overshadowed by the mass-production, impersonal factory system, as in the illustrations on pages 315 and 317.

hour day, higher wages, and tolerable working conditions, they demanded public education for their children and an end to the inhuman practice of imprisonment for debt.

Employers, abhorring the rise of the "rabble" in politics, fought the ten-hour day to the last ditch. They argued that reduced hours would lessen production, increase costs, and demoralize the workers. Laborers would have so much leisure time that the Devil would lead them into mischief. A red-letter gain was at length registered for labor in 1840, when President Van Buren established the ten-hour day for federal employees on public works. In ensuing years a number of states gradually fell into line by reducing the hours of workingpeople.

Day laborers at last learned that their strongest weapon was to lay down their tools, even at the risk of prosecution under the law. Dozens of strikes erupted in the 1830s and 1840s, most of them for higher wages, some for the ten-hour day, and a few for such unusual goals as the right to smoke on the job. The workers usually lost more strikes than they won, for the employer could resort to such tactics as the importing of strikebreakers—often derisively called "scabs" or "rats," and often fresh off the boat from the Old World. Labor long raised its voice against the unrestricted inpouring of wage-depressing and union-busting immigrant workers.

Labor's early and painful efforts at organization had netted some 300,000 trade unionists by 1830. But such encouraging gains were dashed on the rocks of hard times following the severe depression of 1837. As unemployment spread, union membership shriveled. Yet toilers won a promising legal victory in 1842. The supreme court of Massachusetts ruled in the case of *Commonwealth* v. *Hunt* that labor unions were not illegal conspiracies, provided that their methods were "honorable and peaceful." This enlightened decision did not legalize the strike overnight throughout the country, but it was a significant signpost of the times. Trade unions still had a rocky row to hoe, stretching ahead for about a century, before they could meet management on relatively even terms.

Women and the Economy

Women were also sucked into the clanging mechanism of factory production. They typically toiled six days a week, earning a pittance for dreary stints of twelve or thirteen hours—"from dark to dark." The Boston Associates pridefully pointed to their textile mill at Lowell, Massachusetts, as a showplace factory. The workers were virtually all New England

---

Violence broke out along the New York waterfront in 1836 when laborers striking for higher wages attacked "scabs." Philip Hone's diary records,

"The Mayor, who acts with vigour and firmness, ordered out the troops, who are now on duty with loaded arms. . . . These measures have restored order for the present, but I fear the elements of disorder are at work; the bands of Irish and other foreigners, instigated by the mischievous councils of the trades-union and other combinations of discontented men, are acquiring strength and importance which will ere long be difficult to quell."

A woman worker in the Lowell mills wrote a friend in 1844:

"You wish to know minutely of our hours of labor. We go in [to the mill] at five o'clock; at seven we come out to breakfast; at half-past seven we return to our work, and stay until half-past twelve. At one, or quarter-past one four months in the year, we return to our work, and stay until seven at night. Then the evening is all our own, which is more than some laboring girls can say, who think nothing is more tedious than a factory life."

Another worker wrote in 1845:

"I am here, among strangers—a factory girl—yes, a factory girl; that name which is thought so degrading by many, though, in truth, I neither see nor feel its degradation. But here I am. I toil day after day in the noisy mill. When the bell calls I must go: and must I always stay here, and spend my days within these pent-up walls, with this ceaseless din my only music?"

The Sewing Floor of Thompson's Skirt Factory, 1859   The burgeoning textile industry provided employment for thousands of women in antebellum America—and also produced the clothes that women wore. This view of a New York City shop in 1859 illustrates the transition from hand-sewing (on the right) to machine-stitching (on the left). It also vividly illustrates the contrast between the kinds of "sewing circles" in which women had traditionally sought companionship to the impersonal mass-production line of the modern manufacturing plant. Note especially the stark exhortation on the wall: "Strive to Excel." Contrast this impersonal scene with the workplace depicted on page 313.

farm girls, carefully supervised on and off the job by watchful matrons. Escorted regularly to church from their company boardinghouses, forbidden to form unions, they were as disciplined and docile a labor force as any employer could wish.

But factory jobs of any kind were still unusual for women. Opportunities for women to be economically self-supporting were scarce and consisted mainly of nursing, domestic service, and especially teaching. The dedicated Catharine Beecher, unmarried daughter of a famous preacher and sister of Harriet Beecher Stowe, tirelessly urged women to enter the teaching profession. She eventually succeeded beyond her dreams, as men left teaching for other lines of work and schoolteaching became a thoroughly "feminized" occupation. Other work "opportunities" for women beckoned in household service. Perhaps one white family in ten employed servants at midcentury, most of whom were poor white, immigrant, or black women. About 10 percent of white women were working for pay

outside their own homes in 1850, and estimates are that about 20 percent of all women had been employed at some time prior to marriage.

The vast majority of working women were single. Upon marriage, they left their paying jobs and took up their new work (without wages) as wives and mothers. In the home they were enshrined in a "cult of domesticity," a widespread cultural creed that glorified the customary functions of the homemaker. From their pedestal, married women commanded immense moral power, and they increasingly made decisions that altered the character of the family itself.

Women's changing roles and the spreading industrial revolution brought some important changes in the life of the nineteenth-century home—the traditional "women's sphere." Love, not parental "arrangement," more and more frequently determined the choice of a spouse—yet parents often retained the power of veto. Families thus became more closely knit and affectionate, providing the

York, Pennsylvania, Family with Negro Servant, by an unknown American artist, c.1828
This portrait of a Pennsylvania family presents a somewhat idealized picture of the home as the woman's sphere. The wife and mother sits at the center of activity; while she reads to the children, the husband and father stands by somewhat superfluously. A black servant cares for an infant in the corner, suggesting the prosperous status of this household.

emotional refuge that made the threatening impersonality of big-city industrialism tolerable to many people.

Most striking, families grew smaller. The average household had nearly six members at the end of the eighteenth century but fewer than five members a century later. The "fertility rate," or number of births among women aged 14 to 45, dropped sharply among white women in the years after the Revolution and, in the course of the nineteenth century as a whole, fell by half. Birth control was still a taboo topic for polite conversation, and contracep-

tive technology was primitive, but clearly some form of family limitation was being practiced quietly and effectively in countless families, rural and urban alike. Women undoubtedly played a large part—perhaps the leading part—in decisions to have fewer children. This newly assertive role for women has been called "domestic feminism," because it signified the growing power and independence of women, even while they remained wrapped in the "cult of domesticity."

Smaller families, in turn, meant child-centered families, since where children are fewer, parents can lavish more care on them individually. European visitors to the United States in the nineteenth century often complained about the unruly behavior of American "brats." But though American parents may have increasingly spared the rod, they did not spoil their children. Lessons were enforced by punishments other than the hickory stick. When the daughter of novelist Harriet Beecher Stowe neglected to do her homework, her mother sent her from the dinner table and gave her "only bread and water in her own apartment." What Europeans saw as permissiveness was in reality the consequence of an emerging new idea of child rearing, in which the child's will was not to be simply broken, but rather shaped. In the little republic of the family, as in the Republic at large, good citizens were raised not to be meekly obedient to authority, but to be independent individuals who could make their own decisions on the basis of internalized moral standards. Thus the outlines of the "modern" family were clear by midcentury: it was small, affectionate, child-centered, and provided a special arena for the talents of women. Feminists of a later day might decry the stifling atmosphere of the nineteenth-century home, but to many women of the time it seemed a big step upward from the conditions of grinding toil—often alongside men in the fields—in which their mothers had lived.

Western Farmers Reap a Revolution in the Fields

As smoke-belching factories altered the eastern skyline, flourishing farms were changing the face of the West. The trans-Allegheny region—especially the Ohio-Indiana-Illinois tier—was fast becoming the nation's breadbasket. Before long, it would become a granary to the world.

Pioneer families first hacked a clearing out of the forest and then planted their painfully furrowed fields to corn. The yellow grain was amazingly versatile. It could be fed to hogs ("corn on the hoof") or distilled into liquor ("corn in the bottle"). Both these products could be transported more easily than the bulky grain itself, and they became the early western farmer's staple market items. So many hogs were butchered, traded, or shipped at Cincinnati that the city was known as the "Porkopolis" of the West.

Most western produce was at first floated down the Ohio-Mississippi river system, to feed the lusty appetite of the booming Cotton Kingdom. But western farmers were as hungry for profits as southern slaves and planters were for food. These tillers, spurred on by the easy availability of seemingly boundless acres, sought ways to bring more and more land into cultivation.

Ingenious inventors came to their aid. One of the first obstacles that frustrated the farmers was the thickly matted soil of the West, which snagged and snapped fragile wooden plows. John Deere of Illinois in 1837 finally produced a steel plow that broke the virgin soil. Sharp and effective, it was also light enough to be pulled by horses, rather than oxen.

In the 1830s Virginia-born Cyrus McCormick contributed the most wondrous contraption of all: a mechanical mower-reaper. The clattering cogs of McCormick's horse-drawn machine were to the western farmers what the cotton gin was to the southern planters. Seated on his red-chariot reaper, a single husbandman could do the work of five men with sickles and scythes.

No other American invention cut so wide a swath. It made ambitious capitalists out of humble plowmen, who now scrambled for more acres on which to plant more fields of billowing wheat. Subsistence farming gave way to production for the market, as large-scale ("extensive"), specialized, cash-crop agriculture came to dominate the trans-Allegheny West. With it followed mounting indebtedness, as farmers bought more land and more machinery to work it. Soon hustling farmer-businesspeople were annually harvesting a larger crop than the South—which was becoming self-sufficient in food production—could devour. They began to dream of markets elsewhere—in the mushrooming factory towns of the East, or across the faraway Atlantic. But they were still largely landlocked. Commerce moved north and south on the river systems. Before it could begin to move east-west in bulk, a transportation revolution would have to occur.

McCormick Reaper Works, 1850s Contrast this scene of "mass production" with the workplace depicted in "The Master Craftsman" on p. 313.

McCormick's Miraculous Reaper
This illustration shows an early test of Cyrus McCormick's mechanical reaper near his home in Virginia in 1831. The reaper was best suited, however, to the horizonless fields of wheat on the rolling prairies of the Midwest; by the 1850s McCormick's Chicago factory was cranking out more than 20,000 reapers a year for midwestern farmers.

Highways and Steamboats

In 1789, when the Constitution was launched, primitive methods of travel were still in use. Waterborne commerce, whether along the coast or on the rivers, was slow, uncertain, and often dangerous. Stagecoaches and wagons lurched over bone-shaking roads. Passengers would be routed out to lay nearby fence rails across muddy stretches, and occasionally horses would drown in muddy pits while wagons sank slowly out of sight.

Cheap and efficient carriers were imperative if raw materials were to be transported to factories and if finished products were to be delivered to consumers. On December 3, 1803, a firm in Providence, Rhode Island, sent a shipment of yarn to a point 60 miles (97 kilometers) away, notifying the purchaser that the consignment could be expected to arrive in "the course of the winter."

A promising improvement came in the 1790s, when a private company completed the Lancaster turnpike in Pennsylvania. It was a broad, hard-surfaced highway that thrust 62 miles (100 kilometers) westward, from Philadelphia to Lancaster. As drivers approached the toll gate, they were confronted with a barrier of sharp pikes, which were turned aside when they paid their toll. Hence the term *turnpike*.

The Lancaster turnpike proved to be a highly successful venture, returning as high as 15 percent annual dividends to its stockholders. It attracted a rich trade to Philadelphia and touched off a turnpike-building boom that lasted about twenty years. It also stimulated western development. The turnpikes beckoned to the canvas-covered Conestoga wagons, whose creakings heralded a westward advance that would know no real retreat.

Western road building, always expensive, encountered many obstacles. One pesky roadblock was the noisy states' righters, who opposed federal aid to local projects. Eastern states also protested against being bled of their populations by the westward-reaching arteries.

Westerners scored a notable triumph in 1811 when the federal government began to construct the elongated National Road, or Cumberland Road. This highway ultimately stretched from Cumberland, in western Maryland, to Vandalia, in Illinois, a distance of 591 miles (952 kilometers). The War of 1812 interrupted construction, and states' rights shackles on internal improvements hampered federal grants. But the thoroughfare was belatedly brought to its destination, in 1852, by a combination of aid from the states and the federal government.

The steamboat craze, which overlapped the turnpike craze, was touched off by an ambitious painter-engineer named Robert Fulton. He installed

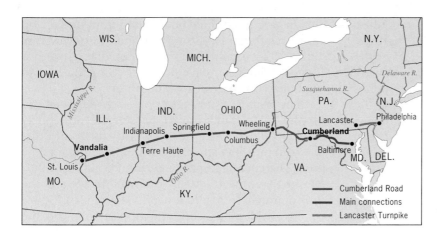

Cumberland (National) Road and Main Connections
Note also the Lancaster Turnpike.

a powerful steam engine in a vessel that posterity came to know as the *Clermont* but that a dubious public dubbed "Fulton's Folly." On a historic day in 1807, the quaint little ship, belching sparks from its single smokestack, churned steadily from New York City up the Hudson River toward Albany. It made the run of 150 miles (242 kilometers) in 32 hours.

The success of the steamboat was sensational. People could now in large degree defy wind, wave, tide, and downstream current. Within a few years Fulton had changed all of America's navigable streams into two-way arteries, thereby doubling their carrying capacity. Hitherto keelboats had been pushed up the Mississippi, with quivering poles and raucous profanity, at less than one mile an hour—a process that was prohibitively expensive. Now the steamboats could churn rapidly against the current, ultimately attaining speeds in excess of 10 miles (16 kilometers) an hour. The mighty Mississippi had now met its master.

By 1820 there were some sixty steamboats on the Mississippi and its tributaries; by 1860, about one thousand, some of them luxurious river palaces. Keen rivalry among the swift and gaudy steamers led to memorable races. Excited passengers would urge the captain to pile on wood at the

Mississippi in Time of Peace, by Mrs. Frances Flora Bond Palmer, 1865
By the mid-nineteenth century, steamboats had made the Mississippi a bustling river highway—as it remains today.

risk of bursting the boilers, which all too often exploded with tragic results for the floating firetraps.

Chugging steamboats played a vital role in the opening of the West and South, both of which were richly endowed with navigable rivers. Like bunches of grapes on a vine, population clustered along the banks of the broad-flowing streams. Cotton growers and other farmers made haste to take up and turn over the now-profitable virgin soil. Not only could they float their produce out to market but, hardly less important, they could ship in at low cost their shoes, hardware, and other manufactured necessities.

"Clinton's Big Ditch" in New York

A canal-cutting craze paralleled the boom in turnpikes and steamboats. A few canals had been built around falls and elsewhere in colonial days, but ambitious projects lay in the future. Resourceful New Yorkers, cut off from federal aid by states' righters, themselves dug the Erie Canal, linking the Great Lakes with the Hudson River. They were blessed with the driving leadership of Governor DeWitt Clinton, whose grandiose project was scoffingly called "Clinton's Big Ditch" or "the Governor's Gutter."

Begun in 1817, the canal eventually ribboned 363 miles (585 kilometers). On its completion in 1825, a garlanded canal boat glided from Buffalo, on Lake Erie, to the Hudson River and on to New York harbor. There, with colorful ceremony, Governor Clinton emptied a cask of water from the lake to symbolize "the marriage of the waters."

The water from Clinton's keg baptized an Empire State. Mule-drawn passengers and bulky freight could now be handled with thrift and dispatch, at the dizzy speed of 5 miles (8 kilometers) an hour. The cost of shipping a ton of grain from Buffalo to New York City fell from $100 to $5, and the time of transit from about twenty days to six.

Ever-widening economic ripples followed the completion of the Erie Canal. The value of land along the route skyrocketed, and new cities—such as Rochester and Syracuse—blossomed. Industry in the state boomed. The new profitability of farming in the Old Northwest—notably in Ohio, Michigan, Indiana, Illinois—attracted thousands of European immigrants to the unaxed and untaxed lands now available. Flotillas of steamships soon plied the Great Lakes, connecting with canal barges at Buffalo. Interior waterside villages like Cleveland, Detroit, and Chicago exploded into mighty cities.

Other profound economic and political changes followed the canal's completion. The price of potatoes in New York City was cut in half, and many dispirited New England farmers, no longer able to face the ruinous competition, abandoned their rocky holdings and went elsewhere. Some became mill hands, thus speeding the industrialization of

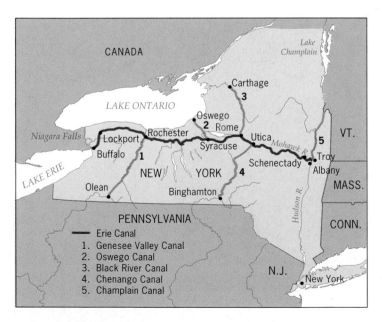

Erie Canal and Main Branches
The Erie Canal system, and others like it, tapped the fabulous agricultural potential of the Midwest, while canal construction and maintenance provided employment for displaced eastern farmers squeezed off the land by competition from their more productive midwestern cousins. The transportation revolution thus simultaneously expanded the nation's acreage under cultivation and speeded the shift of the work force from agricultural to manufacturing and "service" occupations. In 1820 more than three-quarters of American workers labored on farms; by 1850 only a little more than half of them were so employed. (Also see the map on the top of page 321.)

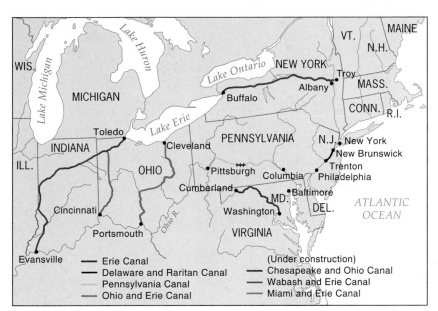

Principal Canals in 1840
Note that the canals mainly facilitated east-west traffic, especially along the great Lake Erie artery. No comparable network of canals existed in the South—a disparity that helps to explain Northern superiority in the Civil War that came two decades later.

America. Others, finding it easy to go west over the Erie Canal, took up new farmlands south of the Great Lakes, where they were joined by thousands of New Yorkers and other northerners. Still others shifted to fruit, vegetable, and dairy farming. The transformations in the Northeast—canal consequences—showed how long-established local market structures could be swamped by the emerging behemoth of a continental economy.

Pioneer Railroad Promoters

The most significant contribution to the development of such an economy proved to be the railroad. It was fast, reliable, cheaper than canals to construct, and not frozen over in winter. Able to go almost anywhere, even through the Allegheny barrier, it defied terrain and weather. The first railroad appeared in the United States in 1828. By 1860, only thirty-two years later, the United States boasted 30,000 miles (48,000 kilometers) of railroad track, three-fourths of it in the rapidly industrializing North.

At first the railroad faced strong opposition from vested interests, especially canal backers. Anxious to protect its investment in the Erie Canal, the New York legislature in 1833 prohibited the railroads from carrying freight—at least temporarily. Early railroads were also considered a dangerous public menace, for flying sparks could set fire to nearby

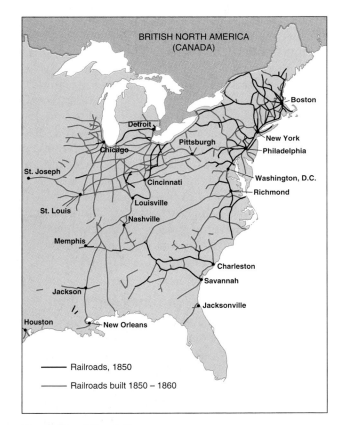

The Railroad Revolution
Note the explosion of new railroad construction in the 1850's, and its heavy concentration in the North.

The Stourbridge Lion
On August 8, 1829, at Honesdale, Pennsylvania, this smoke-belching beast made the first successful trip in America by a steam locomotive.

haystacks and houses, and appalling railway accidents could turn the wooden "miniature hells" into flaming funeral pyres for their riders.

Railroad pioneers had to overcome other obstacles as well. Brakes were so feeble that the engineer might miss the station twice, both arriving and backing up. Arrivals and departures were conjectural, and numerous differences in gauge (the distance between the rails) meant frequent changes of trains for passengers. In 1840 there were seven transfers between Philadelphia and Charleston. But gauges gradually became standardized, better brakes did brake, safety devices were adopted, and the Pullman "sleeping palace" was introduced in 1859. America at long last was being bound together with braces of iron, later to be made of steel.

The Transport Web Binds the Union

More than anything else, the desire of the East to tap the West stimulated the "transportation revolution." Until about 1830 the produce of the western region drained southward to the cotton belt or to the heaped-up wharves of New Orleans. The steamboat vastly aided the reverse flow of finished goods up the watery western arteries and helped bind West and South together. But the truly revolutionary changes in commerce and communication came in the three decades before the Civil War, as canals and

railroad tracks radiated out from the East, across the Alleghenies and into the blossoming heartland. The ditch-diggers and tie-layers were attempting nothing less than a conquest of nature itself. They would offset the "natural" flow of trade on the interior rivers by laying down an impressive grid of "internal improvements."

The builders succeeded beyond their wildest dreams. The Mississippi was increasingly robbed of its traffic, as goods moved eastward on chugging trains, puffing lake boats, and mule-tugged canal barges. Governor Clinton had in effect picked up the mighty Father of Waters and flung it over the Alleghenies, forcing it to empty into the sea at New York City. By the 1840s the city of Buffalo handled more western produce than New Orleans. Between 1836 and 1860, grain shipments through Buffalo increased a staggering sixtyfold. New York City became the seaboard queen of the nation, a gigantic port through which a vast hinterland poured its wealth and to which it daily paid economic tribute.

By the eve of the Civil War, a truly continental economy had emerged. The principle of division of labor, which spelled productivity and profits in the factory, applied on a national scale as well. Each region now specialized in a particular type of economic activity. The South raised cotton for export to New England and Old England; the West grew grain and livestock to feed factory workers in the East and in Europe; the East made machines and textiles for the South and the West.

The economic pattern thus woven had fateful political and military implications. Many southerners regarded the Mississippi as a silver chain that naturally linked together the upper valley states and the Cotton Kingdom. They were convinced, as secession approached, that some or all of these states would have to secede with them or be strangled. But they overlooked the man-made links that now bound the upper Mississippi Valley to the East in intimate commercial union. Southern rebels would have to fight not only Northern armies but the tight bonds of an interdependent continental economy. Economically, the two northerly sections were Siamese twins.

The emergence of a specialized, continental-scale economy also had far-reaching social effects. As more and more Americans—mill hands as well as farm hands, women as well as men—linked their economic fate to the burgeoning market economy, the self-sufficient households of colonial days were transformed. Most families had once raised all their own food, spun their own wool, and bartered with their neighbors for the few necessities they could not make themselves. In growing numbers they now scattered to work for wages in the mills, or they planted just a few crops for sale at market and used the money to buy goods made by strangers in far-off factories. As store-bought fabrics, candles, and soap replaced homemade products, a quiet revolution occurred in the household division of labor and status. Traditional women's work was rendered superfluous and devalued. The home itself, once a center of economic production in which all family members cooperated, grew into a place of refuge from the world of work, a refuge that became increasingly the special and separate sphere of women.

Wealth and Poverty

Revolutionary advances in manufacturing and transportation brought increased prosperity to all Americans, but they also widened the gulf between the rich and the poor. Millionaires had been rare in the early days of the Republic, but by the eve of the Civil War several specimens of colossal financial success were strutting across the national stage.

The Levee at New Orleans   With the expansion of cotton growing into the new states of the trans-Appalachian Southwest and the coming of the steamboat, the entire Cotton Kingdom paid economic tribute to New Orleans, Queen City of the South.

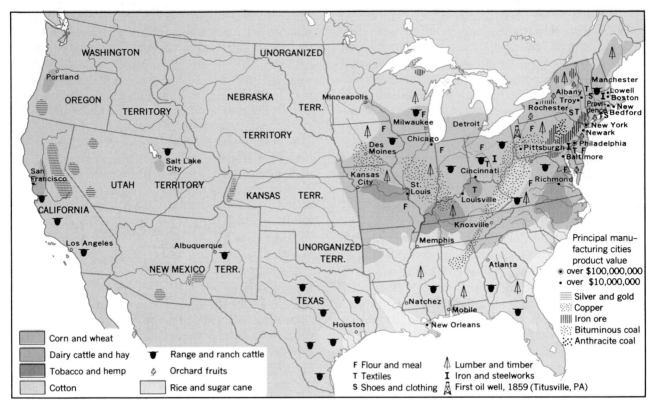

Industry and Agriculture, 1860   Still a nation of farmers on the eve of the Civil War, Americans had nevertheless made an impressive start on their own industrial revolution, especially in the Northeast.

Spectacular was the case of fur-trader and real estate speculator John Jacob Astor, who left an estate of $30 million on his death in 1848.

Cities bred the greatest extremes of economic inequality. Unskilled workers, then as always, fared worst. Many of them came to make up a floating mass of "drifters," buffeted from town to town by the shifting prospects for menial jobs. These wandering workers accounted at various times for up to half the population of the brawling industrial centers. Although their numbers were large, they left little behind them but the homely fruits of their transient labor. Largely unstoried and unsung, they are among the forgotten men and women of American history.

Many myths about "social mobility" grew up over the buried memories of these unfortunate day laborers. Mobility did exist in industrializing America—but not in the proportions that legend often portrays. Rags-to-riches success stories were relatively few.

Yet America, with its dynamic society and wide-open spaces, undoubtedly provided more "opportunity" than did the contemporary countries of the Old World—which is why millions of immigrants packed their bags and headed for New World shores. Moreover, a rising tide lifts all boats, and the improvement in overall standards of living was real. Wages for unskilled workers in a labor-hungry America rose about 1 percent a year from 1820 to 1860. This general prosperity helped defuse the potential class conflict that might otherwise have exploded—and that did explode in many European countries.

Cables, Clippers, and Pony Riders

Though businesspeople concentrated on developing the wondrously rewarding domestic market, a new pattern of American foreign trade also emerged in the antebellum years. (Foreign commerce seldom added up to more than 7 percent of the national product.) Abroad as at home, cotton was king and regularly accounted for more than half the value of all American exports. After the repeal of the British exclusionary Corn Laws in 1846, the wheat gathered by McCormick's reapers began to play an increasingly important role in trade with Great Britain. Americans generally exported agricultural products and imported manufactured goods—and they generally imported more than they exported, running up substantial debts to foreign creditors.

A crucial step came in 1858 when Cyrus Field, called "the greatest wire puller in history," finally stretched a cable under the deep North Atlantic waters from Newfoundland to Ireland. Although this initial cable went dead after three weeks of public rejoicing, a heavier cable laid in 1866 permanently linked the American and European continents.

The United States merchant marine encountered rough sailing during much of the early nineteenth century. American vessels had been repeatedly laid up by the embargo, the War of 1812, and the panics of 1819 and 1837. American naval designers made few contributions to maritime progress. A pioneer American steamer, the *Savannah,* had crept across the Atlantic in 1819, but it used sail most of the time and was pursued for a day by a British captain who thought it afire.

In the 1840s and 1850s, a golden age dawned for American shipping. Yankee naval yards, notably Donald McKay's at Boston, began to send down the ways sleek new craft called clipper ships. Long, narrow, and majestic, they glided across the sea under towering masts and clouds of canvas. In a fair breeze they could outrun any steamer.

The stately clippers sacrificed cargo space for speed, and their captains made killings by hauling high-value cargoes in record times. They wrested much of the tea-carrying trade between the Far East and England from their slower-sailing British competitors, and they sped thousands of impatient adventurers to the gold fields of California and Australia.

Chariot of Fame Clipper Ship, by Duncan McFarlane, 1854

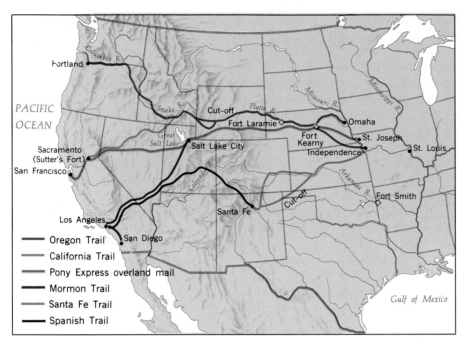

Main Routes West Before the Civil War Mark Twain described his stagecoach trip to California in the 1860s: "We began to get into country, now, threaded here and there with little streams. These had high, steep banks on each side, and every time we flew down one bank and scrambled up the other, our party inside got mixed somewhat. First we would all be down in a pile at the forward end of the stage, . . . and in a second we would shoot to the other end, and stand on our heads. And . . . as the dust rose from the tumult, we would all sneeze in chorus, and the majority of us would grumble, and probably say some hasty thing, like: 'Take your elbow out of my ribs!—can't you quit crowding?'"

But the hour of glory for the clipper was relatively brief. On the eve of the Civil War, the British had clearly won the world race for maritime ascendancy with their iron tramp steamers ("teakettles"). Although slower and less romantic than the clipper, these vessels were steadier, roomier, more reliable, and hence more profitable.

No story of rapid American communication would be complete without including the Far West. By 1858, horse-drawn overland stagecoaches, immortalized by Mark Twain's *Roughing It,* were a familiar sight. Their dusty tracks stretched from the bank of the muddy Missouri River clear to California.

As late as 1877, stagecoach passengers were advised in print,

"Never shoot on the road as the noise might frighten the horses. . . . Don't point out where murders have been committed, especially if there are women passengers. . . . Expect annoyances, discomfort, and some hardships."

Even more dramatic was the Pony Express, established in 1860 to carry mail speedily the 2,000 lonely miles (3,220 kilometers) from St. Joseph, Missouri, to Sacramento, California. Daring, lightweight riders, leaping onto wiry ponies saddled at stations approximately 10 miles (16 kilometers) apart, could make the trip in an amazing ten days. These unarmed horsemen galloped on, summer or winter, day or night, through dust or snow, past Indians and bandits. The speeding postmen missed only one trip, though the whole enterprise lost money heavily and folded after only eighteen legend-leaving months.

Just as the clippers had succumbed to steam, so were the express riders unhorsed by Morse's clacking keys, which began tapping messages to California in 1861. The swift ships and the fleet ponies ushered out a dying technology of wind and muscle. In the future, machines would be in the saddle.

Chronology

c. 1750	Industrial revolution begins in Britain
1791	Samuel Slater builds first U. S. textile factory
1793	Eli Whitney invents the cotton gin
1798	Whitney develops interchangeable parts for muskets
1807	Robert Fulton's first steamboat Embargo spurs American manufacturing
1811	Cumberland Road construction begins
1817	Erie Canal construction begins
1825	Erie Canal completed
1828	First railroad in United States
1830s	Cyrus McCormick invents mechanical mower-reaper
1834	Anti-Catholic riot in Boston
1837	John Deere develops steel plow
1840	President Van Buren establishes ten-hour day for federal employees
1842	Massachusetts declares labor unions legal in *Commonwealth* v. *Hunt*
c. 1843– 1868	Era of clipper ships
1844	Samuel Morse invents telegraph Anti-Catholic riot in Philadelphia
1845– 1849	Potato famine in Ireland
1846	Elias Howe invents sewing machine
1848	First general incorporation laws in New York Democratic revolutions collapse in Germany
1849	Order of the Star-Spangled Banner (Know-Nothing party) formed
1852	Cumberland Road completed
1858	Cyrus Field lays first transatlantic cable
1860	Pony Express established
1861	First transcontinental telegraph
1866	Permanent transatlantic cable established

SUGGESTED READINGS

PRIMARY SOURCE DOCUMENTS

Seth Luther, *An Address to the Working-Men of New England** (1833), is the eloquent appeal of an uneducated working-class labor reformer. On the transportation revolution, see John H. B. Latrobe, *Western Waters** (1871), and Mark Twain's classic *Life on the Mississippi** (1883). Lemuel Shaw's decision of 1842 in *Commonwealth* v. *Hunt*, 4 Metc. III (in Henry Steele Commager, *Documents of American History*) is regarded as the "Magna Carta of American labor organization." Thomas

Dublin has edited *Farm to Factory: Women's Letters, 1830–1860.* Richard H. Dana Jr.'s personal narrative, *Two Years Before the Mast* (1840), describes the romance of the clipper ships.

SECONDARY SOURCES

Charles Sellers offers a sweeping interpretation of the era in *The Market Revolution: Jacksonian America, 1815–1846* (1991). On immigration, see Maldwyn Jones, *American Immigration* (1960); John Bodnar, *The Transplanted: A History of Immigrants in Urban America* (1985); Carl Wittke, *Refugees of Revolution: The German Forty-Eighters in America* (1952); Hasia Diner, *Erin's Daughters in America* (1983); and Kerby A. Miller, *Emigrants and Exiles: Ireland and the Irish Exodus to North*

---

* An asterisk indicates that the document, or an excerpt from it, can be found in Thomas A. Bailey and David M. Kennedy, eds., *The American Spirit: United States History as Seen by Contemporaries,* 9th ed. (Boston: Houghton Mifflin, 1998).

America (1985). Solid introductions are George R. Taylor, *The Transportation Revolution, 1815–1860* (1951); Clarence H. Danhoff, *Change in Agriculture: The Northern United States, 1820–1870* (1969); and Douglas C. North, *Economic Growth in the United States, 1790–1860* (1961). See also North's *Growth and Welfare in the American Past* (rev. ed., 1974). The events of the period are placed in a larger context of economic history in Stuart Bruchey, *The Roots of American Economic Growth, 1607 –1861* (1965), and Albert W. Niemi, *U.S. Economic History: A Survey of the Major Issues* (1975). Thomas C. Cochran, *Frontiers of Change: Early Industrialism in America* (1981), sees industrialization as culturally inspired change. Two fascinating case studies of the coming of industrialism are Alan Dawley, *Class and Community: The Industrial Revolution in Lynn* (1977), and Anthony F. C. Wallace, *Rockdale: The Growth of an American Village in the Early Industrial Revolution* (1978). The laboring classes are chronicled in Bruce Laurie, *Artisans into Workers: Labor in Nineteenth-Century America* (1989). Consult also Herbert Gutman's pathbreaking *Work, Culture, and Society in Industrializing America* (1976); Sean Wilentz's insightful *Chants Democratic: New York City and the Rise of the American Working Class, 1788–1850* (1984); and David R. Roediger, *The Wages of Whiteness: Race and the Making of the American Working Class* (1991). The experiences of women workers are the focus of Thomas Dublin, *Women at Work: The Transformation of Work and Community in Lowell, Massachusetts, 1826–1860* (1979), and Christine Stansell, *City of Women: Sex and Class in New York, 1789–1860* (1986). On the introduction of technology, see David H. Hounshell, *From the American System to Mass Production, 1800–1932: The Development of Manufacturing Technology in the United States* (1984), and David F. Hawke, *Nuts and Bolts of the Past: A History of American Technology, 1776–1860* (1988). Ideological aspects of this process are described in John F. Kassen, *Civilizing the Machine: Technology and Republican Values in America, 1776–1900* (1976). The canal era is comprehensively described in Carter Goodrich, *Government Promotion of American Canals and Railroads, 1800–1890* (1960), and in Ronald E. Shaw, *Canals for a Nation: The Canal Era in the United States, 1790–1860* (1990). On railroads, consult Robert Fogel, *Railroads and American Economic Growth* (1964), which presents the startling thesis that the iron horse in fact did little to promote growth. For a different view, see Albert Fishlow, *American Railroads and the Transformation of the Ante-Bellum Economy* (1965). The organization and management of railroad corporations is treated in Alfred D. Chandler, Jr., *The Visible Hand: The Managerial Revolution in American Business* (1977). The legal foundation of the market revolution is discussed in Morton Horwitz, *The Transformation of American Law, 1780–1860* (1977). Steven Hahn and Jonathan Prude, eds., *The Countryside in the Age of Capitalist Transformation: Essays in the Social History of Rural America* (1985), is a provocative look at the impact of the transportation and industrial revolutions on the countryside. See also Christopher Clark, *The Roots of Rural Capitalism: Western Massachusetts, 1780–1860* (1990), and Alan Kulikoff, *The Agrarian Origins of American Capitalism* (1992). On urbanization, see Allan R. Pred, *Urban Growth and the Circulation of Information: The United States System of Cities, 1790–1840* (1973), and Elizabeth Blackmar, *Manhattan for Rent, 1785–1850* (1989).

16

The Ferment of Reform and Culture

1790–1860

We [Americans] will walk on our own feet; we will work with our own hands; we will speak our own minds.

RALPH WALDO EMERSON, "THE AMERICAN SCHOLAR," 1837

Reviving Religion

Church attendance was still a regular ritual for about three-fourths of the 23 million Americans in 1850. Alexis de Tocqueville declared that there was "no country in the world where the Christian religion retains a greater influence over the souls of men than in America." Yet the religion of these years was not the old-time religion of colonial days. The austere Calvinist rigor had long been seeping out of the American churches. The rationalist ideas of the French Revolutionary era had done much to soften the older orthodoxy. Thomas Paine's widely circulated book *The Age of Reason* (1794) had shockingly declared that all churches were "set up to terrify and enslave mankind, and monopolize power and profit." American anticlericalism was seldom that virulent, but many of the Founding Fathers, includ-

ing Jefferson and Franklin, embraced the liberal doctrines of Deism that Paine promoted. Deists relied on reason rather than revelation, on science rather than the Bible. They rejected the concept of original sin and denied Christ's divinity. Yet Deists believed in a Supreme Being who had created a knowable universe and endowed human beings with a capacity for moral behavior.

Deism helped to inspire an important spin-off from the severe Puritanism of the past—the Unitarian faith, which began to gather momentum in New England at the end of the eighteenth century. Unitarians held that God existed in only *one* person (hence *uni*tarian), and not in the orthodox Trinity (God the Father, God the Son, and God the Holy Spirit). Although denying the deity of Jesus, Unitarians stressed the essential goodness of human nature rather than its vileness; they proclaimed their belief in free will and the possibility of salvation through good works; they pictured God not as a stern Creator but as a loving Father. Embraced by many leading thinkers (including Ralph Waldo Emerson), the Unitarian movement appealed mostly to intellectuals whose rationalism and optimism contrasted sharply with the hellfire doctrines of Calvinism, especially predestination and human depravity.

A boiling reaction against the growing liberalism in religion set in about 1800. A fresh wave of roaring revivals, beginning on the southern frontier but soon rolling even into the cities of the Northeast, sent a Second Great Awakening surging across the land. Sweeping up even more people than the First Great Awakening (see p. 94) almost a century earlier, the Second Awakening was one of the most momentous episodes in the history of American religion. This tidal wave of spiritual fervor left in its wake countless converted souls, many shattered and reorganized churches, and numerous new sects. It also encouraged an effervescent evangelicalism that bubbled up into innumerable areas of American life—including prison reform, the temperance cause, the women's movement, and the crusade to abolish slavery.

The Second Great Awakening was spread to the masses on the frontier by huge "camp meetings." As many as twenty-five thousand people would gather for an encampment of several days to drink the hellfire gospel as served up by an itinerant preacher. Thousands of spiritually starved souls "got religion" at these gatherings and in their ecstasy engaged in frenzies of rolling, dancing, barking, and jerking. Many of the "saved" soon backslid into their former sinful ways, but the revivals boosted church membership and stimulated a variety of humanitarian reforms. Responsive Easterners were moved to do missionary work in the West with Indians, in Hawaii, and in Asia.

Methodists and Baptists reaped the most abundant harvest of souls from the fields fertilized by revivalism. Both sects stressed personal conversion (contrary to predestination), a relatively democratic control of church affairs, and a rousing emotionalism. As a frontier jingle ran,

> *The devil hates the Methodist*
> *Because they sing and shout the best.*

Powerful Peter Cartwright (1785–1872) was the best known of the Methodist "circuit riders," or traveling frontier preachers. This ill-educated but sinewy servant of the Lord ranged for a half-century from Tennessee to Illinois, calling upon sinners to repent. With bellowing voice and flailing arms, he converted thousands of souls to the Lord. Not only did he lash the Devil with his tongue, but with his fists he knocked out rowdies who tried to break up his meetings. His Christianity was definitely muscular.

Bell-voiced Charles Grandison Finney was the greatest of the revival preachers. Trained as a lawyer,

A Camp Meeting at Eastham, Massachusetts, 1851
At huge, days-long encampments like this, repentant sinners dedicated themselves to lives of personal rectitude and social reform. Out of this religious upheaval grew many of the movements for social improvement in the pre–Civil War decades, including the abolitionist crusade.

Finney abandoned the bar to become an evangelist after a deeply moving conversion experience as a young man. Tall and athletically built, Finney held huge crowds spellbound with the power of his oratory and the pungency of his message. He led massive revivals in Rochester and New York City in 1830 and 1831. Finney preached a version of the old-time religion, but he was also an innovator. He devised the "anxious bench," where repentant sinners could sit in full view of the congregation, and he encouraged women to pray aloud in public. Holding out the promise of a perfect Christian kingdom on earth, Finney denounced both alcohol and slavery. He eventually served as president of Oberlin College in Ohio, which he helped to make a hotbed of revivalist activity and abolitionism.

Denominational Diversity

Revivals also furthered the fragmentation of religious faiths. Western New York, where many descendants of New England Puritans had settled, was so blistered by sermonizers preaching "hellfire and damnation" that it came to be known as the "Burned-Over District."

Millerites, or Adventists, who mustered several hundred thousand adherents, rose from the superheated soil of the Burned-Over region in the 1830s. Named after the eloquent and commanding William Miller, they interpreted the Bible to mean that Christ would return to earth on October 22, 1844. Donning their go-to-meeting clothes, they gathered in prayerful assemblies to greet their Redeemer. The failure of Jesus to descend on schedule dampened but did not destroy the movement.

Like the First Great Awakening, the Second Great Awakening tended to widen the lines between classes and regions. The more prosperous and conservative denominations in the East were little touched by revivalism, and Episcopalians, Presbyterians, Congregationalists, and Unitarians continued to rise mostly from the wealthier, better-educated levels of society. Methodists, Baptists, and the members of the other new sects spawned by the swelling evangelistic fervor tended to come from less prosperous, less "learned" communities in the rural South and West.

Religious diversity further reflected social cleavages when the churches faced up to the slavery issue. By 1844–1845 both the southern Baptists and

Charles Grandison Finney, 1792–1875

the southern Methodists had split with their northern brethren over human bondage. The Methodists came to grief over the case of a slaveowning bishop in Georgia, whose second wife added several household slaves to his estate. In 1857 the Presbyterians, North and South, parted company. The secession of

---

In his lecture "Hindrances to Revivals," delivered in the 1830s, Charles Grandison Finney (1792–1875) proposed the excommunication of drinkers and slaveholders:

"Let the churches of all denominations speak out on the subject of temperance, let them close their doors against all who have anything to do with the death-dealing abomination, and the cause of temperance is triumphant. A few years would annihilate the traffic. Just so with slavery. . . . It is a great national sin. It is a sin of the church. The churches by their silence, and by permitting slaveholders to belong to their communion, have been consenting to it. . . . The church cannot turn away from this question. It is a question for the church and for the nation to decide, and God will push it to a decision."

the southern churches foreshadowed the secession of the southern states. First the churches split, then the political parties split, and then the Union split.

A Desert Zion in Utah

The smoldering spiritual embers of the Burned-Over District kindled one especially ardent flame in 1830. In that year Joseph Smith—a rugged visionary, proud of his prowess at wrestling—reported that he had received some golden plates from an angel. When deciphered, they constituted the Book of Mormon, and the Church of Jesus Christ of Latter-Day Saints (Mormons) was launched. It was a native American product, a new religion, destined to spread its influence worldwide.

After establishing a religious oligarchy, Smith ran into serious opposition from his non-Mormon neighbors, first in Ohio and then in Missouri and Illinois. His cooperative sect rasped rank-and-file Americans, who were individualistic and dedicated to free enterprise. The Mormons aroused further antagonism by voting as a unit and by openly but understandably drilling their militia for defensive purposes. Accusations of polygamy likewise arose and increased in intensity, for Joseph Smith was reputed to have several wives.

Continuing hostility finally drove the Mormons to desperate measures. In 1844 Joseph Smith and his brother were murdered and mangled by a mob

> *Polygamy was an issue of such consequence that it was bracketed with slavery in the Republican national platform of 1856:*
>
> "It is both the right and the imperative duty of Congress to prohibit in the Territories those twin relics of barbarism—Polygamy and Slavery."

in Carthage, Illinois, and the movement seemed near collapse. The falling torch was seized by a remarkable Mormon Moses named Brigham Young. Stern and austere in contrast to Smith's charm and affability, the barrel-chested Brigham Young had received only eleven days of formal schooling. But he quickly proved to be an aggressive leader, an eloquent preacher, and a gifted administrator. Determined to escape further persecution, Young in 1846–1847 led his oppressed and despoiled Latter-Day Saints over vast rolling plains to Utah as they sang "Come, Come, Ye Saints."

Overcoming pioneer hardships, the Mormons soon made the desert bloom like a new Eden by means of ingenious and cooperative methods of irrigation. The crops of 1848, threatened by hordes of crickets, were saved when flocks of gulls appeared, as if by a miracle, to gulp down the invaders. (A monument to the sea gulls stands in Salt Lake City today.)

Mormon Pioneers Determined Mormons tamed some of the most forbidding and inhospitable terrain in America, including the "Desert Zion" of Utah. Their polygamous practices, apparent in this photograph, created much friction with non-Mormon "gentiles" in early days.

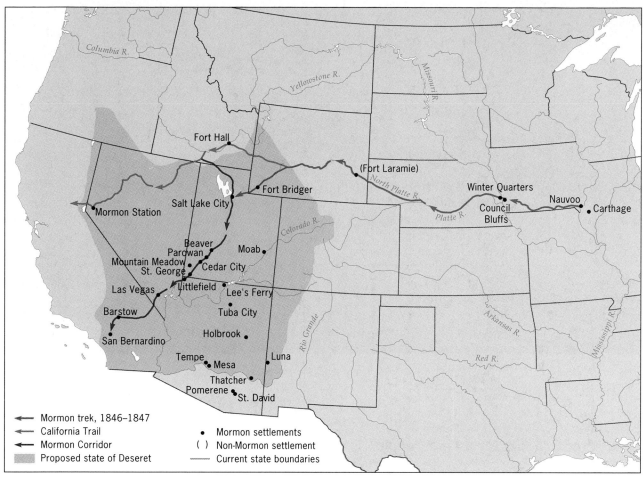

The Mormon World   After Joseph Smith's murder at Carthage in 1844, the Mormons abandoned their thriving settlement at Nauvoo, Illinois (which had about 20,000 inhabitants in 1845), and set out for the valley of the Great Salt Lake, then still part of Mexico. When the Treaty of Guadalupe Hidalgo (see p. 394) in 1848 brought the vast Utah Territory into the United States, the Mormons rapidly expanded their desert colony, which they called Deseret, especially along the "Mormon Corridor" that stretched from Salt Lake to southern California.

Semiarid Utah grew remarkably. By the end of 1848 some five thousand settlers had arrived, and other large bands were to follow them. Many dedicated Mormons in the 1850s actually made the 1,300-mile (2,090-kilometer) trek across the plains pulling two-wheeled carts.

Under the rigidly disciplined management of Brigham Young, the community became a prosperous frontier theocracy and a cooperative commonwealth. Young married as many as twenty-seven women—some of them wives in name only—and begot fifty-six children. The population was further swelled by thousands of immigrants from Europe,

where the Mormons had established a flourishing missionary movement.

A crisis developed when the Washington government was unable to control the hierarchy of Brigham Young, who had been made territorial governor in 1850. A federal army marched in 1857 against the Mormons, who harassed its lines of supply and rallied to die in their last dusty ditch. Fortunately, the quarrel was finally adjusted without serious bloodshed. The Mormons later ran afoul of the antipolygamy laws passed by Congress in 1862 and 1882, and their unique marital customs delayed statehood for Utah until 1896.

The Country School, by Winslow Homer, 1871   Stark and simple by latter-day standards, the one-room schoolhouse nevertheless contributed richly to the development of the young Republic.

Free Schools for a Free People

Tax-supported primary schools were scarce in the early years of the Republic. They had the odor of pauperism about them, since they existed chiefly to educate the children of the poor—the so-called ragged schools. Advocates of "free" public education met stiff opposition. A midwestern legislator cried that he wanted only this simple epitaph when he died: "Here lies an enemy of public education."

Well-to-do, conservative Americans gradually saw the light. If they did not pay to educate "other folkses brats," the "brats" might grow up into a dangerous, ignorant rabble—armed with the vote. Taxation for education was an insurance premium that the wealthy paid for stability and democracy.

Tax-supported public education, though miserably lagging in the slavery-cursed South, triumphed between 1825 and 1850. Grimy-handed laborers wielded increased influence and demanded instruction for their children. Most important was the gaining of manhood suffrage for whites in Jackson's day. A free vote cried aloud for free education. A civilized

nation that was both ignorant and free, declared Thomas Jefferson, "never was and never will be."

The famed little red schoolhouse—with one room, one stove, one teacher, and often eight grades—became the shrine of American democracy. Regrettably, it was an imperfect shrine. Early free schools stayed open only a few months of the year. Schoolteachers, most of them men in this era, were too often ill trained, ill tempered, and ill paid. They frequently put more stress on "lickin'" (with a hickory stick) than on "larnin'." These knights of the blackboard often "boarded around" in the community, and some knew scarcely more than their older pupils. They usually taught only the "three Rs"— "readin', 'ritin', and 'rithmetic." To many rugged Americans, suspicious of "book larnin'," this was enough.

Reform was urgently needed. Into the breach stepped Horace Mann (1796–1859), a brilliant and idealistic graduate of Brown University. As secretary of the Massachusetts Board of Education, he campaigned effectively for more and better schoolhouses, longer school terms, higher pay for teachers, and an expanded curriculum. His influence radiated out to other states, and impressive improvements were chalked up. Yet education remained an expensive luxury for many communities. As late as 1860, the nation counted only about a hundred public secondary schools—and nearly a million white adult illiterates. Black slaves in the South were legally forbidden to receive instruction in reading or writing, and even free blacks, in the North as well as the South, were usually excluded from the schools.

Educational advances were aided by improved textbooks, notably those of Noah Webster (1758–1843), a Yale-educated Connecticut Yankee who was known as the "Schoolmaster of the Republic." His "reading lessons," used by millions of children in the nineteenth century, were partly designed to promote patriotism. Webster devoted twenty years to his famous dictionary, published in 1828, which helped to standardize the American language.

Equally influential was Ohioan William H. McGuffey (1800–1873), a teacher-preacher of rare power. His grade-school readers, first published in the 1830s, sold 122 million copies in the following decades. *McGuffey's Readers* hammered home lasting lessons in morality, patriotism, and idealism. One copy-exercise ran

> *Beautiful hands are they that do*
> *Deeds that are noble good and true;*
> *Beautiful feet are they that go*
> *Swiftly to lighten another's woe.*

Abraham Lincoln (1809–1865) wrote of his education (1859),

"There were some schools so-called [in Indiana], but no qualification was ever required of a teacher beyond 'readin', writin' and cipherin' to the rule of three. . . . There was absolutely nothing to excite ambition for education. Of course, when I came of age I did not know much. Still, somehow, I could read, write and cipher to the rule of three, but that was all. I have not been to school since. The little advance I now have upon this store of education, I have picked up from time to time under the pressure of necessity. I was raised to work, which I continued till I was twenty-two."

Higher Goals for Higher Learning

Higher education was likewise stirring. The religious zeal of the Second Great Awakening led to the planting of many small, denominational, liberal arts colleges, chiefly in the South and West. Too often they were academically anemic, established more to satisfy local pride than genuinely to advance the cause of learning. Like their more venerable, ivy-draped brethren, the new colleges offered a narrow, tradition-bound curriculum of Latin, Greek, mathematics, and moral philosophy. On new and old campuses alike there was little intellectual vitality and much boredom.

The first state-supported universities sprang up in the South, beginning with North Carolina in 1795. Federal land grants nourished the growth of state institutions of higher learning. Conspicuous among the early group was the University of Virginia, founded in 1819. It was largely the brainchild of Thomas Jefferson, who designed its beautiful architecture and who at times watched its construction through a telescope from his hilltop home. He dedicated the university to freedom from religious or political shackles, and modern languages and the sciences received unusual emphasis.

Women's higher education was frowned upon in the early decades of the nineteenth century. A woman's place was believed to be in the home, and training in needlecraft seemed more important than training in algebra. In an era when the clinging-vine bride was the ideal, coeducation was regarded as frivolous. Prejudices also prevailed that too much learning injured the feminine brain, undermined health, and rendered a young lady unfit for marriage. The teachers of Susan B. Anthony, the future feminist, refused to instruct her in long division.

Women's schools at the secondary level began to attain some respectability in the 1820s, thanks in part to the dedicated work of Emma Willard (1787–1870). In 1821 she established the Troy (New York) Female Seminary. Oberlin College, in Ohio, jolted traditionalists in 1837 when it opened its doors to women as well as men. (Oberlin had already created shock waves by admitting black students.) In the same year, Mary Lyon established an outstanding women's school, Mount Holyoke Seminary (later College), in South Hadley, Massachusetts. Mossback critics scoffed that "they'll be educatin' cows next."

Mary Lyon (1797–1849), by Joseph Goodhue Chandler, 1844   An intrepid pioneer in the field of higher education for women, Mary Lyon was a gifted teacher who achieved an important breakthrough when, in the face of much antagonism, she managed to raise enough money to launch her "Female Seminary," now Mount Holyoke College. It opened in 1837, and the year after, she had to turn away some four hundred applicants. She served as principal for twelve years.

Adults who craved more learning satisfied their thirst for knowledge at private subscription libraries or, increasingly, at tax-supported libraries. House-to-house peddlers also did a lush business in feeding the public appetite for culture. Traveling lecturers helped to carry learning to the masses through the lyceum lecture associations, which numbered about three thousand by 1835. The lyceums provided platforms for speakers in such areas as science, literature, and moral philosophy. Talented talkers like Ralph Waldo Emerson journeyed thousands of miles on the lyceum circuits, casting their pearls of civilization before appreciative audiences.

Magazines flourished in the pre–Civil War years, but most of them withered after a short life. The *North American Review,* founded in 1815, was the long-lived leader of the intellectuals. *Godey's Lady's Book,* founded in 1830, survived until 1898 and attained the enormous circulation (for those days) of 150,000. It was devoured devotedly by countless millions of women.

An Age of Reform

As the young Republic grew, reform campaigns of all types flourished in sometimes bewildering abundance. There was not "a reading man" who was without some scheme for a new utopia in his "waistcoat pocket," claimed Ralph Waldo Emerson. Reformers promoted rights for women as well as miracle medicines, communal living, polygamy, celibacy, rule by prophets, and guidance by spirits. Societies were formed against alcohol, tobacco, profanity, and the transit of mail on the Sabbath. Fad diets proved popular, including the whole-wheat bread and crackers regimen of Sylvester Graham. Eventually overshadowing all other reforms was the crusade against slavery (see pp. 371–376).

Many reformers were simply crackbrained cranks. But most were intelligent, inspired idealists, usually touched by the fire of evangelical religion then licking through the pews and pulpits of American churches. The optimistic promises of the Second Great Awakening inspired countless souls to do battle against earthly evils. These modern idealists dreamed anew the old Puritan vision of a perfected society: free from cruelty, war, intoxicating drink, discrimination, and—ultimately—slavery. Women were particularly prominent in these reform crusades, especially in their own struggle for suffrage. For many middle-class women, the reform campaigns provided a unique opportunity to escape the confines of the home and enter the arena of public affairs.

In part, the practical, activist Christianity of these reformers resulted from their desire to reaffirm traditional values as they plunged ever further into a world disrupted and transformed by the turbulent forces of a market economy. Mainly middle-class descendants of pioneer farmers, they were often blissfully unaware that they were witnessing the dawn of the industrial era, which posed unprecedented problems and called for novel ideas. They either ignored the factory workers, for example, or blamed their problems on bad habits. With naive single-mindedness, reformers sometimes applied conventional virtue to refurbishing an older order—while events hurtled them headlong into the new.

Imprisonment for debt continued to be a nightmare, though its extent has been exaggerated. As late as 1830, hundreds of penniless people were languishing in filthy holes, sometimes for owing less than one dollar. The poorer working classes were especially hard hit by this merciless practice. But as the embattled laborer won the ballot and asserted himself, state legislatures gradually abolished debtors' prisons.

Criminal codes in the states were likewise being softened, in accord with more enlightened European practices. The number of capital offenses was being reduced, and brutal punishments, such as whipping and branding, were being slowly eliminated. A refreshing idea was taking hold that prisons should reform as well as punish—hence "reformatories," "houses of correction," and "penitentiaries" (for penance).

Sufferers from so-called insanity were still being treated with incredible cruelty. The medieval concept had been that the mentally deranged were cursed with unclean spirits; the nineteenth-century idea was that they were willfully perverse and depraved—to be treated only as beasts. Many crazed persons were chained in jails or poorhouses with sane people.

Into this dismal picture stepped a formidable New England teacher-author, Dorothea Dix (1802–1887). A physically frail woman afflicted with persistent lung trouble, she possessed infinite compassion and willpower. She traveled some 60,000 miles (97,000 kilometers) in eight years and assembled her damning reports on insanity and asylums from firsthand observations. Though she never raised her voice, Dix's message was loud and clear. Her classic petition of 1843 to the Massachusetts legislature, describing cells so foul that visitors were driven back by the stench, turned legislative stomachs and hearts. Her persistent prodding resulted in improved conditions and in a gain for the concept that the demented were not willfully perverse but mentally ill.

Agitation for peace also gained some momentum in the pre–Civil War years. In 1828 the American

Dorothea Dix (1802–1887)   A tireless reformer, she worked mightily to improve the treatment of the mentally ill. At the outbreak of the Civil War she was appointed superintendent of women nurses for the Union forces.

In presenting her case to the Massachusetts legislature for more humane treatment for the mentally ill, Dorothea Dix (1802–1887) quoted from the notebook she carried with her as she traveled around the state:

"*Lincoln.* A woman in a cage. *Medford.* One idiotic subject chained, and one in a close stall for seventeen years. *Pepperell.* One often doubly chained, hand and foot; another violent; several peaceable now. . . . *Dedham.* The insane disadvantageously placed in the jail. In the almshouse, two females in stalls . . .; lie in wooden bunks filled with straw; always shut up. One of these subjects is supposed curable. The overseers of the poor have declined giving her a trial at the hospital, as I was informed, on account of expense."

Peace Society was formed, with a ringing declaration of war on war. A leading spirit was William Ladd, who orated when his legs were so badly ulcerated that he had to sit on a stool. His ideas were finally to bear some fruit in the international organizations for collective security of the twentieth century. The American peace crusade, linked with a European counterpart, was making promising progress by midcentury, but it was set back by the bloodshed of the Crimean War in Europe and the Civil War in America.

Demon Rum—The "Old Deluder"

The ever-present drink problem attracted dedicated reformers. Custom, combined with a hard and monotonous life, led to the excessive drinking of hard liquor, even among women, clergymen, and members of Congress. Weddings and funerals all too often became disgraceful brawls, and occasionally a drunken mourner would fall into the open grave with the corpse. Heavy drinking decreased the efficiency of labor, and poorly safeguarded machinery operated under the influence of alcohol increased the danger of accidents occurring at work. Drunkenness also fouled the sanctity of the family, threatening the spiritual welfare—and physical safety—of women and children.

After earlier and feebler efforts, the American Temperance Society was formed at Boston in 1826. Within a few years about a thousand local groups sprang into existence. They implored drinkers to sign the temperance pledge and organized children's clubs, known as the "Cold Water Army." Temperance crusaders also made effective use of pictures, pamphlets, and lurid lecturers, some of whom were reformed drunkards. A popular temperance song ran,

> *We've done with our days of carousing,*
> *Our nights, too, of frolicsome glee;*
> *For now with our sober minds choosing,*
> *We've pledged ourselves never to spree.*

The most popular anti-alcohol tract of the era was T. S. Arthur's melodramatic novel, *Ten Nights in a Barroom and What I Saw There* (1854). It described in shocking detail how a once-happy village was ruined by Sam Slade's tavern. The book was second only to Stowe's *Uncle Tom's Cabin* as a best-

Temperance Banner Lithograph, by Kellogg and Comstock, c.1848–1850 Among the many evils of alcohol, reformers fulminated especially against its corrupting effects on family life. Here a young man is torn between a drink-bearing temptress and a maiden who exemplifies the virtues of womanly purity.

seller in the 1850s, and it enjoyed a highly successful run on the stage. Its touching theme song began with the words of a little girl:

> *Father, dear father, come home with me now,*
> *The clock in the belfry strikes one.*

Early foes of Demon Drink adopted two major lines of attack. One was to stiffen the individual's will to resist the wiles of the little brown jug. The moderate reformers thus stressed "temperance" rather than "teetotalism," or the total elimination of intoxicants. But less patient zealots came to believe that temptation should be removed by legislation. Prominent among this group was Neal S. Dow of

Maine, a blue-nosed reformer who, as a mayor of Portland and an employer of labor, had often witnessed the debauching effect of alcohol—to say nothing of the cost to his pocketbook of work time lost because of drunken employees.

Dow—the "Father of Prohibition"—sponsored the so-called Maine Law of 1851. This drastic new statute, hailed as "the law of Heaven Americanized," prohibited the manufacture and sale of intoxicating liquor. Other states in the North followed Maine's example, and by 1857 about a dozen had passed various prohibitory laws. But these figures are deceptive, for within a decade some of the statutes were repealed or declared unconstitutional, if not openly flouted.

It was clearly impossible to legislate thirst for alcohol out of existence, especially in localities where public sentiment was hostile. Yet on the eve of the Civil War the prohibitionists had registered inspiriting gains. There was much less drinking among women than earlier in the century and probably much less per capita consumption of hard liquor.

Women in Revolt

When the nineteenth century opened, it was still a man's world, both in America and Europe. A wife was supposed to immerse herself in her home and subordinate herself to her lord and master (her husband). Like black slaves, she could not vote; like black slaves, she could be legally beaten by her overlord "with a reasonable instrument." When she married, she could not retain title to her property; it passed to her husband.

Yet American women, though legally regarded as perpetual minors, fared better than their European cousins, partly because of their scarcity in frontier communities. A western woman could warn her spouse to be respectful, for "if you don't, there's plenty will." Few American husbands were brutes; and women always had quiet ways of protecting themselves, regardless of law.

Despite these relative advantages, women were still "the submerged sex" in America in the early part of the century. But as the decades unfolded, women increasingly surfaced to breathe the air of freedom and self-determination. In contrast to colonial times, many women avoided marriage altogether—about 10 percent of adult women remained "spinsters" at the time of the Civil War.

Gender differences were strongly emphasized in nineteenth-century America—largely because the burgeoning market economy was increasingly separating women and men into sharply distinct economic roles. Women were thought to be physically and emotionally weak, but also artistic and refined. Endowed with finely tuned moral sensibilities, they were the keepers of society's conscience, with special responsibility to teach the young how to be good and productive citizens of the Republic. Men were considered strong but crude, always in danger of slipping into some savage or beastly way of life if not guided by the gentle hands of their loving ladies.

But if gender roles were sharply separated, men and women could still be regarded as equals. As a sign of the prestigious position of American women, French visitor Alexis de Tocqueville noted that in his native France rape was punished only lightly, whereas in America it was one of the few crimes punishable by death.

The home was a woman's special sphere, the centerpiece of the "cult of domesticity." Even reformers like Catharine Beecher, who urged her sisters to seek employment as teachers, endlessly celebrated the role of the good homemaker. But some women increasingly felt that the glorified sanctuary of the home was in fact a gilded cage. They yearned to tear down the bars that separated the private world of women from the public world of men.

Clamorous female reformers began to gather strength as the century neared its halfway point. Most were broad-gauge battlers; while demanding rights for women, they joined in the general reform movement of the age, fighting for temperance and the abolition of slavery. Like men, they had been touched by the evangelical spirit that offered the promise of earthly reward for human endeavor. Neither foul eggs nor foul words, when hurled by disapproving men, could halt women heartened by these doctrines.

The women's rights movement was mothered by some arresting characters. Prominent among them was Lucretia Mott, a sprightly Quaker whose ire had been aroused when she and her fellow female delegates to the London antislavery convention of 1840 were not recognized. Elizabeth Cady Stanton, a mother of seven who had insisted on

Stellar Suffragists   Elizabeth Cady Stanton (left) and Susan B. Anthony (right) were two of the most persistent battlers for women's rights. Their National Woman Suffrage Association fought for women's equality in courts and workplaces as well as at the polls.

ters, Sarah and Angelina, championed antislavery. Lucy Stone retained her maiden name after marriage—hence the latter-day "Lucy Stoners," who follow her example. Amelia Bloomer revolted against the current "street sweeping" female attire by donning a semimasculine short skirt with Turkish trousers—"bloomers," they were called—amid much bawdy ridicule about "Bloomerism" and "loose habits." A jeering male rhyme of the times jabbed,

> *Gibbey, gibbey gab*
> *The women had a confab*
> *And demanded the rights*
> *To wear the tights*
> *Gibbey, gibbey gab.*

Fighting feminists met at Seneca Falls, New York, in a memorable Woman's Rights Convention (1848). The defiant Stanton read a "Declaration of Sentiments," which in the spirit of the Declaration of Independence declared that "all men *and women* are created equal." One resolution formally demanded the ballot for females. Amid scorn and denunciation from press and pulpit, the Seneca Falls meeting launched the modern women's rights movement.

The crusade for women's rights was eclipsed by the campaign against slavery in the decade before the Civil War. Any white male, even an idiot, over the

leaving "obey" out of her marriage ceremony, shocked fellow feminists by going so far as to advocate suffrage for women. Quaker-reared Susan B. Anthony, a militant lecturer for women's rights, fearlessly exposed herself to rotten garbage and vulgar epithets. She became such a conspicuous advocate of female rights that progressive women everywhere were called "Suzy Bs."

Other feminists challenged the man's world. Dr. Elizabeth Blackwell, a pioneer in a previously forbidden profession for women, was the first female graduate of a medical college. Precocious Margaret Fuller edited a transcendentalist journal, *The Dial*, and took part in the struggle to bring unity and republican government to Italy. She died in a shipwreck off New York's Fire Island while returning to the United States in 1850. The talented Grimké sis-

When early feminist Lucy Stone (1818–1893) married fellow abolitionist Henry B. Blackwell in West Brookfield, Massachusetts, in 1855, they added the following vow to their nuptial ceremony:

"While acknowledging our mutual affection by publicly assuming the relation of husband and wife, yet in justice to ourselves and a great principle, we deem it a duty to declare that this act on our part implies no . . . promise of voluntary obedience to such of the present laws of marriage, as refuse to recognize the wife as an independent, rational being, while they confer upon the husband an injurious and unnatural superiority."

What It Would Be If Some Ladies Had Their Own Way The men are sewing, tending the baby, and washing clothes. This scene seemed absurd then, but not a century later.

age of twenty-one could vote; no woman could. Yet women were gradually being admitted to colleges, and some states, beginning with Mississippi in 1839, were even permitting wives to own property after marriage.

Wilderness Utopias

Bolstered by the utopian spirit of the age, various reformers, ranging from the high-minded to the "lunatic fringe," set up more than forty communities of a cooperative, communistic, or "communitarian" nature. Seeking human betterment, a wealthy and idealistic Scottish textile manufacturer, Robert Owen, founded in 1825 a communal society of about a thousand people at New Harmony, Indiana. Little harmony prevailed in the colony, which, in addition to hardworking visionaries, attracted a sprinkling of radicals, work-shy theorists, and outright scoundrels. The colony sank in a morass of contradiction and confusion.

Brook Farm in Massachusetts, comprising two hundred acres of grudging soil, was started in 1841 with the brotherly and sisterly cooperation of about twenty intellectuals committed to the philosophy of transcendentalism (p. 348). They prospered reason-

ably well until 1846, when they lost by fire a large new communal building shortly before its completion. The whole venture in "plain living and high thinking" then collapsed in debt. The Brook Farm experiment inspired Nathaniel Hawthorne's classic novel *The Blithedale Romance* (1852), whose main character was modeled on the feminist writer Margaret Fuller.

A more radical experiment was the Oneida Community, founded in New York in 1848. It practiced free love ("complex marriage"), birth control (through "male continence," or *coitus reservatus*), and the eugenic selection of parents to produce superior offspring. This curious enterprise flourished for more than thirty years, largely because its artisans made superior steel traps and Oneida Community (silver) Plate (see Makers of America, pp. 344–345).

Various communistic experiments, mostly small in scale, have been attempted since Jamestown. But in competition with democratic free enterprise and free land, virtually all of them sooner or later failed or changed their methods. Among the longest-lived sects were the Shakers. Led by Mother Ann Lee, they began in the 1770s to set up the first of a score or so of religious communities. The Shakers attained a membership of about six thousand in 1840, but since their monastic customs

Mountain Meeting, by David Lamson, 1848
Worship was a social activity in Shaker communities. Meetings included the unique Shaker dances—as well as strict segregation of the sexes, as shown here.

prohibited both marriage and sexual relations, they were virtually extinct by 1940.

The Dawn of Scientific Achievement

Early Americans, confronted with pioneering problems, were more interested in practical gadgets than in pure science. Jefferson, for example, was a gifted amateur inventor who won a gold medal for a new type of plow. Noteworthy also were the writings of the mathematician Nathaniel Bowditch (1733–1838) on practical navigation and of the oceanographer Matthew F. Maury (1806–1873) on ocean winds and currents. These writers promoted safety, speed, and economy. But as far as basic science was concerned, Americans were best known for borrowing and adapting the findings of Europeans.

Yet the Republic was not without scientific talent. The most influential American scientist of the first half of the nineteenth century was Professor Benjamin Silliman (1779–1864), a pioneer chemist and geologist who taught and wrote brilliantly at Yale College for more than fifty years. Professor Louis Agassiz (1807–1873), a distinguished French-Swiss immigrant, served for a quarter of a century at Harvard College. A path-breaking student of biology who sometimes carried snakes in his pockets, he insisted on original research and deplored the reigning overemphasis on memory work. Professor Asa Gray (1810–1888) of Harvard College, the Columbus of American botany, published over 350 books, monographs, and papers. His textbooks set new standards for clarity and interest.

Lovers of American bird lore owed much to the French-descended naturalist John J. Audubon (1785–1851), who painted wild fowl in their natural habitat. His magnificently illustrated *Birds of America* attained considerable popularity. The Audubon Society for the protection of birds was named after him, although as a young man he shot much feathered game for sport.

Medicine in America, despite a steady growth of medical schools, was still primitive by modern standards. Bleeding remained a common cure, and a curse as well. Smallpox plagues were still dreaded, and the yellow fever epidemic of 1793 in Philadelphia took several thousand lives. "Bring out your dead!" was the daily cry of the corpse-wagon drivers.

People everywhere complained of ill health—malaria, the "rheumatics," the "miseries," and the chills. Illness often resulted from improper diet, hurried eating, perspiring and cooling off too rapidly, and ignorance of germs and sanitation. "We was sick every fall, regular," wrote the mother of the future President Garfield. Life expectancy was still dismayingly short—about forty years for a white

(left) Passenger Pigeons, by John Audubon; (right) John J. Audubon
An astute naturalist and a gifted artist, Audubon drew the birds of America in loving detail. Ironically, he had to go to England in the 1820s to find a publisher for his pioneering depictions of the unique beauty of American wildlife. Born in Haiti and educated in France, he achieved fame as America's greatest ornithologist.

person born in 1850, and less for blacks. The suffering from decayed or ulcerated teeth was enormous; tooth extraction was often practiced by the muscular village blacksmith.

Self-prescribed patent medicines were common (one dose for people, two for horses) and included Robertson's Infallible Worm Destroying Lozenges. Among home remedies was the rubbing of tumors with dead toads. The use of medicine by the regular doctors was often harmful, and Dr. Oliver Wendell Holmes declared in 1860 that if the medicines, as then employed, were thrown into the sea, humans would be better off and the fish worse off.

Victims of surgical operations were ordinarily tied down, often after a stiff drink of whiskey. The surgeon then sawed or cut with breakneck speed,

An outbreak of cholera occurred in New York City in 1832, and a wealthy businessman, Philip Hone (1780–1851), wrote in his diary for the Fourth of July,

"The alarm about the cholera has prevented all the usual jollification under the public authority. . . . The Board of Health reports to-day twenty new cases and eleven deaths since noon yesterday. The disease is here in all its violence and will increase. God grant that its ravages may be confined, and its visit short."

The Oneida Community

John Humphrey Noyes (1811–1886), the founder of the Oneida Community, repudiated the old Puritan doctrines that God was vengeful and that sinful mankind was doomed to dwell in a vale of tears. Noyes believed in a benign deity, in the sweetness of human nature, and in the possibility of a perfect Christian community on earth. "The more we get acquainted with God," he declared, "the more we shall find it our special duty to be happy."

That sunny thought was shared by many early-nineteenth-century American utopians (a word derived from Greek that slyly combines the meanings of "a good place" and "no such place"). But Noyes added some wrinkles of his own. The key to happiness, he taught, was the suppression of self-ishness. True Christians should possess no private property—nor should they indulge in exclusive emotional relationships, which bred jealousy, quarreling, and covetousness. Material things and sexual partners alike, Noyes preached, should be shared. Marriage should not be monogamous. Instead, all members of the community should be free to love one another in "complex marriage." Noyes called his system "Bible Communism."

Tall and slender, with piercing blue eyes and reddish hair, the charismatic Noyes began voicing these ideas in his hometown of Putney, Vermont, in the 1830s. He soon attracted a group of followers who called themselves the Putney Association, a kind of extended family whose members farmed 500 acres by day and sang and prayed together in the evenings. They sustained their spiritual intensity by submitting to "Mutual Criticism," in which the person being criticized would sit in silence while other members frankly discussed his or her faults and merits. "I was, metaphorically, stood upon my head and allowed to drain till all the self-righteousness had dripped out of me," one man wrote of his experience with Mutual Criticism.

The Putney Associates also indulged in sexual practices that outraged the surrounding community's sense of moral propriety. Indicted for adultery in 1847, Noyes led his followers to Oneida, in the supposedly more tolerant region of New York's Burned-Over District, in the following year. Several affiliated communities were also established, the most important of which was at Wallingford, Connecticut.

The Oneidans struggled in New York until they were joined in the 1850s by Sewell Newhouse, a clever inventor of steel animal traps. The manufacture of Newhouse's traps, and other products such as sewing silk and various types of bags, put the Oneida Community on a sound financial footing. By the 1860s, Oneida was a flourishing commonwealth of some three hundred people. Men and women shared equally in all the community's tasks, from field to factory to kitchen. The members lived under one roof in Mansion House, a sprawling building that boasted central heating, a well-stocked library, and a common dining hall as well as the "Big Hall" where members gathered nightly for prayer and entertainment. Children at the age of three were removed from direct parental care and raised communally in the Children's House until the age of thirteen or fourteen, when they took up jobs in the community's industries. They imbibed their religious doctrines with their school lessons:

> *I-spirit*
> *With me never shall stay,*
> *We-spirit*
> *Makes us happy and gay.*

Oneida's apparent success fed the utopian dreams of others, and for a time it became a great tourist attraction. Visitors from as far away as

Europe came to picnic on the shady lawns, speculating on the sexual secrets that Mansion House guarded, while their hosts fed them strawberries and cream and entertained them with music.

But eventually the same problems that had driven Noyes and his band from Vermont began to shadow their lives at Oneida. Their New York neighbors grew increasingly horrified at the Oneidans' licentious sexual practices, including the selective breeding program by which the community matched mates and gave permission—or orders—to procreate, without regard to the niceties of matrimony. "It was somewhat startling to me," one straight-laced visitor commented, "to hear *Miss _____* speak about her baby."

Yielding to their neighbors' criticisms, the Oneidans gave up complex marriage in 1879. Soon other "communistic" practices withered away as well. The communal dining hall became a restaurant, where meals were bought with money, something many Oneidans had never used before. In 1880, the Oneidans abandoned communism altogether and became a joint-stock company specializing in the manufacture of silver tableware. Led by Noyes's son Pierrepont, Oneida Community, Ltd., grew into the world's leading manufacturer of stainless steel knives, forks, and spoons, with annual sales by the 1990s of some half a billion dollars.

As for Mansion House, it still stands in central New York, but it now serves as a museum and private residence. The "Big Hall" is the site of Oneida, Ltd.'s annual shareholders' meetings. Ironically, what grew from Noyes's religious vision was not utopia but a mighty capitalist corporation.

Mansion House A sprawling, resplendent building, it formed the center of the Oneida Community's life, and was a stunning specimen of mid-nineteenth-century architectural and engineering achievement.

The Founding Father
John Humphrey Noyes (1811–1886).

A Bag Bee on the Lawn of Mansion House The fledgling community supported itself in part by bag manufacturing. Men and women shared equally in the bag-making process.

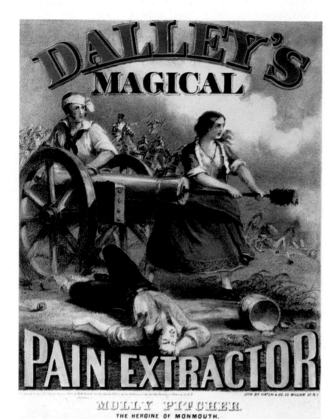

Early Advertising Hawkers of patent medicines pioneered the techniques of modern advertising. Here a pain killer is promoted by invoking the totally irrelevant image of Molly Pitcher. The legendary subject of a poem by John Greenleaf Whittier, Pitcher reputedly took her fallen husband's place at a cannon during the Revolutionary War Battle of Monmouth in 1778. What this exploit had to do with anesthetics is by no means clear, but it supposedly sold the product.

undeterred by the piercing shrieks of the patient. A priceless boon for medical progress came in the early 1840s, when several American doctors and dentists, working independently, successfully employed laughing gas and ether as anesthetics.

Artistic Achievements

Architecturally, America contributed little of note in the first half of the century. The rustic Republic, still under pressure to erect shelters in haste, was con-

tinuing to imitate European models. Public buildings and other important structures followed Greek and Roman lines, which seemed curiously out of place in a wilderness setting. A remarkable Greek revival came between 1820 and 1850, partly stimulated by the heroic efforts of the Greeks in the 1820s to wrest independence from the "terrible Turk." About midcentury strong interest developed in a revival of Gothic forms, with their emphasis on pointed arches and large windows.

Talented Thomas Jefferson, architect of revolution, was probably the ablest American architect of his generation. He brought a classical design to his Virginia hilltop home, Monticello—perhaps the most stately mansion in the nation. The quadrangle of the University of Virginia at Charlottesville, another of Jefferson's creations, remains one of the finest examples of classical architecture in America.

The art of painting continued to be handicapped. It suffered from the dollar grabbing of a raw civilization; from the hustle, bustle, and absence of leisure; from the lack of a wealthy class to sit for portraits—and then pay for them. Some of the earliest painters were forced to go to England, where they found both training and patrons. America exported artists and imported art.

Painting, like the theater, also suffered from the Puritan prejudice that art was a sinful waste of time—and often obscene. John Adams boasted that "he would not give a sixpence for a bust of Phidias or a painting by Raphael." When Edward Everett, the eminent Boston scholar and orator, placed a statue of Apollo in his home, he had its naked limbs draped.

Competent painters nevertheless emerged. Gilbert Stuart (1755–1828), a spendthrift Rhode Islander and one of the most gifted of the early group, wielded his brush in England in competition with the best artists. He produced several portraits of Washington, all of them somewhat idealized and dehumanized. Truth to tell, by the time he posed for Stuart the famous general had lost his natural teeth and some of the original shape of his face. Charles Willson Peale (1741–1827), a Marylander, painted some sixty portraits of Washington, who patiently sat for about fourteen of them. John Trumbull (1756–1843), who had fought in the Revolutionary War, recaptured its scenes and spirit on scores of striking canvases.

During the nationalistic upsurge after the War of 1812, American painters of portraits turned

Autumn—On the Hudson River, by Jasper Francis Cropsey, 1860   This romantic, heroic, sumptuous, mythic rendering of a brooding and beautiful American landscape was typical of the so-called Hudson River School, which flourished in the mid-nineteenth century. Other prominent artists in this group included Thomas Doughty, Asher Brown Durand, Thomas Cole, and George Inness.

increasingly from human landscapes to romantic mirrorings of local landscapes. The Hudson River school excelled in this type of art. At the same time, portrait painters gradually encountered some unwelcome competition from the invention of a crude photograph known as the daguerreotype, perfected about 1839 by a Frenchman, Louis Daguerre.

Music was slowly shaking off the restraints of colonial days, when the prim Puritans had frowned upon nonreligious singing. Rhythmic and nostalgic "darky" tunes, popularized by whites, were becoming immense hits by midcentury. Special favorites were the uniquely American minstrel shows, featuring white actors with blackened faces. "Dixie," later adopted by the Confederates as their battle hymn, was written in 1859, ironically in New York City by an Ohioan. The most famous black songs, also ironically, came from a white Pennsylvanian, Stephen C. Foster (1826–1864). His one excursion into the South occurred in 1852, after he had published "Old Folks at Home." Foster made a valuable contribution to

American folk music by capturing the plaintive spirit of the slaves. An odd and pathetic figure, he finally lost both his art and his popularity and died in a charity ward after drowning his sorrows in drink.

The Blossoming of a National Literature

"Who reads an American book?" sneered a British critic of 1820. The painful truth was that the nation's rough-hewn, pioneering civilization gave little encouragement to "polite" literature. Much of the reading matter was imported or plagiarized from England.

Busy conquering a continent, the Americans poured most of their creative efforts into practical outlets. Praiseworthy were political essays, like *The Federalist* of Hamilton, Jay, and Madison; pamphlets, like Tom Paine's *Common Sense;* and political orations, like the masterpieces of Daniel Webster. In the category of nonreligious books published before 1820, Benjamin Franklin's *Autobiography* (1818) is one of the few that achieved genuine distinction. His narrative is a classic in its simplicity, clarity, and inspirational quality. Even so, it records only a fragment of "Old Ben's" long, fruitful, and amorous life.

A genuinely American literature received a strong boost from the wave of nationalism that followed the War of Independence and especially the War of 1812. By 1820 the older seaboard areas were sufficiently removed from the survival mentality of tree-chopping and butter-churning so that literature could be supported as a profession. The Knickerbocker Group in New York blazed brilliantly across the literary heavens, thus enabling America for the first time to boast of a literature to match its magnificent landscapes.

Washington Irving (1783–1859), born in New York City, was the first American to win international recognition as a literary figure. Steeped in the traditions of New Netherland, he published in 1809 his *Knickerbocker's History of New York*, with its amusing caricatures of the Dutch. When the family business failed, Irving was forced to turn to the goose-feather pen. In 1819–1820 he published *The Sketch Book*, which brought him immediate fame at home and abroad. Combining a pleasing style with delicate charm and quiet humor, he used English as well as American themes and included such immortal Dutch-American tales as "Rip Van Winkle" and "The Legend of Sleepy Hollow." Europe was amazed to find at last an American with a feather in his hand, not in his hair. Later turning to Spanish locales and biography, Irving did much to interpret America to Europe and Europe to America. He was, said the Englishman William Thackeray, "the first ambassador whom the New World of letters sent to the Old."

James Fenimore Cooper (1789–1851) was the first American novelist, as Washington Irving was the first general writer, to gain world fame and to make New World themes respectable. Marrying into a wealthy family, he settled down on the frontier of New York. Reading one day to his wife from an insipid English novel, Cooper remarked in disgust that he could write a better book himself. His wife challenged him to do so—and he did.

After an initial failure, Cooper launched out upon an illustrious career in 1821 with his second novel, *The Spy*—an absorbing tale of the American Revolution. His stories of the sea were meritorious and popular, but his fame rests most enduringly on the *Leatherstocking Tales.* A deadeye rifleman named Natty Bumppo, one of nature's noblemen, meets with Indians in stirring adventures like *The Last of the Mohicans.* James Fenimore Cooper's novels had a wide sale among Europeans, some of whom came to think of all American people as born with tomahawk in hand. Actually Cooper was exploring the viability and destiny of America's republican experiment, by contrasting the undefiled values of "natural men," children of the wooded wilderness, with the artificiality of modern civilization.

A third member of the Knickerbocker group in New York was the belated Puritan William Cullen Bryant (1794–1878), transplanted from Massachusetts. At age sixteen he wrote the meditative and melancholy "Thanatopsis" (published in 1817), which was one of the first high-quality poems produced in the United States. Critics could hardly believe that it had been written on "this side of the water." Although Bryant continued with poetry, he was forced to make his living by editing the influential New York *Evening Post*. For over fifty years he set a model for journalism that was dignified, liberal, and conscientious.

Trumpeters of Transcendentalism

A golden age in American literature dawned in the second quarter of the nineteenth century, when an amazing outburst shook New England. One of the mainsprings of this literary flowering was transcendentalism, especially around Boston, which preened itself as "the Athens of America."

The transcendentalist movement of the 1830s resulted in part from a liberalizing of the straitjacket Puritan theology. It also owed much to foreign influences, including the German romantic philosophers and the religions of Asia. The transcendentalists rejected the prevailing theory, derived from John Locke, that all knowledge comes to the mind through the senses. Truth, rather, "transcends" the senses: it cannot be found by observation alone. Every person possesses an inner light that can illuminate the highest truth and put him or her in direct touch with God, or the "Oversoul."

Ralph Waldo Emerson (1803–1882) Emerson's philosophical observations include such statements as "The less government we have, the better—the fewer laws, and the less confided power"; "To be great is to be misunderstood"; "Every hero becomes a bore at last"; "Shallow men believe in luck"; and "When you strike a king, you must kill him."

> *In 1849 Henry David Thoreau (1817–1862) published* On the Duty of Civil Disobedience, *asserting,*
>
> "I heartily accept the motto, 'That government is best which governs least'; and I should like to see it acted up to more rapidly and systematically. Carried out, it finally amounts to this, which also I believe—'That government is best which governs not at all'; and when men are prepared for it, that will be the kind of government which they will have. Government is at best an expedient; but most governments are usually, and all governments are sometimes, inexpedient."

These mystical doctrines of transcendentalism defied precise definition, but they underlay concrete beliefs. Foremost was a stiff-backed individualism in matters religious as well as social. Closely associated was a commitment to self-reliance, self-culture, and self-discipline. These traits naturally bred hostility to authority and to formal institutions of any kind, as well as to all conventional wisdom. Finally came exaltation of the dignity of the individual, whether black or white—the mainspring of a whole array of humanitarian reforms.

Best known of the transcendentalists was Boston-born Ralph Waldo Emerson (1803–1882). Tall, slender, and intensely blue-eyed, he mirrored serenity in his noble features. Trained as a Unitarian minister, he early forsook his pulpit and ultimately reached a wider audience by pen and platform. He was a never-failing favorite as a lyceum lecturer and for twenty years took a western tour every winter. Perhaps his most thrilling public effort was a Phi Beta Kappa address, "The American Scholar," delivered at Harvard College in 1837. This brilliant appeal was an intellectual Declaration of Independence, for it urged American writers to throw off European traditions and delve into the riches of their own backyards.

Hailed as both a poet and a philosopher, Emerson was not of the highest rank as either. He was more influential as a practical philosopher and through his fresh and vibrant essays enriched countless thousands of humdrum lives. Catching the individualistic mood of the Republic, he stressed self-reliance, self-improvement, self-confidence, optimism, and freedom. The secret of Emerson's popularity lay largely in the fact that his ideals reflected those of an expanding America. By the 1850s he was an outspoken critic of slavery, and he ardently supported the Union cause in the Civil War.

Henry David Thoreau (1817–1862) was Emerson's close associate—a poet, a mystic, a transcendentalist, and a nonconformist. Condemning a government that supported slavery, he refused to pay his Massachusetts poll tax and was jailed for a night.* A gifted prose writer, he is well known for *Walden: Or Life in the Woods* (1854). The book is a

---

*The story (probably apocryphal) is that Emerson visited Thoreau at the jail and asked, "Why are you here?" The reply came, "Why are you *not* here?"

Walt Whitman
This portrait of the young poet appeared in the first edition of *Leaves of Grass* (1855).

Highly romantic, emotional, and unconventional, he dispensed with titles, stanzas, rhymes, and at times even regular meter. He handled sex with shocking frankness, although he laundered his verses in later editions, and his book was banned in Boston.

Whitman's *Leaves of Grass* was at first a financial failure. The only three enthusiastic reviews that it received were written by the author himself—anonymously. But in time the once-withered *Leaves of Grass,* revived and honored, won for Whitman an enormous following in both America and Europe. His fame increased immensely among "Whitmaniacs" after his death.

Leaves of Grass gained for Whitman the informal title "Poet Laureate of Democracy." Singing with transcendental abandon of his love for the masses, he caught the exuberant enthusiasm of an expanding America that had turned its back on the Old World:

> All the Past we leave behind;
> We debouch upon a newer, mightier world,
> varied world;
> Fresh and strong the world we seize—world
> of labor and the march —
> Pioneers! O Pioneers!

Here at last was the native art for which critics had been crying.

record of Thoreau's two years of simple existence in a hut that he built on the edge of Walden Pond, near Concord, Massachusetts. A stiff-necked individualist, he believed that he should reduce his bodily wants so as to gain time for a pursuit of truth through study and meditation. Thoreau's *Walden* and his essay *On the Duty of Civil Disobedience* exercised a strong influence in furthering idealistic thought, both in America and abroad. His writings later encouraged Mahatma Gandhi to resist British rule in India and, still later, inspired the development of American civil rights leader Martin Luther King, Jr.'s thinking about nonviolence.

Bold, brassy, and swaggering was the open-collared figure of Brooklyn's Walt Whitman (1819–1892). In his famous collection of poems *Leaves of Grass* (1855), he gave free rein to his gushing genius with what he called a "barbaric yawp."

In 1876 the London Saturday Review *referred to Walt Whitman (1819–1892) as the author of a volume of*

"so-called poems which were chiefly remarkable for their absurd extravagances and shameless obscenity, and who has since, we are glad to say, been little heard of among decent people."

In 1888 Whitman wrote,

"I had my choice when I commenced. I bid neither for soft eulogies, big money returns, nor the approbation of existing schools and conventions. . . . I have had my say entirely my own way, and put it unerringly on record —the value thereof to be decided by time."

Glowing Literary Lights

Certain other literary giants were not actively associated with the transcendentalist movement, though not completely immune to its influences. Professor Henry Wadsworth Longfellow (1807– 1882), who for many years taught modern languages at Harvard College, was one of the most popular poets ever produced in America. Handsome and urbane, he lived a generally serene life, except for the tragic deaths of two wives, the second of whom perished before his eyes when her dress caught fire. Writing for the genteel classes, he was adopted by the less cultured masses. His wide knowledge of European literature supplied him with many themes, but some of his most admired poems —"Evangeline," "The Song of Hiawatha," and "The Courtship of Miles Standish"— were based on American traditions. Immensely popular in Europe, Longfellow was the only American ever to be honored with a bust in the Poets' Corner of Westminster Abbey.

A fighting Quaker, John Greenleaf Whittier (1807–1892), with piercing dark eyes and swarthy complexion, was the uncrowned poet laureate of the antislavery crusade. Less talented as a writer than Longfellow, he was vastly more important in influencing social action. His poems cried aloud against inhumanity, injustice, and intolerance, against

The outworn rite, the old abuse,
The pious fraud transparent grown.

Undeterred by insults and the stoning of mobs, Whittier helped arouse a calloused America on the slavery issue. A supreme conscience rather than a sterling poet or intellect, Whittier was one of the moving forces of his generation, whether moral, humanitarian, or spiritual. Gentle and lovable, he was preeminently the poet of human freedom.

Many-sided Professor James Russell Lowell (1819–1891), who succeeded Professor Longfellow at Harvard, ranks as one of America's better poets. He was also a distinguished essayist, literary critic, editor, and diplomat—a diffusion of talents that hampered his poetical output. He is remembered as a political satirist in his *Biglow Papers,* especially those of 1846 dealing with the Mexican War. Written partly as poetry in the Yankee dialect, the *Papers* condemned in blistering terms the alleged slavery-expansion designs of the Polk administration.

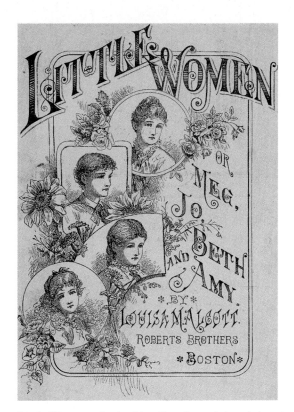

Little Women   Louisa May Alcott's much-loved, largely autobiographical novel for children has remained in print continuously from 1868 until our own day. In search of independence for herself and financial security for her family, Alcott worked as a seamstress, governess, teacher, and housemaid until her writing brought her success.

The scholarly Dr. Oliver Wendell Holmes (1809–1894), who taught anatomy with a sparkle at Harvard Medical School, was a prominent poet, essayist, novelist, lecturer, and wit. A nonconformist and a fascinating conversationalist, he shone among a group of literary lights who regarded Boston as "the hub of the universe." His poem "The Last Leaf," in honor of the last "white Indian" of the Boston Tea Party, came to apply to himself. Dying at the age of eighty-five, he was the "last leaf" among his distinguished contemporaries.*

Two women writers whose work remains enormously popular today were also tied to this New England literary world. Louisa May Alcott (1832–1888) grew up in Concord, Massachusetts, in

---

*Oliver Wendell Holmes had a son with the same name who became a distinguished justice of the Supreme Court (1902–1932) and who lived to be ninety-four, less two days.

the bosom of Transcendentalism, alongside neighbors Emerson, Thoreau, and Fuller. Her philosopher father Bronson Alcott occupied himself more devotedly to ideas than earning a living, leaving his daughter to write *Little Women* (1868) and other books to support her mother and sisters. Not far away in Amherst, Massachusetts, poet Emily Dickinson lived as a recluse but created her own original world through precious gems of poetry. In deceptively spare language and simple rhyme schemes, she explored universal themes of nature, love, death, and immortality. Although she refused during her lifetime to publish any of her poems, when she died, nearly two thousand of them were found among her papers and eventually made their way into print.

The most noteworthy literary figure produced by the South before the Civil War, unless Edgar Allan Poe is regarded as a southerner, was novelist William Gilmore Simms (1806–1870). Quantitatively, at least, he was great: eighty-two books flowed from his ever-moist pen, winning for him the title "the Cooper of the South." His themes dealt with the southern frontier in colonial days and with the South during the Revolutionary War. But he was neglected by his own section, even though he married into the socially elite and became a slaveowner. The high-toned planter aristocracy would never accept the son of a poor Charleston storekeeper.

Literary Individualists and Dissenters

Not all writers in these years believed so keenly in human goodness and social progress. Edgar Allan Poe (1809–1849), who spent much of his youth in Virginia, was an eccentric genius. Orphaned at an early age, cursed with ill health, and married to a child-wife of thirteen who fell fatally ill of tuberculosis, he suffered hunger, cold, poverty, and debt. Failing at suicide, he took refuge in the bottle and dissipated his talent early. Poe was a gifted lyric poet, as "The Raven" attests. A master stylist, he also excelled in the short story, especially of the horror type, in which he shared his alcoholic nightmares with fascinated readers. If he did not invent the modern detective novel, he at least set new high standards in tales like "The Gold Bug."

Poe was fascinated by the ghostly and ghastly, as in "The Fall of the House of Usher" and other stories. He reflected a morbid sensibility distinctly at odds with the usually optimistic tone of American culture. Partly for this reason, Poe has perhaps been even more prized by Europeans than by Americans. His brilliant career was cut short when he was found drunk in a Baltimore gutter and shortly thereafter died.

Two other writers reflected the continuing Calvinist obsession with original sin and with the never-ending struggle between good and evil. In somber Salem, Massachusetts, writer Nathaniel Hawthorne (1804–1864) grew up in an atmosphere heavy with the memories of his Puritan forebears and the tragedy of his father's premature death on an ocean voyage. His masterpiece was *The Scarlet Letter* (1850), which described the Puritan practice of forcing an adultress to wear a scarlet *A* on her clothing. The tragic tale chronicles the psychological effects of sin on the guilty heroine and her secret lover (the father of her baby), a minister of the gospel in Puritan Boston. In *The Marble Faun* (1860), Hawthorne dealt with a group of young American artists who witness a mysterious murder in Rome. The book explored the concepts of the omnipresence of evil and the dead hand of the past weighing upon the present.

Herman Melville (1819–1891), an orphaned and ill-educated New Yorker, went to sea as a youth and served eighteen adventuresome months on a whaler. "A whale ship was my Yale College and my Harvard," he wrote. Jumping ship in the South Seas, he lived among cannibals, from whom he providently escaped uneaten. His fresh and charming tales of the South Seas were immediately popular, but his masterpiece, *Moby Dick* (1851), was not. This epic novel was a complex allegory of good and evil, told in terms of the conflict between a whaling captain, Ahab, and a giant white whale, Moby Dick. Captain Ahab, having lost a leg to the marine monster, lives only for revenge. His pursuit finally ends when Moby Dick rams and sinks Ahab's ship, leaving only one survivor. The whale's exact identity and Ahab's motives remain obscure. In the end the sea, like the terrifyingly impersonal and unknowable universe of Melville's imagination, simply rolls on.

Moby Dick was widely ignored at the time of its publication; people were accustomed to more straightforward and upbeat prose. A disheartened Melville continued to write unprofitably for some years, part of the time eking out a living as a customs

Capturing a Sperm Whale, painted by William Page from a sketch by C. B. Hulsart, 1835
This painting and Melville's *Moby Dick* vividly portray the hazards of whaling. Despite the dangers, it proved to be an important industry from colonial times to the end of the nineteenth century.

inspector, and then died in relative obscurity and poverty. Ironically, his brooding masterpiece about the mysterious white whale had to wait until the more jaded twentieth century for readers and for proper recognition.

Portrayers of the Past

A distinguished group of American historians was emerging at the same time that other writers were winning distinction. Energetic George Bancroft (1800–1891), who as secretary of the navy helped found the Naval Academy at Annapolis in 1845, has deservedly received the title "Father of American History." He published a spirited, superpatriotic history of the United States to 1789 in six (originally ten) volumes (1834–1876), a work that grew out of his vast researches in dusty archives in Europe and America.

Two other historians are read with greater pleasure and profit today. William H. Prescott (1796–1859), who accidentally lost the sight of an eye while in college, conserved his remaining weak vision and published classic accounts of the conquest of Mexico (1843) and Peru (1847). Francis Parkman (1823–1893), whose eyes were so defective that he wrote in darkness with the aid of a guiding machine, penned a brilliant series of volumes, beginning in 1851. In epic style he chronicled the struggle between France and England in colonial times for the mastery of North America.

Early American historians of prominence were almost without exception New Englanders, largely because the Boston area provided well-stocked libraries and a stimulating literary tradition. These writers numbered abolitionists among their relatives and friends and hence were disposed to view unsympathetically the slavery-cursed South. The writing of American history for generations to come was to suffer from an antisouthern bias perpetuated by this early "made in New England" interpretation.

Chronology

1700s	First Shaker communities formed
1794	Thomas Paine publishes *The Age of Reason*
1795	University of North Carolina founded
1800	Second Great Awakening begins
1819	Jefferson founds University of Virginia
1821	Cooper publishes *The Spy,* his first successful novel Emma Willard establishes Troy (New York) Female Seminary
1825	New Harmony commune established
1826	American Temperance Society founded
1828	Noah Webster publishes dictionary American Peace Society founded
1830	Joseph Smith founds Mormon church *Godey's Lady's* Book magazine first published
1830-1831	Finney conducts revivals in eastern cities
1835	Lyceum movement flourishes
1837	Oberlin College admits female students Mary Lyon establishes Mount Holyoke Seminary Emerson delivers "The American Scholar" address
1841	Brook Farm commune established
1843	Dorothea Dix petitions Massachusetts legislature on behalf of the insane
1846-1847	Mormon migration to Utah
1848	Seneca Falls Woman's Rights Convention held Oneida Community established
1850	Hawthorne publishes *The Scarlet Letter*
1851	Melville publishes *Moby Dick* Maine passes first law prohibiting liquor
1855	Whitman publishes *Leaves of Grass*

Reform: Who? What? How? and Why?

Early chronicles of the antebellum period universally lauded the era's reformers, portraying them as idealistic altruistic crusaders intent on improving American society.

After World War II, however, some historians began to detect selfish and even conservative motives underlying the apparent benevolence of the reformers. This view described the advocates of reform as anxious, upper-class men and women threatened by the ferment of life in antebellum America. The pursuit of reforms like temperance, asylums, prisons, and mandatory public education represented a means of asserting "social control." In this vein, one historian described a reform movement as "the anguished protest of an aggrieved class against a world they never made." In Michael Katz's treatment of early educational reform, proponents were community leaders who sought a school system that would ease the traumas of America's industrialization by inculcating business-oriented values and discipline in the working classes.

The wave of reform activity in the 1960s prompted a reevaluation of the reputations of the antebellum reformers. These more recent interpretations found much to admire in the authentic religious commitments of reformers and especially in the participation of women, who sought various social improvements as an extension of their function as protectors of the home and family.

The scholarly treatment of abolitionism is a telling example of how reformers and their campaigns have risen and fallen in the estimation of historians. To Northern historians writing in the late nineteenth century, abolitionists were courageous men and women so devoted to uprooting the evil of slavery that they were willing to dedicate their lives to a cause that often ostracized them from their communities. By the early twentieth century, however, an interpretation more favorable to the South prevailed, one that blamed the fanaticism of the abolitionists for the Civil War. But as the racial climate in the United States began to change by the mid-twentieth century, historians once again showed sympathy for the abolitionist struggle, and by the 1960s abolitionist men and women were revered as ideologically committed individuals dedicated not just to freeing the enslaved but to saving the moral soul of America.

Recently, scholars animated by the modern feminist movement have inspired a reconsideration of women's reform activity. It had long been known, of course, that women were active participants in charitable organizations. But not until Nancy Cott, Kathryn Sklar, Mary Ryan, and other historians began to look more closely at what Cott has called "the bonds of womanhood" did the links between women's domestic lives and their public benevolent behavior fully emerge.

Carroll Smith-Rosenberg showed in her study of the New York Female Moral Reform Society, for example, that members who set out at first to convert prostitutes to evangelical Protestantism and to close down the city's many brothels soon developed an ideology of female autonomy that rejected male dominance. When men behaved in immoral or illegal ways, women reformers claimed that they had the right—even the duty—to leave the confines of their homes and actively work to purify society. More recently, historians Nancy Hewitt and Lori Ginzberg have challenged the assumption that all women reformers embraced a single definition of female identity. Instead, they have emphasized the importance of class differences in shaping women's reform work, which led inevitably to tensions within female ranks. Giving more attention to the historical evolution of female reform ideology, Ginzberg has also detected a shift from an early focus on moral uplift to a more class-based appeal for social control.

Historians of the suffrage movement have emphasized another kind of exclusivity among women reformers, the boundaries of race. Ellen DuBois has shown that after a brief alliance with the abolitionist movement, many female suffrage reformers abandoned the cause of black liberation in an effort to achieve their own goal with less controversy. Whatever historians may conclude about the liberating or leashing character of early reform, it is clear by now that they have to contend with the ways in which class, gender, and race divided reformers, making the plural—*reform movements*—the more accurate depiction of the impulse to "improve" that pervaded American society in the early nineteenth century.

SUGGESTED READINGS

PRIMARY SOURCE DOCUMENTS

Alexis de Tocqueville, *Democracy in America** (1835, 1840), has stood for over a century and a half as the classic analysis of the American character. Joseph Smith, *The Pearl of Great Price** (1829), contains an account of the Mormon leader's religious visions, which capture the religious restiveness of the age. William H. McGuffey, *Fifth Eclectic Reader* (1879), was the most popular school text of the age. On the women's movement, see the "Seneca Falls Manifesto"* (1848), which laid the foundations of the feminist movement. Catharine Beecher and Harriet Beecher Stowe, *The American Woman's Home** (1869), discusses the role of women. Stowe's classic novel, *Uncle Tom's Cabin* (1852), offers an emotional appeal against slavery and a fascinating portrait of slavery, religion, and family life in antebellum America.

SECONDARY SOURCES

A magisterial synthesis is Daniel Boorstin, *The Americans: The National Experience* (1965). Satisfying detail is found in two Russell B. Nye books: *The Cultural Life of the New Nation, 1776–1830* (1960) and *Society and Culture in America, 1830–1860* (1974). Alexis de Tocqueville's classic account of life in the young Republic is brilliantly analyzed by James R. Schlieffer in *The Making of Tocqueville's "Democracy in America"* (1980). On the rise of the middle class, see Karen Halttunen, *Confidence Men and Painted Women* (1982); Richard L. Bushman, *The Refinement of America: Persons, Houses, Cities* (1992); and Stuart M. Blumin, *The Emergence of the Middle Class* (1989). Sydney E. Ahlstrom, *Religious History of the American People* (1972), is sweeping. On revivalism, see Nathan O. Hatch, *The Democratization of American Christianity* (1989), and Paul Johnson, *A Shopkeeper's Millennium: Society and Revivals in Rochester, New York, 1815–1837* (1978), which links revivals to economic change. Bushman describes the origins of Mormonism in *Joseph Smith and the Beginnings of Mormonism* (1984), and Leonard J. Arrington analyzes the most celebrated Mormon leader in *Brigham Young: American Moses* (1984). Ronald Walters, *American Reformers, 1815–1860* (1978), is the best

single volume on that subject. For particular subjects consult David Rothman, *The Discovery of the Asylum* (1971), Gerald Grob, *Mental Institutions in America: Social Policy to 1875* (1973), and David Gallagher, *Voice for the Mad: The Life of Dorothea Dix* (1995); on the development of hospitals, see Charles Rosenberg, *The Care of Strangers: The Rise of America's Hospital System* (1987); on juvenile delinquency, Joseph Hawes, *Children in Urban Society* (1971); and on prohibition, Ian Tyrrell, *Sobering Up: From Temperance to Prohibition in Antebellum America* (1979). On education see Lawrence A. Cremin, *American Education: The National Experience, 1789–1860* (1980); David Nasaw, *Schooled to Order: A Social History of Public Schooling in the United States* (1979); and Carl F. Kaestle and Maris A. Vinovskis, *Education and Social Change in Nineteenth-Century Massachusetts* (1980). An alternative interpretation of the rise of public education can be found in Michael Katz, *The Irony of Early School Reform* (1968), and in Samuel Bowles and Herbert Gintis, *Schooling in Capitalist America* (1976). Vinovskis offers a critique of these "revisionist" authors in *The Origins of Public High Schools: A Reexamination of the Beverly High School Controversy* (1985). Women's history for this period has blossomed in a number of studies, including Carroll Smith-Rosenberg, *Religion and the Rise of the American City* (1971); Nancy Cott, *The Bonds of Womanhood: "Woman's Sphere" in New England; 1780–1835* (1977); Ellen Carol DuBois, *Feminism and Suffrage* (1978); Ruth Bordin, *Women and Temperance* (1981); Estelle B. Freedman, *Their Sisters' Keepers: Women's Prison Reform in America, 1830–1930* (1981); Barbara Epstein, *The Politics of Domesticity* (1981); Nancy Hewitt, *Women's Activism and Social Change: Rochester, New York, 1822–1872* (1984); Lori D. Ginzberg, *Women and the Work of Benevolence* (1990); and, emphasizing intellectual and literary history, Ann Douglas, *The Feminization of American Culture* (1977). Family history is covered in Steven Mintz and Susan Kellogg, *Domestic Revolutions: A Social History of American Family Life* (1988); Jeanne Boydston, *Home and Work: Housework, Wages, and the Ideology of Labor in the Early Republic* (1990); Joseph F. Kett, *Rites of Passage: Adolescence in America* (1976); Lewis Perry, *Childhood, Marriage, and Reform: Henry Clarke Wright, 1797–1870* (1980); Carl N. Degler, *At Odds: Women and the Family in America from the Revolution to the Present* (1980); and Mary P. Ryan, *Cradle of the Middle Class: The Family in Oneida County, New York* (1981). See also Kathryn Kish Sklar, *Catharine Beecher: A Study in Domesticity* (1973). Suzanne Lebsock, *The Free*

*An asterisk indicates that the document, or an excerpt from it, can be found in Thomas A. Bailey and David M. Kennedy, eds., *The American Spirit: United States History as Seen by Contemporaries,* 9th ed. (Boston: Houghton Mifflin, 1998).

Women of Petersburg (1984), discusses these issues in a southern context. For the relationship of nature to the emerging American culture, see Henry Nash Smith, *Virgin Land: The American West as Symbol and Myth* (1950); Leo Marx, *The Machine in the Garden: Technology and the Pastoral Ideal in America* (1964); and Barbara Novak, *Nature and Culture: American Landscape and Painting, 1825–1875* (1980). Studies with a cultural focus include Joseph Ellis, *After the Revolution: Profiles of Early American Culture* (1979); Larzer Ziff, *Literary Democracy: The Declaration of Cultural Independence in America* (1981); and Anne Rose, *Voices of the Marketplace: American Thought and Culture, 1830–1860* (1995).

PART THREE

Testing the New Nation

T he Civil War of 1861–1865 was the awesome trial by fire of American nationhood, and of the American soul. All Americans knew, said Abraham Lincoln, that slavery "was somehow the cause of this war." The war tested, in Lincoln's ringing phrase at Gettysburg, whether any nation "dedicated to the proposition that all men are created equal . . . can long endure." How did this great and bloody conflict come about? And what were its results?

American slavery was by any measure a "peculiar institution." It was rooted in both racism and economic exploitation, and depended for its survival on brutal repression. Yet the American slave population was the only enslaved population in history that grew by means of its own biological reproduction—a fact that suggests to many histori-

ans that conditions under slavery in the United States were somehow less punitive than in other slave societies. Indeed, a distinctive and durable African-American culture managed to flourish under slavery, further suggesting that the slave regime provided some "space" for African-American cultural development. But however benignly it might be painted, slavery remained a cancer in the heart of American democracy, a moral outrage that mocked the nation's claim to be a model of social and political enlightenment. As time went on, more and more voices called more and more stridently for its abolition.

The nation lived uneasily with slavery from the outset. Thomas Jefferson was only one among many in the founding generation who felt acutely the conflict between the high principle of equality and the

Returning from the Cotton Fields in South Carolina
African-American slaves planted and picked virtually all the cotton that formed the foundation of the nineteenth-century southern economy. The white South ferociously defended its "peculiar institution" of slavery, which ended at last only in the fires of the Civil War.

ugly reality of slavery. The federal government in the early Republic took several steps to check the growth of slavery. It banned slavery in the Old Northwest in 1787, prohibited the further importation of slaves after 1808, and declared in the Missouri Compromise of 1820 that the vast western territories secured in the Louisiana Purchase were forever closed to slavery north of the state of Missouri. Antislavery sentiment even abounded in the South in the immediate post-Revolutionary years. But as time progressed, and especially after Eli Whitney's invention of the cotton gin in the 1790s, the southern planter class became increasingly dependent on slave labor to wring profits from the sprawling plantations that carpeted the South. As cotton cultivation spread westward, the South's stake in slavery grew deeper, and the abolitionist outcry grew louder.

The controversy over slavery significantly intensified following the war with Mexico in the 1840s. "Mexico will poison us," predicted the philosopher Ralph Waldo Emerson, and he proved distressingly prophetic. The lands acquired from Mexico—most of the present-day American Southwest, from Texas to California—reopened the question of extending slavery into the western territories. The decade and a half following the Mexican War—from 1846 to 1861—witnessed a series of ultimately ineffective efforts to come to

grips with that question, including the ill-starred Compromise of 1850, the conflict-breeding Kansas-Nebraska Act of 1854, and the Supreme Court's inflammatory decision in the Dred Scott case of 1857. Ultimately, the slavery question was settled by force of arms, in the Civil War itself.

The Civil War, as Lincoln observed, was assuredly about slavery. But as Lincoln also repeatedly insisted, the war was about the viability of the Union as well and about the strength of democracy itself. Could a democratic government, built on the principle of popular consent, rightfully deny some of its citizens the same right to independence that the American Revolutionaries had exercised in seceding from the British Empire in 1776? Southern rebels, calling the conflict "The War for Southern Independence," asked that question forcefully, but ultimately it, too, was answered not in the law courts or in the legislative halls but on the battlefield.

The war unarguably established the supremacy of the Union, and it ended slavery as well. But as the victorious Union set about the task of "reconstruction" after the war's end in 1865, a combination of weak northern will and residual southern power frustrated the goal of making the emancipated blacks full-fledged American citizens. The war in the end brought nothing but freedom—but over time, freedom proved a powerful tool indeed.

The First Virginia Regiment
These Virginia militiamen were photographed in 1859 while attending the trial of the abolitionist John Brown for treason against the State of Virginia. Two years later, their regiment formed part of the Confederate Army that struck for southern independence.

17

The South and the Slavery Controversy
1793–1860

*If you put a chain around the neck of a slave,
the other end fastens itself around your own.*

RALPH WALDO EMERSON, 1841

"Cotton Is King!"

When George Washington first took the presidential oath, the economic wheels of the South were creaking badly. The region was burdened with depressed prices, unmarketable products, overcropped lands, and the dead weight of an unprofitable slave system. Some southern statesmen, including Thomas Jefferson, were talking openly of freeing their slaves and confidently predicting that slavery would gradually die of economic anemia.

But the introduction of Eli Whitney's cotton gin in 1793 changed the scene. The newly popularized short-staple cotton, which brought a premium price, gradually became the dominant southern crop, eclipsing tobacco, rice, and sugar. Slavery was reinvigorated, with the slave being chained to the gin, and the planter being chained to the slave.

As time passed, the Cotton Kingdom developed into a huge agricultural factory, pouring out avalanches of the fluffy fiber. Quick profits drew planters to the virgin bottomlands of the gulf states. As long as the soil was still vigorous, the yield was bountiful and the rewards were high. Caught up in an economic spiral, the planters bought more slaves and land to grow more cotton, so as to buy still more slaves and land.

Northern shippers reaped a large part of the profits from the cotton trade. They would load bulging bales of cotton at southern ports, transport them to England, sell their fleecy cargo for pounds sterling, and buy needed manufactured goods for sale in the United States. To a large degree, the prosperity of both North and South rested on the bent backs of southern slaves.

Cotton accounted for half the value of all American exports after 1840. The South produced more than half of the entire world's supply of cotton—a

The Planter "Aristocracy"

Before the Civil War the South was in some respects not so much a democracy as an oligarchy—or a government by the few, in this case heavily influenced by a planter aristocracy. In 1850 only 1,733 families owned more than 100 slaves each, and this select group provided the cream of the political and social leadership of the section and nation. Here was the mint-julep South of the tall-columned and white-painted plantation mansion—the "big house," where dwelt the "cottonocracy."

The planter aristocrats, with their blooded horses and Chippendale chairs, enjoyed a lion's share of southern wealth. They could educate their children in the finest schools, often in the North or abroad. Their money provided the leisure for study, reflection, and statecraft, as was notably true of men like John C. Calhoun (a Yale graduate) and Jefferson Davis (a West Point graduate). They felt a keen sense of obligation to serve the public. It was no accident that Virginia and the other southern states produced a higher proportion of front-rank statesmen before 1860 than the "dollar-grubbing" North.

But even in its best light, dominance by a favored aristocracy was basically undemocratic. It widened the gap between rich and poor. It hampered tax-supported public education, because the rich planters could and did send their children to private institutions.

A favorite author of elite southerners was Sir Walter Scott, whose manors and castles, graced by

Cotton as King In this Northern Civil War cartoon, the Confederacy appears as a lighted bomb.

fact that held foreign nations in partial bondage. Britain was then the leading industrial power. Its most important single manufacture in the 1850s was cotton cloth, from which about one-fifth of its population, directly or indirectly, drew its livelihood. About 75 percent of this precious supply of fiber came from the white-carpeted acres of the South.

Southern leaders were fully aware that England was tied to them by cotton threads, and this dependence gave them a heady sense of power. In their eyes "Cotton was King," the gin was his throne, and the black bondsmen were his henchmen. If war should ever break out between North and South, northern warships would presumably cut off the outflow of cotton. Fiber-famished British factories would then close their gates, starving mobs would force the London government to break the blockade, and the South would triumph. Cotton was a powerful monarch indeed.

Thomas Jefferson (1743–1826) wrote in 1782,

"The whole commerce between master and slave is a perpetual exercise of the . . . most unremitting despotism on the one part, and degrading submissions on the other. . . . Indeed I tremble for my country when I reflect that God is just; that his justice cannot sleep forever."

Unlike Washington, Jefferson did not free his slaves in his will; he had fallen upon distressful times.

Harvesting Cotton
This Currier and Ives print shows slaves of both sexes harvesting cotton, which is then "ginned," baled, carted to the river-bank, and taken by paddle wheeler downriver to New Orleans.

brave Ivanhoes and fair Rowenas, helped them idealize a feudal society, even when many of their economic activities were undeniably capitalistic. Southern aristocrats, who sometimes staged jousting tournaments, strove to perpetuate a type of medievalism that had died out in Europe—or was rapidly dying out.* Mark Twain later accused Sir Walter Scott of having had a hand in starting the Civil War. The British novelist, Twain said, aroused the southerners to fight for a decaying social structure—"a sham civilization."

The plantation system also shaped the lives of southern women. The mistress of a great plantation commanded a sizable household staff of mostly female slaves. She gave daily orders to cooks, maids, seamstresses, laundresses, and body servants. Relationships between mistresses and slaves ranged from affectionate to atrocious. Some mistresses showed tender regard for their bondswomen, and some slave women took pride in their status as "members" of the household. But slavery strained even the bonds of womanhood. Virtually no slave-holding women believed in abolition, and relatively few protested when the husbands and children of their slaves were sold. One plantation mistress harbored a special affection for her slave Annica but noted in her diary that "I whipt Annica" for insolence.

---

*Oddly enough, by legislative enactment jousting became the official state sport of Maryland in 1962.

Slaves of the Slave System

Unhappily the moonlight-and-magnolia tradition concealed much that was worrisome, distasteful, and sordid. Plantation agriculture was wasteful, largely because King Cotton and his money-hungry subjects despoiled the good earth. Quick profits led to excessive cultivation, or "land butchery," which in turn caused a heavy leakage of population to the West and Northwest.

The economic structure of the South became increasingly monopolistic. As the land wore thin, many small farmers sold their holdings to more prosperous neighbors and went north or west. The big got bigger and the small smaller. When the Civil War finally erupted, a large percentage of southern farms had passed from the hands of the families that had originally cleared them.

Another cancer in the bosom of the South was the financial instability of the plantation system. The temptation to overspeculate in land and slaves caused many planters, including Andrew Jackson in his later years, to plunge in beyond their depth. Although the black slaves might in extreme cases be fed for as little as ten cents a day, there were other expenses. The slaves represented a heavy investment of capital, perhaps $1,200 each in the case of prime field hands; and they might deliberately injure themselves or run away. An entire slave quar-

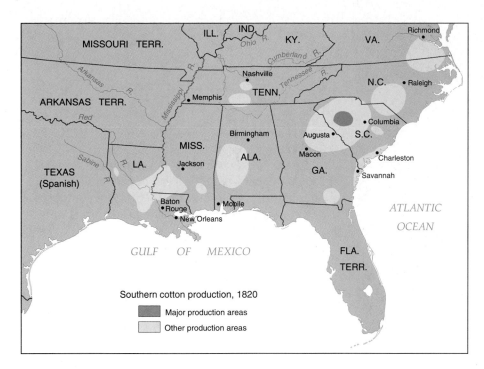

Southern Cotton
Production, 1820

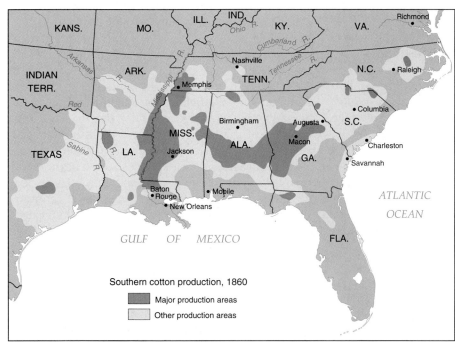

Southern Cotton
Production, 1860

ter might be wiped out by disease or even by lightning, as happened in one instance to twenty ill-fated blacks.

Dominance by King Cotton likewise led to a dangerous dependence on a one-crop economy, whose price level was at the mercy of world conditions. The whole system discouraged a healthy diversification of agriculture and particularly of manufacturing.

Southern planters resented watching the North grow fat at their expense. They were pained by the heavy outward flow of commissions and interest to northern middlemen, bankers, agents, and shippers.

Basil Hall (1788–1844), an Englishman, visited part of the cotton belt on a river steamer (1827–1828). Noting the preoccupation with cotton, he wrote,

"All day and almost all night long, the captain, pilot, crew, and passengers were talking of nothing else; and sometimes our ears were so wearied with the sound of cotton! cotton! cotton! that we gladly hailed a fresh inundation of company in hopes of some change—but alas! . . . 'What's cotton at?' was the first eager inquiry. 'Ten cents [a pound],' 'Oh, that will never do!'"

The White Majority

Only a handful of southern whites lived in Grecian-pillared mansions. Below those 1,733 families in 1850 who owned a hundred or more slaves were the less wealthy slaveowners. They totaled in 1850 some 345,000 families, representing about 1,725,000 white persons. Over two-thirds of these families—255,268 in all—owned fewer than ten slaves each. All told, only about one-fourth of white southerners owned slaves or belonged to a slaveowning family.

The smaller slaveowners did not own a majority of the slaves, but they made up a majority of the masters. These lesser masters were typically small farmers. With the striking exception that their household contained a slave or two, or perhaps an entire slave family, the style of their lives probably resembled that of small farmers in the North more than it did that of the southern planter aristocracy. They lived in modest farmhouses and sweated beside their bondsmen in the cotton fields, laboring callus for callus just as hard as their slaves.

Beneath the slaveowners on the population pyramid was the great body of whites who owned no slaves at all. By 1860 their numbers had swelled to 6,120,825—three-quarters of all southern whites. Shouldered off the richest bottomlands by the mighty planters, they scratched a simple living from the thinner soils of the backcountry and the mountain valleys. To them, the riches of the Cotton Kingdom were a distant dream, and they often sneered at the lordly pretensions of the cotton "snobocracy." These red-necked farmers participated in the market economy scarcely at all. As subsistence farmers, they raised corn and hogs, not cotton, and often lived isolated lives, punctuated periodically by extended socializing and sermonizing at religious camp meetings.

True souls of the South, especially by the 1850s, deplored the fact that when born they were wrapped in Yankee-made swaddling clothes and that they spent the rest of their lives in servitude to Yankee manufacturing. When they died, they were laid in coffins held together with Yankee nails and were buried in graves dug with Yankee shovels. The South furnished the corpse and the hole in the ground.

The Cotton Kingdom also repelled large-scale European immigration, which added so richly to the manpower and wealth of the North. In 1860 only 4.4 percent of the southern population were foreign-born, as compared with 18.7 percent for the North. German and Irish immigration to the South was generally discouraged by the competition of slave labor, by the high cost of fertile land, and by European ignorance of cotton growing. The diverting of non-English immigration to the North caused the white South to become the most Anglo-Saxon section of the nation.

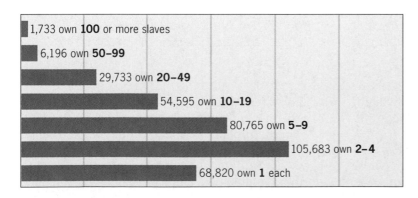

Slaveowning Families, 1850
More than half of all slaveholding families owned fewer than four slaves. In contrast, 2 percent of slaveowners owned more than fifty slaves each. A tiny slaveholding elite held a majority of slave property in the South. The great majority of white southerners owned no slaves at all.

Some of the least prosperous nonslaveholding whites were scorned even by slaves as "poor white trash." Known also as "hillbillies," "crackers," or "clay eaters," they were often described as listless, shiftless, and misshapen. Later investigations have revealed that many of them were not simply lazy, but sick, suffering from malnutrition and parasites, especially hookworm.

All these whites without slaves had no direct stake in the preservation of slavery, yet they were among the stoutest defenders of the slave system. Why? The answer is not far to seek.

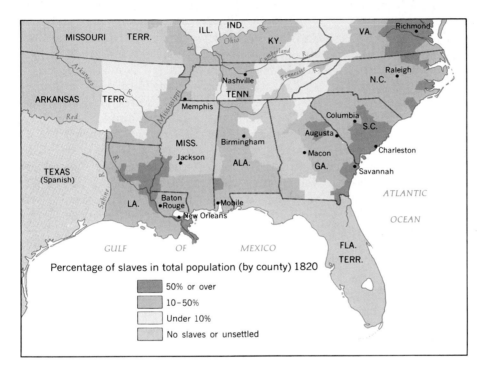

Distribution of Slaves, 1820
The philosopher Ralph Waldo Emerson, a New Englander, declared in 1856, "I do not see how a barbarous community and a civilized community can constitute a state. I think we must get rid of slavery or we must get rid of freedom."

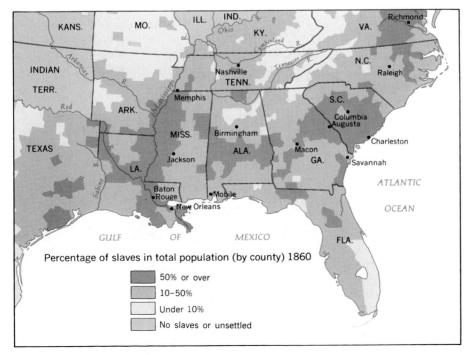

Distribution of Slaves, 1860

The carrot on the stick ever dangling before their eyes was the hope of buying a slave or two and of parlaying their paltry holdings into riches—all in accord with the "American dream" of upward social mobility. They also took fierce pride in their presumed racial superiority, which would be watered down if the slaves were freed. Many of the poorer whites were hardly better off economically than the slaves; some, indeed, were not so well off. But even the most wretched whites could take perverse comfort from the knowledge that they outranked someone in status: the still more wretched African-American slave. Thus did the logic of economics join with the illogic of racism in buttressing the slave system.

In a special category among white southerners were the mountain whites, more or less marooned in the valleys of the Appalachian range that stretched from western Virginia to northern Georgia and Alabama. Civilization had largely passed them by, and they still lived under spartan frontier conditions. They were a kind of living ancestry, for some of them retained Elizabethan speech forms and habits that had long since died out in England.

As independent small farmers, hundreds of miles distant from the heart of the cotton kingdom and rarely if ever in sight of a slave, these mountain whites had little in common with the whites of the flatlands. Many of them, including future president Andrew Johnson of Tennessee, hated both the haughty planters and their gangs of blacks. They looked upon the impending strife between North and South as "a rich man's war but a poor man's fight."

When the war came, the tough-fibered mountain whites constituted a vitally important peninsula of Unionism jutting down into the secessionist Southern sea. They ultimately played a significant role in crippling the Confederacy. Their attachment to the Union party of Abraham Lincoln was such that for generations after the Civil War, the only concentrated Republican strength in the solid South was to be found in the southern highlands.

Free Blacks: Slaves Without Masters

Precarious in the extreme was the standing of the South's free blacks, who numbered about 250,000 by 1860. In the upper South, the free black population traced its origins to a wavelet of emancipation inspired by the idealism of Revolutionary days. In the deeper South, many free blacks were mulattoes, usually the emancipated children of a white planter and his black mistress. Throughout the South were some free blacks who had purchased their freedom with earnings from labor after hours. Many free blacks owned property, especially in New Orleans, where a sizable mulatto community prospered. Some, such as William T. Johnson, the "barber of Natchez," even owned slaves. He was the master of fifteen bondsmen; his diary records that in June 1848 he flogged two slaves and a mule.

The free blacks in the South were a kind of "third race." These people were prohibited from working in certain occupations and forbidden from testifying against whites in court. They were always vulnerable to being highjacked back into slavery by unscrupulous slave traders. As free men and women, they were walking examples of what might be achieved by emancipation and hence were resented and detested by defenders of the slave system.

Free blacks were also unpopular in the North, where about another 250,000 of them lived. Several states forbade their entrance, most denied them the right to vote, and some barred blacks from public schools. In 1835 New Hampshire farmers hitched their oxen to a small schoolhouse that had dared to enroll fourteen black children and dragged it into a swamp. Northern blacks were especially hated by the pick-and-shovel Irish immigrants, with whom they competed for menial jobs. Much of the agitation in the North against the spread of slavery into the new territories in the 1840s and 1850s grew out of race prejudice, not humanitarianism.

> *"Arthur Lee, Freeman,"* petitioned the General Assembly of Virginia in 1835 for permission to remain in the state despite a law against the residency of free blacks. After asserting his upstanding moral character, he implored,
>
> "He therefore most respectfully and earnestly prays that you will pass a law permitting him on the score of long and meritorious service to remain in the State, together with his wife and four children, and not force him in his old age to seek a livelihood in a new Country."

Antiblack feeling was in fact frequently stronger in the North than in the South. The gifted and eloquent former slave Frederick Douglass, an abolitionist and self-educated orator of rare power, was several times mobbed and beaten by northern rowdies. It was sometimes observed that white southerners, who were often suckled and reared by black nurses, liked the black as an individual but despised the race. The white northerner, on the other hand, often professed to like the race but disliked individual blacks.

Plantation Slavery

In society's basement in the South of 1860 were nearly 4 million black human chattels. Their numbers had quadrupled since the dawn of the century, as the booming cotton economy created a seemingly unquenchable demand for slave labor. Legal importation of African slaves into America ended in 1808, when Congress outlawed slave imports. But the price of "black ivory" was so high in the years before the Civil War that uncounted thousands of blacks were smuggled into the South, despite the death penalty for slavers. Although several were captured, Southern juries repeatedly acquitted them. Only one slave trader was ever executed, N. P. Gordon, and this took place in New York in 1862, the second year of the Civil War. Yet the huge bulk of the increase in the slave population came not from imports but instead from natural reproduction—a fact that distinguished slavery in America from other New World societies and that implied much about the tenor of the slave regime and the conditions of family life under slavery.

Above all, the planters regarded the slaves as investments, into which they had sunk nearly $2 billion of their capital by 1860. Slaves were the primary form of wealth in the South, and as such they were cared for as any asset is cared for by a prudent capitalist. Accordingly, they were sometimes, though by no means always, spared dangerous work, like putting a roof on a house. If a neck was going to be broken, the master preferred it to be that of a wage-earning Irish laborer rather than that of a prime field hand, worth $1,800 by 1860 (a price that had quintupled since 1800). Tunnel blasting and swamp draining were often consigned to itinerant gangs of expendable Irishmen because those perilous tasks were "death on niggers and mules."

The Cruelty of Slavery (left) Held captive in a net, a slave sits on the Congo shore, waiting to be sold and shipped. (above) This device was riveted around a slave's neck. Its attached bells, like a cow bell, made it impossible for the wearer to hide from his or her owner.

A Slave Auction   Abraham Lincoln said in 1865, "Whenever I hear anyone arguing for slavery, I feel a strong impulse to see it tried on him personally."

Slavery was profitable for the great planters, though it hobbled the economic development of the region as a whole. The profits from the cotton boom sucked ever more slaves from the upper to the lower South, so that by 1860 the Deep South states of South Carolina, Florida, Mississippi, Alabama, and Louisiana each had a majority or near-majority of blacks and accounted for about half of all slaves in the South.

Breeding slaves in the way that cattle are bred was not openly encouraged. But thousands of blacks from the soil-exhausted slave states of the Old South, especially tobacco-depleted Virginia, were "sold down the river" to toil as field-gang laborers on the cotton frontier of the lower Mississippi Valley. Women who bore thirteen or fourteen babies were prized as "rattlin' good breeders," and some of these fecund females were promised their freedom when they had produced ten. White masters, all too frequently, would force their attentions on female slaves, fathering a sizable mulatto population, most of which remained enchained.

Slave auctions were brutal sights. The open selling of human flesh under the hammer, sometimes with cattle and horses, was among the most revolting aspects of slavery. On the auction block, families were separated with distressing frequency, usually for economic reasons such as bankruptcy or the division of "property" among heirs. The sundering of families in this fashion was perhaps slavery's greatest psychological horror. Abolitionists decried the practice, and Harriet Beecher Stowe seized on the emotional power of this theme by putting it at the heart of the plot of *Uncle Tom's Cabin*.

Life Under the Lash

White southerners often romanticized about the happy life of their singing, dancing, banjo-strumming, joyful "darkies." But how did the slaves actually live? There is no simple answer to this question. Conditions varied greatly from region to region, from large plantation to small farm, and from master to master. Everywhere, of course, slavery meant hard work, ignorance, and oppression. The slaves—both men and women—usually toiled from dawn to dusk in the fields, under the watchful eyes and ready whip-hand of a white overseer or black "driver." They had no civil or political rights, other than minimal protection from arbitrary murder or unusually cruel punishment. Some states offered further protections, such as banning the sale of a child under the age of ten away from his or her mother. But all such laws were difficult to enforce, since slaves were forbidden to testify in court or even to have their marriages legally recognized.

Floggings were common, for the whip was the substitute for the wage-incentive system and the most visible symbol of the planter's mastery. Strong-willed slaves were sometimes sent to "breakers," whose technique consisted mostly in lavish laying on of the lash. As an abolitionist song of the 1850s lamented,

> To-night the bond man, Lord
> Is bleeding in his chains;
> And loud the falling lash is heard
> On Carolina's plains!

But savage beatings made sullen laborers, and lash marks hurt resale values. There are, to be sure, sadistic monsters in any population, and the planter class contained its share. But the typical planter had too much of his own prosperity riding on the backs of his slaves to beat them bloody on a regular basis.

By 1860 most slaves were concentrated in the "black belt" of the Deep South that stretched from South Carolina and Georgia into the new southwest states of Alabama, Mississippi, and Louisiana. This was the region of the southern frontier, into which the explosively growing Cotton Kingdom had burst in a few short decades. As on all frontiers, life was often rough and raw, and in general the lot of the slave was harder here than in the more settled areas of the Old South.

Slave Nurse and Young White Master Southern whites would not allow slaves to own property or exercise civil rights, but, paradoxically, they often entrusted them with the raising of their own precious children. Many a slave "mammy" served as a surrogate mother for the offspring of the planter class.

A majority of blacks lived on larger plantations that harbored communities of twenty or more slaves. In some counties of the Deep South, especially along the lower Mississippi River, blacks accounted for more than 75 percent of the population. There the family life of slaves tended to be relatively stable, and a distinctive African-American slave culture developed. Forced separations of spouses, parents, and children were evidently more common on smaller plantations and in the Upper South. Slave marriage vows sometimes proclaimed, "Until death or *distance* do you part."

With impressive resilience, blacks managed to sustain family life in slavery, and most slaves were raised in stable two-parent households. Continuity of family identity across generations was evidenced in the widespread practice of naming children for grandparents or adopting the surname not of a current master, but of a forebear's master. African-Americans also displayed their African cultural roots when they avoided marriage between first cousins, in contrast to the frequent intermarriage of close relatives among the ingrown planter aristocracy.

African roots were also visible in the slaves' religious practices. Though heavily Christianized by the itinerant evangelists of the Second Great Awakening, blacks in slavery molded their own distinctive religious forms from a mixture of Christian and African elements. They emphasized those aspects of the Christian heritage that seemed most pertinent to their own situation—especially the captivity of the Israelites in Egypt. One of their most haunting spirituals implored,

> *Tell old Pharaoh*
> *"Let my people go."*

And another lamented,

> *Nobody knows de trouble I've had*
> *Nobody knows but Jesus*

African practices also persisted in the "responsorial" style of preaching, in which the congregation frequently punctuates the minister's remarks with assents and amens—an adaptation of the give-and-take between caller and dancers in the African ring-shout dance.

The Burdens of Bondage

Slavery was intolerably degrading to the victims. They were deprived of the dignity and sense of responsibility that come from independence and the right to make choices. They were denied an education, because reading brought ideas, and ideas brought discontent. Many states passed laws forbidding their instruction, and perhaps nine-tenths of adult slaves at the beginning of the Civil War were totally illiterate. For all slaves—indeed for virtually all blacks, slave or free—the "American dream" of bettering one's lot through study and hard work was a cruel and empty mockery.

Not surprisingly, victims of the "peculiar institution" devised countless ways to throw sand in its gears. When workers are not voluntarily hired and adequately compensated, they can hardly be expected to work with alacrity. Accordingly, slaves often slowed the pace of their labor to the barest minimum that would spare them the lash, thus fostering the myth of black "laziness" in the minds of whites. They filched food from the "big house" and pilfered other goods that had been produced or

Plantation Kitchen, by Fanny Palmer, c. 1845 This painting by an English-born illustrator idealizes the opulence and graciousness of plantation life, but accurately puts a black slave—the foundation of the plantation economy—at the focal point of the picture.

purchased by their labor. They sabotaged expensive equipment, stopping the work routine altogether until repairs were accomplished. Occasionally, they even poisoned their master's food.

The slaves also universally pined for freedom. Many took to their heels as runaways, frequently in search of a separated family member. A black girl, asked if her mother was dead, replied, "Yassah, massah, she is daid, but she's free." Others rebelled, though never successfully. In 1800 an armed insurrection led by a slave named Gabriel in Richmond, Virginia, was foiled by informers, and its leaders were hanged. Denmark Vesey, a free black, led another ill-fated rebellion in Charleston in 1822. Also betrayed by informers, Vesey and more than thirty followers were publicly strung from the gallows. In 1831 the semiliterate Nat Turner, a visionary black preacher, led an uprising that slaughtered about sixty Virginians, mostly women and children. Reprisals were swift and bloody.

The dark taint of slavery also left its mark on the whites. It fostered the brutality of the whip, the bloodhound, and the branding iron. White southerners increasingly lived in a state of imagined siege, surrounded by potentially rebellious blacks inflamed by abolitionist propaganda from the North. Their fears bolstered an intoxicating theory of biological racial superiority and turned the South into a reactionary backwater in an era of progress—one of the last bastions of slavery in the Western world. The defenders of slavery were forced to degrade themselves, along with their victims. As Booker T. Washington, a distinguished black leader

and former slave, later observed, whites could not hold blacks in a ditch without getting down there with them.

Early Abolitionism

The inhumanity of the "peculiar institution" gradually caused antislavery societies to sprout forth. Abolitionist sentiment first stirred at the time of the Revolution, especially among Quakers. Because of the widespread loathing of blacks, some of the earliest abolitionist efforts focused on transporting the blacks bodily back to Africa. The American Colonization Society was founded for this purpose in 1817, and in 1822 the Republic of Liberia, on the fever-stricken West African coast, was established for former slaves. Its capital, Monrovia, was named after President Monroe. Some 15,000 freed blacks were transported there over the next four decades. But most blacks had no wish to be transplanted into a strange civilization after having become partially Americanized. By 1860 virtually all southern slaves were no longer Africans, but native-born African-Americans, with their own distinctive history and culture. Yet the colonization idea appealed to some antislaveryites, including Abraham Lincoln, until the time of the Civil War.

In the 1830s the abolitionist movement took on new energy and momentum, mounting to the proportions of a crusade. American abolitionists took heart in 1833 when their British counterparts

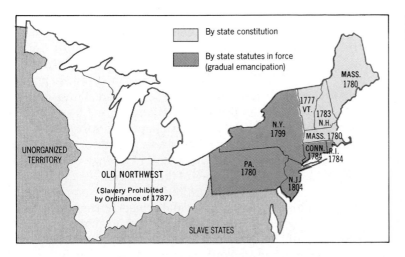

Early Emancipation in the North

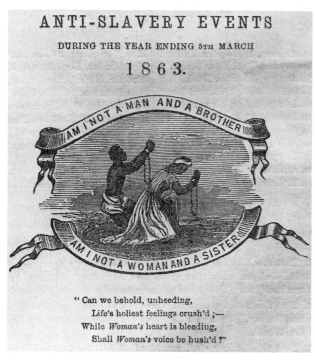

ANTI-SLAVERY EVENTS

DURING THE YEAR ENDING 5TH MARCH

1863.

AM I NOT A MAN AND A BROTHER

AM I NOT A WOMAN AND A SISTER

" Can we behold, unheeding,
Life's holiest feelings crush'd ;—
While *Woman's* heart is bleeding,
Shall *Woman's* voice be hush'd ?"

"Am I Not a Man and a Brother? Am I Not a Woman and a Sister?"   A popular appeal

William Lloyd Garrison (1805–1879)   The most conspicuous and most vilified of the abolitionists, Garrison was a nonresistant pacifist and a poor organizer. He favored northern secession from the South and antagonized both sections with his intemperate language.

unchained the slaves in the West Indies. Most important, the religious spirit of the Second Great Awakening now inflamed the hearts of many abolitionists against the sin of slavery. Prominent among them was lanky, tousle-haired Theodore Dwight Weld, who had been evangelized by Charles Grandison Finney in New York's Burned-Over District in the 1820s. Self-educated and simple in manner and speech, Weld appealed with special power and directness to his rural audiences of untutored farmers.

Spiritually inspired by Finney, Weld was materially aided by two wealthy and devout New York merchants, the brothers Arthur and Lewis Tappan. In 1832 they paid his way to Lane Theological Seminary in Cincinnati, Ohio, which was presided over by the formidable Lyman Beecher, father of a remarkable brood, including novelist Harriet Beecher Stowe, reformer Catharine Beecher, and preacher-abolitionist Henry Ward Beecher. Expelled along with several other students in 1834 for organizing an eighteen-day debate on slavery, Weld and his fellow "Lane Rebels"—full of the energy and idealism of youth—fanned out across the Old Northwest preaching the antislavery gospel. Humorless and deadly earnest, Weld also assembled a potent propaganda pamphlet, *American Slavery As It Is*

(1839). Its compelling arguments made it among the most effective abolitionist tracts and greatly influenced Harriet Beecher Stowe's *Uncle Tom's Cabin*.

Radical Abolitionism

On New Year's Day, 1831, a shattering abolitionist blast came from the bugle of William Lloyd Garrison, a mild-looking reformer of twenty-six. The emotionally high-strung son of a drunken father and a spiritual child of the Second Great Awakening, Garrison published in Boston the first issue of his militantly antislavery newspaper *The Liberator*. With this mighty paper broadside, Garrison triggered a thirty-year war of words and in a sense fired one of the opening barrages of the Civil War.

Stern and uncompromising, Garrison nailed his colors to the masthead of his weekly. He proclaimed in strident tones that under no circumstances would he tolerate the poisonous weed of slavery but would stamp it out at once, root and branch:

Sojourner Truth   Also known simply as "Isabella," she held audiences spellbound with her deep, resonant voice and the religious passion with which she condemned the sin of slavery. This photo was taken about 1870.

Frederick Douglass (c. 1817–1895)   Born a slave in Maryland, Frederick Douglass escaped to the North and became the most prominent of the black abolitionists. Gifted as an orator, writer, and editor, he continued to battle for the civil rights of his people after emancipation. Near the end of a distinguished career, he served as U.S. minister to Haiti.

> I will be as harsh as truth and as uncompromising as justice. . . . I am in earnest—I will not equivocate—I will not excuse—I will not retreat a single inch—and I WILL BE HEARD!

Other dedicated abolitionists rallied to Garrison's standard, and in 1833 they founded the American Anti-Slavery Society. Prominent among them was Wendell Phillips, a Boston patrician known as "abolition's golden trumpet." A man of strict principle, he would eat no cane sugar and wear no cotton cloth, since both were produced by southern slaves.

Black abolitionists distinguished themselves as living monuments to the cause of African-American freedom. Their ranks included David Walker, whose incendiary *Appeal to the Colored Citizens of the World* (1829) advocated a bloody end to white supremacy. Also noteworthy were Sojourner Truth, a freed black woman in New York who fought tirelessly for black emancipation and women's rights, and Martin Delaney, one of the few black leaders to

take seriously the notion of mass recolonization of Africa. In 1859 he visited West Africa's Niger Valley seeking a suitable site for relocation.

The greatest of the black abolitionists was Frederick Douglass. Escaping from bondage in 1838 at

> *Frederick Douglass (1817?–1895), the remarkable ex-slave, told of Mr. Covey, a white owner who bought a single female slave "as a breeder." She gave birth to twins at the end of the year.*
>
> "At this addition to the human stock Covey and his wife were ecstatic with joy. No one dreamed of reproaching the woman or finding fault with the hired man, Bill Smith, the father of the children, for Mr. Covey himself had locked the two up together every night, thus inviting the result."

After hearing Frederick Douglass speak in Bristol, England, in 1846, Mary A. Estlin wrote to an American abolitionist:

"[T]here is but one opinion of him. Wherever he goes he arouses sympathy in your cause and love for himself. . . . Our expectations were highly roused by his narrative, his printed speeches, and the eulogisms of the friends with whom he has been staying: but he far exceeds the picture we had formed both in outward graces, intellectual power and culture, and eloquence."*

the age of twenty-one, he was "discovered" by the abolitionists in 1841 when he gave a stunning impromptu speech at an antislavery meeting in Massachusetts. Thereafter he lectured widely for the cause, despite frequent beatings and threats against his life. In 1845 he published his classic autobiography, *Narrative of the Life of Frederick Douglass.* It depicted his remarkable origins as the son of a black slave woman and a white father, his struggle to learn to read and write, and his eventual escape to the North.

Douglass was as flexibly practical as Garrison was stubbornly principled. Garrison often appeared to be more interested in his own righteousness than in the substance of the slavery evil itself. He repeatedly demanded that the "virtuous" North secede from the "wicked" South. Yet he did not explain how the creation of an independent slave republic would bring an end to the "damning crime" of slavery. Renouncing politics, on the Fourth of July, 1854, he publicly burned a copy of the Constitution as "a covenant with death and an agreement with hell" (a phrase he borrowed from a Shaker condemnation of marriage). Critics, including some of his former supporters, charged that Garrison was cruelly probing the moral wound in America's underbelly but offering no acceptable balm to ease the pain.

Douglass, on the other hand, along with other abolitionists, increasingly looked to politics to end the blight of slavery. These political abolitionists backed the Liberty party in 1840, the Free Soil party

*From Clare Taylor, ed., *British and American Abolitionists, An Episode in Transatlantic Understanding* (Edinburgh University Press, 1974), p. 282.

in 1848, and eventually the Republican party in the 1850s. In the end, most abolitionists, including even the pacifistic Garrison himself, followed out the logic of their beliefs and supported a frightfully costly fratricidal war as the price of emancipation.

High-minded and courageous, the abolitionists were men and women of goodwill and various colors who faced the cruel choice that people in many ages have had thrust upon them: when is evil so enormous that it must be denounced, even at the risk of precipitating bloodshed and butchery?

The South Lashes Back

Antislavery sentiment was not unknown in the South, and in the 1820s antislavery societies were more numerous south of Mason and Dixon's line* than north of it. But after about 1830 the voice of white southern abolitionism was silenced. In a last gasp of southern questioning of slavery, the Virginia legislature debated and eventually defeated various emancipation proposals in 1831–1832. That debate marked a turning point. Thereafter all the slave states tightened their slave codes and moved to prohibit emancipation of any kind, voluntary or compensated. Nat Turner's rebellion in 1831 sent a wave of hysteria sweeping over the snowy cotton fields, and planters in growing numbers slept with pistols by their pillows. Although Garrison had no demonstrable connection with the Turner conspiracy, his *Liberator* appeared at about the same time, and he was bitterly condemned as a terrorist and an inciter of murder. The state of Georgia offered $5,000 for his arrest and conviction.

The nullification crisis of 1832 further implanted haunting fears in white southern minds, conjuring up nightmares of black incendiaries and abolitionist devils. Jailings, whippings, and lynchings now greeted rational efforts to discuss the slavery problem in the South.

Proslavery whites responded by launching a massive defense of slavery as a positive good. In doing so they forgot their own section's previous doubts about the morality of the "peculiar institution." Slavery, they claimed, was supported by the authority of the Bible and the wisdom of Aristotle. It was good for the Africans, who were lifted from the

*Originally the southern boundary of colonial Pennsylvania.

barbarism of the jungle and clothed with the blessings of Christian civilization. Slavemasters did indeed encourage religion in the slave quarters. A catechism for blacks contained such passages as,

Q. *Who gave you a master and a mistress?*
A. *God gave them to me.*
Q. *Who says that you must obey them?*
A. *God says that I must.*

White apologists also pointed out that master-slave relationships really resembled those of a family. On many plantations, especially those of the Old South of Virginia and Maryland, this argument had a certain plausibility. A slave's tombstone bore this touching inscription:

JOHN:
A faithful servant:
 and true friend:
Kindly, and considerate:
Loyal, and affectionate:
The family he served
Honours him in death:
But, in life they gave him love:
For he was one of them

Southern whites were quick to contrast the "happy" lot of their "servants" with that of the overworked northern wage slaves, including sweated women and stunted children. The blacks mostly toiled in the fresh air and sunlight, not in dark and stuffy factories. They did not have to worry about slack times or unemployment, as did the "hired hands" of the North. Provided with a jail-like form of Social Security, they were cared for in sickness and old age, unlike northern workers, who were set adrift when they had outlived their usefulness.

These curious proslavery arguments only widened the chasm between a backward-looking South and a forward-looking North—and indeed much of the rest of the Western world. The southerners reacted defensively to the pressure of their own fears and bristled before the merciless nagging of the northern abolitionists. Increasingly the white South turned in upon itself and grew hotly intolerant of any embarrassing questions about the status of slavery.

Regrettably, also, the controversy over free people endangered free speech in the entire country. Piles of petitions poured in upon Congress from the antislavery reformers; and in 1836 sensitive southerners drove through the House the so-called gag resolution. It required all such antislavery appeals to be tabled without debate. This attack on the right of petition aroused the sleeping lion in the aged ex-president, Representative John Quincy Adams, and he waged a successful eight-year fight for its repeal.

Southern whites likewise resented the flooding of their mails with incendiary abolitionist literature. Even if blacks could not read, they could interpret the inflammatory drawings, such as those that showed masters knocking out slaves' teeth with clubs. In 1835 a mob in Charleston, South Carolina, looted the post office and burned a pile of abolitionist propaganda. Capitulating to southern pressures, the Washington government in 1835 ordered southern postmasters to destroy abolitionist material and

A Two-Way Proslavery Cartoon
Published in New York, the cartoon shows a chilled and rejected free black in the North (left) disconsolately passing a grogshop, while (right) a happy southern slave enjoys life with a fishing rod in the company of a white youth.

called on southern state officials to arrest federal postmasters who did not comply. Such was "freedom of the press" as guaranteed by the Constitution.

The Abolitionist Impact in the North

Abolitionists—especially the extreme Garrisonians—were for a long time unpopular in many parts of the North. Northerners had been brought up to revere the Constitution and to regard the clauses on slavery as a lasting bargain. The ideal of Union, hammered home by the thundering eloquence of Daniel Webster and others, had taken deep root; and Garrison's wild talk of secession grated harshly on northern ears.

The North also had a heavy economic stake in Dixieland. By the late 1850s, the southern planters owed northern bankers and other creditors about $300 million, and much of this immense sum would be lost—as, in fact, it later was—should the Union dissolve. New England textile mills were fed with cotton raised by the slaves, and a disrupted labor system might cut off this vital supply and bring unemployment. The Union during these critical years was partly bound together with cotton threads, tied by lords of the loom in collaboration with the so-called lords of the lash. It was not surprising that strong hostility developed in the North against the boat-rocking tactics of the radical antislaveryites.

Repeated tongue-lashings by the extreme abolitionists provoked many mob outbursts in the North, some led by respectable gentlemen. A gang of young toughs broke into Lewis Tappan's New York house in 1834 and demolished its interior, while a crowd in the street cheered. In 1835 Garrison, with a rope tied around him, was dragged through the streets of Boston by the so-called Broadcloth Mob but escaped almost miraculously. Reverend Elijah P. Lovejoy, of Alton, Illinois, not content to assail slavery, impugned the chastity of Catholic women. His printing press was destroyed four times, and in 1837 he was killed by a mob, and became "the martyr abolitionist." So unpopular were the antislavery zealots that ambitious politicians, like Lincoln, usually avoided the taint of Garrisonian abolition like the plague.

Yet by the 1850s the abolitionist outcry had made a deep dent in the northern mind. Many citizens had come to see the South as the land of the unfree and the home of a hateful institution. Few northerners were prepared to abolish slavery out-

right, but a growing number, including Lincoln, opposed extending it to the western territories. People of this stamp, commonly called "free-soilers," swelled their ranks as the Civil War approached.

Chronology

1793	Whitney's cotton gin transforms southern economy
1800	Gabriel slave rebellion in Virginia
1808	Congress outlaws slave trade
1817	American Colonization Society formed
1820	Missouri Compromise
1822	Vesey slave rebellion in Charleston Republic of Liberia established in Africa
1829	Walker publishes *Appeal to the Colored Citizens of the World*
1831	Nat Turner slave rebellion in Virginia Garrison begins publishing *The Liberator*
1831-1832	Virginia legislature debates slavery and emancipation
1833	British abolish slavery in the West Indies American Anti-Slavery Society founded
1834	Abolitionist students expelled from Lane Theological Seminary
1835	U.S. Post Office orders destruction of abolitionist mail "Broadcloth Mob" attacks Garrison
1836	House of Representatives passes "Gag Resolution"
1837	Mob kills abolitionist Lovejoy in Alton, Illinois
1839	Weld publishes *American Slavery As It Is*
1840	Liberty party organized
1845	Douglass publishes *Narrative of the Life of Frederick Douglass*
1848	Free Soil party organized

What Was the True Nature of Slavery?

By the early twentieth century, the predictable accounts of slavery written by partisans of the North or South had receded in favor of a romantic vision of the Old South conveyed through popular literature, myth, and, increasingly, scholarship. That vision was persuasively validated by the publication of Ulrich Bonnell Phillips's landmark study, *American Negro Slavery* (1918). Phillips made three key arguments. First, he claimed that slavery was a dying economic institution, unprofitable to the slaveowner and an obstacle to the economic development of the South as a whole. Second, he contended that slavery was a rather benign institution and that the planters, contrary to abolitionist charges of ruthless exploitation, treated their chattels with kindly paternalism. Third, he reflected the dominant racial attitudes of his time in his belief that blacks were inferior and submissive by nature, and did not abhor the institution that enslaved them.

For nearly a century, historians have debated these assertions, sometimes heatedly. More sophisticated economic analysis has refuted Phillips's claim that slavery would have withered away without a war. Economic historians have demonstrated that slavery was a viable, profitable, expanding economic system and that slaves constituted a worthwhile investment for their owners. The price of a prime field hand rose dramatically, even in the 1850s.

No such definitive conclusion has yet been reached in the disputes over slave treatment. Beginning in the late 1950s, historians came increasingly to emphasize the harshness of the slave system. One study, Stanley Elkin's *Slavery* (1959), went so far as to compare the "peculiar institu-tion" to the Nazi concentration camps of World War II. Both were "total institutions," Elkins contended, which "infantilized" their victims.

More recently, scholars such as Eugene Genovese have moved beyond debating whether slavery was kind or cruel. Without diminishing the deprivations and pains of slavery, Genovese has conceded that slavery embraced a strange form of paternalism, a system that reflected not the benevolence of southern slaveholders but their need to control and coax work out of their reluctant and often recalcitrant "investments." Furthermore, within this paternalist system, black slaves were able to make reciprocal demands of their white owners, and to protect a "cultural space" of their own in which family and religion particularly could flourish. The crowning paradox of slaveholder paternalism was that in treating their property more humanely, slave owners implicitly recognized the humanity of their slaves and thereby subverted the racist underpinnings upon which their slave society existed.

The revised conceptions of the master-slave relationship also spilled over into the debate about slave personality. Elkins accepted Phillips's portrait of the slave as a child-like "Sambo," but saw it as a consequence of slavery rather than a congenital attribute of the African-Americans. Kenneth Stampp, rejecting the Sambo stereotype, stressed the frequency and variety of slave resistance, both mild and militant. A third view, imaginatively documented in the work of Lawrence Levine, argues that the Sambo character was an act, an image that slaves used to confound their masters without incurring punishment. Levine's *Black Culture and Black Consciousness* (1977) shares with books by John Blassingame and Herbert Gutman an emphasis on the tenacity with which slaves maintained their own culture and kin relations, despite the hardships of bondage. Most recently, historians have attempted to avoid the polarity of repression versus autonomy. They assert the debasing oppression of slavery, while also acknowledging slaves' ability to resist the dehumanizing effects of enslavement. The challenge before historians today is to capture the vibrancy of slave culture and its legacy for African-American society after emancipation, without diminishing the brutality of life under the southern slave regime.

A new sensitivity to gender, spurred by the growing field of women's history, has also expanded the horizons of slavery studies. Historians such as Elizabeth Fox-Genovese, Jacqueline Jones, and Catherine Clinton have focused on the ways in which slavery differed for men and women, both slaves and slaveholders. Enslaved black women, for example, had the unique task of negotiating an identity out of their dual responsibilities as plantation laborer, even sometimes caretaker of white women and children, and anchor of the black family. By tracing the interconnectedness of race and gender in the American South, these historians have also shown how slavery shaped conceptions of masculinity and femininity within southern society, further distinguishing its culture from that of the North.

SUGGESTED READINGS

PRIMARY SOURCE DOCUMENTS

Two influential abolitionist documents are Theodore Dwight Weld, *American Slavery As It Is** (1839), and the inaugural editorial of William Lloyd Garrison, *The Liberator** (1831). Roy P. Basler, ed., *The Collected Works of Abraham Lincoln* (1933), contains the Great Emancipator's assessment of abolitionism in 1854. For southern perspectives, see James Henry Hammond's famous "Cotton Is King" speech, *Congressional Globe*, 36 Cong., 1 sess. p. 961 (March 3, 1858).* Famous first-hand accounts of slavery include Frederick Douglass, *Narrative of the Life of Frederick Douglass* (1845), and Solomon Northrup, *Twelve Years a Slave* (1853). John W. Blassingame, ed., *Slave Testimony* (1977), offers a rich collection of slave narratives.

SECONDARY SOURCES

A good introduction to southern history is Clement Eaton, *A History of the Old South: The Emergence of a Reluctant Nation* (1975). Wilbur J. Cash, *The Mind of the South* (1941), is an engagingly written classic. Always incisive is C. Vann Woodward, *The Burden of Southern History* (1960). On white politics and society, see Bruce Collins, *White Society in the Antebellum South* (1985); Bertram Wyatt-Brown, *Honor and Violence in the Old South* (1986); and Drew Gilpin Faust's perceptive biography, *James Henry Hammond and the Old South: A Design for Mastery* (1982). Nonslaveholding whites are documented in Frank L. Owsley, *Plain Folk of the Old South*

(1949), and Stephanie McCurry, *Masters of Small Worlds: Yeoman Households, Gender Relations, and the Political Culture of the Antebellum South Carolina Low Country* (1995). Important interpretations of the "peculiar institution" include Eugene Genovese, *The Political Economy of Slavery* (1965); Barbara Jeanne Fields, *Slavery and Freedom on the Middle Ground: Maryland During the Nineteenth Century* (1985); Gavin Wright, *The Political Economy of the Cotton South* (1978); and Eugene Genovese and Elizabeth Fox-Genovese, *Fruits of Merchant Capital* (1983). James Oakes has questioned many of Genovese's interpretations in *The Ruling Race: A History of American Slaveholders* (1982) and *Slavery and Freedom: An Interpretation of the Old South* (1990). Catherine Clinton examines *The Plantation Mistress* (1982); Elizabeth Fox-Genovese discusses southern women more generally in *Within the Plantation Household: Black and White Women of the Old South* (1988). See also Deborah Gray White, *Ar'n't I a Woman? Female Slaves in the Plantation South* (1985); Melton Alonza McLaurin, *Celia, a Slave* (1991); and Brenda E. Stevenson, *Life in Black and White: Family and Community in the Slave South* (1996). The literature on slavery and African-Americans is enormous; the best place to start is John Hope Franklin, *From Slavery to Freedom* (5th ed., 1980); see also Peter J. Parish, *Slavery: History and Historians* (1989). The modern debate on slavery began with Ulrich B. Phillips's classic *American Negro Slavery* (1918); a darker view of the same subject is found in Kenneth M. Stampp, *The Peculiar Institution* (1956). Consult also Stanley Elkins's controversial essay, *Slavery* (2d ed., 1968), which also has interesting observations on the abolitionists. More recently, considerable furor has surrounded the publication of Robert Fogel and Stanley Engerman, *Time on the Cross: The Economics of American Slavery* (2 vols., 1974). For contrasting views and

---

*An asterisk indicates that the document, or an excerpt from it, can be found in Thomas A. Bailey and David M. Kennedy, eds., *The American Spirit: United States History as Seen by Contemporaries*, 9th ed. (Boston: Houghton Mifflin, 1998).

rebuttals, see John W. Blassingame, *The Slave Community* (rev. ed., 1979); Herbert Gutman, *The Black Family in Slavery and Freedom, 1750–1925* (1976); Paul David, *Reckoning with Slavery* (1976); Eugene Genovese, *Roll, Jordan, Roll* (1974); Lawrence Levine, *Black Culture and Black Consciousness: Afro-American Folk Thought from Slavery to Freedom* (1977); and Albert J. Raboteau, *Slave Religion: The "Invisible Institution" in the Antebellum South* (1978); and Sterling Stuckey, *Slave Culture: Nationalist Theory and the Foundations of Black America* (1987). Vincent Harding, *There Is a River: The Black Struggle for Freedom in America* (1981), discusses slave resistance and revolt, a subject handled rather differently in Peter Kolchin's fascinating comparative study, *Unfree Labor: American Slavery and Russian Serfdom* (1987). A study that compares the development of race relations in South Africa and the United States is George M. Frederickson, *White Supremacy: A Comparative Study in American and South African History* (1981). Robert Starobin examines *Industrial Slavery in the Old South* (1970), and Ira Berlin tells the story of free blacks in *Slaves Without Masters* (1975), which should be supplemented by Michael P. Johnson and James L. Roark, *Black Masters: A Free Family of Color in the Old South* (1984). See also Leon Litwack, *North of Slavery* (1961), for the situation of blacks outside the South. Valuable community studies include Charles Joyner, *Down by the Riverside: A South Carolina Slave Community* (1984); Suzanne Lebsock, *The Free Women of Petersburg: Status and Culture in a Southern Town, 1784–1860* (1984); and Orville Vernon Burton, *In My Father's House Are Many Mansions: Family and Community in Edgefield, South Carolina* (1985). David B. Davis provides indispensable background to the history of abolitionism in *The Problem of Slavery in Western Culture* (1966) and *The Problem of Slavery in the Age of Revolution* (1975), as does Thomas Bender, ed., in *The Antislavery Debate* (1992). The best brief history of the abolitionists is James B. Stewart, *Holy Warriors* (1976). Ronald E. Walters emphasizes the constraints that American culture placed on the abolitionists in *The Antislavery Appeal: American Abolitionism After 1830* (1976). James B. Stewart focuses on *Wendell Phillips: Liberty's Hero* (1987). Aileen Kraditor is favorably disposed toward Garrison in *Means and Ends in American Abolitionism: Garrison and His Critics* (1967). For provocative new approaches, see Lewis Perry and Michael Fellman, eds., *Antislavery Reconsidered: New Perspectives on the Abolitionists* (1979). Benjamin Quarles examines *Black Abolitionists* (1969), as do Jane H. Pease and William H. Pease in *They Who Would Be Free: Blacks Search for Freedom, 1830–1861* (1974), and Shirley J. Yee, *Black Women Abolitionists: A Study in Activism, 1828–1860* (1992). Sojourner Truth is the subject of Nell Irvin Painter, *Sojourner Truth: A Life, A Symbol* (1996). The most prominent black abolitionist is portrayed in Waldo E. Martin, Jr., *The Mind of Frederick Douglass* (1984), and William S. McFeely, *Frederick Douglass* (1990).

18

Manifest Destiny and Its Legacy

1841–1848

Our manifest destiny [is] to overspread the continent allotted by Providence for the free development of our yearly multiplying millions.

JOHN L. O'SULLIVAN, 1845*

The Accession of "Tyler Too"

A horde of hard-ciderites descended upon Washington early in 1841, clamoring for the spoils of office. Newly elected President Harrison, bewildered by the uproar, was almost hounded to death by Whig spoilsmen.

The real leaders of the Whig party regarded "Old Tippecanoe" as little more than an impressive figurehead. Daniel Webster, as secretary of state, and Henry Clay, the uncrowned king of the Whigs and their ablest spokesman in the Senate, would grasp the helm. The aging general was finally forced to rebuke the overzealous Clay and pointedly remind

him that he, William Henry Harrison, was president of the United States.

Unluckily for Clay and Webster, their schemes soon hit a fatal snag. Before the new term had fairly started, Harrison contracted pneumonia. Wearied by official functions and plagued by office seekers, the enfeebled old warrior died after only four weeks in the White House—by far the shortest administration in American history, following by far the longest inaugural address.

The "Tyler too" part of the Whig ticket, hitherto only a rhyme, now claimed the spotlight. What manner of man did the nation now find in the presidential chair? Six feet (1.83 meters) tall, slender, blue-eyed, and fair-haired, with classical features and a high forehead, John Tyler was a Virginia gentleman of the old school—gracious and kindly, yet stubbornly attached to principle. He had earlier resigned from the Senate, quite unnecessarily,

---

*Earliest known use of the term *manifest destiny,* sometimes called "manifest desire."

rather than accept distasteful instructions from the Virginia legislature. Still a lone wolf, he had forsaken the Jacksonian Democratic fold for that of the Whigs, largely because he could not stomach the dictatorial tactics of Jackson.

Tyler's enemies accused him of being a Democrat in Whig clothing, but this charge was only partially true. The Whig party, like the Democratic party, was something of a catchall, and the accidental president belonged to the minority wing, which embraced a number of Jeffersonian states' righters. Tyler had in fact been put on the ticket partly to attract the vote of this fringe group, many of whom were influential southern gentry.

Yet Tyler, high-minded as he was, should never have consented to run on the ticket. Although the dominant Clay-Webster group had published no platform, every alert politician knew what the unpublished platform contained. And on virtually every major issue the obstinate Virginian was at odds with the majority of his adoptive Whig party, which was pro-bank, pro–protective tariff, and pro–internal improvements. "Tyler too" rhymed with "Tippecanoe," but there the harmony ended. As events turned out, President Harrison, the Whig, served for only 4 weeks, whereas Tyler, the ex-Democrat who was still largely a Democrat at heart, served for 204 weeks.

John Tyler: A President Without a Party

After their hard-won, hard-cider victory, the Whigs brought their not-so-secret platform out of Clay's waistcoat pocket. To the surprise of no one, it outlined a strongly nationalistic program.

Financial reform came first. The Whig Congress hastened to pass a law ending the independent treasury system, and President Tyler, disarmingly agreeable, signed it. Clay next drove through Congress a bill for a "Fiscal Bank," which would establish a new Bank of the United States.

Tyler's hostility to a centralized bank was notorious, and Clay—the "Great Compromiser"—would have done well to conciliate him. But the Kentuckian, robbed repeatedly of the presidency by lesser men, was in an imperious mood and riding for a fall. When the bank bill reached the presidential desk,

President John Tyler (1790–1862), by George P. A. Healy, 1859   The first "accidental president," he was faithful to his states' rights convictions until death. A member of the Virginia secession convention in 1861, he served in the provisional congress of the Confederacy and was elected to a seat in the Confederate house of representatives. Invading Northern troops vengefully despoiled his beautiful Virginia estate, Sherwood Forest.

Tyler flatly vetoed it on both practical and constitutional grounds. A drunken mob gathered late at night near the White House and shouted insultingly, "Huzza for Clay!" "A Bank! A Bank!" "Down with the Veto!"

The stunned Whig leaders tried once again. Striving to pacify Tyler's objections to a "Fiscal Bank," they passed another bill providing for a "Fiscal Corporation." But the president, still unbending, vetoed the offensive substitute. Democrats were jubilant: they had been saved from another financial "monster" only by the pneumonia that had felled Harrison.

Whig extremists, seething with indignation, condemned Tyler as "His Accidency" and as an

"Executive Ass." Widely burned in effigy, he received numerous letters threatening him with death. A wave of influenza then sweeping the country was called the "Tyler grippe." To the delight of Democrats, the stiff-necked Virginian was formally expelled from his party by a caucus of Whig congressmen, and a serious attempt to impeach him was broached in the House of Representatives. His entire cabinet resigned in a body, except Secretary of State Webster, who was then in the midst of delicate negotiations with England.

The proposed Whig tariff also felt the prick of the president's well-inked pen. Tyler appreciated the necessity of bringing additional revenue to the Treasury. But old Democrat that he was, he looked with a frosty eye on the major tariff scheme of the Whigs because it provided, among other features, for a distribution among the states of revenue from the sale of public lands in the West. Tyler could see no point in squandering federal money when the federal Treasury was not overflowing, and he again wielded an emphatic veto.

Chastened Clayites redrafted their tariff bill. They chopped out the offensive dollar-distribution scheme and pushed down the rates to about the moderately protective level of 1832, roughly 32 percent on dutiable goods. Tyler had no fondness for a protective tariff, but realizing the need for addi-tional revenue, he reluctantly signed the law of 1842. In subsequent months the pressure for higher customs duties slackened as the country gradually edged its way out of the depression. The Whig slogan, "Harrison, Two Dollars a Day and Roast Beef," was reduced by unhappy Democrats to, "Ten Cents a Day and Bean Soup."

A War of Words with England

Hatred of England during the nineteenth century came to a head periodically and had to be lanced by treaty settlement or by war. The poison had festered ominously by 1842.

Anti-British passions were composed of many ingredients. At bottom lay the bitter, red-coated memories of the two Anglo-American wars. In addition, the genteel pro-British Federalists had died out, eventually yielding to the boisterous Jacksonian Democrats. British travelers, sniffing with aristocratic noses at the crude scene, wrote acidly of American tobacco spitting, slave auctioneering, lynching, eye gouging, and other unsavory features of the rustic Republic. Travel books penned by these critics, whose views were avidly read on both sides of the Atlantic, stirred up angry outbursts in America.

Life in an American Hotel, 1856
An English caricature of American rudeness and readiness with the pistol.

But the literary fireworks did not end here. British magazines added fuel to the flames when, enlarging on the travel books, they launched sneering attacks on Yankee shortcomings. American journals struck back with "you're another" arguments, thus touching off the "Third War with England." Fortunately, this British-American war was fought with paper broadsides, and only ink was spilled. British authors, including Charles Dickens, entered the fray with gall-dipped pens, for they were being denied rich royalties by the absence of an American copyright law.*

Sprawling America, with expensive canals to dig and railroads to build, was a borrowing nation in the nineteenth century. Imperial Britain, with its overflowing coffers, was a lending nation. The well-heeled creditor is never popular with the down at the heels debtor, and the phrase "bloated British bond-holder" rolled bitterly from many an American tongue. When the panic of 1837 broke and several states defaulted on their bonds or repudiated them openly, honest Englishmen assailed Yankee trickery. One of them offered a new stanza for an old song:

> Yankee Doodle borrows cash,
> Yankee Doodle spends it,
>   And then he snaps his fingers at
> The jolly flat [simpleton] who lends it.

Troubles of a more dangerous sort came closer to home in 1837, when a short-lived insurrection erupted in Canada. It was supported by such a small minority of Canadians that it never had a real chance of success. Yet hundreds of hot-blooded Americans, hoping to strike a blow for freedom against the hereditary enemy, furnished military supplies or volunteered for armed service. The Washington regime tried arduously, though futilely, to uphold its weak neutrality regulations. But again, as in the case of Texas, it simply could not enforce unpopular laws in the face of popular opposition.

A provocative incident on the Canadian frontier brought passions to a boil in 1837. An American steamer, the *Caroline*, was carrying supplies to the insurgents across the swift Niagara River. It was finally attacked on the New York shore by a determined British force, which set the vessel on fire. Lurid American illustrators showed the flaming ship, laden with shrieking souls, plummeting over

the Niagara Falls. The craft in fact sank short of the plunge, and only one American was killed.

This unlawful invasion of American soil—a counterviolation of neutrality—had alarming aftermaths. The Washington officials lodged vigorous but ineffective protests. Three years later, in 1840, the incident was dramatically revived in the state of New York. A Canadian named McLeod, after allegedly boasting in a tavern of his part in the *Caroline* raid, was arrested and indicted for murder. The London Foreign Office, which regarded the *Caroline* raiders as members of a sanctioned armed force and not as criminals, made clear that his execution would mean war. Fortunately, McLeod was freed after establishing an alibi. It must have been airtight, for it was good enough to convince a New York jury. The tension forthwith eased, but it snapped taut again in 1841, when British officials in the Bahamas offered asylum to 130 Virginia slaves who had rebelled and captured the American ship *Creole*.

Manipulating the Maine Maps

An explosive controversy of the early 1840s involved the Maine boundary dispute. The St. Lawrence River is icebound several months of the year, as the British, remembering the War of 1812, well knew. They were determined, as a defensive precaution against the Yankees, to build a road westward from the seaport of Halifax to Quebec. But the proposed route ran through disputed territory—claimed also by Maine under the misleading peace treaty of 1783. Tough-knuckled lumberjacks from both Maine and Canada entered the disputed no-man's-land of the tall-timbered Aroostook River Valley. Ugly fights flared up and both sides summoned the local militia. The small-scale lumberjack clash, which was dubbed the "Aroostook War," threatened to widen into a full-dress shooting war.

As the crisis deepened in 1842, the London Foreign Office took an unusual step. It sent to Washington a nonprofessional diplomat, the conciliatory financier Lord Ashburton, who had married a wealthy American woman. He speedily established cordial relations with Secretary Webster, who had recently been lionized during a visit to England.

The two statesmen, their nerves frayed by protracted negotiations in the heat of a Washington summer, finally agreed to compromise on the

---

*Not until 1891 did Congress extend copyright privileges to foreign authors.

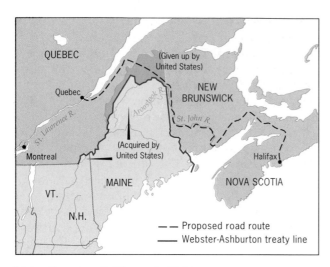

Maine Boundary Settlement, 1842

Maine boundary. On the basis of a rough, split-the-difference arrangement, the Americans were to retain some 7,000 square miles (18,130 square kilometers) of the 12,000 square miles (31,080 square kilometers) of wilderness in dispute. The British got less land but won the desired Halifax-Quebec route. During the negotiations the *Caroline* affair, malingering since 1837, was patched up by an exchange of diplomatic notes.

An overlooked bonus sneaked by in the small print of the same treaty: the British, in adjusting the U.S.-Canadian boundary farther west, surrendered 6,500 square miles (16,835 square kilometers). The area was later found to contain the priceless Mesabi iron ore of Minnesota.

The London Morning Chronicle *greeted the Webster-Ashburton treaty thus:*

"See the feeling with which the treaty has been received in America; mark the enthusiasm it has excited. What does this mean? Why, either that the Americans have gained a great diplomatic victory over us, or that they have escaped a great danger, as they have felt it, in having to maintain their claim by war."

The Lone Star of Texas Shines Alone

During the uncertain eight years since 1836, Texas had led a precarious existence. Mexico, refusing to recognize Texas's independence, regarded the Lone Star Republic as a province in revolt, to be reconquered in the future. Mexican officials loudly threatened war if the American eagle should ever gather the fledgling republic under its protective wings.

The Texans were forced to maintain a costly military establishment. Vastly outnumbered by their Mexican foe, they could not tell when he would strike again. Mexico actually did make two half-hearted raids that, though ineffectual, foreshadowed more fearsome efforts. Confronted with such perils, Texas was driven to open negotiations with England and France, in the hope of securing the defensive shield of a protectorate. In 1839 and 1840, the Texans concluded treaties with France, Holland, and Belgium.

Britain was intensely interested in an independent Texas. Such a republic would check the southward surge of the American colossus, whose bulging biceps posed a constant threat to nearby British possessions in the New World. A puppet Texas, dancing to strings pulled by Britain, could be turned upon the Yankees. Subsequent clashes would create a smoke-screen diversion, behind which foreign powers could move into the Americas and challenge the insolent Monroe Doctrine. French schemers were likewise attracted by the hoary game of divide and conquer. These actions would result, they hoped, in the fragmentation and militarization of America.

Dangers threatened from other foreign quarters. British abolitionists were busily intriguing for a foothold in Texas. If successful in freeing the few blacks there, they presumably would inflame the nearby slaves of the South. In addition, British merchants regarded Texas as a potentially important free-trade area—an offset to the tariff-walled United States. British manufacturers likewise perceived that those vast Texan plains constituted one of the great cotton-producing areas of the future. An independent Texas would relieve British looms of their chronic dependence on American fiber—a supply that might be cut off in time of crisis by embargo or war.

The Belated Texas Nuptials

Partly because of the fears aroused by British schemers, Texas became a leading issue in the presidential campaign of 1844. The foes of expansion assailed annexation, while southern hotheads cried, "Texas or Disunion." The proexpansion Democrats under James K. Polk finally triumphed over the Whigs under Henry Clay, the hardy perennial candidate. Lame-duck President Tyler thereupon interpreted the narrow Democratic victory, with dubious accuracy, as a "mandate" to acquire Texas.

Eager to crown his troubled administration with this splendid prize, Tyler deserves much of the credit for shepherding Texas into the fold. Many "conscience Whigs" feared that Texas in the Union would be red meat to nourish the lusty "slave power." Aware of their opposition, Tyler despaired of securing the needed two-thirds vote for a treaty in the Senate. He therefore arranged for annexation by a joint resolution. This solution required only a simple majority in both houses of Congress. After a spirited debate, the resolution passed early in 1845, and Texas was formally invited to become the twenty-eighth star on the American flag.

Mexico angrily charged that the Americans had despoiled it of Texas. This was to some extent true in 1836, but hardly true in 1845, for the area was no longer Mexico's to be despoiled of. As the years stretched out, realistic observers could see that the Mexicans would not be able to reconquer their lost province. Yet Mexico left the Texans dangling by denying their right to dispose of themselves as they chose.

By 1845 the Lone Star Republic had become a danger spot, inviting foreign intrigue that menaced the American people. The continued existence of Texas as an independent nation threatened to involve the United States in a series of ruinous wars, both in America and in Europe. Americans were in a "lick all creation" mood when they sang "Uncle Sam's Song to Miss Texas":

> *If Mexy back'd by secret foes,*
> *Still talks of getting you, gal;*
> *Why we can lick 'em all you know*
> *And then annex 'em too, gal.*

What other power would have spurned the imperial domain of Texas? The bride was so near, so rich, so fair, so willing. Whatever the peculiar circumstances of the Texas revolution, the United States can hardly be accused of unseemly haste in achieving annexation. Nine long years were surely a decent wait between the beginning of the courtship and the consummation of the marriage.

Oregon Fever Populates Oregon

The so-called Oregon Country was an enormous wilderness. It sprawled magnificently west of the Rockies to the Pacific Ocean, and north of California to the line of 54° 40'—the present southern tip of the Alaska panhandle. All or substantial parts of this immense area were claimed at one time or another by four nations: Spain, Russia, Britain, and the United States.

Two claimants dropped out of the scramble. Spain, though the first to raise its banner in Oregon, bartered away its claims to the United States in the so-called Florida Treaty of 1819. Russia retreated to the line of 54° 40' by the treaties of 1824 and 1825 with America and Britain. These two remaining rivals now had the field to themselves.

British claims to Oregon were strong—at least to that portion north of the Columbia River. They were based squarely on prior discovery and exploration, on treaty rights, and on actual occupation. The most important colonizing agency was the far-flung Hudson's Bay Company, which was trading profitably with the Indians of the Pacific Northwest for furs.

In winning Oregon the Americans had great faith in their procreative powers. Boasted one congressman in 1846,

"Our people are spreading out with the aid of the American multiplication table. Go to the West and see a young man with his mate of eighteen; after the lapse of thirty years, visit him again, and instead of two, you will find twenty-two. That is what I call the American multiplication table."

St. Louis in 1846, by Henry Lewis   Thousands of pioneers like these pulling away from St. Louis said farewell to civilization as they left the Mississippi River and headed across the untracked plains to Oregon in the 1840s.

Americans, for their part, could also point pridefully to exploration and occupation. Captain Robert Gray in 1792 had stumbled upon the majestic Columbia River, which he named after his ship; and the famed Lewis and Clark expedition of 1804–1806 had ranged overland through the Oregon Country to the Pacific. This shaky American toehold was ultimately strengthened by the presence of missionaries and other settlers, a sprinkling of whom reached the grassy Willamette River Valley, south of the Columbia, in the 1830s. These men and women of God, in saving the soul of the Indian, were instrumental in saving the soil of Oregon for the United States. They stimulated interest in a faraway domain that countless Americans had earlier assumed would not be settled for centuries.

Scattered American and British pioneers in Oregon continued to live peacefully side by side. At the time of negotiating the Treaty of 1818 (see p. 250), the United States had sought to divide the vast domain at the forty-ninth parallel. But the British, who regarded the Columbia River as the St. Lawrence of the West, were unwilling to yield this vital artery. A scheme for peaceful "joint occupation" was thereupon adopted, pending future settlement.

The handful of Americans in the Willamette Valley was suddenly multiplied in the early 1840s, when "Oregon fever" seized hundreds of restless pioneers. In increasing numbers their creaking covered wagons jolted over the 2,000-mile (3,200-kilometer) Oregon Trail as the human rivulet widened into a stream.* By 1846 about five thousand Americans had settled south of the Columbia River, some of them tough "border ruffians," expert with bowie knife and "revolving pistol."

The British, in the face of this rising torrent of humanity, could muster only seven hundred or so subjects north of the Columbia. Losing out lopsidedly in the population race, they were beginning to

---

*The average rate of progress in covered wagons was 1 to 2 miles an hour. This amounted to about 100 miles (161 kilometers) a week, or about five months for the entire journey. Thousands of humans, in addition to horses and oxen, died en route. One estimate is seventeen deaths a mile for men, women, and children.

The National Wagon Road Guide, 1858
By the 1850s, official guidebooks, like the one shown here, helped travelers make their way along the Overland Trail to the West.

see the wisdom of arriving at a peaceful settlement before being engulfed by their neighbors.

A curious fact is that only a relatively small segment of the Oregon Country was in actual controversy by 1845. The area in dispute consisted of the rough quadrangle between the Columbia River on the south and east, the forty-ninth parallel on the north, and the Pacific Ocean on the west. Britain had repeatedly offered the line of the Columbia; America had repeatedly offered the forty-ninth parallel. The whole fateful issue was now tossed into the presidential election of 1844, where it was largely overshadowed by the question of annexing Texas.

A Mandate (?) for Manifest Destiny

The two major parties nominated their presidential standard-bearers in May 1844. Ambitious but often frustrated Henry Clay, easily the most popular man in the country, was enthusiastically chosen by the Whigs at Baltimore. The Democrats, meeting there later, seemed hopelessly deadlocked. Finally the expansionists, dominated by the pro-Texas southerners, trotted out and nominated James K. Polk of Tennessee, America's first "dark horse" or "surprise" presidential candidate.

Polk may have been a dark horse, but he was hardly an unknown or decrepit nag. Speaker of the House of Representatives for four years and governor of Tennessee for two terms, he was a determined, industrious, ruthless, and intelligent public servant. Sponsored by Andrew Jackson, his friend and neighbor, he was rather implausibly touted by Democrats as yet another "Young Hickory." Whigs attempted to jeer him into oblivion with the taunt, "Who is James K. Polk?" They soon found out.

The campaign of 1844 was in part an expression of the mighty emotional upsurge known as Manifest Destiny. Countless citizens in the 1840s and 1850s, feeling a sense of mission, believed that Almighty God had "manifestly" destined the American people for a hemispheric career. They would irresistibly spread their uplifting and ennobling democratic institutions over at least the entire continent, and possibly over South America as well. Land greed and ideals—"empire" and "liberty"—were thus conveniently conjoined.

Expansionist Democrats were strongly swayed by the intoxicating spell of Manifest Destiny. They came out flat-footedly in their platform for the "Reannexation of Texas"* and the "Reoccupation of Oregon," all the way to 54° 40'. Outbellowing the Whig log-cabinites in the game of slogans, they shouted "All of Oregon or None." They also condemned Clay as a "corrupt bargainer," a dissolute character, and a slaveowner. (Their own candidate, Polk, also owned slaves—a classic case of the pot calling the kettle black.)

---

*The United States had given up its claims to Texas in the so-called Florida Purchase Treaty with Spain in 1819 (see p. 251). The slogan "Fifty-four forty or fight" was evidently not coined until two years later, in 1846.

The Whigs, as noisemakers, took no back seat. They countered with such slogans as "Hooray for Clay" and "Polk, Slavery, and Texas, or Clay, Union, and Liberty." They also spread the lie that a gang of Tennessee slaves had been seen on their way to a southern market branded with the initials J. K. P. (James K. Polk).

On the crucial issue of Texas, the acrobatic Clay tried to ride two horses at once. The "Great Compromiser" appears to have compromised away the presidency when he wrote a series of confusing letters. They seemed to say that while he personally favored annexing slaveholding Texas (an appeal to the South), he also favored postponement (an appeal to the North). He might have lost more ground if he had not "straddled," but he certainly alienated the more ardent antislaveryites.

In the stretch drive, "Dark Horse" Polk nipped Henry Clay at the wire, 170 to 105 votes in the Electoral College and 1,338,464 to 1,300,097 in the popular column. Clay would have won if he had not lost New York State by a scant 5,000 votes. There the tiny antislavery Liberty party absorbed nearly 16,000 votes, many of which would otherwise have gone to the unlucky Kentuckian. Ironically, the anti-Texas Liberty party, by spoiling Clay's chances and helping to ensure the election of pro-Texas Polk, hastened the annexation of Texas.

Land-hungry Democrats, flushed with victory, proclaimed that they had received a mandate from the voters to take Texas. But a presidential election is seldom, if ever, a clear-cut mandate on anything. The only way to secure a true reflection of the voters' will is to hold a special election on a given issue. The picture that emerged in 1844 is one not of mandate but of muddle. What else could there have been when the results were so close, the personalities so colorful, and the issues so numerous—including Oregon, Texas, the tariff, slavery, the bank, and internal improvements? Yet this unclear "mandate" was interpreted by President Tyler as a crystal-clear charge to annex Texas—and he signed the joint resolution three days before leaving the White House.

Polk the Purposeful

"Young Hickory" Polk, unlike "Old Hickory" Jackson, was not an impressive figure. Of middle height (5 feet, 8 inches; 1.72 meters), lean, white-haired (worn long), gray-eyed, and stern-faced, he took life seriously and drove himself mercilessly into a premature grave. His burdens were increased by an unwillingness to delegate authority. Methodical and hardworking but not brilliant, he was shrewd,

Westward the Course of Empire Takes Its Way   This romantic tribute to the spirit of Manifest Destiny was commissioned by Congress in 1860 and may still be seen in the Capitol.

President James K. Polk (1795–1849), by George P. A. Healy, 1858   Distinguished for both determination and deviousness, Polk added more territory to the United States (by questionable means) than any other president. In tenaciously pursuing his goals, he broke himself down with overwork and died 103 days after his single term ended. His somewhat priggish wife (and secretary) banned all drinking and dancing in the White House.

House Vote on Tariff of 1846*

Regions	For	Against
New England	9	19
Middle states	18	44
West and Northwest	29	10
South and Southwest	58	20
TOTAL	114	93

*Compare vote on 1832 tariff, p. 274.

narrow-minded, conscientious, and persistent. "What he went for he fetched," wrote a contemporary. Purposeful in the highest degree, he developed a positive four-point program and with remarkable success achieved it completely in less than four years.

One of Polk's goals was a lowered tariff. His secretary of the treasury, wispy Robert J. Walker, devised a tariff-for-revenue bill that reduced the average rates of the Tariff of 1842 from about 32 percent to 25 percent. With the strong support of low-tariff southerners, Walker lobbied the measure through Congress, though not without loud complaints from the Clayites, especially in New England and the middle states, that American manufacturing would be ruined. But these prophets of doom missed the mark. The Walker Tariff of 1846 proved to be an excellent revenue producer, largely because it was followed by boom times and heavy imports.

A second objective of Polk was the restoration of the independent treasury, unceremoniously dropped by the Whigs in 1841. Pro-bank Whigs in Congress raised a storm of opposition, but victory at last rewarded the president's efforts in 1846.

The third and fourth points on Polk's "must list" were the acquisition of California and the settlement of the Oregon dispute.

"Reoccupation" of the "whole" of Oregon had been promised northern Democrats in the campaign of 1844. But southern Democrats, once they had annexed Texas, rapidly cooled off. Polk, himself a southerner, had no intention of insisting on the 54° 40' pledge of his own platform. But feeling bound by the three offers of his predecessors to London, he again proposed the compromise line of 49°. The British minister in Washington, on his own initiative, brusquely spurned this olive branch.

The next move on the Oregon chessboard was up to Britain. Fortunately for peace, the ministry began to experience a change of heart. British anti-expansionists ("Little Englanders") were now persuaded that the Columbia River was not after all the St. Lawrence of the West and that the turbulent American hordes might one day seize the Oregon Country. Why fight a hazardous war over this wilderness on behalf of an unpopular monopoly, the Hudson's Bay Company, which had already "furred out" much of the area anyhow?

Early in 1846 the British, hat in hand, came around and themselves proposed the line of 49°. President Polk, irked by the previous rebuff, threw the decision squarely into the lap of the Senate. The senators speedily accepted the offer and approved the subsequent treaty, despite a few diehard shouts of "Fifty-four forty forever!" and "Every foot or not

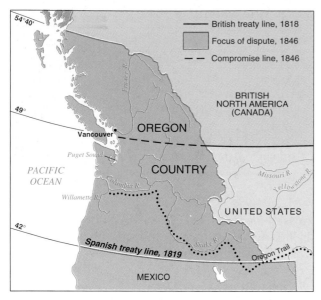

The Oregon Controversy, 1846

an inch!" The fact that the United States was then a month deep in a war with Mexico doubtless influenced the Senate's final vote.

Satisfaction with the Oregon settlement among Americans was not unanimous. The northwestern states, hotbed of Manifest Destiny and "fifty-four fortyism," joined the antislavery forces in condemning what they regarded as a base betrayal by the South. Why *all* of Texas but not *all* of Oregon? Because, retorted the expansionist Senator Benton of Missouri, "Great Britain is powerful and Mexico is weak."

So Polk, despite all the campaign bluster, got neither "fifty-four forty" nor a fight. But he did get something that in the long run was better: a reasonable compromise without a rifle being raised.

Misunderstandings with Mexico

Faraway California was another worry of Polk's. He and other disciples of Manifest Destiny had long coveted its verdant valleys, and especially the spacious bay of San Francisco. This splendid harbor was widely regarded as America's future gateway to the Pacific Ocean.

The population of California in 1845 was curiously mixed. It consisted of perhaps 13,000 sun-

blessed Spanish-Mexicans, and as many as 75,000 dispirited Indians. There were fewer than a thousand "foreigners," mostly Americans, some of whom had "left their consciences" behind them as they rounded Cape Horn. Given time, these transplanted Yankees might yet bring California into the Union by "playing the Texas game."

Polk was eager to buy California from Mexico, but relations with Mexico City were dangerously embittered. Among other friction points, the United States had claims against the Mexicans for some $3 million in damages to American citizens and their property. The revolution-riddled regime in Mexico had formally agreed to assume most of this debt but had been forced to default on its payments.

A more serious bone of contention was Texas. The Mexican government, after threatening war if the United States should acquire the Lone Star Republic, had recalled its minister from Washington following annexation. Diplomatic relations were completely severed.

Deadlock with Mexico over Texas was further tightened by a question of boundaries. During the long era of Spanish-Mexican occupation, the southwestern boundary of Texas had been the Nueces River. But the expansive Texans, on rather farfetched grounds, were claiming the more southerly Rio Grande instead. Polk, for his part, felt a strong moral obligation to defend Texas in its claim, once it was annexed.

The Mexicans were far less concerned about this boundary quibble than was the United States. In their eyes all of Texas was still theirs, although temporarily in revolt, and a dispute over the two rivers seemed pointless. Yet Polk was careful to keep American troops out of virtually all of the explosive no-man's-land between the Nueces and the Rio Grande, as long as there was any real prospect of peaceful adjustment.

The golden prize of California continued to cause Polk much anxiety. Disquieting rumors (now known to have been ill-founded) were circulating that Britain was about to buy or seize California—a grab that Americans could not tolerate under the Monroe Doctrine. In a last desperate throw of the dice, Polk dispatched John Slidell to Mexico City as minister late in 1845. The new envoy, among other alternatives, was instructed to offer a maximum of $25 million for California and territory to the east. But the proud Mexican people would not even permit Slidell to present his "insulting" proposition.

El Patrón, by James Walker, c. 1840   The California ranchero's way of life was soon to be extinguished when California became part of the United States in 1848 and thousands of American gold-seekers rushed into the state in the following year.

American Blood on American (?) Soil

A frustrated Polk was now prepared to force a showdown. On January 13, 1846, he ordered four thousand men, under General Zachary Taylor, to march from the Nueces River to the Rio Grande, provocatively near Mexican forces. Polk's presidential diary reveals that he expected at any moment to hear of a clash. When none occurred after an anxious wait, he informed his cabinet on May 9, 1846, that he proposed to ask Congress to declare war on the basis of (1) unpaid claims and (2) Slidell's rejection. These, at best, were rather flimsy pretexts. Two cabinet members spoke up and said that they would feel better satisfied if Mexican troops should fire first.

That very evening, as fate would have it, news of bloodshed arrived. On April 25, 1846, Mexican troops had crossed the Rio Grande and attacked General Taylor's command, with a loss of sixteen Americans killed or wounded.

Polk, further aroused, sent a vigorous war message to Congress. He declared that despite "all our efforts" to avoid a clash, hostilities had been forced upon the country by the shedding of "American blood on the American soil." A patriotic Congress overwhelmingly voted for war, and enthusiastic volunteers cried, "Ho for the Halls of the Montezumas!" and "Mexico or Death!" Inflamed by the war fever, even antislavery Whig bastions melted and joined with the rest of the nation, though they later condemned "Jimmy Polk's war." As James Russell Lowell of Massachusetts lamented,

Massachusetts, God forgive her,
She's akneelin' with the rest.

In his message to Congress, Polk was making history—not writing it. If he had been a historian, he would have explained that American blood had been shed on soil that the Mexicans had good reason to regard as their own. A gangling, rough-featured Whig congressman from Illinois, one Abraham Lincoln, introduced certain resolutions that requested information as to the precise "spot" on American soil where American blood had been shed. He pushed his "spot" resolutions with such persistence that he came to be known as the "spotty Lincoln," who could die of "spotted fever." The more extreme antislavery agitators of the North, many of them Whigs, branded the president a liar—"Polk the Mendacious."

Did Polk provoke war? California was an imperative point in his program, and Mexico would not sell it at any price. The only way to get it was to use force or wait for an internal American revolt. Yet delay seemed dangerous, for the claws of the British lion might snatch the ripening California fruit from the talons of the American eagle. Grievances against

On June 1, 1860, less than a year before he became president, Abraham Lincoln (1809–1865) wrote,

"The act of sending an armed force among the Mexicans was unnecessary, inasmuch as Mexico was in no way molesting or menacing the United States or the people thereof; and . . . it was unconstitutional, because the power of levying war is vested in Congress, and not in the President."

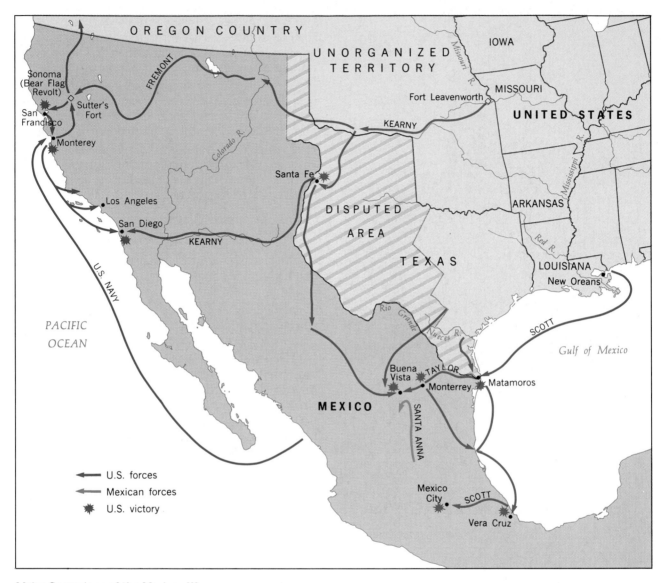

Major Campaigns of the Mexican War

Mexico were annoying yet tolerable; in later years America endured even worse ones. But in 1846 patience had ceased to be a virtue, as far as Polk was concerned. Bent on grasping California by fair means or foul, he pushed the quarrel to a bloody showdown.

Both sides, in fact, were spoiling for a fight. Feisty Americans, especially southwestern expansionists, were eager to teach the Mexicans a lesson. The Mexicans, in turn, were burning to humiliate the "Bullies of the North." Possessing a considerable standing army, heavily overstaffed with generals, they boasted of invading the United States, freeing the black slaves, and lassoing whole regiments of Americans. They were hoping that the quarrel with Britain over Oregon would blossom into a full-dress war, as it came near doing, and further pin down the hated *yanquis*. A conquest of Mexico's vast and arid expanses seemed fantastic, especially in view of the bungling American invasion of Canada in 1812.

Both sides were fired by moral indignation. The Mexican people could fight with the flaming sword of righteousness, for had not the "insolent" Yankee picked a fight by polluting their soil? Many earnest Americans, on the other hand, sincerely believed that Mexico was the aggressor.

The Mastering of Mexico

Polk wanted California—not war. But when war came, he hoped to fight it on a limited scale and then pull out when he had captured the prize. The dethroned Mexican dictator Santa Anna, then exiled with his teenage bride in Cuba, let it be known that if the American blockading squadron would permit him to slip into Mexico, he would sell out his country. Incredibly, Polk agreed to this discreditable intrigue. But the double-crossing Santa Anna, once he returned to Mexico, proceeded to rally his countrymen to a desperate defense of their soil.

American operations in the Southwest and in California were completely successful. In 1846 General Stephen W. Kearny led a detachment of seventeen hundred troops over the famous Santa Fe trail from Fort Leavenworth to Santa Fe. This sunbaked outpost, with its drowsy plazas, was easily captured. But before Kearny could reach California, the fertile province was won. When war broke out, Captain John C. Frémont, the dashing explorer, just "happened" to be there with several dozen well-armed men. In helping to overthrow Mexican rule in 1846, he collaborated with American naval officers and with the local Americans, who had hoisted the banner of the short-lived California Bear Flag Republic.

General Zachary Taylor meanwhile had been spearheading the main thrust. Known as "Old Rough and Ready" because of his iron constitution and incredibly unsoldierly appearance—he sometimes wore a Mexican straw hat—he fought his way across the Rio Grande into Mexico. After several gratifying victories, he reached Buena Vista. There, on February 22–23, 1847, his weakened force of 5,000 men was attacked by some 20,000 march-weary troops under Santa Anna. The Mexicans were finally repulsed with extreme difficulty, and

War News from Mexico, by Richard Caton Woodville The new-fangled telegraph kept the nation closely informed of events in far-off Mexico.

overnight Zachary Taylor became the "Hero of Buena Vista." One Kentuckian was heard to say that "Old Zack" would be elected president in 1848 by "spontaneous combustion."

Sound American strategy now called for a crushing blow at the enemy's vitals—Mexico City. General Taylor, though a good leader of modest-sized forces, could not win decisively in the semi-deserts of northern Mexico. The command of the main expedition, which pushed inland from the coastal city of Vera Cruz early in 1847, was entrusted to General Winfield Scott. A handsome giant of a man, Scott had emerged as a hero from the War of 1812 and had later earned the nickname of "Old Fuss and Feathers" because of his resplendent uniforms and strict discipline. He was severely handicapped in the Mexican campaign by inadequate numbers of troops, by expiring enlistments, by a more numerous enemy, by mountainous terrain, by disease, and by political backbiting at home. Yet he succeeded in battling his way up to Mexico City by September 1847 in one of the most brilliant campaigns in American military annals. He proved to be the most distinguished general produced by his country between 1783 and 1861.

Fighting Mexico for Peace

Polk was anxious to end the shooting as soon as he could secure his territorial goals. Accordingly, he sent along with Scott's invading army the chief clerk of the State Department, Nicholas P. Trist, who among other weaknesses was afflicted with an over-fluid pen. Trist and Scott arranged for an armistice with Santa Anna, at a cost of $10,000. The wily dictator pocketed the bribe and then used the time to bolster his defenses.

Negotiating a treaty with a sword in one hand and a pen in the other was ticklish business. Polk, disgusted with his blundering envoy, abruptly recalled Trist. The wordy diplomat then dashed off a sixty-five-page letter explaining why he was not coming home. The president was furious. But Trist, grasping a fleeting opportunity to negotiate, signed the Treaty of Guadalupe Hidalgo on February 2, 1848, and forwarded it to Washington.

The terms of the treaty were breathtaking. They confirmed the American title to Texas and yielded the enormous area stretching westward to Oregon and the ocean and embracing coveted California. This total expanse, including Texas, was about one-half of Mexico. The United States agreed to pay $15 million for the land and to assume the claims of its citizens against Mexico in the amount of $3,250,000 (see "Makers of America: The Californios," pp. 396–397).

Polk submitted the treaty to the Senate. Although Trist had proved highly annoying, he had generally followed his original instructions. And speed was imperative. The antislavery Whigs in Congress— dubbed "Mexican Whigs" or "Conscience Whigs"— were denouncing this "damnable war" with increasing heat. Having secured control of the House in 1847, they were even threatening to vote down supplies for the armies in the field. If they had done so, Scott probably would have been forced to retreat, and the fruits of victory might have been tossed away.

Another peril impended. A swelling group of expansionists, intoxicated by Manifest Destiny, was clamoring for all of Mexico. If America had seized it, the nation would have been saddled with an expensive and vexatious policing problem. Farseeing southerners like Calhoun, alarmed by the mounting anger of antislavery agitators, realized that the South would do well not to be too greedy. The treaty was finally approved by the Senate, 38 to 14. Oddly enough, it was condemned both by those opponents who wanted all of Mexico and by opponents who wanted none of it.

Victors rarely pay an indemnity, especially after a costly conflict has been "forced" on them. Yet Polk,

Early in 1848 the New York Evening Post *demanded,*

"Now we ask, whether any man can coolly contemplate the idea of recalling our troops from the [Mexican] territory we at present occupy . . . and . . . resign this beautiful country to the custody of the ignorant cowards and profligate ruffians who have ruled it for the last twenty-five years? Why, humanity cries out against it. Civilization and Christianity protest against this reflux of the tide of barbarism and anarchy."

Such was one phase of Manifest Destiny.

who had planned to offer $25 million before fighting the war, arranged to pay $18,250,000 after winning it. Cynics have charged that the Americans were pricked by guilty consciences; apologists have pointed proudly to the "Anglo-Saxon spirit of fair play." A decisive factor was the need for haste, while there was still a responsible Mexican government to carry out the treaty and before political foes in the United States, notably the antislavery zealots, sabotaged Polk's expansionist program.

Profit and Loss in Mexico

As wars go, the Mexican War was a small one. It cost some thirteen thousand American lives, most of them taken by disease. But the fruits of the fighting were enormous.

America's total expanse, already vast, was increased by about one-third (counting Texas)—an addition even greater than that of the Louisiana Purchase. A sharp stimulus was given to the spirit of Manifest Destiny, for as the proverb has it, the appetite comes with eating.

As fate ordained, the Mexican War was the blood-splattered schoolroom of the Civil War. The campaigns provided priceless field experience for most of the officers destined to become leading generals in the forthcoming conflict, including Captain Robert E. Lee and Lieutenant Ulysses S. Grant. The Military Academy at West Point, founded in 1802, fully justified its existence through the well-trained officers. Useful also was the navy, which did valuable work in throwing a crippling blockade around Mexican ports. The Marine Corps, in existence since 1798, won new laurels and to this day sings in its stirring hymn about the Halls of Montezuma.

The army waged war without defeat and without a major blunder, despite formidable obstacles and a half-dozen or so achingly long marches. Chagrined British critics, as well as other foreign skeptics, reluctantly revised upward their estimate of Yankee military prowess. Opposing armies, moreover, emerged with increased respect for each other. The Mexicans, though poorly led, fought heroically. At Chapultepec, near Mexico City, the teenage lads of the military academy there *(los niños)* perished to a boy.

Long-memoried Mexicans have never forgotten that their northern enemy tore away about half of their country. The argument that they were lucky not to lose all of it, and that they had been paid something for their land, has scarcely lessened their bitterness. The war also marked an ugly turning

PLUCKED:

THE MEXICAN EAGLE BEFORE THE WAR!   THE MEXICAN EAGLE AFTER THE WAR!

A Cartoon from *Yankee Doodle,* 1847   This satiric drawing was symbolic of the "lick all creation" spirit of the times.

The Californios

In 1848 the United States, swollen with the spoils of war, reckoned the costs and benefits of the conflict with Mexico. Thousands of Americans had fallen in battle, and millions of dollars had been invested in a war machine. For this expenditure of blood and money, the nation was repaid with ample land—and with people, the former citizens of Mexico who now became, whether willingly or not, Americans. The largest single addition to American territory in history, the Mexican Cession stretched the United States from sea to shining sea. It secured Texas, brought in vast tracts of the desert Southwest, and included the great prize—the fruited valleys and port cities of California. There, at the conclusion of the Mexican War, dwelled some thirteen thousand

Californios—descendants of the Spanish and Mexican conquerors who had once ruled California.

The Spanish had first arrived in California in 1769, extending their New World empire and outracing Russian traders to bountiful San Francisco Bay. Father Junipero Serra, an enterprising Franciscan friar, soon established twenty-one missions along the coast. Indians in the iron grip of the missions were encouraged to adopt Christianity and were often forced to toil endlessly as farmers and herders, in the process suffering disease and degradation. These frequently maltreated mission Indians occupied the lowest rungs on the ladder of Spanish colonial society.

Upon the loftiest rungs perched the Californios. Pioneers from the Mexican heartland of New Spain, they had trailed Serra to California, claiming land and civil offices in their new home. Yet even the proud Californios had deferred to the all-powerful Franciscan missionaries until Mexico threw off the Spanish colonial yoke in 1821, whereupon the infant Mexican government turned an anxious eye toward its frontier outpost.

Mexico now emptied its jails to send settlers to the sparsely populated north, built and garrisoned fortresses, and, most important, transferred authority from the missions to secular (that is, governmental) authorities. This "secularization" program attacked and eroded the immense power of the

Mission San Gabriel,
Founded in 1771

California Indians Dancing at the Mission in San José, by Sykes, 1806

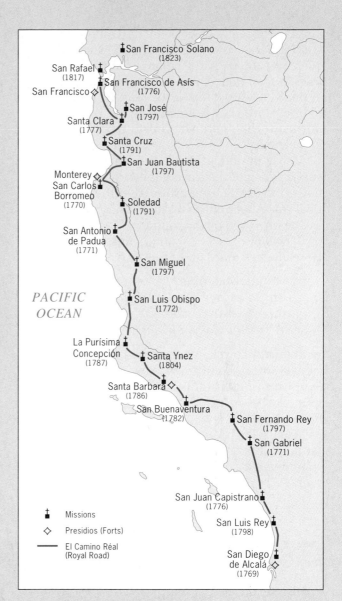

Spanish Missions and Presidios

missions and of their Franciscan masters—with their bawling herds of cattle, debased Indian workers, millions of acres of land, and lucrative foreign trade. The frocked friars had commanded their fiefdoms so self-confidently that earlier reform efforts had dared to go no further than levying a paltry tax on the missions and politely requesting that the missionaries limit their floggings of Indians to fifteen lashes per week. But during the 1830s, the power of the missions weakened, and much of their land and their assets were confiscated by the Californios. Vast *ranchos* (ranches) formed, and from those citadels the Californios ruled in their turn until the Mexican War.

The Californios' glory faded in the wake of the American victory, even though in some isolated places they clung to their political offices for a decade or two. Overwhelmed by the inrush of Anglo golddiggers—some eighty-seven thousand after the discovery at Sutter's Mill in 1848—and undone by the waning of the pastoral economy, the Californios saw their recently acquired lands and their recently established political power slip through their fingers. When the Civil War broke out in 1861, so harshly did the word *Yankee* ring in their ears that many Californios supported the South.

By 1870 the Californios' brief ascendancy had utterly vanished—a short and sad tale of riches to rags in the face of the Anglo onslaught. Half a century later, beginning in 1910, hundreds of thousands of young Mexicans would flock into California and the Southwest. They would enter a region liberally endowed with Spanish architecture and artifacts, bearing the names of Spanish missions and Californio *ranchos*. But they would find it a land dominated by Anglos, a place far different from that which their Californio ancestors had settled so hopefully in earlier days.

point in the relations between the United States and Latin America as a whole. Hitherto, Uncle Sam had been regarded with some complacency, even friendliness. Henceforth, he was increasingly feared as the "Colossus of the North." Suspicious neighbors to the south condemned him as a greedy and untrustworthy bully, who might next despoil them of their soil.

Most ominous of all, the war rearoused the snarling dog of the slavery issue, and the beast did not stop yelping until drowned in the blood of the Civil War. Abolitionists assailed the Mexican conflict as one provoked by the southern "slavocracy" for its own evil purposes. As James Russell Lowell had Hosea Biglow drawl in his Yankee dialect,

> They jest want this Californy
>   So's to lug new slave-states in
> To abuse ye, an' to scorn ye,
>   An' to plunder ye like sin.

In line with Lowell's charge, the bulk of the American volunteers were admittedly from the South and Southwest. But, as in the case of the Texan revolution, the basic explanation was proximity rather than conspiracy.

Quarreling over slavery extension also erupted on the floors of Congress. In 1846, shortly after the shooting started, Polk had requested an appropriation of $2 million with which to buy a peace. Representative David Wilmot of Pennsylvania, fearful of the southern "slavocracy," introduced a fateful amendment. It stipulated that slavery should never exist in any of the territory to be wrested from Mexico.

The disruptive Wilmot amendment twice passed the House, but not the Senate. Southern members, unwilling to be robbed of prospective slave states, fought the restriction tooth and nail. Antislavery men, in Congress and out, battled no less bitterly for the exclusion of slaves. The "Wilmot Proviso," eventually endorsed by the legislatures of all but one of the free states, soon came to symbolize the burning issue of slavery in the territories.

In a broad sense, the opening shots of the Mexican War were the opening shots of the Civil War. President Polk left the nation the splendid physical heritage of California and the Southwest but also the ugly moral heritage of an embittered slavery dispute. "Mexico will poison us," said the philosopher Ralph Waldo Emerson. Even the great champion of the South, John C. Calhoun, had prophetically warned that "Mexico is to us the forbidden fruit . . . the penalty of eating it would be to subject our institutions to political death." Mexicans could later take some satisfaction in knowing that the territory wrenched from them had proved to be a venomous apple of discord that could well be called Santa Anna's revenge.

Chronology

1837	Canadian rebellion and *Caroline* incident
1841	Harrison dies after four weeks in office Tyler assumes presidency
1842	Aroostook War over Maine boundary Webster-Ashburton treaty
1844	Polk defeats Clay in "Manifest Destiny" election
1845	United States annexes Texas
1846	Walker Tariff Independent Treasury restored United States settles Oregon dispute with Britain
1846	United States and Mexico clash over Texas boundary Kearny takes Santa Fe Frémont conquers California Wilmot Proviso passes House of Representatives
1846–1848	Mexican War
1847	Battle of Buena Vista Scott takes Mexico City
1848	Treaty of Guadalupe Hidalgo

SUGGESTED READINGS

PRIMARY SOURCE DOCUMENTS

The colorful reminiscences of the pioneers are collected in Dale Morgan, ed., *Overland in 1846: Diaries and Letters of the California-Oregon Trail** (1963). For women's perspectives see Sandra Myres, *Ho for California! Women's Overland Diaries from the Huntington Library* (1980). The outbreak and conduct of the Mexican War come alive in the fascinating *Diary of James K. Polk,** edited by Milo Milton Quaife (1910).

SECONDARY SOURCES

A brief introduction is Ray A. Billington, *The Far Western Frontier, 1830–1860* (1956); more comprehensive is his *Westward Expansion* (rev. ed., 1974). Still useful is Albert K. Weinberg, *Manifest Destiny* (1935), though it should be supplemented by Frederick Merk, *Manifest Destiny and Mission in American History* (1963). See also Reginald Horsman, *Race and Manifest Destiny: The Origins of American Racial Anglo-Saxonism* (1981); Patricia Nelson Limerick, *The Legacy of Conquest: The Unbroken Past of the American West* (1987); and the early chapters of Richard D. White, *"It's Your Misfortune and None of My Own": A History of the American West* (1992). Paul Horgan, *Great River* (1954), is a magnificent history of the Southwest and the Rio Grande. *The Texas Revolution* is

the subject of William C. Binkley's 1952 study. It should be supplemented by Frederick W. Merk, *Slavery and the Annexation of Texas* (1972). For the Pacific region, see Francis Parkman's classic *The California and Oregon Trail* (1849); Norman A. Graebner's general account, *Empire on the Pacific* (1955); and Theodore J. Karamanski, *Fur Trade and Exploration: Opening the Far Northwest, 1821–1852* (1983). On the conflict with Mexico, see K. Jack Bauer, *The Mexican-American War, 1846–1848* (1974), and James McCaffrey, *Army of Manifest Destiny: The American Soldier in the Mexican War* (1992). The other side's perspective is given in Gene M. Brack, *Mexico Views Manifest Destiny, 1821–1846* (1976), and David J. Weber, *The Mexican Frontier, 1821–1846: The American Southwest under Mexico* (1982). John H. Schroeder analyzes an important aspect of the conflict in *Mr. Polk's War: American Opposition and Dissent, 1846–1848* (1973). Paul H. Bergeron scrutinizes Polk's administration in *The Presidency of James K. Polk* (1987). David M. Pletcher gives an overall view in *The Diplomacy of the Annexation of Texas, Oregon, and the Mexican War* (1973). Robert W. Johansen uses the war to investigate American culture in *To the Halls of the Montezumas: The Mexican War in the American Imagination* (1985). Unusually colorful social history of the westward movement is provided in John Mack Faragher, *Women and Men on the Overland Trail* (1979), and John D. Unruh, Jr., *The Plains Across: The Overland Emigrants and the Trans-Mississippi West, 1840–1860* (1979). Julie Roy Jeffrey focuses on *Frontier Women* (1979), as does Glenda Riley, in *The Female Frontier* (1988), and the contributors to Susan Armitage and Elizabeth Jameson, eds., *The Women's West* (1987).

---

*An asterisk indicates that the document, or an excerpt from it, can be found in Thomas A. Bailey and David M. Kennedy, eds., *The American Spirit: United States History as Seen by Contemporaries,* 9th ed. (Boston: Houghton Mifflin, 1998).

19

Renewing the
Sectional Struggle

1848–1854

―❧―

*Secession! Peaceable secession! Sir, your eyes and
mine are never destined to see that miracle.*

―❦―

DANIEL WEBSTER,
SEVENTH OF MARCH SPEECH, 1850

The Popular Sovereignty Panacea

The year 1848, highlighted by a rash of revolutions
in Europe, was filled with unrest in America. The
Treaty of Guadalupe Hildalgo had officially ended
the war with Mexico, but it had initiated a new and
perilous round of political warfare in the United
States. The vanquished Mexicans had been forced to
relinquish an enormous tract of real estate, including Texas, California, and all the area between. The
acquisition of this huge domain raised anew the
burning issue of extending slavery into the territories. Northern antislaveryites had rallied behind the
Wilmot Proviso, which flatly prohibited slavery in
any territory acquired in the Mexican War. Southern
senators had blocked the passage of the proviso, but
the issue would not die. Ominously, debate over

slavery in the area of the Mexican Cession threatened to disrupt the ranks of both Whigs and Democrats and split national politics along North-South
sectional lines.

Each of the two great political parties was a vital
bond of national unity, for each enjoyed powerful
support in both North and South. If they should be
replaced by two purely sectional groupings, the
Union would be in peril. To politicians, the wisest
strategy seemed to be to sit on the lid of the slavery
issue and ignore the boiling beneath. Even so, the
cover bobbed up and down ominously in response
to the agitation of zealous northern abolitionists
and impassioned southern "fire-eaters."

Anxious Democrats were forced to seek a new
standard-bearer in 1848. President Polk, broken in
health by overwork and chronic diarrhea, had
pledged himself to a single term. The Democratic
National Convention at Baltimore turned to an

aging leader, General Lewis Cass, a veteran of the War of 1812. Although a senator and diplomat of wide experience and considerable ability, he was sour-visaged and somewhat pompous. His enemies dubbed him General "Gass" and quickly noted that *Cass* rhymed with *jackass*. The Democratic platform, in line with the lid-sitting strategy, was silent on the burning issue of slavery in the territories.

But Cass himself had not been silent. His views on the extension of slavery were well known because he was the reputed father of "popular sovereignty." This was the doctrine that stated that the sovereign people of a territory, under the general principles of the Constitution, should themselves determine the status of slavery.

Popular sovereignty had a persuasive appeal. The public liked it because it accorded with the democratic tradition of self-determination. Politicians liked it because it seemed a comfortable compromise between the abolitionist bid for a ban on slavery in the territories and southern demands that Congress protect slavery in the territories. Popular sovereignty tossed the slavery problem into the laps of the people in the various territories. Advocates of the principle thus hoped to dissolve the most stubborn national issue of the day into a series of local issues. Yet popular sovereignty had one fatal defect: it might serve to spread the blight of slavery.

Political Triumphs for General Taylor

The Whigs, meeting in Philadelphia, cashed in on the "Taylor fever." They nominated frank and honest Zachary Taylor, the "Hero of Buena Vista," who had never held civil office or even voted for president. Henry Clay, the living embodiment of Whiggism, should logically have been nominated. But Clay had made too many speeches—and too many enemies.

As usual, the Whigs pussyfooted in their platform. Eager to win at any cost, they dodged all troublesome issues and merely extolled the homespun virtues of their candidate. The self-reliant old frontier fighter had not committed himself on the issue of slavery extension. But as a wealthy resident of Louisiana, living on a sugar plantation, he owned scores of slaves.

Ardent antislavery men in the North, distrusting both Cass and Taylor, organized the Free Soil party. Aroused by the conspiracy of silence in the Demo-

General Zachary Taylor (1784–1850) This Democratic campaign cartoon of 1848 charges that Taylor's reputation rested on Mexican skulls.

cratic and Whig platforms, the Free-Soilers made no bones about their own stand. They came out foursquare for the Wilmot Proviso and against slavery in the territories. Going beyond other antislavery groups, they broadened their appeal by advocating federal aid for internal improvements and by urging free government homesteads for settlers.

The new party assembled a strange assortment of new fellows in the same political bed. It attracted industrialists miffed at Polk's reduction of protective tariffs. It appealed to Democrats resentful of Polk's settling for part of Oregon while insisting on all of Texas—a disparity that suggested a menacing southern dominance in the Democratic party. It harbored many northerners whose hatred was directed not so much at slavery as at blacks and who gagged at the prospect of sharing the newly acquired western territories with African-Americans. It also contained a large element of "conscience Whigs," heavily influenced by the abolitionist crusade, who condemned slavery on moral grounds. The Free-Soilers trotted out wizened former President Van Buren and marched into the fray, shouting, "Free soil, free speech, free labor, and free men." These freedoms provided the bedrock on which the Free-Soilers built their party. Free-Soilers condemned slavery not so much for enslaving blacks but for destroying the chances of free white workers to rise up from wage-earning dependence to the esteemed status of self-employment. Free-Soilers argued that only with free soil in the West could a traditional American commitment to upward mobility continue to flourish. If forced to compete with slave labor, more costly wage labor would inevitably wither away, and with it the chance for the American worker to own property. As the first widely inclusive party organized around the issue of slavery and confined to a single section, the Free Soil party foreshadowed the emergence of the Republican party six years later.

With the slavery issue officially shoved under the rug by the two major parties, the politicians on both sides opened fire on personalities. The amateurish Taylor had to be carefully watched, lest his indiscreet pen puncture the reputation won by his sword. His admirers puffed him up as a gallant knight and a Napoleon, and sloganized his remark, allegedly uttered during the Battle of Buena Vista, "General Taylor never surrenders." Taylor's wartime popularity pulled him through. He harvested 1,360,967 popular and 163 electoral votes, as compared with Cass's 1,222,342 popular and 127 electoral votes. Free-Soiler Van Buren, although winning no state, polled 291,263 ballots and apparently diverted enough Democratic strength from Cass in the crucial state of New York to throw the election to Taylor.

"Californy Gold"

Tobacco-chewing President Taylor—with his stumpy legs, rough features, heavy jaw, black hair, ruddy complexion, and squinty gray eyes—was a military square peg in a political round hole. He would have been spared much turmoil if he could

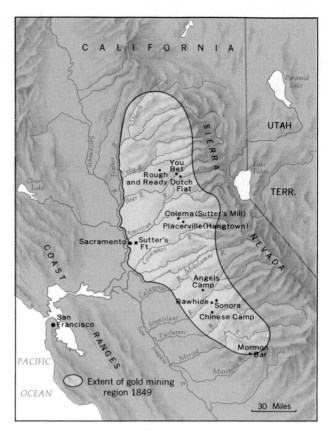

California Gold Rush Country   Miners from all over the world swarmed over the rivers that drained the western slope of California's Sierra Nevada mountains. Their nationalities and religions, their languages and their ways of life, are recorded in the colorful place names they left behind.

have continued to sit on the slavery lid. But the discovery of gold in California, early in 1848, blew the cover off.

A horde of adventurers poured into the valleys of California. Singing "O Susannah!" and shouting "Gold! Gold! Gold!" they began tearing frantically at the yellow-graveled streams and hills. A fortunate few of the bearded miners "struck it rich" at the "diggings." But the luckless many, who netted blisters instead of nuggets, probably would have been money well ahead if they had stayed at home unaffected by the "gold fever," which was often followed by more deadly fevers. The most reliable profits were made by those who mined the miners, notably by charging outrageous rates for laundry and other personal services. Some soiled clothing was even sent as far away as the Hawaiian Islands for washing.

Placer Miners in California
Cheap but effective, placer mining consisted of literally "washing" the gold out of surface deposits. No deep excavation was required. This crew of male and female miners in California in 1852 was using a "long tom" sluice that washed relatively large quantities of ore.

The overnight inpouring of tens of thousands of people into the future Golden State completely overwhelmed the one-horse government of California. A distressingly high proportion of the newcomers were lawless men, accompanied or followed by virtueless women. A contemporary song ran,

Oh what was your name in the States?
Was it Thompson or Johnson or Bates?
Did you murder your wife,
And fly for your life?
Say, what was your name in the States?

A married woman wrote from the California goldfields to her sister in New England in 1853:

"i tell you the woman are in great demand in this country no matter whether they are married or not   you need not think strange if you see me coming home with some good looking man some of these times with a pocket full of rocks. . . . it is all the go here for Ladys to leave there Husbands   two out of three do it   there is a first rate Chance for a single woman   she can have her choice of thousands   i wish mother was here she could marry a rich man and not have to lift her hand to do her work. . . ."

An outburst of crime inevitably resulted from the presence of so many miscreants and outcasts. Robbery, claim jumping, and murder were commonplace; and such violence was only partly discouraged by rough vigilante justice. In San Francisco, from 1848 to 1856, there were scores of lawless killings but only three semilegal hangings.

A majority of Californians, as decent and law-abiding citizens needing protection, grappled earnestly with the problem of erecting an adequate state government. Privately encouraged by President Taylor, they drafted a constitution in 1849 that excluded slavery and then boldly applied to Congress for admission. California would thus bypass the usual territorial stage, thwarting southern congressmen seeking to block free soil. Southern politicians, alarmed by the Californians' "impertinent" stroke for freedom, arose in violent opposition. Would California prove to be the golden straw that broke the back of the Union?

The idea that many ne'er-do-wells went west is found in the Journals *(January 1849) of Ralph Waldo Emerson (1803–1882):*

"If a man is going to California, he announces it with some hesitation; because it is a confession that he has failed at home."

Blacksmith Shop, by Francis A. Beckett, c. 1880 This blacksmith shop in gold-rush California was exceptionally well outfitted. The leather-aproned owner sports a stovepipe hat, while his assistants wear mere derbies. Note the massive bellows suspended from the high ceiling. It could heat the fire to blast-furnace temperatures.

Sectional Balance and the Underground Railroad

The South of 1850 was relatively well off. It then enjoyed, as it had from the beginning, more than its share of the nation's leadership. It had seated in the White House the war hero Zachary Taylor, a Virginia-born, slaveowning planter from Louisiana. It boasted a majority in the cabinet and on the Supreme Court. If outnumbered in the House, the South had equality in the Senate, where it could at least neutralize northern maneuvers. Its cotton fields were expanding, and cotton prices were profitably high. Few sane people, North or South, believed that slavery was seriously threatened where it already existed below the Mason-Dixon line. The fifteen slave states could easily veto any proposed constitutional amendment.

Yet the South was deeply worried, as it had been for several decades, by the ever-tipping political balance. There were then fifteen slave states and fifteen free states. The admission of California would destroy the delicate equilibrium in the Senate, perhaps forever. Potential slave territory under the American flag was running short, if it had not in fact disappeared. Agitation had already developed in the territories of New Mexico and Utah for admission as nonslave states. The fate of California might well establish a precedent for the rest of the Mexican Cession territory—an area purchased largely with southern blood.

Texas nursed an additional grievance of its own. It claimed a huge area east of the Rio Grande and north to the forty-second parallel, embracing in part about half the territory of present-day New Mexico. The federal government was proposing to detach this prize, while hot-blooded Texans were threatening to descend upon Santa Fe and seize what they regarded as rightfully theirs. The explosive quarrel foreshadowed shooting.

Many southerners were also angered by the nagging agitation in the North for the abolition of slavery in the District of Columbia. They looked with alarm on the prospect of a ten-mile-square oasis of free soil, thrust between slaveholding Maryland and slaveholding Virginia.

Even more disagreeable to the South was the loss of runaway slaves, many of whom were assisted north by the Underground Railroad. This virtual freedom train consisted of an informal chain of "stations" (anti-slavery homes), through which scores of "passengers" (runaway slaves) were spirited by "conductors" (usually white and black abolitionists) from the slave states to the free-soil sanctuary of Canada.

The most amazing of these "conductors" was an illiterate runaway slave from Maryland, fearless Harriet Tubman. During nineteen forays into the South, she rescued more than three hundred slaves, including her aged parents, and deservedly earned the title "Moses." Lively imaginations later exaggerated the role of the Underground Railroad and its "station masters," but its existence was a fact.

By 1850 southerners were demanding a new and more stringent fugitive-slave law. The old one, passed by Congress in 1793, had proved inadequate to cope with runaways, especially since unfriendly state authorities failed to provide needed cooperation. Unlike cattle thieves, the abolitionists who ran the Underground Railroad did not gain personally from their lawlessness. But to the slaveowners the loss was infuriating, whatever the motives. The moral judgments of the abolitionists seemed, in some ways, more galling than outright theft. They reflected not only a holier-than-thou attitude but a refusal to obey the laws solemnly passed by Congress.

Estimates indicate that the South in 1850 was losing perhaps 1,000 runaways a year, out of its total of some 4 million slaves. In fact, more blacks probably gained their freedom by self-purchase or voluntary emancipation than ever escaped. But the principle weighed heavily with the slavemasters. They rested their argument on the Constitution, which protected slavery, and on the laws of Congress, which provided for slave-catching. "Although the loss of property is felt," said a southern senator, "the loss of honor is felt still more."

Harriet Tubman, Premier Assistant of Runaway Slaves
John Brown called her "General Tubman" for her effective work in helping slaves escape to Canada on the Underground Railroad. During the Civil War she served as a Union spy behind Confederate lines. Herself illiterate, she worked after the war to bring education to the freed slaves in North Carolina.

Texas and the Disputed Area Before the Compromise of 1850

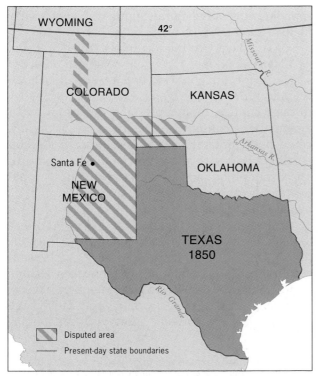

Twilight of the Senatorial Giants

Southern fears were such that Congress was confronted with catastrophe in 1850. Free-soil California was banging on the door for admission, and "fire-eaters" in the South were voicing ominous threats of secession. The crisis brought into the congressional forum the most distinguished assemblage of statesmen since the Constitutional Convention of 1787—the Old Guard of the dying generation and the young gladiators of the new. That "immortal trio"—Clay, Calhoun, and Webster—appeared together for the last time on the public stage.

Henry Clay, now seventy-three years of age, played a crucial role. The "Great Pacificator" had come to the Senate from Kentucky to engineer his third great compromise. The once-glamorous statesman—though disillusioned, enfeebled, and racked by a cruel cough—was still eloquent, conciliatory, and captivating. He proposed and skillfully defended a series of compromises. He was ably seconded by thirty-seven-year-old Senator Stephen A. Douglas of Illinois, the "Little Giant" (5 feet, 4 inches; 1.62 meters), whose role was less spectacular but even more important. Clay urged with all his persuasiveness that the North and South both make concessions and that the North partially yield by enacting a more feasible fugitive-slave law.

Senator John C. Calhoun, the "Great Nullifier," then sixty-eight and dying of tuberculosis, championed the South in his last formal speech. Too weak to deliver it himself, he sat bundled up in the Senate chamber, his eyes glowing within a stern face, while a younger colleague read his fateful words. Although approving the purpose of Clay's proposed concessions, Calhoun rejected them as not providing adequate safeguards. His impassioned plea was to leave slavery alone, return runaway slaves, give the South its rights as a minority, and restore the political balance. He had in view, as was later revealed, an utterly unworkable scheme of electing two presidents, one from the North and one from the South, each wielding a veto.

Calhoun died in 1850, before the debate was over, murmuring the sad words, "The South! The South! God knows what will become of her!" Appreciative fellow citizens in Charleston erected to his memory an imposing monument which bore the inscription "Truth, Justice, and the Constitution." Calhoun had labored to preserve the Union and had taken his stand on the Constitution, but his proposals in their behalf almost undid both.

Daniel Webster next took the Senate spotlight to uphold Clay's compromise measures in his last great speech, a three-hour effort. Now sixty-eight years old and suffering from a liver complaint aggravated by high living, he had lost some of the fire in his magnificent voice. Speaking deliberately and before overflowing galleries, he urged all reasonable concessions to the South, including a new fugitive-slave law with teeth.

As for slavery in the territories, asked Webster, why legislate on the subject? To do so was an act of sacrilege, for Almighty God had already passed the Wilmot Proviso. The good Lord had decreed—through climate, topography, and geography—that a plantation economy, and hence a slave economy, could not profitably exist in the Mexican Cession territory.* Webster sanely concluded that compromise, concession, and sweet reasonableness would provide the only solutions. "Let us not be pygmies," he pleaded, "in a case that calls for men."

If measured by its immediate effects, Webster's famed Seventh of March speech, 1850, was his finest. It helped turn the tide in the North toward compromise. The clamor for printed copies became so great that Webster mailed out more than 100,000, remarking that 200,000 would not satisfy the demand. His tremendous effort visibly strength-

---

Ralph Waldo Emerson, the philosopher and moderate abolitionist, was outraged by Webster's support of concessions to the South in the Fugitive Slave Act. In February 1851 he wrote in his Journal,

"I opened a paper to-day in which he [Webster] pounds on the old strings [of liberty] in a letter to the Washington Birthday feasters at New York. 'Liberty! liberty!' Pho! Let Mr. Webster, for decency's sake, shut his lips once and forever on this word. The word *liberty* in the mouth of Mr. Webster sounds like the word *love* in the mouth of a courtesan."

---

*Webster was wrong here; within one hundred years, California had become one of the great cotton-producing states of the Union.

Compromise of 1850

Concessions to the North	Concessions to the South
California admitted as a free state	The remainder of the Mexican Cession area to be formed into the territories of New Mexico and Utah, without restriction on slavery, hence open to popular sovereignty
Territory disputed by Texas and New Mexico to be surrendered to New Mexico	Texas to receive $10 million from the federal government as compensation
Abolition of the slave trade (but not slavery) in the District of Columbia	A more stringent Fugitive Slave Law, going beyond that of 1793

ened Union sentiment. It was especially pleasing to the banking and commercial centers of the North, which stood to lose millions of dollars by secession. One prominent Washington banker canceled two notes of Webster's, totaling $5,000, and sent him a personal check for $1,000 and a message of congratulations.

But the abolitionists, who had assumed Webster was one of them, upbraided him as a traitor, worthy of bracketing with Benedict Arnold. The poet Whittier lamented,

> *So fallen! so lost! the light withdrawn*
> *   Which once he wore!*
> *The glory from his gray hairs gone*
> *   For evermore!*

These reproaches were most unfair. Webster, who had long regarded slavery as evil but disunion as worse, had, in fact, always despised the abolitionists and never joined their ranks.

Deadlock and Danger on Capitol Hill

The stormy congressional debate of 1850 was not finished, for the Young Guard from the North were yet to have their say. This was the group of newer leaders who, unlike the aging Old Guard, had not grown up with the Union. They were more interested in purging and purifying it than in patching and preserving it.

William H. Seward, the wiry and husky-throated freshman senator from New York, was the able spokesman for many of the younger northern radicals. A strong antislaveryite, he came out unequivocally against concession. He seemed not to realize that compromise had brought the Union together and that when the sections could no longer compromise, they would have to part company.

Seward argued earnestly that Christian legislators must obey God's moral law as well as man's mundane law. He therefore appealed, with reference to excluding slavery in the territories, to an even "higher law" than the Constitution. This alarming phrase, wrenched from its context, may have cost him the presidential nomination and the presidency in 1860.

A Seward Caricature
He later became Lincoln's foremost rival for the presidency, and still later his secretary of state.

As the great debate in Congress ran its heated course, deadlock seemed certain. Blunt old President Taylor, who had allegedly fallen under the influence of men like "Higher Law" Seward, seemed bent on vetoing any compromise passed by Congress. His military ire was aroused by the threats of Texas to seize Santa Fe. He appeared to be doggedly determined to "Jacksonize" the dissenters, if need be, by leading an army against the Texans in person and hanging all "damned traitors." If troops had begun to march, the South probably would have rallied to the defense of Texas, and the Civil War might have erupted in 1850.

Breaking the Congressional Logjam

At the height of the controversy in 1850, President Taylor unknowingly helped the cause of concession by dying suddenly, probably of an acute intestinal disorder. Portly, round-faced Vice President Millard Fillmore, a colorless and conciliatory New York lawyer-politician, took over the reins. As presiding officer of the Senate, he had been impressed with the arguments for conciliation, and he gladly signed the series of compromise measures that passed Congress after seven long months of stormy debate. The balancing of interests in the Compromise of 1850 was delicate in the extreme.

The struggle to get these measures accepted by the country was hardly less heated than in Congress. In the northern states, "Union savers" like Senators Clay, Webster, and Douglas orated on behalf of the compromise. The ailing Clay himself delivered more than seventy speeches, as a powerful sentiment for acceptance gradually crystallized in the North. It was strengthened by a growing spirit of goodwill, which sprang partly from a feeling of relief and partly from an upsurge of prosperity enriched by California gold.

But the "fire-eaters" of the South were still violently opposed to concessions. One extreme South Carolina newspaper avowed that it loathed the Union and hated the North as much as it did Hell itself. A movement in the South to boycott northern goods gained some headway, but in the end the southern Unionists, assisted by the warm glow of prosperity, prevailed.

In mid-1850 an assemblage of southern extremists had met in Nashville, Tennessee, ironically near the burial place of Andrew Jackson. The delegates not only took a strong position in favor of slavery but condemned the compromise measures then being hammered out in Congress. Meeting again later in the year after the bills had passed, the convention proved to be a dud. By that time southern opinion had reluctantly accepted the verdict of Congress.

Like the calm after a storm, a second Era of Good Feelings dawned. Disquieting talk of secession subsided. Peace-loving people, both North and South, were determined that the compromises should be a "finality" and that the explosive issue of slavery should be buried. But this placid period of reason proved all too brief.

Balancing the Compromise Scales

Who got the better deal in the Compromise of 1850? The answer is clearly the North. California, as a free state, tipped the Senate balance permanently against the South. The territories of New Mexico and Utah were open to slavery on the basis of popular sovereignty. But the iron law of nature—the "highest law" of all—had loaded the dice in favor of free soil. The southerners urgently needed more slave territory to restore the "sacred balance." If they could not carve new states out of the recent conquests from Mexico, where else might they get them? In the Caribbean, was one answer.

Even the apparent gains of the South rang hollow. Disgruntled Texas was to be paid $10 million toward discharging its indebtedness, but in the long run this was a modest sum. The immense area in dispute had been torn from the side of slaveholding Texas and was almost certain to be free. The South had halted the drive toward abolition in the District of Columbia, at least temporarily, by permitting the outlawing of the slave *trade* in the federal district. But even this move was an entering wedge toward complete emancipation in the nation's capital.

Most alarming of all, the drastic new Fugitive Slave Law of 1850—"the Bloodhound Bill"—stirred up a storm of opposition in the North. The fleeing slaves could not testify in their own behalf, and they were denied a jury trial. These harsh practices, some citizens feared, threatened to create dangerous precedents for white Americans. The federal commissioner who handled the case of a fugitive would receive five dollars if the runaway were freed and ten dollars if not—an arrangement that strongly

Free
Slave
Decision left to territory

Slavery After the Compromise of 1850   Regarding the Fugitive Slave Act provisions of the Compromise of 1850, Ralph Waldo Emerson declared (May 1851) at Concord, Massachusetts, "The act of Congress . . . is a law which every one of you will break on the earliest occasion—a law which no man can obey, or abet the obeying, without loss of self-respect and forfeiture of the name of gentleman." Privately he wrote in his *Journal*, "This filthy enactment was made in the nineteenth century, by people who could read and write. I will not obey it, by God."

resembled a bribe. Freedom-loving northerners who aided the slave to escape were liable to heavy fines and jail sentences. They might even be ordered to join the slave-catchers, and this possibility rubbed salt into old sores.

So savage was this "Man-Stealing Law" that it touched off an explosive chain reaction in the North.

Many shocked moderates, hitherto passive, were driven into the swelling ranks of the antislaveryites. When a runaway slave from Virginia was captured in Boston in 1854, he had to be removed from the city under heavy federal guard through streets lined with sullen Yankees and shadowed by black-draped buildings festooned with flags flying upside down.

A Ride for Liberty, by Eastman Johnson In this famous painting, Johnson, a New England artist, brilliantly evokes the anxiety of fleeing slaves.

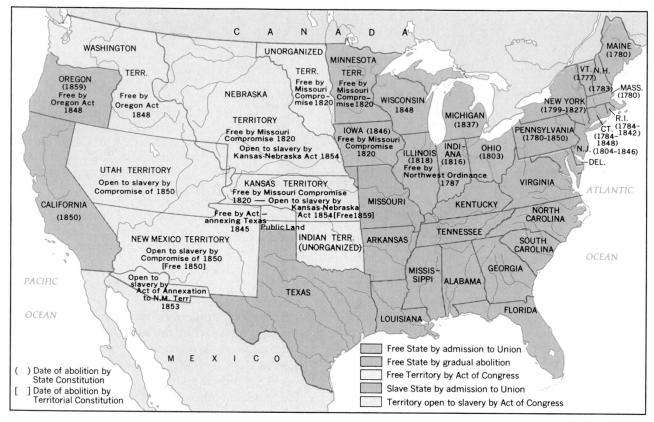

The Legal Status of Slavery, from the Revolution to the Civil War

One prominent Bostonian who witnessed this grim spectacle wrote that "we went to bed one night old-fashioned, conservative, Compromise Union Whigs and waked up stark mad Abolitionists."

The Underground Railroad stepped up its timetable, and infuriated northern mobs rescued slaves from their pursuers. Massachusetts, in a move toward nullification suggestive of South Carolina in 1832, made it a penal offense for any state official to enforce the new federal statute. Other states passed "personal liberty laws," which denied local jails to federal officials and otherwise hampered enforcement. The abolitionists rent the heavens with their protests against the man-stealing statute. A meeting presided over by William Lloyd Garrison in 1851 declared, "We execrate it, we spit upon it, we trample it under our feet."

Beyond question, the Fugitive Slave Law was an appalling blunder on the part of the South. No single irritant of the 1850s was more persistently galling to both sides, and none did more to awaken in the North a spirit of antagonism against the South. The southerners in turn were embittered because the northerners would not in good faith execute the law—the one real and immediate southern "gain" from the Great Compromise. Slave-catchers, with some success, redoubled their efforts.

Should the shooting showdown have come in 1850? From the standpoint of the secessionists, yes; from the standpoint of the Unionists, no. Time was fighting for the North. With every passing decade this huge section was forging further ahead in population and wealth—in crops, factories, foundries, ships, and railroads.

Delay also added immensely to the moral strength of the North—to its will to fight for the Union. In 1850 countless thousands of northern moderates were unwilling to pin the South to the rest of the nation with bayonets. But the inflammatory events of the 1850s did much to bolster the Yankee will to resist secession, whatever the cost. This one feverish decade gave the North time to accumulate the material and moral strength that provided the margin of victory. Thus the Compromise of 1850, from one point of view, won the Civil War for the Union.

Defeat and Doom for the Whigs

Meeting in Baltimore, the Democratic nominating convention of 1852 startled the nation. Hopelessly deadlocked, it finally stampeded to the second "dark horse" candidate in American history, an unrenowned lawyer-politician, Franklin Pierce, from the hills of New Hampshire. The Whigs tried to jeer him back into obscurity with the cry, "Who is Frank Pierce?" Democrats replied, "The Young Hickory of the Granite Hills."

Pierce was a weak and indecisive figure. Youngish, handsome, militarily erect, smiling, and convivial, he had served without real distinction in the Mexican War. As a result of a painful groin injury that caused him to fall off a horse, he was known as the "Fainting General," though scandalmongers pointed to a fondness for alcohol. But he was enemyless because he had been inconspicuous, and as a prosouthern northerner he was acceptable to the slavery wing of the Democratic party. His platform came out emphatically for the finality of the Compromise of 1850, Fugitive Slave Law and all.

The Whigs, also convening in Baltimore, missed a splendid opportunity to capitalize on their record in statecraft. Able to boast of a praiseworthy achievement in the Compromise of 1850, they might logically have nominated President Fillmore or Senator Webster, both of whom were associated with it. But having won in the past only with military heroes, they turned to another, "Old Fuss and Feathers" Winfield Scott, perhaps the ablest American general of his generation. Although he was a huge and impressive figure, his manner bordered on haughtiness. His personality not only repelled the masses but eclipsed his genuinely statesmanlike achievements. The Whig platform praised the Compromise of 1850 as a lasting arrangement, though less enthusiastically than the Democrats.

With slavery and sectionalism to some extent soft-pedaled, the campaign again degenerated into a dull and childish attack on personalities. Democrats ridiculed Scott's pomposity; Whigs charged that Pierce was the hero of "many a well-fought *bottle.*" Democrats cried exultantly, "We Polked 'em in '44; we'll Pierce 'em in '52."

Luckily for the Democrats, the Whig party was hopelessly split. Antislavery Whigs of the North swallowed Scott as their nominee but deplored his platform, which endorsed the hated Fugitive Slave Law. The current phrase ran, "We accept the candidate but spit on the platform." Southern Whigs, who doubted Scott's loyalty to the Compromise of 1850 and especially the Fugitive Slave Law, accepted the platform but spat on the candidate. More than five thousand Georgia Whigs—"finality men"—voted in vain for Webster, although he had died nearly two weeks before the election.

General Scott, victorious on the battlefield, met defeat at the ballot box. His friends remarked whimsically that he was not used to "running." Actually, he was stabbed in the back by his fellow Whigs, notably in the South. The pliant Pierce won in a landslide, 254 electoral votes to 42, although the popular count was closer, 1,601,117 to 1,385,453.

The election of 1852 was fraught with frightening significance, though it may have seemed tame at the time. It marked the effective end of the disorganized Whig party and, within a few years, its complete death. The Whigs' demise augured the eclipse of *national* parties and the worrisome rise of purely *sectional* political alignments. The Whigs were governed at times by the crassest opportunism, and they won only two presidential elections (1840, 1848) in their colorful career, both with war heroes. They finally choked to death trying to swallow the distasteful Fugitive Slave Law. But their great contribution—and a noteworthy one indeed—was to help uphold the ideal of the Union through their electoral strength in the South and through the eloquence of leaders like Henry Clay and Daniel Webster. Both of these statesmen, by unhappy coincidence, died during the 1852 campaign. But the good they had done lived after them and contributed powerfully to the eventual preservation of a united United States.

President Pierce the Expansionist

At the outset the Pierce administration displayed vigor. The new president, standing confidently before some fifteen thousand people on inauguration day, delivered from memory a clear-voiced inaugural address. His cabinet contained aggressive southerners, including as secretary of war one Jefferson Davis, future president of the Confederacy. The people of Dixie were determined to acquire more slave territory, and the compliant Pierce was prepared to be their willing tool.

The intoxicating victories of the Mexican War stimulated the spirit of Manifest Destiny. The conquest of a Pacific frontage, and the discovery of gold on it, aroused lively interest in the transisthmian land routes of Central America, chiefly in Panama and Nicaragua. Many Americans were looking even further ahead to potential canal routes and to the islands flanking them, notably Spain's Cuba.

These visions especially fired the ambitions of the "slavocrats." They lusted for new territory after the Compromise of 1850 seemingly closed most of the lands of the Mexican Cession to the "peculiar institution." In 1856 a Texan proposed a toast that was drunk with gusto: "To the Southern republic bounded on the north by the Mason and Dixon line and on the South by the Isthmus of Tehuantepec [southern Mexico], including Cuba and all other lands on our Southern shore."

Southerners took a special interest in Nicaragua. A brazen American adventurer, William Walker, tried repeatedly to grab control of this Central American country in the 1850s. (He had earlier attempted and failed to seize Baja California from Mexico and turn it into a slave state.) Backed by an armed force recruited largely in the South, he installed himself as president in July 1856 and promptly legalized slavery. One southern newspaper proclaimed to the planter aristocracy that Walker—the "gray-eyed man of destiny"—"now offers Nicaragua to you and your slaves, at a time when you have not a friend on the face of the earth." But a coalition of Central American nations formed an alliance to overthrow him. President Pierce withdrew diplomatic recognition, and the gray-eyed man's destiny was to crumple before a Honduran firing squad in 1860.

Nicaragua was also of vital concern to Great Britain, the world's leading maritime and commercial power. Fearing that the grasping Yankees would monopolize the trade arteries there, the British made haste to secure a solid foothold at Greytown, the eastern end of the proposed Nicaraguan canal route. This challenge to the Monroe Doctrine forthwith raised the ugly possibility of an armed clash. The crisis was surmounted in 1850 by the Clayton-Bulwer Treaty, which stipulated that neither America nor Britain would fortify or secure exclusive control over any future isthmian waterway. This agreement, at the time, seemed necessary to halt the British, but to American canal promoters in later years, it proved to be a ball and chain.

America had become a Pacific power with the acquisition of California and Oregon, both of which faced Asia. The prospects of a rich trade with the Far East now seemed rosier. Americans had already established contacts with China, and shippers were urging Washington to push for commercial intercourse with Japan. The mikado's empire, after some

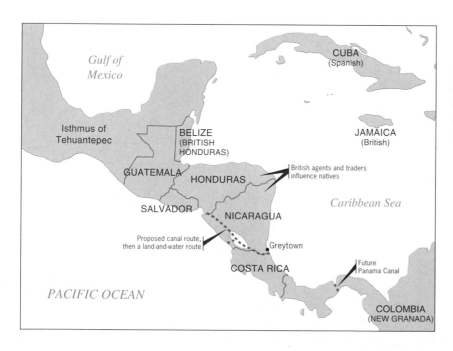

Central America, c. 1850, Showing British Possessions and Proposed Canal Routes   Until President Theodore Roosevelt swung into action with his big stick in 1903, a Nicaraguan canal, closer to the United States, was generally judged more desirable than a canal across Panama.

Commodore Perry and Flag Bearer, by an anonymous Japanese artist, c. 1853 (detail)   Painted at the time of the opening of Japan, this scene shows Perry and his steward from the point of view of a Japanese artist.

Coveted Cuba: Pearl of the Antilles

Sugar-rich Cuba, lying off the nation's southern doorstep, was the prime objective of Manifest Destiny in the 1850s. Supporting a large population of enslaved blacks, it was coveted by the South as the most desirable slave territory available. Carved into several states, it would once more restore the political balance in the Senate.

Cuba was a kind of heirloom—the most important remnant of Spain's once-mighty New World empire. Polk, the expansionist, had taken steps to offer $100 million for it, but the sensitive Spaniards had replied that they would see it sunk into the ocean before they would sell it to the Americans at any price. With purchase completely out of the question, seizure was apparently the only way to pluck the ripening fruit.

Private adventurers from the South now undertook to shake the tree of Manifest Destiny. During 1850–1851 two "filibustering" expeditions (from the Spanish *filibustero*, meaning "freebooter" or "pirate"), each numbering several hundred armed men, descended upon Cuba. Both feeble efforts were repelled, and the last one ended in tragedy when the leader and fifty followers—some of them from the "best families" of the South—were summarily shot or strangled. So outraged were the southerners that an angry mob sacked Spain's consulate in New Orleans.

Spanish officials in Cuba rashly forced a showdown in 1854, when they seized an American steamer, *Black Warrior*, on a technicality. Now was the time for President Pierce, dominated as he was by the South, to provoke a war with Spain and seize Cuba. The major powers of Europe—England, France, and Russia—were about to become bogged down in the Crimean War and hence were unable to aid Spain.

An incredible cloak-and-dagger episode followed. The secretary of state instructed the American ministers in Spain, England, and France to prepare confidential recommendations for the acquisition of Cuba. Meeting initially at Ostend, Belgium, the three envoys drew up a top-secret dispatch, soon known as the Ostend Manifesto. This startling document urged that the administration offer $120 million for Cuba. If Spain refused, and if its continued ownership endangered American

disagreeable experiences with the European world, had withdrawn into a cocoon of isolationism and had remained there for over two hundred years. The Japanese were so protective of their insularity that they prohibited shipwrecked foreign sailors from leaving and refused to readmit to Japan their own sailors who had been washed up on the West Coast of North America. But by 1853, as events proved, Japan was ready to emerge from reclusion, partly because of the Russian menace.

The Washington government was now eager to pry open the bamboo gates of Japan. It dispatched a fleet of awesome, smoke-belching warships, commanded by Commodore Matthew C. Perry, brother of the hero of the Battle of Lake Erie in 1813. By a judicious display of force and tact, he persuaded the Japanese in 1854 to sign a memorable treaty. It provided for only a commercial foot in the door, but it was the beginning of an epochal relationship between the Land of the Rising Sun and the Western world. Ironically, this achievement attracted little notice at the time, partly because Perry devised no memorable slogan.

> *The first platform of the newly born (antislavery) Republican party in 1856 lashed out at the Ostend Manifesto, with its transparent suggestion that Cuba be seized. The plank read,*
>
> "*Resolved,* That the highwayman's plea, that 'might makes right', embodied in the Ostend Circular, was in every respect unworthy of American diplomacy, and would bring shame and dishonor upon any Government or people that gave it their sanction."

interests, the United States would "be justified in wresting" the island from the Spanish.

The secret Ostend Manifesto quickly leaked out. Northern free-soilers, already angered by the Fugitive Slave Law and other gains for slavery, rose in an outburst of wrath against the "manifesto of brigands." Confronted with disruption at home, the red-faced Pierce administration was forced to drop its brazen schemes for Cuba.

Clearly the slavery issue, like a two-headed snake with the heads at each other's throat, deadlocked territorial expansion in the 1850s. The North, flushed with Manifest Destiny, was developing a renewed appetite for Canada. The South coveted Cuba. Neither section would permit the other to get the apple of its eye, so neither got either. The shackled black hands of Harriet Beecher Stowe's Uncle Tom, whose plight had already stung the conscience of the North, now held the South back from Cuba. The internal distresses of the United States were such that, for once, it could not take advantage of Europe's distresses—in this case the Crimean War.

Pacific Railroad Promoters and the Gadsden Purchase

Acute transportation problems were another legacy of the Mexican War. The newly acquired prizes of California and Oregon might just as well have been islands some 8,000 miles (13,000 kilometers) west of the nation's capital. The sea routes to and from the isthmus of Panama, to say nothing of those around South America, were too long. Covered-wagon travel past bleaching animal bones was possible, but slow and dangerous. A popular song recalled,

> *They swam the wide rivers and crossed the tall peaks,*
> *And camped on the prairie for weeks upon weeks.*
> *Starvation and cholera and hard work and slaughter,*
> *They reached California spite of hell and high water.*

Feasible land transportation was imperative—or the newly won possessions on the Pacific Coast might break away. Camels were even proposed as the answer. Several score of these temperamental beasts—"ships of the desert"—were imported from the Near East, but mule-driving Americans did not adjust to them. A transcontinental railroad was clearly the only real solution to the problem.

Railroad promoters, both North and South, had projected many drawing-board routes to the Pacific Coast. But the estimated cost in all cases was so great that for many years there could obviously be only one line. Should its terminus be in the North or in the South? The favored section would reap rich rewards in wealth, population, and influence. The South, losing the economic race with the North, was eager to extend a railroad through adjacent southwestern territory all the way to California.

Another chunk of Mexico now seemed desirable, because the campaigns of the recent war had shown that the best railway route ran slightly south of the Mexican border. Secretary of War Jefferson Davis, a Mississippian, arranged to have James Gadsden, a prominent South Carolina railroad man, appointed minister to Mexico. Finding Santa Anna in power for the sixth and last time, and as usual in need of money, Gadsden made gratifying headway. He negotiated a treaty in 1853, which ceded to the United States the Gadsden Purchase area for $10 million. The transaction aroused much criticism among northerners, who objected to paying a huge sum for a cactus-strewn desert nearly the size of Gadsden's South Carolina. Undeterred, the Senate approved the pact, in the process shortsightedly eliminating a window on the Sea of Cortez.

No doubt the Gadsden Purchase enabled the South to claim the coveted railroad with even greater insistence. A southern track would be easier to build because the mountains were less high and

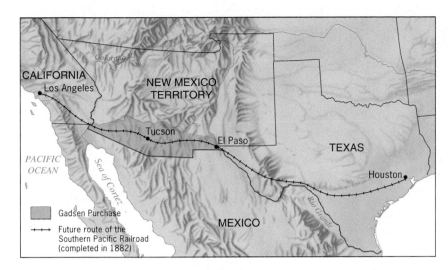

The Gadsden Purchase, 1853

because the route, unlike the proposed northern lines, would not pass through unorganized territory. Texas was already a state at this point, and New Mexico (with the Gadsden Purchase added) was a formally organized territory, with federal troops available to provide protection against marauding tribes of Indians. Any northern or central railroad line would have to be thrust through the unorganized territory of Nebraska, where the buffalo and Indians roamed.

Northern railroad boosters quickly replied that if organized territory were the test, then Nebraska should be organized. Such a move was not premature, because thousands of land-hungry pioneers were already poised on the Nebraska border. But all schemes proposed in Congress for organizing the territory were greeted with apathy or hostility by many southerners. Why should the South help create new free-soil states and thus cut its own throat by facilitating a northern railroad?

Douglas's Kansas-Nebraska Scheme

At this point in 1854, Senator Stephen A. Douglas of Illinois delivered a counterstroke to offset the Gadsden thrust for southern expansion westward. A squat, bull-necked, and heavy-chested figure, the "Little Giant" radiated the energy and breezy optimism of the self-made man. An ardent booster for the West, he longed to break the North-South deadlock over westward expansion and stretch a line of settlements across the continent. He had also invested heavily in Chicago real estate and in railway stock and was eager to have the Windy City become the eastern terminus of the proposed Pacific railroad. He would thus endear himself to the voters of Illinois, benefit his section, and enrich his own purse.

A veritable "steam engine in breeches," Douglas threw himself behind a legislative scheme that would enlist the support of a reluctant South. The proposed Territory of Nebraska would be sliced into two territories, Kansas and Nebraska. Their status regarding slavery would be settled by popular sovereignty—a democratic concept to which Douglas and his western constituents were deeply attached. Kansas, which lay due west of slaveholding Missouri, would presumably choose to become a slave state. But Nebraska, lying west of free-soil Iowa, would presumably become a free state.

Douglas's Kansas-Nebraska scheme ran headlong into a formidable political obstacle. The Missouri Compromise of 1820 had forbidden slavery in the proposed Nebraska Territory, which lay north of the sacred 36° 30' line; and the only way to open the region to popular sovereignty was to repeal the ancient compact outright. This bold step Douglas was prepared to take, even at the risk of shattering the uneasy truce patched together by the Compromise of 1850.

Many southerners, who had not conceived of Kansas as slave soil, rose to the bait. Here was a chance to gain one more slave state. The pliable President Pierce, under the thumb of southern

Stephen A. Douglas (1813–1861)   Despite having stirred up sectional bitterness, Douglas was so devoted to the Union that he warmly supported his rival, Lincoln, when war broke out. He attended the inauguration and reportedly held Lincoln's stovepipe hat while the president spoke.

Douglas Hatches a Slavery Problem   Note the already hatched Missouri Compromise, Squatter Sovereignty, and Filibuster (in Cuba), and the about-to-hatch Free Kansas and Dred Scott decision. So bitter was the outcry against Douglas at the time of the Kansas-Nebraska controversy that he claimed with exaggeration that he could have traveled from Boston to Chicago at night by the light from his burning effigies.

advisers, threw his full weight behind the Kansas-Nebraska Bill.

But the Missouri Compromise, now thirty-four years old, could not be brushed aside lightly. Whatever Congress passes it can repeal, but by this time the North had come to regard the sectional pact as almost as sacred as the Constitution itself. Free-soil members of Congress struck back with a vengeance. They met their match in the violently gesticulating Douglas, who was the ablest rough-and-tumble debater of his generation. Employing twisted logic and oratorical fireworks, he rammed the bill through Congress, with strong support from many southerners. So heated were political passions that bloodshed was barely averted. Some members carried a concealed revolver or a bowie knife—or both.

Douglas's motives in prodding anew the snarling dog of slavery have long puzzled historians. His personal interests have already been mentioned. In addition, his foes accused him of angling for the presidency in 1856. Yet his admirers have argued plausibly in his defense that if he had not championed the ill-omened bill, someone else would have.

The truth seems to be that Douglas acted somewhat impulsively and recklessly. His heart did not bleed over the issue of slavery, and he declared repeatedly that he did not care whether it was voted up or down in the territories. What he failed to perceive was that hundreds of thousands of his fellow citizens in the North *did* feel deeply on this moral issue. They regarded the repeal of the Missouri Compromise as an intolerable breach of faith, and they would henceforth resist to the last trench all future southern demands for slave territory. As Abraham

Lincoln said, the North wanted to give to pioneers in the West "a clean bed, with no snakes in it."

Genuine leaders, like skillful chess players, must foresee the possible effects of their moves. Douglas predicted a "hell of a storm," but he grossly underestimated its proportions. His critics in the North, branding him a "Judas" and a "traitor," greeted his name with frenzied boos, hisses, and "three groans for Doug." But he still enjoyed a high degree of popularity among his following in the Democratic party, especially in Illinois, a stronghold of popular sovereignty.

Congress Legislates a Civil War

The Kansas-Nebraska Act—a curtain raiser to a terrible drama—was one of the most momentous measures ever to pass Congress. By one way of reckoning, it greased the slippery slope to Civil War.

Antislavery northerners were angered by what they condemned as an act of bad faith by the "Nebrascals" and their "Nebrascality." All future compromise with the South would be immeasurably more difficult, and without compromise there was bound to be conflict.

Henceforth the Fugitive Slave Law of 1850, previously enforced in the North only halfheartedly, was

> *The Massachusetts senator Charles Sumner (1811–1874) described the Kansas-Nebraska Bill as "at once the worst and the best Bill on which Congress ever acted." It was the worst because it represented a victory for the slave power in the short run. But it was the best, he said prophetically, because*
>
> "[It] annuls all past compromises with slavery, and makes all future compromises impossible. Thus it puts freedom and slavery face to face, and bids them grapple. Who can doubt the result?"

a dead letter. The Kansas-Nebraska Act wrecked two compromises: that of 1820, which it repealed specifically, and that of 1850, which northern opinion repealed indirectly. Emerson wrote, "The Fugitive [Slave] Law did much to unglue the eyes of men, and now the Nebraska Bill leaves us staring." Northern abolitionists and southern "fire-eaters" alike saw less and less they could live with. The growing legion of antislaveryites gained numerous recruits, who resented the grasping move by the "slavocracy" for Kansas. The southerners, in turn, became inflamed

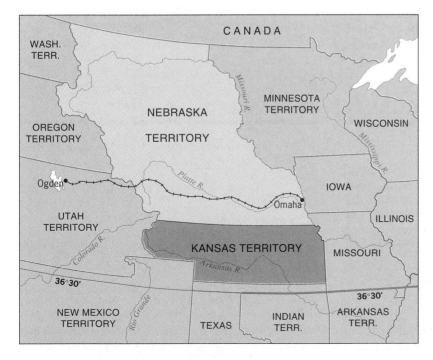

Kansas and Nebraska, 1854
The future Union Pacific Railroad (completed in 1869) is shown. Note the Missouri Compromise line of 36°30' (1820).

when the free-soilers tried to control Kansas, contrary to the presumed "deal."

The proud Democrats—a party now over half a century old—were shattered by the Kansas-Nebraska Act. They did elect a president in 1856, but he was the last one they were to boost into the White House for twenty-eight long years.

Undoubtedly the most durable offspring of the Kansas-Nebraska blunder was the new Republican party. It sprang up spontaneously in the Middle West, notably in Wisconsin and Michigan, as a mighty moral protest against the gains of slavery. Gathering together dissatisfied elements, it soon included disgruntled Whigs (among them Abraham Lincoln), Democrats, Free-Soilers, Know-Nothings, and other foes of the Kansas-Nebraska Act. The hodgepodge party spread eastward with the swiftness of a prairie fire and with the zeal of a religious crusade. Unheard of and unheralded at the beginning of 1854, it elected a Republican Speaker of the House of Representatives within two years. Never really a third-party movement, it erupted with such force as to become almost overnight the second major political party—and a purely sectional one at that.

At long last the dreaded sectional rift had appeared. The new Republican party would not be allowed south of the Mason-Dixon line. Countless southerners subscribed wholeheartedly to the sentiment that it was "a nigger stealing, stinking, putrid, abolition party." The Union was in dire peril.

Chronology

1848 Treaty of Guadalupe Hidalgo ends U.S.-Mexican War

Taylor defeats Cass and Van Buren for presidency

1849 California gold rush

1850 Fillmore assumes presidency after Taylor's death
Compromise of 1850, including Fugitive Slave Law
Clayton-Bulwer Treaty with Britain

1852 Pierce defeats Scott for presidency

1853 Gadsden Purchase from Mexico

1854 Commodore Perry opens Japan
Ostend Manifesto proposes seizure of Cuba
Kansas-Nebraska Act
Republican party organized

1856 William Walker becomes president of Nicaragua and legalizes slavery

SUGGESTED READINGS

PRIMARY SOURCE DOCUMENTS

The *Congressional Globe* for 1850 contains the dramatic orations of a dying generation of American statesmen on the Compromise of 1850. See the speeches by Webster,* Calhoun,* and Clay (in Richard Hofstadter, ed., *Great Issues in American History*). The debate on the Kansas-Nebraska Bill can be found in the 1854 volume of the same source, which includes addresses by Stephen A. Douglas* and his Republican opponent, Salmon P. Chase.*

SECONDARY SOURCES

Earlier interpretations of the sectional crisis include the relevant portions of James Ford Rhodes, *History of the United States* (1893–1906), and Charles A. and Mary R. Beard, *The Rise of American Civilization* (1927); see also Avery Craven, *The Repressible Conflict, 1830–1861* (1939). The best account of the events of the 1850s is David M. Potter's masterful *The Impending Crisis,*

---

*An asterisk indicates that the document, or an excerpt from it, can be found in Thomas A. Bailey and David M. Kennedy, eds., *The American Spirit: United States History as Seen by Contemporaries*, 9th ed. (Boston: Houghton Mifflin, 1998).

1848–1861 (1976). A concise summary of the events leading to the war is also available in the opening chapters of James M. McPherson, *Battle Cry of Freedom: The Civil War Era* (1988). Comprehensive treatments may be found in James G. Randall and David Donald, *The Civil War and Reconstruction* (rev. ed., 1969); William J. Cooper, *The South and the Politics of Slavery* (1978); Kenneth Stampp, ed., *The Imperiled Union: Essays on the Background of the Civil War* (1980); Richard H. Sewell, *A House Divided: Sectionalism and Civil War, 1848–1860* (1988); and William Freehling, *Road to Disunion: Secessionists at Bay, 1776–1854* (1990). The standard work is Holman Hamilton, *Prologue to Conflict: The Crisis and Compromise of 1850* (1964). On the southern view of events, see Kenneth S. Greenberg, *Masters and Statesmen: The Political Culture of American Slavery* (1985); and Eugene Genovese, *The World the Slaveholders Made* (1969). The emergence of the Republican party can be studied in Eric Foner's brilliant discussion of ideology, *Free Soil, Free Labor, Free Men* (1970); William Gienapp, *The Origins of the Republican Party, 1852–1856* (1987); Michael Holt's perceptive *Forging a Majority: The For-*

mation of the Republican Party in Pittsburgh (1969); Paul Kleppner, *The Third Electoral System, 1853–1892: Parties, Voters and Political Cultures* (1979); and Bruce Levine, *Half Slave and Half Free: The Roots of the Civil War* (1992). On the Know-Nothing party, see Tyler Anbinder, *Nativism and Slavery: The Northern Know-Nothings and the Politics of the 1850s* (1992). Holt has developed his views in *The Political Crisis of the 1850s* (1978), an unusually provocative book. Party politics are treated in two books by Joel H. Silbey, *The Shrine of Party: Congressional Voting Behavior, 1841–1852* (1967) and his unorthodox *Partisan Imperative: The Dynamics of American Politics Before the Civil War* (1985). Richard H. Sewell, *Ballots for Freedom: Antislavery Politics in the United States, 1837–1860* (1976), is a standard work. A biographical approach is taken in Merrill Peterson, *The Great Triumvirate: Webster, Clay, and Calhoun* (1987). Robert Trennert examines the impact of westward migration and the gold rush on U.S. Indian policy in *Alternative to Extinction: Federal Indian Policy and the Beginnings of the Reservation System, 1846–1851* (1975).

20

Drifting Toward Disunion

1854–1861

A house divided against itself cannot stand. I believe this government cannot endure permanently half slave and half free.

ABRAHAM LINCOLN, 1858

Stowe and Helper: Literary Incendiaries

Sectional tensions were further strained in 1852, and later, by an inky phenomenon. Harriet Beecher Stowe, a wisp of a woman and the mother of a half-dozen children, published her heartrending novel *Uncle Tom's Cabin*. Dismayed by the passage of the Fugitive Slave Law, she was determined to awaken the North to the wickedness of slavery by laying bare its terrible inhumanity, especially the cruel splitting of families. Her wildly popular book relied on powerful imagery and touching pathos. "God wrote it," she explained in later years—a reminder that the deeper sources of her antislavery sentiments lay in the evangelical religious crusades of the Second Great Awakening.

The success of the novel at home and abroad was sensational. Several hundred thousand copies were published in the first year, and the totals soon ran into the millions as the tale was translated into more than a score of languages. It was also put on the stage in "Tom shows" for lengthy runs. No other novel in American history—perhaps in all history—can be compared with it as a political force. To millions of people it made slavery appear almost as evil as it really was.

When Mrs. Stowe was introduced to President Lincoln in 1862, he reportedly remarked with twinkling eyes, "So you're the little woman who wrote the book that made this great war." The truth is that *Uncle Tom's Cabin* did help start the Civil War—and win it. The South condemned that "vile wretch in petticoats" when it learned that hundreds of thousands of fellow Americans were reading and believing her "unfair" indictment. Mrs. Stowe had never

Harriet Beecher Stowe (1811–1896), daguerreotype by Southworth and Hawes   She was a remarkable woman whose pen helped to change the course of history.

135,000 SETS, 270,000 VOLUMES SOLD.

UNCLE TOM'S CABIN

FOR SALE HERE.

AN EDITION FOR THE MILLION, COMPLETE IN 1 Vol., PRICE 37 1-2 CENTS.
"   "   IN GERMAN, IN 1 Vol., PRICE 50 CENTS.
"   "   IN 2 Vols., CLOTH, 6 PLATES, PRICE $1.50.
SUPERB ILLUSTRATED EDITION, IN 1 Vol., WITH 153 ENGRAVINGS,
PRICES FROM $2.50 TO $5.00.

The Greatest Book of the Age.

"The Book That Made This Great War"   Lincoln's celebrated remark to author Harriet Beecher Stowe reflected the enormous emotional impact of her impassioned novel.

witnessed slavery at first hand in the Deep South, but she had seen it briefly during a visit to Kentucky, and she had lived for many years in Ohio, a center of Underground Railway activity.

Uncle Tom, endearing and enduring, left a profound impression on the North. Uncounted thousands of readers swore that henceforth they would have nothing to do with the enforcement of the Fugitive Slave Law. The tale was devoured by millions of impressionable youths in the 1850s—some of whom later became the Boys in Blue who volunteered to fight the Civil War through to its grim finale. The memory of a beaten and dying Uncle Tom helped sustain them in their determination to wipe out the plague of slavery.

The novel was immensely popular abroad, especially in England and France. Countless readers wept over the kindly Tom and the angelic Eva, while deploring the brutal Simon Legree. When the guns in America finally began to boom, the common people of England sensed that the triumph of the North would spell the end of the black curse. The governments in London and Paris seriously considered intervening in behalf of the South, but they were sobered by the realization that many of their own people, aroused by the "Tom-mania," might not support them.

Another trouble-brewing book appeared in 1857, five years after the debut of Uncle Tom. Entitled *The Impending Crisis of the South,* it was written by Hinton R. Helper, a nonaristocratic white from North Carolina. Hating both slavery and blacks, he attempted to prove by an array of statistics that indirectly the nonslaveholding whites were the ones who suffered most from the millstone of slavery. Unable to secure a publisher in the South, he finally managed to find one in the North.

Helper's influence was negligible among the poorer whites to whom he addressed his message. His book, with its "dirty allusions," was banned in the South, where book-burning parties were held. But in the North, untold thousands of copies, many

> *In the closing scenes of Harriet Beecher Stowe's novel, Uncle Tom's brutal master, Simon Legree, orders the $1,200 slave savagely beaten (to death) by two fellow slaves. Through tears and blood Tom exclaims,*
>
> "No! no! no! my soul an't yours Mas'r! You haven't bought it—ye can't buy it! It's been bought and paid for by One that is able to keep it. No matter, no matter, you can't harm me!" "I can't" said Legree, with a sneer; "we'll see—we'll see! Here, Sambo, Quimbo, give this dog such a breakin' in as he won't get over this month!"

in condensed form, were distributed as campaign literature by the Republicans. Southerners were further embittered when they learned that their northern brethren were spreading these wicked "lies." Thus did southerners, reacting much as they did to *Uncle Tom's Cabin,* become increasingly unwilling to sleep under the same federal roof with their hostile Yankee bedfellows.

The North-South Contest for Kansas

The rolling plains of Kansas had meanwhile been providing an example of the worst-possible workings of popular sovereignty, although admittedly under abnormal conditions.

Newcomers who ventured into Kansas were a motley lot. Most of the northerners were just ordinary westward-moving pioneers in search of richer lands beyond the sunset. But a small part of the inflow was financed by groups of northern abolitionists or free-soilers. The most famous of these antislavery organizations was the New England Emigrant Aid Company, which sent about two thousand people to the troubled area to forestall the South—and also to make a profit. Shouting "Ho for Kansas," many of them carried the deadly new breech-loading Sharps rifles, nicknamed "Beecher's Bibles" after the Reverend Henry Ward Beecher (Harriet Beecher Stowe's brother), who had helped raise money for their purchase. Many of the Kansas-bound pioneers sang Whittier's marching song (1854):

> *We cross the prairie as of old*
> *The pilgrims crossed the sea,*
> *To make the West, as they the East,*
> *The homestead of the free!*

Southern spokesmen, now more than ordinarily touchy, raised furious cries of betrayal. They had supported the Kansas-Nebraska scheme of Douglas with the unspoken understanding that Kansas would become slave and Nebraska free. The northern "Nebrascals," allegedly by foul means, were now apparently out to "abolitionize" *both* Kansas and Nebraska.

A few southern hotheads, quick to respond in kind, attempted to "assist" small groups of well-armed slaveowners to Kansas. Some carried banners proclaiming,

> *Let Yankees tremble, abolitionists fall,*
> *Our motto is, "Give Southern Rights to All."*

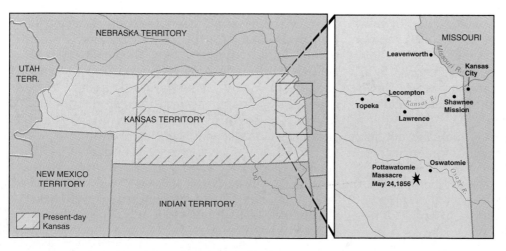

Bleeding Kansas, 1854–1860 "Enter every election district in Kansas . . . and vote at the point of a bowie knife or revolver," one proslavery agitator exhorted a Missouri crowd. Proslavery Missouri senator David Atchison declared that "there are 1,100 men coming over from Platte County to vote, and if that ain't enough we can send 5,000—enough to kill every Goddamned abolitionist in the Territory."

But planting blacks on Kansas soil was a losing game. Slaves were valuable and volatile property, and foolish indeed were owners who would take them where bullets were flying and where the soil might be voted free under popular sovereignty. The census of 1860 found only 2 slaves among 107,000 souls in all Kansas Territory and only 15 in Nebraska. There was much truth in the charge that the whole quarrel over slavery in the territories revolved around "an imaginary Negro in an impossible place."

Crisis conditions in Kansas rapidly worsened. When the day came in 1855 to elect members of the first territorial legislature, proslavery "border ruffians" poured in from Missouri to vote early and often. The slavery supporters triumphed and then set up their own puppet government at Shawnee Mission. The free-soilers, unable to stomach this fraudulent conspiracy, established an extralegal regime of their own in Topeka. The confused Kansans thus had their choice between two governments—one based on fraud, the other on illegality.

Tension mounted as settlers also feuded over conflicting land claims. The breaking point came in 1856 when a gang of proslavery raiders, alleging provocation, shot up and burned a part of the free-soil town of Lawrence. This outrage was but the prelude to a bloodier tragedy.

Kansas in Convulsion

The fanatical figure of John Brown now stalked upon the Kansas battlefield. Spare, gray-bearded, and iron-willed, he was obsessively dedicated to the abolitionist cause. The power of his glittering gray eyes was such, so he claimed, that his stare could force a dog or cat to slink out of a room. Becoming involved in dubious dealings, including horse stealing, he moved to Kansas from Ohio with a part of his large family. Brooding over the recent attack on Lawrence, "Old Brown" of Osawatomie led a band of his followers to Pottawatomie Creek, in May 1856. There they literally hacked to pieces five surprised men, presumed to be proslaveryites. This fiendish butchery, clearly the product of a deranged mind, besmirched the free-soil cause and brought vicious retaliation from the proslavery forces.

Civil war in Kansas, which thus flared forth in 1856, continued intermittently until it merged with the large-scale Civil War of 1861–1865. Altogether, the Kansas conflict destroyed millions of dollars'

John Brown (1800–1859)   A militant abolitionist, Brown became perhaps the most sung-about man up to that time, except Jesus. From a primitive photograph (daguerreotype) taken in 1856.

worth of property, paralyzed agriculture in certain areas, and cost scores of lives.

Yet by 1857 Kansas had enough people, chiefly free-soilers, to apply for statehood on a popular-sovereignty basis. The proslavery forces, then in the saddle, devised a tricky document known as the Lecompton Constitution. The people were not allowed to vote for or against the constitution as a whole, but for the constitution either "with slavery" or "with no slavery." If they voted against slavery, one of the remaining provisions of the constitution would protect the owners of slaves already in Kansas. So whatever the outcome, there would still be black bondage in Kansas. Many free-soilers, infuriated by this ploy, boycotted the polls. Left to themselves, the slaveryites approved the constitution with slavery late in 1857.

The scene next shifted to Washington. President Pierce had been succeeded by the no-less-pliable James Buchanan, who was also strongly under southern influence. Blind to sharp divisions within his own Democratic party, Buchanan threw the

The Little Giant in the Character of the Gladiator, 1858
Champion of popular sovereignty, Stephen A. Douglas (nicknamed the "Little Giant") is shown as a gladiator, doing battle for the Kansas-Nebraska Act.

weight of his administration behind the notorious Lecompton Constitution. But Senator Douglas, who had championed true popular sovereignty, would have none of this semipopular fraudulency. Deliberately tossing away his strong support in the South for the presidency, he fought courageously for fair play and democratic principles. The outcome was a compromise that, in effect, submitted the *entire* Lecompton Constitution to a popular vote. The free-soil voters thereupon thronged to the polls and snowed it under. Kansas remained a territory until 1861, when the southern secessionists left Congress.

President Buchanan, by antagonizing the numerous Douglas Democrats in the North, hopelessly divided the once-powerful Democratic party. Until then, it had been the only remaining *national* party, for the Whigs were dead and the Republicans were sectional. With the disruption of the Democrats

came the snapping of one of the last important strands in the rope that was barely binding the Union together.

"Bully" Brooks and His Bludgeon

"Bleeding Kansas" also splattered blood on the floor of the Senate in 1856. Senator Charles Sumner of Massachusetts, a tall and imposing figure, was a leading abolitionist—one of the few prominent in political life. Highly educated but cold, humorless, intolerant, and egotistical, he had made himself one of the most disliked men in the Senate. Brooding over the turbulent miscarriage of popular sovereignty, he delivered a blistering speech entitled "The Crime against Kansas." Sparing few epithets, he condemned the proslavery men as "hirelings picked from the drunken spew and vomit of an uneasy civilization." He also referred insultingly to South Carolina and to its white-haired Senator Andrew Butler, one of the best-liked members of the Senate.

Hot-tempered Congressman Preston S. Brooks of South Carolina now took vengeance into his own hands. Ordinarily gracious and gallant, he resented the insults to his state and to its senator, a distant cousin. His code of honor called for a duel, but in the South one fought only with one's social equals. And had not the coarse language of the Yankee, who probably would reject a challenge, dropped him to a lower order? To Brooks, the only alternative was to chastise the senator as one would beat an unruly dog. On May 22, 1856, he approached Sumner, then sitting at his Senate desk, and pounded the orator with an eleven-ounce cane until it broke. The victim fell bleeding and unconscious to the floor, while several nearby senators refrained from interfering.

Sumner had been provocatively insulting, but this counteroutrage put Brooks in the wrong. The House of Representatives could not muster enough votes to expel the South Carolinian, but he resigned and was triumphantly reelected. Southern admirers deluged Brooks with canes, some of them gold-headed, to replace the one that had been broken. The injuries to Sumner's head and nervous system were serious. He was forced to leave his seat for three and a half years and go to Europe for treatment that was both painful and costly. Meanwhile, Massachusetts defiantly reelected him, leaving his seat eloquently empty. Bleeding Sumner was thus joined with bleeding Kansas as a political issue.

The free-soil North was mightily aroused against the "uncouth" and "cowardly" "Bully" Brooks. Copies of Sumner's abusive speech, otherwise doomed to obscurity, were sold by the tens of thousands. Every blow that struck the senator doubtless made thousands of Republican votes. The South, although not unanimous in approving Brooks, was angered not only because Sumner had made such an intemperate speech but because it had been so extravagantly applauded in the North.

The Sumner-Brooks clash and the ensuing reactions revealed how dangerously inflamed passions were becoming, North and South. It was ominous that the cultured Sumner should have used the language of a barroom bully and that the gentlemanly Brooks should have employed the tactics and tools of a thug. Emotion was displacing thought. The blows rained on Sumner's head were, broadly speaking, among the first blows of the Civil War.

"Old Buck" versus "The Pathfinder"

With bullets whining in Kansas, the Democrats met in Cincinnati to nominate their presidential standard-bearer of 1856. They shied away from both the weak-kneed President Pierce and the dynamic Douglas. Each was too indelibly tainted by the Kansas-Nebraska Act. The delegates finally chose James Buchanan (pronounced by many *Buck-anan*), who was muscular, white-haired, and tall (6 feet; 1.83 meters), with a short neck and a protruding chin. Because of an eye defect, he carried his head cocked to one side. A well-to-do Pennsylvania lawyer, he had been serving as minister to London during the recent Kansas-Nebraska uproar. He was therefore "Kansasless," and hence relatively enemyless. But in a crisis that called for giants, "Old Buck" Buchanan was mediocre, irresolute, and confused.

Delegates of the fast-growing Republican party met in Philadelphia with bubbling enthusiasm. "Higher Law" Seward was their most conspicuous leader, and he probably would have arranged to win the nomination had he been confident that this was a "Republican year." The final choice was Captain John C. Frémont, the so-called Pathfinder of the West—a dashing but erratic explorer-soldier-surveyor who was supposed to find the path to the White House. The black-bearded and flashy young adventurer was virtually without political experience, but like Buchanan he was not tarred with the Kansas brush. The Republican platform came out vigorously against the extension of slavery into the territories, while the Democrats declared no less emphatically for popular sovereignty.

An ugly dose of antiforeignism was injected into the campaign, even though slavery extension loomed largest. The recent influx of immigrants from Ireland and Germany had alarmed "nativists," as many old-stock Protestants were called. They organized the American party, known also as the Know-Nothing party because of its secretiveness, and in 1856 nominated the lackluster ex-president Fillmore. Antiforeign and anti-Catholic, these superpatriots adopted the slogan "Americans Must Rule America." Remnants of the dying Whig party likewise endorsed Fillmore, and they and the Know-Nothings threatened to cut into Republican strength.

Republicans fell in behind Frémont with the zeal of crusaders. Shouting "We Follow the Pathfinder" and "We Are Buck Hunting," they organized glee clubs which sang (to the tune of the "Marseillaise"),

> *Arise, arise ye brave!*
> *And let our war-cry be,*
> *Free speech, free press, free soil, free men,*
> *Fré-mont and victory!*

"And free love," sneered the Buchanan supporters ("Buchaneers").

Mudslinging bespattered both candidates. "Old Fogy" Buchanan was assailed because he was a bachelor: the fiancée of his youth had died after a lovers' quarrel. Frémont was reviled because of his illegitimate birth, for his young mother had left her elderly husband, a Virginia planter, to run away with a French adventurer. In due season she gave birth to John in Savannah, Georgia—further to shame the South. More harmful to Frémont was the allegation, which alienated many bigoted Know-Nothings and other "nativists," that he was a Roman Catholic.

The Electoral Fruits of 1856

A bland Buchanan, although polling less than a majority of the popular vote, won handily. His tally in the Electoral College was 174 to 114 for Frémont, with Fillmore garnering 8. The popular vote was 1,832,955 for Buchanan to 1,339,932 for Frémont, and 871,731 for Fillmore.

Why did the rousing Republicans go down to defeat? Frémont lost much ground because of grave doubts as to his honesty, capacity, and sound judgment. Perhaps more damaging were the violent threats of the southern "fire-eaters" that the election of a sectional "Black Republican" would be a declaration of war on them, forcing them to secede. Many northerners, anxious to save both the Union and their profitable business connections with the South, were thus intimidated into voting for Buchanan. Innate conservatism triumphed, assisted by so-called southern bullyism.

It was probably fortunate for the Union that secession and civil war did not come in 1856, following a Republican victory. Frémont, an ill-

A Know-Nothing Party Mob, Baltimore, c. 1856–1860 These armed ruffians were campaigning in Baltimore for their ultranationalistic, anti-immigrant, anti-Catholic candidate.

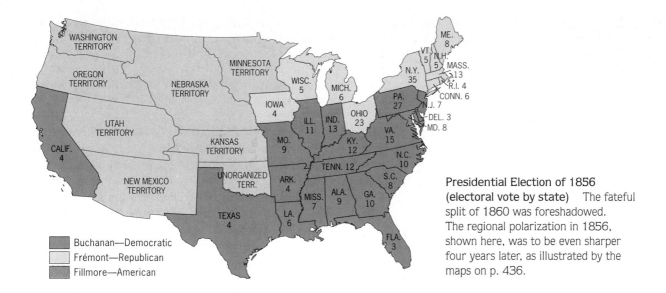

Presidential Election of 1856 (electoral vote by state)   The fateful split of 1860 was foreshadowed. The regional polarization in 1856, shown here, was to be even sharper four years later, as illustrated by the maps on p. 436.

balanced and second-rate figure, was no Abraham Lincoln. And in 1856 the North was more willing to let the South depart in peace than in 1860. Dramatic events from 1856 to 1860 were to arouse hundreds of thousands of still-apathetic northerners to a fighting pitch.

Yet the Republicans in 1856 could rightfully claim a "victorious defeat." The new party—a mere two-year-old toddler—had made an astonishing showing against the well-oiled Democratic machine. Whittier exulted:

> *Then sound again the bugles,*
> *Call the muster-roll anew;*
> *If months have well-nigh won the field,*
> *What may not four years do?*

The election of 1856 cast a long shadow forward, and politicians, North and South, peered anxiously toward 1860.

The Dred Scott Bombshell

The Dred Scott decision, handed down by the Supreme Court on March 6, 1857, abruptly ended the two-day presidential honeymoon of the unlucky bachelor, James Buchanan. This pronouncement was one of the opening paper-gun blasts of the Civil War.

Basically, the case was simple. Dred Scott, a black slave, had lived with his master for five years in Illinois and Wisconsin Territory. Backed by interested abolitionists, he sued for freedom on the basis of his long residence on free soil.

The Supreme Court proceeded to twist a simple legal case into a complex political issue. It ruled, not surprisingly, that Dred Scott was a black slave and not a citizen, and hence could not sue in federal courts.* The tribunal could then have thrown out the case on these technical grounds alone. But a majority decided to go further, under the leadership of emaciated Chief Justice Taney from the slave state of Maryland. A sweeping judgment on the larger issue of slavery in the territories seemed desirable, particularly to forestall arguments by two free-soil justices who were preparing dissenting opinions. The prosouthern majority evidently hoped in this way to lay the odious question to rest.

Taney's thunderclap rocked the free-soilers back on their heels. A majority of the Court decreed that because a slave was private property, he or she could be taken into *any* territory and legally held there in slavery. The reasoning was that the Fifth Amendment clearly forbade Congress to deprive people of their property without due process of law. The Court, to be consistent, went further. The Missouri Compromise, banning slavery north of 36° 30', had been repealed three years earlier by the Kansas-

---

*This part of the ruling, denying blacks their citizenship, seriously menaced the precarious position of the South's quarter-million free blacks.

Dred Scott This lone slave's long legal battle for his freedom, culminating in the Dred Scott decision by the Supreme Court in 1857, helped to start the Civil War.

The decision of Chief Justice Roger B. Taney (1777–1864) in the case of Dred Scott referred to the status of slaves when the Constitution was adopted:

"They had for more than a century before been regarded as beings of an inferior order; and altogether unfit to associate with the white race, either in social or political relations; and so far inferior that they had no rights which the white man was bound to respect. . . . This opinion was at that time fixed and universal in the civilized portion of the white race."

Taney's statement accurately described historical attitudes, but it deeply offended antislaveryites when applied to conditions in 1857.

Nebraska Act. But its spirit was still venerated in the North. Now the Court ruled that the Compromise of 1820 had been unconstitutional all along: Congress had no power to ban slavery from the territories, regardless even of what the territorial legislatures themselves might want.

Southerners were delighted with this unexpected victory. Champions of popular sovereignty were aghast, including Senator Douglas and a host of northern Democrats. Another lethal wedge was thus driven between the northern and southern wings of the once-united Democratic party.

Foes of slavery extension, especially the Republicans, were infuriated by the Dred Scott setback. Their chief rallying cry had been the banishing of bondage from the territories. They now insisted that the ruling of the Court was merely an opinion, not a decision, and no more binding than the views of a "southern debating society." Republican defiance of the exalted tribunal was intensified by an awareness that a majority of its members were southerners and by the conviction that it had debased itself—"sullied the ermine"—by wallowing in the gutter of politics.

Southerners in turn were inflamed by all this defiance. They began to wonder anew how much longer they could remain joined to a section that refused to honor the Supreme Court, to say nothing of the constitutional compact that had established it.

The Financial Crash of 1857

Bitterness caused by the Dred Scott decision was deepened by hard times, which dampened a period of feverish prosperity. Late in 1857 a panic burst about Buchanan's harassed head. The storm was not so bad economically as the panic of 1837, but psychologically it was probably the worst of the nineteenth century.

What caused the crash? Inpouring California gold played its part by helping to inflate the currency. The demands of the Crimean War had overstimulated the growing of grain, while frenzied speculation in land and railroads had further ripped the economic fabric. When the collapse came, over five thousand businesses failed within a year. Unemployment, accompanied by hunger meetings in urban areas, was widespread. "Bread or Death" stated one desperate slogan.

The North, including its grain growers, was hardest hit. The South, enjoying favorable cotton prices abroad, rode out the storm with flying colors. Panic conditions seemed further proof that cotton *was* king and that its economic kingdom was stronger than that of the North. This fatal delusion helped drive the overconfident southerners closer to a shooting showdown.

Financial distress in the North, especially in agriculture, gave a new vigor to the demand for free farms of 160 acres from the public domain. For several decades interested groups had been urging the federal government to abandon its ancient policy of selling the land for revenue. Instead, the argument ran, acreage should be given outright to the sturdy pioneers as a reward for risking health and life to develop it.

A scheme to make outright gifts of homesteads encountered two-pronged opposition. Eastern industrialists had long been unfriendly to free land; some of them feared that their underpaid workers would be drained off to the West. The South was even more bitterly opposed, partly because gang-labor slavery could not flourish on a mere 160 acres. Free farms would merely fill up the territories more rapidly with free-soilers and further tip the political balance against the South. In 1860, after years of debate, Congress finally passed a homestead act—one that made public lands available at a nominal sum of twenty-five cents an acre. But the homestead act was stabbed to death by the veto pen of President Buchanan, near whose elbow sat leading southern sympathizers.

The panic of 1857 also created a clamor for higher tariff rates. Several months before the crash, Congress, embarrassed by a large Treasury surplus, had enacted the Tariff of 1857. The new law, responding to pressures from the South, reduced duties to about 20 percent on dutiable goods—the lowest point since the War of 1812. Hardly had the revised rates been placed on the books when financial misery descended like a black pall. Northern manufacturers, many of them Republicans, noisily blamed their misfortunes on the low tariff. As the surplus melted away in the Treasury, industrialists in the North pointed to the need for higher duties. But what really concerned them was their desire for increased protection. Thus the panic of 1857 gave the Republicans two surefire economic issues for the election of 1860: protection for the unprotected and farms for the farmless.

Wall Street, Half Past Two O'clock, October 13, 1857, by James H. Cafferty and Charles G. Rosenberg The panic of 1857 further burdened President Buchanan, already reeling from the armed clashes in Kansas and the controversy over the Dred Scott decision.

An Illinois Rail-Splitter Emerges

The Illinois senatorial election of 1858 now claimed the national spotlight. Senator Douglas's term was about to expire, and the Republicans decided to run against him a rustic Springfield lawyer, one Abraham Lincoln. The Republican candidate—6 feet, 4 inches (1.93 meters) in height and 180 pounds (81.7 kilograms) in weight—presented an awkward but arresting figure. Lincoln's legs, arms, and neck were grotesquely long; his head was crowned by coarse, black, and unruly hair; and his face was sad, sunken, and weather-beaten.

Lincoln was no silver-spoon child of the elite. Born in 1809 in a Kentucky log cabin to impoverished parents, he attended a frontier school for not more than a year; being an avid reader, he was mainly self-educated. All his life he said, "git," "thar," and "heered." Although narrow-chested and somewhat stoop-shouldered, he shone in his frontier community as a wrestler and weight lifter, and spent

Abraham Lincoln, a Most Uncommon Common Man
This daguerreotype of Lincoln was done by Mathew B. Brady, a distinguished photographer of the era.

In 1832, when Abraham Lincoln (1809–1865) became a candidate for the Illinois legislature, he delivered a speech at a political gathering:

"I presume you all know who I am. I am humble Abraham Lincoln. I have been solicited by many friends to become a candidate for the Legislature. My [Whiggish] politics are short and sweet, like the old woman's dance. I am in favor of a national bank. I am in favor of the internal-improvement system, and a high protective tariff. These are my sentiments and political principles. If elected, I shall be thankful; if not, it will be all the same."

He was elected two years later.

some time, among other pioneering pursuits, as a splitter of logs for fence rails. A superb teller of earthy and amusing stories, he would oddly enough plunge into protracted periods of melancholy.

Lincoln's private and professional life was not especially noteworthy. He married "above himself" socially, into the influential Todd family of Kentucky; and the temperamental outbursts of his high-strung wife, known by her enemies as the "she wolf," helped to school him in patience and forbearance. After reading a little law, he gradually emerged as one of the dozen or so better-known trial lawyers in Illinois, although still accustomed to carrying important papers in his stovepipe hat. He was widely referred to as "Honest Abe," partly because he would refuse cases that he had to suspend his conscience to defend.

The rise of Lincoln as a political figure was less than rocketlike. After making his mark in the Illinois legislature as a Whig politician of the logrolling variety, he served one undistinguished term in Congress, 1847–1849. Until 1854, when he was forty-five years of age, he had done nothing to establish a claim to statesmanship. But the passage of the Kansas-Nebraska Act in that year lighted within him unexpected fires. After mounting the Republican bandwagon, he emerged as one of the foremost politicians and orators of the Northwest. At the Philadelphia convention of 1856, where John Frémont was nominated, Lincoln actually received 110 votes for the vice-presidential nomination.

The Great Debate: Lincoln versus Douglas

Lincoln, as Republican nominee for the Senate seat, boldly challenged Douglas to a series of joint debates. This was a rash act, because the stumpy senator was probably the nation's most devastating debater. Douglas promptly accepted Lincoln's challenge, and seven meetings were arranged from August to October 1858.

At first glance the two contestants seemed ill matched. The well-groomed and polished Douglas, with bearlike figure and bullhorn voice, presented a striking contrast to the lanky Lincoln, with his baggy clothes and unshined shoes. Moreover, "Old Abe," as he was called in both affection and derision, had a piercing, high-pitched voice and was often ill at ease when he began to speak. But as he threw himself into an argument, he seemed to grow in height, while his glowing eyes lighted up a rugged face. He relied on logic rather than on table-thumping.

The most famous debate came at Freeport, Illinois, where Lincoln nearly impaled his opponent on the horns of a dilemma. Suppose, he queried, the people of a territory should vote slavery down? The Supreme Court in the Dred Scott decision had decreed that they could not. Who would prevail, the Court or the people?

Legend to the contrary, Douglas and some southerners had already publicly answered the Freeport question. The "Little Giant" therefore did not hesitate to meet the issue head on, honestly and consistently. His reply to Lincoln became known as the "Freeport Doctrine." No matter how the Supreme Court ruled, Douglas argued, slavery would stay down if the people voted it down. Laws to protect slavery would have to be passed by the territorial legislatures. These would not be forthcoming in the absence of popular approval, and black bondage would soon disappear. Douglas, in

Lincoln expressed his views on the relation of the black and white races in 1858, in his first debate with Stephen A. Douglas:

"I, as well as Judge Douglas, am in favor of the race to which I belong, having the superior position. I have never said anything to the contrary, but I hold that notwithstanding all this, there is no reason in the world why the negro is not entitled to all the natural rights enumerated in the Declaration of Independence, the right to life, liberty, and the pursuit of happiness. I hold that he is as much entitled to those rights as the white man. I agree with Judge Douglas he is not my equal in many respects—certainly not in color, perhaps not in moral or intellectual endowment. But in the right to eat the bread, without leave of anybody else, which his own hand earns, he is my equal and the equal of Judge Douglas, and the equal of every living man."

Lincoln and Douglas Debate, 1858   Thousands attended each of the seven Lincoln-Douglas debates. Douglas is shown here sitting to Lincoln's right in the debate at Charleston, Illinois, in September. On one occasion, Lincoln quipped that Douglas's logic would prove that a horse chestnut was a chestnut horse.

truth, had American history on his side. Where public opinion does not support the federal government, as in the case of Jefferson's embargo, the law is almost impossible to enforce.

The upshot was that Douglas defeated Lincoln for the Senate seat. The "Little Giant's" loyalty to popular sovereignty, which still had a powerful appeal in Illinois, probably was decisive. Senators were then chosen by state legislatures; and in the general election that followed the debates, more pro-Douglas members were elected than pro-Lincoln members. Yet thanks to inequitable apportionment, the districts carried by Douglas supporters represented a smaller population than those carried by Lincoln supporters. "Honest Abe" thus won a clear moral victory.

Lincoln possibly was playing for larger stakes than just the senatorship. Although defeated, he had shambled into the national limelight in company with the most prominent northern politicians. Newspapers in the East published detailed accounts

of the debates, and Lincoln began to emerge as a potential Republican nominee for president. But Douglas, in winning Illinois, hurt his own chances of winning the presidency, while further splitting his splintering party. After his opposition to the Lecompton Constitution for Kansas and his further defiance of the Supreme Court at Freeport, southern Democrats were determined to break up the party (and the Union) rather than accept him. The Lincoln-Douglas debate platform thus proved to be one of the preliminary battlefields of the Civil War.

John Brown: Murderer or Martyr?

The gaunt, grim figure of John Brown of bleeding Kansas infamy now appeared again in an even more terrible way. His crackbrained scheme was to invade the South secretly with a handful of followers, call upon the slaves to rise, furnish them with arms, and

Last Moments of John Brown, by Thomas Hovenden   Sentenced to be hanged, John Brown wrote to his brother, "I am quite cheerful in view of my approaching end, being fully persuaded that I am worth inconceivably more to hang than for any other purpose. . . . I count it all joy. 'I have fought the good fight,' and have, as I trust, 'finished my course.'" This painting of Brown going to his execution may have been inspired by the journalist Horace Greeley, who was not present but wrote that "a black woman with a little child stood by the door. He stopped for a moment, and stooping, kissed the child." That scene never took place, as Brown was escorted from the jail only by a detachment of soldiers. But this painting has become famous as a kind of allegorical expression of the pathos of Brown's martyrdom for the abolitionist cause.

establish a kind of black free state as a sanctuary. Brown secured several thousand dollars for firearms from northern abolitionists and finally arrived in hilly western Virginia with some twenty men, including several blacks. At scenic Harpers Ferry he seized the federal arsenal in October 1859, incidentally killing seven innocent people, including a free black, and injuring ten or so more. But the slaves, largely ignorant of Brown's strike, failed to rise, and the wounded Brown and the remnants of his tiny band were quickly captured by U.S. Marines under the command of Lieutenant Colonel Robert E. Lee. Ironically, within two years Lee became the preeminent general in the Confederate army.

"Old Brown" was convicted of murder and treason, after a hasty but legal trial. His presumed insanity was supported by affidavits from seventeen friends and relatives, who were trying to save his neck. Actually thirteen of his near relations were regarded as insane, including his mother and grandmother. Governor Wise of Virginia would have been most wise, so his critics say, if he had only clapped the culprit into a lunatic asylum.

But Brown—"God's angry man"—was given every opportunity to pose and to enjoy martyrdom. Though probably of unsound mind, he was clever enough to see that he was worth much more to the abolitionist cause dangling from a rope than in any other way. His demeanor during the trial was dignified and courageous, his last words ("this *is* a beautiful country") were to become legendary, and he marched up the scaffold steps without flinching. His conduct was so exemplary, his devotion to freedom so inflexible, that he took on an exalted character, however deplorable his previous record may have been. So the hangman's trap was sprung, and Brown plunged not into oblivion but into world fame. A memorable marching song of the impending Civil War ran,

John Brown's body lies a-mould'ring in the grave,
His soul is marching on.

The effects of Harpers Ferry were calamitous. In the eyes of the South, already embittered, "Osawatomie Brown" was a wholesale murderer and an apostle of treason. Many southerners asked how they could possibly remain in the Union while a "murderous gang of abolitionists" were financing armed bands to "Brown" them. Moderate northerners, including Republican leaders, openly deplored this mad exploit. But the South naturally concluded that the violent abolitionist view was shared by the entire North, dominated by "Brown-loving" Republicans.

Abolitionists and other ardent free-soilers were infuriated by Brown's execution. Many of them were ignorant of his bloody past and his even more bloody purposes, and they were outraged because the Virginians had hanged so earnest a reformer who was working for so righteous a cause. On the day of his execution, free-soil centers in the North tolled bells, fired guns, lowered flags, and held rallies. Some spoke of "Saint John" Brown, and the serene Ralph Waldo Emerson compared the new martyr-hero with Jesus. The gallows became a cross. E. C. Stedman wrote,

And Old Brown,
Osawatomie Brown,
May trouble you more than ever,
* when you've nailed his coffin down!*

The ghost of the martyred Brown would not be laid to rest.

Upon hearing of John Brown's execution, escaped slave and abolitionist Harriet Tubman (c. 1820–1913) paid him the highest tribute for his self-sacrifice.

"I've been studying, and studying upon it, and its clar to me, it wasn't John Brown that died on that gallows. When I think how he gave up his life for our people, and how he never flinched, but was so brave to the end; its clar to me it wasn't mortal man, it was God in him."

Not all opponents of slavery, however, shared Tubman's reverence for Brown. Republican presidential candidate Abraham Lincoln dismissed Brown as deluded:

"[The Brown] affair, in its philosophy, corresponds with the many attempts, related in history, at the assassination of kings and emperors. An enthusiast broods over the oppression of a people till he fancies himself commissioned by Heaven to liberate them. He ventures the attempt, which ends in little else than his own execution."

It cant stop me for I built it

You find me in dis yer Fence Massa Duglis.

How can I get over this Rail Fence.

Lincoln and Douglas Race for the White House, 1860
Both Lincoln's height and Douglas's diminutive stature are exaggerated. The black youth crouched in the (split-rail) fence that stands between them and the prize is a reminder of the centrality of the slavery question in the campaign.

The Disruption of the Democrats

Beyond question the presidential election of 1860 was the most fateful in American history. On it hung the issue of peace or civil war.

Deeply divided, the Democrats met in Charleston, South Carolina, with Douglas the leading candidate of the northern wing of the party. But the southern "fire-eaters" regarded him as a traitor, as a result of his unpopular stand on the Lecompton Constitution and the Freeport Doctrine. After a bitter wrangle over the platform, the delegates from most of the cotton states walked out. When the remainder could not scrape together the necessary two-thirds vote for Douglas, the entire body dissolved. The first tragic secession was the secession of southerners from the Democratic National Convention. Departure became habit-forming.

The Democrats tried again in Baltimore. This time the Douglas Democrats, chiefly from the North, were firmly in the saddle. Many of the cotton-state delegates again took a walk, and the rest of the convention enthusiastically nominated their hero. The platform came out squarely for popular sovereignty and, as a sop to the South, against obstruction of the Fugitive Slave Law by the states.

Angered southern Democrats promptly organized a rival convention in Baltimore, in which many of the northern states were unrepresented. They selected as their leader the stern-jawed vice president, John C. Breckinridge, a man of moderate

Alexander H. Stephens (1812–1883), destined the next year to become vice president of the new Confederacy, wrote privately in 1860 of the anti-Douglas Democrats who seceded from the Charleston convention:

"The seceders intended from the beginning to rule or ruin; and when they find they cannot rule, they will then ruin. They have about enough power for this purpose; not much more; and I doubt not but they will use it. Envy, hate, jealousy, spite . . . will make devils of men. The secession movement was instigated by nothing but bad passions."

Election of 1860

Candidate	Popular Vote	Percentage of Popular Vote	Electoral Vote
Lincoln	1,865,593	39.79%	180 (every vote of the free states except for 3 of New Jersey's 7 votes)
Douglas	1,382,713	29.40	12 (only Missouri and 3 of New Jersey's 7 votes)
Breckinridge	848,356	18.20	72 (all the cotton states)
Bell	592,906	12.61	39 (Virginia, Kentucky, Tennessee)

views from the border state of Kentucky. The platform favored the extension of slavery into the territories and the annexation of slave-populated Cuba.

A middle-of-the-road group, fearing for the Union, hastily organized the Constitutional Union party, sneered at as the "Do Nothing" or "Old Gentleman's" party. It consisted mainly of former Whigs and Know-Nothings, a veritable "gathering of graybeards." Desperately anxious to elect a compromise candidate, they met in Baltimore and nominated for the presidency John Bell of Tennessee. They went into battle ringing hand bells for Bell and waving handbills for "The Union, the Constitution, and the Enforcement of the Laws."

A Rail-Splitter Splits the Union

Elated Republicans were presented with a heaven-sent opportunity. Scenting victory in the breeze as their opponents split hopelessly, they gathered in Chicago in a huge, boxlike wooden structure called the Wigwam. William H. Seward was by far the best known of the contenders. But his radical utterances, including his "irrepressible conflict" speech at Rochester in 1858, had ruined his prospects.* His numerous enemies coined the slogan "Success Rather than Seward." Lincoln, the favorite son of Illinois, was definitely a "Mr. Second Best," but he was a stronger candidate because he had made fewer enemies. Overtaking Seward on the third

---

*Seward had referred to an "irrepressible conflict" between slavery and freedom, though not necessarily a bloody one.

ballot, he was nominated amid scenes of the wildest excitement.

The Republican platform had a seductive appeal for just about every important nonsouthern group: for the free-soilers, nonextension of slavery; for the northern manufacturers, a protective tariff; for the immigrants, no abridgment of rights; for the Northwest, a Pacific railroad; for the West, internal improvements at federal expense; and for the farmers, free homesteads from the public domain. Alluring slogans included "Vote Yourselves a Farm" and "Land for the Landless."

Southern secessionists promptly served notice that the election of the "baboon" Lincoln—the "abolitionist" rail-splitter—would split the Union. In fact, "Honest Abe," though hating slavery, was no outright abolitionist. As late as February 1865, he was inclined to favor cash compensation to the owners of freed slaves. But for the time being, he saw fit, perhaps mistakenly, to issue no statements to quiet southern fears. He had already put himself on record; and fresh statements might stir up fresh antagonisms.

As the election campaign ground noisily forward, Lincoln enthusiasts staged roaring rallies and parades, complete with pitch-dripping torches and oilskin capes. They extolled "High Old Abe," the "Woodchopper of the West," and the "Little Giant Killer," while groaning dismally for "Poor Little Doug." Enthusiastic "Little Giants" and "Little Dougs" retorted with "We want a statesman, not a rail-splitter, as President." Douglas himself waged a vigorous speaking campaign, even in the South, and threatened to put the hemp with his own hands around the neck of the first secessionist.

The returns, breathlessly awaited, proclaimed a sweeping victory for Lincoln (see the table above).

The Electoral Upheaval of 1860

Awkward "Abe" Lincoln had run a curious race. To a greater degree than any other holder of the nation's highest office (except John Quincy Adams), he was a minority president. Sixty percent of the voters preferred some other candidate. He was also a sectional president, for in ten southern states, where he was not allowed on the ballot, he polled no popular votes. The election of 1860 was virtually two elections: one in the North, the other in the South. South Carolinians rejoiced over Lincoln's victory; they now had their excuse to secede. In winning the North, the "rail-splitter" had split off the South.

Douglas, though scraping together only twelve electoral votes, made an impressive showing. Boldly breaking with tradition, he campaigned energetically for himself. (Presidential candidates customarily maintained a dignified silence.) He drew important strength from all sections and ranked a fairly close second in the popular-vote column. In fact, the Douglas Democrats and the Breckinridge Democrats together amassed 366,484 more votes than did Lincoln.

A myth persists that if the Democrats had only united behind Douglas, they would have triumphed. Yet the cold figures tell a different story. Even if the "Little Giant" had received all the electoral votes cast for all three of Lincoln's opponents, the "rail-splitter" would have won, 169 to 134 instead of 180 to 123. Lincoln still would have carried the populous states of the North and the Northwest. On the other hand, if the Democrats had not broken up, they could have entered the campaign

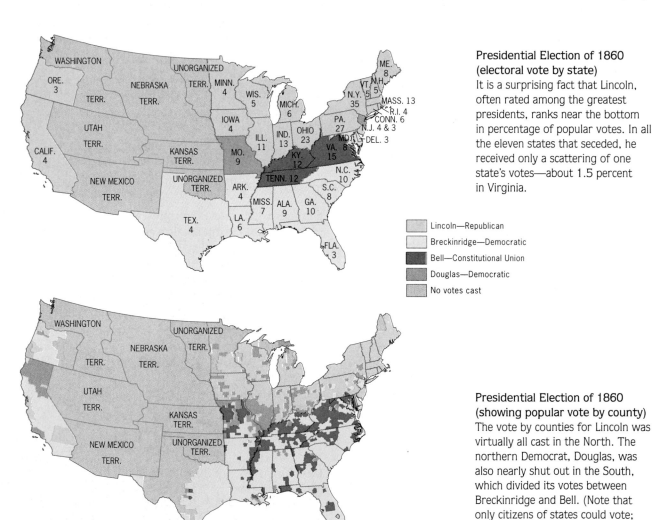

Presidential Election of 1860 (electoral vote by state)
It is a surprising fact that Lincoln, often rated among the greatest presidents, ranks near the bottom in percentage of popular votes. In all the eleven states that seceded, he received only a scattering of one state's votes—about 1.5 percent in Virginia.

Legend:
- Lincoln—Republican
- Breckinridge—Democratic
- Bell—Constitutional Union
- Douglas—Democratic
- No votes cast

Presidential Election of 1860 (showing popular vote by county)
The vote by counties for Lincoln was virtually all cast in the North. The northern Democrat, Douglas, was also nearly shut out in the South, which divided its votes between Breckinridge and Bell. (Note that only citizens of states could vote; inhabitants of territories could not.)

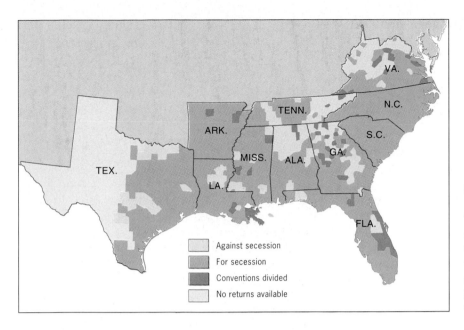

Southern Opposition to Secession, 1860–1861 (showing vote by county) This county vote shows the opposition of the antiplanter, antislavery mountain whites in the Appalachian region. There was also considerable resistance to secession in Texas, where Governor Sam Houston, who led the Unionists, was deposed by secessionists.

Map legend:
- Against secession
- For secession
- Conventions divided
- No returns available

with higher enthusiasm and better organization and might have won.

Significantly, the verdict of the ballot box did not indicate a strong sentiment for secession. Breckinridge, while favoring the extension of slavery, was no disunionist. Although the candidate of the "fire-eaters," in the slave states he polled fewer votes than the combined strength of his opponents, Douglas and Bell. He even failed to carry his own Kentucky.

Yet the South, despite its electoral defeat, was not badly off. It still had a five-to-four majority on the Supreme Court. Although the Republicans had elected Lincoln, they controlled neither the Senate nor the House of Representatives. The federal government could not touch slavery in those states where it existed except by a constitutional amendment, and such an amendment could be defeated by one-fourth of the states. The fifteen slave states numbered nearly one-half of the total—a fact not fully appreciated by southern firebrands.

The Secessionist Exodus

But a tragic chain reaction of secession now began to erupt. South Carolina, which had threatened to go out if the "sectional" Lincoln came in, was as good as its word. Four days after the election of the

"Illinois baboon" by "insulting" majorities, its legislature voted unanimously to call a special convention. Meeting at Charleston in December 1860, South Carolina unanimously voted to secede. During the next six weeks, six other states of the lower South, though somewhat less united, followed the leader over the precipice: Alabama, Mississippi, Florida, Georgia, Louisiana, and Texas. Four more were to join them later, bringing the total to eleven.

Three days after Lincoln's election, Horace Greeley's influential New York Tribune *(November 9, 1860) had declared,*

"If the cotton States shall decide that they can do better out of the Union than in it, we insist on letting them go in peace. The right to secede may be a revolutionary one, but it exists nevertheless. . . . Whenever a considerable section of our Union shall deliberately resolve to go out, we shall resist all coercive measures designed to keep it in. We hope never to live in a republic, whereof one section is pinned to the residue by bayonets."

After the secession movement got well under way, Greeley's Tribune *changed its tune.*

With the eyes of destiny upon them, the seven seceders, formally meeting at Montgomery, Alabama, in February 1861 created a government known as the Confederate States of America. As their president they chose Jefferson Davis, a dignified and austere recent member of the U.S. Senate from Mississippi. He was a West Pointer and a former cabinet member with wide military and administrative experience; but he suffered from chronic ill-health, as well as from a frustrated ambition to be a Napoleonic strategist.

The crisis, already critical enough, was deepened by the "lame duck"* interlude. Lincoln, although elected president in November 1860, could not take office until four months later, March 4, 1861. During this period of protracted uncertainty, when he was still a private citizen in Illinois, seven of the eleven deserting states pulled out of the Union.

President Buchanan, the aging incumbent, has been blamed for not holding the seceders in the Union by sheer force—for wringing his hands instead of secessionist necks. Never a vigorous man and habitually conservative, he was now nearly seventy, and although devoted to the Union, he was surrounded by prosouthern advisers. As an able lawyer wedded to the Constitution, he did not believe that the southern states could legally secede. Yet he could find no authority in the Constitution for stopping them with guns.

"Oh for one hour of Jackson!" cried the advocates of strong-arm tactics. But "Old Buck" Buchanan was not "Old Hickory," and he was faced with a far more complex and serious problem. One important reason why he did not resort to force was that the tiny standing army of some fifteen thousand men, then widely scattered, was urgently needed to control the Indians in the West. Public opinion in the North, at that time, was far from willing to unsheathe the sword. Fighting would merely shatter all prospects of adjustment, and until the guns began to boom, there was still a flickering hope of reconciliation rather than a contested divorce. The weakness lay not so much in Buchanan as in the Constitution and in the Union itself. Ironically, when Lincoln became president in March, he essentially continued Buchanan's wait-and-see policy.

*The "lame duck" period was shortened to ten weeks in 1933 by the Twentieth Amendment (see the Appendix).

Jefferson Davis (1808–1889), by George Lethbridge Saunders, 1849   Faced with grave difficulties, he was probably as able a man for the position as the Confederacy could have chosen. Ironically, Davis and Lincoln were both sprung from the same Kentucky soil. The Davis family had moved south from Kentucky; the Lincoln family, north.

The Collapse of Compromise

Impending bloodshed spurred final and frantic attempts at compromise—in the American tradition. The most promising of these efforts was sponsored by Senator James Henry Crittenden of Kentucky, on whose shoulders had fallen the mantle of a fellow Kentuckian, Henry Clay.

The proposed Crittenden amendments to the Constitution were designed to appease the South. Slavery in the territories was to be prohibited north of 36° 30', but south of that line it was to be given federal protection in all territories existing or "hereafter to be acquired" (such as Cuba). Future states, north or south of 36° 30', could come into the Union with or without slavery, as they should choose. In short, the slavery supporters were to be guaranteed

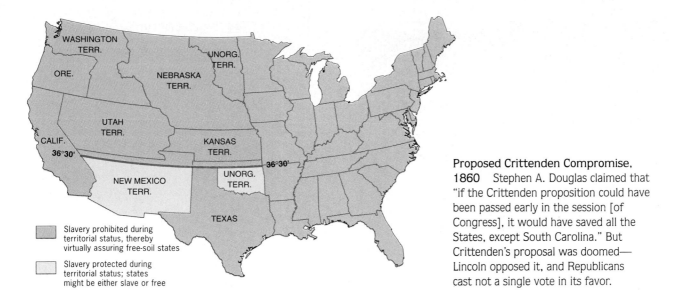

Slavery prohibited during territorial status, thereby virtually assuring free-soil states

Slavery protected during territorial status; states might be either slave or free

Proposed Crittenden Compromise, 1860 Stephen A. Douglas claimed that "if the Crittenden proposition could have been passed early in the session [of Congress], it would have saved all the States, except South Carolina." But Crittenden's proposal was doomed—Lincoln opposed it, and Republicans cast not a single vote in its favor.

full rights in the southern territories, as long as they were territories, regardless of the wishes of the majority under popular sovereignty. Federal protection in a territory south of 36° 30' might conceivably, though improbably, turn the entire area permanently to slavery.

Lincoln flatly rejected the Crittenden scheme, which offered some slight prospect of success, and all hope of compromise evaporated. For this refusal he must bear a heavy responsibility. Yet he had been elected on a platform that opposed the extension of slavery, and he felt that as a matter of principle he could not afford to yield, even though gains for slavery in the territories might be only temporary. Larger gains might come later in Cuba and Mexico. Crittenden's proposal, said Lincoln, "would amount to a perpetual covenant of war against every people, tribe, and state owning a foot of land between here and Tierra del Fuego."

As for the supposedly spineless "Old Fogy" Buchanan, how could he have prevented the Civil War by starting a civil war? No one has yet come up with a satisfactory answer. If he had used force on South Carolina in December 1860, the fighting almost certainly would have erupted three months sooner than it did, and under less favorable circumstances for the Union. The North would have appeared as the heavy-handed aggressor. And the crucial Border States, so vital to the Union, probably would have been driven into the arms of their "wayward sisters."

One reason why the Crittenden Compromise failed in December 1860 was the prevalence of an attitude reflected in a private letter of Senator James Henry Hammond (1807–1864) of South Carolina on April 19:

"I firmly believe that the slave-holding South is now the controlling power of the world—that no other power would face us in hostility. Cotton, rice, tobacco, and naval stores command the world; and we have sense to know it, and are sufficiently Teutonic to carry it out successfully. The North without us would be a motherless calf, bleating about, and die of mange and starvation."

Farewell to Union

Secessionists who parted company with their sister states left for a number of avowed reasons, mostly relating in some way to slavery. They were alarmed by the inexorable tipping of the political balance against them—"the despotic majority of numbers." The "crime" of the North, observed James Russell Lowell, was the census returns. Southerners were

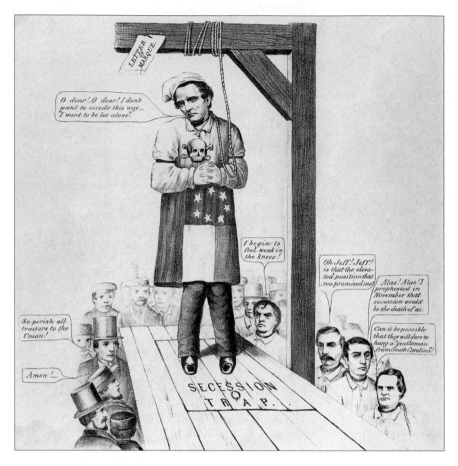

Jeff Davis on His Own Platform, or The Last "Act of Secession," c. 1861 This northern cartoon expressed the sentiment of many people north of the Mason-Dixon line that secession was a self-defeating move, doomed to failure.

also dismayed by the triumph of the new sectional Republican party, which seemed to threaten their rights as a slaveholding minority. They were weary of free-soil criticism, abolitionist nagging, and northern interference, ranging from the Underground Railroad to John Brown's raid. "All we ask is to be let alone," declared Confederate president Jefferson Davis in an early message to his congress.

Many southerners supported secession because they felt sure that their departure would be unopposed, despite "Yankee yawp" to the contrary. They were confident that the clodhopping and codfishing Yankee would not or could not fight. They believed that northern manufacturers and bankers, so heavily dependent on southern cotton and markets, would not dare to cut their own economic throats with their own unionist swords. But should war come, the immense debt owed to northern creditors by the South—happy thought—could be promptly repudiated, as it later was.

Southern leaders regarded secession as a golden opportunity to cast aside their generations of "vassalage" to the North. An independent Dixieland could develop its own banking and shipping, and trade directly with Europe. The low Tariff of 1857, passed largely by southern votes, was not in

> *Regarding the Civil War, the London* Times *(November 7, 1861) editorialized,*
>
> "The contest is really for empire on the side of the North, and for independence on that of the South, and in this respect we recognize an exact analogy between the North and the Government of George III, and the South and the Thirteen Revolted Provinces."

itself menacing. But who could tell when the "greedy" Republicans would win control of Congress and drive through their own oppressive protective tariff? For decades this fundamental friction had pitted the North, with its manufacturing plants, against the South, with its agricultural exports.

Worldwide impulses of nationalism—then stirring in Italy, Germany, Poland, and elsewhere—were fermenting in the South. This huge area, with its distinctive culture, was not so much a section as a subnation. It could not view with complacency the possibility of being lorded over, then or later, by what it regarded as a hostile nation of northerners.

The principles of self-determination—of the Declaration of Independence—seemed to many southerners to apply perfectly to them. Few, if any, of the seceders felt that they were doing anything wrong or immoral. The thirteen original states had voluntarily entered the Union, and now seven—ultimately eleven—southern states were voluntarily withdrawing from it.

Historical parallels ran even deeper. In 1776, thirteen American colonies, led by the rebel George Washington, had seceded from the British Empire by throwing off the yoke of King George III. In 1860–1861, eleven American states, led by the rebel Jefferson Davis, were seceding from the Union by throwing off the yoke of "King" Abraham Lincoln. With that burden gone, the South was confident that it could work out its own peculiar destiny more quietly, happily, and prosperously.

James Russell Lowell (1819–1891), the northern poet and essayist, wrote in the Atlantic Monthly *shortly after the secessionist movement began:*

"The fault of the free States in the eyes of the South is not one that can be atoned for by any yielding of special points here and there. Their offense is that they are free, and that their habits and prepossessions are those of freedom. Their crime is the census of 1860. Their increase in numbers, wealth, and power is a standing aggression. It would not be enough to please the Southern States that we should stop asking them to abolish slavery: what they demand of us is nothing less than that we should abolish the spirit of the age. Our very thoughts are a menace."

Chronology

1852 Harriet Beecher Stowe publishes *Uncle Tom's Cabin*

1854 Kansas-Nebraska Act
Republican party forms

1856 Buchanan defeats Frémont and Fillmore for presidency
Sumner beaten by Brooks in Senate chamber
Brown's Pattawatomie Creek massacre

1856-1860 Civil war in "bleeding Kansas"

1857 Dred Scott decision
Lecompton Constitution rejected

1857 Panic of 1857
Tariff of 1857
Hinton R. Helper publishes *The Impending Crisis of the South*

1858 Lincoln-Douglas debates

1859 Brown raids Harpers Ferry

1860 Lincoln wins four-way race for presidency
South Carolina secedes from the Union
Crittenden Compromise fails

1861 Seven seceding states form the Confederate States of America

The Civil War: Repressible or Irrepressible?

Few topics have generated as much controversy among American historians as the causes of the Civil War. The very names employed to describe the conflict—notably "Civil War" or "War Between the States," or even "War for Southern Independence"—reveal much about the various authors' points of view. Interpretations of the great conflict have naturally differed according to section, and have been charged with both emotional and moral fervor. Yet despite long and keen interest in the origins of the conflict, the causes of the Civil War remain as passionately debated today as they were a century ago.

The so-called nationalist school of the late nineteenth century, typified in the work of historian James Ford Rhodes, claimed that slavery caused the Civil War. Defending the necessity and inevitability of the war, these northern-oriented historians credited the conflict with ending slavery and preserving the Union. But in the early twentieth century, progressive historians, led by Charles and Mary Beard, presented a more skeptical interpretation. The Beards argued that the war was not fought over slavery per se, but rather was a deeply rooted economic struggle between an industrial North and an agricultural South. Anointing the Civil War the "Second American Revolution," the Beards claimed that the war precipitated vast changes in American class relations and shifted the political balance of power by magnifying the influence of business magnates and industrialists while destroying the plantation aristocracy of the South.

Shaken by the disappointing results of World War I, a new wave of historians argued that the Civil War, too, had actually been a big mistake. Rejecting the nationalist interpretation that the clash was inevitable, James G. Randall and Avery Craven asserted that the war had been a "repressible conflict." Neither slavery nor the economic differences between North and South were sufficient causes for war. Instead, Craven and others attributed the bloody confrontation to the breakdown of political institutions, the passion of overzealous reformers, and the ineptitude of a blundering generation of political leaders.

Following the Second World War, however, a neonationalist view regained authority, echoing the earlier views of Rhodes in depicting the Civil War as an unavoidable conflict between two societies, one slave and one free. For Allan Nevins and David M. Potter, irreconcilable differences in morality, politics, culture, social values, and economies increasingly eroded the ties between the sections and inexorably set the United States on the road to Civil War.

Eric Foner and Eugene Genovese have emphasized each section's nearly paranoid fear that the survival of its distinctive way of life was threatened by the expansion of the other section. In *Free Soil, Free Labor, Free Men* (1970), Foner emphasized that most northerners detested slavery not because it enslaved blacks but because its existence—and particularly its rapid extension—threatened the position of free white laborers. This "free labor ideology" increasingly became the foundation stone upon which the North claimed its superiority over the South. Eugene Genovese has argued that the South felt similarly endangered. Convinced that the southern labor system was more humane than the northern factory system, southerners saw northern designs to destroy their way of life lurking at every turn—and every territorial battle.

Some historians have placed party politics at the center of their explanations for the war. For them, no event was more consequential than the breakdown of the Jacksonian party system. When the slavery issue tore apart both the Democratic and Whig parties, the last ligaments binding the nation together were snapped, and the war inevitably came.

More recently, historians of the "ethnocultural school," especially Michael Holt, have acknowledged the significance of the collapse of the established parties, but have offered a different analysis of how that breakdown led to war. They note that the two great national parties before the 1850s had focused attention on issues such as the tariff, banking, and internal improvements, thereby muting sectional differences over slavery. According to this argument, the erosion of the traditional party system is blamed not on growing differences over slavery but on a temporary *consensus* between the two parties in the 1850s on almost all national issues *other* than slavery. In this peculiar political atmosphere, the slavery issue rose to the fore, encouraging the emergence of Republicans in the North and secessionists in the South. In the absence of regular, national, two-party conflict over economic issues, purely regional parties (like the Republicans) coalesced. They identified their opponents not simply as competitors for power but as threats to their way of life, even to the life of the Republic itself.

SUGGESTED READINGS

PRIMARY SOURCE DOCUMENTS

Harriet Beecher Stowe, *Uncle Tom's Cabin** (1852), and Hinton R. Helper, *The Impending Crisis of the South** (1857), are vivid and important. The Lincoln-Douglas debates* (1858) frame the issues of the 1850s and remain classics of American oratory.

SECONDARY SOURCES

For comprehensive treatments of events leading up to the Civil War, refer to Chapter 19 for the titles by David M. Potter, James M. McPherson, James G. Randall and David Donald, William J. Cooper, Kenneth Stampp, and Richard H. Sewell. Richly detailed is Allan Nevins, *The Ordeal of the Union* (2 vols., 1947). David Donald, *Charles Sumner and the Coming of the Civil War* (1960), is an outstanding biography. See also his able *Charles Sumner and the Rights of Man* (1970). On the literary attack on slavery, see Thomas F. Gossett, *Uncle Tom's Cabin and American Culture* (1985). Lincoln's rise is developed in Don E. Fehrenbacher, *Prelude to Greatness* (1962), and in Carl Sandburg, *Abraham Lincoln: The Prairie Years* (2 vols., 1926). On Mary Todd Lincoln, see Jean H. Baker, *Mary Todd Lincoln: A Biography* (1987).

The explosive Kansas issue is dealt with in James A. Rawley, *Race and Politics: "Bleeding Kansas" and the Coming of the Civil War* (1969). On the Buchanan administration, see Kenneth M. Stampp, *America in 1857: A Nation on the Brink* (1990). On the Lincoln-Douglas debates, see Harry V. Jaffa, *Crisis of the House Divided* (1959). Don E. Fehrenbacher brilliantly and thoroughly dissects *The Dred Scott Case* (1978). The final moments before fighting began are scrutinized in David M. Potter, *Lincoln and His Party in the Secession Crisis* (1942), and in Kenneth M. Stampp, *And the War Came* (1950). The southern side of the question appears in Steven A. Channing, *Crisis of Fear: Secession of South Carolina* (1970); William L. Barney, *The Secessionist Impulse: Alabama and Mississippi* (1974); William J. Evitts, *A Matter of Allegiances: Maryland from 1850 to 1861* (1974); and Ralph A. Wooster, *The Secessionist Convention of the South* (1962). See also Michael P. Johnson, *Toward a Patriarchal Republic: The Secession of Georgia* (1977); J. Mills Thornton III, *Power and Politics in a Slave Society: Alabama 1820–1860* (1978); and Marc W. Kruman, *Parties and Politics in North Carolina, 1836–1865* (1983). Stephen B. Oates paints a vivid portrait of John Brown in *To Purge This Land with Blood* (1970), as Joan Hedrick does of Harriet Beecher Stowe in *Harriet Beecher Stowe: A Life* (1994). Thomas J. Pressley reviews the copious literature about the war in *Americans Interpret Their Civil War* (1954). George Forgie offers a psychoanalytic explanation of the coming of the war in *Patricide in the House Divided: A Psychological Interpretation of Lincoln and His Age* (1979).

---

*An asterisk indicates that the document, or an excerpt from it, can be found in Thomas A. Bailey and David M. Kennedy, eds., *The American Spirit: United States History as Seen by Contemporaries,* 9th ed. (Boston: Houghton Mifflin, 1998).

21

Girding for War:
The North and the South
1861–1865

I consider the central idea pervading this struggle is the necessity that is upon us, of proving that popular government is not an absurdity. We must settle this question now, whether in a free government the minority have the right to break up the government whenever they choose. If we fail it will go far to prove the incapability of the people to govern themselves.

ABRAHAM LINCOLN, MAY 7, 1861

President of the Disunited States of America

Abraham Lincoln solemnly took the oath of office on March 4, 1861, after having slipped into Washington at night, partially disguised to thwart assassins. He thus became president, not of the *United* States of America, but of the disunited states of America. Seven had departed; eight more were

teetering on the edge. The girders of the unfinished Capitol dome loomed nakedly in the background, as if to symbolize the imperfect state of the Union.

Lincoln's inaugural address was firm yet conciliatory: there would be no conflict unless the South provoked it. Secession, the president declared, was wholly impractical, because "Physically speaking, we cannot separate."

Here Lincoln put his finger on a profound geographical truth. The North and South were Siamese twins, bound inseparably together. If they had been

444

divided by the Pyrenees Mountains or the Danube River, a sectional divorce might have been more feasible. But the Appalachian Mountains and the mighty Mississippi River both ran the wrong way.

Uncontested secession would create new controversies. What share of the national debt should the South be forced to take with it? What portion of the jointly held federal territories, if any, should the Confederate states be allotted—areas so largely won with Southern blood? How would the fugitive-slave issue be resolved? The Underground Railroad would certainly redouble its activity, and it would have to transport its passengers only across the Ohio River, not all the way to Canada. Was it conceivable that all such problems could have been solved without ugly armed clashes?

A united United States had hitherto been the paramount republic in the Western Hemisphere. If this powerful democracy should break into two hostile parts, the European nations would be delighted. They could gleefully transplant to America their ancient concept of the balance of power. Playing the no less ancient game of divide and conquer, they could incite one snarling fragment of the dis-United States against the other. The colonies of the European powers in the New World, notably those of Britain, would thus be made safer against the rapacious Yankees. And European imperialists, with no unified republic to stand across their path, could more easily defy the Monroe Doctrine and seize territory in the Americas.

South Carolina Assails Fort Sumter

The issue of the divided Union came to a head over the matter of federal forts in the South. As the seceding states left, they had seized the United States arsenals, mints, and other public property within their borders. When Lincoln took office, only two significant forts in the South still flew the Stars and Stripes. The more important of the pair was square-walled Fort Sumter, in Charleston Harbor, with fewer than a hundred men.

Ominously, the choices presented to Lincoln by Fort Sumter were all bad. This stronghold had provisions that would last only a few weeks—until the middle of April 1861. If no supplies were forthcoming, its commander would have to surrender without firing a shot. Lincoln, quite understandably, did

not feel that such a weak-kneed course squared with his obligation to protect federal property. But if he sent reinforcements, the South Carolinians would undoubtedly fight back; they could not tolerate a federal fort blocking the mouth of their most important Atlantic seaport.

After agonizing indecision, Lincoln adopted a middle-of-the-road solution. He notified the South Carolinians that an expedition would be sent to *provision* the garrison, though not to *reinforce* it. But to Southern eyes "provision" spelled "reinforcement."

A Union naval force was next started on its way to Fort Sumter—a move that the South regarded as an act of aggression. On April 12, 1861, the cannons of the Carolinians opened fire on the fort, while crowds in Charleston applauded and waved handkerchiefs. After a thirty-four-hour bombardment, which took no lives, the dazed garrison surrendered.

The shelling of the fort electrified the North, which at once responded with cries of "Remember Fort Sumter" and "Save the Union." Hitherto countless Northerners had been saying that if the Southern states wanted to go, they should not be pinned to the rest of the nation with bayonets. "Wayward sisters, depart in peace" was a common sentiment, expressed even by the commander of the army, war hero General Winfield Scott, now so feeble at seventy-five that he had to be boosted onto his horse.

But the assault on Fort Sumter provoked the North to a fighting pitch: the fort was lost, but the

Fort Sumter, South Carolina, April 12–13, 1861
The Confederate battery at Fort Moultrie bombards Fort Sumter in this contemporary Currier and Ives lithograph.

Union was saved. Lincoln had turned a tactical defeat into a calculated victory. Southerners had wantonly fired upon the glorious Stars and Stripes, and honor demanded an armed response. Lincoln promptly (April 15) issued a call to the states for 75,000 militiamen; and volunteers sprang to the colors in such enthusiastic numbers that many were turned away—a mistake that was not often repeated. On April 19 and 27, the president proclaimed a leaky blockade of Southern seaports.

The call for troops, in turn, aroused the South much as the attack on Fort Sumter had aroused the North. Lincoln was now waging war—from the Southern view an aggressive war—on the Confederacy. Virginia, Arkansas, and Tennessee, all of which had earlier voted down secession, reluctantly joined their embattled sister states, as did North Carolina. Thus the seven states became eleven as the "submissionists" and "Union shriekers" were overcome. Richmond, Virginia, replaced Montgomery, Alabama, as the Confederate capital—too near Washington for strategic comfort on either side.

Brothers' Blood and Border Blood

The only slave states left were the crucial Border States. This group consisted of Missouri, Kentucky, Maryland, Delaware, and later West Virginia—the "mountain white" area that somewhat illegally tore itself from the side of Virginia in mid-1861. If the North had fired the first shot, some or all of these doubtful states probably would have seceded, and the South might well have succeeded. The border group actually contained a white population more than half that of the entire Confederacy. Maryland, Kentucky, and Missouri would almost double the manufacturing capacity of the South and increase by nearly half its supply of horses and mules. The strategic prize of the Ohio River flowed along the northern border of Kentucky and West Virginia. Two of its navigable tributaries, the Cumberland and Tennessee Rivers, penetrated deep into the heart of Dixie, where much of the Confederacy's grain, gunpowder, and iron was produced. Small wonder that Lincoln reportedly said he *hoped* to have God on his side, but he *had* to have Kentucky.

Abraham Lincoln (1809–1865), Kentucky-born like Jefferson Davis, was aware of Kentucky's crucial importance. In September 1861 he remarked,

"I think to lose Kentucky is nearly the same as to lose the whole game. Kentucky gone, we cannot hold Missouri, nor, I think, Maryland. These all against us, and the job on our hands is too large for us. We would as well consent to separation at once, including the surrender of this capital [Washington]."

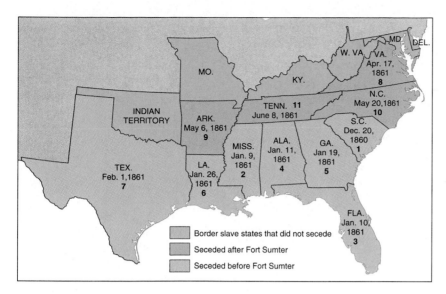

Seceding States (with dates and order of secession) Note the long interval —nearly six months—between the secession of South Carolina, the first state to go, and that of Tennessee, the last state to leave the Union. These six months were a time of terrible trial for moderate Southerners. When a Georgia statesman pleaded for restraint and negotiations with Washington, he was rebuffed with the cry, "Throw the bloody spear into this den of incendiaries!"

In dealing with the Border States, President Lincoln did not rely solely on moral suasion but successfully used methods of dubious legality. In Maryland he declared martial law where needed and sent in troops, because this state threatened to cut off Washington from the North. Lincoln also deployed Union soldiers in western Virginia and notably in Missouri, where they fought beside Unionists in a local civil war within the larger Civil War.

Any official statement of the North's war aims was profoundly influenced by the teetering Border States. At the very outset, Lincoln was obliged to declare publicly that he was not fighting to free the blacks. An antislavery declaration would no doubt have driven the Border States into the welcoming arms of the South. An antislavery war was also extremely unpopular in the so-called Butternut region of southern Ohio, Indiana, and Illinois. That area had been settled largely by Southerners who had carried their racial prejudices with them when they crossed the Ohio River (see "Makers of America: Settlers of the Old Northwest," pp. 246–247). It was to be a hotbed of pro-Southern sentiment throughout the war. Sensitive to this delicate political calculus, Lincoln insisted repeatedly—even though undercutting his moral high ground—that his paramount purpose was to save the Union at all costs. Thus the war began not as one between slave soil and free soil, but one for the Union—with slaveholders on both sides and many proslavery sympathizers in the North.

Slavery also colored the character of the war in the West. In the Indian Territory (present-day Oklahoma), most of the Five Civilized Tribes, the Cherokees, Creeks, Choctaws, Chickasaws, and Seminoles, sided with the Confederacy. Some of these Indians, notably the Cherokees, owned slaves and thus felt themselves to be making common cause with the slaveowning South. To secure their loyalty, the Confederate government agreed to take over federal payments to the tribes and invited the Native Americans to send delegates to the Confederate Congress. In return the tribes supplied troops to the Confederate Army. Meanwhile, a rival faction of Cherokees and most of the Plains Indians sided with the Union, only to be rewarded after the war with a relentless military campaign to herd them onto reservations or into oblivion.

Lincoln wrote to the antislavery editor Horace Greeley in August 1862, even as he was about to announce the Emancipation Proclamation:

"If I could save the Union without freeing any slave, I would do it; and if I could save it by freeing all the slaves, I would do it; and if I could do it by freeing some and leaving others alone, I would also do that."

Unhappily, the conflict between "Billy Yank" and "Johnny Reb" was a brothers' war. There were many Northern volunteers from the Southern states and many Southern volunteers from the Northern states. The "mountain whites" of the South sent north some 50,000 men, and the loyal slave states contributed some 300,000 soldiers to the Union. In many a family of the Border States, one brother rode north to fight with the Blue, another south to fight with the Gray. Senator Crittenden of Kentucky, who fathered the abortive Crittenden Compromise, fathered two sons: one became a general in the Union army, the other a general in the Confederate army. Lincoln's own Kentucky-born wife had four brothers who fought for the Confederacy.

The Balance of Forces

When war broke out, the South seemed to have great advantages. The Confederacy could fight defensively behind interior lines. The North had to invade the vast territory of the Confederacy, conquer it, and drag it bodily back into the Union. In fact, the South did not have to win the war in order to win its independence. If it merely fought the invaders to a draw and stood firm, Confederate independence would be won. Fighting on their own soil for self-determination and preservation of their way of life, Southerners at first enjoyed an advantage in morale as well.

Militarily, the South from the opening volleys of the war had the most talented officers. Most conspicuous among a dozen or so first-rate commanders was gray-haired General Robert E. Lee, whose knightly bearing and chivalric sense of honor embodied the Southern ideal. Lincoln had unofficially offered him command of the Northern armies, but when Virginia seceded, Lee felt honor-bound to go with his native state. Lee's chief lieutenant for much of the war was black-bearded Thomas J. ("Stonewall") Jackson, a gifted tactical theorist and a master of speed and deception.

Besides their brilliant leaders, ordinary Southerners were also bred to fight. Accustomed to managing horses and bearing arms from boyhood, they made excellent cavalrymen and foot soldiers. Their high-pitched "rebel yell" ("yeeeahhh") was designed to strike terror into the hearts of fuzz-chinned Yankee recruits. "There is nothing like it on this side of

Friendly Enemies   The man on the right is George Armstrong Custer. The youngest general in the Union army, this brilliant young officer survived the Civil War only to lose his life and that of every soldier under his command to Sioux warriors at the battle of the Little Big Horn River in 1876— "Custer's Last Stand." The man on the left is a Southern soldier and prisoner of war. He and Custer had been classmates at West Point.

the infernal region," one Northern soldier declared. "The peculiar corkscrew sensation that it sends down your backbone can never be told. You have to feel it."

As one immense farm, the South seemed to be handicapped by the scarcity of factories. Yet by seizing federal weapons, running Union blockades, and developing their own ironworks, Southerners managed to obtain sufficient weaponry. "Yankee ingenuity" was not confined to Yankees.

Nevertheless, as the war dragged on, grave shortages of shoes, uniforms, and blankets disabled the South. Even with immense stores of food on Southern farms, civilians and soldiers often went hungry because of supply problems. "Forward, men! They have cheese in their haversacks," cried one Southern officer as he attacked the Yankees. Much of the hunger was caused by a breakdown of the South's rickety transportation system, especially

Stonewall Jackson   The legendary Confederate general lost his life as a result of accidental injuries he suffered in the Battle of Chancellorsville.

nation's wealth, including three-fourths of the 30,000 miles (48,000 kilometers) of the railroads.

The North also controlled the sea. With its vastly superior navy, it established a blockade that, though a sieve at first, soon choked off Southern supplies and eventually shattered Southern morale. Its sea power also enabled the North to exchange huge quantities of grain for munitions and supplies from Europe, thus adding the output from the factories of Europe to its own.

The Union also enjoyed a much larger reserve of manpower. The loyal states had a population of some 22 million; the seceding states had 9 million people, including about 3.5 million slaves. Adding to the North's overwhelming supply of soldiery were ever-more immigrants from Europe, who continued to pour into the North even during the war (see table p. 450). Over 800,000 newcomers arrived between 1861 and 1865, most of them British, Irish, and German. Large numbers of them were induced to enlist in the Union armies. Altogether about one-fifth of the Union forces were foreign born, and in some units military commands were given in four different languages.

Whether immigrant or native, ordinary Northern boys were much less prepared than their Southern counterparts for military life. Yet the Northern "clodhoppers" and "shopkeepers" eventually adjusted themselves to soldiering and became known for their discipline and determination.

The North was much less fortunate in its higher commanders. Lincoln was forced to use a costly trial-and-error method to sort out effective leaders from the many incompetent political officers, until he finally uncovered a general, Ulysses Simpson Grant, who would crunch his way to victory.

where the railroad tracks were cut or destroyed by the Yankee invaders.

The economy was the greatest Southern weakness; it was the North's greatest strength. The North was not only a huge farm but a sprawling factory as well. Yankees boasted about three-fourths of the

Manufacturing by Sections, 1860

Section	Number of Establishments	Capital Invested	Average Number of Laborers	Annual Value of Products	Percentage of Total Value
New England	20,671	$ 257,477,783	391,836	$ 468,599,287	24%
Middle states	53,387	435,061,964	546,243	802,338,392	42
Western states	36,785	194,212,543	209,909	384,606,530	20
Southern states	20,631	95,975,185	110,721	155,531,281	8
Pacific states	8,777	23,380,334	50,204	71,229,989	3
Territories	282	3,747,906	2,333	3,556,197	1
TOTAL:	140,533	$1,009,855,715	1,311,246	$1,885,861,676	

Immigration to United States, 1860–1866

Year	Total	Britain	Ireland	Germany	All Others
1860	153,640	29,737	48,637	54,491	20,775
1861	91,918	19,675	23,797	31,661	16,785
1862	91,985	24,639	23,351	27,529	16,466
1863	176,282	66,882	55,916	33,162	20,322
1864	193,418	53,428	63,523	57,276	19,191
1865*	248,120	82,465	29,772	83,424	52,459
1866	318,568	94,924	36,690	115,892	71,062

*Only the first three months of 1865 were war months

Recruiting Immigrants for the Union Army
This poster in several languages appeals to immigrants to enlist. Immigrant manpower provided the Union with both industrial and military muscle.

In the long run, as the Northern strengths were brought to bear, they outweighed those of the South. But when the war began, the chances for Southern independence were unusually favorable—certainly better than the prospects for success of the thirteen colonies in 1776. The turn of a few events could easily have produced a different outcome.

The might-have-beens are fascinating. *If* the Border States had seceded, *if* the uncertain states of the upper Mississippi Valley had turned against the Union, *if* a wave of Northern defeatism had demanded an armistice, and *if* England and/or France had broken the blockade, the South might well have won. All of these possibilities almost became realities, but none of them actually occurred, and lacking their impetus, the South could not hope to win.

The American minister to Britain wrote,

"The great body of the aristocracy and the commercial classes are anxious to see the United States go to pieces [but] the middle and lower class sympathise with us [because they] see in the convulsion in America an era in the history of the world, out of which must come in the end a general recognition of the right of mankind to the produce of their labor and the pursuit of happiness."

Dethroning King Cotton

Successful revolutions, including the American Revolution of 1776, have generally succeeded because of foreign intervention. The South counted on it, did not get it, and lost. Of all the Confederacy's potential assets, none counted more weightily than the prospect of foreign intervention. Europe's ruling classes were openly sympathetic to the Confederate cause. They had long abhorred the incendiary example of the American democratic experiment, and they cherished a kind of fellow-feeling for the South's semifeudal, aristocratic social order.

In contrast, the masses of workingpeople in England, and to some extent in France, were pulling and praying for the North. Many of them had read *Uncle Tom's Cabin,* and they sensed that the war—though at the outset officially fought only over the question of union—might extinguish slavery if the North emerged victorious. The common folk of Britain could not yet cast the ballot, but they could cast the brick. Their certain hostility to any official intervention on behalf of the South evidently had a sobering effect on the British government. Thus the dead hands of Uncle Tom helped Uncle Sam by restraining the British and French ironclads from piercing the Union blockade. Yet the fact remained that British textile mills depended on the American South for 75 percent of their cotton supplies. Wouldn't silent looms force London to speak? Humanitarian sympathies aside, Southerners counted on hard economic need to bring Britain to their aid. Why did King Cotton fail them?

He failed in part because he had been so lavishly productive in the immediate prewar years of 1857–1860. Enormous exports of cotton in those years had piled up surpluses in British warehouses. When the shooting started in 1861, English manufacturers had on hand a hefty oversupply of fiber. The real pinch did not come until about a year and a half later, when thousands of hungry operatives were thrown out of work. But by this time Lincoln had announced his slave-emancipation policy, and the "wage slaves" of England were not going to demand a war to defend the slaveowners of the South.

The direst effects of the "cotton famine" in England were relieved in several ways. Hunger among unemployed workers was partially eased when certain kindhearted Americans sent over several cargoes of foodstuffs. As Union armies penetrated the South, they captured or bought considerable supplies of cotton and shipped them to England; and the Confederates also ran a limited quantity

The Confederacy Gets No Help from Europe
Despite repeated pleas from Confederate diplomats for recognition and aid, both France and England refrained from intervening in the American conflict—not least, because of the Union's demonstrated strength on the battlefield and its economic importance to European importers.

> As the Civil War neared the end of its third year, the London Times (January 7, 1864) could boast,
>
> "We are as busy, as rich, and as fortunate in our trade as if the American war had never broken out, and our trade with the States had never been disturbed. Cotton was no King, notwithstanding the prerogatives which had been loudly claimed for him."

through the blockade. In addition, the cotton growers of Egypt and India, responding to high prices, increased their output. Finally, booming war industries in England, which supplied both the North and the South, relieved unemployment.

King Wheat and King Corn—the monarchs of Northern agriculture—proved to be more potent potentates than King Cotton. During these war years, the North, blessed with ideal weather, produced bountiful crops of grain and harvested them with McCormick's mechanical reaper. In the same period, the British suffered a series of bad harvests. They were forced to import huge quantities of grain from America, which happened to have the cheapest and most abundant supply. If the British had broken the blockade to gain cotton, they would have provoked the North to war and would have lost this precious granary. Unemployment for some seemed better than hunger for all. Hence, one Yankee journal could exult,

> Wave the stars and stripes high o'er us,
> Let every freeman sing . . .
> Old King Cotton's dead and buried;
>   brave young Corn is King.

The Decisiveness of Diplomacy

America's diplomatic front has seldom been so critical as during the Civil War. The South never wholly abandoned its dream of foreign intervention, and Europe's rulers schemed to take advantage of America's distress.

The first major crisis with Britain came over the *Trent* affair, late in 1861. A Union warship cruising on the high seas north of Cuba stopped a British mail steamer, the *Trent,* and forcibly removed two Confederate diplomats bound for Europe.

Britons were outraged: upstart Yankees could not so boldly offend the Mistress of the Seas. War preparations buzzed, and red-coated troops embarked for Canada, with bands blaring "I Wish I Was in Dixie." The London Foreign Office prepared an ultimatum demanding surrender of the prisoners and an apology. But luckily, slow communications gave passions on both sides a chance to cool. Lincoln came to see the *Trent* prisoners as "white elephants," and reluctantly released them. "One war at a time," he reportedly said.

Another major crisis in Anglo-American relations arose over the unneutral building in England of Confederate commerce-raiders, notably the *Alabama.* These vessels were not warships within the meaning of loopholed British law because they left their shipyards unarmed and picked up their guns elsewhere. The *Alabama* escaped in 1862 to the Portuguese Azores, and there took on weapons and a crew from two English ships that followed it. Although flying the Confederate flag and officered by Confederates, it was manned by Britons and never entered a Confederate port. England was thus the chief naval base of the Confederacy.

The *Alabama* lighted the skies from Europe to the Far East with the burning hulks of Yankee merchantmen. All told, this "British pirate" captured over sixty vessels. Competing British shippers were delighted, while an angered North had to divert naval strength from its blockade for wild goose chases. The barnacled *Alabama* finally accepted a challenge from a stronger Union cruiser off the coast of France in 1864 and was quickly destroyed.

The *Alabama* was beneath the waves, but the issue of British-built Confederate raiders stayed afloat. Under prodding by the American minister, Charles Francis Adams, the British gradually perceived that allowing such ships to be built was a dangerous precedent that might someday be used against them. In 1863 London openly violated its own leaky laws and seized another raider being built for the South. But despite greater official efforts by Britain to remain truly neutral, Confederate commerce-destroyers, chiefly British-built, captured more than 250 Yankee ships, severely crippling the American merchant marine, which never fully recovered. Glowering Northerners looked farther north and talked openly of securing revenge by grabbing Canada when the war was over.

On the Deck of the *Alabama*
Captain Raphael Semmes leans jauntily against a deck-gun aboard his fearful Confederate raider. The *Alabama* sank sixty-four Union ships before it was sunk by the *U.S.S. Kearsarge* off the coast of Cherbourg, France, in June 1864.

Foreign Flare-Ups

A final Anglo-American crisis was touched off in 1863 by the Laird rams—two Confederate warships being constructed in the shipyard of John Laird and Sons in Great Britain. Designed to destroy the wooden ships of the Union navy with their iron rams and large-caliber guns, they were far more dangerous than the swift but lightly armed *Alabama*. If delivered to the South, they probably would have sunk the blockading squadrons and then brought Northern cities under their fire. In retaliation the North doubtless would have invaded Canada, and a full-dress war with Britain would have erupted. But Minister Adams took a hard line, warning that "this is war" if the rams were released. At the last minute, the London government relented and bought the two ships for the Royal Navy. Everyone seemed satisfied—except the disappointed Confederates. Britain also eventually repented its sorry role in the *Alabama* business. It agreed in 1871 to submit the *Alabama* dispute to arbitration, and in 1872 paid American claimants $15.5 million for damages caused by wartime commerce-raiders.

American rancor was also directed at Canada, where despite the vigilance of British authorities, Southern agents plotted to burn Northern cities. One Confederate raid into Vermont left three banks plundered and one American citizen dead. Hatred of England burned especially fiercely among Irish-Americans, and they unleashed their fury on Canada. They raised several tiny "armies" of a few hundred green-shirted men and launched invasions of Canada, notably in 1866 and 1870. The Canadians condemned the Washington government for permitting such violations of neutrality, but the administration was hampered by the presence of so many Irish-American voters.

As fate would have it, two great nations emerged from the fiery furnace of the American Civil War. One was a reunited United States, and the other was a united Canada. The British Parliament established the Dominion of Canada in 1867. It was partly designed to bolster the Canadians, both politically and spiritually, against the possible vengeance of the United States.

Emperor Napoleon III of France, taking advantage of America's preoccupation with its own internal problems, dispatched a French army to occupy Mexico City in 1863. The following year he installed on the ruins of the crushed republic his puppet, Austrian Archduke Maximilian, as emperor of Mexico. Both sending the army and enthroning Maximilian were flagrant violations of the Monroe Doctrine. Napoleon was gambling that the Union would collapse and thus America would be too weak to enforce its "hands off" policy in the Western Hemisphere.

The North, as long as it was convulsed by war, pursued a walk-on-eggs policy toward France. But when the shooting stopped in 1865, Secretary of State Seward, speaking with the authority of nearly a million war-tempered bayonets, prepared to march south. Napoleon realized that his costly gamble was doomed. He reluctantly took "French leave" of his ill-starred puppet in 1867, and Maximilian soon crumpled ingloriously before a Mexican firing squad.

President Davis versus President Lincoln

The Confederate government, like King Cotton, harbored fatal weaknesses. Its constitution, borrowing liberally from that of the Union, contained one deadly defect. Created by secession, it could not logically deny future secession to its constituent states. Jefferson Davis, while making his bow to states' rights, had in view a well-knit central government. But determined states' rights supporters fought him bitterly to the end. The Richmond regime encountered difficulty even in persuading certain state troops to serve outside their own borders. The governor of Georgia, a belligerent states' righter, at times seemed ready to secede from the secession

and fight both sides. States' rights were no less damaging to the Confederacy than Yankee sabers.

Sharp-featured President Davis—tense, humorless, legalistic, and stubborn—was repeatedly in hot water. Although an eloquent orator and an able administrator, he at no time enjoyed real personal popularity and was often at loggerheads with his congress. At times there was serious talk of impeachment. Unlike Lincoln, Davis was somewhat imperious and inclined to defy rather than lead public opinion. Suffering acutely from neuralgia and other nervous disorders (including a tic), he overworked himself with the details of both civil government and military operations. No one could doubt his courage, sincerity, integrity, and devotion to the South, but the task proved beyond his powers. It was probably beyond the powers of any mere mortal.

Lincoln also had his troubles, but on the whole they were less prostrating. The North enjoyed the prestige of a long-established government, financially stable and fully recognized both at home and abroad. Lincoln, the inexperienced prairie politician, proved superior to the more experienced but less flexible Davis. Able to relax with droll stories at critical times, "Old Abe" grew as the war dragged on. Tactful, quiet, patient, yet firm, he developed a genius for interpreting and leading a fickle public

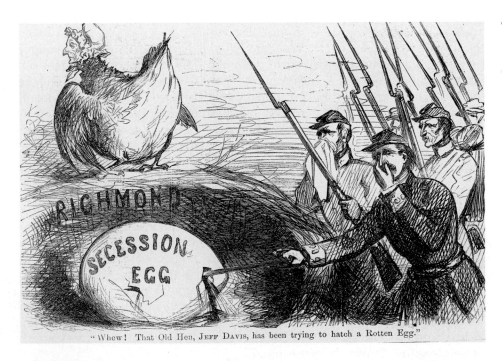

The Stink of Secession Passions ran high in the North against the crime of "secesh."

"Whew! That Old Hen, Jeff Davis, has been trying to hatch a Rotten Egg."

opinion. Holding aloft the banner of Union with inspiring utterances, he demonstrated charitableness toward the South and forbearance toward backbiting colleagues. "Did [Secretary of War Edwin] Stanton say I was a damned fool?" he reportedly replied to a talebearer. "Then I dare say I must be one, for Stanton is generally right and he always says what he means."

Limitations on Wartime Liberties

"Honest Abe" Lincoln, when inaugurated, laid his hand on the Bible and swore a solemn oath to uphold the Constitution. Then, driven by sheer necessity, he proceeded to tear a few holes in that hallowed document. He sagely concluded that if he did not do so, and patch the parchment later, there might not be a Constitution of a *united* United States to mend. The "rail-splitter" was no hair-splitter.

But such infractions were not, in general, sweeping. Congress, as is often true in times of crisis, generally accepted or confirmed the president's questionable acts. Lincoln, though accused of being a "Simple Susan Tyrant," did not believe that his ironhanded authority would continue, once the Union was preserved. As he pointedly remarked in 1863, a man suffering from "temporary illness" would not persist in feeding on bitter medicines for "the remainder of his healthful life."

Congress was not in session when war erupted, so Lincoln gathered the reins into his own hands. Brushing aside legal objections, he boldly proclaimed a blockade. (His action was later upheld by the Supreme Court.) He arbitrarily increased the size of the federal army—something that only Congress can do under the Constitution (see Art. I, Sec. VIII, para. 12). (Congress later approved.) He directed the secretary of the treasury to advance $2 million without appropriation or security to three private citizens for military purposes—a grave irregularity contrary to the Constitution (see Art. I, Sec. IX, para. 7). He suspended the precious privilege of the writ of habeas corpus, so that anti-Unionists might be summarily arrested. In taking this step, he defied a dubious ruling by the chief justice that the safeguards of habeas corpus could be set aside only by authorization of Congress (see Art. I, Sec. IX, para. 2).

Lincoln's regime was guilty of many other high-handed acts. For example, it arranged for "supervised" voting in the Border States. There the intimidated citizen, holding a colored ballot indicating his party preference, had to march between two lines of armed troops. The federal officials also ordered the suspension of certain newspapers and the arrest of their editors on grounds of obstructing the war.

Jefferson Davis was less able than Lincoln to exercise arbitrary power, mainly because of confirmed states' righters who fanned an intense spirit of localism. To the very end of the conflict, the owners of horse-drawn vans in Petersburg, Virginia, prevented the sensible joining of the incoming and outgoing tracks of a militarily vital railroad. The South seemed willing to lose the war before it would surrender local rights—and it did.

Volunteers and Draftees: North and South

Ravenous, the gods of war demanded men—lots of men. Northern armies were at first manned solely by volunteers, with each state assigned a quota based on population. But in 1863, after volunteering had slackened off, Congress passed a federal conscription law for the first time on a nationwide scale in the United States. The provisions were grossly unfair to the poor. Rich boys, including young John D. Rockefeller, could hire substitutes to go in their places or purchase exemption outright by paying $300. "Three-hundred-dollar men" was the scornful epithet applied to these slackers. Draftees who did not have the necessary cash complained that their bandit-like government demanded "three hundred dollars or your life."

The draft was especially damned in the Democratic strongholds of the North, notably in New York City. A frightful riot broke out in 1863, touched off largely by underprivileged and antiblack Irish-Americans, who shouted, "Down with Lincoln!" and "Down with the draft!" For several days the city was at the mercy of a burning, drunken, pillaging mob. Scores of lives were lost, and the victims included many lynched blacks. Elsewhere in the North, conscription met with resentment and an occasional minor riot.

The New York City Draft Riots, 1863   Mostly Irish-American mobs convulsed the city for days, and were in the end put down only by a merciless application of federal firepower.

More than 90 percent of the Union troops were volunteers, since social and patriotic pressures to enlist were strong. As able-bodied men became scarcer, generous bounties for enlistment were offered by federal, state, and local authorities. An enterprising and moneywise volunteer might legitimately pocket more than $1,000.

With money flowing so freely, an unsavory crew of "bounty brokers" and "substitute brokers" sprang up, at home and abroad. They combed the poorhouses of the British Isles and Western Europe; and many an Irishman or German was befuddled with whiskey and induced to enlist. A number of the slippery "bounty boys" deserted, volunteered elsewhere, and netted another handsome haul. The records reveal that one "bounty jumper" repeated his profitable operation thirty-two times. But desertion was by no means confined to "bounty jumpers." The rolls of the Union army recorded about 200,000 deserters of all classes, and the Confederate authorities were plagued with a runaway problem of similar dimensions.

Like the North, the South at first relied mainly on volunteers. But since the Confederacy was much less populous, it scraped the bottom of its manpower barrel much more quickly. Quipsters observed that any man who could see lightning and hear thunder was judged fit for service. The Richmond regime, robbing both "cradle and grave" (ages 17 to 50), was forced to resort to conscription as early as April 1862, nearly a year earlier than the Union.

Confederate draft regulations also worked serious injustices. As in the North, a rich man could hire a substitute or purchase exemption. Slaveowners or overseers with twenty slaves might also claim exemption. These special privileges, later modified, made for bad feelings among the less prosperous, many of whom complained that this was a "a rich man's war but a poor man's fight." Why sacrifice one's life to save an affluent neighbor's slaves? No large-scale draft riots broke out in the South, as in New York City. But the Confederate conscription agents often found it prudent to avoid those areas inhabited by sharp-shooting mountain whites, who were branded "Tories," "traitors," and "Yankee-lovers."

Number of Men in Uniform at Date Given

Date	Union	Confederate
July 1861	186,751	112,040
January 1862	575,917	351,418
March 1862	637,126	401,395
January 1863	918,121	446,622
January 1864	860,737	481,180
January 1865	959,460	445,203

The Economic Stresses of War

Blessed with a lion's share of the wealth, the North rode through the financial breakers much more smoothly than the South. Excise taxes on tobacco and alcohol were substantially increased by Congress. An income tax was levied for the first time in the nation's experience; and although the rates were painlessly low by later standards, they netted millions of dollars.

Customs receipts likewise proved to be important revenue-raisers. Early in 1861, after enough antiprotection Southern members had seceded, Congress passed the Morrill Tariff Act, superseding the low Tariff of 1857. It increased the existing duties some 5 to 10 percent, boosting them to about the moderate level of the Walker Tariff of 1846. But these modest rates were soon pushed sharply upward by the necessities of war. The increases were designed partly to raise additional revenue and partly to provide more protection for the prosperous manufacturers who were being plucked by the new internal taxes. A protective tariff thus became identified with the Republican party, as American industrialists, mostly Republicans, waxed fat on these welcome benefits.

The Washington Treasury also issued greenbacked paper money, totaling nearly $450 million, at face value. This printing-press currency was inadequately supported by gold, and hence its value was determined by the nation's credit. Greenbacks thus fluctuated with the fortunes of Union arms and at one low point were worth only 39 cents on the gold dollar. The holders of the notes, victims of creeping inflation, were indirectly taxed as the value of the currency slowly withered in their hands.

Yet borrowing far outstripped both greenbacks and taxes as a money-raiser. The federal Treasury netted $2,621,916,786 through the sale of bonds, which bore interest and which were payable at a later date. The modern technique of selling these issues to the people directly through "drives" and payroll deductions had not yet been devised. Accordingly, the Treasury was forced to market its bonds through the private banking house of Jay Cooke and Company, which received a commission of three-eighths of 1 percent on all sales. With both profits and patriotism at stake, the bankers succeeded in making effective appeals to citizen purchasers.

A financial landmark of the war was the National Banking System, authorized by Congress in 1863. Launched partly as a stimulant to the sale of government bonds, it was also designed to establish a standard bank-note currency. (The country was then flooded with depreciated "rag money" issued by unreliable bankers.) Banks that joined the National Banking System could buy government bonds and issue sound paper money backed by them. The war-born National Banking Act thus turned out to be the first significant step taken toward a unified banking network since 1836, when the "monster" Bank of the United States was killed by Andrew Jackson. Spawned by the war, this new system continued to function for fifty years, until replaced by the Federal Reserve System in 1913.

An impoverished South was beset by different financial woes. Customs duties were choked off as the coils of the Union blockade tightened. Large issues of Confederate bonds were sold at home and abroad, amounting to nearly $400 million. The Richmond regime also increased taxes sharply and imposed a 10 percent levy on farm produce. But in general the states' rights Southerners were immovably opposed to heavy direct taxation by the central authority: only about 1 percent of the total income was raised in this way.

As revenue began to dry up, the Confederate government was forced to print blue-backed paper money with complete abandon. "Runaway inflation" occurred as Southern presses continued to grind out the poorly backed treasury notes, totaling in all more than $1 billion. The Confederate paper dollar finally sank to the point where it was worth only 1.6 cents when Lee surrendered. Overall, the war inflicted a 9,000 percent inflation rate on the Confederacy, contrasted with 80 percent for the Union.

A contemporary (October 22, 1863) Richmond diary portrays the ruinous effects of inflation:

"A poor woman yesterday applied to a merchant in Carey Street to purchase a barrel of flour. The price he demanded was $70. 'My God!' exclaimed she, 'how can I pay such prices? I have seven children; what shall I do?' 'I don't know, madam,' said he coolly, 'unless you eat your children.'"

The North's Economic Boom

Wartime prosperity in the North was little short of miraculous. The marvel is that a divided nation could fight a costly conflict for four long years and then emerge seemingly more prosperous than ever before.

New factories, sheltered by the friendly umbrella of the new protective tariffs, mushroomed forth. Soaring prices, resulting from inflation, unfortunately pinched the day laborer and the white-collar worker to some extent. But the manufacturers and businesspeople raked in "the fortunes of war."

The Civil War bred a millionaire class for the first time in American history, though a few individuals of extreme wealth could have been found earlier. Many of these newly rich were noisy, gaudy, brassy, and given to extravagant living. Their emergence merely illustrates the truth that some gluttony and greed always mar the devotion and self-sacrifice called forth by war. The story of speculators and peculators was roughly the same in both camps. But graft was more flagrant in the North than in the South, partly because there was more to steal.

Yankee "sharpness" appeared at its worst. Dishonest agents, putting profits above patriotism, palmed off aged and blind horses on government purchasers. Unscrupulous Northern manufacturers supplied shoes with cardboard soles and fast-disintegrating uniforms of reprocessed or "shoddy" wool rather than virgin wool. Hence the reproachful term "shoddy millionaires" was doubly fair. One profiteer reluctantly admitted that his profits were "painfully large."

Newly invented laborsaving machinery enabled the North to expand economically, even though the cream of its manpower was being drained off to the fighting front. The sewing machine wrought wonders in fabricating uniforms and military footwear.

The marriage of military need and innovative machinery largely ended the production of custom-tailored clothing. Graduated standard measurements were introduced, creating "sizes" that were widely used in the civilian garment industry forever after.

Clattering mechanical reapers, which numbered about 250,000 by 1865, proved hardly less potent than thundering guns. They not only released tens of thousands of farm boys for the army but fed them their field rations. They produced vast surpluses of

Nightmare of a War Profiteer, 1861
A dead soldier forces on him the same poisonous food and drink with which he supplied the army.

grain that, when sent abroad, helped dethrone King Cotton. They provided profits with which the North was able to buy munitions and supplies from abroad. They contributed to the feverish prosperity of the North—a prosperity that enabled the Union to weather the war with flying colors.

Other industries were humming. The discovery of petroleum gushers in 1859 had led to a rush of "Fifty-Niners" to Pennsylvania. The result was the birth of a new industry, with its "petroleum plutocracy" and "coal oil Johnnies." Pioneers continued to push westward during the war, altogether an estimated 300,000 people. Major magnets were free gold nuggets and free land under the Homestead Act of 1862. Strong propellants were the federal draft agents. The only major Northern industry to suffer a crippling setback was the ocean-carrying trade, which fell prey to the *Alabama* and other raiders.

The Civil War was a women's war, too. The protracted conflict opened new opportunities for women. When men departed in uniform, women often took their jobs. In Washington, D.C., five hundred women clerks ("government girls") became government workers, with over one hundred in the Treasury Department alone. The booming military demand for shoes and clothing, combined with technological marvels like the sewing machine, likewise drew countless women into industrial employment. Before the war, one industrial worker in four had been female; during the war, the ratio rose to one in three.

Other women, on both sides, stepped up to the fighting front—or close behind it. More than four hundred women accompanied husbands and sweethearts into battle by posing as male soldiers. Other women took on dangerous spy missions. One woman was executed for smuggling gold to the Confederacy. Dr. Elizabeth Blackwell, America's first female physician, helped organize the U.S. Sanitary Commision to assist the Union armies in the field. The commission trained nurses, collected medical supplies, and equipped hospitals. Commission work helped many women to acquire the organizational skills and the self-confidence that would propel the women's movement forward after the war. Heroically energetic Clara Barton and dedicated Dorothea Dix, superintendent of nurses for the Union army, helped transform nursing from a lowly service into a respected profession—and in the process opened up another major sphere of employment for women in the postwar era. Equally renowned in the South was Sally Tompkins, who ran a Richmond infirmary for wounded Confederate soldiers and was awarded the rank of captain by Confederate president Jefferson Davis. Still other women, North as well as South, organized bazaars and fairs that raised millions of dollars for the relief of widows, orphans, and disabled soldiers.

Women at War
During the Civil War women raised money to help soldiers and their families by making handicrafts like these potholders sold at the Northwestern Sanitary Fair in Chicago in 1865.

A Crushed Cotton Kingdom

The South fought to the point of exhaustion. The suffocation caused by the blockade, together with the destruction wrought by invaders, took a terrible toll. Possessing 30 percent of the national wealth in 1860, the South claimed only 12 percent in 1870. Before the war the average per capita income of Southerners (including slaves) was about two-thirds that of Northerners. The Civil War squeezed the average southern income to two-fifths of the Northern level, where it remained for the rest of the century. The South's bid for independence exacted a cruel and devastating cost.

Transportation collapsed. The South was even driven to the economic cannibalism of pulling up rails from the less-used lines to repair the main ones. Window weights were melted down into bullets; gourds replaced dishes; pins became so scarce that they were loaned with reluctance.

To the brutal end, the South mustered remarkable resourcefulness and spirit. Women buoyed up their menfolk, many of whom had seen enough of war at first hand to be heartily sick of it. A proposal was made by a number of women that they cut off their long hair and sell it abroad. But the project was not adopted, partly because of the blockade. The self-sacrificing women took pride in denying themselves the silks and satins of their Northern sisters. The chorus of a song, "The Southern Girl," touched a cheerful note:

> *So hurrah! hurrah! For Southern Rights, hurrah!*
> *Hurrah! for the homespun dress the Southern ladies wear.*

At war's end the Northern Captains of Industry had conquered the Southern Lords of the Manor. A crippled South left the capitalistic North free to work its own way, with high tariffs and other benefits. The manufacturing moguls of the North, ushering in the full-fledged industrial revolution, were destined for increased dominance over American economic and political life. Hitherto the agrarian "slavocracy" of the South had partially checked the ambitions of the rising plutocracy of the North. Now cotton capitalism had lost out to industrial capitalism. The South of 1865 was to be rich in little but amputees, war heroes, ruins, and memories.

Chronology

1861 Confederate government formed Lincoln takes office (March 4) Fort Sumter fired upon (April 12) Four Upper South states secede (April–June) Morrill Tariff Act passed *Trent* affair Lincoln suspends writ of habeas corpus	**1863** Union enacts conscription New York City draft riot National Banking System established
1862 Confederacy enacts conscription Homestead Act	**1863–** **1864** Napoleon III installs Archduke Maximilian as emperor of Mexico
1862– **1864** *Alabama* raids Northern shipping	**1864** *Alabama* sunk by Union warship

SUGGESTED READINGS

PRIMARY SOURCE DOCUMENTS

The Constitution of the Confederacy (1861) makes an interesting contrast to the U.S. Constitution. Three diaries that describe life behind the Confederate lines are those of John B. Jones, published as Earl S. Miers, ed., *A Rebel War Clerk's Diary** (1958); Paul B. Barringer, *The Natural Bent** (1949); and C. Vann Woodward, ed., *Mary Chesnut's Civil War* (1981). Lincoln's Gettysburg Address* (1863) poetically proclaims the president's highest war aims, as does his Second Inaugural Address* (1865).

SECONDARY SOURCES

The best one-volume biography is Stephen B. Oates, *With Malice Toward None: The Life of Abraham Lincoln* (1977). An excellent collection is Don E. Fehrenbacher, *Lincoln in Text and Context: Collected Essays* (1987). See also Garry Wills, *Lincoln at Gettysburg: The Words That Remade America* (1992); and David H. Donald, *Lincoln* (1995). Home-front politics are treated in James A. Rawley, *The Politics of Union* (1974), and in Joel Silbey, *A Respectable Minority: The Democratic Party in the Civil War Era* (1977). See also Jean H. Baker, *Affairs of Party: The Political Culture of the Northern Democrats in the Mid–Nineteenth Century* (1983); and Eric Foner, *Politics and Ideology in the Age of the Civil War* (1980). Lincoln's problems are analyzed in LaWanda Cox, *Lincoln and*

Black Freedom (1981). See also Hans L. Trefousse, *The Radical Republicans: Lincoln's Vanguard for Racial Justice* (1969). Eugene C. Murdoch analyzes the military draft in the North in *One Million Men* (1971). Iver Bernstein treats *The New York City Draft Riots* (1990). Gerald F. Linderman examines the motivations of soldiers in *Embattled Courage: The Experience of Combat in the Civil War* (1987). Mary F. Massey presents the interesting story of women in the Civil War in *Bonnet Brigades* (1966); that topic also figures in Anne Firor Scott, *The Southern Lady* (1970). See also the essays in Catherine Clinton and Nina Silber, eds., *Divided Houses: Gender and the Civil War* (1992), and Drew Gilpin Faust, *Mothers of Invention: Women of the Slaveholding South in the American Civil War* (1996). On the Confederacy see Emory M. Thomas, *The Confederate Nation, 1861–1865* (1979), and Drew Gilpin Faust, *The Creation of Confederate Nationalism* (1988). Economic matters are handled in Ralph L. Andreano, ed., *The Economic Impact of the American Civil War* (1962); David T. Gilchrist and W. David Lewis, eds., *Economic Change in the Civil War Era* (1965); see also the early chapters of Thomas C. Cochran et al., *The Age of Enterprise: A Social History of Industrial America* (1942). Two useful anthologies are David Donald, ed., *Why the North Won the Civil War* (1960), and Robert P. Swierenga, ed., *Beyond the Civil War Synthesis: Political Essays on the Civil War Era* (1975). Richard E. Beringer et al. present a different viewpoint in *Why the South Lost the Civil War* (1986). The war's literary legacy is keenly analyzed in Edmund Wilson's classic *Patriotic Gore* (1962) and in Daniel Aaron's *The Unwritten War: American Writers and the Civil War* (1973). For a fascinating discussion of Northern intellectuals and the conflict, consult George M. Fredrickson, *The Inner Civil War* (1965).

---

*An asterisk indicates that the document, or an excerpt from it, can be found in Thomas A. Bailey and David M. Kennedy, eds., *The American Spirit: United States History as Seen by Contemporaries*, 9th ed. (Boston: Houghton Mifflin, 1998).

22

The Furnace of Civil War

1861–1865

My paramount object in this struggle is to save the Union, and is not either to save or to destroy slavery.

Bull Run Ends the "Ninety-Day War"

When President Lincoln, on April 15, 1861, issued his call to the states for 75,000 militiamen, he envisioned them serving for only ninety days. He reaffirmed that he had "no purpose, directly or indirectly, to interfere with slavery in the States where it exists." With a swift flourish of federal force, he hoped to show the folly of secession and rapidly return the rebellious states to the Union. Northern newspapers, also eager for a quick resolution of the crisis, raised the cry "On to Richmond!"

In this expectant atmosphere, a Union army of some 30,000 men drilled near Washington in the summer of 1861. It was ill prepared for battle, but the press and the public clamored for action. Lincoln eventually concluded that an attack on a smaller

Confederate force at Bull Run (Manassas Junction), some 30 miles (48 kilometers) southwest of Washington, might be worth a try. If successful, it would demonstrate the superiority of Union arms. It might even lead to the capture of the Confederate capital at Richmond, 100 miles to the south. If Richmond fell, secession would be thoroughly discredited and the Union could be restored without damage to the economic and social system of the South.

Raw Yankee recruits swaggered out of Washington toward Bull Run on July 21, 1861, as if they were headed for a sporting event. Congressmen and spectators trailed along with their lunch baskets to witness the fun. At first the battle went well for the Yankees. But "Stonewall" Jackson's gray-clad warriors stood like a stone wall (here he won his nickname), and Confederate reinforcements arrived unexpectedly. Panic seized the green Union troops, many of whom fled in shameful confusion. The

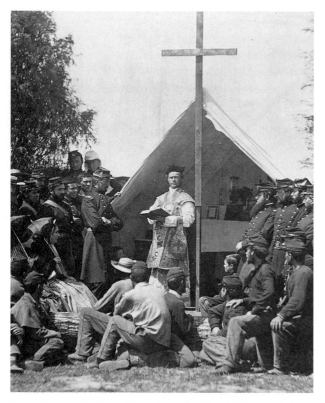

Preparing for Battle   These troops of the 69th New York State Militia, a largely Irish regiment, were photographed attending Sunday morning Mass in May 1861, just weeks before the Battle of Bull Run. Because the regiment was camped near Washington, D.C., women were able to visit.

Confederates, themselves too exhausted or disorganized to pursue, feasted on captured lunches.

The "military picnic" at Bull Run, though not decisive militarily, bore significant psychological and political consequences; many of them paradoxical. Victory was worse than defeat for the South, because it inflated an already dangerous overconfidence. Many of the Southern soldiers promptly deserted, some boastfully to display their trophies, others feeling that the war was now surely over. Southern enlistments fell off sharply, and preparations for a protracted conflict slackened. Defeat was better than victory for the Union, because it dispelled all illusions of a one-punch war and caused the Northerners to buckle down to the staggering task at hand. It also set the stage for a war that would be waged not merely for the cause of Union but also, eventually, for the abolitionist ideal of emancipation.

"Tardy George" McClellan and the Peninsula Campaign

Northern hopes brightened later in 1861, when General George B. McClellan was given command of the Army of the Potomac, as the major Union force near Washington was now called. Red-haired

The Army of the Potomac Marching Up Pennsylvania Avenue, Washington, D.C., 1861   In this painting Union troops parade before the Battle of Bull Run. Colorfully uniformed, they are a regiment of Zouaves, who adopted the name and style of military dress from a legendarily dashing French infantry unit. But bright uniforms were not enough to win battles, and these troops were soon to be routed by the Confederates.

Cocky George McClellan embodied a curious mixture of virtues and defects. He was a superb organizer and drillmaster, and he injected splendid morale into the Army of the Potomac. Hating to sacrifice his troops, he was idolized by his men, who affectionately called him "Little Mac." But he was a perfectionist who seems not to have realized that an army is never ready to the last button and that wars cannot be won without running some risks. He consistently but erroneously believed that the enemy outnumbered him, partly because his intelligence reports from the head of Pinkerton's Detective Agency were unreliable. He was overcautious—Lincoln once accused him of having "the slows"—and he addressed the president in an arrogant tone that a less forgiving person would never have tolerated. Privately the general referred to his chief as a "baboon."

As McClellan doggedly continued to drill his army without moving it toward Richmond, the derisive Northern watchword became "All Quiet along the Potomac." The song of the hour was "Tardy George" (McClellan). After threatening to "borrow" the army if it was not going to be used, Lincoln finally issued firm orders to advance.

A reluctant McClellan at last decided upon a water-borne approach to Richmond, which lies at the western base of a narrow peninsula formed by the James and York Rivers—hence the name given to this historic encounter: the Peninsula Campaign.

and red-mustached, strong and stocky, McClellan was a brilliant, thirty-four-year-old West Pointer. As a serious student of warfare who was dubbed "Young Napoleon," he had seen plenty of fighting, first in the Mexican War and then as an observer of the Crimean War in Russia.

Masterly Inactivity, or Six Months on the Potomac, 1862 McClellan and his Confederate foe view each other cautiously, while their troops engage in visits, weddings, and sports.

Lincoln treated the demands of George McClellan (1826–1885) for reinforcements and his excuses for inaction with infinite patience. One exception came when the general complained that his horses were tired. On October 24, 1862, Lincoln wrote,

"I have just read your dispatch about sore-tongued and fatigued horses. Will you pardon me for asking what the horses of your army have done since the battle of Antietam that fatigues anything?"

Peninsula Campaign, 1862

McClellan warily inched toward the Confederate capital in the spring of 1862 with about 100,000 men. After taking a month to capture historic York-town, which bristled with imitation wooden cannons, he finally came within sight of the spires of Richmond. At this crucial juncture, Lincoln diverted McClellan's anticipated reinforcements to chase "Stonewall" Jackson, whose lightning feints in the Shenandoah Valley seemed to put Washington, D.C., in jeopardy. Stalled in front of Richmond, McClellan was further frustrated when "Jeb" Stuart's Confederate cavalry rode completely around his army on reconnaissance. Then General Robert E. Lee launched a devastating counterattack—the Seven Days' Battles—June 26–July 2, 1862. The Confederates slowly drove McClellan back to the sea. The Union forces abandoned the Peninsula Campaign

Civil War Scene (detail)
A Federal brigade repulses a Confederate assault at Williamsburg, Virginia, in 1862, as the Peninsula Campaign presses toward Richmond. General Winfield Scott Hancock commanded the troops. For his success in this action, Hancock earned the nickname "The Superb."

as a costly failure, and Lincoln temporarily abandoned McClellan as commander of the Army of the Potomac—though Lee's army had suffered some twenty thousand casualties to McClellan's ten thousand.

Lee had achieved a brilliant, if bloody, triumph. Yet the ironies of his accomplishment are striking. If McClellan had succeeded in taking Richmond and ending the war in mid-1862, the Union would probably have been restored with minimal disruption to the "peculiar institution." Slavery would have survived, at least for a time. By his successful defense of Richmond and defeat of McClellan, Lee had in effect ensured that the war would endure until slavery was uprooted and the Old South thoroughly destroyed. Lincoln himself, who had earlier professed his unwillingness to tamper with slavery where it already existed, now declared that the rebels "cannot experiment for ten years trying to destroy the government and if they fail still come back into the Union unhurt." He began to draft an emancipation proclamation.

Union strategy now turned toward total war. As finally developed, the Northern military plan had six components: first, slowly suffocate the South by blockading its coasts; second, liberate the slaves and hence undermine the very economic foundations of the Old South; third, cut the Confederacy in half by seizing control of the Mississippi River backbone; fourth, chop the Confederacy to pieces by sending troops through Georgia and the Carolinas; fifth, decapitate it by capturing its capital at Richmond; and sixth (this was Ulysses Grant's idea, especially), try everywhere to engage the enemy's main strength and to grind it into submission.

> *A Confederate soldier assigned to burial detail after the Seven Days' Battles (1862) wrote,*
>
> "The sights and smells that assailed us were simply indescribable. . . corpses swollen to twice their original size, some of them actually burst asunder with the pressure of foul gasses. . . . The odors were so nauseating and so deadly that in a short time we all sickened and were lying with our mouths close to the ground, most of us vomiting profusely."

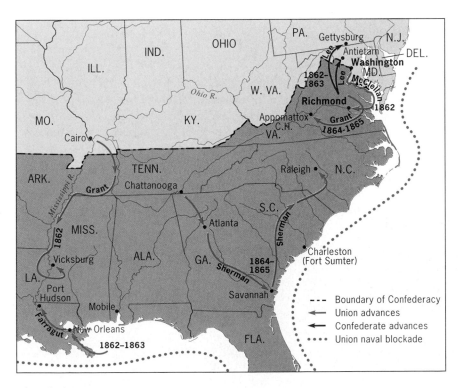

Main Thrusts, 1861–1865
Northern strategists at first believed that the rebellion could be snuffed out quickly by a swift, crushing blow. But the stiffness of Southern resistance to the Union's early probes, and the North's inability to strike with sufficient speed and severity, revealed that the conflict would be a war of attrition, long and bloody.

The War at Sea

The blockade started leakily: it was not clamped down all at once but was extended by degrees. A watertight patrol of some 3,500 miles (5,635 kilometers) of coast was impossible for the hastily improvised Northern navy, which counted converted yachts and ferry boats in its fleet. But blockading was simplified by concentrating on the principal ports and inlets where dock facilities were available for loading bulky bales of cotton.

How was the blockade regarded by the naval powers of the world? Ordinarily, they probably would have defied it, for it was never completely effective and was especially sievelike at the outset. But England, the greatest maritime nation, recognized it as binding and warned its shippers that they ignored it at their peril. An explanation is easy. Blockade happened to be the chief offensive weapon of Britain, which was still Mistress of the Seas. Britain plainly did not want to tie its hands in a future war by insisting that Lincoln maintain impossibly high blockading standards.

Blockade-running soon became riskily profitable, as the growing scarcity of Southern goods drove prices skyward. The most successful blockade runners were swift, gray-painted steamers, scores of which were specially built in Scotland. A leading rendezvous was the West Indian port of Nassau, in the British Bahamas, where at one time thirty-five of the speedy ships rode at anchor. The low-lying craft would take on cargoes of arms brought in by tramp steamers from England, leave with fraudulent papers for "Halifax" (Canada), and then return a few days later with a cargo of cotton. The risks were great, but the profits would mount to 700 percent and more for lucky gamblers. Two successful voyages might well pay for capture on a third. The lush days of blockade-running finally passed as Union squad-rons gradually pinched off the leading Southern ports, from New Orleans to Charleston.

The Northern navy enforced the blockade with high-handed practices. Yankee captains, for example, would seize British freighters on the high seas, if laden with war supplies for the tiny port of Nassau and other halfway stations. The justification was that obviously these shipments were "ultimately" destined, by devious routes, for the Confederacy.

London, although not happy, acquiesced in this disagreeable doctrine of "ultimate destination" or "continuous voyage." British blockaders might need to take advantage of the same far-fetched interpretation in a future war—as in fact they did in the World War of 1914–1918.

The most alarming Confederate threat to the blockade came in 1862. Resourceful Southerners raised and reconditioned a former wooden U.S. warship, the *Merrimack,* and plated its sides with old iron railroad rails. Renamed the *Virginia,* this clumsy but powerful monster easily destroyed two wooden ships of the Union navy in the Virginia waters of Chesapeake Bay; it also threatened catastrophe to the entire Yankee blockading fleet. (Actually the homemade ironclad was not a seaworthy craft.)

A tiny Union ironclad, the *Monitor,* built in about one hundred days, arrived on the scene in the nick of time. For four hours, on March 9, 1862, the little "Yankee cheesebox on a raft" fought the wheezy *Merrimack* to a standstill. Britain and France had already built several powerful ironclads, but the first battle-testing of these new craft heralded the doom of wooden warships. A few months after the historic battle, the Confederates destroyed the *Merrimack* to keep it from the grasp of advancing Union troops.

When news reached Washington that the Merrimack *had sunk two wooden Yankee warships with ridiculous ease, President Lincoln, much "excited," summoned his advisers. Secretary of the Navy Gideon Welles (1802–1878) recorded,*

"The most frightened man on that gloomy day . . . was the Secretary of War [Stanton]. He was at times almost frantic. . . . The *Merrimack,* he said, would destroy every vessel in the service, could lay every city on the coast under contribution, could take Fortress Monroe. . . . Likely the first movement of the *Merrimack* would be to come up the Potomac and disperse Congress, destroy the Capitol and public buildings."

Battle of the *Merrimack* and the *Monitor*, March 9, 1862

The Pivotal Point: Antietam

Robert E. Lee, having broken the back of McClellan's assault on Richmond, next moved northward. At the Second Battle of Bull Run (August 29–30, 1862), he encountered a Federal force under General John Pope. A handsome, dashing, soldierly figure, Pope boasted that in the western theater of war, from which he had recently come, he had seen only the backs of the enemy. Lee quickly gave him a front view, furiously attacking Pope's troops and inflicting a crushing defeat.

Emboldened by this success, Lee daringly thrust into Maryland. He hoped to strike a blow that would not only encourage foreign intervention but also seduce the still wavering Border State and its sisters from the Union. The Confederate troops sang lustily:

> *Thou wilt not cower in the dust,*
> *Maryland! my Maryland!*
> *Thy gleaming sword shall never rust,*
> *Maryland! my Maryland!*

But the Marylanders did not respond to the siren song. The presence among the invaders of so many blanketless, hatless, and shoeless soldiers dampened the state's ardor.

Events finally converged toward a critical battle at Antietam Creek, Maryland. Lincoln, yielding to popular pressure, hastily restored "Little Mac" to active command of the main Northern army. His soldiers tossed their caps skyward and hugged his horse as they hailed his return. Fortune shone upon McClellan when two Union soldiers found a copy of Lee's battle plans wrapped around a packet of three cigars dropped by a careless Confederate officer. With this crucial piece of intelligence in hand, McClellan succeeded in halting Lee at Antietam on September 17, 1862, in one of the bitterest and bloodiest days of the war.

Antietam was more or less a draw militarily. But Lee, finding his thrust parried, retired across the Potomac. McClellan, from whom much more had been hoped, was removed from his field command for the second and final time. His numerous critics, condemning him for not having boldly pursued the ever-dangerous Lee, finally got his scalp.

The landmark Battle of Antietam was one of the decisive engagements of world history—probably the most decisive of the Civil War. Jefferson Davis was perhaps never again so near victory as on that fateful summer day. The British and French

The Killing Fields of Antietam
These Confederate corpses testified to the awful slaughter of the battle. The twelve-hour fight at Antietam Creek ranks as the bloodiest single day of the war, with more than ten thousand Confederate casualties and even more on the Union side. "At last the battle ended," one historian wrote, "smoke heavy in the air, the twilight quivering with the anguished cries of thousands of wounded men."

governments were on the verge of diplomatic mediation, a form of interference sure to be angrily resented by the North. An almost certain rebuff by Washington might well have spurred Paris and London into armed collusion with Richmond. But both capitals cooled off when the Union displayed unexpected power at Antietam, and their chill deepened with the passing months.

Bloody Antietam was also the long-awaited "victory" that Lincoln needed for launching his Emancipation Proclamation. The abolitionists had long been clamoring for action: Wendell Phillips was denouncing the president as a "first-rate second-rate man." By midsummer of 1862, with the Border States safely in the fold, Lincoln was ready to move. But he believed that to issue such an edict on the heels of a series of military disasters would be folly. It would seem like a confession that the North, unable to conquer the South, was forced to call upon the slaves to murder their masters. Lincoln therefore decided to wait for the outcome of Lee's invasion.

Antietam served as the needed emancipation springboard. The halting of Lee's offensive was just enough of a victory to justify Lincoln's issuing, on September 23, 1862, the preliminary Emancipation Proclamation. This hope-giving document announced that on January 1, 1863, the president would issue a final proclamation.

On the scheduled date he fully redeemed his promise, and the Civil War became more of a moral crusade as the fate of slavery and the South it had sustained was sealed. The war now became more of what Lincoln called a "remorseless revolutionary struggle." After January 1, 1863, Lincoln said, "The character of the war will be changed. It will be one of subjugation. . . . The [old] South is to be destroyed and replaced by new propositions and ideas."

A Proclamation Without Emancipation

Lincoln's Emancipation Proclamation of 1863 declared "forever free" the slaves in those Confederate states still in rebellion. Bondsmen in the loyal Border States were not affected, nor were those in specific conquered areas in the South—all told, about 800,000. The tone of the document was dull and legalistic (one historian has said that it had all the moral grandeur of a bill of lading). But if Lincoln stopped short of a clarion call for a holy war to achieve freedom, he pointedly concluded his historic document by declaring that the Proclamation was "an act of justice," and calling for "the considerate judgment of mankind and the gracious favor of Almighty God."

The presidential pen did not formally strike the shackles from a single slave. Where Lincoln could presumably free the slaves—that is, in the loyal Border States—he refused to do so, lest he spur disunion. Where he could not—that is, in the Confederate states—he tried to. In short, where he *could* he would not, and where he *would* he could not. Thus the Emancipation Proclamation was stronger on proclamation than emancipation.

Yet much unofficial do-it-yourself liberation did take place. Thousands of jubilant slaves, learning of the proclamation, flocked to the invading Union armies, stripping already rundown plantations of their work force. In this sense the Emancipation Proclamation was heralded by the drumbeat of running feet. But many fugitives would have come anyhow, as they had from the war's outset. Lincoln's immediate goal was not only to liberate the slaves but also to strengthen the moral cause of the Union at home and abroad. This he succeeded in doing. At the same time, Lincoln's proclamation clearly foreshadowed the ultimate doom of slavery. This was legally achieved by action of the individual states and by their ratification of the Thirteenth Amendment in 1865, eight months after the Civil War had ended. (For text, see the Appendix; see also pp. 493–494.) The Emancipation Proclamation also fundamentally changed the nature of the war because it effectively removed any chance of a negotiated settlement. Both sides now knew that the war would be a fight to the finish.

Public reactions to the long-awaited proclamation of 1863 were varied. "God bless Abraham Lincoln," exulted the antislavery editor Horace Greeley in his New York *Tribune*. But many ardent abolitionists complained that Lincoln had not gone far enough. On the other hand, formidable numbers of Northerners, especially in the "Butternut" regions of

Many of the British aristocrats were unfriendly to the North, and the London Spectator *sneered at Lincoln's so-called Emancipation Proclamation:*

"The Government liberates the enemy's slaves as it would the enemy's cattle, simply to weaken them in the coming conflict. . . . The principle asserted is not that a human being cannot justly own another, but that he cannot own him unless he is loyal to the United States."

the Old Northwest and the Border States, felt that he had gone too far. A cynical Democratic rhymester quipped,

Honest old Abe, when the war first began,
Denied abolition was part of his plan;
Honest old Abe has since made a decree,
The war must go on till the slaves are all free.
As both can't be honest, will some one tell how,
If honest Abe then, he is honest Abe now?

Opposition mounted in the North against supporting an "abolition war"; ex-president Pierce and others felt that emancipation should not be "inflicted" on the slaves. Many Boys in Blue, especially

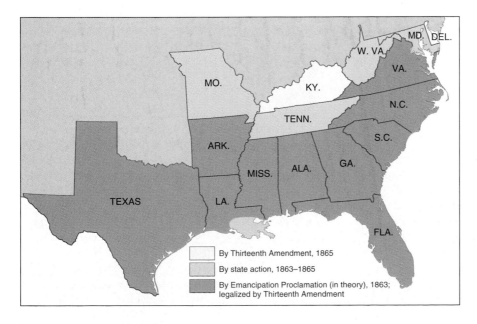

By Thirteenth Amendment, 1865

By state action, 1863–1865

By Emancipation Proclamation (in theory), 1863; legalized by Thirteenth Amendment

Emancipation in the South President Lincoln believed that emancipation of the slaves, accompanied by compensation to their owners, would be fairest to the South. He formally proposed such an amendment to the Constitution in December 1862. What finally emerged was the Thirteenth Amendment of 1865, which freed all slaves *without* compensation.

from the Border States, had volunteered to fight for the Union, not against slavery. Desertions increased sharply. The crucial congressional elections in the autumn of 1862 went heavily against the administration, particularly in New York, Pennsylvania, and Ohio. Democrats even carried Lincoln's Illinois, although they did not secure control of Congress.

The Emancipation Proclamation caused an outcry to rise from the South that "Lincoln the fiend" was trying to stir up the "hellish passions" of a slave insurrection. Aristocrats of Europe, noting that the proclamation applied only to rebel slaveholders, were inclined to sympathize with Southern protests. But the Old World working classes, especially in England, reacted otherwise. They sensed that the proclamation spelled the ultimate doom of slavery, and many laborers were more determined than ever to oppose intervention. Gradually the diplomatic position of the Union improved.

The North now had much the stronger moral cause. In addition to preserving the Union, it had committed itself to freeing the slaves. The moral position of the South was correspondingly diminished.

Blacks Battle Bondage

As Lincoln moved to emancipate the slaves, he also took steps to enlist blacks in the armed forces. Although some African-Americans had served in the Revolution and the War of 1812, the regular army contained no blacks at the war's outset, and the War Department refused to accept those free Northern blacks who tried to volunteer. (The Union navy, however, enrolled many blacks, mainly as cooks, stewards, and firemen.)

Lincoln (1809–1865) defended his policies toward blacks in an open letter to Democrats on August 26, 1863:

"You say you will not fight to free negroes. Some of them seem willing to fight for you; but, no matter. Fight you, then, exclusively to save the Union. I issued the proclamation on purpose to aid you in saving the Union."

But as manpower ran low and emancipation was proclaimed, black enlistees were accepted, sometimes over ferocious protests from Northern as well as Southern whites. By war's end some 180,000 blacks served in the Union armies, most of them from the slave states, but many from the free-soil North. Blacks accounted for about 10 percent of the total enlistments in the Union forces, on land and sea, and included two Massachusetts regiments raised largely through the efforts of the ex-slave Frederick Douglass.

Black fighting men unquestionably had their hearts in the war against slavery that the Civil War had become after Lincoln proclaimed emancipation. Participating in about five hundred engagements, they received twenty-two Congressional

Recruiting Black Troops in Boston, 1863   Led by the white Boston Brahmin Robert Gould Shaw, the 54th Massachusetts Regiment lost nearly half its men, including Shaw, in a futile attack on South Carolina's Fort Wagner in July 1863. A memorial to the regiment stands today on the Boston Common.

"Contraband" Jackson Becomes "Drummer" Jackson This black youth was a "contraband," or refugee slave, who became a drummer in the 79th U.S. Colored Troops.

Medals of Honor—the highest military award. Their casualties were extremely heavy; more than 38,000 died, whether from battle, sickness, or reprisals from vengeful masters. Many, when captured, were put to death as slaves in revolt, for not until 1864 did the South recognize them as prisoners of war. In one notorious case, several black soldiers were massacred after they had formally surrendered at Fort Pillow, Tennessee. Thereafter vengeful black units cried "Remember Fort Pillow" as they swung into battle, and vowed to take no prisoners.

For reasons of pride, prejudice, and principle, the Confederacy could not bring itself to enlist slaves until a month before the war ended, and then it was too late. Meanwhile, tens of thousands were forced into labor battalions, the building of fortifications, the supplying of armies, and other war-connected activities. Slaves moreover were "the stomach of the Confederacy," for they kept the farms going while the white men fought.

Ironically, the great mass of Southern slaves did little to help their Northern liberators, white or black. A thousand scattered torches in the hands of a thousand slaves would have brought the Southern soldiers home, and the war would have ended.

Through the "grapevine," the blacks learned of Lincoln's Emancipation Proclamation. Yet the bulk of them, whether because of fear, loyalty, lack of leadership, or strict policing, did not cast off their chains. But tens of thousands revolted "with their feet" when they abandoned their plantations upon

An affidavit by a Union sergeant described the fate of one group of black Union troops captured by the Confederates:

"All the negroes found in blue uniform or with any outward marks of a Union soldier upon him was killed—I saw some taken into the woods and hung—Others I saw stripped of all their clothing and they stood upon the bank of the river with their faces riverwards and then they were shot—Still others were killed by having their brains beaten out by the butt end of the muskets in the hands of the Rebels."

In August 1863 Lincoln wrote to Grant that enlisting black soldiers

"works doubly, weakening the enemy and strengthening us."

In December 1863 he announced,

"It is difficult to say they are not as good soldiers as any."

In August 1864 he said,

"Abandon all the posts now garrisoned by black men, take 150,000 [black] men from our side and put them in the battlefield or cornfield against us, and we would be compelled to abandon the war in three weeks."

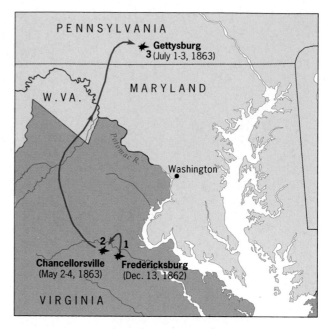

The Road to Gettysburg, December 1862–July 1863

the approach or arrival of Union armies, with or without emancipation proclamations. About 25,000 joined Sherman's march through Georgia in 1864, and their presence in such numbers created problems of supply and discipline.

Lee's Last Lunge at Gettysburg

After Antietam, Lincoln replaced McClellan as commander of the Army of the Potomac with General A. E. Burnside, whose ornate side-whiskers came to be known as "burnsides" or "sideburns." Protesting his unfitness for this responsibility, Burnside proved it when he launched a rash frontal attack on Lee's strong position at Fredericksburg, Virginia, on December 13, 1862. A chicken could not have lived in the line of fire, remarked one Confederate officer. More than 10,000 Northern soldiers were killed or wounded in "Burnside's Slaughter Pen."

A new slaughter pen was prepared when General Burnside yielded his command to "Fighting Joe" Hooker, an aggressive officer but a headstrong subordinate. At Chancellorsville, Virginia, May 2–4, 1863, Lee daringly divided his numerically inferior force and sent "Stonewall" Jackson to attack the Union flank. The strategy worked. Hooker, temporarily dazed by a near hit from a cannonball, was badly beaten but not crushed. This victory was probably Lee's most brilliant, but it was dearly

bought. Jackson was mistakenly shot by his own men in the gathering dusk and died a few days later. "I have lost my right arm," lamented Lee. Southern folklore relates how Jackson outflanked the angels while galloping into Heaven.

Lee now prepared to follow up his stunning victory by invading the North again, this time through Pennsylvania. A decisive blow would add strength to the noisy peace prodders in the North and would also encourage foreign intervention—still a Southern hope. Three days before the battle was joined, Union General George G. Meade—scholarly, unspectacular, abrupt—was aroused from his sleep at 2 A.M. with the unwelcome news that he would replace Hooker.

Quite by accident, Meade took his stand atop a low ridge flanking a shallow valley near quiet little Gettysburg, Pennsylvania. There his 92,000 men in blue locked in furious combat with Lee's 76,000 gray-clad warriors. The battle seesawed across the rolling green slopes for three agonizing days, July 1–3, 1863, and the outcome was in doubt until the very end. The failure of General George Pickett's magnificent but futile charge finally broke the back of the Confederate attack—and broke the heart of the Confederate cause.

Pickett's charge has been called the "high tide of the Confederacy." It defined both the northernmost

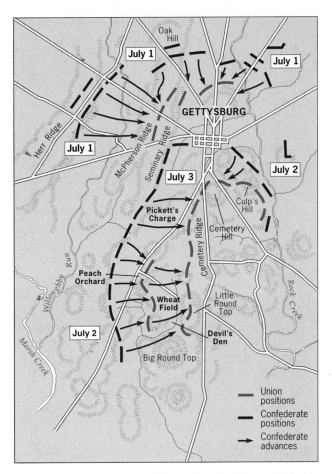

The Battle of Gettysburg, 1863   With the failure of Pickett's charge, the fate of the Confederacy was sealed—though the Civil War dragged on for almost two more bloody years.

In his address at Gettysburg, Lincoln cast the war as a struggle to preserve a nation "conceived in liberty, and dedicated to the proposition that all men are created equal." In his conclusion he declared that

"[T]hese dead shall not have died in vain—that this nation, under God, shall have a new birth of freedom and that government of the people, by the people, and for the people shall not perish from the earth."

address, following a two-hour speech by the orator of the day. Lincoln's noble remarks were branded by the London *Times* as "ludicrous" and by Democratic editors as "dishwatery" and "silly." The address attracted relatively little attention at the time, but the president was speaking for the ages.

The War in the West

Events in the western theater of the war at last provided Lincoln with an able general who did not have to be shelved after every reverse. Ulysses S. Grant had been a mediocre student at West Point, distinguishing himself only in horsemanship, although he did fairly well at mathematics. After fighting creditably in the Mexican War, he was stationed at isolated frontier posts, where boredom and loneliness drove him to drink. Resigning from the army to avoid a court-martial for drunkenness, he failed at various business ventures, and when war came, he was working in his father's leather store in Illinois for $50 a month.

Grant did not cut much of a figure. The shy and silent shopkeeper was short, stooped, awkward, stubble-bearded, and sloppy in dress. He managed with some difficulty to secure a colonelcy in the volunteers. From then on his military experience—combined with his boldness, resourcefulness, and tenacity—catapulted him on a meteoric rise.

Grant's first signal success came in the northern Tennessee theater. After heavy fighting, he captured Fort Henry and Fort Donelson on the Tennessee and Cumberland Rivers in February 1862. When the

point reached by any significant Southern force and the last real chance for the Confederates to win the war. As the Battle of Gettysburg raged, a Confederate peace delegation was moving under a flag of truce toward the Union lines near Norfolk, Virginia. Jefferson Davis hoped his negotiators would arrive in Washington from the south just as Lee's triumphant army marched on it from Gettysburg to the north. But the victory at Gettysburg belonged to Lincoln, who refused to allow the Confederate peace mission to pass through Union lines. From now on the Southern cause was doomed. Yet the men of Dixie fought on for nearly two years longer, through sweat, blood, and weariness of spirit.

Later in that dreary autumn of 1863, with the graves still fresh, Lincoln journeyed to Gettysburg to dedicate the cemetery. He read a two-minute

Confederate commander at Fort Donelson asked for terms, Grant bluntly demanded "an unconditional and immediate surrender."

Grant's triumph in Tennessee was crucial. It not only riveted Kentucky more securely to the Union but also opened the gateway to the strategically important region of Tennessee, as well as to Georgia and the heart of Dixie. Grant next attempted to exploit his victory by capturing the junction of the main Confederate north-south and east-west railroads in the Mississippi Valley at Corinth, Mississippi. But a Confederate force foiled his plans in a gory battle at Shiloh, just over the Tennessee border from Corinth, on April 6-7, 1862. Though Grant successfully counterattacked, the impressive Confederate showing at Shiloh confirmed that there would be no quick end to the war in the West.

Lincoln resisted all demands for the removal of "Unconditional Surrender" Grant, insisting, "I can't spare this man; he fights." When talebearers later told Lincoln that Grant drank too much, the president allegedly replied, "Find me the brand, and I'll send a barrel to each of my other generals." There is no evidence that Grant's drinking habits seriously impaired his military performance.

Other Union thrusts in the West were in the making. In the spring of 1862, a flotilla commanded by David G. Farragut joined with a Northern army to strike the South a blow by seizing New Orleans. With Union gunboats both ascending and descending the Mississippi, the eastern part of the Confederacy was left with a jeopardized back door. Through this narrowing entrance, between Vicksburg, Mississippi, and Port Hudson, Louisiana, flowed herds of vitally needed cattle and other provisions from Louisiana and Texas. The fortress of Vicksburg, located on a hairpin turn of the Mississippi, was the South's sentinel protecting the lifeline to the western sources of supply.

General Grant was now given command of the Union forces attacking Vicksburg and in the teeth of grave difficulties displayed rare skill and daring. The seige of Vicksburg was his best-fought campaign of the war. The beleaguered city at length surrendered, on July 4, 1863, with the garrison reduced to eating mules and rats. Five days later came the fall of Port

General Ulysses S. Grant and General Robert E. Lee
Trained at West Point, Grant (left) proved to be a better general than a president. Oddly, he hated the sight of blood and recoiled from rare beef. Lee (right), a gentlemanly general in an ungentlemanly business, remarked when the Union troops were bloodily repulsed at Fredericksburg. "It is well that war is so terrible, or we should get too fond of it."

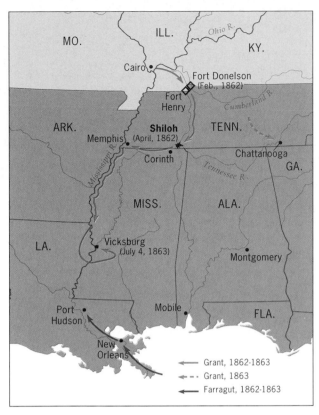

The Mississippi River and Tennessee, 1862–1863

Hudson, the last Southern bastion on the Mississippi. The spinal cord of the Confederacy was now severed and, in Lincoln's quaint phrase, the Father of Waters at last flowed "unvexed to the sea."

The Union victory at Vicksburg (July 4, 1863) came the day after the Confederate defeat at Gettysburg. The political significance of these back-to-back military successes was monumental. Reopening the Mississippi helped to quell the Northern peace agitation in the "Butternut" area of the Ohio River Valley. Confederate control of the Mississippi had cut off that region's usual trade routes down the Ohio-Mississippi river system to New Orleans, thus adding economic pain to that border section's already shaky support for the "abolition war." The twin victories also conclusively tipped the diplomatic scales in favor of the North, as England stopped delivery of the Laird rams to the Confederates and as France killed a deal for the sale of six naval vessels to the Richmond government. By the end of 1863, all Confederate hopes for foreign help were irretrievably lost.

Sherman Scorches Georgia

General Grant, the victor of Vicksburg, was now transferred to the east Tennessee theater, where Confederates had driven Union forces from the battlefield at Chickamauga into the city of Chattanooga, to which they then laid siege. Grant won a series of desperate engagements in November 1863 in the vicinity of besieged Chattanooga, including Missionary Ridge and Lookout Mountain ("the Battle above the Clouds"). Chattanooga was liberated, the state was cleared of Confederates, and the way was thus opened for an invasion of Georgia. Grant was rewarded by being made general-in-chief.

Georgia's conquest was entrusted to General William Tecumseh Sherman. Red-haired and red-bearded, grim-faced and ruthless, he captured Atlanta in September 1864 and burned the city in November of that year. He then daringly left his supply base, lived off the country for some 250 miles (402 kilometers), and weeks later emerged at Savannah on the sea. A rousing Northern song ("Marching through Georgia") put it,

> *"Sherman's dashing Yankee boys will never*
> *reach the coast!"*
> *So the saucy rebels said—and 't was a handsome*
> *boast.*

But Sherman's hated "Blue Bellies," 60,000 strong, cut a 60-mile (97-kilometer) swath of destruction through Georgia. They burned buildings, leaving only the blackened chimneys ("Sherman's Sentinels"). They tore up railroad rails, heated them red-hot, and twisted them into "iron doughnuts" and "Sherman's hairpins." They bayoneted family portraits and ran off with valuable "souvenirs." "War . . . is all hell," admitted Sherman later, and he proved it by his efforts to "make Georgia howl." One of his major purposes was to destroy supplies destined for the Confederate army and to weaken the morale of the men at the front by waging war on their homes.

Sherman was a pioneer practitioner of "total war." His success in "Shermanizing" the South was attested by increasing numbers of Confederate desertions. Although his methods were brutal, he probably shortened the struggle and hence saved lives. But there can be no doubt that the discipline of his army at times broke down, as roving riffraff

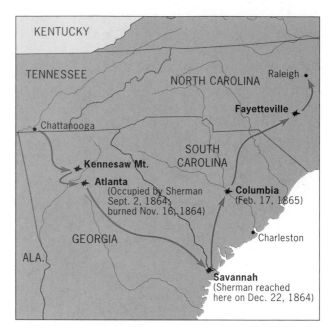

Sherman's March, 1864–1865

(Sherman's "bummers") engaged in an orgy of pillaging. "Sherman the Brute" was universally damned in the South.

After seizing Savannah as a Christmas present for Lincoln, Sherman's army veered north into South Carolina, where the destruction was even more vicious. Many Union soldiers believed that

A Study in Black and White
Soldiers of the 7th Tennessee Cavalry posed with their slaves— whose bondage the Confederacy fought to perpetuate.

this state, the "hell-hole of secession," had wantonly provoked the war. The capital city, Columbia, burst into flames, in all probability the handiwork of the Yankee invader. Crunching northward, Sherman's conquering army had rolled deep into North Carolina by the time the war ended.

The Politics of War

Presidential elections come by the calendar and not by the crisis. As fate would have it, the election of 1864 fell most inopportunely in the midst of war.

Political infighting in the North added greatly to Lincoln's cup of woe. Factions within his own party, distrusting his ability or doubting his commitment to abolition, sought to tie his hands or even remove him from office. Conspicuous among his critics was a group led by the overambitious secretary of the treasury, Salmon Chase. Especially burdensome to Lincoln was the creation of the Congressional Committee on the Conduct of the War, formed in late 1861. It was dominated by "radical" Republicans who resented the expansion of presidential power in wartime and who pressed Lincoln zealously on emancipation.

Most dangerous of all to the Union cause were the Northern Democrats. Deprived of the talent that had departed with the Southern wing of the party, those Democrats remaining in the North were left with the taint of association with the seceders. Tragedy befell the Democrats—and the Union—when their gifted leader, Stephen A. Douglas, died of typhoid fever seven weeks after the war began. Unshakably devoted to the Union, he probably could have kept much of his following on the path of loyalty.

Lacking a leader, the Democrats divided. A large group of "War Democrats" patriotically supported the Lincoln administration, but tens of thousands of "Peace Democrats" did not. At the extreme were the so-called Copperheads, named for the poisonous snake, which strikes without a warning rattle. Copperheads openly obstructed the war through attacks against the draft, against Lincoln, and especially, after 1863, against emancipation. They denounced the president as the "Illinois Ape" and condemned the "Nigger War." They commanded considerable political strength in the southern parts of Ohio, Indiana, and Illinois.

Notorious among the Copperheads was a sometime congressman from Ohio, Clement L. Vallandigham. This tempestuous character possessed brilliant oratorical gifts and unusual talents for stirring up trouble. A Southern partisan, he publicly demanded an end to the "wicked and cruel" war. The civil courts in Ohio were open, and he should

Democracy versus Rebellion   The two American combatants exchange blows while Britain and France look on. Note the copperhead snake that threatens to distract the Union. "Copperhead" was the name given to those Northern Democrats who were willing to settle for a negotiated peace with the Confederacy.

have been tried in them for sedition. But he was convicted by a military tribunal in 1863 for treasonable utterances and was then sentenced to prison. Lincoln decided that if Vallandigham liked the Confederates so much, he ought to be banished to their lines. This was done.

Vallandigham was not so easily silenced. Working his way to Canada, he ran for the governorship of Ohio on foreign soil and polled a substantial but insufficient vote. He returned to his own state before the war ended, and although he defied "King Lincoln" and spat upon a military decree, he was not further prosecuted. The strange case of Vallandigham inspired Edward Everett Hale to write his moving but fictional story of Philip Nolan, "The Man without a Country" (1863), which was immensely popular in the North and which helped stimulate devotion to the Union. Nolan was a young army officer found guilty of participation in the Aaron Burr plot of 1806 (see p. 222). He had cried out in court, "Damn the United States! I wish I may never hear of the United States again!" For this outburst he was condemned to a life of eternal exile on American warships.

The Election of 1864

As the election of 1864 approached, Lincoln's precarious authority depended on his retaining Republican support while spiking the threat from the Peace Democrats and Copperheads.

Fearing defeat, the Republican party executed a clever maneuver. Joining with the War Democrats, it proclaimed itself to be the Union party. Thus the Republican party passed temporarily out of existence.

Lincoln's renomination at first encountered surprisingly strong opposition. Hostile factions whipped up considerable agitation to shelve homely "Old Abe" in favor of his handsome nemesis, Secretary of the Treasury Chase. Lincoln was accused of

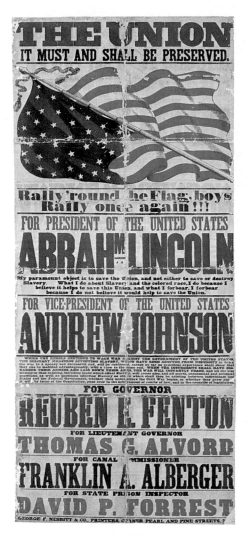

A Lincoln-Johnson Campaign Poster, 1864

lacking force, of being overready to compromise, of not having won the war, and of having shocked many sensitive souls by his ill-timed and earthy jokes. ("Prince of Jesters," one journal called him.) But the "ditch Lincoln" move collapsed, and he was nominated by the Union party without serious dissent.

Union Party, 1864
The blue area represents the Union party.

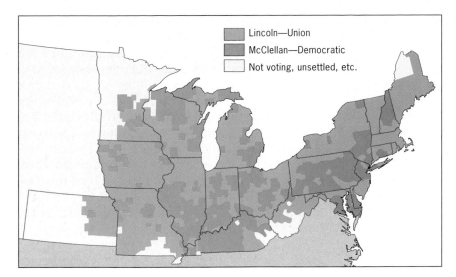

Presidential Election of 1864 (showing popular vote by county) Lincoln also carried California, Oregon, and Nevada, but there was a considerable McClellan vote in each. Note McClellan's strength in the Border States and in the southern tier of Ohio, Indiana, and Illinois—the so-called "Butternut" region.

Lincoln—Union
McClellan—Democratic
Not voting, unsettled, etc.

Lincoln's running mate was ex-tailor Andrew Johnson, a loyal War Democrat from Tennessee who had been a small slaveowner when the conflict began. He was placed on the Union party ticket to "sew up" the election by attracting War Democrats and the voters in the Border States, and, sadly, with no proper regard for the possibility that Lincoln might die in office. Southerners and Copperheads alike condemned both candidates as birds of a feather: two ignorant, third-rate, boorish, back-woods politicians born in log cabins.

Embattled Democrats—regular and Copper-head—nominated the deposed and overcautious war hero, General McClellan. The Copperheads managed to force into the Democratic platform a plank denouncing the prosecution of the war as a failure. But McClellan, who could not otherwise have faced his old comrades-in-arms, repudiated this defeatist declaration.

The campaign was noisy and nasty. The Democrats cried, "Old Abe removed McClellan. We'll now remove Old Abe." They also sang, "Mac Will Win the Union Back." The Union party supporters shouted for "Uncle Abe and Andy" and urged, "Vote as you shot." Their most effective slogan, growing out of a remark by Lincoln, was "Don't swap horses in the middle of the river."

Lincoln's reelection was at first gravely in doubt. The war was going badly, and Lincoln himself gave way to despondency, fearing that political defeat was imminent. The anti-Lincoln Republicans, taking heart, started a new movement to "dump" Lincoln in favor of someone else.

But the atmosphere of gloom was changed electrically, as balloting day neared, by a succession of Northern victories. Admiral Farragut captured Mobile, Alabama, after defiantly shouting the now famous order, "Damn the torpedoes! Go ahead." General Sherman seized Atlanta. General ("Little Phil") Sheridan laid waste the verdant Shenandoah Valley of Virginia so thoroughly that in his words "a crow could not fly over it without carrying his rations with him."

The president pulled through, but nothing more than necessary was left to chance. At election time many Northern soldiers were furloughed home to support Lincoln at the polls. One Pennsylvania veteran voted forty-nine times—once for himself and once for each absent member of his company. Other soldiers were permitted to cast their ballots at the front.

Lincoln, bolstered by the "bayonet vote," vanquished McClellan by 212 electoral votes to 21, losing only Kentucky, Delaware, and New Jersey. But "Little Mac" ran a closer race than the electoral count indicates. He netted a healthy 45 percent of the popular vote, 1,803,787 to Lincoln's 2,206,938, piling up much support in the Southerner-infiltrated states of the Old Northwest, in New York, and also in his native state of Pennsylvania (see map above).

One of the most crushing losses suffered by the South was the defeat of the Northern Democrats in 1864. The removal of Lincoln was the last ghost of a hope for a Confederate victory, and the Southern soldiers would wishfully shout, "Hurrah for McClellan!" When Lincoln triumphed, desertions from the sinking Southern ship increased sharply.

Grant Outlasts Lee

After Gettysburg, Grant was brought in from the West over Meade, who was blamed for failing to pursue the defeated but always dangerous Lee. Lincoln needed a general who, employing the superior resources of the North, would have the intestinal stamina to drive ever forward, regardless of casualties. A soldier of bulldog tenacity, Grant was the man for this meat-grinder type of warfare. His overall basic strategy was to assail the enemy's armies simultaneously, so that they could not assist one another and hence could be destroyed piecemeal. His personal motto was "When in doubt, fight." Lincoln urged him to "chew and choke, as much as possible."

A grimly determined Grant, with more than 100,000 men, struck toward Richmond. He engaged Lee in a series of furious battles in the Wilderness of Virginia, during May and June of 1864, notably in the leaden hurricane of the "Bloody Angle" and "Hell's Half Acre." In this Wilderness Campaign, Grant suffered about fifty thousand casualties, or nearly as many men as Lee commanded at the start. But Lee lost about as heavily in proportion.

In a ghastly gamble, on June 3, 1864, Grant ordered a frontal assault on the impregnable position of Cold Harbor. The Union soldiers advanced to almost certain death with papers pinned on their backs bearing their names and addresses. In a few minutes, about seven thousand men were killed or wounded.

Public opinion in the North was appalled by this "blood and guts" type of fighting. Critics cried that "Grant the Butcher" had gone insane. But his basic strategy of hammering ahead seemed brutally necessary; he could trade two men for one and still beat the enemy to its knees. "I propose to fight it out on this line," he wrote, "if it takes all summer." It did— and it also took all autumn, all winter, and a part of the spring.

In February 1865 the Confederates, tasting the bitter dregs of defeat, tried desperately to negotiate for peace between the "two countries." Lincoln himself met with Confederate representatives aboard a Union ship moored at Hampton Roads, Virginia, to discuss peace terms. But Lincoln could accept nothing short of Union and emancipation, and the Southerners could accept nothing short of independence. So the tribulation wore on—amid smoke and agony—to its terrible climax.

The end came with dramatic suddenness. Rapidly advancing Northern troops captured Richmond and cornered Lee at Appomattox Courthouse in Virginia, in April 1865. Grant—stubble-bearded and informally dressed—met with Lee on the ninth,

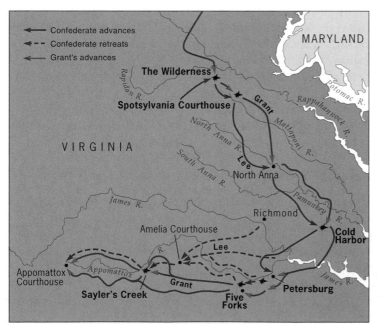

Grant's Virginia Campaign, 1864–1865
The Wilderness Campaign pitted soldier against desperate soldier in some of the most brutal and terrifying fighting of the Civil War. "No one could see the fight fifty feet from him," a Union private recalled of his month spent fighting in Virginia. "The lines were very near each other, and from the dense underbrush and the tops of trees came puffs of smoke, the 'ping' of the bullets and the yell of the enemy. It was a blind and bloody hunt to the death, in bewildering thickets, rather than a battle."

The Burning of Richmond, April 1865   The proud Confederate capital, after holding out against repeated Union assaults, was evacuated and burned in the final days of the war.

Palm Sunday, and granted generous terms of surrender. Among other concessions, the hungry Confederates were allowed to keep their own horses for spring plowing.

Tattered Southern veterans—"Lee's Ragamuffins" —wept as they took leave of their beloved commander. The elated Union soldiers cheered, but they were silenced by Grant's stern admonition, "The war is over; the rebels are our countrymen again."

Lincoln traveled to conquered Richmond and sat in Jefferson Davis's evacuated office just forty hours after the Confederate president had left it. "Thank God I have lived to see this," he said. With a small escort of sailors, he walked the blasted streets of the city. Freed slaves began to recognize him, and crowds gathered to see and touch "Father Abraham." One black man fell to his knees before the Emancipator, who said to him, "Don't kneel to me. This is not right. You must kneel to God only, and thank Him for the liberty you will enjoy hereafter." Sadly, as many freed slaves were to discover, the hereafter of their full liberty was a long time coming.

The Martyrdom of Lincoln

On the night of April 14, 1865 (Good Friday), only five days after Lee's surrender, Ford's Theater in Washington witnessed its most sensational drama. A half-crazed, fanatically pro-Southern actor, John Wilkes Booth, slipped behind Lincoln as he sat in his box and shot him in the head. After lying unconscious all night, the Great Emancipator died the following morning. "Now he belongs to the ages," remarked the once-critical Secretary Stanton— probably the finest words he ever spoke.

Lincoln expired in the arms of victory, at the very pinnacle of his fame. From the standpoint of his reputation, his death could not have been better timed if he had hired the assassin. A large number of his countrymen had not suspected his greatness, and many others had even doubted his ability. But his dramatic death helped to erase the memory of his shortcomings and caused his nobler qualities to stand out in clearer relief.

New York Mourns Lincoln's Death, 1865 Thousands of New Yorkers lined the black-draped urban canyons of Manhattan to observe Lincoln's funeral procession.

The full impact of Lincoln's death was not at once apparent to the South. Hundreds of bedraggled ex-Confederate soldiers cheered, as did some Southern civilians and Northern Copperheads, when they learned of the assassination. This reaction was only natural, because Lincoln had kept the war grinding on to the bitter end. If he had only been willing to stop the shooting, the South would have won.

The powerful London Times, *voice of the upper classes, had generally criticized Lincoln during the war, especially after the Emancipation Proclamation of 1862. He was then condemned as "a sort of moral American Pope" destined to be "Lincoln the Last." When the president was shot, the* Times *reversed itself (April 29, 1865):*

"Abraham Lincoln was as little of a tyrant as any man who ever lived. He could have been a tyrant had he pleased, but he never uttered so much as an ill-natured speech. . . . In all America there was, perhaps, not one man who less deserved to be the victim of the revolution than he who has just fallen."

As time wore on, increasing numbers of Southerners perceived that Lincoln's death was a calamity for them. Belatedly they recognized that his kindliness and moderation would have been the most effective shields between them and vindictive treatment by the victors. The assassination unfortunately increased the bitterness in the North, partly because of the fantastic rumor that Jefferson Davis had plotted it.

A few historians have argued that Andrew Johnson, now president-by-bullet, was crucified in Lincoln's stead. The implication is that if the "rail-splitter" had lived, he would have suffered Johnson's fate of being impeached by the embittered members of his own party who demanded harshness, not forbearance, toward the South.

The crucifixion thesis does not stand up under scrutiny. Lincoln no doubt would have clashed with Congress; in fact, he had already found himself in some hot water. The legislative branch normally struggles to win back the power that has been wrested from it by the executive in time of crisis. But the surefooted and experienced Lincoln could hardly have blundered into the same quicksands that engulfed Johnson. Lincoln was a victorious president, and there is no arguing with victory. In addition to his powers of leadership refined in the war crucible, Lincoln possessed in full measure tact, sweet reasonableness, and an uncommon amount of common sense. Andrew Johnson, hot-tempered and impetuous, lacked all of these price-less qualities.

Ford's Theater, with its tragic murder of Lincoln, set the stage for the wrenching ordeal of Reconstruction.

The Aftermath of the Nightmare

The Civil War took a grisly toll in gore, about as much as all of America's subsequent wars com-bined. Over 600,000 men died in action or of dis-ease, and in all over a million were killed or seriously wounded. To its lasting hurt, the nation lost the cream of its young manhood and potential leader-ship. In addition, tens of thousands of babies went unborn because potential fathers were at the front.

Direct monetary costs of the conflict totaled about $15 billion. But this colossal figure does not include continuing expenses, such as pensions and interest on the national debt. The intangible costs—dislocations, disunities, wasted energies, lowered ethics, blasted lives, bitter memories, and burning hates—cannot be calculated.

The greatest constitutional decision of the cen-tury, in a sense, was written in blood and handed down at Appomattox Courthouse, near which Lee

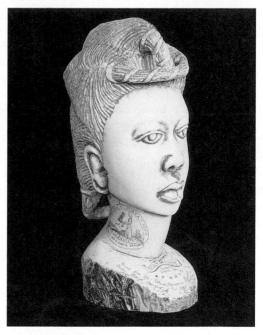

Nora August: The Fruits of Emancipation   An unidentified Union soldier carved this ivory bust of the freedwoman Nora August during the Civil War. Note the elaborately braided hair —a direct adaptation of a West African style. The anonymous sculptor etched the following legend into the base of the statue: "Carved from life. Retreat Plantation. Presented to the Nurses of Darien GA in the year of Our Lord 1865. Nora August (slave). Age 23 years. Purchased from the Market, St. Augustine, Florida, April 17th 1860. Now a Free Woman."

Prisoners from the Front, by Winslow Homer, 1866 This celebrated painting re-flects the artist's firsthand observations of the war. Homer brilliantly captures the enduring depths of sec-tional animosity. The Union officer somewhat disdain-fully asserts his command of the situation; the beaten and disarmed Confederates exhibit on out-at-the-elbows pride and defiance.

surrendered. The extreme states' righters were crushed. The national government, tested in the fiery furnace of war, emerged unbroken. Nullification and secession, those twin nightmares of previous decades, were laid to rest.

Beyond doubt the Civil War—the nightmare of the Republic—was the supreme test of American democracy. It finally answered the question, in the words of Lincoln at Gettysburg, whether a nation dedicated to such principles "can long endure." The preservation of democratic ideals, though not an officially announced war aim, was subconsciously one of the major objectives of the North.

Victory for Union arms also provided inspiration to the champions of democracy and liberalism the world over. The great English Reform Bill of 1867, under which Britain became a true political democracy, was passed two years after the Civil War ended. American democracy had proved itself, and its success was an additional argument used by the disfranchised British masses in securing similar blessings for themselves.

The "Lost Cause" of the South was lost, but few Americans today would argue that the result was not for the best. The shameful cancer of slavery was sliced away by the sword, and African-Americans were at last in a position to claim their rights to life, liberty, and the pursuit of happiness. The nation was again united politically, though for many generations still divided spiritually by the passions of the war. Grave dangers were averted by a Union victory, including the indefinite prolongation of the "peculiar institution," the unleashing of the slave power on weak Caribbean neighbors, and the transformation of the area from Panama to Hudson Bay into an armed camp, with several heavily armed and hostile states constantly snarling and sniping at one another. America still had a long way to go to make the promises of freedom a reality for all its citizens, black and white. But emancipation laid the necessary groundwork, and a united and democratic United States was free to fulfill its destiny as the dominant republic of the hemisphere—and eventually of the world.

Chronology

1861	First Battle of Bull Run
1862	Grant takes Fort Henry and Fort Donelson
	Battle of Shiloh
	McClellan's Peninsula Campaign
	Seven Days' Battle
	Second Battle of Bull Run
	Naval battle of the *Merrimack* (the *Virginia*) and the *Monitor*
	Battle of Antietam
	Preliminary Emancipation Proclamation
	Battle of Fredericksburg
	Northern army seizes New Orleans
1863	Final Emancipation Proclamation
1863	Battle of Chancellorsville
	Battle of Gettysburg
	Fall of Vicksburg
	Fall of Port Hudson
1864	Sherman's march through Georgia
	Grant's Wilderness Campaign
	Battle of Cold Harbor
	Lincoln defeats McClellan for presidency
1865	Hampton Roads Conference
	Lee surrenders to Grant at Appomattox
	Lincoln assassinated
	Thirteenth Amendment ratified

What Were the Consequences of the Civil War?

With the end of the Civil War in 1865, the United States was permanently altered, despite the reunification of the Union and the Confederacy. Slavery was officially banned, secession was a dead issue, and industrial growth surged forward. For the first time, the United States could securely consider itself as a singular nation rather than a union of states. Though sectional differences remained, there would be no return to the unstable days of precarious balancing between Northern and Southern interests. With the Union's victory, power rested firmly with the North, and it would orchestrate the future development of the country. According to historian Eric Foner, the war redrew the economic and political map of the country.

The constitutional impact of the terms of the Union victory created some of the most far-reaching transformations. The first twelve amendments to the Constitution, ratified before the war, had all served to limit government power; in contrast, the Thirteenth Amendment, which abolished slavery, and the revolutionary Fourteenth Amendment, which conferred citizenship and guaranteed civil rights to all those born in the United States, marked unprecedented expansions of federal power.

Historian James McPherson has noted still other ways in which the Civil War extended the authority of the central government. It expanded federal powers of taxation. It encouraged the government to develop a national banking system, print currency, and conscript an army. It made the federal courts more influential. And through the Freedmen's Bureau, which aided former slaves in the South, it instituted the first federal social welfare agency. With each of these actions, the nation moved toward a more powerful federal government, invested with the authority to protect civil rights, aid its citizens, and enforce laws in an aggressive manner that superseded state powers.

Some scholars have disputed whether the Civil War marked an absolute watershed in American history. They correctly note that racial inequality scandalously persisted after the Civil War, despite the abolition of slavery and the supposed protections extended by federal civil rights legislation. Others have argued that the industrial growth of the post–Civil War era had its real roots in the Jacksonian era, and thus cannot be ascribed solely to war. Thomas Cochran has even argued that the Civil War may have retarded over-all industrialization rather than advancing it. Regional differences between North and South endured, moreover, even down to the present day.

Yet the argument that the Civil War launched a modern America remains convincing. The lives of Americans, white and black, North and South, were transformed by the war experience. Industry entered a period of unprecedented growth, having been stoked by the transportation and military needs of the Union army. The emergence of new, national legal and governmental institutions marked the birth of the modern American state. All considered, it is hard to deny that the end of the Civil War brought one chapter of the nation's history to a close, while opening another.

SUGGESTED READINGS

PRIMARY SOURCE DOCUMENTS

Abraham Lincoln's reply in 1862 to Horace Greeley's "Prayer of Twenty Millions"* (*Collected Works of Abraham Lincoln,* edited by Roy P. Basler, 1953) is an early statement of the president's war aims. See also, in the same collection, the Emancipation Proclamation (1863). Reminiscences of the military struggle include Eliza Andrews, *The War-Time Journal of a Georgia Girl** (1908); *Memoirs of General William T. Sherman** (1887); and C. Vann Woodward, ed., *Mary Chesnut's Civil War* (rev. ed., 1981). See also Stephen Crane's classic war novel *The Red Badge of Courage* (1895).

SECONDARY SOURCES

The most compelling single-volume account of the war is James M. McPherson, *Battle Cry of Freedom: The Civil War Era* (1988). Geoffrey C. Ward's *The Civil War* (1990) is beautifully illustrated. An able survey is James G. Randall and David Donald, *The Civil War and Reconstruction* (rev. ed., 1969); greater detail appears in James G. Randall, *Lincoln the President* (4 vols., 1945–1955). Other capable one-volume studies include Peter J. Parish, *The American Civil War* (1975); James M. McPherson, *Ordeal by Fire: The Civil War and Reconstruction* (1982); and Phillip S. Paludan, *"A People's Contest": The Union and the Civil War, 1861–1865* (1988). See also the multivolume study by Shelby Foote, *The Civil War* (3 vols., 1958–1974), and Allan Nevins's monumental *Ordeal of the Union* (8 vols., 1947–1971). Bruce Catton has a series

---

*An asterisk indicates that the document, or an excerpt from it, can be found in Thomas A. Bailey and David M. Kennedy, eds., *The American Spirit: United States History as Seen by Contemporaries,* 9th ed. (Boston: Houghton Mifflin, 1998).

of a dozen or so books on aspects of the Civil War, all readable and knowledgeable, including *A Stillness at Appomattox* (1953) and *This Hallowed Ground* (1956). Herman Hattaway and Archer Jones discuss *How the North Won* (1983). On the homefront, see Reid Mitchell, *The Vacant Chair: The Northern Soldier Leaves Home* (1993). On the "modern" character of the war, see Charles B. Royster, *The Destructive War: William Tecumseh Sherman, Stonewall Jackson, and the Americans* (1991). David P. Crook, *The North, the South, and the Powers* (1974), discusses the relationship of the combatants to England. Bell I. Wiley's descriptions of common soldiers, *The Life of Johnny Reb* (1943) and *The Life of Billy Yank* (1952), are classics. See also Benjamin Quarles, *The Negro in the Civil War* (1953), and James M. McPherson's collection of documents, *The Negro's Civil War* (1965). More recent accounts of the black experience include Ira Berlin et al., *Freedom: A Documentary History of Emancipation, 1861–1867, Series II, The Black Military Experience* (1982), and Joseph Glatthaar, *Forged in Battle: The Civil War Alliance of Black Soldiers and White Officers* (1990). Emancipation is treated in Louis Gerteis, *From Contraband to Freedmen; Federal Policy toward Southern Blacks, 1861–1865* (1973); Herman Belz, *Emancipation and Equal Rights: Politics and Constitutionalism during the Civil War Reconstruction* (1978); LaWanda Cox, *Lincoln and Black Freedom* (1981); and Leon Litwack's powerful *Been in the Storm So Long* (1979). On the abolitionists' role in securing emancipation, see James M. McPherson, *The Struggle for Equality* (1964); see also David W. Blight, *Frederick Douglass' Civil War: Keeping Faith in Jubilee* (1989). The Southern response is discussed in Robert Durden, *The Gray and the Black: The Confederate Debate on Emancipation* (1973). The two leading Civil War generals are masterfully treated in Douglas S. Freeman, *R. E. Lee* (4 vols., 1934–1935), and William S. McFeely, *Grant* (1981).

23

The Ordeal of Reconstruction
1865–1877

With malice toward none, with charity for all, with firmness in the right as God gives us to see the right, let us strive on to finish the work we are in, to bind up the nation's wounds, to care for him who shall have borne the battle and for his widow and orphan, to do all which may achieve and cherish a just and lasting peace among ourselves and with all nations.

ABRAHAM LINCOLN, SECOND INAUGURAL, MARCH 4, 1865

The Problems of Peace

The battle was done, the buglers silent. Bone-weary and bloodied, the American people, North and South, now faced the staggering challenges of peace. Four questions loomed large. How would the South, physically devastated by war and socially revolutionized by emancipation, be rebuilt? How would the liberated blacks fare as free men and women? How would the Southern states be reintegrated into the Union? And who would direct the process of Reconstruction—the Southern states themselves, the president, or Congress?

Other questions also clamored for answers. What should be done with the captured Confederate ringleaders, all of whom were liable to charges of treason? During the war a popular Northern song had been "Hang Jeff Davis to a Sour Apple Tree," and even innocent children had lisped it. Davis was temporarily clapped into irons during the early days of

Richmond Devastated   Charleston, Atlanta, and other Southern cities looked much the same, resembling bombed-out Berlin and Dresden in 1945.

his two-year imprisonment. But he and his fellow "conspirators" were finally released, partly because the odds were that no Virginia jury would convict them. All rebel leaders were finally pardoned by President Johnson as sort of a Christmas present in 1868. But Congress did not remove all remaining civil disabilities until thirty years later and only posthumously restored Davis's citizenship more than a century later.

Dismal indeed was the picture presented by the war-wracked South when the rattle of musketry faded. Not only had an age perished, but a civilization had collapsed, in both its economic and its social structure. The moonlight-and-magnolia Old South, largely imaginary in any case, had forever gone with the wind.

Handsome cities of yesteryear, such as Charleston and Richmond, were rubble-strewn and weed-choked. An Atlantan returned to his once-fair hometown and remarked, "Hell has laid her egg, and right here it hatched."

Economic life had creaked to a halt. Banks and business houses had locked their doors, ruined by runaway inflation. Factories were smokeless, silent, dismantled. The transportation system had broken down completely. Before the war, five different railroad lines had converged on Columbia, South Carolina; now the nearest connected track was 29 miles (47 kilometers) away. Efforts to untwist the rails corkscrewed by Sherman's soldiers proved bumpily unsatisfactory.

Agriculture—the economic lifeblood of the South—was almost hopelessly crippled. Once-white cotton fields now yielded a lush harvest of nothing but green weeds. The slave-labor system had collapsed, seed was scarce, and livestock had been driven off by plundering Yankees. Pathetic instances were reported of men hitching themselves to plows, while women and children gripped the handles. Not until 1870 did the seceded states produce as large a cotton crop as that of the fateful year 1860, and much of that yield came from new acreage in the Southwest.

The princely planter aristocrats were humbled by the war—at least temporarily. Reduced to proud poverty, they faced charred and gutted mansions, lost investments, and almost worthless land. Their investments of more than $2 billion in slaves, their primary form of wealth, had evaporated with emancipation.

Beaten but unbent, many high-spirited white Southerners remained dangerously defiant. They cursed the "damnyankees" and spoke of "your government" in Washington, instead of "our government." One Southern bishop refused to pray for President Andrew Johnson, though Johnson proved to be in sore need of divine guidance. Conscious of no crime, these former Confederates continued to believe that their view of secession was correct and that the "lost cause" was still a just war. One popular anti-Union song ran,

> *I'm glad I fought agin her, I only wish we'd won,*
> *And I ain't axed any pardon for anything I've*
> *done.*

Such attitudes boded ill for the prospects of painlessly binding up the Republic's wounds.

Freedmen Define Freedom

Confusion abounded in the still-smoldering South about the precise meaning of "freedom" for blacks. Emancipation took effect haltingly and unevenly in different parts of the conquered Confederacy. As Union armies marched in and out of various localities, many blacks found themselves emancipated and then re-enslaved. A North Carolina slave estimated that he had celebrated freedom about twelve times. Blacks from one Texas county fleeing to the free soil of the liberated county next door were attacked by slaveowners as they swam across the river that marked the county line. The next day, trees along the riverbank were bent with swinging corpses—a grisly warning to others dreaming of liberty. Other planters resisted emancipation more legalistically, stubbornly protesting that slavery was lawful until state legislatures or the Supreme Court declared otherwise. For many slaves the shackles of bondage were not struck off in a single mighty blow; long-suffering blacks often had to wrench free of their chains link by link.

The variety of responses to emancipation, by whites as well as blacks, illustrated the sometimes startling complexity of the master-slave relationship. Loyalty to the plantation master prompted some slaves to resist the liberating Union armies, while other slaves' pent-up bitterness burst forth violently on the day of liberation. Many newly emancipated slaves, for example, joined Union troops in pillaging their master's possessions. In one instance, a group of Virginia slaves laid twenty lashes on the back of their former master—a painful dose of his own favorite medicine.

Commemorating Emancipation Day
These African-Americans in Richmond, Virginia, in 1888, commemorated the twenty-fifth anniversary of the Emancipation Proclamation by paying their respects to the "Great Emancipator," Abraham Lincoln.

Prodded by the bayonets of Yankee armies of occupation, all masters were eventually forced to recognize their slaves' permanent freedom. The once-commanding planter would assemble his former human chattels in front of the porch of the "big house" and announce their liberty. Though some blacks initially responded to news of their emancipation with suspicion and uncertainty, they soon celebrated their new-found freedom. Many took new names in place of the ones given by their masters and demanded that whites formally address them as "Mr." or "Mrs." Others abandoned the coarse cottons that had been their only clothing as slaves and sought silks, satins, and other finery. Though many whites perceived such behavior as insubordinate, they were forced to recognize the realities of emancipation. "Never before had I a word of impudence from any of our black folk," wrote one white Southerner, "but they are not ours any longer."

Tens of thousands of emancipated blacks took to the roads, some to test their freedom, others to search for long-lost spouses, parents, and children. Emancipation thus strengthened the black family, and many newly freed men and women formalized "slave marriages" for personal and pragmatic reasons, including the desire to make their children legal heirs. Other blacks left their former masters to work in towns and cities, where existing black communities provided protection and mutual assistance. Whole communities sometimes moved together in search of opportunity. From 1878 to 1880, some 25,000 blacks from Louisiana, Texas, and Mississippi surged in a mass exodus to Kansas. The westward flood of these "Exodusters" was stemmed only when steamboat captains refused to transport more black migrants across the Mississippi River.

The church became the focus of black community life in the years following emancipation. As slaves, blacks had worshiped alongside whites, but now they formed their own churches pastored by their own ministers. The black churches grew robustly. The 150,000-member black Baptist Church of 1850 reached 500,000 by 1870, while the African Methodist Episcopal Church quadrupled in size from 100,000 to 400,000 in the first decade after emancipation. These churches formed the bedrock of black community life, and they soon gave rise to other benevolent, fraternal, and mutual aid societies. All these organizations helped blacks protect their newly won freedom.

Emancipation also meant education for many blacks. Learning to read and write had been a privilege generally denied to them under slavery. Freedmen wasted no time establishing societies for self-improvement, which undertook to raise funds to purchase land, build schoolhouses, and hire teachers. One member of a North Carolina education society asserted that "a schoolhouse would be the first proof of their *independence*." Southern blacks soon found, however, that the demand outstripped the supply of qualified black teachers. They accepted the aid of Northern white women sent by the American Missionary Association, who volunteered their services as teachers. They also turned to the federal government for help. The freed blacks were going to need all the friends—and the power—they could muster in Washington.

The Freedmen's Bureau

Abolitionists had long preached that slavery was a degrading institution. Now the emancipators were faced with the brutal reality that the freedmen were overwhelmingly unskilled, unlettered, without property or money, and with scant knowledge of how to survive as free people. To cope with this problem throughout the conquered South, Congress created the Freedmen's Bureau on March 3, 1865.

Houston H. Holloway, aged twenty at the time of his emancipation, recalled his feelings upon hearing of his freedom:

"I felt like a bird out of a cage. Amen. Amen. Amen. I could hardly ask to feel any better than I did that day. . . . The week passed off in a blaze of glory."

The reunion of long-lost relatives also inspired joy; one Union officer wrote home,

"Men are taking their wives and children, families which had been for a long time broken up are united and oh! such happiness. I am glad I am here."

The Faculty of a Freedmen's Bureau School near Norfolk, Virginia Note the racial diversity—but the gender homogeneity—of the teaching staff.

On paper at least, the bureau was intended to be a kind of primitive welfare agency. It was to provide food, clothing, medical care, and education both to freedmen and to white refugees. Heading the bureau was a warmly sympathetic friend of the blacks, Union General Oliver O. Howard, who later founded and served as president of Howard University in Washington, D.C.

Women from the North enthusiastically embraced the opportunity to go South and teach in Freedmen's Bureau schools for emancipated blacks. One volunteer explained her motives:

"I thought I *must* do something, not having money at my command, what could I do but give *myself* to the work. . . . I would go to them, and give them my life if necessary."

The bureau achieved its greatest successes in education. It taught an estimated 200,000 blacks how to read. Many former slaves had a passion for learning, partly because they wanted to close the gap between themselves and the whites and partly because they longed to read the Word of God. In one elementary class in North Carolina sat four generations of the same family, ranging from a six-year-old child to a seventy-five-year-old grandmother.

But in other areas the bureau's accomplishments were meager—or even mischievous. Although the bureau was authorized to settle former slaves on forty-acre tracts confiscated from the Confederates, little land actually made it into blacks' hands. Instead, local administrators often collaborated with planters in expelling blacks from towns and cajoling them into signing labor contracts to work for their former masters. Still, the white South resented the bureau as a meddlesome federal interloper that threatened to upset white racial dominance. President Andrew Johnson, who shared the white-supremacist views of most white Southerners, repeatedly tried to kill it, and it expired in 1872.

Johnson: The Tailor President

Few presidents have ever been faced with a more perplexing sea of troubles than that confronting Andrew Johnson. What manner of man was this medium-built, dark-eyed, black-haired Tennessean, now chief executive by virtue of the bullet that killed Lincoln?

No citizen, not even Lincoln, has ever reached the White House from humbler beginnings. Born to impoverished parents in North Carolina and early orphaned, Johnson never attended school but was apprenticed to a tailor at age ten. Ambitious to get ahead, he taught himself to read, and later his wife taught him to write and do simple arithmetic. Like many another self-made man, he was inclined to overpraise his maker.

Johnson early became active in politics in Tennessee, where he had moved when seventeen years old. He shone as an impassioned champion of the poor whites against the planter aristocrats, although he himself ultimately owned a few slaves. He excelled as a two-fisted stump speaker before angry and heckling crowds, who on occasion greeted his political oratory with cocked pistols, not just cocked

President Andrew Johnson (1808–1875), by Arthur Stumpf An "accidental president," Andrew Johnson was the only chief executive to be impeached by the House, though narrowly acquitted by the Senate. A former U.S. senator from Tennessee, he was reelected in 1875 to the Senate that had formally tried him seven years earlier. As Johnson said in a public speech in 1866, "I love my country. Every public act of my life testifies that is so. Where is the man who can put his finger upon one act of mine . . . to prove the contrary?"

ears. Elected to Congress, he attracted much favorable attention in the North (but not the South) when he refused to secede with his own state. After Tennessee was partially "redeemed" by Union armies, he was appointed war governor and served courageously in an atmosphere of danger.

Political exigency next thrust Johnson into the vice presidency. Lincoln's Union party in 1864 needed to attract support from the War Democrats and other pro-Southern elements, and Johnson, a Democrat, seemed to be the ideal man. Unfortunately, he appeared at the vice-presidential inaugural ceremonies the following March in a scandalous condition. He had recently been afflicted with typhoid fever, and although not known as a heavy drinker, he was urged by his friends to take a stiff bracer of whiskey. This he did—with unfortunate results.

"Old Andy" Johnson was no doubt a man of parts—unpolished parts. He was intelligent, able, forceful, and gifted with homespun honesty. Steadfastly devoted to duty and to the people, he was a

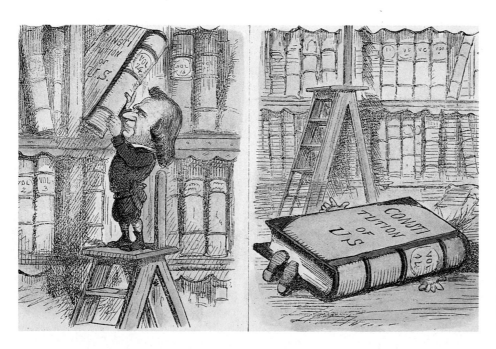

Crushed by the Constitution President Andrew Johnson revered the U.S. Constitution, but eventually felt its awesome weight in his impeachment trial.

dogmatic champion of states' rights and the Constitution. He would often present a copy of the document to visitors, and he was buried with one as a pillow.

Yet the man who had raised himself from the tailor's bench to the president's chair was a misfit. A Southerner who did not understand the North, a Tennessean who had earned the distrust of the South, a Democrat who had never been accepted by the Republicans, a president who had never been elected to the office, he was not at home in a Republican White House. Hotheaded, contentious, and stubborn, he was the wrong man in the wrong place at the wrong time. A Reconstruction policy devised by angels might well have failed in his tactless hands.

Presidential Reconstruction

Even before the shooting war had ended, the political war over Reconstruction had begun. Abraham Lincoln believed that the Southern states had never legally withdrawn from the Union. Their formal restoration to the Union would therefore be relatively simple. Accordingly, Lincoln in 1863 proclaimed his "10 percent" Reconstruction plan. It decreed that a state could be reintegrated into the Union when 10 percent of its voters in the presidential election of 1860 had taken an oath of allegiance to the United States and pledged to abide by emancipation. The next step would be formal erection of a state government. Lincoln would then recognize the purified regime.

Lincoln's proclamation provoked a sharp reaction in Congress, where Republicans feared the restoration of the planter aristocracy to power and the possible re-enslavement of the blacks. Republicans therefore rammed through Congress in 1864 the Wade-Davis Bill. It required that 50 percent of a state's voters take the oath of allegiance and demanded stronger safeguards for emancipation than Lincoln's as the price of readmission. Lincoln "pocket-vetoed" this bill by refusing to sign it after Congress had adjourned. Republicans were outraged. They refused to seat delegates from Louisiana after that state had reorganized its government in accordance with Lincoln's 10 percent plan in 1864.

The controversy surrounding the Wade-Davis Bill had revealed deep differences between the president and Congress. Unlike Lincoln, many in Congress insisted that the seceders had indeed left the Union—had "committed suicide" as republican states—and had therefore forfeited all their rights. They could be readmitted only as "conquered provinces" on such conditions as Congress should decree.

This episode further revealed differences among Republicans. Two factions were emerging. The majority moderate group tended to agree with Lincoln that the seceded states should be restored to the Union as simply and swiftly as reasonable—though on Congress's terms, not the president's. The minority radical group believed that the South should atone more painfully for its sins. Before the South should be restored, the radicals wanted its social structure uprooted, the haughty planters punished, and the newly emancipated blacks protected by federal power.

Some of the radicals were secretly pleased when the assassin's bullet felled Lincoln, for the martyred president had shown tenderness toward the South. Spiteful "Andy" Johnson, who shared their hatred for the planter aristocrats, would presumably also share their desire to reconstruct the South with a rod of iron.

Johnson soon disillusioned them. He agreed with Lincoln that the seceded states had never legally been outside the Union. Thus he quickly recognized several of Lincoln's 10 percent governments, and on May 29, 1865, he issued his own

Before President Andrew Johnson (1808–1875) softened his Southern policy, his views were radical. Speaking on April 21, 1865, he declared,

"It is not promulgating anything that I have not heretofore said to say that traitors must be made odious, that treason must be made odious, that traitors must be punished and impoverished. They must not only be punished, but their social power must be destroyed. If not, they will still maintain an ascendancy, and may again become numerous and powerful; for, in the words of a former Senator of the United States, 'When traitors become numerous enough, treason becomes respectable.'"

Reconstruction proclamation. It disfranchised certain leading Confederates, including those with taxable property worth more than $20,000, though they might petition him for personal pardons. It called for special state conventions, which were required to repeal the ordinances of secession, repudiate all Confederate debts, and ratify the slave-freeing Thirteenth Amendment. States that complied with these conditions, Johnson declared, would be swiftly readmitted to the Union.

Johnson, savoring his dominance over the high-toned aristocrats who now begged his favor, granted pardons in abundance. Bolstered by the political resurrection of the planter elite, the recently rebellious states moved rapidly in the second half of 1865 to organize governments. But as the pattern of the new governments became clear, Republicans of all stripes grew furious.

The Baleful Black Codes

Among the first acts of the new Southern regimes sanctioned by Johnson was the passage of the iron-toothed Black Codes. These laws were designed to regulate the affairs of the emancipated blacks, much as the slave statutes had done in pre–Civil War days. Mississippi passed the first such law in November 1865, and other Southern states soon followed suit. The Black Codes varied in severity from state to state (Mississippi's was the harshest and Georgia's the most lenient), but they had much in common. The Black Codes aimed, first of all, to ensure a stable and subservient labor force. The crushed Cotton Kingdom could not rise from its weeds until the fields were once again put under hoe and plow—and many whites wanted to make sure that they retained the tight control they had exercised over black field hands and plow drivers in the days of slavery.

Dire penalties were therefore imposed by the codes on blacks who "jumped" their labor contracts, which usually committed them to work for the same employer for one year, and generally at pittance wages. Violators could be made to forfeit back wages or could be forcibly dragged back to work by a paid "Negro-catcher." In Mississippi the captured freedmen could be fined and then hired out to pay their fines—an arrangement that closely resembled slavery itself.

The codes also sought to restore as nearly as possible the pre-emancipation system of race relations. Freedom was legally recognized, as were some other privileges, such as the right to marry. But all the codes forbade a black to serve on a jury; some even barred blacks from renting or leasing land. A black could be punished for "idleness" by being sentenced to work on a chain gang. Nowhere were blacks allowed to vote.

These oppressive laws mocked the ideal of freedom, so recently purchased by buckets of blood. The Black Codes imposed terrible burdens on the unfettered blacks, struggling against mistreatment and poverty to make their way as free people. The worst features of the Black Codes would eventually be repealed, but their revocation could not by itself lift the liberated blacks into economic independence. Lacking capital, and with little to offer but their labor, thousands of impoverished former slaves slipped into the status of sharecropper farmers, as did many landless whites. Luckless sharecroppers gradually sank into a morass of virtual peonage and remained there for generations. Formerly slaves to masters, countless blacks as well as poorer whites in effect became slaves to the soil and to their creditors. Yet the dethroned planter aristocracy resented even this pitiful concession to freedom. Sharecropping was the "wrong policy," said one planter. "It makes the laborer too independent; he becomes a partner, and has a right to be consulted."

Early in 1866 one congressman quoted a Georgian:

"The blacks eat, sleep, move, live, only by the tolerance of the whites, who hate them. The blacks own absolutely nothing but their bodies; their former masters own everything, and will sell them nothing. If a black man draws even a bucket of water from a well, he must first get the permission of a white man, his enemy. . . . If he asks for work to earn his living, he must ask it of a white man; and the whites are determined to give him no work, except on such terms as will make him a serf and impair his liberty."

A Family of Sharecroppers at the End of the Civil War
They were free at last, but most freed slaves would have to wait a century or more to escape slavery's cruel legacy of poverty, ignorance, and discrimination.

The Black Codes made an ugly impression in the North. If the former slaves were being re-enslaved, people asked one another, had not the Boys in Blue spilled their blood in vain? Had the North really won the war?

Congressional Reconstruction

These questions grew more insistent when the congressional delegations from the newly reconstituted Southern states presented themselves in the Capitol in December 1865. To the shock and disgust of the Republicans, many former Confederate leaders were on hand to claim their seats.

The appearance of these ex-rebels was a natural but costly blunder. Voters of the South, seeking able representatives, had turned instinctively to their experienced statesmen. But most of the Southern leaders were tainted by active association with the "lost cause." Among them were four former Confederate generals, five colonels, and various members of the Richmond cabinet and Congress. Worst of all, there was the shrimpy but brainy Alexander Stephens, ex–vice president of the Confederacy, still under indictment for treason.

The presence of these "whitewashed rebels" infuriated the Republicans in Congress. The war had been fought to restore the Union, but not on these kinds of terms. The Republicans were in no hurry to embrace their former enemies—virtually all of them Democrats —in the chambers of the Capitol. While the South had been "out" from 1861 to 1865, the Republicans in Congress had enjoyed a relatively free hand. They had passed much legislation that favored the North, such as the Morrill Tariff, the Pacific Railroad Act, and the Homestead Act. Now many Republicans balked at giving up this political advantage. On the first day of the congressional session, December 4, 1865, they banged shut the door in the face of the newly elected Southern delegations.

Looking to the future, the Republicans were alarmed to realize that a restored South would be stronger than ever in national politics. Before the war a black slave had counted as three-fifths of a person in apportioning congressional representation. Now the slave was five-fifths of a person. Eleven Southern states had seceded and been subdued by force of arms. But now, owing to full counting of free blacks, the rebel states were entitled to twelve more votes in Congress, and twelve more presidential electoral votes, than they had previously enjoyed. Again, angry voices in the North raised the cry, Who won the war?

Republicans had good reason to fear that ultimately they might be elbowed aside. Southerners might join hands with Democrats in the North and win control of Congress or maybe even the White House. If this happened, they could perpetuate the Black Codes, virtually re-enslaving the blacks. They could dismantle the economic program of the Republican party by lowering tariffs, rerouting the transcontinental railroad, repealing the free-farm Homestead Act, possibly even repudiating the national debt. President Johnson thus deeply disturbed the congressional Republicans when he announced on December 6, 1865, that the recently rebellious states had satisfied his conditions and that in his view the Union was now restored.

Johnson Clashes with Congress

A clash between president and Congress was now inevitable. It exploded into the open in February 1866, when the president vetoed a bill (later repassed) extending the life of the controversial Freedmen's Bureau.

Aroused, the Republicans swiftly struck back. In March 1866 they passed the Civil Rights Bill, which conferred on blacks the privilege of American citizenship and struck at the Black Codes. President Johnson resolutely vetoed this forward-looking measure on constitutional grounds, but in April congressmen steamrollered it over his veto—something they repeatedly did henceforth. The hapless president, dubbed "Sir Veto" and "Andy Veto," had his presidential wings clipped, as Congress increasingly assumed the dominant role in running the government. One critic called Johnson "the dead dog of the White House."

The Republicans now undertook to rivet the principles of the Civil Rights Bill into the Constitution as the Fourteenth Amendment. They feared that the Southerners might one day win control of Congress and repeal the hated law. The proposed amendment, as approved by Congress and sent to the states in June 1866, was sweeping. It (1) conferred civil rights, including citizenship but excluding the franchise, on the freedmen; (2) reduced proportionately the representation of a state in Congress and in the Electoral College if it denied blacks the ballot; (3) disqualified from federal and state office former Confederates who as federal officeholders had once sworn "to support the Constitution of the United States"; and (4) guaranteed the federal debt, while repudiating all Confederate debts. (See text of Fourteenth Amendment in the Appendix.)

An Inflexible President, 1866   This Republican cartoon shows Johnson knocking blacks out of the Freedmen's Bureau by his veto.

The radical faction was disappointed that the Fourteenth Amendment did not grant the right to vote, but all Republicans were agreed that no state should be welcomed back into the Union fold without first ratifying the Fourteenth Amendment. Yet

Principal Reconstruction Proposals and Plans

Year	Proposal or Plan
1864–1865	Lincoln's 10 percent proposal
1865–1866	Johnson's version of Lincoln's proposal
1866–1867	Congressional plan: 10 percent plan with Fourteenth Amendment
1867–1877	Congressional plan of military Reconstruction: Fourteenth Amendment plus black suffrage, later established nationwide by Fifteenth Amendment

President Johnson advised the Southern states to reject it, and all of the "sinful eleven," except Tennessee, defiantly spurned the amendment. Their spirit was reflected in a Southern song:

> And I don't want no pardon for what I was or
> am,
> I won't be reconstructed and I don't give a damn.

Swinging 'Round the Circle with Johnson

As 1866 lengthened, the battle grew between the Congress and the president. The root of the controversy was Johnson's "10-percent" governments that had passed the most stringent Black Codes. Congress had tried to temper the worst features of the codes by extending the life of the embattled Freedmen's Bureau and passing the Civil Rights Bill. Both measures Johnson had vetoed. Now the issue was whether Reconstruction was to be carried on with or without the Fourteenth Amendment. The Republicans would settle for nothing less.

The crucial congressional elections of 1866—more crucial than some presidential elections—were fast approaching. Johnson was naturally eager to escape from the clutch of Congress by securing a majority favorable to his soft-on-the-South policy. Invited to dedicate a Chicago monument to Stephen A. Douglas, he undertook to speak at various cities en route in support of his views.

Johnson's famous "swing 'round the circle," beginning in the late summer of 1866, was a serio-comedy of errors. The president delivered a series of "give 'em hell" speeches, in which he accused the radicals in Congress of having planned large-scale antiblack riots and murder in the South. As he spoke, hecklers hurled insults at him. Reverting to his stump-speaking days in Tennessee, he shouted back angry retorts, amid cries of "You be damned" and "Don't get mad, Andy." The dignity of his high office sank to a new low, as the old charges of drunkenness were revived.

As a vote-getter, Johnson was highly successful—for the opposition. His inept speechmaking heightened the cry "Stand by Congress" against the "Tailor of the Potomac." When the ballots were counted, the Republicans had rolled up more than a two-thirds majority in both houses of Congress.

Republican Principles and Programs

The Republicans now had a veto-proof Congress and virtually unlimited control of Reconstruction policy. But moderates and radicals still disagreed over the best course to pursue in the South.

The radicals in the Senate were led by the courtly and principled idealist Charles Sumner, long since recovered from his prewar caning on the Senate floor, who tirelessly labored not only for black freedom but for racial equality. In the House the most powerful radical was Thaddeus Stevens, crusty and vindictive congressman from Pennsylvania. Seventy-four years old in 1866, he was a curious figure, with a protruding lower lip, a heavy black wig covering his bald head, and a deformed foot. An unswerving friend of blacks, he had defended runaway slaves in court without fee and, before dying, insisted on burial in a black cemetery. His affectionate devotion to blacks was matched by his vitriolic hatred of rebellious white Southerners. A masterly parliamentarian with a razor-sharp mind and withering wit, Stevens was a leading figure on the Joint (House-Senate) Committee on Reconstruction.

Still opposed to rapid restoration of the Southern states, the radicals wanted to keep them out as long as possible and apply federal power to bring about a drastic social and economic transformation in the South. But moderate Republicans, more attuned to time-honored principles of states' rights and self-government, recoiled from the full implications of the radical program. They preferred policies that restrained the states from abridging citizens' rights, rather than policies that directly involved the federal government in individual lives. The actual

Representative Thaddeus Stevens (1792–1868), in a congressional speech on January 3, 1867, urged the ballot for blacks out of concern for them and out of bitterness against the whites:

"I am for Negro suffrage in every rebel state. If it be just, it should not be denied; if it be necessary, it should be adopted; if it be a punishment to traitors, they deserve it."

Thaddeus Stevens (1792–1868)   Stevens, who regarded the seceded states as "conquered provinces," promoted much of the major Reconstruction legislation, including the Fourteenth (civil rights) Amendment. Reconstruction, he said, must "revolutionize Southern institutions, habits, and manners. . . . The foundation of their institutions . . . must be broken up and relaid, or all our blood and treasure have been spent in vain."

policies adopted by Congress showed the influence of both these schools of thought, though the moderates, as the majority faction, had the upper hand. And one thing both groups had come to agree on by 1867 was the necessity to enfranchise black voters, even if it took federal troops to do it.

Reconstruction by the Sword

Against a backdrop of vicious and bloody race riots that had erupted in several Southern cities, Congress passed the Reconstruction Act on March 2, 1867. Supplemented by later measures, this drastic legislation divided the South into five military districts, each commanded by a Union general and policed by blue-clad soldiers, about twenty thousand all told. The act also temporarily disfranchised tens of thousands of former Confederates.

Congress additionally laid down stringent conditions for the readmission of the seceded states. The wayward states were required to ratify the Fourteenth Amendment, giving the former slaves their rights as citizens. The bitterest pill of all to white Southerners was the stipulation that they guarantee in their state constitutions full suffrage for their former adult male slaves. Yet the act, reflecting moderate sentiment, stopped short of giving the freedmen land or education at federal expense. The overriding purpose of the moderates was to create an electorate in Southern states that would vote those states back into the Union on acceptable terms and thus free the federal government from direct responsibility for the protection of black rights. As later events would demonstrate, this approach proved woefully inadequate to the cause of justice for blacks.

The radical Republicans were still worried. The danger loomed that once the unrepentant states were readmitted, they would amend their constitutions so as to withdraw the ballot from the blacks. The only ironclad safeguard was to incorporate black suffrage in the federal Constitution. This goal was finally achieved by the Fifteenth Amendment, passed by Congress in 1869 and ratified by the required number of states in 1870. (For text, see the Appendix.)

Military Reconstruction of the South not only usurped certain functions of the president as commander in chief but set up a martial regime of dubious legality. The Supreme Court had already ruled, in the case *Ex parte Milligan* (1866), that military tribunals could not try civilians, even during wartime, in areas where the civil courts were open. Peacetime military rule seemed starkly contrary to the spirit of the Constitution. But the circumstances were extraordinary in the Republic's history, and for the time being the Supreme Court avoided offending the Republican Congress.

Prodded into line by federal bayonets, the Southern states got on with the task of constitution making. By 1870 all of them had reorganized their governments and had been accorded full rights. The hated "bluebellies" remained until the new Republican regimes—usually called "radical" regimes—appeared to be firmly entrenched. Yet when the federal troops finally left a state, its government swiftly passed back into the hands of white "Redeemers," or "Home Rule" regimes, which were inevitably Democratic. Finally, in 1877, the last federal muskets were removed from state politics, and the "solid" Democratic South congealed.

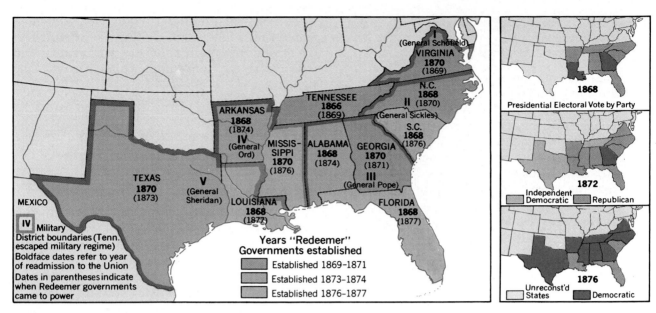

Military Reconstruction, 1867 (five districts and commanding generals)   For many white Southerners, military Reconstruction amounted to turning the knife in the wound of defeat. An often-repeated story of later years had a Southerner remark, "I was sixteen years old before I discovered that damnyankee was two words."

Southern Reconstruction by State

State	Readmitted to Representation in Congress	Home Rule (Democratic or "Redeemer" Regime) Reestablished	Comments
Tennessee	July 24, 1866		Ratified Fourteenth Amendment in 1866 and hence avoided military Reconstruction*
Arkansas	June 22, 1868	1874	
North Carolina	June 25, 1868	1870	
Alabama	June 25, 1868	1874	
Florida	June 25, 1868	1877	Federal troops restationed in 1877, as result of Hayes-Tilden electoral bargain
Louisiana	June 25, 1868	1877	Same as Florida
South Carolina	June 25, 1868	1877	Same as Florida
Virginia	January 26, 1870	1869	
Mississippi	February 23, 1870	1876	
Texas	March 30, 1870	1874	
Georgia	[June 25, 1868] July 15, 1870	1872	Readmitted June 25, 1868, but returned to military control after expulsion of blacks from legislature

*For many years Tennessee was the only state of the secession to observe Lincoln's birthday as a legal holiday. Many Southern states still observe the birthdays of Jefferson Davis and Robert E. Lee.

No Women Voters

The passage of the three Reconstruction-era Amendments—the Thirteenth, Fourteenth, and Fifteenth—delighted former abolitionists but deeply disappointed advocates of women's rights. Women had played a prominent part in the prewar abolitionist movement and had often pointed out that both women and blacks lacked basic civil rights, especially the crucial right to vote. The struggle for black freedom and the crusade for women's rights, therefore, were one and the same in the eyes of many women. Yet during the war, feminist leaders such as Elizabeth Cady Stanton and Susan B. Anthony had temporarily suspended their own demands and worked wholeheartedly for the cause of black emancipation. The Woman's Loyal League had gathered nearly 400,000 signatures on petitions asking Congress to pass a constitutional amendment prohibiting slavery.

Now, with the war ended and the Thirteenth Amendment passed, feminist leaders believed that their time had come. They reeled with shock, however, when the wording of the Fourteenth Amendment, which defined equal national citizenship, for the first time inserted the word *male* into the Constitution in referring to a citizen's right to vote. Both Stanton and Anthony campaigned actively against the Fourteenth Amendment despite the pleas of Frederick Douglass, who had long supported woman suffrage but believed that this was "the Negro's hour." When the Fifteenth Amendment proposed to prohibit denial of the vote on the basis of

The prominent suffragist and abolitionist Susan B. Anthony (1820–1906) was outraged over the proposed exclusion of women from the Fourteenth Amendment. In a conversation with her former male allies, Wendell Phillips and Theodore Tilton, she reportedly held out her arm and declared,

"Look at this, all of you. And hear me swear that I will cut off this right arm of mine before I will ever work for or demand the ballot for the negro and not the woman."

"race, color, or previous condition of servitude," Stanton and Anthony wanted the word *sex* added to the list. They lost this battle, too. Fifty years would pass before the Constitution granted women the right to vote.

The Realities of Radical Reconstruction in the South

The blacks now had freedom, of a sort. Their friends in Congress had only haltingly and somewhat belatedly secured the franchise for them. Both presidents Lincoln and Johnson had proposed to give the ballot gradually to selected blacks who qualified for it through education, property ownership, or military service. Moderate Republicans and even many radicals at first hesitated to bestow suffrage on the freedmen. The Fourteenth Amendment, in many ways the heart of the Republican program for Reconstruction, had fallen short of guaranteeing the right to vote. (It envisioned for blacks the same status as women—citizenship without voting rights.) But by 1867 hesitation had given way to a hard determination to enfranchise the former slaves wholesale and immediately, while thousands of white Southerners were being denied the vote. By glaring contrast most of the Northern states, before ratification of the Fifteenth Amendment in 1870, withheld the ballot from their tiny black minorities. White Southerners naturally concluded that the Republicans were hypocritical in insisting that blacks in the South be allowed to vote.

Having gained their right to suffrage, Southern black men seized the initiative and began to organize politically. Their primary vehicle became the Union League, originally a pro-Union organization based in the North. Assisted by Northern blacks, freedmen turned the League into a network of political clubs that educated members in their civic duties and campaigned for Republican candidates. The League's mission soon expanded to include building black churches and schools, representing black grievances before local employers and government, and recruiting militias to protect black communities from white retaliation.

Though African-American women did not obtain the right to vote, they too assumed new political roles. Black women faithfully attended the parades and rallies common in black communities during the early years of Reconstruction and helped assemble mass meetings in the newly constructed black churches. They even showed up at the constitutional conventions held throughout the South in 1867, monitoring the proceedings and participating in informal votes outside the convention halls.

But black men elected as delegates to the state constitutional conventions held the greater political authority. They formed the backbone of the black political community. At the conventions, they sat down with whites to hammer out new state constitutions, which most importantly provided for universal male suffrage. Though the subsequent elections produced no black governors or majorities in state senates, black political participation expanded exponentially during Reconstruction. Between 1868 and 1876, fourteen black congressmen and two black senators, Hiram Revels and Blanche K. Bruce, both of Mississippi, served in Washington, D.C. Blacks also served in state governments as lieutenant governors and representatives, and in local governments as mayors, magistrates, sheriffs, and justices of the peace.

The sight of former slaves holding office deeply offended their onetime masters, who lashed out

> *At a constitutional convention in Alabama, freed people affirmed their rights in the following declaration:*
>
> "We claim exactly the same rights, privileges and immunities as are enjoyed by white men—we ask nothing more and will be content with nothing less. . . . The law no longer knows white nor black, but simply men, and consequently we are entitled to ride in public conveyances, hold office, sit on juries and do everything else which we have in the past been prevented from doing solely on the ground of color."

with particular fury at the freedmen's white allies, labeling them "scalawags" and "carpetbaggers." The so-called scalawags were Southerners, often former Unionists and Whigs. The former Confederates accused them, often with wild exaggeration, of plundering the treasuries of the Southern states

Freedmen Voting, Richmond, Virginia, 1871   The exercise of democratic rights by former slaves constituted a political and social revolution in the South, and was bitterly resented by whites.

Black Reconstruction
A composite portrait of the first black senators and representatives in the 41st and 42nd congresses. Senator Hiram Revels, on the left, was elected in 1870 to the seat that had been occupied by Jefferson Davis when the South seceded.

through their political influence in the radical governments. The carpetbaggers, on the other hand, were supposedly sleazy Northerners who had packed all their worldly goods into a carpetbag suitcase at war's end and had come South to seek personal power and profit. In fact, most were former Union soldiers and Northern businessmen and professionals who wanted to play a role in modernizing the "New South."

How well did the radical regimes rule? The radical legislatures passed much desirable legislation and introduced many badly needed reforms. For the first time in Southern history, steps were taken toward establishing adequate public schools. Tax systems were streamlined; public works were launched; and property rights were guaranteed to women. Many welcome reforms were retained by the all-white "redeemer" governments that later returned to power.

Despite these achievements, graft ran rampant in many "radical" governments. This was especially true in South Carolina and Louisiana, where conscienceless promoters and other pocket-padders used politically inexperienced blacks as pawns. The worst "black-and-white" legislatures purchased, as "legislative supplies," such "stationery" as hams, perfumes, suspenders, bonnets, corsets, champagne, and a coffin. One "thrifty" carpetbag gover-

nor in a single year "saved" $100,000 from a salary of $8,000. Yet this sort of corruption was by no means confined to the South in these postwar years. The crimes of the Reconstruction governments were no more outrageous than the scams and felonies being perpetrated in the North at the same time, especially in Boss Tweed's New York.

The Ku Klux Klan

Deeply embittered, some Southern whites resorted to savage measures against "radical" rule. Many whites resented the success and ability of black legislators as much as they resented alleged "corruption." A number of secret organizations mushroomed forth, the most notorious of which was the "Invisible Empire of the South," or Ku Klux Klan, founded in Tennessee in 1866. Besheeted night riders, their horses' hoofs muffled, would approach the cabin of an "upstart" black and hammer on the door. In ghoulish tones one thirsty horseman would demand a bucket of water. Then, under pretense of drinking, he would pour it into a rubber attachment concealed beneath his mask and gown, smack his lips, and declare that this was the first water he had tasted since he was killed at the Battle of Shiloh. If

The following excerpt is part of a heartrending appeal to Congress in 1871 by a group of Kentucky blacks:

"We believe you are not familiar with the description of the Ku Klux Klans riding nightly over the country, going from county to county, and in the county towns, spreading terror wherever they go by robbing, whipping, ravishing, and killing our people without provocation, compelling colored people to break the ice and bathe in the chilly waters of the Kentucky River.

"The [state] legislature has adjourned. They refused to enact any laws to suppress Ku-Klux disorder. We regard them [the Ku-Kluxers] as now being licensed to continue their dark and bloody deeds under cover of the dark night. They refuse to allow us to testify in the state courts where a white man is concerned. We find their deeds are perpetrated only upon colored men and white Republicans. We also find that for our services to the government and our race we have become the special object of hatred and persecution at the hands of the Democratic Party. Our people are driven from their homes in great numbers, having no redress only [except] the United States court, which is in many cases unable to reach them."

The Ku Klux Klan, Tennessee, 1868   This nightriding terrorist has even masked the identity of his horse.

fright did not produce the desired effect, force was employed.

Such tomfoolery and terror proved partially effective. Many ex-bondsmen and white "carpetbaggers," quick to take a hint, shunned the polls. Those stubborn souls who persisted in their "upstart" ways were flogged, mutilated, or even murdered. In one Louisiana parish in 1868, the whites in two days killed or wounded two hundred victims; a pile of twenty-five bodies was found half-buried in the woods. By such atrocious practices were blacks "kept in their place"—that is, down. The Klan became a refuge for numerous bandits and cutthroats. Any scoundrel could don a sheet.

Congress, outraged by this night-riding lawlessness, passed the harsh Force Acts of 1870 and 1871.

Federal troops were able to stamp out much of the "lash law," but by this time the Invisible Empire had already done its work of intimidation. Many of the outlawed groups continued their tactics in the guise of "dancing clubs," "missionary societies," and "rifle clubs."

White resistance undermined attempts to empower the blacks politically. The white South, for many decades, openly flouted the Fourteenth and Fifteenth Amendments. Wholesale disfranchisement of the blacks, starting conspicuously about 1890, was achieved by intimidation, fraud, and trickery. Among various underhanded schemes were the literacy tests, unfairly administered by whites to the advantage of illiterate whites. In the eyes of the white Southerners, the goal of white supremacy fully justified these dishonorable devices.

A black leader protested to whites in 1868:

"It is extraordinary that a race such as yours, professing gallantry, chivalry, education, and superiority, living in a land where ringing chimes call child and sire to the Gospel of God—that with all these advantages on your side, you can make war upon the poor defenseless black man."

Johnson Walks the Impeachment Plank

Radicals meanwhile had been sharpening their hatchets for President Johnson. Annoyed by the obstruction of the "drunken tailor" in the White House, they falsely accused him of maintaining there a harem of "dissolute women." Not content with curbing his authority, they decided to remove him altogether by constitutional processes.* Under existing law the president pro tempore of the Senate, the unscrupulous and rabidly radical "Bluff Ben" Wade of Ohio, would then become president.

As an initial step, Congress in 1867 passed the Tenure of Office Act—as usual, over Johnson's veto. Contrary to precedent, the new law required the president to secure the consent of the Senate before he could remove his appointees once they had been approved by that body. One purpose was to freeze into the cabinet the secretary of war, Edwin M. Stanton, a holdover from the Lincoln administration. Although outwardly loyal to Johnson, he was secretly serving as a spy and informer for the radicals.

Johnson provided the radicals with a pretext to begin impeachment proceedings when he abruptly dismissed Stanton early in 1868. The House of Representatives immediately voted 126 to 47 to impeach Johnson for "high crimes and misdemeanors," as required by the Constitution, charging him with various violations of the Tenure of Office Act. Two additional articles related to Johnson's verbal assaults on the Congress, involving "disgrace, ridicule, hatred, contempt, and reproach."

---

*For impeachment, see Art. I, Sec. II, para. 5; Art. I, Sec. III, paras. 6, 7; Art. II, Sec. IV, in the Appendix.

A Not-Guilty Verdict for Johnson

With evident zeal the radical-led Senate now sat as a court to try Johnson on the dubious impeachment charges. The House conducted the prosecution. The trial aroused intense public interest and, with one thousand tickets printed, proved to be the biggest show of 1868. Johnson kept his dignity and sobriety and maintained a discreet silence. His battery of attorneys argued that the president, convinced that the Tenure of Office Act was unconstitutional, had fired Stanton merely to put a test case before the Supreme Court. (That slow-moving tribunal finally ruled indirectly in Johnson's favor fifty-eight years later.) House prosecutors, including oily-tongued Benjamin F. Butler and embittered Thaddeus Stevens, had a harder time building a compelling case for impeachment.

On May 16, 1868, the day for the first voting in the Senate, the tension was electric, and heavy breathing could be heard in the galleries. By a margin of only one vote, the radicals failed to muster the two-thirds majority for Johnson's removal. Seven independent-minded Republican senators, courageously putting country above party, voted "not guilty."

Several factors shaped the outcome. Fears of creating a destabilizing precedent played a role, as did principled opposition to abusing the constitutional mechanism of checks and balances. Political considerations also figured conspicuously. As the vice presidency remained vacant under Johnson, his successor would have been radical Republican Ben Wade, the president pro tempore of the Senate. Wade was disliked by many members of the business community for his high-tariff, soft-money, prolabor views, and distrusted by moderate Republicans. Meanwhile, Johnson indicated through his attorney that he would stop obstructing Republican policies in return for remaining in office.

Die-hard radicals were infuriated by their failure to muster a two-thirds majority for Johnson's removal. "The Country is going to the Devil!" cried the crippled Stevens as he was carried from the hall. But the nation, though violently aroused, accepted the verdict with a good temper that did credit to its political maturity. In a less stable republic, an armed uprising might have erupted against the president.

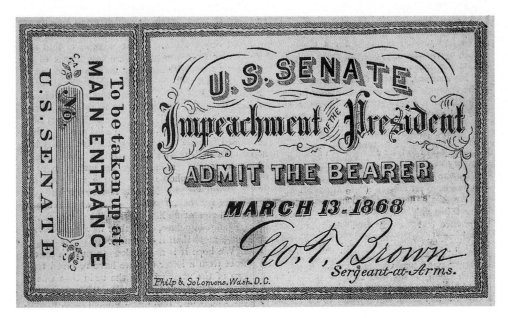

Impeachment Drama
The impeachment proceedings against President Andrew Johnson, among the most severe constitutional crises in the Republic's history, were high political theater, and tickets were in sharp demand.

The nation thus narrowly avoided a dangerous precedent that would have gravely weakened one of the three branches of the federal government. Johnson was clearly guilty of bad speeches, bad judgment, and bad temper, but not of "high crimes and misdemeanors." From the standpoint of the radicals, his greatest crime had been to stand inflexibly in their path.

The Purchase of Alaska

Johnson's administration, though largely reduced to a figurehead, achieved its most enduring success in the field of foreign relations.

The Russians by 1867 were in a mood to sell the vast and chilly expanse of land now known as Alaska. They had already overextended themselves in North America, and they saw that in the likely event of another war with England, they probably would lose their defenseless northern province to the sea-dominant British. Alaska, moreover, had been ruthlessly "furred out" and was a growing economic liability. The Russians were therefore quite eager to unload their "frozen asset" on the Americans, and they put out seductive feelers in Washington. They preferred the United States to any other purchaser, primarily because they wanted to strengthen further the Republic as a barrier against their ancient enemy, Britain.

In 1867 Secretary of State William Seward, an ardent expansionist, signed a treaty with Russia that transferred Alaska to the United States for the bargain price of $7.2 million. But Seward's enthusiasm for these frigid wastes was not shared by his ignorant or uninformed countrymen, who jeered at "Seward's Folly," "Seward's Icebox," "Frigidia," and "Walrussia." The American people, still preoccupied with Reconstruction and other internal vexations, were economy-minded and anti-expansionist.

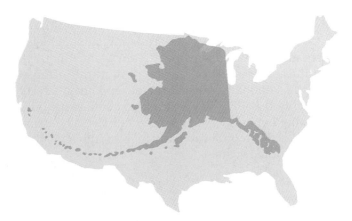

Alaska and the Lower Forty-Eight States
(a size comparison)

Then why did Congress and the American public sanction the purchase? For one thing Russia, alone among the powers, had been conspicuously friendly to the North during the recent Civil War. Americans did not feel that they could offend their great and good friend, the tsar, by hurling his walrus-covered icebergs back into his face. Besides, the territory was rumored to be teeming with furs, fish, and gold, and it might yet "pan out" profitably—as it later did with natural resources, including oil and gas. So Congress and the country accepted "Seward's Polar Bear Garden," somewhat derisively but nevertheless hopefully.

The Heritage of Reconstruction

Many white Southerners regarded Reconstruction as a more grievous wound than the war itself. It left a festering scar that would take generations to heal. They resented the upending of their social and racial system, political empowerment of blacks, and the insult of federal intervention in their local affairs. Yet few rebellions have ended with the victors sitting down to a love feast with the vanquished. Given the explosiveness of the issues that had caused the war, and the bitterness of the fighting, the wonder is that Reconstruction was not far harsher than it was. The fact is that Lincoln, Johnson, and most Republicans had no clear picture at war's end of what federal policy toward the South should be. Policymakers groped for the right policies, influenced as much by Southern responses to defeat and emancipation as by any plans of their own to impose a specific program on the South.

The Republicans acted from a mixture of idealism and political expediency. They wanted both to protect the freed slaves and to promote the fortunes of the Republican party. In the end their efforts backfired badly. Reconstruction conferred only fleeting benefits on the blacks and virtually extinguished the Republican party in the South for nearly one hundred years.

The remarkable ex-slave Frederick Douglass (1817?–1895) wrote in 1882,

"Though slavery was abolished, the wrongs of my people were not ended. Though they were not slaves, they were not yet quite free. No man can be truly free whose liberty is dependent upon the thought, feeling, and action of others, and who has himself no means in his own hands for guarding, protecting, defending, and maintaining that liberty. Yet the Negro after his emancipation was precisely in this state of destitution. . . . He was free from the individual master, but the slave of society. He had neither money, property, nor friends. He was free from the old plantation, but he had nothing but the dusty road under his feet. He was free from the old quarter that once gave him shelter, but a slave to the rains of summer and the frosts of winter. He was, in a word, literally turned loose, naked, hungry, and destitute, to the open sky."

Moderate Republicans never fully appreciated the extensive effort necessary to make the freed slaves completely independent citizens, nor the lengths to which Southern whites would go to preserve their system of racial dominance. Had Thaddeus Stevens's radical program of drastic economic reforms and heftier protection of political rights been enacted, things might well have been different. But deep-seated racism, ingrained American resistance to tampering with property rights, and rigid loyalty to the principle of local self-government, combined with spreading indifference in the North to the plight of the blacks, formed too formidable an obstacle. Despite good intentions by Republicans, the Old South was in many ways more resurrected than reconstructed.

Chronology

1863	Lincoln announces "10 percent" Reconstruction plan
1864	Lincoln vetoes Wade-Davis Bill
1865	Lincoln assassinated
	Johnson issues Reconstruction proclamation
	Congress refuses to seat Southern congressmen
	Freedmen's Bureau established
	Southern states pass Black Codes
1866	Congress passes Civil Rights Bill over Johnson's veto
	Congress passes Fourteenth Amendment
	Johnson-backed candidates lose congressional election
	Ex parte Milligan case
	Ku Klux Klan founded
1867	Reconstruction Act
	Tenure of Office Act
	United States purchases Alaska from Russia
1868	Johnson impeached and acquitted
	Johnson pardons Confederate leaders
1870	Fifteenth Amendment ratified
1870-1871	Force Acts
1872	Freedmen's Bureau ended
1877	Reconstruction ends

How Radical Was Reconstruction?

Few topics have triggered as much intellectual warfare as the "dark and bloody ground" of Reconstruction. The period provoked questions—sectional, racial, and constitutional—about which people felt deeply and remain deeply divided even today. Scholarly argument goes back conspicuously to a Columbia University historian, William A. Dunning, whose students, in the early 1900s, published a series of histories of the Reconstruction South. Dunning and his disciples were influenced by the turn-of-the-century spirit of sectional conciliation as well as by current theories about black racial inferiority. Sympathizing with the white South, they wrote about the Reconstruction period as a kind of national disgrace, foisted upon a prostrate region by vindictive and self-seeking radical Republican politicians. If the South had wronged the North by seceding, the North had wronged the South by reconstructing.

A second cycle of scholarship in the 1920s was impelled by a widespread suspicion that the Civil War itself had been a tragic and unnecessary blunder. Attention now shifted to Northern politicians. Scholars like Howard Beale further questioned the motives of the radical Republicans. To Beale and others, the radicals had masked a ruthless desire to exploit Southern labor and resources behind a false front of "concern" for the freed slaves. Moreover, Northern advocacy of black voting rights was merely a calculated attempt to ensure a Republican political presence in the defeated South. The unfortunate Andrew Johnson, in this view, had valiantly tried to uphold constitutional principles in the face of this cynical Northern onslaught.

Following World War II, Kenneth Stampp, among others, turned this view on its head. Influenced by the modern civil rights movement, he argued that Reconstruction had been a noble attempt to extend American principles of equity and justice. The radical Republicans and the carpetbaggers were now heroes, whereas Andrew Johnson was castigated for his obstinate racism. By the early 1970s, this view had become orthodoxy, and it generally holds sway today. Yet some scholars such as Michael Benedict and Leon Litwack, disillusioned with the inability to achieve full racial justice in the 1960s, began once more to scrutinize the motives of Northern politicians immediately after the Civil War. They claimed to discover that Reconstruction had never been very radical and that the Freedmen's Bureau and other agencies had merely allowed the white planters to maintain their dominance over local politics as well as over the local economy.

More recently, Eric Foner has powerfully reasserted the argument that Reconstruction was a truly radical and noble attempt to establish an interracial democracy. Drawing upon the work of black scholar W. E. B. Du Bois, Foner emphasizes the comparative approach to the American Reconstruction. Clearly, Foner admits, Reconstruction did not create full equality, but it did allow blacks to form political organizations and churches, to vote, and to establish some measure of economic independence. In South Africa, the Caribbean, and other areas once marked by slavery, the freed slaves never received these opportunities. Many of the benefits of Reconstruction were erased by white southerners during the Gilded Age, but in the twentieth century, the constitutional principles and organizations developed during Reconstruction provided the focus and foundation for the modern civil rights movement—which some have called the Second Reconstruction.

SUGGESTED READINGS

PRIMARY SOURCE DOCUMENTS

Booker T. Washington's classic autobiography *Up from Slavery** (1901) records one freedman's experiences. Contemporary comments on Reconstruction include the laments of editor Edwin L. Godkin, *The Nation* (December 7, 1871, p. 364),* and Frederick Douglass, *Life and Times of Frederick Douglass** (1882), as well as the debates in the *Congressional Globe** (1867–1868) between radicals such as Thaddeus Stevens and moderates like Lyman Trumbull.

SECONDARY SOURCES

Eric Foner, *Reconstruction: America's Unfinished Revolution, 1863–1877* (1988), is a superb synthesis of current scholarship. Overall accounts may be found in James G. Randall and David Donald, *The Civil War and Recon-*

struction (rev. ed., 1969), and James McPherson, *Ordeal By Fire: The Civil War and Reconstruction* (1981), perhaps the best brief introduction. Lincoln's early efforts at Reconstruction are handled in Peyton McCrary, *Abraham Lincoln and Reconstruction* (1978), and Herman Belz, *Emancipation and Equal Rights* (1978). Willie Lee Rose engagingly describes a *Rehearsal for Reconstruction: The Port Royal Experiment* (1964). Dan Carter, *When the War Was Over: The Failure of Self-Reconstruction in the South, 1865–1867* (1985), charts the first years of the period. Following up the story of national politics is Eric L. McKitrick, *Andrew Johnson and Reconstruction: Principle and Prejudice, 1865–1866* (1963). Sympathetic to the radical Republicans are James M. McPherson, *The Struggle for Equality* (1964), and Hans L. Trefousse, *The Radical Republicans* (1969). See also David Montgomery, *Beyond Equality: Labor and the Radical Republicans, 1862–1872* (1967). Siding with the radicals in the impeachment fight are Michael L. Benedict, *The Impeachment and Trial of Andrew Johnson* (1973), and Hans L. Trefousse, *Impeachment of a President* (1975). Conditions in the South are analyzed in W. E. B. Du Bois's controversial classic *Black Reconstruction* (1935) and in Leon F. Litwack's brilliantly evocative *Been in the Storm*

---

*An asterisk indicates that the document, or an excerpt from it, can be found in Thomas A. Bailey and David M. Kennedy, eds., *The American Spirit: United States History as Seen by Contemporaries*, 9th ed. (Boston: Houghton Mifflin, 1998).

So Long (1979), a revealing study of the initial responses, by both blacks and whites, to emancipation. An excellent account of the Southern economy after the war is Gavin Wright, *Old South, New South: Revolutions in the Southern Economy Since the Civil War* (1986). It can be usefully supplemented by Roger Ransom and Richard L. Sutch, *One Kind of Freedom: The Economic Consequences of Emancipation* (1977). See also James Roark, *Masters Without Slaves: Southern Planters in the Civil War and Reconstruction* (1977), and Lawrence Powell, *New Masters: Northern Planters During the Civil War and Reconstruction* (1980). Barbara Fields looks at the border state of Maryland in *Slavery and Freedom on the Middle Ground* (1985). William McFeely offers an excellent biography of *Frederick Douglass* (1991). Roger Shugg, *Origins of Class Struggle in Louisiana* (1968); Dewey W. Grantham, *Life and Death of the Solid South* (1988); Edward L. Ayers, *The Promise of a New South: Life After Reconstruction* (1992); Dwight Billings, *Planters and the Making of a "New South": Class, Politics and Development in North Carolina, 1865–1900* (1979); and Jonathan Wiener, *Social Origins of the New South: Alabama, 1860–1885* (1978), elucidate the political economy of the postbellum South. Joel Williamson offers a psychological portrait of race relations in *The Crucible of Race: Black-White Relations in the American South Since Emancipation* (1984). Consult also Thomas Holt, *Black over White: Negro Political Leadership in South Carolina During Reconstruction* (1977). C. Vann Woodward, *The Strange Career of Jim Crow* (rev. ed., 1974), is a classic study of the origins of segregation. His views have drawn criticism in Harold O. Rabinowitz, *Race Relations in the Urban South, 1865–1890* (1977). See also Rabinowitz's *Southern Black Leaders of the Reconstruction Era* (1982). The Freedmen's Bureau has been the subject of several studies, including Peter Kolchin, *First Freedom* (1972); Claude Oubré, *Forty Acres and a Mule: The Freedmen's Bureau and Black Land Ownership* (1978); and Donald Nieman, *To Set the Law in Motion: The Freedmen's Bureau and the Legal Rights of Blacks, 1865–1868* (1979). Nell Irvin Painter follows African-Americans who chose to leave the South altogether in *Exodusters: Black Migration to Kansas After Reconstruction* (1976). Special studies of value are William P. Vaughn, *Schools for All* (1974); William C. Gillette, *The Right to Vote: Politics and the Passage of the 15th Amendment* (1965); Stanley I. Kutler, *Judicial Power and Reconstruction Politics* (1968); and Harold M. Hyman, *A More Perfect Union: The Impact of the Civil War and Reconstruction on the Constitution* (1973). Richard N. Current rehabilitates the maligned carpetbaggers in *Those Terrible Carpetbaggers* (1988). Fresh scholarship is presented in Kenneth M. Stampp and Leon Litwack, eds., *Reconstruction: An Anthology of Revisionist Writings* (1969), and Robert P. Swierenga, ed., *Beyond the Civil War Synthesis* (1975). J. Morgan Kousser and James M. McPherson, eds., *Region, Race, and Reconstruction: Essays in Honor of C. Vann Woodward* (1982), contains some intriguing essays. Eric Foner looks at emancipation in a comparative perspective in *Nothing but Freedom* (1983). A comprehensive study of the climax of this troubled period is William Gillette, *Retreat from Reconstruction, 1869–1879* (1979). Also see Michael Perman, *The Road to Redemption: Southern Politics, 1869–1879* (1984).

PART FOUR

Forging an Industrial Society

A nation of farmers fought the Civil War in the 1860s. By the time the Spanish-American War broke out in 1898, America was an industrial nation. For generations Americans had plunged into the wilderness and plowed their fields. Now they settled in cities and toiled in factories. Between the Civil War and the century's end, economic and technological change came so swiftly and massively that it seemed to many Americans that a whole new civilization had emerged.

In some ways it had. The sheer scale of the new industrial civilization was dazzling. Transcontinental railroads knit the country together from sea to sea. New industries like oil and steel grew to staggering size—and made megamillionaires out of entrepreneurs like oilman John D. Rockefeller and steelmaker Andrew Carnegie.

Drawn by the allure of industrial employment, Americans moved to the city. In 1860 only about 20 percent of the population were city dwellers. By 1900 that proportion doubled, as rural Americans and European immigrants alike flocked to mill town and metropolis in search of steady jobs.

These sweeping changes challenged the spirit of individualism that Americans had celebrated since the seventeenth century. Even on the western frontier, that historic bastion of rugged loners, the hand of government was increasingly felt, as large armies were dispatched to subdue the Plains Indians and federal authority was invoked to regulate the use of natural resources. The rise of powerful monopolies called into question the government's traditional hands-off policy toward business, and a growing band of reformers increasingly clamored for government regulation of private enterprise. The mushrooming cities, with their needs for transport systems, schools, hospitals, sanitation, and fire and police protection, required bigger governments and budgets than an earlier generation could have imagined. As never before, Americans struggled to adapt old ideals of private autonomy to the new realities of industrial civilization.

With economic change came social and political turmoil. Labor violence brought bloodshed to places such as Chicago and Homestead, Pennsylvania. Small farmers, squeezed by debt and foreign competition, rallied behind the People's, or "Populist," party, a radical movement of the 1880s and 1890s that attacked the power of Wall Street, big business, and the banks. Anti-immigrant sentiment swelled. Bitter disputes over tariffs and monetary policy deeply divided the country, setting debtors against lenders, farmers against manufacturers, the West and South against the Northeast. And in this unfamiliar era of big money and expanding government, corruption flourished, from town hall to Congress, fueling loud cries for political reform.

The bloodiest conflict of all pitted Plains Indians against the relentless push of westward expansion. As railroads drove their iron arrows through the heart of the West, the Indians lost their land and life-sustaining buffalo herds. By the 1890s, after

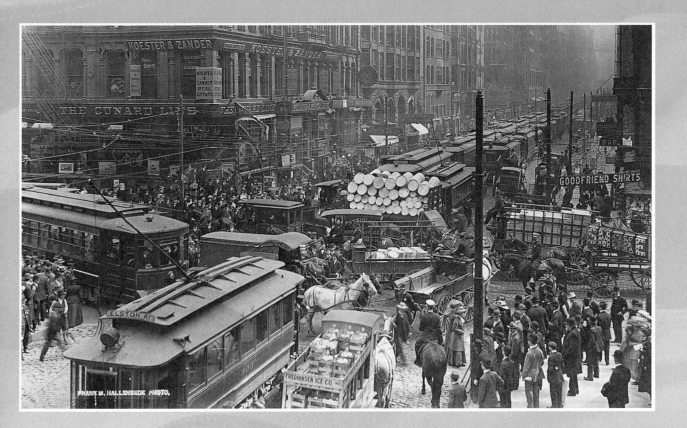

three decades of fierce fighting with the U. S. Army, the Indians who had once roamed across the vast rolling prairies were confined to the open-air prisons called reservations.

The South remained the one region largely untouched by the industrial revolution sweeping the rest of America. A few sleepy southern hamlets did become boomtowns; but for the most part, the South's rural way of life, and its peculiar system of race relations, were largely unperturbed by the changes happening elsewhere. On African-Americans, the vast majority of whom continued to live in the Old South, the post-emancipation era inflicted new forms of racial injustice. State legislatures systematically deprived black Americans of their political rights, including the right to vote. Segregation of schools, housing, and all kinds of public facilities made a mockery of African-Americans' Reconstruction-era hopes for equality before the law.

The new wealth and power of industrial America nurtured a growing sense of national self-confidence. Literature flowered, and a golden age of philanthropy dawned. The reform spirit spread. So did a restless appetite for overseas expansion. In a brief war against Spain in 1898, the United States, born in a revolutionary war of independence and long the champion of colonial peoples yearning to breathe free, seized control of the Philippines and itself became an imperial power. Uncle Sam's venture into empire touched off a bitter national debate about America's role in the world and ushered in a long period of argument over the responsibilities, at home as well as abroad, of a modern industrial state.

Dearborn Street, Chicago Loop, Around 1900
"America is energetic, but Chicago is in a fever," marveled a visiting Englishman about turn-of-the-century Chicago. Street scenes like this were common in America's booming new cities, especially in the "Lord of the Midwest."

24

Politics in the Gilded Age

1869–1889

*Grant . . . had no right to exist. He should have been
extinct for ages. . . . That, two thousand years after
Alexander the Great and Julius Caesar, a man like
Grant should be called—and should actually and truly
be—the highest product of the most advanced
evolution, made evolution ludicrous. . . . The progress
of evolution, from President Washington to President
Grant, was alone evidence enough to upset Darwin. . . .
Grant . . . should have lived in a cave and worn skins.*

HENRY ADAMS, *THE EDUCATION OF HENRY ADAMS*, 1907

The "Bloody Shirt" Elects Grant

Disillusionment ran deep among idealistic Americans in the era after the Civil War. They had spilled their blood for the Union, emancipation, and Abraham Lincoln, who had promised "a new birth of freedom." Instead they got a bitter dose of corruption, petty politics, and Ulysses S. Grant, a great soldier but an inept politician.

Wrangling between Congress and Andrew Johnson had soured the people on professional politicians, and the notion still prevailed that a good general was bound to make a good president. Stubbily bearded General Grant, with his slightly stooped body measuring a shade over 5 feet, 8 inches (1.72 meters), was by far the most popular Northern hero to emerge from the war. Grateful citizens of Philadelphia, Washington, and his hometown of Galena, Illinois, passed the hat around and in each place presented him with a house. New Yorkers tendered him a check for $105,000. The general, silently puffing on his cigar, accepted these gifts with open arms, as if the Republic owed them to him for having rescued the Union.

Unfortunately, this hard-riding soldier was a greenhorn in the political arena. He had almost no political experience, and his one presidential vote had been cast for the Democratic ticket in 1856. A better judge of horseflesh than of humans, his cultural background was breathtakingly narrow. He once reportedly remarked that Venice (Italy) would be a fine city if only it were drained.

The Republicans, now freed from the Union party coalition of war days, enthusiastically nominated Grant for the presidency in 1868. The party's platform sounded a clarion call for continued Reconstruction of the South under the glinting steel of federal bayonets. Yet Grant, always a man of few words, struck a highly popular note in his letter of acceptance when he said, "Let us have peace." This noble sentiment became a leading campaign slogan and was later engraved on his tomb beside the Hudson River.

Expectant Democrats, meeting in their own nominating convention, denounced military Reconstruction but could agree on little else. Wealthy eastern delegates demanded a plank promising that federal bonds, issued during the war, would be redeemed in gold—even though many of the bonds had been purchased with badly depreciated paper greenbacks. Poorer midwestern delegates answered with the "Ohio Idea," forcing a "repudiation" plank into the platform. It called for redemption in greenbacks to the maximum extent possible. Down-on-their-luck agrarian Democrats thus hoped to keep more money in circulation, which would make loans less costly and easier to find.

The midwestern delegates got the platform but not the candidate, who turned out to be the conservative former governor of New York, Horatio Seymour. He promptly repudiated the "repudiation" plank, thereby sinking the Democrats' scant hopes for success at the polls. Republicans whipped up enthusiasm for Grant by energetically "waving the bloody shirt"—that is, reviving gory memories of the Civil War—which became for the first time a prominent feature of a presidential campaign.* "Vote as You Shot" was a powerful Republican slogan aimed at Union army veterans.

Grant won, with 214 electoral votes to 80 for Seymour. But despite his great popularity, the former general scored a majority of only 300,000 in the popular vote (3,013,421 to 2,706,829). Most white voters apparently supported Seymour, and the ballots of three still-unreconstructed southern states (Mississippi, Texas, and Virginia) were not counted. An estimated 500,000 former slaves gave Grant his margin of victory. To remain in power, the Republican party somehow had to continue to control the South—and to keep the ballot in the hands of the grateful freedmen. Republicans could not take future victories "for Granted."

The Era of Good Stealings

The population of the Republic continued to vault upward by vigorous leaps, despite the awful bloodletting of the Civil War. Census takers reported over 39 million people in 1870, a gain of 26.6 percent over the previous decade, as the immigrant tide surged again. The United States was now the third largest nation of the Western world, ranking behind Russia and France.

But the moral stature of the United States fell regrettably short of its physical stature. The Civil War and its aftermath bred waste, extravagance, speculation, and graft. With political and economic aspirants throwing money around with wild abandon, a great deal of it stuck to the wrong fingers.

A few skunks can pollute a large area. Although the great majority of businesspeople and government officials conducted their affairs with decency and honor, the whole atmosphere was fetid. The Man in the Moon, it was said, had to hold his nose when passing over America. Railroad promoters

---

*The expression is said to have derived from a speech by Representative Benjamin F. Butler, who allegedly waved before the House the bloodstained nightshirt of a Klan-flogged carpetbagger.

sometimes left gullible bond buyers with only "two streaks of rust and a right of way." Unscrupulous stock-market manipulators were a cinder in the public eye. Too many judges and legislators put their power up for hire. Cynics defined an honest politician as one who, when bought, would stay bought.

Notorious in the financial world were two millionaires, "Jubilee Jim" Fisk and Jay Gould. The corpulent Fisk—bold, impudent, unprincipled—often paraded in public with "cuddlesome women" behind a span of fast horses. He provided the "brass," and the undersized and cunning Gould provided the brains of the combination. The crafty pair concocted a plot in 1869 to corner the gold market. Their slippery game would work only if the federal Treasury refrained from selling gold. The conspirators worked on President Grant directly and also through his brother-in-law, who received $25,000 for his complicity. On "Black Friday" (September 24, 1869), Fisk and Gould madly bid the price of gold skyward, while scores of honest businesspeople were driven to the wall. The bubble finally broke when the Treasury, contrary to Grant's supposed assurances, was compelled to release gold. A congressional probe concluded that Grant had done nothing crooked, though he had acted stupidly and indiscreetly.

The infamous Tweed Ring in New York City vividly displayed the ethics (or lack of ethics) typical of the age. Burly "Boss" Tweed—240 pounds (109 kilograms) of rascality—employed bribery, graft, and fraudulent elections to milk the metropolis of as much as $200 million. He adopted the cynical rule "Addition, division, and silence." The books once recorded a payment of $138,000 to a plasterer for two days of labor. Honest citizens were cowed into silence. Protesters found their tax assessments raised.

Tweed's luck finally ran out. *The New York Times* secured damning evidence in 1871 and courageously published it, though offered $5 million not to do so. Gifted cartoonist Thomas Nast pilloried Tweed mercilessly, after spurning a heavy bribe to desist. The portly thief reportedly complained that his illiterate followers could not help seeing "them damn pictures." A New York attorney, Samuel J. Tilden, headed the prosecution and gained fame that later paved the path to his presidential nomination. Unbailed and unwept, Tweed died behind bars.

Can the Law Reach Him? 1872
Cartoonist Thomas Nast attacked "Boss" Tweed in a series of cartoons like this one that appeared in *Harper's Weekly* in 1872. Here Nast depicts the corrupt Tweed as a powerful giant, towering over a puny law force.

A Carnival of Corruption

With the atmosphere so badly contaminated, it was small wonder that the easygoing Grant apparently failed to scent some of the worst evildoing in public life. His cabinet was a nest of grafters and incompetents, with one notable exception, Secretary of State Hamilton Fish. Favor seekers haunted the White House, often plying Grant with cigars, wines, and horses. His election was a godsend to his in-laws of the Dent family, several dozen of whom attached themselves to the public payroll.

Grant was tarred by the Crédit Mobilier scandal, though the dirtiest work had been done in

1867–1868, before he took office. The Crédit Mobilier was a railroad construction company, formed by the insiders of the transcontinental Union Pacific Railway. They cleverly hired themselves to build the railroad line and sometimes paid themselves as much as $50,000 a mile for construc-

---

In a famous series of newspaper interviews in 1905, George Washington Plunkitt (1842–1924), a political "boss" in the same Tammany Hall Democratic political "machine" that had spawned William Marcy ("Boss") Tweed, candidly described his ethical and political principles:

"Everybody is talkin' these days about Tammany men growin' rich on graft, but nobody thinks of drawin' the distinction between honest graft and dishonest graft. There's all the difference in the world between the two. Yes, many of our men have grown rich in politics. I have myself. I've made a big fortune out of the game, and I'm gettin' richer every day, but I've not gone in for dishonest graft—blackmailin' gamblers, saloonkeepers, disorderly people, etc.—and neither has any of the men who have made big fortunes in politics.

"There's an honest graft, and I'm an example of how it works. I might sum up the whole thing by sayin': 'I seen my opportunities and I took 'em.'

"Just let me explain by examples. My party's in power in the city, and it's goin' to undertake a lot of public improvements. Well, I'm tipped off, say, that they're going to lay out a new park at a certain place.

"I see my opportunity and I take it. I go to that place and I buy up all the land I can in the neighborhood. Then the board of this or that makes its plan public, and there is a rush to get my land, which nobody cared particular for before.

"Ain't it perfectly honest to charge a good price and make a profit on my investment and foresight? Of course, it is. Well, that's honest graft."

---

tion that actually cost only $30,000 a mile. In one year the Crédit Mobilier paid dividends of 348 percent. Fearing that Congress might blow the whistle, the company furtively distributed shares of its valuable stock to key congressmen.

A New York newspaper finally exposed the scandal in 1872, and a congressional investigation confirmed some of the worst charges. Two members of Congress were formally censured, and the vice president of the United States was shown to have accepted twenty shares of stock and some dividends.

The breath of scandal in Washington also reeked of alcohol. In 1875 the public learned that a sprawling Whiskey Ring had robbed the Treasury of millions in excise-tax revenues. "Let no guilty man escape," insisted President Grant. But when his own private secretary turned up among the culprits, the president speedily changed his views. He volunteered a written statement to the jury, with all the weight of his exalted office behind it, and the thief escaped. News of further rottenness in the Grant administration broke in 1876, when Secretary of War William Belknap was shown to have pocketed some $24,000 by selling the privilege of disbursing supplies—often junk—to the Indians. The House voted unanimously to impeach him. Belknap resigned the same day, thus avoiding conviction by the Senate. Grant, ever loyal to his crooked cronies, accepted his resignation "with great regret."

The Liberal Republican Revolt of 1872

By 1872 a powerful wave of disgust with Grantism was beginning to build up throughout the nation, even before some of the worst scandals had been exposed. Reform-minded citizens banded together in the Liberal Republican party. Voicing the slogan "Turn the Rascals Out," they urged purification of the Washington administration and an end to military Reconstruction.

The Liberal Republicans muffed their chance when their Cincinnati nominating convention, heavily studded with starry-eyed reformers, fell into the hands of amateurish journalists and scheming politicians. This "conclave of cranks" now astounded the country by nominating the brilliant but erratic Horace Greeley for the presidency. Greeley was a mind-boggling choice. Although he was a fearless editor of the *New York Tribune,* he was dogmatic,

Can Greeley and the Democrats "Swallow" Each Other, 1872 This cartoon by Thomas Nast is a Republican gibe at the forced alliance between these former foes. General W. T. Sherman wrote from Paris to his brother, "I feel amazed to see the turn things have taken. Grant who never was a Republican is your candidate; and Greeley who never was a Democrat, but quite the reverse, is the Democratic candidate."

emotional, petulant, and notoriously unsound in his political judgments.

More astonishing still was the action of the office-hungry Democrats, who endorsed Greeley's candidacy. In swallowing Greeley the Democrats "ate crow" in large gulps, for the eccentric editor had long blasted them as traitors, slave shippers, saloon keepers, horse thieves, and idiots. Yet Greeley pleased the Democrats, North and South, when he pleaded for a clasping of hands across "the bloody chasm." The Republicans dutifully renominated Grant, and the voters were thus presented with a choice between two candidates who had made their careers in fields other than politics and who were both eminently unqualified, by temperament and lifelong training, for high political office.

Much mud was spattered along the campaign trail in 1872. Greeley was denounced as an atheist, a communist, a free-lover, a vegetarian, a brown-bread eater, and a cosigner of Jefferson Davis's bail bond, which in fact he had signed. "Grant beat Davis—Greeley bailed him," ran the slogan. The much-defamed Greeley was heard to wonder if he were running for the presidency or the penitentiary. Grant, in turn, was derided as an ignoramus, a drunkard, and a swindler. But the regular Republicans, chanting "Grant us another term," pulled the president through. The count in the electoral column was 286 to 66, in the popular column 3,596,745 to 2,843,446. For Horace Greeley the final outcome was tragic. Within a month he lost the election, his wife, his job, his mind, and his life.

Liberal Republican agitation frightened the regular Republicans into cleaning their own house before they were thrown out of it. The Republican Congress in 1872 passed a general amnesty act, removing political disabilities from all but some five hundred former Confederate leaders. Congress also moved to reduce high Civil War tariffs and to fumigate the Grant administration with mild civil-service reform. Like many American third parties, the Liberal Republicans left some enduring footprints, even in defeat.

Depression and Demands for Inflation

The evil repute of the scandal-scarred Grant years was worsened by the paralyzing panic that broke in 1873. Bursting with startling rapidity, the crash was one of those periodic plummets that roller-coastered the economy in this age of unbridled capitalist expansion. Overreaching promoters had laid more railroad track, sunk more mines, erected more factories, and cleared more grainfields than existing markets could bear. Bankers, in turn, had made too many imprudent loans to finance those enterprises. When profits failed to materialize, loans went unpaid, and the whole credit-based house of cards fluttered down.

The first severe shock came with the failure of the New York banking firm of Jay Cooke & Company, headed by the fabulously rich Jay Cooke, financier of the Civil War. The aftershocks of the Cooke collapse were felt all along the economic fault line. Boom times became gloom times as more than fifteen thousand businesses went bankrupt. In New York City an army of unemployed riotously battled police. Black Americans were hard hit. The Freedman's Savings and Trust Company had made unsecured loans to several companies that went under.

Black depositors who had entrusted over $7 million to the bank lost their savings, and black economic development and black confidence in savings institutions went down with it.

Hard times were especially distressing to debtors, who began to clamor for inflationary policies to lessen the value of their debts. Proponents of inflation breathed new life into the issue of greenbacks. During the war $450 million of the "folding money" had been issued, but it had depreciated under a cloud of popular mistrust and dubious legality.* By 1868 the Treasury had already withdrawn $100 million of the "battle-born currency" from circulation, and "hard-money" people everywhere looked forward to its complete disappearance. But now afflicted agrarian and debtor groups—"cheap-money" supporters—clamored for a reissuance of the greenbacks. With a crude but essentially accurate grasp of monetary theory, they reasoned that more money meant cheaper money and, hence, rising prices and easier-to-pay debts. Creditors, of course, reasoning from the same premises, advocated precisely the opposite policy. They had no desire to see the money they had loaned repaid in depreciated dollars.

The "hard-money" advocates carried the day in 1874 when they persuaded the confused Grant to veto a bill to print more paper money. They scored another victory in the Resumption Act of 1875, which pledged the government to the further withdrawal of greenbacks from circulation and to the redemption of all paper currency in gold at face value, beginning in 1879.

Down but not out, debtors now looked for relief to another precious metal, silver. The "sacred white metal," they claimed, had received a raw deal. In the early 1870s, the Treasury stubbornly and unrealistically maintained that an ounce of silver was worth only 1/16 as much as an ounce of gold, though open-market prices for silver were higher. Silver miners thus stopped offering their shiny product for sale to the federal mints. With no silver flowing into the federal coffers, Congress formally dropped the coinage of silver dollars in 1873. Fate then played a sly joke when new silver discoveries later in the 1870s shot production up and forced silver prices down. Westerners from silver-mining states joined with debtors in assailing the "Crime of '73," demanding a return to the "Dollar of Our Daddies." This demand, like the demand for more greenbacks, was essentially a call for inflation. Republicans resisted this call and counted on Grant to hold the line against it. He did not disappoint them.

Grant's name continued to be associated with sound money, though not with sound government. The Treasury began to accumulate gold stocks against the appointed day for resumption of metallic-money payments. Coupled with the reduction of greenbacks, this policy was called "contraction." It had a noticeable deflationary effect—the amount of money per capita in circulation actually *decreased* between 1870 and 1880, from $19.42 to $19.37. Contraction probably worsened the impact of the depression. But the new policy did restore the government's credit rating, and it brought the embattled greenbacks up to their full face value. When Redemption Day came in 1879, few greenback holders bothered to exchange the lighter and more convenient bills for gold.

A compromise was struck between silver-loving "soft-money" advocates and silver-scorning "sound-money" proponents with the Bland-Allison Act of 1878, masterminded by Representative Richard P. ("Silver Dick") Bland of Missouri. The law instructed the Treasury to buy and coin between $2 million and $4 million worth of silver bullion each month. But the government dampened the hopes of inflationists when it stuck steadfastly to a policy of buying only the legal minimum.

Republican hard-money policy had a political backlash. It helped elect a Democratic House of Representatives in 1874, and in 1878 it spawned a Greenback Labor party that polled over a million votes and elected fourteen members of Congress.

Pallid Politics in the Gilded Age

The political seesaw was delicately balanced throughout most of the Gilded Age (a sarcastic name given to the post–Civil War era by Mark Twain in 1873). Even a slight nudge could tip the teeter-totter to the advantage of the opposition party. Every presidential election was a squeaker, and the

---

*The Supreme Court in 1870 declared the Civil War Legal Tender Act unconstitutional. With the concurrence of the Senate, Grant thereupon added to the bench two justices who could be counted on to help reverse that decision, which happened in 1871. This is how the Court grew to its current size of nine justices.

majority party in the House of Representatives switched six times in the eleven sessions between 1869 and 1891. In only three sessions did the same party control the House, the Senate, and the White House. Wobbling in such shaky equilibrium, politicians were not inclined to take bold, firm stands. They tended, instead, to tiptoe timidly, producing a political record that was often trivial and petty.

Few significant economic issues separated the major parties. Democrats and Republicans saw very nearly eye-to-eye on major questions like the tariff, currency, and civil-service reform. Yet despite their rough agreement on these national matters, the two parties were ferociously competitive with each other. They were tightly and efficiently organized, and they commanded fierce loyalty from their members. Voter turnouts reached heights unmatched before or since. Nearly 80 percent of eligible voters cast their ballots in presidential elections in the three decades after the Civil War. On election days, droves of the party faithful tramped behind marching bands to the polling places, and "ticket splitting," or failing to vote the straight party line, was as rare as a silver dollar.

How can this apparent paradox of political consensus and partisan fervor be explained? The answer lies in the sharp ethnic and cultural differences in the membership of the two parties—in distinctions of style and tone, and especially of religious sentiment. Republican voters tended to adhere to those creeds that traced their lineage to Puritanism. They stressed strict codes of personal morality and believed that government should play a role in regulating both the economic and the moral affairs of the community as a whole. Democrats, among whom immigrant Lutherans and Roman Catholics figured heavily, were more likely to adhere to faiths that took a less stern view of human weakness. Their religions professed toleration of differences in an imperfect world, and they spurned government efforts to impose a single moral standard on the entire society. These differences in temperament and religious values often produced raucous political contests at the local level, where issues like prohibition and education loomed large.

Democrats, still somewhat cursed with the charge of wartime Copperheadism, had a solid electoral base in the South. They also ran well in the northern industrial cities, which were packed with immigrants and controlled by well-oiled political machines. Republicans could usually count on winning the Midwest and the rural and small-town Northeast, still populous enough to swing the northeastern states regularly into the Republican column. Grateful freedmen in the South, considering the party their best hope for change, continued to vote Republican in significant numbers. Another important bloc of Republican ballots came from the members of the Grand Army of the Republic (GAR)—a politically potent fraternal organization of several hundred thousand Union veterans of the Civil War. The initials *GAR* were humorously interpreted to mean "Generally All Republicans." The lifeblood of both parties was patronage—disbursing jobs by the bucketful in return for votes, kickbacks, and party service. In this postwar era of vastly expanded government employment—especially in the postal service —the old practice of awarding the spoils to the victors had mushroomed into a big business. Reformers increasingly assailed the spoils system as both the nemesis of efficient public administration and the nutrient of rampant corruption.

Boisterous infighting beset the Republican party in the 1870s and 1880s. A "Stalwart" faction, led by the handsome and imperious Roscoe ("Lord Roscoe") Conkling, U.S. senator from New York, unblushingly embraced the time-honored system of swapping civil-service jobs for votes. Once needled by a rival as having a "turkey gobbler strut," Conkling was forever after portrayed by cartoonists as a gobbling turkey. Opposed to the Conklingites were the so-called Half-Breeds, who flirted coyly with civil-service reform, but whose real quarrel with the Stalwarts was over who should grasp the ladle that dished out the spoils. The champion of the Half-Breeds was James G. Blaine, a radiantly personable congressman from Maine. Gifted with a photographic memory for names and faces, he was a politician's politician. He had a fine physical presence, flashing eyes, a thrilling speaking voice, and an elastic conscience. A perennial contender for the presidency, Blaine was inclined to demagoguery in his pursuit of the office. He would twist the British lion's tail for Irish votes and wave the bloody shirt for veterans' votes. The fact that he himself had not heard the whine of Confederate bullets led to the gibe, "Invisible in war, invincible in peace." But despite all the color of their personalities, Conkling and Blaine succeeded for the most part only in stalemating each other and deadlocking their party.

The Hayes-Tilden Standoff, 1876

Hangers-on around Grant, like fleas urging their ailing dog to live, begged the "Old Man" to try for a third term in 1876. The general, blind to his own ineptitudes, showed a disquieting willingness. But the House, by a lopsided bipartisan vote of 233 to 18, derailed the third-term bandwagon. It passed a resolution that sternly reminded the country—and Grant—of the antidictator implications of the two-term tradition.

With Grant out of the running and with the Conklingites and Blaineites neutralizing each other, the Republicans turned to a compromise candidate, Rutherford B. Hayes, who was obscure enough to be dubbed "The Great Unknown." Of medium build, he displayed a high-domed forehead above a heavy reddish beard. Wounded several times as an officer in the Civil War, he appealed to veterans. His foremost qualification was the fact that he hailed from the electorally doubtful but potent state of Ohio, where he had served three terms as governor. So crucial were the "swing" votes of Ohio in the cliff-hanging presidential contests of the day that the state produced more than its share of presidential candidates. A political saying of the 1870s went,

> *Some are born great,*
> *Some achieve greatness,*
> *And some are born in Ohio.*

Pitted against the humdrum Hayes was the Democratic nominee, Samuel J. Tilden, who had risen to fame as the man who bagged Boss Tweed in New York. Boyish-faced and smooth-shaven (unusual in that bewhiskered age), Tilden was slightly built, nervous, droopy-eyed, and weak-voiced ("Whispering Sammy"). Campaigning against Republican scandal and for sweeping civil-service reform, Tilden racked up 184 electoral votes of the needed 185, with 20 votes in four states doubtful because of irregular returns (see the map below). Surely Tilden could pick up at least one of these, especially in view of the fact that he had polled 247,448 more popular votes than Hayes, 4,284,020 to 4,036,572.

Both parties scurried to send "visiting statesmen" to the contested southern states of Louisiana, South Carolina, and Florida where Republican regimes had not yet been "redeemed" by Southern Democrats forcing their way back into power. All three disputed states submitted two sets of returns, one Democratic and one Republican. As the weeks drifted by, the paralysis tightened. Here were the makings of an epochal constitutional crisis. The Constitution merely specifies that the electoral returns from the states shall be sent to Congress, and in the presence of the House and Senate they shall be *opened* by the president of the Senate (see the Twelfth Amendment). But who should *count* them? On this point the Constitution was silent. If counted by the president of the Senate (a

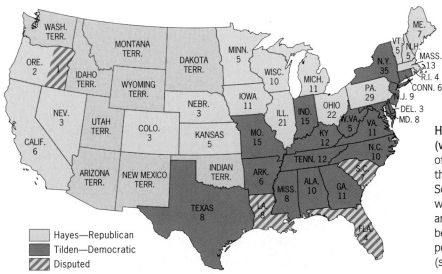

Hayes-Tilden Disputed Election of 1876 (with electoral vote by state)   Nineteen of the twenty disputed votes composed the total electoral count of Louisiana, South Carolina, and Florida. The twentieth was one of Oregon's three votes, cast by an elector who turned out to be ineligible because he was a federal officeholder (a postmaster), contrary to the Constitution (see Art. II, Sec I, para. 2).

Republican), the Republican returns would be selected. If counted by the Speaker of the House (a Democrat), the Democratic returns would be chosen.

The Compromise of 1877 and the End of Reconstruction

Clash or compromise was the stark choice. The danger loomed that there would be no president on Inauguration Day, March 4, 1877. "Tilden or Blood!" cried Democratic hotheads, and some of their "Minute Men" began to drill with arms. But behind the scenes, frantically laboring statesmen gradually hammered out an agreement in the Henry Clay tradition—the Compromise of 1877.

The election deadlock itself was to be broken by the Electoral Count Act, which passed Congress early in 1877. It set up an electoral commission consisting of fifteen men selected from the Senate, the House, and the Supreme Court. The fifteenth member of the commission, according to Democratic schemes, was to have been the giant-sized Justice David Davis, an independent—with Democratic leanings. But at the last moment he resigned from the bench to go to the Senate, and the only remaining members of the Supreme Court were Republicans. One Republican rhymester chortled at the Democrats:

> They digged a pit, they digged it deep,
> They digged it for their brother;
> But through their sin they did fall in
> The pit they digged for t' other.

In February 1877, about a month before Inauguration Day, the Senate and House met together in an electric atmosphere to settle the dispute. The roll of the states was tolled off alphabetically. When Florida was reached—the first of the three southern states with two sets of returns—the disputed documents were referred to the electoral commission, which sat in a nearby chamber. After prolonged discussion the members agreed, by the partisan vote of eight Republicans to seven Democrats, to accept the Republican returns. Outraged Democrats in Congress, smelling defeat, undertook to launch a filibuster "until hell froze over."

Renewed deadlock was avoided by the rest of the complex Compromise of 1877, already partially concluded behind closed doors. The Democrats reluctantly agreed that Hayes might take office in return for his withdrawing intimidating federal troops from the two states in which they remained, Louisiana and South Carolina. Among various concessions, the Republicans assured the Democrats a place at the presidential patronage trough and support for a bill subsidizing the Texas and Pacific Railroad's construction of a southern transcontinental line. Not all of these promises were kept in later years, including the Texas and Pacific subsidy. But the deal held together long enough to break the dangerous electoral standoff. The Democrats permitted Hayes to receive the remainder of the disputed returns—all by the partisan vote of 8 to 7. So close was the margin of safety that the explosive issue was settled only three days before the new president was officially sworn into office. The nation breathed a collective sigh of relief.

The compromise bought peace at a price. Violence was averted by sacrificing the black freedmen in the South. With the Hayes-Tilden deal, the Republican party quietly abandoned its commitment to black equality. That commitment had been weakening, in any case. The Civil Rights Act of 1875 was in a sense the last feeble gasp of the congressional radical Republicans. The act supposedly guaranteed equal accommodations in public places and prohibited racial discrimination in jury selection, but the law was born toothless and stayed that way for nearly a century. The Supreme Court pronounced much of the act unconstitutional in the *Civil Rights Cases* (1883). The Court declared that the Fourteenth Amendment prohibited only *government* violations of civil rights, not the denial of civil rights by *individuals*, unaided by government authority. Hayes clinched the bargain soon after his inauguration, when he appointed a former Confederate officer as postmaster general. Hayes also withdrew the last federal troops that were protecting Reconstructed state governments, and the bayonet-

Composition of the Electoral Commission, 1877

Members	Republicans	Democrats
Senate (Republican majority)	3	3
House (Democratic majority)	2	3
Supreme Court	3	2
TOTAL	8	7

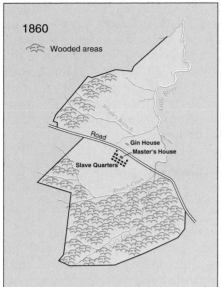
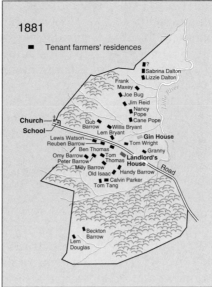

1860

🌳 Wooded areas

1881

■ Tenant farmers' residences

A Southern Plantation, Before and After the Civil War   The emancipated blacks moved out of the slave quarters and into humble cabins dispersed around the plantation. The master had now become the landlord and the employer, and the slaves had become tenant farmers and sharecroppers—but were they better off?

backed Republican regimes collapsed in the wake of the blue-clad soldiers' departure.

The Democratic South speedily solidified and swiftly suppressed the now friendless blacks. Reconstruction, for better or worse, was officially ended. Through fraud and intimidation, white Democrats resumed political power in the South. Blacks who tried to vote faced unemployment, eviction, and physical harm. Moreover, in the 1890s, southern states added literacy requirements, voter-registration laws, and poll taxes to ensure full-scale disfranchisement of the South's black population.

The white South also made blacks economically dependent. Blacks (and poor whites) were forced into sharecropping and tenant farming. Former slaves often found themselves at the mercy of former masters who were now their landlords and merchants. Through the "crop-lien" system, store-keepers extended credit to small farmers for food and supplies and in return took a lien on their

Weighing Cotton   Cotton pickers who once toiled under the lash as slaves now worked for wages as sharecroppers, but they were still beholden to the plantation owner. At this "weigh up," the "Boss Man" carefully calculates his profit as each hamper is filled, while the sharecroppers await their meager payment.

harvests. Shrewd merchants manipulated the system so that farmers remained perpetually in debt to them. For generations to come, southern blacks were condemned to eke out a threadbare living under conditions scarcely better than slavery.

With white southerners back in the political saddle, daily discrimination against blacks grew increasingly oppressive. What had started as informal separation of blacks and whites in the immediate postwar years developed during the 1890s into systematic state-level legal codes of segregation known as Jim Crow laws. The Supreme Court validated the South's segregationist social order in the case of *Plessy* v. *Ferguson* (1896). It ruled that "separate but equal" facilities were constitutional under the "equal protection" clause of the Fourteenth Amendment. But in reality the quality of African-American life was grotesquely unequal to that of whites. Segregated in inferior schools and separated from whites in virtually all public facilities, including railroad cars, theaters, and even restrooms, blacks were assaulted daily by galling reminders of their second-class citizenship. To ensure the stability of this political and economic "new order," southern whites dealt harshly with any black who dared to violate the South's racial code of conduct. A record number of blacks were lynched during the 1890s, sometimes as punishment for crimes against whites, but most often for the "crime" of asserting themselves as equals. It would take a second Reconstruction, nearly a century later, to redress the racist imbalance of southern society.

Class Conflicts and Ethnic Clashes

The year 1877 marked more than the end of Reconstruction. As the curtains officially closed on regional warfare, they opened on scenes of class warfare. The explosive atmosphere was largely a by-product of the long years of depression and deflation following the panic of 1873. Railroad workers faced particularly hard times. When the presidents of the nation's four largest railroads collectively decided in 1877 to cut employees' wages by 10 percent, the workers struck back. President Hayes's decision to call in federal troops to quell the unrest brought the striking laborers an outpouring of working-class support. Work stoppages spread like wildfire in cities from Baltimore to St. Louis. When the battling between workers and soldiers ended after several weeks, over 100 people had died.

The failure of the great railroad strike exposed the weakness of the labor movement. Racial and ethnic fissures among workers fractured labor unity and were particularly acute between the Irish and Chinese in California (see "Makers of America: The Chinese," pp. 524–525). By 1880 the Golden State counted seventy-five thousand Asian newcomers, about 9 percent of its entire population. Mostly poor, uneducated, single males, they derived predominantly from the Taishan district of K'uang-t'ung (Guangdong) province in southern China. They had originally come to America to dig in the gold fields and to sledgehammer the tracks of the transcontinental railroads across the West. When the gold supply petered out and the tracks were laid, many —perhaps half of those who arrived before the 1880s —returned home to China with their meager savings.

Those who remained in America faced extraordinary hardships. They worked at the most menial jobs, often as cooks, laundrymen, or domestic servants. Without women or families, they were

Persons in United States Lynched [by race], 1882–1970*

Year	Whites	Blacks	Total
1882	64	49	113
1885	110	74	184
1890	11	85	96
1895	66	113	179
1900	9	106	115
1905	5	57	62
1910	9	67	76
1915	13	56	69
1920	8	53	61
1925	0	17	17
1930	1	20	21
1935	2	18	20
1940	1	4	5
1945	0	1	1
1950	1	1	2
1965	0	0	0

*There were no lynchings in 1965–1970. In every year from 1882 (when records were first kept) to 1964, the number of lynchings corresponded roughly to the figures given here. The worst year was 1892, when 161 blacks and 69 whites were lynched (total 230); the next worst was 1884, when 164 whites and 51 blacks were lynched (total 211).

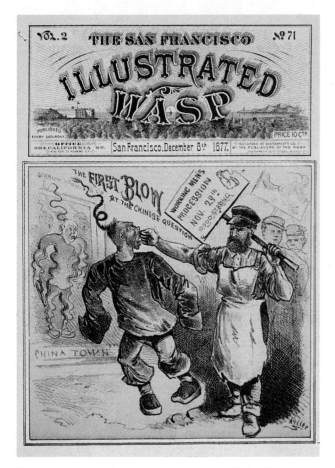

The First Blow at the Chinese Question, 1877   Caucasian workers, seething with economic anxiety and ethnic prejudice, savagely mistreated the Chinese in California in the 1870s.

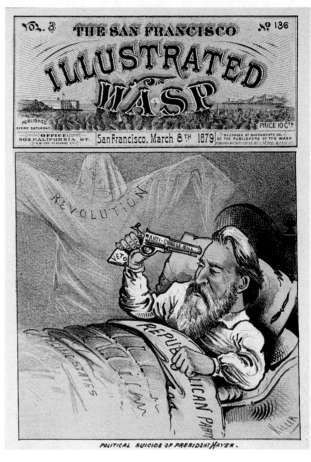

Political Suicide of President Hayes, 1879   The president risked political suicide by his courageous veto of the Chinese Exclusion Act, which was especially popular among anti-Chinese Californians. The bill passed soon after he left office.

marooned in a land where they were neither wanted nor wanted to be. They lived lonely lives, bereft of the children who in other immigrant communities eased their parents' assimilation through their exposure to the English language and American customs in school. The phrase "not a Chinaman's chance" emerged in this era to describe the daunting odds against which they struggled.

In San Francisco, Irish-born demagogue Denis Kearney incited his followers to violent abuse of the hapless Chinese. The Kearneyites, many of whom were recently arrived immigrants from Europe, fiercely resented the competition of cheap labor from the still more recently arrived Chinese. The beef-eater, they claimed, had no chance against the rice-eater in a life-and-death struggle for jobs and wages. The present tens of thousands of Chinese "coolies" were regarded as a menace; the prospective millions, as a calamity. Taking to the streets, gangs of Kearneyites terrorized the Chinese by shearing off precious pigtails. Some victims were murdered outright.

Congress finally responded to all this uproar in 1879, when it passed a bill severely restricting the influx of Chinese immigrants. But Hayes, ever the man of honor, vetoed this discriminatory measure on the grounds that it violated the existing treaty with China. Angry Californians burned the president in effigy. Once the scrupulous Hayes was out of the way, in 1882, Congress slammed the door on Chinese laborers with the enactment of the Chinese Exclusion Act, and it stayed slammed until 1943.

The Chinese

In the late nineteenth century, the burgeoning industries and booming frontier towns of the United States' Pacific coast hungered for laborers to wrench minerals from stubborn rock, to lay down railroad track through untamed wastelands, and to transform dry expanses into fertile fields of fruit and vegetables. In faraway Asia the Chinese answered the call. Contributing their muscle to the building of the West, they dug in the gold mines and helped to lay the transcontinental railroads that stitched together the American nation.

The first Chinese had arrived in Spanish America as early as 1565. But few followed those earliest pioneers until the 1848 discovery of gold in California attracted people from all over the world to

Surviving Central Pacific Railroad Workers   These men, posing in 1919, helped build the railroad during the 1860s.

America's Pacific coast. Among them were many fortune-hungry Chinese who sailed into San Francisco, which Chinese immigrants named the "golden mountain."

The California boom coincided with the culmination of years of tumult and suffering in China. The once great Chinese Empire was disintegrating, while a few ruthless landlords, like looters, grabbed control of nearly every acre of farmland. In destructive complement to this internal disarray, the European imperial powers forced their way into the unstable country, seeking to unlock the riches of a nation that had been closed to outsiders for centuries.

Faced with economic hardship and political turmoil, more than 2 million Chinese left their homeland between 1840 and 1900, for destinations as diverse as Southeast Asia, Peru, Hawaii, and Cuba, with more than three hundred thousand entering the United States. Although their numbers included a few merchants and artisans, most were unskilled country folk. In some cases families pooled their money to send out a son, but most travelers, desperately poor, obtained their passage through Chinese middlemen, who advanced them ship fare in return for the emigrants' promise to work off their debts after they landed. This contracting sometimes led to conditions so cruel that the practice was ignominiously called pig selling.

The Chinese-America of the late-nineteenth-century West was overwhelmingly a bachelor society. Women of good repute rarely made the passage. Of the very few Chinese women who ventured to California at this time, most became prostitutes. Many of them had been deceived by the false promise of honest jobs.

Although a stream of workers returned to their homeland, many Chinese stayed. "Chinatowns" sprang up wherever economic opportunities pre-

Chinese Butcher Shop,
San Francisco, California, c. 1890

sented themselves—in railroad towns, farming villages, and cities. Chinese in these settlements spoke their own language, enjoyed the fellowship of their own compatriots, and sought safety from prejudice and violence, never rare in American society. Many immigrant clubs, American adaptations of Chinese traditions of loyalty to clan or region, were established in these communities. Rivaling such clubs and associations were the secret societies known as tongs. The word *tong*—literally, "meeting hall"— acquired a sinister reputation among non-Chinese, for the tongs counted the poorest and shadiest immigrants among their members. These were people without ties to a clan, those individuals most alienated from traditional Chinese organizations and from American society as well.

After 1882 the Chinese Exclusion Act barred nearly all Chinese from the United States for six decades. Many of the bachelors who had made the long journey to America died or returned home. Slowly, however, those men and the few women who remained raised families and reared a new generation of Chinese Americans. Like their immigrant parents, this second generation suffered from discrimination. They had to eke out a living in jobs despised by Caucasian laborers or take daunting risks in small entrepreneurial ventures. Yet many hardworking Chinese did manage to open their own restaurants, laundries, and other small businesses. The enterprises formed a solid economic foundation for their small community and remain a source of livelihood for many Chinese-Americans even today.

Chinese Population in the Continental United States, 1850–1900

Year	Population	Males per One Female	Percentage U.S.-Born	Total Chinese Immigrants in Preceding Decade[a]
1850	4,018[b]	——	——	——
1860	34,933	19	——	41,397
1870	63,199	13	1	64,301
1880	105,465	21	1	123,201
1890	107,488	27	3	61,711
1900	89,863	19	10	14,799

[a]Includes Chinese immigrants in Hawaii after 1898.   [b]Estimated

"Cold Water" Gets Cold Shoulder

Rutherford ("Rutherfraud") B. Hayes took office with a cloud over his title. Newspapers pilloried him as "Old 8-to-7" and "His Fraudulency," and cartoonists sketched him with "Fraud" on his honest brow. All this cut him deeply. A man of unsullied honor and high ideas—a "Queen Victoria in breeches"—he believed himself rightfully elected. Lucy Webb Hayes, his wife and childhood sweetheart, was a kindred spirit. The family prayed daily; and because both the president and Mrs. Hayes were temprance advocates, "Lemonade Lucy" served no alcohol. The "cold-water administration" swept the fetid, smoke-laden atmosphere out of the wineless White House.

Hayes accomplished little that was lasting—except writing "finished" to Reconstruction. His legislative record was negligible, and his political record was a disaster. As the presidential campaign of 1880 approached, Hayes was a man without a party. Denounced as "Granny" Hayes and a "Goody Two-Shoes" reformer, he was openly repudiated by the old-line politicians. He had earlier declared himself to be a single-termer, and this decision proved to be a face-saver because he probably could not have won renomination in any event.

The Garfield Interlude

Having freed itself of Hayes, the Republican party sought a new standard-bearer for 1880. Deadlocked for thirty-five ballots by the usual Stalwart–Half-Breed standoff, the Republicans finally broke the impasse when they nominated for the presidency a "dark-horse" candidate, James A. Garfield from the electorally powerful state of Ohio. Born in a log cabin, "Boatman Jim" had struggled up from poverty by driving mules along the towpaths of the Ohio Canal. He had served honorably as a Civil War officer, rising to the rank of major general.

Crestfallen spoilsmen received some slight consolation. The delegates chose for the vice presidency a notorious Stalwart, Senator Conkling's henchman Chester A. Arthur of New York. The platform declared emphatically for the protective tariff and somewhat feebly for reform of the civil service, sneeringly labeled the "snivel service" by those who plundered it for political gain. A Republican delegate from Texas blurted, "What are we here for except the offices?"

Wrathful Democrats, still seething over having been robbed of the presidency in 1876, nominated another former Civil War general, Winfield S. Hancock. He appealed to veterans as a hero wounded at Gettysburg, and he was popular in the South, where he had fair-mindedly headed one of the military Reconstruction districts. The Democratic platform called for civil-service reform and a "tariff for revenue only."

The campaigners shunned real controversy like leprosy, as happened in so many electoral contests during this politically cautious era. Turning their backs on the festering problems of debt-burdened farmers and powerless laborers, Republicans strove desperately to wring another president from the bloody shirt by verbally refighting the Civil War. They drenched Indiana with Republican money

President and Mrs. Rutherford B. Hayes   The teetotalling Hayes family symbolized Victorian probity—a welcome change from the flamboyantly corrupt atmosphere of the Grant administration. But Hayes had scant political talents. The historian Henry Adams wrote that Hayes "is a third-rate nonentity, whose only recommendation is that he is obnoxious to no one."

President James A. Garfield (1831–1881)
He was the second president to be killed by an assassin's bullet. He may have had a premonition; two days before the shooting, he called in Lincoln's son for an hour of recollection of the 1865 assassination.

Theodore Roosevelt (1858–1919), an ardent civil-service reformer, condemned the patronage system as

"tending to degrade American politics. . . . The men who are in office only for what they can make out of it are thoroughly unwholesome citizens, and their activity in politics is simply noxious. . . . Decent private citizens must inevitably be driven out of politics if it is suffered to become a mere selfish scramble for plunder, where victory rests with the most greedy, the most cunning, the most brazen. The whole patronage system is inimical to American institutions; it forms one of the gravest problems with which democratic and republican government has to grapple."

Office-hungry Republicans besieged the White House. "My God!" exclaimed an exasperated Garfield. "What is there in this place that a man should ever want to get into it?" He rewarded his chief political benefactor, James G. Blaine, with the prize plum of the secretaryship of state. The Half-Breed Blaine immediately set out to persuade the president to clip the wings of his perennial Stalwart nemesis, the "turkey-gobbler" Senator Roscoe Conkling of New York. Conkling, a colossus of conceit, fought back bitterly, especially when the president appointed a staunch anti-Conklingite to the coveted office of collector of the port of New York.

Then, as the political battle was raging, tragedy struck. A disappointed and mentally deranged office seeker, Charles J. Guiteau, shot President Garfield in the back in a Washington railroad station. Garfield lingered in agony for eleven weeks and died on September 19, 1881. Guiteau, when seized, reportedly cried, "I am a Stalwart. Arthur is now President of the United States." The implication was that now the Conklingites would all get good jobs. Guiteau's attorneys argued that he was not guilty because of his incapacity to distinguish right from wrong—an early instance of the "insanity defense." The defendant himself demonstrated his weak grip on reality when he asked all those who had benefited politically by the assassination to contribute to his defense fund. These tactics

("soap"), helping to grease it into the Republican column. Energetic Democrats, equally oblivious to deepening economic and social injustices, harped on Garfield's alleged receipt of $329 in stock dividends in the Crédit Mobilier scandal. They chalked those telltale figures on buildings, walls, and fences.

Garfield, "the Canal Boy," barely scraped across the electoral reefs. He polled only 39,213 more votes than Hancock—4,453,295 to 4,414,082—but his margin in the electoral column was a comfortable 214 to 155. The new president was an able and generous man and a devoted son who turned and kissed his mother after taking the inaugural oath. But he had one serious weakness. He hated to hurt people's feelings by saying "no."

availed little, as he was found guilty of murder and hanged.

Statesmen are dead politicians, the saying goes, and Garfield's "martyrdom" undoubtedly enhanced his reputation. Brutal though the thought is, Garfield's greatest single service to his country probably was to die when he did and as he did. An unwitting martyr to the evils of spoils seeking, he departed this life in such a way as to shock public servants into taking action to correct flagrant abuses. The nation might well bow its head in shame when it was a case of "an office—or your life."

Chester Arthur Takes Command

Garfield's death was rendered all the more shocking by the low repute of his successor. Arthur had no apparent qualifications for the presidency, though he was well endowed in other ways. The new president was a wealthy, handsome widower who enjoyed a richly stocked wine cellar and a wardrobe that included eighty pairs of trousers. His previous political experience consisted almost entirely of faithful service as a spoilsman in Conkling's sprawling New York political machine.

But observers at first underestimated Arthur. He proved to have unsuspected reserves of intelligence, idealism, and integrity. A Phi Beta Kappa graduate of Union College, he had served as a lawyer for the abolitionist cause while a young man in New York. Now the responsibilities of the highest office in the land lifted "Prince" Arthur to new, unexpected heights. He prosecuted with vigor certain post-office frauds and gave his former Conklingite cronies a frosty reception when they came seeking favors. "For the vice-presidency, I was indebted to Mr. Conkling," he declared, "but for the presidency of the United States my debt is to the Almighty."

Disgust with the circumstances of Garfield's murder churned the public's clamor for civil-service reform into an irresistible wave, and Arthur commendably threw his influence behind the movement. The Republican party itself began to reveal a previously undetected enthusiasm for reform. Republicans lost control of the House in the midterm elections of 1882, and they rightly feared further political hemorrhaging if they failed to find a cure for the ravages that the spoils system was inflicting on the body politic.

The Office Makes the Man, 1881   Besieged by his former New York cronies, Arthur tries to assert the dignity of his new presidential office.

The Pendleton Act of 1883—the so-called Magna Carta of civil-service reform—was the medicine finally applied to the long-suffering organs of the federal government. It prohibited, at least on paper, financial assessments on jobholders, including lowly scrubwomen. It established a merit system of making appointments to office on the basis of aptitude rather than "pull." It set up a Civil Service Commission, charged with administering open competitive examinations to applicants for posts in the classified service. Offices not "classified" by the president remained the fought-over footballs of politics.

Ironically, the success of the new antispoils law depended largely on the cooperation of a seasoned former spoilsman, President Arthur. Fortunately, he cooperated with vigor. By 1884 he had classified

> *New York political "boss" Roscoe Conkling (1829–1888) denounced the civil-service reformers in the New York* World *(1877):*
>
> "[The reformers'] vocation and ministry is to lament the sins of other people. Their stock in trade is rancid, canting self-righteousness. They are wolves in sheep's clothing. Their real object is office and plunder. When Dr. Johnson defined patriotism as the last refuge of a scoundrel, he was unconscious of the then undeveloped capabilities and uses of the word 'Reform.'"

nearly fourteen thousand federal offices, or about 10 percent of the total. A century later about 90 percent of federal offices were classified.

Civil-service reform was a necessary idea whose time had come. Yet like many well-intentioned reforms, it bred unintended problems of its own. The law skimmed off much of the cream of federal patronage and put it safely beyond the reach of grasping politicians. They were now forced to look elsewhere for money, "the mother's milk of politics." Increasingly, they turned to the bulging coffers of the big corporations. A new breed of "boss" emerged—less skilled at mobilizing small armies of immigrants and other voters on election day, but more adept at milking dollars from manufacturers and lobbyists. The Pendleton Act partially divorced

politics from patronage, but it helped drive politicians into "marriages of convenience" with big-business leaders.

One good term deserves another, and President Arthur's surprising display of integrity deserved to be rewarded with a presidential nomination "in his own right." But his reforms had offended too many powerful Republicans. His ungrateful party turned him out to pasture, and in 1886 he died of a cerebral hemorrhage.

The Blaine-Cleveland Mudslingers of 1884

James G. Blaine's persistence in pursuit of the presidential nomination finally paid off in 1884. The dashing Down Easter, blessed with almost every political asset except a reputation for honesty, was the clear choice of the Republican convention in Chicago. But many reform-minded Republicans gagged on Blaine's candidacy. They referred contemptuously to Blaine as the "tattooed man"—tattooed with countless political villainies. Blaine's enemies publicized the fishy-smelling "Mulligan letters," written by Blaine to a Boston businessman and linking the powerful politician to a corrupt deal involving federal favors to a southern railroad. At least one of the damning documents ended with the furtive warning "Burn this letter." Some reformers, unable to swallow Blaine, bolted to the Democrats. They were sneeringly dubbed *Mugwumps,* a word of

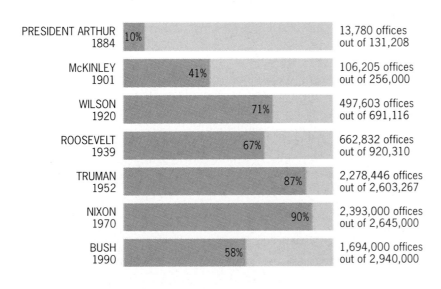

President	%	Offices
PRESIDENT ARTHUR 1884	10%	13,780 offices out of 131,208
McKINLEY 1901	41%	106,205 offices out of 256,000
WILSON 1920	71%	497,603 offices out of 691,116
ROOSEVELT 1939	67%	662,832 offices out of 920,310
TRUMAN 1952	87%	2,278,446 offices out of 2,603,267
NIXON 1970	90%	2,393,000 offices out of 2,645,000
BUSH 1990	58%	1,694,000 offices out of 2,940,000

Growth of Classified Civil Service (subject to competitive requirements) The most recent numbers reflect the changes mandated by the Postal Reorganization Act of 1971, which moved U.S. Postal Service employees from competitive to excepted service.

Little Lost Mugwumps Who Had Gone Astray James G. Blaine, depicted as Little Bo Peep, tries to woo the errant Mugwump reformers back into the Republican fold in 1884.

Indian derivation apparently meaning "great man" or "holier than thou."*

Victory-starved Democrats, scenting their own success in the nomination of a tainted Republican, turned enthusiastically to a noted reformer, Grover Cleveland. A burly bachelor with a soup-straining mustache and a taste for chewing tobacco, Cleveland was a solid but not brilliant lawyer of forty-seven. He had rocketed from the mayor's office in Buffalo to the governorship of New York and the presidential nomination in three short years. He enjoyed a well-deserved reputation for probity in office, gained especially by his veto, while governor, of a popular bill reducing fares on New York City's elevated railroads. Moralistic Americans, hungry for a candidate whose character they could applaud, seemed to have found their man at last in "Grover the Good."

Unfortunately, Cleveland's admirers soon got something of a shock. Resolute Republicans, digging for dirt in the past of bachelor Cleveland, unearthed the report that he had been involved in an amorous affair with a Buffalo widow, to whom an illegitimate son, now eight years old, had been born. Although several other men had been attentive to her at the same time, Cleveland had forthrightly assumed full responsibility and had made financial provision for the unwelcome offspring. Democratic elders, who had launched the campaign on a high ethical plane, were demoralized. They hurried to Cleveland and urged him to lie like a gentleman, but their ruggedly honest candidate insisted, "Tell the truth."

The campaign of 1884 sank to perhaps the lowest level in American experience, as the two parties grunted and shoved for the hog trough of office. Few fundamental differences separated them. Even the bloody shirt had faded to a pale pink.* Personalities, not principles, claimed the headlines. Enormous crowds of Democrats surged through city streets, chanting—to the rhythm of left, left, left, right, left—"Burn, burn, burn this letter!" Republicans taunted in return, "Ma, ma, where's my pa?" Defiant Democrats shouted back, "Gone to the White House, ha, ha, ha!"

The contest hinged on the state of New York, where Blaine blundered badly in the closing days of the campaign. A witless Republican clergyman damned the Democrats in a speech as the party of "Rum, Romanism, and Rebellion"—insulting at one swift stroke the race, the faith, and the patriotism of New York's numerous Irish-American voters. Blaine was present at the time but lacked the presence of

---

*Latter-day punsters gibed that the Mugwumps were priggish politicians who sat on the fence with their "mugs" on one side and their "wumps" on the other.

*Neither candidate served in the Civil War. Cleveland hired a substitute to go in his stead while he supported his widowed mother and two sisters. Blaine was the only candidate nominated by the Republicans from Grant through McKinley (1868 to 1900) who had not been a Civil War officer.

"I Want My Pa!"   Malicious anti-Cleveland cartoon.

dishonesty and private immorality. The desertion of the Mugwumps and Blaine's mishaps in New York were the deciding factors.

"Old Grover" Takes Over

Bull-necked Cleveland in 1885 was the first Democrat to take the oath of presidential office since Buchanan, twenty-eight years earlier. Huge question marks hung over his portly frame (5 feet, 11 inches, 250 pounds; 1.8 meters, 113 kilograms). Could the "party of disunion" be trusted to govern the Union? Would desperate Democrats, ravenously hungry after twenty-four years of exile, trample the frail sprouts of civil-service reform in a stampede to the patronage trough? Could Cleveland restore a measure of respect and power to the maligned and enfeebled presidency?

Cleveland was not a suave or skillful political leader. Inclined to put his foot down rather than slide it down, he could not work well in party harness. His fame had been built on his vetoes, and he at first showed little stomach for taking bold political initiatives. A staunch apostle of the hands-off creed of laissez-faire, the new president caused the hearts of businesspeople and bankers to beat with contentment. He summed up his political philosophy in 1887 when he vetoed a bill to provide seeds for drought-ravaged Texas farmers. "Though the people support the government," he declared, "the govern-

mind to repudiate the statement immediately. The pungent phrase, shortened to "RRR," stung and stuck. Blaine's silence seemed to give assent, and the wavering Irishmen who deserted his camp helped account for Cleveland's paper-thin plurality of about a thousand votes in New York State.

Cleveland swept the solid South and squeaked into office with 219 to 182 electoral votes and 4,879,507 to 4,850,293 popular votes. Basically, the issue narrowed down to a choice between public

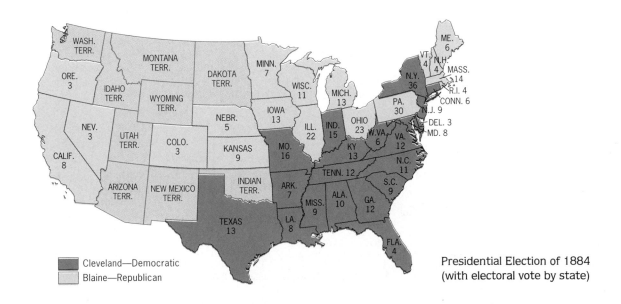

Cleveland—Democratic
Blaine—Republican

Presidential Election of 1884
(with electoral vote by state)

ment should not support the people." As tactless as a mirror and as direct as a bulldozer, he was outspoken, unbending, and profanely hot-tempered.

At the outset Cleveland calmed the disquiet of some of his critics. He narrowed the North-South chasm by naming to his cabinet two former Confederates, but he stopped far short of handing over the government to ex-rebels. As for the civil service, Cleveland was whipsawed between the demands of the Democratic faithful for jobs and the demands of the Mugwumps, who had helped elect him, for reform. Believing in the merit system, Cleveland at first favored the cause of the reformers; but he eventually caved in to the carpings of Democratic bosses and fired almost two-thirds of the 120,000 federal employees, including 40,000 incumbent (Republican) postmasters.

Military pensions gave Cleveland some of his most painful political headaches. The Union had tried to treat its veterans generously, but by the 1880s the pension legislation contained gaping loopholes and was aggressively abused. The prospect of easy access to Treasury dollars attracted grafters as honey attracts flies. Slippery pension attorneys ferreted out able-bodied veterans and induced them to file fraudulent claims. If the Pension Bureau proved uncompliant, the claimant might appeal to his congressman, who, mindful of the politically powerful Grand Army of the Republic (GAR), would often introduce a special bill.

Hundreds of private pension bills were thus logrolled through Congress and sent to the White House. Handouts were granted to deserters, to bounty jumpers, to men who never served, and to former soldiers who in later years had incurred disabilities in no way connected with war service. Cleveland, a slave to his conscience, read the bills carefully, vetoed several hundred of them, and then laboriously penned individual veto messages for Congress. Sometimes he waxed sarcastic, as when referring to one man's "terrific encounter with the measles." A Democrat and a nonveteran, Cleveland was in a vulnerable position when it came to fighting the pension-grabbers. Yet he showed real courage in taking them on. His fortitude was well displayed in 1887 when he risked the retribution of the GAR and vetoed a bill adding several hundred thousand new pensioners to the rolls.

Cleveland Battles for a Lower Tariff

During the Civil War, tariff schedules had been jacked up to new high levels, partly to raise revenues for the insatiable military machine. American industry, which was preponderantly in Republican hands, had profited from this protection and hated to see the sheltering benefits reduced in peacetime. But the high duties continued to pile up revenue at

Grover Cleveland (1837–1908)
A strong supporter of civil-service reform and tariff reduction, President-elect Cleveland was also the country's most eligible bachelor. In this cartoon of 1884, he is shown struggling to avoid office seekers on the one side and potential mothers-in-law on the other.

the customshouses, and by 1881 the Treasury was running an annual surplus amounting to an embarrassing $145 million. Most of the government's income, in those pre–income tax days, came from the tariff.

Congress could reduce the vexatious surplus in two ways. One was to squander it on pensions and "pork-barrel" bills and thus curry favor with veterans and other self-seeking groups. The other was to lower the tariff—something the big industrialists vehemently opposed. Grover Cleveland, the rustic Buffalo attorney, had known little and cared less about the tariff before entering the White House. But as he studied the subject, he was much impressed by the arguments for downward revision of the tariff schedules. Lower barriers would mean lower prices for consumers and less protection for monopolies. Most important, they would mean an end to the Treasury surplus, a standing mockery of Cleveland's professed belief in fiscal orthodoxy and small-government frugality. After much hesitation Cleveland saw his duty and overdid it.

Rejecting the advice of Democratic politicians, Cleveland decided to prod the hornet's nest of the tariff issue. "What's the use," he insisted, "of being elected or reelected unless you stand for something?" With his characteristic bluntness, Cleveland tossed an appeal for lower tariffs like a bombshell into the lap of Congress in late 1887. The annual message of the president had always been devoted to a review of the year's events, but Cleveland aimed his fire solely on the tariff.

The response was electric. Cleveland succeeded admirably in smoking the issue out into the open. Democrats were deeply depressed at the obstinacy of their chief. Republicans rejoiced at his apparent recklessness. The old warrior Blaine gloated, "There's one more President for us in [tariff] protection." For the first time in years, a real issue divided the two parties and would dominate the upcoming presidential election of 1888.

Harrison Ousts Cleveland in 1888

Dismayed Democrats, seeing no alternative, somewhat dejectedly nominated Grover Cleveland in their St. Louis convention. Eager Republicans turned to Benjamin Harrison, whose grandfather was former President William Henry ("Tippecanoe") Harrison. The grandson, "Little Ben," was joyously

hailed as "Young Tippecanoe" and was pictured wearing his grandfather's military hat. Democrats maliciously cartooned the pint-sized Indianan as rattling around ridiculously in the oversize martial headgear.

The campaign proceeded on a fairly high level, despite some feeble flapping of the bloody shirt and some further probing of Cleveland's private life. The "Beast of Buffalo," who had married his beautiful twenty-one-year-old ward (twenty-seven years his junior) during his second year in the White House, was absurdly accused of beating his wife during drunken fits. But the tariff was the prime issue. The two parties flooded the country with some 10 million pamphlets on the subject.

The British lion's tail came in for some energetic twisting, especially when a California man claiming English birth wrote to the British minister in Washington, Sir Lionel Sackville-West, for advice on how to vote. The foolish diplomat replied, in effect, that a vote for Cleveland, with his low-tariff policies, was a vote for England, the champion of "free trade."

Cleveland Files Rough Edges from Tariff, 1888

Weighing the Candidates, 1888
Novelties like this were widely distributed in late-nineteenth-century political campaigns. This toy scale evidently favored the corpulent Democratic candidate, Grover Cleveland.

sial Dawes Act, designed to control the Indians (see p. 604), and the Interstate Commerce Act (see p. 543), designed to curb the railroads, both enacted in 1887. Cleveland's administration also retrieved for the government some 81 million acres of the public domain in the West—land that in many cases had been improperly acquired by the "cattle barons" or the railroad "octopus" (see pp. 536–538).

But for the most part, Cleveland, despite his gruff integrity and occasional courage, was tied down in office by the same threads that held all presidents of the day to Lilliputian levels. Grant, Hayes, Garfield, Arthur, and Harrison are often called the "forgettable presidents." Bewhiskered and bland in person, they left mostly blanks—or blots—on the nation's political record. In this dull galaxy even such a dim light as Cleveland shone like a bright star. What little political vitality existed was found in local settings, or in Congress, which overshadowed the White House during most of the Gilded Age.

As the nineteenth century was drawing to a close, observers were asking, "Why are the 'best men' not in politics?" One answer was that they had been lured away from public life by the lusty attractions of the booming industrial economy. Talented men ached for profits, not the presidency; they dreamed of controlling corporations, not Congress. What the nation lost in political leadership, it gained in an astounding surge of economic growth. Although still in many ways a political dwarf, the United States was about to stand up before the world as an industrial colossus.

Republicans jubilantly trumpeted the indiscreet letter and made it a front-page sensation. The crucial Irish vote in New York, normally Democratic, began to slip away. Cleveland was forced to send the "damned Englishman" packing off to England. Crowds of gleeful Republicans tramped through New York chanting,

> *West, West, Sackville-West*
> *He didn't want to go home*
> *But Cleveland thought it best.*

The specter of a lowered tariff spurred the Republicans to frantic action. In an impressive demonstration of the post–Pendleton Act politics of alliances with big business, they raised a war chest of some $3 million—the heftiest yet—largely by "frying the fat" out of nervous industrialists. The money was widely used to line up corrupt "voting cattle" known as "repeaters" and "floaters." In Indiana, always a crucial "swing" state, votes were shamelessly purchased for as much as $20 each.

On election day Harrison nosed out Cleveland, 233 to 168 electoral votes. A change of about 7,000 ballots in New York would have reversed the outcome. Cleveland actually polled more popular votes, 5,537,857 to 5,447,129. Such are the curiosities of the Electoral College.

Grover Cleveland, the first sitting president to be voted out of his chair since Martin Van Buren in 1840, could count some legislative landmarks during his four-year term. They included the controver-

On the night before the inauguration of Harrison, a crowd of jubilant Republicans tauntingly serenaded the darkened White House with a popular campaign ditty directed at Grover Cleveland:

> Down in the cornfield
> Hear that mournful sound;
> All the Democrats are weeping—
> Grover's in the cold, cold ground!

But Grover was to rise again and serve as president for a second term of four more years.

Chronology

1868	Grant defeats Seymour for the presidency	**1880**	Garfield defeats Hancock for presidency
1869	Fisk and Gould corner the gold market	**1881**	Garfield assassinated; Arthur assumes presidency
1871	Tweed scandal in New York	**1882**	Chinese Exclusion Act
1872	Crédit Mobilier scandal exposed Liberal Republicans break with Grant Grant defeats Greeley for the presidency	**1883**	*Civil Rights Cases* Pendleton Act sets up Civil Service Commission
1873	Panic of 1873	**1884**	Cleveland defeats Blaine for presidency
1875	Whiskey Ring scandal Civil Rights Act of 1875 Resumption Act passed	**1887**	Dawes Act Interstate Commerce Act
1876	Hayes-Tilden election standoff and crisis	**1888**	Harrison defeats Cleveland for presidency
1877	Compromise of 1877 Reconstruction ends Railroad strikes paralyze nation	**1896**	*Plessy* v. *Ferguson* legitimizes "separate but equal" doctrine

SUGGESTED READINGS

PRIMARY SOURCE DOCUMENTS

Henry Adams penned some perceptive and sour observations on the era in his autobiographical *Education of Henry Adams* (1907) and in his novel *Democracy* (1880). See also the classic satire by Mark Twain and Charles Dudley Warner, *The Gilded Age* (1873).

SECONDARY SOURCES

The scandal-rocked Grant era is treated with brevity in James G. Randall and David Donald, *The Civil War and Reconstruction* (rev. ed., 1969), and at greater length in William Gillette, *Retreat from Reconstruction* (1979), and James M. McPherson, *Ordeal by Fire* (1981). On Hayes, See Ari Hoogenboom, *Rutherford B. Hayes: Warrior and President* (1995). A general look at corruption as a political issue is Mark Wahlgren Summers, *The Era of Good Stealings* (1993). Consult also William McFeely, *Grant* (1981). Southern politics is detailed in Otto H. Olsen, *Reconstruction and Redemption in the South* (1980); Terry L. Seip, *The South Returns to Congress* (1983); Michael Perman, *The Road to Redemption* (1984); and J. Morgan Kousser, *The Shaping of Southern Politics* (1974). Barry A. Crouch, *The Freedmen's Bureau and Black Texans* (1992), details the hopes and frustrations of freedom for blacks in post–Civil War Texas. William Gillette, *The Right to Vote* (1965); Dale Baum, *The Civil War Party System: The Case of Massachusetts, 1848–1876* (1984); and James C. Mohr, *The Radical Republicans and Reform in New York During Reconstruction* (1973), discuss the North. Mark W. Summers analyzes *Railroads, Reconstruction and the Gospel of Prosperity* (1984). William Issel and Robert W. Cherny examine the West's largest city in *San Francisco, 1865–1932: Politics, Power, and Urban Development* (1986). On the party systems, see Paul Kleppner, *The Third Electoral System, 1835–1892* (1979); Morton Keller, *Affairs of State: Public Life in Nineteenth-Century America* (1977); Peter McCaffery, *When Bosses Ruled Philadelphia: The Emergence of the Republican Machine, 1867–1933* (1993); Samuel McSeveney, *The Politics of Depression: Political Behavior in the Northeast, 1893–1896* (1972); and Richard Jensen, *The Winning of the Mid-West* (1971). Jon Teaford defends the record of municipal governments in *The Unheralded Triumph: City Government in America, 1870–1900* (1984). Money questions are treated in Irwin Unger, *The Greenback Era* (1964); Walter T. K. Nugent, *Money and American Society, 1865–1880* (1968); and Allen Weinstein's account of the "Crime of '73," *Prelude to Populism* (1970). C. Vann Woodward sharply analyzes the Compromise of 1877 in *Reunion and Reaction* (rev. ed., 1956). California receives special attention in Alexander Saxton, *The Indispensable Enemy: Labor and the Anti-Chinese Movement in California* (1975).

25

Industry Comes of Age
1865–1900

The wealthy class is becoming more wealthy; but the poorer class is becoming more dependent. The gulf between the employed and the employer is growing wider; social contrasts are becoming sharper; as liveried carriages appear, so do barefooted children.

HENRY GEORGE, 1879

The Iron Colt Becomes an Iron Horse

The government-business entanglements that increasingly shaped politics after the Civil War also undergirded the industrial development of the nation. The unparalleled outburst of railroad construction was a crucial case. When Lincoln was shot in 1865, there were only 35,000 miles (56,350 kilometers) of steam railways in the United States, mostly east of the Mississippi. By 1900 the figure had spurted up to 192,556 miles (310,115 kilometers), or more than that for all of Europe combined, and much of the new trackage ran west of the Mississippi.

Transcontinental railroad building was so costly and risky as to require government subsidies. The extension of rails into thinly populated regions was unprofitable until the areas could be built up; and private promoters were unwilling to suffer heavy initial losses. Congress, impressed by arguments pleading military and postal needs, began to advance liberal money loans to two favored cross-continent companies in 1862 and added enormous donations of acreage paralleling the tracks. All told, Washington rewarded the railroads with 155,504,994 acres, and the western states contributed 49 million more—a total area larger than Texas.

Grasping railroads tied up even more land than this for a number of years. Land grants to railroads were made in broad belts along the proposed route. Within these belts the railroads were allowed to choose *alternate* mile-square sections in checkerboard fashion (see the map opposite). But until they determined the precise location of their tracks and

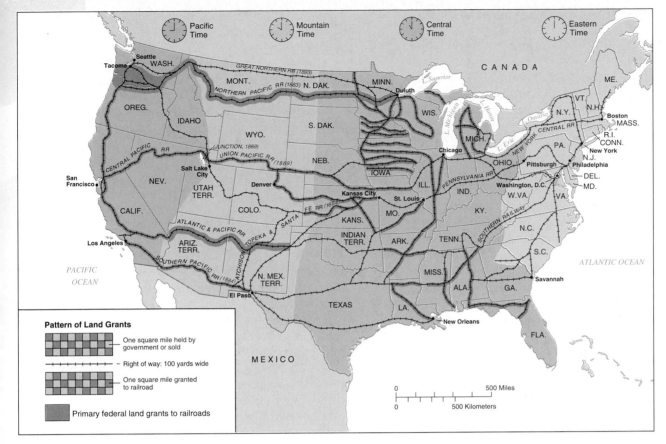

Federal Land Grants to Railroads
The heavy red lines indicate areas within which the railroads might be given specific parcels of land. As shown in the inset, lands were reserved in belts of various widths on either side of a railroad's right of way. Until the railroad selected the individual mile-square sections it chose to possess, *all* such sections within the belt were withdrawn from eligibility for settlement. The "time zones" were introduced in 1883 (see p. 542), and their boundaries have since been adjusted.

decided which sections were the choicest selections, the railroads withheld *all* the land from other users. President Grover Cleveland put an end to this foot-dragging practice in 1887 and threw open to settlement the still-unclaimed public portions of the land-grant areas.

Noisy criticism, especially in later years, was leveled at the "giveaway" of so valuable a birthright to greedy corporations. But the government did receive beneficial returns, including long-term preferential rates for postal service and military traffic. Granting land was also a "cheap" way to subsidize a much-desired transportation system, because it avoided new taxes for direct cash grants. The railroads could turn the land into gold by using it as collateral for loans from private bankers or, later, by selling it. This they often did, at an average price of $3 an acre. Critics were also prone to overlook the fact that the land did not have even that relatively modest value until the railroads had ribboned it with steel.

Frontier villages touched by the magic wand of the iron rail became flourishing cities; those that were bypassed often withered away and became "ghost towns." Little wonder that communities fought one another for the privilege of playing host to the railroads. Ambitious towns customarily held out monetary and other attractions to the builders, who sometimes blackmailed them into contributing more generously.

Spanning the Continent with Rails

Deadlock in the 1850s over the proposed transcontinental railroad was broken when the South seceded, leaving the field to the North. In 1862, the year after the guns first spoke at Fort Sumter, Congress made provision for starting the long-awaited line. One weighty argument for action was the urgency of bolstering the Union, already disrupted, by binding the Pacific Coast—especially gold-rich California—more securely to the rest of the Republic.

The Union Pacific Railroad—note the word *Union*—was thus commissioned by Congress to thrust westward from Omaha, Nebraska. For each mile (1.6 kilometers) of track constructed, the company was granted 20 square miles (51.8 square kilometers) of land, alternating in 640-acre sections on either side of the track. For each mile the builders were also to receive a generous federal loan, ranging from $16,000 on the flat prairie land to $48,000 for mountainous country. The laying of rails began in earnest after the Civil War ended in 1865; and with juicy loans and land grants available, the "ground-hog" promoters made all possible haste. Insiders of the Crédit Mobilier construction company reaped fabulous profits. They slyly pocketed $73 million for some $50 million worth of breakneck construction, spending small change to bribe congressmen to look the other way.

Sweaty construction gangs, containing many Irish "Paddies" (Patricks) who had fought in the Union armies, worked at a frantic pace. On one record-breaking day, a sledge-and-shovel army of some five thousand men laid 10 miles (16 kilometers) of track. A favorite song was

> *Then drill, my Paddies, drill;*
> *Drill, my heroes, drill;*
> *Drill all day,*
> *No sugar in your tay,*
> *Workin' on the U. P. Railway.*

When hostile Indians attacked in futile efforts to protect what once rightfully had been their land, the laborers would drop their picks and seize their rifles. Scores of men—railroad workers and Indians—lost their lives as the rails stretched ever westward. At rail's end, workers tried their best to find relaxation and conviviality in their tented towns, known as "hells on wheels," often teeming with as many as ten thousand men and a sprinkling of painted prostitutes and performers.

Rail laying at the California end was undertaken by the Central Pacific Railroad. This line pushed boldly eastward from boomtown Sacramento, over

Snow Sheds on the Central Pacific Railroad in the Sierra Nevada Mountains, by Joseph H. Becker, c. 1869 Formidable obstacles of climate and terrain confronted the builders of the Central Pacific Railroad in the mountainous heights of California. Note the Chinese laborers in the foreground.

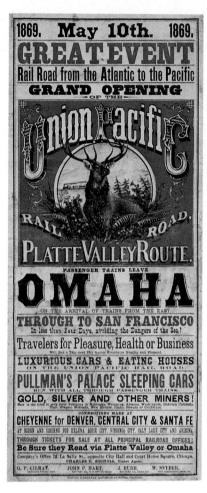

Promoting the Union Pacific Railroad, 1869

premature explosions and other mishaps). The towering Sierra Nevada presented a formidable barrier; and the nerves of the Big Four were strained when their workers could chip only a few inches a day tunneling through solid rock, while the Union Pacific was sledgehammering westward across the open plains.

A "wedding of the rails" was finally consummated near Ogden, Utah, in 1869, as two locomotives—"facing on a single track, half a world behind each back"—gently kissed cowcatchers. The colorful ceremony included the breaking of champagne bottles and the driving of a last ceremonial (golden) spike, with ex-governor Leland Stanford clumsily wielding a silver sledgehammer.* In all, the Union Pacific built 1,086 miles (1,739 kilometers); the Central Pacific, 689 miles (1,110 kilometers).

Completion of the transcontinental line—a magnificent engineering feat for that day—was one of America's most impressive peacetime undertakings. It welded the West Coast more firmly to the Union and facilitated a flourishing trade with Asia. It penetrated the arid barrier of the deserts, paving the way for the phenomenal growth of the Great West. Americans compared this electrifying achievement with the Declaration of Independence and the emancipation of the slaves; jubilant Philadelphians again rang the cracked bell of Independence Hall.

Binding the Country with Railroad Ties

With the westward trail now blazed, four other transcontinental lines were completed before the century's end. None of them secured monetary loans from the federal government, as did the Union Pacific and the Central Pacific. But all of them except the Great Northern received generous grants of land.

The Northern Pacific Railroad, stretching from Lake Superior to Puget Sound, reached its terminus in 1883. The Atchison, Topeka and Santa Fe, stretching through the southwestern deserts to California, was completed in 1884. The Southern Pacific ribboned from New Orleans to San Francisco and was consolidated in the same year.

The last spike of the last of the five transcontinental railroads of the nineteenth century was

and through the towering, snow-clogged Sierra Nevada. Four farseeing men—the so-called Big Four—were the chief financial backers of the enterprise. The quartet included the heavyset, enterprising ex-governor Leland Stanford of California, who had useful political connections, and the burly, energetic Collis P. Huntington, an adept lobbyist. The Big Four cleverly operated through two construction companies, and although they walked away with tens of millions in profits, they kept their hands relatively clean by not becoming involved in the bribery of congressmen.

The Central Pacific, which was granted the same princely subsidies as the Union Pacific, had the same incentive to haste. Some ten thousand Chinese laborers, sweating from dawn to dusk under their basket hats, proved to be cheap, efficient, and expendable (hundreds lost their lives in

---

*The spike was promptly removed and is now exhibited at the Stanford University Museum.

Grading for the Northern Pacific Railroad, 1879
This grading crew sliced a path through the Beaver Creek Valley of western North Dakota in what became known as the "Big Cut." This first rail line to the Pacific Northwest opened in 1883. Railroad trackage grew prodigiously in the 1880s, when an average of more than 7,000 miles of new line was laid each year.

hammered home in 1893. The Great Northern, which ran from Duluth to Seattle north of the Northern Pacific, was the creation of a far-visioned Canadian-American, James J. Hill, a bearlike man who was probably the greatest railroad builder of all. Endowed with a high sense of public duty, he perceived that the prosperity of his railroad depended on the prosperity of the area that it served. He ran agricultural demonstration trains through the "Hill Country" and imported from England blooded bulls,

In 1892 James Baird Weaver (1833–1912), nominee of the Populists, wrote regarding the railroad magnates:

"In their delirium of greed the managers of our transportation systems disregard both private right and the public welfare. Today they will combine and bankrupt their weak rivals, and by the expenditure of a trifling sum possess themselves of properties which cost the outlay of millions. Tomorrow they will capitalize their booty for five times the cost, issue their bonds, and proceed to levy tariffs upon the people to pay dividends upon the fraud."

which he distributed to the farmers. His enterprise was so soundly organized that it rode through later financial storms with flying colors.

Yet the romance of the rails was not without its sordid side. Pioneer builders were often guilty of gross overoptimism. Avidly seeking land bounties and pushing into areas that lacked enough potential population to support a railroad, they sometimes laid down rails that led "from nowhere to nothing." When prosperity failed to smile upon their coming, they went into bankruptcy, carrying down with them the savings of trusting investors. Many of the large railroads in the post–Civil War decades passed through seemingly endless bankruptcies, mergers, or reorganizations.

Railroad Consolidation and Mechanization

The success of the western lines was facilitated by welding together and expanding the older eastern networks, notably the New York Central. The genius in this enterprise was "Commodore" Cornelius Vanderbilt—burly, boisterous, white-whiskered. Having made his millions in steamboating, he daringly turned, in his late sixties, to a new career in railroading. Though ill educated, ungrammatical, coarse,

Cornelius Vanderbilt (1794–1877)
Vanderbilt established a shipping–land transit line across Nicaragua in response to the California gold rush. By the time of his death, his New York Central rail line ran from New York to Chicago and operated along more than 4,500 miles of track.

Traveling First Class   This sumptuously appointed Pullman "Palace Car" offered its prosperous passengers the comforts of home while they were far away from it.

and ruthless, he was clear-visioned. Offering superior railway service at lower rates, he amassed a fortune of $100 million. His name is perhaps best remembered through his contribution of $1 million to the founding of Vanderbilt University in Tennessee.

Two significant new improvements proved a boon to the railroads. One was the steel rail, which Vanderbilt helped popularize when he replaced the old iron tracks of the New York Central with the tougher metal. Steel was safer and more economical because it could bear a heavier load. A standard gauge of track width likewise came into wide use during the postwar years, thus eliminating the expense and inconvenience of numerous changes from one line to another.

Other refinements played a vital role in railroading. The Westinghouse air brake, generally adopted in the 1870s, was a marvelous contribution to efficiency and safety. The Pullman Palace Cars, advertised as "gorgeous traveling hotels," were introduced on a considerable scale in the 1860s. Alarmists condemned them as "wheeled torture chambers" and potential funeral pyres, for the wooden cars were equipped with swaying kerosene lamps. Appalling accidents continued to be almost daily tragedies, despite safety devices like the telegraph ("talking wires"), double-racking, and (later) the block signal.

Revolution by Railways

The metallic fingers of the railroads intimately touched countless phases of American life. For the first time, a sprawling nation became united in a physical sense, bound with ribs of iron and steel. By stitching North America together from sea to sea, the transcontinental lines created an enormous domestic market for American raw materials and manufactured goods—probably the largest integrated national market area in the world. This huge empire of commerce beckoned to foreign and domestic investors alike, as well as to businesspeople who could now dare to dream on a continental scale.

More than any other single factor, the railroad network spurred the amazing industrialization of the post–Civil War years. The puffing locomotives opened up fresh markets for manufactured goods and sped raw materials to factories. The forging of the rails themselves generated the largest single backlog for the adolescent steel industry.

The screeching iron horse likewise stimulated mining and agriculture, especially in the West. It took farmers out to their land, carried the fruits of their toil to market, and brought them their manufactured necessities. Clusters of farm settlements paralleled the railroads, just as earlier they had followed the rivers.

Railways were a boon for cities and played a leading role in the great cityward movement of the last decades of the century. The iron monsters could carry food to enormous concentrations of people and at the same time ensure them a livelihood by providing both raw materials and markets.

Railroad companies also stimulated the mighty stream of immigration. Seeking settlers to whom their land grants might be sold at a profit, they advertised seductively in Europe and sometimes offered to transport the newcomers free to their farms.

The land also felt the impact of the railroad—especially the broad, ecologically fragile midsection of the continent that Thomas Jefferson had purchased from France in 1803. Settlers following the railroads plowed up the tallgrass prairies of Iowa, Illinois, Kansas, and Nebraska and planted well-drained, rectangular cornfields. On the shortgrass prairies of the high plains in the Dakotas and Montana, range-fed cattle rapidly displaced the buffalo, which were hunted to near-extinction. The white pine forests of Michigan, Wisconsin, and Minnesota disappeared into lumber that was rushed by rail to prairie farmers who used it to build houses and fences.

Time itself was bent to the railroads' needs. Until the 1880s every town in the United States had its own "local" time, dictated by the sun's position.

When it was noon in Chicago, it was 11:50 A.M. in St. Louis and 12:18 P.M. in Detroit. For railroad operators worried about keeping schedules and avoiding wrecks, this patchwork of local times was a nightmare. Thus on November 18, 1883, the major rail lines decreed that the continent would henceforth be divided into four "time zones." Most communities quickly adopted railroad "standard" time.

Finally, the railroad, more than any other single factor, was the maker of millionaires. A raw new aristocracy, consisting of "lords of the rail," replaced the old southern "lords of the lash." The multi-webbed lines became the playthings of Wall Street; and colossal wealth was amassed by stock speculators and railroad wreckers.

Wrongdoing in Railroading

Corruption lurks nearby when fabulous fortunes can materialize overnight. The fleecings administered by the railroad construction companies, such as the Crédit Mobilier, were but the first of the bunco games that the railroad promoters learned to play. Methods soon became more refined, as fast-fingered financiers executed multimillion-dollar maneuvers beneath the noses of a bedazzled public. Jay Gould was the most adept of these ringmasters of rapacity. For nearly thirty years he boomed and busted the stocks of the Erie, the Kansas Pacific, the Union Pacific, and the Texas and Pacific in an incredible circus of speculative skullduggery.

One of the favorite devices of the moguls of manipulation was "stock watering." The term originally referred to the practice of making cattle thirsty by feeding them salt and then having them bloat themselves with water before they were weighed in for sale. Using a variation of this technique, railroad stock promoters grossly inflated their claims about a given line's assets and profitability and sold stocks and bonds far in excess of the railroad's actual value. "Promoters' profits" were often the tail that wagged the iron horse itself. Railroad managers were forced to charge extortionate rates and wage ruthless competitive battles in order to pay off the exaggerated financial obligations with which they were saddled.

The public interest was frequently trampled underfoot as the railroad titans waged their brutal wars. Crusty old Cornelius Vanderbilt, when told that the law stood in his way, reportedly exclaimed,

"Law! What do I care about the law? Hain't I got the power?" On another occasion he supposedly threatened some associates: "I won't sue you, for the law is too slow. I'll ruin you." His son, William H. Vanderbilt, when asked in 1883 about the discontinuance of a fast mail train, reportedly snorted, "The public be damned!"

While abusing the public, the railroaders blandly bought and sold people in public life. They bribed judges and legislatures, employed arm-twisting lobbyists, and elected their own "creatures" to high office. They showered free passes on journalists and politicians in profusion. One railroad man noted in 1885 that in the West "no man who has money, or official position, or influence thinks he ought to pay anything for riding on a railroad."

Railroad kings were, for a time, virtual industrial monarchs. As manipulators of a huge natural monopoly, they exercised more direct control over the lives of more people than did the president of the United States—and their terms were not limited to four years. They increasingly shunned the crude bloodletting of cutthroat competition and began to cooperate with one another to rule the railroad dominion. Sorely pressed to show at least some

William H. Vanderbilt, Robber Baron   This caricature from a contemporary newspaper takes aim at railroad magnate Vanderbilt's infamous comment, "The public be damned!"

returns on their bloated investments, they entered into defensive alliances to protect precious profits.

The earliest form of combination was the "pool"—an agreement to divide the business in a given area and share the profits. Other rail barons granted secret rebates or kickbacks to powerful shippers in return for steady and assured traffic. Often they slashed their rates on competing lines, but they more than made up the difference on noncompeting ones, where they might actually charge more for a short haul than for a long one.

Government Bridles the Iron Horse

It was neither healthy nor politically acceptable that so many people should be at the mercy of so few. Impoverished farmers, especially in the Midwest, began to wonder if the nation had not escaped from the slavery power only to fall into the hands of the money power, as represented by the railroad plutocracy.

But the American people, though quick to respond to political injustice, were slow to combat economic injustice. Dedicated to free enterprise and to the principle that competition is the soul of trade, they cherished a traditionally keen pride in progress. They remembered that Jefferson's ideals were hostile to government interference with business. Above all, there shimmered the "American dream": the hope that in a catch-as-catch-can economic system, anyone might become a millionaire.

The depression of the 1870s finally goaded the farmers into protesting against being "railroaded" into bankruptcy. Under pressure from organized agrarian groups like the Grange (Patrons of Husbandry), many midwestern legislatures tried to regulate the railroad monopoly.

The scattered state efforts screeched to a halt in 1886. The Supreme Court, in the famed *Wabash* case, decreed that individual states had no power to regulate *inter*state commerce. If the mechanical monster were to be corralled, the federal government would have to do the job.

Stiff-necked President Cleveland did not look kindly on effective regulation. But Congress ignored his grumbling indifference and passed the epochal Interstate Commerce Act in 1887. It prohibited rebates and pools and required the railroads to publish their rates openly. It also forbade unfair

The Modern Colossus of Railroads, 1879
William H. Vanderbilt, flanked by Cyrus Field (left) and Jay Gould (right), towers over the scene. With the Interstate Commerce Act in 1887, the government began to weaken the magnates' grip over the nation's transportation system.

discrimination against shippers and outlawed charging more for a short haul than for a long one over the same line. Most important, it set up the Interstate Commerce Commission (ICC) to administer and enforce the new legislation.

Despite acclaim, the Interstate Commerce Act emphatically did not represent a popular victory over corporate wealth. One of the leading corporation lawyers of the day, Richard Olney, shrewdly noted that the new commission "can be made of great use to the railroads. It satisfies the popular clamor for a government supervision of railroads, at the same time that such supervision is almost

entirely nominal. . . . The part of wisdom is not to destroy the Commission, but to utilize it."

What the new legislation did do was to provide an orderly forum where competing business interests could resolve their conflicts in peaceable ways. The country could now avoid ruinous rate wars among the railroads and outraged, "confiscatory" attacks on the lines by pitchfork-prodded state legislatures. This was a modest accomplishment but by no means an unimportant one. The Interstate Commerce Act tended to stabilize, not revolutionize, the existing business system.

Yet the act still ranks as a red-letter law. It was the first large-scale attempt by Washington to regulate business in the interest of society at large. It heralded the arrival of a series of independent regulatory commissions in the next century, which would irrevocably commit the government to the daunting task of monitoring and directing the private economy. It foreshadowed the doom of freewheeling, buccaneering business practices and served full notice that there was a public interest in private enterprise that the government was bound to protect.

Miracles of Mechanization

Postwar industrial expansion, partly a result of the railroad network, rapidly began to assume mammoth proportions. When Lincoln was elected in 1860, the Republic ranked only fourth among the manufacturing nations of the world. By 1894 it had bounded into first place. Why the sudden upsurge?

Liquid capital, previously scarce, was now becoming abundant. The word *millionaire* had not been coined until the 1840s, and in 1861 only a handful of individuals comprised this class. But the Civil War, partly through profiteering, created immense fortunes; and these accumulations could now be combined with the customary borrowings from foreign capitalists.

The amazing natural resources of the nation were now about to be fully exploited, including coal, oil, and iron. For example, the Minnesota–Lake Superior region, which had yielded some iron ore by the 1850s, contributed the rich deposits of the Mesabi Range by the 1890s. This priceless bonanza, where mountains of red-rusted ore could be scooped up by steam shovels, ultimately became a cornerstone of a vast steel empire.

Massive immigration helped make unskilled labor cheap and plentiful. Steel, the keystone industry, built its strength largely on the sweat of low-priced immigrant labor from eastern and southern Europe, working in two twelve-hour shifts, seven days a week.

American ingenuity at the same time played a vital role in the second American industrial revolution. Techniques of mass production, pioneered by Eli Whitney, were being perfected by the captains of industry. American inventiveness flowered luxuriantly in the postwar years: between 1860 and 1890 some 440,000 patents were issued. Business operations were facilitated by such machines as the cash register, the stock ticker, and the typewriter ("literary piano"), which attracted women from the confines of home to industry. Urbanization was speeded by the refrigerator car, the electric dynamo, and the electric railway, which displaced animal-drawn cars.

One of the most ingenious inventions was the telephone, introduced by Alexander Graham Bell in 1876. A teacher of the deaf who was given a dead man's ear to experiment with, he remarked that if he could make the mute talk, he could make iron speak. America was speedily turned into a nation of "telephoniacs," as a gigantic communication network was built on his invention. The social impact of this instrument was further revealed when an additional army of "number please" women was attracted from the stove to the switchboard. Telephone boys were at first employed as operators, but their profanity shocked patrons.

The most versatile inventor of all was Thomas A. Edison, who as a boy had been considered so dull-witted that he was taken out of school. This "Wizard of the Wires" ran a veritable invention factory in New Jersey. He is perhaps best known for his perfection in 1879 of the electric light, which he unveiled after trying some six thousand filaments. So deaf that he was not easily distracted, he displayed sleepless energy and a flair for practical money-making schemes rather than pure science. He invented, perfected, or did useful exploratory work on the phonograph, the mimeograph, the dictaphone, and the moving picture. "Genius," he said, "is one percent inspiration and ninety-nine percent perspiration."

The Trust Titan Emerges

Despite pious protests to the contrary, competition was the bugbear of most business leaders of the day. Tycoons like Andrew Carnegie, the steel king, John D. Rockefeller, the oil baron, and J. Pierpont Morgan, the bankers' banker, exercised their genius in devising ways to circumvent competition. Carnegie integrated every phase of his steel-making operation. His miners scratched the ore from the earth in the Mesabi Range; Carnegie ships floated it across the Great Lakes; Carnegie railroads delivered it to the blast furnaces at Pittsburgh. When the molten metal finally poured from the glowing crucibles into the waiting ingot molds, no other hands but those in Carnegie's employ had touched the product. Carnegie thus pioneered the creative entrepreneurial tactic of "vertical integration," combining into one organization all phases of manufacturing from mining to marketing. His goal was to improve efficiency by making supplies more reliable, controlling the quality of the product at all stages of production, and eliminating middlemen's fees.

Less justifiable on grounds of efficiency was the technique of "horizontal integration," which simply meant allying with competitors to monopolize a given market. Rockefeller was a master of this stratagem. He perfected a device for controlling bothersome rivals—the "trust." Stockholders in various smaller oil companies assigned their stock to the board of directors of his Standard Oil Company, formed in 1870. It then consolidated and concerted the operations of the previously competing enterprises. "Let us prey" was said to be Rockefeller's unwritten motto. Ruthlessly wielding vast power, Standard Oil soon cornered virtually the entire world petroleum market. Weaker competitors, left out of the trust agreement, were forced to the wall.

Regarding the exploitation of immigrant labor, Ralph Waldo Emerson (1803–1882) wrote in 1860,

"The German and Irish millions, like the Negro, have a great deal of guano in their destiny. They are ferried over the Atlantic, and carted over America, to ditch and to drudge, to make corn cheap, and then to lie down prematurely to make a spot of green grass on the prairie."

The Octopus, 1904
This cartoon visually captures a feeling of widespread resentment against Standard Oil as a powerful, sprawling "octopus" whose tentacles controlled all branches of government.

Rockefeller's stunning success inspired many imitators, and the word *trust* came to be generally used to describe any large-scale business combination.

The imperial Morgan devised still other schemes for eliminating "wasteful" competition. The depression of the 1890s drove into his welcoming arms many bleeding businesspeople, wounded by cutthroat competition. His prescribed remedy was to consolidate rival enterprises and to ensure future harmony by placing officers of his own banking syndicate on their various boards of directors. These came to be known as "interlocking directorates."

The Supremacy of Steel

"Steel is king!" might well have been the exultant war cry of the new industrialized generation. The mighty metal ultimately held together the new steel civilization, from skyscrapers to coal scuttles, while providing it with food, shelter, and transportation. Steel making, notably rails for railroads, typified the dominance of "heavy industry," which concentrated on making "capital goods," as distinct from the production of "consumer goods" such as clothes and shoes.

Now taken for granted, steel was a scarce commodity in the wood-and-brick America of Abraham Lincoln. Considerable iron went into railroad rails and bridges, but steel was expensive and was used largely for products like cutlery. The early iron horse snorted exclusively (and dangerously) over iron rails; and when in the 1870s "Commodore" Vanderbilt of the New York Central began to use steel rails, he was forced to import them from England.

Yet within an amazing twenty years, the United States had outdistanced all foreign competitors and was pouring out more than one-third of the world's supply of steel. By 1900 the Americans were producing as much as England and Germany combined.

What wrought the transformation? Chiefly the invention in the 1850s of a method of making cheap steel—the Bessemer process. It was named after a derided British inventor, although an American had stumbled on it a few years earlier. William Kelly, a Kentucky manufacturer of iron kettles, discovered that cold air blown on red-hot iron caused the metal to become white-hot by igniting the carbon and thus eliminating impurities. He tried to apply the new "air boiling" technique to his own product, but his customers decried "Kelly's fool steel," and his business declined. Gradually the Bessemer-Kelly process won acceptance, and these two "crazy men" ultimately made possible the present steel civilization.

A revolutionary steel-fabricating process was not the whole story. America was one of the few places in the world where one could find relatively close together abundant coal for fuel, rich iron ore for smelting, and other essential ingredients for making steel. The nation also boasted an abundant labor supply, guided by industrial know-how of a high order. The stage was set for miracles of production.

Carnegie and Other Sultans of Steel

Kingpin among steelmasters was Andrew Carnegie, an undersized, charming Scotsman. As a towheaded lad, he was brought to America by his impoverished parents in 1848 and got a job as a bobbin boy at $1.20 a week. Mounting the ladder of success so fast that he was said to have scorched the rungs, he forged ahead by working hard, doing the extra chore, cheerfully assuming responsibility, and smoothly cultivating influential people.

After accumulating some capital, Carnegie entered the steel business in the Pittsburgh area. A gifted organizer and administrator, he succeeded by picking high-class associates and by eliminating many middlemen. Although inclined to be tough-fisted in business, he was not a monopolist and disliked monopolistic trusts. His remarkable organization was a partnership that involved, at its maximum, about forty "Pittsburgh millionaires." By 1900 he was producing one-fourth of the nation's Bessemer steel, and the partners were dividing profits of $40 million a year, with the "Napoleon of the Smokestacks" himself receiving a cool $25 million. These were the pre–income tax days, when millionaires were really rich, and profits represented take-home pay.

J. P. Morgan (1837–1913)   As the most influential banker of his day, he symbolized to many people the power and arrogance of "finance capitalism." The chronic skin disorder on his nose inspired the taunt, "Johnny Morgan's nasal organ has a purple hue."

Into the picture now stepped the financial giant of the age, J. Pierpont Morgan. "Jupiter" Morgan had made a legendary reputation for himself and his Wall Street banking house by financing the reorganization of railroads, insurance companies, and banks. An impressive figure of a man, with massive shoulders, shaggy brows, piercing eyes, and a bulbous, acne-cursed red nose, he had established an enviable reputation for integrity. He did not believe that "money power" was dangerous, except when in dangerous hands—and he did not regard his own hands as dangerous.

The force of circumstances brought Morgan and Carnegie into collision. By 1900 the canny little Scotsman, weary of turning steel into gold, was eager to sell his holdings. Morgan had meanwhile plunged heavily into the manufacture of steel pipe tubing. Carnegie, cleverly threatening to invade the same business, was ready to ruin his rival if he did not receive his price. The steelmaster's agents haggled with the imperious Morgan for eight agonizing hours, and the financier finally agreed to buy out Carnegie for over $400 million. Fearing that he would die "disgraced" with so much wealth, Carnegie dedicated the remaining years of his life to giving away money for public libraries, pensions for

Andrew Carnegie (1835–1919) wrote in 1889,

"The man who dies leaving behind him millions of available wealth, which was his to administer during life, will pass away 'unwept, unhonored, and unsung,' no matter to what uses he leaves the dross which he cannot take with him. Of such as these the public verdict will then be: 'The man who dies thus rich dies disgraced.'"

professors, and other such philanthropic purposes—in all disposing of about $350 million.

Morgan moved rapidly to expand his new industrial empire. He took the Carnegie holdings, added others, "watered" the stock liberally, and in 1901 launched the enlarged United States Steel Corporation. Capitalized at $1.4 billion, it was America's first billion-dollar corporation—a larger sum than the total estimated wealth of the nation in 1800. The industrial revolution, with its hot Bessemer breath, had come into its own.

Rockefeller Grows an American Beauty Rose

The sudden emergence of the oil industry was one of the most striking developments of the years during and after the Civil War. Traces of oil found on streams had earlier been bottled for back-rub and other patent medicines, but not until 1859 did the first well in Pennsylvania—"Drake's Folly"—pour out its liquid "black gold." Almost overnight an industry was born that was to take more wealth from the earth, and more useful wealth at that, than all of the gold extracted by the forty-niners and their western successors. Kerosene, derived from petroleum, was the first major product of the infant oil industry. Burned from a cotton wick in a glass chimney lamp, kerosene produced a much brighter

flame than whale oil. The oil business boomed; by the 1870s kerosene was America's fourth-most-valuable export. Whaling, in contrast, the lifeblood of ocean-roaming New Englanders since before the days of *Moby Dick*, swiftly became a sick industry.

But what technology gives, technology takes away. By 1885, 250,000 of Thomas Edison's electric light bulbs were in use; fifteen years later, perhaps 15 million. The new electrical industry rendered kerosene obsolete just as kerosene had rendered whale-oil obsolete. Only in rural America and overseas did a market continue for oil-fired lamps.

Oil might thus have remained a modest, even a shrinking, industry but for yet another turn of the technological tide—the invention of the automobile. By 1900 the gasoline-burning internal combustion engine had clearly bested its rivals, steam and electricity, as the superior means of automobile propulsion. As the century of the automobile dawned, the oil business got a new, long-lasting, and hugely profitable lease on life.

John D. Rockefeller—lanky, shrewd, ambitious, abstemious (he neither drank, smoked, nor swore)—came to dominate the oil industry. Born to a family of precarious income, he became a successful businessman at age nineteen. One upward stride led to another, and in 1870 he organized the Standard Oil Company of Ohio, nucleus of the great trust formed in 1882. Locating his refineries in Cleveland, he sought to eliminate the middlemen and squeeze out competitors.

Washington as Seen by the Trusts, 1900 "What a funny little government," John D. Rockefeller observes in this satirical cartoon. His own wealth and power are presumed to dwarf the resources of the federal government.

The Bosses of the Senate
This cartoon charges that the bloated corporate interests dominate even the Senate of the United States. The tiny, compliant senators are overshadowed by the huge "trusts."

Pious and parsimonious, Rockefeller flourished in an era of completely free enterprise. So-called piratical practices were employed by "corsairs of finance," and business ethics were distressingly low. Rockefeller, operating "just to the windward of the law," pursued a policy of rule or ruin. "Sell all the oil that is sold in your district" was the hard-boiled order that went out to his local agents. By 1877 Rockefeller controlled 95 percent of all the oil refineries in the country.

Rockefeller—"Reckafellow," as Carnegie had once called him—showed little mercy. A kind of primitive savagery prevailed in the jungle world of big business, where only the fittest survived. Or so Rockefeller believed. His son later explained that the giant American Beauty rose could be produced "only by sacrificing the early buds that grew up around it." His father pinched off the small buds with complete ruthlessness. Employing spies and extorting secret rebates from the railroads, he even forced the lines to pay him rebates on the freight bills of his competitors!

Rockefeller thought he was simply obeying a law of nature. "The time was ripe" for aggressive consolidation, he later reflected. "It had to come, though all we saw at the moment was the need to save ourselves from wasteful conditions. . . . The day of combination is here to stay. Individualism has gone, never to return."

On the other side of the ledger, Rockefeller's oil monopoly did turn out a superior product at a relatively cheap price. It achieved important economies, both at home and abroad, by its large-scale methods of production and distribution. This, in truth, was the tale of the other trusts, as well. The efficient use of expensive machinery called for bigness, and consolidation proved more profitable than ruinous price wars.

Other trusts blossomed along with the American Beauty of oil. These included the sugar trust, the tobacco trust, the leather trust, and the harvester trust, which amalgamated some two hundred competitors. The meat industry arose on the backs of bawling western herds, and meat kings like Gustavus F. Swift and Philip Armour took their place among the new royalty. Wealth was coming to dominate the commonwealth.

These untrustworthy trusts, and the "pirates" who captained them, were disturbingly new. They eclipsed an older American aristocracy of modestly successful merchants and professionals. An arrogant class of "new rich" was now elbowing aside the patrician families in the mad scramble for power and prestige. Not surprisingly, the ranks of the antitrust crusaders were frequently spearheaded by the "best men"—genteel old-family do-gooders who were not radicals but conservative defenders of their own vanishing influence.

The Gospel of Wealth

Monarchs of yore invoked the divine right of kings, and America's industrial plutocrats took a somewhat similar stance. Some candidly credited heavenly help. "Godliness is in league with riches," preached the Episcopal bishop of Massachusetts, and hardfisted John D. Rockefeller piously acknowledged that "the good Lord gave me my money." Steel baron Andrew Carnegie agreed that the wealthy, entrusted with society's riches, had to prove themselves morally responsible according to a "Gospel of Wealth." But most defenders of wide-open capitalism relied more heavily on the survival-of-the-fittest theories of Charles Darwin. "The millionaires are a product of natural selection," concluded Yale Professor and Social Darwinist William Graham Sumner. "They get high wages and live in luxury, but the bargain is a good one for society." Despite plutocracy and deepening class divisions, the captains of industry provided material progress.

Self-justification by the wealthy inevitably involved contempt for the poor. Many of the rich, especially the newly rich, had pulled themselves up by their own bootstraps; hence they concluded that those who stayed poor must be lazy and lacking in enterprise. The Reverend Russell Conwell of Philadelphia became rich by delivering his lecture "Acres of Diamonds" thousands of times. In it he charged, "There is not a poor person in the United States who was not made poor by his own shortcomings." Such attitudes were a formidable roadblock to social reform.

Plutocracy, like the earlier slavocracy, took its stand firmly on the Constitution. The clause that gave Congress sole jurisdiction over interstate commerce was a godsend to the monopolists; their high-priced lawyers used it time and again to thwart controls by the state legislatures. Giant trusts likewise sought refuge behind the Fourteenth Amendment, which had been originally designed to protect the rights of the ex-slaves as persons. The courts ingeniously interpreted a corporation to be a legal "person" and decreed that, as such, it could not be deprived of its property by a state without "due process of law" (see

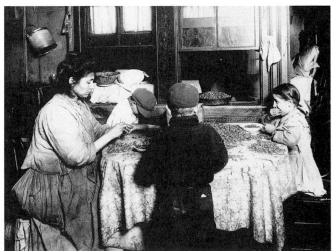

The New Rich and the New Immigrants
A well-to-do family plays chess at its parlor table (left) while a tenement family does "piecework" around its kitchen table—shelling nuts for commercial use (below). The young working girl seems to be "snitching" some nuts for herself. The apparently growing gulf between the rich and the poor deeply worried reformers in the late nineteenth century. They feared that democracy could not survive in the face of such gross inequality.

Industrial millionaires were condemned in the Populist platform of 1892:

"The fruits of the toil of millions are boldly stolen to build up colossal fortunes for a few . . . and the possessors of these, in turn despise the Republic and endanger liberty. From the same prolific womb of governmental injustice we breed the two great classes—tramps and millionaires."

Amendment XIV, para. 1). There is some questionable evidence that slippery corporation lawyers deliberately inserted this loophole when the Fourteenth Amendment was being fashioned in 1866.

Great industrialists likewise sought to incorporate in "easy states," like New Jersey, where the restrictions on big business were mild or nonexistent. For example, the Southern Pacific Railroad, with much of its trackage in California, was incorporated in Kentucky.

Government Tackles the Trust Evil

At long last the masses of the people began to mobilize against monopoly. They first tried to control the trusts through state legislation, as they had earlier attempted to curb the railroads. Failing here, as before, they were forced to appeal to Congress. After prolonged pulling and hauling, the Sherman Anti-Trust Act of 1890 was finally signed into law.

The Sherman Act flatly forbade combinations in restraint of trade, without any distinction between "good" trusts and "bad" trusts. Bigness, not badness, was the sin. The law proved ineffective, largely because it had only baby teeth or no teeth at all, and because it contained legal loopholes through which clever corporation lawyers could wriggle. But it was unexpectedly effective in one respect. Contrary to its original intent, it was used to curb labor unions or labor combinations that were deemed to be restraining trade.

Early prosecutions of the trusts by the Justice Department under the Sherman Act of 1890, as it turned out, were neither vigorous nor successful. The decisions in seven of the first eight cases pre-

sented by the attorney general were adverse to the government. More new trusts were formed in the 1890s under President McKinley than during any other like period. Not until 1914 were the paper jaws of the Sherman Act fitted with reasonably sharp teeth. Until then, there was some question whether the government would control the trusts or the trusts the government.

But the iron grip of monopolistic corporations was being threatened. A revolutionary new principle had been written into the law books by the Sherman Anti-Trust Act of 1890, as well as by the Interstate Commerce Act of 1887. Private greed must henceforth be subordinated to public need.

The South in the Age of Industry

The industrial tidal wave that washed over the North after the Civil War caused only feeble ripples in the backwater of the South. As late as 1900, the South still produced a smaller percentage of the nation's manufactured goods than it had before the Civil War. The plantation system had degenerated into a pattern of absentee land ownership. White and black sharecroppers now tilled the soil for a share of the crop, or they became tenants, in bondage to their landlords who controlled needed credit and supplies.

Southern agriculture received a welcome boost in the 1880s, when machine-made cigarettes replaced the roll-your-own variety and tobacco consumption shot up. James Buchanan Duke took full advantage of the new technology to mass-produce the dainty "coffin nails." In 1890, in what was becoming a familiar pattern, he absorbed his main competitors into the American Tobacco Company. The cigarette czar later showed such generosity to Trinity College, near his birthplace in Durham, North Carolina, that the trustees gratefully changed its name to Duke University.

Industrialists tried to coax the agricultural South out of the fields and into the factories, but with only modest success. The region remained overwhelmingly rural. Prominent among the boosters of a "new South" was silver-tongued Henry W. Grady, editor of the Atlanta *Constitution*. He tirelessly exhorted the ex-Confederates to become "Georgia Yankees" and outplay the North at the commercial and industrial game.

A Virginia Tobacco Factory, c. 1880   The employment of women and children was a common practice in late-nineteenth-century American industry, north as well as south.

Yet formidable obstacles lay in the path of southern industrialization. One was the paper barrier of regional rate-setting systems imposed by the northern-dominated railroad interests. Railroads gave preferential rates to manufactured goods moving southward from the north, but in the opposite direction they discriminated in favor of southern raw materials. The net effect was to keep the South in a kind of "third world" servitude to the Northeast—as a supplier of raw materials to the manufacturing metropolis, unable to develop a substantial industrial base of its own.

A bitter example of this economic discrimination against the South was the "Pittsburgh plus" pricing system in the steel industry. Rich deposits of coal and iron ore near Birmingham, Alabama, worked by low-wage southern labor, should have given steel manufacturers there a competitive edge, especially in southern markets. But the steel lords of Pittsburgh brought pressure to bear on the compli-

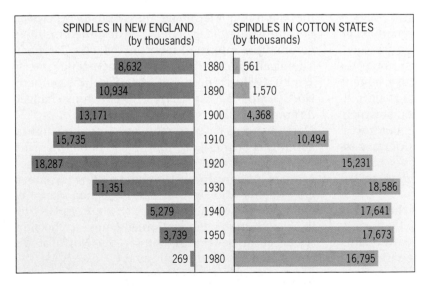

SPINDLES IN NEW ENGLAND (by thousands)		SPINDLES IN COTTON STATES (by thousands)
8,632	1880	561
10,934	1890	1,570
13,171	1900	4,368
15,735	1910	10,494
18,287	1920	15,231
11,351	1930	18,586
5,279	1940	17,641
3,739	1950	17,673
269	1980	16,795

Cotton Manufacturing Moves South, 1880–1980   Textile manufacturing usually looms large in the early stages of industrial development. In later stages it gives way to higher-technology businesses. This trend can be seen here, both in the migration of textile manufacturing to the southern United States and in the decline in the number of spindles in the United States as a whole since the 1930s, as developing Third World countries became major textile producers.

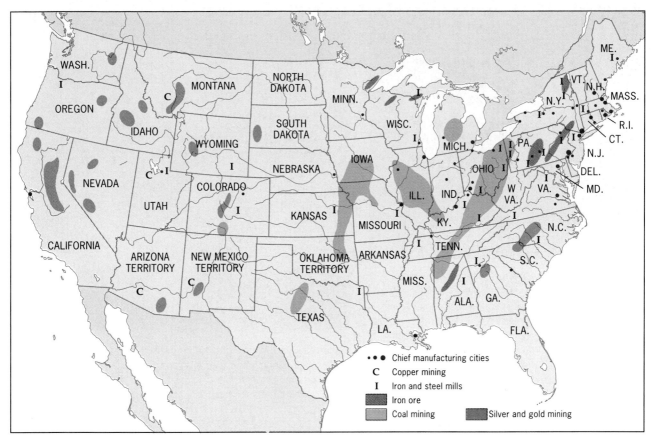

American Industry in 1900   By the end of the nineteenth century, once-rural America boasted the world's largest industrial output—a development with enormous consequences for politics, diplomacy, and family life.

ant railroads. As a result, Birmingham steel, no matter where it was delivered, was charged a fictional fee, as if it had been shipped from Pittsburgh. This stunting of the South's natural economic advantages throttled the growth of the Birmingham steel industry.

In manufacturing cotton textiles, the South fared considerably better. Southerners had long resented shipping their fiber to New England, and now their cry was "Bring the mills to the cotton." Beginning about 1880, northern capital began to erect cotton mills in the South, largely in response to tax benefits and the prospect of cheap and nonunionized labor. (See the chart at left.)

The textile mills proved a mixed blessing to the economically blighted South. They slowly wove an industrial thread into the fabric of southern life, but at a considerable human cost. Cheap labor was the South's major attraction for potential investors, and

Henry W. Grady (1851–1889), editor of the Atlanta Constitution, *urged the new South to industrialize. In a Boston speech in 1889, he described the burial in Georgia of a Confederate veteran:*

"The South didn't furnish a thing on earth for that funeral but the corpse and the hole in the ground. . . . They buried him in a New York coat and a Boston pair of shoes and a pair of breeches from Chicago and a shirt from Cincinnati, leaving him nothing to carry into the next world with him to remind him of the country in which he lived, and for which he fought for four years, but the chill of blood in his veins and the marrow in his bones."

Doffers at the Bibb Mill, No. 1, Macon, Georgia, 1909
The boys' job was to remove fully wound bobbins from the spinning machine, which required dangerous climbing on the whirling mechanism. One quarter of the workers in the southern textile industry were under sixteen years of age. Photographs like this one by Lewis Hine became icons of the reform crusade against child labor, a campaign crowned with success only with the passage of the Fair Labor Standards Act in 1938.

Assembly Line, Westinghouse Foundry, Pittsburgh, 1890
Technological innovations like this continuous assembly line created abundant employment opportunities for semi-skilled workers, many of them immigrants from eastern and southern Europe.

keeping labor cheap became almost a religion among southern industrialists. The mills took root in the chronically depressed piedmont region and came to dominate utterly the communities in which they resided.

Rural southerners—virtually all of them white, for blacks were excluded from all but the most menial jobs in the mills—poured out of the hills and hollows to seek employment in the hastily erected company mill towns. Entire families—often derided as "hillbillies," or "lint-heads"—worked from dawn to dusk amid the whirring spindles. They were paid at half the rate of their northern counterparts and often received their compensation in the form of credit at a company store, to which they were habitually in debt. But despite their depressed working conditions and poor pay, many southerners saw employment in the mills as a salvation, the first steady jobs and wages they had ever known. With many mills anxious to tap the cheap labor of women and children, mill work often offered destitute farm-fugitive families their only chance to remain together.

The Impact of the New Industrial Revolution on America

Economic miracles wrought during the decades after the Civil War enormously increased the wealth of the Republic. The standard of living rose sharply, and well-fed American workers enjoyed more physical comforts than their counterparts in any other industrial nation. Urban centers mushroomed as the insatiable factories demanded more American labor and as immigrants swarmed like honeybees to the new jobs (see "Makers of America: The Poles," pp. 750–751).

Early Jeffersonian ideals were withering before the smudgy blasts from the smokestacks. As agriculture declined in relation to manufacturing, America could no longer aspire to be a nation of small freehold farms. Jefferson's concepts of free enterprise, with neither help nor hindrance from Washington, were being thrown out the factory window. Tariffs had already provided assistance, but the long arm of federal authority was now committed to decades of corporation curbing and "trust-busting."

Older ways of life also wilted in the heat of the factory furnaces. The very concept of time was revolutionized. Rural American migrants and peasant European immigrants, used to living by the languid clock of nature, now had to regiment their lives by the factory whistle. The seemingly arbitrary discipline of industrial labor did not come easily and sometimes had to be forcibly taught. One large corporation simultaneously instructed its Polish immigrant workers in the English language and in the obligations of factory work schedules:

> I hear the whistle. I must hurry.
> I hear the five-minute whistle.
> It is time to go into the shop. . . .
> I change my clothes and get ready to work.
> The starting whistle blows.
> I eat my lunch.
> It is forbidden to eat until then. . . .
> I work until the whistle blows to quit.
> I leave my place nice and clean.
> I put all my clothes in the locker.
> I must go home.

Probably no single group was more profoundly affected by the new industrial age than women. Propelled into industry by recent inventions, chiefly the typewriter and the telephone switchboard, millions of stenographers and "hello girls" discovered new economic and social opportunities. The "Gibson Girl," a magazine image of an independent and athletic "new woman" created in the 1890s by Charles Dana Gibson, became the romantic ideal of the age. For these middle-class women, careers often meant delayed marriages and smaller families. Most women workers, however, toiled neither for independence nor for glamour, but out of economic necessity. They faced the same long hours and dangerous working conditions as did their mates and brothers, and they earned less, as wages for "women's jobs" were usually set below men's.

The clattering machine age likewise accentuated class division. "Industrial buccaneers" flaunted bloated fortunes, and their rags-to-riches spouses displayed glittering diamonds. Such extravagances evoked bitter criticism. Some of it was envious, but much of it rose from a small but increasingly vocal group of socialists and other radicals, many of whom were recent European immigrants. The existence of an oligarchy of money was amply demon-

strated by the fact that by 1900 about one-tenth of the people owned and controlled nine-tenths of the nation's wealth.

A nation of farmers and independent producers was becoming a nation of wage earners. In 1860 half of all workers were self-employed; by the century's end, two of every three working Americans depended on wages. Real wages were rising, and times were good for workers who were working. But with dependence on wages came vulnerability to the swings of the economy and the whims of the employer. The fear of unemployment was never distant. A breadwinner's illness could mean catastrophe for an entire family. Nothing more sharply

Gibson Girl, 1899 Illustrator Charles Dana Gibson created a sensation with his drawings of healthy, athletic, young women. The image of the "Gibson Girl" inspired new standards of female fashion as the twentieth century opened, and came to symbolize women's growing independence and assertiveness.

defined the growing difference between working-class and middle-class conditions of life than the precariousness of the laborer's lot. Reformers struggled to introduce a measure of security—job and wage protection, and provision for temporary unemployment—into the lives of the working class.

Finally, strong pressures for foreign trade developed as the tireless industrial machine threatened to flood the domestic market. American products radiated out all over the world—notably the five-gallon kerosene can of the Standard Oil Company. The flag follows trade, and empire tends to follow the flag—a harsh lesson that America was soon to learn.

In Unions There Is Strength

Sweat of the laborer lubricated the vast new industrial machine. Yet the wage workers did not share proportionally with their employers in the benefits of the age of big business.

The worker, suggestive of the Roman galley slave, was becoming a lever-puller in a giant mechanism. Individual originality and creativity were being stifled, and less value than ever before was being placed on manual skills. Before the Civil War, the worker might have toiled in a small plant whose owner hailed the employee in the morning by first name and inquired after the family's health. But now the factory hand was employed by a corporation—depersonalized, bodiless, soulless, and often conscienceless. The directors knew the worker not; and in fairness to their stockholders they were not inclined to engage in large-scale private philanthropy.

New machines displaced employees, and though in the long run more jobs were created than destroyed, in the short run the manual worker was often hard hit. A glutted labor market, moreover, severely handicapped wage earners. Employers could take advantage of the vast new railroad network and bring in unemployed workers, from the four corners of the country and beyond, to beat down high wage levels. During the 1880s and 1890s, several hundred thousand unskilled workers a year poured into the country from Europe, creating a labor market more favorable to the boss than the worker.

Individual workers were powerless to battle single-handedly against giant industry. Forced to organize and fight for basic rights, they found the dice heavily loaded against them. The corporation could dispense with the individual worker much more easily than the worker could dispense with the corporation. Employers could pool vast wealth through thousands of stockholders, retain high-priced lawyers, buy up the local press, and put pressure on the politicians. They could import strikebreakers ("scabs") and employ thugs to beat up labor organizers. In 1886 Jay Gould reputedly boasted, "I can hire one-half of the working class to kill the other half."

Corporations had still other weapons in their arsenals. They could call upon the federal courts—presided over by well-fed and conservative judges—to issue injunctions ordering the strikers to cease striking. If defiance and disorders ensued, the company could request the state and federal authorities to bring in troops. Employers could lock their doors against rebellious workers—a procedure called the "lockout"—and then starve them into submission. They could compel them to sign "ironclad oaths" or "yellow dog contracts," both of which were solemn agreements not to join a labor union. They could put the names of agitators on a "black list" and circulate it among fellow employers. A corporation might even own the "company town," with its high-priced grocery stores and "easy" credit. Often the worker sank into perpetual debt—a status that strongly resembled serfdom. Countless thousands of blackened coal miners were born in a company house, nurtured by a (high-priced) company store, and buried in a company graveyard—prematurely dead.

The middle-class public, annoyed by recurrent strikes, grew deaf to the outcry of the worker. Ameri-

The Reverend Henry Ward Beecher (1813–1887) of Brooklyn, the most distinguished (and notorious) clergyman of the era after the Civil War, said,

"The trade union, which originated under the European system, destroys liberty. I do not say a dollar a day is enough to support a working man, but it is enough to support a man. Not enough to support a man and five children if a man insists on smoking and drinking beer."

The Strike, by Robert Koehler, 1886   Scenes like this were becoming more typical of American life in the late nineteenth century as industrialism advanced spectacularly and sometimes ruthlessly. Here Koehler (1850–1917) shows an entire community of men, women, and children—many of them apparently immigrant newcomers—challenging the power of the "boss." The scene is tense but orderly, though violence seems to be imminent as one striker reaches for a rock.

can wages were perhaps the highest in the world, although a dollar a day for pick-and-shovel labor does not now seem excessive. Carnegie and Rockefeller had battled their way to the top, and the view was common that the laborer could do likewise. Somehow the strike seemed like a foreign importation—socialistic and hence unpatriotic. Big business might combine into trusts to raise prices, but the worker must not combine into unions to raise wages. Unemployment seemed to be an act of God, who somehow would take care of the laborer.

Labor Limps Along

Labor unions, which had been few and disorganized in 1861, were given a strong boost by the Civil War. This bloody conflict, with its drain on human resources, put more of a premium on labor; and the mounting cost of living provided an urgent incentive to unionization. By 1872 there were several

hundred thousand organized workers and thirty-two national unions, representing such crafts as bricklayers, typesetters, and shoemakers.

The National Labor Union, organized in 1866, represented a giant bootstride by workers. The union lasted six years and attracted the impressive total of some 600,000 members, including the skilled, unskilled, and farmers, though in keeping with the times, it excluded the Chinese and made only nominal efforts to include women and blacks. Black workers organized their own Colored National Labor Union as an adjunct, but their support for the Republican party and the persistent racism of white unionists prevented the two national unions from working together. The National Labor Union agitated for the arbitration of industrial disputes and the eight-hour workday, and won the latter for government workers. But the devastating depression of the 1870s dealt it a knockout blow. Labor was generally rocked back on its heels during the tumultuous years of the depression, but it never completely toppled. Wage reductions in 1877 touched off such disruptive strikes on the railroads that nothing short of federal troops could restore order.

A new organization—the Knights of Labor—seized the torch dropped by the defunct National Labor Union (see "Makers of America: The Knights of Labor," pp. 560–561). Officially known as The Noble and Holy Order of the Knights of Labor, it began inauspiciously in 1869 as a secret society, with a private ritual, passwords, and a grip. Secrecy, which continued until 1881, would forestall possible reprisals by employers.

The Knights of Labor, like the National Labor Union, sought to include all workers in "one big union." Their slogan was "An injury to one is the concern of all." A welcome mat was rolled out for the skilled and unskilled, for men and women, for whites and underprivileged blacks, some 90,000 of whom joined. The Knights barred only "nonproducers"—liquor dealers, professional gamblers, lawyers, bankers, and stockbrokers.

Setting up broad goals, the embattled Knights refused to thrust their lance into politics. Instead they campaigned for economic and social reform, including producers' cooperatives and codes for safety and health. Voicing the war cry "Labor is the only creator of values and capital," they frowned upon industrial warfare while fostering industrial arbitration. The ordinary workday was then ten hours or more, and the Knights waged a determined campaign for the eight-hour stint. A favorite song of these years ran,

> *Hurrah, hurrah, for labor,*
> *it is mustering all its powers,*
> *And shall march along to victory*
> *with the banner of eight hours.*

Under the eloquent but often erratic leadership of Terence V. Powderly, an Irish-American of nimble wit and fluent tongue, the Knights won a number of strikes for the eight-hour day. When the Knights staged a successful strike against Jay Gould's Wabash Railroad in 1885, membership mushroomed, to about three-quarters of a million workers.

Unhorsing the Knights of Labor

Despite their outward success, the Knights were riding for a fall. They became involved in a number of May Day strikes in 1886, about half of which failed. A focal point was Chicago, home to about eighty thousand Knights. The city was also honeycombed with a few hundred anarchists, many of them foreign-born, who were advocating a violent overthrow of the American government.

Tensions rapidly built up to the bloody Haymarket Square episode. Labor disorders had broken out, and on May 4, 1886, the Chicago police advanced on a meeting called to protest alleged brutalities by the authorities. Suddenly a dynamite bomb was thrown that killed or injured several dozen people, including police.

Hysteria swept the Windy City. Eight anarchists were rounded up, although nobody proved that they had anything to do directly with the bomb. But the judge and jury held that since they had preached incendiary doctrines, they could be charged with conspiracy. Five were sentenced to death, one of whom committed suicide, and the other three were given stiff prison terms.

Agitation for clemency mounted. In 1892, some six years later, John P. Altgeld, a German-born Democrat of strong liberal tendencies, was elected governor of Illinois. After studying the Haymarket case exhaustively, he pardoned the three survivors. Violent abuse was showered on him by conservatives, unstinted praise by those who thought the men innocent. He was defeated for reelection and died a few years later in relative obscurity, "The Eagle Forgotten." Whatever the merits of the case, Altgeld displayed courage in opposing what he regarded as a gross injustice.

The Haymarket Square bomb helped blow the props from under the Knights of Labor. They were associated in the public mind, though mistakenly, with the anarchists. The eight-hour movement suffered correspondingly, and subsequent strikes by the Knights met with scant success.

Another fatal handicap of the Knights was their inclusion of both skilled and unskilled workers. Unskilled labor could easily be replaced by strike-breaking "scabs." High-class craft unionists, who enjoyed a semimonopoly of skills, could not readily be supplanted and hence enjoyed a superior bargaining position. They finally wearied of sacrificing this advantage on the altar of solidarity with their unskilled coworkers and sought refuge in a federation of exclusively skilled craft unions—the American Federation of Labor. The desertion of the skilled craft unionists dealt the Knights a body blow. By the 1890s they had melted away to 100,000 members, and these gradually fused with other protest groups of that decade.

The AF of L to the Fore

The elitist American Federation of Labor, born in 1886, was largely the brainchild of squat, square-jawed Samuel Gompers. This colorful Jewish cigar maker, born in a London tenement and removed from school at age ten, was brought to America when thirteen. Taking his turn at reading informative literature to fellow cigar makers in New York, he was pressed into overtime service because of his strong voice. Rising spectacularly in the labor ranks, he was elected president of the American Federation of Labor every year except one from 1886 to 1924.

Significantly, the American *Federation* of Labor was just what it called itself—a federation. It consisted of an association of self-governing national unions, each of which kept its independence, with the AF of L unifying overall strategy. No individual laborer as such could join the central organization.

Gompers adopted a down-to-earth approach, soft-pedaling attempts to engineer sweeping social reform. A bitter foe of socialism, he shunned politics for economic strategies and goals. Gompers had no quarrel with capitalism, but he demanded a fairer share for labor. All he wanted, he said, was "more." Promoting what he called a "pure and simple" unionism, he sought better wages, hours, and working conditions. Unlike the somewhat utopian Knights of Labor, he was not concerned with the sweet by-and-by, but with the bitter here and now. A major goal of Gompers was the "trade agreement" authorizing the "closed shop"—or all-union labor. His chief weapons were the walkout and the boycott, enforced by "We don't patronize" signs. The stronger craft unions of the federation, by pooling funds, were able to amass a war chest that would enable them to ride out prolonged strikes.

The AF of L thus established itself on solid but narrow foundations. Although attempting to speak for all workers, it fell far short of being representative of them. Composed of skilled crafts, like the carpenters and the bricklayers, it was willing to let unskilled laborers, including women and especially blacks, fend for themselves. Though hard-pressed by big industry, the federation was basically nonpolitical. But it did attempt to persuade members to reward friends and punish foes at the polls. The AF of L weathered the panic of 1893 reasonably well, and by 1900 it could boast a membership of 500,000.

Samuel Gompers (1850–1924) Samuel Gompers declared, "Show me the country in which there are no strikes and I'll show you that country in which there is no liberty." In later years this was notably true of authoritarian countries.

Critics referred to it, with questionable accuracy, as "the labor trust."

Labor disorders continued, peppering the years from 1881 to 1900 with an alarming total of over 23,000 strikes. These disturbances involved 6,610,000 workers, with a total loss to both employers and employees of $450 million. The strikers lost about half their strikes, and won or compromised the remainder. Perhaps the gravest weakness of organized labor was that it still embraced only a small minority of all working people—about 3 percent in 1900.

But attitudes toward labor had begun to change perceptibly by 1900. The public was beginning to concede the right of workers to organize, to bargain collectively, and to strike. As a sign of the times,

The Knights of Labor

It was 1875. The young worker was guided into a room, where his blindfold was removed. Surrounding him were a dozen men, their faces covered by hoods. One of the masked figures solemnly asked three questions: "Do you believe in God?" "Do you gain your bread by the sweat of your brow?" "Are you willing to take a solemn vow, binding you to secrecy, obedience, and mutual assistance?" Yes, came the reply. The men doffed their hoods and joined hands in a circle. Their leader, the Master Workman, declared: "On behalf of the toiling millions of earth, I welcome you to this Sanctuary, dedicated to the service of God, by serving humanity." Then the entire group burst into song:

"Mother Jones"

> Storm the fort, ye Knights of Labor,
> Battle for your cause;
> Equal rights for every neighbor,
> Down with tyrant laws!

The carefully staged pageantry then drew to a close. The worker was now a full-fledged member of the Knights of Labor.

He had just joined a loose-knit organization of some 100,000 working people, soon to swell to nearly one million after the Knights led several successful strikes in the 1880s. The first women Knights joined in 1881, when an all-female local was established in the shoe trade in Philadelphia, and one in ten members were women by 1885. They were organizers, too. Fiery Mary Harris ("Mother") Jones got her start agitating for the Knights in the Illinois coal fields. The first all-black local was founded among coal miners in Ottumwa, Iowa. The Knights preached tolerance and the solidarity of all working men and women, and they meant it; but even their inclusionary spirit had its limits. Chinese workers were barred from joining, and the Knights vigorously supported the Chinese Exclusion Act of 1882. They also championed the Contract Labor Law of 1885, which aimed to restrain competition from low-wage immigrant workers—though immigrants, especially the Irish, were themselves disproportionately represented among the Knights' membership.

Terence V. Powderly, born to Irish immigrant parents in Carbondale, Pennsylvania, in 1849, became the Grand Master Workman of the Knights in 1879. Slightly built, with mild blue eyes behind glasses, he had dropped out of school at age thirteen to take a job guarding railroad track-switches and rose to mayor of Scranton, Pennsylvania, in the 1870s. In 1894 he became a lawyer—despite the fact that the Knights excluded lawyers from membership. A complex, colorful, and sometimes cynical man, he denounced the "multimillionaires [for] laying the foundation for their colossal fortunes on the bodies and souls of living men." In the eyes of

Powderly and his Knights, only the economic and political independence of American workers could preserve republican traditions and institutions from corruption by monopolists and other "parasites."

Powderly denounced "wage-slavery" and dedicated the Knights to achieving the "cooperative commonwealth." Shunning socialism, which advocated government ownership of the means of production, Powderly urged laborers to save enough from their wages to purchase mines, factories, railroads, and stores. They would thereby create a kind of toilers' utopia; because labor would own and operate those enterprises, workers themselves would be owner-producers, and the conflict between labor and capital would evaporate. The Knights actually did operate a few businesses, including coal mines in Indiana, but all eventually failed.

Powderly's vision of the cooperative commonwealth reflected the persistent dream of many nineteenth-century American workers that they would all one day become producers. As expectant capitalists, they lacked "class consciousness"—that is, a sense of themselves as a permanent working class that must organize to coax what benefits it could out of the capitalist system. Samuel Gompers, by contrast, accepted the framework of American capitalism and his American Federation of Labor sought to work within that framework, not to overturn it. Gompers's conservative strategy, not Powderly's utopian dream, eventually carried the day. The swift decline of the Knights in the 1890s underscored the obsolescence of their unrealistic, even naive, view that a bygone age of independent producers could be restored. Yet the Knights' commitment to unify-

Machinist Frank J. Ferrell, Black Delegate of District Assembly No. 49, Introducing General Master Workman Terence Powderly to the 10th Annual Convention of the Knights of Labor, Held in Richmond, Virginia, 1886

ing all workers in one union—regardless of race, gender, ethnicity, or skill level—provided a blueprint for the eventual success of similarly committed unions like the Congress of Industrial Organizations in the 1930s.

Women Delegates to the 1886 Convention of the Knights of Labor

Labor Day was made a legal holiday by act of Congress in 1894. A few enlightened industrialists had come to perceive the wisdom of avoiding costly economic warfare by bargaining with the unions and signing agreements. But the vast majority of employers continued to fight organized labor, which achieved its grudging gains only after recurrent strikes and frequent reverses. Nothing was handed to it on a silver platter. Management still held the whip hand, and several trouble-fraught decades were to pass before labor was to gain a position of relative equality with capital. If the age of big business had dawned, the age of big labor was still some distance over the horizon.

Chronology

1862	Congress authorizes a transcontinental railroad
1866	National Labor Union organized
1869	Transcontinental railroad joined near Ogden, Utah Knights of Labor organized
1870	Standard Oil Company organized
1876	Bell invents the telephone
1879	Edison invents the electric light
1886	Haymarket Square bombing *Wabash* case American Federation of Labor formed
1887	Interstate Commerce Act
1890	Sherman Anti-Trust Act
1901	United States Steel Corporation formed

Industrialization: Boon or Blight?

The capitalists who forged an industrial America in the late nineteenth century were once called captains of industry—a respectful title that bespoke the awe due their wondrous material accomplishments. But these economic innovators have never been universally admired. During the Great Depression of the 1930s, when the entire industrial order they had created seemed to have collapsed utterly, it was fashionable to speak of them as robber barons—a term implying scorn for their high-handed methods. This sneer often issued from the lips and pens of leftist critics like Matthew Josephson, who sympathized with the working classes that were allegedly brutalized by the factory system.

Criticism has also come from writers nostalgic for a preindustrial past. These critics believe that industrialization stripped away the traditions, values, and pride of native farmers and immigrant craftspeople. Conceding that economic development elevated the material standard of living for working Americans, this interpretation contends that the industrial revolution diminished their spiritual "quality of life." Accordingly, historians like Herbert Gutman and David Montgomery portray labor's struggle for control of the workplace as the central drama of industrial expansion.

Nevertheless, even these historians concede that class-based protest has never been as powerful a force in the United States as in certain European countries. Many historians believe that this is so because greater social mobility in America dampened class tensions. The French observer Alexis de Tocqueville noted in the 1830s that America had few huge inherited fortunes and that most of its wealthy men were self-made. For two centuries a majority of Americans have believed that greater opportunity distinguished the New World from the Old.

In the 1960s, historians led by Stephan Thernstrom began to test this long-standing belief. Looking at such factors as occupation, wealth, and geographic mobility, they tried to gauge the nature and extent of social mobility in the United States. Most of these historians concluded that although relatively few Americans made rags-to-riches leaps like those heralded in the Horatio Alger stories, large numbers experienced small improvements in their economic and social status. Few sons of laborers became corporate tycoons, but many more became line bosses and white-collar clerks. These studies also have found that race and ethnicity often affected one's chance for success. For instance, the children and grandchildren of Jewish immigrants tended to rise faster in the professions than Americans of Italian and Irish descent. Throughout the nineteenth and early twentieth centuries, blacks lagged far behind other groups in almost every category.

In recent years such studies have been criticized by certain historians who point out the difficulties involved in defining social status. For instance, some white-collar clerical workers received lower wages than manual laborers did. Were they higher or lower on the social scale? Furthermore, James Henretta has pointed out that different groups defined success differently: whereas Jewish immigrants often scrapped to give their sons professional educations, the Irish put more emphasis on acquiring land, and Italians, on building small family-run businesses.

Meanwhile, leftist historians such as Michael Katz have argued that the degree of social mobility in America has been overrated. These historians argue that industrial capitalism created two classes: a working class that sold its labor, and a business class that controlled resources and bought labor. Although most Americans took small steps upward, they generally remained within the class in which they began. Thus, these historians argue, the inequality of a capitalistic class system persisted in America's seemingly fluid society.

SUGGESTED READINGS

PRIMARY SOURCE DOCUMENTS

Andrew Carnegie, "Wealth,"* *North American Review* (June 1889), gives the philosophy of the Gilded Age's greatest entrepreneur. Henry Grady's Boston speech (1889), in Joel C. Harris, *Life of Henry W. Grady* (1890), dramatizes the plight of the South. Samuel Gompers penned his "Letter on Labor in Industrial Society," an open letter to Judge Peter Grossup, in 1894 (in Richard Hofstadter, *Great Issues in American History*). William Dean Howell's novel *The Rise of Silas Lapham* (1885) treats the moral impact of the new business culture on one New England businessman and his family.

---

*An asterisk indicates that the document, or an excerpt from it, can be found in Thomas A. Bailey and David M. Kennedy, eds., *The American Spirit: United States History as Seen by Contemporaries*, 9th ed. (Boston: Houghton Mifflin, 1998).

SECONDARY SOURCES

A useful survey is Samuel P. Hays's penetrating study, *The Response to Industrialism, 1885–1914* (1957). Stuart Bruchey puts the period in context in *The Growth of the Modern Economy* (1975). Business is the subject of Alfred D. Chandler, Jr., *The Visible Hand: The Managerial Revolution in American Business* (1978); Saul Engelbourg, *Power and Morality: American Business Ethics, 1840–1914* (1980); and Naomi R. Lamoreaux, *The Great Merger Movement in American Business, 1895–1904* (1985). Olivier Zunz surveys the development of corporate culture in *Making America Corporate, 1870–1920* (1990), while Scott M. Cutlip examines *The Unseen Power: Public Relations, a History* (1994). Thomas K. McCraw assesses government regulation in *Prophets of Regulation: Charles Francis Adams, Louis D. Brandeis, James M. Landis, Alfred E. Kahn* (1984). In *Control Through Communication: The Rise of System in American Management* (1989), Joanne

Yates argues that big business was more efficient than Brandeis believed. The thought and attitudes characteristic of the new industrial age are examined by Richard Hofstadter, *Social Darwinism in American Thought* (rev. ed., 1955); Daniel T. Rodgers, *The Work Ethic in Industrial America, 1850–1920* (1978); and Alan Trachtenberg, *The Incorporation of America: Culture and Society in the Gilded Age* (1982). On the railroads see George R. Taylor and Irene D. Neu, *The American Railroad Network, 1861–1890* (1956), and Robert Fogel's provocative *Railroads and American Economic Growth* (1964). C. Vann Woodward has provided a masterful analysis of *Origins of the New South, 1877–1913* (1951), which can be profitably supplemented by Jonathan M. Wiener, *Social Origins of the New South* (1978), and Don H. Doyle, *New Men, New Cities, New South: Atlanta, Nashville, Charleston, Mobile, 1860–1910* (1980). Also see Gaines M. Foster, *Ghosts of the Confederacy: Defeat, the Lost Cause and the Emergence of the New South, 1865–1913* (1987). For more on race relations in the post-Reconstruction South, see Joel Williamson, *The Crucible of Race* (1984); Howard Rabinowitz, *Race Relations in the Urban South, 1865–1890* (1978); and Neil R. McMillen, *Dark Journey: Black Mississippians in the Age of Jim Crow* (1989). Labor is the subject of Gerald Grob, *Workers and Utopia* (1961), and David Montgomery's innovative *The Fall of the House of Labor: The Workplace, the State, and American Labor Activism, 1865–1925* (1987). Paul Krause details *The Battle for Homestead, 1880–1892* (1992). Especially stimulating are two volumes by Herbert Gutman, *Work, Culture, and Society in Industrializing America* (1976) and *Power and Culture: Essays on the American Working Class* (1987). On female workers see David Katzman, *Seven Days a Week: Women and Domestic Service in Industrializing America* (1978); Philip Foner, *Women and the American Labor Movement* (1979); and Alice Kessler-Harris, *Out to Work: A History of Wage-Earning Women in the United States* (1982). For a discussion of labor and race, see Gerald David Jaynes, *Branches Without Roots: Genesis of the Black Working Class in the American South, 1862–1882* (1986).

26

America Moves to the City

1865–1900

*What shall we do with our great cities? What will
our great cities do with us . . . ? [T]he question . . .
does not concern the city alone. The whole country
is affected . . . by the condition of its great cities.*

LYMAN ABBOTT, 1891

The Urban Frontier

Born in the country, America moved to the city in
the decades following the Civil War. By the year 1900
the United States' upsurging population nearly doubled from its level of some 40 million souls enumerated in the census of 1870. Yet in the very same
period the population of American cities *tripled*. By
the end of the nineteenth century, 4 out of 10 Americans were city dwellers, in striking contrast to the
rustic population of stagecoach days.

  This cityward drift affected not only the United
States but most of the Western world. European
peasants, pushed off the land in part by competition
from cheap American foodstuffs, were pulled into

cities—in both Europe and America—by the new
lure of industrial jobs. A revolution in agriculture
thus fed the industrial and urban revolutions.

  The growth of American metropolises was spectacular. In 1860 no city in the United States could
boast a million inhabitants; by 1890 New York,
Chicago, and Philadelphia had vaulted past the million mark. By 1900 New York, with some 3.5 million
people, was the second largest city in the world, outranked only by London.

  Cities grew both up and out. The cloud-brushing skyscraper allowed more people and workplaces
to be packed onto a parcel of land. Appearing first as
a ten-story building in Chicago in 1885, the skyscraper was made usable by the perfecting of the
electric elevator. An opinionated Chicago architect,
Louis Sullivan (1856–1924), contributed formidably

Lower Broadway, 1875   Horses still abounded in New York and other cities when this lithograph was made, but they would soon be displaced by street railways and automobiles.

to the further development of the skyscraper with his famous principle that "form follows function." Nesting loftily above city streets in the new steel-skeleton high-rises that Sullivan helped to make popular, many Americans were becoming modern cliff dwellers.

Americans were also becoming commuters, carted daily between home and job on the mass-transit lines that radiated out from central cities to surrounding suburbs. Electric trolleys, powered by wagging antennae from overhead wires, propelled city limits explosively outward. The compact and communal "walking city," its boundaries fixed by the limits of leg-power, gave way to the immense and impersonal megalopolis, carved into distinctly different districts for business, industry, and residential neighborhoods—which were in turn segregated by race, ethnicity, and social class.

Rural America could not compete with the siren song of the city. Industrial jobs, above all, drew

country folks off the farms and into factory centers. But the urban lifestyle also held powerful attractions. The predawn milking of cows had little appeal when compared with the late-night glitter of city lights. Electricity, indoor plumbing, and telephones—whose numbers leapt from some 50,000 in 1880 to over 1 million in 1900—all made life in the big city more alluring. Engineering marvels like the skyscraper and New York's awesome Brooklyn Bridge, a harplike suspension span dedicated in 1883, further added to the seductive glamour of the gleaming cities.

Cavernous department stores such as Macy's in New York and Marshall Field's in Chicago attracted urban middle-class shoppers and provided urban working-class jobs, many of them for women. The bustling emporiums also heralded a dawning era of consumerism and accentuated widening class divisions. When Carrie Meeker, novelist Theodore Dreiser's fictional heroine in *Sister Carrie* (1900),

The Brooklyn Bridge, 1890
Completed in 1883, the bridge was an engineering marvel in its day and has inspired poets ever since. The twentieth-century poet Hart Crane called it "O harp and altar!"

escapes from rural boredom to Chicago just before the turn of the century, it is the spectacle of the city's dazzling department stores that awakens her fateful yearning for a richer, more elegant way of life—for entry into the privileged urban middle class, whose existence she had scarcely imagined in the rustic countryside.

The move to the city introduced Americans to new ways of life. Country dwellers produced little household waste. Domestic animals or scavenging pigs ate food scraps on the farm. Rural women mended and darned worn clothing rather than discard it. Household products were sold in bulk at the local store, without wrapping. Mail-order houses such as Sears and Montgomery Ward, which increasingly displaced the rural "general store" in the late nineteenth century, at first did not list trash barrels or garbage cans in their catalogues. In the city, however, goods came in throw-away bottles, boxes, bags, and cans. Apartment houses had no adjoining barnyards where residents might toss garbage to the hogs. Cheap ready-to-wear clothing

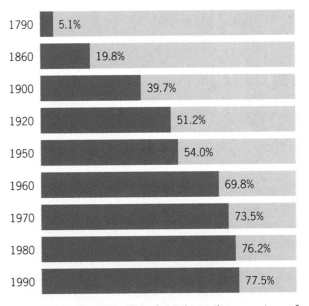

Year	Percentage
1790	5.1%
1860	19.8%
1900	39.7%
1920	51.2%
1950	54.0%
1960	69.8%
1970	73.5%
1980	76.2%
1990	77.5%

The Shift to the City   This chart shows the percentage of total population living in locales with a population of twenty-five hundred or more. Note the slowing of the cityward trend from 1970s onward.

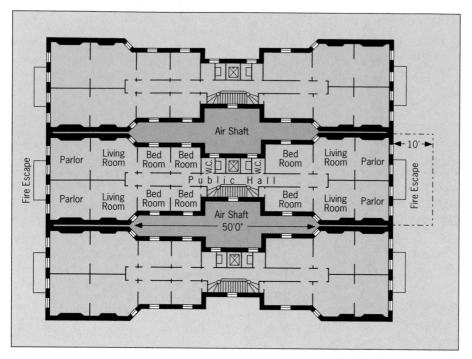

Dumbbell Tenement This was the standard architectural plan for the human warehouses on New York's Lower East Side. Despite the innovation of an air shaft to bring light and ventilation to the middle of the building, only one room in each of the apartments was directly exposed to sunlight and open air. All families on a floor shared the toilet ("W.C.") in the hallway.

and swiftly changing fashions pushed old suits and dresses out of the closet and onto the trash heap. Waste disposal, in short, was an issue new to the urban age. And the mountains of waste that urbanites generated further testified to a cultural shift away from the virtues of thrift to the conveniences of consumerism.

The jagged skyline of America's perpendicular civilization could not fully conceal the canker sores of a feverish growth. Criminals flourished like lice in the teeming asphalt jungles. Sanitary facilities could not keep pace with the mushrooming population explosion. Impure water, uncollected garbage, unwashed bodies, and droppings from draft animals enveloped many cities in a satanic stench. Baltimore was described as smelling like a billion polecats.

The cities were monuments of contradiction. They represented "humanity compressed," remarked one observer, "the best and the worst combined, in a strangely composite community." They harbored merchant princes and miserable paupers, stately banks and sooty factories, green-grassed suburbs and treeless ghettos, towering skyscrapers and stinking tenements. The glaring contrasts that assaulted the eye in New York reminded one visitor of "a lady in ball costume, with diamonds in her ears, and her toes out at the boots."

Worst of all were the human pigsties known as slums. They seemed to grow ever more crowded, more filthy, and more rat-infested, especially after the perfection in 1879 of the "dumbbell" tenement. So named because of the outline of its floor plan, the dumbbell was usually seven or eight stories high, with shallow, sunless, and ill-smelling air shafts providing minimal ventilation. Several families were sardined onto each floor of the barracks-like structures, and they shared a malodorous toilet in the hall. In these fetid warrens, conspicuously in New York's "Lung Block," hundreds of unfortunate urbanites coughed away their lives. "Flophouses" abounded where the half-starved and unemployed might sleep for a few cents on verminous mattresses. Small wonder that slum dwellers strove mightily to escape their wretched surroundings—as many of them did. The slums remained foul places, inhabited by successive waves of newcomers. To a remarkable degree hard-working people moved up and out of them. But although they escaped the old ghetto, they generally resettled in other urban neighborhoods alongside people of the same ethnicity or religion. The wealthiest left the cities altogether and headed for the semirural suburbs. These leafy "bedroom communities" eventually ringed the brick-and-concrete cities with a greenbelt of affluence.

The New Immigration

The powerful pull of the American urban magnet was felt even in faraway Europe. A brightly colored stream of immigrants continued to pour in from the old "mother continent." In each of the three decades from the 1850s through the 1870s, more than 2 million migrants had stepped onto America's shores. By the 1880s the stream had swelled to a rushing torrent, as more than 5 million cascaded into the country. A new high for a single year was reached in 1882, when 788,992 arrived—or more than 2,100 a day.

Until the 1880s most immigrants had come from the British Isles and western Europe, chiefly Germany and Scandinavia. They were typically fair-skinned Anglo-Saxon and Teutonic types; and they were usually Protestant, except for the Catholic Irish and many Catholic Germans. Many of them boasted a comparatively high rate of literacy and were accustomed to some kind of representative government. Their Old Country ways of life were such that they fitted relatively easily into American society, especially when they took up farming, as many did.

But in the 1880s the character of the immigrant stream changed drastically. The so-called New Immigrants came from southern and eastern Europe. Among them were Italians, Croats, Slovaks, Greeks, and Poles; many of them worshiped in orthodox churches or synagogues. They came from countries with little history of democratic government, where people had grown accustomed to cringing before despotism and where opportunities for advancement were few. Largely illiterate and impoverished, most new immigrants preferred to seek industrial jobs in jam-packed cities rather than move out to farms (see "Makers of America: The Italians," pp. 572–573).

These new peoples totaled only 19 percent of the inpouring immigrants in the 1880s; but by the first decade of the twentieth century, they constituted an astonishing 66 percent of the total inflow. They hived together in cities like New York and Chicago, where the "Little Italys" and "Little Polands" soon claimed more inhabitants than many of the largest cities of the same nationality in the

Annual Immigration, 1860–1994 The 1989 total includes 478,814 people granted permanent residence status under the "amnesty" provisions of the 1986 Immigration Reform and Control Act. The 1990 total includes 880,372 people granted permanent residence under these provisions. The peak came in 1991, when 1,123,162 people were affected. (Source: *Statistical Abstracts of the United States,* relevant years.)

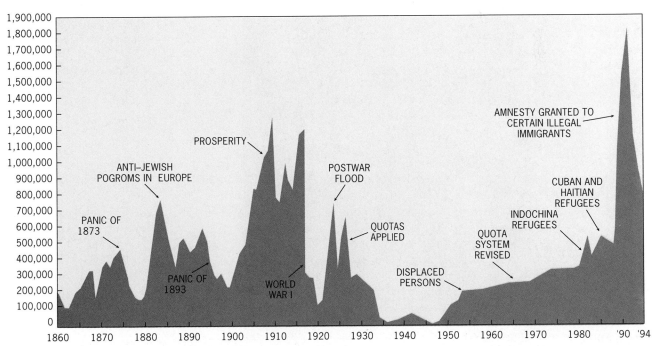

Old World. Some Americans feared that these New Immigrants would not—or could not—assimilate to life in their new land, and they began asking if the nation had become a melting pot or a dumping ground.

Southern Europe Uprooted

Why were these bright-shawled and quaint-jacketed strangers hammering on the gates? In part, they left their native countries because Europe seemed to have no room for them. The population of the Old World was growing vigorously. It nearly doubled in the century after 1800, thanks in part to abundant supplies of fish and grain from America and to the widespread cultivation in Europe of that humble New World transplant, the potato. American food

imports and the galloping pace of European industrialization shook the peasantry loose from its ancient habitats and customary occupations, creating a vast, footloose army of the unemployed. Europeans by the millions drained out of the countryside and into European cities. Most stayed there, but some kept moving and left Europe altogether. About 60 million Europeans abandoned the Old Continent in the nineteenth and early twentieth centuries. More than half of them moved to the United States. But that striking fact should not obscure the important truth that masses of people were already in motion in Europe before they felt the tug of the American magnet. Immigration to America was, in many ways, a by-product of the urbanization of Europe.

"America fever" proved highly contagious in Europe. The United States was often painted as a land of fabulous opportunity in the "America let-

The Lower East Side of Manhattan, New York, c. 1900   Population densities in America's immigrant neighborhoods were among the highest in the world.

ters" sent by friends and relatives already transplanted—letters that were soiled by the hands of many readers. "We eat here every day," wrote one jubilant Pole, "what we get only for Easter in our [native] country." The land of the free was also blessed with freedom from military conscription and institutionalized religious persecution.

Profit-seeking Americans trumpeted throughout Europe the attractions of the new promised land. Industrialists wanted low-wage labor, railroads wanted buyers for their land grants, states wanted more population, and steamship lines wanted more human cargo for their holds. In fact, the ease and cheapness of steam-powered shipping greatly accelerated the transoceanic surge.

As the century lengthened, savage persecutions of minorities in Europe drove many shattered souls to American shores. In the 1880s the Russians turned violently upon their own Jews, chiefly in the Polish areas. Tens of thousands of these battered refugees, survivors of centuries of harassment as hated outcasts, fled their burning homes. They made their way to the seaboard cities of the Atlantic Coast, notably New York. Jews had experienced city life in Europe—a circumstance that made them virtually unique among the New Immigrants. Many of them brought their urban skills of tailoring or shopkeeping to American cities. Destitute and devout, eastern European Jews were frequently given a

Mary Antin (1881–1949), who came to America from Russian Poland in 1894, when thirteen years of age, later wrote in The Promised Land *(1912),*

"So at last I was going to America! Really, really going, at last! The boundaries burst. The arch of heaven soared. A million suns shone out for every star. The winds rushed in from outer space, roaring in my ears, 'America! America!'"

frosty reception not only by old-stock Americans but also by those German Jews who had arrived decades earlier and prospered in the United States, some as garment manufacturers who now condescendingly employed their coreligionists as cheap labor.

Many of the immigrants never intended to become Americans in any case. A large number of them were single men who worked in the United States for several months or years and then returned home with their hard-earned roll of American dollars. Some 25 percent of the nearly 20 million people who arrived between 1820 and 1900 were "birds of

Jewish Women Working in a Sweatshop, c. 1910 Countless immigrant women found their first American employment in shops like this.

The Italians

Who were the "New Immigrants"? Who were these southern and eastern European birds of passage that flocked to the United States between 1880 and 1920? Prominent and typical among them were Italians, some 4 million of whom sailed to the United States during the four decades of the New Immigration.

They came from the southern provinces of their native land, the heel and toe of the Italian boot. These areas had lagged behind the prosperous, industrial region of northern Italy. The north had

been the seat of earlier Italian glory, as well as the fountainhead of the successful movement to unify the country in 1860. There industry had been planted and agriculture modernized. Unification raised hopes of similar progress in the downtrodden south, but it was slow in coming. Southern Italian peasants tilled their fields without fertilizer or machinery, using hand plows and rickety hoes that had been passed down for generations.

From such disappointed and demeaned conditions, southern Italians set out for the New World. Almost all of them were young men who intended to spend only a few months in America, stuff their pockets with dollars, and return home. Almost half

Italian Immigrants Arriving at Ellis Island, c. 1910

Pietro Learning to Write on Jersey Street
"The sons shall teach the fathers," the old saying goes. Many immigrants learned English from their children who attended American schools, like this youngster and parent in early-twentieth-century New Jersey.

Italian Immigrant Women Doing Piecework at Home in New York, c. 1910

Italian Construction Workers, c. 1910

of Italian immigrants did indeed repatriate—as did comparable numbers of the other New Immigrants, with the conspicuous exception of the Jews, who had fled their native lands to escape religious persecution. Almost all Italian immigrants sailed through New York harbor, sighting the Statue of Liberty as they debarked from crowded ships. Many soon moved on to other large cities, but so many remained that in the early years of the twentieth century, more Italians resided in New York than in the Italian cities of Florence, Venice, and Genoa combined.

Since the immigrant Italians, with few exceptions, had been peasant farmers in the Old Country, the U.S. government encouraged them to practice their ancestral livelihood here, believing they would more rapidly assimilate in the countryside than in the ethnic enclaves of the cities. But almost all such ventures failed. The farmers lacked capital, and they were in any case more interested in earning quick money than in permanently sinking roots. Although they huddled in the cities, Italian immigrants did not, however, abandon their rural upbringings entirely. Much to their neighbors' consternation, they often kept chickens in vacant lots and raised vegetables in small garden plots nestled between decaying tenement houses.

Those who bade a permanent farewell to Italy clustered in tightly knit communities that boasted opera clubs, Italian-language newspapers, and courts for playing bocci—a version of lawn bowling imported from the Old Country. Pizza emerged from the hot wood-burning ovens of these Little Italies, its aroma and flavor wafting its way into the hearts and stomachs of all Americans.

Italians typically earned their daily bread as industrial laborers—most famously as longshoremen and construction workers. They owed their prominence in the building trades to the "padrone system." The *padrone*, or labor boss, met immigrants upon arrival and secured jobs for them in New York, Chicago, or wherever there was an immediate demand for industrial labor. The padrone owed his power to his ability to speak both Italian and English, and he often found homes as well as jobs for the newcomers.

Lacking education, the Italians, as a group, remained in blue-collar jobs longer than some of their fellow New Immigrants. Many Italians, valuing vocation over schooling, sent their children off to work as early in their young lives as possible. Before World War I, less than 1 percent of Italian children enrolled in high school. Over the next fifty years, Italian-Americans and their offspring gradually prospered, moving out of the cities into the more affluent suburbs. Many served heroically in World War II and availed themselves of the GI Bill to finance the college educations and professional training their immigrant forebears had lacked.

passage" who eventually returned to their country of origin. For them the grip of the American magnet was never strong.

Even those who stayed in America struggled heroically to preserve their traditional culture. Catholics expanded their parochial-school system and Jews established Hebrew schools. Foreign-language newspapers abounded. Yiddish theaters, kosher food stores, Polish parishes, Greek restaurants, and Italian social clubs all attested to the desire to keep old ways alive. Yet time took its toll on these efforts to conserve the customs of the Old World in the New. The children of the immigrants grew up speaking fluent English, sometimes mocking the broken grammar of their parents. They often rejected the Old Country manners of their mothers and fathers in their desire to plunge headlong into the mainstream of American life.

Reactions to the New Immigration

America's government system, nurtured in wide-open spaces, was ill suited to the cement forests of the great cities. Beyond minimal checking to weed out criminals and the insane, the federal government did virtually nothing to ease the assimilation of immigrants into American society. State governments, usually dominated by rural representatives, did even less. City governments, overwhelmed by the sheer scale of rampant urban growth, proved woefully inadequate to the task. By default, the business of ministering to the immigrants' needs fell to the unofficial "governments" of the urban political machines, led by "bosses" like New York's notorious Boss Tweed.

Taking care of the immigrants was big business, indeed. Trading jobs and services for votes, a powerful boss might claim the loyalty of thousands of followers. In return for their support at the polls, the boss provided jobs on the city's payroll, found housing for new arrivals, tided over the needy with gifts of food and clothing, patched up minor scrapes with the law, and helped get schools, parks, and hospitals built in immigrant neighborhoods. Reformers gagged at this cynical exploitation of the immigrant vote, but the political boss gave valuable assistance that was forthcoming from no other source.

The nation's social conscience, slumbering since the antislavery crusade, gradually awakened to the plight of the cities, and especially their immi-

grant masses. Prominent in this awakening were several Protestant clergymen, who sought to apply the lessons of Christianity to the slums and factories. Noteworthy among them was Walter Rauschenbusch, who in 1886 became pastor of a German Baptist church in New York City. Also conspicuous was Washington Gladden, who took over a Congregational church in Columbus, Ohio, in 1882. Preaching the "social gospel," they both insisted that the churches tackle the burning social issues of the day. The Sermon on the Mount, they declared, was the science of society, and many social gospelers predicted that socialism would be the logical outcome of Christianity. These "Christian socialists" did much to prick calloused middle-class consciences, thus preparing the path for the progressive reform movement after the turn of the century.

One middle-class woman who was deeply dedicated to uplifting the urban masses was Jane Addams (1860–1935). Born into a prosperous Illinois family, Addams was one of the first generation of college-educated women. Upon her graduation she sought other outlets for her large talents than could be found in teaching or charitable volunteer work, then the only permissible occupations for a young woman of her social class. Inspired by a visit to England, in 1889 she acquired the decaying Hull mansion in Chicago. There she established Hull House, the most prominent (though not the first) American settlement house.

Soft-spoken but tenacious, Jane Addams became a kind of urban American saint in the eyes of many admirers. The philosopher William James told her, "You utter instinctively the truth we others vainly seek." She was a broad-gauge reformer who courageously condemned war as well as poverty, and she eventually won the Nobel Peace Prize in 1931. But her pacifism also earned her the enmity of some Americans, including the Daughters of the American Revolution, who choked on her antiwar views and expelled her from membership in their august organization.

Located in a poor immigrant neighborhood of Greeks, Italians, Russians, and Germans, Hull House offered instruction in English, counseling to help newcomers cope with American big-city life, child-care services for working mothers, and cultural activities for neighborhood residents. Following Jane Addams's lead, women founded settlement houses in other cities as well. Conspicuous among the houses was Lillian Wald's Henry Street Settlement in New York, which opened its doors in 1893.

Jane Addams (1860–1935)   Although Addams never married or bore children of her own, she "mothered" hundreds of youngsters like this one at Hull House, the Chicago settlement house she founded in 1889.

The settlement houses became centers of women's activism and of social reform. The women of Hull House successfully lobbied in 1893 for an Illinois antisweatshop law that protected women workers and prohibited child labor. They were led in this case by the black-clad Florence Kelley, a guerrilla warrior in the urban jungle. Armed with the insights of socialism and endowed with the voice of an actress, Kelley was a lifelong battler for the welfare of women, children, blacks, and consumers. She later moved to the Henry Street Settlement in New York and served for three decades as general secretary of the National Consumers League.

The pioneering work of Addams, Wald, and Kelley helped blaze the trail that many women—and some men—later followed into careers in the new profession of social work. These reformers vividly demonstrated the truth that the city was the frontier of opportunity for women, just as the wilderness had been for men.

The urban frontier opened new possibilities for women. More than a million women joined the work force in the single decade of the 1890s. Strict social codes prescribed which women might work and what jobs they might hold. Because employment for wives and mothers was considered taboo, the vast majority of working women were single. Their jobs depended on their race, ethnicity, and class. Black women had few opportunities beyond domestic service. White-collar jobs as social workers, secretaries, department store clerks, and telephone operators were largely reserved for native-born women. Immigrant women tended to cluster in particular industries, as Jewish women did in the garment trades. Although hours were often long, pay low, and advancement limited, a job still bought working women some economic and social independence. After contributing a large share of their earnings to their families, many women still had enough money in their pocketbooks to enter a new urban world of sociability—excursions to amusement parks with friends on days off, Saturday night dances with the "fellas."

Narrowing the Welcome Mat

Antiforeignism, or "nativism," earlier touched off by the Irish and German arrivals in the 1840s and 1850s, bared its ugly face in the 1880s with fresh ferocity. The New Immigrants had come for much the same reasons as the Old—to escape the poverty and squalor of Europe and to seek new opportunities in America. But "nativists" viewed the eastern and southern Europeans as culturally and religiously exotic hordes and often gave them a rude reception. The newest newcomers aroused widespread alarm. Their high birthrate, common among people with a low standard of living and sufficient youth and vigor to pull up stakes, raised worries that the original Anglo-Saxon stock would soon be outbred and outvoted. Still more horrifying was the prospect that it would be mongrelized by a mixture of "inferior" southern European blood and that the fairer Anglo-Saxon types would disappear. One New England writer cried out in anguish,

O Liberty, white Goddess! is it well
To leave the gates unguarded?

Looking Backward
Older immigrants, trying to keep their own humble arrival in America "in the shadows," sought to close the bridge that had carried them and their ancestors across the Atlantic.

"Native" Americans voiced additional fears. They blamed the immigrants for the degradation of urban government. Trade unionists assailed the alien arrivals for their willingness to work for "starvation" wages that seemed to them like princely sums and for importing in their intellectual baggage such dangerous doctrines as socialism, communism, and anarchism. Many business leaders, who had welcomed the flood of cheap manual labor, began to fear that they had embraced a Frankenstein's monster.

Antiforeign organizations, reminiscent of the "Know-Nothings" of antebellum days, were now revived in a different guise. Notorious among them was the American Protective Association (APA), which was created in 1887 and soon claimed a million members. In pursuing its nativist goals, the APA urged voting against Roman Catholic candidates for office and sponsored the publication of lustful fantasies about runaway nuns.

Organized labor was quick to throw its growing weight behind the move to choke off the rising tide of foreigners. Frequently used as strikebreakers, the wage-depressing immigrants were hard to unionize because of the language barrier. Labor leaders argued, not illogically, that if American industry was entitled to protection from foreign goods, American workers were entitled to protection from foreign laborers.

Congress finally nailed up partial bars against the inpouring immigrants. The first restrictive law, passed in 1882, banged the gate shut in the faces of paupers, criminals, and convicts, all of whom had to be returned at the expense of the greedy or careless shipper. Congress further responded to pained outcries from organized labor when in 1885 it prohibited the importation of foreign workers under contract—usually for substandard wages.

In later years other federal laws lengthened the list of undesirables to include the insane, polygamists, prostitutes, alcoholics, anarchists, and people carrying contagious diseases. A proposed literacy test, long a favorite of nativists because it favored the Old Immigrants over the New, met vigorous opposition. It was not enacted until 1917, after three

Sociologist E. A. Ross (1866–1951) wrote in 1914,

"Observe immigrants . . . in their gatherings. You are struck by the fact that from ten to twenty per cent are hirsute, low-browed, big-faced persons of obviously low mentality. . . . They . . . clearly belong in skins, in wattled huts at the close of the Great Ice Age. These oxlike men are descendants of those who always stayed behind."

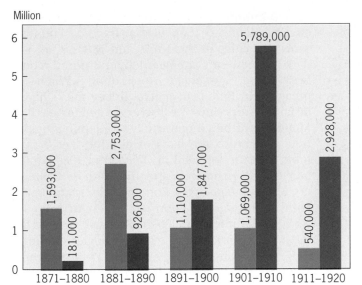

Million

| 1871–1880 | 1881–1890 | 1891–1900 | 1901–1910 | 1911–1920 |

1,593,000 / 181,000
2,753,000 / 926,000
1,110,000 / 1,847,000
1,069,000 / 5,789,000
540,000 / 2,928,000

Old and New Immigration (by decade)
In the 1970s the sources of immigration to the United States shifted yet again. The largest number of immigrants came from Latin America (especially Mexico), the next-largest from Asia. The old "mother continent" of Europe accounted for only 10 percent of the immigrants to America in the 1990s. (See the chart on p. 1033.)

Leading nations of the Old Immigration: England, Ireland, Germany

Leading nations of the New Immigration: Italy, Austria– Hungary, Russia

presidents had vetoed it on the grounds that literacy was more a measure of opportunity than of intelligence.

The year 1882, in addition to the first federal restrictions on immigration, brought forth a law to bar completely one ethnic group—the Chinese (see p. 523). Hitherto America, at least officially, had embraced the oppressed and underprivileged of all races and creeds. Hereafter the gates would be padlocked against defective undesirables—plus the Chinese.

Four years later, in 1886, the Statue of Liberty arose in New York harbor, a gift from the people of France. On its base were inscribed the words of Emma Lazarus:

> *Give me your tired, your poor*
> *Your huddled masses yearning to breathe free,*
> *The wretched refuse of your teeming shore.*

To many nativists, those noble words described only too accurately the "scum" washed up by the New Immigrant tides. Yet the uprooted immigrants, unlike "natives" lucky enough to have had parents who caught an earlier ship, became American citizens the hard way. These new immigrants stepped off the boat, many of them full-grown and well muscled, ready to put their shoulders to the nation's industrial wheels. The Republic owes much to these latercomers—for their brawn, their brains, their courage, and the yeasty diversity they brought to American society.

Lady Liberty Being Readied for Travel A centennial "birthday present" from the French people, the Statue of Liberty arrived from France in 1886.

Churches Confront the Urban Challenge

The swelling size and changing character of the urban population posed sharp challenges to American churches, which, like other national institutions, had grown up in the country. Protestant churches, in particular, suffered heavily from the shift to the city, where many of their traditional doctrines and pastoral approaches seemed irrelevant. Some of the larger houses of worship, with their stained-glass windows and thundering pipe organs, were tending to become merely sacred diversions or amusements. Reflecting the wealth of their prosperous parishioners, many of the old-line churches were distressingly slow to raise their voices against social and economic vices. John D. Rockefeller was a pillar of the Baptist church; J. Pierpont Morgan, of the Episcopal church. Trinity Episcopal Church in New York actually owned some of the city's worst slum property. Cynics remarked that the Episcopal church had become "the Republican party at prayer." Some religious leaders began to worry that in the age-old struggle between God and the Devil, the Wicked One was registering dismaying gains. The mounting emphasis was on materialism; too many devotees worshiped at the altar of avarice. Money was the accepted measure of achievement, and the new gospel of wealth proclaimed that God caused the righteous to prosper.

Into this spreading moral vacuum stepped a new generation of urban revivalists. Most conspicuous was a former Chicago shoe salesman, Dwight Lyman Moody. Like many of those to whom he preached, Moody was a country boy who had made good in the big city. Proclaiming a gospel of kind-ness and forgiveness, Moody was a modern urban circuit rider who took his message to countless American cities in the 1870s and 1880s. Clad in a dark business suit, the bearded and rotund Moody held huge audiences spellbound. When he preached in Brooklyn, special trolley tracks had to be laid to carry the crowds who wanted to hear him. Moody contributed powerfully to adapting the old-time religion to the facts of city life. The Moody Bible Institute founded in Chicago in 1889 continued to carry on his work after his death in 1899.

Simultaneously, the Roman Catholic and Jewish faiths were gaining enormous strength from the New Immigration. By 1900 the Roman Catholics had increased their lead as the largest single denomination, numbering nearly 9 million communicants. Roman Catholic and Jewish groups kept the common touch better than many of the leading Protestant churches. Cardinal Gibbons (1834–1921), an urban Catholic leader devoted to American unity, was immensely popular with Roman Catholics and Protestants alike. Acquainted with every president from Johnson to Harding, he employed his liberal sympathies to assist the American labor movement.

By 1890 the variety-loving Americans could choose from 150 religious denominations, 2 of them newcomers. One was the band-playing Salvation Army, whose soldiers without swords invaded America from England in 1879 and established a beachhead on the street corners. Appealing frankly to the down-and-outers, the boldly named Salvation Army did much practical good, especially with free soup.

The other important new faith was the Church of Christ, Scientist (Christian Science), founded by Mary Baker Eddy in 1879, after she had suffered much ill health. Preaching that the true practice of Christianity heals sickness, she set forth her views in a book entitled *Science and Health with Key to the Scriptures* (1875), which sold an amazing 400,000 copies before her death. A fertile field for converts was found in America's hurried, nerve-racked, and urbanized civilization, to which Eddy held out the hope of relief from discords and diseases through prayer as taught by Christian Science. By the time she died in 1910, she had founded an influential church that embraced several hundred thousand devoted worshippers.

Urbanites also participated in a new kind of religious-affiliated organization, the Young Men's and Women's Christian Associations. The YMCA and the

Mary Baker Eddy (1821–1910) The founder of the Christian Science Church declared in her *Science and Health*, "We classify disease as error, which nothing but Truth or Mind can heal, and this Mind must be divine, not human."

YWCA, established in the United States before the Civil War, grew by leaps and bounds. Combining physical and other kinds of education with religious instruction, the "Y's" appeared in virtually every major American city by the end of the nineteenth century.

Darwin Disrupts the Churches

The old-time religion received many blows from modern trends, including a booming sale of books on comparative religion and on historical criticism as applied to the Bible. Most unsettling of all was *On the Origin of Species,* a highly controversial volume published in 1859, on the eve of the Civil War, by the

Charles Darwin (1809–1882) wrote in 1871,

"Man is descended from a hairy, tailed quadruped, probably arboreal in its habits. . . . For my part I would as soon be descended from a baboon . . . as from a savage who delights to torture his enemies, . . . treats his wives like slaves, . . . and is haunted by the grossest superstitions."

English naturalist Charles Darwin. He set forth in lucid form the sensational theory that humans had slowly evolved from lower forms of life—a theory that was soon summarized to mean "the survival of the fittest."

Evolution cast serious doubt on a literal interpretation of the Bible, which relates how God created the heaven and the earth in six days. The Conservatives, or "Fundamentalists," stood firmly on the Scripture as the inspired and infallible Word of God, and they condemned what they thought was the "bestial hypothesis" of the Darwinians. "Modernists" parted company with the "Fundamentalists" and flatly refused to accept the Bible in its entirety as either history or science.

This furious battle over Darwinism created rifts in the churches and colleges of the post–Civil War era. "Modernist" clergymen were removed from their pulpits; teachers of biology who embraced evolution were dismissed from their chairs. But as time wore on, an increasing number of liberal thinkers were able to reconcile Darwinism with Christianity. They heralded the revolutionary theory as a newer and grander revelation of the ways of the Almighty. As one commentator observed,

Some call it Evolution,
And others call it God.

But Darwinism undoubtedly did much to loosen religious moorings and to promote unbelief among the gospel-glutted. The most bitterly denounced skeptic of the era was a golden-tongued orator, Colonel Robert G. Ingersoll, who lectured widely on "Some Mistakes of Moses" and "Why I Am an Agnostic." He might have gone far in public life if he had stuck to politics and refrained from attacking orthodox religion by "giving hell hell," as he put it.

> *A famous and vehement evangelist, Billy Sunday (1862–1935), declared in 1908,*
>
> "I have studied the Bible from Genesis to Revelation, I have read everything that Bob Ingersoll ever spouted. . . . And if Bob Ingersoll isn't in hell, God is a liar and the Bible isn't worth the paper it is printed on."

The Lust for Learning

Public education continued its upward climb. The ideal of tax-supported elementary schools, adopted on a nationwide basis before the Civil War, was still gathering strength. Americans were accepting the truism that a free government cannot function successfully if the people are shackled by ignorance. Beginning about 1870, more and more states were making at least a grade-school education compulsory, and this gain, incidentally, helped check the frightful abuses of child labor.

Spectacular indeed was the spread of high schools, especially by the 1880s and 1890s. Before the Civil War, private academies at the secondary level were common, and tax-supported high schools were rare, numbering only a few hundred. But the concept was now gaining impressive support that a high-school education, as well as a grade-school education, was the birthright of every citizen. By 1900 there were some six thousand high schools. In addition, free textbooks were being provided in increasing quantities by the taxpayers of the states during the last two decades of the century.

Other trends were noteworthy. Teacher-training schools, then called "normal schools," experienced a striking expansion after the Civil War. In 1860 there were only twelve of them; in 1910, over three hundred. Kindergartens, earlier borrowed from Germany, also began to gain strong support. The New Immigration in the 1880s and 1890s brought vast new strength to the private Catholic parochial schools, which were fast becoming a major pillar of the nation's educational structure.

Public schools, though showering benefits on children, excluded millions of adults. This deficiency was partially remedied by the Chautauqua movement, a successor to the lyceums, which was launched in 1874 on the shores of Lake Chautauqua, in New York. The organizers achieved gratifying success through nationwide public lectures, often held in tents and featuring well-known speakers, including the witty Mark Twain. In addition, there were extensive Chautauqua courses of home study, for which 100,000 people enrolled in 1892 alone.

Crowded cities, despite their cancers, generally provided better educational facilities than the old one-room, one-teacher red schoolhouse. The success of the public schools is confirmed by the falling of the illiteracy rate from 20 percent in 1870 to 10.7 percent in 1900. Americans were developing a profound faith, often misplaced, in formal education as the sovereign remedy for their ills.

Booker T. Washington and Education for Black People

War-torn and impoverished, the South lagged far behind other regions in public education, and African-Americans suffered most severely. A staggering 44 percent of nonwhites were illiterate in 1900. Some help came from northern philanthropists, but the foremost champion of black education was an ex-slave, Booker T. Washington, who had slept under a board sidewalk to save pennies for his schooling. Called in 1881 to head the black normal and industrial school at Tuskegee, Alabama, he began with forty students in a tumbledown shanty. Undaunted, he taught black students useful trades so that they could gain self-respect and economic security. Washington's self-help approach to solving the nation's racial problems was labeled "accommodationist" because it stopped short of directly challenging white supremacy. Recognizing the depths of southern white racism, Washington avoided the issue of *social* equality. Instead he grudgingly acquiesced in segregation in return for the right to develop—however modestly and painstakingly— the economic and educational resources of the black community. Economic independence would ultimately be the ticket, Washington believed, to black political and civil rights.

Washington's commitment to training young blacks in agriculture and the trades guided the curriculum at Tuskegee Institute and made it an ideal place for slave-born George Washington Carver to

Booker T. Washington in His Office at Tuskegee Institute, c. 1902   In a famous speech in Atlanta, Washington accepted social separateness for blacks: "In all things that are purely social, we can be as separate as the fingers, yet one as the hand in all things essential to mutual progress."

W. E. B. Du Bois   At the end of a long lifetime of struggle for racial justice in the United States, Du Bois renounced his American citizenship in 1961, at the age of 93, and took up residence in the newly independent African state of Ghana.

teach and research. After Carver joined the faculty in 1896, he became an internationally famous agricultural chemist who provided a much-needed boost to the southern economy by discovering hundreds of new uses for the lowly peanut (shampoo, axle grease), sweet potato (vinegar), and soybean (paint).

Other black leaders, notably Dr. W. E. B. Du Bois, assailed Booker T. Washington as an "Uncle Tom" who was condemning their race to manual labor and perpetual inferiority. Born in Massachusetts, Du Bois was a mixture of African, French, Dutch, and Indian blood ("Thank God, no Anglo-Saxon," he would add). After a determined struggle, he earned a Ph.D. at Harvard, the first of his race to achieve this goal. ("The honor, I assure you, was Harvard's," he said.) He demanded complete equality for blacks, social as well as economic, and helped to found the National Association for the Advancement of Colored People (NAACP) in 1910. Rejecting Washington's gradualism and separatism, he demanded that the "talented tenth" of the black community be given full and immediate access to the mainstream of American life. An exceptionally

skilled historian, sociologist, and poet, he died as a self-exile in Africa in 1963, at the age of ninety-five. Many of Du Bois's differences with Washington reflected the contrasting life experiences of southern and northern blacks.

W. E. B. Du Bois (1868–1961) wrote in his 1903 classic, The Souls of Black Folk,

"It is a peculiar sensation, this double-consciousness, this sense of always looking at one's self through the eyes of others, of measuring one's self through the eyes of others. . . . One ever feels his two-ness—an American, a Negro; two souls, two thoughts, two unreconciled strivings; two warring ideals in one dark body, whose dogged strength alone keeps it from being torn asunder."

The Hallowed Halls of Ivy

Colleges and universities also shot up like lusty young saplings in the decades after the Civil War. A college education increasingly seemed indispensable in the scramble for the golden apple of success. The educational battle for women, only partially won before the war, now turned into a rout of the masculine diehards. Women's colleges such as Vassar were gaining ground; and universities open to both genders were blossoming, notably in the Midwest. By 1900 every fourth college graduate was a woman. By the turn of the century as well the black institutes and academies planted during Reconstruction had blossomed into a crop of southern black colleges. Howard University in Washington, D.C., Hampton Institute in Virginia, Atlanta University, and numerous others nurtured higher education for blacks until the civil rights movement of the 1960s made attendance at white institutions possible.

The truly phenomenal growth of higher education owed much to the Morrill Act of 1862. This enlightened law, passed after the South had seceded, provided a generous grant of the public lands to the states for support of education. "Land-grant colleges," most of which became state universities, in turn bound themselves to provide certain services, such as military training. The Hatch Act of 1887, extending the Morrill Act, provided federal funds for the establishment of agricultural experiment stations in connection with the land-grant colleges.

Private philanthropy richly supplemented federal grants to higher education. Many of the new industrial millionaires, developing tender social consciences, donated immense fortunes to educational enterprises. A philanthropist was cynically described as "one who steals privately and gives publicly." In the twenty years from 1878 to 1898, these money barons gave away about $150 million. Noteworthy among the new private universities of high quality to open were Cornell (1865) and Leland Stanford Junior (1891), the latter founded in memory of the deceased fifteen-year-old only child of a builder of the Central Pacific Railroad. The University of Chicago, opened in 1892, speedily forged into a front-rank position, owing largely to the lubricant of John D. Rockefeller's oil millions. Rockefeller died

Educational Levels, 1870–1990

Year	Number Graduating From High School	Number Graduating From College	Median School Years Completed Completed (Years)*	High School Graduates As A Percentage Of 17-Year-Old Population
1870	16,000	9,371		2.0%
1880	24,000	12,896		2.5
1890	44,000	15,539		3.5
1900	95,000	27,410		6.4
1910	156,000	37,199	8.1†	8.8
1920	311,000	48,622	8.2†	16.8
1930	667,000	122,484	8.4†	29.0
1940	1,221,000	186,500	8.6	50.8
1950	1,199,700	432,058	9.3	59.0
1960	1,858,000	392,440	10.5	69.5
1970	2,889,000	792,656	12.2	76.9
1980	3,043,000	929,417	12.5	71.4
1990	2,587,000	1,049,657 (est.)	12.7	74.2

*People twenty-five years and over.
†1910–1930 based on retrogressions of 1940 data; 1940 was the first year measured. (Folger and Nam, *Education of the American Population*, a 1960 Census Monograph.)
(Sources: *Digest of Education Statistics*, 1992 a publication of the National Center for Education Statistics, and *Statistical Abstracts of the United States*, relevant years.)

at 97, after having given some $550 million for philanthropic purposes.

Significant also was the sharp increase in professional and technical schools, where modern laboratories were replacing the solo experiment performed by instructors in front of their classes. Towering among the specialized institutions was the Johns Hopkins University, opened in 1876, which maintained the nation's first high-grade graduate school. Several generations of American scholars, repelled by snobbish English cousins and attracted by painstaking Continental methods, had attended German universities. Johns Hopkins ably carried on the Germanic tradition of profusely footnoted tomes. Reputable scholars no longer had to go abroad for a gilt-edged graduate degree; and Dr. Woodrow Wilson, among others, received his Ph.D. from Johns Hopkins.

The March of the Mind

Cut-and-dried, the old classical curriculum in the colleges was on the way out, as the new industrialization brought insistent demands for "practical" courses and specialized training in the sciences. The elective system, which permitted students to choose more courses in cafeteria fashion, was gaining popularity. It received a powerful boost in the 1870s, when Dr. Charles W. Eliot, a vigorous young chemist, became president of Harvard College and embarked upon a lengthy career of educational statesmanship.

Medical schools and medical science after the Civil War were prospering. Despite the enormous sale of patent medicines and so-called Indian remedies—"good for man or beast"—the new scientific gains were reflected in improved public health. Revolutionary discoveries abroad, such as those of the French scientist Louis Pasteur and the English physician Joseph Lister, left their imprint on America.* The popularity of heavy whiskers waned as the century ended; such hairy adornments were now coming to be regarded as germ traps. As a result of new health-promoting precautions, including campaigns against public spitting, life expectancy at birth was measurably increased.

---

*From Pasteur came the word *pasteurize;* from Lister came *Listerine.*

One of America's most brilliant intellectuals, the slight and sickly William James (1842–1910), served for thirty-five years on the Harvard faculty. Through his numerous writings he made a deep mark on many fields. His *Principles of Psychology* (1890) helped to establish the modern discipline of behavioral psychology. In *The Will to Believe* (1897) and *Varieties of Religious Experience* (1902), he explored the philosophy and psychology of religion. In his most famous work, *Pragmatism* (1907), he colorfully described America's greatest contribution to the history of philosophy. The concept of pragmatism held that truth was to be tested, above all, by the practical consequences of an idea, by action rather than theories. This kind of reasoning aptly expressed the philosophical temperament of a nation of doers.

The Appeal of the Press

Books continued to be a major source of edification and enjoyment, for both juveniles and adults. Bestsellers of the 1880s were generally old favorites like *David Copperfield* and *Ivanhoe.*

Well-stocked public libraries—the poor person's university—were making encouraging progress, especially in Boston and New York. The magnificent Library of Congress building, which opened its doors in 1897, provided thirteen acres of floor space in the largest and costliest edifice of its kind in the world. A new era was inaugurated by the generous gifts of Andrew Carnegie. This openhanded Scotsman, book-starved in his youth, contributed $60 million for the construction of public libraries all over the country. By 1900 there were about nine thousand free circulating libraries in America, each with at least three hundred books.

Roaring newspaper presses, spurred by the invention of the Linotype in 1885, more than kept pace with the demands of a word-hungry public. But the heavy investment in machinery and plant was accompanied by a growing fear of offending advertisers and subscribers. Bare-knuckle editorials were, to an increasing degree, being supplanted by feature articles and noncontroversial syndicated material. The day of slashing journalistic giants like Horace Greeley was passing.

Sensationalism, at the same time, was capturing the public taste. The semiliterate immigrants,

The "Penny Press"
The Chicago *Daily News* was but one of several cheap, mass-circulation newspapers that flourished in the new urban environment of Gilded Age America.

A DAILY PAPER FOR ONE CENT A DAY.

A DAILY NEWSPAPER NOW COSTS BUT LITTLE MORE THAN THE OLD-TIME WEEKLY.

"NEARLY EVERYBODY WHO READS THE ENGLISH LANGUAGE IN AROUND AND ABOUT CHICAGO, READS THE CHICAGO DAILY NEWS."

FROM THE PRESS OFFICE REVIEW

THE CHICAGO DAILY NEWS

DAILY MARKET REPORTS

OVER 200,000 A DAY.

THE CHICAGO DAILY NEWS.

CHICAGO WEEKLY NEWS.

SUBSCRIPTIONS RECEIVED HERE.

combined with straphanging urban commuters, created a profitable market for news that was simply and punchily written. Sex, scandal, and other human-interest stories burst into the headlines, as a vulgarization of the press accompanied the growth of circulation. Critics now complained in vain of these "presstitutes."

Two new journalistic tycoons emerged. Joseph Pulitzer, Hungarian-born and near-blind, was a leader in the techniques of sensationalism in St. Louis and especially with the New York *World.* His use of the colored comic supplements, featuring the "Yellow Kid," gave the name of *yellow journalism* to his lurid sheets. A close and ruthless competitor was youthful William Randolph Hearst, who had been expelled from Harvard College for a crude prank. Able to draw on his California father's mining millions, he ultimately built up a powerful chain of

newspapers, beginning with the San Francisco *Examiner* in 1887.

Unfortunately, the overall influence of Pulitzer and Hearst was not altogether wholesome. Although both championed many worthy causes, both prostituted the press in their struggle for increased circulation; both "stooped, snooped, and scooped to conquer." Their flair for scandal and sensational rumor was happily somewhat offset by the introduction of syndicated material and by the strengthening of the news-gathering Associated Press, which had been founded in the 1840s.

Apostles of Reform

Magazines partially satisfied the public appetite for good reading, notably old standbys like *Harper's,* the *Atlantic Monthly,* and *Scribner's Monthly.* Possibly the most influential journal of all was the liberal and highly intellectual New York *Nation,* which was read largely by professors, preachers, and publicists as "the weekly Day of Judgment." Launched in 1865 by the Irish-born Edwin L. Godkin, a merciless critic, it crusaded militantly for civil-service reform, honesty in government, and a moderate tariff. The *Nation* attained only a modest circulation—about 10,000 in the nineteenth century—but Godkin believed that if he could reach the right 10,000 leaders, his ideas through them might reach the 10 millions.

Another journalist-author, Henry George, was an original thinker who left an enduring mark. Poor in formal schooling, he was rich in idealism and in the milk of human kindness. After seeing poverty at its worst in India, and land-grabbing at its greediest in California, he took pen in hand. His classic treatise *Progress and Poverty* undertook to solve "the great enigma of our times"—"the association of progress with poverty." According to George, the pressure of growing population on a fixed supply of land unjustifiably pushed up property values, showering unearned profits on owners of land. A single 100 percent tax on those windfall profits would eliminate unfair inequalities and stimulate economic growth.

George soon became a most controversial figure. His single-tax ideas were so horrifying to the propertied classes that his manuscript was rejected by numerous publishers. Finally brought out in 1879, the book gradually broke into the best-seller lists and ultimately sold some 3 million copies.

> *Henry George (1839–1897), in* Progress and Poverty *(1879), wrote,*
>
> "Our boasted freedom necessarily involves slavery, so long as we recognize private property in land. Until that is abolished, Declarations of Independence and Acts of Emancipation are in vain. So long as one man can claim the exclusive ownership of the land from which other men must live, slavery will exist, and as material progresses on, must grow and deepen!"

George also lectured widely in America, where he influenced thinking about the maldistribution of wealth, and in Britain, where he left an indelible mark on English Fabian socialism.

Edward Bellamy, a quiet Massachusetts Yankee, was another journalist-reformer of remarkable power. In 1888 he published a socialistic novel, *Looking Backward,* in which the hero, falling into a hypnotic sleep, awakens in the year 2000. He "looks backward" and finds that the social and economic injustices of 1887 have melted away under an idyllic government, which has nationalized big business to serve the public interest. To a nation already alarmed by the trust evil, the book had a magnetic appeal and sold over a million copies. Scores of Bellamy Clubs sprang up to discuss this mild utopian socialism, and they heavily influenced American reform movements near the end of the century.

Postwar Writing

As literacy increased, so did book reading. Post–Civil War Americans devoured millions of "dime novels," usually depicting the wilds of the woolly West. Paint-bedaubed Indians and quick-triggered gunmen like "Deadwood Dick" shot off vast quantities of powder, and virtue invariably triumphed. These lurid "paperbacks" were frowned upon by parents, but goggle-eyed youths read them in haylofts or in schools behind the broad covers of geography books. The king of dime novelists was Harlan F. Halsey, who made a fortune by dashing off about 650 novels, often one in a day.

General Lewis Wallace—lawyer-soldier-author—was a colorful figure. Having fought with distinction in the Civil War, he sought to combat the prevailing wave of Darwinian skepticism with his novel *Ben Hur: A Tale of the Christ* (1880). A phenomenal success, the book sold an estimated 2 million copies in many languages, including Arabic and Chinese, and later appeared on stage and screen. It was the *Uncle Tom's Cabin* of the anti-Darwinists, who found in it support for the Holy Scriptures.

An even more popular writer was Horatio ("Holy Horatio") Alger, a Puritan-reared New Englander, who in 1866 forsook the pulpit for the pen. Deeply interested in New York newsboys, he wrote more than a hundred volumes of juvenile fiction that sold over 100 million copies. His stock formula was that virtue, honesty, and industry are rewarded by success, wealth, and honor—a kind of survival of the purest, especially nonsmokers, nondrinkers, nonswearers, and nonliars. Although Alger's own bachelor life was criticized, he implanted morality and the conviction that there is always room at the top (especially if one is lucky enough to save the life of the boss's daughter and marry her).

In poetry Walt Whitman was one of the few luminaries of yesteryear who remained active. Although shattered in health by service as a Civil War nurse, he brought out successive—and purified—revisions of his hardy perennial, *Leaves of Grass.* The assassination of Lincoln inspired him to write two of the most moving poems in American literature, "O Captain! My Captain!" and "When Lilacs Last in the Dooryard Bloom'd."

The curious figure of Emily Dickinson, one of America's most gifted lyric poets, did not emerge until 1886, when she died and her poems were discovered. A Massachusetts recluse, she wrote over a thousand short lyrics on scraps of paper. Only two were published during her lifetime, and those without her consent. As she wrote,

> *How dreary to be somebody!*
> *How public, like a frog*
> *To tell your name the livelong June*
> *To an admiring bog!*

Among the lesser poetical lights was a tragic southerner, Sidney Lanier (1842–1881). He was oppressed by poverty and ill health, and torn between flute playing and poetry. Dying young of tuberculosis, he wrote some of his finest poems while afflicted with a temperature of 104 degrees Fahrenheit (40 degrees Celsius). He is perhaps best

Emily Dickinson (1830–1886)   A great American poet, she pursued intense intellectual relationships with several literary and cultural figures, including the abolitionist Thomas Wentworth Higginson.

Mark Twain (1835–1910)   Born Samuel Langhorne Clemens, he was not only America's most popular author but also a renowned platform lecturer.

known for his "The Marshes of Glynn," a poem of faith inspired by the current clash between Darwinism and orthodox religion.

Literary Landmarks

In novel writing the romantic sentimentality of a youthful era was giving way to a rugged realism that reflected more faithfully the materialism of an industrial society. American authors now turned increasingly to the coarse human comedy and drama of the world around them to find their subjects.

Two Missouri-born authors with deep connections to the South brought altogether new voices to the late-nineteenth-century literary scene. The daring feminist author Kate Chopin (1851–1904) wrote candidly about adultery, suicide, and women's ambitions in *The Awakening* (1899). Largely ignored in her own day, Chopin was rediscovered by later readers, who cited her work as suggestive of the feminist yearnings that stirred beneath the surface of "respectability" in the Gilded Age.

Mustachioed Mark Twain (1835–1910) had leapt to fame with *The Celebrated Jumping Frog of Calaveras County* (1867) and *The Innocents Abroad* (1869). He teamed up with Charles Dudley Warner in 1873 to write *The Gilded Age*. An acid satire on post–Civil War politicians and speculators, the book gave a name to an era. With his scanty formal schooling in frontier Missouri, Twain typified a new breed of American authors in revolt against the elegant refinements of the old New England school of writing. Christened Samuel Langhorne Clemens, he had served for a time as a Mississippi riverboat pilot and later took his pen name, Mark Twain, from the boatman's cry that meant two fathoms. After a brief stint in the armed forces, Twain journeyed westward to California, a trip he described, with a mixture of truth and tall tales, in *Roughing It* (1872).

Many other books flowed from Twain's busy pen. His *The Adventures of Tom Sawyer* (1876) and *The Adventures of Huckleberry Finn* (1884) rank among American masterpieces, though initially regarded as "trash" by snobbish Boston critics. His later years were soured by bankruptcy growing out of unwise investments, and he was forced to take to the lecture platform and amuse what he called "the damned human race." A great tribute was paid to his self-tutored genius—and to American letters—when England's Oxford University awarded him an honorary degree in 1907. Journalist, humorist, satirist, and foe of social injustice, he made his most enduring contribution in recapturing frontier realism and humor in the authentic American dialect.

Another author who wrote out of the West and achieved at least temporary fame and fortune was Bret Harte (1836–1902). A foppishly dressed New Yorker, Harte struck it rich in California with gold-rush stories, especially "The Luck of Roaring Camp" and "The Outcasts of Poker Flat." Catapulted suddenly into notoriety by those stories, he never again matched their excellence or their popularity. He lived out his final years in London as little more than a hack writer.

William Dean Howells (1837–1920), a printer's son from Ohio, could boast of little schoolhouse education, but his busy pen carried him high into the literary circles of the East. In 1871 he became the editor in chief of the prestigious Boston-based *Atlantic Monthly* and was subsequently presented with honorary degrees from six universities, including Oxford. He wrote about ordinary people and about contemporary and sometimes controversial social themes. *A Modern Instance* (1882) deals with the once-taboo subject of divorce; *The Rise of Silas Lapham* (1885) describes the trials of a newly rich

paint manufacturer caught up in the caste system of Brahmin Boston. *A Hazard of New Fortunes* (1890) portrays the reformers, strikers, and Socialists in Gilded Age New York.

Stephen Crane (1871–1900), the fourteenth son of a Methodist minister, also wrote about the seamy underside of life in urban, industrial America. His *Maggie: A Girl of the Streets* (1893), a brutal tale about a poor prostitute driven to suicide, was too grim to find a publisher. Crane had to have it printed privately. He rose quickly to prominence with *The Red Badge of Courage* (1895), the stirring story of a bloodied young Civil War recruit ("fresh fish") under fire. Crane himself had never seen a battle and wrote entirely from the printed Civil War records. He died of tuberculosis in 1900, when only twenty-nine.

Henry James (1843–1916), brother of Harvard philosopher William James, was a New Yorker who turned from law to literature. Taking as his dominant theme the confrontation of innocent Americans with subtle Europeans, James penned a remarkable number of brilliant novels, including *Daisy Miller* (1879), *The Portrait of a Lady* (1881), and *The Wings of the Dove* (1902). In *The Bostonians* (1886) he wrote one of the first novels about the rising feminist movement. James frequently made women his central characters, exploring their inner reactions to complex situations with a deftness that marked him as a master of "psychological realism." Long resident in England, he became a British subject shortly before his death.

Candid portrayals of contemporary life and social problems were the literary order of the day by the turn of the century. Jack London (1876–1916), famous as a nature writer in such books as *The Call of the Wild* (1903), turned to depicting a possible fascistic revolution in *The Iron Heel* (1907). Frank

---

In 1935 Ernest Hemingway (1899–1961) wrote,

"All modern American literature comes from one book by Mark Twain called *Huckleberry Finn*. . . ." All American writing comes from that. There was nothing before. There has been nothing as good since."

Jack London (1876–1916), the Socialist who hated strikebreakers known as "scabs," said,

"No man has a right to scab so long as there is a pool of water to drown his carcass in, or a rope long enough to hang his body with. Judas Iscariot was a gentleman compared with a scab. For betraying his master, he had character enough to hang himself. A scab has not."

Norris (1870–1902), like London a Californian, wrote *The Octopus* (1901), an earthy saga of the stranglehold of the railroad and corrupt politicians on California wheat ranchers. A sequel, *The Pit* (1903), dealt with the making and breaking of speculators on the Chicago wheat exchange.

Two black writers, Paul Laurence Dunbar (1872–1906) and Charles W. Chesnutt (1858–1932), brought another kind of realism to late-nineteenth-century literature. Dunbar through poetry—particularly his acclaimed *Lyrics of Lowly Life* (1896)—and Chesnutt through fiction—short stories in *The Atlantic Monthly* and *The Conjure Women* (1899)—embraced the use of black dialect and folklore, previously shunned by black authors, to capture the spontaneity and richness of southern black culture.

Conspicuous among the new "social novelists" rising in the literary firmament was Theodore Dreiser (1871–1945), a homely, gangling writer from Indiana. He burst upon the literary scene in 1900 with *Sister Carrie,* a graphically realistic narrative of a poor working girl in Chicago and New York. She becomes one man's mistress, then elopes with another, and finally strikes out on her own to make a career on the stage. The fictional Carrie's disregard for prevailing moral standards so offended Dreiser's publisher that the book was soon withdrawn from circulation.

Sister Carrie, 1900
Theodore Dreiser published his first novel after having worked as a journalist in Chicago. His immersion in big-city life and in the techniques of modern magazine writing imparted a gritty realism to his prose. His portrait of Carrie Meeber in "Sister Carrie" displays his deep understanding of urban America and especially of the "new women" who peopled it.

The New Morality

Victoria Woodhull, who was real flesh and blood, also shook the pillars of conventional morality when she publicly proclaimed her belief in free love in 1871. Woodhull was a beautiful and eloquent divorcée, sometime stockbroker, and tireless feminist propagandist. Together with her sister, Tennessee Claflin, she published a far-out periodical, *Woodhull and Claflin's Weekly.* The sisters again shocked "respectable" society in 1872 when their journal struck a blow for the new morality by charging that Henry Ward Beecher, the most famous preacher of his day, had for years been carrying on an adulterous affair.

Pure-minded Americans sternly resisted these affronts to their moral principles. Their foremost champion was a portly crusader, Anthony Comstock, who made lifelong war on the "immoral." Armed after 1873 with a federal statute—the notorious "Comstock Law"—this self-appointed defender of sexual purity boasted that he had confiscated no fewer than 202,679 "obscene pictures and photos"; 4,185 "boxes of pills, powders, etc., used by abortionists"; and 26 "obscene pictures, framed on walls of saloons." His proud claim was that he had driven at least fifteen people to suicide.

The antics of the Woodhull sisters and Anthony Comstock exposed to daylight the battle going on in late-nineteenth-century America over sexual attitudes and the place of women. Switchboards and typewriters in the booming cities became increasingly the tools of women's liberation. Economic freedom encouraged sexual freedom, and the "new morality" began to be reflected in soaring divorce rates, the spreading practice of birth control, and increasingly frank discussion of sexual topics. By 1913, said one popular magazine, the chimes had struck "sex o'clock in America."

Families and Women in the City

The new urban environment was hard on families. Paradoxically, the crowded cities were emotionally isolating places. Urban families had to go it alone, separated from clan, kin, and village. As families increasingly became the virtually exclusive arena for intimate companionship and for emotional and psychological satisfaction, they were subjected to unprecedented stress. Many families cracked under the strain. The urban era launched the era of divorce. From the late nineteenth century dates the beginning of the "divorce revolution" that transformed the United States' social landscape in the twentieth century (see the table below).

Urban life also dictated changes in work habits and even in family size. Not only fathers but mothers and even children as young as ten years old often worked, and usually in widely scattered locations. On the farm having many children meant having more hands to help with hoeing and harvesting; but in the city more children meant more mouths to feed, more crowding in sardine-tin tenements, and more human baggage to carry in the uphill struggle for social mobility. Not surprisingly, birthrates were still dropping and family size continued to shrink as the nineteenth century lengthened. Marriages were being delayed, and more couples learned the techniques of birth control. The decline in family size in fact affected rural Americans as well as urban dwellers, and old-stock "natives" as well as new immigrant groups.

Women were growing more independent in the urban environment, and in 1898 they heard the voice of a major feminist prophet, Charlotte Perkins Gilman. In that year the freethinking and original-minded Gilman published *Women and Economics,* a classic of feminist literature. A distant relative of Harriet Beecher Stowe and Catharine Beecher, Gilman displayed the restless temperament and reforming zeal characteristic of the remarkable Beecher clan. Strikingly handsome, she shunned traditional feminine frills and instead devoted herself to a vigorous regimen of physical exercise and philosophical meditation.

In her masterwork of 1898, Gilman called on women to abandon their dependent status and contribute to the larger life of the community through productive involvement in the economy. Rejecting all claims that biology gave women a fundamentally different character from men, she argued that "our highly specialized motherhood is not so advantageous as believed." She advocated centralized nurseries and cooperative kitchens to facilitate women's participation in the work force—anticipating by more than half a century the day-care centers and convenience-food services of a later day.

Fiery feminists also continued to insist on the ballot. They had been demanding the vote since before the Civil War, but many high-minded female reformers had temporarily shelved the cause of women to battle for the rights of blacks. In 1890 militant suffragists formed the National American Woman Suffrage Association. Its founders included aging pioneers like Elizabeth Cady Stanton, who had helped organize the first women's rights convention in 1848, and her long-time comrade Susan

Marriages and Divorces, 1890–1990

Year	Marriages	Divorces	Ratio of Divorces to Marriages
1890	570,000	33,461	1 : 17
1900	709,000	55,751	1 : 12
1910	948,166	83,045	1 : 11
1920	1,274,476	170,505	1 : 7
1930	1,126,856	195,961	1 : 5
1940	1,595,879	264,000	1 : 6
1950	1,667,231	385,144	1 : 4.3
1960	1,523,381	393,000	1 : 3.8
1970	2,159,000	708,000	1 : 3
1980	2,390,000	1,189,000	1 : 2
1990	2,443,000	1,182,000	1 : 2

(Sources: *Statistical Abstracts of the United States,* relevant years.)

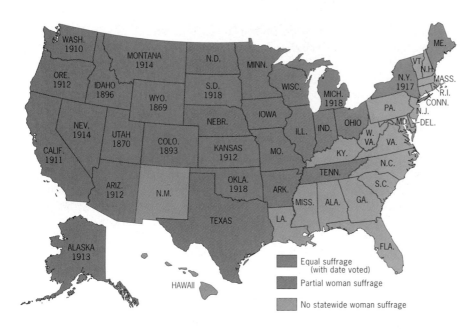

Woman Suffrage Before the Nineteenth Amendment
Dates show when a state or territory adopted woman suffrage. Note the concentration of woman-suffrage states in the West.

Equal suffrage (with date voted)

Partial woman suffrage

No statewide woman suffrage

B. Anthony, the radical Quaker spitfire who had courted jail by trying to cast a ballot in the 1872 presidential election.

By 1900 a new generation of women had taken command of the suffrage battle. Their most effective leader was Carrie Chapman Catt, a pragmatic and businesslike reformer of relentless dedication. Significantly, under Catt the suffragists deemphasized the argument that women deserved the vote as a matter of right, because they were in all respects the equals of men. Instead Catt stressed the desirability of giving women the vote if they were to continue to discharge their traditional duties as homemakers and mothers in the increasingly public world of the city. Women had special responsibility for the health of the family and the education of children, the argument ran. On the farm, women could discharge these responsibilities in the separate sphere of the isolated homestead. But in the city, they needed a voice on boards of public health, police commissions, and school boards.

By thus linking the ballot to a traditional definition of women's role, suffragists registered encouraging gains as the new century opened, despite continuing showers of rotten eggs and the jeers of male critics who insisted that women were made for loving, not for voting. Women were increasingly permitted to vote in local elections, particularly on issues related to the schools. Wyoming Territory—later called "the Equality State"—granted the first unrestricted suffrage to women in 1869. This important

Woman Suffrage, by Evelyn Rumsey Cary
After a century of struggle, women finally won a constitutionally guaranteed right to vote in 1920.

In 1906, progressive reformer Jane Addams argued that granting women the vote would improve the social and political condition of American cities:

"City housekeeping has failed partly because women, the traditional housekeepers, have not been consulted as to its multiform activities. The men have been carelessly indifferent to much of the civic housekeeping, as they have been indifferent to the details of the household. . . . City government demands the help of minds accustomed to detail and a variety of work, to a sense of obligation to the health and welfare of young children, and to a responsibility for the cleanliness and comfort of other people."

Ida B. Wells   In 1892 Wells spearheaded a protest against the heinous lynching of three respected black businessmen in Memphis. Faced with threats on her own life, Wells fled from the South, perservering with her tenacious anti-lynching campaign from the North and from England.

breach in the dike once made, many states followed Wyoming's example. Paralleling these triumphs, most of the states by 1890 had passed laws to permit wives to own or control their property after marriage. City life also fostered the growth of a spate of women's organizations, including the General Federation of Women's Clubs, which counted some 200,000 members in 1900.

The reborn suffrage movement and other women's organizations excluded black women from their ranks. Fearful that an integrated campaign would compromise its efforts to get the vote, the National American Women Suffrage Association limited membership to whites. Black women, however, created their own associations. Journalist and teacher Ida B. Wells inspired black women to mount a nationwide antilynching crusade. She also helped launch the black women's club movement, which culminated in the establishment of the National Association of Colored Women in 1896.

Prohibition of Alcohol and Social Progress

Alarming gains by Demon Rum spurred the temperance reformers to redoubled zeal. Especially obnoxious to them was the shutter-doored corner saloon, appropriately called "the poor man's club." The

barroom helped keep both him and his family poor. Liquor consumption had increased during the nerve-racking days of the Civil War; and immigrant groups, accustomed to alcohol in the Old Country, were hostile to restraints. Whiskey-loving foreigners in Boston would rudely hiss temperance lecturers. Many tipplers charged, with some accuracy, that temperance reform amounted to a middle-class assault on working-class lifestyles.

The National Prohibition party, organized in 1869, polled a sprinkling of votes in some of the ensuing presidential elections. Among the favorite songs of these sober souls were "I'll Marry No Man If He Drinks," "Vote Down the Vile Traffic," and "The

Drunkard's Doom." Typical was

> *Now, all young men, a warning take,*
> *And shun the poisoned bowl;*
> *'Twill lead you down to hell's dark gate,*
> *And ruin your own soul.*

Militant women entered the alcoholic arena, notably when the Woman's Christian Temperance Union (WCTU) was organized in 1874. The white ribbon was its symbol of purity; the saintly Frances E. Willard—also a champion of planned parenthood—was its leading spirit. Less saintly was a muscular and mentally deranged "Kansas Cyclone," Carrie A. Nation, whose first husband had died of alcoholism. With her hatchet she boldly smashed saloon bottles and bars, and her "hatchetations" brought considerable disrepute to the prohibition movement by the violence of her one-woman crusade.

But rum was now on the run. The potent Anti-Saloon League was formed in 1893, with its members singing "The Saloon Must Go" and "Vote for Cold Water, Boys." Female supporters sang "The Lips That Touch Liquor Must Never Touch Mine." Statewide prohibition, which had made surprising gains in Maine and elsewhere before the Civil War, was sweeping new states into the "dry" column. The great triumph—but only a temporary one—came in 1919, when the national prohibition amendment (Eighteenth) was attached to the Constitution.

Banners of other social crusaders were aloft. The American Society for the Prevention of Cruelty to Animals was created in 1866, after its founder had witnessed brutality to horses in Russia. The American Red Cross was launched in 1881, with the dynamic 5-foot (1.52-meter) Clara Barton, an "angel" of Civil War battlefields, at the helm.

Carrie Nation Advertised as a Lecturer
She holds her famous hatchet. Carrie Nation took her antidrink crusade to several universities, including Harvard and Yale, which she denounced as "hellholes." Predictably, the students greeted her with wild burlesque.

Clara Barton (1821–1912)
A shy Massachusetts school-teacher, she was afflicted with attacks of nervous prostration during the first half of her life. She established the American Red Cross, which she headed from 1881 to 1904.

Artistic Triumphs

John Adams had anticipated that his generation's preoccupation with nation-building would allow art to flourish in the future, but the results long proved unspectacular. Portrait painting continued to appeal, as it had since the colonial era, but many of America's finest painters made their livings abroad. James Whistler (1834–1903) did much of his work, including the celebrated portrait of his mother, in England. This eccentric and quarrelsome Massachusetts Yankee had earlier been dropped from West Point after failing chemistry. "Had silicon been a gas," he later jested, "I would have been a major general." Another gifted portrait painter, likewise self-exiled in England, was John Singer Sargent (1856–1925). His flattering but somewhat superficial likenesses of the British nobility were highly prized. Mary Cassatt, an American-in-exile in Paris, painted sensitive portrayals of women and children that earned her a place in the pantheon of the French impressionist painters.

Other brush wielders, no less talented, brightened the artistic horizon. Self-taught George Inness (1825–1894), who looked like a fanatic with his long hair and piercing gaze, became America's leading landscapist. Thomas Eakins (1844–1916) attained a high degree of realism in his paintings, a quality not appreciated by portrait sitters who wanted their moles overlooked. Boston-born Winslow Homer (1836–1910), who as a youth had secretly drawn sketches in school, was perhaps the greatest painter of the group. Earthily American and largely resistant to foreign influences, he revealed rugged realism and boldness of conception. His canvases of the sea and of fisherfolk were masterly, and probably no American artist has excelled him in portraying the awesome power of the ocean.

Probably the most gifted sculptor yet produced by America was Augustus Saint-Gaudens (1848–1907). Born in Ireland of an Irish mother and a French father, he became an adopted American. Among his most moving works is the Robert Gould Shaw memorial, erected in Boston in 1897. It depicts Colonel Shaw, a young white "Boston Brahmin" officer, leading his black troops into battle in the Civil War.

Music, too, was gaining popularity. America of the 1880s and 1890s was assembling high-quality symphony orchestras, notably in Boston and Chicago. The famed Metropolitan Opera House of New York was erected in 1883. In its fabled "Diamond Horseshoe" the newly rich, often under the pretense of enjoying the imported singers, would flaunt their jewels, gowns, and furs. While symphonies and operas were devoted to bringing European music to elite American audiences, new strains of homegrown American music were sprouting in the South. Black folk traditions like spirituals and "ragged music" were evolving into the blues, ragtime, and jazz that would transform American popular music in the twentieth century.

A marvelous discovery was the reproduction of music by mechanical means. The phonograph, though a squeakily imperfect instrument when invented by the deaf Edison, had by 1900 reached over 150,000 homes. Americans were rapidly being dosed with "canned music," as the "sitting room" piano increasingly gathered dust.

In addition to skyscraper builder Louis Sullivan, a famous American architect of the age was Henry H. Richardson. Born in Louisiana and educated at Harvard and in Paris, Richardson settled in Boston and from there spread his immense influence throughout the eastern half of the United States. He popularized a distinctive, ornamental style that came to be known as "Richardsonian." High-vaulted arches, like those on Gothic churches, were his trademark. His masterpiece and most famous work was the Marshall Field Building (1885) in Chicago. Enjoying his success, Richardson was noted for his capacity for champagne, his love of laughter, and the bright yellow vests he sported.

A revival of classical architectural forms—and a setback for realism—came with the great Columbian Exposition. Held in Chicago in 1893, it honored the four-hundredth anniversary of Columbus's first

---

Hamlin Garland (1860–1940), the well-known novelist and writer of short stories, was immensely impressed by the cultural value of the Chicago Columbian Exposition. He wrote to his aged parents on their Dakota farm:

"Sell the cook stove if necessary and come. You *must* see this fair."

Buffalo Bill's Wild West Show, c. 1907   By the late 1800s, the "wild" West was already passing into the realm of myth—and popular entertainment. Famed frontiersman William F. ("Buffalo Bill") Cody made his fortune showing off his tame cowboys and Indians to urban audiences.

voyage. This so-called dream of loveliness, which was visited by 27 million people, did much to raise American artistic standards and promote city planning, although many of the spectators were attracted primarily by the contortions of a hootchy-kootchy dancer, "Little Egypt."

The Business of Amusement

Fun and frolic were not neglected by the workaday American. The pursuit of happiness, heralded in the Declaration of Independence, had by century's end become a frenzied scramble. People sought their pleasures fiercely, as they had overrun their continent fiercely. And now they had more time to play.

Varied diversions beckoned. As a nation of "joiners" contemptuous of royalty, Americans in-

consistently sought to escape from democratic equality in the aristocratic hierarchies of lodges. The legitimate stage still flourished, as appreciative audiences responded to the lure of the footlights. Vaudeville, with its coarse jokes and graceful acrobats, continued to be immensely popular during the 1880s and 1890s, as were minstrel shows in the South, now performed by black singers and dancers rather than by blackfaced whites as in the North before the Civil War.

The circus—high-tented and multiringed—finally emerged full-blown. Phineas T. Barnum, the master showman who had early discovered that "the public likes to be humbugged," joined hands with James A. Bailey in 1881 to stage the "Greatest Show on Earth."*

---

*Now Ringling Bros. and Barnum & Bailey Circus.

Colorful "Wild West" shows, first performed in 1883, were even more distinctively American. Headed by the knightly, goateed, and free-drinking William F. ("Buffalo Bill") Cody, the troupe included war-whooping Indians, live buffalo, and deadeye marksmen. Among them was the girlish Annie Oakley. Rifle in hand, at thirty paces she could perforate a tossed-up card half a dozen times before it fluttered to the ground (hence the term *Annie Oakley* for a punched ticket, later for a free pass).

Baseball, already widely played before the Civil War, was clearly emerging as the national pastime, if not a national mania. A league of professional players was formed in the 1870s, and in 1888 an all-star baseball team toured the world, using the pyramids as a backstop while in Egypt.

A gladiatorial trend toward spectator sports, rather than participative sports, was exemplified by football. This rugged game, with its dangerous flying wedge, had become popular well before 1889, when Yaleman Walter C. Camp chose his first "All American" team. The Yale-Princeton game of 1893 drew fifty thousand cheering fans, while foreigners jeered that the nation was getting sports "on the brain."

Even pugilism, with its long background of bare-knuckle brutality, gained a new and gloved respectability in 1892. Agile "Gentleman Jim" Corbett, a scientific boxer, wrestled the world championship from the aging and alcoholic John L. Sullivan, the fabulous "Boston Strong Boy."

Two crazes swept the country in the closing decades of the century. Croquet became all the rage, though condemned by moralists of the "naughty nineties" because it exposed feminine ankles and promoted flirtation. The low-framed "safety" bicycle came to replace the high-seated model. By 1893 a million bicycles were in use, and thousands of young women, jokesters remarked, were turning to this new "spinning wheel," one that offered freedom, not tedium.

Basketball was invented in 1891 by James Naismith, a YMCA instructor in Springfield, Massachusetts. Designed as an active indoor sport that could be played during the winter months, it spread rapidly and enjoyed enormous popularity in the next century.

The land of the skyscraper was plainly becoming more standardized, owing largely to the new industrialization. Although race and ethnicity assigned urban Americans to distinctive neighborhoods and workplaces, to an increasing degree they shared a common popular culture—playing, reading, shopping, and talking alike. As the century drew to a close, the explosion of cities paradoxically made Americans more diverse and more similar at the same time.

The New Woman, by Edward Lamson Henry, 1892 Bicycling appealed to young women eager to escape nineteenth-centruy strictures against female exercise and bodily exposure. This young female cyclist, pedaling on her own and free of corsets and elaborate clothing, both shocked and amused an older generation.

Chronology

1859 Charles Darwin publishes *On the Origin of Species*

1862 Morrill Act provides public land for higher education

1866 The American Society for the Prevention of Cruelty to Animals (ASPCA) created

1869 Wyoming Territory grants women the right to vote

1871 *Woodhull and Claflin's Weekly* published

1873 Comstock Law passed

1874 Woman's Christian Temperance Union (WCTU) organized
Chautauqua education movement launched

1876 Johns Hopkins University graduate school established

1879 Henry George publishes *Progress and Poverty*
Dumbbell tenement introduced
Mary Baker Eddy establishes Christian Science
Salvation Army begins work in America

1881 Booker T. Washington becomes head of Tuskegee Institute
American Red Cross founded
Barnum and Bailey first join to stage the "Greatest Show on Earth"

1882 First immigration-restriction laws passed

1883 Brooklyn Bridge completed
Metropolitan Opera House built in New York

1884 Mark Twain publishes *The Adventures of Huckleberry Finn*

1885 Louis Sullivan builds the first skyscraper, in Chicago
Linotype invented

1886 Statue of Liberty erected in New York harbor

1887 American Protective Association (APA) formed
Hatch Act supplements Morrill Act

1888 Edward Bellamy publishes *Looking Backward*
American all-star baseball team tours the world

1889 Jane Addams founds Hull House in Chicago
Moody Bible Institute established in Chicago

1890 National American Women's Suffrage Association formed

1891 Basketball invented

1893 Lillian Wald opens Henry Street Settlement in New York
Anti-Saloon League formed
Columbian Exposition held in Chicago

1897 Library of Congress opens

1898 Charlotte Perkins Gilman publishes *Women and Economics*

1899 Kate Chopin publishes *The Awakening*

1900 Theodore Dreiser publishes *Sister Carrie*

1910 National Association for the Advancement of Colored People (NAACP) founded

SUGGESTED READINGS

PRIMARY SOURCE DOCUMENTS

Jacob Riis, *How the Other Half Lives** (1890), is a vivid account of life in America's slums. In *A Hazard of New Fortunes* (1890), William Dean Howells penned one of the first "urban novels" in American literature. Frances Willard, *Glimpses of Fifty Years** (1880), is the memoir of a leading prohibitionist. Victoria Woodhull, *The Scarecrows of Sexual Slavery** (1874), provocatively illustrates some changing ideas about women's roles. Henry James's novel *The Bostonians* (1886) vividly portrays feminists and suffragists.

*An asterisk indicates that the document, or an excerpt from it, can be found in Thomas A. Bailey and David M. Kennedy, eds., *The American Spirit: United States History as Seen by Contemporaries*, 9th ed. (Boston: Houghton Mifflin, 1998).

SECONDARY SOURCES

The Rise of the City, 1878–1898 (1933) is a classic study by Arthur M. Schlesinger. More recent are Gunther Barth, *City People: The Rise of Modern City Culture in Nineteenth-Century America* (1980); Howard Chudacoff, *The Evolution of American Urban Society* (1975); the opening chapters of Kenneth T. Jackson, *Crabgrass Frontier: The Suburbanization of America* (1985); and Eric H. Monkkonen, *America Becomes Urban: The Development of Cities and Towns, 1780–1980* (1988). Specific cities are discussed in Sam Bass Warner Jr.'s *The Private City: Philadelphia in Three Periods of Its Growth* (1968) and in his study of Boston, *Streetcar Suburbs* (1962). See also Edward K. Spann, *The New Metropolis: New York City, 1840–1857* (1981), and Karen Sawislak's graceful and insightful *Smoldering City: Chicagoans and the Great Fire, 1871–1874* (1995). On architecture see Robert Twombly, *Louis Sullivan: His Life and Work* (1986). On new urban spaces and their use by city dwellers, see Roy Rosenzweig and Elizabeth Blackmar, *The Park and The People: A History of Central Park* (1992); Kathy Peiss, *Cheap Amusements: Working Women and Leisure in Turn-of-the Century New York* (1986); and David Nasaw, *Going Out: The Rise and Fall of Public Amusements* (1993). Oscar Handlin introduced the study of immigrant communities in American cities with his *Boston's Immigrants* (rev. ed., 1959). More recent studies of the same topic include John Bodnar, *The Transplanted: A History of Immigrants in Urban America* (1985); Jon Gjerde, *From Peasants to Farmers: The Migration from Norway to the Upper Middle West* (1985); Kerby A. Miller, *Emigrants and Exile: Ireland and the Irish Exodus to North America* (1985); Donna Gabaccia, *From the Other Side: Women, Gender, and Immigrant Life in the U.S., 1820–1990* (1994). Thomas Kessner, *The Golden Door: Italian and Jewish Mobility in New York City, 1880–1915* (1977); Stephan Thernstrom, *The Other Bostonians* (1973); Virginia Yans-McLaughlin, *Family and Community: Italian Immigrants in Buffalo, 1880–1930* (1975); Dino Cinel, *From Italy to San Francisco: The Immigrant Experience* (1982); Humbert Nelli, *Italians of Chicago, 1880–1920* (1970); Ronald Takaki, *Strangers from a Different Shore: A History of Asian Americans* (1989); and Irving Howe's monumental and moving account of Jewish immigration, *World of Our Fathers* (1976). Maldwyn Jones, *American Immigration* (1960), is a well-written introduction, as is Thomas J. Archdeacon, *Becoming American* (1983). Oscar Handlin, *The Uprooted* (1951), is an imaginative account of the immigrant experience. John Higham examines the "nativist" reaction in *Strangers in the Land* (1955). On medicine consult Morris J. Vogel, *The Invention of the Modern Hospital: Boston, 1870–1930* (1980); Paul Starr, *The Social Transformation of American Medicine* (1982); and John Duffy, *The Sanitarians: A History of American Public Health* (1990). On education see Lawrence Cremin, *The Transformation of the School* (1961), and Laurence Veysey, *The Emergence of the American University* (1965). Black thought for this period is illuminated by three studies: August Meier, *Negro Thought in America, 1880–1915* (1963); Louis R. Harlan, *Booker T. Washington: The Making of a Black Leader, 1865–1901* (1972); and David Levering Lewis, *W. E. B. Du Bois: Biography of a Race, 1868–1919* (1993). For blacks in northern cities before World War I, see Allan H. Spear, *Black Chicago: The Making of a Negro Ghetto, 1890–1920* (1967), and James Borchert, *Alley Life in Washington: Family, Community, Religion, and Folklife in the City* (1980). On religion see Susan Curtis, *A Consuming Faith: The Social Gospel and Modern American Culture* (1991). On women and the family, consult Carl Degler, *At Odds: Women and the Family from the Revolution to the Present* (1980); Steven Mintz, *A Prison of Expectations: The Family in Victorian Culture* (1983); Mari Jo Buhle, *Women and American Socialism, 1870–1920* (1981); Margaret W. Rossiter, *Women Scientists in America* (1982); Elisabeth Griffith, *In Her Own Right: The Life of Elizabeth Cady Stanton* (1984); Rosalind Rosenberg, *Beyond Separate Spheres* (1982); the same author's *Divided Lives* (1992); Allen F. Davis, *American Heroine: The Life and Legend of Jane Addams* (1973); Elaine May, *Great Expectations: Marriage and Divorce in Post-Victorian America* (1980); Carroll Smith-Rosenberg, *Disorderly Conduct: Visions of Gender in Victorian America* (1985); and Estelle B. Freedman, *Their Sisters' Keepers: Women's Prison Reform in America, 1830–1930* (1981). John L. Thomas considers *Alternative America: Henry George, Edward Bellamy, Henry Demarest Lloyd, and the Adversary Tradition* (1983). Bruce Kuklick examines Harvard's star-studded philosophy department in *The Rise of American Philosophy* (1977). James Turner probes one aspect of the conflict between science and religion in *Without God, Without Creed: The Origins of Unbelief in America* (1985). Three fascinating studies document the rise of a "new" middle-class mentality: Burton J. Bledstein, *The Culture of Professionalism* (1976); Thomas Haskell, *The Emergence of Professional Social Science* (1977); and Stuart M. Blumin, *The Emergence of the Middle Class: Social Experience in the American City, 1760–1900* (1989). See also Alexandra Oleson and John Voss, eds., *The Organization of Knowledge in Modern America, 1860–1920* (1979).

27

The Great West and the Agricultural Revolution

1865–1890

Up to our own day American history has been in a large degree the history of the colonization of the Great West. The existence of an area of free land, its continuous recession, and the advance of American settlement westward, explain American development.

FREDERICK JACKSON TURNER, 1893

Indians Embattled in the West

When the Civil War crashed to a close, the frontier line was still wavering westward. A long fringe of settlement, bulging outward here and there, ran roughly north through central Texas and on to the Canadian border. Between this jagged line and the settled areas on the Pacific slope, there were virtually no white people. The few exceptions were the islands of Mormons in Utah, occasional trading posts and gold camps, and several scattered Spanish-Mexican settlements throughout the Southwest.

Sprawling in expanse, the Great West was a rough square that measured about 1,000 miles (1,600 kilometers) on each side. Embracing mountains, plateaus, deserts, and plains, it was the habitat of the Indian, the buffalo, the wild horse, the prairie dog, and the coyote. Twenty-five years later—that is, by 1890—the entire domain had been carved into states and the four territories of Utah, Arizona, New Mexico, and the "Indian Territory," or Oklahoma. Pioneers flung themselves greedily on this enormous prize, as if to ravish it. Never before in human experience, probably, had so huge an area been transformed so rapidly.

On the Southern Plains, by Frederic Remington, 1907

Native Americans numbered about 360,000 in 1860, most of them still ranging freely over the vast, vacant trans-Mississippi West. But to their misfortune, the Indians stood in the path of the advancing white American settlers. Like the blades of mighty scissors, two lines of onward-moving pioneers were closing in simultaneously—one from the Pacific coast, the other from the trans-Mississippi East. An inevitable clash loomed between an acquisitive civilization and a traditional culture as the march of modernity crushed under its feet the hunting grounds, and hence the food supply, of the native inhabitants.

Diverse tribes of buffalo-hunting Indians roamed the spacious western plains in 1860. In three centuries the Spanish-introduced horse had transformed the culture of the Plains Indians, causing the tribes to become more nomadic and more warlike. The Plains Indians had become superbly skilled riders and fighters.

When white soldiers and settlers had edged onto the plains in the two or three decades before the Civil War, they triggered an environmental cycle that set the Indian tribes against one another and ultimately undermined the foundations of Native American culture. White intruders unwittingly spread cholera, typhoid, and smallpox among the native peoples of the plains, with devastating results. Worse still, by hunting and by grazing their own livestock on the prairie grasses, whites steadily shrank the Great Plains bison population. As the mammoth buffalo herds dwindled, the Plains tribes warred among themselves over ever-scarcer hunting grounds. The Sioux, displaced by Chippewas from their ancestral lands at the headwaters of the Mississippi in the late eighteenth century, were aggressively expanding at the expense of the Crows, Kiowas, and Pawnees when whites began arriving in force in the 1850s. "These lands once belonged to the Kiowas and Crows," explained a Sioux spokesman, "but we whipped those nations out of them and in this we did what the white men do when they want the lands of the Indians." When the Sioux killed more than one hundred Pawnee men, women, and children in a battle in 1873, the Pawnees finally sought refuge on a tiny reservation in the Indian Territory.

Pawnee Indians in Front of Their Lodge, c. 1868
The Pawnees of central Nebraska never made war on the United States, which they regarded as an ally in their own struggles against the marauding Sioux.

The federal government tried to pacify the Plains Indians by signing treaties with the "chiefs" of various "tribes" at Fort Laramie in 1851 and at Fort Atkinson in 1853. The treaties marked the beginnings of the reservation system in the West. They established boundaries for the territory of each tribe and attempted to separate the Indians into two great "colonies" to the north and south of a corridor of intended white settlement.

But the white treaty makers misunderstood both Indian government and Indian society. "Tribes" and "chiefs" were often fictions of the white imagination, which could not grasp the fact that Native Americans, living in scattered bands, usually recognized no authority outside their immediate family, or perhaps a village elder. And the nomadic culture of the Plains Indians was utterly alien to the concept of living out one's life in the confinement of a defined territory.

In the 1860s the federal government intensified this policy and herded the Indians into still smaller confines, principally the "Great Sioux reservation" in the Dakota Territory, and the Indian Territory of present-day Oklahoma, into which dozens of southern Plains tribes were forced.

The Indians surrendered their ancestral lands only when they had received solemn promises from Washington that they would be left alone and provided with food, clothing, and other supplies. Regrettably, the federal Indian agents were often corrupt. They palmed off moth-eaten blankets, spoiled beef, and other defective provisions on the friendless Indians. One of these cheating officials, on an annual salary of $1,500, returned home after four years with an estimated "savings" of $50,000.

Grasping white men were guilty of many additional provocations. They flagrantly disregarded treaty promises, openly seized the Indians' land, wantonly slaughtered their game, and occasionally debauched the women. During the Civil War the Sioux of Minnesota, facing starvation and taking advantage of the sectional quarrel, went on the warpath and murdered several hundred settlers. The uprising was finally crushed by federal troops, and nearly forty of the Sioux Indians, after a summary trial, were hanged at a well-attended mass execution.

One disheartened Indian complained to the white Sioux Commission created by Congress:

"Tell your people that since the Great Father promised that we should never be removed we have been moved five times. . . . I think you had better put the Indians on wheels and you can run them about wherever you wish."

From 1868 to about 1890, almost incessant warfare raged in various parts of the West between Indians and whites. A printed list of the names of the engagements alone covers over a hundred pages. The fighting was fierce and harrowing, especially the winter campaigning in subzero weather. Many of the regular troops were veterans of the Civil War. A disproportionate number were immigrants, many of whom, ironically, had fled Europe to avoid military service. Their ranks also embraced four crack black units, including the famous Tenth Cavalry. All told, about one-fifth of all soldiers assigned to the frontier during these years were black men attracted to steady monthly pay and the opportunity to escape limited options at home. Generals Sherman, Sheridan ("the only good Indian is a dead Indian"), and Custer, all of whom had won their spurs in the Civil War, gathered further laurels in the West. They were matched against formidable adversaries, for the Indians of the plains, unlike those first encountered by the American colonists, rode swift ponies and enjoyed baffling mobility. To the disgust of the American soldiers, the "hostiles" were often better armed, with repeating rifles provided by fur-traders, than were the federal troops sent against them, who usually toted clumsy muzzle-loaders.

Receding Native Population

The Indian wars in the West were often savage clashes. Aggressive whites sometimes shot peaceful Indians on sight, just to make sure they would give no trouble. At Sand Creek, Colorado, in 1864, Colonel J. M. Chivington's militia massacred in cold blood some four hundred Indians who apparently thought they had been promised immunity. Women were shot praying for mercy, children had their brains dashed out, and braves were tortured, scalped, and unspeakably mutilated. On several notorious occasions, innocent Indians were killed for outrages committed by their fellow tribesmen; sometimes they were shot just for "sport."

Cruelty begot cruelty. In 1866 a Sioux war party attempting to block construction of the Bozeman Trail to the Montana goldfields ambushed Captain William J. Fetterman's command of eighty-one soldiers and civilians in Wyoming's Big Horn Mountains. The Indians left not a single survivor and grotesquely mutilated the corpses. One trooper's face was spitted with 105 arrows. George Armstrong

> *A young lieutenant told Colonel Chivington that to attack the Indians would be a violation of pledges.*
>
> "His reply was, bringing his fist down close to my face, 'Damn any man who sympathizes with Indians.' I told him what pledges were given the Indians. He replied that he 'had come to kill Indians, and believed it to be honorable to kill Indians under any and all circumstances.'"

Custer, the buckskin-clad "boy general" of Civil War fame, now demoted to colonel and turned Indian fighter, wrote that Fetterman's annihilation "awakened a bitter feeling toward the savage perpetrators." The cycle of ferocious warfare intensified.

The Fetterman massacre led to one of the few—though short-lived—Indian triumphs in the plains wars. In another Treaty of Fort Laramie, signed in 1868, the government abandoned the Bozeman Trail. The sprawling "Great Sioux reservation" was guaranteed to the Sioux tribes.

Then in 1874, Colonel Custer led a "scientific" expedition into the Black Hills of South Dakota (part of the Sioux reservation) and announced that he had discovered gold. Hordes of greedy gold-seekers rushed to the Dakota Territory. The aggrieved Sioux, their lands invaded despite treaty guarantees, took to the warpath. Conspicuous among their leaders was Sitting Bull, a medicine man as wily as he was influential.

Colonel Custer's Seventh Cavalry, nearly half of whose troopers were foreign-born immigrants, set out to suppress the Indians and to return them to the reservation. Attacking what turned out to be a superior force of some 2,500 well-armed warriors camped along the Little Big Horn River in present-day Montana, the "White Chief with Yellow Hair" and his 264 officers and men were completely wiped out in 1876 when two supporting columns failed to come to their rescue.* But white reinforcements later arrived, and the Indians who defeated Custer

---

*When the whites wiped out Indians, the engagement (in white history books) was usually a "battle"; when the Indians wiped out whites, it was a "massacre." "Strategy," when practiced by Indians, was "treachery."

were relentlessly hunted and crushed in a series of battles across the northern plains over the next several months.

The Nez Percé Indians of Idaho were also goaded into warfare in 1877, when gold discoveries on their reservation prompted the federal government to shrink its size by 90 percent. Chief Joseph finally surrendered his renegade band of some seven hundred Indians after a tortuous, 1,700-mile, three-month trek across the Continental Divide toward Canada. There the Nez Percés hoped to rendezvous with Sitting Bull, who had taken refuge north of the border after the Battle of the Little Big Horn. Betrayed into believing they would be returned to their ancestral lands in Idaho, the Nez Percés instead were sent to a dusty reservation in Kansas, where 40 percent of them perished from disease. The survivors were eventually allowed to return to Idaho.

Fierce Apache tribes of Arizona and New Mexico were the most difficult to subdue. Led by Geronimo, whose eyes blazed hatred of the whites, they were pursued into Mexico by federal troops using the sun-flashing heliograph, a communication device, which impressed the Indians as "big medicine." Scattered remnants of the warriors were finally persuaded to

Indian Wars, 1860–1890   Surrendering in 1877, Chief Joseph of the Nez Percé declared, "Our chiefs are killed. . . . The old men are all dead. . . . The little children are freezing to death. . . . I want to have time to look for my children. . . . Hear me, my chiefs. My heart is sick and sad. From where the sun now stands I will fight no more forever."

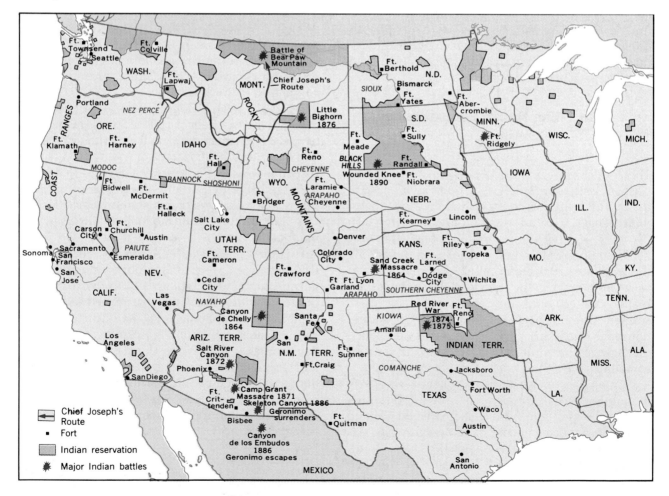

diseases, to which they showed little resistance, and by their firewater, to which they showed almost no resistance. Above all, the virtual extermination of the buffalo resulted in the near-extermination of the Plains Indians.

Bellowing Herds of Bison

Tens of millions of buffalo—described by early Spaniards as "hunchback cows"—blackened the western prairies when the white Americans first arrived. These shaggy, lumbering animals were the staff of life for Native Americans (see "Makers of America: The Plains Indians," pp. 606–607). Their flesh provided food; their dried dung provided fuel ("buffalo chips"); their hides provided clothing, lariats, and harnesses.

When the Civil War closed, some 15 million of these meaty beasts were still grazing on the western plains. In 1868 a Kansas Pacific locomotive had to wait eight hours for a herd to amble across the tracks; experience had shown that trying to smash through would produce only mangled flesh and derailment. Much of the food supply of the railroad construction gangs came from leathery buffalo steaks. William "Buffalo Bill" Cody—sinewy, telescope-eyed, and a crack shot—killed over 4,000 animals in eighteen months while employed by the Kansas Pacific.

With the building of the railroad, the massacre of the herds began in deadly earnest. Most of the creatures were slain for their hides in response to the insatiable demand for buffalo robes, then highly fashionable. Others were felled merely for their tongues or a few other choice cuts, while the rest of the carcass was left to be picked by the vultures. Countless buffalo were shot with repeating rifles for sheer amusement. "Sportsmen" on lurching railroad trains would lean out the windows and blaze away at the animals to satisfy their lust for slaughter or excitement.

Such wholesale butchery could have only one end. By 1885 fewer than a thousand buffalo were left, and the once-numerous beasts were in danger of complete extermination. A few thousand of the beefy animals have been kept alive, largely as living museum pieces for tourists in Yellowstone National Park. The whole story is a shocking example of the greed and waste that accompanied the conquest of the continent.

Geronimo (c. 1829–1909)   He was the most famous Apache leader.

surrender after the Apache women had been exiled to Florida. The Apaches ultimately became successful farmers in Oklahoma.

This relentless fire-and-sword policy of the whites at last shattered the spirit of the Indians. The vanquished Native Americans were finally ghettoized in "human zoos," known as reservations, there to eke out a sullen existence as wards of the government. Their white masters had at last discovered that the Indians were much cheaper to feed than to fight. Even so, for many decades they were almost ignored to death.

The "taming" of the Indians was engineered by a number of factors. Of cardinal importance was the railroad, which shot an iron arrow through the heart of the West. Locomotives ("bad medicine wagons") could bring out unlimited numbers of troops, farmers, cattlemen, sheepherders, and settlers. The Indians were also ravaged by the white people's

The Buffalo Hunt, by Frederic Remington, 1890 A New Yorker who first went west at the age of nineteen as a cowboy and ranch cook, Remington (1861–1909) became the foremost artist of the vanishing way of life of the old Far West. Once a common sight on the high plains, the kind of buffalo kill that Remington records here was a great rarity by the time he painted this scene in 1890. The once-vast herds of bison had long since been reduced to a pitiful few by the white man's rifles.

The End of the Trail

By the 1880s the national conscience began to stir uneasily over the plight of the Indians. Helen Hunt Jackson, a Massachusetts writer of children's literature, pricked the moral sense of Americans in 1881, when she published *A Century of Dishonor.* The book chronicled the sorry record of government ruthlessness and chicanery in dealing with the Indians. Her later novel *Ramona* (1884), a love story of injustice to the California Indians, sold some 600,000 copies and further inspired sympathy for the Indians.

Debate seesawed. Humanitarians wanted to treat the Indians kindly and persuade them thereby to "walk the white man's road." Yet hard-liners insisted on the current policy of forced containment and brutal punishment. Neither side showed much respect for traditional Native American culture. Christian reformers, who often administered educational facilities on the reservations, sometimes withheld food to force the Indians to give up their tribal religion and assimilate to white society. In 1884 these zealous white souls joined with military men in successfully persuading the federal government to outlaw the sacred Sun Dance. When the "Ghost Dance" cult later spread to the Dakota Sioux, the army bloodily stamped it out in 1890 at the so-

called Battle of Wounded Knee. In the fighting thus provoked, an estimated two hundred Indian men, women, and children were killed, as well as twenty-nine invading soldiers.

The misbegotten offspring of the movement to reform Indian policy was the Dawes Severalty Act of 1887. Reflecting the forced-civilization views of the reformers, the act dissolved many tribes as legal entities, wiped out tribal ownership of land, and set up individual Indian family heads with 160 free acres. If the Indians behaved themselves like "good white settlers," they would get full title to their holdings, as well as citizenship, in twenty-five years. The probationary period was later extended, but full citizenship was granted to all Indians in 1924.

Civil War veteran and long-time Indian fighter General Philip Sheridan (1831–1888) reflected on the wars against the Indians:

"We took away their country and their means of support, broke up their mode of living, their habits of life, introduced disease and decay among them, and it was for this and against this they made war. Could anyone expect less?"

Arapaho Chief Hail Wearing Ghost Dance Shirt, c. 1890
The Ghost Dance cult originated among the Paiute Indians in the 1870s, and spread swiftly throughout the western tribes. It held out the promise of a revival of traditional Indian culture and revenge on the invading whites, but it was ruthlessly suppressed by the U.S. authorities. Ghost Dance shirts like this one were thought by their wearers to be impermeable to bullets.

Reservation land not allotted to the Indians under the Dawes Act was to be sold to railroads and white settlers, with the proceeds used by the federal government to educate and "civilize" the native peoples. In 1879 the government had already funded the Carlisle Indian School in Pennsylvania, where Native American children, separated from their tribe, were taught English and inculcated with white values and customs. "Kill the Indian and save the man" was the school founder's motto. In the 1890s the government expanded its network of Indian boarding schools and sent "field matrons" to the reservations to teach Native American women the art of sewing and to preach the virtues of chastity and hygiene.

> *The Indian spokesman Plenty Coups said in 1909,*
>
> "I see no longer the curling smoke rising from our lodge poles. I hear no longer the songs of the women as they prepare the meal. The antelope have gone; the buffalo wallows are empty. Only the wail of the coyote is heard. The white man's medicine is stronger than ours. . . . We are like birds with a broken wing."

The Dawes Act struck directly at tribal organization and tried to make rugged individualists out of the Indians. This legislation ignored the inherent reliance of traditional Indian culture on tribally held land, literally pulling the land out from under them. By 1900 Indians had lost 50 percent of the 156 million acres they had held just two decades earlier. The forced-assimilation doctrine of the Dawes Act remained the cornerstone of the government's official Indian policy for nearly half a century, until the Indian Reorganization Act (the "Indian New Deal") of 1934 partially reversed the individualistic approach and belatedly tried to restore the tribal basis of Indian life (see p. 807).

Under these new federal policies, defective though they were, the Indian population started to mount slowly. The total number had been reduced by 1887 to about 243,000—the result of bullets, bottles, and bacteria—but the census of 1990 counted some 1.5 million Native Americans, urban and rural.

Mining: From Dishpan to Ore Breaker

The conquest of the Indians and the coming of the railroad were life-giving boons to the mining frontier. The golden gravel of California continued to yield "pay dirt," and in 1858 an electrifying discovery convulsed Colorado. Avid "fifty-niners" or "Pike's Peakers" rushed west to rip at the ramparts of the Rockies. But there were more miners than minerals; and many gold-grubbers, with "Pike's Peak or Bust" inscribed on the canvas of their covered wagons, creaked wearily back with the added inscription, "Busted, by Gosh." Yet countless bearded fortune

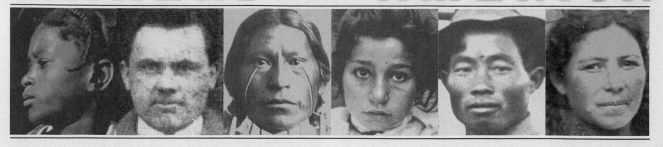

The Plains Indians

The last of the native peoples of North America to bow before the military might of the whites, the Indians of the northern Great Plains long defended their lands and their ways of life against the American cavalry. After the end of the Indian wars, toward the close of the nineteenth century, the Plains tribes struggled on, jealously guarding their communities against white encroachment. Crowded onto reservations, subject to ever-changing federal Indian policies, assailed by corrupt settlers and Indian agents, the Plains Indians have nonetheless preserved much of their ancestral culture to this day.

Before Europeans first appeared in North America in the sixteenth century, the vast plain from northern Texas to Saskatchewan was home to some thirty different tribes. There was no typical Plains Indian; each tribe spoke a distinct language, practiced its own religion, and formed its own government. When members of different bands met on the prairies, communication depended on a special sign language.

Indians had first trod the arid plains to pursue sprawling herds of antelope, elk, and especially buffalo. But these early peoples of the plains were not exclusively hunters: the women were expert farmers, coaxing lush gardens of pumpkins, squash, corn, and beans from the dry but fertile soil. Still,

A Comanche Village, by George Catlin, 1834

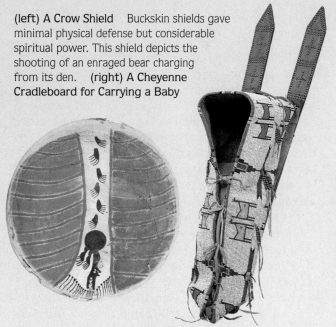

(left) A Crow Shield Buckskin shields gave minimal physical defense but considerable spiritual power. This shield depicts the shooting of an enraged bear charging from its den. (right) A Cheyenne Cradleboard for Carrying a Baby

Chan-Chä-Uiá-Teüin, Teton Sioux Woman, by Karl Bodmer, c. 1830s Bodmer, a German artist, painted this woman's portrait during an expedition to the Great Plains. Her name means "Woman of the Crow Nation," which seems to suggest that she was taken captive from the Sioux's mortal enemies, the Crow.

the shaggy pelt and heavy flesh of the buffalo constituted the staff of life on the plains. Hunted by men, the great bison were butchered by women, who used every part of the beast. They fashioned horns and hooves into spoons, and intestines into containers. They stretched sinews into strong bowstrings and wove buffalo hair into ropes. Meat not immediately eaten was pounded into pemmican—thin strips of smoked or sun-dried buffalo flesh mixed with berries and stuffed into rawhide bags.

The nomadic Plains Indians roamed the countryside in small bands throughout the winter, gathering together in summer for religious ceremonies, socializing, and communal buffalo hunts. At first these seasonal migrations required arduous loading and carting. The Indians carried all their possessions or heaped them on wheelless carts called travois, which were dragged by dogs—their only beasts of burden.

Then in the sixteenth century, the mounted Spanish *conquistadores* ventured into the New World. Their steeds—some of them escaping to become mustangs, the wild horses of the American West, and others acquired by the Indians in trade —quickly spread over the plains. The horse revolutionized Indian societies, turning the Plains tribes into efficient hunting machines that promised to banish hunger from the prairies. But the plains pony also ignited a furious competition for grazing lands, for trade goods, and for ever more horses, so that wars of aggression and of revenge became increasingly bitter and frequent.

The European invasion soon eclipsed the short-lived era of the horse. After many battles the Plains Indians found themselves crammed together on tiny reservations, clinging with tired but determined fingers to their traditions. Although much of Plains Indian culture persists to this day, the Indians' free-ranging way of life has passed into memory. As Black Elk, an Ogalala Sioux, put it, "Once we were happy in our own country and we were seldom hungry, for then the two-leggeds and the four-leggeds lived together like relatives, and there was plenty for them and for us. But then the Wasichus [white people] came, and they made little islands for us . . . and always these islands are becoming smaller, for around them surges the gnawing flood of Wasichus."

Dance-Hall Girl, Virginia City, Nevada, c. 1890
Women as well as men sought their fortunes in the frontier West—especially in wide-open mining towns like Virginia City.

third cabin was a saloon, where sweat-stained miners drank adulterated liquor ("rotgut") in the company of accommodating women. Lynch law and hempen vigilante justice, as in early California, preserved a crude semblance of order in the towns. And when the "diggings" petered out, the gold-seekers decamped, leaving eerily picturesque "ghost towns," such as Virginia City, Nevada, silhouetted in the desert. Begun with a boom, these towns ended with a whimper.

Once the loose surface gold was gobbled up, ore-breaking machinery was imported to smash the gold-bearing quartz. This operation was so expensive that it could ordinarily be undertaken only by corporations pooling the wealth of stockholders. Gradually the age of big business came to the mining industry. Dusty, bewhiskered miners, dishpans in hand, were replaced by the impersonal corporations, with their costly machinery and trained engineers. The once-independent gold-washer became just another day laborer.

Yet the mining frontier had played a vital role in subduing the continent. Magnetlike, it attracted population and wealth, while advertising the wonders of the Wild West. Women as well as men found opportunity, running boardinghouses or working as prostitutes. They won a kind of equality on the rough frontier that earned them the vote in Wyoming (1869), Utah (1870), Colorado (1893), and Idaho (1896) long before their sisters in the East could cast a ballot.

The amassing of precious metals helped finance the Civil War, facilitated the building of railroads, and intensified the already bitter conflict between whites and Indians. The outpouring of silver and gold enabled the Treasury to resume specie payments in 1879 and injected the silver issue into American politics. "Silver Senators," representing the thinly peopled "acreage states" of the West, used their disproportionate influence to promote the interests of the silver miners. Finally, the mining frontier added to American folklore and literature, as the writings of Bret Harte and Mark Twain so colorfully attest.

Beef Bonanzas and the Long Drive

When the Civil War ended, the grassy plains of Texas supported several million tough, long-horned cattle. These scrawny beasts, whose horn spread

seekers stayed on, some to strip away the silver deposits, others to extract nonmetallic wealth from the earth in the form of golden grain.

"Fifty-niners" also poured feverishly into Nevada in 1859, after the fabulous Comstock Lode had been uncovered. A fantastic amount of gold and silver, worth more than $340 million, was mined by the "Kings of the Comstock" from 1860 to 1890. The scantily populated state of Nevada, "child of the Comstock Lode," was prematurely railroaded into the Union in 1864, partly to provide three electoral votes for President Lincoln.

Smaller "lucky strikes" drew frantic gold- and silver-seekers into Montana, Idaho, and other western states. Boomtowns, known as "Helldorados," sprouted from the desert sands like magic. Every

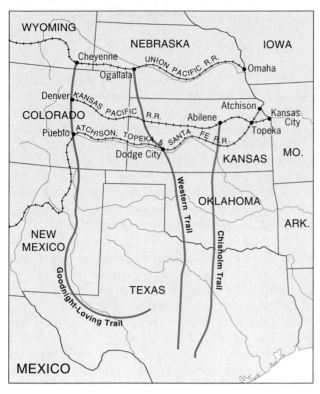

Cattle Trails

Dressed to Kill   Cowboys came in all varieties and sizes in the wild and woolly frontier West—and in all kinds of garb, as well.

sometimes reached 8 feet (2.4 meters), were killed primarily for their hides. There was no way of getting their meat profitably to market.

The problem of marketing was neatly solved when the transcontinental railroads thrust their iron fingers into the West. Cattle could now be shipped bodily to the stockyards, and under "beef barons" like the Swifts and Armours, the highly industrialized meat-packing business sprang into existence as a main pillar of the economy. Drawing upon the gigantic stockyards at Kansas City and Chicago, the meat packers could ship their fresh products to the East Coast in the newly perfected refrigerator cars.

A spectacular feeder of the new slaughter-houses was the "Long Drive." Texas cowboys—black, white, and Mexican—drove herds numbering from one thousand to ten thousand head slowly over the unfenced and unpeopled plains until they reached a railroad terminal. The bawling beasts grazed en route on the free government grass. Favorite terminal points were flyspecked "cow towns" like Dodge City—"the Bibulous Babylon of the Frontier"—and Abilene (Kansas), Ogallala (Nebraska), and Cheyenne (Wyoming). At Abilene,

order was maintained by Marshal James B. ("Wild Bill") Hickok, a fabulous gunman who reputedly killed only in self-defense or in the line of duty and who was fatally shot in the back in 1876, while playing poker.*

As long as lush grass was available, the Long Drive proved profitable—that is, to the luckier cattlemen who escaped the Indians, stampedes, cattle fever, and other hazards. From 1866 to 1888, bellowing herds, totaling over 4 million steers, were driven northward from the beef bowl of Texas. In peak years the profits to some cattlemen would soar as high as 40 percent. The steer was king in a Cattle Kingdom richly carpeted with grass.

What the Lord giveth, the Lord also can taketh away. The railroad made the Long Drive; and the railroad unmade the Long Drive, primarily because the locomotives ran both ways. The same rails that bore the cattle from the open range to the kitchen range brought out the homesteader and the sheepherder. Both of these intruders, amid flying bullets, built

---

*Frontier marshals like Hickok, Wyatt Earp, and "Bat" Masterson have been highly romanticized; some were little better than criminals who shot men from behind curtains: hooligans, not heroes. They were less "fast on the draw" and less accurate with their "six-guns" than legend commonly portrays. A western saying was that God did not make all men equal; Colonel Colt did.

barbed-wire fences that were too numerous to be cut down by the cowboys. Furthermore the terrible winter of 1886–1887, with blinding blizzards reaching 68 degrees below zero (-56 degrees Celsius), left thousands of dazed cattle starving and freezing. Overexpansion and overgrazing likewise took their toll, as the cowboys slowly gave way to plowboys.

The only escape for the stockmen was to make cattle raising a big business and avoid the perils of overproduction. Breeders learned to fence their ranches, lay in winter feed, import blooded bulls, and produce fewer and meatier animals. They also learned to organize. The Wyoming Stock-Growers' Association, especially in the 1880s, virtually controlled the state and its legislature.

This was the heyday of the cowboy. The equipment of the cowhand—from "shooting irons" and ten-gallon hat to chaps and spurs—served a useful, not an ornamental, function. A "genuwine" gun-toting cowpuncher, riding where men were men and smelled like horses, could justifiably boast of his toughness.

These bowlegged Knights of the Saddle, with their colorful trappings and cattle-lulling songs, became part of American folklore. Many of them, perhaps five thousand, were blacks, who especially enjoyed the newfound freedom of the open range.

Free Land for Free Families

A new day dawned for western farmers with the Homestead Act of 1862—an epochal measure vigorously opposed by the South before secession. The law provided that a settler could acquire as much as 160 acres of land (a quarter-section) by living on it five years, improving it, and paying a nominal fee averaging about $30.00. As an alternative, land might be acquired after only six months' residence at $1.25 an acre. Lands acquired in either fashion were to be exempt from attachment for debt.

The Homestead Act marked a drastic departure from previous policy. Before the act, public land had been sold primarily for revenue; now it was to be given away to encourage a rapid filling of empty spaces and to provide a stimulus to the family farm—"the backbone of democracy." The new law was a godsend to a host of farmers who could not afford to buy large holdings. During the forty years after its passage, about half a million families took advantage of the Homestead Act to carve out new homes in the vast open stretches. Yet five times that many families *purchased* their land from the railroads, the land companies, or the states.

The Homesteader's Wife, by Harvey Dunn   Women as well as men toiled without shade or respite on the sun-scorched and wind-parched Great Plains.

The Homestead Act often turned out to be a cruel hoax. The standard 160 acres, quite adequate in the well-watered Mississippi basin, frequently proved pitifully inadequate on the rain-scarce Great Plains. Thousands of homesteaders, perhaps two out of three, were forced to give up the one-sided struggle against drought. Uncle Sam, it was said, bet 160 acres against ten dollars that the settlers could not live on their homesteads for five years. One of these unsuccessful gambles in Greer County, western Oklahoma, inspired a folk song:

> *Hurrah for Greer County! The land of the free,*
> *The land of the bedbug, grasshopper, and flea;*
> *I'll sing of its praises, I'll tell of its fame,*
> *While starving to death on my government*
> *   claim.*

Naked fraud was spawned by the Homestead Act and similar laws. Perhaps ten times more of the public domain wound up in the clutches of land-grabbing promoters than in the hands of bona fide farmers. Unscrupulous corporations would use "dummy" homesteaders—often aliens bribed with cash or a bottle of beer—to grab the best properties containing timber, minerals, and oil. Settlers would later swear that they had "improved" the property by erecting a "twelve by fourteen" dwelling, which turned out to measure twelve by fourteen *inches.* In later years federal officials were only partially successful in unraveling the tangled skein of deceit. So functioned the government's first big "giveaway" program.

In making the arduous journey across the western prairies, many women settlers discovered new confidence in their abilities. Early on in her trek, Mary Richardson Walker (1811–1897) confided in her diary that

". . . my circumstances are rather trying. So much danger attends me on every hand. A long journey before me, going I know not whither, without mother or sister to attend me, can I expect to survive it all?"

Only a month later she recorded that

"in the afternoon we rode thirty-five miles without stopping. Pretty well tired out, all of us. Stood it pretty well myself."

Taming Western Deserts

The life-giving railways also played a major role in developing the agricultural West, largely through the profitable marketing of crops. In addition, some railroad companies induced Americans and European immigrants to buy the cheap lands earlier granted by the government. A leader in such "induced colonization" was the Northern Pacific Railroad, which at one time had nearly a thousand paid agents in Europe distributing roseate leaflets in various languages.

A shattering of the myth of the Great American Desert opened the gateways to the agricultural West even wider. The windswept prairies were for the most part treeless, and the tough sod had been pounded solid by millions of buffalo hooves. Pioneer explorers and trappers had assumed that the soil must be sterile, simply because it was not heavily watered and did not support immense forests. But once the prairie sod was broken with heavy iron plows pulled by four yokes of oxen—the "plow that broke the plains"—the earth proved astonishingly fruitful. "Sodbusters" poured onto the prairies. Lacking trees for lumber and fuel, they built homes from the very sod they dug from the ground, and burned corncobs for warmth.

Lured by higher wheat prices resulting from crop failures elsewhere in the world, settlers in the 1870s rashly pushed still farther west, onto the poor, marginal lands beyond the 100th meridian. That imaginary line, running north to south from the Dakotas through west Texas, separated two climatological regions—a well-watered area to the east, and a semiarid area to the west. Bewhiskered and one-armed geologist John Wesley Powell, explorer of the Colorado River's Grand Canyon and director of the U.S. Geological Survey, warned in 1874 that beyond the 100th meridian so little rain fell that agriculture was impossible without massive irrigation.

Ignoring Powell's advice, farmers heedlessly chewed up the crusty earth in western Kansas, eastern Colorado, and Montana. They quickly went broke as a six-year drought in the 1880s further desiccated the already dusty region. Western Kansas lost half its population between 1888 and 1892. "There is no God west of Salina," one hapless homesteader declared.

In the wake of the devastating drought, the new technique of "dry farming" took root on the plains.

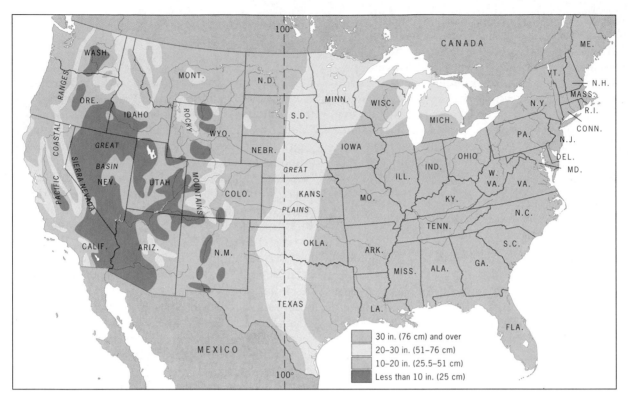

Average Annual Precipitation   In the Northern Hemisphere, storms usually circle the globe in a west-to-east direction. Much of the life-nourishing water in these storms is dumped as rainfall on the western slopes of the cloud-high Pacific coastal ranges and the Rocky Mountains. This weather pattern creates deep, dry "rain-shadows" in the Great Basin and in the plains area immediately east of the Rockies.

Its methods of frequent shallow cultivation supposedly were adapted to the arid western environment, but over time "dry farming" created a finely pulverized surface soil that contributed to the notorious "Dust Bowl" several decades later (see p. 807).

Other adaptations to the western environment were more successful. Tough strains of wheat, resistant to cold and drought, were imported from Russia and blossomed into billowing yellow carpets. Wise farmers abandoned corn in favor of sorghum and other drought-resistant grains. Barbed wire, perfected by Joseph F. Glidden in 1874, solved the problem of how to build fences on the treeless prairies.

Eventually, federally financed irrigation projects—on a colossal scale, beyond even what John Wesley Powell had dreamed—caused the Great American Desert to bloom. A century after Powell's predictions, arching dams had tamed the Missouri and Columbia Rivers and had so penned up and diverted the canyon-gnawing Colorado that its mouth in the Gulf of California was dry. More than

45 million acres were irrigated in seventeen western states. In the long run, the hydraulic engineers had more to do with shaping the modern West than all the trappers, miners, cavalrymen, and cowboys there ever were. As one engineer boasted, "We enjoy pushing rivers around."

The Far West Comes of Age

The Great West experienced a fantastic growth in population from the 1870s to the 1890s. A current quip was that one could not tell the truth about the West without lying. Confederate and Union veterans alike moved into the sunset with their families, as did a certain fraction of the inpouring immigrants.

A parade of new western states proudly joined the Union. Boomtown Colorado, offspring of the Pike's Peak gold rush, was greeted in 1876 as "the Centennial State." In 1889–1890 a Republican

Congress, eagerly seeking more Republican electoral and congressional votes, admitted in a wholesale lot six new states: North Dakota, South Dakota, Montana, Washington, Idaho, and Wyoming. The Mormon church formally and belatedly banned polygamy in 1890, but not until 1896 was Utah deemed worthy of admission. Only Oklahoma, New Mexico, and Arizona remained to be lifted into statehood from contiguous territory on the mainland of North America.

In a last gaudy fling, the federal government made available to settlers vast stretches of fertile plains formerly occupied by the Indians in the district of Oklahoma ("the Beautiful Land"). Scores of overeager and well-armed "sooners," illegally jumping the gun, had entered Oklahoma Territory. They had to be evicted repeatedly by federal troops, who on occasion would shoot the intruders' horses. On April 22, 1889, all was in readiness for the legal opening, and some 50,000 "boomers" were poised expectantly on the boundary line. At high noon the bugle shrilled, and a horde of "eighty-niners" poured in on lathered horses or careening vehicles. That night a lonely spot on the prairie had mushroomed into the tent city of Guthrie, with over 10,000 people. By the end of the year, Oklahoma boasted 60,000 inhabitants, and Congress made it a territory. In 1907 it became the "Sooner State."

The mad haste of the "boomers" underscored the fact that fertile free land was no longer abundant. In 1890—a watershed date—the superintendent of the census announced that for the first time in America's experience a frontier line was no longer discernible. All the unsettled areas were now broken into by isolated bodies of settlement. The "closing" of the frontier inspired one of the most influential essays ever written about American history—Frederick Jackson Turner's "The Significance of the Frontier in American History," in 1893.

Actually, few Americans in 1890 realized that the fading frontier line had disappeared. The Homestead Act remained on the books—and still does—and more millions of acres were taken up after 1890 than between 1862 and 1890. But in general the new lands were less desirable, and many sterile or parched farms, though well watered with sweat, had to be abandoned. To this day the federal government, which owns nearly one-fourth of all U.S. soil, has many millions of acres that may be homesteaded. But they are mostly grazing lands and other marginal areas incapable of sustaining a decent standard of living. From time to time, considerable acreage was rendered attractive for homesteading by the completion of irrigation or reclamation projects. In these ways the frontier survived its "death" by several decades.

As the nineteenth century neared its sunset, the westward-tramping American people were disturbed to find that their fabled free land was going or had gone. The secretary of war had prophesied in 1827 that five hundred years would be needed to fill the West. But as the nation finally recognized that its land was not inexhaustible, seeds were planted to preserve the vanishing resource. The government set aside land for national parks—first Yellowstone in 1872, followed by Yosemite and Sequoia in 1890.

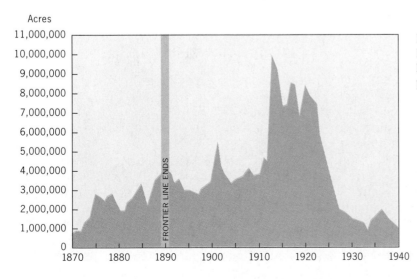

Homesteads from the Public Lands (acreage legally transferred to private ownership)

The Folding Frontier

The frontier was more than a place: it was also a state of mind and a symbol of opportunity. Its passing ended a romantic phase of the nation's internal development and created new economic and psychological problems.

Traditionally footloose, Americans have been notorious for their mobility; the automobile trailer is a typically American vehicle. The nation's farmers, unlike the peasants of Europe, have seldom remained rooted to their soil. The land, sold for a profit as settlement closed in, was often the settler's most profitable crop.

Much has been said about the frontier as a "safety valve." The theory is that when hard times came, the unemployed who cluttered the city pavements merely moved west, took up farming, and prospered.

In truth, relatively few city dwellers, at least in the populous eastern centers, migrated to the frontier during depressions. Most of them did not know how to farm; few of them could raise enough money to transport themselves west and then pay for livestock and expensive machinery. The initial outlay for equipment had become so heavy by the 1880s and 1890s that the West was decreasingly a land of opportunity for farmers, though it might be for ranchers, miners, and day laborers. A large proportion of the settlers who moved west came from farms on the older frontier, which was within striking distance of the new frontier.

But the safety-valve theory does have some validity. Free acreage did lure to the West a host of immigrant farmers, who otherwise might have remained in the eastern cities to clog the job markets and to crowd the festering and already overpopulated slums. And the very *possibility* of westward migration may have induced urban employers to maintain wage rates high enough to discourage workers from leaving. Ironically, however, the real safety valve by the late nineteenth century was the city. Failed farmers, busted miners, and erstwhile easterners made Chicago America's "second city" (after New York), and they found San Francisco a better place to seek their fortunes than the goldfields nearby.

United States history cannot be properly understood unless it is viewed in light of the westward-moving experience. As Frederick Jackson Turner wrote, "American history has been in a large degree the history of the colonization of the Great West." The story of settling and taming the trans-Mississippi West in the late nineteenth century was but the last chapter in the saga of colonizing various American "wests" since Columbus's day—from the West Indies to the Chesapeake shore, from the valleys of the Hudson and Connecticut Rivers to the valleys of the Tennessee and Ohio Rivers.

And yet the trans-Mississippi West formed a distinct chapter in that saga and retains even to this day much of its uniqueness. There the Native Amer-

Harvesting in Washington State   Humans, horses, and machine join forces in this turn-of-the-century scene.

ican peoples made their last and most desperate struggle against colonization, and there most Native Americans live today. There "Anglo" culture collided most directly with Hispanic culture—the historic rival of the Anglo-Americans for dominance in the New World—and the Southwest remains the most Hispanicized region in America. There America faced across the Pacific to Asia, and there most Asian-Americans dwell today. There the scale and severity of the environment posed their largest challenges to human ambitions, and there the environment, with its aridity and still-magical emptiness, continues to mold social and political life, and the American imagination, as in no other part of the nation. And in no other region has the federal government, with its vast land holdings, its subsidies to the railroads, and its massive irrigation projects, played so conspicuous a role in economic and social development.

The westward-moving pioneers and the country they confronted have assumed mythic proportions in the American mind. They have been immortalized by such writers as Bret Harte, Mark Twain, Helen Hunt Jackson, and Francis Parkman, and by such painters as George Catlin, Frederic Remington, and Albert Bierstadt. For better or worse, those pioneers planted the seeds of civilization in the immense western wilderness. The life we live, they dreamed of; the life they lived, we can only dream.

The Farm Becomes a Factory

The situation of American farmers, once Jacks-and-Jills-of-all-trades, was rapidly changing. They had once raised their own food, fashioned their own clothing, and bartered for other necessities with neighbors. Now high prices persuaded farmers to concentrate on growing single "cash" crops, such as wheat or corn, and use their profits to buy foodstuffs at the general store and manufactured goods in town or by mail order. The Chicago firm of Aaron Montgomery Ward sent out its first catalogue—a single sheet—in 1872.

American Agriculture in 1900

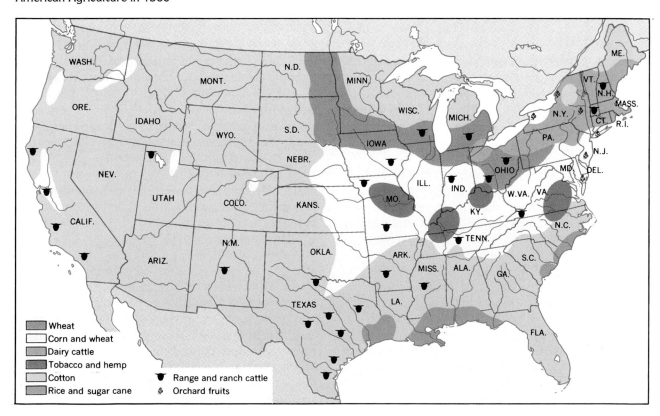

Large-scale farmers, especially in the immense grain-producing areas of the Mississippi Valley, were now both specialists as well as business-people. As cogs in the vast industrial machine, these farmers were intimately tied to banking, rail-roading, and manufacturing. They had to buy expensive machinery in order to plant and to harvest their crops. A powerful steam engine could drag behind it simultaneously the plow, seeder, and harrow. The speed of harvesting wheat was dramat-ically increased in the 1870s by the invention of the twine binder and then in the 1880s by the "com-bine"—the combined reaper-thresher, which was drawn by twenty to forty horses and which both reaped and bagged the grain. Widespread use of such costly equipment naturally called for first-class management. But the farmers, often unskilled as businesspeople, were inclined to blame the banks and railroads, rather than their own short-comings, for their losses.

This amazing mechanization of agriculture in the postwar years was almost as striking as the mechanization of industry. In fact, agricultural modernization drove many marginal farmers off the land, thus swelling the ranks of the new industrial work force. As the rural population steadily decreased, those farmers who remained achieved miracles of production, making America the world's breadbasket and butcher shop. The farm was attain-ing the status of a factory—an outdoor grain factory. Bonanza wheat farms of the Minnesota–North Dakota area, for example, were enormous. By 1890 at least a half-dozen of them were larger than fifteen thousand acres, with communication by telephone from one part to another. These bonanza farms foreshadowed the gigantic agribusinesses of the next century.

Agriculture was a big business from its earliest days in California's phenomenally productive (and phenomenally irrigated) Central Valley. California farms, carved out of giant Spanish-Mexican land grants and the railroads' huge holdings, were from the outset more than three times larger than the national average. The reformer Henry George in 1871 described the Golden State as "not a country of farms but a country of plantations and estates." With the advent of the railroad refrigerator car in the 1880s, California fruit and vegetable crops, raised on sprawling tracts by ill-paid migrant Mexican and Chinese farmhands, sold at a handsome profit in the rich urban markets of the East.

Deflation Dooms the Debtor

Once the farmers became chained to a one-crop economy—wheat or corn—they were in the same leaky boat with the southern cotton growers. As long as prices stayed high, all went well. But when they skidded in the 1880s, bankruptcy fell like a blight on the farm belts.

The grain farmers were no longer the masters of their own destinies. They were engaged in one of the most fiercely competitive of businesses, for the price of their product was determined in a world market by the world output. If the wheat fields of Argentina, Russia, and other foreign countries flour-ished, the price of the farmers' grain would fall and American sodbusters would face ruin, as they did in the 1880s and 1890s.

Low prices and a deflated currency were the chief worries of the frustrated farmers—North, South, and West. If a family had borrowed $1,000 in 1855, when wheat was worth about a dollar a bushel, they expected to pay back the equivalent of 1,000 bushels, plus interest, when the mortgage fell due. But if they let their debt run to 1890, when wheat had fallen to about fifty cents a bushel, they would have to pay back the price of 2,000 bushels for the $1,000 they had borrowed, plus interest. This unexpected burden struck them as unjust, though their steely-eyed creditors often branded the com-plaining farmers as slippery and dishonest rascals.

The deflationary pinch on the debtor flowed partly from the static money supply. There were simply not enough dollars to go around, and as a result, prices were forced down. In 1870 the cur-rency in circulation for each person was $19.42; in 1890 it was only $22.67. Yet during these twenty years, business and industrial activity, increasing manyfold, had intensified the scramble for available currency.

The forgotten farmers were caught on a tread-mill. Despite unremitting toil, they operated year after year at a loss and lived off their fat as best they could. In a vicious circle, their farm machinery increased their output of grain, lowered the price, and drove them even deeper into debt. Mortgages engulfed homesteads at an alarming rate; by 1890 Nebraska alone reported more than 100,000 farms blanketed with mortgages. The repeated crash of the sheriff-auctioneer's hammer kept announcing

Nebraska Homesteaders in Front of Their Sod House, 1887 These two brothers and their families had escaped to Canada from the slave South during the Civil War. Returning to the United States in the 1880s, they took advantage of the Homestead Act to stake out farms in Custer County, Nebraska.

to the world that another sturdy American farmer had become landless in a landed nation.

Ruinous rates of interest, running from 8 to 40 percent, were charged on mortgages, largely by agents of eastern loan companies. The windburned sons and daughters of the sod, who felt that they deserved praise for developing the country, cried out in despair against the loan sharks and the Wall Street octopus.

Farm tenancy rather than farm ownership was spreading like stinkweed. The trend was especially marked in the sharecropping South, where cotton prices also sank dismayingly. By 1880 one-fourth of all American farms were operated by tenants. The United States was ready to feed the world, but under the new industrial feudalism the farmers were about to sink into a status suggesting Old World serfdom.

A contemporary farm protest song, "The Kansas Fool," ran,

The bankers followed us out west;
And did in mortgages invest;
They looked ahead and shrewdly planned,
And soon they'll have our Kansas land.

Unhappy Farmers

Even Mother Nature ceased smiling, as her powerful forces conspired against agriculture. Mile-wide clouds of grasshoppers, leaving "nothing but the mortgage," periodically ravaged prairie farms. The terrible cotton-boll weevil was also wreaking havoc in the South by the early 1890s.

The good earth was going sour. Floods added to the waste of erosion, which had already washed the topsoil off millions of once-lush southern acres. Expensive fertilizers were urgently needed. A long succession of droughts seared the trans-Mississippi West, beginning in the summer of 1887. Whole towns were abandoned. "Going home to the wife's folks" and "In God we trusted, in Kansas we busted" were typical laments of many impoverished farmers, as they fled their weather-beaten shacks and sun-baked sod houses. One irate "poet" snarled,

Fifty miles to water,
A hundred miles to wood,
To hell with this damned country,
I'm going home for good.

To add to their miseries, the soil-tillers were gouged by their government—local, state, and national. Their land was overassessed and they paid painful local taxes, whereas wealthy easterners concealed their stocks and bonds in safe-deposit boxes. Protective tariffs of these years, while pouring profits into the pockets of the manufacturer, imposed heavy burdens on agriculture, especially in the South. Cotton producers or grain growers had to sell their low-priced, unprotected product in a fiercely competitive world market, while buying high-priced manufactured goods in a protected home market.

The farmers were also "farmed" by the corporations and processors. They were at the mercy of the harvester trust, the barbed-wire trust, and the fertilizer trust, all of which could control output and raise prices to extortionate levels. Middlemen took a juicy "cut" from the selling price of the goods that the farmers bought, while operators pushed storage rates to the ceiling at grain warehouses and elevators.

In addition, the railroad octopus had the grain growers in its grip. Freight rates could be so high that the farmers sometimes lost less if they burned their corn for fuel than if they shipped it. If they raised their voices in protest, the ruthless railroad operators might let their grain spoil in damp places or refuse to provide them with cars when needed.

Farmers still made up nearly one-half the population in 1890, but they were hopelessly disorganized. The manufacturers and the railroad barons knew how to combine to promote their interests, and so, increasingly, did industrial workers. But the farmers were by nature independent and individualistic—dead set against consolidation or regimentation. No really effective Carnegie or Gompers arose among them to preach the gospel of economic integration and concentration. They never did organize successfully to restrict production until forced to by the federal government nearly half a century later, in Franklin Roosevelt's New Deal days. What they did manage to organize was a monumental political uprising.

The Farmers Take Their Stand

Agrarian unrest had flared forth earlier, in the Greenback movement shortly after the Civil War. Prices sagged in 1868, and a host of farmers unsuccessfully sought relief from low prices and high indebtedness by demanding an inflation of the currency with paper money.

The National Grange of the Patrons of Husbandry—better known as the Grange—was organ-

ized in 1867. Its leading spirit was Oliver H. Kelley, a shrewd and energetic Minnesota farmer then working as a clerk in Washington. Kelley's first objective was to enhance the lives of isolated farmers through social, educational, and fraternal activities. Farm men and women, cursed with loneliness in widely separated farmhouses, found the Grange's picnics, concerts, and lectures a godsend. Kelley, a Mason, even found farmers receptive to his mumbo-jumbo of passwords and secret rituals, as well as his four-ply hierarchy, ranging (for men) from Laborer to Husbandman and (for women) from Maid to Matron. The Grange spread like an old-time prairie fire and by 1875 claimed 800,000 members, chiefly in the Midwest and South. Buzzing with gossip, these calicoed and calloused folk often met in red schoolhouses around potbellied stoves.

The Grangers gradually raised their goals from individual self-improvement to improvement of the farmers' collective plight. In a determined effort to escape the clutches of the trusts, they established cooperatively owned stores for consumers and cooperatively owned grain elevators and warehouses for producers. Their most ambitious experiment was an attempt to manufacture harvesting machinery, but this venture, partly as a result of mismanagement, ended in financial disaster.

Embattled Grangers also went into politics, enjoying their most gratifying success in the grain-growing regions of the upper Mississippi Valley, chiefly in Illinois, Wisconsin, Iowa, and Minnesota. There, through state legislation, they strove to regulate railway rates and the storage fees charged by railroads and by the operators of warehouses and grain elevators. Many of the state courts, notably in Illinois, were disposed to recognize the principle of public control of private business for the general welfare. A number of the so-called Granger Laws, however, were badly drawn, and they were bitterly fought through the high courts by the well-paid lawyers of the "interests." Following judicial reverses, most severely at the hands of the Supreme Court in the famous *Wabash* decision of 1886 (see p. 543), the Grangers' influence faded. But their organization has lived on as a vocal champion of farm interests, while brightening rural life with social activities.

Farmers' grievances likewise found a vent in the Greenback Labor party, which combined the inflationary appeal of the earlier Greenbackers with a program for improving the lot of labor. In 1878, the high-water mark of the movement, the Greenback-

The Grange Awakening the Sleepers
The farmer tries to arouse the apathetic public to the dangers of the onrushing railroad monopoly.

Laborites polled over a million votes and elected fourteen members of Congress. In the presidential election of 1880, the Greenbackers ran General James B. Weaver, an old Granger who was a favorite of the Civil War veterans and who possessed a remarkable voice and bearing. He spoke to perhaps a half-million citizens in a hundred or so speeches but polled only 3 percent of the total popular vote.

Prelude to Populism

A striking manifestation of rural discontent came through the Farmers' Alliance, founded in Texas in the late 1870s. Farmers came together in the Alliance to socialize, but more importantly to break the strangling grip of the railroads and manufacturers through cooperative buying and selling. Local chapters spread throughout the South and the Great Plains during the 1880s, until by 1890 members numbered more than a million hard-bitten souls, who gathered together to sing "Toilers Unite" and "Where Will the Farmer Be?"

For all its collective spirit, the Alliance suffered from internal divisions. Its programs were targeted primarily at those who owned their own land, there-by ignoring the plight of landless tenant farmers, sharecroppers, and farmworkers. Even more debilitating was the Alliance's exclusion of blacks, who counted for nearly half the agricultural population of the South. In the 1880s a separate Colored Farmers' National Alliance emerged to attract black farmers, and by 1890 membership numbered more than 250,000. The long history of racial division in the South, however, made it difficult for white and black farmers to work together in the same organization.

White Alliance members from different regions found more in common. They agreed on the need to nationalize railroads, abolish national banks, institute a graduated income tax, and create a new federal subtreasury—a scheme to provide farmers with government-owned warehouses where they could store their crops until market prices rose. Meanwhile, farmers would be able to take out government loans against their stored crops, to be repaid when the crops were sold.

Numerous fiery prophets sprang forward to lead the Populists. Among these assorted characters loomed an eloquent red-haired "spellbinder," Ignatius Donnelly from the state of Minnesota, who was three times elected to Congress.

The queen of the "calamity howlers" was undeniably Mary Elizabeth ("Mary Yellin'") Lease, a tall, athletically built woman who was called "the Kansas Pythoness." In 1890 she made an estimated 160 speeches. Upbraiding the moneyed aristocracy and denouncing the government "of Wall Street, by Wall Street, and for Wall Street," she reportedly cried that the Kansans should raise "less corn and more hell." They did. The big-city New York *Evening Post* snarled, "We don't want any more states until we can civilize Kansas." To many easterners, complaint, not corn, was the chief crop of the westerners.

Yet the Alliance, despite its peculiarities, was not to be brushed aside. In deadly earnest its members were leading an impassioned crusade to relieve the misfortunes of the farmer. Smiles faded from Republican and Democratic faces alike as the Alliance's political victories mounted. Four governors and more than forty congressmen in the South, as well as legislators in Nebraska, Kansas, and South Dakota, were no laughing matter. Yawning eastern plutocrats would have done well to heed these western "hayseeds," for at long last the hardship-hardened farmers of the South and West were marshaling their political strength. In the coming decade, they would combine in a new People's party (Populists) to launch a ferocious attack on the northeastern citadels of power.

Mary E. Lease (1853–1933)   She was so eloquent as to be called a "Patrick Henry in petticoats."

Chronology

1858 Pike's Peak gold rush	**1887** Dawes Severalty Act
1859 Nevada Comstock Lode discovered	**1889** Oklahoma opened to settlement
1862 Homestead Act	**1889–1890** North Dakota, South Dakota, Montana, Washington, Idaho, and Wyoming admitted to the Union
1864 Sand Creek massacre Nevada admitted to the Union	
1867 National Grange organized	**1890** Census Bureau declares frontier line ended Emergence of People's party (Populists) Battle of Wounded Knee
1876 Battle of Little Big Horn Colorado admitted to the Union	**1893** Frederick Jackson Turner publishes "The Significance of the Frontier in American History"
1877 Nez Percé Indian War	
1881 Helen Hunt Jackson publishes *A Century of Dishonor*	**1896** Utah admitted to the Union
	1907 Oklahoma admitted to the Union
1884 Federal government outlaws Indian Sun Dance	**1924** Indians granted U.S. citizenship
1885–1890 Farmers' Alliances formed	**1934** Indian Reorganization Act

Was the West Really "Won"?

For more than half a century, the Turner thesis dominated historical writing about the West. In his famous essay of 1893, "The Significance of the Frontier in American History," historian Frederick Jackson Turner argued that the frontier experience molded both region and nation. Not only the West, Turner insisted, but the national character had been uniquely shaped by the westward movement. Pioneers had brought the raw West into the embrace of civilization. And the struggle to overcome the hazards of the western wilderness—including distance, deserts, drought, and Indians—had transformed *Europeans* into tough, inventive, and self-reliant *Americans.*

Turner's thesis raised a question that Americans found especially intriguing in 1893. Just three years earlier, the superintendent of the census declared that the frontier, defined as a zone with little or no settled population, had closed forever. What new forces, Turner now asked, would shape a distinctive American national character, now that the testing ground of the frontier had been plowed and tamed?

Turner's hypothesis that the American character was forged in the western wilderness is surely among the most provocative statements ever made about the formative influences on the nation's development. But as the frontier era recedes ever further into the past, scholars are less persuaded that Turner's thesis adequately explains the national character. American society is still conspicuously different from European and other cultures, even though Turner's frontier disappeared more than a century ago.

Modern scholars charge that Turner based his thesis on several questionable assumptions. Historian David J. Weber, for example, suggests that the line of the frontier did not define the quavering edge of "civilization" but marked the boundary between diverse cultures, each with its own claims to legitimacy and, indeed, to legitimate possession of the land. The frontier should therefore be understood not as the place where "civilization" triumphed over "savagery," but as the principal site of interaction between those cultures.

Several so-called New Western historians take this argument still further. Scholars such as Patricia Nelson Limerick, Richard White, and Donald Worster suggest that the cultural and ecological damage inflicted by advancing "civilization" must be reckoned with in any final accounting of what the pioneers accomplished. These same scholars insist that the West did not lose its regional identity after the frontier line was no longer recognizable in 1890. The West, they argue, is still a unique part of the national mosaic, a region whose history, culture, and identity remain every bit as distinctive as those of New England or the Old South.

But where Turner saw the frontier as the principal shaper of the region's character, the New Western historians emphasize the effects of ethnic and racial confrontation, topography, climate, and the roles of government and big business as the factors that have made the modern West. The New Western historians thus reject Turner's emphasis on the triumphal civilizing of the wilderness. As they see the matter, European and American settlers did not tame the West but rather conquered it, by suppressing the Native American and Hispanic peoples who had preceded them into the region. But those conquests were less than complete, so the argument goes, and the West therefore remains, uniquely among American regions, an unsettled arena of commingling and competition among those groups. Moreover, in these accounts the West's distinctively challenging climate and geography yielded to human habitation not through the efforts of heroic individual pioneers, but only through massive corporate—and especially federal government—investments in transportation systems (like the transcontinental railroad) and irrigation projects (like the watering of California's Central Valley). Such developments still give western life its special character today.

SUGGESTED READINGS

PRIMARY SOURCE DOCUMENTS

Black Elk Speaks, edited by John G. Neihardt (1932), is an eloquent Indian statement about the Sioux experience. Indian perspectives on the westward movement can be found in Jerome A. Greene, ed., *Lakota and Cheyenne: Indian Views of the Great Sioux Wars, 1876–1877** (1994). Theodore Roosevelt, *Hunting Trips of a Ranchman** (1885), offers the future president's views on the Indian question. Mary Lease's famous call to arms is recorded in William E. Connelley, ed., *History of Kansas, State and People** (1928).

SECONDARY SOURCES

Vivacious chapters appear in Ray A. Billington, *Westward Expansion* (rev. ed., 1974). Walter Prescott Webb, *The Great Plains* (1931), is a classic. Robert V. Hine, *The American West* (2d ed., 1984), is a useful survey. Patricia Nelson Limerick traces regional themes across time in *Legacy of Conquest: The Unbroken Past of the American West* (1987). Richard White's fresh account, *"It's Your Misfortune and None of My Own": A New History of the American West* (1991), emphasizes the role of the federal government, corporations, and the market economy in the region's development and pays special attention to the twentieth century, as do Donald Worster, *Rivers of Empire: Water, Aridity, and the Growth of the American West* (1986), and Donald J. Pisani, *To Reclaim a Divided West: Water, Law, and Policy, 1848–1902* (1992). Women in the West are discussed in Glenda Riley, *The Female Frontier: A Comparative View of Women on the Prairie and Plains* (1988), and Beverly Beeton, *Women Vote in the West: The Woman Suffrage Movement, 1869–1896* (1986). Native Americans are discussed in Robert Utley, *The Indian Frontier of the American West, 1846–1890* (1984), and in Dee Brown's *Bury My Heart at Wounded Knee: An Indian History of the American West* (1970).

Consult also Francis P. Prucha, *The Great Father: The United States Government and the American Indians* (1984); Frederick E. Hoxie, *A Final Promise: The Campaign to Assimilate the Indians* (1984); Joe S. Sando, *Pueblo Nations: Eight Centuries of Pueblo Indian History* (1992); Thomas Berger's novel *Little Big Man* (1964); and Albert Hurtado, *Indian Survival on the California Frontier* (1988). The military history of the "Indian Wars" is covered in S. L. A. Marshall, *Crimsoned Prairie* (1972). Two intriguing studies of cross-cultural perception are Robert F. Berkhofer, Jr., *The White Man's Indian* (1978), and Richard Drinnon, *Facing West: The Metaphysics of Indian Hating and Empire Building* (1980). A sweeping look at Chicano history is Juan Gómez-Quiñones, *Roots of Chicago Politics, 1600–1940* (1994). David Alan Johnson explores *Founding the Far West: California, Oregon, and Nevada, 1840–1890* (1992). William Cronon explores the relationship between Chicago and the development of the "Great West" in *Nature's Metropolis* (1991), a book nicely complemented by John C. Hudson, *Making the Corn Belt* (1994). Donald J. Pisani looks at western agriculture in *From the Family Farm to Agribusiness: The Irrigation Crusade in California and the West, 1850–1931* (1984). For beef see Philip Durham and Everett L. Jones, *The Negro Cowboys* (1965); Robert Dykstra, *The Cattle Town* (1968); and Gene M. Gressley, *Bankers and Cattlemen* (1966). See also David J. Weber, *The Spanish Frontier in North America* (1992). A powerful work on the farmers' protest is Lawrence Goodwyn, *Democratic Promise* (1976), abridged as *The Populist Moment* (1978). See also John D. Hicks's classic *The Populist Revolt* (1931); Walter T. K. Nugent, *The Tolerant Populists* (1963); Steven Hahn, *The Roots of Southern Populism* (1983); William A. Link, *The Paradox of Southern Progressivism, 1880–1930* (1992); and Bruce Palmer, *"Man over Money": The Southern Populist Critique of American Capitalism* (1980). Kevin Starr probes the cultural history of California in both *Americans and the California Dream, 1850–1915* (1973) and *Inventing the Dream: California Through the Progressive Era* (1985). Henry Nash Smith, *Virgin Land: The American West as Symbol and Myth* (1950), is a landmark study of particular interest to students of literature.

---

*An asterisk indicates that the document, or excerpt from it, can be found in Thomas A. Bailey and David M. Kennedy, eds., *The American Spirit: United States History as Seen by Contemporaries,* 9th ed. (Boston: Houghton Mifflin, 1998).

28

The Revolt of the Debtor
1889–1900

*You come to us and tell us that the great cities
are in favor of the gold standard. We reply that
the great cities rest upon our broad and fertile
prairies. Burn down your cities and leave our
farms, and your cities will spring up again as if by
magic. But destroy our farms, and the grass will
grow in the streets of every city in the country.*

WILLIAM JENNINGS BRYAN, CROSS OF GOLD SPEECH, 1896

The Republicans Return Under Harrison

Benjamin Harrison—stocky, heavily bearded, and dignified—was inaugurated president under weeping heavens on March 4, 1889. The outgoing Grover Cleveland obligingly held an umbrella over him. The incoming president was an honest and earnest party man, but he was also brusque and abrupt. He could charm a crowd of ten thousand people with his speechcraft, but he would chill them individually with a clammy handshake. He came to be known, rather unfairly, as "the White House Ice Chest."

After a four-year fast, Republicans licked their lips hungrily for the bounty of federal office. James G. Blaine, the headstrong and still-ambitious "Plumed Knight," again received the secretaryship of state as a consolation prize for failing to attain the presidency. Harrison also named to the Civil Service Commission a bespectacled and violently energetic New Yorker, Theodore Roosevelt, as a reward for the eager-beaver politician's oratory in the campaign.

Republicans in the House of Representatives could hardly expect smooth sailing; they had only three votes more than the necessary quorum of 163 members. If the Democrats continued their practice of refusing to answer roll calls, the Republicans could muster a quorum only with difficulty. The

Democrats were also prepared to make numerous delaying motions. These included time-consuming demands for a roll call to determine the presence of a quorum, even though one was obviously present. For their part the Republicans were eager to get on with squandering money and thus safeguard the high tariff that was producing a surplus.

Into this explosive cockpit stepped the new Republican Speaker of the House, Thomas B. Reed of Maine. A hulking figure who towered 6 feet, 3 inches (1.91 meters), he had already made his mark as a masterful debater. Cool and collected, he spoke with a harsh nasal drawl and wielded a verbal harpoon of sarcasm. One congressman who had declaimed that he would "rather be right than President," like Henry Clay, was silenced by Reed's sneer that he would "never be either." Opponents cringed at "the crack of his quip."

Early in 1890 the redoubtable Reed undertook single-handedly to change the House rules. He believed that the majority should legislate, in accord with democratic practices, and not be crippled by a filibustering minority. He therefore ignored Democratic speakers who sprang to their feet and sought to establish the absence of a quorum. In piecing out quorums, he counted as present certain Democrats in the chamber who had not answered the roll and who, rule book in hand, furiously denied that they were legally present. For three days pandemonium rocked the House, while Reed held his ground, reputedly counting as present congressmen who were in the barbershop or on trains headed for home.

The gavel rule of "Czar" Reed finally prevailed. The Fifty-first, or "Billion-Dollar," Congress*—the first in peacetime to appropriate approximately this sum—gave birth to a bumper crop of expensive legislative babies. When the Democrats won control of the House two years later, they paid Reed the compliment of adopting some of his reforms for speedier action.

Political Gravy for All

President Harrison, himself a Civil War general, was disposed to deal generously with his old comrades-in-arms. He appointed as commissioner of pensions a Civil War amputee, who promised to drive a

---

*By the 1990s Congress was appropriating an average of more than a billion dollars *a day!*

President Harrison Disposes of Surplus, 1892

six-mule team through the Treasury and to wring "from the hearts of some the prayer, 'God help the surplus.'" He cut a wide swath, and a Treasury surplus has never been a problem since his day.

This "Billion-Dollar" Congress cooperated by opening wide the federal purse in the Pension Act of 1890. It showered pensions on all Union Civil War veterans who had served for ninety days and who were now unable to do manual labor. Between 1891 and 1895 the host of pensioners was thus raised from 676,000 to 970,000, and by the time Harrison left office in 1893, the annual bill had shot up from $81 million to $135 million. Thus was faintly foreshadowed the government-financed "welfare state" of the twentieth century.

This policy of liberality toward old soldiers had special attractions for Republican politicians. It helped solve the problem of the Treasury surplus—a problem that had bedeviled President Cleveland. It helped save the protective tariff by making plausible, even necessary, the continuance of high customs duties. It helped secure Republican votes, for the aging veterans of the GAR (Grand Army of the Republic) were grateful to the GOP (Grand Old Party) for its handouts.

"Czar" Reed's gavel, pounding imperiously, drove through Congress additional bills, conspicuous among which was the Sherman Anti-Trust Act of 1890. This pioneering law, though a feeble bludgeon, helped to quiet the mounting uproar against bloated corporations (see p. 551).

Noteworthy also was the Sherman Silver Purchase Act of 1890. Western miners were acutely unhappy over the limited silver-purchase program under the Bland-Allison Law of 1878, and many of the silverites were demanding unrestricted government buying of the "beloved white metal." At the same time, many debt-burdened western and southern farmers were clamoring for the unlimited coinage of silver. They continued to believe that the addition of an immense amount of metallic money would inflate the currency and thus make for higher prices and easier debt payments. The "Gold Bug" East looked with conservative horror on any such tampering with the money supply but hungered for the profits that might be reaped from a boost in the tariff schedules.

Thus the stage was set for a huge logrolling operation. Western silver agitators agreed to support a protective tariff, which they detested; eastern protectionists agreed to support a silver bill, which they distrusted. As a part of the resulting Sherman Silver Purchase Act of 1890, the Treasury was to buy a total of 4.5 million ounces (127,800 kilograms) monthly—about all that was being mined—and pay for it in notes redeemable in either silver or gold. This new law, while boosting the price for the miners, would approximately double the minimum amount of silver that could be acquired under the old Bland-Allison Law.

High-tariff Republicans reaped their political reward with the McKinley Tariff Bill of 1890, which boosted rates to their highest peacetime level yet—an average of 48.4 percent on dutiable goods. Sponsored in the House by William McKinley of Ohio, the "high priest of high protection," the bill disposed of the troublesome surplus by giving a bounty of two cents a pound to American sugar producers. It also raised tariffs on agricultural products—a hollow gesture to farmers, because foreign growers could never compete with soil-rich Americans.

These new duties on manufactured goods, as fate would have it, actually brought new woes to the

Corn-husking
Hard-working farmers like the Krueger family, pictured in Wisconsin around the turn of the century, sought relief from their heavy debt burdens in the 1890s by clamoring for various inflationary schemes, including the monetization of silver.

farmers. Some eastern manufacturers raised their prices even before the law went into effect. Tin peddlers—some reportedly in the pay of the Democrats—went systematically from house to house in the Midwest, displaying their wares to homemakers. They would cleverly but dishonestly say that yesterday a pie pan sold for ten cents, but today for twenty-five cents—all because of the wicked Republican tariff.

Mounting discontent against "Bill" McKinley and his McKinley Bill caused voters to rise in wrath, especially in the midwestern farm belt. The congressional landslide of 1890 reduced the Republican membership of the House from 166 to a scant 88 members, as compared with 235 Democrats. Even the highly publicized McKinley lost his seat in the House. Ominously for conservatives, the new Congress also included nine members of the Farmers' Alliance, the militant organization of southern and western farmers.

The Populist Challenge in 1892

Discontent over Republican high-tariff policies gave the Democrats high hopes as the presidential election of 1892 approached. Their man of destiny was portly but energetic former president Grover Cleveland. He had built up a profitable law practice in New York City and, after hobnobbing with his wealthy clientele, had become increasingly conservative. Yet his reputation was such that he was nominated in Chicago on the first ballot.

Gathering in Minneapolis, the Republicans renominated cold-fish President Harrison, even though he was cordially disliked by party bosses. With seemingly arrogant disregard for the political consequences, their platform championed the protective tariff.

Politics was no longer "as usual" in 1892, when the newly formed People's party (Populists) burst on the scene. Rooted in the Farmers' Alliance of frustrated farmers in the West and South, the Populists met in Omaha to adopt a scorching platform that denounced the "prolific womb of governmental injustice." Addressing many of the Alliance's grievances, the platform demanded free and unlimited coinage of silver at the ratio of sixteen to one, a graduated income tax, and government ownership of the telephone, telegraph, and railroads. The Populists sought a simpler and purer democracy by

advocating the direct election of United States Senators, a one-term limit on the presidency, and the use of the initiative and referendum to allow citizens to propose and review legislation. In a bid for labor's support, the Populists demanded a shorter workday and immigration restriction. As their presidential candidate, the Populists uproariously nominated the eloquent old Greenbacker, General James B. Weaver.

An epidemic of nationwide strikes in the summer of 1892 raised the prospect that the Populists could bring aggrieved workers together with indebted farmers in a revolutionary joint assault on the capitalist order. At Andrew Carnegie's Homestead steel plant near Pittsburgh, company officials called in 300 armed Pinkerton detectives in July to crush a strike by steelworkers angry over pay cuts. Defiant strikers, armed with rifles and dynamite, forced their assailants to surrender after a vicious

The Homestead Strike, 1892   Three hundred armed Pinkerton detectives floated on barges down the Monongahela River to the site of the Carnegie steel plant at Homestead. Met by a defiant and disciplined force of strikers, they were compelled to surrender. Here, the Pinkerton men are shown disembarking from their barges after their capitulation, while the jeering strikers ashore exult in their victory.

battle in which ten people were killed and some sixty wounded. Troops were eventually summoned, and both the strike and the union were broken. That same month, federal troops had to be dispatched to crush a strike among silver miners in Idaho's Coeur d'Alene district.

The Populists made a remarkable showing in the 1892 presidential election. Singing "Good-by, Party Bosses," they rolled up 1,029,846 popular votes and 22 electoral votes for General Weaver. They thus became one of the few third parties in U.S. history to break into the electoral column. But they fell far short of an electoral majority. Industrial laborers, especially in the urban East, did not rally to the Populist banner in appreciable numbers. Populist electoral votes came from only six midwestern and western states, four of which (Kansas, Colorado, Idaho, and Nevada) fell completely into the Populist basket.

The South, although a hotbed of agrarian agitation, proved especially unwilling to throw in its lot with a new party. Race was the reason. The more than one million southern black farmers now organized in the Colored Farmers' National Alliance shared a host of complaints with poor white farmers, and for a time their common economic goals promised to overcome their racial differences. Recognizing the crucial edge that black votes could give them in the South, Populist leaders like Georgia's Tom Watson reached out to the black community; this wiry redhead who could "talk like the thrust of a Bowie knife" declared, "There is no reason why the black man should not understand that the law that hurts me, as a farmer, hurts him, as a farmer." Many blacks were disillusioned enough with the Republican party to respond. Alarmed, the conservative white "Bourbon" elite in the South played cynically upon historic racial antagonisms to counter the Populists' appeal for interracial solidarity and woo back poor whites.

Southern blacks were heavy losers. The Populist-inspired reminder of potential black political strength led to the near-total extinction of what little

The Kansas Legislature, 1893 Rifle-bearing Populists seized the Kansas capitol after the election of 1892 to make good their claim that they had won at the polls. Republicans disagreed and eventually prevailed when sergeants-at-arms, shown here, restored order.

Thomas Edward Watson (1865–1922) Populist leader Tom Watson of Georgia promoted interracial political cooperation, though he despaired that many poor white farmers preferred to "hug the chains of . . . wretchedness rather than do any experimenting on [the race] question."

African-American suffrage remained in the South. Literacy tests and poll taxes were used to deny blacks the ballot. The notorious "grandfather clause" exempted from those requirements anyone whose forebear had voted in 1860—when, of course, black slaves had not voted at all. More than half a century would pass before southern blacks could again vote in considerable numbers. Accompanying this disfranchisement were more severe Jim Crow laws, designed to enforce racial segregation in public places, including hotels and restaurants, and backed up by atrocious lynchings and other forms of intimidation.

The conservative crusade to eliminate the black vote also had dire consequences for the Populist party itself. Even Tom Watson abandoned his interracial appeals and, in time, became a vociferous racist himself. After 1896 the Populist party lapsed increasingly into vile racism and staunchly advocated black disfranchisement. Such were the bitterly ironic fruits of the Populist campaign in the South.

"Old Grover" Cleveland Again

With the Populists divided and the Republicans discredited, Grover Cleveland took office once again in 1893, the only president ever reelected after defeat. He was the same old bull-necked and

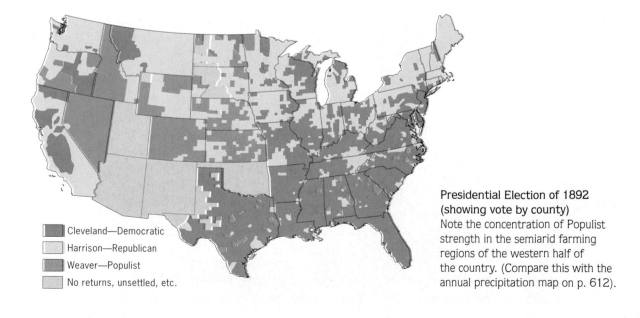

Cleveland—Democratic

Harrison—Republican

Weaver—Populist

No returns, unsettled, etc.

Presidential Election of 1892 (showing vote by county) Note the concentration of Populist strength in the semiarid farming regions of the western half of the country. (Compare this with the annual precipitation map on p. 612).

bull-headed Cleveland, with a little more weight, polish, conservatism, and self-assertiveness. But though it was the same old Cleveland, it was not the same old country; debtors were up in arms, and the advance shadows of panic were falling.

Hardly had Cleveland seated himself in the presidential chair when the depression of 1893 burst about his burly frame. Lasting for about four years, it was the most devastating economic downturn of the century. As the first large-scale depression in the new urban and industrial age, it brought unprecedented hardships to the masses in the cities. Contributing causes were the splurge of overbuilding and overspeculation, labor disorders, and the current agricultural depression. Free-silver agitation had also damaged American credit abroad, and the usual pinch on American finances had come when European banking houses, after earlier failures, began to call in loans from the United States.

Distress was acute and widespread. About eight thousand American business houses collapsed in six months, and dozens of railroad lines went into the hands of receivers. Business executives "died like flies under the strain," wrote Henry Adams. Soup kitchens were set up for the unemployed, and gangs of hoboes ("tramps") wandered aimlessly about the country. Local charities did their feeble best, but the federal government, bound by the let-nature-take-its-course philosophy of the times, was unwilling to relieve the suffering masses.

Cleveland, who had earlier been bothered by a surplus, was now burdened with a deficit. Under the Sherman Silver Purchase Act, the Treasury was required to issue legal tender notes for the silver bullion that it bought. Owners of the paper currency would then present it for gold, and by law the notes had to be reissued. New holders would repeat the process, thus draining away gold in an "endless-chain" operation.

Alarmingly, the gold reserve in the Treasury dropped below $100 million, which was popularly regarded as the safe minimum for supporting about $350 million in outstanding paper money. Cleveland saw no alternative but to halt the bleeding away of gold by engineering a repeal of the Sherman Silver Purchase Act of 1890. For this purpose he summoned Congress into an extra session in the summer of 1893.

Unknown to the country, complications threatened from another quarter. A malignant growth had

> *In his special message to Congress (1893), President Grover Cleveland (1837–1908) warned,*
>
> "Unless Government bonds are to be constantly issued and sold to replenish our exhausted gold, only to be again exhausted, it is apparent that the operation of the silver-purchase law now in force leads in the direction of the entire substitution of silver for the gold in the Government Treasury, and that this must be followed by the payment of all Government obligations in depreciated silver."

developed on the roof of Cleveland's mouth, and it had to be removed on a private yacht with extreme secrecy. If the president had died under the knife his place would have been taken by the "soft-money" vice president, Adlai E. Stevenson—an eventuality that would have deepened the crisis.

In Congress the debate over the repeal of the silver act was meanwhile running its heated course. A silver-tongued young congressman from Nebraska, thirty-three-year-old William Jennings Bryan, held the galleries spellbound for three hours as he championed the cause of free silver. The friends of silver announced that "hell would freeze over" before Congress passed the repeal measure. But an angered Cleveland used his office-giving power to break the filibuster in the Senate. He thus alienated the Democratic silverites and disrupted his party at the very outset of his administration.

Gold Shortages and Job Shortages

The hemorrhaging of gold from the Treasury was only partially stopped by the repeal of the Sherman Silver Purchase Act. Other currency was still being presented for redemption, and in February 1894 the gold reserve sank to a dismaying $41 million. The United States was now in grave danger of going off the gold standard—a move that would render the nation's currency volatile and unreliable as a measure of value and that could also mortally cripple America's international trade.

Coxey's Army on the Outskirts of Washington, D.C., 1894 Jacob Sechler Coxey arrived at the nation's capital with 500 men, not the 100,000 he predicted, to make a "living petition" of the unemployed.

Again Cleveland was forced to act vigorously. As a champion of sound money, he could see no alternative but to sell government bonds for gold and deposit the proceeds in the Treasury. Two bond issues were floated in 1894, totaling over $100 million; but the "endless-chain" operations continued relentlessly.

Early in 1895 Cleveland turned in desperation to J. P. Morgan, "the bankers' banker," and a Wall Street syndicate. After tense negotiations at the White House, the bankers agreed to lend the government $65 million in gold. They were obviously in business for profit, so they charged a commission amounting to about $7 million. But they did make a significant concession when they agreed to obtain one-half of the gold abroad and take the necessary steps to dam it up in the leaky Treasury. The loan, at least temporarily, helped restore confidence in the nation's finances.

But the bond deal stirred up a storm. The Wall Street ogre, especially in the eyes of the silverites and other debtors, symbolized all that was wicked and grasping. President Cleveland's secretive dealings with the mighty "Jupiter" Morgan were savagely condemned as a "sellout" of the national government. But Cleveland was certain that he had done no wrong. Sarcastically denying that he was "Morgan's errand boy," Cleveland asserted, "Without shame and without repentance I confess my share of the guilt."

Ragged armies of the unemployed, victims of the depression, meanwhile demonstrated for help. The most famous of these marches was that of "General" Jacob S. Coxey, a wealthy Ohio quarry owner, who started for Washington in 1894 with several score of supporters, accompanied by a swarm of newspaper reporters. His platform included a demand that the government relieve unemployment by an inflationary public works program, supported by some $500 million in legal tender notes to be issued by the Treasury. Coxey himself rode in a carriage with his wife and infant son, appropriately named Legal Tender Coxey, while his tiny "army" tramped along behind, singing

We're coming, Grover Cleveland,
500,000 strong,
We're marching on to Washington
to right the nation's wrong.

The "Commonweal Army" of Coxeyites finally straggled into the nation's capital. But the invasion took on the aspects of a comic opera when "General" Coxey and his "lieutenants" were arrested for walking on the grass. Other armies—"petitions in boots"—were less well behaved and accounted for considerable disorder and pillage.

Cleveland Crushes the Pullman Strike

Violent flare-ups accompanied labor protests, notably in Chicago. Most frightening was the crippling Pullman strike of 1894. Eugene V. Debs, an impetuous but personally lovable labor leader, had helped organize the American Railway Union of about 150,000 members. The Pullman Palace Car Company, which maintained a model town near Chicago for its employees, was hit hard by the depression and cut wages about one-third, while holding the line on rent for the company houses. The workers finally struck—in some places overturning Pullman cars—and paralyzed railway traffic from Chicago to the Pacific Coast.

This turmoil in Chicago was serious but not completely out of hand. At least this was the judgment of Governor John Peter Altgeld of Illinois, a friend of the downtrodden, who had pardoned the Haymarket Square anarchists the year before (see p. 558). But Attorney General Richard Olney, an arch-conservative and an ex–railroad attorney, urged the dispatch of federal troops. His legal grounds were that the strikers were interfering with the transit of the U.S. mail. Cleveland supported Olney with the ringing declaration, "If it takes the

> *After the Pullman strike collapsed, Eugene Debs (1855–1926) said,*
>
> "No strike has ever been lost."
>
> *In 1897 he declared,*
>
> "The issue is Socialism versus Capitalism. I am for Socialism because I am for humanity."

entire army and navy to deliver a postal card in Chicago, that card will be delivered."

To the delight of conservatives, the Pullman strike was crushed by bayonet-supported intervention from Washington. Debs and his leading associates, who had defied a federal court injunction to cease striking, were sentenced to six months' imprisonment for contempt of court. Ironically, the lean labor agitator spent much of his enforced leisure reading radical literature, which had much to do with his later leadership of the Socialist movement in America.

Embittered cries of "government by injunction" now burst from organized labor. This was the first time that such a legal weapon had been used conspicuously by Washington to break a strike, and it

The Pullman Strike, 1894
Police clubs and U.S. Army bayonets finally broke the back of a strike that halted railroads throughout the country.

was all the more distasteful because defiant laborites who were held in contempt could be imprisoned without jury trial. Signs multiplied that employers were striving to smash labor unions by court action. Nonlabor elements of the country, including the Populists and other debtors, were likewise incensed. They saw in the brutal Pullman episode further proof of an unholy alliance between big business and the courts.

Democratic Tariff Tinkering

The McKinley Tariff of 1890 had been designed to keep protection high and the surplus low. It succeeded remarkably in achieving both goals. By 1894 the Treasury was faced with an alarming deficit of $61 million.

In Congress the Democrats undertook to frame a tariff that would provide adequate revenue with moderate protection, as they had promised in the Cleveland-Harrison campaign of 1892. A bill aimed at securing these objectives was introduced in the House. As a concession to the Populists and other foes of "plutocracy," the measure included a tax of 2 percent on incomes over $4,000. Joseph H. Choate, a wealthy lawyer, growled, "Communistic, socialistic."

When the new tariff bill reached the Senate, it ran afoul of a swarm of lobbyists in the pay of big industry. After much buttonholing and vote trading, the Wilson-Gorman Bill was drastically revamped by the addition of over 630 amendments. The sugar trust stirred up a scandal when it inserted benefits to itself worth a sweet $20 million a year. As a result of such backstairs pressures, the Wilson-Gorman Tariff Act of 1894 fell scandalously short of establishing a low tariff, even though it did reduce the existing McKinley rates from 48.4 percent to 41.3 percent on dutiable goods. (See the Appendix.)

Cleveland was outraged by what he regarded as a gross betrayal of Democratic campaign pledges. In an angry outburst, he denounced the bill as "party perfidy and party dishonor"—to the glee of the Republicans. But to veto the patchwork affair would leave the even higher McKinley Tariff on the books, so Cleveland grudgingly let the bill become law without his signature. The Wilson-Gorman hodgepodge at least had the redeeming feature of the income tax, which was highly popular among the masses.

Crying for Protection, 1896
Uncle Sam is called on in this cartoon to nurse so-called infant industries—some of which had in fact long since grown into vigorous adulthood.

But the income tax lasted less than a year. In 1895 the Supreme Court, by a five-to-four decision, struck down this part of the Wilson-Gorman Act.* The only popular feature of the unpopular tariff law thus perished under the judicial hatchet. A chorus of denunciation rose from the Populists and other impoverished groups, who found further proof that the courts were only the tools of the plutocrats.

Democratic political fortunes naturally suffered. The tariff dynamite that had blasted the Republicans out of the House in 1890 now dislodged the Democrats, with a firm nudge from the depression. Revitalized Republicans, singing "The Soup House" and "Times Are Mighty Hard," won the congressional elections of 1894 in a landslide and now had 244 votes to 105 for the Democrats. The prospects of the Republicans for 1896 seemed propitious. They were openly boasting that they had

---

*It violated the "direct tax" clause. See Art. I, Sec. IX, para. 4, Appendix. The Sixteenth Amendment to the Constitution, adopted in 1913, permitted an income tax.

only to nominate a "rag baby" or a "yaller dog," and they could put it in the White House. Such optimism misread the signs of the times.

Discontented debtors, especially the Populists, were turning in throngs to free silver as a cure-all. An enormously popular pamphlet entitled *Coin's Financial School* (1894) was being distributed by the hundreds of thousands of copies. Written by William Hope Harvey, it was illustrated by clever woodcuts, one of which depicted the gold ogre beheading the beautiful silver maiden. In fiction parading as fact, the booklet showed how the "little professor"—"Coin" Harvey—overwhelmed the bankers and professors of economics with his brilliant sallies in behalf of free silver. The belief was gaining momentum among silverites and debtors that there was a foul conspiracy on foot, both nationally and internationally, to elevate gold above silver.

McKinley: Hanna's Fair-Haired Boy

The leading candidate for the Republican presidential nomination in 1896 was ex-congressman William McKinley of Ohio, sponsor of the ill-starred tariff bill of 1890. He had established a creditable Civil War record, having risen to the rank of major; he hailed from the electorally potent state of Ohio; and he could point to long years of honorable service in Congress, where he had made many friends with his kindly and conciliatory manner. His physical resemblance to Napoleon Bonaparte—seized upon by the cartoonists—earned him the nicknames "the Napoleon of Protection" and "the Advance Agent of Prosperity."

As a presidential candidate, McKinley was peculiarly the creation of a fellow Ohioan, Marcus Alonzo Hanna. The latter had made his fortune in the iron business, and he now coveted the role of president-maker. He was personally attracted to McKinley; "I love McKinley," he once said. When the overgenerous Ohio congressman faced bankruptcy after unwisely endorsing a friend's notes for about $100,000, Hanna and his wealthy associates paid off the obligation.

Hanna, as a wholehearted Hamiltonian, believed that a prime function of government was to aid business. Honest, earnest, rough, and direct, he became the personification of big industry in politics. He was often caricatured in cartoons, quite

McKinley Campaign Headquarters, Chicago, 1896 Those few black Americans who could exercise their right to vote in the 1890s still remained faithful to "the party of Lincoln."

unfairly, as a bloated bully in a loud checkered suit with a dollar sign in each square. As a conservative in business, he was a confirmed "standpatter," content not to rock the boat. He believed that in some measure prosperity "trickled down" to the laborer, whose dinner pail was full when business flourished. Critics assailed this idea as equivalent to feeding the horses in order to feed the sparrows.

A hardheaded Hanna, although something of a novice in politics, organized his preconvention campaign for McKinley with consummate skill and with a liberal outpouring of his own money. The convention steamroller, well lubricated with Hanna's dollars, nominated McKinley on the first ballot at St. Louis in June 1896.

The Republican platform cleverly straddled the monetary question. It declared for the gold standard, even though McKinley's voting record in Congress had been embarrassingly friendly to silver. But the platform made a gesture toward the silverites when it came out for international bimetallism, or a worldwide gold-silver standard. The catch was that all the leading nations of the world would have had to agree to such a scheme, and this obviously they would not do. Additionally, the platform condemned hard times and Democratic incapacity, while pouring praise on the protective tariff.

Bryan: Silverite Messiah

Dissension riddled the Democratic camp. Cleveland no longer led his party; dubbed "the Stuffed Prophet," he was undeniably the most unpopular man in the country. Labor-debtor groups remembered too vividly the silver-purchase repeal, the Pullman strike, and the backstairs Morgan bond deal. Ultraconservative in finance, Cleveland was now more a Republican than a Democrat on the silver issue.

Rudderless, the Democratic convention met in Chicago in July 1896, with the silverites in command. Shouting insults at the absent Cleveland, they refused, by a suicidal vote of 564 to 357, to endorse their own administration. They had the enthusiasm and the numbers; all they lacked was a leader.

A new Moses suddenly appeared in the person of William Jennings Bryan of Nebraska. Then only thirty-six years of age and known as "the Boy Orator of the Platte,"* he stepped confidently onto the platform before fifteen thousand people. His masterful presence was set off by handsome features, a smooth-shaven jaw, and raven-black hair. He radiated honesty, sincerity, and energy. He had a good mind but not a brilliant one; he was less a student of books than of human nature; and he possessed broad human sympathies.

In Chicago the setting was made to order for a magnificent oratorical effort. A hush fell over the convention as Bryan stood before it. With an organ-like voice that rolled into the outer corners of the huge hall, he delivered a fervent plea for silver. Rising to supreme heights of eloquence, he thundered, "We will answer their demands for a gold standard by saying to them: 'You shall not press down upon

William Jennings Bryan, 1896 The premier orator of his day, the spellbinding speaker was the presidential candidate of both the Democratic and Populist parties in 1896.

the brow of labor this crown of thorns, you shall not crucify mankind upon a cross of gold.'"

The Cross of Gold speech was a sensation. Swept off its feet in a tumultuous scene, the Democratic convention nominated Bryan the next day on the fifth ballot. The platform declared for the unlimited coinage of silver at the ratio of 16 ounces of silver to 1 of gold, though the market ratio was about 32 to 1. This meant that the silver in a dollar would be worth about fifty cents.

Democratic "Gold Bugs," unable to swallow Bryan, bolted their party over the silver issue. A conservative senator from New York, when asked if he

---

*One contemporary sneered that Bryan, like the Platte River, was "six inches deep and six miles wide at the mouth."

was a Democrat still, reportedly replied, "Yes, I am a Democrat still—*very* still." The Democratic minority, including Cleveland, charged that the Populist-silverites had stolen both the name and the clothes of their party. They nominated a lost-cause ticket of their own, and many of them, including Cleveland, hoped for a McKinley victory.

Populists were left out in the cold, for the Democratic majority had appropriated their main plank— "16 to 1," that "heaven-born ratio." The bulk of the Populists, fearing a hard-money McKinley victory, endorsed both "fusion" with the Democrats and Bryan for president, sacrificing their identity in the mix. Singing "The Jolly Silver Dollar of the Dads," they became in effect the "Demo-Pop" party. But many of the original Populists refused to support Bryan and went down with their colors nailed to the mast.

Hanna Leads the "Gold Bugs"

Mark Hanna smugly assumed that he could make the tariff the focus of the campaign. But Bryan, a dynamo of energy, forced the free-trade issue into a back seat when he took to the stump in behalf of free silver. Sweeping through twenty-seven states and traveling 18,000 miles (29,000 kilometers), he made between five and six hundred speeches—thirty-six in one day—and even invaded the East, "the enemy's country." Vachel Lindsay caught the spirit of his oratorical orgy:

> *Prairie avenger, mountain lion,*
> * Bryan, Bryan, Bryan, Bryan,*
> *Gigantic troubadour, speaking like a siege*
> * gun,*
> *Smashing Plymouth Rock with his*
> * boulders from the West.**

Free silver became almost as much a religious as a financial issue. Hordes of fanatical free-silverites hailed Bryan as the messiah to lead them out of the wilderness of debt. They sang "We'll All Have Our Pockets Lined with Silver" and "No Crown of Thorns, No Cross of Gold."

---

*Reprinted with permission of Simon & Schuster from *Collected Poems of Vachel Lindsay*. Copyright 1920 by Macmillan Publishing Company, renewed 1948 by Elizabeth C. Lindsay.

William Jennings Bryan created panic among eastern conservatives with his threat of converting their holdings overnight into fifty-cent dollars. The "Gold Bugs" vented their alarm in abusive epithets, which ranged all the way from "fanatic" and "madman" to "traitor" and "murderer." "In God We Trust, with Bryan We Bust," the Republicans sneered, while one eastern clergyman cried, "That platform was made in Hell."

Widespread fear of Bryan and the "silver lunacy" enabled "Dollar Mark" Hanna, now chairman of the Republican National Committee, to shine as a money raiser. He "shook down" the trusts and plutocrats and piled up an enormous "slush fund" for a "campaign of education"—or of propaganda, depending on one's point of view. The Republicans amassed the most formidable political campaign chest thus far in American history. At all levels—national, state, and local—it amounted to

The Sacrilegious Candidate   A hostile cartoonist makes sport of Bryan's notorious Cross of Gold speech in 1896.

about $16 million, as contrasted with about $1 million for the poorer Democrats (roughly "16 to 1"). With some justification, the Bryanites accused Hanna of "buying" the election and of floating McKinley into the White House on a tidal wave of greenbacks. The Republicans definitely had the edge in money and mud.

Appealing to the Pocketbook Vote

With gold gushing into his money bags, Hanna waged a high-pressure campaign against silver. He distributed tens of millions of pamphlets, tracts, leaflets, and posters, many of them in the native languages of immigrant groups. He sent hundreds of "spellbinders" out onto the stump, where they engaged in the free and unlimited coinage of wordage. There was a maximum of shouting and a minimum of thinking, primarily because only a few trained economists were able to grasp fully the implications of silver-and-gold bimetallism—and even they disagreed. "The whole currency question," wrote the humorist "Mr. Dooley" (Finley Peter Dunne), "is a matter of lungs."

Republicans harped constantly on their promise of prosperity. Reminding the voters of Cleveland's "Democratic panic," they appealed to the "belly vote" with their prize slogan: "McKinley and the Full Dinner Pail." McKinley, though an effective orator, was no match for Bryan in the rough-and-tumble of stump speaking. He remained at his Ohio home, conducting a quiet and dignified front-porch campaign. Stressing prosperity, he read calm and confident little speeches to delegations of visiting Republicans.

Bryan's cyclonic campaign, launched with irresistible enthusiasm, began to lose steam as the weeks passed. Just before the election, the price of wheat rose sharply, owing largely to crop failures abroad. Hostility to the Republican party in the vast wheat belt began to wane, even though agriculture generally remained depressed.

Fear was probably the strongest ally of Hanna, the worst enemy of Bryan, who allegedly had "silver on the brain." Republican businesspeople placed contracts with manufacturers, contingent on the election of McKinley. A few factory owners, with thinly veiled intimidation, paid off their workers

and told them not to come to work on Wednesday morning if Bryan won. Reports were also current that employers were threatening to pay their employees in fifty-cent pieces, instead of in dollars, if Bryan triumphed. Such were some of the "dirty tricks" of the "Stop Bryan, Save America" crusade.

Class Conflict: Plowholders versus Bondholders

Hanna's campaign methods paid off, for on election day McKinley triumphed decisively. The vote was 271 to 176 in the Electoral College, and 7,102,246 to 6,492,559 in the popular column. Driven by fear, hope, and excitement, an unprecedented outpouring of voters flocked to the polls. McKinley ran strongly in the populous East, where he carried every county of New England, and in the upper Mississippi Valley. Bryan's states, concentrated in the debt-burdened South and the trans-Mississippi West, involved more acreage than McKinley's but less population—only the South and the desert, cynics said.

The free-silver election of 1896 was probably the most significant since Lincoln's victories in 1860 and 1864. Despite Bryan's strength in the South and West, the results vividly demonstrated his lack of appeal to the unmortgaged farmer and especially the eastern urban laborer. Many wage earners in the East voted for their jobs and full dinner pails, threatened as they were by free silver, free trade, and fireless factories. Living precariously on a fixed wage, the factory workers had no reason to favor inflation, which was the heart of the Bryanites' program.

In gold-standard England there was much relief over McKinley's victory. The London Standard *commented,*

"The hopelessly ignorant and savagely covetous waifs and strays of American civilization voted for Bryan, but the bulk of the solid sense, business integrity, and social stability sided with McKinley. The nation is to be heartily congratulated."

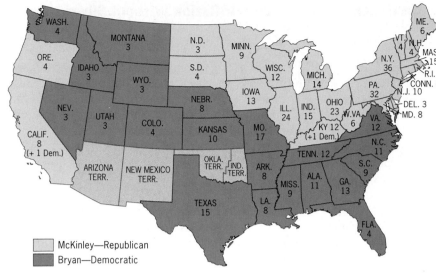

Presidential Election of 1896 (with electoral vote by state) This election tolled the death knell of the Gilded Age political party system, with its razor-close elections, strong party loyalties, and high voter turnouts. For years after 1896, Republicans predominated; and citizens showed declining interest in either joining parties or voting.

Campaign Gimcrack, 1896 This McKinley paper hat was distributed in a Boston Sunday newspaper.

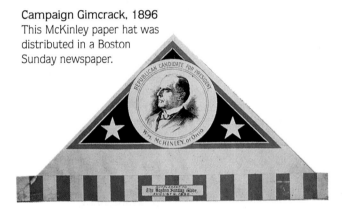

The Bryan-McKinley battle heralded the advent of a new era in American politics. At first glance the election seemed to be the age-old story of the underprivileged many against the privileged few, of the indebted backcountry against the wealthier seaboard, of the country against the city, of the agrarians against the industrialists, of Main Street against Wall Street, of the nobodies against the somebodies. Yet when Bryan made his evangelical appeal to all those supposed foes of the social order, there were simply not enough of them.

The outcome was instead a resounding victory for big business, the big cities, middle-class values, and financial conservatism. Bryan's defeat marked the last serious effort to win the White House with mostly agrarian votes. The future of presidential politics lay not on the farms, with their dwindling population, but in the mushrooming cities.

The smashing Republican victory of 1896 also heralded a Republican grip on the White House for sixteen consecutive years—indeed, for all but eight of the next thirty-six years. McKinley's election thus imparted a new character to the American political system. The long reign of Republican political dominance that it ushered in was accompanied by diminishing voter participation in elections, a weakening of party organizations, and the fading away of issues like the money question and civil-service reform, which came to be replaced by concern for industrial regulation and the welfare of labor. Scholars have dubbed this new political era the period of the "fourth party system."*

---

*The first party system, marked by doubts about the very legitimacy of parties, embraced the Federalist-Republican clashes of the 1790s and early 1800s. The second party system took shape with the emergence of mass-based politics in the Jacksonian era, pitting Democrats against Whigs. The third party system was characterized by the precarious equilibrium between Republicans and Democrats, as well as the high electoral participation, that lasted from the end of the Civil War to McKinley's election. The fourth party system is described above. The fifth party system emerged in Franklin Roosevelt's New Deal, which initiated a long period of Democratic ascendancy. Each "system," except the fifth, has lasted about forty years. Debate continues as to whether the nation has now entered or is about to enter the era of the sixth party system.

Republican Standpattism Enthroned

An eminently "safe" McKinley took the inaugural oath in 1897. Though a man of considerable ability, he was an ear-to-the-ground politician who seldom got far out of line with majority opinion. His cautious, conservative nature caused him to shy away from the flaming banner of reform. Business was given a free rein, and the trusts, which had trusted him in 1896, were allowed to develop more mighty muscles without serious restraints.

McKinley, unlike Cleveland, was able to work smoothly in party harness. With impeccable white vest, he seemed never to perspire, even in oppressively muggy Washington. Able to get along well with Congress—he had served there for many years—he shone best at reconciling conflicting interests. Conciliatory and warm-handed, he would send an angry-faced caller away beaming, sometimes wearing a carnation from the presidential desk. McKinley continued to maintain intimate relations with Hanna, but he was by no means under the thumb of his mentor, despite Vachel Lindsay's cruel query:

> *Where is McKinley, Mark Hanna's McKinley,*
> *His slave, his echo, his suit of clothes?*

The tariff issue, which had played second fiddle to silver in the "Battle of '96," quickly forced itself to the fore. The current Wilson-Gorman law was not raising enough revenue to cover the annual Treasury deficits, and the Republican trusts had purchased additional protection by their lush contributions to Hanna's war chest.

In due course the Dingley Tariff Bill was jammed through the House in 1897, under the pounding gavel of the rethroned "Czar" Reed. The proposed new rates were high, but not high enough to satisfy the paunchy lobbyists, who once again descended upon the Senate. Over 850 amendments were tacked onto the overburdened bill. The resulting piece of patchwork finally established the average rates at 46.5 percent, substantially higher than the Democratic Wilson-Gorman Act of 1894 and in some categories even higher than the McKinley Act of 1890. (See the chart in the Appendix.)

Inflation Without Silver

Prosperity, long lurking around the corner, began to return with a rush in 1897, the first year of McKinley. The depression of 1893 had run its course, and farm prices rose. Paint-thirsty midwestern barns blossomed in new colors, and the wheels of industry increased their hum. Republican politicians, like crowing roosters believing they caused the sun to rise, claimed credit for attracting the sunlight of prosperity.

The Gold Standard Act, loudly demanded by hard-moneyites, was not passed by the Republicans until 1900, when many silverites had left Congress. It provided that the paper currency was to be redeemed freely in gold. Last-ditch silverites fought the bill with bitterness but without success. The cries of the inflationists, further choked by returning prosperity, gradually died away. Thus ended some twenty years of attempts to "do something" for the debtor.

In retrospect, a controlled expansion of American currency in the 1880s and 1890s was clearly desirable. Prices were depressed, money was tight, and the volume of currency in circulation lagged far behind the increasing volume of business. Agrarian debtors therefore had a good cause: relief from social and economic hardship through an inflation of the dollar supply. But free silver, which aroused exaggerated fears, was a poor sword. By brandishing this tinseled weapon, William Jennings Bryan actually defeated his own ends. The free-silver fixation not only discredited the case for needed currency expansion but seriously set back the movement for agrarian reform.

Nature and science gradually provided an inflation that the "Gold Bug" East had fought so frantically to prevent. Electrifying discoveries of new gold deposits in Canada (Klondike), Alaska, South Africa, and Australia eased the pressure, as did the perfecting of the cheap cyanide process for extracting gold from low-grade ore. Moderate inflation thus took care of the currency needs of an explosively expanding nation, as its circulatory system greatly improved. The tide of "silver heresy" rapidly receded, and the "Popocratic" fish were left gasping high and dry on a golden-sanded beach.

Chronology

1889	Harrison assumes the presidency
1890	"Billion-Dollar" Congress Pension Act of 1890 Sherman Silver Purchase Act of 1890 (repealed 1893) McKinley Tariff Bill
1892	Cleveland defeats Harrison and Weaver for presidency Homestead steel strike
1893	Depression of 1893 begins
1894	Coxey's "Commonweal Army" marches on Washington
1894	Pullman strike Wilson-Gorman Tariff Act

1895	Morgan's banking syndicate loans $65
	  million in gold to federal government
	Supreme Court declares income tax
	  unconstitutional
	Income tax struck down

1896	McKinley defeats Bryan for presidency
1897	Dingley Tariff Bill
1900	Gold Standard Act

The Populists: Radicals or Reactionaries?

Taking their cue from contemporary satirical commentaries like Mark Twain and Charles Dudley Warner's *The Gilded Age* (1873), the first historians who wrote about the post–Civil War era judged it harshly. They condemned its politicians as petty and corrupt, lamented the emergence of a new plutocratic class, and railed against the arrogance of corporate power. Such a view is conspicuous in Charles and Mary Beard's *The Rise of American Civilization* (4 vols., 1927–1942), perhaps the most influential American history textbook ever written. It is equally evident in Vernon Louis Parrington's classic literary history, *Main Currents of American Thought* (3 vols., 1927–1930), in which the entire post–Civil War period is contemptuously dismissed as the time of "The Great Barbecue."

The Beards and Parrington were leaders of the so-called progressive school of historical writing that flourished in the early years of the twentieth century. Progressive historians, many of whom grew up in the Gilded Age, shared in a widespread disillusionment that the Civil War had failed to generate a rebirth of American idealism. Their political sympathies were chillingly antibusiness and warmly prolabor, profarmer, and proreform.

Historians of the progressive persuasion identified populism as virtually the only organized opposition to the social, economic, and political order that took shape in the last decades of the nineteenth century. The Populists thus became heroes to several generations of writers who bemoaned that order and looked back longingly at American's agrarian past. John D. Hicks, *The Populist Revolt* (1931), is the classic portrayal of the Populists as embattled farmers hurling defiance at Wall Street and the Robber Barons in a last-ditch defense of their simple, honest way of life. Bowed but unbroken by the defeat of their great champion, William Jennings Bryan, in the presidential election of 1896, the Populists, Hicks claimed, left a reforming legacy that flourished again in the Progressive Era and the New Deal.

Hicks's point of view was the dominant one until the 1950s, when it was sharply criticized by Richard Hofstadter in *The Age of Reform* (1955). Hofstadter charged that the progressive historians had romanticized the Populists, who were best understood not as picturesque protesters, but as "harassed little country businessmen," bristling with provincial prejudices. The city-born-and-bred Hofstadter argued that the Populist revolt was aimed not just at big business and the money power, but somewhat irrationally at urbanism, immigrants, the East, and modernity itself. Hofstadter thus exposed a "dark side" of Populism, which contained elements of backwoods anti-intellectualism, paranoia, and even anti-Semitism.

In the 1960s, several scholars, inspired by the work of C. Vann Woodward, as well as by sympathy with the protest movements of the turbulent sixties decade, began to rehabilitate the Populists as authentic reformers with genuine grievances. Especially notable in this vein was Lawrence Goodwyn's *Democratic Promise: The Populist Moment in America* (1976). Goodwyn depicted the Populists as reasonable radicals who were justifiably resentful of their eclipse by urban industrialism and finance capitalism. He also portrayed populism as the last gasp of popular political participation, a democratic "moment" in American history that expired with the Populists' absorption into the Democratic party.

Two more recent works, Edward L. Ayers's *Promise of the New South* (1992) and Robert C. McMath's *American Populism* (1993), synthesize many of the older perspectives and present a balanced view of the Populists as radical in many ways, yet also limited by their nostalgia for a lost agrarian past.

SUGGESTED READINGS

PRIMARY SOURCE DOCUMENTS

William H. Coin Harvey, *Coin's Financial School** (1894), expounded the silverite position. William Jennings Bryan's Cross of Gold speech* won him the Democratic nomination in 1896 and a hallowed place in the annals of American oratory.

SECONDARY SOURCES

Valuable background can be found in the books by Hicks, Hahn, and Goodwyn cited in Chapter 27. A comprehensive account is Harold U. Faulkner, *Politics, Reform and Expansion, 1890–1900* (1959). Carl N. Degler, *The Age of Economic Revolution, 1876–1900* (1977), is a brief survey. Placing the period within a larger context are Robert H. Wiebe, *The Search for Order, 1877–1920* (1967), and Richard Hofstadter's stimulating *The Age of Reform* (1955). Paolo Coletta's biography of *William Jennings Bryan* (3 vols., 1964–1969) is rich in detail. On politics see R. Hal Williams, *Years of Decision:*

American Politics in the 1890s (1978), and Robert D. Marcus, *Grand Old Party: Political Structure in the Gilded Age* (1971). A later school of historians concentrated on local issues. Their works include Richard Jensen, *The Winning of the Midwest* (1971); Samuel T. McSeveney, *The Politics of Depression* (1972); and Paul Kleppner, *The Third Electoral System, 1853–1892* (1979). Labor issues are cogently and compellingly discussed in Paul Krause, *The Battle for Homestead, 1880–1892: Politics, Culture, and Steel* (1992). Charles Hoffman examines *The Depression of the Nineties* (1970), an issue given much attention in David P. Thelen, *The New Citizenship: Origins of Progressivism in Wisconsin, 1885–1900* (1972). The election of 1896 is examined in Robert F. Durden, *The Climax of Populism: The Election of 1896* (1965), and Stanley L. Jones, *The Presidential Election of 1896* (1964). Also informative are Paul W. Glad, *McKinley, Bryan and the People* (1964), and H. Wayne Morgan, *William McKinley and His America* (1963). Three intriguing cultural histories of the period are Alan Trachtenberg, *The Incorporation of America: Culture and Society in the Gilded Age* (1982); Richard Slotkin, *The Fatal Environment: The Myth of the Frontier in American History, 1800–1890* (1985); and Lawrence Levine, *Highbrow/Lowbrow: The Emergence of Cultural Hierarchy in America* (1988).

---

*An asterisk indicates that the document, or an excerpt from it, can be found in Thomas A. Bailey and David M. Kennedy, eds., *The American Spirit: United States History as Seen by Contemporaries,* 9th ed. (Boston: Houghton Mifflin, 1998).

29

The Path of Empire
1890–1899

*We assert that no nation can long endure half
republic and half empire, and we warn the
American people that imperialism abroad will
lead quickly and inevitably to despotism at home.*

<small>Democratic National Platform, 1900</small>

Imperialist Stirrings

From the end of the Civil War to the 1880s, the indifference of most Americans to the outside world was almost unbelievable. But then in the sunset decades of the nineteenth century, a momentous shift occurred in U.S. foreign policy. The new diplomacy mirrored the far-reaching changes that were reshaping industry, agriculture, and the social structure.

The Republic was becoming increasingly outward-looking as exports of both manufactured goods and agricultural products shot up. Many Americans believed that the United States had to expand or explode. Their country was bursting with a new sense of power generated by the booming increase in population, wealth, and industrial production—and it was trembling from the hammer blows of labor violence and agrarian unrest. Overseas markets might provide a safety valve to relieve such pressures.

Other forces also stimulated overseas expansion. The lurid "yellow press" of Joseph Pulitzer and William Randolph Hearst whetted the popular taste for excitement abroad. Missionaries, inspired by books like the Reverend Josiah Strong's *Our Country: Its Possible Future and Its Present Crisis*, looked overseas for new fields to till. Strong trumpeted the superiority of Anglo-Saxon civilization and summoned Americans to spread their religion and their values to the "backward" peoples. He cast his seed on fertile ground. At the same time, aggressive Americans like Theodore Roosevelt and Congressman Henry Cabot Lodge were interpreting Darwinism to mean that the earth belonged to the strong and the fit—that is, to Uncle Sam. This view was strengthened as latecomers to the colonial scramble scooped up leavings from the banquet table of

The Imperial Menu
A pleased Uncle Sam gets ready to place his order with headwaiter William McKinley. Swallowing some of these possessions eventually produced political indigestion.

earlier diners. Africa, previously unexplored and mysterious, was partitioned by the Europeans in the 1880s in a pell-mell rush of colonial conquest. In the 1890s Japan, Germany, and Russia all extorted concessions from the anemic Chinese Empire. If America was to survive in the competition of modern nation-states, perhaps it, too, would have to become an imperial power.

The development of a new steel navy also focused attention overseas. Captain Alfred Thayer Mahan's book of 1890, *The Influence of Sea Power upon History, 1660–1783*, argued that control of the sea was the key to world dominance. Read by the English, Germans, and Japanese, as well as by his fellow Americans, Mahan helped stimulate the naval race among the great powers that gained momentum around the turn of the century. Red-blooded Americans joined in the demands for a mightier navy and for an American-built isthmian canal between the Atlantic and the Pacific.

America's new international interest manifested itself in several ways. As secretary of state, first in the Garfield administration and later in the Harrison administration, James G. Blaine pushed his "Big Sister" policy. It aimed to rally the Latin American nations behind Uncle Sam's leadership and to open Latin American markets to Yankee traders. Blaine's efforts bore modest fruit in 1889, when he presided over the first Pan-American Conference, held in Washington, D.C. Although the frock-coated delegates did little more than sketch a vague plan for economic cooperation through reciprocal tariff reduction, they succeeded in blazing the way for a long and increasingly important series of inter-American assemblages.

A number of diplomatic crises or near-wars also marked the path of American diplomacy in the late 1880s and early 1890s. The American and German navies nearly came to blows in 1889 over the far-away Samoan Islands in the South Pacific. The lynching of eleven Italians in New Orleans in 1891 brought America and Italy to the brink of war; the crisis was defused when the United States agreed to pay compensation. In the ugliest affair, American demands on Chile after the deaths of two American sailors in the port of Valparaiso in 1892 made hostilities between the two countries seem inevitable. The threat of attack by Chile's modern navy spread alarm on the Pacific Coast, until American power finally forced the Chileans to pay an indemnity. A simmering argument between the United States and Canada over seal hunting near the Pribilof Islands off the coast of Alaska was resolved by arbitration in 1893. The willingness of Americans to risk war over such distant and minor disputes demonstrated the aggressive new national mood.

Monroe's Doctrine and the Venezuelan Squall

America's anti-British feeling, which periodically came to a head, flared ominously in 1895–1896 over Venezuela. For more than a half-century, the jungle boundary between British Guiana and Venezuela had been in dispute. The Venezuelans, whose claims on the whole were extravagant, had repeatedly urged arbitration. But the prospect of a peaceful settlement faded when gold was discovered in the contested area.

President Cleveland, a champion of righteousness and no lover of Britain, at length decided upon a strong protest. His no less pugnacious Secretary of State Richard Olney was authorized to present to London a smashing note, which Cleveland later dubbed a "twenty-inch gun" blast. Olney declared in effect that the British, by attempting to dominate Venezuela in this quarrel and acquire more territory, were flouting the Monroe Doctrine. London should therefore submit the dispute to arbitration. Not content to stop here, Olney haughtily informed the world's number one naval power that the United States was now calling the tune in the Western Hemisphere.

British officials, unimpressed, took four months to prepare their reply. Preoccupied elsewhere, they were inclined to shrug off Olney's lengthy salvo as just another twist of the lion's tail designed to elicit cheers from Irish-American voters. When London's answer finally came, it flatly denied the relevance of the Monroe Doctrine, while no less emphatically

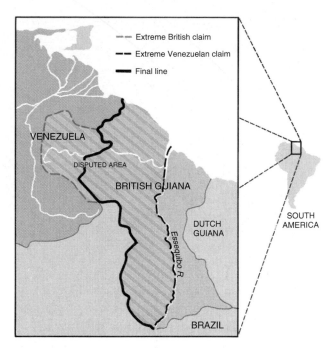

The Venezuela–British Guiana Boundary Dispute

spurning arbitration. In short, said John Bull, the affair was none of Uncle Sam's business.

President Cleveland—"mad clear through," as he put it—sent a bristling special message to Congress. He urged an appropriation for a commission of experts, who would run the line where it ought to go. Then, he implied, if the British would not accept this rightful boundary, the United States would fight for it.

The entire country, irrespective of political party, was swept off its feet in an outburst of hysteria. War seemed inevitable, even though Britain had thirty-two warships of the battleship class to only five flying Old Glory.

Fortunately, sober second thoughts prevailed on both sides of the Atlantic. The British, though vastly annoyed by their upstart cousins, had no real urge to fight. Canada was vulnerable to yet-to-be-raised American armies, and Britain's rich merchant marine was vulnerable to American commerce raiders. The European atmosphere was menacing, for Britain's traditional policy of "splendid isolation" was bringing insecure isolation. Russia and France were unfriendly; and Germany, under the saber-rattling Kaiser Wilhelm II, was about to challenge British naval supremacy.

The undiplomatic note to Britain of Secretary of State Richard Olney (1835–1917) read,

"To-day the United States is practically sovereign on this continent, and its fiat is law upon the subjects to which it confines its interposition. . . . Its infinite resources combined with its isolated position render it master of the situation and practically invulnerable as against any or all other powers."

The World's Plunderers, 1885

The German kaiser, blunderingly and unwittingly, increased chances of a peaceful solution to the Venezuelan crisis. An unauthorized British raiding party of six hundred armed men was captured by the Dutch-descended Boers in South Africa, and Wilhelm forthwith cabled his congratulations to the victors. Overnight, British anger against America was largely deflected to Germany, and London consented to arbitrate the Venezuelan dispute. The final decision, ironically, awarded the British the bulk of what they had claimed from the beginning.

America had skated close to the thin ice of a terrible war, but the results on the whole were favorable. The prestige of the Monroe Doctrine was immensely enhanced. Europe was irked by Cleveland's claim to domination in this hemisphere, but he had made his claim stick. Many Latin American republics were pleased by the determination of the United States to protect them, and when Cleveland died in 1908, some of them lowered their flags to half-mast.

The chastened British, their eyes fully opened to the European peril, were now determined to cultivate Yankee friendship. The British inaugurated an era of "patting the eagle's head," which replaced a century or so of America's "twisting the lion's tail." Sometimes called the Great Rapprochement—or reconciliation—between the United States and Britain, the new Anglo-American cordiality became a cornerstone of both nations' foreign policies as the twentieth century opened.

Spurning the Hawaiian Pear

Enchanted Hawaii had early attracted the attention of Americans. In the morning years of the nineteenth century, the breeze-brushed islands were a way station and provisioning point for Yankee shippers, sailors, and whalers. In 1820 came the first New England missionaries, who preached the twin

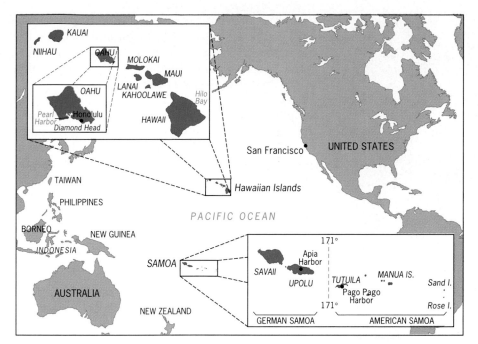

The Pacific
The enlargements show the Hawaiian Islands and the Samoas, both areas of American imperialistic activity in the late nineteenth century.

blessings of Protestant Christianity and protective calico. They came to do good—and did well; their children did even better. In some respects Honolulu took on the earmarks of a typical New England town.

Americans gradually came to regard the Hawaiian Islands as a virtual extension of their own coastline. The State Department, beginning in the 1840s, sternly warned other powers to keep their grasping hands off. America's grip was further tightened in 1875 by a commercial reciprocity agreement and in 1887 by a treaty with the native government guaranteeing priceless naval-base rights at spacious Pearl Harbor.

But trouble, both economic and political, was brewing in the insular paradise. Sugar cultivation, which had become immensely profitable, went somewhat sour in 1890 when the McKinley Tariff raised barriers against the Hawaiian product. White planters, mostly Americans, quickly concluded that the best way to overcome the tariff was to annex Hawaii to the United States. But that ambition was blocked by the strong-willed Queen Liliuokalani, who insisted that native Hawaiians should control the islands. Desperate whites, though only a tiny minority, organized a successful revolt early in 1893. It was openly assisted by American troops, who

landed under the unauthorized orders of the expansionist American minister in Honolulu. "The Hawaiian pear is now fully ripe," he wrote exultantly to his superiors in Washington, "and this is the golden hour for the United States to pluck it."

Hawaii, like Texas of earlier years, seemed ready for annexation—at least in the eyes of the ruling American whites. An appropriate treaty was rushed to Washington. But before it could be railroaded through the Senate, Republican President Harrison's term expired and Democratic President Cleveland came in. "Old Grover," who set great store by "national honesty," suspected that his powerful nation had gravely wronged the deposed Queen Liliuokalani.

Cleveland abruptly withdrew the treaty from the Senate early in 1893 and then sent a special investigator to Hawaii. The subsequent probe revealed the damning fact that a majority of the Hawaiian natives did not favor annexation at all. But the white revolutionists were firmly in the saddle, and Cleveland could not unhorse them without using armed force—a step American public opinion would not have tolerated. Although Queen Liliuokalani could not be reinstated, the sugarcoated move for annexation had to be abandoned temporarily—until 1898.

Queen Liliuokalani (1838–1917)   She was the last reigning queen of Hawaii, whose defense of native Hawaiian self-rule led to revolt by white settlers and to her dethronement. She wrote many songs, the most famous of which was "Aloha Oe" or Farewell to Thee, played countless times by Hawaiian bands for departing tourists.

The question of annexing Hawaii touched off the first full-fledged imperialistic debate in American experience. Cleveland was savagely criticized for trying to stem the new Manifest Destiny, and a popular jingle ran

> ... *Liliuokalani,*
> *Give us your little brown hannie.*

But Cleveland's motives, in a day of international land-grabbing, were honorable both to himself and to his country. The Hawaiian pear continued to ripen for five more years.

Cubans Rise in Revolt

Cuba's masses, frightfully misgoverned, again rose against their Spanish oppressor in 1895. The roots of their revolt were partly economic, with partial origins in the United States. Sugar production—the backbone of the island's prosperity—was crippled when the American tariff of 1894 restored high duties on the toothsome product.

Driven to desperation, the insurgents now adopted a scorched-earth policy. They reasoned that if they did enough damage, Spain might be willing to move out. Or the United States might move in and help the Cubans win their independence. In pursuance of this destructive strategy, the *insurrectos* torched cane fields and sugar mills; they even dynamited passenger trains.

American sympathies, ever on the side of patriots fighting for freedom, went out to the Cuban underdogs. Aside from pure sentiment, the United States had an investment stake of about $50 million in Cuba and an annual trade stake of about $100 million. Moreover, Spanish misrule in Cuba menaced the shipping routes of the West Indies and the Gulf, and less directly the future isthmian canal.

Fuel was added to the Cuban conflagration in 1896 with the coming of the Spanish General ("Butcher") Weyler. He undertook to crush the rebellion by herding many civilians into barbed-wire reconcentration camps, where they could not give assistance to the armed *insurrectos*. Lacking proper sanitation, these enclosures turned into deadly pestholes; the victims died like dogs.

An outraged American public demanded action. Congress in 1896 overwhelmingly passed a resolution that called upon President Cleveland to recognize the belligerency of the revolted Cubans. But as the government of the insurgents consisted of hardly more than a few fugitive leaders, Cleveland—an antijingoist and anti-imperialist—refused to budge. He defiantly vowed that if Congress declared war, the commander in chief would not issue the necessary order to mobilize the army.

The Mystery of the *Maine* Explosion

Atrocities in Cuba were made to order for the sensational new "yellow journalism." William R. Hearst and Joseph Pulitzer, then engaged in a titanic duel for circulation, attempted to outdo each other with screeching headlines and hair-raising "scoops." Lesser competitors zestfully followed suit.

The Explosion of the *Maine*, February 15, 1898   Encouraged and amplified by the "yellow press," the outcry over the tragedy of the *Maine* helped drive the country into an impulsive war against Spain.

Where atrocity stories did not exist, they were invented. Hearst sent the gifted artist Frederic Remington to Cuba to draw sketches, and when the latter reported that conditions were not bad enough to warrant hostilities, Hearst is alleged to have replied, "You furnish the pictures and I'll furnish the war." Among other outrages, Remington depicted Spanish customs officials brutally disrobing and searching an American woman. Most readers of Hearst's *Journal*, their indignation soaring, had no way of knowing that such tasks were performed by female attendants. "Butcher" Weyler was removed in 1897, yet conditions steadily worsened. There was some talk in Spain of granting the restive island a type of self-government, but such a surrender was so bitterly opposed by many Spaniards in Cuba that they engaged in furious riots. Early in 1898 Washington sent the battleship *Maine* to Cuba, ostensibly for a "friendly visit" but actually to protect and evacuate Americans if a dangerous flare-up should again occur.

This already explosive situation suddenly grew acute, on February 9, 1898, when Hearst sensationally headlined a private letter written by the Spanish minister in Washington, Dupuy de Lôme. The indiscreet epistle, which had been stolen from the mails, described President McKinley as an ear-to-the-ground politician who lacked good faith. The resulting uproar was so violent that Dupuy de Lôme was forced to resign.

A tragic climax came a few days later, on February 15, 1898, when the *Maine* mysteriously blew up in Havana harbor, with a loss of 260 officers and men. Two investigations of the iron coffin were undertaken, one by U.S. naval officers, and the other by Spanish officials, whom the Americans would not trust near the wreck. The Spanish commission stated that the explosion had been internal and presumably accidental; the American commission reported that the blast had been caused by a submarine mine. Washington, not unmindful of popular indignation, spurned Spanish proposals of arbitration.

Various theories have been advanced as to how the *Maine* was blown up. The least convincing explanation of all is that the Spanish officials in Cuba were guilty, for they were under the American gun and Spain was far away. Not until 1976 did Admiral H. G. Rickover, under U.S. Navy auspices, give what appears to be the final answer. He presented overwhelming evidence that the initial explosion had resulted from spontaneous combustion in one of the coal bunkers adjacent to a powder magazine. Ironically, this is essentially what the Spanish commission had deduced in 1898.

But Americans in 1898, now war-mad, blindly accepted the least likely explanation. Lashed to fury by the yellow press, they leapt to the conclusion that the Spanish government had been guilty of intolerable treachery. The battle cry of the hour became

Remember the Maine!
To hell with Spain!

Nothing would do but to hurl the "dirty" Spanish flag from the hemisphere.

Many Spaniards felt that accusations about their blowing up the Maine *reflected on Spanish honor. One Madrid newspaper spoke up:*

"The American jingoes . . . imagine us capable of the most foul villainies and cowardly actions. Scoundrels by nature, the American jingoes believe that all men are made like themselves. What do they know about noble and generous feelings? . . . We should not in any way heed the jingoes: they are not even worth our contempt, or the saliva with which we might honor them in spitting at their faces."

McKinley Unleashes the Dogs of War

The national war fever burned higher, even though American diplomats had already gained Madrid's agreement to Washington's two basic demands: an end to the reconcentration camps and an armistice with Cuban rebels. The cautious McKinley did not want hostilities. The hesitant chief executive was condemned by jingoes as "Wobbly Willie" McKinley, while fight-hungry Theodore Roosevelt reportedly snarled that the "white-livered" occupant of the White House did not have "the backbone of a chocolate éclair." The president, whose shaken nerves required sleeping pills, was even being hanged in effigy. Many critics did not realize that backbone was needed to stay out of war, not to plunge into it.

McKinley's private desires clashed sharply with opinions now popular with the public. He did not want hostilities, for he had seen enough bloodshed as a major in the Civil War. Mark Hanna and Wall Street did not want war, for business might be unsettled. But the public, prodded by the yellow press and the appeals of Cuban exiles in the United States, clamored for a fight. The president, recognizing the inevitable, finally yielded and gave the people what they wanted.

But public pressures did not fully explain McKinley's course. He had no faith in Spain's promises regarding Cuba; Madrid had spoken them and broken them before. He was certain that a showdown would have to come sooner or later. He believed in the democratic principle that the people should rule, and he hesitated to deny Americans what they demanded—even if it was not good for them. He also perceived that if he stood out against war, the Democrats would make political capital out of his stubbornness. Bryan might sweep into the presidency two years later under a banner inscribed "Free Cuba and Free Silver." Gold-standard McKinley was a staunch party man, and to him it seemed better to break up the remnants of Spain's once-glorious empire than to break up the Grand Old Party—especially since war seemed inevitable.

On April 11, 1898, McKinley sent his war message to Congress, urging armed intervention to free the oppressed Cubans. The legislators responded uproariously with what was essentially a declaration of war. In a burst of self-righteousness, they likewise

"Cuba Libre," by Captain Fritz W. Guerin of St. Louis, 1898   This elaborately staged tableau depicts Confederate and Union officers reconciled three decades after the Civil War as they join hands to liberate innocent Cuba from her chains of bondage to Spain.

adopted the hand-tying Teller Amendment. This proviso proclaimed to the world that when the United States had overthrown Spanish misrule, it would give the Cubans their freedom—a declaration that caused imperialistic Europeans to smile skeptically.

Dewey's May Day Victory at Manila

The American people plunged into the war light-heartedly, like schoolchildren off to a picnic. Bands blared incessantly "There'll Be a Hot Time in the Old Town Tonight" and "Hail, Hail, the Gang's All Here," thus leading foreigners to believe that those were national anthems.

But such jubilation seemed premature to European observers. The regular army, which was commanded by corpulent Civil War oldsters, was unprepared for a war under tropical skies. It num-

bered only 2,100 officers and 28,000 men, as compared with some 200,000 Spanish troops in Cuba. The American navy, at least to transatlantic experts, seemed slightly less powerful than Spain's. European powers, moreover, were generally friendly to their Old World associate. The only conspicuous exception was the ally-seeking British, who now were ardently wooing their American cousins.

Yet in one important respect, Spain's apparent superiority was illusory. Its navy, though formidable on paper, was in wretched condition. It labored under the added handicap of having to operate thousands of miles from its home base. But the new American steel navy, now fifteen years old and ranking about fifth among the fleets of the world, was in fairly good trim, though the war was to lay bare serious defects.

The readiness of the navy owed much to two men: the easygoing navy secretary John D. Long and his bellicose assistant secretary, Theodore Roosevelt. The secretary hardly dared leave his desk for fear that his overzealous underling would stir up a hornet's nest. On February 25, 1898, while Long was away for a weekend, Roosevelt had cabled Commodore George Dewey, commanding the American Asiatic Squadron at Hong Kong, to descend upon Spain's Philippines in the event of war. McKinley subsequently confirmed these instructions, even though an attack in the distant Far East seemed like a strange way to free nearby Cuba.

Dewey carried out his orders magnificently on May 1, 1898. Sailing boldly with his six warships at night into the fortified harbor of Manila, he trained his guns the next morning on the ten-ship Spanish fleet, one of whose craft was only a moored hulk without functioning engines. The entire collection of antiquated and overmatched vessels was quickly destroyed, with a loss of nearly four hundred Spaniards killed and wounded, and without the loss of a single life in Dewey's fleet. An American consul who was there wrote that all the American sailors needed was cough drops for throats made raw by cheers of victory.

Dewey's Route in the Philippines, 1898

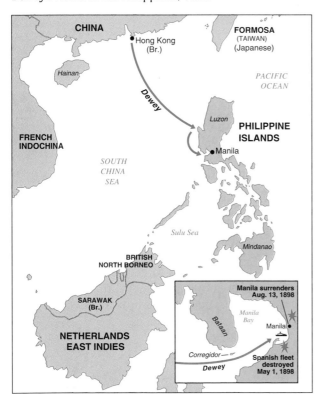

Unexpected Imperialistic Plums

Taciturn George Dewey became a national hero overnight. He was promptly promoted to the rank of admiral, as the price of flags rose sharply. An amateur poet blossomed forth with

> *Oh, dewy was the morning*
> *Upon the first of May,*
> *And Dewey was the Admiral,*
> *Down in Manila Bay.*
> *And dewy were the Spaniards' eyes,*
> *Them orbs of black and blue;*
> *And dew we feel discouraged?*
> *I dew not think we dew!*

Yet Dewey was in a perilous position. He had destroyed the enemy fleet, but he could not storm the forts of Manila with his sailors. His nerves frayed, he was forced to wait in the steaming-hot bay while troop reinforcements were slowly assembled in America.

Foreign warships meanwhile had begun to gather in the harbor, ostensibly to safeguard their nationals in Manila. The Germans sent five vessels—a naval force more powerful than Dewey's—and their haughty admiral defied the American blockade regulations. After several disagreeable incidents, Dewey lost his temper and threatened the arrogant German with war "as soon as you like." Happily, the storm blew over. The British commander, by contrast, was conspicuously successful in carrying out London's new policy of friendliness. A false tale subsequently circulated that the British dramatically interposed their ships to prevent the Germans from blowing the Americans out of the water.

Long-awaited American troops, finally arriving in force, captured Manila on August 13, 1898. They collaborated with the Filipino insurgents, commanded by their well-educated, part-Chinese leader, Emilio Aguinaldo. Dewey, to his later regret, had brought this shrewd and magnetic revolutionary from exile in Asia, so that he might weaken Spanish resistance.

These thrilling events in the Philippines had meanwhile focused attention on Hawaii. An impression spread that America needed the archipelago as a coaling and provisioning way station, in order to send supplies and reinforcements to Dewey. The

Emilio Aguinaldo (c. 1869–1964)   Aguinaldo had a colorfully checkered career. Exiled from the Philippines by the Spanish in 1897, he was brought back in 1898 to assist the American invasion. A year later he led the Filipino insurrection against the new American rulers. Captured in 1901, he declared his loyalty to the United States. During World War II, he collaborated with the Japanese when they occupied the Philippines. After a lifetime of political intrigue and armed struggle, Aguinaldo died peacefully in Manila in 1964 in his ninety-fifth year.

truth is that the United States could have used these island "Crossroads of the Pacific" without annexing them, so eager was the white-dominated Honolulu government to compromise its neutrality and risk the vengeance of Spain. But an appreciative American public would not leave Dewey in the lurch. A joint resolution of annexation was rushed through Congress and approved by McKinley on July 7, 1898.

The residents of Hawaii were granted U.S. citizenship with annexation and received full territorial status in 1900. These events in the idyllic islands, though seemingly sudden, were but the culmination of nearly a century of Americanization by sailors, whalers, traders, and missionaries.

The Confused Invasion of Cuba

Shortly after the outbreak of war, the Spanish government ordered a fleet of warships to Cuba. It was commanded by Admiral Cervera, who protested that his wretchedly prepared ships were flirting with suicide. Four armored cruisers finally set forth (one without its main battery of guns). They were accompanied by six torpedo boats, three of which had to be abandoned en route.

Panic seized the eastern seaboard of the United States. American vacationers abandoned their seashore cottages, while nervous investors moved their securities to inland depositories. Demands for protection poured in on Washington from nervous citizens, and the Navy Department was forced to dispatch some useless old Civil War ships to useless places for morale purposes. Cervera finally found refuge in bottle-shaped Santiago harbor, Cuba, where he was blockaded by the much more powerful American fleet.

Sound strategy seemed to dictate that an American army be sent in from the rear to drive out Cervera. Leading the invading force was the grossly overweight General William R. Shafter, a leader so blubbery and gout-stricken that he had to be carried about on a door. The ill-prepared Americans were unequipped for war in the tropics; they had been amply provided with heavy woolen underwear and uniforms designed for subzero operations against the Indians.

The "Rough Riders," a part of the invading army, now charged onto the stage of history. This colorful regiment of volunteers, short on discipline but long on dash, consisted largely of western cowboys and other hardy characters, with a sprinkling of ex–polo players and ex-convicts. Commanded by Colonel Leonard Wood, the group was organized principally by the glory-hungry Theodore Roosevelt, who had resigned from the Navy Department to serve as lieutenant colonel. Although totally without military experience, he used his strong political pull to secure his commission and to bypass physical standards. He was so nearsighted that as a safeguard he

Colonel Theodore Roosevelt with Some of the "Rough Riders" Roosevelt later described his first encounter with the Spanish enemy: "Soon we came to the brink of a deep valley. There was a good deal of cracking of rifles way off in front of us, but as they used smokeless powder we had no idea as to exactly where they were, or who they were shooting at. Then it dawned on us that we were the target. The bullets began to come overhead, making a sound like the ripping of a silk dress, with sometimes a kind of pop. . . . We advanced, firing at them, and drove them off."

took along a dozen pairs of spectacles, cached in handy spots on his person or nearby.

About the middle of June a bewildered American army of seventeen thousand men finally embarked at congested Tampa, Florida, amid scenes of indescribable confusion. The Rough Riders, fearing that they would be robbed of glory, rushed one of the transports and courageously held their place for almost a week in the broiling tropical sun. About half of them finally got to Cuba without

With a mixture of modesty and immodesty, Colonel Theodore Roosevelt (1858–1919) wrote privately in 1903 of his "Rough Riders":

"In my regiment nine-tenths of the men were better horsemen than I was, and probably two-thirds of them better shots than I was, while on the average they were certainly hardier and more enduring. Yet after I had had them a very short while they all knew, and I knew too, that nobody else could command them as I could."

most of their horses, and the bowlegged regiment then came to be known as "Wood's Weary Walkers."

Shafter's landing near Santiago, Cuba, was made without serious opposition. Defending Spaniards, even more disorganized than the Americans, were unable to muster at this spot more than two thousand men. Brisk fighting broke out on July 1 at El Caney and San Juan Hill, up which Colonel Roosevelt and his horseless Rough Riders charged, with strong support from two crack black regiments. They suffered heavy casualties, but the colorful colonel, having the time of his life, shot a Spaniard with his revolver, and rejoiced to see his victim double up like a jackrabbit. He later wrote a book on his exploits, which, "Mr. Dooley" remarked, ought to have been entitled *Alone in Cubia* [*sic*].

Curtains for Spain in America

The American army, fast closing in on Santiago, spelled doom for the Spanish fleet. Admiral Cervera, again protesting against suicide, was flatly ordered to fight for the honor of the flag. The odds against him were heavy: the guns of the U.S.S. *Oregon* alone threw more metal than his four armored cruisers

Charge of the Rough Riders at San Juan Hill, by Frederic Remington (detail)
Theodore Roosevelt thought it a "bully fight."

combined. After a running chase, on July 3, the foul-bottomed Spanish fleet was entirely destroyed, as the wooden decks caught fire and the blazing infernos were beached. About five hundred Spaniards were killed, as compared with one death for the Americans. "Don't cheer, men," admonished Captain Philip of the *Texas*, "The poor devils are dying." Shortly thereafter Santiago surrendered.

Hasty preparations were now made for a descent upon Puerto Rico before the war should end. The American army, commanded by the famed Indian-fighter General Nelson A. Miles, met little resistance, as most of the population greeted the invaders as liberating heroes. "Mr. Dooley" was led to refer to "Gin'ral Miles' Gran' Picnic an' Moonlight Excursion." By this time Spain had satisfied its honor, and on August 12, 1898, it signed an armistice.

If the Spaniards had held out a few months longer in Cuba, the American army might have melted away. The inroads of malaria, typhoid, dysentery, and yellow fever became so severe that hundreds were incapacitated—"an army of convalescents." Others suffered from odorous canned meat known as "embalmed beef." Fiery and

The Cuban Campaign, 1898

insubordinate Colonel Roosevelt, who had no regular military career to jeopardize, was a ringleader in making "round-robin"* demands on Washington that the army be moved before it perished. About twenty-five thousand men, 80 percent of them ill, were transferred to chilly Long Island, where their light summer clothing finally arrived.

One of the war's worst scandals was the high death rate from sickness, especially typhoid fever. This disease was rampant in the unsanitary training camps in the United States. All told, nearly four hundred men lost their lives to bullets; over five thousand succumbed to bacteria and other causes.

McKinley Heeds Duty, Destiny, and Dollars

Late in 1898 the Spanish and American negotiators met in Paris, there to begin heated discussions. McKinley had sent five commissioners, including three senators, who would have a final vote on their own handiwork. War-racked Cuba, as expected, was freed from its Spanish overlords. The Americans had little difficulty in securing the remote Pacific island of Guam, which they had captured early in the conflict from astonished Spaniards who, lacking a cable, had not known that a war was on. They also picked up Puerto Rico, the last remnant of what had been Spain's vast New World empire. In the decades to come, American investment in the island and Puerto Rican immigration to the United States would make this acquisition one of the weightier consequences of this somewhat carefree war (see "Makers of America: The Puerto Ricans," pp. 658–659).

Knottiest of all was the problem of the Philippines, a veritable apple of discord. These lush islands not only embraced an area larger than the British Isles but also contained a completely alien population of some 7 million souls. McKinley was confronted with a devil's dilemma. He did not feel that America could honorably give the islands back to Spanish misrule, especially after it had fought a

Uncle Sam's White Elephant, 1898

war to free Cuba. And America would be turning its back upon its responsibilities in a cowardly fashion, he believed, if it simply pulled up anchor and sailed away.

McKinley viewed other alternatives open to him as trouble-fraught. The Filipinos, if left to govern themselves, might fall into anarchy. One of the major powers, possibly aggressive Germany, might then try to seize them, and the result might be a world war into which the United States would be sucked. Seemingly the least of the evils consistent with national honor and safety was to acquire all the Philippines and then perhaps give the Filipinos their freedom later.

President McKinley, ever sensitive to public opinion, kept a carefully attuned ear to the ground. The rumble that he heard seemed to call for the entire group of islands. Zealous Protestant missionaries were eager for new converts from Spanish Catholicism*; and the invalid Mrs. McKinley, to

---

*A "round robin" is a document signed in circular form around the edges so that no one person can be identified (and punished) as the first signer.

---

*The Philippines had been substantially Christianized by Catholics before the founding of Jamestown in 1607.

whom her husband was devoted, expressed deep concern about the welfare of the Filipinos. Wall Street had generally opposed the war; but awakened by the booming of Dewey's guns, it was clamoring for profits in the Philippines. "If this be commercialism," cried Mark Hanna, then "for God's sake let us have commercialism."

A tormented McKinley, so he was later reported as saying, finally went down on his knees seeking divine guidance. An inner voice seemed to tell him to take all the Philippines and Christianize and civilize them. This solution apparently coincided with the demands of the American people as well as with the McKinley-Hanna outlook. The mixture of things spiritual and material in McKinley's reasoning was later slyly summarized by a historian: "God directs us—perhaps it will pay." Profits thus joined hands with piety.

Fresh disputes broke out with the Spanish negotiators in Paris, once McKinley had reached the thorny decision to keep the Philippines. Manila had been captured the day *after* the armistice was signed, and the islands could not properly be listed among the spoils of war. The deadlock was broken when the Americans at length agreed to pay Spain $20 million for the Philippine Islands—one of the best bargains the Spaniards ever drove and their last great haul from the New World. Ex-Speaker

President William McKinley (1843–1901) later described his decision to annex the Philippines:

"When next I realized that the Philippines had dropped into our laps, I confess I did not know what to do with them. . . . I went down on my knees and prayed Almighty God for light and guidance. . . . And one night late it came to me this way. . . . That there was nothing left for us to do but to take them all, and to educate the Filipinos, and uplift and civilize and Christianize them and by God's grace do the very best we could by them, as our fellow men, for whom Christ also died. And then I went to bed and went to sleep, and slept soundly."

"Czar" Reed sneered at America's having acquired millions of Malays, at three dollars a head, "in the bush."

America's Course (Curse?) of Empire

The signing of the pact of Paris touched off one of the most impassioned debates in American history. Except for glacial Alaska, coral-reefed Hawaii, and a handful of Pacific atolls acquired mostly for whaling stations, the Republic had hitherto acquired only contiguous territory on the continent. All previous acquisitions had been thinly peopled and capable of ultimate statehood. But in the Philippines the nation had on its hands a distant tropical area, thickly populated by Asians of alien race, culture, tongue, religion, and government institutions.

An Anti-Imperialist League sprang into being to fight the McKinley administration's expansionist moves. The organization counted among its members some of the most prominent people in the United States including the presidents of Stanford and Harvard universities, the philosopher William James, and the novelist Mark Twain. The anti-imperialist blanket even stretched over such strange bedfellows as the labor leader Samuel Gompers and steel titan Andrew Carnegie. "God-damn the United States for its vile conduct in the Philippine Isles!" burst out the usually mild-mannered Professor James. The Harvard philosopher could not believe that the United States could "puke up its ancient soul in five minutes without a wink of squeamishness."

Anti-imperialists had still other arrows in their quiver. The Filipinos panted for freedom; and to annex them would violate the "consent of the governed" philosophy in the Declaration of Independence. Despotism abroad might well beget despotism at home. Finally, annexation would propel the United States into the political and military cauldron of the Far East.

Yet the expansionists or imperialists could sing a seductive song. They appealed to patriotism and to the glory of annexation—"don't let any dastard dishonor the flag by hauling it down." Stressing the opportunities for exploiting the islands, they played up possible trade profits. Manila, in fact, might become another Hong Kong. The richer the natural resources of the islands appeared to be, the less capable of self-government the Filipinos seemed to be. Rudyard Kipling, the British poet laureate of imperialism, urged America down the slippery path:

> *Take up the White Man's burden—*
> *Ye dare not stoop to less—*
> *Nor call too loud on Freedom*
> *To cloak your weariness.*

In short, the wealthy Americans must help to uplift (and exploit) the underprivileged, underfed, and underclad of the world.

In the Senate the Spanish treaty ran into such heated opposition that it seemed doomed to defeat. But at this juncture the silverite Bryan unexpectedly sallied forth as its champion. As a Democratic volunteer colonel whom the Republicans had kept out of Cuba, he apparently had no reason to help the McKinley administration out of a hole. But free silver was dead as a political issue. Bryan's foes assumed that he was preparing to fasten the stigma of imperialism on the Republicans and then sweep into the presidency in 1900 under the flaming banner of anti-imperialism.

Bryan could support the treaty on plausible grounds. He argued that the war would not officially end until America had ratified the pact. It already had the islands on its hands, and the sooner it accepted the document, the sooner it could give the Filipinos their independence. After Bryan had used

his personal influence with certain Democratic senators, the treaty was approved, on February 6, 1899, with only one vote to spare. But the responsibility, as Bryan had foreseen, rested primarily with the Republicans.

Perplexities in Puerto Rico and Cuba

Many of Puerto Rico's one million inhabitants lived in poverty. The island's population grew faster than its economy. By the Foraker Act of 1900, Congress accorded the Puerto Ricans a limited degree of popular government and, in 1917, granted them U.S. citizenship. Although the American regime worked wonders in education, sanitation, transportation, and other tangible improvements, many of the inhabitants still aspired to independence. Great numbers of Puerto Ricans ultimately moved to New York City, where they added to the diversity of its immigrant culture.

A thorny legal problem was posed by the question: did the Constitution follow the flag? Did American laws, including tariff laws, apply with full force to the newly acquired possessions, chiefly the Philippines and Puerto Rico? Beginning in 1901 with the *Insular Cases*, a badly divided Supreme Court decreed, in effect, that the flag did outrun the Con-

Uncle Sam: "By Gum, I Rather Like Your Looks," 1900

stitution, and that the outdistanced document did not necessarily extend with full force to the new windfalls. The Congress was therefore left with a free hand to determine the degree of applicability.

Cuba, scorched and chaotic, presented another headache. An American military government, set up under the administrative genius of General Leonard Wood of Rough Rider fame, wrought miracles in government, finance, education, agriculture, and public health. Under his leadership a frontal attack was launched on yellow fever. Spectacular experiments were performed by Dr. Walter Reed and others upon American soldiers, who volunteered as human guinea pigs; and the stegomyia mosquito was proved to be the lethal carrier. A cleanup of breeding places for mosquitoes wiped out yellow fever in Havana, while removing the recurrent fear of epidemics in cities of the South and Atlantic seaboard.

The United States, honoring its self-denying Teller Amendment of 1898, withdrew from Cuba in 1902. Old World imperialists could scarcely believe their eyes. But the Washington government could not turn this rich and strategic island completely loose on the international sea; a grasping power like Germany might secure dangerous lodgment near America's soft underbelly. The Cubans were therefore forced to write into their own constitution of 1901 the so-called Platt Amendment.

The hated restriction severely hobbled the Cubans. They reluctantly bound themselves not to impair their independence by treaty or by contracting a debt beyond their resources. They further agreed that the United States might intervene with troops to restore order and to provide mutual protection. Finally, the Cubans promised to sell or lease needed coaling or naval stations, ultimately two and then only one (Guantanamo), to their powerful "benefactor." The United States still occupies its twenty-eight-thousand acre beachhead under an agreement that can be revoked only by the consent of both parties.

New Horizons in Two Hemispheres

In essence the Spanish-American War was a kind of colossal coming-out party. Despite a common misconception, the conflict did not cause the United States to become a world power. Dewey's thunder-

The New Jingoism   An enthusiastic Uncle Sam cheers the U.S. Navy in the "splendid little war" of 1898. Many Americans, however, were less than enthused about America's new imperial adventure.

ing guns merely advertised the fact that the nation was already a world power.

The war itself was short (113 days), spectacular, low in casualties, and uninterruptedly successful—despite the bungling. American prestige rose sharply, and the European powers grudgingly accorded the Republic more respect. In Germany, Prince Bismarck reportedly growled that there was a special Providence that looked after drunkards, fools, and the United States of America. At times it seemed as though not only Providence but the Spaniards were fighting on the side of the Yankees. So great, in fact, was America's good fortune that rejoicing citizens found in the victories further support—misleading support—for their indifference to adequate preparedness.

An exhilarating new spirit thrilled America. National pride was touched and cockiness was

The Puerto Ricans

At dawn on July 26, 1898, the U.S. warship *Gloucester* steamed into Puerto Rico's Guánica harbor, fired at the Spanish blockhouse, and landed some 3,300 troops. Within days, the Americans had taken possession of the militarily strategic Caribbean island 1,000 miles southeast of Florida. In so doing they set in motion changes on the island that ultimately brought a new wave of immigrants to U.S. shores.

Puerto Rico had been a Spanish possession since Christopher Columbus claimed it for Castile in 1493. The Spaniards enslaved many of the island's 40,000 Taino Indians and set them to work on farms and in mines. Many Tainos died of exhaustion and disease, and in 1511 the Indians rebelled. The Spaniards crushed the uprising, killed thousands of Indians, and began importing African slaves—thus establishing the basis for Puerto Rico's multiracial society.

The first Puerto Rican immigrants to the United States arrived as political exiles in the nineteenth century. From their haven in America, they agitated for the island's independence from Spain. In 1897 Spain finally granted the island local autonomy; ironically, however, the Spanish-American War the following year placed it in American hands. Puerto Rican political émigrés in the United States returned home, but they were soon replaced by poor islanders looking for work.

Changing conditions in Puerto Rico after the U.S. takeover had driven these new immigrants north. Although slow to grant Puerto Ricans U.S. citizenship, the Americans quickly improved health and sanitation on the island, triggering a population surge in the early twentieth century. At the same time, growing monopoly control of Puerto Rico's sugar cane plantations undermined the island's subsistence economy, and a series of hurricanes devastated the coffee plantations that had employed large numbers of people. With almost no industry to provide wage labor, Puerto Rico's unemployment rate soared.

Thus when Congress finally granted Puerto Ricans U.S. citizenship in 1917, thereby eliminating immigration hurdles, many islanders hurried north to find jobs. Over the ensuing decades, Puerto Ricans went to work in Arizona cotton fields, New

The First Puerto Ricans   The Spanish *conquistadores* treated the native Taino Indian peoples in Puerto Rico with extreme cruelty, and the Indians were virtually extinct by the mid-1500s.

Preparing for *Carnaval* (Carnival)   Artist making *máscaras de cartón* (papier-mâché masks) for the annual Puerto Rican festival. Masked figures at *Carnaval* have been part of Puerto Rican tradition for more than two centuries.

Carnaval in New York   Puerto Rican Americans making music in New York City.

Jersey soup factories, and Utah mines. The majority, however, clustered in New York City and found work in the city's cigar factories, shipyards, and garment industry. Migration slowed somewhat after the 1920s as the Great Depression shrank the job market on the mainland and as World War II made travel hazardous.

When World War II ended in 1945, the sudden advent of cheap air travel sparked an immigration explosion. As late as the 1930s, the tab for a boat trip to the mainland exceeded the average Puerto Rican's yearly earnings. But with an airplane surplus after World War II, the six-hour flight from Puerto Rico to New York cost under fifty dollars. The Puerto Rican population on the mainland quadrupled between 1940 and 1950 and tripled again by 1960. In 1970, 1.5 million Puerto Ricans lived in the United States, one-third of the island's total population.

U.S. citizenship and affordable air travel made it easy for Puerto Ricans to return home. Thus to a far greater degree than most immigrant groups, Puerto Ricans kept one foot in the United States and the other on their native island. By some estimates, 2 million people a year journeyed to and from the island during the postwar period. Puerto Rico's gubernatorial candidates sometimes campaigned in New York for the thousands of voters who were expected to return to the island in time for the election.

This transience worked to keep Puerto Ricans' educational attainment and English proficiency far below the national average. At the same time, the immigrants encountered a deep-seated racism in America unlike anything on their multiracial island. Throughout the postwar years, Puerto Ricans remained one of the poorest groups in the United States, with a median family income below that of African-Americans and Mexican-Americans.

Still, Puerto Ricans have fared better economically in the United States than on the island, where, in 1970, 60 percent of all inhabitants lived below the poverty line. In recent years Puerto Ricans have attained more schooling, and many have attended college. Invigorated by the civil rights movement of the 1960s, Puerto Ricans also have become more politically active, electing growing numbers of congressmen and state and city officials.

Three years after the Spanish-American War ended, a foreign diplomat in Washington remarked,

"I have seen two Americas, the America before the Spanish American War and the America since."

increased by what John Hay called a "splendid little war."* Enthusiasm over these triumphs made easier the rush down the thorny path of empire. America did not start the war with imperialistic motives, but after falling through the cellar door of imperialism in a drunken fit of idealism, it wound up with imperialistic and colonial fruits in its grasp. The much-criticized British imperialists were pleased, partly because of the newfound friendship, partly because misery loves company. But America's German rival was envious, and Latin American neighbors were deeply suspicious of Yankee greed.

---

*Anti-imperialist William James called it "our squalid war with Spain."

By taking on the Philippine Islands, the United States became a full-fledged Far Eastern power. Hereafter these distant islands were to be a "heel of Achilles"—a kind of indefensible hostage given to Japan, as events proved in 1941. With singular shortsightedness, the Americans assumed dangerous commitments that they were later unwilling to defend by proper naval and military outlays.

But the lessons of unpreparedness were not altogether lost. Captain Mahan's big-navyism seemed vindicated, and pride in the exploits of the navy energized popular support for more and better battleships. A masterly organizer, Elihu Root, took over the reins at the War Department. He established a general staff and founded the War College in Washington. His genius later paid dividends when the United States found itself involved in the World War of 1914–1918.

One of the happiest results of the conflict was the further closing of the "bloody chasm" between North and South. Thousands of patriotic southerners had flocked to the Stars and Stripes, and the gray-bearded General Joseph ("Fighting Joe") Wheeler—a Confederate cavalry hero of about a thousand Civil War skirmishes and battles—was given a command in Cuba. He allegedly cried, in the heat of battle, "To hell with the Yankees! Dammit, I mean the Spaniards."

Chronology

1820	New England missionaries arrive in Hawaii		1898	*Maine* explosion in Havana harbor Spanish-American War Teller Amendment Dewey's victory at Manila Bay Hawaii annexed
1889	Samoa crisis with Germany Pan-American Conference			
1890	Mahan publishes *The Influence of Sea Power upon History*		1899	Senate ratifies treaty acquiring the Philippines
1891	New Orleans crisis with Italy		1900	Hawaii receives full territorial status Foraker Act for Puerto Rico
1892	Valparaiso crisis with Chile			
1893	Pribilof Islands dispute with Canada White planter revolt in Hawaii Cleveland refuses Hawaii annexation		1901	Supreme Court *Insular Cases* Platt Amendment
1895	Cubans revolt against Spain		1902	U.S. troops leave Cuba
1895-1896	Venezuelan boundary crisis with Britain		1917	Puerto Ricans granted U.S. citizenship

SUGGESTED READINGS

PRIMARY SOURCE DOCUMENTS

Examples of "yellow journalism" include Joseph Pulitzer's New York *World* and William R. Hearst's New York *Journal*. Particularly interesting is the editorial in the *World* of February 13, 1897,* and the article by Charles Duval in the *Journal* of October 10, 1897.* McKinley's War Message,* James D. Richardson, ed., *Messages and Papers of the Presidents* (1899), vol. X, pp. 139ff., outlines the American rationale for intervention. The anti-imperialist answer can be found in Charles E. Norton's article in *Public Opinion*, June 23, 1898, pp. 775–776.*

SECONDARY SOURCES

Main outlines are sketched in Thomas G. Paterson, *American Foreign Policy: A Brief History* (2d ed., 1983). Two general (and quite contrasting) interpretations of modern American foreign policy are George F. Kennan, *American Diplomacy* (1951), and William Appleman Williams, *The Tragedy of American Diplomacy* (1959). Consult also Ernest R. May, *American Imperialism: A Speculative Essay* (1968); and Walter LaFeber, *The New Empire* (1963) and *Inevitable Revolutions* (1983). E. S.

---

*An asterisk indicates that the document, or an excerpt from it, can be found in Thomas A. Bailey and David M. Kennedy, eds., *The American Spirit: United States History as Seen by Contemporaries*, 9th ed. (Boston: Houghton Mifflin, 1998).

Rosenberg's *Spreading the American Dream* (1982) examines U.S. economic and cultural expansion from 1890 to 1945. Thoughtful perceptions can be found in Robert Seager II, *Alfred Thayer Mahan* (1977), and James L. Abrahamson, *America Arms for a New Century* (1981). On the Spanish-American War, see Frank Freidel, *The Splendid Little War* (1958), and David F. Trask, *The War with Spain in 1898* (1981). Fascinating reading is Hyman G. Rickover, *How the Battleship* Maine *Was Destroyed* (1976). Helpful studies of the opponents of expansion are Robert L. Beisner, *Twelve Against Empire: The Anti-Imperialists, 1898–1900* (1968); E. Berkeley Tompkins, *Anti-Imperialism in the United States: The Great Debates, 1890–1920* (1970); and Kendrick A. Clements, *William Jennings Bryan: Missionary Isolationist* (1983). Thomas McCormick sees a design for "informal" imperialism in *The China Market* (1967). David F. Healey examines *The United States in Cuba, 1898–1902* (1963), and Leon Wolff paints a grim picture of American involvement in the Philippines in *Little Brown Brother* (1961). For more on the Philippine imbroglio, see Peter W. Stanley, *A Nation in the Making: The Philippines and the United States, 1899–1921* (1975); H. W. Brands, *Bound to Empire: The United States and the Philippines* (1992); Richard E. Welch, Jr., *Response to Imperialism: The United States and the Philippine-American War, 1899–1902* (1979); Stuart C. Miller, *"Benevolent Assimilation": The American Conquest of the Philippines, 1899–1903* (1982); and Stanley Karnow, *In Our Image: America's Empire in the Philippines* (1989).

PART FIVE

Struggling for Justice
At Home and Abroad

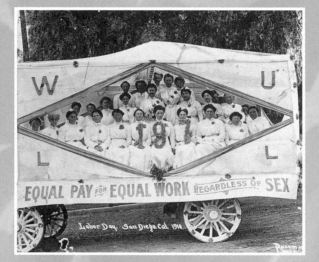

The new century brought astonishing changes to America. Victory in the Spanish-American War made it clear that the United States was now a world power. Industrialization ushered in giant corporations, sprawling factories, sweatshop labor, and the ubiquitous automobile. A huge wave of immigration was altering the face of the nation, especially the cities, where a majority of Americans lived by 1920. With bigger cities came bigger fears—of crime, vice, poverty, and disease.

Changes of such magnitude raised vexing questions. What role should the United States play in the world? How could the enormous power of industry be controlled? How would the millions of new immigrants make their way in America? What should the country do about poverty, disease, and the continuing plague of racial inequality? All these issues turned on a fundamental point: should government remain narrowly limited in its powers, or did the times require a more potent government that would actively shape society and secure American interests abroad?

The progressive movement represented the first attempt to answer those questions. Reform-minded men and women from all walks of life and from both major parties shared in the progressive crusade for greater government activism. Buoyed by this outlook, Presidents Theodore Roosevelt, William Howard Taft, and Woodrow Wilson enlarged the capacity of government to fight graft, "bust" business trusts, regulate corporations, and promote fair labor practices, child welfare, conservation, and consumer protection. Progressive reformers, convinced that women would bring greater morality to politics, bolstered the decades-long struggle for female suffrage. Women finally secured the vote in 1920 with the ratification of the Nineteenth Amendment.

Progressive era presidents also challenged America's tradition of isolationism in foreign policy.

Labor Day Parade Wagon, 1910
Reformers fought on many fronts in the Progressive Era. These San Diego trade unionists demanded government protection for women workers.

They felt the country had a moral obligation to spread democracy and an economic opportunity to reap profits in foreign markets. Roosevelt and Taft launched diplomatic initiatives in the Caribbean, Central America, and East Asia. Wilson aspired to "make the world safe for democracy" by rallying support for American intervention in the First World War.

The progressive spirit waned, however, as the United States retreated during the 1920s into what President Harding called "normalcy." Isolationist sentiment revived with a vengeance. Blessed with a booming economy, Americans turned their gaze inward to baseball heroes, radio, jazz, movies, and the first mass-produced American automobile, the Model T Ford. Presidents Harding, Coolidge, and Hoover backed off from the economic regulatory zeal of their predecessors.

"Normalcy" also had a brutal side. Thousands of suspected radicals were jailed or deported in the Red Scare of 1919 and 1920. Anti-immigrant passions flared until immigration quotas in 1924 squeezed the flow of newcomers to a trickle. Race riots scorched several northern cities in the summer of 1919, a sign of how embittered race relations had become in the wake of the "great migration" of southern blacks to wartime jobs in northern industry. A reborn Ku Klux Klan staged a comeback, not just in the South but in the North and West as well.

"Normalcy" itself soon proved short-lived, a casualty of the stock market crash of 1929 and the Great Depression that followed. As Americans watched banks fail, businesses collapse, and millions

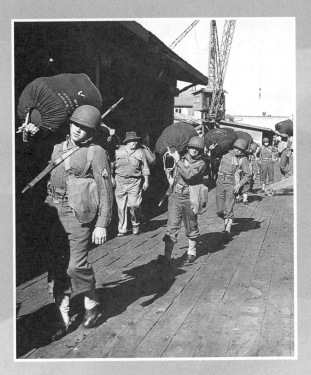

of people lose their jobs, they asked with renewed urgency what role the government should play in rescuing the nation. President Franklin D. Roosevelt's answer was the "New Deal"—an ambitious array of relief programs, public works, and economic regulations that failed to cure the Depression but furnished an impressive legacy of social reforms.

Most Americans came to accept an expanded federal governmental role at home under FDR's leadership in the 1930s, but they still clung stubbornly to isolationism. The United States did little in the 1930s to check the rising military aggression of Japan and Germany. By the early 1940s events forced Americans to reconsider. Once Hitler's Germany had seized control of most of Europe, Roosevelt, who had long opposed the isolationists, found ways to aid a beleaguered Britain. When Japan attacked the American naval base at Pearl Harbor in December 1941, isolationists at last fell silent. Roosevelt led a stunned but determined nation into the Second World War, and victory in 1945 positioned the United States to assume a commanding position in the postwar world order.

The Great Depression and the Second World War brought to a head a half century of debate over the role of government and the place of the United States in the world. In the name of a struggle for justice, FDR established a new era of government activism at home and internationalism abroad. The New Deal's legacy set the terms of debate in American political life for the rest of the century.

Bound for Guadalcanal, 1942
These troops were headed for one of the bloodiest battles of World War II, in the southwest Pacific's Solomon Islands. America threw some fifteen million men and the full weight of its enormous economy into the struggle against German and Japanese aggression.

30

America on the World Stage

1899–1909

---

*I never take a step in foreign policy unless I am
assured that I shall be able eventually to carry
out my will by force.*

THEODORE ROOSEVELT, 1905

"Little Brown Brothers" in the Philippines

Unhappily, the liberty-loving Filipinos were tragically deceived. They had assumed that they, like the Cubans, would be granted their freedom after the war. A clear-cut pledge by Congress to this effect probably would have averted the sorry sequel, but the Senate by the narrowest of margins refused to pass such a resolution. Bitterness toward the American troops continued to mount and finally erupted into open insurrection on February 4, 1899, under Emilio Aguinaldo.

The war with the Filipinos, unlike the "splendid" little set-to with Spain, was sordid and prolonged. It involved more savage fighting, more soldiers killed, and far more scandal. Anti-imperialists redoubled their protests. In their view the United States, having

plunged into war with Spain to free Cuba, was now fighting 10,000 miles (16,000 kilometers) away to rivet shackles on a people who asked for nothing but liberty—in the American tradition.

As the ill-equipped Filipino armies were defeated, they melted into the jungle to wage vicious guerrilla warfare. Many of the outgunned Filipinos used barbarous methods, and the infuriated American troops responded in kind. A brutal soldier song betrayed inner feelings:

> *Damn, damn, damn the Filipinos!*
> *Cross-eyed kakiak ladrones* [*thieves*]*!*
> *Underneath the starry flag*
> *Civilize 'em with a Krag* [*rifle*]*,*
> *And return us to our own beloved homes.*

Atrocity tales shocked and rocked the United States, for such methods did not reflect America's better self. Uncle Sam's soldiers resorted to such

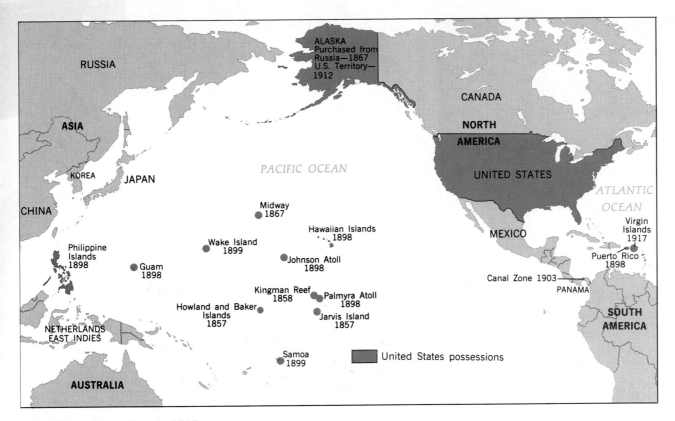

United States Possessions to 1917

extremes as the painful "water cure"—that is, forcing water down victims' throats until they yielded information or died. Reconcentration camps were even established that strongly suggested those of "Butcher" Weyler in Cuba. America, having begun the Spanish war with noble ideals, now dirtied its hands. One New York newspaper published a reply to Rudyard Kipling's famous poem:

> *We've taken up the white man's burden*
> *Of ebony and brown;*
> *Now will you kindly tell us, Rudyard,*
> *How we may put it down?*

The backbone of the Filipino insurrection was finally broken in 1901, when American soldiers cleverly infiltrated a guerrilla camp and captured Aguinaldo. But sporadic fighting dragged on for many dreary months.

The problem of a government for the conquered islanders worried President McKinley, who, in 1899, appointed a Philippine Commission to make appropriate recommendations. In its second year, this body was headed by future president William H. Taft, an able and amiable lawyer-judge from Ohio who weighed about 350 pounds (159 kilograms). Forming a strong attachment for the Filipinos, he called them his "little brown brothers" and danced light-footedly with their tiny women. But among the American soldiers, sweatily combing the jungles, a different view of the insurgent prevailed:

> *He may be a brother of Big Bill Taft,*
> *But he ain't no brother of mine.*

McKinley's "benevolent assimilation" of the Philippines proceeded with painful slowness. Millions of American dollars were poured into the islands to improve roads, sanitation, and public health. Important economic ties, including trade in sugar, developed between the two peoples. American teachers—"pioneers of the blackboard"—set up an unusually good school system and helped make English a second language. But all this vast expenditure, which profited America little, was ill received. The Filipinos, who hated compulsory American-

Captured Filipino Insurrectionists, c. 1899   For three years after its annexation of the Philippine Islands in 1898, the United States fought a savage war to suppress a Filipino rebellion against American rule. Some 600,000 Filipinos perished. There was bitter irony in this clash, as the Americans had claimed to be "liberating" the Filipinos from their oppressive Spanish masters; now the Yankee liberators appeared to be no less oppressive than the Spaniards they had ousted.

A growing group of Americans viewed the vivisection of China with alarm. Churches worried about their missionary strongholds; manufacturers and exporters feared that Chinese markets would be monopolized by Europeans. An alarmed American public, openly prodded by the press and slyly nudged by certain free-trade Britons, demanded that Washington do something. Secretary of State John Hay, a quiet but witty poet-novelist-diplomat with a flair for capturing the popular imagination, finally decided upon a dramatic move.

In the summer of 1899, Hay dispatched to all the great powers a communication soon known as the Open Door note. He urged them to announce that in their leaseholds or spheres of influence they would respect certain Chinese rights and the ideal of fair competition. In short, in their dealings with foreign traders the intruding powers would observe the Open Door. The principle was not new, for America had tried repeatedly to make it the basis of its commercial dealings with China in the nineteenth century. But the phrase *Open Door* quickly caught the public fancy and gained wide acceptance.

Hay's proposal of this self-denying policy caused much squirming in the leading capitals of the world. It was like asking all those who did not have thieving designs to stand up and be counted. Italy alone accepted the Open Door unconditionally; it was the only major power that had no lease-

izaiton, preferred liberty. Like caged hawks, they beat against their gilded bars until they finally got their freedom, on the Fourth of July, 1946. In the meantime, thousands of Filipinos emigrated to the United States (see "Makers of America: The Filipinos," pp. 668–669).

John Hay Defends China (and U.S. Interests)

Exciting events had meanwhile been brewing in faraway and enfeebled China. Following its defeat by Japan in 1894–1895, the imperialistic European powers, notably Russia and Germany, moved in. Like vultures descending upon a wounded whale, they began to tear away valuable leaseholds and economic spheres of influence from the Manchu government.

The commercial interests of both Britain and America were imperiled by the power grabs in China, and a close concert between the two powers would have helped both. Yet as Secretary of State John Hay (1838–1905) wrote privately in June 1900,

"Every Senator I see says, 'For God's sake, don't let it appear we have any understanding with England.' How can I make bricks without straw? That we should be compelled to refuse the assistance of the greatest power in the world [Britain], in carrying out our own policy, because all Irishmen are Democrats and some [American] Germans are fools—is enough to drive a man mad."

American Missionary Grace Roberts Teaching in China, 1903   A long history of American missionary involvement in China nurtured a sentimental affection for that country among Americans that persisted well into the twentieth century.

hold or sphere of influence in China. Britain, Germany, France, and Japan all accepted, but subject to the condition that the others acquiesce unconditionally. Russia, with covetous designs on China's Manchuria, in effect politely declined. But John Hay, rather than run the risk of flat rejection, artfully interpreted the Russian refusal as an acceptance and proclaimed that the Open Door was in effect. Under such dubious midwifery was the infant born, and no one should have been surprised when the child proved to be sickly and relatively short-lived.

Hinging the Open Door in China

Open Door or not, patriotic Chinese did not care to be used as a doormat by the Europeans. In 1900 a superpatriotic group known as the "Boxers" broke loose with the cry, "Kill Foreign Devils." Over two hundred missionaries and other ill-fated whites were murdered, and a number of foreign diplomats were besieged in the capital, Beijing (Peking).

A rescue force of some eighteen thousand soldiers, hastily assembled, arrived in the nick of time and quelled the rebellion. This multinational contingent consisted of Japanese, Russian, British, French, German, and American troops, with the American contribution some twenty-five hundred men. Such participation in a joint military operation, especially in Asia, was plainly contrary to the nation's time-honored principles of nonentanglement and noninvolvement. But America had not been a Far Eastern power in the days of the Founding Fathers.

The victorious allied invaders acted angrily and vindictively. They assessed prostrate China an excessive indemnity of $333 million, of which America's share was to be $24.5 million. When Washington discovered that this sum was much more than enough to pay damages and expenses, it remitted about $18 million. The Beijing government, appreciating this gesture of goodwill, set aside the money to educate a selected group of Chinese students in the United States. These bright young scholars later played a significant role in the westernization of Asia.

Secretary Hay now let fly another paper broadside, for he feared that the triumphant powers might use the Boxer outrages as a pretext for carving up China outright. His new circular note to the powers in 1900 announced that henceforth the Open Door would embrace the territorial integrity of China, in addition to its commercial integrity. Hay,

The Filipinos

At the beginning of the twentieth century, the United States, its imperial muscles just flexed in the war with Spain, found itself in possession of the Philippines. Uncertain of how to manage this empire, which seethed resentfully against its new masters, the United States promised to build democracy in the Philippines and to ready the islanders for home rule. Almost immediately after annexation, the American governor of the archipelago sent a corps of Filipino students to the United States, hoping to forge future leaders steeped in American

Filipino Laborers at Work on a Hawaiian Pineapple Plantation, 1930s

ways who would someday govern an independent Philippines. Yet this small student group found little favor in their adopted country, although in their native land many went on to become respected citizens and leaders.

Most Filipino immigrants to the United States in these years, however, came not to study but to toil. With Chinese immigration banned, Hawaii and the Pacific coast states turned to the Philippines for cheap agricultural labor. Beginning in 1906, the Hawaiian Sugar Planters Association aggressively recruited Filipino workers. Enlistments grew slowly at first, but by the 1920s thousands of young Filipino men had reached the Hawaiian Islands and been assigned to sugar plantations or pineapple fields.

Typically, a young Filipino wishing to emigrate first made his way to Manila, where he signed a contract with the growers that promised three years' labor in return for transportation to Hawaii, wages, free housing and fuel, and return passage at the end of the contract. Not all of the emigrants returned; there remain in Hawaii today some former field workers still theoretically eligible for free transport back to their native land.

Those Filipinos venturing as far as the American mainland found work less arduous but also less certain than did their countrymen on Hawaiian plantations. Many mainlanders worked seasonally—in winter as domestic servants, busboys, or bellhops; in summer journeying to the fields to harvest lettuce, strawberries, sugar beets, and potatoes. Eventually, Filipinos, along with Mexican immigrants, shared the dubious honor of making up California's agricultural work force.

A mobile society, Filipino America was also overwhelmingly male; there was only one Filipino woman for every fourteen Filipino men in California in 1930. Thus the issue of intermarriage became acutely sensitive. California and many other states prohibited the marriage of Asians and Caucasians in demeaning laws that remained on the books until 1948. And if a Filipino so much as approached a Caucasian woman, he could expect reprisals—sometimes violent. For example, white vigilante groups roamed the Yakima Valley in Washington and the San Joaquin and Salinas Valleys in California, intimidating and even attacking Filipinos whom they accused of improperly accosting white women. In 1930 one Filipino was murdered and others wounded after they invited some Caucasian women to a dance. Undeterred, the Filipinos challenged the restrictive state laws and the hooligans who found in them an excuse for mayhem. But Filipinos, who did not become eligible for American citizenship until 1946, long lacked political leverage.

After World War II, Filipino immigration accelerated. Between 1950 and 1970, the number of Filipinos in the United States nearly doubled, with women and men stepping aboard the new transpacific airliners in roughly equal numbers. Many of these recent arrivals sprang from sturdy middle-class stock and sought in America a better life for their children than the Philippines seemed able to offer. Today the war-torn and perpetually depressed archipelago sends more immigrants to American shores than does any other Asian nation.

Filipino Workers Arriving in Honolulu, 1940s Tags around their necks indicated the plantations to which they had been assigned.

A Filipino Day Parade, New York City

The Boxer Rebellion, 1900   Chinese nationalists, known as "Boxers," rose up against foreign domination of China in 1900. This map illustrates the Boxers' resentment against Russian, British, Japanese, and American incursions in China. Note the Russian bear and the American eagle.

remembering his previous rebuff, did not ask for formal acceptances this time.

Defenseless China was spared partition during these troubled years. But its salvation was probably not due to Hay's fine phrases, which the American people were reluctant to back up with muscle. China owed its preservation far more to the strength of the competing powers; none of them could trust the others not to try to gain an advantage.

Kicking "Teddy" Roosevelt Upstairs

President McKinley's renomination by the Republicans in 1900 was a foregone conclusion. He had piloted the country through a victorious war; he had

acquired rich, though burdensome, real estate; he had established the gold standard; and he had brought the promised prosperity of the full dinner pail. "We'll stand pat!" was the poker-playing counsel of Mark Hanna, since 1897 a senator from Ohio. McKinley was renominated at Philadelphia on a platform that smugly endorsed prosperity, the gold standard, and overseas expansion.

An irresistible vice-presidential boom had developed for "Teddy" Roosevelt (TR), the cowboy-hero of San Juan Hill. Capitalizing on his war-born popularity, he had been elected governor of New York, where the local political bosses had found him headstrong and difficult to manage. They therefore devised a scheme to kick the colorful colonel upstairs into the vice presidency.

This plot to railroad Roosevelt worked beautifully. Gesticulating wildly, he attended the nominating convention, where his western-style cowboy hat had made him stand out like a white crow. He had no desire to die of slow rot in the vice-presidential "burying ground," but he was eager to prove that he could get the nomination if he wanted it. He finally gave in when, to a chanting chorus of "We want Teddy!" he received a unanimous vote, except for his own. A frantic Hanna reportedly moaned that there would be only one heartbeat between that wild-eyed "madman"—"that damned cowboy"—and the presidency of the United States.

William Jennings Bryan was the odds-on choice of the Democrats, meeting at Kansas City. The free-silver issue was now as defunct as an abandoned mine, but Bryan, a slave to consistency, forced a silver plank down the throats of his protesting associates. Choking on its candidate's obstinacy, the Democratic platform proclaimed, as did Bryan, that the paramount issue was Republican overseas imperialism.

Imperialism or Bryanism in 1900?

Campaign history partially repeated itself in 1900. McKinley, the soul of dignity, sat safely on his front porch, as before. Bryan, also as before, took to the stump in a cyclonic campaign, assailing both imperialism and Republican-fostered trusts.

The superenergetic, second-fiddle Roosevelt out-Bryaned Bryan. He toured the country with revolver-shooting cowboys, and his popularity cut heavily into Bryan's support in the Midwest. Flashing his magnificent teeth and pounding his fist fiercely into his palm, Roosevelt denounced all dastards who would haul down Old Glory.

Bryanites loudly trumpeted their "paramount" issue of imperialism. Lincoln, they charged, had abolished slavery for 3.5 million Africans; McKinley had reestablished it for 7 million Malayans. But the question of imperialism was actually stale; it had been agitating the novelty-loving American people for more than two years. The Republic had the Philippines on its hands anyhow, and the real question was not "Should it keep them?" but "What should it do with them in the future?" Besides, anti-imperialists like Bryan were merely encouraging the Filipinos to resist.

Republicans responded by charging that "Bryanism," not imperialism, was the paramount issue. By this accusation they meant that Bryan would rock the boat of prosperity, once he got into office with his free-silver lunacy and other dangerous ideas. The voters were much less concerned about imperialism than about "Four Years More of the Full Dinner Pail" and "Let Well Enough Alone." Prosperity at home seemed more important than freedom abroad. When the smoke cleared, McKinley had triumphed by a much wider margin than in 1896; 7,218,491 to 6,356,734 popular votes, and 292 to 155 electoral votes.

Victory for the Republicans was not a mandate for or against imperialism, legend to the contrary. The confused voters were not asked to decide this issue but, basically, to select either McKinley or Bryan. Many citizens who favored Bryan's anti-imperialism feared his free silver; many who favored McKinley's "sound money" hated his imperialism. One citizen wrote to ex-president Cleveland: "It is a choice between evils, and I am going to shut my eyes, hold my nose, vote, go home and disinfect myself." If there was any mandate at all it was for the two *P*s: prosperity and protection. Content with good times, the country anticipated four more years of a full dinner pail crammed with fried chicken. "Boss" Platt of New York gleefully looked forward to Inauguration Day, when he would see Roosevelt exit Albany and "take the veil" as vice president.

TR: Brandisher of the Big Stick

Kindly William McKinley had scarcely served another six months when, in September 1901, he was murdered by a deranged anarchist. Roosevelt became president at age forty-two, the youngest thus far in American history. Knowing he had a reputation for impulsiveness and radicalism, he sought to reassure the country by proclaiming that he would carry out the policies of his predecessor. Cynics sneered that he would indeed carry them out—to the garbage heap.

What manner of man was Theodore Roosevelt, the red-blooded blue blood? Born into a wealthy and distinguished New York family, he had fiercely built up his spindly, asthmatic body by a stern and self-imposed routine of exercise. Graduating from Harvard with Phi Beta Kappa honors, he published at the age of twenty-four the first of some thirty volumes of muscular prose. Then came busy years, which involved duties as a ranch owner and bespectacled cowboy ("Four Eyes") in the Dakotas, followed by various political posts. When fully developed, he was a barrel-chested 5 feet, 10 inches (1.76 meters), with prominent teeth, squinty eyes, droopy mustache, and piercing voice.

A Too-Continuous Performance By the election of 1900, William Jennings Bryan's promotion of free-silver was a stale—and largely irrelevant—act.

A TOO-CONTINUOUS PERFORMANCE

The Rough Rider's high-voltage energy was electrifying. Believing that it was better to wear out than to rust out, he would shake the hands of some six thousand people at one stretch or ride horseback many miles in a day as an example for portly cavalry officers. Not surprisingly, he gathered about him a group of athletic, tennis-playing cronies, who were popularly dubbed "the tennis cabinet."

Incurably boyish and bellicose, Roosevelt loved to fight—"an elegant row." He never ceased to preach the virile virtues and to denounce civilized softness, with its pacifists and other "flubdubs" and "mollycoddles." An ardent champion of military and naval preparedness, he adopted as his pet proverb, "Speak softly and carry a big stick, [and] you will go far." If statesmen had the big stick, they could work their will among foreign nations without shouting; if they lacked it, shouting would do no good. TR had both a big stick and a shrill voice.

Wherever Roosevelt went, there was a great stir. At a wedding he eclipsed the bride; at a funeral, the corpse. Shockingly unconventional, he loved to break hoary precedents—the hoarier the better. He was a colossal egoist, and his self-confidence merged with self-righteousness. So sure was he of the correctness of his convictions that he impetuously branded people liars who disagreed with him. As a true cosmopolite, he loved people and mingled with those of all ranks, from Catholic cardinals to professional prizefighters, one of whom blinded a Rooseveltian eye in a White House bout.

An outspoken moralizer and reformer, Roosevelt preached virtue from the White House pulpit. Yet he was an opportunist who would cut a deal rather than butt his head against a stone wall. He was, in reality, much less radical than his blustery actions would indicate. A middle-of-the-roader, he stood just a little left of center and bared his mulelike molars at liberals and reactionaries alike.

Roosevelt rapidly developed into a master politician with an idolatrous personal following. After visiting him, a journalist wrote, "You go home and wring the personality out of your clothes." TR—as he was called—had an enormous popular appeal, partly because the common people saw in him a fiery champion. A magnificent showman, he was always front-page copy; and his cowboyism, his bear shooting, his outsize teeth, and his pincenez glasses were ever the delight of cartoonists. Though a staunch party man, he detested many of the dirty-handed bosses; but he learned, as Cleve-

Theodore Roosevelt   Roosevelt gives a speech with both voice and body language in North Carolina in 1902.

land never did, to hold his nose and work with them.

Above all, Roosevelt was a direct-actionist. He believed that the president should lead; and although he made mistakes, he kept things noisily moving—generally forward. Never a lawyer, he condemned the law and the courts as too slow. He had no real respect for the delicate checks and balances among the three branches of the government. Finding the Constitution too rigid, he would on occasion ignore it; finding Congress too rebellious, he tried a mixture of coercion and compromise on it. The president, he felt, may take any action in the general interest that is not specifically forbidden by the laws of the Constitution. As one poet noted,

The Constitution rides behind
And the Big Stick rides before,
(Which is the rule of precedent
In the reign of Theodore.)

Colombia Blocks the Canal

Foreign affairs absorbed much of Roosevelt's bullish energy. Having traveled extensively in Europe, he enjoyed a far more intimate knowledge of the outside world than most of his predecessors.

The Spanish-American War had emphasized the need for the long-talked-about canal across the Central American isthmus, through which only printer's ink had ever flowed. Americans had learned a sobering lesson when the battleship *Oregon,* stationed on the Pacific Coast at the outbreak of war in 1898, had to steam all the way around South America to join the fleet in Cuban waters. Alarmists speculated on what might have happened if it had not arrived in time for the Battle of Santiago and if the Spanish fleet had been stronger. An isthmian canal would plainly augment the strength of the navy by increasing its mobility. Such a waterway would also make easier the defense of such recent acquisitions as Puerto Rico, Hawaii, and the Philippines, while facilitating the operations of the American merchant marine.

Initial obstacles in the path of the canal builders were legal rather than geographical. By the terms of the ancient Clayton-Bulwer Treaty, concluded with Britain in 1850, the United States could not secure exclusive control over such a route. But by 1901 America's British cousins were willing to yield ground. Confronted with an unfriendly Europe and bogged down in the South African Boer War, they consented to the Hay-Pauncefote Treaty in 1901. It not only gave the United States a free hand to build the canal but conceded the right to fortify it as well.

Legal barriers now removed, the next question was, Where should the canal be dug? Many American experts favored the Nicaraguan route, but agents of the old French Canal Company were eager to salvage something from their costly failure at S-shaped Panama. Represented by a young, energetic, and unscrupulous engineer, Philippe Bunau-Varilla, the New Panama Canal Company suddenly dropped the price of its holdings from $109 million to the fire-sale price of $40 million.

The Nicaragua-versus-Panama issue was hotly debated in Congress, where a serious objection to Nicaragua was its volcanic activity. Providentially for Bunau-Varilla, Mount Pelée, on the West Indian island of Martinique, blew its top in May 1902 and wiped out some thirty thousand people. The clever Frenchman hastily secured ninety Nicaraguan postage stamps, each bearing a picture of the country's most fearsome volcano, and sent one to each senator. Hanna delivered a persuasive Senate speech, in which he stressed the engineering advantages of the Panama route. In June 1902 Congress finally accepted his views.

The scene now shifted to Colombia, of which Panama was an unwilling part. A treaty highly favorable to the United States was negotiated in Washington with the agent of the Colombian government in Bogota. It granted the lease of a 6-mile-wide (9.66-kilometer) zone in perpetuity, in return for $10 million and an annual payment of $250,000. But when the pact was submitted to the Bogota Senate, it was unanimously rejected. The isthmian strip was regarded as one of Colombia's most valuable natural assets, and many Colombians felt short-changed by the small purse. Evidence later unearthed indicates that if Washington had been willing to pay an additional $15 million, the pact would have been approved.

Roosevelt was infuriated by his setback at the hands of what he called "those dagoes." Frantically eager to be elected president "in his own right" in 1904, he was anxious to "make the dirt fly" to impress the voters. "Damn the law," he reportedly cried in private, "I want the canal built!" He assailed "the blackmailers of Bogota" who, like armed highwaymen, were blocking the onward march of civilization. He failed to note that the United States Senate also rejects treaties.

Uncle Sam Creates
Puppet Panama

Impatient Panamanians, who had rebelled numerous times, were ripe for another revolt. They had counted on a wave of prosperity to follow construction of the canal, and they feared that the United States would now turn to the Nicaraguan route. Scheming Bunau-Varilla was no less disturbed by the prospect of losing the company's $40 million. Working hand in glove with the Panama revolutionists, he raised a tiny "patriot" army consisting largely of members of the Panamanian fire department, plus five hundred "bought" Colombian troops—for a reported price of $100,000.

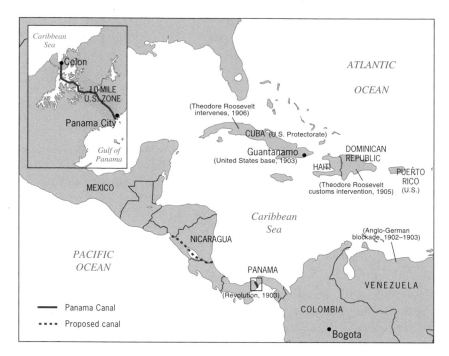

Big Stick in the Caribbean
In 1901 Roosevelt declared, "If a man continually blusters . . . a big stick will not save him from trouble; and neither will speaking softly avail, if back of the softness there does not lie strength, power. . . . If the boaster is not prepared to back up his words, his position becomes absolutely contemptible."

The Panama revolution occurred on November 3, 1903, with the incidental killing of a Chinese civilian and a donkey. Colombian troops were gathered to crush the uprising, but U.S. naval forces would not let them cross the isthmus. Roosevelt justified this highly questionable interference by a strained interpretation of the treaty of 1846 with Colombia. (This pact obligated Washington to maintain the "perfect neutrality" of the isthmus, obviously against outsiders.)

Roosevelt moved rapidly to make steamy Panama a virtual outpost of the United States. Three days after the uprising, he hastily extended the right hand of recognition. Fifteen days later, Bunau-Varilla, who was now the Panamanian minister despite his French citizenship, signed the Hay–Bunau-Varilla treaty in Washington. The price of the canal strip was left the same, but the zone was widened from 6 to 10 miles (9.66 to 16 kilometers). The French company gladly pocketed its $40 million from the U.S. Treasury.

Roosevelt, it seems clear, did not actively plot to tear Panama from the side of Colombia. But the conspirators knew of his angrily expressed views, and they counted on his using the big stick to hold Colombia at bay. Yet the Rough Rider became so indiscreetly involved in the Panama affair as to

Roosevelt in Panama   When he visited the Panama Canal construction site in 1906 to see "the dirt fly," Roosevelt was the first president to leave the United States for foreign soil.

create the impression that he had been a secret party to the intrigue.

Unhappily, the United States suffered a black eye as a result of Roosevelt's "cowboy diplomacy." European imperialists, who were old hands at this sort of thing, could now raise their eyebrows in scorn at America's superior moral pretensions—and they did.

Completing the Canal and Appeasing Colombia

The so-called rape of Panama marked an ugly downward lurch in U.S. relations with Latin America. Much fear had already been aroused by the recent seizure of Puerto Rico and by the Yankee stranglehold on Cuba. The fate of Colombia, when it dared defy the Colossus of the North, indicated that its weak fellow republics were not safe. The era of the bullying "Big Brother" policy was brazenly launched.

Roosevelt heatedly defended himself against all charges of evildoing. He claimed that he had received a "mandate from civilization" to start the canal and that Colombia had wronged the United States by not permitting itself to be benefited. To deal with these "blackmailers," he insisted, was like "nailing currant jelly to the wall."

But TR was not completely candid. He failed to point out that the Nicaragua route was about equally feasible and that it was available without a revolution. Yet this alternative would have involved some delay, and the presidential election of 1904 was fast approaching.

Active work was begun on "making the dirt fly" in 1904, but grave difficulties were encountered, ranging from labor troubles to landslides. The organization was finally perfected under an energetic but autocratic West Point engineer, Colonel George Washington Goethals. At the outset, sanitation proved to be more important than excavation. Colonel William C. Gorgas, the quiet and determined exterminator of yellow fever in Havana, ultimately made the Canal Zone "as safe as a health resort."

Americans finally succeeded where the French had failed. In 1914 the colossal canal project was completed at an initial cost of about $400 million,

> *In 1911 Theodore Roosevelt (1858–1919) made a costly boast in a speech in Berkeley, California:*
>
> "I am interested in the Panama Canal because I started it. If I had followed traditional, conservative methods I would have presented a dignified state paper . . . to Congress and the debates on it would have been going on yet; but I took the Canal Zone and let Congress debate; and while the debate goes on the Canal does also."

just as World War I was breaking out. The whole enterprise, in the words of the English writer James Bryce, was "the greatest liberty Man has ever taken with Nature."

TR's Perversion of Monroe's Doctrine

Latin American debt defaults created the conditions for further Rooseveltian involvement in affairs south of the border. Nations such as Venezuela and the Dominican Republic were chronically in arrears in their payments to European creditors, particularly Britain and Germany. Seeking to force payment, German warships sank two Venezuelan gunboats and bombarded a town in early 1903.

This ironfisted intervention aroused Roosevelt. He feared that if the Germans or British got their foot in the door as bill collectors, they might remain in Latin America, in flagrant violation of the Monroe Doctrine. Roosevelt therefore devised a devious policy of "preventive intervention," better known as the Roosevelt Corollary to the Monroe Doctrine. He declared that in the event of future financial malfeasance by the Latin American nations, the United States itself would intervene, take over the customshouses, pay off the debts, and keep the troublesome powers on the other side of the Atlantic. The United States had a moral obligation to do so, Roosevelt argued, because it would not permit the European nations themselves to intervene in the bankrupt banana republics. In short, no outsiders could push around the Latin nations except Uncle Sam, Policeman of the Caribbean.

This new brandishing of the big stick in the Caribbean became effective in 1905, when the United States took over the management of tariff collections in the Dominican Republic, an arrangement formalized in a treaty with the Dominicans two years later. Dominican officials, who had raked in much juicy graft, were not happy with such interference, and they acquiesced only after some strenuous arm-twisting from Washington. But from a debt-collecting point of view, the customshouse intervention was a success.

Roosevelt's corollary, though tacked onto the Monroe Doctrine, bore only a strained relation to the original dictum of 1823. Monroe had in effect said to the European powers, "Thou shalt not intervene." TR changed this warning to mean, "We shall intervene to prevent you from intervening." The Roosevelt doctrine was actually so radical as to be a completely new policy, but it gained readier acceptance by being associated with the honored name of Monroe. Yet in its own right the corollary had considerable merit as a preemptive stroke.

Roosevelt's rewriting of Monroe's doctrine had its dark side. It probably did more than any other single step to promote the "Bad Neighbor" policy begun in these years. As time wore on, the new corollary was used to justify wholesale interventions and repeated landings of the marines, all of which helped turn the Caribbean into a "Yankee lake." Latin Americans mistakenly cursed the unoffending

Roosevelt wrote to a correspondent in February 1904:

"I have been hoping and praying for three months that the Santo Domingans would behave so that I would not have to act in any way. I want to do nothing but what a policeman has to do. . . . As for annexing the island, I have about the same desire to annex it as a gorged boa-constrictor might have to swallow a porcupine wrong-end-to."

Monroe, when they should have cursed the offending Roosevelt. To them it seemed as though the Monroe Doctrine, far from providing a shield, was a cloak behind which the United States sought to strangle them.

The shadow of the big stick likewise fell on Cuba in 1906. Revolutionary disorders brought an appeal from the Cuban president, and "necessity being the mother of invention," U.S. Marines were landed. These police forces were withdrawn temporarily in 1909, but in Latin American eyes the episode was but another example of the creeping power of the Colossus of the North.

Uncle Sam Gets Cocky, 1901 American policy toward Latin America grew more assertive, even aggressive, around the turn of the century, alarming both Latin Americans and Europeans. In this cartoon, the European chickens complain to a giant Uncle Sam that "you're not the only rooster in South America," to which he replies, "I was aware of that when I cooped you up!" (with the Monroe Doctrine). The Latin American republics themselves, meanwhile, are dwarfed by the American rooster.

Theodore Roosevelt and His Big Stick in the Caribbean, 1904 Roosevelt's policies seemed to be turning the Caribbean into a Yankee pond.

Roosevelt on the World Stage

Booted and spurred, Roosevelt charged into international affairs far beyond Latin America. The outbreak of war between Russia and Japan in 1904 gave him a chance to perform as a global statesman. The Russian bear, having lumbered across Asia, was seeking to bathe its frostbitten paws in the ice-free ports of China's Manchuria, particularly Port Arthur. In Japanese eyes, Manchuria and Korea in tsarist hands were pistols pointed at Japan's strategic heart. Russian troops had invaded Manchuria during the Boxer outburst of 1900 and, despite solemn promises, were not withdrawing. The tsar was obviously stalling until his trans-Siberian railroad could be finished, as it would be in a few months. With the clock ticking against them, the Japanese suddenly began war in 1904 with a devastating surprise pounce on the Russian fleet at Port Arthur. They proceeded to administer a humiliating series of beatings to the inept Russians—the first serious military setback to a European power by a non-European force since the Turkish invasions of the sixteenth century. But as the war dragged on, Japan began to run short of men and yen—a weakness it did not want to betray to the enemy. Tokyo officials therefore approached Roosevelt in the deepest secrecy and asked him to help sponsor peace negotiations.

Roosevelt agreed and shepherded the delegates of the two sides together at Portsmouth, New Hampshire, in 1905. The Japanese presented stern demands for a huge indemnity and the entire strategic island of Sakhalin, while the Russians stubbornly refused to admit the depths of their defeat. Blustering at both sides behind the scenes, Roosevelt forced through an accord in which the Japanese received no indemnity for the losses and only the southern half of Sakhalin.

For achieving this agreement, as well as for helping arrange an international conference at Algeciras, Spain, in 1906 to mediate North African disputes, Roosevelt received the Nobel Peace Prize in 1906. But the price of TR's diplomatic glory was

Roosevelt at Portsmouth Conference Roosevelt meets with the two Russian and two Japanese delegates in 1905. Roosevelt wrote that dealing with U.S. senators was a tough job, but dealing with these peace envoys was even tougher. He had to be "polite and sympathetic and patient in explaining for the hundredth time something perfectly obvious . . . when I really want to give utterance to whoops of rage and jump up and knock their heads together."

high for U.S. foreign relations. Two historic friendships withered on the windswept plains of Manchuria. American relations with Russia, once friendly, soured as the Russians implausibly accused Roosevelt of robbing them of military victory. Revelations about savage massacres of Russian Jews further poisoned American feeling against Russia. Japan, once America's protégé, felt robbed of its due compensation. Both newly powerful, Japan and America now became rivals in Asia, as fear and jealousy between them grew. To many Americans, the Japanese were getting too big for their kimonos.

Japanese Laborers in California

The population of America's Pacific Coast was directly affected by the Russo-Japanese War. A new restlessness swept over the rice paddies of Japan, largely as a result of the dislocations and tax bur-

dens caused by the recent conflict. Numerous Japanese laborers, with their wives and children, began to pour into the spacious valleys of California. By 1906 approximately seventy thousand Japanese dwelt along the Pacific Coast. Nervous Californians, confronted by another "yellow peril," feared being drowned in an Asian sea.

A showdown on the Japanese influx came in 1906. Following the frightful earthquake and fire of that year in San Francisco, the local school authorities, pressed for space, decreed that Japanese children should attend a special school.

Instantly, the Japanese school incident boiled into an international crisis. The people of Japan, who were highly sensitive on questions of race, regarded this discrimination as an insult to them and their beloved children. On both sides of the Pacific, irresponsible war talk sizzled in the yellow press—the real "yellow peril." Roosevelt, who as a Rough Rider had relished shooting, was less happy over the prospect that California might stir up a war that all the other states would have to wage. He therefore invited the entire San Francisco Board of Education, headed by a bassoon-playing mayor under indictment for graft, to come to the White House.

TR finally broke the deadlock, but not until he had brandished his big stick and bared his big teeth. The Californians were induced to repeal the offensive school order and to accept what came to be known as the "Gentlemen's Agreement." This secret understanding was worked out, during 1907–1908, by an exchange of diplomatic notes between Washington and Tokyo. The Japanese, for their part, agreed to stop the flow of laborers to the American mainland by withholding passports. Caucasian Californians, their anxiety allayed, henceforth slept more easily.

Roosevelt worried that his intercession between California and Japan might be interpreted in Tokyo as prompted by fear of the Japanese. Accordingly, he hit upon a dramatic scheme to impress the Japanese with the heft of his big stick. He daringly decided to send the entire battleship fleet on a highly visible voyage around the world.

Late in 1907, sixteen sparkling-white, smoke-belching battleships started from Virginia waters. Their commander pointedly declared that he was ready for "a feast, a frolic, or a fight." The Great White Fleet—saluted by cannonading champagne corks—received tumultuous welcomes in Latin America, Hawaii, New Zealand, and Australia.

As events turned out, an overwhelming reception in Japan was the high point of the trip. Tens of thousands of kimonoed schoolchildren had been trained to wave tiny American flags and sing "The Star-Spangled Banner"—reportedly in English. In the warm diplomatic atmosphere created by the visit of the fleet, the Root-Takahira agreement of 1908 was reached with Japan. The United States and Japan solemnly pledged themselves to respect each other's territorial possessions in the Pacific and to uphold the Open Door in China. The once fight-thirsty Roosevelt, who thus went out of his way to avoid a war with Japan, regarded the battleship cruise as his most important contribution to peace. The voyage of the white fleet also gave Uncle Sam a new recruiting slogan: "Join the Navy and See the World."

Japanese Workers Building a Road in California, c. 1910

Chronology

1899   Aguinaldo launches rebellion against
United States in the Philippine Islands
First American Open Door note

1900   Boxer Rebellion and U.S. expedition to
China
Second Open Door note
McKinley defeats Bryan for presidency

1901   McKinley assassinated; Roosevelt assumes
presidency
Filipino rebellion defeated
Hay-Pauncefote Treaty

1902   Colombian Senate rejects canal treaty

1903   Panamanian revolution against Colombia
Hay–Bunau-Varilla treaty

1904   Roosevelt Corollary to the Monroe
Doctrine

**1904-
1914**   Construction of the Panama Canal

1905   United States takes over Dominican
Republic customs
Roosevelt mediates Russo-Japanese peace
treaty

1906   San Francisco Japanese education crisis
Roosevelt arranges Algeciras conference

**1906-
1909**   U.S. Marines occupy Cuba

1907   Great White Fleet

**1907-
1908**   "Gentlemen's Agreement" with Japan

1908   Root-Takahira agreement

Why Did America Become a World Power?

American imperialism has long been an embarrassing topic for students of American history, who remember the Republic's own revolutionary origins and anti-colonial tradition. Perhaps for that reason, many historians have tried to explain the dramatic overseas expansionism of the 1890s as some kind of aberration—a sudden, singular, and short-lived departure from time-honored American principles and practices. Various explanations have been offered to account for this spasmodic lapse. Scholars such as Julius Pratt pointed to the irresponsible behavior of the yellow press. Richard Hofstadter ascribed America's imperial fling to the "psychic crisis of the 1890s," a crisis brought on, he argued, by the strains of the decade's economic depression and the Populist upheaval. Howard K. Beale emphasized the contagious scramble for imperial possessions by the European powers, as well as Japan, in these years.

In Beale's argument, the United States—and Theodore Roosevelt in particular—succumbed to a kind of international peer pressure: if other countries were expanding their international roles and even establishing colonies around the globe, could the United States safely refrain from doing the same? In Beale's view, Theodore Roosevelt was no simple-minded imperial swashbuckler, but a coolly calculating diplomatic realist who perceived that if the United States did not hold its own against other powers, it would soon risk being pushed around, even in its own hemisphere, despite the Monroe Doctrine.

Perhaps the most controversial interpretation of American imperialism has come from a so-called New Left school of writers, inspired by William Appleman Williams (and before him by V. I. Lenin's 1916 book *Imperialism: The Highest Stage of Capitalism*). Historians such as Williams and Walter LaFeber argue that the explanation for political and military expansion abroad is to be found in economic expansion at home. These scholars try to link the two most striking developments of the age: the amazing industrialization of the United States in the half-century after the Civil War and the Republic's sudden emergence as a world power. Increasing industrial output, so the argument goes, required ever more raw materials and, especially, overseas markets. To meet those needs, the nation adopted a strategy of "informal empire," shunning formal territorial possessions (with the conspicuous exception of the Philippines), but seeking economic dominance over foreign markets, materials, and investment outlets.

That "revisionist" interpretation, in turn, has been sharply criticized by scholars who point out that foreign trade, especially in this period, accounted for only a tiny share of American output. Critics of the New Left view also insist that the exceedingly complex diplomacy of the period was far too diverse in its motives, methods, and goals to be reduced to the elementary explanation of "economic need."

SUGGESTED READINGS

PRIMARY SOURCE DOCUMENTS

Theodore Roosevelt's corollary* to the Monroe Doctrine, in *A Compilation of the Messages and Papers of the Presidents,* vol. XVI, pp. 7053–7054, found its first expression in 1904. *The Annual Report* of the secretary of commerce and labor for 1908* contains the "Gentlemen's Agreement" with Japan. For the intrigue surrounding the independence of Panama and the building of the canal, see *Foreign Relations of the United States** (1903) and Theodore Roosevelt to Albert Shaw, October 10, 1903,* in *The Letters of Theodore Roosevelt,* edited by Elting E. Morison (1951), vol. 3, p. 628.

SECONDARY SOURCES

Howard K. Beale describes *Theodore Roosevelt and the Rise of America to World Power* (1956). See also the work of William Appleman Williams, cited in Chapter 29. Analytical and sympathetic is John M. Blum, *The Republican Roosevelt* (new ed., 1977). John M. Cooper, Jr., contrasts Roosevelt and Woodrow Wilson in *The Warrior and the Priest* (1983). An outstanding single-volume biography of TR is William H. Harbaugh, *Power and Responsibility* (rev. ed., 1975). Lewis L. Gould focuses on *The Presidency of Theodore Roosevelt* (1991), while especially good on the youthful Roosevelt is David McCullough, *Mornings on Horseback* (1981). For the Open Door, consult Marilyn B. Young, *The Rhetoric of Empire: America's China Policy, 1895–1901* (1968), and Jerry Israel, *Progressivism and the Open Door: America and China 1905–1921* (1971). On relations with Japan, see Charles E. Neu, *An Uncertain Friendship: Theodore Roosevelt and Japan, 1906–1909* (1967) and *The Troubled Encounter: The United States and Japan* (1975). Also valuable are two books by Akira Iriye, *Across the Pacific* (1967) and *Pacific Estrangement: Japanese and American Expansion, 1897–1911* (1972). James Reed discusses *The Missionary Mind and American East Asian Policy, 1911–1915* (1983). Also see William R. Hutchinson, *Errand to the World: American Protestant Thought and Foreign Missions* (1987). On the treatment of the Japanese in the United States, see Ronald Takaki, *Strangers from a Different Shore* (1989). The canal issue is analyzed in David McCullough, *The Path Between the Seas* (1977); Walter LaFeber, *The Panama Canal* (1978); and Richard H. Collin, *Theodore Roosevelt's Caribbean: The Panama Canal, the Monroe Doctrine, and the Latin American Context* (1990).

---

*An asterisk indicates that the document, or an excerpt from it, can be found in Thomas A. Bailey and David M. Kennedy, eds., *The American Spirit: United States History as Seen by Contemporaries,* 9th ed. (Boston: Houghton Mifflin, 1998).

31

Progressivism and the Republican Roosevelt
1901–1912

When I say I believe in a square deal I do not mean . . . to give every man the best hand. If the cards do not come to any man, or if they do come, and he has not got the power to play them, that is his affair. All I mean is that there shall be no crookedness in the dealing.

THEODORE ROOSEVELT, 1905

Progressive Roots

Nearly 76 million Americans greeted the new century in 1900. Of them, almost 1 in 7 was foreign-born. In the fourteen years of peace that remained before the Great War of 1914 engulfed the globe, 13 million more migrants would carry their bundles down the gangplanks to the land of promise.

Hardly had the twentieth century dawned on the ethnically and racially mixed American people than they were convulsed by a reform movement, the like of which the nation had not seen since the 1840s. The new crusaders, who called themselves "progressives," waged war on many evils, notably monopoly, corruption, inefficiency, and social injustice. The progressive army was large, diverse, and widely deployed, but it had a single battle cry: "Strengthen the State." The "real heart of the movement," explained one of the progressive reformers, was "to use government as an agency of human welfare."

The ground swell of the new reformist wave went far back—to the Greenback Labor party of the 1870s and the Populists of the 1890s, to the mounting unrest throughout the land as grasping industrialists concentrated more and more power in fewer and fewer hands. An outworn philosophy of hands-off individualism seemed increasingly out of place in the modern machine age. Social and economic problems were now too complex for the intentionally feeble Jeffersonian organs of government. Progressive theorists were insisting that society could no longer afford the luxury of a limitless "let-alone" policy (laissez-faire). The people, through government, must substitute mastery for drift.

Well before 1900, perceptive politicians and writers had begun to pinpoint targets for the progressive attack. Bryan, Altgeld, and the Populists loudly branded the "bloated trusts" with the stigma of corruption and wrongdoing. In 1894 Henry Demarest Lloyd charged headlong into the Standard Oil Company with his book entitled *Wealth Against Commonwealth.* Eccentric Thorstein Veblen assailed the new rich with his prickly pen in *The Theory of the Leisure Class* (1899), a savage attack on "predatory wealth" and "conspicuous consumption."

Other pen-wielding knights likewise entered the fray. The keen-eyed and keen-nosed Danish immigrant Jacob A. Riis, a reporter for the New York *Sun,* shocked middle-class Americans in 1890 with *How the Other Half Lives.* His account was a damning indictment of the dirt, disease, vice, and misery of the rat-gnawed human rookeries known as New York slums. The book deeply influenced a future New York City police commissioner, Theodore Roo-

Saluting the Flag   Flooded with immigrant children, many of whom could scarcely speak English, schools like this one in New York in 1892 cultivated loyalty to the newcomers' adopted land by teaching courses in "civics" and encouraging patriotic rituals like the Pledge of Allegiance to the U.S. flag.

sevelt. Novelist Theodore Dreiser used his blunt prose to batter promoters and profiteers in *The Financier* (1912) and *The Titan* (1914).

Caustic critics of social injustice issued from several other corners. Socialists, many of whom were European immigrants inspired by the strong

Room in a Tenement Flat, 1910 Tenement life on the Lower East Side of New York City was exposed by the camera of Jacob Riis, who compiled a large photographic archive of turn-of-the-century urban life. Many families counted themselves lucky to share a single room, no matter how squalid.

movement for state socialism in the Old World, began to register appreciable strength at the ballot box. High-minded messengers of the social gospel promoted a brand of progressivism based in Christian teachings. They used religious doctrine to demand better housing and living conditions for the urban poor. Feminists in multiplying numbers added social justice to suffrage on their list of needed reforms. With urban pioneers like Jane Addams in Chicago and Lillian Wald in New York blazing the way, women entered the fight to clean up corrupt city governments, to win pensions for single mothers with dependent children, to protect women on the hazardous factory floor, to keep children out of smudgy mills and sooty mines, and to ensure that only safe food products found their way to the family table (see pages 574–575). Much of progressivism, in fact, reflected the new public commitment of women to improve the lots of families living and working in the festering cities.

Raking Muck with the Muckrakers

Muckraker Ida M. Tarbell, 1921   As a younger woman, in 1904, Tarbell made her reputation by publishing a scathing history of the Standard Oil Company, the "Mother of Trusts."

Beginning about 1902 the exposing of evil became a flourishing industry among American publishers. A group of aggressive ten- and fifteen-cent popular magazines surged to the front, notably *McClure's, Cosmopolitan, Collier's,* and *Everybody's.* Waging fierce circulation wars, they dug deep for the dirt that the public loved to hate. Enterprising editors financed extensive research and encouraged pugnacious writing by their bright young reporters, whom President Roosevelt branded as "muckrakers" in 1906. Annoyed by their excess of zeal, he compared the mudslinging magazine dirt-diggers to the figure in Bunyan's *Pilgrim's Progress* who was so intent on raking manure that he could not see the celestial crown dangling overhead.

Despite presidential scolding, these muckrakers boomed circulation, and some of their most scandalous exposures were published as best-selling books. The reformer-writers ranged far, wide, and deep in their crusade to lay bare the muck of iniquity in American society. In 1902 a brilliant New York reporter, Lincoln Steffens, launched a series of articles in *McClure's* entitled "The Shame of the Cities." He fearlessly unmasked the corrupt alliance between big business and municipal government. Steffens was followed in the same magazine by Ida

M. Tarbell, a pioneering woman journalist who published a devastating but factual exposé of the Standard Oil Company. (Her father had been ruined by the oil interests.) Fearing legal reprisals, the muckraking magazines went to great pains and expense to check their material—paying as much as three thousand dollars to verify a single Tarbell article.

Plucky muckrakers fearlessly tilted their penlances at varied targets. They assailed the malpractices of life insurance companies and tariff lobbies. They roasted the beef trust, the "money trust," the railroad barons, and the corrupt amassing of American fortunes. Thomas W. Lawson, an erratic speculator who had himself made $50 million on the stock market, laid bare the practices of his accomplices in "Frenzied Finance." This series of articles, appearing in 1905–1906, rocketed the circulation of *Everybody's.* Lawson, by fouling his own nest, made many enemies among his rich associates, and he died a poor man.

David G. Phillips shocked an already startled nation by his series in *Cosmopolitan* entitled "The Treason of the Senate" (1906). He boldly charged that seventy-five of the ninety senators did not represent the people at all but the railroads and trusts. This withering indictment, buttressed by facts, impressed President Roosevelt. Phillips continued his attacks through novels and was fatally shot in 1911 by a deranged young man whose family he had allegedly maligned.

Some of the most effective fire of the muckrakers was directed at social evils. The ugly list included the immoral "white slave" traffic in women, the rickety slums, and the appalling number of industrial accidents. The sorry subjugation of America's 9 million blacks—of whom 90 percent still lived in the South, and one-third were illiterate—was spotlighted in Ray Stannard Baker's *Following the Color Line* (1908). The abuses of child labor were brought luridly to light by John Spargo's *The Bitter Cry of the Children* (1906).

Vendors of potent patent medicines (often heavily spiked with alcohol) likewise came in for bitter criticism. These conscienceless vultures sold incredible quantities of adulterated or habit-forming drugs, while "doping" the press with lavish advertising. Muckraking attacks in *Collier's* were ably reinforced by Dr. Harvey W. Wiley, chief chemist of the Department of Agriculture, who with his famous "Poison Squad" performed experiments on himself.

In his muckraker speech (1906), Theodore Roosevelt (1858–1919) said,

"Now, it is very necessary that we should not flinch from seeing what is vile and debasing. There is filth on the floor and it must be scraped up with the muck-rake; and there are times and places where this service is the most needed of all the services that can be performed. But the man who never does anything else, who never thinks or speaks or writes, save of his feats with the muck-rake, speedily becomes, not a help to society, not an incitement to good, but one of the most potent forces for evil."

Full of sound and fury, the muckrakers signified much about the nature of the progressive reform movement. They were long on lamentation and short on sweeping remedies. To right social wrongs they counted on publicity and an aroused public conscience, not drastic political change. They sought not to overthrow capitalism but to cleanse it. The cure for the ills of American democracy, they earnestly believed, was more democracy.

Breaker Boys, 1900
Photographer Lewis Hine captured the grimness of these West Virginia mine helpers' lives. For hours they sat on benches above a moving belt kicking large pieces of coal with their feet, breaking the lumps to uniform size for shipment.

Political Progressivism

Progressive reformers were mainly middle-class men and women who felt themselves squeezed from above and below. They sensed pressure from the new giant corporations, the restless immigrant hordes, and the aggressive labor unions. The progressives simultaneously sought two goals: to use state power to curb the trusts and to stem the Socialist threat by generally improving the common person's conditions of life and labor. Progressives emerged in both major parties, in all regions, and at all levels of government. The truth is that progressivism was less a minority movement and more a majority mood.

One of the first objectives of progressives was to regain the power that had slipped from the hands of the people into those of the "interests." These ardent reformers pushed for direct primary elections so as to undercut power-hungry party bosses. They favored the "initiative" so that voters could directly propose legislation themselves, thus bypassing the boss-bought state legislatures. Progressives also agitated for the "referendum." This device would place laws on the ballot for final approval by the people, especially laws that had been railroaded through a compliant legislature by free-spending agents of big business. The "recall" would enable the voters to remove faithless elected officials, particularly those who had been bribed by bosses or lobbyists.

> *In his muckraking classic,* The Shame of the Cities *(1904), Lincoln Steffens (1866–1936) decried the great threat posed by New York City's Tammany machine:*
>
> "Bribery is no ordinary felony, but treason; . . . 'corruption which breaks out here and there and now and then' is not an occasional offense, but a common practice, and . . . the effect of it is literally to change the form of our government from one that is representative of the people to an oligarchy, representative of special interests."

Rooting out graft also became a prime goal of earnest progressives. A number of the state legislatures passed corrupt-practices acts, which limited the amount of money that candidates could spend for their election. Such legislation also restricted huge gifts from corporations, for which the donors would expect special favors. The secret Australian ballot was likewise being introduced more widely in the states to counteract boss rule. Bribery was less feasible when bribers could not tell if they were getting their money's worth from the bribed.

Direct election of U.S. senators became a favorite goal of progressives, especially after the muckrakers had exposed the scandalous intimacy between greedy corporations and Congress. By 1900 the Senate had so many rich men that it was often sneered at as the "Millionaires' Club." Too many of these prosperous solons, elected as they then were by trust-dominated legislatures, heeded the voice of their "masters" rather than the voice of the masses.

A constitutional amendment to bring about the popular election of senators had rough sledding in Congress, for the plutocratic members of the Senate were happy with existing methods. But a number of states established primary elections in which the voters expressed their preferences for the Senate. The local legislatures, when choosing senators, found it politically wise to heed the voice of the people. Partly as a result of such pressures, the Seventeenth Amendment to the Constitution, approved in 1913, established the direct election of U.S. senators. (See the Appendix.) But the expected improvement in caliber was slow in coming.

Woman suffrage, the goal of feminists for many decades, likewise received powerful new support from the progressives early in the 1900s. The political reformers believed that women's votes would elevate the political tone, and the foes of the saloon felt that they could count on the support of enfranchised females. The suffragists, with their cry of "Votes for Women" and "Equal Suffrage for Men and Women," protested bitterly against "Taxation without Representation." Many of the states, especially the more liberal ones in the West, gradually extended the vote to women. But by 1910 nationwide female suffrage was still a decade away; and a suffragist could still be sneeringly defined as "one who has ceased to be a lady and has not yet become a gentleman."

Suffragists Put the Pressure on Washington Success finally crowned their effort with the ratification of the Nineteenth Amendment in 1920.

> *The suffrage campaign of the early twentieth century benefited from a new generation of women who considered themselves "feminists." At a mass meeting in New York in 1914, Marie Jenny Howe (1870–1934), a minister by training as well as a prominent early feminist, proclaimed,*
>
> "We intend simply to be ourselves, not just our little female selves, but our whole big human selves."

Progressivism in the Cities and States

Progressives scored some of their most impressive gains in the cities. Frustrated by the inefficiency and corruption of machine-oiled city government, many localities followed the pioneering example of Galveston, Texas. In 1901 it had appointed expert-staffed commissions to manage urban affairs. Other communities adopted the city-manager system, also designed to take politics out of municipal administration. Some of these "reforms" obviously valued efficiency more highly than democracy, as control of civic affairs was further removed from the people's hands.

Urban reformers likewise attacked "slumlords," juvenile delinquency, and wide-open prostitution (vice-at-a-price), which flourished in red-light districts unchallenged by bribed police. Public-spirited city dwellers also moved to halt the corrupt sale of franchises for streetcars and other public utilities.

Progressivism naturally bubbled up to the state level, notably in Wisconsin, which became a yeasty laboratory of reform. The governor of the state, pompadoured Robert M. ("Fighting Bob") La Follette, was an undersized but overbearing crusader who emerged as the most militant of the progressive Republican leaders. After a desperate fight with entrenched monopoly, he reached the governor's chair in 1901. Routing the lumber and railroad "interests," he wrested considerable control from the crooked corporations and returned it to the people. He also perfected a scheme for regulating public utilities, while laboring in close association with experts on the faculty of the state university at Madison.

Other states marched steadily toward the progressive camp, as they undertook to regulate railroads and trusts, chiefly through public utilities commissions. Oregon was not far behind Wisconsin, and California made giant bootstrides under the stocky Hiram W. Johnson. Elected Republican governor in 1910, this dynamic prosecutor of grafters helped break the dominant grip of the Southern Pacific Railroad on California politics and then, like La Follette, set up a political machine of his own. Heavily whiskered Charles Evans Hughes, the able and audacious reformist Republican governor of New York, had earlier gained national fame as an investigator of malpractices by gas and insurance companies and by the coal trust.

Battling Social Ills

In these and other states, fired-up progressives tackled head-on a whole array of social problems. One of the most remarkable features of this era was the energy and confidence with which reformers did battle with a host of evils. They finally secured the enactment of safety and sanitation codes for industry and closed certain harmful trades to juveniles. Progressives further protected the toiler with workmen's compensation laws, thus relieving the injured laborer from the burden of lawsuits to prove negligence on the part of the employer. The reformers also secured laws setting maximum hours and minimum wages.

Steaming and unsanitary sweatshops were a public scandal in many cities. The issue was thrust into the public eye in 1911, when a fire at the Triangle Shirtwaist Company in New York City incinerated 146 female workers, mostly young women. Lashed by the public outcry, the legislature of New York and later other legislatures passed laws regulating the hours and conditions of toil in such firetraps. In the landmark case of *Muller* v. *Oregon* (1908), crusading attorney Louis D. Brandeis persuaded the Supreme Court to accept the constitutionality of laws protecting women workers by presenting evidence of the harmful effects of factory labor on women's weaker bodies. Although this argument calling for special protection for women seemed discriminatory by later standards and closed many "male" jobs to women, progressives at the time hailed Brandeis's achievement as a triumph over existing legal doctrine, which afforded employers total control over the workplace.

But crusaders for these humane measures did not always have smooth sailing. One dismaying setback came in 1905, when the Supreme Court, in *Lochner* v. *New York,* invalidated a New York law establishing a ten-hour day for bakers. Yet the

reformist progressive wave finally washed up into the judiciary, and in 1917 the Court upheld a ten-hour law for factory workers. Gradually, the concept of the employer's responsibility to society was replacing the old dog-eat-dog philosophy of unregulated free enterprise.

Corner saloons, with their shutter doors, naturally attracted the ire and fire of progressives. Alcohol was intimately connected with prostitution in red-light districts, with the drunken voter, with crooked city officials dominated by "booze" interests, and with the blowsy "boss" who counted poker chips by night and miscounted ballots by day (including the "cemetery vote"). By 1900 cities like New York and San Francisco had one saloon for about every two hundred people.

Antiliquor campaigners received powerful support from several militant organizations, notably the Woman's Christian Temperance Union (WCTU). Founder Frances E. Willard, who would fall to her knees in prayer on saloon floors, mobilized nearly one million women to "make the world homelike"

Out of Work and the Reason Why, 1899 This temperance propaganda from an 1899 magazine illustrates the role of women in the temperance movement. Alcohol abuse threatened the stability of the family, still predominantly the "woman's sphere" in the late nineteenth century.

and built the WCTU into the largest organization of women in the world. She found a vigorous ally in the Anti-Saloon League, which was aggressive, well organized, and well financed.

Caught up in the crusade, some states and numerous counties passed "dry" laws, which controlled, restricted, or abolished alcohol. The big cities were generally "wet," for they had a large immigrant vote accustomed in the Old Country to the free flow of wine and beer. When World War I erupted in 1914, nearly one-half of the population lived in "dry" territory, and nearly three-fourths of the total area had outlawed saloons. Demon Rum was groggy and about to be floored—temporarily—by the Eighteenth Amendment in 1919.

TR's Square Deal for Labor

Theodore Roosevelt, although something of an imperialistic busybody abroad, was touched by the progressive wave at home. Like other reformers, he feared that the "public interest" was being submerged in the drifting seas of indifference. Everybody's interest was nobody's interest. Roosevelt decided to make it his. His sportsman's instincts spurred him into demanding a "Square Deal" for capital, labor, and the public at large. Broadly speaking, the president's program embraced three *C*s: control of the corporations, consumer protection, and conservation of natural resources.

The Square Deal for labor received its acid test in 1902, when a crippling strike broke out in the anthracite coal mines of Pennsylvania. Some 140,000 besooted workers, many of them illiterate immigrants, had long been frightfully exploited and accident-plagued. They demanded, among other improvements, a 20 percent increase in pay and a reduction of the working day from ten to nine hours.

Unsympathetic mine owners, confident that a chilled public would react against the miners, refused to arbitrate or even negotiate. One of their spokesmen, multimillionaire George F. Baer, reflected the high-and-mighty attitude of certain ungenerous employers. Workers, he wrote, would be cared for "not by the labor agitators, but by the Christian men to whom God in His infinite wisdom has given the control of the property interests of this country."

As coal supplies dwindled, factories and schools were forced to shut down, and even hospitals felt the icy grip of winter. Desperately seeking a solution, Roosevelt summoned representatives of the striking miners and the mine owners to the White House. He was profoundly annoyed by the "extraordinary stupidity and bad temper" of the "woodenheaded gentry" who operated the mines. As he later confessed, if it had not been for the dignity of his high office, he would have taken one of them "by the seat of the breeches" and "chucked him out of the window."

Roosevelt finally resorted to his trusty big stick when he threatened to seize the mines and operate them with federal troops. Faced with this first-time-ever threat to use federal bayonets against capital, rather than labor, the owners grudgingly consented to arbitration. A compromise decision ultimately gave the miners a 10 percent pay boost and a working day of nine hours. But their union was not officially recognized as a bargaining agent.

Keenly aware of the mounting antagonisms between capital and labor, Roosevelt urged Congress to create a new Department of Commerce and Labor. This goal was achieved in 1903. (Ten years later the agency was split in two.) An important arm of the newborn Cabinet body was the Bureau of Corporations, which was authorized to probe businesses engaged in interstate commerce. The bureau was highly useful in helping to break the stranglehold of monopoly and in clearing the road for the era of "trust-busting."

Roosevelt was a charismatic figure who made a powerful impression on his contemporaries. The journalist William Allen White (1868–1944) later wrote of his first meeting with TR in 1897:

"He sounded in my heart the first trumpet call of the new time that was to be. . . . I had never known such a man as he, and never shall again. He overcame me. And in the hour or two we spent that day at lunch, and in a walk down F Street, he poured into my heart such visions, such ideals, such hopes, such a new attitude toward life and patriotism and the meaning of things, as I had never dreamed men had. . . . After that I was his man."

TR Corrals the Corporations

The sprawling railroad octopus sorely needed restraint. The Interstate Commerce Commission, created in 1887 as a feeble sop to the public, had proved woefully inadequate. Railroad barons could simply appeal the commission's decisions on rates to the federal courts—a process that might take ten years.

Spurred by the former-cowboy president, Congress passed effective railroad legislation, beginning with the Elkins Act of 1903. This curb was aimed primarily at the rebate evil. Heavy fines could now be imposed both on the railroads that gave rebates and on the shippers that accepted them.

Still more effective was the Hepburn Act of 1906. Free passes, with their hint of bribery, were severely restricted. The once-infantile Interstate Commerce Commission was expanded, and its reach was extended to include express companies, sleeping-car companies, and pipelines. For the first time, the commission was given real molars when it was authorized, on complaint of shippers, to nullify existing rates and stipulate maximum rates.

Railroads also provided Roosevelt with an opportunity to brandish his antitrust bludgeon. *Trusts* had come to be a fighting word in the progressive era. Roosevelt believed that these industrial behemoths, with their efficient means of production, had arrived to stay. He concluded that there were "good" trusts, with public consciences, and "bad" trusts, which lusted greedily for power. He was determined to respond to the popular outcry against the trusts but was also determined not to throw out the baby with the bathwater by indiscriminately smashing all large businesses.

Roosevelt, as a trustbuster, first burst into the headlines in 1902 with an attack on the Northern Securities Company, a railroad holding company organized by financial titan J. P. Morgan and empire builder James J. Hill. These Napoleonic moguls of money sought to achieve a virtual monopoly of the railroads in the Northwest. Roosevelt was therefore challenging the most regal potentates of the industrial aristocracy.

The railway promoters appealed to the Supreme Court, which in 1904 upheld Roosevelt's antitrust suit and ordered the Northern Securities Company to be dissolved. The *Northern Securities* decision jolted Wall Street and angered big business

Roosevelt Turns the Screws on the Trusts   This cartoon exaggerates Roosevelt's impact on the corporate giants. He wanted to bring the trusts under government control, but not necessarily wring them dry of their wealth.

but greatly enhanced Roosevelt's reputation as a trust smasher.

Roosevelt's big stick crashed down on other giant monopolies, as he initiated over forty legal proceedings against them. The Supreme Court in 1905 declared the beef trust illegal, and the heavy fist of justice fell upon monopolists controlling sugar, fertilizer, harvesters, and other key products.

Much mythology has inflated Roosevelt's reputation as a trustbuster. The Rough Rider understood the political popularity of monopoly-smashing, but he did not consider it sound economic policy. Combination and integration, he felt, were the hallmarks of the age, and to try to stem the tide of economic progress by political means he considered the rankest folly. Bigness was not necessarily badness; so why punish success? Roosevelt's real purpose in assaulting the Goliaths of industry was symbolic: to prove conclusively that the government, not private business, ruled the country. He believed in regulating, not fragmenting, the big business combines. The threat of dissolution, he felt, might make the sultans of the smokestacks more amenable to federal regulation—as it did.

In truth, Roosevelt never swung his trust-crushing stick with maximum force. In many ways the huge industrial behemoths were healthier—though perhaps more "tame"—at the end of Roosevelt's reign than they had been before. His successor, William Howard Taft, actually "busted" more trusts than TR did. In one celebrated instance in 1907, Roosevelt even gave his personal blessing to J. P. Morgan's plan to have U.S. Steel absorb the Tennessee Coal and Iron Company, without fear of antitrust reprisals. When Taft then launched a suit against U.S. Steel in 1911, the political reaction from TR was explosive.

Caring for the Consumer

Roosevelt backed a noteworthy measure in 1906 that benefited both corporations and consumers. Big meat packers were being shut out of certain European markets because some American meat—from the small packinghouses, claimed the giants—had been found to be tainted. Foreign governments were even threatening to ban all American meat imports by throwing out the good beef with the bad botulism.

At the same time, American consumers hungered for safer canned products. Their appetite for reform was whetted by Upton Sinclair's sensational novel *The Jungle*, published in 1906. Sinclair intended his revolting tract to focus attention on the plight of the workers in the big canning factories, but instead he appalled the public with his description of disgustingly unsanitary food products. (As he put it, he aimed for the nation's heart, but hit its stomach.) The book described in noxious detail the filth, disease, and putrefaction in Chicago's damp, ill-ventilated slaughterhouses. Many readers, including Roosevelt, were so sickened that for a time they found meat unpalatable. The president was moved by the loathsome mess in Chicago to appoint a special investigating commission, whose cold-blooded report almost outdid Sinclair's novel. It related how piles of poisoned rats, rope ends, splinters, and other debris were scooped up and canned as potted ham. A cynical jingle of the time ran,

> *Mary had a little lamb,*
> *And when she saw it sicken,*
> *She shipped it off to Packingtown,*
> *And now it's labeled chicken.*

Backed by a nauseated public, Roosevelt induced Congress to pass the Meat Inspection Act of 1906. It decreed that the preparation of meat

Sausage-Making, c. 1906
White-jacketed inspectors like these on the right made some progress in cleaning up the septic slaughterhouses after the passage of the Meat Inspection Act in 1906.

shipped over state lines would be subject to federal inspection from corral to can. Although the largest packers resisted certain features of the act, they grudgingly accepted it as an opportunity to drive their smaller, fly-by-night competitors out of business. At the same time, they could receive the government's seal of approval on their exports. As a companion to the Meat Inspection Act, the Pure Food and Drug Act of 1906 was designed to prevent the adulteration and mislabeling of foods and pharmaceuticals.

Earth Control

Wasteful Americans, assuming that their natural resources were inexhaustible, had looted and polluted their incomparable domain with unparalleled speed and greed. Westerners were especially eager to accelerate the destructive process, for they panted to build up the country, and the environmental consequences be hanged. But even before the end of the nineteenth century, far-visioned leaders saw that such a squandering of the nation's birthright would have to be halted or America would sink from resource richness to despoiled dearth.

A first feeble step toward conservation had been taken with the Desert Land Act of 1877, under which the federal government sold arid land cheaply on the condition that the purchaser irrigate the thirsty soil within three years. More successful was the Forest Reserve Act of 1891, authorizing the president to set aside public forests as national parks and other

High Point for Conservation   Conservationist Roosevelt and famed naturalist-conservationist John Muir visit Glacier Point, on the rim of Yosemite Valley, California. In the distance is Yosemite Falls; a few feet behind Roosevelt is a sheer drop of 3,254 feet (992 meters).

In his annual message to Congress (1907), Roosevelt declared prophetically,

"We are prone to speak of the resources of this country as inexhaustible; this is not so. The mineral wealth of the country, the coal, iron, oil, gas, and the like, does not reproduce itself, and therefore is certain to be exhausted ultimately; and wastefulness in dealing with it to-day means that our descendants will feel the exhaustion a generation or two before they otherwise would."

reserves. Under this statute some 46 million acres of magnificent trees were rescued from the lumberman's saw in the 1890s and preserved for posterity. The Carey Act of 1894 distributed federal land to the states on the condition that it be irrigated and settled. The law led to the cultivation of about a million barren acres, in a fruitful marriage of desert and water.

A new day in the history of conservation dawned with the advent of Roosevelt. Huntsman, naturalist, rancher, lover of the great outdoors, he was appalled by the pillaging of timber and mineral resources. Other dedicated conservationists, notably Gifford Pinchot, head of the federal Division of Forestry, had broken important ground before him. But Roosevelt seized the banner of leadership and charged into the fray with all the weight of his prestige, his

Logging in California, c. 1890 It took the sweat and skill of many men to conquer a giant California redwood like this one. An ax-wielding "sniper" had rounded the edges of this log so that a team of oxen, driven by a "bullwhacker," could more easily drag it out of the woods along a "skid road." *Skid road* (sometimes corrupted as *skid row*) was also a name for the often-sleazy sections of logging towns, where loggers spent their time in the off-season.

energy, his firsthand knowledge, and his slashing invective.

The thirst of the desert still unslaked, Congress responded to the whip of the Rough Rider by passing the landmark Newlands Act of 1902. Washington was authorized to collect money from the sale of public lands in the sun-baked western states and then use these funds for the development of irrigation projects. Settlers repaid the cost of reclamation from their now-productive soil, and the money was put into a revolving fund to finance more such enterprises. The giant Roosevelt Dam, constructed on Arizona's Salt River, was appropriately dedicated by Roosevelt in 1911. Thanks to this epochal legislation, dozens of dams were thrown across virtually every major western river in the ensuing decades.

Roosevelt pined to preserve the nation's shrinking forests. By 1900 only about a quarter of the once-vast virgin timberlands remained standing. Lumbermen had already logged off most of the first-growth timber from Maine to Michigan, and the sharp thud of their axes was beginning to split the silence in the great fir forests of the Pacific slope. Roosevelt proceeded to set aside in federal reserves some 125 million acres, or almost three times the acreage thus saved from the saw by his three predecessors. He similarly earmarked millions of acres of coal deposits, as well as water resources useful for irrigation and power. To set a shining example, in 1902 he banned Christmas trees from the White House.

Conservation, including reclamation, may have been Roosevelt's most enduring tangible achievement. The superactive president took conservation out of the conversation stage, threw the force of his colorful personality behind it, dramatized it, and aroused public opinion to a constructive crusade. He was buoyed in this effort by an upwelling national mood of concern about the disappearance of the frontier—believed to be the source of such national characteristics as individualism and

Gifford Pinchot (1865–1946), a foremost conservationist in the Roosevelt administration, wrote,

"The object of our forest policy is not to preserve the forests because they are refuges for the wild creatures of the wilderness, but the making of prosperous homes. Every other consideration comes as secondary. . . . The test of utility . . . implies that no lands will be permanently reserves which can serve the people better in any other way."

democracy. An increasingly citified people worried that too much civilization might not be good for the national soul. City dwellers snapped up Jack London's *Call of the Wild* (1903) and other books about nature, and urban youngsters made the outdoor-oriented Boy Scouts of America the country's largest youth organization. The Sierra Club, founded in 1892, dedicated itself to preserving the wildness of the western landscape.

The preservationists lost a major battle in 1913 when the federal government allowed the city of San Francisco to build a dam for its municipal water supply in the spectacular, high-walled Hetch Hetchy Valley in Yosemite National Park. The Hetch Hetchy controversy laid bare a deep division among conservationists that persists to the present day. To the preservationists of the Sierra Club, including famed naturalist John Muir, Hetch Hetchy was a "temple" of nature that should be held inviolable by the civilizing hand of humanity. But other conservationists, among them President Roosevelt's chief forester, Gifford Pinchot, believed that "wilderness was waste." Pinchot and Roosevelt wanted to *use* the nation's natural endowment intelligently. In their eyes they had to battle on two fronts: against greedy commercial interests who abused nature as well as against romantic preservationists in thrall to simple "woodman-spare-that-tree" sentimentality.

Under Roosevelt, professional foresters and engineers developed a policy of "multiple-use resource management." They sought to combine recreation, sustained-yield logging, watershed protection, and summer stock grazing on the same expanse of federal land.

Sunrise, Yosemite Valley, by Albert Bierstadt, c. 1870
A German-born artist, Bierstadt romanticized the already awesome beauty of the American West.

The Machine and Nature   These hardy sightseers at the Grand Canyon in 1911 ironically and probably unwittingly foreshadowed the age of mass tourism that arrived with the dawning automobile age. Soon millions of motorized Americans would regularly flee from the cities and suburbs to "get away from it all" in wilderness sites increasingly overrun by their fellow refugees from "civilization."

Campaigning in Kansas in 1910, ex-president Roosevelt said,

"Of all the questions which can come before this nation, short of its existence in a great war, there is none which compares in importance with the central task of leaving this land even a better land for our descendants than it is for us, and training them into a better race to inhabit the land and pass it on. Conservation is a great moral issue, for it involves the patriotic duty of insuring the safety and continuance of the nation."

The "Roosevelt Panic" of 1907

Roosevelt was handily elected president "in his own right" in 1904 and entered his new term buoyed by his enormous personal popularity—the cuddly "teddy bear" honored one of his bear-hunting exploits (when he saved the life of a cub), and children piped vigorously on whistles modeled on his famous teeth. Yet the conservative Republican bosses considered him as dangerous and unpredictable as a rattlesnake. They grew increasingly restive as Roosevelt in his second term called ever more loudly for regulating the corporations, taxing incomes, and protecting workers. Roosevelt, meanwhile, had partly defanged himself after his election in 1904 by announcing that under no circumstances would he be a candidate for a third term. This was a tactical blunder, for the power of the king wanes when the people know he will be dead in four years.

Roosevelt suffered a sharp setback in 1907, when a short but punishing panic descended on Wall Street. The financial flurry featured frightened "runs" on banks, suicides, and criminal indictments against speculators.

The financial world hastened to blame Roosevelt for the storm. It cried that this "quack" had unsettled industry with his boat-rocking tactics. Conservatives damned him as "Theodore the Meddler" and branded the current distress the "Roosevelt panic." The hot-tempered president angrily lashed back at his critics when he accused "certain

Rational use of resources meant large-scale and long-term planning as well as efficient administrative techniques. Roosevelt's conservation program, like many of his business policies, meant working hand in glove with the biggest resource users. The one-man-and-a-mule logger, or the one-man-and-a-dog sheepherder, could not be counted upon to cooperate with the new resources bureaucracy. Single-person enterprises were inevitably shouldered aside, in the interests of efficiency, by the combined bulk of big business and big government.

malefactors of great wealth" of having deliberately engineered the monetary crisis to force the government to relax its assaults on trusts.

Fortunately, the panic of 1907 paved the way for long-overdue fiscal reforms. Precipitating a currency shortage, the flurry laid bare the need for a more elastic medium of exchange. In a crisis of this sort, the hard-pressed banks were unable to increase the volume of money in circulation, and those with ample reserves were reluctant to lend to their less fortunate competitors. Congress in 1908 responded by passing the Aldrich-Vreeland Act, which authorized national banks to issue emergency currency backed by various kinds of collateral. The path was thus smoothed for the momentous Federal Reserve Act of 1913 (see p. 708).

The Rough Rider Thunders Out

Still warmly popular in 1908, Roosevelt could easily have won a second presidential nomination and almost certainly the election. But he felt bound by his impulsive postelection promise after his victory in 1904.

The departing president thus naturally sought a successor who would carry out "my policies." The man of his choice was amiable, ample-girthed, and huge-framed (6 feet tall; 1.83 meters) William Howard Taft, secretary of war and a mild progressive. As an heir apparent, he had often been called upon in Roosevelt's absence to "sit on the lid"—all 350 pounds (159 kilograms) of him. At the Republican convention of 1908 in Chicago, Roosevelt used his control of the party machinery—the "steamroller"—to push through Taft's nomination on the first ballot. Three weeks later, in mile-high Denver, in the heart of silver country, the Democrats nominated twice-beaten William Jennings Bryan.

The dull campaign of 1908 featured the rotund Taft and the now-balding "Boy Orator" both trying to don the progressive Roosevelt mantle. The solid Judge Taft read cut-and-dried speeches while Bryan griped that Roosevelt had stolen his policies from the Bryanite camp. A majority of voters chose stability with Roosevelt-endorsed Taft, who polled 321 electoral votes to 162 for Bryan. The victor's popular count was 7,675,320 to 6,412,294. The election's only surprise came from the Socialists, who amassed 420,793 votes for Eugene V. Debs, the hero of the Pullman strike of 1894 (see p. 631).

Baby, Kiss Papa Good-bye   Theodore Roosevelt leaves his baby, "My Policies," in the hands of his chosen successor, William Howard Taft. Friction between Taft and Roosevelt would soon erupt, however, prompting Roosevelt to return to politics and challenge Taft for the presidency.

Roosevelt, ever in the limelight, left soon after the election for a lion hunt in Africa. His numerous enemies clinked glasses while toasting "Health to the lions," and a few irreverently prayed that some big cat would "do its duty." But TR survived, still bursting with energy at the age of fifty-one in 1909.

Roosevelt was branded by his adversaries as a wild-eyed radical, but his reputation as an eater of errant industrialists now seems inflated. He fought many a sham battle, and the number of laws he inspired was certainly not in proportion to the amount of noise he emitted. He was often under attack from the reigning business lords, but the more enlightened of them knew that they had a friend in the White House. Roosevelt should be remembered first and foremost as the cowboy who started to tame the bucking bronco of adolescent capitalism, thus ensuring it a long adult life.

resource-predators, was probably his most typical and his most lasting achievement.

Several other contributions of Roosevelt lasted beyond his presidency. First, he greatly enlarged the power and prestige of the presidential office—and masterfully developed the technique of using the big stick of publicity as a political bludgeon. Second, he helped shape the progressive movement and beyond it the liberal reform campaigns later in the century. His Square Deal, in a sense, was the grandfather of the New Deal later launched by his fifth cousin, Franklin D. Roosevelt. Finally, to a greater degree than any of his predecessors, TR opened the eyes of Americans to the fact that they shared the world with other nations. As a great power they had fallen heir to responsibilities—and had been seized by ambitions—from which there was no escaping.

Taft Campaigning   A powerful voice was a political necessity in the pre-electronic age.

Taft: A Round Peg in a Square Hole

William Howard Taft, with his ruddy complexion and upturned mustache, at first inspired widespread confidence. "Everybody loves a fat man," the saying goes, and the jovial Taft, with "mirthquakes" of laughter bubbling up from his abundant abdomen, was personally popular. He had graduated second in his class at Yale and had established an enviable reputation as a lawyer and judge, though he was widely regarded as hostile to labor unions. He had been a trusted administrator under Roosevelt—in the Philippines, at home, and in Cuba, where he had served capably as a troubleshooter.

But "good old Will" suffered from lethal political handicaps. Roosevelt had led the conflicting elements of the Republican party by the sheer force of his personality. Taft, in contrast, had none of the arts of a dashing political leader and none of Roosevelt's zest for the fray. Recoiling from the clamor of controversy, he generally adopted an attitude of passivity toward Congress. He was a poor judge of public opinion, and his candor made him a chronic victim of "foot-in-mouth" disease.

"Peaceful Bill" was no doubt a mild progressive, but at heart he was more wedded to the status quo than to change. Significantly, his cabinet did not contain a single representative of the party's "insurgent" wing, which was on fire for reform of current abuses, especially the tariff.

TR's enthusiasm and perpetual youthfulness, like an overgrown Boy Scout's, appealed to the young of all ages. "You must always remember," a British diplomat cautioned his colleagues, "that the president is about six." He served as a political lightning rod to protect capitalists against popular indignation—and against socialism, which Roosevelt regarded as "ominous." He strenuously sought the middle road between unbridled individualism and paternalistic collectivism. His conservation crusade, which tried to mediate between the romantic wilderness-preservationists and the rapacious

Roosevelt, who preached the doctrine of the "strenuous life," practiced it until almost the end. In 1913 he sent a political message on a still-preserved phonograph recording to the Boy's Progressive League:

"Don't flinch, don't foul, and hit the line hard."

Ex-President Theodore Roosevelt Watches President Taft Struggle With the Demands of Government, 1910

The Dollar Goes Abroad as a Diplomat

Though ordinarily lethargic, Taft bestirred himself to use the lever of American investments to boost American political interests abroad, an approach to foreign policy that his critics denounced as "dollar diplomacy." Washington warmly encouraged Wall Street bankers to sluice their surplus dollars into foreign areas of strategic concern to the United States, especially in the Far East and in the regions critical to the security of the Panama Canal. Otherwise, investors from rival powers, such as Germany, might take advantage of financial chaos and secure a lodgment inimical to Uncle Sam's interests, both physical and commercial. New York bankers would thus strengthen American defenses and foreign policies, while bringing further prosperity to their homeland—and to themselves. The almighty dollar thereby supplanted the big stick.

China's Manchuria was the object of Taft's most spectacular effort to inject the reluctant dollar into the Far Eastern theater. Newly ambitious Japan and imperialistic Russia, recent foes, controlled the railroads of this strategic province. President Taft saw in the Manchurian railway monopoly a possible strangulation of Chinese economic interests and a consequent slamming of the Open Door in the faces of U.S. merchants. In 1909 Secretary of State Philander C. Knox blunderingly proposed that a group of American and foreign bankers buy the Manchurian railroads and then turn them over to China under a self-liquidating arrangement. Both Japan and Russia, unwilling to be jockeyed out of their dominant position, bluntly rejected Knox's overtures. Taft was showered with ridicule.

Another dangerous new trouble spot was the revolution-riddled Caribbean—now virtually a Yankee lake. Hoping to head off trouble, Washington urged Wall Street bankers to pump dollars into the financial vacuums in Honduras and Haiti to keep out foreign funds. The United States, under the Monroe Doctrine, would not permit foreign nations to intervene, and consequently felt obligated to put its money where its mouth was to prevent economic and political instability.

Again necessity was the mother of armed Caribbean intervention. Sporadic disorders in palm-fronded Cuba, Honduras, and the Dominican Republic brought American forces to these countries to restore order and protect American investment. A revolutionary upheaval in Nicaragua, regarded as perilously close to the nearly completed Panama Canal, resulted in the landing of twenty-five hundred marines in 1912. The marines remained in Nicaragua for thirteen years. (See map, p. 711.)

Taft the Trustbuster

Taft managed to gain some fame as a smasher of monopolies. The ironic truth is that the colorless Taft brought 90 suits against the trusts during his 4 years in office, as compared with some 44 for Roosevelt in $7\frac{1}{2}$ years.

By fateful happenstance the most sensational judicial actions during the Taft regime came in 1911. In that year the Supreme Court ordered the dissolution of the mighty Standard Oil Company, which was judged to be a combination in restraint of trade in violation of the Sherman Anti-Trust Act of 1890. At the same time, the Court handed down its famous "rule of reason." This doctrine held that only those combinations that "unreasonably" restrained trade were illegal. This fine-print proviso ripped a huge hole in the government's antitrust net.

Even more explosively, in 1911 Taft decided to press an antitrust suit against the U.S. Steel Corporation. This initiative infuriated Roosevelt, who had personally been involved in one of the mergers that prompted the suit. Once Roosevelt's protégé, President Taft was increasingly taking on the role of his antagonist. The stage was being set for a bruising confrontation.

Taft Splits the Republican Party

Lowering the barriers of the formidable protective tariff—the "Mother of Trusts"—was high on the agenda of the progressive members of the Republican party, and they at first thought they had a friend and ally in Taft. True to his campaign promises to reduce tariffs, Taft called Congress into special session in March 1909. The House proceeded to pass a moderately reductive bill, but senatorial reactionaries, led by Senator Nelson W. Aldrich of Rhode Island, tacked on hundreds of upward tariff revisions. Only such items as hides, sea moss, and canary-bird seed were left on the duty-free list.

After much handwringing, Taft signed the Payne-Aldrich Bill, thus betraying his campaign promises and outraging the progressive wing of his party, heavily drawn from the Midwest. Taft rubbed salt in the wound by proclaiming it "the best bill that the Republican party ever passed."

Taft revealed a further knack for shooting himself in the foot in his handling of conservation. The portly president was a dedicated conservationist, and his contributions actually equaled or surpassed those of Roosevelt. He established the Bureau of Mines to control mineral resources, rescued millions of acres of western coal lands from exploitation, and protected water-power sites from private development.

But those praiseworthy accomplishments were largely erased in the public mind by the noisy Ballinger-Pinchot quarrel that erupted in 1910. When Secretary of the Interior Richard Ballinger opened public lands in Wyoming, Montana, and Alaska to corporate development, he was sharply criticized by Gifford Pinchot, chief of the Agriculture Department's Division of Forestry and a stalwart Rooseveltian. When Taft dismissed Pinchot on the narrow grounds of insubordination, a storm of protest arose from conservationists and from Roosevelt's friends, who were legion. The whole unsavory episode further widened the growing rift between the president and the former president, one-time bosom political partners.

The reformist wing of the Republican party was now up in arms. It had been aroused mostly by the unpopular Payne-Aldrich Tariff and by White House support for Ballinger. Taft was being pushed increasingly into the embrace of the standpat Old Guard. When he deserted the progressives in their attack on the leading Old Guard mouthpiece in the House of Representatives, the coarse and profane Speaker, "Uncle Joe" Cannon, the breach was complete.

By the spring of 1910, the Grand Old Party was split wide open, owing largely to the clumsiness of Taft. A suspicious Roosevelt returned triumphantly to New York in June 1910 and shortly thereafter stirred up a tempest. Unable to keep silent, he took to the stump at Osawatomie, Kansas, and shocked the Old Guard with a flaming speech. The doctrine that he proclaimed—popularly known as the "New Nationalism"—urged the national government to increase its power to remedy economic and social abuses.

Weakened by these internal divisions, the Republicans lost badly in the congressional elections of 1910. In a victory of landslide proportions, the Democrats emerged with 228 seats, leaving the

Roosevelt the Take-Back Giver

once-dominant Republicans with only 161. In a further symptom of the reforming temper of the times, a Socialist representative, Austrian-born Victor L. Berger, was elected from Milwaukee.* The Republicans, by virtue of holdovers, retained the Senate, 51 to 41, but the insurgents in their midst were numerous enough to make that hold precarious.

The Taft-Roosevelt Rupture

The sputtering uprising in Republican ranks had now blossomed into a full-fledged revolt. Early in 1911 the National Progressive Republican League was formed, with the fiery, white-maned Senator La Follette of Wisconsin its leading candidate for the Republican presidential nomination. The assumption was that Roosevelt, an anti–third termer, would not permit himself to be "drafted."

But the restless Rough Rider began to change his views about third terms as he saw Taft, hand in glove with the hated Old Guard, discard "my policies." In February 1912 Roosevelt formally wrote to seven state governors that he was willing to accept

the Republican nomination. His reasoning was that the third-term tradition applied to three *consecutive elective* terms. Exuberantly he cried, "My hat is in the ring!" and "The fight is on and I am stripped to the buff!"

Roosevelt forthwith seized the Progressive banner, while La Follette, who had served as a convenient pathbreaker, was protestingly elbowed aside. Girded for battle, the Rough Rider came clattering into the presidential primaries then being held in many states. He shouted through half-clenched teeth that the president had fallen under the thumb of the reactionary bosses and that, although Taft "means well, he means well feebly." The once-genial Taft, now in a fighting mood, retorted by branding Roosevelt supporters "emotionalists and neurotics."

A Taft-Roosevelt explosion was near in June 1912, when the Republican convention met in Chicago. The Rooseveltites, who were about 100 delegates short of winning the nomination, challenged the right of some 250 Taft delegates to be seated. Most of these contests were arbitrarily settled in favor of Taft, whose supporters held the throttle of the convention steamroller. The Roosevelt adherents, crying "fraud" and "naked theft," in the end refused to vote, and Taft triumphed.

Roosevelt, the supposedly good sportsman, refused to quit the game. Having tasted for the first time the bitter cup of defeat, he was now on fire to lead a third-party crusade.

*He was eventually denied his seat in 1919, during a wave of antired hysteria.

Chronology

1901	Commission system established in Galveston, Texas
	Progressive Robert La Follette elected governor of Wisconsin
1902	Lincoln Steffens and Ida Tarbell publish muckraking exposés
	Anthracite coal strike
	Newlands Act
1903	Department of Commerce and Labor established
	Elkins Act
1904	*Northern Securities* case
	Roosevelt defeats Alton B. Parker for presidency
1905	*Lochner* v. *New York*
1906	Hepburn Act
	Upton Sinclair publishes *The Jungle*
	Meat Inspection Act
1906	Pure Food and Drug Act
1907	"Roosevelt panic"
1908	*Muller* v. *Oregon*
	Taft defeats Bryan for presidency
	Aldrich-Vreeland Act
1909	Payne-Aldrich Tariff
1910	Ballinger-Pinchot affair
1911	Triangle Shirtwaist Company fire
	Standard Oil antitrust case
	U.S. Steel Corporation antitrust suit
1912	Taft wins Republican nomination over Roosevelt
1913	Seventeenth Amendment passed (direct election of U.S. senators)
	Federal Reserve Act

SUGGESTED READINGS

PRIMARY SOURCE DOCUMENTS

Lincoln Steffens, *The Shame of the Cities** (1904), is an exemplary muckraking document, as is Upton Sinclair's notorious novel *The Jungle* (1906). For a less than gracious assessment of the muckrakers, see Theodore Roosevelt, "The Man with the Muckrake,"* *Putnam's Monthly and The Critic,* vol. I (October 1906), pp. 42–43. A revealing account of municipal politics is George Washington Plunkitt, *Plunkitt of Tammany Hall** (1905). See also the decision of the Supreme Court on state bakery regulations in *Lochner* v. *New York,* 198 U.S. 45 (1905). Oliver Wendell Holmes, Jr.'s thundering dissent in the *Lochner* case is reprinted in Richard Hofstadter, *Great Issues in American History.*

---

*An asterisk indicates that the document, or an excerpt from it, can be found in Thomas A. Bailey and David M. Kennedy, eds., *The American Spirit: United States History as Seen by Contemporaries,* 9th ed. (Boston: Houghton Mifflin, 1998).

SECONDARY SOURCES

A brief introduction is John W. Chambers, *The Tyranny of Change: America in the Progressive Era, 1900–1917* (1980). Perceptive interpretations are Samuel P. Hays, *The Response to Industrialism, 1885–1914* (1957); Robert H. Wiebe, *The Search for Order* (1967); and Richard Hofstadter, *The Age of Reform* (1955). Valuable analyses of progressivism at the state level include Richard McCormick's exceptionally good *From Realignment to Reform: Political Change in New York State, 1893–1910* (1981); David Thelen's study of Wisconsin, *The New Citizenship* (1972); and Dewey W. Grantham, *Southern Progressivism* (1983). Especially provocative are James Weinstein, *The Corporate Ideal in the Liberal State* (1968), and Gabriel Kolko, *The Triumph of Conservatism* (1963). Consult also Alfred D. Chandler, Jr., *The Visible Hand* (1977), and Morton Keller, *Regulating a New Economy: Public Policy and Economic Change in America, 1900–1933* (1990). On pure food and drugs, see James Harvey Young, *Pure Food: Securing the Federal Food and*

Drugs Act of 1906 (1989), and Oscar E. Anderson, Jr., *The Health of a Nation: Harvey H. Wiley and the Fight for Pure Food* (1958). Other social issues of importance are treated in James H. Timberlake, *Prohibition and the Progressive Movement* (1963); David J. Rothman, *Conscience and Convenience: The Asylum and Its Alternatives in Progressive America* (1980); Allen F. Davis, *Spearheads for Reform: The Social Settlements and the Progressive Movement, 1890–1914* (1967); Mina Carson, *Settlement Folk: Social Thought and the American Settlement Movement, 1885–1930* (1990); James Patterson, *America's Struggle Against Poverty, 1900–1980* (1981); David B. Tyack, *The One Best System: A History of American Urban Education* (1974); and Lynn Gordon, *Gender and Higher Education in the Progressive Era* (1990). On religion see Martin E. Marty, *Modern American Religion: The Irony of It All, 1893–1919* (1986); T. J. Jackson Lears takes a different perspective in *No Place of Grace: Antimodernism and the Transformation of American Culture* (1981). Municipal reform is the subject of Martin J. Schiesl, *The Politics of Efficiency* (1977), and two useful anthologies, Bruce Stave, ed., *Urban Bosses, Machines and Progressive Reformers* (1972), and Blaine A. Brownell and Warren E. Stickle, eds., *Bosses and Reformers* (1973). On conservation see Samuel P. Hays, *Conservation and the Gospel of Efficiency* (1959); Elmo Richardson, *The Politics of Conservation* (1962); and James Penick, Jr., *Progressive Politics and Conservation* (1968). Socialism is discussed in Nick Salvatore, *Eugene V. Debs: Citizen and Socialist* (1982); James Weinstein, *The Decline of Socialism in America, 1912–1925* (1967); and Mari Jo Buhle, *Women and American Socialism, 1897–1920* (1981). Another perspective on women in this period is given in Rosalind Rosenberg, *Beyond Separate Spheres* (1982). Jacqueline Jones focuses on black women in *Labor of Love, Labor of Sorrow: Black Women, Work, and the Family from Slavery to the Present* (1985). The Taft era is summarized in Paolo Coletta, *The Presidency of William Howard Taft* (1973). See also Norman Wilensky, *Conservatives in the Progressive Era* (1965), and James Holt, *Congressional Insurgents and the Party System, 1909–1916* (1968). Otis Graham traces the progressive legacy in *Encore for Reform: The Old Progressives and the New Deal* (1967).

32

Wilsonian Progressivism at Home and Abroad

1912–1916

This is not a day of triumph; it is a day of dedication. Here muster not the forces of party, but the forces of humanity. . . . I summon all honest men, all patriotic, all forward-looking men, to my side. God helping me, I will not fail them, if they will but counsel and sustain me!

THOMAS WOODROW WILSON, INAUGURAL, 1913

The Emergence of Dr. Thomas Woodrow Wilson

Office-hungry Democrats—the "outs" since 1897—were jubilant over the disruptive Republican brawl at Chicago. If they could come up with an outstanding reformist leader, they had an excellent chance to win the White House. Such a leader appeared in Dr. Woodrow Wilson, once a mild conservative but now a militant progressive. Beginning professional life as a brilliant academic lecturer on government, he had

risen in 1902 to the presidency of Princeton University, where he had achieved some sweeping educational reforms.

Wilson entered politics in 1910 when New Jersey bosses, needing a respectable "front" candidate for the governorship, offered him the nomination. They expected to lead the academic novice by the nose, but to their surprise, Wilson waged a passionate reform campaign in which he assailed the "predatory" trusts and promised to return state government to the people. Riding the crest of the progressive wave, the "Schoolmaster in Politics" was swept into office.

GOP Divided by Bull Moose Equals Democratic Victory, 1912

Once in the governor's chair, Wilson drove through the legislature a sheaf of forward-looking measures that made reactionary New Jersey one of the more liberal states. Filled with righteous indignation, Wilson revealed irresistible reforming zeal, burning eloquence, superb powers of leadership, and a refreshing habit of appealing over the heads of the scheming bosses to the sovereign people. Now a figure of national eminence, Wilson was being widely mentioned for the presidency.

When the Democrats met at Baltimore in 1912, Wilson was nominated on the forty-sixth ballot, aided by William Jennings Bryan's switch to his side. The Democrats gave Wilson a strong progressive platform to run on; dubbed the "New Freedom" program, it included calls for stronger antitrust legislation, banking reform, and tariff reductions.

The "Bull Moose" Campaign of 1912

Surging events had meanwhile been thrusting Roosevelt to the fore as a candidate for the presidency on a third-party Progressive Republican ticket. The fighting ex-cowboy, angered by his recent rebuff, was eager to lead the charge. A pro-Roosevelt Progressive convention, with about two thousand delegates from forty states, assembled in Chicago during August 1912. Dramatically symbolizing the rising political status of women, as well as Progressive support for the cause of social justice, settlement-house pioneer Jane Addams placed Roosevelt's name in nomination for the presidency. Roosevelt was applauded tumultuously as he cried in a vehement speech, "We stand at Armageddon,

and we battle for the Lord!" The hosanna spirit of a religious revival meeting suffused the convention, as the hoarse delegates sang "Onward Christian Soldiers" and "Battle Hymn of the Republic." William Allen White, the caustic Kansas journalist, later wrote, "Roosevelt bit me and I went mad."

Fired-up Progressives entered the campaign with righteousness and enthusiasm. Roosevelt boasted that he felt "as strong as a bull moose," and the bull moose took its place with the donkey and the elephant in the American political zoo. As one poet whimsically put it,

> I want to be a Bull Moose,
> And with the Bull Moose stand
> With antlers on my forehead
> And a Big Stick in my hand.

Roosevelt and Taft were bound to slit each other's political throats; by dividing the Republican vote, they virtually guaranteed a Democratic victory. The two antagonists tore into each other as only former friends can. "Death alone can take me out now," cried the once-jovial Taft, as he branded Roosevelt a "dangerous egotist" and a "demagogue." Roosevelt, fighting mad, assailed Taft as a "fathead" with the brain of a "guinea pig."

Beyond the clashing personalities, the overshadowing question of the 1912 campaign was which of two varieties of progressivism would prevail—Roosevelt's New Nationalism or Wilson's New Freedom. Both men favored a more active government role in economic and social affairs, but they disagreed sharply over specific strategies. Roosevelt preached the theories spun out by the progressive thinker Herbert Croly in his book *The Promise of American Life* (1910). Croly and TR both favored continued consolidation of trusts and labor unions, paralleled by the growth of powerful regulatory agencies in Washington. Roosevelt and his "bull moosers" also campaigned for woman suffrage and a broad program of social welfare, including minimum-wage laws and "socialistic" social insurance. Clearly, the bull moose Progressives looked forward to the kind of activist welfare state that Franklin Roosevelt's New Deal would one day make a reality.

Wilson's New Freedom, by contrast, favored small enterprise, entrepreneurship, and the free functioning of unregulated and unmonopolized markets. The Democrats shunned social-welfare proposals and pinned their economic faith on competition—on the "man on the make," as Wilson put it. The keynote of Wilson's campaign was not regulation but fragmentation of the big industrial combines, chiefly by means of vigorous enforcement of the antitrust laws. The election of 1912 thus offered the voters a choice not merely of policies but of political and economic philosophies—a rarity in United States history.

The heat of the campaign cooled a bit when, in Milwaukee, Roosevelt was shot in the chest by a fanatic. The Rough Rider suspended active campaigning for more than two weeks after delivering, with bull moose gameness and a bloody shirt, his scheduled speech.

Woodrow Wilson: A Minority President

Former professor Wilson won handily, with 435 electoral votes and 6,296,547 popular votes. The "third-party" candidate, Roosevelt, finished second, receiving 88 electoral votes and 4,118,571 popular votes. Taft won only 8 paltry electoral votes and 3,486,720 popular votes (see the map on p. 706).

The election figures are fascinating. Wilson, with only 41 percent of the popular vote, was clearly a minority president, though his party won a majority in Congress. His popular total was actually smaller than Bryan had amassed in any of his three defeats, despite the increase in population. Taft and Roosevelt together polled over one-and-a-quarter million more votes than the Democrats. Progressivism rather than Wilson was the runaway winner. Although the Democratic total obviously included many conservatives in the solid South, still the combined progressive vote for Wilson and Roosevelt exceeded the tally of the more conservative Taft. To the progressive tally must be added some support for the Socialist candidate, persistent Eugene V. Debs, who rolled up 900,672 votes, or more than twice as many as he had netted four years earlier. Starry-eyed Socialists dreamed of being in the White House within eight years.

Roosevelt's lone-wolf course was tragic both for himself and for his former Republican associates. Perhaps, to rephrase William Allen White, he had bitten himself and gone mad. The Progressive party, which was primarily a one-man show, had no future because it had elected few candidates to state and local offices; the Socialists, in contrast, elected more than a thousand. Without patronage plums to hand out to the faithful workers, death by slow starvation was inevitable for the upstart party. Yet the Progressives made a tremendous showing for a hastily organized third party and helped spur the enactment of many of their pet reforms by the Wilsonian Democrats.

As for the Republicans, they were thrust into unaccustomed minority status in Congress for the next six years and were frozen out of the White

The Presidential Vote, 1912

Candidate	Party	Electoral Vote	Popular Vote	Approximate Percentage
Woodrow Wilson	Democratic	435	6,296,547	41%
Theodore Roosevelt	Progressive	88	4,118,571	27
William H. Taft	Republican	8	3,486,720	23
Eugene V. Debs	Socialist	—	900,672	6
E. W. Chafin	Prohibition	—	206,275	1
A. E. Reimer	Socialist-Labor	—	28,750	0.2

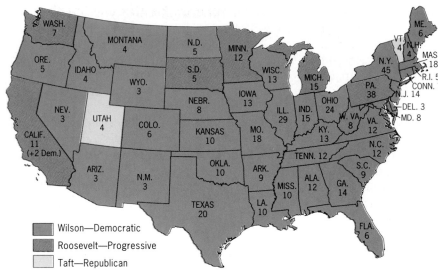

Presidential Election of 1912 (with electoral vote by state) The Republican split surely boosted Wilson to victory, as he failed to win a clear majority in any state outside the old Confederacy. The election gave the Democrats solid control of the White House and both houses of Congress for the first time since the Civil War.

House for eight years. Taft himself had a fruitful old age. He taught law for eight pleasant years at Yale University and in 1921 became chief justice of the Supreme Court—a job for which he was far more happily suited than the presidency.

Wilson: The Idealist in Politics

(Thomas) Woodrow Wilson, the second Democratic president since 1861, looked like the ascetic intellectual he was, with his clean-cut features, pinched-on eyeglasses, and trim figure (5 feet, 11 inches, and 179 pounds; 1.8 meters, 81.2 kilograms). Born in Virginia shortly before the Civil War and reared in Georgia and the Carolinas, the professor-politician was the first man from one of the seceded southern states to reach the White House since Zachary Taylor, sixty-four years earlier.

The impact of Dixieland on young "Tommy" Wilson was profound. He sympathized with the Confederacy's gallant attempt to win its independence, a sentiment that partly inspired his ideal of self-determination for people of other countries. Steeped in the traditions of Jeffersonian democracy, he shared Jefferson's faith in the masses—if they were properly informed.

Son of a Presbyterian minister, Wilson was reared in an atmosphere of fervent piety. He later used the presidential pulpit to preach his inspirational political sermons. A moving orator, Wilson could rise on the wings of spiritual power to soaring eloquence. Skillfully using a persuasive voice, he relied not on arm-waving but on sincerity and moral appeal. As a lifelong student of finely chiseled words, he turned out to be a "phraseocrat" who coined many noble epigrams. Someone has remarked that he was born halfway between the Bible and the dictionary, and never strayed far from either.

A profound student of government, Wilson believed that the chief executive should play a dynamic role. He was convinced that Congress could not function properly unless the president, like a kind of prime minister, got out in front and provided leadership. He enjoyed dramatic success, both as governor and as president, in appealing over the heads of legislators to the sovereign people.

Splendid though Wilson's intellectual equipment was, he suffered from serious defects of personality. Though jovial and witty in private, he could be cold and standoffish in public. Incapable of unbending and acting the showman, like "Teddy" Roosevelt, he lacked the common touch. He loved humanity in the mass rather than the individual in person. His academic background caused him to feel most at home with scholars, although he had to work with politicians. An austere and somewhat arrogant intellectual, he looked down his nose through pince-nez glasses upon lesser minds,

President Woodrow Wilson (1856–1924), by Sir William
Orpen   A realist-idealist, Wilson wrote some six years before
coming to the White House, "The President is at liberty, both
in law and conscience, to be as big a man as he can." Fighting
desperately later for the League of Nations and breaking himself down, he said, "I would rather fail in a cause that I know
some day will triumph than to win in a cause that I know
some day will fail."

including journalists. He was especially intolerant
of stupid senators, whose "bungalow" minds made
him "sick."

Wilson's burning idealism—especially his desire
to reform ever-present wickedness—drove him forward faster than lesser spirits were willing to go. His
sense of moral righteousness was such that he often
found compromise difficult; black was black, wrong
was wrong, and one should never compromise with
wrong. President Wilson's Scottish Presbyterian
ancestors had passed on to him an inflexible stubbornness. When convinced that he was right, the
principled Wilson would break before he would
bend, unlike the pragmatic Roosevelt.

Wilson Tackles the Tariff

Few presidents have arrived at the White House
with a clearer program than Wilson's or one destined to be so completely achieved. The new president called for an all-out assault on what he called
"the triple wall of privilege": the tariff, the banks,
and the trusts.

He tackled the tariff first, summoning Congress
into special session in early 1913. In a precedent-
shattering move, he did not send his presidential
message over to the Capitol to be read loudly by a
bored clerk, as had been the custom since Jefferson's
day. Instead he appeared in person before a joint
session of Congress and presented his appeal with
stunning eloquence and effectiveness.

Moved by Wilson's aggressive leadership, the
House swiftly passed the Underwood Tariff Bill,
which provided for a substantial reduction of rates.
When a swarm of lobbyists descended on the Senate
seeking to disembowel the bill, Wilson promptly
issued a combative message to the people, urging
them to hold their elected representatives in line.
The tactic worked. The force of public opinion,
aroused by the president's oratory, secured final
approval late in 1913 of the bill Wilson wanted.

The new Underwood tariff substantially reduced import fees. It also was a landmark in tax legislation. Under authority granted by the recently
ratified Sixteenth Amendment, Congress enacted a
graduated income tax, beginning with a modest
levy on incomes over $3,000 (then considerably
higher than the average family's income). By 1917
revenue from the income tax shot ahead of receipts
from the tariff. This gap has since been vastly
widened.

Wilson Battles the Bankers

A second bastion of the "triple wall of privilege" was
the antiquated and inadequate banking and currency system, long since outgrown by the Republic's
lusty economic expansion. The country's financial
structure, still creaking along under the Civil War
National Banking Act, revealed glaring defects. Its
most serious shortcoming, as exposed by the panic
of 1907, was the inelasticity of the currency. Banking

reserves were heavily concentrated in New York and a handful of other large cities and could not be mobilized in times of financial stress into areas that were badly pinched.

In 1908 Congress had authorized an investigation headed by a mossback banker, Republican Senator Aldrich. Three years later Aldrich's special commission recommended a gigantic bank with numerous branches—in effect, a third Bank of the United States.

For their part, Democratic banking reformers heeded the findings of a House committee chaired by Congressman Arsene Pujo, which traced the tentacles of the "money monster" into the hidden vaults of American banking and business. President Wilson's confidant, progressive-minded Massachusetts attorney Louis D. Brandeis, further fanned the flames of reform with his incendiary though scholarly book *Other People's Money and How the Bankers Use It* (1914).

In June 1913, in a second dramatic personal appearance before both houses of Congress, the president delivered a stirring plea for sweeping reform of the banking system. He ringingly endorsed Democratic proposals for a decentralized bank in government hands, as opposed to Republican demands for a huge private bank with fifteen branches.

Again appealing to the sovereign people, Wilson scored another triumph. In 1913 he signed the epochal Federal Reserve Act, the most important piece of economic legislation between the Civil War and the New Deal. The new Federal Reserve Board, appointed by the president, oversaw a nationwide system of twelve regional reserve districts, each with its own central bank. Although these regional banks were actually bankers' banks, owned by member financial institutions, the final authority of the Federal Reserve Board guaranteed a substantial measure of public control. The board was also empowered to issue paper money—"Federal Reserve Notes"—backed by commercial paper, such as promissory notes of businesspeople. Thus the amount of money in circulation could be swiftly increased as needed for the legitimate requirements of business.

The Federal Reserve Act was a red-letter achievement. It carried the nation with flying banners through the financial crises of the World War of 1914–1918. Without it, the Republic's progress toward the modern economic age would have been seriously retarded.

The President Tames the Trusts

Without pausing for breath, Wilson pushed toward the last remaining rampart in the "triple wall of privilege"—the trusts. Early in 1914 he again went before Congress in a personal appearance that still carried drama.

Nine months and thousands of words later, Congress responded with the Federal Trade Commission Act of 1914. The new law empowered a presidentially appointed commission to turn a searchlight on industries engaged in interstate commerce, such as the meatpackers. The commissioners were expected to crush monopoly at the source by rooting out unfair trade practices, including unlawful competition, false advertising, mislabeling, adulteration, and bribery.

The knot of monopoly was further cut by the Clayton Anti-Trust Act of 1914. It lengthened the shopworn Sherman Act's list of business practices that were deemed objectionable, including price discrimination and interlocking directorates (whereby the same individuals served as directors of supposedly competing firms).

The Clayton Act also conferred long-overdue benefits on labor. Conservative courts had unexpectedly been ruling that trade unions fell under the antimonopoly restraints of the Sherman Act. A classic case involved striking hatmakers in Danbury, Connecticut, who were assessed triple damages of more than $250,000, which resulted in the loss of their savings and homes. The Clayton Act therefore sought to exempt labor and agricultural organiza-

Organization of Holding Companies Keep in mind that the voting stock of a corporation is often only a fraction of the total stock.

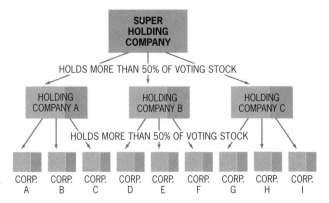

Wilson the Trustbuster   A prominent part of Woodrow Wilson's reform program involved strengthening the Sherman Anti-Trust Law of 1890. Congress obliged him by passing the Clayton Anti-Trust Act in 1914.

tions from antitrust prosecution, while explicitly legalizing strikes and peaceful picketing.

Union leader Samuel Gompers hailed the act as the Magna Carta of labor because it legally lifted human labor out of the category of "a commodity or article of commerce." But the rejoicing was premature, as conservative judges in later years continued to clip the wings of the union movement.

Wilsonian Progressivism at High Tide

Energetically scaling the "triple wall of privilege," Woodrow Wilson had treated the nation to a dazzling demonstration of vigorous presidential leadership. He proved nearly irresistible in his first eighteen months in office. For once, a political creed was matched by deed, as the progressive reformers racked up victory after victory.

Standing at the peak of his powers at the head of the progressive forces, Wilson pressed ahead with further reforms. The Federal Farm Loan Act of 1916 made credit available to farmers at low rates of interest—as long demanded by the Populists. The Warehouse Act of 1916 authorized loans on the security of staple crops—another Populist idea. Other laws benefited rural America by providing for highway construction and the establishment of agricultural extension work in the state colleges.

Sweaty laborers also made gains as the progressive wave foamed forward. Sailors, treated brutally from cat-o'-nine-tails days onward, were given relief by the La Follette Seamen's Act of 1915. It required decent treatment and a living wage on American merchant ships. One unhappy result of this well-intentioned law was the crippling of America's merchant marine, as freight rates spiraled upward with the crew's wages.

Wilson further helped the workers with the Workingmen's Compensation Act of 1916, granting assistance to federal civil-service employees during periods of disability. In the same year, the president approved an act restricting child labor on products flowing into interstate commerce, though the standpat Supreme Court soon invalidated the law. Railroad workers, numbering about 1.7 million, were not sidetracked. The Adamson Act of 1916 established an eight-hour day for all employees on trains in interstate commerce, with extra pay for overtime.

Wilson earned the enmity of businesspeople and bigots but endeared himself to progressives when in 1916 he nominated for the Supreme Court the prominent reformer Louis D. Brandeis—the first Jew to be called to the high bench. Yet even Wilson's progressivism had its limits, and it clearly stopped short of better treatment for blacks. The southern-bred Wilson actually presided over accelerated segregation in the federal bureaucracy. When a delegation of black leaders personally protested to him, the schoolmasterish president virtually froze them out of his office.

Despite these limitations, Wilson knew that to be reelected in 1916, he needed to identify himself clearly as the candidate of progressivism. He appeased businesspeople by making conservative appointments to the Federal Reserve Board and the Federal Trade Commission, but he devoted most of his energies to cultivating progressive support. Wilson's election in 1912 had been something of a fluke, owing largely to the Taft-Roosevelt split in the Republican ranks. To remain in the White House, the president would have to woo the bull moose voters into the Democratic fold.

New Directions in Foreign Policy

In one important area, Wilson chose not to answer the trumpet call of the bull moosers. In contrast to Roosevelt and even Taft, Wilson recoiled from an aggressive foreign policy. Hating imperialism, he was repelled by TR's big stickism. Suspicious of Wall Street, he detested the so-called dollar diplomacy of Taft.

In office only a week, Wilson declared war on dollar diplomacy. He proclaimed that the government would no longer offer special support to American investors in Latin America and China. Shivering from this Wilsonian bucket of cold water, American bankers pulled out of the Taft-engineered six-nation loan to China the next day.

In a similarly self-denying vein, Wilson persuaded Congress in early 1914 to repeal the Panama Canal Tolls Act of 1912, which had exempted American coastwise shipping from tolls and thereby provoked sharp protests from injured Britain. The president further chimed in with the anti-imperial song of Bryan and other Democrats when he signed the Jones Act in 1916. It granted to the Philippines the boon of territorial status and promised independence as soon as a "stable government" could be established. That glad day came thirty years later, on July 4, 1946.

Wilson also partially defused a menacing crisis with Japan in 1913. The California legislature, still seeking to rid the Golden State of Japanese settlers, prohibited them from owning land. Tokyo, understandably irritated, lodged vigorous protests. At Fortress Corregidor, in the Philippines, American gunners were put on around-the-clock alert. But when Wilson dispatched Secretary of State William Jennings Bryan to plead with the California legislature to soften its stand, tensions eased somewhat.

Political turmoil in Haiti soon forced Wilson to eat some of his anti-imperialist words. The climax of the disorders came in 1914–1915, when an outraged populace literally tore to pieces the brutal Haitian president. In 1915 Wilson reluctantly dispatched marines to protect American lives and property. In 1916 he stole a page from Roosevelt's corollary to the Monroe Doctrine and concluded a treaty with Haiti providing for U.S. supervision of finances and the police. In the same year, he sent the leather-necked marines to quell riots in the Dominican Republic, and that debt-cursed land came under the shadow of the American eagle's wings for the next eight years. In 1917 Wilson purchased from Denmark the Virgin Islands, in the West Indies,

U.S. Marines in Haiti, 1919
The United States sent the marines to Haiti in 1915 to protect American economic interests. They remained for nineteen years.

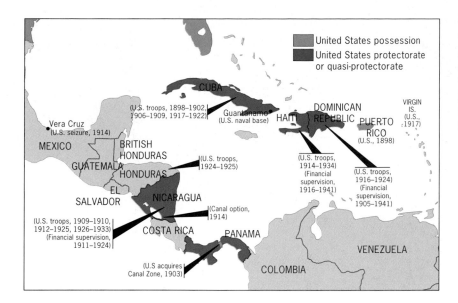

The United States in the Caribbean
This map explains why many Latin Americans accused the United States of turning the Caribbean Sea into a Yankee lake. It also suggests that Uncle Sam was much less "isolationist" in his own backyard than he was in faraway Europe or Asia.

tightening the grip of Uncle Sam in these shark-infested waters. Increasingly the Caribbean Sea, with its vital approaches to the now navigable Panama Canal, was taking on the earmarks of a Yankee preserve.

Moralistic Diplomacy in Mexico

Rifle bullets whining across the southern border served as a constant reminder that all was not quiet in Mexico. For decades Mexico had been sorely exploited by foreign investors in oil, railroads, and mines. By 1913 American capitalists had sunk about a billion dollars into the underdeveloped but generously endowed country, and about fifty thousand U.S. citizens had taken up residence south of the Rio Grande.

But if Mexico was rich, the Mexicans were poor. Fed up with their miserable lot, they at last revolted. Their revolution took an ugly turn in 1913, when a conscienceless clique murdered the popular new revolutionary president and installed General Victoriano Huerta, a full-blooded Indian, in the president's chair. All this chaos accelerated a massive migration of Mexicans to the United States. More than a million Spanish-speaking newcomers tramped across the southern border in the first three decades of the twentieth century. Settling mostly in Texas, New Mexico, Arizona, and California, they swung picks building highways and rail-roads or followed the fruit harvests as pickers. Though often segregated in Spanish-speaking enclaves, they helped to create a unique borderland culture that blended Mexican and American folkways.

The revolutionary bloodshed also menaced American lives and property in Mexico. Cries for intervention burst from the lips of American jingoes. Prominent among those chanting for war was the influential chain-newspaper publisher William Randolph Hearst, whose views presumably were colored by his ownership of a Mexican ranch larger than Rhode Island. Yet President Wilson stood firm against demands to step in. It was "perilous," he

A Republican congressman voiced complaints against Wilson's Mexican policy in 1916:

"It is characterized by weakness, uncertainty, vacillation, and uncontrollable desire to intermeddle in Mexican affairs. He has not had the courage to go into Mexico nor the courage to stay out. . . . I would either go into Mexico and pacify the country or I would keep my hands entirely out of Mexico. If we are too proud to fight, we should be too proud to quarrel. I would not choose between murderers."

Thorny Problems in Mexico   President Huerta clung to power for more than a year in 1913–1914, despite Woodrow Wilson's strong disapproval of his regime.

Calling Uncle Sam's Bluff   Though Woodrow Wilson had supported Mexican president Carranza's rise to power, Carranza vehemently protested General Pershing's pursuit of "Pancho" Villa into Mexico in 1917. The complicated tangle of the Mexican situation, 1913–1917, baffled and frustrated American diplomats, whose sometimes confused and contradictory decisions reaped a lasting harvest of ill will in Mexico.

declared, to determine foreign policy, "in the terms of material interest."

But though he refused to intervene, Wilson also refused to recognize officially the murderous government of "that brute" Huerta, even though most foreign powers acknowledged Huerta's bloody-handed regime. "I am going to teach the South American republics to elect good men," the former professor declared. He put his munitions where his mouth was in 1914, when he allowed American arms to flow to Huerta's principal rivals, white-bearded Venustiano Carranza and the firebrand Francisco ("Pancho") Villa.

The Mexican volcano erupted at the Atlantic seaport of Tampico in April 1914, when a small party of American sailors was arrested. The Mexicans promptly released the captives and apologized, but they refused the affronted American admiral's demand for a salute of twenty-one guns. Wilson, heavy-hearted but stubbornly determined to eliminate Huerta, asked Congress for authority to use force against Mexico. Before Congress could act, Wilson ordered the navy, which was seeking to intercept a German ship bearing arms to Huerta, to seize the Mexican port of Vera Cruz. Huerta as well as Carranza hotly protested against this high-handed Yankee maneuver.

Just as a full-dress shooting conflict seemed inevitable, Wilson was rescued by an offer of mediation from the ABC Powers—Argentina, Brazil, and Chile. Huerta collapsed in July 1914 under pressure from within and without. He was succeeded by his archrival, Venustiano Carranza, still fiercely resentful of Wilson's military meddling. The whole sorry

"Pancho" Villa with His Ragtag Army in Mexico, c. 1916
His daring, impetuosity, and horsemanship made Villa a hero to the masses of northern Mexico. Yet he proved to be a violent and ineffective crusader against social abuses, and he was assassinated in 1923.

episode did not augur well for the future of United States–Mexican relations.

"Pancho" Villa, a combination of bandit and Robin Hood, had meanwhile stolen the spotlight. He emerged as the chief rival to President Carranza, who was now reluctantly supported with arms and diplomatic recognition by Wilson. Challenging Carranza's authority while also punishing the gringos, Villa's men ruthlessly hauled sixteen young American mining engineers off a train traveling through northern Mexico in January 1916 and killed them. The culminating outrage came a month later when Villa and his followers, hoping to provide a war between Wilson and Carranza, blazed across the border into Columbus, New Mexico, and murdered another nineteen Americans.

General John J. ("Black Jack"*) Pershing, a grim-faced and ramrod-erect veteran of the Cuban and Philippine campaigns, was ordered to break up the bandit band. His hastily organized force of several thousand mounted troops penetrated deep into rugged Mexico with surprising speed. They clashed with Carranza's forces and mauled the Villistas but missed capturing Villa himself. As the threat of war with Germany loomed larger, the invading army was withdrawn in January 1917.

---

*So called from his earlier service as an officer with the crack black Tenth Cavalry.

Thunder Across the Sea

Europe's powder magazine, long smoldering, blew up in the summer of 1914, when the flaming pistol of a Serb patriot killed the heir to the throne of Austria-Hungary in Sarajevo. An outraged Vienna government, backed by Germany, forthwith presented a stern ultimatum to neighboring Serbia.

An explosive chain reaction followed. Tiny Serbia, backed by its powerful Slav neighbor Russia, refused to bend the knee sufficiently. The Russian tsar began to mobilize his ponderous war machine, menacing Germany on the east, even as his ally, France, confronted Germany on the west. In alarm, the Germans struck suddenly at France through unoffending Belgium; their objective was to knock their ancient enemy out of action so that they would have two free hands to repel Russia. Great Britain, its coastline jeopardized by the assault on Belgium, was sucked into the conflagration on the side of France.

Almost overnight most of Europe was locked in a fight to the death. On one side were arrayed the Central Powers: Germany and Austria-Hungary, and later Turkey and Bulgaria. On the other side were the Allies, principally France, Britain, and Russia, and later Japan and Italy.

Americans thanked God for the ocean moats and self-righteously congratulated themselves on having had ancestors wise enough to have abandoned the hell pits of Europe. America felt strong, snug, smug, and secure—but not for long.

A Precarious Neutrality

President Wilson's grief at the outbreak of war was compounded by the recent death of his wife. He sorrowfully issued the routine neutrality proclamation and called on Americans to be neutral in thought as well as deed. But such scrupulous evenhandedness proved difficult.

Both sides wooed the United States, the great neutral in the West. The British enjoyed the boon of close cultural, linguistic, and economic ties with America and had the added advantage of controlling most of the transatlantic cables. Their censors sheared away war stories harmful to the Allies and drenched the United States with tales of German bestiality.

The Germans and the Austro-Hungarians counted on the natural sympathies of their transplanted countrymen in America. Including persons with at least one foreign-born parent, people with blood ties to the Central Powers numbered some 11 million in 1914. Some of these recent immigrants expressed noisy sympathy for the fatherland, but most were simply grateful to be so distant from the fray.

Most Americans were anti-German from the outset. With his villainous upturned mustache,

The Kaiser and His Wolves   Resentment against German submarine attacks inflamed anti-German opinion in America.

Kaiser Wilhelm II seemed the embodiment of arrogant autocracy, an impression strengthened by Germany's ruthless strike at neutral Belgium. German and Austrian agents further tarnished the image of the Central Powers in American eyes when they

Principal Foreign Elements in the United States (Census of 1910; Total U.S. Population: 91,972,266)

Country of Origin		Foreign-Born	Natives with Two Foreign-Born Parents	Natives with One Foreign-Born Parent	Total
Central Powers	Germany	2,501,181	3,911,847	1,869,590	8,282,618
	Austria-Hungary	1,670,524	900,129	131,133	2,701,786
Allied Powers	Great Britain	1,219,968	852,610	1,158,474	3,231,052
	(Ireland)*	1,352,155	2,141,577	1,010,628	4,504,360
	Russia	1,732,421	949,316	70,938	2,752,675
	Italy	1,343,070	695,187	60,103	2,098,360
TOTAL (for all foreign countries, including those not listed)		13,345,545	12,916,311	5,981,526	32,243,282

*Ireland was not yet independent.

resorted to violence in American factories and ports. When a German operative in 1915 absent-mindedly left his briefcase on a New York elevated car, its documents detailing plans for industrial sabotage were quickly discovered and publicized. American opinion, already ill disposed, was further inflamed against the kaiser and Germany. Yet the great majority of Americans earnestly hoped to stay out of the horrible war.

America Earns Blood Money

When Europe burst into flames in 1914, the United States was bogged down in a worrisome business recession. But as fate would have it, British and French war orders soon pulled American industry out of the morass of hard times and onto a peak of war-born prosperity. Part of this boom was financed by American bankers, notably the Wall Street firm of J. P. Morgan and Company, which eventually advanced to the Allies the enormous sum of $2.3 billion during the period of American neutrality. The Central Powers protested bitterly against the immense trade between America and the Allies, but this traffic did not in fact violate the international neutrality laws. Germany was technically free to trade with the United States. It was prevented from doing so not by American policy but by geography and the British navy. Trade between Germany and America had to move across the Atlantic; but the British controlled the sea lanes, and they threw a noose-tight blockade of mines and ships across the North Sea, gateway to German ports. Over the unavailing protests of American shippers, farmers, and manufacturers, the British began forcing Amer-

> *The* Fatherland, *the chief German-American propaganda newspaper in the United States, cried,*
>
> "We [Americans] prattle about humanity while we manufacture poisoned shrapnel and picric acid for profit. Ten thousand German widows, ten thousand orphans, ten thousand graves bear the legend 'Made in America.'"

ican vessels off the high seas and into their ports. This harassment of American shipping proved highly effective, as trade between Germany and the United States virtually ceased.

Hard-pressed Germany did not tamely consent to being starved out. In retaliation for the British blockade, in February 1915 Berlin announced a submarine war area around the British Isles. The submarine was a weapon so new that existing international law could not be made to fit it. The old rule that a warship must stop and board a merchantman could hardly apply to submarines, which could easily be rammed or sunk if they surfaced.

The cigar-shaped marauders posed a dire threat to the United States—so long as Wilson insisted on maintaining America's neutral rights. Berlin officials declared that they would try not to sink *neutral* shipping, but they warned that mistakes would probably occur. Wilson now determined on a policy of calculated risk. He would continue to claim profitable neutral trading rights, while hoping that no high-seas incident would force his hand to grasp the sword of war. Setting his peninsular jaw, he emphat-

U.S. Exports to Belligerents, 1914–1916

Belligerent	1914	1915	1916	1916 Figure as a Percentage of 1914 Figure
Britain	$594,271,863	$911,794,954	$1,526,685,102	257%
France	159,818,924	369,397,170	628,851,988	393
Italy*	74,235,012	184,819,688	269,246,105	364
Germany	344,794,276	28,863,354	288,899	0.08

*Italy joined the Allies in April 1915.

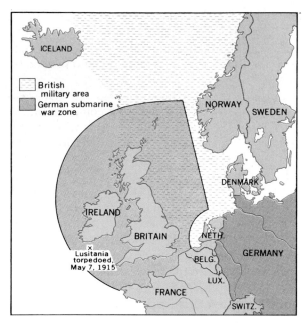

British Military Area (declared November 3, 1914), and German Submarine War Zone (declared February 4, 1915)

A German U-Boat   This deadly new weapon rendered useless existing rules of naval warfare, eventually forcing the United States to declare war against Germany in 1917.

ically warned Germany that it would be held to "strict accountability" for any attacks on American vessels or citizens.

The German submarines (known as U-boats from the German *Unterseeboot,* or "underseaboat") meanwhile began their deadly work. In the first months of 1915, they sank about ninety ships in the war zone. Then the submarine issue became acute when the British passenger liner *Lusitania* was torpedoed and sank off the coast of Ireland on May 7, 1915, with the loss of 1,198 lives, including 128 Americans.

The *Lusitania* was carrying forty-two hundred cases of small-arms ammunition, a fact the Germans used to justify the sinking. But Americans were swept by a wave of shock and anger at this act of "mass murder" and "piracy." The eastern United States, closer to the war, seethed with talk of fighting, but the rest of the country showed a strong distaste for hostilities. The peace-loving Wilson had no stomach for leading a disunited nation into war. He well remembered the mistake in 1812 of his fellow Princetonian, James Madison. Instead, by a series of increasingly strong notes, Wilson attempted to bring the German warlords sharply to book. Even this measured approach was too much for Secretary

of State Bryan, who resigned rather than sign a protestation that might spell shooting. But Wilson resolutely stood his ground. "There is such a thing," he declared, "as a man being too proud to fight." This kind of talk incensed the war-thirsty Theodore Roosevelt. The Rough Rider assailed the spineless simperers who heeded the "weasel words" of the pacifistic professor in the White House.

Yet Wilson, sticking to his verbal guns, made some diplomatic progress. After another British liner, the *Arabic,* was sunk in August 1915, with the loss of two American lives, Berlin reluctantly agreed not to sink unarmed and unresisting passenger ships *without warning.*

This pledge appeared to be violated in March 1916, when the Germans torpedoed a French pas-

Advertisement from the New York *Herald*, May 1, 1915
Six days later the *Lusitania* was sunk. Note the German warning.

senger steamer, the *Sussex*. The infuriated Wilson informed the Germans that unless they renounced the inhuman practice of sinking merchant ships without warning, he would break diplomatic relations—an almost certain prelude to war.

Germany reluctantly knuckled under to President Wilson's *Sussex* ultimatum, agreeing not to sink passenger ships and merchant vessels without giving warning. But the Germans attached a long string to their *Sussex* pledge: the United States would have to persuade the Allies to modify what Berlin regarded as their illegal blockade. This, obviously, was something that Washington could not do. Wilson promptly accepted the German pledge, without accepting the "string." He thus won a temporary but precarious diplomatic victory—precarious because Germany could pull the string whenever it chose, and the president might suddenly find himself tugged over the cliff of war.

Wilson Wins Reelection in 1916

Against this ominous backdrop, the presidential campaign of 1916 gathered speed. Both the bull moose Progressives and the Republicans met in Chicago. The Progressives uproariously renominated Theodore Roosevelt, but the Rough Rider, who loathed Wilson and all his works, had no stomach for splitting the Republicans again and ensuring the reelection of his hated rival. In refusing to run, he sounded the death knell of the Progressive party.

Roosevelt's Republican admirers also clamored for "Teddy," but the Old Guard detested the renegade who had ruptured the party in 1912. Instead they drafted Supreme Court Justice Charles Evans Hughes, a cold intellectual who had achieved a solid liberal record when he was governor of New York. The Republican platform condemned the Democratic tariff, assaults on the trusts, and Wilson's wishy-washiness in dealing with Mexico and Germany.

The thick-whiskered Hughes ("an animated feather duster") left the bench for the campaign stump, where he was not at home. In anti-German areas of the country, he assailed Wilson for not standing up to the kaiser, whereas in isolationist areas he took a softer line. This fence-straddling operation led to the jeer, "Charles Evasive Hughes."

Theodore Roosevelt, War Hawk
The former president clamored for American intervention in the European war, but the country preferred peace in 1916. Ironically, Roosevelt's archrival, Woodrow Wilson, would take the country into the war just months after the 1916 election.

Hughes was further plagued by Roosevelt, who was delivering a series of skin-'em-alive speeches against "that damned Presbyterian hypocrite Wilson." Frothing for war, TR privately scoffed at Hughes as a "whiskered Wilson"; the only difference between the two, he said, was "a shave."

Wilson, nominated by acclamation at the Democratic convention in St. Louis, ignored Hughes on the theory that one should not try to murder a man who is committing suicide. His campaign was built on the slogan, "He Kept Us Out of War."

Democratic orators warned that by electing Charles Evans Hughes, the nation would be electing a fight—with a certain frustrated Rough Rider leading the charge. A Democratic advertisement appealing to the American workingpeople read,

> *You are Working;*
> *—Not Fighting!*
> *Alive and Happy;*
> *—Not Cannon Fodder!*
> *Wilson and Peace with Honor?*
> *or*
> *Hughes with Roosevelt and War?*

On election day Hughes swept the East and looked like a surefire winner. Wilson went to bed that night prepared to accept defeat, while the New York newspapers displayed huge portraits of "The President-Elect—Charles Evans Hughes."

But the rest of the country turned the tide. Midwesterners and westerners, attracted by Wilson's progressive reforms and antiwar policies, flocked to the polls for the president. The final result, in doubt for several days, hinged on California, which Wilson carried by some 3,800 votes out of about a million cast.

During the 1916 campaign, J. A. O'Leary, the head of a pro-German and pro-Irish organization, sent a scorching telegram to Wilson condemning him for having been pro-British in approving war loans and ammunition traffic. Wilson shot back an answer:

"Your telegram received. I would feel deeply mortified to have you or anybody like you vote for me. Since you have access to many disloyal Americans and I have not, I will ask you to convey this message to them."

President Wilson's devastating and somewhat insulting response probably won him more votes than it lost.

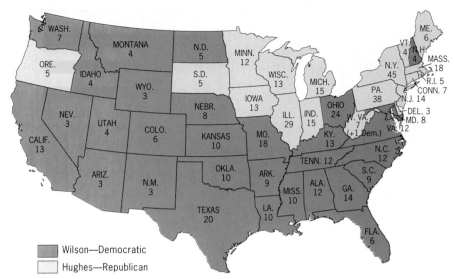

Presidential Election of 1916 (with electoral vote by state) Wilson was so worried about being a lame-duck president in a time of great international tensions that he drew up a plan whereby Hughes, if victorious, would be appointed secretary of state, Wilson and the vice president would resign, and Hughes would thus succeed immediately to the presidency.

Wilson barely squeaked through, with a final vote of 277 to 254 in the Electoral College, and 9,127,695 to 8,533,507 in the popular column. The prolabor Wilson had received strong support from the working class and from renegade bull moosers, whom Republicans failed to lure back into their camp. Wilson had not specifically promised to keep the country out of war, but probably enough voters relied on such implicit assurances to ensure his victory. Their hopeful expectations were soon rudely shattered.

Chronology

1912 Wilson defeats Taft and Roosevelt for presidency

1913 Underwood Tariff Act
Sixteenth Amendment (income tax) passed
Federal Reserve Act
Huerta takes power in Mexico
Seventeenth Amendment passed (direct election of senators)

1914 Clayton Anti-Trust Act
Federal Trade Commission established
U.S. occupation of Vera Cruz, Mexico
World War I begins in Europe

1915 La Follette Seamen's Act
Lusitania torpedoed and sunk by German U-boat

1915 U.S. Marines sent to Haiti

1916 *Sussex* ultimatum and pledge
Workingmen's Compensation Act
Federal Farm Loan Act
Warehouse Act
Adamson Act
Pancho Villa raids New Mexico
Brandeis appointed to Supreme Court
Jones Act
U.S. Marines sent to Dominican Republic
Wilson defeats Hughes for presidency

1917 United States buys Virgin Islands from Denmark

Who Were
the Progressives?

Debate about progressivism has revolved mainly around a question that is simple to ask but devilishly difficult to answer: who were the progressives? It was once taken for granted that progressive reformers were simply the heirs of the Jeffersonian-Jacksonian-Populist reform crusades; they were the oppressed and downtrodden common folk who finally erupted in wrath and demanded their due.

But in his influential *Age of Reform* (1955), Richard Hofstadter astutely challenged that view. Progressive leaders, he argued, were not drawn from the ranks of society's poor and marginalized. Rather, they were middle-class people threatened from above by the emerging power of new corporate elites and from below by a restless working class. It was not economic deprivation, but "status anxiety," Hofstadter insisted, that prompted these people to become reformers. Their psychological motivation, Hofstadter concluded, rendered many of their reform efforts quirky and ineffectual.

By contrast, "New Left" historians, notably Gabriel Kolko, argue that progressivism was dominated by established business leaders who successfully directed "reform" to their own conservative ends. In this view, government regulation (as embodied in new agencies like the Federal Reserve Board and the Federal Tariff Commission, and in legislation like the Meat Inspection Act) simply accomplished what two generations of private efforts had failed to accomplish: dampening cutthroat competition, stabilizing markets, and making America safe for monopoly capitalism.

Still other scholars, notably Robert H. Wiebe and Samuel P. Hays, argue that the progressives were neither the psychologically or economically disadvantaged, not the old capitalist elite, but were, rather, members of a rapidly emerging, self-confident social class possessed of the new techniques of scientific management, technological expertise, and organizational know-how. This "organizational school" of historians does not see progressivism as a struggle of the "people" against the "interests," nor as a confused and nostalgic campaign by status-threatened reformers, nor a conservative coup d'état. The progressive movement, in this view, was by and large an effort to rationalize and modernize many social institutions, by introducing the wise and impartial hand of government regulation.

This view has much to recommend it. Yet despite its widespread acceptance among historians, it is an explanation that cannot adequately account for the titanic political struggles of the progressive era over the very reforms that the "organizational school" regards as simple adjustments to modernity. The organizational approach also brushes over the deep philosophical differences that divided progressives themselves—such as the ideological chasm that separated Roosevelt's New Nationalism from Wilson's New Freedom. Nor can the organizational approach sufficiently explain why, as demonstrated by Otis Graham in *An Encore for Reform*, so many progressives—perhaps a majority—who survived into the New Deal era criticized that agenda for being too bureaucratic, and for laying too heavy a regulatory hand on American society.

Recently, scholars such as Robyn Muncie, Linda Gordon, and Theda Skocpol have stressed the role of women in advocating progressive reforms. Building the American welfare state in the early twentieth century, they argue, was fundamentally a gendered activity inspired by a "female dominion" of social workers and "social feminists." Moreover, in contrast to many European countries where labor movements sought a welfare state to benefit the working class, American female reformers promoted welfare programs specifically to protect women and children.

SUGGESTED READINGS

PRIMARY SOURCE DOCUMENTS

Theodore Roosevelt's "Acceptance Speech"* at the Progressive convention of 1912, and Woodrow Wilson's collection of campaign speeches, *The New Freedom** (1913), give the substance and flavor of the critical 1912 campaign. Louis D. Brandeis, *Other People's Money and How the Bankers Use It** (1914), expresses the philosophy of a key Wilson adviser. On the *Lusitania* incident, see *Foreign Relations of the United States,* 1915, Supplement, pp. 394–395, 420.

SECONDARY SOURCES

See the titles by John W. Chambers, Samuel P. Hays, Richard Hofstadter, and Robert H. Wiebe cited in Chapter 31. John M. Cooper, Jr., *The Warrior and the Priest* (1983), deftly contrasts Wilson and Theodore Roosevelt. Biographies of Wilson include August Heckscher's voluminous *Woodrow Wilson: A Biography* (1991), Arthur Link's five-volume *Wilson* (1947–1965), and John M. Blum, *Woodrow Wilson and the Politics of Morality* (1956). Particularly interesting is Alexander and Juliette George's psychological study, *Woodrow Wilson and*

---

*An asterisk indicates that the document, or an excerpt from it, can be found in Thomas A. Bailey and David M. Kennedy, eds., *The American Spirit: United States History as Seen by Contemporaries,* 9th ed. (Boston: Houghton Mifflin, 1998).

Colonel House (1956). For a sharply contrasting view, see Edwin A. Weinstein, *Woodrow Wilson: A Medical and Psychological Biography* (1981). The road to World War I finds comprehensive treatment in Ernest May, *The World War and American Isolation, 1914–1917* (1959). Consult also Ross Gregory, *The Origins of American Intervention in the First World War* (1971), and Patrick Devlin, *Too Proud to Fight: Woodrow Wilson's Neutrality* (1975). Mira Wilkins traces *The History of Foreign Investment in the United States to 1914* (1989). Superb biographies of prominent intellectuals include David Levy, *Herbert Croly of the New Republic: The Life and Thought of an American Progressive* (1985); Edward A. Stettner, *Shaping Modern Liberalism: Herbert Croly and Progressive Thought* (1993); and Philippa Strum, *Brandeis: Justice for the People* (1984). Special studies of value include Thomas A. Bailey and Paul B. Ryan, *The* Lusitania *Disaster* (1975); Jeffrey J. Safford, *Wilsonian Maritime Diplomacy* (1978); Ronald Radosh, *American Labor and Foreign Policy* (1969), and Burton I. Kaufman, *Efficiency and Expansion* (1974). For the European background, see Laurence Lafore, *The Long Fuse* (1965), and Fritz Fisher, *Germany's Aims in the First World War* (1967). Social and intellectual currents are described in Henry F. May, *The End of American Innocence: A Study of the First Years of Our Own Time, 1912–1917* (1959). Michael C. Adams, *The Great Adventure: Male Desire and the Coming of World War I* (1990), is a provocative work that tries to link Victorian gender ideology to the martial enthusiasms of the early twentieth century.

33

The War to End War

1917–1918

The world must be made safe for democracy. Its peace must be planted upon the tested foundations of political liberty. We have no selfish ends to serve. We desire no conquest, no dominion. We seek no indemnities for ourselves, no material compensation for the sacrifices we shall freely make.

WOODROW WILSON, WAR MESSAGE, APRIL 2, 1917

War by Act of Germany

Destiny dealt cruelly with Woodrow Wilson. The lover of peace, as fate would have it, was forced to lead a hesitant and peace-loving nation into war. As the last days of 1916 slipped through the hourglass, the president made one final, futile attempt to mediate between the embattled belligerents. On January 22, 1917, he delivered one of his most moving addresses, realistically declaring that only a negotiated "peace without victory" would prove durable.

Germany's warlords responded with a blow of the mailed fist. On January 31, 1917, they announced to an astonished world that they intended to wage *unlimited* submarine warfare, sinking *all* ships, including America's, in the war zone.

The Germans thus jerked viciously on the string they had attached to their *Sussex* pledge in 1916. Wilson, his bluff now called, broke diplomatic relations but refused to move toward war unless the Germans undertook "overt" acts against American lives and property. To defend American interests short of war, the president asked Congress for authority to arm American merchant ships. When a band of midwestern senators launched a filibuster to block the measure, Wilson denounced them as a "little group of willful men" who were rendering a great nation "helpless and contemptible." But their obstruction was a powerful reminder of the continuing strength of American isolationism.

Meanwhile, the sensational Zimmermann note was intercepted and published on March 1, 1917, infuriating Americans, especially westerners. German foreign secretary Arthur Zimmermann had secretly proposed a German-Mexican alliance, tempting anti-Yankee Mexico with veiled promises of recovering Texas, New Mexico, and Arizona.

On the heels of this provocation came the long-dreaded "overt" acts in the Atlantic, where German U-boats sank four unarmed American merchant vessels in the first two weeks of March. As one Philadelphia newspaper observed, "the difference between war and what we have now is that now we aren't fighting back." Simultaneously came the rousing news that a revolution in Russia had toppled the cruel regime of the tsars. America could now fight foursquare for democracy on the side of the Allies, without the black sheep of Russian despotism in the Allied fold.

Subdued and solemn, Wilson at last stood before a hushed joint session of Congress on the evening of April 2, 1917, and asked for a declaration of war. He had lost his gamble that America could pursue the profits of neutral trade without being sucked into the ghastly maelstrom. A myth developed in later years that America was dragged unwittingly into war by munitions makers and Wall Street

I Dare You to Come Out, 1917 The kaiser defies American rights, national honor, freedom of the seas, and international law.

War! Attacks by German submarines finally forced Wilson's hand, and he asked Congress for a declaration of war on April 2, 1917. Four days later, after considerable debate and with fifty-six dissenting votes, Congress obliged the president.

---

bankers, desperate to protect their profits and loans. Yet the weapons merchants and financiers were already thriving, unhampered by wartime government restrictions and heavy taxation. Their slogan might well have been "Neutrality Forever." The simple truth is that British harassment of American commerce had been galling but endurable; Germany had resorted to the mass killing of civilians. The difference was like that between a gang of thieves and a gang of murderers. President Wilson had drawn a clear, if risky, line against the depredations of the submarine. The German high command, in a last desperate throw of the dice, chose to cross it. In a figurative sense, America's war declaration of April 6, 1917, bore the unambiguous trademark "Made in Germany."

Wilsonian Idealism Enthroned

"It is a fearful thing to lead this great peaceful people into war," Wilson said in his war message. It was fearful indeed, not least of all because of the formidable challenge it posed to Wilson's leadership skills. Ironically, it fell to the scholarly Wilson, deeply respectful of American traditions, to shatter one of the most sacred of those traditions by entangling America in a distant European war.

How could the president arouse the American people to shoulder this unprecedented burden? For more than a century, they had prided themselves on their isolationism from the periodic outbursts of militarized violence that afflicted the Old World. Since 1914 their pride had been reinforced by the bountiful profits gained through neutrality. German U-boats had now roughly shoved a wavering America into the abyss, but ominously, no fewer than six senators and fifty representatives (including the first congresswoman, Jeannette Rankin of Montana) had voted against the war resolution. Wilson could whip up no enthusiasm, especially in the landlocked Midwest, by fighting to make the world safe from the submarine. To galvanize the country, Wilson would have to proclaim more glorified aims.

Wilson's burning idealism led him instinctively to an inspired decision. Radiating the spiritual fervor of his Presbyterian ancestors, he declared the twin goals of "a war to end war" and a crusade "to make the world safe for democracy." Brandishing the sword of righteousness, Wilson virtually hypno-

tized the nation with his lofty ideals. He contrasted the selfish war aims of the other belligerents, Allied and enemy alike, with America's shining altruism. America, he preached, did not fight for the sake of riches or territorial conquest. The Republic sought only to shape an international order in which democracy could flourish without fear of power-crazed autocrats and militarists.

In Wilsonian idealism the personality of the president and the necessities of history were perfectly matched. The high-minded Wilson genuinely believed in the principles he so eloquently intoned. And probably no other appeal could have successfully converted the American people from their historic hostility to involvement in European squabbles. Americans, it seemed, could be either isolationists or crusaders, but nothing in between.

Wilson's appeal worked—perhaps too well. Holding aloft the torch of idealism, the president fired up the public mind to a fever pitch. "Force, force to the utmost, force without stint or limit," he cried, while the country responded less elegantly with "Hang the kaiser." Lost on the gale was Wilson's earlier plea for "peace without victory."

Fourteen Potent Wilsonian Points

Wilson quickly came to be recognized as the moral leader of the Allied cause. He scaled a summit of inspiring oratory on January 8, 1918, when he delivered his famed Fourteen Points Address to an enthusiastic Congress. Although one of his primary purposes was to keep reeling Russia in the war, Wilson's vision inspired all the drooping Allies to make mightier efforts and demoralized the enemy governments by holding out alluring promises to their dissatisfied minorities.

The first five of the Fourteen Points were broad in scope. (1) A proposal to abolish secret treaties pleased liberals of all countries. (2) Freedom of the seas appealed to the Germans, as well as to Americans who distrusted British sea power. (3) A removal of economic barriers among nations was comforting to Germany, which feared postwar vengeance. (4) Reduction of armament burdens was gratifying to taxpayers everywhere. (5) An adjustment of colonial claims in the interests of both native peoples and the colonizers was reassuring to the anti-imperialists.

Other points among the fourteen proved to be no less seductive. They held out the hope of independence ("self-determination") to oppressed minority groups, such as the Poles, millions of whom lay under the heel of Germany and Austria-Hungary. The capstone point, number fourteen, foreshadowed the League of Nations—an international organization that Wilson dreamed would provide a system of collective security. Wilson earnestly prayed that this new scheme would effectively guarantee the political independence and territorial integrity of all countries, whether large or small.

Yet Wilson's appealing points, though raising hopes the world over, were not everywhere applauded. Certain leaders of the Allied nations, with an eye to territorial booty, were less than enthusiastic. Hard-nosed Republicans at home grumbled, and some of them openly mocked the "fourteen commandments" of "God Almighty Wilson."

Creel Manipulates Minds

Mobilizing people's minds for war, both in America and abroad, was an urgent task facing the Washington authorities. For this purpose the Committee on Public Information was created. It was headed by a youngish journalist, George Creel, who, though outspoken and tactless, was gifted with zeal and imagination. His job was to sell America on the war and sell the world on Wilsonian war aims.

The Creel organization, employing some 150,000 workers at home and overseas, proved that words were indeed weapons. It sent out an army of 75,000 "four-minute men"—often longer-winded than that—who delivered countless speeches containing much "patriotic pep."

Creel's propaganda took varied forms. Posters were splashed on billboards in the "Battle of the Fences," as artists "rallied to the colors." Millions of leaflets and pamphlets, which contained the most pungent Wilsonisms, were showered like confetti upon the world. Propaganda booklets with red-white-and-blue covers were printed by the millions.

Hang-the-kaiser movies, carrying such titles as *The Kaiser, the Beast of Berlin* and *To Hell with the Kaiser,* revealed the helmeted "Hun" at his bloodiest. Arm-waving conductors by the thousands led huge audiences in songs that poured scorn on the enemy and glorified the "boys" in uniform.

Anti-German Propaganda   The government relied extensively on emotional appeals and hate propaganda to rally support for the First World War, which most Americans regarded as a distant "European" affair.

The entire nation, catching the frenzied spirit of a religious revival, burst into song. This was undoubtedly America's singingest war. Most memorable was George M. Cohan's spine-tingling "Over There":

Over there, over there
Send the word, send the word over there,
That the Yanks are coming, the Yanks are coming
The drums rum-tumming ev'rywhere.

Creel typified American war mobilization, which relied more on aroused passion and voluntary compliance than on formal laws. But he oversold the ideals of Wilson and led the world to expect too much. When the president proved to be a mortal and not a god, the resulting disillusionment both at home and abroad was disastrous.

Enforcing Loyalty and Stifling Dissent

German-Americans numbered over 8 million, counting those with at least one parent foreign-born, out of a total population of 100 million. On the whole they proved to be dependably loyal to the United States. Yet rumormongers were quick to spread tales of spying and sabotage: even trifling epidemics of diarrhea were blamed on German agents. A few German-Americans were tarred, feathered, and beaten; in one extreme case a German Socialist in Illinois was lynched by a drunken mob.

As emotion mounted, hysterical hatred of Germans and things Germanic swept the nation. Orchestras found it unsafe to present German-composed music, like that of Wagner or Beethoven. The teaching of the German language was short-sightedly discontinued in many high schools and colleges. Sauerkraut became "liberty cabbage," and hamburger became "liberty steak."

Both the Espionage Act of 1917 and the Sedition Act of 1918 reflected current fears about Germans and antiwar Americans. Especially visible among the 1,900 prosecutions undertaken under these laws were antiwar Socialists and members of the radical union Industrial Workers of the World (IWWs). King-pin Socialist Eugene V. Debs was convicted under the Espionage Act in 1918 and sentenced to ten years in a federal penitentiary. IWW leader William D. ("Big Bill") Haywood and ninety-nine associates were similarly convicted. There was also mild press censorship, and some leftist papers such as *The Masses* were denied mailing privileges.

These prosecutions form an ugly chapter in the history of American civil liberty. With the dawn of peace, presidential pardons were rather freely granted, including President Harding's to Eugene Debs in 1921. Yet a few victims lingered behind bars into the 1930s.

The Nation's Factories Go to War

Victory was no foregone conclusion, especially since the Republic, despite ample warning, was caught flat-footedly unready for its leap into global war. The pacifistic Wilson had only belatedly backed some mild preparedness measures beginning in 1915, including the creation of a civilian Council of National Defense to study problems of economic mobilization. He had also launched a shipbuilding program (as much to capture the belligerents' war-disrupted foreign trade as to anticipate America's

Socialist Leader Eugene V. Debs Addresses an Antiwar Rally in Columbus, Ohio, 1918 For his remarks in this speech, Debs was convicted under the Espionage Act of 1917 and sent to federal prison. He ran as a presidential candidate in 1920 while still incarcerated in his cell and received nearly a million votes.

possible entry into the war) and endorsed a modest beefing-up of the army, which with 100,000 regulars then ranked about fifteenth among the armies of the world, in the same category with Persia. It would take a herculean effort to marshal America's daunting but disorganized resources and throw them into the field quickly enough to bolster the Allied war effort.

Towering obstacles confronted economic mobilizers. Sheer ignorance was among the biggest roadblocks. No one knew precisely how much steel or explosive powder the country was capable of producing. Old ideas also proved to be liabilities, as traditional fears of big government hamstrung efforts to orchestrate the economy from Washington. States' rights Democrats and businesspeople alike balked at federal economic controls, even though the embattled nation could ill afford the freewheeling, hit-or-miss chaos of the peacetime economy.

Late in the war, and after some bruising political battles, Wilson succeeded in imposing some order on this economic confusion. In March 1918 he appointed lone-eagle stock speculator Bernard Baruch to head the War Industries Board. But the War Industries Board never had more than feeble formal powers, and it was disbanded within days after the armistice. Even in a globe-girdling crisis, the American preference for laissez-faire and for a weak central government proved amazingly strong.

The War, Workers, and Women

Spurred by the slogan, "Labor Will Win the War," American workers sweated their way to victory. In part they were driven by the War Department's "work or fight" rule of 1918, which threatened any unemployed male with being immediately drafted —a powerful discouragement to go on strike. But, for the most part, government tried to treat labor fairly. The National War Labor Board, chaired by former president Taft, exerted itself to head off labor disputes that might hamper the war effort. While pressing employers to grant concessions to labor, including high wages and the eight-hour day, the board stopped short of supporting labor's most important demand: a government guarantee of the right to organize into unions.

Fortunately for the Allied cause, Samuel Gompers and his American Federation of Labor (AF of L)

loyally supported the war, though some smaller and more radical labor organizations, including the Industrial Workers of the World, did not. The IWWs, known as the "Wobblies" and sometimes derided as the "I Won't Works," engineered some of the most damaging industrial sabotage, and not without reason. As transient laborers in such industries as fruit and lumber, the Wobblies were victims of some of the shabbiest working conditions in the country. When they protested, many were viciously beaten, arrested, or run out of town.

Mainstream labor's loyalty was rewarded. At war's end, the AF of L had more than doubled its membership, to over 3 million, and in the most heavily unionized sectors—coal mining, manufacturing, and transportation—real wages (after adjusting for inflation) had risen more than 20

A Universal Draft, 1917   The prewar song "I Didn't Raise My Boy to Be a Soldier" was changed to "I Didn't Raise My Boy to Be a Slacker," which in turn inspired the cruel parody: "I Didn't Raise My Dog to Be a Sausage."

percent over prewar levels. A new day seemed to be dawning for the long-struggling union movement.

Yet labor harbored grievances. Recognition of the right to organize still eluded labor's grasp. Wartime inflation threatened to eclipse wage gains (prices more than doubled between 1914 and 1920). Not even the call of patriotism and Wilsonian idealism could defuse all labor disputes. Some six thousand strikes, several stained by blood, broke out in the war years. In 1919, the greatest strike in American history rocked the steel industry. More than a quarter of a million steelworkers walked off their jobs in a bid to force their employers to recognize their right to organize and bargain collectively. The steel companies resisted mercilessly. They refused to negotiate with union representatives, and brought in thirty thousand African-American strikebreakers to keep the mills running. After bitter confrontations that left more than a dozen

workers dead, the steel strike collapsed, a grievous setback that crippled the union movement for more than a decade.

The black workers who entered the steel mills in 1919 were but a fraction of the tens of thousands of southern blacks drawn to the North in wartime by the magnet of war-industry employment. These migrants made up the small-scale beginnings of a great northward African-American trek that would eventually grow to massive proportions. Their sudden appearance in previously all-white areas sometimes sparked interracial violence. An explosive riot in East St. Louis, Missouri, in July 1917 left nine whites and at least forty blacks dead. An equally gruesome race riot ripped through Chicago. The wartime Windy City was taut with racial tension as a growing black population expanded into white working-class neighborhoods, and as African-Americans found jobs as strikebreakers in meat-packing plants. Triggered by an incident at a bathing beach in July 1919, a reign of terror descended on the city for nearly two weeks. Black and white gangs

Suppressing the Steel Strike: Pittsburgh, 1919   The big steel producers ferociously resisted the unionization of their industry. In Pittsburgh, compliant local officials bent to the steelmakers' will and issued an order banning all outdoor meetings of strikers. These mounted police enforced the order with flailing billy clubs. The steelworkers' strike eventually failed, leaving the steel industry un-unionized until the New Deal championed labor's cause in the Depression decade of the 1930s.

Race Riot, Chicago, 1919   The policeman apparently arrived too late to spare this victim from being pelted by stones from an angry mob.

roamed Chicago's streets, eventually killing fifteen whites and twenty-three blacks.

Women also heeded the call of patriotism and opportunity. Thousands of female workers flooded into factories and fields, taking up jobs vacated by men who left the assembly line for the front line. Women's war work helped convince President Wilson to endorse woman suffrage as "a vitally necessary war measure." Nearly a century of struggle was crowned with success when women received the right to vote with the passage of the Nineteenth Amendment in 1920. (For text, see the Appendix). Yet women's wartime economic gains proved fleeting. Although a permanent Women's Bureau did emerge after the war in the Department of Labor to protect women in the workplace, most women workers soon gave up their war jobs. Meanwhile, Congress affirmed its support for women in their traditional role as mothers when it passed the Sheppard-Towner Maternity Act of 1921, providing federally financed instruction in maternal and infant health care.

Feminists continued to flex their political muscle in the postwar decade, especially in campaigns for laws to protect women in the workplace and prohibit child labor. Complete success often eluded them in those crusades, but the developments of the World War I era nevertheless foreshadowed a future when women's wage-labor and political power would re-shape the American way of life.

Women Working on the Railroad, 1918   The First World War created many new job opportunities for women, as illustrated by this 1918 photograph of the Union Pacific yards in Cheyenne, Wyoming. But the war ended too quickly for many women to secure a permanent foothold in occupations traditionally dominated by men.

Suffragists Picket the White House, 1917   Militant feminists sometimes handcuffed themselves to the White House fence to dramatize their appeal to the president.

Forging a War Economy

Mobilization relied more on the heated emotions of patriotism than on the cool majesty of the laws. The largely voluntary and somewhat haphazard character of economic war organization testified unequivocally to ocean-insulated America's safe distance from the fighting—as well as to the still-modest scale of government powers in the progressive-era Republic.

As the larder of democracy, America had to feed itself and its allies. By a happy inspiration, the man chosen to head the Food Administration was the Quaker-humanitarian Herbert C. Hoover. He was already considered a hero because he had successfully led a massive charitable drive to feed the starving people of war-racked Belgium.

In common with other American war administrators, Hoover preferred to rely on voluntary compliance rather than on compulsory edicts. He deliberately rejected issuing ration cards, a practice used in Europe. Instead he waged a whirlwind propaganda campaign through posters, billboards, newspapers, pulpits, and movies. To save food for export, Hoover proclaimed wheatless Wednesdays and meatless Tuesdays—all on a voluntary basis. Even children, when eating apples, were urged to be "patriotic to the core."

The country soon broke out in a rash of vegetable "victory gardens," as perspiring patriots hoed their way to victory in backyards and vacant lots. Congress severely restricted the use of foodstuffs for manufacturing alcoholic beverages, and the war-spawned spirit of self-denial helped accelerate the wave of prohibition that was sweeping the country. Many leading brewers were German-descended, and this taint made the drive against alcohol all the more popular. The reformers' dream of a saloonless nation was finally achieved—temporarily—in 1919, with the passage of the Eighteenth Amendment, prohibiting all alcoholic drinks.

Thanks to the fervent patriotic wartime spirit, Hoover's voluntary approach worked. Farm production increased by one-fourth, and food exports to the Allies tripled in volume. Hoover's methods were widely imitated in other war agencies. The Fuel Administration exhorted Americans to save fuel with "heatless Mondays," "lightless nights," and "gasless Sundays." The Treasury Department spon-

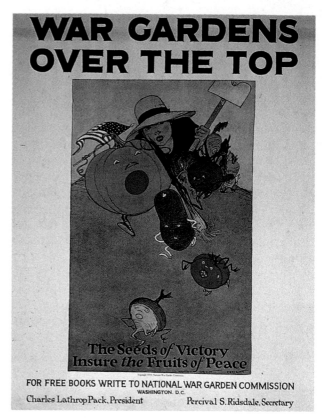

Food for Thought The wartime Food Administration flooded the country with posters like this in 1917–1918, exhorting households to "grow their own" and thus ease the pressure on food supplies.

sored huge parades and invoked slogans like "Halt the Hun" to promote four great Liberty Loan drives, followed by a Victory Loan campaign in 1919. Together, these efforts netted the then-fantastic sum of about $21 billion, or two-thirds of the current cost of the war to the United States. The remainder was raised by increased taxes, which, unlike the loan subscriptions, were obligatory. (The ultimate bill, including interest and veterans' benefits, mounted to some $112 billion.)

Pressures of various kinds, patriotic and otherwise, were used to sell bonds. The unfortunate German-American who could not display a Liberty Bond button might find his or her house bedaubed with yellow paint. A number of reluctant investors in war bonds were roughly handled. In at least one instance a man signed for a bond with a rope around his neck.

Miracles in Shipbuilding

Despite the Wilson administration's preference for voluntary means of mobilizing the economy, the government on occasion reluctantly exercised its sovereign formal power, notably when it took over the nation's railroads following indescribable traffic snarls in late 1917. Washington also hustled to get its hands on ships. It seized enemy merchant vessels trapped in America's harbors and orchestrated a gigantic drive to construct new tonnage. A few concrete vessels were launched, including one appropriately named *Faith*. A wooden-ship program was undertaken, though after months of war, birds were still nesting in the trees from which the vessels were to be hammered.

Making Plowboys into Doughboys

Most citizens, at the outset, did not dream of sending a mighty force to France. As far as fighting went, America would use its navy to uphold freedom of the seas. It would continue to ship war materials to the Allies and supply them with loans, which finally totaled nearly $10 billion. But in April and May of 1917, the European associates laid their cards on the table. They confessed that they were scraping the bottom not only of their money chests but, more ominously, of their manpower barrels. A huge American army would have to be raised, trained, and transported, or the whole western front would collapse.

Conscription was the only answer to the need for raising an immense army with all possible speed. Wilson disliked a draft, as did many other Americans with Civil War memories; but he eventually accepted and eloquently supported conscription as a disagreeable and temporary necessity.

The proposed draft bill immediately ran into a barrage of criticism in Congress. A congressman from Missouri, deploring compulsion, cried out in protest that there was "precious little difference between a conscript and a convict." Prophets of doom predicted that on draft-registration day the streets would run red with blood. At length Congress—six weeks after declaring war—grudgingly got around to passing conscription.

The draft act required the registration of all males between the ages of eighteen and forty-five. No "draft dodger" could purchase his exemption or hire a substitute, as in the days of the Civil War, though the law exempted men in key industries, such as shipbuilding.

The draft machinery, on the whole, worked effectively. Registration day proved to be a day of patriotic pilgrimages to flag-draped registration centers, and the sign-up saw no shedding of blood, as some had gloomily predicted. Despite precautions, some 337,000 "slackers" escaped the draft, and about 4,000 conscientious objectors were excused.

Within a few frantic months the army grew to over 4 million men. For the first time, women were admitted to the armed forces; some 11,000 to the navy and 269 to the marines. African-Americans also served in the armed forces, though in strictly segregated units and usually under white officers. Reflecting racial attitudes of the time, military authories hesitated to train black men for combat, and the majority of black soldiers were assigned to "construction battalions" or put to work unloading ships.

Recruits were supposed to receive six months of training in America and two more months overseas. But so great was the urgency that many doughboys were swept swiftly into battle scarcely knowing how to handle a rifle, much less a bayonet.

Fighting in France—Belatedly

Russia's collapse underscored the need for haste. The communistic Bolsheviks, after seizing power late in 1917, ultimately withdrew their beaten country from the "capitalistic" war early in 1918. This sudden defection released hundreds of thousands of battle-tested Germans from the eastern front facing Russia for the western front in France, where, for the first time in the war, they were developing a dangerous superiority in manpower.

Berlin's calculations as to American tardiness were surprisingly accurate. Germany had counted on knocking out Britain six months after the declaration of unlimited submarine warfare, long before America could get into the struggle. No really effective American fighting force reached France until about a year after Congress declared war. Berlin had also reckoned on the inability of the Americans to transport their army, assuming that they were able to raise one. Here again the German predictions were not far from the mark as shipping shortages plagued the Allies.

Nevertheless, France gradually began to bustle with American doughboys. The first trainees to reach the front were used as replacements in the Allied armies and were generally deployed in quiet sectors with the British and French. The newcomers soon made friends with the French girls—or tried to—and one of the most sung-about women in history was the fabled "Mademoiselle from Armentières." One of the printable stanzas ran

> *She was true to me, she was true to you,*
> *She was true to the whole damned army, too.*

American operations were not confined solely to France; small detachments fought in Belgium, Italy, and notably Russia. The United States, hoping to keep stores of munitions from falling into German hands when Bolshevik Russia quit fighting, contributed some 5,000 troops to an Allied invasion of northern Russia at Archangel. Wilson likewise sent nearly 10,000 troops to Siberia as part of an Allied expedition, which included more than 70,000 Japanese. Major American purposes were to prevent Japan from getting a stranglehold on Siberia, to rescue some 45,000 marooned Czechoslovak troops, and to snatch military supplies from Bolshevik

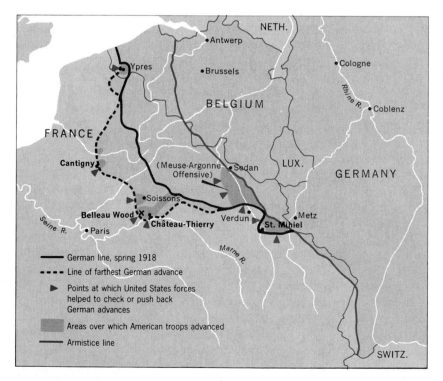

Major U.S. Operations in France, 1918 One doughboy recorded in his diary his baptism of fire at St. Mihiel: "Hiked through dark woods. No lights allowed, guided by holding on the pack of the man ahead. Stumbled through underbrush for about half mile into an open field where we waited in soaking rain until about 10:00 P.M. We then started on our hike to the St. Mihiel front, arriving on the crest of a hill at 1:00 A.M. I saw a sight which I shall never forget. It was the zero hour and in one instant the entire front as far as the eye could reach in either direction was a sheet of flame, while the heavy artillery made the earth quake."

control. Sharp fighting at Archangel and in Siberia involved casualties on both sides, including several hundred Americans. The Bolsheviks long resented these "capitalistic" interventions, which they regarded as high-handed efforts to suffocate their infant communist revolution in its cradle.

America Helps Hammer the "Hun"

The dreaded German drive on the western front exploded in the spring of 1918. Spearheaded by about half a million troops, the enemy rolled forward with terrifying momentum. So dire was the peril that the Allied nations for the first time united under a supreme commander, the quiet French Marshal Foch, whose axiom was "To make war is to attack." Until then the Allies had been fighting imperfectly coordinated actions.

At last the ill-trained "Yanks" were coming—and not a moment too soon. Late in May 1918, the German juggernaut, smashing to within 40 miles (64 kilometers) of Paris, threatened to knock out France. Newly arrived American troops, numbering fewer than 30,000, were thrown into the breach at Château-Thierry, right in the teeth of the German advance. This was a historic moment—the first significant engagement of American troops in a European war. Battle-fatigued French soldiers watched incredulously as the roads filled with endless truckloads of American doughboys, singing New World songs at the top of their voices, a seemingly inexhaustible flood of fresh and gleaming youth. With their arrival it was clear that a new American giant had arisen in the West to replace the dying Russian titan in the East.

American weight in the scales was now being felt. By July 1918 the awesome German drive had spent its force, and keyed-up American men participated in a Foch counteroffensive in the Second Battle of the Marne. This engagement marked the beginning of a German withdrawal that was never effectively reversed. In September 1918 nine American divisions (about 243,000 men) joined four French divisions to push the Germans from the St. Mihiel salient, a German dagger in France's flank.

The Americans, dissatisfied with merely bolstering the British and French, had meanwhile been demanding a separate army. General John J. ("Black

Over There American troops man a trench gun in a bomb-blasted forest.

Gassed, by John Singer Sargent   The noted artist captures the horror of trench warfare in World War I. The enemy was often distant and unseen, and death came impersonally from gas or artillery fire. American troops, entering the line only in the war's final days, were only briefly exposed to this kind of brutal fighting.

Jack") Pershing was finally assigned a front of 85 miles (137 kilometers), stretching northwestward from the Swiss border to meet the French lines.

As a part of the last mighty Allied assault, involving several million men, Pershing's army undertook the Meuse-Argonne offensive, from September 26 to November 11, 1918. One objective was to cut the German railroad lines feeding the western front. This battle, the most gargantuan thus far in American history, lasted forty-seven days and engaged 1.2 million American troops. With especially heavy fighting in the rugged Argonne Forest, the killed and wounded mounted to 120,000, or 10

Approximate Comparative Losses in World War I

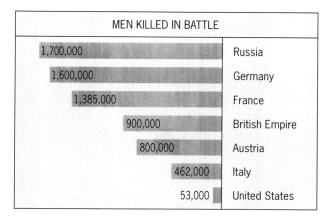

MEN KILLED IN BATTLE	
1,700,000	Russia
1,600,000	Germany
1,385,000	France
900,000	British Empire
800,000	Austria
462,000	Italy
53,000	United States

percent of the Americans involved. The slow progress and severe losses from machine guns resulted in part from inadequate training, in part from dashing open-field tactics, with the bayonet liberally employed. Tennessee-bred Alvin C. York, a member of an antiwar religious sect, became a hero when he single-handedly killed 20 Germans and captured 132 more.

Victory was in sight—and fortunately so. The slowly advancing American armies in France were eating up their supplies so rapidly that they were in grave danger of running short. But the battered Germans were ready to stagger out of the trenches and cry "Kamerad" ("Comrade"). Their allies were deserting them; the British blockade was causing critical food shortages; and the sledgehammer blows of the Allies rained down relentlessly. Propaganda leaflets, containing seductive Wilsonian promises, rained upon their crumbling lines from balloons, shells, and rockets.

The Fourteen Points Disarm Germany

Berlin was now ready to hoist the white flag. Warned of imminent defeat by the generals, it turned to the presumably softhearted Wilson in October 1918, seeking a peace based on the Fourteen Points. In stern responses the president made it clear that the kaiser must be thrown overboard before an armistice could be negotiated. War-weary Germans, whom Wilson had been trying to turn against their "military masters," took the hint. The kaiser was forced to flee to Holland, where he lived out his remaining twenty-three years, "unwept, unhonored, and unhung."

The exhausted Germans were through. They laid down their arms at eleven o'clock on the eleventh day of the eleventh month of 1918, and an eerie, numbing silence fell over the western front. War-taut America burst into a delirium of around-the-clock rejoicing, as streets were jammed with laughing, whooping, milling, dancing masses. The war to end wars had ended.

The United States' main contributions to the ultimate victory had been foodstuffs, munitions, credits, oil for this first mechanized war, and manpower—but not battlefield victories. The Yanks fought only two major battles, at St. Mihiel and the Meuse-Argonne, both in the last two months of the four-year war, and they were still grinding away in the Meuse-Argonne, well short of their objectives, when the war ended. It was the *prospect* of endless U.S. troop reserves, rather than America's actual military performance, that eventually demoralized the Germans.

Ironically enough, General Pershing in some ways depended more on the Allies than they depended on him. His army purchased more of its supplies in Europe than it shipped from the United States. Fewer than five hundred of Pershing's artillery pieces were of American manufacture. Virtually all his aircraft were provided by the British and French. Britain and France transported a majority of the doughboys to Europe. The United States, in short, was no arsenal of democracy in this war; that role awaited it in the next global conflict, two decades later.

Wilson Steps Down from Olympus

Woodrow Wilson had helped to win the war. What part would he now play in shaping the peace? Expectations ran extravagantly high. As the fighting in Europe crashed to a close, the American president towered at the peak of his popularity and power. In lonely huts in the mountains of Italy, candles burned before poster-portraits of the revered American prophet. In Poland starry-eyed university

German "Repentance," 1918   A prophetic reflection of the view that the failure to smash Germany completely would lead to another world war.

students would meet on the streets, clasp hands, and utter only one word: "Wilson." No other man had over occupied so dizzy a pinnacle as moral leader of the world. Wilson also had behind him the prestige of victory and the economic resources of the mightiest nation on earth. But at this fateful moment, his sureness of touch deserted him, and he began to make a series of tragic fumbles.

Under the slogan "Politics Is Adjourned," partisan political strife had been kept below the surface

Theodore Roosevelt (1858–1919) favored the Germans' unconditional surrender. Referring to Wilson's practice of drafting diplomatic notes on his own typewriter, Roosevelt telegraphed several senators (October 24, 1918):

"Let us dictate peace by the hammering guns and not chat about peace to the accompaniment of clicking typewriters. The language of the fourteen points and the subsequent statements explaining or qualifying them are thoroughly mischievous."

Heroes' Welcome 1917
The people of Harlem gathered to welcome home the black regiment known as the "Hell-fighters of Harlem." Black troops were confined to segregated units in World War I, and segregation followed some of them even into death. When Congress appropriated money in 1930 to send "Gold Star Mothers" to visit the graves of their slain soldier-sons in France, it provided for separate ships, hotels, and trains for African-American women. Several black mothers, preferring "to remain at home and retain our honor and self-respect," reluctantly refused to make the trip.

during the war crisis. Hoping to strengthen his hand at the Paris peace table, Wilson broke the truce by personally appealing for a Democratic victory in the congressional elections of November 1918. But the maneuver backfired when voters instead returned a narrow Republican majority to Congress. Having staked his reputation on the outcome, Wilson went to Paris as a diminished leader. Unlike all the parliamentary statesmen at the table, he did not command a legislative majority at home.

Wilson's decision to go in person to Paris to help make the peace infuriated Republicans. At that time no president had traveled to Europe, and Wilson's journey looked to his critics like flamboyant grandstanding. He further ruffled Republican feathers when he snubbed the Senate in assembling his peace delegation and neglected to include a single Republican senator in his official party. The logical choice was the new chairman of the Senate Committee on Foreign Relations, slender and aristocratically bewhiskered Henry Cabot Lodge of Massachusetts, a Harvard Ph.D. But including Lodge would have been problematic for the president. The senator's mind, quipped one critic, was like the soil of his native New England: "naturally barren but highly cultivated." Wilson loathed him, and the feeling was hotly reciprocated. An accom-

plished author, Lodge had been known as the "scholar in politics" until Wilson came on the scene. The two men were at daggers drawn, personally and politically.

An Idealist Battles the Imperialists in Paris

Woodrow Wilson, the great prophet arisen in the West, received tumultuous welcomes from the masses of France, England, and Italy late in 1918 and early in 1919. They saw in his idealism the promise of a better world. But the statesmen of France and Italy were careful to keep the new messiah at arm's length from worshipful crowds. He might so arouse the people as to prompt them to overthrow their leaders and upset finespun imperialistic plans.

The Paris Conference of great and small nations fell into the hands of an inner clique, known as the Big Four. Wilson, representing the richest and freshest great power, more or less occupied the driver's seat. He was joined by genial Premier Vittorio Orlando of Italy and by the brilliant Prime Minister David Lloyd George of Britain. Perhaps the most realistic of the quartet was cynical, hard-bitten Premier Georges Clemenceau of France, the seventy-eight-year-old "organizer of victory" known as "the Tiger."

Speed was urgent when the conference opened on January 18, 1919. Europe seemed to be slipping into anarchy; the red tide of communism was licking westward from Bolshevist Russia.

Wilson's ultimate goal was a world parliament to be known as the League of Nations, but he first bent his energies to preventing any vengeful parceling out of the former colonies and protectorates of the vanquished powers. He forced through a compromise between naked imperialism and Wilsonian idealism. The victors would not take possession of the conquered territory outright, but would receive

Grave concern was expressed by General Tasker H. Bliss (1853–1930), one of the five American peace commissioners (December 18, 1918):

"I am disquieted to see how hazy and vague our ideas are. We are going to be up against the wiliest politicians in Europe. There will be nothing hazy or vague about their ideas."

it as trustees of the League of Nations. Strategic Syria, for example, was awarded to France, and oil-rich Iraq went to Britain. But in practice this half-loaf solution was little more than the old prewar colonialism, thinly disguised.

Meanwhile, Wilson had been serving as midwife for the League of Nations, which he envisioned as containing an assembly with seats for all nations and a council to be controlled by the great powers. He gained a signal victory over the skeptical Old World diplomats in February 1919, when they agreed to make the League Covenant, Wilson's brainchild, an integral part of the final peace treaty. At one point he spoke with such ardor for his plan that even the hardboiled newspaper reporters forgot to take notes.

Hammering Out the Treaty

Domestic duties now required Wilson to make a quick trip to America, where ugly storms were brewing in the Senate. Certain Republican senators, Lodge in the lead, were sharpening their knives for Wilson. To them the League was either a useless "sewing circle" or an overpotent "super-state." Their hard core was composed of a dozen or so militant isolationists, led by senators William Borah of Idaho and Hiram Johnson of California, who were known as "irreconcilables" or "the Battalion of Death."

Thirty-nine Republican senators or senators-elect—enough to defeat the treaty—proclaimed that the Senate would not approve the League of Nations in its existing imperfect form. These difficulties delighted Wilson's Allied adversaries in Paris. They were now in a stronger bargaining position because Wilson would have to beg them for changes in the

Wilson in Dover, England, 1919   Hailed by many Europeans in early 1919 as the savior of the Western world, Wilson was a fallen idol only a few months later, when Americans repudiated the peace treaty he had help to craft.

Pilgrim Landing in America, 1919

Wilson's next battle was with Italy over Fiume, a valuable seaport inhabited by both Italians and Yugoslavs. When Italy demanded Fiume, Wilson insisted that the seaport go to Yugoslavia and appealed over the heads of Italy's leaders to the country's masses. The maneuver fell flat. The Italian delegates went home in a huff, while the Italian masses turned savagely against Wilson.

Another crucial struggle was with Japan over China's Shantung peninsula and the German islands in the Pacific, which the Japanese had seized during the war. Japan was conceded the strategic Pacific islands under a League of Nations mandate,* but Wilson staunchly opposed Japanese control of Shantung as a violation of self-determination for its 30 million Chinese residents. But when the Japanese threatened to walk out, Wilson reluctantly accepted a compromise whereby Japan kept Germany's economic holdings in Shantung and pledged to return the peninsula to China at a later date. The Chinese were outraged by this imperialistic solution, while Clemenceau jeered that Wilson "talked like Jesus Christ and acted like Lloyd George."

The Peace Treaty That Bred a New War

A completed Treaty of Versailles, after more weeks of wrangling, was handed to the Germans in June 1919—almost literally on the point of a bayonet. Germany had capitulated on the strength of assurances that it would be granted a peace based on the Fourteen Points. A careful analysis of the treaty shows that only about four of the twenty-three original Wilsonian points and subsequent principles were fully honored. Loud and bitter cries of betrayal burst from German throats—charges that Adolf Hitler would soon reiterate during his meteoric rise to power.

Wilson, of course, was guilty of no conscious betrayal. But the Allied powers were torn by conflicting aims, many of them sanctioned by secret treaties. There had to be compromise at Paris—or there would be no agreement. Faced with hard reali-

covenant that would safeguard the Monroe Doctrine and other American interests dear to the senators.

As soon as Wilson was back in Paris, hardheaded Premier Clemenceau pressed French demands for the German-inhabited Rhineland and the Saar Valley, a rich coal area. Faced with fierce Wilsonian opposition to this violation of self-determination, France settled for a compromise whereby the Saar Basin would remain under the League of Nations for fifteen years and then a popular vote would determine its fate.* In exchange for dropping its demands for the Rhineland, France got a Security Treaty in which both Britain and America pledged to come to its aid in the event of another German invasion. The French later felt betrayed when this pact was quickly pigeonholed by the U.S. Senate, which shied away from all entangling alliances.

---

*The Saar population voted overwhelmingly to rejoin Germany in 1935.

*In due time the Japanese illigally fortified these islands—the Marshalls, Marianas, and Carolines—and used them as bases against the United States in World War II.

ties, Wilson was forced to compromise away some of his less cherished Fourteen Points in order to salvage the more precious League of Nations. He was much like the mother who had to throw her sickly younger children to the pursuing wolves to save her sturdy firstborn.

A troubled Wilson was not happy with the results. Greeted a few months earlier with frenzied acclaim in Europe, he was now a fallen idol, condemned alike by disillusioned liberals and frustrated imperialists. He was keenly aware of some of the injustices that had been forced into the treaty. But he was hoping that the League of Nations—a potent League with America as a leader—would iron out the inequities.

Yet the loudly condemned treaty had much to commend it. Not least among its merits was its liberation of millions of minority peoples, such as the Poles, from the yoke of an alien dynasty. Disappointing though Wilson's handiwork was, he saved the pact from being an old-time peace of grasping imperialism. His critics to the contrary, the settlement was almost certainly a fairer one because he had gone to Paris.

The Domestic Parade of Prejudice

Returning for the second and final time to America, Wilson sailed straight into a political typhoon. Isolationists raised a whirlwind of protest against the treaty, especially against Wilson's commitment to usher the United States into his newfangled League of Nations. Invoking the revered advice of Washington and Jefferson, they wanted no part of any "entangling alliance."

Nor were the isolationists Wilson's only problem. Critics showered the Treaty of Versailles with abuse from all sides.

Rabid Hun-haters, regarding the pact as not harsh enough, voiced their discontent. Principled liberals, like the editors of the New York *Nation,* thought it too harsh—and a gross betrayal to boot. German-Americans, Italian-Americans, and other "hypehenated" Americans were aroused because the peace settlement was not sufficiently favorable to their native lands.

Irish-Americans, traditional twisters of the British lion's tail, also denounced the League. They felt that with the additional votes of the five over-

seas British dominions, it gave Britain undue influence; and they feared that it could be used to force the United States to crush any rising for Irish independence. Crowds of Irish-American zealots hissed and booed Wilson's name.

Wilson's Tour and Collapse (1919)

Despite mounting discontent, the president had reason to feel optimistic. When he brought home the treaty, with the "Wilson League" firmly riveted in as Part I, a strong majority of the people still seemed favorable. At this time—early July 1919—Senator Lodge had no real hope of defeating the Treaty of Versailles. His strategy was merely to amend it in such a way as to "Americanize," "Republicanize," or "senatorialize" it. The Republicans could then claim political credit for the changes.

Lodge effectively used delay to muddle and divide public opinion. He read the entire 264-page treaty aloud in the Senate Foreign Relations Committee and held protracted hearings in which people of various nationalities aired their grievances.

Wilson fretted increasingly as the hot summer of 1919 wore on. The bulky pact was bogged down in the Senate, while the nation was drifting into confusion and apathy. He therefore decided to go to the country in a spectacular speechmaking tour. He would appeal over the heads of the Senate to the sovereign people—as he often had in the past.

The strenuous barnstorming campaign was undertaken in the face of protests by physicians and friends. Wilson had never been robust; he had entered the White House nearly seven years before with a stomach pump and with headache pills for his neuritis. His frail body had begun to sag under the strain of partisan strife, a global war, and a stressful peace conference. But he declared that he was willing to die, like the soldiers he had sent into battle, for the sake of the new world order.

The presidential tour, begun in September 1919, got off to a rather lame start. The Midwest received Wilson lukewarmly, partly because of strong German-American influence. Trailing after him like bloodhounds came two "irreconcilable" senators, Borah and Johnson, who spoke in the same cities a few days later. Hat-tossing crowds answered their attacks on Wilson, crying, "Impeach him, impeach him!"

Going to Talk to
the Boss, 1919

But the reception was different in the Rocky Mountain region and on the Pacific Coast. These areas, which had elected Wilson in 1916, welcomed him with heartwarming outbursts. The high point—and the breaking point—of the return trip was at Pueblo, Colorado, September 25, 1919. Wilson, with tears coursing down his cheeks, pleaded for the League of Nations as the only real hope of preventing future wars. That night he collapsed from physical and nervous exhaustion.

Wilson was whisked back in the "funeral train" to Washington, where several days later a stroke paralyzed one side of his body. During the next few weeks he lay in a darkened room in the White House, as much a victim of the war as the unknown soldier buried at Arlington. For $7\frac{1}{2}$ months he did not meet his cabinet.

Wilson Rejects the Lodge Reservations

Senator Lodge, coldly calculating, was now at the helm. After failing to amend the treaty outright, he finally came up with fourteen formal reservations to it—a sardonic slap at Wilson's Fourteen Points. These safeguards reserved the rights of the United States under the Monroe Doctrine and the Constitution and otherwise sought to protect American sovereignty. Senator Lodge and other critics were especially alarmed by Article X of the League because it *morally* bound the United States to aid any member victimized by external aggression. A jealous Congress wanted to reserve for itself the constitutional war-declaring power.

Wilson, hating Lodge, saw red at the mere suggestion of the *Lodge* reservations. He was quite willing to accept somewhat similar reservations sponsored by his faithful Democratic followers, but

The Coonskin on the Wall   Senator Henry Cabot Lodge is here "credited" with killing Woodrow Wilson's dream of a peace treaty incorporating the League of Nations.

he insisted that the Lodge reservations "emasculated" the entire pact.

Although too feeble to lead, Wilson was still strong enough to obstruct. When the day finally came for the voting in the Senate, he sent word to all true Democrats to vote *against* the treaty with the odious Lodge reservations attached. Wilson hoped that when these were cleared away, the path would be open for ratification without reservations or with only some mild Democratic reservations.

Loyal Democrats in the Senate, on November 19, 1919, blindly did Wilson's bidding. Combining with the "irreconcilables," mostly Republicans, they rejected the treaty with the Lodge reservations appended, 55 to 39.

Defeat Through Deadlock

The nation was too deeply shocked to accept the verdict as final. About four-fifths of the senators professed to favor the treaty, with or without reservations, yet a simple majority could not agree on a single proposition. So strong was public indignation that the Senate was forced to act a second time. In March 1920 the treaty was brought up again, with the Lodge reservations tacked on.

There was only one possible path to success. Unless the Senate approved the pact with the Lodge reservations, the entire document would be rejected. But the sickly Wilson, still sheltered behind

---

Senator Gilbert M. Hitchcock (1859–1934), the Democratic leader, later told of one of his brief visits to Wilson and his suggestion of compromise with Lodge.

"'Let Lodge compromise,' he replied.

'Well, of course,' I added, he must compromise also, but we might well hold out the olive branch.'

'Let Lodge hold out the olive branch,' he retorted, and that ended it for that day, for he was too sick a man to argue with in the presence of his anxious doctor and his more anxious wife."

---

drawn curtains and blind to disagreeable realities, again sent word to all loyal Democrats to vote down the treaty with the obnoxious Lodge reservations. He thus signed the death warrant of the treaty as far as America was concerned. On a fateful March 19, 1920, the treaty netted a simple majority but failed to get the necessary two-thirds majority by a count of 49 yeas to 35 nays.

Who defeated the treaty? The Lodge-Wilson personal feud, traditionalism, isolationism, disillusionment, and partisanship all contributed to the confused picture. But Wilson himself must bear a substantial share of the responsibility. He asked for all or nothing—and got nothing. One Democratic senator angrily charged that the president had strangled his own brainchild with his own palsied hands rather than let the Senate straighten its crooked limbs. Isolationist Republicans taunted opponents with a parody of the noble 1916 slogan: "He Kept Us Out of Peace."

The "Solemn Referendum" of 1920

Wilson had his own pet solution for the deadlock, and this partly explains why he refused to compromise on Lodge's terms. He proposed to settle the treaty issue in the forthcoming presidential campaign of 1920 by appealing to the people for a "solemn referendum." This was sheer folly, for a true mandate on the League in the noisy arena of politics was clearly an impossibility.

Jubilant Republicans gathered in Chicago in June 1920 with wayward bull moosers back in the corral (after Theodore Roosevelt's death in 1919) and the senatorial Old Guard back in the saddle. The convention devised a masterfully ambiguous platform that could appeal to both pro-League and anti-League sentiment in the party. The nominee would run on a teeter-totter rather than a platform.

As the leading presidential contestants jousted with one another, the political weathervane began to veer toward genial Senator Warren G. Harding of Ohio. A group of Senate bosses, meeting rather casually in the historic "smoke-filled" Room 404 of the Hotel Blackstone, informally decided on the affable and malleable Ohioan. Their fair-haired boy was a prosperous, backslapping, small-town newspaper editor of the "folksy" type, quite the opposite of Wilson, who had earlier noted the senator's

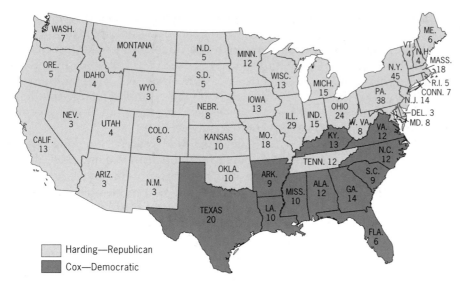

Presidential Election of 1920 (with electoral vote by state) Cox rashly claimed that "traitors" would vote Republican. But Harding and Coolidge ran successfully as small-town boys who had made good. Harding celebrated his fifty-fifth birthday on election day, and the voters presented him with the largest victory margin to date in a U.S. presidential election.

"disturbingly dull" mind. For vice president the party nominated frugal, grim-faced Governor Calvin ("Silent Cal") Coolidge of Massachusetts, who had attracted conservative support by breaking a police strike in Boston.

Meeting in San Francisco, Democrats nominated earnest Governor James M. Cox of Ohio, who strongly supported the League. His running mate was assistant navy secretary Franklin D. Roosevelt, a young, handsome, vibrant New Yorker.

Democratic attempts to make the campaign a referendum on the League were thwarted by Senator Harding, who issued muddled and contradictory statements on the issue from his front porch. Pro-League and anti-League Republicans both claimed that Harding's election would advance their cause, while the candidate suggested that if elected he would work for a vague Association of Nations—*a* league but not *the* League.

With newly enfranchised women swelling the vote totals, Harding was swept into power with a prodigious plurality of over 7 million votes—16,143,407 to 9,130,328 for Cox. The electoral count was 404 to 127. Eugene V. Debs, federal prisoner number 9653 at the Atlanta Penitentiary, rolled up the largest vote ever for the left-wing Socialist party—919,799.

Public desire for a change found vent in a resounding repudiation of "high and mighty" Wilsonism. People were tired of professional high-browism, star-reaching idealism, bothersome do-goodism, moral overstrain, and constant self-sacrifice. Eager to lapse back into "normalcy," they were willing to accept a second-rate president—and they got a third-rate one.

Although the election could not be considered a true referendum, Republican isolationists successfully turned Harding's victory into a death sentence for the League. Politicians increasingly shunned the League as they would a leper. When the legendary Wilson died in 1924, admirers knelt in the snow outside his Washington home. His "great vision" of a league for peace had perished long before.

The Betrayal of Great Expectations

America's spurning of the League was tragically shortsighted. The Republic had helped to win a costly war, but it foolishly kicked the fruits of victory under the table. Whether a strong international organization would have averted World War II in 1939 will always be a matter of dispute. But there can be no doubt that the orphaned League of Nations was undercut at the start by the refusal of the mightiest power on the globe to join it. The

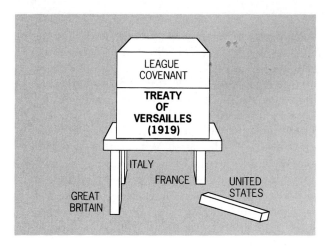

An Unstable Peace   America's failure to join the League of Nations knocked an indispensable prop from under Woodrow Wilson's design for the postwar world.

Covenant, was a top-heavy structure designed to rest on a four-legged table. The fourth leg, the United States, was never put into place. This rickety structure teetered for over a decade and then crashed in ruins—a debacle that played into the hands of German demagogue Adolf Hitler.

No less ominous events were set in motion when the Senate spurned the Security Treaty with France. The French, fearing that a new generation of Germans would follow in their fathers' goose steps, undertook to build up a powerful military force. Predictably resenting the presence of strong French armies, Germany began to rearm illegally. The seething cauldron of uncertainty and suspicion brewed an intoxicant that helped inflame the fanatical following of dictator Adolf Hitler.

The United States, as the tragic sequel proved, hurt its own cause when it buried its head in the sand. Granted that the conduct of its Allies had been disillusioning, it had its own ends to serve by carrying through the Wilsonian program. It would have been well advised if it had forthrightly assumed its war-born responsibilities and had resolutely embraced the role of global leader proffered by the hand of destiny. In the interests of its own security, if for no other reason, the United States should have used its enormous strength to shape world-shaking events. Instead it permitted itself blithely to drift toward the abyss of a second and even more bloody international disaster.

Allies themselves were largely to blame for the new world conflagration that flared up in 1939, but they found a convenient justification for their own shortcomings by pointing an accusing finger at Uncle Sam.

The ultimate collapse of the Treaty of Versailles must be laid, at least in some degree, at America's doorstep. This complicated pact, tied in with the four other peace treaties through the League

Chronology

1915	Council of National Defense established
1917	Germany resumes unrestricted submarine warfare Zimmermann note United States enters World War I Espionage Act of 1917
1918	Wilson proposes the Fourteen Points Sedition Act of 1918 Battle of Château-Thierry Second Battle of the Marne Meuse-Argonne offensive
1918	Armistice ends World War I
1919	Paris Peace Conference and Treaty of Versailles Wilson's pro-League tour and collapse Eighteenth Amendment (prohibition of alcohol) passed
1920	Final Senate defeat of Versailles Treaty Nineteenth Amendment (women's suffrage) passed Harding defeats Cox for presidency

Woodrow Wilson: Realist or Idealist?

As the first president to take the United States into a foreign war, Woodrow Wilson was obliged to make a systematic case to the American people to justify his unprecedented European intervention. His ideas have largely defined the character of American foreign policy ever since—for better or worse.

"Wilsonianism" comprises three closely related principles: (1) the era of American isolation from world affairs has irretrievably ended; (2) the United States must infuse its own founding political and economic ideas—including democracy, the rule of law, free trade, and national self-determination (or anticolonialism)—into the international order; and (3) American influence can eventually steer the world away from rivalry and warfare toward a cooperative and peaceful international system, maintained by the League of Nations or, later, the United Nations.

Whether that Wilsonian vision constitutes hard-nosed realism or starry-eyed idealism has excited scholarly debate for nearly a century. "Realists," such as George F. Kennan and Henry Kissinger, insist Wilson was anything but. They criticize the president as a naive, impractical dreamer who failed to understand that the international order is, and always will be, an anarchic, unruly arena, outside the rule of law, where only military force can effectively protect the nation's security. In a sharp critique in his 1950 study, *American Diplomacy,* Kennan condemned Wilson's vision as "moralism-legalism." In this view, Wilson dangerously threatened to sacrifice American self-interests on the altar of his admirable but ultimately unworkable ideas.

Wilson's defenders, including conspicuously his principal biographer, Arthur S. Link, argue that Wilson's idealism was in fact a kind of higher realism, recognizing as it did that armed conflict on the scale of World War I could never again be tolerated, and that some framework of peaceful international relations simply had to be found. The development of nuclear weapons in a later generation gave this argument still more force. This "liberal" defense of Wilsonianism derives from the centuries-old liberal faith that, given sufficient intelligence and willpower, the world can be made into a better place. Realists reject this notion of moral and political progress as hopelessly innocent, especially as applied to international affairs.

Some leftist scholars, such as William Appleman Williams, have argued that Wilson was in fact a realist of another kind: a subtle and wily imperialist whose stirring rhetoric cloaked a grasping ambition to make the United States the world's dominant economic power. Sometimes called "the imperialism of free trade," this strategy allegedly sought to decolonialize the world and open up international commerce, not for the good of peoples elsewhere, but to create a system in which American economic might would irresistibly prevail. This criticism itself rests on a naive assumption that international relations are a "zero-sum game," in which one nation's gain must necessarily be another nation's loss. In a Wilsonian world, Wilson's defenders claim, *all* parties would be better off; altruism and self-interest are not mutually exclusive.

Still other scholars, especially John Milton Cooper, Jr., emphasize the absence of economic factors in shaping Wilson's diplomacy. Isolationism, so this argument goes, held such sway over American thinking precisely because the United States had such a puny financial stake abroad—no hard American economic interests were mortally threatened in 1917, nor for a long time thereafter. In these circumstances, Wilson—and the Wilsonians who came after him, such as Franklin D. Roosevelt—had no choice but to appeal to abstract ideals and high principles. The "idealistic" Wilsonian strain in American diplomacy, in this view, may be an unavoidable heritage of America's historically isolated situation. If so, it was Wilson's genius to make practical use of those ideas in his bid for popular support of his diplomacy.

SUGGESTED READINGS

PRIMARY SOURCE DOCUMENTS

John J. Pershing, *My Experiences in the World War** (1931), recounts American fighting tactics. Woodrow Wilson's "Fourteen Points Address" to Congress on January 8, 1918* (*Congressional Record,* 65 Cong., 2 sess., p. 691), defined the nation's war aims. William E. Borah, *"Speech on the League of Nations"* (1919), in Richard Hofstadter, *Great Issues in American History,* reveals the isolationist position. Ernest Hemingway's *A Farewell to Arms* (1929) is an outstanding war novel.

SECONDARY SOURCES

The home front is emphasized in David M. Kennedy, *Over Here: The First World War and American Society* (1980). Economic mobilization is covered in Robert Cuff, *The War Industries Board* (1973), and Daniel R. Beaver, *Newton D. Baker and the American Financing of World War I* (1970). On labor see Frank L. Grubbs, Jr., *The Struggle for Labor Loyalty* (1968); David Brody, *Labor in Crisis: The Steel Strike of 1919* (1965); and Michael Kazin, *Barons of Labor: The San Francisco Building Trades and Union Power in the Progressive Era* (1987). Politics is treated in Seward Livermore, *Politics Is Adjourned: Woodrow Wilson and the War Congress, 1916–1918* (1966). American propaganda efforts are colorfully portrayed in James R. Mock and Cedric Larson, *Words That Won the War* (1939), and Stephen L. Vaughn, *Holding Fast the Inner Lines: Democracy, Nationalism, and the Committee on Public Information* (1980). The abuse of civil liberties is luridly described in H. C. Peterson and Gilbert C. Fite, *Opponents of War, 1917–1918* (1957), and is more soberly analyzed in Harry N. Scheiber, *The Wilson Administration and Civil Liberties, 1917–1921* (1960), and Paul L. Murphy, *World War I and the Origin of Civil Liberties in the United States* (1979). Military matters are handled in Edward M. Coffman, *The War to End All Wars: The American Military Experience in World War I* (1968); Arthur E. Barbeau and Florette Henri, *Unknown Soldiers: Black American Troops in World War One* (1974); and John Whiteclay Chambers II, *To Raise an Army: The Draft Comes to Modern America* (1987). The war experiences of women are captured in Maurine W. Greenwald, *Women, War, and Work* (1980). Gerd Hardach, *The First World War, 1914–1918* (1977), is a broad economic history. On Wilson's foreign economic policies, see Jeffrey J. Safford, *Wilsonian Maritime Diplomacy* (1978), and Burton I. Kaufman, *Efficiency and Expansion: Foreign Trade Organization in the Wilson Administration* (1974). The postwar international economic position of the United States is discussed in Carl Parrini, *Heir to Empire* (1969); Michael Hogan, *Informal Entente* (1977); and Joan Hoff Wilson, *American Business and Foreign Policy, 1920–1933* (1973). Paul P. Abrahams examines *The Foreign Expansion of American Finance and Its Relationship to the Foreign Economic Policies of the United States, 1907–1921* (1976). Works of cultural history include Stanley Cooperman, *World War I and the American Novel* (1966); Stuart Rochester, *American Liberal Disillusionment in the Wake of World War I* (1977); and Paul Fussell, *The Great War and Modern Memory* (1975). On the peace see Arthur S. Link, *Woodrow Wilson: Revolution, War, and Peace* (1979), and two studies by Thomas A. Bailey, *Woodrow Wilson and the Lost Peace* (1944) and *Woodrow Wilson and the Great Betrayal* (1945). Consult also N. Gordon Levin, Jr., *Woodrow Wilson and World Politics* (1968); Arno J. Mayer, *Politics and Diplomacy of Peacemaking* (1967); Thomas J. Kuock, *To End All Wars: Woodrow Wilson and the Quest for a New World Order* (1992); Robert H. Ferrell, *Woodrow Wilson and World War I, 1917–1921* (1985); and Lloyd C. Gardner, *Safe for Democracy: The Anglo-American Response to Revolution, 1913–1923* (1984). Lodge is somewhat rehabilitated in John A. Garraty, *Henry Cabot Lodge* (1953), and especially in William C. Widenor, *Henry Cabot Lodge and the Search for an American Foreign Policy* (1980). The end of this troubled period is sketched in Burl Noggle, *Into the Twenties: The U.S. from Armistice to Normalcy* (1974).

---

*An asterisk indicates that the document, or an excerpt from it, can be found in Thomas A. Bailey and David M. Kennedy, eds., *The American Spirit: United States History as Seen By Contemporaries,* 9th ed. (Boston: Houghton Mifflin, 1998).

34

American Life in the "Roaring Twenties"
1919–1929

America's present need is not heroics but healing;
not nostrums but normalcy; not revolution but
restoration; . . . not surgery but serenity.

WARREN G. HARDING, 1920

Insulating America from the Radical Virus

Bloodied by the war and disillusioned by the peace, Americans turned inward in the 1920s. Shunning diplomatic commitments to foreign countries, they also denounced "radical" foreign ideas, condemned "un-American" lifestyles, and clanged shut the immigration gates against foreign peoples. They partly sealed off the domestic economy from the rest of the world and plunged headlong into a dizzying decade of homegrown prosperity.

Hysterical fears of red Russia continued to color American thinking for several years after the Bolshevik revolution of 1917, which spawned a tiny Communist party in America. Tensions were heightened by an epidemic of strikes that convulsed the Republic at war's end, many of them the result of high prices and frustrated union-organizing drives. Upstanding Americans jumped to the conclusion that labor troubles were fomented by bomb-and-whisker Bolsheviks. A general strike in Seattle in 1919, though modest in its demands and orderly in its methods, prompted a call from the mayor for federal troops, to head off "the anarchy of Russia." Fire-and-brimstone evangelist "Billy" Sunday struck a responsive chord when he described a Bolshevik as "a guy with a face like a porcupine and a breath that would scare a pole cat. . . . If I had my way, I'd fill the jails so full of them that their feet would stick out the window."

The big "red scare" of 1919–1920 resulted in a nationwide crusade against left-wingers whose Americanism was suspect. Attorney General A.

Radicals on the Run, 1919 In the aftermath of the war, the American Legion, superpatriotic voice of veterans, joined the anti-Bolshevik chorus zealously attacking political leftists in the United States as "enemy reds."

Mitchell Palmer, who "saw red" too easily, earned the title of the "Fighting Quaker" by his excess of zeal in rounding up suspects. They ultimately totaled about six thousand. This drive to root out radicals was redoubled in June 1919, when a bomb shattered both the nerves and the Washington home of Palmer. The "Fighting Quaker" was thereupon dubbed the "Quaking Fighter."

Other events highlighted the red scare. Late in December 1919, a shipload of 249 alleged alien radicals was deported on the *Buford* ("Soviet Ark") to the "workers' paradise" of Russia. One zealot cried, "My motto for the Reds is S.O.S.—ship or shoot." Hysteria was temporarily revived in September 1920, when a still-unexplained bomb blast in Wall Street killed thirty-eight people and wounded several hundred others.

Various states joined the pack in the outcry against radicals. In 1919–1920 a number of legisla-tures, reflecting the anxiety of "solid" citizens, passed criminal syndicalism laws. These antired statutes, some of which were born of the war, made unlawful the mere *advocacy* of violence to secure social change. Critics protested that mere words were not criminal deeds, that there was a great gulf between throwing fits and throwing bombs, and that "free screech" was for the nasty as well as the nice. Violence was done to traditional American concepts of free speech as IWWs and other radicals were vigorously prosecuted. The hysteria went so far that in 1920 five members of the New York legislature, all lawfully elected, were denied their seats simply because they were Socialists.

The red scare was a godsend to conservative businesspeople, who used it to break the backs of the fledgling unions. Labor's call for the "closed," or all-union, shop was denounced as "Sovietism in disguise." Employers, in turn, hailed their own anti-union campaign for the "open" shop as "the American plan."

Antiredism and antiforeignism were reflected in a notorious case regarded by liberals as a "judicial lynching." Nicola Sacco, a shoe-factory worker, and Bartolomeo Vanzetti, a fish peddler, were convicted in 1921 of the murder of a Massachusetts paymaster and his guard. The jury and judge were prejudiced in some degree against the defendants because they were Italians, atheists, anarchists, and draft dodgers.

Liberals and radicals the world over rallied to the defense of the two aliens doomed to die. The case dragged on for six years until 1927, when the condemned men were electrocuted. Communists and other radicals were thus presented with two martyrs in the "class struggle," while many American liberals hung their heads. The evidence against the accused, though damaging, betrayed serious weaknesses. If the trial had been held in an atmosphere less surcharged with antiredism, the outcome might well have been only a prison term.

An author-soldier (Guy Empey) applauded the "deportation delirium" when he wrote,

"I believe we should place them [the Reds] all on a ship of stone, with sails of lead, and that their first stopping place should be hell."

Hooded Hoodlums of the KKK

A new Ku Klux Klan, spawned by the postwar reaction, mushroomed fearsomely in the early 1920s. Despite the familiar sheets and hoods, it more closely resembled the antiforeign "nativist" movements of the 1850s than the antiblack night riders of the 1860s. It was antiforeign, anti-Catholic, antiblack, anti-Jewish, antipacifist, anti-Communist, anti-internationalist, antievolutionist, antibootlegger, antigambling, antiadultery, and anti–birth control. It was also pro–Anglo-Saxon, pro-"native" American, and pro-Protestant. In short, the besheeted Klan betokened an extremist, ultraconservative uprising against many of the forces of diversity and modernity that were transforming American culture.

As reconstituted, the Klan spread with astonishing rapidity, especially in the Midwest and the "Bible Belt" South. At its peak in the mid-1920s, it claimed about 5 million dues-paying members and wielded potent political influence. It capitalized on the typically American love of on-the-edge adventure and

KKK Parade of 40,000 Men in Washington, 1925

in-group camaraderie, to say nothing of the adolescent ardor for secret ritual. "Knights of the Invisible Empire" included among their officials Imperial Wizards, Grand Goblins, King Kleagles, and other horrendous "kreatures." The most impressive displays were "konclaves" and huge flag-waving parades. The chief warning was the blazing cross. The principal weapon was the bloodied lash, supplemented by tar and feathers. Rallying songs were "The Fiery Cross on High," "One Hundred Percent American," and "The Ku Klux Klan and the Pope" (against kissing the Pope's toe). One brutal slogan was "Kill the Kikes, Koons, and Katholics."

This reign of hooded horror, so repulsive to the best American ideals, collapsed rather suddenly in the late 1920s. Decent people at last recoiled from the orgy of ribboned flesh and terrorism, while scandalous embezzling by Klan officials launched a congressional investigation. The bubble was punctured when the movement was exposed, not as a crusade, but as a vicious racket based on a $10 initiation fee, $4 of which was kicked back to local organizers as an incentive to recruit. The KKK was an alarming manifestation of the intolerance and prejudice plaguing people anxious about the dizzying pace of social change in the 1920s. America needed no such cowardly apostles, whose white sheets concealed dark purposes.

Stemming the Foreign Flood

Isolationist America of the 1920s, ingrown and provincial, had little use for the immigrants who began to flood into the country again as peace settled soothingly, on the war-torn world. Some 800,000 stepped ashore in 1920–1921, about two-thirds of them from southern and eastern Europe. The "one-hundred-percent Americans," recoiling at the sight of this resumed "New Immigration," once again cried that the famed poem at the base of the Statue of Liberty was all too literally true: they claimed that a sickly Europe was indeed vomiting on America "the wretched refuse of its teeming shore."

Congress temporarily plugged the breach with the Emergency Quota Act of 1921. Newcomers from Europe were restricted in any given year to a definite quota, which was set at 3 percent of the people of their nationality who had been living in the

The Only Way to Handle It

United States in 1910. This national-origins system was relatively favorable to the immigrants from southern and eastern Europe, for by 1910 immense numbers of them had already arrived.

This stopgap legislation of 1921 was replaced by the Immigration Act of 1924. Quotas for foreigners were cut from 3 percent to 2 percent. The national-origins base was shifted from the census of 1910 to that of 1890, when comparatively few southern Europeans had arrived.* Great Britain and Northern Ireland, for example, could send 65,721 a year as against 5,802 for Italy. Southern Europeans bitterly denounced the device as unfair and discriminatory—a triumph for the "nativist" belief that blue-eyed and fair-haired northern Europeans were of better blood. The purpose was clearly to freeze America's existing racial composition, which was largely northern European. A flagrantly discriminatory section of the Immigration Act of 1924 slammed the door absolutely against Japanese immigrants. Mass "Hate America" rallies erupted in Japan, and one Japanese superpatriot expressed his outrage by committing suicide near the American embassy in Tokyo. Exempt from the quota system were Canadians and Latin Americans, whose proximity made them easy to attract for jobs when times were good and just as easy to send back home when they were not.

The quota system effected a pivotal departure in American policy. It claimed that the nation was filling up and that a "No Vacancy" sign was needed.

Immigration henceforth dwindled to a mere trickle. By 1931, probably for the first time in American experience, more foreigners left than arrived. Quotas thus caused America to sacrifice something of its tradition of freedom and opportunity, as well as its future ethnic diversity.

The Immigration Act of 1924 marked the end of an era—a period of virtually unrestricted immigration that in the preceding century had brought some 35 million newcomers to the United States, mostly from Europe. The immigrant tide was now cut off; but it left on American shores by the 1920s a patchwork of ethnic communities separated from each other and from the larger society by language, religion, and customs. Many of the most recent arrivals, including the Italians, Jews, and Poles, lived in isolated enclaves with their own houses of worship, newspapers, and theaters (see Makers of America: The Poles, pp. 750–751). Efforts to organize labor unions repeatedly foundered on the rocks of ethnic differences. Immigrant workers on the same shop floor might share a common interest in wages and working conditions, but they often had no

---

*Five years later the Act of 1929, using 1920 as the quota base, virtually cut immigration in half by limiting the total to 152,574 a year. In 1965 Congress abolished the national-origins quota system.

MAKERS OF AMERICA

The Poles

The Poles were among the largest immigrant groups to respond to industrializing America's call for badly needed labor after the Civil War. Between 1870 and World War I, some 2 million Polish-speaking peasants boarded steamships bound for the United States. By the 1920s, when antiforeign feeling led to restrictive legislation that choked the immigrant stream to a trickle, Polish immigrants and their American-born children began to develop new identities as Polish-Americans.

The first Poles to arrive in the New World had landed in Jamestown in 1608 and helped to develop that colony's timber industry. Over the ensuing two and a half centuries, scattered religious dissenters and revolutionary nationalists also made their way from Poland to America. During the Revolution about one hundred Poles, including two officers recruited by Benjamin Franklin, served in the Continental army.

But the Polish hopefuls who poured into the United States in the late-nineteenth century came primarily to stave off starvation and to earn money to buy land. Known in their homeland as *za chlebem* ("for bread") emigrants, they belonged to the mass of central and eastern European peasants who had been forced off their farms by growing competition from the large-scale, mechanized agriculture of western Europe and the United States. An exceptionally high birthrate among the Catholic Poles compounded this economic pressure, creating an army of the land-poor and landless, who left their homes seasonally or permanently in search of work. In 1891 farm workers and unskilled laborers in the United States earned about $1 a day, more than eight times as much as agricultural workers in

the Polish province of Galicia. Such a magnet was irresistible.

These Polish-speaking newcomers emigrated not from a unified nation but from a weakened country that had been partitioned in the eighteenth century by three great European powers: Prussia (later Germany), Austria-Hungary, and Russia. The Prussian Poles, driven from their homeland in part by the anti-Catholic policies that the German imperial government pursued in the 1870s, arrived in America first. Fleeing religious persecution as well as economic turmoil, many of these early immigrants arrived in the United States intending to stay. By contrast, most of those who came later from Austrian and Russian Poland simply hoped to earn enough American dollars to return home and to buy land.

Some of the Polish peasants learned of America from propaganda spread throughout Europe by agents for U.S. railroad and steamship lines. But many more were lured by glowing letters from friends and relatives already living in the United States. The first wave of Polish immigrants had established a thriving network of self-help and fraternal associations, organized around Polish Catholic parishes. Often Polish-American entrepreneurs helped their European compatriots make travel arrangements or find jobs in the United States. One of the most successful of these, the energetic Chicago grocer Anton Schermann, is credited with "bringing over" 100,000 Poles and causing the Windy City to earn the nickname the "American Warsaw."

Most of the Poles arriving in the United States in the late-nineteenth century headed for booming industrial cities such as Buffalo, Pittsburgh, Detroit, Milwaukee, and Chicago. In 1907, four-fifths of the men toiled as unskilled laborers in coal mines, meatpacking factories, textile and steel mills, oil refineries, and garment-making shops. Although married women usually stayed home and contributed to the family's earnings by taking in laundry and boarders, children and single girls often joined their fathers and brothers on the job.

By putting the whole family to work, America's Polish immigrants saved tidy sums. By 1901 about one-third of all Poles in the United States owned real estate, and they sent so much money to relatives in Austria and Russia that American and European authorities fretted about the consequences: in 1907 a nativist U.S. immigration commission groused that the huge outflow of funds to eastern Europe was weakening the U.S. economy.

When an independent Poland was created after World War I, few Poles chose to return to their Old World homeland. Instead, like other immigrant groups in the 1920s, they redoubled their effort to integrate into American society. Polish institutions like churches and fraternal organizations, which had served to perpetuate a distinctive Polish culture in the New World, now facilitated the transformation of Poles into Polish-Americans. When Poland was absorbed into the Communist bloc after World War II, Polish-Americans clung still more tightly to their American identity, pushing for landmarks like Chicago's Pulaski Road to memorialize their culture in the New World.

Polish Coal Miners, c. 1905 It was common practice in American mines to segregate mining crews by ethnicity and race.

Solidarity Still, 1984 Even after generations of removal from their mother country, many Polish Americans took a keen interest in the fate of their ancestral land, as shown by this pro-"Solidarity" banner at a Polish festival in Chicago.

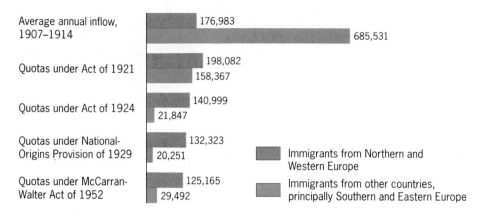

Average annual inflow, 1907–1914	176,983	
		685,531
Quotas under Act of 1921	198,082	
	158,367	
Quotas under Act of 1924	140,999	
	21,847	
Quotas under National-Origins Provision of 1929	132,323	
	20,251	
Quotas under McCarran-Walter Act of 1952	125,165	
	29,492	

■ Immigrants from Northern and Western Europe

■ Immigrants from other countries, principally Southern and Eastern Europe

Annual Immigration and the Quota Laws   The national-origins quota system was abolished in 1965. Legislation in that year capped the level of immigration at 170,000 per year but made exceptions for children, spouses, and parents of persons already arrived. It also restricted immigration from any single country to 20,000 people per year. The immigration laws were again significantly revised in 1986 (see p. 948 and p. 1033).

common language with which to forge common cause; indeed, cynical employers often played upon ethnic rivalries to keep their workers divided and powerless. Ethnic variety thus undermined class and political solidarity. It was an old American story, but one that some reformers hoped would not go on forever.

The Prohibition "Experiment"

One of the last peculiar spasms of the progressive reform movement was prohibition, loudly supported by crusading churches and by many women. The arid new order was authorized in 1919 by the Eighteenth Amendment (for text, see the Appendix), as implemented by the Volstead Act passed by Congress later that year. Together these laws made the world "safe for hypocrisy."

The legal abolition of alcohol was fairly popular in the Midwest, and especially so in the South. Southern whites were eager to keep stimulants out of the hands of the blacks, lest they burst out of "their place." But despite the overwhelming ratification of the "dry" amendment, strong opposition persisted in the larger eastern cities. For many "wet" foreign-born people, Old World styles of sociability were built around drinking in beer gardens and corner taverns. Yet most Americans now assumed that prohibition had come to stay. Everywhere carousers

indulged in last wild flings, as the nation prepared to enter upon a permanent "alcoholiday."

But prohibitionists were naive in the extreme. They overlooked the tenacious American tradition of strong drink and of weak control by the central government, especially over private lives. They forgot that the federal authorities had never satisfactorily enforced a law where the majority of the people—or a strong minority—were hostile to it. They ignored the fact that one cannot make a crime overnight out of something that millions of people have never regarded as a crime. Lawmakers could not legislate away a thirst.

Automaker Henry Ford (1863–1947), an ardent prohibitionist, posted this notice in his Detroit factory in 1922:

"From now on it will cost a man his job . . . to have the odor of beer, wine or liquor on his breath, or to have any of these intoxicants on his person or in his home. The Eighteenth Amendment is a part of the fundamental laws of this country. It was meant to be enforced. Politics has interfered with the enforcement of this law, but so far as our organization is concerned, it is going to be enforced to the letter."

Peculiar conditions hampered the enforcement of prohibition. Profound disillusionment over the aftermath of the war raised serious questions as to the wisdom of further self-denial. Slaking thirst became a cherished personal liberty, and many ardent wets believed that the way to bring about repeal was to violate the law on a large enough scale. Hypocritical, hip-flasked legislators spoke or voted dry while privately drinking wet. ("Let us strike a blow for liberty" was an ironic toast.) Frustrated soldiers, returning from France, complained that prohibition had been "put over" on them while they were "over there." Grimy workers bemoaned the loss of their cheap beer, while pointing out that the idle rich could buy all the illicit alcohol they wanted. Flaming youth of the jazz age thought it "smart" to swill bootleg liquor—"liquid tonsillectomies." Millions of older citizens likewise found forbidden fruit fascinating, as they engaged in "bar hunts."

Prohibition might have started off on a better foot if there had been a larger army of enforcement officials. But the state and federal agencies were understaffed, and their snoopers, susceptible to bribery, were underpaid. The public was increasingly distressed as scores of people, including innocent bystanders, were killed by quick-triggered dry agents.

Prohibition simply did not prohibit. The old-time "men only" corner saloons were replaced by thousands of "speakeasies," each with its tiny grilled window through which the thirsty spoke softly before the barred door was opened. Hard liquor, especially the cocktail, was drunk in staggering volume by both men and women. Largely because of the difficulties of transporting and concealing bottles, beverages of high alcoholic content were popular. Foreign rumrunners, often from the West Indies, had their inning, and countless cases of liquor leaked down from Canada. The zeal of American prohibition agents on occasion strained diplomatic relations with Uncle Sam's northern neighbor.

"Home brew" and "bathtub gin" became popular, as law-evading adults engaged in "alky cooking" with toy stills. The worst of the homemade "rotgut" produced blindness, even death. The affable bootlegger worked in silent partnership with the friendly undertaker.

Yet the "noble experiment" was not entirely a failure. Bank savings increased, and absenteeism in

Texas Guinan, Queen of the Nightclubs, in One of the "Speakeasies" That She Operated in New York City During Prohibition

Federal Agents Destroy Booze in Brooklyn

industry decreased, presumably because of the newly sober ways of formerly soused barflies. On the whole, probably less alcohol was consumed than in the days before prohibition, though strong drink continued to be available. As the legendary tippler remarked, prohibition was "a darn sight better than no liquor at all."

The Golden Age of Gangsterism

Prohibition spawned shocking crimes. The lush profits of illegal alcohol led to bribery of the police, many of whom were induced to see and smell no evil. Violent gang wars broke out in the big cities between rivals seeking to corner the rich market in booze. Rival triggermen used their sawed-off shotguns and chattering "typewriters" (machine guns) to "erase" bootlegging competitors who were trying to "muscle in" on their "racket." In the gang wars of the 1920s in Chicago, about five hundred low characters were murdered. Arrests were few and convictions were even fewer, as the button-lipped gangsters covered for one another with the underworld's code of silence.

Chicago was by far the most spectacular example of lawlessness. In 1925 "Scarface" Al Capone, a grasping and murderous booze distributor, began six years of gang warfare that netted him millions of blood-spattered dollars. He zoomed through the streets in an armor-plated car with bulletproof windows. A Brooklyn newspaper quipped,

And the pistols' red glare,
Bombs bursting in air
Give proof through the night
That Chicago's still there.

Capone, though branded "Public Enemy Number One," could not be convicted of the cold-blooded massacre, on St. Valentine's Day in 1929, of seven disarmed members of a rival gang. But after serving most of an eleven-year sentence in a federal penitentiary for income-tax evasion, he was released as a syphilitic wreck.

Gangsters rapidly moved into other profitable and illicit activities: prostitution, gambling, and narcotics. Honest merchants were forced to pay "protection money" to the organized thugs; otherwise their windows would be smashed, their trucks

The King Still Reigns, 1930   Gangster Al Capone, headquartered in Chicago, was reported as saying, "Everybody calls me a racketeer. I call myself a businessman. When I sell liquor, it's bootlegging. When my patrons serve it on a silver tray on Lake Shore Drive, it's hospitality."

overturned, or their employees or themselves beaten up. Racketeers even invaded the ranks of local labor unions as organizers and promoters. Organized crime had come to be one of the nation's most gigantic businesses. By 1930 the annual "take" of the underworld was estimated to be from $12 billion to $18 billion—several times the income of the Washington government.

Criminal callousness sank to new depths in 1932 with the kidnapping for ransom, and eventual murder, of the infant son of aviator-hero Charles A. Lindbergh. The entire nation was inexpressibly shocked and saddened, causing Congress in 1932 to pass the so-called Lindbergh Law, making interstate abduction in certain circumstances a death-penalty offense.

Monkey Business in Tennessee

Education in the 1920s continued to make giant bootstrides. More and more states were requiring young people to remain in school until age sixteen or eighteen, or until graduation from high school. The proportion of seventeen-year-olds who finished high school almost doubled in the 1920s, to more than one in four.

The most revolutionary contribution to educational theory during these yeasty years was made by mild-mannered Professor John Dewey, who was on the faculty of Columbia University from 1904 to 1930. By common consent one of America's few front-rank philosophers, he set forth the principles of "learning by doing" that formed the foundation of so-called progressive education, with its greater "permissiveness." He believed that the workbench was as essential as the blackboard, and that "education for life" should be a primary goal of the teacher.

This new emphasis on creating socially useful adults rendered many schools more attractive. No longer was the schoolhouse a kind of juvenile jail, from which the pupils burst at the end of the year chanting, as young Dewey had when a youngster in Vermont, "Good-bye school, good-bye teacher, damned old fool."

Science also scored wondrous advances in these years. A massive public-health program, launched by the Rockefeller Foundation in the South in 1909, had virtually wiped out the ancient affliction of hookworm by the 1920s. Better nutrition and health care helped to increase the life expectancy of a newborn infant from fifty years in 1901 to fifty-nine years in 1929.

Yet both science and progressive education in the 1920s were subjected to unfriendly fire from the Fundamentalists. These old-time religionists charged that the teaching of Darwinian evolution was destroying faith in God and the Bible, while contributing to the moral breakdown of youth in the jazz age. Numerous attempts were made to secure laws prohibiting the teaching of evolution, "the bestial hypothesis," in the public schools, and three southern states adopted such shackling measures. The trio of states included Tennessee, in the heart of the so-called Bible Belt South, where the spirit of evangelical religion was still robust.

The stage was set for the memorable "Monkey Trial" at the hamlet of Dayton, eastern Tennessee, in 1925. A likable high-school biology teacher, John T. Scopes, was indicted for teaching evolution. Batteries of newspaper reporters, armed with notebooks and cameras, descended upon the quiet town to witness the spectacle. Scopes was defended by nationally known attorneys, while former presidential candidate William Jennings Bryan, an ardent

Hiram Wesley Evans, imperial wizard of the Ku Klux Klan, in 1926 poignantly described the cultural grievances that fueled the Klan and lay behind much of the Fundamentalist revolt against "Modernism":

"Nordic Americans for the last generation have found themselves increasingly uncomfortable and finally deeply distressed. . . . One by one all our traditional moral standards went by the boards, or were so disregarded that they ceased to be binding. The sacredness of our Sabbath, of our homes, of chastity, and finally even of our right to teach our own children in our own schools fundamental facts and truths were torn away from us. Those who maintained the old standards did so only in the face of constant ridicule. . . . We found our great cities and the control of much of our industry and commerce taken over by strangers. . . . We are a movement of the plain people, very weak in the matter of culture, intellectual support, and trained leadership. . . . This is undoubtedly a weakness. It lays us open to the charge of being 'hicks' and 'rubes' and 'drivers of second-hand Fords.'"

The bombastic Fundamentalist evangelist W. A. (Billy) Sunday (1862–1935) declared in 1925,

"If a minister believes and teaches evolution, he is a stinking skunk, a hypocrite, and a liar."

The Fundamentalist Outcry, 1925   Radicalism and science are both condemned as blasphemers.

Presbyterian Fundamentalist, joined the prosecution. Taking the stand as an expert on the Bible, Bryan was made to appear foolish by the famed criminal lawyer Clarence Darrow. Five days after the trial was over, Bryan died of a stroke, no doubt brought on by the wilting heat and witness-stand strain.

This historic clash between theology and biology proved inconclusive. Scopes, the forgotten man of the drama, was found guilty and fined $100. But the supreme court of Tennessee, while upholding the law, set aside the fine on a technicality.* The Fundamentalists at best won only a hollow victory, for the absurdities of the trial cast ridicule on their cause. Yet even though increasing numbers of Christians were coming to reconcile the revelations of religion with the findings of modern science, Fundamentalism, with its emphasis on literal reading of the Bible, remained a vibrant force in American spiritual life. It was especially strong in the Baptist church and in the rapidly growing Churches of Christ, organized in 1906.

---

*The Tennessee law was not formally repealed until 1967.

The Mass-Consumption Economy

Prosperity—real, sustained, and widely shared—put much of the "roar" into the twenties. The economy kicked off its war harness in 1919, faltered a few steps in the recession of 1920–1921, and then sprinted forward for nearly seven years. Both the recent war and Treasury Secretary Andrew Mellon's tax policies favored the rapid expansion of capital investment. Ingenious machines, powered by relatively cheap energy from newly tapped oil fields, dramatically increased the productivity of the laborer. Assembly-line production reached such perfection in Henry Ford's famed Rouge River plant near Detroit that a finished automobile emerged every ten seconds.

Great new industries suddenly sprouted forth. Supplying electrical power for the humming new machines became a giant business in the 1920s. Above all, the automobile, once the horseless chariot of the rich, now became the carriage of the common citizen. By 1930 Americans owned almost 30 million cars.

The nation's deepening "love affair" with the automobile headlined a momentous shift in the character of the economy. American manufacturers seemed to have mastered the problems of production; their worries now focused on consumption. Could they find the mass markets for the goods they had contrived to spew forth in such profusion?

Responding to this need, a new arm of American commerce came into being: advertising. By persuasion and ploy, seduction and sexual suggestion, advertisers sought to make Americans chronically discontented with their paltry possessions and want more, more, more. A founder of this new "profession" was Bruce Barton, prominent New York partner in a Madison Avenue firm. In 1925 Barton published a best-seller, *The Man Nobody Knows*, setting forth the provocative thesis that Jesus Christ was the greatest adman of all time. "Every advertising man ought to study the parables of Jesus," Barton preached. "They are marvelously condensed, as all good advertising should be." Barton even had a good word to say for Christ's executive ability: "He picked up twelve men from the bottom ranks of business and forged them into an organization that conquered the world."

In this commercialized atmosphere, even sports were becoming a big business. Ballyhooed by the "image makers," home-run heroes like George H. ("Babe") Ruth were far better known than most statesmen. The fans bought tickets in such numbers that Babe's hometown park, Yankee Stadium, became known as "the house that Ruth built." In 1921 the slugging heavyweight champion, Jack Dempsey, knocked out the dapper French light heavyweight, Georges Carpentier. The Jersey City crowd in attendance had paid more than a million dollars—the first in a series of million-dollar "gates" in the golden 1920s.

Buying on credit was another innovative feature of the postwar economy. "Possess today and pay tomorrow" was the message directed at buyers. Once-frugal descendants of Puritans went ever deeper into debt to own all kinds of newfangled marvels—refrigerators, vacuum cleaners, and especially cars and radios—now. Prosperity thus accumulated an overhanging cloud of debt, and the economy became increasingly vulnerable to disruptions of the credit structure.

"Babe" Ruth: The "Sultan of Swat"

Putting America on Rubber Tires

A new industrial revolution slipped into high gear in America in the 1920s. Thrusting out steel tentacles, it changed the daily life of the people in unprecedented ways. Machinery was the new messiah—and the automobile was its principal prophet.

Of all the inventions of the era, the automobile cut the deepest mark. It heralded an amazing new industrial system, based on assembly-line methods and mass-production techniques.

Americans adapted rather than invented the gasoline engine; Europeans can claim the original honor. By the 1890s a few daring American inventors and promoters, including Henry Ford and Ransom E. Olds (Oldsmobile), were developing the infant automotive industry. By 1910 sixty-nine car companies rolled out a total annual production of 181,000 units. The early contraptions were neither speedy nor reliable. Many a stalled motorist, profanely cranking a balky automobile, had to endure the jeer "Get a horse" from the occupants of a passing dobbin-drawn carriage.

An enormous industry sprang into being, as Detroit became the motorcar capital of America. The mechanized colossus owed much to the stopwatch efficiency techniques of Frederick W. Taylor, a prominent inventor, engineer, and tennis player, who sought to eliminate wasted motion. His epitaph reads "Father of Scientific Management."

Best known of the new crop of industrial wizards was Henry Ford, who more than any other individual put America on rubber tires. His high and hideous Model T ("Tin Lizzie") was cheap, rugged, and reasonably reliable, though rough and clattering. The parts of Ford's "flivver" were highly standardized, but the behavior of this rattling good car was so eccentric that it became the butt of numberless jokes.

Lean and silent Henry Ford, who was said to have wheels in his head, erected an immense personal empire on the cornerstone of his mechanical genius, though his associates provided much of the organizational talent. Ill educated, this multimillionaire mechanic was socially and culturally narrow; "History is bunk," he once testified. But he dedicated himself with one-track devotion to the gospel of standardization. After two early failures, he grasped and applied fully the techniques of assembly-line production—"Fordism." He is supposed to have

Henry Ford in His First Car, Built in 1896   He has been called "Father of the Traffic Jam."

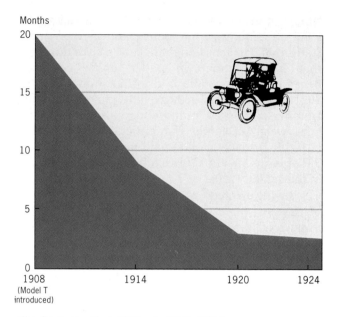

The Cost of a Model T Ford, 1908–1924
Henry Ford's mass-production techniques cut the costs of production dramatically and put the automobile within reach of the workingperson's purse. (Cost is shown in months of labor for an employee at the average national wage.)

remarked that the purchaser could have his automobile any color he desired—just as long as it was black. So economical were his methods that in the mid-1920s he was selling the Ford roadster for $260—well within the purse of a thrifty worker.

The flood of Fords was phenomenal. In 1914 the "Automobile Wizard" turned out his 500,000th Model T. By 1930 his total had risen to 20 million, or, on a bumper-to-bumper basis, more than enough to encircle the globe. A national newspaper and magazine poll conducted in 1923 revealed Ford to be the people's choice for the presidential nomination in 1924.

By 1929, when the great bull market collapsed, 26 million motor vehicles were registered in the United States. This figure, averaging 1 for every 4.9 Americans, represented far more automobiles than existed in all the rest of the world.

The Advent of the Gasoline Age

The impact of the self-propelled carriage on various aspects of American life was tremendous. A gigantic new industry emerged, dependent on steel, but displacing steel from its kingpin role. Employing directly or indirectly about 6 million people by 1930, it was a major wellspring of the nation's prosperity. Thousands of new jobs, moreover, were created by supporting industries. The lengthening list would include rubber, glass, and fabrics, to say nothing of highway construction and thousands of service stations and garages. America's standard of living, responding to this infectious vitality, rose to an enviable level.

New industries boomed lustily; older ones grew sickly. The petroleum business experienced an explosive development. Hundreds of oil derricks shot up in California, Texas, and Oklahoma, as these states expanded wondrously and the wilderness frontier became an industrial frontier. The once-feared railroad octopus, on the other hand, was hard hit by the competition of passenger cars,

Gas Station, New York City, 1923 Gas stations like this one began to appear about 1913; before that the nation's handful of automobile owners bought fuel from their local oil companies and stored it in tanks in their own yards.

buses, and trucks. An age-old story was repeated: one industry's gains were another industry's pains.

Other effects were widely felt. Speedy marketing of perishable foodstuffs, such as fresh fruits, was accelerated. A new prosperity enriched outlying farms, as city dwellers were provided with produce at attractive prices. Countless new roads ribboned out to meet the demand of the American motorist for smoother and faster highways, often paid for by taxes on gasoline. The era of mud ended as the nation made haste to construct the finest network of hard-surfaced roadways in the world. Lured by sophisicated advertising, and encouraged by tempting installment-plan buying, countless Americans

with shallow purses acquired the habit of riding as they paid.

Zooming motorcars were agents of social change. At first a luxury, they rapidly became a necessity. Essentially devices for needed transportation, they soon developed into a badge of freedom and equality—a necessary prop for self-respect. To some, ostentation seemed more important than transportation. Leisure hours could now be spent more pleasurably, as tens of thousands of cooped-up souls responded to the call of the open road on joyriding vacations. Women were further freed from clinging-vine dependence on men. Isolation among the sections was broken down, and the less attractive

The Ford Model A: New Wheels for the Masses In 1927 Ford Motor Company ceased making its classic Model T, the first of its mass-produced automobiles. After shutting down its entire production line for several months in order to retool, Ford eventually unveiled its new product, the Model A, in 1928.

states lost population at an alarming rate. By the late 1920s, Americans owned more automobiles than bathtubs. "I can't go to town in a bathtub," one homemaker explained.

Other social by-products of the automobile were visible. Autobuses made possible the consolidation of schools and to some extent of churches. The sprawling suburbs spread out still farther from the urban core, as America became a nation of commuters.

The demon machine, on the other hand, exacted a terrible toll by catering to the American mania for speed. Citizens were becoming statistics. Not counting the hundreds of thousands of injured and crippled, the one millionth American had died in a motor vehicle accident by 1951—more than all those killed on all the battlefields of all the nation's wars to that date. "The public be rammed" seemed to be the motto of the new age.

Virtuous home life partially broke down as joyriders of all ages forsook the parlor for the highway. The morals of flaming youth sagged correspondingly—at least in the judgment of their elders. Even the disgraceful crime waves of the 1920s and 1930s were partly stimulated by the motorcar, for gangsters could now make quick getaways.

Yet no sane American would plead for a return of the old horse and buggy, complete with fly-breeding manure. The automobile contributed notably to improved air and environmental quality, despite its later notoriety as a polluter. Life might be cut short on the highways, and smog might poison the air, but the automobile brought more convenience, pleasure, and excitement into more people's lives than almost any other single invention.

Humans Develop Wings

Gasoline engines also provided the power that enabled humans to fulfill the age-old dream of sprouting wings. After near-successful experiments by others with heavier-than-air craft, the Wright brothers, Orville and Wilbur, performed "the miracle at Kitty Hawk," North Carolina. On a historic day—December 17, 1903—Orville Wright took aloft a feebly engined plane that stayed airborne for 12 seconds and 120 feet (37 meters). Thus the air age was launched by two obscure bicycle repairmen.

As aviation gradually got off the ground, the world slowly shrank. The public was made increasingly air-minded by unsung heroes—often martyrs—who appeared as stunt fliers at fairs and other public gatherings. Airplanes—"flying coffins"—were used with marked success for various purposes during the Great War of 1914–1918. Shortly thereafter private companies began to operate passenger lines with airmail contracts, which were in effect a subsidy from Washington. The first transcontinental airmail route was established from New York to San Francisco in 1920.

"Lucky Lindy"   Charles A. Lindbergh (1902–1974), the first person to fly solo across the Atlantic, became a roving ambassador of goodwill for the United States after his historic 1927 flight, as the flags on his airplane attested. On a trip to Latin America in 1928, he met his future wife, Anne Morrow, daughter of the U.S. ambassador to Mexico.

In 1927 modest and skillful Charles A. Lindbergh, the so-called Flyin' Fool, electrified the world by the first solo west-to-east conquest of the Atlantic. Seeking a prize of $25,000, the lanky stunt flier courageously piloted his single-engined plane, the *Spirit of St. Louis,* from New York to Paris in a grueling thirty-three hours and thirty-nine minutes.

Lindbergh's exploit swept Americans off their feet. Fed up with the cynicism and debunking of the jazz age, they found in this wholesome and handsome youth a genuine hero. They clasped the soaring "Lone Eagle" to their hearts much more warmly than the bashful young man desired. "Lucky Lindy" received an uproarious welcome in the "hero canyon" of lower Broadway, as eighteen hundred tons of ticker tape and other improvised confetti showered upon him. Lindbergh's achievement—it was more than a "stunt"—did much to dramatize and popularize flying, while giving a strong boost to the infant aviation industry.

The impact of the airship was tremendous. It provided the restless American spirit with yet another dimension. At the same time, it gave birth to a giant new industry. Unfortunately, the accident rate in the pioneer stages of aviation was high, though hardly more so than on the early railroads. But by the 1930s and 1940s, travel by air on regularly scheduled airlines was significantly safer than on many overcrowded highways.

Humanity's new wings also increased the tempo of an already breathless civilization. The floundering railroad received another setback through the loss of passengers and mail. A lethal new weapon was given to the gods of war; and with the coming of city-busting aerial bombs, people could well debate whether the conquest of the air was a blessing or a curse. The Atlantic Ocean was shriveling to about the size of the Aegean Sea in the days of Socrates, while isolation behind ocean moats was becoming a bygone dream.

The Radio Revolution

The speed of the airplane was far eclipsed by the speed of radio waves. Guglielmo Marconi, an Italian, invented wireless telegraphy in the 1890s, and his brainchild was used for long-range communication during World War I.

Next came the voice-carrying radio, a triumph of many minds. A red-letter day was posted in

"Radioing" Three generations gathered for an evening of radio listening, c. 1925.

November 1920, when the Pittsburgh station KDKA broadcast the news of the Harding landslide. Later miracles were achieved in transatlantic wireless photographs, radiotelephones, and television. The earliest radio programs reached only local audiences. But by the late 1920s, technological improvements made long-distance broadcasting possible, and national commercial networks drowned out much local programming. Meanwhile, advertising "commercials" made radio another vehicle for American free enterprise, as contrasted with the government-owned systems of Europe.

While other marvels of the era—like the automobile—were luring Americans away from home, the radio was drawing them back. For much of the decade family and neighbors gathered around a household's sole radio as they once had around the toasty hearth. Radio knitted the nation together. Various regions heard voices with standardized accents, and countless millions "tuned in" to perennial comedy favorites like "Amos 'n' Andy." Programs sponsored by manufacturers and distributors of brand-name products, like the "A&P Gypsies" and

> *Radio came in with a bang in the winter of 1921–1922. A San Francisco newspaper reported a discovery that countless citizens were making:*
>
> "There is radio music in the air, every night, everywhere. Anybody can hear it at home on a receiving set, which any boy can put up in an hour."

the "Eveready Hour," helped to make radio-touted labels household words, and purchases.

Educationally and culturally, the radio made a significant contribution. Sports were further stimulated. Politicians had to adjust their speaking techniques to the new medium, and millions rather than thousands of voters heard their promises and pleas. A host of listeners swallowed the gospel of their favorite newscaster or were even ringside participants in world-shaking events. Finally, the music of famous artists and symphony orchestras was beamed into countless homes.

Hollywood's Filmland Fantasies

The flickering movie was the fruit of numerous geniuses, including Thomas A. Edison. As early as the 1890s this novel contraption, though still in crude form, had attained some popularity in the naughty peep-show penny arcades. The real birth of the movie came in 1903, when the first story sequence reached the screen. This breathless melodrama—*The Great Train Robbery*—was featured in the five-cent theaters, popularly called "nickelodeons." Spectacular among the first full-length classics was D. W. Griffith's *The Birth of a Nation* (1915), which glorified the Ku Klux Klan of Reconstruction days and defamed both blacks and Northern carpetbaggers. White southerners would fire guns at the screen during the attempted "rape" scene.

A fascinating industry was thus launched. Hollywood, in southern California, quickly became the movie capital of the world, for it enjoyed a maximum of sunshine and other advantages. Early producers featured nudity and heavy-lidded female

vampires ("vamps"), and an outraged public forced the screen magnates to set up their own rigorous code of censorship. The motion picture really arrived during the World War of 1914–1918, when it was used as an engine of anti-German propaganda. Specially prepared "hang the kaiser" films aided powerfully in selling war bonds and in boosting morale.

A new era began in 1927 with the success of the first "talkie"—*The Jazz Singer,* starring the white performer Al Jolson in blackface. The age of the "silents" was ushered out as theaters everywhere were "wired for sound." At about the same time, reasonably satisfactory color films were being produced.

Movies eclipsed all other new forms of amusement in the phenomenal growth of their popularity. Movie "stars" of the first pulchritude commanded much larger salaries than the president of the United States, in some cases as much as $100,000 for a single picture. Many actors and actresses were far more widely known than the nation's political leaders.

Critics bemoaned the vulgarization of popular tastes wrought by the new technologies of radio and motion pictures. But the effects of the new mass media were not all negative. The parochialism of insular ethnic communities eroded as the immigrants' children, especially, forsook the neighborhood vaudeville theater for the downtown movie palace or turned away from Grandma's Yiddish storytelling to tune in "Amos 'n' Andy." Much of the rich diversity of the immigrants' Old Country cultures was lost, but the standardization of tastes and

> *In the face of protests against sex in the movies, the industry appointed a "movie czar," Will H. Hays (1879–1954), who issued the famous "Hays Code" in 1934. As he stated in a speech,*
>
> "This industry must have toward that sacred thing, the mind of a child, toward that clean virgin thing, that unmarked slate, the same responsibility, the same care about the impressions made upon it, that the best clergyman or the most inspired teacher of youth would have."

of language hastened entry into the American mainstream—and set the stage for the emergence of a working-class political coalition that, for a time, would overcome the divisive ethnic differences of the past.

The Dynamic Decade

Far-reaching changes in lifestyles and values paralleled the dramatic upsurge of the economy. The census of 1920 revealed that for the first time most Americans no longer lived in the countryside but in urban areas. Women continued to find opportunities for employment in the cities, though they tended to cluster in a few low-paying jobs (such as retail clerking and office typing) that became classified as "women's work." An organized birth-control movement, led by fiery feminist Margaret Sanger, openly championed the use of contraceptives. A National Women's Party began in 1923 to campaign for an Equal Rights Amendment to the Constitution. (The campaign was still stalled short of success seven decades later.) To some defenders of traditional ways, it seemed that the world had suddenly gone mad.

Even the churches were affected. The Fundamentalist champions of the old-time religion lost ground to the Modernists, who liked to think that God was a "good guy" and the universe a pretty chummy place.

Some churches tried to fight the Devil with worldly weapons. Competing with joyriding automobiles and golf links, they turned to quality entertainment of their own, including wholesome moving pictures for young people. One uptown house of the Lord in New York advertised on a billboard, "Come to Church: Christian Worship Increases Your Efficiency."

Even before the war, one observer thought the chimes had "struck sex o'clock in America," and the 1920s witnessed what many old-timers regarded as a veritable erotic eruption. Advertisers exploited sexual allure to sell everything from soap to car tires. Once-modest maidens now proclaimed their new freedom as "flappers" in bobbed tresses and dresses. Young women appeared with hemlines elevated, stockings rolled, breasts taped flat, cheeks rouged, and lips a "crimson gash" that held a dangling cigarette. Thus did the "flapper" symbolize a yearned-for and devil-may-care independence (some said wild abandon) in some American women. Still more adventuresome females shocked their elders when they sported the new one-piece bathing suits.

Justification for this new sexual frankness could be found in the recently translated writings of Dr. Sigmund Freud. This Viennese physician appeared to argue that sexual repression was responsible for a variety of nervous and emotional ills. Thus not pleasure alone, but health, demanded sexual gratification and liberation.

Many taboos flew out the window as sex-conscious Americans let themselves go. As unknow-

The Flapper New dance styles, like the "Charleston," flamboyantly displayed the new social freedom of the "flapper," whose dress and antics frequently flummoxed the guardians of respectability.

The Guardian of Morality   Women's new one-piece bathing suits were a sensation in the 1920s. Here a check is carefully made to ensure that not too much leg is showing.

ing Freudians, teenagers pioneered the sexual frontiers. Glued together in rhythmic embrace, they danced to jazz music squeaking from phonographs. In an earlier day a kiss had been the equivalent of a proposal of marriage. But in the new era,

exploratory young folk sat in darkened movie houses or took to the highways and byways in automobiles—branded "houses of prostitution on wheels" by straitlaced elders. There, the youthful "neckers" and "petters" poached upon the forbidden territory of each other's bodies.

If the flapper was the goddess of the "era of wonderful nonsense," jazz was its sacred music. With its virtuoso wanderings and tricky syncopation, jazz moved up from New Orleans along with the migrating blacks during World War I. Tunes like W. C. Handy's "St. Louis Blues" became instant classics, as the wailing saxophone became the trumpet of the new era. Blacks such as Handy, "Jelly Roll" Morton, and Joseph ("Joe") King Oliver gave birth to jazz, but the entertainment industry soon spawned all-white bands—notably Paul Whiteman's. Caucasian impresarios cornered the profits, though not the creative soul, of America's most native music.

A new racial pride also blossomed in the northern black communities that burgeoned during and after the war. Harlem in New York City, counting some 100,000 African-American residents in the 1920s, was one of the largest black communities in the world. Harlem sustained a vibrant, creative culture that nourished poets like Langston Hughes, whose first volume of verses, *The Weary Blues*, appeared in 1926. Harlem in the 1920s also spawned a charismatic political leader, Marcus Garvey. Jamaican-born Garvey founded the United Negro

King Oliver's Creole Jazz Band, Early 1920s   Joseph ("Joe") King Oliver arrived in Chicago from New Orleans in 1918. His band became the first important black jazz ensemble and made Chicago's Royal Garden Cafe a magnet for jazz lovers. Left to right: Honoré Dutrey, trombone; Baby Dodds, drums; King Oliver, cornet; Lil Hardin, piano; Bill Johnson, banjo; and Johnny Dodds, clarinet. Kneeling in the foreground is the young Louis Armstrong.

Improvement Association (UNIA) to promote the resettlement of American blacks in their own "African homeland." Within the United States, the UNIA sponsored stores and other businesses, like the Black Star Line Steamship Company, to keep blacks' dollars in black pockets. Most of Garvey's enterprises failed financially, and Garvey himself was convicted in 1927 for alleged mail fraud and deported by a nervous United States government. But the race pride that Garvey inspired among the 4 million blacks who counted themselves UNIA followers at the movement's height helped these newcomers to northern cities gain self-confidence and self-reliance. And his example proved important to the later founding of the Nation of Islam (Black Muslim) movement.

Langston Hughes (1902–1967)   Raised in the Midwest, Hughes arrived in New York City in 1921 to attend Columbia University. He spent most of his life in Harlem, making it so much the center of his prolific and versatile literary career that he was often introduced as "the Poet Laureate of Harlem."

Literary Liberation

Likewise in literature an older era seemed to have ground to a halt with the recent war. By the dawn of the 1920s, most of the custodians of an aging genteel culture had died—Henry James in 1916, Henry Adams in 1918, and William Dean Howells (the "Dean of American literature") in 1920. A few novelists who had been popular in the previous decades continued to thrive, notably the well-to-do, cosmopolitan New Yorker Edith Wharton and the Virginia-born Willa Cather, esteemed for her stark but sympathetic portrayals of pioneering on the prairies.

But in the decade after the war, a new generation of writers burst upon the scene. Many of them hailed from ethnic and regional backgrounds different from that of the Protestant New Englanders who traditionally had dominated American cultural life. The newcomers exhibited the energy of youth, the ambition of excluded outsiders, and in many cases the smoldering resentment of ideals betrayed. They bestowed on American literature a new vitality, imaginativeness, and artistic quality.

A patron saint of many young authors was H. L. Mencken, the "Bad Boy of Baltimore," who admired their critical attitude toward American society. But few went so far in their faultfinding as Mencken himself. Little escaped his acidic wit. In the pages of his green-covered monthly *American Mercury,* he wielded a slashing rapier as much as a pen. He assailed marriage, patriotism, democracy, prohibition, Rotarians, and the middle-class American "booboisie." The South he contemptuously dismissed as "the Sahara of the Bozart" (a bastardization of *beaux arts,* French for the "fine arts"), and he scathingly attacked do-gooders as "Puritans." Puritanism, he jibed, was "the haunting fear that someone, somewhere, might be happy."

The war had jolted many young writers out of their complacency about traditional values and literary standards. With their pens they probed for new codes of morals and understanding, as well as fresh forms of expression. F. Scott Fitzgerald, a handsome Minnesota-born Princetonian then only twenty-four years old, became an overnight celebrity when he published *This Side of Paradise* in 1920. The book became a kind of Bible for the young. It was eagerly devoured by aspiring flappers and their ardent wooers, many of whom affected an

F. Scott Fitzgerald and His Wife, Zelda   They are shown here in the happy, early days of their stormy marriage.

Farewell to Arms (1929), he crafted one of the finest novels in any language about the war experience. A troubled soul, he finally blew out his brains with a shotgun blast in 1961.

Other writers turned to a caustic probing of American small-town life. Sherwood Anderson dissected various fictional personalities in *Winesburg, Ohio* (1919), finding them all in some way warped by their cramped psychological surroundings. But the chief chronicler of midwestern life was spindly, red-haired, heavy-drinking Sinclair Lewis, a hot-headed journalistic product of Sauk Centre, Minnesota. A master of satire, he sprang into prominence in 1920 with *Main Street,* the story of one woman's unsuccessful war against provincialism. In *Babbitt* (1922) he affectionately pilloried George F. Babbitt, a prosperous, vulgar, middle-class real estate broker who slavishly conformed to the respectable materialism of his group. The word *Babbittry* was quickly coined to describe his all-too-familiar lifestyle.

William Faulkner, a dark-eyed, pensive Mississippian, penned a bitter war novel, *Soldier's Pay,* in 1926. He then turned his attention to a fictional chronicle of an imaginary, history-rich Deep South county. In powerful books like *The Sound and the Fury* (1929) and *As I Lay Dying* (1930), Faulkner peeled back layers of time and consciousness from the constricted souls of his ingrown southern characters.

air of bewildered abandon toward life. Catching the spirit of the hour (often about 4 A.M.), Fitzgerald found "All gods dead, all wars fought, all faiths in man shaken." He followed this melancholy success with *The Great Gatsby* (1925), a brilliant evocation of the glamour and cruelty of an achievement-oriented society. Theodore Dreiser's masterpiece of 1925 explored much the same theme: *An American Tragedy* dealt with the murder of a pregnant working girl by her socially ambitious young lover.

Ernest Hemingway, who had seen action on the Italian front in 1917, was among the writers most affected by the war. He responded to pernicious propaganda and the overblown appeal to patriotism by devising his own lean, word-sparing but word-perfect style. Hemingway spoke with a voice that was to have many imitators but no equals. In *The Sun Also Rises* (1926), he told of disillusioned, spiritually numb American expatriates in Europe. In *A*

In A Farewell to Arms *(1929), Ernest Hemingway's (1899–1961) hero, Frederic Henry, confessed,*

"I was always embarrassed by the words sacred, glorious, and sacrifice and the expression in vain. . . . There were many words that you could not stand to hear and finally only the names of places had dignity. Certain numbers were the same way and certain dates and these with the names of the places were all you could say and have them mean anything. Abstract words such as glory, honor, courage, or hallow were obscene beside the concrete names of villages, the numbers of roads, the names of rivers, the numbers of regiments, and the dates."

Nowhere was innovation in the 1920s more obvious than in poetry. Ezra Pound, a brilliantly erratic Idahoan who deserted America for Europe, rejected what he called "an old bitch civilization, gone in the teeth" and proclaimed his doctrine: "Make It New." Pound strongly influenced the Missouri-born and Harvard-educated T. S. Eliot, who took up residence in England. In "The Waste Land" (1922), Eliot produced one of the most impenetrable but influential poems of the century. Robert Frost, a San Francisco–born poet, wrote hauntingly about his adopted New England. The most daringly innovative of all was e.e. cummings, who relied on unorthodox diction and peculiar typesetting to produce startling poetical effects.

On the stage, Eugene O'Neill, a New York dramatist and Princeton dropout of globe-trotting background, laid bare Freudian notions of sex in plays like *Strange Interlude* (1928). A prodigious playwright, he authored more than a dozen productions in the 1920s and won the Nobel Prize in 1936.

O'Neill arose from New York's Greenwich Village, which before and after the war was a seething cauldron of writers, painters, musicians, actors, and other would-be artists. After the war a black cultural renaissance also took root uptown in Harlem, led by such gifted writers as Claude McKay, Langston Hughes, and Zora Neale Hurston, and by jazz artists like Louis Armstrong and Eubie Blake. In an outpouring of creative expression called the Harlem Renaissance, they proudly exulted in their black culture and argued for a "New Negro" who was a full citizen and a social equal to whites.

Architecture also married itself to the new materialism and functionalism. Long-range city planning was being intelligently projected, and architects like Frank Lloyd Wright were advancing the theory that buildings should grow from their

Langston Hughes (1902–1967) celebrated Harlem's role in energizing a generation of artists and writers in his poem "Esthete in Harlem" (1930):

> *Strange,*
> *That in this nigger place*
> *I should meet life face to face;*
> *When, for years, I had been seeking*
> *Life in places gentler-speaking,*
> *Until I came to this vile street*
> *And found Life stepping on my feet!**

sites and not slavishly imitate Greek and Roman importations. The machine age outdid itself in New York City when it thrust upward the cloud-brushing Empire State Building, 102 stories high. Dedicated in 1931, the "Empty State Building" towered partially vacant during the depressed 1930s.

Wall Street's Big Bull Market

The boom of the golden twenties showered genuine benefits on Americans. Their incomes and living standards assuredly rose, but there always seemed to be something fantastic about it all. People sang, somewhat incredulously,

> *My sister she works in the laundry,*
> *My father sells bootlegger gin,*
> *My mother she takes in the washing,*
> *My God! how the money rolls in!*

Signals abounded that the economic joyride might end in a crash; even in the best years of the 1920s, several hundred banks failed annually. This something-for-nothing craze was well illustrated by real estate speculation, especially the fantastic Florida boom that culminated in 1925. Numerous underwater lots were sold to eager purchasers for preposterous sums. The whole wildcat scheme collapsed when the peninsula was devastated by a West

William Faulkner (1897–1962) said in 1956,

"The writer's only responsibility is to his art. He will be completely ruthless if he is a good one. He has a dream. It anguishes him so much he must get rid of it. He has no peace until then. Everything goes by the board: honor, pride, decency, security, happiness, all to get the book written."

---

*From *Collected Poems* by Langston Hughes. Copyright © 1994 by the Estate of Langston Hughes. Reprinted by permission of Alfred A. Knopf, Inc.

Calvin Coolidge Presides over the "Jazz Age"
His hands-off policies were sweet music to big business.

Indian hurricane, which belied advertisements of a "soothing tropical wind."

The stock exchange provided even greater sensations. Speculation ran wild, and an orgy of boom-or-bust trading pushed the market up to dizzy peaks. "Never sell America short" and "Be a bull on America" were favorite catchwords, as Wall Street bulls gored one another and fleeced greedy lambs. The stock market became a veritable gambling den.

As the 1920s lurched forward, everybody seemed to be buying stocks "on margin"—that is, with a small down payment. Barbers, stenographers, and elevator operators cashed in on "hot tips" picked up while on duty. One valet was reported to have parlayed his wages into a quarter of a million dollars. "The cash register crashed the social register" as rags-to-riches Americans reverently worshiped at the altar of the ticker-tape machine. So powerful was the intoxicant of quick profits that few heeded the voices raised in certain quarters to warn that this kind of tinsel prosperity could not last forever.

Little was done by Washington to curb money-mad speculators. In the wartime days of Wilson, the national debt had rocketed from the 1914 figure of $1,188,235,400 to the 1921 peak of $23,976,250,608. Conservative principles of money management pointed to a diversion of surplus funds to reduce this financial burden.

A businesslike move toward economic sanity was made in 1921, when a Republican Congress created the Bureau of the Budget. The bureau's director was to assist the president in preparing careful estimates of receipts and expenditures for submission to Congress as the annual budget. This new reform, long overdue, was designed in part to prevent haphazardly extravagant appropriations.

The burdensome taxes inherited from the war were especially distasteful to Secretary of the Treasury Mellon, as well as to his fellow millionaires. Their theory was that such high levies forced the rich to invest in tax-exempt securities rather than in the factories that provided prosperous payrolls. The Mellonites also argued, with considerable persuasiveness, that high taxes not only discouraged business but, in so doing, also brought a smaller net return to the Treasury than moderate taxes.

Seeking to succor the "poor" rich people, Mellon helped engineer a series of tax reductions from 1921 to 1926. Congress followed his lead by repealing the excess-profits tax, abolishing the gift tax, and reducing excise taxes, the surtax, the income tax, and estate taxes. In 1921 a wealthy person with an income of $1 million had paid $663,000 in income taxes; in 1926 the same person paid about $200,000. Secretary Mellon's spare-the-rich policies thus shifted much of the tax burden from the wealthy to the middle-income groups.

Mellon, lionized by conservatives as the "greatest secretary of the treasury since Hamilton," remains a controversial figure. True, he reduced the national debt by $10 billion—from about $26 billion to $16 billion. But foes of the emaciated multimillionaire charged that he should have bitten an even larger chunk out of the debt, especially while the country was pulsating with prosperity. He was also accused of indirectly encouraging the bull market. If he had absorbed more of the national income in taxes, there would have been less money left for frenzied speculation. His refusal to do so typified the single-mindedly probusiness regime that dominated the political scene throughout the postwar decade.

Chronology

1903	Wright brothers fly the first airplane
	First story-sequence motion picture
1919	Eighteenth Amendment (prohibition) ratified
	Volstead Act
	Seattle general strike
	Anderson publishes *Winesburg, Ohio*
1919-	
1920	"Red scare"
1920	Radio broadcasting begins
	Fitzgerald publishes *This Side of Paradise*
	Lewis publishes *Main Street*
1921	Sacco-Vanzetti trial
	Emergency Quota Act of 1921
	Bureau of the Budget created
1922	Lewis publishes *Babbitt*
	Eliot publishes "The Waste Land"

1923	Equal Rights Amendment (ERA) proposed
1924	Immigration Act of 1924
1925	Scopes trial
	Florida real estate boom
	Fitzgerald publishes *The Great Gatsby*
	Dreiser publishes *An American Tragedy*
1926	Hughes publishes *The Weary Blues*
	Hemingway publishes *The Sun Also Rises*
1927	Lindbergh flies the Atlantic solo
	First talking motion pictures
	Sacco and Vanzetti executed
1929	Faulkner publishes *The Sound and the Fury*
	Hemingway publishes *A Farewell to Arms*

SUGGESTED READINGS

PRIMARY SOURCE DOCUMENTS

For the fallout from the red scare, see Walter Lippmann's eloquent plea for the lives of the Italian-American radicals Sacco and Vanzetti in the New York *World** (August 19, 1927). For caustic fictional versions of the decade's social conditions, see the novels of Sinclair Lewis, *Main Street* (1920), *Babbitt* (1922), and *Arrowsmith* (1925).

SECONDARY SOURCES

The best introduction to the 1920s is William Leuchtenburg, *The Perils of Prosperity, 1914–1932* (1958). Also strong is Michael E. Parrish, *Anxious Decades: America in Prosperity and Depression, 1920–1941* (1992). Frederick Lewis Allen, *Only Yesterday* (1931), is an evocative recollection of the texture of life in the decade. Equally informative are Robert S. Lynd and Helen M. Lynd's classic sociological studies, *Middletown* (1929) and *Middletown*

*An asterisk indicates that the document, or an excerpt from it, can be found in Thomas A. Bailey and David M. Kennedy, eds., *The American Spirit: United States History as Seen by Contemporaries,* 9th ed. (Boston: Houghton Mifflin, 1998).

in Transition (1937). Robert K. Murray, *Red Scare* (1955), is authoritative; on the same subject, see Stanley Coben, *A. Mitchell Palmer* (1963). Immigration restriction is dealt with in John Higham, *Strangers in the Land* (1955). The standard work on the revived Klan is David M. Chalmers, *Hooded Americanism* (rev. ed., 1981). Also valuable is Kenneth T. Jackson, *The Ku Klux Klan in the City, 1915–1930* (1967), and Nancy MacLean, *Behind the Mask of Chivalry: The Making of the Second KKK* (1993). The changing experiences of women are discussed in Winnifred Wandersee, *Women's Work and Family Values, 1920–1940* (1981); Lois Scharf and Joan M. Jensen, eds., *Decades of Discontent: The Women's Movement, 1920–1940* (1983); Nancy F. Cott, *The Grounding of Modern Feminism* (1987); and Phyllis Palmer, *Domesticity and Dirt: Housewives and Domestic Servants in the United States, 1920–1945* (1990). Prohibition is handled in Norman H. Clark's highly readable *Deliver Us from Evil* (1976). On a related subject, see Humbert S. Nelli, *The Business of Crime* (1976). Revealing on the Scopes trial are Ray Ginger, *Six Days or Forever?* (1958), and Lawrence W. Levine's sensitive study of William Jennings Bryan, *Defender of the Faith* (1965). On the economy see Alfred D. Chandler, Jr., *Strategy and Structure: Chapters in the History of Industrial Enterprise* (1962); Irving

Bernstein, *The Lean Years: A History of the American Worker, 1920–1933* (1960); and Daniel Nelson, *Frederick Winslow Taylor and the Rise of Scientific Management* (1980). On advertising consult Stuart Ewen, *Captains of Consciousness* (1976); Daniel Pope, *The Making of Modern Advertising* (1983); and Roland Marchand, *Advertising the American Dream: Making Way for Modernity* (1985). Movies are featured in Lary May, *Screening Out the Past: The Birth of Mass Culture and the Motion Picture Industry* (1980), and Robert Sklar, *Movie-Made America* (1975). The "youth culture" is the subject of Paula Fass, *The Damned and the Beautiful: American Youth in the 1920s* (1977). Changing sexual attitudes are analyzed in David M. Kennedy, *Birth Control in America: The Career of Margaret Sanger* (1970), and Linda Gordon, *Woman's Body, Woman's Right: A Social History of Birth Control in America* (1976). See also Ellen Chesler, *Woman of Valor: Margaret Sanger and the Birth Control Movement in America* (1992). Gilbert Osofsky describes the background of the Harlem Renaissance in *Harlem: The Making of a Ghetto, 1890–1930* (1966). See also David Lewis, *When Harlem Was in Vogue* (1981). William M. Tuttle, *Race Riot: Chicago in the Red Summer of 1919* (1970), describes the violent side of race relations in the 1920s. The "Great Migration" of blacks to the North is described in James R. Grossman's *Land of Hope: Chicago, Black Southerners, and the Great Migration* (1989). Judith Stein, *The World of Marcus Garvey* (1986), discusses the most popular black leader of the period. Richard W. Fox and T. J. Jackson Lears have edited a fascinating collection of essays on American culture, *The Culture of Consumption: Critical Essays in American History, 1880–1980* (1983). Also see Warren I. Susman, *Culture as History: The Transformation of American Society in the Twentieth Century* (1984). David M. Kennedy, *Over Here: The First World War and American Society* (1980), pays special attention to the literature that emerged from the war experience.

35

The Politics of Boom and Bust

1920–1932

We in America today are nearer to the final triumph over poverty than ever before in the history of any land. We have not yet reached the goal—but . . . we shall soon, with the help of God, be in sight of the day when poverty will be banished from this nation.

HERBERT HOOVER, 1928

The Republican "Old Guard" Returns

Handsome President Warren Harding—with erect figure (6 feet; 1.83 meters), broad shoulders, high forehead, bushy eyebrows, and graying hair—was one of the best-liked men of his generation. An easygoing, warm-handed first-namer, he exuded graciousness and love of people. So kindly was his nature that he would brush off ants rather than crush them.

Yet the charming, smiling exterior concealed a weak, inept interior. With a mediocre mind, Harding quickly found himself beyond his depth in the presidency. "God! What a job!" was his anguished cry on one occasion.

Harding, like Grant, was unable to detect moral halitosis in his evil associates, and he was soon surrounded by his poker-playing, shirt-sleeved cronies of the "Ohio Gang." "A good guy," Harding was "one of the boys." He hated to hurt people's feelings, especially those of his friends, by saying "no"; and designing political leeches capitalized on this weakness. The difference between George Washington and Warren Harding, ran a current quip, was that while Washington could not tell a lie, Harding could not tell a liar. He "was not a bad man," said one Washington observer. "He was just a slob."

771

The Harding Scandals
This 1924 cartoon satirizing the misdemeanors of the Harding administration shows the sale of the Capitol, the White House, and even the Washington Monument.

Candidate Harding, who admitted his scanty mental furnishings, had promised to gather about him the "best minds" of the party. Charles Evans Hughes—masterful, imperious, incisive, brilliant—brought to the secretaryship of state a dominating if somewhat conservative leadership. The new secretary of the treasury was a lean and elderly Pittsburgh aluminum king, Andrew W. Mellon, multimillionaire collector of the paintings that are now displayed in Washington as his gift to the nation. Chubby-faced Herbert Hoover, famed feeder of the Belgians and wartime food administrator, became secretary of commerce. An energetic businessman and engineer, he raised his second-rate cabinet post to first-rate importance, especially in drumming up foreign trade for U.S. manufacturers.

But the "best minds" of the cabinet were largely offset by two of the worst. Senator Albert B. Fall of New Mexico, a scheming anticonservationist, was appointed secretary of the interior. As guardian of the nation's natural resources, he resembled the wolf hired to protect the sheep. Harry M. Daugherty, a small-town lawyer but a big-time crook in the "Ohio Gang," was supposed to prosecute wrongdoers as attorney general.

GOP Reaction at the Throttle

Well intentioned but weak-willed, Harding was a perfect "front" for enterprising industrialists. A McKinley-style old order settled back into place with a heavy thud at war's end, crushing the reform seedlings that had sprouted in the progressive era. A blowsy, nest-feathering crowd moved into Washington and proceeded to hoodwink Harding, whom many regarded as an "amiable boob."

This new Old Guard hoped to improve on the old business doctrine of laissez-faire. Their plea was not simply for government to keep hands off business, but for government to help guide business along the path to profits. They subtly and effectively achieved their ends by putting the courts and the administrative bureaus into the safekeeping of fellow standpatters. Harding initiated these practices and set the tone of Republican economic policies for the rest of the decade.

The Supreme Court was a striking example of this trend. Harding lived less than three years as president, but he appointed four of the nine justices. Several of his choices were or became deep-dyed reactionaries, and they buttressed the dike against popular currents for nearly two decades. Harding's fortunate choice for chief justice was ex-president Taft, who not only performed his duties ably but surprisingly was more liberal than some of his cautious associates.

In the first years of the 1920s, the Supreme Court axed progressive legislation. It killed a federal child-labor law, stripped away many of labor's hard-won gains, and rigidly restricted government intervention in the economy. In the landmark case of *Adkins* v. *Children's Hospital* (1923), the Court reversed its own reasoning in *Muller* v. *Oregon* (see p. 688), which had declared women to be deserving of special protection in the workplace, and invalidated a minimum-wage law for women. Its strained ruling was that because women now had the vote (Nineteenth Amendment), they were the legal equals of men and could no longer be protected by special legislation. The contradictory premises of the *Muller* and *Adkins* cases framed a debate over gender differences that would continue for the rest of the century: were women sufficiently different from men that they merited special legal and social treatment, or were they effectively equal in the eyes of the law and therefore undeserving of special protections and preferences? (An analogous debate over *racial* differences haunted affirmative-action policies later in the century.)

Corporations, under Harding, could once more relax and expand. Antitrust laws were often ignored, circumvented, or feebly enforced by friendly prosecutors in the attorney general's office. The Interstate Commerce Commission, to single out one agency, came to be dominated by men who were personally sympathetic to the managers of the railroads. Harding reactionaries might well have boasted, "We care not what laws the Democrats pass as long as we are permitted to administer them."

Big industrialists, striving to reduce the rigors of competition, now had a free hand to set up trade associations. Cement manufacturers, for example, would use these agencies to agree upon standardization of product, publicity campaigns, and a united front in dealing with the railroads and labor. Although many of these associations ran counter to the spirit of existing antitrust legislation, their formation was encouraged by Secretary Hoover. His sense of engineering efficiency led him to condemn the waste resulting from cutthroat competition, and his commitment to voluntary cooperation led him to urge businesses to regulate themselves rather than be regulated by big government.

Justice Oliver Wendell Holmes (1841–1935), wryly dissenting in the Adkins *case, said,*

"It would need more than the Nineteenth Amendment to convince me that there are no differences between men and women, or that legislation cannot take those differences into account."

The Aftermath of War

Wartime government controls on the economy were swiftly dismantled. The War Industries Board disappeared with almost indecent haste. With its passing, progressive hopes for more government regulation of big business evaporated.

Washington likewise returned the railroads to private management in 1920. Reformers had hoped that wartime government operation of the lines might lead to their permanent nationalization. Instead Congress passed the Esch-Cummins Transportation Act of 1920, which encouraged private consolidation of the railroads and pledged the Interstate Commerce Commission to guarantee their profitability. The new philosophy was not to save the country from the railroads, as in the days of the Populists, but to save the railroads for the country.

The federal government also tried to pull up anchor and get out of the shipping business. The Merchant Marine Act of 1920 authorized the Shipping Board, which controlled about fifteen hundred vessels, to dispose of much of the hastily built wartime fleet at bargain-basement prices. The board operated the remaining vessels without conspicuous success. Under the La Follette Seaman's Act of 1915, American shipping could not thrive in competition with foreigners, who all too often provided their crews with wretched food and starvation wages.

Labor, suddenly deprived of its wartime crutch of friendly government support, limped along badly in the postwar decade. A bloody strike in the steel industry was ruthlessly broken in 1919, partly by exploiting ethnic and racial divisions among the steelworkers and partly by branding the strikers as dangerous "reds." The Railway Labor Board, a successor body to the wartime labor boards, ordered a wage cut of 12 percent in 1922, provoking a two-month strike. It ended when Attorney General Daugherty, who fully shared Harding's big-business bias, clamped on the strikers one of the most sweeping injunctions in American history. Unions wilted in this hostile political environment, and membership shriveled by nearly 30 percent between 1920 and 1930.

Needy veterans were among the few nonbusiness groups to reap lasting gains from the war. Congress in 1921 generously created the Veterans'

Bureau, authorized to operate hospitals and provide vocational rehabilitation for the disabled.

Veterans quickly organized into pressure groups. The American Legion had been founded in Paris in 1919 by Colonel Theodore Roosevelt, Jr. Legionnaires met periodically to renew old hardships and let off steam in good-natured horseplay. The legion soon became distinguished for its militant patriotism, rock-ribbed conservatism, and zealous antiradicalism.

The legion also became notorious for its aggressive lobbying for veterans' benefits. The chief grievance of the former "doughboys" was monetary—they wanted their "dough." The former servicemen demanded "adjusted compensation" to make up for the wages they had "lost" when they turned in their factory overalls for military uniforms during the Great War.

Critics denounced this demand as a holdup "bonus," but the millions of veterans deployed heavy political artillery. They browbeat Congress into passing a bonus bill in 1922, which Harding promptly vetoed. Re-forming their lines, the repulsed veterans gathered for a final attack. In 1924 Congress again hoisted the white flag and passed the Adjusted Compensation Act. It gave every former soldier a paid-up insurance policy due in twenty years—adding about $3.5 billion to the total cost of the war. Penny-pinching Calvin Coolidge sternly vetoed the measure, but Congress overrode him, leaving the veterans with their loot.

America Seeks Benefits Without Burdens

Making peace with the fallen foe was the most pressing problem left on Harding's doorstep. The United States, having rejected the Treaty of Versailles, was still technically at war with Germany, Austria, and Hungary nearly three years after the armistice. Peace was finally achieved by lone-wolf tactics. In July 1921 Congress passed a simple joint resolution that declared the war officially ended.

Isolation was enthroned in Washington. The Harding administration, with the Senate "irreconcilables" holding a hatchet over its head, continued to regard the League of Nations as a thing unclean. Harding at first refused even to support the League's world health program. But the new world body was much too important to be completely ignored. "Unofficial observers" were sent to its seat in Geneva, Switzerland, to hang around like detectives shadowing a suspected criminal.

Harding could not completely turn his back on the outside world, especially the Middle East, where a sharp rivalry developed between America and Britain for oil-drilling concessions. Remembering that the Allies had floated to victory on a flood of oil, experts recognized that liquid "black gold" would be as necessary as blood in the battles of tomorrow. Secretary Hughes eventually secured for American oil companies the right to share in the exploitation of the sandy region's oil riches.

Disarmament was one international issue on which Harding, after much indecision, finally seized the initiative. He was prodded by businesspeople unwilling to dig deeper into their pockets for money to finance the ambitious naval building program started during the war. A deadly contest was shaping up with Britain and Japan, which watched with alarm as the oceans filled with American vessels. Britain still commanded the world's largest navy, but the clatter of American riveters proclaimed that the United States would soon overtake it. Tensions ran especially high in the Far East, where the Japanese were growing increasingly restive. Anxieties were further heightened by a long-standing Anglo-Japanese alliance (signed in 1902), which supposedly obligated the British to join with Japan in the event of war between Japan and the United States.

Ship-Scrapping at the Washington Conference

Public agitation in America, fed by these worries, brought about the headline-making Washington "Disarmament" Conference in 1921–1922. Invitations went to all the major naval powers—except Bolshevik Russia, whose government the United States refused officially to recognize. The double agenda included naval disarmament and the situation in the Far East.

At the outset, Secretary Hughes startled the delegates, who were expecting the usual diplomatic fence-straddling, with a comprehensive, concrete plan for declaring a ten-year "holiday" on construction of battleships and even for scrapping some of

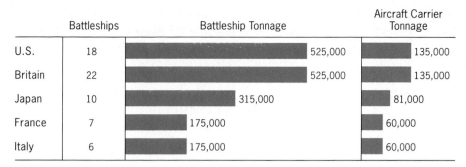

	Battleships	Battleship Tonnage	Aircraft Carrier Tonnage
U.S.	18	525,000	135,000
Britain	22	525,000	135,000
Japan	10	315,000	81,000
France	7	175,000	60,000
Italy	6	175,000	60,000

Limits Imposed by Washington Conference, 1921–1922   The pledge of the British and Americans to refrain from fortifying their Far Eastern possessions, while Japan was allowed to fortify its possessions, was the key to the naval limitation treaty. The United States and Great Britain thus won a temporary victory but later paid a horrendous price when they had to dislodge the well-entrenched Japanese from the Pacific in World War II.

the huge dreadnoughts already built or being built. He proposed that the scaled-down navies of America and Britain should enjoy parity in battleships and aircraft carriers, with Japan on the small end of a 5:5:3 ratio. This arrangement sounded to the sensitive Japanese ambassador like "Rolls-Royce, Rolls-Royce, Ford."

Complex bargaining followed in the wake of Hughes's proposals. The Five-Power Naval Treaty of 1922 embodied Hughes's ideas on ship ratios, but only after face-saving compensation was offered to the insecure Japanese. The British and Americans both conceded that they would refrain from fortifying their Far Eastern possessions, including the Philippines. The Japanese were not subjected to such restraints in their possessions. In addition, a Four-Power Treaty replaced the twenty-year-old Anglo-Japanese alliance. The new pact bound Britain, Japan, France, and the United States to preserve the status quo in the Pacific—another concession to the jumpy Japanese. Finally, the Washington Conference gave chaotic China—"the Sick Man of the Far East"—a shot in the arm with the Nine-Power Treaty of 1922, whose signatories agreed to nail wide open the Open Door in China.

When the final gavel banged, the Hardingites boasted with much fanfare—and some justification—of their globe-shaking achievement in disarmament. But their satisfaction was somewhat illusory. No restrictions had been placed on small warships, and the other powers churned ahead with the construction of cruisers, destroyers, and submarines, while penny-pinching Uncle Sam lagged

dangerously behind. Congress also pointedly declared that it was making no commitment to the use of armed force or any kind of joint action when it ratified the Four-Power Treaty. These reservations, in effect, rendered the treaty a dead letter. Ominously, the American people seemed content to rely for their security on words and wishful thinking rather than on weapons and hardheaded realism.

A similar sentimentalism welled up later in the decade, when Americans clamored for the "outlawry of war." The conviction spread that if quarreling nations would only take the pledge to foreswear war as an instrument of national policy, swords could be beaten into plowshares. Calvin Coolidge's secretary of state, Frank B. Kellogg, who later won the Nobel Peace Prize for his role, was lukewarm about the idea. But after petitions bearing more than 2 million signatures cascaded into Washington, he signed with the French foreign minister in 1928 the famed Kellogg-Briand Pact. Officially known as the Pact of Paris, it was ultimately ratified by sixty-two nations.

As for the burdens of armament, the New York Independent, *a prominent magazine, noted in January 1921 that*

"[The country is] more afraid of the tax collector than of any more distant foe."

This new parchment peace was delusory in the extreme. Defensive wars were still permitted, and what scheming aggressor could not cook up an excuse of self-defense? Lacking both muscles and teeth, the pact was a diplomatic derelict—and virtually useless in a showdown. Yet it accurately—and dangerously—reflected the American mind in the 1920s, which was all too willing to be lulled into a false sense of security. This mood took even deeper hold in the ostrichlike neutralism of the 1930s.

Hiking the Tariff Higher

A comparable lack of realism afflicted foreign economic policy in the 1920s. Businesspeople, shortsightedly obsessed with the dazzling prospects in the prosperous home market, sought to keep that market to themselves by flinging up insurmountable tariff walls around the United States. They were spurred into action by their fear of a flood of cheap goods from recovering Europe, especially during the brief but sharp recession of 1920–1921.

In 1922 Congress passed the comprehensive Fordney-McCumber Tariff Law. Glib lobbyists once more descended upon Washington and helped boost schedules from the average of 27 percent under Wilson's Underwood Tariff of 1913 to an average of 38.5 percent, which was almost as high as Taft's Payne-Aldrich Tariff of 1909. (See the Appendix.) Duties on farm produce were increased, and the principle was proclaimed that the general rates were designed to equalize the cost of American and foreign production. A promising degree of flexibility was introduced for the first time, when the president was authorized, with the advice of the fact-finding Tariff Commission, to reduce or increase duties by as much as 50 percent.

Presidents Harding and Coolidge, true to their big-industry sympathies, were far more friendly to tariff increases than to reductions. In six years they authorized thirty-two upward changes, including on their list vital commodities like dairy products, chemicals, and pig iron. During the same period, the White House ordered only five reductions. These included mill feed and such trifling items as bobwhite quail, paintbrush handles, phenol, and cresylic acid.

The high-tariff course thus charted by the Republican regimes set off an ominous chain reaction. European producers felt the squeeze, for the American tariff walls prolonged their postwar chaos. An impoverished Europe needed to sell its manufactured goods to the United States, particularly if it hoped to achieve economic recovery and to pay its huge war debt to Washington. America needed to give foreign nations a chance to make a profit from it so that they could buy its manufactured articles and repay debts. International trade, Americans were slow to learn, is a two-way street. In general, they could not sell to others in quantity unless they bought from them in quantity—or lent them more U.S. dollars.

Erecting tariff walls was a game that two could play. The American example spurred European nations, throughout the feverish 1920s, to pile up higher barriers themselves. These artificial obstacles were doubly bad: they hurt not only American-made goods but the products of European countries as well. The whole vicious circle further deepened the international economic distress, providing one more rung on the ladder by which Adolf Hitler scrambled to power.

The Stench of Scandal

The loose morality and get-rich-quickism of the Harding era manifested themselves spectacularly in a series of scandals.

Early in 1923 Colonel Charles R. Forbes, onetime deserter from the army, was caught with his hand in the till and resigned as head of the Veterans' Bureau. An appointee of the gullible Harding, he and his accomplices looted the government to the tune of about $200 million, chiefly in connection with the building of veterans' hospitals. He was sentenced to two years in a federal penitentiary.

Most shocking of all was the Teapot Dome scandal, an affair that involved priceless naval oil reserves at Teapot Dome (Wyoming) and Elk Hills (California). In 1921 the slippery secretary of the interior, Albert B. Fall, induced his careless colleague, the secretary of the navy, to transfer these valuable properties to the Interior Department. Harding indiscreetly signed the secret order. Fall then quietly leased the lands to oilmen Harry F. Sinclair and Edward L. Doheny, but not until he had received a bribe ("loan") of $100,000 from Doheny and about three times that amount in all from Sinclair.

Teapot Dome, no tempest in a teapot, finally came to a whistling boil. Details of the crooked transaction gradually began to leak out in March 1923, two years after Harding took office. Fall, Sinclair, and Doheny were indicted the next year, but the case dragged through the courts until 1929. Finally, Fall was found guilty of taking a bribe and was sentenced to one year in jail. By a curious quirk of justice, the two bribe givers were acquitted while the bribe taker was convicted, although Sinclair served several months in jail for having "shadowed" jurors and for refusing to testify before a Senate committee.

The oily smudge from Teapot Dome polluted the prestige of the Washington government. Right-thinking citizens wondered what was going on when public officials could sell out the nation's vital resources, especially those reserved for the U.S. Navy. The acquittal of Sinclair and Doheny undermined faith in the courts, while giving further currency to the cynical sayings, "You can't put a million dollars in jail" and "In America everyone is assumed guilty until proven rich."

Still more scandals erupted. Persistent reports as to the underhanded doings of Attorney General Daugherty prompted a Senate investigation in 1924 of the illegal sale of pardons and liquor permits.

Washington Officials Trying to Outpace the Teapot Dome Scandal, c. 1922

Forced to resign, the accused official was tried in 1927 but was released after a jury twice failed to agree. During the trial, Daugherty hid behind the trousers of the now-dead Harding by implying that persistent probing might uncover crookedness in the White House.

Harding was mercifully spared the full revelation of these iniquities, though his worst suspicions were aroused. While news of the scandals was beginning to break, he embarked upon a speech-making tour across the country all the way to Alaska. On the return trip he died in San Francisco, on August 2, 1923, of pneumonia and thrombosis. His death may have been hastened by a broken heart resulting from the disloyalty of designing friends. Mourning millions, not yet fully aware of the graft in Washington, expressed genuine sorrow.

The brutal fact is that Harding was not a strong enough man for the presidency—as he himself privately admitted. Such was his weakness that he tolerated people and conditions that subjected the Republic to its worst disgrace since the days of President Grant.

Calvin Coolidge: A Yankee in the White House

News of Harding's death was sped to Vice President Coolidge, then visiting at his father's New England farmhouse. By the light of two kerosene lamps the elder Coolidge, a justice of the peace, used the old family Bible to administer the presidential oath to his son.

This homespun setting was symbolic of Coolidge. Quite unlike Harding, the stern-faced Vermonter, with his thin nose and tightly set lips, embodied the New England virtues of honesty, morality, industry, and frugality. As a youth, his father reported, he seemed to get more sap out of a maple tree than did any of the other boys. Practicing a rigid economy in both money and words, "Silent Cal" came to be known in Washington conversational circles for his brilliant flashes of silence. His dour, serious visage prompted the acid observation that he had been "weaned on a pickle."

Coolidge seemed to be a crystallization of the commonplace. A painfully shy individual of average height (5 feet, 10 inches; 1.77 meters), he was blessed with only mediocre powers of leadership.

Farm-Bred Calvin Coolidge Revisits Vermont

He would occasionally display a dry wit in private; but his speeches, delivered in a nasal New England twang, were invariably boring. A staunch apostle of the status quo, he was no knight in armor riding forth to tilt at wrongs. His only horse, in fact, was an electric-powered steed on which he took his exercise. True to Republican philosophy, he became the "high priest of the great god Business." He believed that "the man who builds a factory builds a temple" and that "the man who works there worships there."

The hands-off temperament of "Cautious Cal" Coolidge suited the times perfectly. His thrifty nature caused him to sympathize fully with Secretary of the Treasury Mellon's efforts to reduce both taxes and debts. No foe of industrial bigness, he let business have its head. "Coolidge luck" held during his five and a half prosperity-blessed years.

Ever a profile in caution, Coolidge slowly gave the Harding regime a badly needed moral fumigation. Teapot Dome had scalded the Republican party badly, but so transparently honest was the vinegary Vermonter that the scandalous oil did not rub off on him. The public, though at first shocked by the scandal, quickly simmered down; and an alarming tendency developed in certain quarters to excuse some of the wrongdoers on the grounds that "they had gotten away with it." Some critics even condemned the government prosecutors for continuing to rock the boat. America's moral sensibility was evidently being dulled by prosperity.

Frustrated Farmers

Sun-bronzed farmers were caught squarely in a boom-or-bust cycle in the postwar decade. While the fighting had raged, they had raked in money hand over gnarled fist; by the spring of 1920, the price of wheat had shot up to an incredible three dollars a bushel. But peace brought an end to government-guaranteed high prices and to massive purchases by other nations, as foreign production reentered the stream of world commerce.

Machines also threatened to plow the farmers under an avalanche of their own overabundant crops. The gasoline-engine tractor was working a revolution on American farms. This steel mule was to cultivation and sowing what the McCormick reaper was to harvesting. Blue-denimed farmers no longer had to plod after the horse-drawn plow with high-footed gait. They could sit erect on their chugging mechanized chariots and turn under and harrow many acres in a single day. They could grow bigger crops on larger areas, using fewer horses and hired hands. The wartime boom had encouraged

Cash Register Chorus   Business croons its appreciation of "Coolidge prosperity."

WHAT A FRIEND WE HAVE IN COOLIDGE!

Have you placed a Sentimental Value on your Horses out of proportion to the work they are able to perform?

BAILOR MOTOR CULTIVATORS

Mechanizing Agriculture
Just as the automobile replaced the horse on city streets, so did the gas-engine tractor replace horses and mules on the nation's farms in the 1920s. American farmers owned ten times more tractors in 1930 than they had owned in 1920. The smoke-belching tractors bolstered productivity—and also increased the farmers' debt burden, as the Great Depression made tragically clear.

them to bring vast new tracts under cultivation, especially in the "wheat belt" of the upper Midwest. But such improved efficiency and expanded agricultural acreage helped to pile up more price-dampening surpluses. A withering depression swept through agricultural districts in the 1920s, when one farm in four was sold for debt or taxes. As a plaintive song of the period ran,

No use talkin', any man's beat,
With 'leven-cent cotton and forty-cent meat.

Schemes abounded for bringing relief to the hard-pressed farmers. A bipartisan "farm bloc" from the agricultural states coalesced in Congress in 1921 and succeeded in driving through some helpful laws. Noteworthy was the Capper-Volstead Act, which exempted farmers' marketing cooperatives from antitrust prosecution. The farm bloc's favorite proposal was the McNary-Haugen Bill, pushed energetically from 1924 to 1928. It sought to keep agricultural prices high by authorizing the government to buy up surpluses and sell them abroad. Government losses were to be made up by a special tax on the farmers. Congress twice passed the bill, but frugal Coolidge twice vetoed it. Farm prices stayed down, and farmers' political temperatures stayed high, reaching fever pitch in the election of 1924.

A Three-Way Race for the White House in 1924

Self-satisfied Republicans, chanting "Keep Cool and Keep Coolidge," nominated "Silent Cal" for the presidency at their convention in Cleveland in the simmering summer of 1924. Squabbling Democrats had more difficulty choosing a candidate when they met in New York's sweltering Madison Square Garden. Reflecting many of the cultural tensions of the decade, the party was hopelessly split between "wets" and "drys," urbanites and farmers, Fundamentalists and Modernists, northern liberals and southern standpatters, immigrants and old-stock Americans. In one symptomatic spasm of discord, the conventioneers failed by just one vote to pass a resolution condemning the Ku Klux Klan.

Deadlocked for an unprecedented 102 ballots, the convention at last turned wearily, sweatily, and unenthusiastically to John W. Davis. A wealthy corporation lawyer connected with the Wall Street banking house of J. P. Morgan and Company, the polished nominee was no less conservative than cautious Calvin Coolidge.

The field was now wide open for a liberal candidate. The white-pompadoured Senator ("Fighting

Bob") La Follette from Wisconsin, perennial aspirant to the presidency and now sixty-nine years of age, sprang forward to lead a new Progressive grouping. He gained the endorsement of the American Federation of Labor and enjoyed the support of the shrinking Socialist party, but his major constituency was made up of the price-pinched farmers. La Follette's new Progressive party, fielding only a presidential ticket, with no candidates for local office, was a head without a body. It proved to be only a shadow of the robust Progressive coalition of prewar days. Its platform called for government ownership of railroads and relief for farmers, lashed out at monopoly and antilabor injunctions, and urged a constitutional amendment to limit the Supreme Court's power to invalidate laws passed by Congress.

La Follette turned in a respectable showing, polling nearly 5 million votes. But "Cautious Cal" and the oil-smeared Republicans slipped easily back into office, overwhelming Davis, 15,718,211 votes to 8,385,283. The electoral count stood at 382 for Coolidge, 136 for Davis, and 13 for La Follette, all from his home state of Wisconsin (see the map below). As the so-called conscience of the calloused 1920s, La Follette injected a badly needed liberal tonic into a decade drugged on prosperity. But times were too good for too many for his reforming message to carry the day.

Foreign-Policy Flounderings

Isolation continued to reign in the Coolidge era. Despite presidential proddings, the Senate proved unwilling to allow America to adhere to the World Court—the judicial arm of the still-suspect League of Nations. Coolidge only half-heartedly—and unsuccessfully—pursued further naval disarmament after the loudly trumpeted agreements worked out at the Washington Conference in 1922.

A glaring exception to the United States' inward-looking indifference to the outside world was the armed interventionism in the Caribbean and Central America. American troops were withdrawn (after an eight-year stay) from the Dominican Republic in 1924, but they remained in Haiti from 1914 to 1934. President Coolidge in 1925 briefly removed American bayonets from troubled Nicaragua, where they had glinted intermittently since 1909, but in 1926 he sent them back, five thousand strong, and they stayed until 1933. American oil companies clamored for a military expedition to Mexico in 1926 when the Mexican government began to assert its sovereignty over oil resources. Coolidge kept cool and defused the Mexican crisis with some skillful diplomatic negotiating. But his mailed-fist tactics elsewhere bred sore resentments

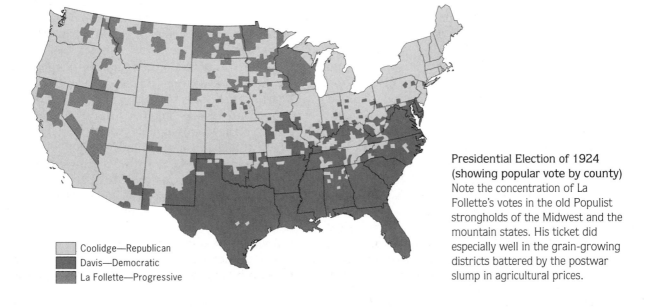

Coolidge—Republican
Davis—Democratic
La Follette—Progressive

Presidential Election of 1924 (showing popular vote by county) Note the concentration of La Follette's votes in the old Populist strongholds of the Midwest and the mountain states. His ticket did especially well in the grain-growing districts battered by the postwar slump in agricultural prices.

Harmony in Europe, 1932

south of the Rio Grande, where angry critics loudly assailed "*yanqui* imperialism."

Overshadowing all other foreign-policy problems in the 1920s was the knotty issue of international debts, a complicated tangle of private loans, Allied war debts, and German reparations payments. Almost overnight, World War I had reversed the international financial position of the United States. In 1914 America had been a debtor nation in the sum of about $4 billion; by 1922 it had become a creditor nation in the sum of about $16 billion. The almighty dollar rivaled the pound sterling as the financial giant of the world. American investors loaned some $10 billion to foreigners in the 1920s, though even this huge river of money could not fully refloat the war-shelled world economy. Americans, bewitched by lucrative investment opportunities in their domestic economy, did not lend nearly so large a fraction of their national income overseas as had the British in the prewar period.

The key knot in the debt tangle was the $10 billion that the U.S. Treasury had loaned to the Allies during and immediately after the war. Uncle Sam held their IOUs—and he wanted to be paid. The Allies, in turn, protested that the demand for repayment was grossly unfair. The French and the British

pointed out, with much justice, that they had held up a wall of flesh and bone against the common foe until America the Unready had finally entered the fray. America, they argued, should write off its loans as war costs, just as the Allies had been tragically forced to write off the lives of millions of young men. The debtors also complained that the real effect of their borrowed dollars had been to fuel the boom in the already roaring wartime economy in America, where nearly all their purchases had been made. And the final straw, protested the Europeans, was that America's postwar tariff walls made it almost impossible for them to sell the goods to earn the dollars to pay their debts.

Unraveling the Debt Knot

America's tightfisted insistence on getting its money back helped to harden the hearts of the Allies against conquered Germany. The French and the British demanded that the Germans make enormous reparations payments, totaling some $32 billion, as compensation for war-inflicted damages. The Allies hoped to settle their debts to the United States with the money received from Germany. The French, seeking to extort lagging reparations payments, sent troops into Germany's industrialized Ruhr Valley in 1923. Berlin responded by permitting its currency to inflate astronomically. At one point in October 1923, a loaf of bread cost 480 million marks, or about $120 million in preinflation money. German society teetered on the brink of mad anarchy, and the whole international house of financial cards threatened to flutter down in colossal chaos.

Sensible statesmen now urged that war debts and reparations alike be drastically scaled down or even canceled outright. But to Americans such proposals smacked of "welshing" on a debt. "We went across, but they won't come across," cried a prominent politician. Scroogelike, Calvin Coolidge turned aside suggestions of debt cancellation with a typically terse question: "They hired the money, didn't they?" The Washington administration proved especially unrealistic in its dogged insistence that there was no connection whatever between debts and reparations.

Reality finally dawned in the Dawes Plan of 1924. Negotiated largely by Charles Dawes, about to be nominated as Coolidge's running mate, it

Pundit Walter Lippmann (1889–1974) wrote in the New York World *(1926),*

"International debts are like bills submitted to pay for the damage done on a wild party by one's grandfather. The payment seems to the debtor like pure loss, and when it is paid by one nation to another it seems like tribute by the conquered to the conqueror. Money borrowed to build a railroad earns money to pay for itself. But money borrowed to fight a war produces nothing."

rescheduled German reparations payments and opened the way for further American private loans to Germany. The whole financial cycle now became still more complicated, as U.S. bankers loaned money to Germany, Germany paid reparations to France and Britain, and the former Allies paid war debts to the United States. Clearly the source of this monetary merry-go-round was the flowing well of American credit. When that well dried up after the great crash in 1929, the jungle of international finance quickly turned into a desert. President Herbert Hoover declared a one-year debt moratorium in 1931, and before long all the debtors had defaulted—except "honest little Finland," which struggled along making payments until the last of its debt was discharged in 1976.

The United States never did get its money, but it harvested a bumper crop of ill will. Irate French crowds on occasion attacked American tourists, and throughout Europe Uncle Sam was caricatured as Uncle Shylock, greedily whetting his knife for the last pound of Allied flesh. The bad taste left in American mouths by the whole sorry episode contributed powerfully to the storm-cellar neutrality legislation passed by Congress in the 1930s.

The Triumph of Herbert Hoover, 1928

Poker-faced Calvin Coolidge, the tight-lipped "Sphinx of the Potomac," bowed himself out of the 1928 presidential race when he announced, "I do not choose to run." His logical successor was super-Secretary (of Commerce) Herbert Hoover, unpopular with the political bosses but the much-admired darling of the masses, who asked "Hoo but Hoover?" He was nominated on a platform that clucked contentedly over both prosperity and prohibition.

Still-squabbling Democrats nominated Alfred E. Smith, four-time governor of New York and one of the most colorful personalities in American politics. He was a wisecracking, glad-handing liberal who suffered from several fatal political handicaps. "Al(cohol)" Smith was soakingly and drippingly "wet" at a time when the country was still devoted to the "noble experiment" of prohibition. To a nation that had only recently moved to the city,

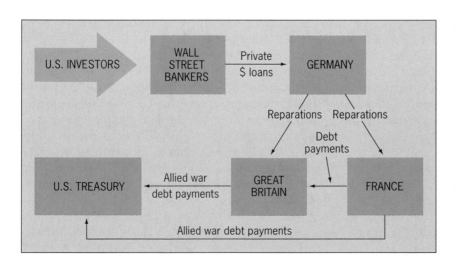

Aspects of the Financial Merry-go-round, 1921–1933 Great Britain, with a debt of over $4 billion owed to the U.S. Treasury, had a huge stake in proposals for inter-Allied debt cancellation; but France's stake was even larger. Less prosperous than Britain in the 1920s and more battered by the war, which had been fought on its own soil, France owed nearly $3.5 billion to the United States and additional billions to Britain.

native New Yorker Smith seemed too abrasively urban. He was a Roman Catholic in an overwhelmingly Protestant—and unfortunately prejudiced—land. Many dry, rural, and Fundamentalist Democrats gagged on his candidacy, and they saddled the wet Smith with a dry running mate and a dry platform. Jauntily sporting a brown derby and a big cigar, Smith, "the Happy Warrior," tried to carry alcohol on one shoulder and water on the other. But his effort was doomed from the start.

Radio figured prominently in this campaign for the first time, and it helped Hoover more than Smith. The New Yorker had more personal sparkle, but he could not project it through the radio (which in his Lower East Side twang he pronounced "radd-dee-o," grating on the ears of many listeners). Iowa-born Hoover, with his double-breasted dignity, came out of the microphone better than he went in. Decrying un-American "socialism" and preaching "rugged individualism," he sounded both grass-rootish and statesmanlike.

Chubby-faced, ruddy-complexioned Herbert Hoover, with his painfully high starched collar, was a living example of the American success story and an intriguing mixture of two centuries. As a poor orphan boy who had worked his way through Stanford University, he had absorbed the nineteenth-century copybook maxims of industry, thrift, and self-reliance. As a fabulously successful mining engineer and a brilliant businessman, he had honed to a high degree the efficiency doctrines of the progressive era.

A small-town boy from Iowa and Oregon, he had traveled and worked abroad extensively. Long years of self-imposed exile had deepened his determination, abundantly supported by national tradition, to avoid foreign entanglements. His experiences abroad had further strengthened his faith in American individualism, free enterprise, and small government.

With his unshaken dignity and Quaker restraint, Hoover was a far cry from the typical backslapping politician. Though a citizen of the world and laden with international honors, he was quite shy, stand-offish, and stiff. Personally colorless in public, he had been accustomed during much of his life to giving orders to subordinates and not to soliciting votes. Never before elected to public office, he was thin-skinned in the face of criticism, and he did not adapt readily to the necessary give-and-take of political accommodation. His real power lay in his integrity, his humanitarianism, his passion for

Herbert Hoover on the Road "Whistle-stop" campaigns, with candidates speaking from the rear platforms of trains, were a standard feature of American politics before the advent of television. Herbert Hoover here greets a crowd in Newark, New Jersey, during the 1928 campaign.

assembling the facts, his efficiency, his talents for administration, and his ability to inspire loyalty in close associates. They called him "the Chief."

As befitted America's newly mechanized civilization, Hoover was the ideal businessperson's candidate. A self-made millionaire, he recoiled from anything suggesting socialism, paternalism, or "planned economy." Yet as secretary of commerce, he had exhibited some progressive instincts. He endorsed labor unions and supported federal regulation of the new radio broadcasting industry. He even flirted for a time with the idea of government-owned radio, similar to the British Broadcasting Corporation (BBC).

As bands blared Smith's theme song, "The Sidewalks of New York," the campaign sank into the

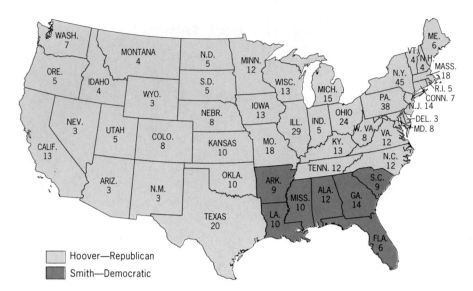

Presidential Election of 1928 (with electoral vote by state) Smith, despite his defeat, managed to poll almost as many votes as the victorious Coolidge had in 1924. By attracting to the party an immense urban or "sidewalk" vote, the breezy New Yorker foreshadowed Roosevelt's New Deal victory in 1932, when the Democrats patched together the solid South and the urban North. A cruel joke had Smith cabling the Pope a single word after the election: "Unpack."

sewers beneath the sidewalks. Despite the best efforts of Hoover and Smith, below-the-belt tactics were employed to a disgusting degree by lower-level campaigners. Religious bigotry raised its hideous head over Smith's Catholicism. An irresponsible whispering campaign claimed that "A Vote for Al Smith Is a Vote for the Pope" and that the White House, under Smith, would become a branch of the Vatican—complete with "Rum, Romanism, and Ruin." Hoover's attempts to quash such rumors were in vain.

The proverbially solid South—"100 percent American" and a stronghold of Protestant Ku Klux Klanism—shied away from "city slicker" Al Smith. It might have accepted a Catholic, or a wet, or the descendant of Irish grandparents, or an urbanite. But a concoction of Catholicism, wettism, foreignism, and liberalism brewed on the sidewalks of New York was too bitter a dose for southern stomachs. Smith's theme song was a constant and rasping reminder that his upbringing had not been convincingly American.

Hoover triumphed in a landslide. He bagged 21,391,993 popular votes to 15,016,169 for his embittered opponent, while rolling up an electoral count of 444 to 87. A huge Republican majority was returned to the House of Representatives. Tens of thousands of dry southern Democrats—"Hoovercrats"—rebelled against Al Smith, and Hoover proved to be the first Republican candidate in fifty-two years, except for Harding's Tennessee victory in 1920, to carry a state that had seceded. He swept five states of the former Confederacy, as well as all the Border States.

President Hoover's First Moves

Prosperity in the late 1920s smiled broadly as the Hoover years began. Soaring stocks on the bull market continued to defy the laws of financial gravitation. But two immense groups of citizens were not getting their share of the riches flowing from the national cornucopia: the unorganized wage earners and especially the disorganized farmers.

Hoover's administration, in line with its philosophy of promoting self-help, responded to the outcry of the wounded farmers with legislative aspirin. The Agricultural Marketing Act, passed by Congress in June 1929, was designed to help the farmers help themselves, largely through producers' cooperatives. It set up a Federal Farm Board, with a revolving fund of half a billion dollars at its disposal. Money was lent generously to farm organizations seeking to buy, sell, and store agricultural surpluses.

In 1930 the Farm Board itself created both the Grain Stabilization Corporation and the Cotton Stabilization Corporation. The prime goal was to bolster sagging prices by buying up surpluses. But the two agencies were soon suffocated by an avalanche of farm produce, as wheat dropped to fifty-seven cents a bushel and cotton to five cents a pound.

Farmers had meanwhile clutched at the tariff as a possible straw to help keep their heads above the waters of financial ruin. During the recent presidential campaign, Hoover, an amateur in politics, had been stampeded into a politically unwise pledge. He had promised to call Congress into special session to consider agricultural relief and, specifically, to bring about "limited" changes in the tariff. These hope-giving assurances no doubt won many votes for Hoover in the midwestern farm belt.

The Hawley-Smoot Tariff of 1930 followed the well-worn pattern of Washington horse trading. It started out in the House as a fairly reasonable protective measure, designed to assist the farmers. But by the time the high-pressure lobbyists had pushed it through the Senate, it had acquired about a thousand amendments. It thus turned out to be the highest protective tariff in the nation's peacetime history. The average duty on nonfree goods was raised from 38.5 percent, as established by the Fordney-McCumber Act of 1922, to nearly 60 percent.

To angered foreigners, the Hawley-Smoot Tariff was a blow below the trade belt. It seemed like a declaration of economic warfare on the entire outside world. It reversed a promising worldwide trend toward reasonable tariffs and widened the yawning trade gaps. It plunged both America and other nations deeper into the terrible depression that had already begun. It increased international financial chaos and forced the United States further into the bog of economic isolationism. And economic isolationism, both at home and abroad, was playing directly into the hands of a hate-filled German demagogue, Adolf Hitler.

The Great Crash Ends the Golden Twenties

When Herbert Hoover confidently took the presidential oath on March 4, 1929, there were few black clouds on the economic horizon. The "long boom" seemed endless, with the painful exception of the debt-blanketed farm belt. America's productive colossus—stimulated by the automobile, radio, movie, and other new industries—was roaring along at a dizzy speed that suggested a permanent plateau of prosperity. Few people sensed that it might smother its own fires by pouring out too much.

The speculative bubble was actually near the bursting point. Prices on the stock exchange continued to spiral upward and create a fool's paradise of paper profits, despite Hoover's early but fruitless efforts to curb speculation through the Federal Reserve Board. A few prophets of disaster were bold enough to sound warnings, but were drowned out by the mad chatter of the ticker-tape machine.

A catastrophic crash came in October 1929. It was partially triggered by the British, who raised their interest rates in an effort to bring back capital lured abroad by American investments. Foreign investors and wary domestic speculators began to dump their "insecurities," and an orgy of selling followed. Tension built up to the panicky "Black Tuesday" of October 29, 1929, when 16,410,030 shares of

The Great Crash of 1929
The stock-market collapse caused fear to run like wildfire through the financial world. These anxious depositors lined up outside a New York bank, clamoring to withdraw their deposits before the bank failed. Ironically, "runs" on banks like this actually sped the downward economic spiral.

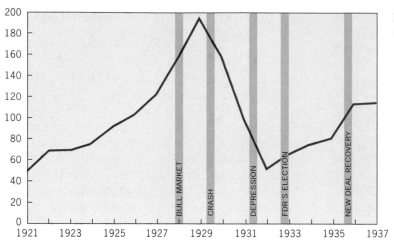

Index of Common Stock Prices
(1926 = 100)

stocks were sold in a save-who-may scramble. Wall Street became a wailing wall as gloom and doom replaced boom, and suicides increased alarmingly. A "sick joke" of the time had hotel room clerks ask registrants, "For sleeping or jumping?"

Losses, even in blue-chip securities, were unbelievable. By the end of 1929—two months after the initial crash—stockholders had lost $40 billion in paper values, or more than the total cost of World War I to the United States.

The stock-market collapse heralded a business depression, at home and abroad, that was the most prolonged and prostrating in American or world experience. No other industrialized nation suffered so severe a setback. By the end of 1930, more than 4 million workers in the United States were jobless; two years later the figure had about tripled. Hungry and despairing workers pounded pavements in search of nonexistent jobs ("We're firing, not hiring"). Where employees were not discharged, wages and salaries were often slashed. A current jingle ran,

> Mellon pulled the whistle,
> Hoover rang the bell
> Wall Street gave the signal
> And the country went to hell.

The misery and gloom were incalculable, as forests of dead chimneys stood stark against the sky. Over five thousand banks collapsed in the first three years of the depression, carrying down with them the life savings of tens of thousands of ordinary citizens. Countless thousands of honest, hardworking people lost their homes and farms to the forecloser's hammer. Bread lines formed, soup kitchens dis-

pensed food, and apple sellers stood shivering on street corners trying to peddle their wares for five cents. Families felt the stress, as jobless fathers nursed their guilt and shame at not being able to provide for their households. Breadless breadwinners often blamed themselves for their plight, despite abundant evidence that the economic system, not individual initiative, had broken down. Mothers meanwhile nursed fewer babies, as hard times reached even into the nation's bedrooms, precipitating a decade-long dearth of births. As cash registers gathered cobwebs, the song "My God, How the Money Rolls In" was replaced with "Brother, Can You Spare a Dime?"

The Depression spectacle of want in the shadow of surplus moved an observer to write in Current History *(1932):*

"We still pray to be given each day our daily bread. Yet there is too much bread, too much wheat and corn, meat and oil and almost every commodity required by man for his subsistence and material happiness. We are not able to purchase the abundance that modern methods of agriculture, mining and manufacture make available in such bountiful quantities. Why is mankind being asked to go hungry and cold and poverty stricken in the midst of plenty?"

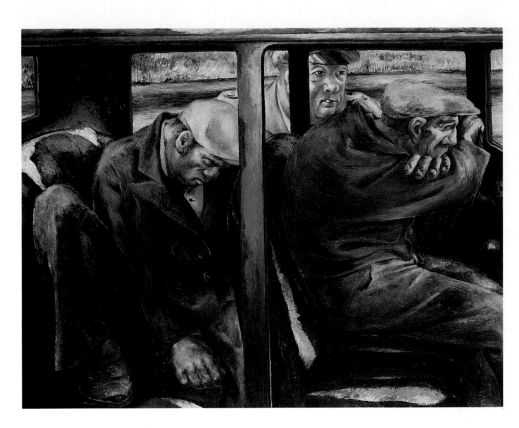

The Unemployed, by John
Langley Howard, 1937
In this painting Howard
soberly evokes the dispirited
state of millions of unemployed Americans during
the depression.

Hooked on the Horn of Plenty

What caused the Great Depression? One basic
explanation was overproduction by both farm and
factory. Ironically, the depression of the 1930s was
one of abundance, not want. It was the "great glut"
or the "plague of plenty."

The nation's ability to produce goods had clearly
outrun its capacity to consume or pay for them. Too
much money was going into the hands of a few
wealthy people, who in turn invested it in factories
and other agencies of production. Not enough was
going into salaries and wages, where revitalizing
purchasing power could be more quickly felt.

Other maladies were at work. Overexpansion of
credit through installment-plan buying overstimulated production. Paying on so-called easy terms
caused many consumers to dive in beyond their
depth. Normal technological unemployment, resulting from new laborsaving machines, also added
its burden to the abnormal unemployment of the
"threadbare thirties."

This already bleak picture was further darkened
by economic anemia abroad. Britain and the Continent had never fully recovered from the upheaval of
World War I. Depression in America was given a further downward push by a chain-reaction financial
collapse in Europe, following the failure in 1931 of a
prominent Vienna banking house. A drying up of
international trade, moreover, had been hastened
by the shortsighted Hawley-Smoot Tariff of 1930.
European uncertainties over reparations, war debts,
and defaults on loans owed to America caused tensions that reacted unfavorably on the United States.
Many of these conditions had been created or worsened by Uncle Sam's own narrow-visioned policies,
but it was now too late to unscramble the omelet.

As if man-made disasters were not enough, a
terrible drought scorched the Mississippi Valley in
1930. Thousands of farms were sold at auction for
taxes, though in some cases kind neighbors would
intimidate prospective buyers, bid one cent, and
return the property to its original owner. Farm
tenancy or rental—a species of peonage—was
spreading at an alarming rate among both whites
and blacks.

"Hooverville" in Seattle, 1934   In the early years of the depression, desperate, homeless people constructed shacks out of scavenged materials. These shanty-towns sprang up in cities across the country.

By 1930 the depression had become a national calamity. Through no fault of their own, a host of industrious citizens had lost everything. They wanted to work—but there was no work. The insidious effect of all this dazed despair on the nation's spirit was incalculable and long-lasting. America's "uniqueness" no longer seemed so unique or its Manifest Destiny so manifest. Hitherto the people had grappled with storms, trees, stones, and other physical obstacles. But the depression was a baffling wraith they could not grasp. Initiative and self-respect were stifled, as panhandlers begged for food or "charity soup." In extreme cases "ragged individualists" slept under "Hoover blankets" (old newspapers), fought over the contents of garbage cans, or cooked their findings in old oil drums in tin-and-paper shantytowns cynically named "Hoovervilles." The very foundations of America's social and political structure trembled.

Rugged Times for Rugged Individualists

Hoover's exalted reputation as a wonder-worker and efficiency engineer crashed about as dismally as the stock market. He doubtless would have shone in the prosperity-drenched Coolidge years, when he had

foreseen the abolition of poverty and poorhouses. But damming the Great Depression proved to be a task beyond his engineering talents.

The perplexed president was impaled on the horns of a cruel dilemma. As a deservedly famed humanitarian, he was profoundly distressed by the widespread misery about him. Yet as a "rugged individualist," deeply rooted in an earlier era of free enterprise, he shrank from the heresy of government handouts. Convinced that industry, thrift, and self-reliance were the virtues that had made Amer-

> *Hoover spoke approvingly in a campaign speech in 1928 of "the American system of Rugged Individualism." In 1930 he referred to Cleveland's 1887 veto of a bill to appropriate seed grain for the drought-stricken farmers of Texas:*
>
> "I do not believe that the power and duty of the General Government ought to be extended to the relief of individual suffering. . . . The lesson should be constantly enforced that though the people support the Government the Government should not support the people."

Home Relief Station, by Louis Ribak, 1935–1936 Destitute and despairing, millions of hardworking Americans like these had to endure the degradation and humiliation of going on relief as the pall of depression descended over the land.

ica great, President Hoover feared that a government doling out doles would weaken, perhaps destroy, the national fiber.

Hoover had deep faith in the efficiency of the industrial machine, which itself was undamaged by depression. From time to time he would attempt to encourage the public by issuing optimistic statements, which often were followed by a fresh decline. He was accused of saying, although he did not use these precise words, that prosperity was hovering just around the corner. "Hoovering," critics sniped.

As the depression nightmare steadily worsened, relief by local government agencies broke down. Hoover was finally forced to turn reluctantly from his doctrine of log-cabin individualism and accept the proposition that the welfare of the people in a nationwide catastrophe is a direct concern of the national government.

The president at last worked out a compromise between the old hands-off philosophy and the "soul-destroying" direct dole then being used in England. He would assist the hard-pressed railroads, banks, and rural credit corporations, in the hope that if financial health were restored at the top of the economic pyramid, unemployment would be relieved at the bottom on a trickle-down basis.

Partisan critics sneered at the "Great Humanitarian"—he who had fed the faraway Belgians but would not use federal funds to feed needy Americans. Hostile commentators remarked that he was willing to lend government money to the big bankers, who allegedly had plunged the country into the mess. He would likewise lend money to agricultural organizations to feed pigs—but not people. Pigs, the cynics of the time noted, had no character to undermine.

Much of this criticism was unfair. Although continued suffering seemed to mock the effectiveness of Hoover's measures, his efforts probably prevented a more serious collapse than did occur. And his expenditures for relief, revolutionary for that day, paved the path for the enormous federal outlays of his New Deal successor, Franklin Roosevelt. Hoover proved that the old bootstrap-pulling techniques would no longer work in a crisis of this magnitude, especially when people lacked boots.

Herbert Hoover: Pioneer for the New Deal

President Hoover, in line with his "trickle-down" philosophy, at last recommended that Congress vote immense sums for useful public works. Though at heart an antispender, he secured from Congress appropriations totaling $2.25 billion for such projects. To alarmists, the Washington ship of state seemed in danger of sinking in a red-ink sea of unbalanced budgets and mounting debts. Hoover warned, "Prosperity cannot be restored by raids on the public treasury."

Most imposing of the public enterprises was the gigantic Hoover Dam on the Colorado River. Voted by Congress in the days of Coolidge, it was begun in 1930 under Hoover and completed in 1936 under Roosevelt. It succeeded in creating a huge man-made lake for purposes of irrigation, flood control, and electric power.

But Hoover sternly fought all schemes that he regarded as "socialistic." Conspicuous among them was the Muscle Shoals Bill, designed to dam the Tennessee River and ultimately embraced by Franklin Roosevelt's Tennessee Valley Authority. Hoover emphatically vetoed this measure, primarily because he opposed the government's selling electricity in competition with its own citizens in private companies.

Early in 1932 Congress, responding to Hoover's belated appeal, established the Reconstruction Finance Corporation (RFC). With an initial working capital of half a billion dollars, this agency became a government lending bank. It was designed to provide indirect relief by assisting insurance companies, banks, agricultural organizations, railroads, and even hard-pressed state and local governments. But to preserve individualism and character, there would be no loans to individuals from this "billion-dollar soup kitchen."

"Pump-priming" loans by the RFC were no doubt of widespread benefit, though the organization was established many months too late for maximum usefulness. Projects that it supported were largely self-liquidating, and the government as a banker actually profited to the tune of many millions of dollars. Giant corporations so obviously benefited from this assistance that the RFC was dubbed—rather unfairly—"the millionaires' dole."

The irony is that the thrifty and individualistic Hoover had sponsored the project, though with initial reluctance. It actually had a strong New Dealish flavor.

Hoover's administration also provided some indirect benefits for labor. After stormy debate, Congress passed the Norris–La Guardia Anti-Injunction Act in 1932, and Hoover signed it. The measure outlawed "yellow dog" (antiunion) contracts and forbade the federal courts to issue injunctions to restrain strikes, boycotts, and peaceful picketing.

The truth is that Herbert Hoover, despite criticism of his "heartlessness," did inaugurate a significant new policy. In previous panics the masses had been forced to "sweat it out." Slow though Hoover was to abandon this nineteenth-century bias, by the end of his term he had started down the road toward government assistance for needy citizens—a road that Franklin Roosevelt would travel much farther.

Hoover's woes were increased by a hostile Congress. At critical times during his first two years, the Republican majority proved highly uncooperative. Friction worsened during his last two years. A depression-cursed electorate, rebelling in the congressional elections of 1930, so reduced the Republican majority that Democrats controlled the new House and almost controlled the Senate. Insurgent Republicans could—and did—combine with opposition Democrats to harass Hoover. Some of the president's troubles were deliberately manufactured by Congress, who, in his words, "played politics with human misery."

Routing the Bonus Army in Washington

Many veterans of World War I were numbered among the hard-hit victims of the depression. Industry had secured a "bonus"—though a dubious one—in the Hawley-Smoot Tariff. So the thoughts of the former soldiers naturally turned to what the government owed them for their services in 1917–1918, when they had "saved" democracy. A drive developed for the premature payment of the deferred bonus voted by Congress in 1924 and payable in 1945.

Thousands of impoverished veterans, both of war and of unemployment, were now prepared to move on to Washington, there to demand of Congress the immediate payment of their *entire* bonus. The "Bonus Expeditionary Force" (BEF), which mustered about twenty thousand souls, converged on the capital in the summer of 1932. These supplicants promptly set up unsanitary public camps and erected shacks on vacant lots—a gigantic "Hooverville." They thus created a menace to the public health, while attempting to intimidate Congress by their presence in force. After the pending bonus bill had failed in Congress by a narrow margin, Hoover arranged to pay the return fare of about six thousand bonus marchers. The rest refused to decamp, though ordered to do so.

Following riots that cost two lives, Hoover responded to the demands of the Washington authorities by ordering the army to evacuate the unwanted guests. Although Hoover charged that the "Bonus Army" was led by riffraff and reds, in fact only a sprinkling of them were former convicts and Communist agitators. The eviction was carried out by General Douglas MacArthur with bayonets and tear gas, and with far more severity than Hoover had planned. A few of the former soldiers were injured as the torch was put to their pathetic shanties in the inglorious "Battle of Anacostia Flats." An eleven-month-old "bonus baby" allegedly died from exposure to tear gas.

This brutal episode brought down additional abuse on the once-popular Hoover, who by now was the most loudly booed man in the country. The Democrats, not content with Hoover's vulnerable record, employed professional "smear" artists to drive him from office. Cynics sneered that the "Great Engineer" had in a few months "ditched, drained, and damned the country." The existing panic was unfairly branded "the Hoover depression." In truth, Hoover had been oversold as a wizard—and the public grumbled when his magician's wand failed to produce rabbits. The time was ripening for the Democratic party—and Franklin D. Roosevelt—to cash in on Hoover's calamities.

Japanese Militarists Attack China

The Great Depression, which brewed enough distress at home, added immensely to difficulties abroad.

Militaristic Japan stole the Far Eastern spotlight. In September 1931 the Japanese imperialists, noting that the Western world was badly mired in depression, lunged into Manchuria. Alleging provocation, they rapidly overran the coveted Chinese province and proceeded to bolt shut the Open Door in the conquered area.

Japanese Aggression in Manchuria   These Chinese troops marched to counter the Japanese incursion into Manchuria in 1931. Chinese resistance was in vain, however, and the Japanese set up the puppet state of Manchukuo in September 1932.

Peaceful peoples were stunned by this act of naked aggression. It was a flagrant violation of the League of Nations covenant, as well as of various other international agreements solemnly signed by Tokyo. Far-visioned observers feared that unless the major powers, acting through the League of Nations, could force Japan to disgorge, the League would perish. Failure would kill collective security and wipe out the best hope of averting another global conflagration.

Meeting in Geneva, the League was eager to strengthen itself by luring the United States into its camp. In response to an urgent invitation, an American sat for the first time, though unofficially, with the council of the League during its discussions of the Manchurian crisis. An American also served on the firsthand investigating commission appointed by the League.

Intervention by the League, however, availed nothing. Its five-man commission of probers reported in 1932 that the Japanese incursion was unjustified. But this censure, instead of driving Japan out of Manchuria, merely drove Japan out of the League. Another nail was thus hammered into the coffin of collective security.

Numerous indignant Americans, though by no means a majority, urged strong measures, ranging from boycotts to blockades. Possibly a tight blockade by the League, backed by the United States, would have brought Japan sharply to book. But Hoover reflected the isolationist sentiments of most Americans, who wanted no part of the Far Eastern mess. One newspaper remarked that America did not "give a hoot in a rain barrel" about who controlled Manchuria.

The League was handicapped in taking two-fisted action by the nonmembership of the United States. Washington flatly rebuffed initial attempts in 1931 to secure American cooperation in applying economic pressure. But Secretary of State Henry Stimson, who was much more internationalist-minded than Hoover, indicated that the United States probably would not interfere with a League embargo. The next year Stimson was more eager to take vigorous steps, but the president cautiously restrained him.

Washington in the end decided to fire only paper bullets at the Japanese aggressors. The so-called Stimson doctrine, proclaimed in 1932, declared that the United States would not recognize any territorial acquisitions that were achieved by

> *Hoover later wrote of his differences with Secretary of State Stimson over economic boycotts:*
>
> "I was soon to realize that my able Secretary was at times more of a warrior than a diplomat. To him the phrase 'economic sanctions' was the magic wand of force by which all peace could be summoned from the vasty deep. . . . Ever since Versailles I had held that 'economic sanctions' meant war when applied to any large nation."

force. Righteous indignation—or a preach-and-run policy—would substitute for solid initiatives.

This verbal slap on the wrist from America did not deter the march of the Japanese militarists. Smarting under a Chinese boycott, they bombed Shanghai in 1932, with shocking losses to civilians. Outraged Americans launched informal boycotts of Japanese goods, chiefly dime-store knickknacks. But there was no real sentiment for armed intervention among a depression-ridden people, who remained strongly isolationist during the 1930s. President Hoover, who fully shared their views, believed that boycotts and embargoes spelled bayonets and bombs.

In a broad sense, collective security died and World War II was born in 1931 on the windswept plains of Manchuria. The League members had the economic and naval power to halt Japan but lacked the courage to act. One reason—though not the only one—was that they could not count on America's support. Even so, the Republic came closer to stepping into the chill waters of internationalism than American prophets would have dared to predict in the early 1920s.

Hoover Pioneers the Good Neighbor Policy

Hoover's arrival at the White House brought a more hopeful turn to relations with America's southern neighbors. The new president was deeply interested in the often troubled nations below the Rio Grande; shortly after his election in 1928 he had undertaken a goodwill tour of Latin America—on a U.S. battleship.

World depression softened an age-old aggressive attitude in the United States toward weak Latin neighbors. Following the stock-market collapse of 1929, Americans had less money to invest abroad. As millions of dollars' worth of investments in Latin America went sour, many Yankees felt as though they were more preyed upon than preying. Economic imperialism—so called—became much less popular in the United States than it had been in the golden twenties.

As an advocate of international goodwill, Hoover strove to abandon the interventionist twist given to the Monroe Doctrine by Theodore Roosevelt. In 1932 he negotiated a new treaty with the French-speaking republic of Haiti, and this pact, later supplanted by an executive agreement, provided for the complete withdrawal of American platoons by 1934. Further pleasing omens came early in 1933, when the last marine "leathernecks" sailed away from Nicaragua after an almost continuous stay of some twenty years.

Herbert Hoover, the engineer in politics, thus happily engineered the foundation stones of the "Good Neighbor" policy. Upon them rose an imposing edifice in the days of his successor, Franklin Roosevelt.

Chronology

1919 American Legion founded
Chicago race riot

1920 Esch-Cummins Transportation Act
Merchant Marine Act

1921 Veterans' Bureau created
Capper-Volstead Act

1922 Five-Power Naval Treaty
Four-Power and Nine-Power Treaties on the
Far East
Fordney-McCumber Tariff Law

1923 *Adkins* v. *Children's Hospital*
Teapot Dome scandal
Harding dies; Coolidge assumes presidency

1924 Adjusted Compensation Act for veterans
Dawes Plan for international finance
U.S. troops leave the Dominican Republic
Coolidge wins three-way presidential election

1926 U.S. troops occupy Nicaragua

1928 Kellogg-Briand Pact
Hoover defeats Smith for presidency
Hoover takes goodwill tour of Latin America

1929 Agricultural Marketing Act sets up Federal
Farm Board
Stock-market crash

1930 Hawley-Smoot Tariff

1931 Japanese invade Manchuria

1932 Reconstruction Finance Corporation (RFC)
established
Norris–La Guardia Anti-Injunction Act
"Bonus Army" dispersed from
Washington, D.C.

SUGGESTED READINGS

PRIMARY SOURCE DOCUMENTS

Herbert Hoover, *American Individualism* (1922), contains the philosophy of the man and his times. See also Hoover's "Rugged Individualism" speech (1928), in Richard Hofstadter, *Great Issues in American History*. As the Great Depression descended, Hoover fought to maintain his principles in a noteworthy speech at New York's Madison Square Garden.* (*The New York Times*, November 1, 1932.) On foreign affairs see the "Stimson Doctrine" (1931), in Henry Steele Commager, ed., *Documents of American History*.

SECONDARY SOURCES

A lively introduction to the postwar decade is Burl Noggle, *Into the Twenties: The United States from Armistice to Normalcy* (1974). On Harding see Robert K. Murray's balanced *The Harding Era* (1969); consult also his *Politics of Normalcy: Government Theory and Practice in the Harding-Coolidge Era* (1973). John D. Hicks presents the standard liberal interpretation of the decade in *Republican Ascendancy* (1960). Burl Noggle looks at the chief scandal of the period in *Teapot Dome* (1962). David M. Kennedy, *Over Here: The First World War and American Society* (1980), discusses postwar race relations and demobilization as well as the international economic aftermath of the war, a subject treated at greater length in Joan Hoff Wilson, *American Business and Foreign Policy, 1920–1933* (1971). Robert Cohen explores *When the Old Left Was Young: Student Radicals and America's First Mass Student Movement, 1929–1941* (1993). On labor see Robert H. Zieger, *American Worker, American Unions, 1920–1985* (1986), for a concise summary. For background on the Washington disarmament conference, consult Roger Dingman, *Power in the Pacific: The Origins of Naval Arms Limitation, 1914–1922* (1976). For the conference itself, see Thomas H. Buckley, *The United States and the Washington Conference, 1921–1922* (1970). The Democratic party is analyzed in David Burner, *The Politics of Provincialism* (1967). The complicated international financial tangle of the 1920s is deftly discussed in Herbert Feis, *The Diplomacy of the Dollar* (1950), and in the early chapters of Charles Kindleberger, *The World in Depression* (1973). The drama of the 1928 election is captured in Allan J. Lichtman, *Prejudice and the Old Politics: The Presidential Election of 1928* (1979), and in Oscar Handlin, *Al Smith and His America* (1958). The election is placed in a larger context in Samuel Lubell's classic *The Future of American Politics* (1952), and in Paul Kleppner, *Who Voted? The Dynamics of Electoral Turnout, 1870–1980* (1982). George H. Nash's multivolume biography, *The Life of Herbert Hoover* (1988), is detailed, while the best brief biography of Hoover is Joan Hoff Wilson, *Herbert Hoover, Forgotten Progressive* (1975). Brilliantly unsympathetic toward Hoover is Arthur M. Schlesinger, Jr., *The Crisis of the Old Order, 1919–1933* (1957). On the depression itself, consult John K. Galbraith's breezy *The Great Crash, 1929* (1955); Peter Temin's trenchant *Did Monetary Factors Cause the Great Depression?* (1976); Robert McElvaine, *The Great Depression* (1984); and Lester V. Chandler's comprehensive *America's Greatest Depression* (1970).

*An asterisk indicates that the document, or an excerpt from it, can be found in Thomas A. Bailey and David M. Kennedy, eds., *The American Spirit: United States History as Seen by Contemporaries*, 9th ed. (Boston: Houghton Mifflin, 1998).

36

The Great Depression and the New Deal

1933–1938

The country needs and . . . demands bold, persistent experimentation. It is common sense to take a method and try it. If it fails, admit it frankly and try another. But above all, try something.

FRANKLIN D. ROOSEVELT, 1932 CAMPAIGN SPEECH

FDR: A Politician in a Wheelchair

Voters were in an ugly mood as the presidential campaign of 1932 neared. Countless factory chimneys remained ominously cold, while more than 11 million unemployed workers and their families sank ever deeper into the pit of poverty. Herbert Hoover may have won the 1928 election by promising "A chicken in every pot," but three years later that chicken seemed to have laid a discharge slip in every pay envelope.

Hoover, sick at heart, was renominated by the Republican convention in Chicago without great enthusiasm. The platform indulged in extravagant praise of Republican antidepression policies, while halfheartedly promising to repeal national prohibition and return control of liquor to the states.

The rising star of the Democratic firmament was Governor Franklin Delano Roosevelt of New York, a fifth cousin of Theodore Roosevelt. Like the Rough Rider, he had been born to a wealthy New York family, had graduated from Harvard, had been elected as a kid-gloved politician to the New York legislature, had served as governor of the Empire State, had been nominated for the vice presidency (though not elected), and had served capably as assistant secretary of the navy. Although both men were master politicians, adept with the colorful phrase, FDR was suave and conciliatory, whereas TR was pugnacious and confrontational.

Eleanor Roosevelt (1884–1962)   She was America's most active First Lady and commanded enormous popularity and influence during FDR's presidency. Here she emerges, miner's cap in hand, from an Ohio coal mine.

Infantile paralysis, while putting steel braces on Franklin Roosevelt's legs, put additional steel into his soul. Until 1921, when the dread disease struck, young Roosevelt—tall (6 feet, 2 inches; 1.88 meters), athletic, classic-featured, and handsome—impressed observers as charming and witty yet at times a superficial and arrogant "lightweight." But suffering humbled him to the level of common clay. In courageously fighting his way back from complete helplessness to a hobbling mobility, he schooled himself in patience, tolerance, compassion, and strength of will. He once remarked that after trying for two years to wiggle one big toe, all else seemed easy.

Another of Roosevelt's great personal and political assets was his wife, Eleanor. The niece of Theodore Roosevelt, she was Franklin Roosevelt's distant cousin as well as his spouse. Tall, ungainly, and toothy, she overcame the misery of an unhappy childhood and emerged as a champion of the dispossessed—and ultimately, as the "conscience of the New Deal." FDR's political career was as much hers as it was his own. She traveled countless miles with him or on his behalf in all his campaigns, beginning with his run for the New York legislature before World War I, later considering herself "his legs." She was to become the most active First Lady in history. Through her lobbying of her husband, her speeches, and her syndicated newspaper column, she powerfully influenced the policies of the national government. Always, she battled for the impoverished and the oppressed. At one meeting in Birmingham, Alabama, she confounded local authorities and flouted the segregation statutes by deliberately straddling the aisle separating the black and white seating sections. Sadly, her personal relationship with her husband was often rocky, due to his occasional infidelity. Condemned by conservatives and loved by liberals, she was one of the most controversial—and consequential—public figures of the twentieth century.

Roosevelt's political appeal was amazing. His commanding presence and his golden speaking voice, despite a sophisticated accent, combined to make him the premier American orator of his generation. He could turn on charm in private conversations as one would turn on a faucet. As a popular depression governor of New York, he had sponsored heavy state spending to relieve human suffering. Though favoring frugality, he believed that money, rather than humanity, was expendable. He revealed a deep concern for the plight of the "forgotten man"—a phrase he used in a 1932 speech—although he was assailed by the rich as a "traitor to his class."

Exuberant Democrats met in Chicago in June 1932 and speedily nominated Roosevelt. Fellow New Yorker Al Smith felt entitled to a second chance; and a beautiful friendship wilted when he was elbowed aside for Franklin Roosevelt. The Democratic platform came out more forthrightly than the Republican for repeal of prohibition, assailed the so-called Hoover depression, and promised not only a balanced budget but sweeping social and economic reforms. Roosevelt flew daringly through stormy weather to Chicago, where he smashed precedent by accepting the nomination in person. He electrified the delegates and the public with these words: "I pledge you, I pledge myself to a new deal for the American people."

> *In his successful campaign of 1928 for the governorship of New York, Franklin Roosevelt (1882–1945) had played down alleged Democratic "socialism:"*
>
> "We often hear it said that government operation of anything under the sun is socialistic. If that is so, our postal service is socialistic, so is the parcel post which has largely taken the place of the old express companies; so are the public highways which took the place of the toll roads."

Presidential Hopefuls of 1932

In the campaign that followed, Roosevelt seized the offensive with a slashing attack on the Republican Old Dealers. He was especially eager to prove that he was not an invalid ("Roosevelt Is Robust") and to display his magnificent torso and radiant personality to as many voters as possible.

Roosevelt consistently preached a New Deal for the "forgotten man," but he was annoyingly vague and somewhat contradictory. Many of his speeches were "ghostwritten" by the "Brains Trust" (popularly the "Brain Trust"), a small group of reform-minded intellectuals. They were predominantly youngish college professors, who, as a kind of kitchen cabinet, later authored much of the New Deal legislation. Roosevelt rashly promised a balanced budget and berated heavy Hooverian deficits, amid cries of "Throw the Spenders Out!" and "Out of the Red with Roosevelt." All of this was to make ironic reading in later months.

The high spirits of the Democrats found expression in the catchy air "Happy Days Are Here Again." This theme song fit FDR's indestructible smile, his jauntily angled cigarette holder, his breezy optimism, and his promises to do something, even at the risk of bold experimentation.

Grim-faced Herbert Hoover remained in the White House, conscientiously battling the depression through short lunches and long hours. Out on the firing line, his supporters halfheartedly assured half-listening voters, "The Worst Is Past," "It Might Have Been Worse," and "Prosperity Is Just Around

the Corner." Hoover never ceased to insist that the uncertainty and fear produced by Roosevelt's impending victory plunged the nation deeper into the depression.

With the campaign going badly for the Republicans, a weary and despondent Hoover was persuaded to take to the stump. He stoutly reaffirmed his faith in American free enterprise and individual initiative, and gloomily predicted that if the Hawley-Smoot Tariff were repealed, the grass would grow "in the streets of a hundred cities." Such down-at-the-mouthism contrasted sharply with Roosevelt's tooth-flashing optimism and sparkling promises.

The Humiliation of Hoover in 1932

Hoover had been swept into office on the rising tide of prosperity; he was swept out of office by the receding tide of depression. The flood of votes totaled 22,809,638 for Roosevelt and 15,758,901 for Hoover; the electoral count stood at 472 to 59. In all, the loser carried only six rock-ribbed Republican states.

One striking feature of the election was the beginning of a distinct shift of blacks, traditionally grateful to the Republican party of Lincoln, over to the Roosevelt camp. As the "last hired and first fired," black Americans had been among the worst sufferers from the depression. Beginning with the election of 1932, they became, notably in the great urban centers of the North, a vital element in the Democratic party.

Hard times unquestionably ruined the Republicans, for the electoral upheaval in 1932 was as much anti-Hoover as it was pro-Roosevelt. Democrats had only to harness the national grudge and let it pull them to victory. An overwhelming majority appear to have voiced a demand for change: *a* new deal rather than *the* New Deal, for the latter was only a gleam in the eyes of its sponsors. Any upstanding Democratic candidate probably could have won.

The preinauguration lame duck period now ground slowly to an end. Hoover, though defeated and repudiated, continued to be president for four long months, until March 4, 1933. But he was helpless to embark upon any long-range policies without the cooperation of Roosevelt—and the victorious president-elect proved rather uncooperative. Hoover at length succeeded in arranging two meetings with him to discuss the war-debt muddle.

But Roosevelt, who airily remarked to the press, "It's not my baby," fought shy of assuming responsibility without authority. As Hoover privately confessed, he was trying to bind his successor to an anti-inflationary policy that would have made impossible many of the later New Deal experiments. But in politics the winner, not the loser, calls the tune.

With Washington deadlocked, the vast and vaunted American economic machine clanked to a virtual halt. One worker in four tramped the streets, feet weary and hands idle. Banks were locking their doors all over the nation, as people nervously stuffed paper money under their mattresses. Hooverites, then and later, accused Roosevelt of deliberately permitting the depression to worsen, so that he could emerge the more spectacularly as a savior.

FDR and the Three R's: Relief, Recovery, Reform

Great crises often call forth gifted leaders; and the hand of destiny tapped Roosevelt on the shoulder. On a dreary Inauguration Day, March 4, 1933, his vibrant voice, broadcast nationally from a bullet-proof stand, provided the American people with inspirational new hope. He denounced the "money changers" who had brought on the calamity and declared that the government must wage war on the Great Depression as it would wage war on an armed foe. His clarion note was, "Let me assert my firm belief that the only thing we have to fear is fear itself."

Roosevelt moved decisively. Now that he had full responsibility, he boldly declared a nationwide banking holiday, March 6–10, as a prelude to opening the banks on a sounder basis. He then summoned the overwhelmingly Democratic Congress into special session to cope with the national emergency. For the so-called Hundred Days (March 9–June 16, 1933), members hastily cranked out an unprecedented basketful of remedial legislation. Some of it derived from earlier progressivism, but these new measures mostly sought to deal with a desperate emergency.

Roosevelt's New Deal programs aimed at three *R*'s—relief, recovery, and reform. Short-range goals were relief and immediate recovery, especially in the first two years. Long-range goals were permanent recovery and reform of current abuses, particularly those that had produced the boom-or-bust catastrophe. The three-*R* objectives often overlapped and got in one another's way. But amid all the topsy-turvy haste, the gigantic New Deal program lurched forward.

Firmly ensconced in the driver's seat, President Roosevelt cracked the whip. A green Congress so fully shared the panicky feeling of the country that it

The Inauguration of Franklin D. Roosevelt, March 4, 1933, by Covarrubias   This highly stylized painting triumphantly celebrates FDR's inaugural.

was ready to rubber-stamp bills drafted by White House advisers—measures that Roosevelt called "must legislation." More than that, Congress gave the president extraordinary blank-check powers: some of the laws it passed expressly delegated legislative authority to the chief executive. One senator complained that if FDR asked Congress "to commit suicide tomorrow, they'd do it."

Roosevelt was delighted to exert executive leadership, and Congress responded to it, although he did

Principal New Deal Acts During Hundred Days Congress, 1933*
(Items in parentheses indicate secondary purposes)

Recovery	Relief	Reform
FDR closes banks, March 6, 1933		
Emergency Banking Relief Act, March 9, 1933		
(Beer Act)	(Beer Act)	Beer and Wine Revenue Act, March 22, 1933
(CCC)	Unemployment Relief Act, March 31, 1933, creates Civilian Conservation Corps (CCC)	
FDR orders gold surrender, April 5, 1933		
FDR abandons gold standard, April 19, 1933		
(FERA)	Federal Emergency Relief Act, May 12, 1933, creates Federal Emergency Relief Administration (FERA)	
(AAA)	Agricultural Adjustment Act (AAA), May 12, 1933	
(TVA)	(TVA)	Tennessee Valley Authority Act (TVA), May 18, 1933 Federal Securities Act, May 27, 1933
Gold-payment clause repealed, June 5, 1933		
(HOLC)	Home Owners' Refinancing Act, June 13, 1933, creates Home Owners' Loan Corporation (HOLC)	
National Industrial Recovery Act, June 16, 1933, creates National Recovery Administration (NRA), Public Works Administration (PWA)	(NRA, PWA)	(NRA)
(Glass-Steagall Act)	(Glass-Steagall Act)	Glass-Steagall Banking Reform Act, June 16, 1933, creates Federal Deposit Insurance Corporation

*For later New Deal measures, see p. 802.

The Champ: FDR Chatting with Reporters   Roosevelt mastered the press as few presidents before or since have been able to do.

Roosevelt Tackles Money and Banking

Banking chaos cried aloud for immediate action. Congress pulled itself together and in an incredible eight hours had the Emergency Banking Relief Act of 1933 ready for Roosevelt's busy pen. The new law invested the president with power to regulate banking transactions and foreign exchange and to reopen solvent banks.

Roosevelt, the master showman, next turned to the radio to deliver the first of his thirty famous "fireside chats." As some 35 million people hung on his soothing words, he gave assurances that it was now safer to keep money in a reopened bank than "under the mattress." Confidence returned with a gush, and the banks began to unlock their doors.

The Emergency, or Hundred Days, Congress buttressed public reliance on the banking system by enacting the memorable Glass-Steagall Banking Reform Act. This measure provided for the Federal Deposit Insurance Corporation, which insured indi-

not always know precisely where he was going. He was inclined to do things by intuition—off the cuff. He was like the quarterback, as he put it, whose next play depends on the outcome of the previous play. So desperate was the mood of an action-starved public that *any* movement, even in the wrong direction, seemed better than no movement at all.

The frantic Hundred Days Congress passed many essentials of the New Deal "three *R*'s," though important long-range measures were added in later sessions. These reforms owed much to the legacy of the pre–World War I progressive movement. Many of them were long overdue, sidetracked by the war in Europe and the Old Guard reaction of the 1920s. The New Dealers, sooner or later, embraced such progressive ideas as unemployment insurance, old-age insurance, minimum-wage regulations, conservation and development of natural resources, and restrictions on child labor. A few such reforms had already made limited gains in some of the states. Many of these forward-looking measures had been adopted a generation or so earlier by the more advanced countries of western Europe. In the area of social welfare, the United States, in the eyes of many Europeans, remained a "backward nation."

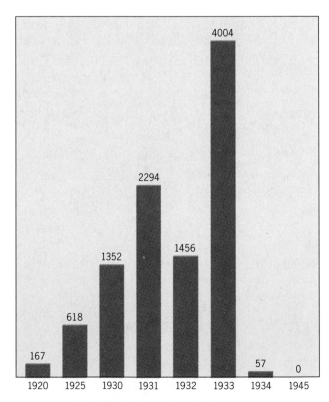

Bank Failures Before and After the Glass-Steagall Banking Reform Act of 1933

vidual deposits up to $5,000 (later raised). Thus ended the disgraceful epidemic of bank failures, which dated back to the "wildcat" days of Andrew Jackson.*

Roosevelt moved swiftly elsewhere on the financial front, seeking to protect the melting gold reserve and to prevent panicky hoarding. He ordered all private holdings of gold to be surrendered to the Treasury in exchange for paper currency and then took the nation off the gold standard. The Emergency Congress responded to his recommendation by canceling the gold-payment clause in all contracts and authorizing repayment in paper money. A "managed currency" was well on its way.

The goal of Roosevelt's "managed currency" was inflation, which he believed would relieve debtors' burdens and stimulate new production. Roosevelt's principal instrument for achieving inflation was gold buying. He instructed the Treasury to purchase gold at increasing prices, ratcheting the dollar price of gold up from $21 an ounce in 1933 to $35 an ounce in early 1934, a price that held for nearly four decades. This policy did increase the amount of dollars in circulation, as holders of gold cashed it in at the elevated prices. But this inflationary result also provoked the wrath of "sound-money" critics, who gagged on the "baloney dollar." The gold-buying scheme came to an end in February 1934, when FDR returned the nation to a limited gold standard for purposes of international trade only. Thereafter (until 1971—see p. 972), the United States pledged itself to pay foreign bills, if requested, in gold at the rate of one ounce of gold for every $35 due. But domestic circulation of gold continued to be prohibited, and gold coins became collectors' items.

Creating Jobs for the Jobless

Overwhelming unemployment, even more than banking, clamored for prompt remedial action. One out of every four workers was jobless when FDR took his inaugural oath—the highest level of unemployment in the nation's history, before or since. Roosevelt had no hesitancy about using federal money to assist the unemployed and at the same time to "prime the pump" of industrial recovery. (A

A CCC Camp in Idaho, 1930s   These Mexican-Americans from Los Angeles joined some 3 million of their countrymen at such camps in the 1930s. The CCC was among the most popular of all the New Deal programs. While undertaking valuable conservation projects, it provided employment, job training, and a healthy respite in the great outdoors from the conditions of urban life.

farmer has to pour a little water into a dry pump—that is, "prime it"—to start the flow.)

The Hundred Days Congress responded to Roosevelt's spurs when it created the Civilian Conservation Corps (CCC), which proved to be perhaps the most popular of all the New Deal "alphabetical agencies." This law provided employment in fresh-air government camps for about 3 million uniformed young men, many of whom might otherwise have been driven by desperation into criminal habits. Their work was useful—including reforestation, fire fighting (forty-seven lost their lives), flood control, and swamp drainage. The recruits were required to help their parents by sending home most of their pay. Both human resources and natural resources were thus conserved, though there were minor complaints of "militarizing" the nation's youth. Critics charged that CCC "soldiers" would later claim pensions for exposure to poison ivy.

The first major effort of the new Congress to grapple with the millions of adult unemployed was the Federal Emergency Relief Act. Its chief aim was

---

*When FDR was inaugurated in 1933, not a single Canadian bank had failed.

Later Major New Deal Measures, 1933–1939 (Items in parentheses indicate secondary purposes)

Recovery	Relief	Reform
(CWA)	FDR establishes Civil Works Administration (CWA), November 9, 1933	
Gold Reserve Act, January 30, 1934, authorizes FDR's devaluation, January 31, 1934		
		Securities and Exchange Commission (SEC) authorized Congress, June 6, 1934
(Reciprocal Trade Agreements)	(Reciprocal Trade Agreements)	Reciprocal Trade Agreements Act, June 12, 1934 (see pp. 827–828)
		Indian Reorganization Act, June 18, 1934
(FHA)	National Housing Act, June 28, 1934, authorizes Federal Housing Administration (FHA)	(FHA)
(Frazier-Lemke Act)	Frazier-Lemke Farm Bankruptcy Act, June 28, 1934	
(Resettlement Administration)	FDR creates Resettlement Administration, April 30, 1935	
(WPA)	FDR creates Works Progress Administration (WPA), May 6, 1935, under act of April 8, 1985	
(Wagner Act)	(Wagner Act)	(Wagner) National Labor Relations Act, July 5, 1935
		Social Security Act, August 14, 1935
		Public Utility Holding Company Act, August 26, 1935
(Soil Conservation Act)	Soil Conservation and Domestic Allotment Act, February 29, 1936	
(USHA)	(USHA)	United States Housing Authority (USHA) established by Congress, September 1, 1937
(Second AAA)	Second Agricultural Adjustment Act, February 16, 1938	
(Fair Labor Standards)	(Fair Labor Standards)	Fair Labor Standards Act (Wages and Hours Bill), June 25, 21938
		Reorganization Act, April 3, 1939
		Hatch Act, August 2, 1939

immediate relief rather than long-range recovery. The resulting Federal Emergency Relief Administration (FERA) was handed over to zealous Harry L. Hopkins, a painfully thin, shabbily dressed, chain-smoking New York social worker who had earlier won Roosevelt's friendship and who became one of his most influential advisers. Hopkins's agency in all granted about $3 billion to the states for direct dole payments or preferably for wages on work projects.*

Immediate relief was also given two large and hard-pressed special groups by the Hundred Days Congress. One section of the Agricultural Adjustment Act (AAA) made available many millions of dollars to help farmers meet their mortgages. Another law created the Home Owners' Loan Corporation (HOLC). Designed to refinance mortgages on nonfarm homes, it ultimately assisted about a million badly pinched households. The agency not only bailed out mortgage-holding banks, it also bolted the political loyalties of relieved middle-class homeowners securely to the Democratic party.

Harassed by the continuing plague of unemployment, FDR himself established the Civil Works Administration (CWA) late in 1933. As a branch of the FERA, it also fell under the direction of Hopkins. Designed to provide purely temporary jobs during the cruel winter emergency, it served a useful purpose. Tens of thousands of jobless were employed at leaf raking and other make-work tasks, which were dubbed "boondoggling." As this kind of labor put a premium on shovel-leaning slow motion, the scheme was widely criticized. "The only thing we have to fear," scoffers remarked, "is work itself."

Direct relief from Washington to needy families helped pull the nation through the ghastly winter of 1933–1934. But the disheartening persistence of unemployment and suffering demonstrated that emergency relief measures had to be not only continued but supplemented. One danger signal was the appearance of various demagogues, notably a magnetic "microphone messiah," Father Charles Coughlin, a Catholic priest in Michigan who began broadcasting in 1930 and whose slogan was "Social Justice." His anti–New Deal harangues to some 40 million radio fans finally became so anti-Semitic, fascistic, and demagogic that he was silenced in 1942 by his ecclesiastical superiors.

---

*A boast attributed to Hopkins in 1938 was, "We will spend and spend, tax and tax, and elect and elect."

Huey Long (1893–1935)   Long pursued progressive policies as governor of Louisiana, even while he ruled the state with a dictatorial hand. A flamboyant and unpredictable populist, he set the orthodox political establishment on its ear, especially after he became a U.S. senator in 1930. Long's admirers called him the "Kingfish"; Franklin Roosevelt called him "one of the two most dangerous men in the country." (The other, said Roosevelt, was General Douglas MacArthur.)

Also notorious among the new brood of agitators were those who capitalized on popular discontent to make pie-in-the-sky promises. Most conspicuous of these individuals was Senator Huey P. ("Kingfish") Long of Louisiana, who was said to have more brass than a government mule. He used his abundant rabble-rousing talents to publicize his "Share Our Wealth" program, which promised to make "Every Man a King." Every family was to receive $5,000, supposedly at the expense of the prosperous. H. L. Mencken called Long's chief lieutenant, former clergyman Gerald L. K. Smith, "the gutsiest, goriest, loudest and lustiest, the deadliest and damndest orator ever heard on this or any other earth, the champion boob-bumper of all time." Fear

Mary McLeod Bethune (1875–1955)
The daughter of ex-slaves and founder of a college in Florida, Bethune became the highest ranking African-American in the Roosevelt administration when she was appointed director of the Office of Minority Affairs in the National Youth Administration. From this base, she organized the "Black Cabinet" to make sure blacks benefited from the New Deal programs along with whites. Here she is meeting with First Lady Eleanor Roosevelt and Aubrey Williams, executive director of the NYA.

of Long's becoming a fascist dictator ended when he was shot by an assassin in the Louisiana state capitol in 1935.

Another Pied Piper was gaunt Dr. Francis E. Townsend of California, a retired physician whose savings had recently been wiped out. He attracted the trusting support of perhaps 5 million "senior citizens" with his fantastic plan which nonetheless spoke to earthly need. Each oldster sixty years of age or over was to receive $200 a month, provided that the money be spent within the month. One estimate had the scheme costing one-half of the national income.

Partly to quiet the ground swell of unrest produced by such crackbrained proposals, Congress authorized the Works Progress Administration (WPA) in 1935. The objective was employment on useful projects. Launched under the supervision of the ailing but energetic Hopkins, this remarkable agency ultimately spent about $11 billion on thousands of public buildings, bridges, and hard-surfaced roads. Not every WPA project strengthened the infrastructure: for instance, one controlled crickets in Wyoming while another built a monkey pen in Oklahoma City. Predictably, missions like these caused critics to sneer that WPA meant "We Provide Alms." But the fact is that over a period of eight years nearly 9 million people were given jobs, not handouts.

Agencies of the WPA also found part-time occupations for needy high school and college students and for such unemployed white-collar workers as actors, musicians, and writers. John Steinbeck, future Nobel Prize novelist, counted dogs in his California county. Cynical taxpayers condemned lessons in tap dancing, as well as the painting of murals on post office walls. But much precious talent was nourished, self-respect was preserved, and more than a million pieces of art were created, many of them publicly displayed.

A Helping Hand for Industry and Labor

A daring attempt to stimulate a nationwide comeback was initiated when the Emergency Congress authorized the National Recovery Administration (NRA). This ingenious scheme was by far the most complex and far-reaching effort by the New Dealers to combine immediate relief with long-range recovery and reform. Triple-barreled, it was designed to assist industry, labor, and the unemployed.

Individual industries—over two hundred in all—were to work out codes of "fair competition," under which hours of labor would be reduced so that employment could be spread over more people.

A ceiling was placed on the maximum hours of labor; a floor was placed under wages to establish minimum levels.

Labor, under the NRA, was granted additional benefits. Workers were formally guaranteed the right to organize and bargain collectively through representatives *of their own choosing*—not through handpicked agents of the company's choosing. The hated "yellow dog," or antiunion, contract was expressly forbidden, and certain safeguarding restrictions were placed on the use of child labor.

Industrial recovery through the NRA "fair competition" codes would at best be painful, for these called for self-denial by both management and labor. Patriotism was aroused by mass meetings and monster parades, which included 200,000 marchers on New York City's Fifth Avenue. A handsome blue eagle was designed as the symbol of the NRA, and merchants subscribing to a code displayed it in their windows with the slogan "We Do Our Part." A newly formed professional football team was christened the Philadelphia Eagles. Such was the enthusiasm for the NRA that for a brief period there was a marked upswing in business activity, although Roosevelt had warned, "We cannot ballyhoo our way to prosperity."

But the high-flying eagle gradually fluttered to earth. Too much self-sacrifice was expected of labor, industry, and the public for such a scheme to work. Critics began to brand NRA "National Run Around" and "Nuts Running America," symbolized by what Henry Ford called "that damn Roosevelt buzzard." A new "age of chiselry" dawned as certain unscrupulous businesspeople ("chiselers") publicly displayed the blue bird on their windows but secretly violated the codes. Complete collapse was imminent when, in 1935, the Supreme Court shot down the dying eagle in the famed *Schechter* "sick chicken" decision. The learned justices unanimously held that Congress could not "delegate legislative powers" to the executive. They further declared that congressional control of interstate commerce could not properly apply to a local fowl business, like that of the Schechter brothers in Brooklyn, New York. Roosevelt was incensed by this "horse and buggy" interpretation of the Constitution, but actually the Court helped him out of a bad jam.

The same act of Congress that hatched the NRA eagle also authorized the Public Works Administration (PWA), likewise intended both for industrial recovery and for unemployment relief. The agency was headed by the secretary of the interior, acid-tongued Harold L. Ickes, a free-swinging former bull mooser. Long-range recovery was the primary purpose of the new agency, and in time over $4 billion was spent on some thirty-four thousand projects, which included public buildings, highways, and parkways. One spectacular achievement was the Grand Coulee Dam on the Columbia River—the largest structure erected by humans since the Great Wall of China. Speed was essential if the jobless were to be put back to work, but "Honest Harold" Ickes was so determined to prevent waste and extravagance that he blocked maximum relief.

Special stimulants aided the recovery of one segment of business—the liquor industry. The imminent repeal of the prohibition amendment afforded an opportunity to raise needed federal revenue and at the same time to provide a measure of employment. Prodded by Roosevelt, the Hundred Days Congress, in one of its earliest acts, legalized

Frances Perkins (1882–1965) The first woman cabinet member, she served as secretary of labor under Roosevelt. She was subjected to much undeserved criticism from male businessmen, laborites, and politicians. They sneered that FDR kept her in labor for many years.

light wine and beer with an alcoholic content (presumably nonintoxicating) not exceeding 3.2 percent by weight, and levied a tax of $5 on every barrel so manufactured. Disgruntled drys, unwilling to acknowledge the breakdown of law and order begotten by bootlegging, damned Roosevelt as "a 3.2 percent American." Prohibition was officially repealed by the Twenty-first Amendment late in 1933 (see Appendix)—and the saloon doors swung open.

Paying Farmers Not to Farm

Ever since the war-boom days of 1918, farmers had suffered from low prices and overproduction, especially in grain. During the depression conditions became desperate as innumerable mortgages were foreclosed, as corn was burned for fuel, and as embattled farmers tried to prevent shipment of crops to glutted markets. In Iowa several volatile counties were placed under martial law.

A radical new approach to farm recovery was embraced when the Emergency Congress established the Agricultural Adjustment Administration (AAA). Through "artificial scarcity" this agency was to establish "parity prices" for basic commodities. "Parity" was the price set for a product that gave it the same real value, in purchasing power, that it had enjoyed during the period from 1909 to 1914. The AAA would eliminate price-depressing surpluses by paying growers to reduce their crop acreage. The millions of dollars needed for these payments were to be raised by taxing processors of farm products, such as flour millers, who in turn would shift the burden to consumers.

Unhappily, the AAA got off to a wobbly start. It was begun after much of the cotton crop for 1933 had been planted, and balky mules, trained otherwise, were forced to plow under countless young plants. Several million squealing pigs were purchased and slaughtered. Much of their meat was distributed to people on relief, but some of it was used for fertilizer. This "sinful" destruction of food, at a time when thousands of citizens were hungry, increased condemnation of the American economic system by many left-leaning voices.

"Subsidized scarcity" did have the effect of raising farm income, but the whole confused enterprise met with acid criticism. Farmers, food processors,

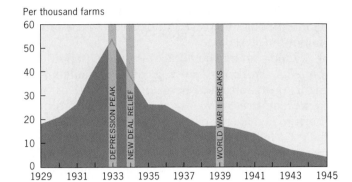

Farm Foreclosures and Defaults, 1929–1945

consumers, and taxpayers were all to some degree unhappy. Paying the farmers not to farm actually increased unemployment, at a time when other New Deal agencies were striving to decrease it. When the Supreme Court finally killed the AAA in 1936 by declaring its regulatory taxation provisions unconstitutional, foes of the plow-under program rejoiced loudly.

Quickly recovering from this blow, the New Deal Congress hastened to pass the Soil Conservation and Domestic Allotment Act of 1936. The withdrawal of acreage from production was now achieved by paying farmers to plant soil-conserving crops, like soybeans, or to let their land lie fallow. With the emphasis thus on conservation, the Supreme Court placed the stamp of its approval on the revamped scheme.

The Second Agricultural Adjustment Act of 1938, passed two years later, was a more comprehensive substitute, although it continued conservation payments. If growers observed acreage

Novelist John Steinbeck (1902–1968) relates in his novel, The Grapes of Wrath *(1939), that when the "Okies" and "Arkies" reached California, they found the big growers unwilling to pay more than twenty-five cents an hour for work in the fields. One owner mutters,*

"A Red is any son-of-a-bitch that wants thirty cents an hour when we're paying twenty-five!"

restrictions on specified commodities like cotton and wheat, they would be eligible for parity payments. Other provisions of the new AAA were designed to give farmers not only a fairer price but a more substantial share of the national income. Both goals were partially achieved.

Dust Bowls and Black Blizzards

Nature meanwhile had been providing some unplanned scarcity. Late in 1933 a prolonged drought struck the states of the trans-Mississippi Great Plains. Rainless weeks were followed by furious, whining winds, while the sun was darkened by millions of tons of powdery topsoil torn from homesteads in Missouri, Texas, Kansas, Arkansas, and Oklahoma—an area soon dubbed the Dust Bowl. Despondent citizens sat on front porches with protective masks on their faces, watching their farms swirl by. A seven-year-old boy in Kansas suffocated. Overawed victims of the Dust Bowl disaster predicted the end of the world or the second coming of Christ.

Drought and wind triggered the dust storms, but they were not the only culprits. The human hand had also worked its mischief. High grain prices during World War I had enticed farmers to bring countless acres of marginal land under cultivation. Worse, dry-farming techniques and mechanization had revolutionized Great Plains agriculture. The steam tractor and the disk plow tore up infinitely more sod than a team of oxen ever could, leaving the powdery topsoil to be swept away at nature's whim.

Burned and blown out of the Dust Bowl, tens of thousands of refugees fled their ruined acres (see "Makers of America: The Dust Bowl Migrants," pp. 808–809). In five years about 350,000 Oklahomans and Arkansans—"Okies" and "Arkies"—trekked to southern California in "junkyards on wheels." The dismal story of these human tumbleweeds was realistically portrayed in John Steinbeck's best-selling novel *The Grapes of Wrath* (1939), which proved to be the *Uncle Tom's Cabin* of the Dust Bowl.

Zealous New Dealers, sympathetic toward the soil-tillers, made various other efforts to relieve their burdens. The Frazier-Lemke Farm Bankruptcy Act, passed in 1934, made possible a suspension of mortgage foreclosures for five years, but it was voided the next year by the Supreme Court. A revised law, limiting the grace period to three years,

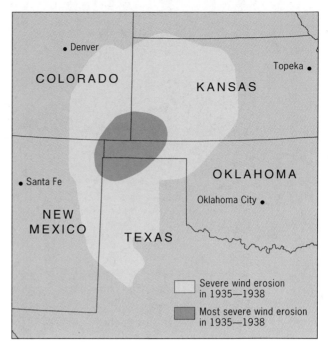

The Extent of Erosion in the 1930s   Note the extensive wind erosion in the western Oklahoma "panhandle" region, which was dubbed the "Dust Bowl" in the 1930s. Mechanized farmers had "busted" the sod of the southern plains so thoroughly that they literally broke the back of the land. Tons of dust blew out of the Dust Bowl in the 1930s and blotted the sun from the skies as far away as New York. A Kansas newspaperman reported in 1935 that in his dust-darkened town "Lady Godiva could ride through streets without even the horse seeing her."

was unanimously upheld. In 1935 the president set up the Resettlement Administration, charged with the task of removing near-farmless farmers to better land. And more than 200 million young trees were successfully planted on the bare prairies as windbreaks by the young men of the Civilian Conservation Corps, even though one governor jeered at trying to "grow hair on a bald head."

Native Americans also felt the far-reaching hand of New Deal reform. Commissioner of Indian Affairs John Collier ardently sought to reverse the forced-assimilation policies in place since the Dawes Act of 1887 (see p. 604). Inspired by a sojourn among the Pueblo Indians in Taos, New Mexico, Collier promoted the Indian Reorganization Act of 1934 (the "Indian New Deal"). The new law encouraged tribes to establish local self-government and to

The Dust Bowl Migrants

Black dust clouds rolled across the southern Great Plains in the 1930s, darkening the skies above a landscape already desolated by the Great Depression. Its soil depleted by erosion, exhausted by over-intensive farming, and parched by drought, the prairie of Oklahoma, Arkansas, northern Texas, and western Missouri became a dust bowl. The thirsty land offered up neither crops nor livelihood to the sturdy people whose forebears had staked out homesteads there. The desiccated earth exhaled only black dust and a dry wind that blew hundreds of thousands of people—the so-called Okies and Arkies—out of the Dust Bowl forever.

They headed mainly for California, piling aboard buses, hopping freight trains, or buying space in westbound cars. Most journeyed in their own autos, cramming their meager possessions into old jalopies and sputtering onto the highway. But unlike the aimless, isolated Joad family of John Steinbeck's classic novel *The Grapes of Wrath,* most Dust Bowl migrants knew where they were headed. Although many had lost everything in the depression, most knew relatives or friends who had migrated to California before the great crash and had sent back word about its abundant promise.

The earliest Okies had migrated under better circumstances in better times, and they often bragged of the good life in California. In the two decades preceding the Great Depression, more than a million people had left the states of Oklahoma, Texas, Arkansas, and Missouri. At least a quarter of them turned toward California, lured by advertisements that painted a life of leisure and plenty amid the palms.

Their ears so long filled with glowing reports from this earlier exodus, the Dust Bowl migrants refused to believe that the depression could sully the bright promise of California. Not even an ominous sign posted by the state of California on the highway just west of Tulsa deterred them. Indeed, the billboard proclaimed its warning in vain—"NO JOBS in California . . . If YOU are looking for work—KEEP OUT."

Some Okies and Arkies made their way past the sign to California cities, but many of them favored the San Joaquin Valley, the southern part of central California's agricultural kingdom. The migrants chose it for its familiarity. The valley shared much in common with the southern plains—arid climate, cotton growing, newfound oil deposits, and abundant land.

An Okie Family Hits the Road in the 1930s

During the 1930s the San Joaquin Valley also proved all too familiar in its poverty; in 1939 the median income for migrants from the southern plains hovered just below the official poverty line. Food, shelter, and clothing were scarce; the winter months, without work and without heat, proved nearly unendurable for the migrants. John Steinbeck, writing in a San Francisco newspaper, exposed the tribulations of the Dust Bowl refugees: "First the gasoline gives out. And without gasoline a man cannot go to a job even if he could get one. Then the food goes. And then in the rains, with insufficient food, the children develop colds. . . ."

Eventually, the Farm Security Administration— a New Deal agency—set up camps to house the Okies. A fortunate few purchased land and erected makeshift homes, creating tiny "Okievilles" or "Little Oklahomas." During World War II, most Okies escaped the deprivation and uncertainty of seasonal farm labor, securing regular jobs in defense industries. But the "Okievilles" remained, to form the bedrock of a still-thriving subculture in California—one that has brought the Dust Bowl's country and western music, pecan pie, and evangelical religion to the Far West.

Factories in the Fields Many Okies became migrant farm workers in the 1930s, drifting about the country to harvest different crops, like the pea-pickers shown here.

The Grapes of Wrath, 1939 Steinbeck's novel followed the Joad family on their epic trek from the drought-devastated farms of Oklahoma to the migrant labor camps of California. That so many Americans were forced to endure this misery aroused intense indignation among millions of readers.

A Dust Storm Envelops Baca County, Colorado, in the 1930s

Drouth Stricken Area, by Alexandre Hogue
A combination of stingy nature and exploitative agricultural practices laid waste much of the southern Great Plains in the 1930s. Artist Alexandre Hogue rendered this grim depiction of the damage done by the desolating dust storms.

preserve their native crafts and traditions. The act also helped to stop the loss of Indian lands and revived tribes' interest in their identity and culture. Yet not all Indians applauded it. Some denounced the legislation as a "back-to-the-blanket" measure that sought to make museum pieces out of Native Americans. Seventy-seven tribes refused to organize under its provisions, though nearly two hundred others did establish tribal governments.

Battling Bankers and Big Business

Reformist New Dealers were determined from the outset to curb the "money changers" who had played fast and loose with gullible investors before the Wall Street crash of 1929. The Hundred Days Congress passed the "Truth in Securities Act" (Federal Securities Act), which required promoters to transmit to the investor sworn information regarding the soundness of their stocks and bonds. An old saying was thus reversed to read, "Let the seller beware," although the buyer might never read the fine print.

In 1934 Congress took further steps to protect the public against fraud, deception, and inside manipulation. It authorized the Securities and Exchange Commission (SEC), which was designed as a watchdog administrative agency. Stock markets henceforth were to operate more as trading marts and less as gambling casinos.

New Dealers likewise directed their fire at public utility holding companies, those supercorporations. Citizens had seen one of these incredible colossi collapse during the spring of 1932, when the Chicagoan Samuel Insull's multibillion-dollar financial empire crashed. Possibilities of controlling, with a minimum of capital, a half-dozen or so pyramided layers of big business suggested to Roosevelt "a ninety-six-inch dog being wagged by a four-inch tail." The Public Utility Holding Company Act of 1935 finally delivered a "death sentence" to this type of bloated growth, except where it might be deemed economically needful.

The TVA Harnesses the Tennessee River

Inevitably, the sprawling electric-power industry attracted the fire of New Deal reformers. Within a few decades it had risen from nothingness to a behemoth with an investment of $13 billion. As a public utility, it reached directly and regularly into

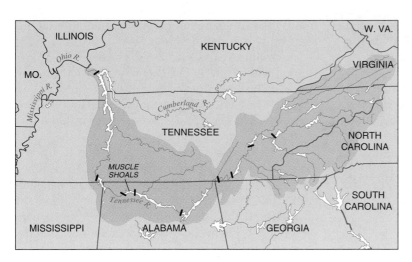

TVA Area   Only the nine dams on the Tennessee River are shown here. More than twenty dams were constructed on the river's tributaries as part of a massive project to control flooding, generate hydroelectric power, and revitalize the Tennessee Valley region, while also creating jobs for the unemployed. The shaded area represents the area served by TVA electric power.

the pocketbooks of millions of consumers for vitally needed services. Ardent New Dealers accused it of gouging the public with excessive rates, especially since it owed its success to having secured, often for a song, priceless waterpower sites from the public domain.

The tempestuous Tennessee River provided New Dealers with a rare opportunity. With its tributaries, the river drained a badly eroded area about the size of England, and one containing some 2.5 million of the most poverty-stricken people in America. The federal government already owned valuable properties at Muscle Shoals, where it had erected plants for needed nitrates in World War I. By developing the hydroelectric potential of the entire area, Washington could combine the immediate advantage of putting thousands of people to work with a long-term project for reforming the power monopoly.

An act creating the Tennessee Valley Authority (TVA) was passed in 1933 by the Hundred Days Congress. This far-ranging enterprise was largely a result of the steadfast vision and unflagging zeal of Senator George W. Norris of Nebraska, after whom one of the mighty dams was named. From the standpoint of "planned economy," the TVA was by far the most revolutionary of all the New Deal schemes.

This new agency was determined to discover precisely how much the production and distribution of electricity cost, so that a "yardstick" could be set up to test the fairness of rates charged by private companies. Utility corporations lashed back at this entering wedge of government control, charging that the low cost of TVA power was due to dishonest bookkeeping and the absence of taxes. Critics complained that the whole dream was "creeping socialism in concrete."

But the New Dealers, shrugging off such outcries, pointed a prideful finger at the amazing achievements of the TVA. The gigantic project brought to the area not only full employment and the blessings of cheap electric power, but low-cost housing, abundant cheap nitrates, the restoration of eroded soil, reforestation, improved navigation, and flood control. Rivers ran blue instead of brown; and a once-poverty-cursed area was being transformed into one of the most flourishing regions in the United States. Foreigners were greatly impressed with the possibilities of similar schemes in their own lands, and exulting New Dealers agitated for parallel enterprises in the valleys of the Columbia, Colorado, and Missouri Rivers. Federally built dams one day would span all those waterways,

In the early 1980s, then–Atlanta mayor Andrew Young (b. 1932) observed that the Tennessee Valley Authority created the economic structure for the later civil rights movement:

"It was the presence of the cheap electricity, lower interest rates, water projects, that laid the foundation for the New South."

impounding more than 30 percent of the total annual run-off from the "roof of America" in the Rocky Mountains. Hydroelectric power from those dams would drive the growth of the urban West, and the waters they diverted would nurture agriculture in the previously bone-dry western deserts. But conservative reaction against the "socialistic" New Deal would confine the TVA's brand of federally guided resource management and comprehensive regional development to the Tennessee Valley.

Housing Reform and Social Security

The New Deal had meanwhile framed sturdy new policies for housing construction. To speed recovery and better homes, Roosevelt set up the Federal Housing Administration (FHA) as early as 1934. The building industry was to be stimulated by small loans to householders, both for improving their dwellings and for completing new ones. So popular did the FHA prove to be that it was one of the few "alphabetical agencies" to outlast the age of Roosevelt.

Congress bolstered the program in 1937 by authorizing the United States Housing Authority (USHA)—an agency designed to lend money to states or communities for low-cost construction. Although units for about 650,000 low-income people were started, new building fell tragically short of needs. New Deal efforts to expand the project collided with brick-wall opposition from real estate promoters, builders, and landlords ("slumlords"), to say nothing of anti–New Dealers who attacked what they considered down-the-rathole spending. Nonetheless, for the first time in a century the slum areas in America ceased growing and even shrank.

Incomparably more important was the success of New Dealers in the field of unemployment insurance and old-age pensions. Their greatest victory was the epochal Social Security Act of 1935—one of the most complicated and far-reaching laws ever to pass Congress. To cushion future depressions, the measure provided for federal-state unemployment insurance. To provide security for old age, specified categories of retired workers were to receive regular payments from Washington. These payments ranged from $10 to $85 a month (later raised) and were financed by a payroll tax on both employers and employees. Provision was also made for the blind, the physically handicapped, delinquent children, and other dependents.

Republican opposition to the sweeping new legislation was bitter. "Social Security," insisted Hoover, "must be builded upon a cult of work, not a cult of leisure." The GOP national chairman falsely charged that every worker would have to wear a metal dog tag for life.

Social Security was largely inspired by the example of some of the more highly industrialized nations of Europe. In the agricultural America of an earlier day, there had always been farm chores for all ages, and the large family had cared for its own dependents. But in an urbanized economy, at the mercy of boom-or-bust cycles, the government was now recognizing its responsibility for the welfare of its citizens. By 1939 over 45 million people were eligible for Social Security benefits, and in subsequent years further categories of workers were added and the payments to them were periodically increased. In contrast to Europe, where benefits generally were universal, American workers had to be employed to get coverage.

A New Deal for Unskilled Labor

The NRA blue eagles, with their call for collective bargaining, had been a godsend to organized labor. As New Deal expenditures brought some slackening of unemployment, labor began to feel more secure and hence more self-assertive. A rash of walkouts occurred in the summer of 1934, including a paralyzing general strike in San Francisco (following a "Bloody Thursday"), which was broken only when outraged citizens resorted to vigilante tactics.

When the Supreme Court axed the blue eagle, a Congress sympathetic to labor unions undertook to fill the vacuum. The fruit of its deliberations was the Wagner, or National Labor Relations, Act of 1935. This trailblazing law created a powerful new National Labor Relations Board for administrative purposes and reasserted the right of labor to engage in self-organization and to bargain collectively through representatives of its own choice. The Wagner Act proved to be one of the real milestones on the rocky road of the U.S. labor movement.

Under the encouragement of a highly sympathetic National Labor Relations Board, a host of unskilled workers began to organize themselves into effective unions. The leader of this drive was

Labor Triumphant   After generations of struggle, organized labor made dramatic gains in membership and bargaining power during the New Deal years.

John L. Lewis (1880–1969) Inciting Textile Workers to Strike, 1937   A miner, Lewis worked his way up to the presidency of the United Mine Workers of America. He then founded the Congress of Industrial Organizations in the mid-1930s to unite all industrial workers in a powerful bloc of "big labor" to stand up to "big business."

beetle-browed, domineering, and melodramatic John L. Lewis, boss of the United Mine Workers. In 1935 he succeeded in forming the Committee for Industrial Organization (CIO) within the ranks of the skilled-craft American Federation of Labor. But skilled workers, ever since the days of the ill-fated Knights of Labor in the 1880s, had shown only lukewarm sympathy for the cause of unskilled labor, especially blacks. In 1936, following inevitable friction with the CIO, the older federation suspended the upstart unions associated with the newer organization.

Undaunted, the rebellious CIO moved on a concerted scale into the huge automobile industry. Late in 1936 the workers resorted to a revolutionary technique (earlier used in both Europe and America) known as the sit-down strike: they refused to leave the factory building of General Motors at Flint, Michigan, and thus prevented the importation of strikebreakers. Conservative respecters of private

property were scandalized. The CIO finally won a resounding victory when its union, after heated negotiations, was recognized by General Motors as the sole bargaining agency for its employees.

A worker at a Chevrolet plant in Flint, Michigan, wrote after the United Auto Workers–CIO victory in 1937:

"The inhuman high speed is *no more.* We now have a voice, and have slowed up the speed of the line. And [we] are now treated as human beings, and not as part of the machinery. The high pressure is taken off. . . . It proves clearly that united we stand, divided or alone we fall."

General Motors Sit-down Strikers, Flint, Michigan, 1937 Strikers like these sometimes kept their spirits up with the song "Sit Down":

When the boss won't talk
Don't take a walk;
Sit down, sit down.

Roosevelts "Coddling" of Labor

Unskilled workers now pressed their advantage. The United States Steel Company, hitherto an impossible nut for labor to crack, averted a costly strike when it voluntarily granted rights of unionization to its CIO-organized employees. But the "little steel" companies fought back savagely. Citizens were shocked in 1937 by the Memorial Day massacre at the plant of the Republic Steel Company in South Chicago. In a bloody fracas, police fired upon pickets and workers, leaving the area strewn with several score dead and wounded.

A better deal for labor continued when Congress, in 1938, passed the memorable Fair Labor Standards Act (Wages and Hours Bill). Industries involved in interstate commerce were to set up minimum-wage and maximum-hour levels. The eventual goals were forty cents an hour (later raised) and a forty-hour week. Labor by children under sixteen was forbidden; under eighteen, if the occupation was dangerous. These reforms were bitterly though futilely opposed by many industrialists, especially by those southern textile manufacturers who had profited from low-wage labor. But the exclusion of agricultural, service, and domestic workers meant that blacks, Mexican-Americans, and women—who were concentrated in these fields—did not benefit from the act.

In later New Deal days, labor unionization thrived; "Roosevelt wants you to join a union" was the rallying cry of professional organizers. The president received valuable support at ballot-box time from labor leaders and many appreciative working men and women. One mill worker remarked that Roosevelt was "the only man we ever had in the White House who would know that my boss is a s.o.b."

The CIO surged forward, breaking completely with the AF of L in 1938. On that occasion the *Committee* for Industrial Organization was formally reconstituted as the *Congress* of Industrial Organizations (the new CIO), under the high-handed presidency of John L. Lewis. By 1940 the CIO could claim about 4 million members in its constituent unions, including some 200,000 blacks. Nevertheless, bitter and annoying jurisdictional feuding, involving strikes, continued with the AF of L. At times labor seemed more bent on costly civil war than on its age-old war with management.

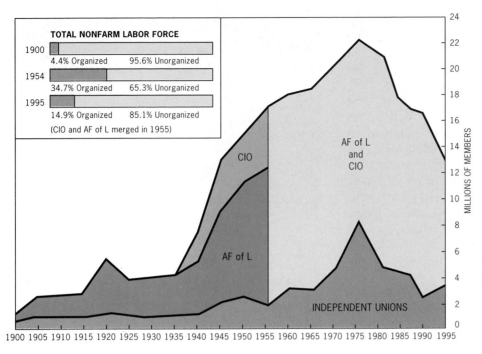

TOTAL NONFARM LABOR FORCE		
1900	4.4% Organized	95.6% Unorganized
1954	34.7% Organized	65.3% Unorganized
1995	14.9% Organized	85.1% Unorganized

(CIO and AF of L merged in 1955)

The Rise and Decline of Organized Labor, 1900–1995 The percentage of the total labor force that was organized increased until 1954, and it has declined ever since.

Landon Challenges "the Champ" in 1936

As the presidential campaign of 1936 neared, the New Dealers were on top of the world. They had achieved considerable progress, and millions of "reliefers" were grateful to their bountiful government. The exultant Democrats, meeting in Philadelphia, pushed through the renomination of Roosevelt in a brief rubber-stamp ceremony. Their platform stood squarely on the record of the New Deal years.

The Republicans, assembling in Cleveland, were hard pressed to find someone to feed to "the Champ." They finally settled on the colorless and mildly liberal Governor Alfred M. Landon of the Sunflower State of Kansas, a wealthy oilman, whose chief claim to distinction was that he had balanced the budget of his state in an era of unbalanced budgets. The Republican platform, though promising relief benefits that would cost many millions, condemned the New Deal of Franklin "Deficit" Roosevelt—its radicalism, experimentation, confusion, and "frightful waste." Popular watchwords were

"Defeat the New Deal and Its Reckless Spending," "Let's Get Another Deck," "Life, Liberty, and Landon," and "Let's Make It a Landon-Slide."

Landon—"the Kansas Coolidge"—was honest, sincere, homespun, "commonsensical," and as American as cherry pie. But he had a poor radio voice and seemed schoolboyish on the stump. Surrounded by imitation Kansas sunflowers, Landon stressed "deeds, not deficits" and condemned New Deal largesse. Though opposing the popular Social Security Act, he advocated just enough reform to cause the Democrats to retort that he would continue the New Deal—a secondhand New Deal—in his own way. He was, they snickered, "the poor man's Hoover."

Democrats denounced the GOP as the party of big moneyed interests and the big depression and amid loud choruses of boos cried, "Remember Hoover!" The embittered ex-president called for a "holy crusade for liberty." A group of wealthy Republicans and conservative Democrats had in 1934 formed the American Liberty League to fight "socialistic" New Deal schemes, and they vented their reactionary spleen against "that man" Roosevelt, "the New Dealocrat." But they hurt their own cause by becoming a made-to-order target for FDR.

Angry enough to stretch sheet iron, Roosevelt took to the stump and denounced the "economic royalists" who sought to "hide behind the flag and the Constitution." "I welcome their hatred," he proclaimed.

A landslide overwhelmed Landon, as the demoralized Republicans carried only two states, Maine and Vermont. This dismal showing caused political wiseacres to make the old adage read, "As Maine goes, so goes Vermont."* The popular vote was 27,752,869 to 16,674,665; the electoral count was 523 to 8—the most lopsided in 116 years. Democratic majorities, riding in on Roosevelt's magic coattails, were again returned to Congress. Jubilant Democrats could now claim more than two-thirds of the seats in the House and a like proportion in the Senate.

The battle of 1936, perhaps the most bitter since Bryan's defeat in 1896, partially bore out Republican charges of class warfare. Even more than in 1932, the needy economic groups were lined up against the so-called greedy economic groups. CIO units contributed generously to FDR's campaign chest. Many left-wingers turned to Roosevelt, as the customary third-party protest vote sharply declined. Blacks, several million of whom had also appreciated welcome relief checks, had by now largely shaken off their traditional allegiance to the Republican party. To them, Lincoln was "finally dead."

FDR won primarily because he appealed to the "forgotten man," whom he never forgot. Some of the president's support was only pocketbook-deep: "relievers" were not going to bite the hand that doled out the government checks. No one, as Al Smith remarked, "shoots at Santa Claus." But Roosevelt in fact had forged a powerful and enduring coalition of the South, the blacks, the urbanites, and the poor. He proved especially effective in marshaling the support of the multitudes of "New Immigrants"—mostly the Catholics and Jews who had swarmed into the great cities since the turn of the century. These once-scorned newcomers, with their now-numerous sons and daughters, had at last come politically of age. In the 1920s one out of every twenty-five federal judgeships went to a Catholic; Roosevelt appointed Catholics to one out of every four.

---

*Maine, which traditionally held its state elections in September, was long regarded as a political weathervane. Hence the expression "As Maine goes, so goes the nation."

Three days before the 1936 election, Roosevelt took the moral high ground in his speech at New York's Madison Square Garden:

"I should like to have it said of my first Administration that in it the forces of selfishness and of lust for power met their match. I should like to have it said of my second Administration that in it these forces met their master."

Nine Old Men on the Supreme Bench

Bowing his head to the sleety blasts, Roosevelt took the presidential oath on January 20, 1937, instead of the traditional March 4. The Twentieth Amendment to the Constitution had been ratified in 1933. (See the Appendix.) It swept away the post-election lame duck session of Congress and shortened by six weeks the awkward period before inauguration.

Flushed with victory, Roosevelt interpreted his reelection as a mandate to continue New Deal reforms. But in his eyes the cloistered old men on the supreme bench, like fossilized stumbling blocks, stood stubbornly in the pathway of progress. In nine major cases involving the New Deal, the Roosevelt administration had been thwarted seven times. The Court was ultraconservative, and six of the nine oldsters in black were over seventy. As luck would have it, not a single member had been appointed by FDR in his first term.

Roosevelt—his "Dutch up"—viewed with mounting impatience what he regarded as the obstructive conservatism of the Court. Some of these Old Guard appointees were hanging on with a senile grip, partly because they felt it their patriotic duty to curb the "socialistic" tendencies of that radical in the White House. Roosevelt believed that the voters in three successive elections—the presidential elections of 1932 and 1936 and the midterm congressional elections of 1934—had returned a smashing verdict in favor of his program of reform. Democracy, in his view, meant rule by the people. If the American way of life was to be preserved, Roosevelt argued, the Supreme Court ought to get in line with the supreme court of public opinion.

Roosevelt finally hit upon a Court scheme that he regarded as "the answer to a maiden's prayer." In fact, it proved to be one of the most costly political misjudgments of his career. When he sprang his brainstorm on a shocked nation, early in 1937, he caught the country and Congress completely by surprise. Roosevelt bluntly asked Congress for legislation to permit him to add a new justice to the Supreme Court for every member over seventy who would not retire. The maximum membership could then be fifteen. Roosevelt pointed to the necessity of injecting vigorous new blood, for the Court, he alleged, was far behind in its work. This charge, which turned out to be false, brought heated accusations of dishonesty. At best, Roosevelt was headstrong and not fully aware of the fact that the Court, in popular thinking, had become something of a sacred cow.

The Supreme Court Under Pressure, 1937
FDR regarded the justices as horse-and-buggy legalists.

The Court Changes Course

Congress and the nation were promptly convulsed over the scheme to "pack" the Supreme Court with a "dictator bill," which one critic called "too damned slick." Franklin "Double-crossing" Roosevelt was vilified for attempting to break down the delicate checks and balances among the three branches of the government. He was accused of grooming himself as a dictator by trying to browbeat the judiciary. In the eyes of countless citizens, mostly Republicans but including many Democrats, basic liberties seemed to be in jeopardy. "God Bless the Supreme Court" was a fervent prayer.

The Court had meanwhile seen the ax hanging over its head. Whatever his motives, Justice Owen J. Roberts, formerly regarded as a conservative, began to vote on the side of his liberal colleagues. "A switch in time saves nine" was the classic witticism inspired by this ideological change. By a five to four decision, the Court, in March 1937, upheld the principle of a state minimum wage for women, thereby reversing its stand on a different case a year earlier. In succeeding decisions a Court more sympathetic to the New Deal upheld the National Labor Relations Act (Wagner Act) and the Social Security Act. Roosevelt's "Court-packing" was further undermined when Congress voted full pay for justices over seventy who retired, whereupon one of the oldest conservative members resigned, to be replaced by a New Dealer, Justice Hugo Black.

Congress finally passed a court reform bill, but this watered-down version applied only to lower courts. Roosevelt, the master politician, thus suffered his first major legislative defeat at the hands of his own party in Congress. Americans have never viewed lightly a tampering with the Supreme Court by the president, no matter how popular their chief executive may be. Yet in losing this battle, Roosevelt incidentally won his campaign. The Court, as he had hoped, became markedly more friendly to New Deal reforms. Furthermore, a succession of deaths and resignations enabled him in time to make nine appointments to the tribunal—more than any of his predecessors since George Washington. The clock "unpacked" the Court.

Yet in a sense FDR lost both the Court battle and the war. He so aroused conservatives of both parties in Congress that few New Deal reforms were passed after 1937, the year of the fight to "pack" the bench. With this catastrophic miscalculation, he squandered much of the political goodwill that had carried him to such a resounding victory in the 1936 election.

The Twilight of the New Deal

Roosevelt's first term, from 1933 to 1937, did not banish the depression from the land. Unemployment stubbornly persisted in 1936 at about 15 percent, down from the grim 25 percent of 1933 but still miserably high. Despite the inventiveness of New Deal programs and the billions of dollars in "pump-priming," recovery had been dishearteningly modest, though the country seemed to be inching its way back to economic health.

Then in 1937 the economy took another sharp downturn, a surprisingly severe depression-within-the-depression that the president's critics quickly dubbed the "Roosevelt recession." In fact, government policies had caused the nosedive, as new Social Security taxes began to bite into payrolls and as the administration cut back on spending out of continuing reverence for the orthodox economic doctrine of the balanced budget.

Only at this late date did Roosevelt at last frankly and deliberately embrace the recommendations of the British economist John Maynard

> *A basic objective of the New Deal was featured in Roosevelt's second inaugural address (1937):*
>
> "I see one-third of a nation ill-housed, ill-clad, ill-nourished. . . . The test of our progress is not whether we add more to the abundance of those who have much; it is whether we provide enough for those who have too little."

Keynes. The New Deal had run deficits for several years, but all of them had been rather small and none was intended. Now, in April 1937, Roosevelt announced a bold program to stimulate the economy by planned deficit spending. Although the deficits were still undersized for the herculean task of conquering the depression, this abrupt policy reversal marked a major turning point in the government's relation to the economy. "Keynesianism" became the new economic orthodoxy and remained so for decades.

Roosevelt had meanwhile been pushing the remaining reform measures of the New Deal. Early in 1937 he urged Congress—a Congress growing more conservative—to authorize a sweeping reorganization of the national administration in the interests of streamlined efficiency. But the issue became tangled up with his presumed autocratic

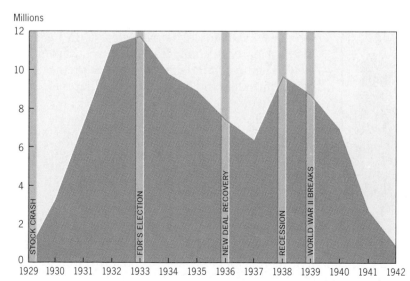

Unemployment, 1929–1942

These cold figures can only begin to suggest the widespread human misery caused by mass unemployment. One man wrote to a newspaper in 1932, "I am forty-eight; married twenty-one years; four children, three in school. For the last eight years I was employed as a Pullman conductor. Since September, 1930, they have given me seven months part-time work. Today I am an object of charity. . . . My small, weak, and frail wife and two small children are suffering and I have come to that terrible place where I could easily resort to violence in my desperation."

Employment Agency, by Isaac Soyer, 1937   Millions of jobless Americans felt the despair Soyer captured in this painting, as depression-era unemployment reached levels never seen before or since in American history.

ambitions in regard to the Supreme Court, and he suffered another stinging defeat. Two years later, in 1939, Congress partially relented and in the Reorganization Act gave him limited powers for administrative reforms, including the key new Executive Office in the White House.

The New Dealers were accused of having the richest campaign chest in history; and in truth government relief checks had a curious habit of coming in bunches just before ballot time. To remedy such practices, which tended to make a farce of free elections, Congress adopted the much-heralded Hatch Act of 1939. This act barred federal administrative officials, except the highest policy-making officers, from active political campaigning and soliciting. It also forbade the use of government funds for political purposes as well as the collection of campaign contributions from people receiving relief payments. The Hatch Act was broadened in 1940 to place limits on campaign contributions and expenditures, but such clever ways of getting around it were found that on the whole the legislation proved disappointing.

By 1938 the New Deal had clearly lost most of its early momentum. Magician Roosevelt could find few dazzling new reform rabbits to pull out of his tall silk hat. In the congressional elections of 1938, the Republicans, for the first time, cut heavily into the New Deal majorities in Congress, though failing to gain control of either house. The international crisis that came to a boil in 1938–1939 shifted public attention away from domestic reform and no doubt helped save the political hide of the Roosevelt "spendocracy." The New Deal, for all practical purposes, had shot its bolt.

New Deal or Raw Deal?

Foes of the New Deal condemned its alleged waste, incompetence, confusion, contradictions, and cross-purposes, as well as the chiseling and graft in the alphabetical agencies—"alphabet soup," sneered Al Smith. Roosevelt had done nothing, cynics said, that an earthquake could not have done better. Critics deplored the employment of "crackpot" college professors, leftist "pinkos," and outright Communists. Such subversives, it was charged, were trying to make America over in the Bolshevik-

Marxist image under "Rooseveltski." The Hearst newspapers lambasted

The Red New Deal with a Soviet seal
Endorsed by a Moscow hand,
   The strange result of an alien cult
In a liberty-loving land.

Roosevelt was further accused by conservatives of being Jewish ("Rosenfield") and of tapping too many bright young Jewish leftists ("The Jew Deal") for his "Drain Trust."

Hardheaded businesspeople, who "had met a payroll," were shocked by the leap-before-you-look, try-anything-once spirit of Roosevelt, the jolly improviser. They accused him of confusing noise and movement with progress. Others appreciated the president's do-something approach. Humorist Will Rogers, the rope-twirling "poet lariat" of the era, remarked that if Roosevelt were to burn down the Capitol, people would say, "Well, we at least got a fire started, anyhow."

"Bureaucratic meddling" and "regimentation" were also bitter complaints of anti–New Dealers; and in truth, bureaucracy did blossom. The federal government, with its hundreds of thousands of employees, became incomparably the largest single business in the country, as the states faded further into the background.

Promises of budget balancing, to say nothing of other promises, had flown out the window—so foes of the New Deal pointed out. The national debt had stood at the already enormous figure of $19,487,000,000 in 1932, and had skyrocketed to $40,440,000,000 by 1939. America was becoming, its critics charged, a "handout state" trying to squander itself into prosperity—*U.S.* stood for "unlimited spending." Such lavish benefactions were undermining the old virtues of thrift and initiative. Ordinary Americans, once self-reliant citizens, were getting a bad case of the "gimmies": their wishbones were becoming larger than their backbones. In the nineteenth century, hard-pressed workers went West; now they went on relief.

Business was bitter. Accusing the New Deal of fomenting class strife, conservatives insisted that the laborer and the farmer—especially the big operator—were being pampered. Why "soak the successful"? Countless businesspeople, especially Republicans, declared that they could pull themselves out of the depression if they could only get the federal government—an interventionist big government—off their backs. Private enterprise, they charged, was being stifled by "planned economy," "planned bankruptcy," "creeping socialism," and the philosophy "Washington can do it better," with a federal pill for every ill. States' rights were being ignored, while the government was competing in business with its own citizens, under a "dictatorship of do-gooders."

The aggressive leadership of Roosevelt—"one-man supergovernment"—also came in for denunciation. Heavy fire was especially directed at his attempts to browbeat the Supreme Court and to create a "dummy Congress." Roosevelt had even tried in the 1938 elections, with backfiring results, to "purge" members of Congress who would not lockstep with him. The three senators whom he publicly opposed were all triumphantly reelected.

The most damning indictment of the New Deal was that it had failed to cure the depression. Afloat in a sea of red ink, it had merely administered aspirin, sedatives, and Band-Aids. Many economists came to believe that better results would have been achieved by much greater deficit spending. Despite some $20 billion poured out in six years of deficit spending and lending, of leaf raking and pump priming, the gap was not closed between production and consumption. There were even more mountainous farm surpluses under Roosevelt than under Hoover. Millions of dispirited men and women were still unemployed in 1939, after six years of drain, strain, and pain. Not until World War II blazed forth in Europe was the unemployment headache solved. The sensational increase in the national debt was caused by World War II, not the New Deal. The national debt was only $40 billion in 1939 but $258 billion in 1945.

FDR's Balance Sheet

New Dealers staunchly defended their record. Admitting that there had been some waste, they pointed out that relief—not economy—had been the primary object of their multifront war on the depression. Conceding also that there had been some graft, they argued that it had been trivial in view of the immense sums spent and the obvious need for haste.

Apologists for Roosevelt further declared that the New Deal had relieved the worst of the crisis in 1933. It promoted the philosophy of "balancing the

Our Skipper   This pro-FDR cartoon depicts a confident Roosevelt ignoring his critics while heading cheerily toward economic recovery. In fact, FDR's New Deal brought neither the recovery he promised nor the ruin his detractors prophesied. The depression dragged on with only periodic improvement for nearly eight years under his leadership, until the cataclysmic emergency of World War II finally banished unemployment from the land.

human budget" and accepted the principle that the federal government was morally bound to prevent mass hunger and starvation by "managing" the economy. The Washington regime was to be used, not feared. The collapse of America's economic system was averted; a fairer distribution of the national income was achieved; and the citizens were enabled to regain and retain their self-respect. "Nobody is going to starve" was Roosevelt's promise.

Though hated by business tycoons, FDR should have been their patron saint, so his admirers claimed. He deflected popular resentments against business and may have saved the American system of free enterprise. Roosevelt's quarrel was not with capitalism but with capitalists; he purged American capitalism of some of its worst abuses so that it might be saved from itself. He may even have headed off a more radical swing to the left by a mild dose of what was mistakenly reviled as "socialism." The head of the American Socialist party, when once asked if the New Deal had carried out the Socialist program, reportedly replied that it had indeed—on a stretcher.

Roosevelt, like Jefferson, provided bold reform without a bloody revolution—at a time in history when some foreign nations were suffering armed uprisings and when many Europeans were predicting either communism or fascism for America. He was upbraided by the left-wing radicals for not going far enough; by the right-wing radicals for going too far. Choosing the middle road, he has been called the greatest American conservative since Hamilton. He was in fact Hamiltonian in his espousal of big government, but Jeffersonian in his concern for the "forgotten man." Demonstrating anew the value of powerful presidential leadership, he exercised that power to relieve the erosion of the nation's greatest physical resource—its people. He helped preserve democracy in America in a time when democracies abroad were disappearing down the sinkhole of dictatorship. And in playing this role, he unwittingly girded the nation for its part in the titanic war that loomed on the horizon—a war in which democracy the world over would be at stake.

In his acceptance speech at the 1936 Democratic convention Roosevelt stated,

"Governments can err; presidents do make mistakes, . . . but better the occasional faults of a Government that lives in a spirit of charity than the consistent omissions of a Government frozen in the ice of its own indifference."

Chronology

1932 Roosevelt defeats Hoover for presidency

1933 Bank holiday
Emergency Banking Relief Act
Beer and Wine Revenue Act
The Hundred Days Congress enacts AAA,
   TVA, HOLC, NRA, and PWA
Federal Securities Act
Glass-Steagall Banking Reform Act
CWA established
Twentieth Amendment (changed calendar
   of congressional sessions and date of
   presidential inauguration)
Twenty-first Amendment (prohibition repealed)

1934 Gold Reserve Act
Securities and Exchange Commission
   authorized
Indian Reorganization Act
FHA established
Frazier-Lemke Farm Bankruptcy Act

1935 WPA established
Wagner Act
Resettlement Administration
Social Security Act
Public Utility Holding Company Act
Schechter "sick-chicken" case
CIO organized

1936 Soil Conservation and Domestic Allotment
   Act
Roosevelt defeats Landon for presidency

1937 USHA established
Roosevelt announces "Court-packing" plan

1938 Second AAA
Fair Labor Standards Act

1939 Reorganization Act
Hatch Act

How Radical Was the New Deal?

The Great Depression was both a great calamity and a great opportunity. How effectively Franklin Roosevelt responded to the calamity and what use he made of the opportunity are the two great questions that have animated historical debate about the New Deal.

Some historians have actually denied that there was much of a connection between the depression and the New Deal. Arthur M. Schlesinger, Jr., for example, who believes in "cycles" of reform and reaction in American history, has written that "there would very likely have been some sort of New Deal in the 1930s even without the Depression." But most of the first generation of historians who wrote about the New Deal (in the 1940s, '50s, and early '60s) agreed with Carl Degler's judgment that the New Deal was "a revolutionary response to a revolutionary situation." In this view, though Roosevelt never found a means short of war to bring about economic recovery, he shrewdly utilized the stubborn economic crisis as a means to enact sweeping reforms. A handful of scholars, notably Edgar Eugene Robinson, condemned Roosevelt's record as a "socialistic" break with American traditions. But until the 1960s, the great majority of historians approved the political values of the new Deal and praised its accomplishments.

Some leftist scholars writing in the 1960s, however, notably Barton J. Bernstein, charged that the New Deal did not reach far enough. This criticism echoed the socialist complaint in the 1930s that the depression represented the total collapse of American capitalism, and that the New

Deal had muffed the chance truly to re-make American society. Roosevelt had the chance, these historians argue, to redistribute wealth, improve race relations, and bring the giant corporations to heel. Instead, say these critics, the New Deal simply represented a conservative holding action to shore up a sagging and corrupt capitalist order.

Those charges against the New Deal stimulated another generation of scholars in the 1970s, '80s, and '90s to look closely at the concrete institutional, attitudinal, and economic circumstances in which the New Deal unfolded. Historians including James Patterson, Alan Brinkley, Kenneth Jackson, Harvard Sitkoff, and Lizabeth Cohen—sometimes loosely referred to as the "constraints school"—conclude that the New Deal offered just about as much reform as circumstances allowed, and as the majority of Americans wanted. The findings of these historians are impressive: the system of checks and balances limited presidential power; the disproportionate influence of southern Democrats in Congress stalled attempts to move toward racial justice; the federal system, in fact, inhibited all efforts to initiate change from

Washington. Most importantly, a majority of the American people at the time wanted to reform capitalism, not overthrow it. Industrial workers, for example, were not hapless pawns upon whom the New Deal was foisted, frustrating their yearning for more radical change. Instead, they sought security and self-determination in ways quite compatible with the New Deal's programs for unemployment insurance, old-age pensions, and guarantees of labor's right to organize.

The best proof of the soundness of that conclusion is probably the durability of the political alliance that Roosevelt assembled. The great "New Deal coalition" that dominated American politics for nearly four decades after Roosevelt's election in 1932 represented a broad consensus in American society about the legitimate limits of government efforts to shape the social and economic order. William Leuchtenburg has offered the most balanced historical assessment in his description of the New Deal as a "half-way revolution," neither radical nor conservative, but accurately reflecting the American people's needs and desires in the 1930s—and for a long time thereafter.

SUGGESTED READINGS

PRIMARY SOURCE DOCUMENTS

James Agee and Walker Evans, *Let Us Now Praise Famous Men* (1940), brilliantly evokes the misery of the depression in words and photographs. Franklin D. Roosevelt's dramatic "First Inaugural Address" (1933), in Henry Steele Commager, ed., *Documents of American History*, captured the imagination of the distressed nation. Less successful was Roosevelt's "Radio Address on Supreme Court Reform" (1937), in Richard Hofstadter, *Great Issues in American History* (1982). See also Dorothy Thompson's attack on the Court plan in the Washington *Star*, February 10, 1937.* Clifford Odets's play *Waiting for Lefty* (1935) and John Steinbeck's novel *The Grapes of Wrath* (1939) exemplify the literature stimulated by the Great Depression. Robert S. McElvaine has collected a compelling set of letters in *Down and Out in the Great Depression* (1983).

---

*An asterisk indicates that the document, or an excerpt from it, can be found in Thomas A. Bailey and David M. Kennedy, eds., *The American Spirit: United States History as Seen by Contemporaries*, 9th ed. (Boston: Houghton Mifflin, 1998).

SECONDARY SOURCES

A masterly summation is William E. Leuchtenburg, *Franklin D. Roosevelt and the New Deal, 1932–1940* (1963). Briefer and more critical of the limitations of reform is Paul Conkin, *The New Deal* (rev. ed., 1975). A detailed biography is Frank Freidel, *Franklin D. Roosevelt* (4 vols., 1952–1973). Brilliantly pro-FDR are the three volumes of Arthur M. Schlesinger, Jr., *Age of Roosevelt: The Crisis of the Old Order* (1957), *The Coming of the New Deal* (1959), and *The Politics of Upheaval* (1960). John M. Blum, *From the Morgenthau Diaries* (3 vols., 1959–1967), gives the perspective of an important New Deal insider, as does T. H. Watkins, *Righteous Pilgrim: The Life and Times of Harold L. Ickes, 1874–1952* (1990). The views of other contemporaries may be found in Frances Perkins, *The Roosevelt I Knew* (1946); Rexford G. Tugwell, *In Search of Roosevelt* (1972); and Raymond Moley, *After Seven Years* (1939). A concise biography is Frank Freidel, *Franklin D. Roosevelt: Rendezvous with Destiny* (1990). The social impact of the depression is vividly etched in Studs Terkel, *Hard Times* (1970), Ann Banks, *First Person America* (1980), and James N.

Gregory, *American Exodus: The Dust Bowl Migration and Okie Culture in California* (1989). Two volumes by Lois Scharf are of interest: *To Work and to Wed: Female Employment, Feminism, and the Great Depression* (1980) and *Eleanor Roosevelt: First Lady of American Liberalism* (1987). Also see Susan Ware, *Beyond Suffrage: Women in the New Deal* (1981), and Blanche Wiesen Cook, *Eleanor Roosevelt: A Life* (1992). Alan Brinkley brilliantly chronicles *Voices of Protest: Huey Long, Father Coughlin, and the Great Depression* (1982). See also his treatment of the later New Deal in *The End of Reform* (1995). For a sharply critical portrayal, see William Ivy Hair, *The Kingfish and His Realm: The Life and Times of Huey P. Long* (1991). Greg Mitchell describes *The Campaign of the Century: Upton Sinclair's Race for Governor of California and the Birth of Media Politics* (1992). Labor is dealt with in Irving Bernstein, *Turbulent Years* (1970), and Lizabeth Cohen, *Making a New Deal: Industrial Workers in Chicago, 1919–1939* (1990). Ellis Hawley, *The New Deal and the Problem of Monopoly* (1966), is a superb analysis of the conflicting currents of economic policy in the Roosevelt administration. W. Andrew Achenbaum examines one of the era's most important pieces of legislation in *Social Security: Visions and Revisions* (1986). On the TVA, see Erwin C. Hargrave, *Prisoners of Myth, The Leadership of the Tennessee Valley Authority, 1933–1990* (1994). A comprehensive assessment by several noted scholars is Harvard Sitkoff, ed., *Fifty Years Later: The New Deal Evaluated* (1985). James Patterson, *The New Deal and the States* (1969), examines the local impact of the Roosevelt measures, as does Charles H. Trout, *Boston, the Great Depression, and the New Deal* (1977). Indians receive special attention in Graham D. Taylor, *The New Deal and American Indian Tribalism* (1980), and Kenneth R. Philip, *John Collier's Crusade for Indian Reform* (1977). On blacks see Harvard Sitkoff, *A New Deal for Blacks* (1978), and Nancy J. Weiss, *Farewell to the Party of Lincoln: Black Politics in the Age of FDR* (1983). Richard Lowitt analyzes *The New Deal and the West* (1984). On the impact of the Great Depression and the New Deal in the South, see Gavin Wright, *Old South, New South: Revolutions in the Southern Economy Since the Civil War* (1986); Bruce Schulman, *From Cotton Belt to Sunbelt* (1990); and James Cobb and Michael Namaroto, eds., *The New Deal and the South* (1984). Especially good on intellectual history is Richard H. Pells, *Radical Visions and American Dreams: Culture and Social Thought in the Depression Years* (1973). A trenchant appraisal of the New Deal legacy is Steven Fraser and Gary Gerstle, eds., *The Rise and Fall of the New Deal Order* (1989).

37

Franklin D. Roosevelt and the Shadow of War

1933–1941

The epidemic of world lawlessness is spreading. When an epidemic of physical disease starts to spread, the community approves and joins in a quarantine of the patients in order to protect the health of the community against the spread of the disease. . . . There must be positive endeavors to preserve peace.

FRANKLIN D. ROOSEVELT,
CHICAGO "QUARANTINE SPEECH," 1937

The London Conference

The sixty-six-nation London Economic Conference, meeting in the summer of 1933, revealed how thoroughly Roosevelt's early foreign policy was subordinated to his strategy for domestic economic recovery. The delegates to the London Conference hoped to organize a coordinated international attack on the global depression. They were particularly eager to stabilize the values of the various nations' currencies, and the rates at which they could be exchanged. Exchange-rate stabilization was essential to the revival of world trade, which had all but evaporated by 1933.

Roosevelt at first agreed to send an American delegation to the conference, including Secretary of State Cordell Hull. But the president soon began to have second thoughts about the conference's agenda. He wanted to pursue his gold juggling and other inflationary policies at home as a means of stimulating American recovery. An international agreement to maintain the value of the dollar in terms of other currencies might tie his hands, and at bottom Roosevelt was unwilling to sacrifice the possibility of domestic recovery for the sake of international cooperation. While vacationing on a yacht along the New England coast, he dashed off a radio message to London, scolding the conference for attempting to stabilize currencies and essentially declaring America's withdrawal from the negotiations.

Roosevelt's bombshell announcement yanked the rug from under the London Conference. The delegates adjourned empty-handed, amid cries of American bad faith. Whether the conference could have arrested the worldwide economic slide is debatable, but Roosevelt's every-man-for-himself attitude plunged the planet even deeper into economic crisis. The collapse of the London Conference also strengthened the global trend toward extreme nationalism, making international cooperation ever more difficult as the dangerous decade of the 1930s unfolded. Reflecting the powerful persistence of American isolationism, Roosevelt's action played directly into the hands of the power-mad dictators who were determined to shatter the peace of the world. Americans themselves would eventually pay a high price for the narrow-minded belief that the United States could go it alone in the modern world.

Freedom for (from?) the Filipinos and Recognition for the Russians

Roosevelt matched isolationism from Europe with withdrawal from Asia. The Great Depression burst the fragile bubble of President McKinley's imperialistic dream in the Far East. With the descent into hard times, American taxpayers were eager to throw overboard their expensive tropical liability in the Philippine Islands. Organized labor demanded the exclusion of low-wage Filipino workers, and American sugar producers clamored for the elimination of Philippine competition.

Remembering its earlier promises of freedom for the Philippines, Congress passed the Tydings-McDuffie Act in 1934. The act provided for the independence of the Philippines after a twelve-year period of economic and political tutelage—that is, by 1946. The United States agreed to relinquish its army bases, but naval bases were reserved for future discussion—and retention.

Just Another Customer, 1933   The United States recognizes the Soviet Union.

In truth, the American people were not so much giving freedom to the Philippines as they were freeing themselves *from* the Philippines. With a selfish eye to their own welfare, and with apparent disregard for the political situation in Asia, they proposed to leave the Philippines to their fate, while imposing upon the Filipinos economic terms so ungenerous as to threaten the islands with economic prostration. Once again, American isolationists rejoiced. Yet in Tokyo, Japanese militarists were calculating that they had little to fear from an inward-looking America that was abandoning its principal possession in Asia.

At the same time, Roosevelt made at least one internationalist gesture when he formally recognized the Soviet Union in 1933. Over the noisy protests of anticommunist conservatives, as well as Roman Catholics offended by the Kremlin's antireligious policies, Roosevelt extended the hand of diplomatic recognition to the sixteen-year-old Bolshevik regime. He was motivated in part by the hope for trade with Soviet Russia, as well as by the desire to bolster the Soviet Union as a friendly counterweight to the possible threat of German power in Europe and Japanese power in Asia.

Becoming a Good Neighbor

Closer to home, Roosevelt inaugurated a refreshing new era in relations with Latin America. He proclaimed in his inaugural address: "I would dedicate this nation to the policy of the Good Neighbor." Taken together, Roosevelt's noninvolvement in Europe and withdrawal from Asia, along with this brotherly embrace of his New World neighbors, suggested that the United States was giving up its ambition to be a world power, and would content itself instead with being merely a regional power, its interests and activities confined exclusively to the Western Hemisphere.

Old-fashioned intervention by bayonet in the Caribbean had not paid off, except in an evil harvest of resentment, suspicion, and fear. The Great Depression had cooled off Yankee economic aggressiveness, as thousands of investors in Latin American securities became sackholders rather than stockholders. There were now fewer dollars to be protected by the rifles of the hated marines.

With war-thirsty dictators seizing power in Europe and Asia, Roosevelt was eager to line up the Latin Americans to help defend the Western Hemisphere. Embittered neighbors would be potential tools of transoceanic aggressors. President Roosevelt made clear at the outset that he was going to renounce armed intervention, particularly the vexatious corollary of the Monroe Doctrine devised by his cousin Theodore Roosevelt. Late in 1933, at the Seventh Pan-American Conference in Montevideo, Uruguay, the U.S. delegation formally endorsed nonintervention.

Deeds followed words. The last marines departed from Haiti in 1934. In the same year restive Cuba was released from the hobbles of the Platt Amendment, under which the United States had been free to intervene, although the naval base at Guantánamo was retained. The tiny country of Panama received a similar uplift in 1936, when Washington relaxed its grip on the isthmus nation.

The hope-inspiring Good Neighbor policy, with the accent on consultation and nonintervention, received its acid test in Mexico. When the Mexican government seized Yankee oil properties in 1938, American investors vehemently demanded armed intervention to repossess their confiscated businesses. But Roosevelt successfully resisted the badgering, and a settlement was finally threshed out in 1941, even though the oil companies lost much of their original stake.

Spectacular success crowned Roosevelt's Good Neighbor policy. His earnest attempts to usher in a new era of friendliness, though hurting some U.S. bondholders, paid rich dividends in goodwill among the peoples to the south. No other citizen of the United States has ever been held in such high esteem in Latin America during his lifetime. Roosevelt was cheered with tumultuous enthusiasm when, as a "traveling salesman for peace," he journeyed to the special Inter-American Conference at Buenos Aires, Argentina, in 1936. The Colossus of the North now seemed less a vulture and more an eagle.

Secretary Hull's Reciprocal Trade Agreements

Intimately associated with Good Neighborism, and also popular in Latin America, was the reciprocal trade policy of the New Dealers. Its chief architect was idealistic Secretary of State Hull, a high-minded Tennessean of the low-tariff school. Like Roosevelt, he believed that trade was a two-way street; that a nation can sell abroad only as it buys abroad; that tariff barriers choke off foreign trade; and that trade wars beget shooting wars.

Responding to the Hull-Roosevelt leadership, Congress passed the Reciprocal Trade Agreements Act in 1934. Designed in part to lift American export trade from the depression doldrums, this enlightened measure was aimed at both relief and recovery. At the same time, it activated the low-tariff policies of the New Dealers. (See the tariff chart in the Appendix.)

The Reciprocal Trade Agreements Act avoided the dangerous uncertainties of a wholesale tariff revision; it merely whittled down the most objectionable schedules of the Hawley-Smoot law by amending them. Roosevelt was empowered to lower existing rates by as much as 50 percent, provided that the other country involved was willing to respond with similar reductions. The resulting pacts, moreover, were to become effective without the formal approval of the Senate. This novel feature not only ensured speedier action but sidestepped the twin evils of high-stakes logrolling and high-pressure lobbying in Congress.

Secretary Hull, whose zeal for reciprocity was unflagging, succeeded in negotiating pacts with twenty-one countries by the end of 1939. During these same years, U.S. foreign trade increased appreciably, presumably in part as a result of the Hull-Roosevelt policies. Trade agreements undoubtedly bettered economic and political relations with Latin America and proved to be an influence for peace in a war-bent world.

The Reciprocal Trade Agreements Act was a landmark piece of legislation. It reversed the traditional high-protective-tariff policy that had persisted almost unbroken since Civil War days and that had so damaged the American and international economies following World War I. It paved the way for the American-led free-trade international economic system that took shape after World War II, a period that witnessed the most robust growth in the history of international trade.

One of Our Quaint Ideas About Foreign Trade

Impulses Toward Storm-Cellar Isolationism

Post-1918 chaos in Europe, followed by the Great Depression, spawned the ominous spread of totalitarianism. The individual was nothing; the state was everything. The Communist USSR led the way, with the crafty and ruthless Joseph Stalin finally emerging as dictator. Blustery Benito Mussolini, a swaggering Fascist, seized the reins of power in Italy during 1922. And Adolf Hitler, a fanatic with a toothbrush mustache, plotted and harangued his way into control of Germany in 1933 with liberal use of the "big lie."

Hitler was the most dangerous of the dictators, because he combined tremendous power with impulsiveness. A frustrated Austrian painter, with hypnotic talents as an orator and a leader, he had secured control of the Nazi party by making political capital of the Treaty of Versailles and Germany's depression-spawned unemployment. He was thus a misbegotten child of the shortsighted postwar policies of the victorious Allies, including the United States. The desperate German people had fallen in behind the new Pied Piper, for they saw no other hope of escape from the plague of economic chaos and national disgrace. In 1936 the Nazi Hitler and the Fascist Mussolini allied themselves in the Rome-Berlin Axis.

International gangsterism was likewise spreading in the Far East, where imperial Japan was on the make. Like Germany and Italy, Japan was a so-called have-not power. Like them, it resented the ungenerous Treaty of Versailles. Like them, it demanded additional space for its teeming millions, cooped-up in their crowded island nation.

Japanese navalists were not to be denied. Determined to find a place in the Asiatic sun, Tokyo gave notice in 1934 of the termination of the twelve-year-old Washington Naval Treaty. A year later at London, the Japanese torpedoed all hope of effective naval disarmament. Upon being denied complete parity, they walked out on the multipower conference and accelerated their construction of giant battleships.

Jut-jawed Mussolini, seeking both glory and empire in Africa, brutally attacked Ethiopia in 1935 with bombers and tanks. The brave defenders, armed with spears and ancient firearms, were speedily crushed. Members of the League of Nations could have caused Mussolini's war machine

The Wages of Despair Disillusioned and desperate, millions of Germans in the 1930s looked to Adolf Hitler as their savior from the harsh terms of the Treaty of Versailles that concluded World War I. This Nazi poster reads "Our Last Hope: Hitler."

The thirst of Benito Mussolini (1883–1945) for national glory in primitive Ethiopia is indicated by his remark in 1940,

"To make a people great it is necessary to send them to battle even if you have to kick them in the pants." (The Italians were notoriously unwarlike.)

In 1934 Mussolini proclaimed in a public speech,

"We have buried the putrid corpse of liberty."

If attacked again by aggressors, these delinquents could "stew in their own juices."

Mired down in the Great Depression, Americans had no real appreciation of the revolutionary forces being harnessed by the dictators. The "have-not" powers were out to become "have" powers. Americans were not so much afraid that totalitarian aggression would cause trouble as they were fearful that they might be drawn into it. Strong nationwide sentiment welled up for a constitutional amendment to forbid a declaration of war by Congress—except in case of invasion—unless there was a favorable popular referendum. With a mixture of seriousness and frivolity, a group of Princeton University students began to agitate in 1936 for a bonus to be paid to the Veterans of Future Wars (VFWs) while the prospective front-liners were still alive.

Congress Legislates Neutrality

As the gloomy 1930s lengthened, an avalanche of lurid articles and books condemning the munitions manufacturers as war-fomenting "merchants of death" poured from American presses. A Senate committee, headed by Senator Gerald Nye of North Dakota, was appointed in 1934 to investigate the "blood business." By sensationalizing evidence regarding America's entry into World War I, the senatorial probers tended to shift the blame away from the German submarines onto the American bankers and arms manufacturers. Because the munitions makers had obviously made money out of the war,

to creak to a halt—if they had only dared to embargo oil. But when the League quailed rather than risk global hostilities, it merely signed its own death warrant.

Isolationism, long festering in America, received a strong boost from these alarms abroad. Though disapproving of the dictators, Americans still believed that their encircling seas conferred a kind of mystic immunity. They were continuing to suffer the disillusionment born of their participation in World War I, which they now regarded as a colossal blunder. They likewise nursed bitter memories of the ungrateful and defaulting debtors. As early as 1934 a spiteful Congress passed the Johnson Debt Default Act, which prevented debt-dodging nations from borrowing further in the United States.

many a naive citizen leaped to the illogical conclusion that these soulless scavengers had *caused* the war in order to make money. This kind of reasoning suggested that if the profits could only be removed from the arms traffic—"one hell of a business"—the country could steer clear of any world conflict that might erupt in the future.

Responding to overwhelming popular pressure, Congress made haste to legislate the nation out of war. Action was spurred by the danger that Mussolini's Ethiopian assault would plunge the world into a new bloodbath. The Neutrality Acts of 1935, 1936, and 1937, taken together, stipulated that *when the president proclaimed* the existence of a foreign war, certain restrictions would automatically go into effect. No American could legally sail on a belligerent ship, or sell or transport munitions to a belligerent, or make loans to a belligerent.

This head-in-the-sand legislation in effect marked an abandonment of the traditional policy of freedom of the seas—a policy for which America had professedly fought two full-fledged wars and several undeclared wars. The Neutrality Acts, so called, were specifically tailored to keep the nation out of a conflict like World War I. If they had been in effect at that time, America probably would not have been sucked in—at least not in April 1917. Congress was one war too late with its legislation. What had seemed dishonorable to Wilson seemed honorable and desirable to a later disillusioned generation.

Storm-cellar neutrality proved to be tragically shortsighted. America falsely assumed that the decision for peace or war lay in its own hands, not in those of the satanic forces already unleashed in the world. Prisoner of its own fears, it failed to recognize that it should have used its enormous power to control international events in its own interest. Instead, it remained at the mercy of events controlled by the dictators.

Statutory neutrality, though of undoubted legality, was of dubious morality. America served notice that it would make no distinction whatever between brutal aggressors and innocent victims. By striving to hold the scales even, it actually overbalanced them in favor of the dictators, who had armed themselves to the teeth. By declining to use its vast industrial strength to aid its democratic friends and defeat its totalitarian foes, it helped goad the aggressors along their blood-spattered path of conquest.

America Dooms Loyalist Spain

The Spanish Civil War of 1936–1939—a proving ground and dress rehearsal in miniature for World War II—was a painful object lesson in the folly of neutrality-by-legislation. Spanish rebels, who rose against the left-leaning republican government in Madrid, were headed by Fascistic General Francisco Franco. Generously aided by his fellow conspirators Hitler and Mussolini, he undertook to overthrow the established Loyalist regime, which in turn was assisted on a smaller scale by the Soviet Union. This pipeline from communist Moscow chilled the natural sympathies of many Americans, especially Roman Catholics.

Washington continued official relations with the Loyalist government. In accordance with previous American practice, this regime should have been free to purchase desperately needed munitions from the United States. But Congress, with the encouragement of Roosevelt and with only one dissenting vote, amended the existing neutrality legislation so as to apply an arms embargo to both Loyalists and rebels. "Roosevelt," remarked dictator Franco, "behaved in the manner of a true gentleman." FDR later regretted being so gentlemanly.

Uncle Sam thus sat on the sidelines while Franco, abundantly supplied with arms and men by his fellow dictators, strangled the republican government of Spain. The democracies, including the United States, were so determined to stay out of war

---

America's policy toward Spain "had been a grave mistake," Roosevelt told his cabinet in early 1939.

"The policy we should have adopted was to forbid the transportation of munitions of war in American bottoms [ships]. This could have been done and Loyalist Spain would still have been able to come to us for what she needed to fight for her life against Franco—to fight for her life," Roosevelt concluded prophetically, "and for the lives of some of the rest of us as well, as events will very likely prove."

that they helped to condemn a fellow democracy to death. In so doing they further encouraged the dictators to take the dangerous road that led over the precipice to World War II.

Such peace-at-any-price-ism was further cursed with illogic. Although determined to stay out of war, America declined to build up its armed forces to a point where it could deter the aggressors. In fact, it allowed its navy to decline in relative strength. It had been led to believe that huge fleets cause huge wars; it was also trying to spare the complaining taxpayer during the grim days of the Great Depression. When President Roosevelt repeatedly called for preparedness, he was branded a warmonger. Not until 1938, the year before World War II exploded, did Congress come to grips with the problem when it passed a billion-dollar naval construction act. The calamitous story was repeated of too little, and too late.

Appeasing Japan and Germany

Sulfurous war clouds had meanwhile been gathering in the tension-taut Far East. In 1937 the Japanese militarists, at the Marco Polo Bridge near Beijing (Peking), touched off the explosion that led to an all-out invasion of China. In a sense this attack was the curtain raiser of World War II.

Roosevelt shrewdly declined to invoke the recently passed neutrality legislation, by refusing to call the so-called China incident an officially declared *war.* If he had put the existing restrictions into effect, he would have cut off the trickle of munitions on which the Chinese were desperately dependent. The Japanese, of course, could continue to buy mountains of war supplies in the United States.

In Chicago—unofficial isolationist "capital" of America—President Roosevelt delivered his sensational "Quarantine Speech" in the autumn of 1937. Alarmed by the recent aggressions of Italy and Japan, he called for "positive endeavors" to "quarantine" the aggressors—presumably by economic embargoes.

The speech triggered a cyclone of protest from isolationists and other foes of involvement; they feared that a moral quarantine would lead to a shooting quarantine. Startled by this angry response, Roosevelt retreated and sought less direct means to curb the dictators.

America's isolationist mood intensified, especially in regard to China. In December 1937 Japanese aviators bombed and sank an American gunboat, the *Panay,* in Chinese waters, with a loss of two killed and thirty wounded. In the days of 1898, when the *Maine* went down, this outrage might have provoked war. But after Tokyo hastened to make the necessary apologies and pay a proper indemnity, Americans breathed a deep sigh of relief. Japanese militarists were thus encouraged to vent their anger against the "superior" white race by subjecting American civilians in China, both male and female, to humiliating slappings and strippings.

Adolf Hitler meanwhile grew louder and bolder in Europe. In 1935 he had openly flouted the Treaty of Versailles by introducing compulsory military service in Germany. The next year he brazenly marched into the demilitarized German Rhineland, likewise contrary to the detested treaty, while France and Britain looked on in an agony of indecision. Lashing his following to a frenzy, Hitler undertook to persecute and then exterminate the Jewish population in the areas under his control. In the end, he wiped out about 6 million innocent victims, mostly in gas chambers (see Makers of America: Refugees from the Holocaust, pp. 834–835). Calling upon his people to sacrifice butter for guns, he whipped the new German air force and mechanized ground divisions into the most devastating military machine the world had yet seen.

Suddenly, in March 1938, Hitler bloodlessly occupied German-speaking Austria, his birthplace. The democratic powers, wringing their hands in despair, prayed that this last grab would satisfy his passion for conquest.

But like a drunken reveler calling for madder music and stronger wine, Hitler could not stop. Intoxicated by his recent gains, he began to make bullying demands for the German-inhabited Sudetenland of neighboring Czechoslovakia. The leaders of Britain and France, eager to appease Hitler, sought frantically to bring the dispute to the conference table. President Roosevelt, also deeply alarmed, kept the wires hot with personal messages to both Hitler and Mussolini urging a peaceful settlement.

A conference was finally held in Munich, Germany, in September 1938. The Western European democracies, badly unprepared for war, betrayed Czechoslovakia to Germany when they consented to the shearing away of the Sudetenland. They

What Next? 1938   The Western European democracies looked on helplessly as Nazi Germany swallowed up Austria and part of Czechoslovakia in 1938, and Hitler's juggernaut seemed unstoppable.

hoped—and these hopes were shared by the American people—that the concessions at the conference table would slake Hitler's thirst for power and bring "peace in our time." Indeed, Hitler publicly promised that the Sudetenland "is the last territorial claim I have to make in Europe."

"Appeasement" of the dictators, symbolized by the ugly word *Munich,* turned out to be merely surrender on the installment plan. It was like giving a cannibal a finger in the hope of saving an arm. In March 1939, scarcely six months later, Hitler suddenly erased the rest of Czechoslovakia from the map, contrary to his solemn vows. The democratic world was again stunned.

Hitler's Belligerency and U.S. Neutrality

Joseph Stalin, the sphinx of the Kremlin, was a key to the peace puzzle. In the summer of 1939, the British and French were busily negotiating with Moscow, hopeful of securing a mutual-defense treaty that would halt Hitler. But mutual suspicions proved insuperable. Then the Soviet Union astounded the world by signing, on August 23, 1939, a nonaggression treaty with the German dictator.

The notorious Hitler-Stalin pact meant that the Nazi German leader now had a green light to make war on Poland and the Western democracies, without fearing a stab in the back from the Soviet Union—his Communist arch-foe. Consternation struck those wishful thinkers in Western Europe who had fondly hoped that Hitler might be egged upon Stalin so that the twin menaces would bleed each other to death. It was as plain as the mustache on Stalin's face that the wily Soviet dictator was plotting to turn his German accomplice against the Western democracies. The two warring camps would then kill each other off—and leave Stalin bestriding Europe like a colossus.

With the signing of the Nazi-Soviet pact, World War II was only hours away. Hitler now demanded from neighboring Poland a return of the areas wrested from Germany after World War I. Failing to secure satisfaction, he sent his mechanized divisions crashing into Poland at dawn on September 1, 1939.

Britain and France, honoring their commitments to Poland, promptly declared war. At long last they perceived the folly of continued appeasement. But they were powerless to aid Poland, which succumbed in three weeks to Hitler's smashing strategy of terror. Stalin, as prearranged secretly in his fateful pact with Hitler, came in on the kill for his share of old Russian Poland. Long-dreaded World War II was now fully launched, and the long truce of 1919–1939 had come to an end.

President Roosevelt speedily issued the routine proclamations of neutrality. Americans were overwhelmingly anti-Nazi and anti-Hitler; they fervently

President Franklin Roosevelt (1882–1945) was roused at 3 A.M. on September 1, 1939, by a telephone call from Ambassador William Bullitt (1891–1967) in Paris:

"Mr. President, several German divisions are deep in Polish territory. . . . There are reports of bombers over the city of Warsaw."

"Well, Bill," FDR replied, "it has come at last. God help us all."

hoped that the democracies would win; they fondly believed that the forces of righteousness would triumph, as in 1918. But they were desperately determined to stay out: they were not going to be "suckers" again.

Neutrality promptly became a heated issue in the United States. Ill-prepared Britain and France urgently needed American airplanes and other weapons, but the Neutrality Act of 1937 raised a sternly forbidding hand. Roosevelt summoned Congress in special session, shortly after the invasion of Poland, to consider lifting the arms embargo. After six hectic weeks of debate, a makeshift law emerged.

The Neutrality Act of 1939 provided that henceforth the European democracies might buy American war materials, but only on a "cash-and-carry basis." This meant that they would have to transport the munitions in their own ships, after paying for them in cash. America would thus avoid loans, war debts, and the torpedoing of American arms-carriers. While Congress thus loosened former restrictions in response to interventionist cries, it added others in response to isolationist fears. Roosevelt was now also authorized to proclaim danger zones into which American merchant ships would be forbidden to enter.

Despite its defects, this unneutral neutrality law clearly favored the democracies against the dictators—and was so intended. As the British and French navies controlled the Atlantic, the European aggressors could not send their ships to buy America's munitions. The United States not only improved its moral position but simultaneously helped its economic position. Overseas demand for war goods brought a sharp upswing from the recession of 1937–1938 and ultimately solved the decade-long unemployment crisis (see the chart on p. 818).

Aftermath of the Fall of France

The months following the collapse of Poland, while France and Britain marked time, were known as the "phony war." An ominous silence fell on Europe, as Hitler shifted his victorious divisions from Poland for a knockout blow at France. Inaction during this anxious period was relieved by the Soviets, who wantonly attacked neighboring Finland in an effort to secure strategic buffer territory. The debt-paying

> *In 1924, while briefly imprisoned, Adolf Hitler (1889–1945) prepared a remarkable book,* Mein Kampf (My Struggle), *which brazenly set forth his objectives and techniques. He was a past master of the "big lie." As he wrote,*
>
> "The primitive simplicity of their minds [the masses] renders them a more easy prey to a big lie than a small one, for they themselves often tell little lies but would be ashamed to tell big ones." He also said, "The victor will never be asked if he told the truth," and "Success is the sole earthly judge of right and wrong."

Finns, who had a host of admirers in America, were speedily granted $30 million by an isolationist Congress for *nonmilitary* supplies. But despite heroic resistance, Finland was finally flattened by the Soviet steamroller.

An abrupt end to the "phony war" came in April 1940 when Hitler, again without warning, overran his weaker neighbors Denmark and Norway. Hardly pausing for breath, the next month he attacked the Netherlands and Belgium, followed by a paralyzing blow at France. By late June, France was forced to surrender, but not until Mussolini had pounced on its rear for a jackal's share of the loot. In a pell-mell but successful evacuation from the French port of Dunkirk, the British managed to salvage the bulk of their shattered and partially disarmed army. The crisis providentially brought forth an inspired leader in Prime Minister Winston Churchill, the bulldog-jawed orator who nerved his people to fight off the fearful air bombings of their cities.

France's sudden collapse shocked Americans out of their daydreams. Stouthearted Britons, singing "There'll Always Be an England," were all that stood between Hitler and the death in Europe of constitutional government. If Britain went under, Hitler would have at his disposal the workshops, shipyards, and slave labor of Western Europe. He might even have the powerful British fleet as well. This frightening possibility, which seemed to pose a dire threat to American security, steeled the American people to a tremendous effort.

Refugees from the Holocaust

Fed by Adolf Hitler's genocidal delusions, anti-Semitism bared its fangs in the 1930s, spreading across Europe as Nazi Germany seized Austria and Czechoslovakia. Eluding the jackboots of Hitler's bloodthirsty SS (*Schutzstaffel*, an elite military and police force), Jews tried to flee from the Nazi juggernaut. Some succeeded, including the world's premier nuclear physicist, Albert Einstein, the Nobel laureate whose plea to Franklin Roosevelt helped initiate the top-secret atomic bomb project; the philosopher Hannah Arendt; the painter Marc Chagall; and the composer Kurt Weill. In all, some 150,000 Jews fled the Third Reich for America in the 1930s—a tiny fraction of the millions of Jews who eventually came under Hitler's heel. Why did America not make room for more?

For one thing, those exiled luminaries who managed to make it out of Germany found a divided Jewish community in America. Before the closing of unrestricted immigration in 1924, Jews had arrived in two stages—a trickle from Germany in the mid-nineteenth century, followed by a flood from Eastern Europe in the decades after 1890. Both groups had migrated as families and without a thought of return to the old country. But beyond that experience and their shared religious heritage, the two waves had relatively little in common, especially when it came to coping with the refugee crisis of the 1930s. The settled and prosperous German-Jewish community, organized in the American Jewish Committee, had fought hard to convince their fellow Americans of their loyalty, and many now feared that bold advocacy for refugees from Hitler's Germany would touch off an outburst of anti-Semitism

in America. The notorious "Radio Priest," Father Charles Coughlin, was already preaching venomous pronouncements against the Jews, though his audience remained small—for the time being. The more numerous but less wealthy and influential East European Jews, organized in the American Jewish

Nazi Anti-Semitism This widely distributed German poster attacks "The Jew—Purveyor of war, prolonger of war."

Albert Einstein Arriving in America, 1933   Sadly, the United States admitted only a trickle of refugees from Nazism, while some 6 million European Jews died.

Hannah Arendt, 1933   A brilliant political theorist, she fled the Nazis and continued her career in the United States.

A Survivor of the Holocaust   A Polish Jew is reunited with his sister in the United States in 1946. He was lucky to have lived; most Polish Jews perished at Hitler's hands.

Congress, were intent on pressuring the Roosevelt administration to rescue Europe's Jews. This internal discord compromised the political effectiveness of the American Jewish community in the face of the refugee dilemma.

Other factors also helped to keep America's doors shut against Jews seeking refuge in the United States. The restrictive American immigration law of 1924 set rigid national quotas and made no provisions for seekers of asylum from racial, religious, or political persecution. The Great Depression made it impossible to provide employment for workers already in the United States, much less make room in the job line for newcomers. And opening America's gates to Germany's half-million Jews raised the daunting prospect that such action would unleash a deluge of millions more Jews from countries like Poland and Romania, which were advertising their eagerness to be rid of their Jewish populations. No one, of course, yet knew just how fiendish a destiny Hitler was preparing for Europe's Jews.

Many Jews and Gentiles alike, including Congressman Emmanuel Celler and Senator Robert Wagner, both of New York, nevertheless lobbied Roosevelt's government to extend a welcoming hand to Jews seeking asylum—to no avail. In 1941 Congress rejected a Wagner bill to bring 20,000 German-Jewish children to the United States out-side the quota restrictions. An even more desperate plan to settle refugees in Alaska also foundered.

Once the United States entered the war, the State Department went so far as to suppress early reports of Hitler's plan to exterminate all European Jewry. After the Führer's sordid final solution became known in America, the War Department rejected pleas to bomb the rail lines leading to the gas chambers. Military officials maintained that a raid on the death camps like Auschwitz would divert essential military resources and needlessly extend the war. Thus only a lucky few escaped the Nazi terror, while 6 million died in one of history's most ghastly testimonials to the human capacity for evil.

European War Narrows
the Atlantic

Just So There'll Be No Misunderstanding   Hitler and
Mussolini are warned not to seize orphaned colonies in America.

Roosevelt moved with electrifying energy and dispatch. He called upon an already debt-burdened nation to build huge airfleets and a two-ocean navy, which could also check Japan. Congress, jarred out of its apathy toward preparedness, within a year appropriated the astounding sum of $37 billion. This figure was more than the total cost of fighting World War I and about five times larger than any New Deal annual budget.

Congress also passed a conscription law, approved September 6, 1940. Under this measure—America's first peacetime draft—provision was made for training each year 1.2 million troops and 800,000 reserves. The act was later adapted to the requirements of a global war.

The Latin American bulwark likewise needed bracing. The Netherlands, Denmark, and France, all crushed under the German jackboot, had orphaned colonies in the New World. Would these fall into German hands? At the Havana Conference of 1940, the United States agreed to share with its twenty New World neighbors the responsibility of upholding the Monroe Doctrine. This ancient dictum, hitherto unilateral, had been a bludgeon brandished only in the hated Yankee fist. Now multilateral, it was to be wielded by twenty-one pairs of American hands—at least in theory.

Bolstering Britain with the Destroyer Deal (1940)

Before the fall of France in June 1940, Washington had generally observed a technical neutrality. But now, as Britain alone stood between Hitler and his dream of world domination, the wisdom of neutrality seemed increasingly questionable. Hitler launched air attacks against Britain in August 1940, preparatory to an invasion scheduled for September. For months the Battle of Britain raged in the air over the British Isles. The Royal Air Force's tenacious defense of its native islands eventually led Hitler to postpone his planned invasion indefinitely.

During the precarious months of the Battle of Britain, debate intensified in the United States over what foreign policy to embrace. Radio broadcasts from London brought the drama of the nightly German air raids directly into millions of American homes. Sympathy for Britain grew, but it was not yet sufficient to push the United States into war.

Roosevelt faced a historic decision: whether to hunker down in the Western Hemisphere, assume a "Fortress America" defensive posture, and let the rest of the world go it alone; or to bolster beleaguered Britain by all means short of war itself. Both sides had their advocates.

Supporters of aid to Britain formed propaganda groups, the most potent of which was the Committee to Defend America by Aiding the Allies. Its argument was double-barreled. To interventionists, it could appeal for direct succor to the British by such slogans as "Britain Is Fighting Our Fight." To the isolationists, it could appeal for assistance to the democracies by "All Methods Short of War," so that the terrible conflict would be kept in faraway Europe.

The isolationists, both numerous and sincere, were by no means silent. Determined to avoid American bloodshed at all costs, they organized the America First Committee and proclaimed, "England Will Fight to the Last American." They contended that America should concentrate what strength it had to defend its own shores, lest a victorious Hitler, after crushing Britain, plot a transoceanic assault. Their basic philosophy was "The Yanks Are Not Coming," and their most effective speechmaker was the famed aviator Colonel Charles A. Lindbergh, who, ironically, had narrowed the Atlantic in 1927.

Britain was in critical need of destroyers, for German submarines were again threatening to

Pro-British Propaganda   This patriotic poster was put out by the Committee to Defend America by Aiding the Allies.

starve it out with attacks on shipping. Roosevelt moved boldly when, on September 2, 1940, he agreed to transfer to Great Britain fifty old-model, four-funnel destroyers left over from World War I. In return, the British promised to hand over to the United States eight valuable defensive base sites, stretching from Newfoundland to South America. These strategically located outposts were to remain under the Stars and Stripes for ninety-nine years.

Transferring fifty destroyers to a foreign navy was a highly questionable disposal of government property, despite a strained interpretation of existing legislation. The exchange was achieved by a simple presidential agreement, without so much as a "by your leave" to Congress. Applause burst from the aid-to-Britain advocates, many of whom had been urging such a step. But condemnation arose from America Firsters and other isolationists, as well as from antiadministration Republicans. Some of them approved the transfer but decried Roosevelt's secretive and arbitrary methods. Yet so grave was the crisis that the president was unwilling to submit the scheme to the uncertainties and delays of a full-dress debate in the Congress.

Shifting warships from a neutral United States to a belligerent Britain was, beyond question, a flagrant violation of neutral obligations—at least neutral obligations that had existed before Hitler's barefaced aggressions rendered foolish such old-fashioned concepts of fair play. Public-opinion polls demonstrated that a majority of Americans were determined, even at the risk of armed hostilities, to provide the battered British with "all aid short of war."

FDR Shatters the Two-Term Tradition (1940)

A distracting presidential election, as fate decreed, came in the midst of this crisis. The two leading Republican aspirants were round-faced and flat-voiced Senator Robert A. Taft of Ohio, son of the ex-president, and the energetic boy wonder, lawyer-prosecutor Thomas E. Dewey of New York. But in one of the miracles of American political history, the Philadelphia convention was swept off its feet by a colorful latecomer, Wendell L. Willkie, a German-descended son of Hoosier Indiana. This dynamic lawyer—tousled-headed, long-lipped, broad-faced, and large-framed—had until recently been a Democrat and the head of a huge public utilities corporation. A complete novice in politics, he had rocketed from political nothingness in a few short weeks. His great appeal lay in his personality, for he was magnetic, transparently trustful, and honest in a homespun, Lincolnesque way.

With the galleries in Philadelphia wildly chanting "We Want Willkie," the delegates finally accepted this political upstart as the only candidate who could possibly beat Roosevelt. The Republican platform condemned FDR's alleged dictatorship, as well as the costly and confusing zigzags of the New Deal. Willkie, an outspoken liberal, was opposed not so much to the New Deal as to its extravagances and inefficiencies. Democratic critics branded him "the rich man's Roosevelt" and "the simple barefoot Wall Street lawyer."

While the rumor pot boiled, Roosevelt delayed to the last minute the announcement of his decision to challenge the sacred two-term tradition. Despite what he described as his personal yearning for retirement, he avowed that in so grave a crisis he owed his experienced hand to the service of his country and humanity. The Democratic delegates in Chicago, realizing that only with "the Champ" could they defeat Willkie, drafted him by a technically unanimous vote. "Better a Third Term Than a Third-Rater" was the war cry of many Democrats.

> *The old-line Republican bosses were not happy over having a recent Democrat head their ticket. A former senator reportedly told Willkie to his face,*
>
> "You have been a Democrat all your life. I don't mind the church converting a whore, but I don't like her to lead the choir the first night."

A Campaign Poster from the Election of 1940 Roosevelt emerged as the only president ever to break the two-term tradition.

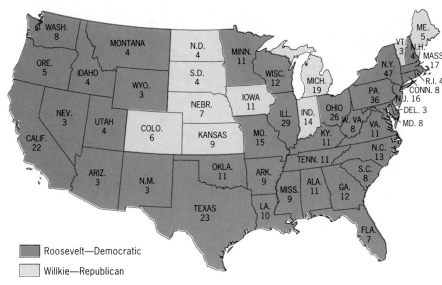

Presidential Election of 1940 (with electoral vote by state) Willkie referred to Roosevelt only as "the third-term candidate." On election eve, FDR hinted that communists and fascists were among Willkie's supporters. Despite these campaign conflicts, the two men respected each other. FDR later asked Willkie to serve as his emissary abroad and even suggested that they run together on a coalition ticket in 1944.

Burning with sincerity and energy, Willkie launched out upon a whirlwind, Bryanesque campaign in which he delivered over five hundred speeches. At times his voice became a hoarse croak. The country was already badly split between interventionists and isolationists, and Willkie might have widened the breach dangerously by a violent attack on Roosevelt's aid-to-Britain polices. But seeing eye-to-eye with FDR on the necessity of bolstering the beleaguered democracies, he refrained from assailing the president's interventionism, though objecting to his methods.

In the realm of foreign affairs, there was not much to choose between the two candidates. Both promised to stay out of the war; both promised to strengthen the nation's defenses. Yet Willkie, with a mop of black hair in his eyes, hit hard at Rooseveltian "dictatorship" and the third term. His enthusiastic followers cried, "Win with Willkie," "No Fourth Term Either," and "There's No Indispensable Man."

Roosevelt, busy at his desk with mounting problems, made only a few speeches. Stung by taunts that he was leading the nation by the back door into the European slaughterhouse, he repeatedly denied any such intention. His most specific statement was at Boston, where he emphatically declared, "Your boys are not going to be sent into any foreign wars"—a pledge that later came back to plague him. He and his supporters vigorously defended the New Deal as well as all-out preparations for the defense of America and aid to the Allies.

Roosevelt triumphed, although Willkie ran a strong race. The popular total was 27,307,819 to 22,321,018, and the electoral count was 449 to 82. This contest was much less of a walkaway than in 1932 or 1936; Democratic majorities in Congress remained about the same.

Jubilant Democrats hailed their triumph as a mandate to abolish the two-term tradition. But the truth is that Roosevelt won in spite of the third-term handicap. Voters generally felt that should war come, the experienced hand of the tried leader was needed at the helm. Less appealing was the completely inexperienced hand of the well-intentioned Willkie, who had never held public office.

The time-honored argument that one should not change horses in the middle of a stream was strong, especially in an era of war-pumped prosperity. Roosevelt might not have won if there had not been a war crisis. On the other hand, he probably would not have run if foreign perils had not loomed so ominously. In a sense, his opponent was Adolf Hitler, not Willkie.

Congress Passes the Landmark Lend-Lease Law

By late 1940 embattled Britain was nearing the end of its financial tether; its credits in America were being rapidly consumed by insatiable war orders. But Roosevelt, who had bitter memories of the wrangling over the Allied debts of World War I, was determined, as he put it, to eliminate "the silly, foolish, old dollar sign." He finally hit on the scheme of lending or

Main Flow of Lend-Lease Aid (width of arrows indicates relative amount) The proud but desperate British prime minister, Winston Churchill, declared in early 1941, "Give us the tools and we will finish the job." Lend-lease eventually provided the British and other Allies with $50 billion worth of "tools."

leasing American arms to the reeling democracies. When the shooting was over, to use his comparison, the guns and tanks could be returned, just as one's next-door neighbor would return a garden hose when a threatening fire was put out. But isolationist Senator Taft (who was reputed to have the finest mind in Washington until he made it up) retorted that lending arms was like lending chewing gum: "You don't want it back." Who wants a chewed-up tank?

The lend-lease bill, patriotically numbered 1776, was entitled "An Act Further to Promote the Defense of the United States." Sprung on the country after the election was safely over, it was praised by the administration as a device that would keep the nation out of the war rather than drag it in. The underlying concept was "Send guns, not sons" or "Billions, not bodies." America, so President Roosevelt promised, would be the "arsenal of democracy." It would send a limitless supply of arms to the victims of aggression, who in turn would finish the job and keep the war on their side of the Atlantic. Accounts would be settled by returning the used weapons or their equivalents to the United States when the war was ended.

Lend-lease was heatedly debated throughout the land and in Congress. Most of the opposition came, as might be expected, from isolationists and anti-Roosevelt Republicans. The scheme was assailed as "the blank-check bill" and, in the words of isolationist Senator Burton Wheeler, as "the new Triple-A [Agricultural Adjustment Act] bill"—a measure designed to "plow under every fourth American boy." Nevertheless, lend-lease was finally

approved in March 1941 by sweeping majorities in both houses of Congress.

Lend-lease was one of the most momentous laws ever to pass Congress; it was a challenge hurled squarely into the teeth of the Axis dictators. America pledged itself, to the extent of its vast resources, to bolster those nations that were indirectly defending it by fighting aggression. When the gigantic operation ended in 1945, America had sent about $50 billion worth of arms and equipment—much more than the cost to the country of World War I—to those nations fighting aggressors. The passing of lend-lease was in effect an economic declaration of war; now a shooting declaration could not be very far around the corner.

By its very nature, the lend-lease bill marked the abandonment of any pretense of neutrality. It was no destroyer deal arranged privately by President Roosevelt. The bill was universally debated, over drugstore counters and cracker barrels, from California all the way to Maine; and the sovereign citizen at last spoke through convincing majorities in Congress. Most people probably realized that they were tossing the old concepts of neutrality out the window. But they also recognized that they would play a suicidal game if they bound themselves by the oxcart rules of the nineteenth century—especially while the Axis aggressors themselves openly spurned international obligations. Lend-lease would admittedly involve a grave risk of war, but most Americans were prepared to take that chance rather than see Britain collapse and then face the diabolical dictators alone.

No to Lend-Lease These protesting mothers feared that America's increasing involvement with the Allied cause would eventually draw their sons into battle—as it did, despite President Roosevelt's assurances to the contrary.

Lend-lease had the somewhat incidental result of gearing U.S. factories for all-out war production. The enormously increased capacity thus achieved helped save America's own skin when, at long last, the shooting war burst around its head.

Hitler evidently recognized lend-lease as an unofficial declaration of war. Until then, Germany had avoided attacking U.S. ships; memories of America's decisive intervention in 1917–1918 were still fresh in German minds. But after the passing of lend-lease, there was less point in trying to curry favor with the United States. On May 21, 1941, the *Robin Moor,* an unarmed American merchantman, was torpedoed and destroyed by a German submarine in the South Atlantic, outside a war zone. The sinkings had started, but on a limited scale.

Hitler's Assault on the Soviet Union Spawns the Atlantic Charter

Two globe-shaking events marked the course of World War II before the assault on Pearl Harbor in December 1941. One was the fall of France in June 1940; the other was Hitler's invasion of the Soviet Union, almost exactly one year later, in June 1941.

The scheming dictators Hitler and Stalin had been uneasy yoke-fellows under the ill-begotten Nazi-Soviet pact of 1939. As masters of the double cross, neither trusted the other. They engaged in prolonged dickering in a secret attempt to divide potential territorial spoils between them, but Stalin balked at dominant German control of the Balkans. Hitler thereupon decided to crush his coconspirator, seize the oil and other resources of the Soviet Union, and then have two free hands to snuff out Britain. He assumed that his invincible armies would subdue Stalin's "Mongol half-wits" in a few short weeks.

Out of a clear sky, on June 22, 1941, Hitler launched a devastating attack on his Soviet neighbor. This timely assault was an incredible stroke of good fortune for the democratic world—or so it seemed at the time. The two fiends could now slit

Senator (later president) Harry S Truman (1884–1972) expressed a common reaction to Hitler's invasion of the Soviet Union in 1941:

"If we see that Germany is winning, we ought to help Russia, and if we see Russia is winning, we ought to help Germany, and that way let them kill as many as possible."

each other's throats on the icy steppes of Russia. Or they would if the Soviets did not quickly collapse, as many military experts predicted.

Sound American strategy seemed to dictate speedy aid to Moscow while it was still afloat. Roosevelt immediately promised assistance and backed up his words by making some military supplies available. Several months later, interpreting the lend-lease law to mean that the defense of the USSR was now essential for the defense of the United States, he extended $1 billion in lend-lease—the first installment on an ultimate total of $11 billion. Meanwhile, the valor of the Red Army, combined with the white paralysis of an early Russian winter, had halted Hitler's invaders at the gates of Moscow.

With the surrender of the Soviet Union still a dread possibility, the drama-charged Atlantic Conference was held in August 1941. British Prime Minister Winston Churchill, with cigar embedded in his cherubic face, secretly met with Roosevelt on a warship off the foggy coast of Newfoundland. This was the first of a series of history-making conferences between the two statesmen for the discussion of common problems, including the menace of Japan in the Far East.

The most memorable offspring of this get-together was the eight-point Atlantic Charter. It was formally accepted by Roosevelt and Churchill and endorsed by the Soviet Union later that year. Suggestive of Wilson's Fourteen Points, the new covenant outlined the aspirations of the democracies for a better world at war's end.

Surprisingly, the Atlantic Charter was rather specific. While opposing imperialistic annexations, it promised that there would be no territorial changes contrary to the wishes of the inhabitants (self-determination). It further affirmed the right of a people to choose their own form of government and, in particular, to regain the governments abolished by the dictators. Among various other goals, the charter declared for disarmament and a peace of security, pending a "permanent system of general security" (a new League of Nations).

Liberals the world over took heart from the Atlantic Charter, as they had taken heart from Wilson's comparable Fourteen Points. It was especially gratifying to subject populations, like the Poles, who were then ground under the iron heel of a conqueror. But the agreement was roundly condemned in the United States by isolationists and others hostile to Roosevelt. What right, they charged, had "neutral" America to confer with belligerent Britain on common policies? Such critics missed the point: the nation was in fact no longer neutral.

U.S. Destroyers and Hitler's U-Boats Clash

Lend-lease shipments of arms to Britain on British ships were bound to be sunk by German wolfpack submarines. If the intent was to get the munitions to England, not to dump them into the ocean, the freighters would have to be escorted by U.S. warships. Britain simply did not have enough destroyers. The dangerous possibility of being "convoyed into war" had been mentioned in Congress during the lengthy debate on lend-lease, but administration spokespeople had brushed the idea aside. Their strategy was to make only one commitment at a time.

Roosevelt made the fateful decision to convoy in July 1941. By virtue of his authority as commander in chief of the armed forces, the president issued orders to the navy to escort lend-lease shipments as

Unexpected Guest, 1941
Stalin joins the democracies, Britain and America.

far as Iceland. The British would then shepherd them the rest of the way.

Inevitable clashes with submarines ensued on the Iceland run, even though Hitler's orders were to strike at American warships only in self-defense. In September 1941 the U.S. destroyer *Greer,* provocatively trailing a German U-boat, was attacked by the undersea craft, without damage to either side. Roosevelt then proclaimed a shoot-on-sight policy. On October 17 the escorting destroyer *Kearny,* while engaged in a battle with U-boats, lost eleven men when it was crippled but not sent to the bottom. Two weeks later the destroyer *Reuben James* was torpedoed and sunk off southwestern Iceland, with the loss of more than a hundred officers and enlisted men.

Neutrality was still inscribed on the statute books, but not in American hearts. Congress, responding to public pressures and confronted with a shooting war, voted in mid-November 1941 to pull the teeth from the now-useless Neutrality Act of 1939. Merchant ships could henceforth be legally armed, and they could enter the combat zones with munitions for Britain. Americans braced themselves for wholesale attacks by Hitler's submarines.

Heading for the Surprise Assault at Pearl Harbor

The blowup came, not in the Atlantic, but in the far-away Pacific. This explosion should have surprised no close observer, for Japan, since September 1940, had been a formal military ally of Nazi Germany—America's shooting foe in the North Atlantic.

Japan's position in the Far East had grown more perilous by the hour. It was still mired down in the costly and exhausting "China incident," from which it could extract neither honor nor victory. Its war machine was fatally dependent on immense shipments from the United States of steel, scrap iron, oil, and aviation gasoline. Such assistance to the Japanese aggressor was highly unpopular in America. But Roosevelt had resolutely held off an embargo, lest he goad the Tokyo warlords into a descent upon the oil-rich but defense-poor Dutch East Indies.

Washington, late in 1940, finally imposed the first of its embargoes on Japan-bound supplies. This blow was followed in mid-1941 by a freezing of Japanese assets in the United States and a cessation of all shipments of gasoline and other sinews of war. As the oil gauge dropped, the squeeze on Japan grew steadily more nerve-racking. Protracted delay was on the side of the United States. Japanese leaders were faced with two painful alternatives. They could either knuckle under to the Americans or break out of the embargo ring by a desperate attack on the oil supplies and other riches of Southeast Asia. The ticking of the clock, although soothing to American ears, drove the Japanese to madness.

Final tense negotiations with Japan took place in Washington during November and early December of 1941. The State Department insisted that the Japanese clear out of China, but to sweeten the pill offered to renew trade relations on a limited basis. Japanese imperialists, after waging a bitter war against the Chinese for more than four years, were unwilling to lose face by withdrawing at the behest of the United States. Faced with capitulation or continued conquest, they chose the sword. They had to put up or shut up, as the American press noted. They put up, believing that the war had been forced on them.

Officials in Washington, having "cracked" the top-secret code of the Japanese, knew that Tokyo's decision was for war. But the United States, as a democracy committed to public debate and action by Congress, could not shoot first. Roosevelt, misled by Japanese ship movements in the Far East, evidently expected the blow to fall on British Malaya or on the Philippines. No one in high authority in Washington seems to have believed that the Japanese were either strong enough or foolhardy enough to strike Hawaii.

But the paralyzing blow struck Pearl Harbor, while Tokyo was deliberately prolonging negotiations in Washington. Japanese bombers, winging in from distant aircraft carriers, attacked without warning on the "Black Sunday" morning of December 7, 1941. It was a date, as Roosevelt told Congress, "which will live in infamy." About three thousand casualties were inflicted on American personnel; many aircraft were destroyed; the battleship fleet was virtually wiped out when all eight of the craft were sunk or otherwise immobilized; and numerous small vessels were damaged or destroyed. Fortunately for America, the three priceless aircraft carriers happened to be outside the harbor.

An angered Congress, the next day, officially recognized the war that had been "thrust" upon the United States. The roll call in the Senate and House fell only one vote short of unanimity. Germany and

embargo—stop trade
perilous—dangerous

The Battleship *West Virginia,*
wrecked at Pearl Harbor

Italy, allies of Japan, spared Congress the indecision of debate by declaring war on December 11, 1941. This challenge was formally accepted on the same day by a unanimous vote of both Senate and House. The unofficial war, already of many months' duration, was now official.

America's Transformation from Bystander to Belligerent

Japan's hara-kiri gamble in Hawaii paid off only in the short run. True, the Pacific fleet was largely destroyed or immobilized, but the sneak attack aroused and united America as almost nothing else could have done. To the very day of the blowup, a strong majority of Americans still wanted to keep out of war. But the bombs that pulverized Pearl Harbor blasted the isolationists into silence. The only thing left to do, growled isolationist Senator Wheeler, was "to lick hell out of them."

But Pearl Harbor was not the full answer to the question of why the United States went to war. This treacherous attack was but the last explosion in a long chain reaction. Following the fall of France, Americans were confronted with a devil's dilemma. They desired above all to stay out of the conflict; yet

they did not want Britain to be knocked out. They wished to halt Japan's conquests in the Far East—conquests that menaced not only American trade and security but international peace as well. To keep Britain from collapsing, the Roosevelt administration felt compelled to extend the unneutral aid that invited attacks from German submarines. To keep Japan from expanding, Washington undertook to cut off vital Japanese supplies with embargoes that invited possible retaliation. Rather than let democracy die and dictatorship rule supreme, most citizens were evidently determined to support a policy that might lead to war. It did.

Clearheaded Americans had come to the conclusion that no nation was safe in an era of international anarchy. Appeasement—the tactic of

---

Roosevelt's war message to Congress began with these famous words:

"Yesterday, December 7, 1941—a date which will live in infamy—the United States of America was suddenly and deliberately attacked by naval and air forces of the Empire of Japan."

throwing the weaker persons out of the sleigh to the pursuing wolves—had been tried, but the devoured victims had merely whetted dictatorial appetites. Power-drunk dictators had flouted international law and decency. Asserting the philosophy that might makes right, they had cynically negotiated nonag-gression treaties with their intended targets, merely to lull them into a false sense of security. Most Americans were determined to stand firm—and let war come if it must—because they were convinced that with ruthless dictators on the loose, the world could not long remain half-enchained and half-free.

Chronology

1933	FDR torpedoes the London Economic Conference United States recognizes the Soviet Union FDR declares Good Neighbor policy toward Latin America
1934	Tydings-McDuffie Act provides for Philippine independence on July 4, 1946 Reciprocal Trade Agreements Act
1935	Mussolini invades Ethiopia First U.S. Neutrality Act
1936	Second U.S. Neutrality Act
1936-1939	Spanish Civil War
1937	U.S. Neutrality Act of 1937 *Panay* incident Japan invades China
1938	Hitler seizes Austria Munich Conference
1939	Hitler seizes all of Czechoslovakia Nazi-Soviet pact World War II begins in Europe with Hitler's invasion of Poland U.S. Neutrality Act of 1939
1940	Fall of France Hitler invades Denmark, Norway, the Netherlands, and Belgium United States invokes first peacetime draft Havana Conference Battle of Britain Bases-for-destroyers deal with Britain FDR defeats Willkie for presidency
1941	Lend-Lease Act Hitler attacks the Soviet Union Atlantic Charter Japan attacks Pearl Harbor

SUGGESTED READINGS

PRIMARY SOURCE DOCUMENTS

For background on the date that will live in infamy, see *Pearl Harbor Attack: Hearings Before the Joint Committee on the Investigation of the Pearl Harbor Attack*, 79th Congress, 1st Session* (1946) Franklin D. Roosevelt's "Quarantine the Aggressors" speech (1937), in Richard Hofstadter, *Great Issues in American History* (1982), revealed what would become the goal of the president's foreign policy in succeeding years. See also Roosevelt's "Press Conference on Lend-Lease" (1940), in *The Public Papers and Addresses of Franklin D. Roosevelt, 1940 Volume* (1941), pp. 606–608.* For opposition to lend-lease, see the speech of January 12, 1941, by Montana Senator Burton K. Wheeler, *Congressional Record*, 77 Cong., 1 sess., Appendix, pp. 178–179.* Charles A. Lindbergh elaborated the isolationist position in *The New York Times*, April 24, 1941, p. 12.* Warren F. Kimball, ed., *Churchill and Roosevelt: The Complete Correspondence* (1984), is enlightening on many topics.

*An asterisk indicates that the document, or an excerpt from it, can be found in Thomas A. Bailey and David M. Kennedy, eds., *The American Spirit: United States History as Seen by Contemporaries*, 9th ed. (Boston: Houghton Mifflin, 1998).

SECONDARY SOURCES

Indispensable and comprehensive is Robert Dallek, *Franklin D. Roosevelt and American Foreign Policy, 1932–1945* (1979). Also strong is Kenneth S. Davis, *FDR: Into the Storm, 1937–1940; A History* (1993). A useful brief survey is John E. Wiltz, *From Isolation to War, 1931–1941* (1968). More specialized is Lloyd Gardner, *Economic Aspects of New Deal Diplomacy* (1964). Isolationism is ably handled in Manfred Jonas, *Isolationism in America, 1935–1941* (1966); Thomas Guinsburg, *The Pursuit of Isolationism in the United States Senate from Versailles to Pearl Harbor* (1982); and Robert A. Divine, *The Reluctant Belligerent* (1965). Sympathetic to the isolationists is Wayne S. Cole, *Roosevelt and the Isolationists, 1932–1945* (1983) and *Charles A. Lindbergh and the Battle Against American Intervention in World War II* (1974). On Good Neighborism consult Bryce Wood, *The Making of the Good Neighbor Policy* (1961), and Irwin F. Gellman, *Good Neighbor Diplomacy* (1979). The Spanish Civil War is dealt with in Allen Guttmann, *The Wound in the Heart: America and the Spanish Civil War* (1962), and Douglas Little, *Malevolent Neutrality: The United States, Great Britain, and the Origins of the Spanish Civil War* (1985). For the Far East, see Dorothy Borg, *The United States and the Far Eastern Crisis of 1933–1938* (1964), P. W. Schroeder, *The Axis Alliance and Japanese-American Relations, 1941* (1958), and Akira Iriye and Warren Cohen, eds., *American, Chinese, and Japanese Perspectives on Wartime Asia, 1931–49* (1990). Warren F. Kimball analyzes *The Most Unsordid Act: Lend Lease, 1939–1941* (1969). David L. Porter examines *The Seventy-Sixth Congress and World War II, 1939–1940* (1979). The Japanese attack on Pearl Harbor is considered in Gordon W. Prange, *At Dawn We Slept* (1981), and Michael Slackman, *Target: Pearl Harbor* (1990). A provocative analysis of the reasons (or lack of them) for U.S. entry into the conflict is Bruce Russett, *No Clear and Present Danger* (1972). See also Donald Cameron Watt, *How War Came: The Immediate Origins of the Second World War, 1938–1939* (1989).

38

America in World War II

1941–1945

Never before have we had so little time in which to do so much.

FRANKLIN D. ROOSEVELT, 1942

The Allies Trade Space for Time

The United States was plunged into the inferno of World War II with the most stupefying and humiliating military defeat in its history. In the dismal months that ensued, the democratic world teetered on the edge of disaster.

Japan's fanatics forgot that whoever stabs a king must stab to kill. A wounded but still potent American giant pulled itself out of the mud of Pearl Harbor, grimly determined to avenge the bloody treachery. "Get Japan first" was the cry that rose from millions of infuriated Americans, especially on the Pacific Coast. These outraged souls regarded America's share in the global conflict as a private war of vengeance in the Pacific, with the European front a kind of holding operation.

But Washington, in the so-called ABC-1 agreement with the British, had earlier and wisely adopted the grand strategy of "getting Germany first." If America diverted its main strength to the Pacific, Hitler might crush both the Soviet Union and Britain and then emerge unconquerable in Fortress Europe. But if Germany was knocked out first, the combined Allied forces could be concentrated on Japan, and its daring game of conquest would be up. Meanwhile, just enough American strength would be sent to the Pacific to prevent Japan from digging in too deeply.

The get-Germany-first strategy was the solid foundation on which all American military strategy was built. But it encountered much ignorant criticism from two-fisted Americans who thirsted for revenge against Japan. Aggrieved protests were also registered by shorthanded American commanders in the Pacific and by Chinese and Australian allies.

Throwing in an Extra Charge, 1941   The Japanese attack on Pearl Harbor in 1941 excited virulent hatred of Japan among Americans, who called for a war of vengeance against the treacherous aggressor. Anti-Japanese sentiment remained stronger than anti-German sentiment throughout the war.

But President Roosevelt, a competent strategist in his own right, wisely resisted these pressures.

Given time, the Allies seemed bound to triumph. But would they be given time? True, they had on their side the great mass of the world's population, but the wolf is never intimidated by the number of the sheep. The United States was the mightiest military power on earth—potentially. But wars are won with bullets, not blueprints. Indeed America came perilously close to losing the war to the well-armed aggressors before it could begin to throw its full weight onto the scales.

Time, in a sense, was the most needed munition. Expense was no limitation. The overpowering problem confronting America was to retool itself for all-out war production, while praying that the dictators would not meanwhile crush the democracies. Haste was all the more imperative because the highly skilled German scientists might turn up with unbeatable secret weapons, including rocket bombs and perhaps even atomic arms.

America's task was far more complex and backbreaking than during World War I. It had to feed, clothe, and arm itself, as well as transport its forces to regions as far separated as Britain and Burma. More than that, it had to send a vast amount of food and munitions to its hard-pressed allies, who stretched all the way from the USSR to Australia. Could the American people, reputedly "gone soft," measure up to this Herculean task? Was democracy "rotten" and "decadent," as the dictators sneeringly proclaimed?

The Shock of War

National unity was no worry, thanks to the electrifying blow by the Japanese at Pearl Harbor. American Communists had denounced the Anglo-French "imperialist" war before Hitler attacked Stalin in 1941, but they now clamored for an unmitigated assault on the Axis powers. The handful of strutting pro-Hitlerites in the United States melted away, while millions of Italian-Americans and German-Americans loyally supported the nation's war program. In contrast to World War I, when the patriotism of millions of immigrants was hotly questioned, World War II actually speeded the assimilation of many ethnic groups into American society. Immigration had been choked off for almost two decades before 1941, and America's ethnic communities were now composed of well-settled members, whose votes were crucial to Franklin Roosevelt's Democratic party. Consequently, there was virtually no government witch-hunting of minority groups, as had happened in World War I.

A painful exception was the plight of some 110,000 Japanese-Americans, concentrated on the

American song titles aimed at the Japanese after Pearl Harbor were "Goodby, Mamma, I'm Off to Yokohama," "We Are the Sons of the Rising Guns," "Oh, You Little Son of an Oriental," "To Be Specific, It's Our Pacific," and "The Sun Will Soon Be Setting on the Land of the Rising Sun."

Pacific Coast (see "Makers of America: The Japanese," pp. 850–851). The Washington top command, fearing that they might act as saboteurs for Japan in case of invasion, forcibly herded them together in concentration camps, though about two-thirds of them were American-born U.S. citizens. This brutal precaution was both unnecessary and unfair, as the loyalty and combat record of Japanese-Americans proved to be admirable. But a wave of post–Pearl Harbor hysteria, backed by the long historical swell of anti-Japanese prejudice on the West Coast, temporarily robbed many Americans of their good sense—and their sense of justice. The internment camps deprived these uprooted Americans of dignity and basic rights; the internees also lost hundreds of millions of dollars in property and foregone earnings. The wartime Supreme Court in 1944 upheld the constitutionality of the Japanese relocation in *Korematsu* v. *U.S.* But more than four decades later, in 1988, the U.S. government officially apologized for its actions and approved the payment of reparations of $20,000 to each camp survivor.

The war prompted other changes in the American mood. Many programs of the once-popular New Deal—including the Civilian Conservation Corps, the Works Progress Administration, and the National Youth Administration—were wiped out by the conservative Congress elected in 1942. Roosevelt declared in 1943 that "Dr. New Deal" was going into retirement, to be replaced by "Dr. Win-the-War." His announcement acknowledged not only the urgency of the war effort but the power of the revitalized conservative forces in the country. The era of New Deal reform was over.

World War II was no idealistic crusade, as World War I had been. The Washington government did make some effort to propagandize at home and

Enemy Aliens   When the United States suddenly found itself at war with Germany, Italy, and Japan in December 1941, non-citizen German, Italian, and Japanese immigrants became "enemy aliens" and were required to register with the authorities. Several hundred resident Germans and Italians were detained in internment camps, but the harshest treatment was meted out to the Japanese, some 110,000 of whom, non-citizens and citizens alike, were eventually interned. Ironically, the two Japanese-American Boy Scouts posting this notice in Los Angeles would soon be on their way to a government detention camp.

abroad with the Atlantic Charter, but the accent was on action. Opinion polls in 1942 revealed that nine out of ten Americans could cite no provisions of the Atlantic Charter. A majority then, and a near-majority two years later, confessed to having "no clear idea what the war is about." All Americans knew was that they had a dirty job on their hands and that the only way out was forward. They went about their bloody task with astonishing efficiency.

Building the War Machine

The war crisis caused the drooping American economy to snap to attention. Massive military orders—over $100 billion in 1942 alone—almost instantly soaked up the idle industrial capacity of the still-lingering Great Depression. Orchestrated by the War Production Board, American factories poured forth

> *A young Japanese-American recorded in his diary on May 3, 1942, some of his first impressions of his hastily thrown-together "detention center":*
>
> "I saw a soldier in a tall guardhouse near the barbed wire and did not like it because it reminds me of a concentration camp."

The Japanese

In 1853 the American commodore Matthew Perry sailed four gunboats into Japan's Uraga Bay and demanded that the nation open itself to diplomatic and commercial exchange with the United States. Perry's arrival ended two centuries of Japan's self-imposed isolation, and eventually led to the overthrow of the last Japanese shogun (military ruler) and the restoration of the emperor. Within two decades of Perry's arrival, Japan's new "Meiji" government had launched the nation on an ambitious program of industrialization and militarization designed to make it the economic and political equal of the Western powers.

As Japan rapidly modernized, its citizens increasingly took ship for America. A steep land tax imposed by the Meiji government to pay for its reforms drove more than 300,000 Japanese farmers off their land. In 1884 the Meiji government permitted Hawaiian planters to recruit contract laborers from among this displaced population. By the 1890s many Japanese were sailing beyond Hawaii to the ports of Long Beach, San Francisco, and Seattle.

Between 1885 and 1924, roughly 200,000 Japanese migrated to Hawaii, and around 180,000 more ventured to the U.S. mainland. They were a select group: because the Meiji government saw overseas Japanese as representatives of their homeland, it strictly regulated emigration. Thus Japanese immigrants to America arrived with more money than their European counterparts. Also, because of Japan's system of compulsory education, Japanese immigrants on average were better educated and more literate than European immigrants.

Women as well as men migrated. The Japanese government, wanting to avoid the problems of an itinerant bachelor society that it observed among the Chinese in the United States, actively promoted women's migration. Although most Japanese immigrants were young men in their twenties and thirties, thousands of women also ventured to Hawaii and the mainland as contract laborers or "picture brides," so called because their courtship had consisted exclusively of an exchange of photographs with their prospective husbands.

Like many Chinese and European immigrants, most Japanese who came to America expected to stay only temporarily. They planned to work hard for wages that were high by Japanese standards and then to return home and buy land. In Hawaii most Japanese labored on the vast sugar cane planta-

Pledging in Vain   These Japanese-American school children in San Francisco were soon evacuated along with their parents.

Japanese-Owned Loganberry Farm, Centerville, California, 1942 Successful farmers for generations before World War II, many Japanese-Americans lost their land forever as a consequence of wartime internment.

Japanese-American Evacuees, 1942 This farm family in Los Angeles County was "relocated" shortly after this photograph was taken.

tions. On the mainland they initially found migratory work on the railroads or in fish, fruit, or vegetable canneries. A separate Japanese economy of restaurants, stores, and boardinghouses soon sprang up in cities to serve the immigrant's needs.

From such humble beginnings, many Japanese—particularly those on the Pacific Coast—quickly moved into farming. In the late-nineteenth century, the spread of irrigation shifted California agriculture from grain to fruits and vegetables, and the invention of the refrigerated railcar opened hungry new markets in the East. The Japanese, with centuries of experience in intensive farming, arrived just in time to take advantage of these developments. As early as 1910, Japanese farmers produced 70 percent of California's strawberries, and by 1940 they grew 95 percent of the state's snap beans and more than half its tomatoes. One Japanese farmer, known as the Potato King, sent his children to Harvard and Stanford universities and died in 1926 with an estate valued at $15 million.

But the very success of the Japanese proved a lightning rod for trouble. On the West Coast, Japanese immigrants had long endured racist barbs and social segregation. Increasingly, white workers and farmers, jealous of Japanese success, pushed for immigration restrictions. Bowing to this pressure, President Theodore Roosevelt in 1908 negotiated

the "Gentleman's Agreement," under which the Japanese government voluntarily agreed to limit emigration. In 1913 the California legislature denied Japanese immigrants already living in the United States the right to own land.

Discriminated against in their adopted homeland, Japanese immigrants (the "Issei," from the Japanese word for *first*) became more determined than ever that their American-born children (the "Nissei," from the Japanese word for *second*) would succeed. Japanese parents encouraged their children to learn English, to excel in school, and to get college educations. Many Nissei grew up in two worlds, a fact they often recognized by Americanizing their Japanese names. Although education and acculturation did not protect the Nissei from the hysteria of World War II, those assets did give them a springboard to success in the postwar era.

OURS...to fight for

Freedom of Speech   *Freedom of Worship*

Freedom from Want   *Freedom from Fear*

The Four Freedoms, by Norman Rockwell   In his speech to Congress of January 6, 1941, requesting lend-lease aid to the Allies, President Roosevelt spoke eloquently of the "four freedoms" then threatened by Nazi and Japanese aggression. They are here given pictorial representation by Norman Rockwell, probably the most popular and best-loved American artist of the time.

an avalanche of weaponry: 40 billion bullets, 300,000 aircraft, 76,000 ships, 86,000 tanks, and 2.6 million machine guns. Miracle-man shipbuilder Henry J. Kaiser was dubbed "Sir Launchalot" for his prodigies of ship construction; one of his ships was fully assembled in fourteen days, complete with life jackets and coat hangers.

The War Production Board halted manufacture of nonessential items such as passenger cars. It assigned priorities for transportation and access to raw materials. When the Japanese invasion of British Malaya and the Dutch East Indies snapped America's lifeline of natural rubber, the government imposed a national speed limit and gasoline

rationing in order to conserve rubber and built fifty-one synthetic-rubber plants. By war's end they were far outproducing the prewar supply.

Farmers, too, rolled up their sleeves and increased their output. The armed forces drained the farms of workers, but heavy new investment in agricultural machinery and improved fertilizers more than made up the difference. In 1944 and 1945, blue-jeaned farmers hauled in record-breaking billion-bushel wheat harvests.

These wonders of production also brought economic strains. Full employment and scarce consumer goods fueled a sharp inflationary surge in 1942. The Office of Price Administration eventually brought ascending prices under control with extensive regulations. Rationing held down the consumption of critical goods such as meat and butter, though some "black marketeers" and "meatleggers" cheated the system. The War Labor Board (WLB) imposed ceilings on wage increases.

Labor unions, whose membership grew from about 10 million to more than 13 million workers during the war, fiercely resented the government-dictated wage ceilings. Despite the no-strike pledges of most of the major unions, a rash of labor walkouts plagued the war effort. Prominent among the strikers were the United Mine Workers, who several times were called off the job by their crusty and iron-willed chieftain, John L. Lewis.

Threats of lost production through strikes became so worrisome that Congress, in June 1943, passed the Smith-Connally Anti-Strike Act. This act authorized the federal government to seize and operate tied-up industries. Strikes against any government-operated industry were made a criminal offense. Under the act, Washington took over the coal mines and, for a brief period, the railroads. Yet work stoppages, although dangerous, actually accounted for less than 1 percent of the total working hours of the United States' wartime laboring force—a record better than blockaded Britain's. American workers, on the whole, were commendably committed to the war effort.

Manpower and Womanpower

The armed services enlisted nearly 15 million men in World War II—and some 216,000 women, who were employed for noncombat duties. Best known of these "women in arms" were the WAACS (army),

WAVES (navy), and SPARS (Coast Guard). As the draft net was tightened after Pearl Harbor, millions of young men were plucked from their homes and clothed in "GI" (government issue) outfits. As the arsenal of democracy, the United States exempted certain key categories of industrial and agricultural workers from the draft, in order to keep its mighty industrial and food-producing machines humming.

But even with these exemptions, the draft left the nation's farms and factories so short of personnel that new workers had to be found. An agreement with Mexico in 1942 brought thousands of Mexican agricultural workers, called *braceros,* across the border to harvest the fruit and grain crops of the West. The *bracero* program outlived the war by some twenty years, becoming a fixed feature of the agricultural economy in many western states.

Even more dramatic was the march of women onto the factory floor. More than 6 million women took up jobs outside the home; over half of them had never before worked for wages. Many of them were mothers, and the government was obliged to

> *Poster appeals and slogans urging women to enlist in the WAACS (Women's Army Auxiliary Corps) were "Speed Them Back, Join the WAAC," "I'd Rather Be with Them— than Waiting for Them," "Back the Attack, Be a WAAC! For America Is Calling," and (a song throwback to World War I) "The WAACS and WAVES Will Win the War, Parlez Vous."*

set up some 3,000 day-care centers to care for "Rosie the Riveter's" children while she drilled the fuselage of a heavy bomber or joined the links of a tank track. When the war ended, Rosie and many of her sisters were in no hurry to put down their tools. They wanted to keep on working and often did. The war thus foreshadowed an eventual revolution in the roles of women in American society.

War Workers   More than 6 million women—3 million of them homemakers who had never before worked for wages—entered the work force during World War II. In contrast to the experience of women workers in World War I, many of these newly employed women continued as wage workers after the war ended.

Yet the war's immediate impact on women's lives has frequently been exaggerated. The great majority of American women—especially those with husbands present in the home or with small children to care for—did not work for wages in the wartime economy but continued in their traditional roles. In both Britain and the Soviet Union, a far greater percentage of women, including mothers, were pressed into industrial employment as the gods of war laid a much heavier hand on those societies than they did on the United States. A poll in 1943 revealed that a majority of American women would not take a job in a war plant if it were offered.

At war's end, two-thirds of women war-workers left the labor force. Many of these were forced out of their jobs by employers and unions eager to re-employ returning servicemen. But half of them told census takers that they quit their jobs voluntarily because of family obligations. The immediate post-war period witnessed not a permanent widening of women's employment opportunities, but a wide-spread rush into suburban domesticity and the mothering of the "baby boomers" who were born by the tens of millions in the decade and a half after 1945. America was destined to experience a thoroughgoing revolution in women's status later in the postwar period, but that epochal change was only beginning to gather momentum in the war years.

Wartime Migrations

The war also proved to be a demographic cauldron, churning and shifting the American population. Many of the 15 million men and women in uniform, having seen new sights and glimpsed new horizons, chose not to go home again at war's end. War industries sucked people into boomtowns like Los Angeles, Detroit, Seattle, and Baton Rouge. California's population grew by nearly 2 million. The South experienced especially dramatic changes. Franklin Roosevelt had called the South "the nation's number one economic problem" in 1938; when war came, he seized the opportunity to accelerate the region's

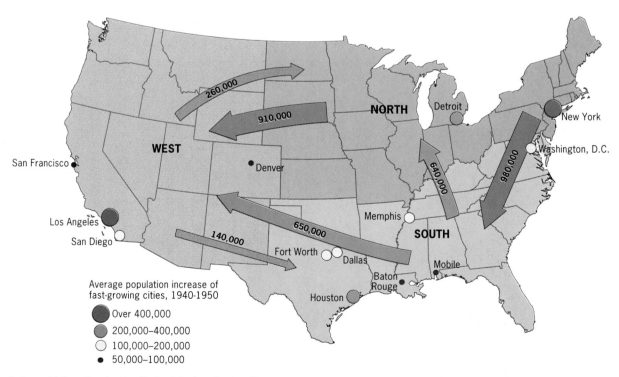

Internal Migration in the United States During World War II   Few events in American history have moved the American people about so massively as World War II. The West and the South boomed, and several war-industry cities grew explosively. A majority of migrants from the South were blacks; 1.6 million African-Americans left the region in the 1940s. (United States Department of Labor, Bureau of Labor Statistics.)

economic development. The states of the old Confederacy received a disproportionate share of defense contracts, including nearly $6 billion of federally financed industrial facilities. Here were the seeds of the postwar blossoming of the "Sunbelt."

Despite this economic stimulus in the South, some 1.6 million blacks left the land of their ancient enslavement to seek jobs in the war plants of the West and North (see "Makers of America: The Great African-American Migration," pp. 856–857). Forever after, race relations constituted a national, not a regional, issue. Explosive tensions developed over employment, housing, and segregated facilities. Black leader A. Philip Randolph, head of the Brotherhood of Sleeping Car Porters, threatened a massive "Negro March on Washington" in 1941 to demand equal opportunities for blacks in war jobs and in the armed forces. Roosevelt's response was to issue an executive order forbidding discrimination in defense industries. In addition, the president established the Fair Employment Practices Commission (FEPC) to monitor compliance with his edict. Blacks were also drafted into the armed forces, though they were still generally assigned to service branches rather than combat units and subjected to petty degradations such as segregated blood banks for the wounded. But in general the war helped to embolden blacks in their long struggle for equality. They rallied behind the slogan "Double V"—victory over the dictators abroad and over racism at home. Membership in the National Association for the Advancement of Colored People (NAACP) shot up almost to the half-million mark, and a new militant organization, the Congress of Racial Equality (CORE), was founded in 1942.

The northward migration of African-Americans accelerated after the war, thanks to the advent of the mechanical cotton picker—an invention whose impact rivaled that of Eli Whitney's cotton gin. Introduced in 1944, this new mechanical marvel did the work of fifty people at about one-eighth the cost. Overnight, the Cotton South's historic need for cheap labor disappeared. Their muscle no longer required in Dixie, some 5 million black tenant farmers and sharecroppers headed north in the three decades after the war. Theirs was one of the great migrations in American history, comparable in size to the immigrant floods from Ireland, Italy, and Poland. Within a single generation, a near majority of African-Americans gave up their historic homeland and their rural way of life. By 1970 half of all blacks lived outside of the South, and *urban* had become almost a synonym for *black*. The speed and scale of these changes jolted the migrants and sometimes convulsed the communities that received them.

The war also prompted an exodus of Native Americans from the reservations. Thousands of

Segregation in the Military
These pilots belonged to the 99th Fighter Pursuit Squadron, an all-black wing of the Army Air Corps. Virtually all military units were racially segregated in World War II, and the 99th was one of the few black outfits in any service to see combat. Trained at the Institute founded in Alabama by Booker T. Washington in 1881, they were known as the "Tuskegee Airmen."

The Great African-American Migration

So many black southerners took to the roads during World War II that local officials could not keep track of the migrants passing through their towns. Black workers on the move—a vast population with no addresses or telephone numbers—crowded into boardinghouses, camped out in cars, and clustered in the juke joints of roadside America en route to a new, uncertain future in northern and western cities.

Southern cotton fields and tobacco plantations had yielded but slender sustenance to African-American farmers, few of whom owned their own land. Instead, most had struggled on as tenants and sharecroppers. The Great Depression had been yet another setback, for when the New Deal farm program paid growers to leave land fallow, many landlords pocketed the money, evicting the tenants from the now-fallow fields. Initially, the wartime defense boom only worsened matters, as new military bases and armories ate up farmland, uprooting still more tenants. With few other opportunities in the depression-ravaged country, dispossessed former sharecroppers toiled as seasonal farm laborers or found themselves without work, without shelter, and without hope for the future.

The shiny new war plants and busy shipyards of the South offered little solace to African-Americans.

The Migration of the Negro, by Jacob Lawrence, 1940–1941   Artist Jacob Lawrence depicted the migration of southern blacks to the North during and after World War II in a series of paintings. The first panel of the series bears the description: "During the World War there was a great migration north by southern Negroes."

The Home Front   Though often fighting against prejudice and discrimination, many African-American migrants from the rural South during World War II found their first industrial jobs in wartime defense plants.

In 1940 and 1941, the labor-hungry war machine soaked up white unemployment but commonly denied jobs to southerners who had the "wrong" skin color. Government training programs in the South, designed to teach skills necessary for work in aircraft, shipbuilding, machine manufacture, electronics, and other war industries, enrolled few blacks. When the army constructed a camp near Petersburg, Virginia, it imported white carpenters from all parts of the United States, although hundreds of available black carpenters resided nearby. Nor was discrimination restricted to skilled positions. Federal investigators discovered that even unskilled jobs in defense industries were closed to black applicants. Fed up with such injustices, many African-Americans headed for shipyards, factories, foundries, and fields north of the Mason-Dixon line, where their willing hands found waiting work in abundance.

Angered by the racism that drove their people from the South, black leaders pressured President Roosevelt into declaring that "there shall be no discrimination in the employment of workers in defense industries or government because of race, creed, color, or national origin." This executive order was but a tenuous, rudimentary step; still, many blacks were heartened to see a presidential response to their protests. The war experience emboldened the civil rights movement, adding momentum and tactical knowledge to the cause. NAACP leader Walter White concluded that the war "immeasurably magnified the Negro's awareness of the disparity between the American profession and practice of democracy. . . ."

By war's end many African-Americans made new homes in the North and Far West, shifting the heart of America's black community from southern plantations to northern cities. There they competed for scarce housing in overcrowded slums and paid outrageous rents to secure a foothold in the few neighborhoods of northern cities that would admit them.

The entire nation was now grappling with the evil of racism, as bloody World War II–era riots in Detroit, New York, and other cities tragically revealed. And the trek to northern cities, while an economic boon for most African-Americans, did not end the intractable national problem of black poverty. African-Americans found themselves the first to be fired when the war plants closed down. And black teenage unemployment, a scourge to this day, dates from World War II. Southern farms, though providing the barest subsistence, had been all too generous in dispensing work to all members of the family—work not so readily found by African-American youth in today's decaying northern cities.

Detroit Race Riot, 1943   A black passenger is dragged from a streetcar.

The Mechanical Cotton Picker   The advent of this new machine in the 1940s deprived millions of southern blacks of their traditional meager employment in the cotton fields. Their massive displacement by the mechanical picker set off one of the greatest migrations in American history.

The Covered Wagon, 1934   The war uprooted and shifted millions of Americans, including Navajos like these.

Indian men and women found war work in the major cities, and thousands more answered Uncle Sam's call to arms. More than 90 percent of Indians resided on reservations in 1940; four decades later almost half lived in cities, with a large concentration in southern California.

Some 25,000 Native American men served in the armed forces. Comanches in Europe and Navajos in the Pacific made especially valuable contributions as "code talkers." They transmitted radio messages in their native languages, which were incomprehensible to the Germans and the Japanese.

The sudden rubbing against one another of unfamiliar peoples produced some distressingly violent friction. In 1943 young "zoot-suit"–clad Mexicans and Mexican-Americans in Los Angeles were viciously attacked by Anglo sailors who cruised the streets in taxicabs, searching for victims. Order was restored only after the Mexican ambassador made an emotional plea, pointing out that such outbreaks were grist for Nazi propaganda mills. At almost the same time, an even more brutal race riot that killed twenty-five blacks and nine whites erupted in Detroit.

Holding the Home Front

Despite these ugly episodes, Americans on the home front suffered little from the war, compared to the peoples of the other fighting nations. By war's end much of the planet was a smoking ruin. But in America the war invigorated the economy and lifted the country out of a decade-long depression. The gross national product vaulted from less than $100 billion in 1940 to more than $200 billion in 1945. Corporate profits rose from about $6 billion in 1940 to almost twice that amount four years later. ("If you are going to try to go to war in a capitalist country," said Secretary of War Henry Stimson, "you have to let business make money out of the process, or business won't work.") Despite wage ceilings, overtime pay fattened pay envelopes. Disposable personal income, even after payment of wartime taxes, more than doubled. On December 7, 1944, the third anniversary of Pearl Harbor, Macy's department store rang up the biggest sales day in its history. Americans had never had it so good—and they wanted it a lot better. When price controls were finally lifted in 1946, America's pent-up lust to consume pushed prices up 33 percent in less than two years. The rest of the world, meanwhile, was still clawing its way out from under the rubble of war.

The hand of government touched more American lives more intimately during the war than ever before. The war, perhaps even more than the New Deal, pointed the way to the post-1945 era of big-government interventionism. Every household felt the constraints of the rationing system. Millions of men and women worked for Uncle Sam in the armed forces. Millions more worked for him in the defense industries, where their employers and unions were monitored by the FEPC and the WLB, and their personal needs were cared for by government-sponsored housing projects, day-care facilities, and health plans. The Office of Scientific Research and Development channeled hundreds of millions of dollars into university-based scientific research, establishing the partnership between the government and universities that underwrote America's technological and economic leadership in the postwar era.

The flood of war dollars—not the relatively modest rivulet of New Deal spending—at last swept the plague of unemployment from the land. War, not enlightened social policy, cured the depression. As the postwar economy continued to depend dangerously on military spending for its health, many observers looked back to the years 1941–1945 as the origins of a "warfare-welfare state."

The conflict was phenomenally expensive. The wartime bill amounted to more than $330 billion—ten times the direct cost of World War I and twice as much as *all* previous federal spending since 1776. Roosevelt would have preferred to follow a pay-as-you-go policy to finance the war, but the costs were simply too gigantic. The income-tax net was expanded to catch about four times as many people as before, and maximum tax rates rose as high as 90 percent. But despite such drastic measures, only about two-fifths of the war costs were paid from current revenues. The remainder was borrowed. The national debt skyrocketed from $49 billion in 1941 to $259 billion in 1945. When production finally slipped into high gear, the war was costing about $10 million an hour. This was the price of victory over such implacable enemies.

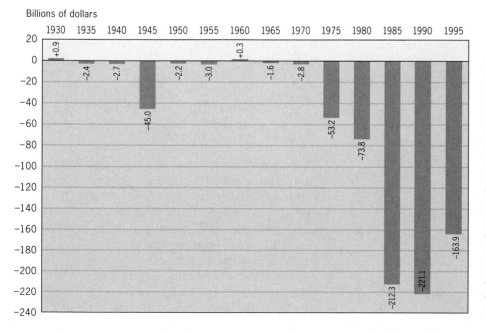

Surpluses and Deficits in the Federal Budget, 1930–1995 British economist John Maynard Keynes had urged massive deficit spending by the government as a cure for the Great Depression. Never seriously tried in the 1930s, deficit spending prompted by World War II proved a surefire tonic for depression-spawned unemployment. The federal budget remained in chronic deficit in the post–World War II years and mounted to staggering sums in the 1980s and 1990s. (*Historical Statistics of the United States* and *Statistical Abstract of the United States* relevant years.)

The Rising Sun in the Pacific

Early successes of the efficient Japanese militarists were breathtaking: they realized that they would have to win quickly or lose slowly. Seldom, if ever, has so much territory been conquered so rapidly with so little loss.

Simultaneously with the assault on Pearl Harbor, the Japanese launched widespread and uniformly successful attacks on various Far Eastern bastions. These included the American outposts of Guam, Wake, and the Philippines. In a dismayingly short time, the Japanese invader seized not only the British-Chinese port of Hong Kong but also British Malaya, with its critically important supplies of rubber and tin.

Nor did the Japanese tide stop there. The overambitious soldiers of the emperor, plunging into the snake-infested jungles of Burma, cut the famed Burma road. This was the route over which the United States had been trucking a trickle of munitions to the armies of the Chinese Generalissimo Jiang Jieshi (Chiang Kai-shek), who was still resisting the Japanese invader in China. Thereafter, intrepid American aviators were forced to fly a handful of war supplies to Jiang "over the hump" of the towering Himalaya Mountains from the India-Burma theater. Meanwhile, the Japanese had lunged southward against the oil-rich Dutch East Indies. The jungle-matted islands speedily fell to the assailants, after the combined British, Australian, Dutch, and American naval and air forces had been smashed at an early date by their numerically superior foe.

Better news came from the Philippines, which succeeded dramatically in slowing down the mikado's warriors for five months. The Japanese promptly landed a small but effective army, and General Douglas MacArthur, the eloquent and egotistical American commander, withdrew to a strong defensive position at Bataan, not far from Manila. There about twenty thousand American troops, supported by a much larger force of ill-trained Filipinos, held off violent Japanese attacks until April 9, 1942. The defenders, reduced to eating mules and monkeys, heroically traded their lives for time in the face of hopeless odds. They grimly joked while vainly hoping for reinforcements:

We're the battling bastards of Bataan;
No Mamma, no Papa, no Uncle Sam. . . .

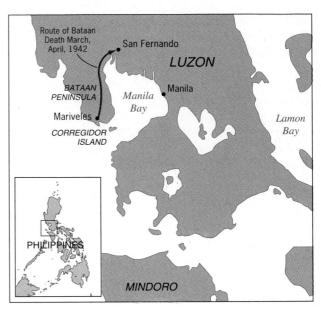

Corregidor and Bataan

Before the inevitable American surrender, General MacArthur was ordered by Washington to depart secretly for Australia, there to head the resistance against the Japanese. Leaving by motorboat and airplane, he proclaimed, "I shall return." After the battered remnants of his army had hoisted the white flag, they were treated with vicious cruelty in the infamous 85-mile (137-kilometer) Bataan death march to prisoner-of-war camps. The island fortress of Corregidor, in Manila Harbor, held out until May 6, 1942, when it too surrendered and left Japanese forces in complete control of the Philippine archipelago.

Japan's High Tide at Midway

The aggressive warriors from Japan, making hay while the Rising Sun shone, pushed relentlessly southward. They invaded the turtle-shaped island of New Guinea, north of Australia, and landed on the Solomon Islands, from which they threatened Australia itself. Their onrush was finally checked by a crucial naval battle fought in the Coral Sea, in May 1942. An American carrier task force, with Australian support, inflicted heavy losses on the victory-flushed Japanese. For the first time in history,

Hell in the Pacific   Assaulting Japanese island-fortresses in the Pacific was a bloody, costly business. These American soldiers perished as they stepped ashore at Buna beach in New Guinea in 1942. Their damaged landing craft wallows in the surf behind them.

the fighting was all done by carrier-based aircraft, and neither fleet saw or fired a shot directly at the other.

Japan next undertook to seize Midway Island, more than 1,000 miles (1,600 kilometers) northwest of Honolulu. From this strategic base, it could launch devastating assaults on Pearl Harbor and perhaps force the weakened American Pacific fleet into destructive combat—possibly even compel the United States to negotiate a cease-fire in the Pacific. An epochal naval battle was fought near Midway from June 3–6, 1942. Admiral Chester W. Nimitz, a high-grade naval strategist, directed a smaller but skillfully maneuvered carrier force, under Admiral Raymond A. Spruance, against the powerful invad-

ing fleet. The fighting was all done by aircraft, and the Japanese broke off action after losing four vitally important carriers.

Midway was a pivotal victory. Combined with the Battle of the Coral Sea, the U.S. success at Midway halted Japan's juggernaut. But the thrust of the Japanese into the eastern Pacific did net them America's fog-girt islands of Kiska and Attu, in the Aleutian archipelago, off Alaska. This easy conquest aroused fear of an invasion of the United States from the northwest. Much American strength was consequently diverted to the defense of Alaska, including the construction of the "Alcan" highway through Canada.

Yet the Japanese imperialists, overextended in 1942, suffered from "victory disease." Their appetites were bigger than their stomachs. If they had only dug in and consolidated their gains, they would have been much more difficult to dislodge once the tide turned.

American Leapfrogging Toward Tokyo

Following the heartening victory at Midway, the United States for the first time was able to seize the initiative in the Pacific. In August 1942 American ground forces gained a toehold on Guadalcanal Island, in the Solomons, in an effort to protect the lifeline from America to Australia through the Southwest Pacific. An early naval defeat inflicted by the Japanese shortened American supplies dangerously, and for weeks the U.S. troops held onto the malarial island only by their fingernails. After several desperate sea battles for naval control, the Japanese troops evacuated Guadalcanal in February 1943. Japanese losses were 20,000, compared to 1,700 for the Americans. That casualty ratio of more than ten to one, Japanese to American, persisted throughout the Pacific war.

American and Australian forces, under General MacArthur, meanwhile had been hanging on courageously to the southeastern tip of New Guinea, the last buffer protecting Australia. The scales of war gradually began to tip as the American navy, including submarines, inflicted lethal losses on Japanese supply ships and troop carriers. Conquest of the north coast of New Guinea was completed by August 1944, after General MacArthur had fought his way westward through tropical jungle hells. This hard-won victory was the first leg on his long return journey to the Philippines.

The United States Navy, with marines and army divisions doing the meat-grinder fighting, had meanwhile been "leapfrogging" the Japanese-held islands in the Pacific. Old-fashioned strategy dictated that the American forces, as they drove toward Tokyo, should reduce the fortified Japanese outposts on their flank. This course would have taken many bloodstained months, for the holed-in defenders were prepared to die to the last man in their caves. The new strategy of island hopping called for bypassing some of the most heavily fortified Japanese posts, capturing nearby islands, setting up airfields on them, and then neutralizing the enemy bases through heavy bombing. Deprived of essential supplies from the homeland, Japan's outposts would slowly wither on the vine—as they did.

Brilliant success crowned the American attacks on the Japanese island strongholds in the Pacific, where Admiral Nimitz skillfully coordinated the efforts of naval, air, and ground units. In May and August of 1943, Attu and Kiska in the Aleutians were easily retaken. In November 1943, "bloody Tarawa" and Makin, both in the Gilbert Islands, fell after suicidal resistance. In January and February 1944, the key outposts of the Marshall Islands group succumbed after savage fighting.

Especially prized were the Marianas, including America's conquered Guam. From bases in the Marianas, the United States' new B-29 superbombers could carry out round-trip bombing raids on Japan's home islands. The assault on the Marianas opened on June 19, 1944, with what American pilots called the "Great Marianas Turkey Shoot." A combination of the combat superiority of the recently developed American "Hellcat" fighter plane and the new technology of the antiaircraft proximity fuse destroyed nearly 250 Japanese aircraft, with a loss of only 29 American planes. The following day, in the Battle of

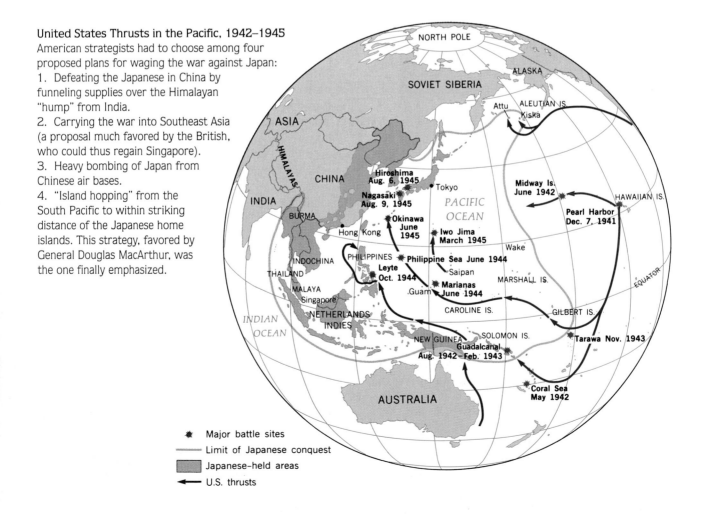

United States Thrusts in the Pacific, 1942–1945
American strategists had to choose among four proposed plans for waging the war against Japan:
1. Defeating the Japanese in China by funneling supplies over the Himalayan "hump" from India.
2. Carrying the war into Southeast Asia (a proposal much favored by the British, who could thus regain Singapore).
3. Heavy bombing of Japan from Chinese air bases.
4. "Island hopping" from the South Pacific to within striking distance of the Japanese home islands. This strategy, favored by General Douglas MacArthur, was the one finally emphasized.

the Philippine Sea, U.S. naval forces sank several Japanese carriers. The Japanese navy never recovered from these massive losses of planes, pilots, and ships.

After fanatical resistance, including a mass suicide leap of surviving Japanese soldiers and civilians from "Suicide Cliff" on Saipan, the major islands of the Marianas fell to the U.S. attackers in July and August 1944. With these unsinkable aircraft carriers now available, virtual round-the-clock bombing of Japan began in November 1944.

The Allied Halting of Hitler

Early setbacks for America in the Pacific were paralleled in the Atlantic. Hitler had entered the war with a formidable fleet of ultramodern submarines, which ultimately operated in "wolf packs" with frightful effect, especially in the North Atlantic, the Caribbean, and the Gulf of Mexico. During ten months of 1942 more than 500 merchant ships were reported lost—111 in June alone—as ship destruction far outran construction.

The tide of subsea battle turned with agonizing slowness. Old techniques, such as escorting convoys of merchant vessels and dropping depth bombs from destroyers, were strengthened by air patrol, the newly invented technology of radar, and the bombing of submarine bases. "Keep 'Em Sailing" was the motto of oil-begrimed merchant seamen, hundreds of whom perished as unsung heroes in icy seas. Eventually, Allied antisubmarine tactics improved substantially, thanks especially to British code-breakers, who had cracked the Germans' "Enigma" codes and could therefore pinpoint the locations of the U-boats lurking in the North Atlantic.

Not until the spring of 1943 did the Allies clearly have the upper hand against the U-boat. If they had not won the battle of the Atlantic, Britain would have been forced under, and a second front could not have been launched from its island springboard. Victory over the undersea raiders was nerve-rackingly narrow. When the war ended, Hitler was about to mass-produce a fearsome new submarine —one that could remain underwater indefinitely and cruise at seventeen knots when submerged.

Meanwhile, the turning point of the land-air war against Hitler had come late in 1942. The British had launched a thousand-plane raid on Cologne in

> *British Prime Minister Winston Churchill (1874–1965) observed in a speech (May 1943),*
>
> "The proud German Army has by its sudden collapse, sudden crumbling and breaking up . . . once again proved the truth of the saying, 'The Hun [German] is always either at your throat or at your feet.'"

May. In August 1942 they were joined by the American air force and were cascading bombs on German cities. The Germans under Marshal Erwin Rommel—the "Desert Fox"—had driven eastward across the hot sands of North Africa into Egypt, perilously close to the Suez Canal. A breakthrough would have spelled disaster for the Allies. But late in October 1942, British General Bernard Montgomery delivered a withering attack at El Alamein, west of Cairo. With the aid of several hundred hastily shipped American Sherman tanks, he speedily drove the enemy back to Tunisia, more than 1,000 miles (1,600 kilometers) away.

On the Soviet front, the unexpected successes of the red army gave a new lift to the Allied cause. In September 1942 the Russians stalled the German steamroller at rubble-strewn Stalingrad, graveyard of Hitler's hopes. More than a score of invading divisions, caught in an icy noose, later surrendered or were "mopped up." In November 1942 the resilient Russians unleashed a crushing counteroffensive, which was never seriously reversed. A year later, Stalin had regained about two-thirds of the blood-soaked Soviet motherland wrested from him by the German invader.

The North African Second Front

Soviet leaders meanwhile continued to plead for the British and the Americans to open a "second front" in the west. Soviet losses were already staggering in 1942: millions of soldiers and civilians lay dead, and Hitler's armies had overrun most of the western USSR. Anglo-American losses at this time could be counted in the thousands. By war's end, in fact, the grave had closed over some 20 million Soviets, and

Women at War   Members of the Women's Army Corps disembark in North Africa in 1944.

their country had been laid waste to an extent equaling the utter devastation of the United States from Chicago to the Atlantic seaboard. It is small wonder the Kremlin leaders impatiently insisted that their western Allies get into the European war and divert their fair share of German strength.

Many Americans, including FDR, were eager to begin a diversionary invasion of France in 1942 or 1943. They feared that the Soviets, unable to hold out forever against Germany, might make a separate peace, as they had in 1918, and leave the western Allies to face Hitler's fury alone. Some American leaders had other concerns as well. If the Soviets did all the fighting, Secretary of War Stimson reflected, "I think that will be dangerous business for us at the end of the war. Stalin won't have much of an opinion of people who have done that and we will not be able to share much of the postwar world with him."

But British military planners, remembering their appalling losses in 1914–1918, were not enthusiastic about a frontal assault on German-held France. It might end in complete disaster. They preferred to attack Hitler's Fortress Europe through the "soft underbelly" of the Mediterranean, while gathering strength for an eventual thrust across the English Channel. Faced with British reluctance and the woeful lack of adequate shipping and other resources, the Americans reluctantly agreed to postpone a massive invasion of Europe.

An invasion of French-held North Africa was a compromise second front. It seemed less risky than a premature descent upon the coast of France, yet it would serve as a partial answer to the Kremlin's demands for a diversion. If successful, it would open the Axis-dominated Mediterranean to lifeline communication with India and other parts of Asia.

The highly secret Allied attack on North Africa, launched in November 1942, was headed by a gifted and easy-smiling American general, Dwight D. ("Ike") Eisenhower, a master of organization and conciliation. As a joint Allied operation ultimately involving some 400,000 men (British, Canadian, French, and chiefly American) and about 850 ships, the invasion was the mightiest waterborne effort up to that time in history.

At the outset the surprise landing in North Africa was highly successful. The neutralized French put up only token resistance. After savage fighting with the Germans, who inflicted a sharp setback on the green Americans at Kasserine Pass, the remnants of the German-Italian army were finally trapped in Tunisia. Some 266,000 dazed survivors surrendered in May 1943.

The North African campaign, though redeeming one continent, in itself was not conclusive. It was not the beginning of the end, but "the end of the beginning." Skeptical Soviets scoffed at this second-rate second front, but valuable lessons were learned for the full-fledged invasion of France.

The Rough Road to Rome

New blows were now planned by the Allies. At Casablanca, in newly occupied French Morocco, President Roosevelt, who had boldly flown the Atlantic, met in a historic conference with Winston Churchill in January 1943. The Big Two agreed to step up the Pacific war, invade Sicily, increase pressure on Italy, and insist upon an "unconditional surrender" of the enemy—a phrase earlier popularized by General Grant during the Civil War. Such an unyielding policy would presumably hearten the ultrasuspicious Soviets, who professed to fear separate Allied peace negotiations. It would also forestall charges of broken armistice terms, such as had come after 1918. Paradoxically, the tough-sounding unconditional surrender declaration was an admission of the weakness of the western Allies. Still unable in 1943 to mount the kind of second front their Soviet partner desperately demanded, the British and the Americans had little but words to offer Stalin.

"Unconditional surrender" proved to be one of the most controversial moves of the war. The main criticism was that it steeled the enemy to fight to a last-bunker resistance, while discouraging antiwar groups in Germany from revolting. Although there was some truth in these charges, no one can prove that "unconditional surrender" either shortened or lengthened the war. But by helping to destroy the German government utterly, the harsh policy immensely complicated the problems of post-war reconstruction.

The victorious Allied forces—American, British, and Canadian—now turned against the not-so-soft underbelly of Europe. Sicily fell, in August 1943, after sporadic but sometimes bitter resistance. Shortly before the conquest of the island, Mussolini was deposed and a new Rome government was set up. Italy surrendered unconditionally early in September 1943, while Allied troops were pouring onto the toe of the Italian boot. President Roosevelt, referring to the three original Axis accomplices—Germany, Italy, and Japan—joked grimly that it was now one down and two to go. Two years later Mussolini, together with his mistress, was brutally lynched by his own people. Both bodies were ingloriously hung up by the heels for public display.

But if Italy dropped out of the war, the Germans did not drop out of Italy. Hitler's well-trained troops resisted the Allied invaders with methodical and infuriating stubbornness. The luckless Italians, turning their coats, declared war on Germany in October 1943. "Sunny Italy" proceeded to belie its name, for in the snow-covered and mud-caked mountains of its elongated peninsula occurred some of the filthiest, bloodiest, and most frustrating fighting of the war.

For many months Italy appeared to be a dead end, as the Allied advance was halted by a seemingly impregnable German defense centered around the ancient monastery of Monte Cassino. After a touch-and-go assault on the Anzio beachhead, Rome was finally taken on June 4, 1944. Two days later, when the tremendous cross-channel invasion of France began, Italy became a kind of sideshow. But the Allies, with limited manpower, continued to fight their way slowly and painfully into northern Italy. On May 2, 1945, only five days before Germany's official surrender, several hundred thousand Axis troops in Italy laid down their arms and became prisoners of war.

The Italian campaign, though agonizingly slow, was by no means fruitless. It opened the Mediterranean, diverted some German divisions from the blazing Soviet and French fronts, and provided air bases for bombing assaults on German Austria and southern Germany. Yet it may also have delayed the main Allied invasion of Europe, from England across the English Channel to France, by many months—allowing more time for the Soviet army to advance into Eastern Europe.

The Big Two British Prime Minister Winston Churchill and U.S. President Franklin D. Roosevelt meet at the Casablanca Conference in Morocco, January 1943.

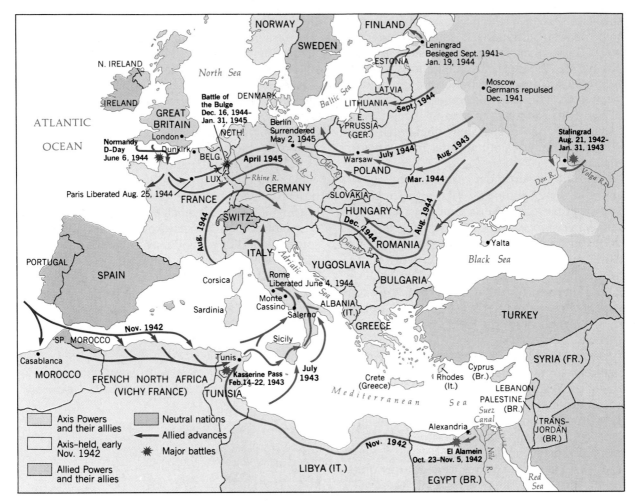

World War II in Europe and North Africa, 1939–1945

Eisenhower's D-Day Invasion of France

The Soviets had never ceased their clamor for an all-out second front, and the time rapidly approached for Churchill, Roosevelt, and Stalin to meet in person to coordinate the promised effort. Marshal Joseph Stalin, with a careful eye on Soviet military operations, balked at leaving Moscow. President Roosevelt, who jauntily remarked in private, "I can handle that old buzzard," was eager to confer with him. The president seemed confident that Rooseveltian charm could woo the hardened conspirator of the Kremlin from his nasty communist ways.

Teheran, the capital of Iran (Persia), was finally chosen as the meeting place. To this ancient city Roosevelt riskily flew, after a stopover conference in Cairo with Britain's Churchill and China's Jiang Jieshi regarding the war against Japan. At Teheran the discussions among Stalin, Roosevelt, and Churchill—from November 28 to December 1, 1943—progressed smoothly. Perhaps the most important achievement was agreement on broad plans, especially those for launching Soviet attacks on Germany from the east simultaneously with the prospective Allied assault from the west.

Preparations for the cross-channel invasion of France were gigantic. Britain's fast-anchored isle virtually groaned with munitions, supplies, and troops, as nearly 3 million fighting men were read-

Allies Landing in Normandy, June 6, 1944   Nine-foot ocean swells on invasion day made loading the assault landing craft, such as the one pictured here, treacherous business. Many men were injured or tossed into the sea as the bathtublike amphibious vessels bobbed wildly up and down alongside the troop transports. As the vulnerable boats churned toward the beach, some officers led their tense, grim-faced troops in prayer. One major, recalling the remarkable Battle of Agincourt in 1415, quoted from Shakespeare's *Henry V:* "He that outlives this day, and comes safe home / Will stand a tip-toe when this day is named."

ied. Because the United States was to provide most of the Allied warriors, the overall command was entrusted to an American, General Eisenhower. He had already distinguished himself in the North African and Mediterranean campaigns, not only for his military capacity but also for his gifts as a conciliator of clashing Allied interests.

French Normandy, less heavily defended than other parts of the European coast, was pinpointed for the invasion assault. On D-Day, June 6, 1944, the enormous operation, which involved some 4,600 vessels, unwound. Stiff resistance was encountered from the Germans, who had been misled by a feint into expecting the blow to fall farther north. The Allies had already achieved mastery of the air over France. They were thus able to block reinforcements by crippling the railroads, while worsening German fuel shortages by bombing gasoline-producing plants.

The Allied beachhead, at first clung to with fingertips, was gradually enlarged, consolidated, and reinforced. After desperate fighting, the invaders finally broke out of the German iron ring that enclosed the Normandy landing zone. Most spectacular were the lunges across France by American armored divisions, brilliantly commanded by blustery and profane General George S. ("Blood 'n' Guts") Patton. The retreat of the German defenders was hastened when an American-French force landed in August 1944 on the southern coast of France and swept northward. With the assistance of the French "underground," Paris was liberated in

Liberating France
Two GIs (U.S. soldiers) hustled these captured Germans off to a prisoner-of-war camp during the fighting for the French port of Brest in 1944.

August 1944, amid exuberant manifestations of joy and gratitude.

Allied forces rolled irresistibly toward Germany, and many of the Americans encountered places, like Château-Thierry, familiar to their fathers in 1918. "Lafayette, we are here again," quipped some of the American soldiers. The first important German city (Aachen) fell to the Americans in October 1944, and the days of Hitler's "thousand-year *Reich*" were numbered.

FDR: The Fourth-Termite of 1944

The presidential campaign of 1944, which was bound to divert energy from the war program, came most awkwardly as the awful conflict roared to its climax. But the normal electoral processes continued to function, despite some loose talk of suspending them "for the duration."

Victory-starved Republicans met in Chicago with hopeful enthusiasm. They quickly nominated the short, mustachioed, and dapper Thomas E. Dewey, popular vote-getting governor of New York. Regarded as a liberal, he had already made a national reputation as a prosecutor of grafters and racketeers in New York City. His shortness and youth—he was only forty-two—had caused one veteran New Dealer to sneer that the candidate had cast his diaper into the ring. To offset Dewey's mild internationalism, the convention nominated for the vice presidency a strong isolationist, handsome and white-maned Senator John W. Bricker of Ohio. Yet the platform called for an unstinted prosecution of the war and for the creation of a new international organization to maintain peace.

FDR, aging under the strain, was the "indispensable man" of the Democrats. No other major figure was available, and the war was apparently grinding to its finale. He was nominated at Chicago on the first ballot by acclamation. But in a sense he was the "forgotten man" of the convention, for in view of his age, an unusual amount of attention was focused on the vice presidency.

The scramble for the vice-presidential plum turned into something of a free-for-all. Henry A. Wallace, onetime "plow 'em under" secretary of agriculture, had served four years as vice president and desired a renomination. But conservative Democrats distrusted him as an ill-balanced and unpredictable liberal. A "ditch Wallace" move developed tremendous momentum, despite the popularity of Wallace with large numbers of voters and many of the delegates. With Roosevelt's blessing, the vice-presidential nomination finally went to smiling and self-assured Senator Harry S Truman of Missouri ("the new Missouri Compromise"). Hitherto inconspicuous, he had recently attained national visibility as the efficient chairman of a Senate committee conducting an investigation of wasteful war expenditures. Nobody had much against him or on him.

Roosevelt Defeats Dewey

A dynamic Dewey took the offensive, for Roosevelt was too consumed with directing the war to spare much time for speechmaking. The vigorous young "crime buster," with his beautiful baritone voice and polished diction, denounced the tired and quarrelsome "old men" in Washington. He proclaimed repeatedly that after "twelve long years" of New Dealism, it was "time for a change." As for the war, Dewey would not alter the basic strategy but would fight it better—a type of "me-tooism" ridiculed by the Democrats. The fourth-term issue did not figure prominently, now that the ice had been broken by Roosevelt's third term. But "Dewey-eyed" Republicans, half-humorously, professed to fear fifth and sixth terms by the "lifer" in the White House.

In the closing weeks of the campaign, Roosevelt left his desk for the stump. He was stung by certain Republican charges, including alleged aspersions on his pet Scottie dog, Fala. He was also eager to show himself, even in chilling rains, to spike well-founded rumors of failing health.

Substantial assistance came from the new Political Action Committee of the CIO, which was organized to get around the law banning the direct use of union funds for political purposes. Zealous CIO members, branded as Communists by the Republicans, rang countless doorbells and asked, with pointed reference to the recent depression, "What were you doing in 1932?" At times Roosevelt seemed to be running again against Hoover. As in every one of his previous three campaigns, FDR was opposed by a majority of the newspapers, which were owned chiefly by Republicans. Roosevelt, as customary, won a sweeping victory: 432 to 99 in the Electoral College; 25,606,585 to 22,014,745 in the popular totals. Elated, he quipped that "the first twelve years are the hardest."

> *During the bitter campaign of 1944, Roosevelt's pre–Pearl Harbor policies came under sharp attack from Congresswoman Clare Boothe Luce (1903–1987) (the "Blonde Bombshell"), who violently blasted Roosevelt:*
>
> "[He] lied us into war because he did not have the political courage to lead us into it."

Roosevelt won primarily because the war was going well. A winning pitcher is not ordinarily pulled from the game. Foreign policy was a decisive factor with untold thousands of voters, who concluded that Roosevelt's experienced hand was needed in fashioning a future organization for world peace. The dapper Dewey, cruelly dubbed "the little man on top of the wedding cake," had spoken smoothly of international cooperation, but his isolationist running mate, Bricker, had implanted serious doubts. The Republican party was still suffering from the taint of isolationism fastened on it by the Hardingites.

The Last Days of Hitler

By mid-December 1944, the month after Roosevelt's fourth-term victory, Germany seemed to be wobbling on its last legs. The Soviet surge had penetrated eastern Germany. Allied aerial "blockbuster" bombs, making the "rubble bounce" with around-the-clock attacks, were falling like giant explosive hailstones on cities, factories, and transportation arteries. The German western front seemed about to buckle under the sledgehammer blows of the United States and its Allies.

Hitler then staked everything on one last throw of his reserves. Secretly concentrating a powerful force, he hurled it, on December 16, 1944, against the thinly held American lines in the heavily befogged and snow-shrouded Ardennes forest. His objective was the Belgian port of Antwerp, key to the Allied supply operation. Caught off guard, the outmanned Americans were driven back, creating a deep "bulge" in the Allied line. The ten-day penetration was finally halted after the 101st Airborne Division had stood firm at the vital bastion of Bastogne.

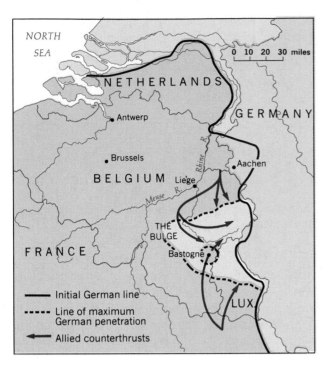

Battle of the Bulge,
December 1944–January 1945

even to bomb the rail lines that carried the victims to the camps. But until the war's end, the full dimensions of the "Holocaust" had not been known. When the details were revealed, the whole world was aghast.

The vengeful Soviets, clawing their way forward from the east, reached Berlin in April 1945. After desperate house-to-house fighting, followed by an orgy of pillage and rape, they captured the bomb-shattered city. Adolf Hitler, after a hasty marriage to his mistress, committed suicide in an underground bunker on April 30, 1945.

Tragedy had meanwhile struck the United States. President Roosevelt, while relaxing at Warm Springs, Georgia, suddenly died from a massive cerebral hemorrhage on April 12, 1945. The crushing burden of twelve depression and war years in the White House had finally taken its toll. Knots of confused, leaderless citizens gathered to discuss the future anxiously, as a bewildered, unbriefed Vice President Truman took the helm.

On May 7, 1945, what was left of the German government surrendered unconditionally. May 8 was officially proclaimed V-E Day—Victory in Europe Day—and was greeted with frenzied rejoicing in the Allied countries.

The commander, Brigadier General A. C. McAuliffe, defiantly answered the German demand for surrender with one word: "Nuts." Reinforcements were rushed up, and the last-gasp Hitlerian offensive was at length bloodily stemmed in the Battle of the Bulge.

In March 1945, forward-driving American troops reached Germany's Rhine River, where, by incredibly good luck, they found one strategic bridge undemolished. Pressing their advantage, General Eisenhower's troops reached the river Elbe in April 1945. There, a short distance south of Berlin, American and Soviet advance guards dramatically clasped hands, amid cries of *"Amerikanskie tovarishchi"* (American comrades). The conquering Americans were horrified to find blood-bespattered and still-stinking concentration camps, where the German Nazis had engaged in scientific mass murder of "undesirables," including an estimated 6 million Jews. The Washington government had long been informed about Hitler's campaign of genocide against the Jews and had been reprehensibly slow to take steps against it. Roosevelt's administration had bolted the door against large numbers of Jewish refugees, and his military commanders declined

American and Soviet Soldiers Meet in Germany, 1945
Such friendly sights soon became rare as mutual suspicion deepened.

A Nazi Death Camp   These gaunt survivors of the Nazi concentration camp at Evensee, Austria, greeted their liberators from the U.S. Third Army on May 7, 1945. Scanty food and wretched sanitation claimed almost as many lives in the death camps as the horrid gas chambers. Although the world had some knowledge of these conditions before the war's end, the full revelation of Hitler's atrocities as the Allies overran Germany in the spring of 1945 stunned and sickened the invading troops.

Japan Dies Hard

Japan's rickety bamboo empire meanwhile was tottering to its fall. American submarines—"the silent service"—were sending the Japanese merchant marine to the bottom so fast they were running out of prey. All told, these undersea craft destroyed 1,042 ships, or about 50 percent of Japan's entire life-sustaining merchant fleet.

Giant bomber attacks were more spectacular. Launched from Saipan and other captured Mariana Islands, they were reducing the enemy's fragile cities to cinders. The massive fire-bomb raid on Tokyo, March 9–10, 1945, was annihilating. It destroyed over 250,000 buildings, gutted a quarter of the city, and killed an estimated 83,000 people—a loss comparable to that later inflicted by atomic bombs.

General MacArthur was also on the move. Completing the conquest of jungle-draped New Guinea, he headed northwest for the Philippines, en route to Japan, with six hundred ships and 250,000 men. In a scene well staged for the photographers, he splashed ashore at Leyte Island, on October 20, 1944, with the summons, "People of the Philippines, I have returned. . . . Rally to me."

Japan's navy—still menacing—now made one last-chance effort to destroy MacArthur by wiping out his transports and supply ships. A gigantic clash at Leyte Gulf, fought on the sea and in the air, was actually three battles (October 23–26, 1944). The Americans won all of them, though the crucial engagement was almost lost when Admiral William F. ("Bull") Halsey was decoyed away by a feint.

Japan was through as a sea power: it had lost about sixty ships in the greatest naval battle of all time. American fleets, numbering more than four thousand vessels, now commanded the western Pacific. Several battleships, raised from the mud of Pearl Harbor, were exacting belated but sweet revenge.

Overrunning Leyte, MacArthur next landed on the main Philippine island of Luzon, in January 1945. Manila was his major objective; the ravaged city fell in March, but the Philippines were not conquered until July. Victory was purchased only after bitter fighting against holed-in Japanese, who took a toll of over sixty thousand American casualties.

America's steel vise was tightening mercilessly around Japan. The tiny island of Iwo Jima, needed as a haven for damaged American bombers returning from Japan, was captured in March 1945. This desperate twenty-five-day assault cost over four thousand American dead.

The Flag Raising at Iwo Jima   Atop Mt. Suribachi, press photographer Joe Rosenthal snapped this dramatic picture, probably the most famous of the war.

Okinawa, a well-defended Japanese island, was next on the list: it was needed for closer bases from which to blast and burn enemy cities and industries. Fighting dragged on from April to June of 1945. Japanese soldiers, fighting with incredible courage from their caves, finally sold Okinawa for fifty thousand American casualties, while suffering far heavier losses themselves.

The American navy, which covered the invasion of Okinawa, sustained severe damage. Japanese suicide pilots ("kamikazes") in an exhibition of mass hara-kiri for their god-emperor, crashed their bomb-laden planes onto the decks of the invading fleet. All told, the death squads sank over thirty ships and badly damaged scores more.

Atomic Awfulness

Strategists in Washington were meanwhile planning an all-out invasion of the main islands of Japan—an invasion that presumably would cost hundreds of thousands of American (and even more Japanese)

casualties. Tokyo, recognizing imminent defeat, had secretly sent peace feelers to Moscow, which had not yet entered the Far Eastern war. The Americans, having broken the secret Japanese radio codes, knew of these feelers. But bomb-scorched Japan still showed no outward willingness to surrender *unconditionally* to the Allies.

The Potsdam conference, held near Berlin in July 1945, sounded the death knell of the Japanese. There President Truman, still new on his job, met in a seventeen-day parley with Joseph Stalin and the British leaders. The conferees issued a stern ultimatum to Japan: surrender or be destroyed. American bombers showered the dire warning on Japan in tens of thousands of leaflets, but no encouraging response was forthcoming.

America had a fantastic ace up its sleeve. Early in 1940, after Hitler's wanton assault on Poland, Roosevelt was persuaded by American and exiled scientists, notably German-born Albert Einstein, to push ahead with preparations for unlocking the secret of an atomic bomb. Congress, at Roosevelt's blank-check request, blindly made available nearly $2 billion. Many military minds were skeptical of this "damned professor's nonsense," but fears that the Germans might first acquire such an awesome weapon provided a powerful spur to action. Ironically, Germany eventually abandoned its own atomic project as too costly. And as it happened, the war against Germany ended before the American weapon was ready. In a cruel twist of fate, Japan—not Germany, the original target—suffered the fate of being the first nation subjected to atomic bombardment.

The huge atomic project was pushed feverishly forward, as American know-how and industrial power were combined with the most advanced scientific knowledge. Much technical skill was provided by British and refugee scientists, who had fled to America to escape the torture chambers of the dictators. Finally, in the desert near Alamogordo, New Mexico, on July 16, 1945, the experts detonated the first awesome and devastating atomic device.

With Japan still refusing to surrender, the Potsdam threat was fulfilled. On August 6, 1945, a lone American bomber dropped one atomic bomb on the military-base city of Hiroshima, Japan. In a blinding flash of death, followed by a funnel-shaped cloud, about 180,000 people were left killed, wounded, or missing. Some 70,000 of them died instantaneously. Sixty thousand more soon perished from burns and radiation disease.

Two days later, on August 8, Stalin entered the war against Japan, exactly on the deadline date previously agreed upon with his allies. Soviet armies speedily overran the depleted Japanese defenses in Manchuria and Korea in a six-day "victory parade" that involved several thousand Russian casualties. Stalin was evidently determined to be in on the kill, lest he lose a voice in the final division of Japan's holdings.

Fanatically resisting Japanese, though facing atomization, still did not surrender. American aviators, on August 9, dropped a second atomic bomb on the naval-base city of Nagasaki. The explosion took a horrible toll of about eighty thousand people killed or missing.

At last the Japanese nation could endure no more. On August 10, 1945, Tokyo sued for peace on one condition: that Hirohito, the bespectacled Son of Heaven, be allowed to remain on his ancestral throne as nominal emperor. Despite their "unconditional surrender" policy, the Allies accepted this condition on August 14, 1945. The Japanese, though losing face, were able to save both their exalted ruler and what was left of their native land.

The formal end came, with dramatic force, on September 2, 1945. Official surrender ceremonies were conducted by General MacArthur on the battleship *Missouri* in Tokyo Bay. At the same time

Hiroshima, Japan, August 1945   Two stunned survivors walk through the unbelievable destruction. The single atomic blast at Hiroshima killed an estimated 130,000 Japanese.

The Japanese Surrender Representatives of the Japanese government sign the surrender instrument on the deck of the battle-ship *Missouri* in Tokyo harbor, September 2, 1945. General Douglas MacArthur is standing in front of the microphones.

Americans at home hysterically celebrated V-J Day—Victory in Japan Day—after the most horrible war in history had ended in mushrooming atomic clouds.

The Allies Triumphant

World War II proved to be terribly costly. American forces suffered some 1 million casualties, about one-third of which were deaths. Compared with other wars, the proportion killed by wounds and disease was sharply reduced, owing in part to the use of blood plasma and "miracle" drugs, notably penicillin. Yet heavy though American losses were, the Soviet allies suffered casualties many times greater—perhaps 20 million people killed.

America was fortunate in emerging with its mainland virtually unscathed. Two Japanese submarines, using shells and bombers, had rather harmlessly attacked the California and Oregon coast, and a few balloons, incendiary and otherwise, had drifted across the Pacific. But that was about all.

Much of the rest of the world was utterly destroyed and destitute. America alone was untouched and healthy—oiled and muscled like a prize bull, standing astride the world's ruined landscape.

This complex conflict was the best-fought war in America's history. Though unprepared for it at the outset, the nation was better prepared than for the others, partly because it had begun to buckle on its armor about a year and a half before the war officially began. It was actually fighting German submarines in the Atlantic months before the explosion in the Pacific at Pearl Harbor. In the end the United States showed itself to be resourceful, tough, adaptable—able to accommodate itself to the tactics of an enemy who was relentless and ruthless.

American military leadership proved to be of the highest order. A new crop of war heroes emerged in brilliant generals like Eisenhower, MacArthur, and Marshall (chief of staff) and in imaginative admirals like Nimitz and Spruance. President Roosevelt and Prime Minister Churchill, as kindred spirits, collaborated closely in planning strategy. "It is fun to be in the same decade with you," FDR once cabled Churchill.

Industrial leaders were no less skilled, for marvels of production were performed almost daily. Assembly lines proved as important as battle lines; and victory went again to the side with the most smokestacks. The enemy was almost literally smothered by bayonets, bullets, bazookas, and bombs. Hitler and his Axis coconspirators had chosen to make war with machines, and the ingenious Yankees could ask for nothing better. They demonstrated again, as they had in World War I, that the American way of war was simply more—more men, more weapons, more machines, more technology, and more money than any enemy could hope to match. From 1940 to 1945, the output of American factories was simply phenomenal. As Winston Churchill remarked, "Nothing succeeds like excess."

Hermann Goering, a Nazi leader, had sneered, "The Americans can't build planes—only electric iceboxes and razor blades." Democracy had given its answer, as the dictators, despite long preparation, were overthrown and discredited. It is true that an unusual amount of direct control was exercised over the individual by the Washington authorities during the war emergency. But the American people preserved their precious liberties without serious impairment.

V-J Day: Crowds Cheering at Times Square, by Edward Dancig, 1947 Russian-born American artist Edward Dancig captured the feelings of triumph and relief that Americans felt at the end of World War II. His painting shows the V-J (Victory in Japan) Day celebration of August 15, 1945, in New York's Times Square.

Chronology

1941 The United States declares war on Japan
Germany declares war on the United States
Randolph plans black march on Washington
Fair Employment Practices Commission
(FEPC) established

1942 Japanese-Americans sent to internment
camps
Japan conquers the Philippines
Battle of the Coral Sea
Battle of Midway
United States invades North Africa
Congress of Racial Equality (CORE) founded

1943 Allies hold Casablanca conference
Allies invade Italy
Smith-Connally Anti-Strike Act
"Zoot-suit" riots in Los Angeles
Race riot in Detroit

1943 Japanese driven from Guadalcanal
Teheran conference

1944 *Korematsu* v. *U.S.*
D-Day invasion of France
Battle of Marianas
Roosevelt defeats Dewey for presidency

1944-
1945 Battle of the Bulge

1945 Roosevelt dies; Truman assumes presidency
Germany surrenders
Battles of Iwo Jima and Okinawa
Potsdam conference
Atomic bombs dropped on Hiroshima and
Nagasaki
Japan surrenders

World War II: Triumph or Tragedy?

After World War II ended in 1945, many historians were convinced that the tragedy could have been averted if only the United States had awakened earlier from its isolationist illusions. These scholars condemned the policies and attitudes of the 1930s as a "retreat from responsibility." Much of the historical writing in the postwar period contained the strong flavor of medicine to ward off another infection by the isolationist virus.

This approach fell into disfavor during the Vietnam War in the 1960s, when many U.S. policymakers defended their actions in Southeast Asia by making dubious comparisons to the decade before World War II. Some scholars responded by arguing that the "lessons" of the 1930s—especially about the need to avoid "appeasement" and to take quick and decisive action against "aggressors"—could not properly be applied to any and all subsequent situations. Ho Chi Minh, they pointed out, was not Hitler, and Vietnam was not Nazi Germany. One controversial product of this line of thinking was Bruce Russett's *No Clear and Present Danger* (1972), which argued that the United States had no clearly defined national interests at stake in 1941, and that both the nation and the world might have been better off without U.S. intervention. This analysis paralleled "revisionist" commentaries written in the 1930s about U.S. participation in World World I.

Although few scholars fully accept Russett's conclusions, more recently writing on American entry into World War II has tended to avoid finding in that episode lessons for posterity. Attention has focused, rather, on the wisdom or folly of specific policies, such as Washington's hard line toward Tokyo throughout 1941, when the possibil-

ity of a negotiated settlement with Japan perhaps existed. P. W. Schroeder's *The Axis Alliance and Japanese-American Relations, 1941* makes that point with particular force. Other issues include Franklin Roosevelt's diplomatic role. Was the president a bold internationalist struggling heroically against an isolationist Congress and public opinion, or did he share much of the traditional isolationist credo? Robert Dallek's encyclopedic study of Roosevelt's foreign policy portrays Roosevelt as a shrewd and calculating internationalist, whereas Donald Cameron Watts's *How War Came* depicts him as a myopic and ill-informed leader who overestimated his own peacemaking abilities and, like most other Americans, only belatedly awakened to the menace of totalitarianism.

No decision of the war era has provoked sharper controversy than the atomic bombings of Japan in August 1945. Lingering moral questions about the nuclear incineration of Hiroshima and Nagasaki have long threatened to tarnish the crown of military victory. America is the only nation ever to have used an atomic weapon in war; and some critics have even claimed to find elements of racism in the fact that the bombs were dropped on people of a nonwhite race. The fact is, however, that Germany surrendered before the bombs were ready; had the war in Europe lasted just a few months longer, some German city would probably have suffered the fate of Hiroshima.

Some scholars, notably Gar Alperovitz, have further charged that the atomic holocausts at Hiroshima and Nagasaki were not the last shots of World War II, but the first salvos in the emerging Cold War. Alperovitz argues that the Japanese were already defeated in the summer of 1945, and were in fact attempting to arrange a *conditional* surrender. President Truman ignored those attempts and unleashed his horrible new weapons, so the argument goes, not simply to defeat Japan but to frighten the Soviets into submission to America's will, and to keep them out of the final stages of the war—and postwar reconstruction—in Asia.

Could the use of the atomic bombs have been avoided? As Martin J. Shewin's studies have shown, few policymakers at the time seriously asked that question. American leaders wanted to end the war as quickly as possible. Intimidating the Soviets might have been a "bonus" to using the bomb against Japan, but influencing Soviet behavior was never the *primary* reason for the fateful decision. American military strategists had always assumed the atomic bomb would be dropped as soon as it was available. That moment came on August 6, 1945. Yet misgivings and remorse about the atomic conclusion of World War II have plagued the American conscience ever since.

SUGGESTED READINGS

PRIMARY SOURCE DOCUMENTS

Vivid portraits of the fighting are found in Ernie Pyle, *Here Is Your War* (1943) and *Brave Men* (1944). On the atomic bomb, consult the reactions of the *Nippon Times** (August 10, 1945), *The Christian Century** (August 29, 1945), and President Truman's justification of the bombing in *Memoirs of Harry S Truman** (1955).

SECONDARY SOURCES

A scholarly discussion of the home front is John M. Blum, *V Was for Victory: Politics and American Culture During World War II* (1976). Consult also Doris Kearns Goodwin, *No Ordinary Time* (1994); William L. O'Neill, *A Democracy at War: America's Fight at Home and Abroad in World War II* (1993); Richard Polenberg, *War and Society: The United States, 1941–1945* (1972); and Harold G. Vatter, *The U.S. Economy in World War II* (1985). Studs Terkel has compiled an interesting oral history of the war experience in *The Good War* (1984). On women see William H. Chafe, *The American Woman: Her Changing Social, Economic, and Political Roles, 1920–1970* (1972); Susan M. Hartmann, *The Home Front and Beyond* (1982); and D'Ann Campbell, *Women at War with America: Private Lives in a Patriotic Era* (1984). On the internment of the Japanese-Americans, consult Roger Daniels, *Concentration Camps U.S.A.: Japanese-Americans and World War II* (1971); Peter Irons, *Justice at War: The Story of the Japanese-American Internment Cases* (1983); and the oral histories provided in John Tateishi, ed., *And Justice for All* (1984). On blacks see Neil A. Wynn, *The Afro-Americans and the Second World War* (1976), and Nicholas Lemann, *The Promised Land: The Great Black Migration and How It Changed America* (1991). Nelson Lichtenstein examines *Labor's War at Home: The CIO in World War II* (1983), and Gerald Nash describes *The*

American West Transformed: The Impact of the Second World War (1985). The military history of the war is capably summarized in H. P. Willmott, *The Great Crusade: A New Complete History of the Second World War* (1990), and in Gerhard Weinberg's massively detailed *A World at Arms* (1994). See also Russell F. Weigley, *Eisenhower's Lieutenants: The Campaigns of France and Germany, 1944–1945* (1981); Eric Larrabee, *Commander in Chief: Franklin Delano Roosevelt, His Lieutenants, and Their War* (1987); and David Eisenhower, *Eisenhower at War: 1943–45* (1986). Ed Cray profiles *General of the Army: George C. Marshall, Soldier and Statesman* (1990). A good introduction to wartime diplomacy is Gaddis Smith, *American Diplomacy During the Second World War* (1965). More detailed are Herbert Feis's three volumes: *Churchill, Roosevelt, Stalin* (2d ed., 1967), *Between War and Peace: The Potsdam Conference* (1960), and *The Atomic Bomb and the End of World War II* (1966). Also valuable are Robert Dallek's work, cited in Chapter 37; John L. Gaddis, *The United States and the Origins of the Cold War, 1941–1947* (1972); and two "revisionist" studies that are highly critical of American policy: Gabriel Kolko, *The Politics of War: The World and United States Foreign Policy, 1943–1945* (1968), and Lloyd Gardner, *Architects of Illusion: Men and Ideas in American Foreign Policy, 1941–1949* (1970). The war in Asia is covered in Ronald H. Spector's gracefully written *Eagle Against the Sun: The American War with Japan* (1985). John W. Dower explores the racial ideas that underlay the war against Japan in *War Without Mercy: Race and Power in the Pacific War* (1986). Paul Fussell contrasts actual combat and wartime rhetoric in *Wartime: Understanding and Behavior in the Second World War* (1989). On the atomic bomb, the most comprehensive account is Richard Rhodes, *The Making of the Atomic Bomb* (1986). Also see Richard G. Hewlett and Oscar E. Anderson, Jr., *The New World* (1962); Martin J. Sherwin, *A World Destroyed: The Atomic Bomb and the Grand Alliance* (1975); and Gar Alperovitz's questionable critique of American nuclear strategy, *Atomic Diplomacy* (rev. ed., 1985). Paul Boyer, *By the Bomb's Early Light* (1985), analyzes the bomb's impact on the American mind.

---

*An asterisk indicates that the document, or an excerpt from it, can be found in Thomas A. Bailey and David M. Kennedy, eds., *The American Spirit: United States History as Seen by Contemporaries,* 9th ed. (Boston: Houghton Mifflin, 1998).

PART SIX

Making Modern America

W orld War II broke the back of the Great Depression in the United States and also ended the century-and-a-half-old American tradition of isolationism in foreign affairs. Alone among the warring powers, the United States managed to emerge from the great conflict physically unscarred, economically healthy, and diplomatically strengthened. Yet if Americans faced a world full of promise at the war's end, it was also a world full of dangers, none more disconcerting than Soviet communism. These two themes of promise and menace mingled uneasily throughout the nearly five decades of the Cold War era, from the end of World War II in 1945 to the collapse of the Soviet Union in 1991.

At home, unprecedented prosperity in the postwar quarter-century nourished a robust sense of national self-confidence and fed a revolution of rising expectations. Invigorated by the prospect of endlessly spreading affluence, Americans in the 1940s, '50s, and '60s had record numbers of babies, aspired to ever-higher standards of living, generously expanded the welfare state (especially for the elderly), widened opportunities for women, welcomed immigrants, and even found the will to grapple at long last with the nation's grossest legacy of injustice, its treatment of African-Americans. With the exception of Dwight Eisenhower's presidency in the 1950s, Americans elected liberal Democratic presidents (Harry Truman in 1948, John F. Kennedy in 1960, and Lyndon Johnson in 1964). The Democratic party, the party of the liberal New Deal at home and of an activist foreign policy abroad, comfortably remained the nation's majority party.

The Suburban Society
In the phenomenally affluent post–World War II years, newly prosperous Americans flocked to the freshly built suburbs.

Americans trusted their government and had faith in the American dream that their children would lead a richer life than their parents had done. Anything and everything seemed possible.

The rising curve of ascending expectations, propelled by economic growth, bounded upward through the 1950s. It peaked in the 1960s, an exceptionally stormy decade during which faith in government, in the wisdom of American foreign policy, and in the American dream itself, began to sour. Lyndon Johnson's "Great Society" reforms, billed as the completion of the unfinished work of the New Deal, foundered on the rocks of fiscal limitations and stubborn racial resentments. Johnson, the most ambitious reformer in the White House since Franklin Roosevelt, eventually saw his presidency destroyed by the furies unleashed over the Vietnam War.

When economic growth flattened in the 1970s, the horizon of hopes for the future seemed to sink as well. The nation entered a frustrating period of stalled expectations, increasingly rancorous racial tensions, disillusion with government, and political stalemate. With the exceptions of Jimmy Carter in the 1970s and Bill Clinton in the 1990s, Americans after 1968 elected conservative Republicans to the White House (Richard Nixon in 1968 and 1972, Ronald Reagan in 1980 and 1984, George Bush in 1988), but continued to elect Democratic congresses. Yet by the 1990s, a newly invigorated conservative Republican party was bidding to achieve long-term majority status.

Abroad, the competition with the Soviet Union, and after 1949 with Communist China as well, colored every aspect of America's foreign relations, and shaped domestic American life too. Unreasoning fear of communists at home unleashed the destructive force of McCarthyism in the 1950s—a modern-day witch-hunt in which careers were capsized and lives ruined by reckless accusations of communist sympathizing. The FBI encroached on sacred American liberties in its zeal to uncover communist "subversives."

The Cold War remained cold, in the sense that no shooting conflict broke out between the great power rivals. But the United States did fight two shooting wars, in Korea in the 1950s and Vietnam in the 1960s. Vietnam, the only foreign war in which the United States has ever been defeated, cruelly convulsed American society, ending not only Lyndon Johnson's presidency but the thirty-five year era of the Democratic party's political dominance as well. Vietnam also touched off the most vicious inflationary cycle in American history, and embittered and disillusioned an entire generation.

Uncle Sam in the Cold War era also built a fearsome arsenal of nuclear weapons, great air and missile fleets to deliver them, a two-ocean navy, and, for a time, a large army raised by conscription. Whether the huge expenditures necessary to maintain that gigantic defense establishment stimulated or distorted the economy is a question that remains controversial.

Suburbia's Children
The bitter Vietnam War in the 1960s shattered the confidence of the post–World War II generation, and ushered in an era of national self-doubt and reduced expectations, especially among the "baby boomers" who had been born into suburban affluence in the postwar years.

39

The Cold War Begins
1945–1952

America stands at this moment at the summit of the world.

Winston Churchill, 1945

Postwar Economic Anxieties

The American people, 140 million strong, cheered the blinding atomic climax of World War II in 1945. But when the shouting faded away, countless men and women began to worry about their future. Four fiery years of global war had not entirely driven from their minds the painful memories of twelve desperate years of the Great Depression.

The decade of the 1930s had left deep scars. Joblessness and insecurity had pushed up the suicide rate and dampened the marriage rate. Babies went unborn as pinched budgets and sagging self-esteem wrought a sexual depression in American bedrooms. The war had banished the blight of depression, but would the respite last? Grim-faced observers were warning that the war had only temporarily lifted the pall of economic stagnation and that peace would bring the return of hard times. Homeward-bound GIs, so the gloomy predictions

ran, would step out of the army's chow lines and back into the breadlines of the unemployed.

The faltering economy in the initial postwar years threatened to confirm the worst predictions of the doomsayers who foresaw another Great Depression. Real gross national product (GNP) slumped sickeningly in 1946 and 1947 from its wartime peak. With the removal of wartime price controls, prices giddily levitated by 33 percent in 1946–1947. An epidemic of strikes swept the country. During 1946 alone some 4.6 million laborers laid down their tools. Especially crippling were work stoppages in such basic industries as steel making, automobile manufacturing, and bituminous coal mining.

The growing muscle of organized labor deeply annoyed many conservatives. They had their revenge against labor's New Deal gains in 1947, when a Republican-controlled Congress (the first in fourteen years) passed the Taft-Hartley Act over President Truman's vigorous veto. Labor leaders condemned the Taft-Hartley Act as a "slave-labor law." It outlawed the "closed" (all-union) shop, made unions liable for damages that resulted from jurisdictional disputes among themselves, and required union leaders to take a non-Communist oath.

Taft-Hartley was only one of several obstacles that slowed the growth of organized labor in the years after World War II. In the heady days of the New Deal, unions had spread swiftly in the industrialized Northeast, especially in huge manufacturing industries like steel and automobiles. But labor's postwar efforts to organize in the historically anti-union regions of the South and West proved frustrating. The CIO's "Operation Dixie," aimed at unionizing southern textile and steel workers, failed miserably in 1948 to overcome lingering fears of racial mixing. And workers in the rapidly growing service sector of the economy—many of them middle-aged women, often working only part-time in small shops, widely separated from one another—proved much more difficult to organize than the thousands of assembly-line workers who in the 1930s had poured into the auto and steel unions. Union membership would peak in the 1950s, and then begin a long, unremitting decline.

The Democratic administration meanwhile took some steps of its own to forestall an economic downturn. It sold war factories and other government installations to private businesses at fire-sale prices. It secured passage in 1946 of the Employ-

ment Act, making it government policy "to promote maximum employment, production, and purchasing power." The act created a three-member Council of Economic Advisers to provide the president with the data and the recommendations to make that policy a reality.

Most dramatic was the passage of the Servicemen's Readjustment Act of 1944—better known as the GI Bill of Rights, or the GI Bill. Enacted partly out of fear that the employment markets would never be able to absorb 15 million returning veterans at war's end, the GI Bill made generous provisions for sending the former soldiers to school. In the postwar decade, some 8 million veterans advanced their education at Uncle Sam's expense. The majority attended technical and vocational schools, but colleges and universities were crowded to the blackboards as more than 2 million ex-GIs stormed the halls of higher learning. The total eventually spent for education was some $14.5 billion in taxpayer dollars. The act also enabled the Veterans' Administration (VA) to guarantee about $16 billion in loans for veterans to buy homes, farms, and small businesses. By raising educational levels and stimulating the construction industry, the GI Bill powerfully nurtured the robust and long-lived economic expansion that eventually took hold in the late 1940s—and that profoundly shaped the entire history of the postwar era.

The GI Bill Financed by the federal government, thousands of World War II veterans crowded into college classrooms in the 1940s. Here a fresh crop of ex-soldier students lays in supplies for the new term.

The Long Economic Boom, 1950–1970

Gross national product began to climb haltingly in 1948. Then, beginning about 1950, the American economy surged onto a dazzling plateau of sustained growth that was to last virtually uninterrupted for two decades. America's economic performance became the envy of the world. National income nearly doubled in the 1950s and almost doubled again in the 1960s, shooting through the trillion-dollar mark in 1973. Americans, some 6 percent of the world's people, were enjoying about 40 percent of the planet's wealth.

As the gusher of postwar prosperity poured forth its riches, Americans drank deeply from the gilded goblet. Millions of depression-pinched souls sought to make up for the sufferings of the 1930s. They determined to "get theirs" while the getting was good. A people who had once considered a

Coca-Colonizing the World   American consumerism—and American products—flooded over the globe after World War II, as this 1950 cover from *Time* Magazine illustrates.

chicken in every pot the standard of comfort and security now hungered for two cars in every garage, swimming pools in their backyards, vacation homes, and gas-guzzling recreational vehicles. The size of the "middle class," defined as households earning between $3,000 and $10,000 a year, doubled from pre–Great Depression days and included 60 percent of the American people by the mid-1950s. By the end of that decade, the vast majority of American families owned their own car and washing machine, and nearly 90 percent owned a television set—a gadget invented in the 1920s but virtually unknown until the late 1940s. In another revolution of sweeping consequences, almost 60 percent of American families owned their own homes by 1960, compared with less than 40 percent in the 1920s.

Of all the beneficiaries of postwar prosperity, none reaped greater rewards than women. More than ever, urban offices and shops provided a bonanza of employment for female workers. The great majority of new jobs created in the postwar era went to women, as the service sector of the economy dramatically outgrew the old industrial and manufacturing sectors. Women accounted for a quarter of the American work force at the end of World War II, and for nearly half the labor pool five decades later. Yet even as women continued their march into the workplace in the 1940s and 1950s, popular culture glorified the traditional feminine roles of homemaker and mother. The clash between the demands of suburban housewifery and the realities of employment eventually sparked a feminist revolt in the 1960s.

Nothing loomed larger in the history of the post–World War II era than this fantastic eruption of affluence. It did not enrich all Americans, and it did not touch all people evenly, but it transformed the lives of a majority of citizens and molded the agenda of politics and society for at least two generations. Prosperity underwrote social mobility; it paved the way for the eventual success of the civil rights movement; it funded vast new welfare programs, like Medicare; and it gave Americans the confidence to exercise unprecedented international leadership in the Cold War era. What propelled this unprecedented economic explosion?

The Second World War itself provided a powerful stimulus. While other countries had been ravaged by years of fighting, the United States had used the war crisis to fire up its smokeless factories and rebuild its depression-plagued economy. Invigor-

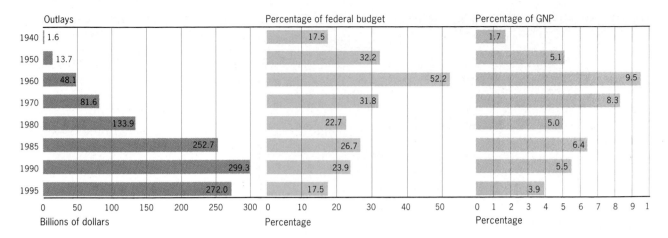

National Defense Budget, 1940–1995
(Budget, Historical Tables, and Statistical Abstract of the United States relevant years.)

ated by battle, America had almost effortlessly come to dominate the ruined global landscape of the postwar period.

Ominously, much of the glittering prosperity of the 1950s and 1960s rested on the underpinnings of colossal military budgets, leading some critics to speak of a "permanent war economy." The economic upturn of 1950 was fueled by massive appropriations for the Korean War, and defense spending accounted for some 10 percent of the GNP throughout the ensuing decade. Pentagon dollars primed the pumps of high-technology industries such as aerospace, plastics, and electronics—areas in which the United States reigned supreme over all foreign competitors. The military budget also financed much scientific research and development ("R and D"—hence the name of one of the most famous "think tanks," the Rand Corporation). More than ever before, unlocking the secrets of nature was the key to unleashing economic growth.

Cheap energy also fed the economic boom. American and European companies thoroughly dominated the international oil business. They controlled the flow of abundant petroleum from the sandy expanses of the Middle East, and they kept prices low. Americans doubled their consumption of inexpensive and seemingly inexhaustible oil in the quarter-century after the war. Anticipating a limitless future of low-cost fuels, they flung out endless ribbons of highways, installed air-conditioning in their homes, and engineered a sixfold increase in the country's electricity-generating capacity between 1945 and 1970. Spidery grids of electrical

cables carried the pent-up power of oil, gas, coal, and falling water to activate the tools of workers on the factory floor.

With the forces of nature increasingly harnessed in their hands, workers chalked up spectacular gains in productivity—the amount of output per hour of work. In the two decades after the outbreak of the Korean War in 1950, productivity increased at an average rate of more than 3 percent per year. Gains in productivity were also enhanced by the rising educational level of the work force. By 1970 nearly 90 percent of the school-age population was enrolled in educational institutions—a dramatic contrast with the opening years of the century, when only half of this age group had attended school. Better educated and better equipped, American workers in 1970 could produce nearly twice as much in an hour's labor as they had in 1950. Productivity was the key to prosperity. Rising productivity in the 1950s and 1960s virtually doubled the average American's standard of living in the postwar quarter-century.

Also contributing to the vigor of the postwar economy were some momentous changes in the nation's basic economic structure. Conspicuous was the accelerating shift of the work force out of agriculture, which achieved productivity gains virtually unmatched by any other economic sector. The family farm nearly became an antique artifact as consolidation produced giant agribusinesses able to employ costly machinery. Thanks largely to mechanization and to rich new fertilizers—as well as to government subsidies and price supports—one

Agribusiness Expensive machinery of the sort shown here made most of American agriculture a capital-intensive, phenomenally productive big business by the 1990s—and sounded the death knell for many small-scale family farms.

farmworker by the century's end could produce food for over fifty people, compared with about fifteen people in the 1940s. Farmers whose forebears had busted sod with oxen or horses now plowed their fields in air-conditioned tractor cabs, listening on their stereophonic radios to weather forecasts or the latest Chicago commodities market quotations. Once the mighty backbone of the agricultural Republic, and still some 15 percent of the labor force at the end of World War II, farmers made up a slim 2 percent of the American population by the 1990s—yet they fed much of the world.

The Smiling Sunbelt

The convulsive economic changes of the post-1945 period shook and shifted the American people, amplifying the population redistribution set in motion by World War II. As immigrants and westward-trekking pioneers, Americans had always been a people on the move, but they were astonishingly footloose in the postwar years. For some three decades after 1945, an average of 30 million people changed residences every year. Families especially felt the strain, as distance divided parents from children, and brothers and sisters from one another. One sign of this sort of stress was the phenomenal popularity of advice books on child-rearing, especially Dr. Benjamin Spock's *The Common Sense Book of Baby and Child Care.* First published in 1945, it instructed millions of parents during the ensuing decades in the kind of homely wisdom that was

once transmitted naturally from grandparent to parent, and from parent to child. In fluid postwar neighborhoods, friendships were also hard to sustain. Mobility could exact a high human cost in loneliness and isolation.

Especially striking was the growth of the "Sunbelt"—a fifteen-state area stretching in a smiling crescent from Virginia through Florida and Texas to Arizona and California. This region increased its population at a rate nearly double that of the old industrial zones of the Northeast (the "Frostbelt"). In the 1950s California alone accounted for one-fifth of the entire nation's population growth and by 1963 had outdistanced New York as the most populous state—a position it still held in the 1990s, with more than 30 million people, or one out of every eight Americans.

The South and the Southwest were a new frontier for Americans after World War II. These modern pioneers came in search of jobs, a better climate, and lower taxes. Jobs they found in abundance, especially in the California electronics industry, in the aerospace complexes in Florida and Texas, and in the huge military installations that powerful southern congressional representatives secured for their districts.

A Niagara of federal dollars accounted for much of the Sunbelt's prosperity, though, ironically, southern and western politicians led the cry against government spending. By the 1990s the South and West were annually receiving some $125 billion more in federal funds than the Northeast and Midwest. A new economic war between the states seemed to be shaping up. Northeasterners and their allies from

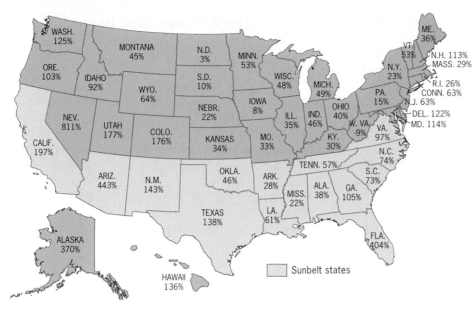

Population Increase in the Sunbelt States, 1950–1994

States with figures higher than 50 percent were growing faster than the national average. Note that "Sunbelt" is a loose geographical concept, as some Deep South states had very little population growth, whereas the mountain and Pacific states were booming. *(Statistical Abstract of the United States and Historical Abstract of the United States, relevant years.)*

the hard-hit heavy-industry region of the Ohio Valley (the "Rustbelt") tried to rally political support with the sarcastic slogan "The North shall rise again."

These dramatic shifts of population and wealth further broke the historic grip of the North on the nation's political life. Every elected occupant of the White House since 1964 has hailed from the Sunbelt, and the region's congressional representation rose as its population grew. With their frontier ethic of unbridled individualism and their devotion to unregulated economic growth, the Sunbelters were redrawing the Republic's political map.

The Rush to the Suburbs

In all regions, America's modern migrants—if they were white—fled from the cities to the burgeoning new suburbs (see "Makers of America: The Suburbanites," pp. 888–889). Government policies encouraged this momentous movement. Federal Housing Authority (FHA) and Veterans' Administration (VA) home-loan guarantees made it more economically attractive to own a home in the suburbs

Sunbelt Prosperity

The old and new West are evident in this view of booming Dallas.

than to rent an apartment in the city. Tax deductions for interest payments on home mortgages provided additional financial incentive. And government-built highways that sped commuters from suburban homes to city jobs further facilitated this mass migration. By 1960 one of every four Americans dwelt in suburbia, and the same leafy neighborhoods held more than half the nation's population as the century neared its end.

The construction industry boomed in the 1950s and 1960s to satisfy this demand. Pioneered by innovators like the Levitt brothers, whose first "Levittown" sprouted on New York's Long Island in the 1940s, builders revolutionized the techniques of home construction. Erecting hundreds or even thousands of dwellings in a single project, specialized crews working from standardized plans laid foundations, while others raised factory-assembled framing modules, put on roofs, strung wires, installed plumbing, and finished the walls in record time and with cost-cutting efficiency. Snooty critics wailed about the aesthetic monotony of the suburban "tract" developments, but eager home-buyers nevertheless moved into them by the millions.

"White flight" to the leafy green suburbs left the inner cities—especially those in the Northeast and Midwest—black, brown, and broke. Migrating blacks from the South filled up the urban neighborhoods that were abandoned by the departing white middle class (see "Makers of America: The Great African-American Migration," pp. 856–857). In effect, the incoming blacks imported the grinding poverty of the rural South into the inner cores of northern cities. Taxpaying businesses fled with their affluent customers from downtown shops to suburban shopping malls (another post–World War II invention).

Government policies sometimes aggravated this spreading pattern of residential segregation. FHA administrators, citing the "risk" of making loans to blacks and other "unharmonious racial or nationality groups," often refused them mortgages for private home purchases, thus limiting black mobility out of inner cities and driving many minorities into public housing projects. Even public housing programs frequently followed a so-called neighborhood composition rule, which effectively built housing for blacks in neighborhoods that were already identified as predominantly black—thus solidifying racial separation.

The Postwar Baby Boom

Of all the upheavals in postwar America, none was more dramatic than the "baby boom"—the huge leap in the birthrate in the decade and a half after 1945. Confident young men and women tied the nuptial knot in record numbers at war's end, and they began immediately to fill the nation's empty cradles. They thus touched off a demographic explosion that added more than 50 million bawling babies to the nation's population by the end of the 1950s. The soaring birthrate finally crested in 1957 and was followed by a deepening birth dearth. By 1973 fertility rates had dropped below the point necessary to maintain existing population figures. If the downward trend persisted, only further immigration would lift the U.S. population above its 1996 level of some 264 million.

This boom-or-bust cycle of births begot a bulging wave along the American population curve. As the oversize postwar generation grew to maturity, it was destined—like the fabled pig passing through the python—to strain and distort many aspects of American life. Elementary-school enrollments, for example, swelled to nearly 34 million pupils in 1970. Then began a steady decline, as the onward-marching age group left in its wake closed schools and unemployed teachers.

The maturing babies of the postwar boom sent economic shock waves undulating through the decades. As tykes and toddlers in the 1940s and 1950s, they made up a lucrative market for manufacturers of canned food and other baby products. As teenagers in the 1960s, the same youngsters spent an estimated $20 billion a year for clothes and recorded rock music—and their sheer numbers laid the basis of the much-ballyhooed "youth culture" of that tumultuous decade. In the 1970s the consumer tastes of the aging baby boomers changed again, and the most popular jeans maker began marketing pants with a fuller cut for those former "kids" who could no longer squeeze into their size-thirty Levi's. In the 1980s the horde of baby boomers bumped and jostled one another in the job market, struggling to get a foothold on the crowded ladder of social mobility. In the 1990s the boom generation began to enter middle age, raising its own "secondary boom" of children—a faint demographic echo of the postwar population explosion. The impact of the huge postwar generation will continue to ripple through American society well into the next century, when its members pass eventually into retirement, placing enormous strains on the Social Security system.

Truman: the "Gutty" Man from Missouri

Presiding over the opening of the postwar period was an "accidental president"—Harry S Truman. "The moon, the stars, and all the planets" had fallen on him, he remarked when he was called upon to shoulder the dead Roosevelt's awesome burdens of leadership. Trim and owlishly bespectacled, with his graying hair and friendly, toothy grin, Truman was called "the average man's average man." Even his height—5 feet, 9 inches (1.75 meters)—was average. The first president in many years without a college education, he had farmed, served as an artillery officer in France during World War I, and failed as a haberdasher. He then tried his hand at precinct-level Missouri politics, through which he rose from a judgeship to the U.S. Senate. Though a protégé of a notorious political machine in Kansas City, he had managed to keep his own hands clean.

The problems of the postwar period were staggering, and the suddenly burdened new president at first approached his tasks with becoming humility. But gradually he evolved from a shrinking pipsqueak into a scrappy little cuss, gaining confidence to the point of cockiness. When the Soviet foreign minister complained, "I have never been talked to like that in my life," Truman shot back, "Carry out your agreements and you won't get talked to like that." Truman later boasted: "I gave him the one-two, right to the jaw."

A smallish man thrust suddenly into a giant job, Truman permitted designing old associates of the "Missouri gang" to gather around him and, like Grant, was stubbornly loyal to them when they were caught with cream on their whiskers. On occasion he would send critics hot-tempered and profane "s.o.b." letters. Most troubling, in trying to demonstrate to a skeptical public his decisiveness and power of command, he was inclined to go off half-cocked or stick mulishly to a wrongheaded notion. "To err is Truman," cynics gibed.

What Next? 1946   This cartoon expresses the feeling of many Americans that their new president was overwhelmed, even bamboozled, by his job.

But if he was sometimes small in the small things, he was often big in the big things. He had down-home authenticity, few pretensions, rock-solid probity, and a lot of that old-fashioned character trait called moxie. Not one to dodge responsibility, he placed a sign on his White House desk that read, "The buck stops here." Among his favorite sayings was, "If you can't stand the heat, get out of the kitchen."

Yalta: Bargain or Betrayal?

Vast and silent, the Soviet Union continued to be the great enigma. The conference at Teheran in 1943, where Roosevelt had first met Stalin man to man, had done something to clear the air; but much had remained unresolved—especially questions about the postwar fates of Germany, Eastern Europe, and Asia.

The Suburbanites

Few images evoke more vividly the prosperity of the postwar era than aerial photographs of sprawling suburbs. Neat rows of look-alike tract houses, each with driveway and lawn and here and there a backyard swimming pool, came to symbolize the capacity of the economy to deliver the "American Dream" to millions of families.

Suburbanization was hardly new. Well-off city dwellers had beaten paths to leafy outlying neighborhoods since the nineteenth century. But after

The Suburban Dream of Two Cars in Every Garage

1945 the steady flow became a stampede. The baby boom, new highways, government guarantees for mortgage lending, and favorable tax policies all made suburbia blossom.

Who were the Americans racing to the new postwar suburbs? War veterans led the way in the late 1940s, aided by Veterans' Administration mortgages that featured tiny down payments and low interest rates. The general public soon followed. The Federal Housing Administration (FHA) offered insured mortgages with low down payments and 2–3 percent interest rates on thirty-year loans. With deals like this, it was hardly surprising that American families flocked into "Levittowns," built by William and Alfred Levitt, and other similar suburban developments.

People of all kinds found their way to suburbia, heading for neighborhoods that varied from the posh to the plain. Yet for all this diversity the overwhelming majority of suburbanites were white and middle-class. In 1967, sociologist Herbert Gans published *The Levittowners,* based on his own move to a Levitt-built community outside Philadelphia. He described suburban families in tract developments as predominantly third- or fourth-generation Americans with some college education and at least two children.

Men tended to work in either white-collar jobs or upper-level blue-collar positions such as foremen. Women usually worked in the home, so much so that suburbia came to symbolize the domestic confinement that feminists in the 1960s and 1970s decried in their campaign for women's rights.

The house itself became more important than ever as postwar suburbanites built their leisure lives around television, home improvement projects, and barbecues on the patio. The center of family life shifted to the fenced-in backyard as neighborly city habits of visiting on the front stoop, gabbing on the sidewalk, and strolling to local stores disappeared. Institutions that had thrived as social centers in the city—churches, women's clubs, fraternal organizations, taverns—had a tougher time attracting patrons in the privatized world of postwar suburbia.

Life in the suburbs was a boon to the automobile, as parents jumped behind the wheel to shuttle children, groceries, and golf clubs to and fro. The second car, once an unheard-of luxury, became a practical "necessity" for suburban families constantly "on the go." A car culture sprang up with new destinations, like drive-thru restaurants and drive-in movies. Roadside shopping centers edged out downtowns as places to shop. Meanwhile, the new interstate highway system enabled breadwinners to live farther and farther from their jobs and still commute to work daily.

Many suburbanites continued to depend on cities for jobs, though by the 1980s the suburbs themselves became important sites of employment. Wherever they worked, suburbanites turned their backs on the city and its problems. They fought to maintain their communities as secluded retreats, independent municipalities with their own taxes, schools, and zoning restrictions designed to keep out public housing and the poor. Even the naming of towns and streets reflected a pastoral ideal. Poplar Terrace and Mountainview Drive were popular street names; East Paterson, New Jersey, was renamed Elmwood Park in 1973. With a majority of Americans living in suburbs by the 1980s, cities lost their political clout. Bereft of state and federal aid, cities festered with worsening social problems: poverty, drug addiction, and crime.

Drive-in Café in Los Angeles, the Mother and Model of all Suburbias

Middle-class African-Americans began to move to the suburbs in substantial numbers by the 1980s, but even that migration failed to alter dramatically the racial divide of metropolitan America. Black suburbanites settled in towns like Rolling Oaks outside Miami or Brook Glen near Atlanta—black middle-class towns in white-majority counties. By the end of the twentieth century, suburbia as a whole was more racially diverse than at mid-century. But old patterns of urban "white flight" and residential segregation endured.

The Suburbanization of America After World War II, Americans by the millions moved to suburban housing developments like this one at Levittown, New York. Although criticized for their architectural monotony and cultural barrenness, the suburbs provided inexpensive and spacious housing for growing families seeking to escape the crowded confines of the cities.

A final fateful conference of the Big Three had taken place in February 1945 at Yalta. At this former tsarist resort on the relatively warm shores of the Black Sea, Stalin, Churchill, and the fast-failing Roosevelt reached momentous agreements, after pledging their faith with vodka. Final plans were laid for smashing the buckling German lines and shackling the beaten Axis foe. Stalin agreed that Poland, with revised boundaries, should have a representative government based on free elections—a pledge he soon broke. Bulgaria and Romania were likewise to have free elections—a promise also flouted. The Big Three further announced that they had decided to hold a multipower conference, this time in San Francisco, for the purpose of fashioning a new international peacekeeping organization—the United Nations.

Of all the grave decisions at Yalta, the most controversial concerned the Far East. The atomic bomb had not yet been tested, and Washington strategists expected frightful American casualties in the projected assault on Japan. From Roosevelt's standpoint it seemed highly desirable that Stalin should enter the Asian war, pin down Japanese troops in Manchuria and Korea, and lighten American losses. But Soviet casualties had already been enormous, and Moscow presumably needed inducements to bring it into the Far Eastern conflagration.

Horse trader Stalin was in a position at Yalta to exact a high price. He agreed to attack Japan within three months after the collapse of Germany; and he later redeemed this pledge in full. In return, the Soviets were promised the southern half of Sakhalin Island, lost by Russia to Japan in 1905, and Japan's Kurile Islands as well. The Soviet Union was also granted joint control over the railroads of China's Manchuria and, in a revival of tsarist imperialism, received special privileges in the two key seaports of that area, Dairen and Port Arthur. These concessions evidently would give Stalin control over vital industrial centers of America's weakening Chinese ally.

The Soviet Union's last-minute entry into the war against Japan was hailed in the United States with delight. But critics quickly concluded that Stalin's aid had not been needed, and that in any case his desire to grab his share of the spoils would have brought him into the conflict without concessions. Foes of the dead Roosevelt charged angrily that he had sold Jiang Jieshi (Chiang Kai-shek) down the river when he conceded control of China's Manchuria to Stalin. The consequent undermining of Chinese morale, so the accusation ran, con-

The Big Three   From left to right, Churchill, Roosevelt, and Stalin take time out from their fateful meeting at Yalta in February 1945.

tributed powerfully to Jiang's overthrow by the communists four years later. The critics also assailed the "sellout" of Poland and other East European countries.

Defenders of the departed Roosevelt countered that Stalin, with his mighty Red Army, could have secured much more of China if he wished, and that the Yalta conference really set limits to his ambitions. Apologists for Roosevelt also contended that if Stalin had kept his promise to support free elections in Poland and the liberated Balkans, the sorry sequel would have been different. Actually, Soviet troops had then occupied much of Eastern Europe, and a war to throw them out was unthinkable.

The fact is that the Big Three at Yalta were not drafting a comprehensive peace settlement; at most they were sketching general intentions and testing one another's reactions. Later critics who howled about broken promises overlooked that fundamental point. In the case of Poland, Roosevelt admitted that the Yalta agreement was "so elastic that the Russians can stretch it all the way from Yalta to Washington without ever technically breaking it." More specific understandings among the wartime allies—especially the two emerging superpowers, the United States and the Soviet Union—awaited the arrival of peace.

The United States and The Soviet Union

History provided little hope that the United States and the Soviet Union would reach cordial understandings about the shape of the postwar world. Mutual suspicions were ancient, abundant, and abiding. Communism and capitalism were historically hostile social philosophies. The United States had refused officially to recognize the Bolshevik revolutionary government in Moscow until it was sixteen years old, in 1933. Soviet skepticism toward the West was nourished by the British and American delays in opening up a second front against Germany, while the Soviet army paid a grisly price to roll the Nazi invaders back across Russia and Eastern Europe. Britain and America had also frozen their Soviet "ally" out of the project to develop atomic weapons, further feeding Stalin's mistrust. The Washington government rubbed salt in Soviet wounds when it abruptly terminated vital lend-lease aid to a battered USSR in 1945 and spurned Moscow's plea for a $6 billion reconstruction loan—while approving a similar loan of $3.75 billion to Britain in 1946.

Different visions of the postwar world also separated the two superpowers. Stalin aimed above all to guarantee the security of the Soviet Union. The USSR had twice in the twentieth century been stabbed in its heartland by attacks across the windswept plains of Eastern Europe. Stalin made it clear from the outset of the war that he was determined to have friendly governments along the Soviet western border, especially in Poland. By maintaining an extensive Soviet sphere of influence in Eastern and Central Europe, the USSR could protect itself and consolidate its revolutionary base as the world's leading communist country.

To many Americans, that "sphere of influence" looked like an ill-gained "empire." Doubting that Soviet goals were purely defensive, they remembered the earlier Bolshevik call for world revolution. Stalin's emphasis on "spheres" also clashed with Franklin Roosevelt's Wilsonian dream of an "open world," decolonized, demilitarized, and democratized, with a strong international organization to oversee global peace.

Even the ways in which the United States and the Soviet Union resembled each other were troublesome. Both countries had been largely isolated from world affairs before World War II—the United States through choice, the Soviet Union through rejection by the other powers. Both nations also had a history of conducting a kind of "missionary" diplomacy—of trying to export to all the world the political doctrines precipitated out of their respective revolutionary origins.

Unaccustomed to their great-power roles, unfamiliar with or even antagonistic to each other, and each believing in the universal applicability of its own particular ideology, America and the USSR suddenly found themselves staring eyeball-to-eyeball over the prostrate body of battered Europe—a Europe that had been the traditional center of international affairs. In these circumstances, some sort of confrontation was virtually unavoidable. The wartime "Grand Alliance" of the United States, the Soviet Union, and Britain had been a misbegotten child of necessity, kept alive only until the mutual enemy was crushed. When the hated Hitler fell, suspicion and rivalry between communistic, despotic Russia and capitalistic, democratic America were all but inevitable. In a fateful progression of events, marked often by misperceptions as well as by genuine conflicts of interest, the two powers provoked each other into a tense standoff known as the Cold War. Enduring four and a half decades, the Cold War not only shaped Soviet-American relations; it overshadowed the entire postwar international order in every corner of the globe. The Cold War also molded societies and economies and the lives of individual people all over the planet.

Shaping the Postwar World

Despite these obstacles the United States did manage at war's end to erect some of the structures that would support Roosevelt's vision of an open world. Meeting at Bretton Woods, New Hampshire, in 1944, the Western Allies established the International Monetary Fund (IMF) to encourage world trade by regulating currency exchange rates. They also founded the International Bank for Reconstruction and Development (World Bank) to promote economic growth in war-ravaged and underdeveloped areas. In contrast to its behavior after World War I, the United States took the lead in creating these important international bodies and supplied most of their funding. The stubborn Soviets declined to participate.

As flags wept at half-mast, the United Nations Conference opened on schedule, April 25, 1945, despite Roosevelt's dismaying death thirteen days earlier. Unlike Woodrow Wilson, Roosevelt had displayed political tact by choosing both Republican and Democratic senators for the American delegation. Meeting at the San Francisco War Memorial Opera House, representatives from fifty nations fashioned a United Nations charter that strongly resembled the old League of Nations Covenant. It featured a Security Council dominated by the Big Five powers (the United States, Britain, the USSR, France, and China), each of whom had the right of veto, and an Assembly that could be controlled by smaller countries. In contrast with the chilly American reception of the League in 1919, the Senate overwhelmingly approved the document on July 28, 1945, by a vote of eighty-nine to two.

The United Nations, setting up its permanent glass home in New York City, had some gratifying initial successes. It helped preserve peace in Iran,

> *Bernard Baruch (1870–1965), in presenting his plan for the control of atomic energy to the United Nations, in June 1946 said,*
>
> "We are here to make a choice between the quick and the dead. That is our business. Behind the black portent of the new atomic age lies a hope which, seized upon with faith, can work our salvation. If we fail, then we have damned every man to be the slave of fear. Let us not deceive ourselves; we must elect world peace or world destruction."

Kashmir, and other trouble spots. It played a large role in creating the new Jewish state of Israel. The U.N. Trusteeship Council guided former colonies to independence. Through such arms as UNESCO (United Nations Educational, Scientific, and Cultural Organization), FAO (Food and Agricultural Organization), and WHO (World Health Organization), the U.N. brought benefits to peoples the world over.

Far less heartening was the failure of the United Nations to control the fearsome new technology of the atom. United States delegate Bernard Baruch called in 1946 for a U.N. agency, free from the great-power veto, to inspect all nuclear facilities to prevent the manufacture of nuclear weapons. Fearful of giving up their veto and opposed to capitalist "spies" snooping around the USSR, the Soviets rejected the Baruch plan. A priceless opportunity to tame the nuclear monster in its infancy was forever lost. The atomic clock ticked ominously on, overshadowing all relations between the Soviet Union and the United States for the next forty-five years and casting a pall over the future of the human race.

The Problem of Germany

Hitler's ruined *Reich* posed especially thorny problems for all the wartime Allies. They agreed only that the cancer of Nazism had to be cut out of the German body politic, which involved punishing Nazi leaders for war crimes. The Allies joined in trying twenty-two top culprits at Nuremberg, Germany,

Witnesses for the Prosecution, 1945

during 1945–1946. Accusations included committing crimes against the laws of war and humanity and plotting aggressions contrary to solemn treaty pledges.

Justice, Nuremberg-style, was harsh. Twelve of the accused Nazis swung from the gallows, and seven were sentenced to long jail terms. "Foxy Hermann" Goering, whose blubbery chest had once blazed with ribbons, cheated the hangman a few hours before his scheduled execution by swallowing a hidden cyanide capsule. The trials of several small-fry Nazis continued for years. Legal critics in America condemned these proceedings as judicial lynchings, because the victims were tried for offenses that had not been clear-cut crimes when the war began.

Beyond punishing the top Nazis, the Allies could agree on little about postwar Germany. Some American Hitler-haters, noting that an industrialized Germany had been a brutal aggressor, at first wanted to dismantle German factories and reduce the country to a potato patch. The Soviets, denied American economic assistance, were determined to rebuild their shattered land by extracting enormous reparations from the Germans. Both these desires

clashed headlong with the reality that an industrial, healthy German economy was indispensable to the recovery of Europe. The Americans soon came to appreciate that fact. But the Soviets, deeply fearful of another blitzkrieg, resisted all efforts to revitalize Germany.

Along with Austria, Germany had been divided at war's end into four military occupation zones, each assigned to one of the Big Four powers (France, Britain, America, and the USSR). The Western Allies refused to allow Moscow to bleed their zones of the reparations that Stalin insisted he had been promised at Yalta. They also began to promote the idea of a reunited Germany. The communists responded by tightening their grip on their Eastern zone. Before long, it was apparent that Germany would remain indefinitely divided. West Germany eventually became an independent country, wedded to the West. East Germany, along with other Soviet-dominated East European countries, such as Poland and Hungary, became nominally independent "satellite" states, bound to the Soviet Union. East Europe virtually disappeared from Western sight behind the "iron curtain" of secrecy and isolation that Stalin clanged down across Europe from the Baltic to the Adriatic. The division of Europe would endure for more than four decades.

With Germany now split in two, there remained the problem of the rubble heap known as Berlin. Lying deep within the Soviet zone (see map on p. 894), this beleaguered isle in a red sea had been broken, like Germany as a whole, into sectors occupied by troops of each of the four victorious powers. In 1948, following controversies over German currency reform and four-power control, the Soviets abruptly choked off all rail and highway access to Berlin. They evidently reasoned that the Allies would be starved out.

Former Prime Minister Winston Churchill (1874–1965), in a highly controversial speech at Fulton, Missouri (March 1946), warned of Soviet expansionism:

"From Stettin in the Baltic to Trieste in the Adriatic an iron curtain has descended across the Continent."

Postwar Partition of Germany
Germany lost much of its territory in the east to Poland and to the Soviet Union. The military occupation zones composed the bases for the formation of two separate countries in 1949, when the British, French, and American zones became West Germany, and the Soviet zone became East Germany. (The two Germanies were reunited in 1990.) Berlin remained under joint four-power occupation from 1945 to 1990, and became a focus and symbol of Cold War tensions.

Berlin became a hugely symbolic issue for both sides. At stake was not only the fate of the city but a test of wills between Moscow and Washington. The Americans organized a gigantic airlift in the midst of hair-trigger tension. For nearly a year, flying some of the very aircraft that had recently dropped bombs on Berlin, American pilots ferried thousands of tons of supplies a day to the grateful Berliners, their former enemies. Western Europeans took heart from this vivid demonstration of America's determination to honor its commitments in Europe. The Soviets, their bluff dramatically called, finally lifted their blockade in May 1949. In the same year, the governments of the two Germanies, East and West, were formally established. The Cold War had icily congealed.

Crystallizing the Cold War

A crafty Stalin also probed the West's resolve at other sensitive points, including oil-rich Iran. Seeking to secure oil concessions similar to those held by the British and Americans, Stalin in 1946 broke an agreement to remove his troops from Iran's northernmost province, which the USSR had occupied, with British and American approval, during World War II. Instead, he used the troops to aid a rebel

Berliners Watch Incoming U.S. Relief Airplane, 1948

movement. Truman sent off a stinging protest, and the Soviet dictator backed down.

Moscow's hard-line policies in Germany, Eastern Europe, and the Middle East wrought a psychological Pearl Harbor. The eyes of Americans were jarred wide open by the Kremlin's apparent unwillingness to continue the wartime partnership. Any remaining goodwill from the period of comradeship-in-arms evaporated in a cloud of dark distrust. "I'm tired of babying the Soviets," Truman remarked privately in 1946, as attitudes on both sides began to harden frostily.

Truman's piecemeal responses to various Soviet challenges took on intellectual coherence in 1947, with the formulation of the "containment doctrine." Crafted by a brilliant young diplomat and Soviet specialist, George F. Kennan, this concept held that Russia, whether tsarist or communist, was relentlessly expansionary. But the Kremlin was also cautious, Kennan argued, and the flow of Soviet power into "every nook and cranny available to it" could be stemmed by "firm and vigilant containment."

Kennan's advice seemed to require a globe-girdling strategy of military and political preparedness. Truman embraced this advice when he formally and publicly adopted a "get-tough-with-Russia" policy in 1947. His first dramatic move was triggered by word that heavily burdened Britain could no longer bear the financial and military load of defending Greece against communist pressures. If Greece fell, Turkey would presumably collapse and the strategic eastern Mediterranean would pass into the Soviet orbit.

In a surprise appearance, the president went before Congress, on March 12, 1947, and requested support for what came to be known as the Truman Doctrine. Specifically, he asked for $400 million to bolster Greece and Turkey, which Congress quickly granted. More generally, he declared that "it must be the policy of the United States to support free peoples who are resisting attempted subjugation by armed minorities or by outside pressures"—a sweeping and open-ended commitment of vast and worrisome proportions. Critics then and later charged that Truman had overreacted by promising unlimited support to any tinhorn despot who claimed to be resisting "Communist aggression." Critics also complained that the Truman Doctrine needlessly polarized the world into pro-Soviet and pro-American camps and unwisely construed the Soviet threat as primarily military in nature. Apolo-

Where To? 1947
A satirical view of the Truman Doctrine.

gists for Truman have explained that it was Truman's fear of a revived isolationism that led him to exaggerate the Soviet threat and to cast his message in the charged language of a holy global war against godless communism—a description of the Cold War that straitjacketed future policymakers who would seek to tone down Soviet-American competition and animosity.

A threat of a different sort loomed in Western Europe—especially France, Italy, and Germany. These key nations were still suffering from the hunger and economic chaos spawned by war. They were in grave danger of being taken over from the inside by Communist parties that could exploit these hardships.

Truman responded with a bold policy. In a commencement address at Harvard University on June 5, 1947, Secretary of State George C. Marshall invited the Europeans to get together and work out a *joint* plan for their economic recovery. If they did so, the United States would provide substantial financial assistance. This forced cooperation constituted a powerful nudge on the road to the eventual creation of the European Community (EC).

The Marshall Plan Turns Enemies into Friends   The poster in this 1950 photograph in Berlin reads: "Berlin Rebuilt with Help from the Marshall Plan."

The democratic nations of Europe rose enthusiastically to the life-giving bait of the so-called Marshall Plan. They met in Paris in July 1947 to thrash out the details. The contemptuous Soviets spurned a golden opportunity to share in the plan—or to snarl it hopelessly—when they walked out of the conference.

The Marshall Plan called for spending $12.5 billion over four years in sixteen cooperating countries. Congress at first balked at this mammoth sum. It looked even more huge when added to the nearly $2 billion the United States had already contributed to European relief through the United Nations Relief and Rehabilitation Administration (UNRRA) and the hefty American contributions to the United Nations, IMF, and World Bank. But a Soviet-sponsored communist coup in Czechoslovakia finally awakened the legislators to reality, and they voted the initial appropriations in April 1948. Congress evidently concluded that if Uncle Sam did not get the Europeans back on their feet, they would never get off his back.

United States Foreign Aid, Military and Economic, 1945–1954   Marshall Plan aid swelled the outlay for Europe. Note the emphasis on the "developed" world, with relatively little aid going to what are now called "Third World" countries.

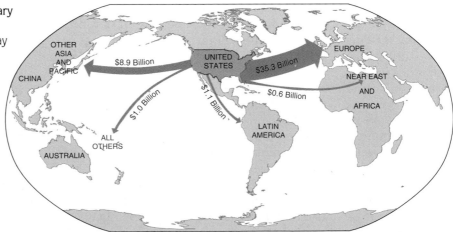

American Motor of the Latest Type   In this Russian view, the conquering Truman uses U.S. moneybags to induce dollar-hungry European nations to draw the U.S. capitalistic chariot.

Truman's Marshall Plan was a spectacular success. American dollars pumped reviving blood into the economic veins of the anemic Western European nations. Within a few years, most of them were exceeding their prewar outputs, as an "economic miracle" drenched Europe in prosperity. The Communist parties in Italy and France lost ground, and these two keystone countries were saved from the westward thrust of communism.

A resolute Truman made another fateful decision in 1948. Access to Middle Eastern oil was crucial to the European recovery program, and it would become increasingly crucial to the health of the U.S. economy, too, as domestic American oil reserves dwindled. Yet the Arab oil countries adamantly opposed the creation of the Jewish state of Israel in the British mandate territory of Palestine. Should Israel be born, a Saudi Arabian leader warned Truman, the Arabs "will lay siege to it until it dies of famine." Defying Arab wrath as well as the objections of his own State and Defense departments and the European Allies, all of them afraid to antagonize the oil-endowed Arabs, Truman officially recognized the state of Israel on its birthday, May 14, 1948. Humanitarian sympathy for the Jewish sur-vivors of the Holocaust ranked high among his reasons, as did his wishes to preempt Soviet influence in the Jewish state and to retain the support of American Jewish voters. Truman's policy of strong support for Israel would vastly complicate U.S. relations with the Arab world in the decades ahead.

America Begins to Rearm

The Cold War, the struggle to contain Soviet communism, was not war, yet it was not peace. The standoff with the Kremlin banished the dreams of tax-fatigued Americans that tanks could be beaten into automobiles.

The Soviet menace spurred the unification of the armed services as well as the creation of a huge new national security apparatus. Congress in 1947 passed the National Security Act, creating the Department of Defense. The department was to be housed in the sprawling Pentagon building on the banks of the Potomac and to be headed by a new cabinet officer, the secretary of defense. Under the secretary, but now without cabinet status, were the civilian secretaries of the navy, the army (replacing the old secretary of war), and the air force (a recognition of the rising importance of air power). The uniformed heads of each service were brought together as the Joint Chiefs of Staff. Unification was a large and necessary step toward more efficient military management, but it did not end interservice rivalry, as reflected in the annual football contests between the academies at West Point, Annapolis, and Colorado Springs.

The National Security Act also established a National Security Council (NSC) to advise the president on security matters and a Central Intelligence Agency (CIA) to coordinate the government's foreign fact-gathering. The "Voice of America," authorized by Congress in 1948, began beaming American radio broadcasts behind the iron curtain. In the same year, Congress resurrected the military draft, providing for the conscription of selected young men from nineteen to twenty-five years of age. The forbidding presence of the Selective Service System shaped millions of young people's educational, marital, and career plans in the following quarter-century. One shoe at a time, a war-weary America was reluctantly returning to a war footing.

Reintegrating Europe
In the shadow of the Eiffel Tower, West Germany is admitted to NATO in 1955. The Western powers' embrace of their World War II enemy reflected the pressures of the Cold War, when West Germany was needed in the alliance to defend Western Europe against a possible Soviet Russian attack.

The Soviet threat was also forcing the divided democracies of Western Europe into an unforeseen degree of unity that was both economic and political. In 1948, Britain, France, Belgium, the Netherlands, and Luxembourg signed a path-breaking treaty of defensive alliance at Brussels. They then invited the United States to join them.

The proposal confronted the United States with an historic decision. America had traditionally avoided entangling alliances, especially in peacetime (if the Cold War could be considered peacetime). Yet American participation in the emerging coalition could serve many purposes: it would strengthen the policy of containing the Soviet Union; it would provide a framework for the reintegration of Germany into the European family; and it would reassure jittery Europeans that a traditionally isolationist Uncle Sam was not about to abandon them to the marauding Russian bear—or to a resurgent and domineering Germany.

The Truman administration decided to join the European pact, called the North Atlantic Treaty Organization in recognition of its transatlantic character. With white-tie pageantry, the NATO treaty was signed in Washington on April 4, 1949. The twelve original signatories pledged to regard an attack on one as an attack on all, and promised to respond with "armed force" if necessary. Despite last-ditch howls from immovable isolationists, the Senate approved the treaty on July 21, 1949, by a vote of eighty-two to thirteen. Membership was boosted to fourteen in 1952 by the inclusion of Greece and Turkey; to fifteen in 1955 by the addition of West Germany.

The NATO pact was epochal. It marked a dramatic departure from American diplomatic convention, a gigantic boost for European unification, and a significant step in the militarization of the Cold War. NATO became the cornerstone of all Cold War American policy toward Europe. With good reason, pundits summed up NATO's threefold purpose: "to keep the Russians out, the Germans down, and the Americans in."

Reconstruction and Revolution in Asia

Reconstruction in Japan was simpler than in Germany, primarily because it was largely a one-man show. The occupying American army, under the supreme Allied commander, five-starred General Douglas MacArthur, sat in the driver's seat. In the teeth of violent protests from the Soviet officials,

MacArthur went inflexibly ahead with his program for the democratization of Japan. Following the pattern in Germany, top Japanese "war criminals" were tried in Tokyo from 1946 to 1948. Eighteen of them were sentenced to prison terms, and seven were hanged.

General MacArthur, as a kind of Yankee mikado, enjoyed a stunning success. He made a tremendous impression on the Japanese with his aloof, Greek-god bearing; and the vanquished people cooperated with their conqueror to an astonishing degree. They were clever enough to see that good behavior and the adoption of democracy would speed the end of the occupation—as it did. A MacArthur-dictated constitution was adopted in 1946. It renounced militarism and introduced Western-style democratic government—paving the way for a phenomenal economic recovery that within a few decades made Japan one of the world's mightiest industrial powers.

If Japan was a success story for American policymakers, the opposite was true in China, where a bitter civil war had raged for years between Nationalists and communists. Washington had half-heartedly supported the Nationalist government of Generalissimo Jiang Jieshi in his struggle with the communists under Mao Zedong (Mao Tse-tung). But ineptitude and corruption within the generalissimo's regime gradually began to corrode the confidence of his people. Communist armies swept south overwhelmingly, and late in 1949 Jiang was forced to flee with the remnants of his once-powerful force to the last-hope island of Formosa (Taiwan).

The collapse of Nationalist China was a depressing defeat for America and its allies in the Cold War—the worst to date. At one fell swoop nearly one-fourth of the world's population—some 500 million people—was swept into the communist camp. The so-called fall of China became a bitterly partisan issue in the United States. The Republicans, seeking "goats" who had "lost China," assailed President Truman and his bristly mustached, British-appearing secretary of state, Dean Acheson. They insisted that Democratic agencies, wormy with communists, had deliberately withheld aid from Jiang Jieshi so that he would fall. Democrats heatedly replied that when a regime has forfeited the support of its people, no amount of outside help will save it. Truman, the argument ran, did not "lose" China because he never had China to lose. Jiang himself had never controlled all of China.

More bad news came in September 1949, when President Truman shocked the nation by announcing that the Soviets had exploded an atomic bomb—approximately three years earlier than many experts had thought possible. American strategists since 1945 had counted on keeping the Soviets in line by threats of a one-sided aerial attack with nuclear weapons. America's monopoly of this lethal weapon may in fact have restrained the USSR from launching out on a course of armed aggression. But atomic bombing was now a game that two could play.

To outpace the Soviets in nuclear weaponry, Truman ordered the development of the "H-bomb" (hydrogen bomb)—a city-smashing device many times more deadly than the atomic bomb. The United States exploded its first hydrogen device on a South Pacific atoll in 1952, despite warnings from some scientists that the H-bomb was so powerful that "it becomes a weapon which in practical effect is almost one of genocide." Famed physicist Albert Einstein, whose theories had helped give birth to the atomic age, declared that "annihilation of any life on earth has been brought within the range of technical possibilities." Not to be outdone, the Soviets exploded their first H-bomb in 1953, and the nuclear arms race entered a perilously competitive cycle. Nuclear "superiority" became a dangerous and delusive dream, as each side tried to outdo the other in the scramble to build more destructive weapons. If the Cold War should ever blaze into a hot war, there might be no world left for the

---

In August 1949 Secretary of State Dean Acheson (1893–1971) explained publicly why America had "dumped" Jiang Jieshi:

"The unfortunate but inescapable fact is that the ominous result of the civil war in China was beyond the control of the government of the United States. Nothing that this country did or could have done within the reasonable limits of its capabilities could have changed that result; nothing that was left undone by this country has contributed to it. It was the product of internal Chinese forces, forces which this country tried to influence but could not."

The Hydrogen Bomb
This test blast at Bikini Atoll in the Marshall Islands in 1954 was so powerful that one Japanese fisherman was killed and all twenty-two of his crewmates were seriously injured by radioactive ash that fell on their vessel some eighty miles away. Fishing boats 1,000 miles from Bikini later brought in radioactively contaminated catches.

communists to communize or the democracies to democratize—a chilling thought that constrained both camps. Peace through mutual terror brought a shaky stability to the superpower standoff.

Ferreting Out Alleged Communists

One of the most active Cold War fronts was at home, where a new antired chase was in full cry. Many nervous citizens feared that communist spies, paid with Moscow gold, were undermining the government and treacherously misdirecting foreign policy. In 1947 Truman launched a massive "loyalty" program. The attorney general drew up a list of ninety supposedly disloyal organizations, none of which was given the opportunity to prove its innocence. A Loyalty Review Board investigated more than 3 million federal employees, some 3,000 of whom either resigned or were dismissed, none under formal indictment.

Individual states likewise became intensely security-conscious. Loyalty oaths in increasing numbers were demanded of employees, especially teachers. The gnawing question for many earnest Americans was, Could the nation continue to enjoy traditional freedoms—especially freedom of speech, freedom of thought, and the right of political dissent—in a Cold War climate?

In 1949 eleven communists were brought before a New York jury for violating the Smith Act of 1940, the first peacetime antisedition law since 1798. Hiding behind the very Constitution they were attempting to destroy, the defendants were convicted of advocating the overthrow of the American government by force and were sent to prison. The Supreme Court upheld their convictions in *Dennis* v. *United States* (1951).

The House of Representatives in 1938 had established a Committee on Un-American Activities (popularly known as "HUAC"), to investigate "subversion." In 1948 committee member Richard M. Nixon, an ambitious red-catcher, led the chase after Alger Hiss, a prominent ex–New Dealer and a distinguished member of the "eastern establishment." Accused of being a communist agent in the 1930s, Hiss demanded the right to defend himself. He dramatically met his chief accuser before the Un-American Activities Committee in August 1948. Hiss denied everything but was caught in embarrassing falsehoods, convicted of perjury in 1950, and sentenced to five years in prison.

In February 1950 a new and madly reckless anticommunist crusader burst upon the scene. Senator Joseph R. McCarthy, a Wisconsin Republican, spectacularly charged that there were scores of known communists in the State Department. He proved utterly unable to substantiate his accusation, and many Americans, including President Truman, began to fear that the red-hunt was turning into a witch-hunt. In 1950 Truman vetoed the McCarran Internal Security Bill, which among other provisions authorized the president to arrest and detain suspicious people during an "internal security emergency." Critics protested that the bill smacked of police-state, concentration-camp tactics. But the congressional guardians of the Republic's liberties enacted the bill over Truman's veto.

The stunning success of the Soviet scientists in developing an atomic bomb was presumably due, at least in part, to the cleverness of communist spies in stealing American secrets. Notorious among those Americans and Britishers who had allegedly "leaked" atomic data to Moscow were two American citizens, Julius and Ethel Rosenberg. They were convicted in 1951 of espionage and, after prolonged

> *In his inaugural address, January 1949, President Harry S Truman (1884–1972) said,*
>
> "Communism is based on the belief that man is so weak and inadequate that he is unable to govern himself, and therefore requires the rule of strong masters. . . . Democracy is based on the conviction that man has the moral and intellectual capacity, as well as the inalienable right, to govern himself with reason and justice."

appeals, went to the electric chair in 1953—the only people in American history ever executed in peacetime for espionage. Their sensational trial and electrocution, combined with sympathy for their two orphaned children, began to sour some sober citizens on the excesses of the red-hunters.

Democratic Divisions in 1948

Attacking high prices and "High-Tax Harry" Truman, the Republicans had won control of Congress in the congressional elections of 1946. Their prospects had seldom looked rosier as they gathered in Philadelphia to choose their 1948 presidential candidate. They noisily renominated warmed-over New York Governor Thomas E. Dewey, still as debonair as if he had stepped out of a bandbox.

Also gathering in Philadelphia, Democratic politicos looked without enthusiasm on their hand-me-down president and sang, "I'm Just Mild about Harry." But their "dump Truman" movement collapsed when war hero Dwight D. Eisenhower refused to be drafted. The peppery president, unwanted but undaunted, was then chosen in the face of vehement opposition by southern delegates. They were alienated by his strong stand in favor of civil rights for blacks, who now mustered many votes in the big-city ghettos of the North.

Truman's nomination split the party wide open. Embittered southern Democrats from thirteen states, like their fire-eating forebears of 1860, next met in their own convention, in Birmingham, Alabama, with Confederate flags brashly in evidence. Amid scenes of heated defiance, these "Dixiecrats"

Richard Nixon, Red-Hunter   Congressman Nixon examines the microfilm that figured as important evidence in Alger Hiss's conviction for perjury in 1950.

The Harried Piano Player, 1948   Besieged by the left and right wings of his own party, and by a host of domestic and foreign problems, Truman was a long shot for reelection in 1948. But the scrappy president surprised his legions of critics by handily defeating his opponent, Thomas E. Dewey.

nominated Governor J. Strom Thurmond of South Carolina on a States' Rights party ticket.

To add to the confusion within Democratic ranks, former Vice President Henry A. Wallace threw his hat into the ring. Having parted company with the administration over its get-tough-with-Russia policy, he was nominated at Philadelphia by the new Progressive party—a bizarre collection of disgruntled former New Dealers, starry-eyed pacifists, well-meaning liberals, and communist-fronters.

Wallace, a vigorous if misguided liberal, assailed Uncle Sam's "dollar imperialism" from the stump. This so-called Pied Piper of the Politburo took an apparently pro-Soviet line that earned him drenchings with rotten eggs in hostile cities. But to many Americans, Wallace raised the only hopeful voice in the deepening gloom of the Cold War.

With the Democrats ruptured three ways and the Republican congressional victory of 1946 just past, Dewey's victory seemed assured. Succumbing to overconfidence engendered by his massive lead in public-opinion polls, the cold, smug Dewey confined himself to dispensing soothing-syrup trivialities like "Our future lies before us."

The seemingly doomed Truman, with little money and few active supporters, had to rely on his "gut-fighter" instincts and folksy personality. Traveling the country by train to deliver some three hundred "give 'em hell" speeches, he lashed out at the Taft-Hartley "slave labor" law and the "do-nothing" Republican Congress while whipping up support for his program of civil rights, improved labor benefits, and health insurance. "Pour it on 'em, Harry!" cried increasingly large and enthusiastic crowds, as the pugnacious president rained a barrage of verbal uppercuts on his opponent.

On election night the Chicago *Tribune* ran off an early edition with the headline "DEWEY DEFEATS TRUMAN." But in the morning it turned out that "President" Dewey had embarrassingly snatched defeat from the jaws of victory. Truman had swept to a stunning triumph, to the complete bewilderment of politicians, pollsters, prophets, and pundits. Even though Thurmond took away 39 electoral votes in the South, Truman won 303 electoral votes, primarily from the South, Midwest, and West. Dewey's 189 electoral votes came principally from the East. The popular vote was 24,179,345 for Truman, 21,991,291 for Dewey, 1,176,125 for Thurmond, and 1,157,326 for Wallace. To make the victory sweeter, the Democrats regained control of Congress as well.

Truman's victory rested on farmers, workers, and blacks, all of whom were Republican-wary. Republican overconfidence and Truman's lone-wolf, never-

That Ain't the Way I Heard It!   Truman wins.

say-die campaign also won him the support of many Americans who admired his "guts." No one wanted him, someone remarked, except the people. Dewey, in contrast, struck many voters as arrogant, evasive, and wooden. When Dewey took the platform to give a speech, said one commentator, "he comes out like a man who has been mounted on casters and given a tremendous shove from behind."

Smiling and self-assured, Truman sounded a clarion note, in the fourth point of his inaugural address, when he called for a "bold new program" ("Point Four"). The plan was to lend U.S. money and technical aid to underdeveloped lands to help them help themselves. Truman wanted to spend millions to keep underprivileged peoples from becoming communists rather than spend billions to shoot them after they had become communists. This farseeing program was officially launched in 1950, and it brought badly needed assistance to impoverished countries, notably in Latin America, Africa, the Near East, and the Far East.

At home, Truman outlined a sweeping "Fair Deal" program in his 1949 message to Congress. It called for improved housing, full employment, a higher minimum wage, better farm price supports, new TVAs, and an extension of Social Security. But most of the Fair Deal fell victim to Congressional opposition from Republicans and southern Democrats. The only major successes came in raising the minimum wage, providing for public housing in the Housing Act of 1949, and extending old-age insurance to many more beneficiaries in the Social Security Act of 1950.

The Korean Volcano Erupts (1950)

Korea, the Land of the Morning Calm, heralded a new and more disturbing phase of the Cold War—a shooting phase—in June 1950.

When Japan collapsed in 1945, Soviet troops had accepted the Japanese surrender north of the thirty-eighth parallel on the Korean peninsula, and American troops had done likewise south of that line. Both superpowers professed to want the reunification of Korea, but, as in Germany, each helped to set up rival regimes above and below the parallel.

By 1949, when the Soviets and Americans had both withdrawn their forces, the entire peninsula was a bristling armed camp, with two hostile regimes eyeing each other suspiciously. Secretary of State Acheson seemed to wash his hands of the dispute early in 1950, when he declared in a memorable speech that Korea was outside the essential United States defense perimeter in the Pacific.

The explosion came on June 25, 1950. Spearheaded by Soviet-made tanks, North Korean army columns rumbled across the thirty-eighth parallel. Caught flat-footed, the South Korean forces were shoved back southward to a dangerously tiny defensive area around Pusan, their weary backs to the sea.

President Truman sprang quickly into the breach, for he remembered that the old League of Nations had died from inaction. The invasion seemed to provide devastating proof of a fundamental premise in the "containment doctrine" that shaped Washington's foreign policy: that even a slight relaxation of America's guard was an invitation to communist aggression somewhere.

The Korean invasion also provided the occasion for a vast expansion of the American military. Truman's National Security Council had recommended in a famous document of 1950 (known as National Security Council Memorandum Number 68, or NSC-68) that the United States should quadruple its defense spending. Buried at the time because it was considered politically impossible to implement, NSC-68 was resurrected by the Korean crisis. "Korea saved us," Secretary of State Acheson later commented. Truman now ordered a massive military buildup, well beyond what was necessary for the immediate purposes of the Korean war. Soon the United States had 3.5 million men under arms and was spending $50 billion per year on the defense budget—some 13 percent of the GNP.

NSC-68 was a key document of the Cold War period, not only because it marked a major step in the militarization of American foreign policy, but also because it vividly reflected the sense of almost limitless possibility that pervaded postwar American society. NSC-68 rested on the assumption that the enormous American economy could bear without strain the huge costs of a gigantic rearmament program. Said one NSC-68 planner: "There was practically nothing the country could not do if it wanted to do it."

Truman took full advantage of temporary Soviet absence from the United Nations Security Council on June 25, 1950, when he obtained a unanimous condemnation of North Korea as an aggressor. (Why the Soviets were absent remains controversial. Scholars once believed that the Soviets were just as surprised as the Americans by the attack. It now

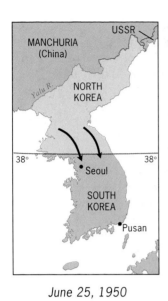

June 25, 1950

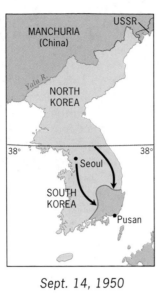

Sept. 14, 1950

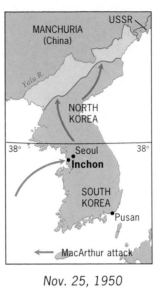

Nov. 25, 1950

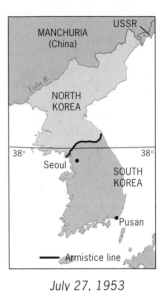

July 27, 1953

The Shifting Front in Korea

appears that Stalin had given his reluctant approval to North Korea's strike plan, but believed that the fighting would be brief and that the United States would take little interest in it.) The Council also called upon all U.N. members, including the United States, to "render every assistance" to restore peace. Two days later, without consulting Congress, Truman ordered American air and naval units to support South Korea. Before the week was out, he also ordered General Douglas MacArthur's Japan-based occupation troops into action alongside the beleaguered South Koreans.

Officially, the United States was simply participating in a United Nations "police action." But in fact, the United States made up the overwhelming bulk of the U.N. contingents, and General MacArthur, appointed U.N. commander of the entire operation, took his orders from Washington, not from the Security Council.

The Military Seesaw in Korea

Rather than fight his way out of the southern Pusan perimeter, MacArthur launched a daring amphibious landing behind the enemy's lines at Inchon. This bold gamble, on September 15, 1950, succeeded brilliantly; within two weeks the North Koreans had scrambled back behind the "sanctuary" of

the thirty-eighth parallel. Truman's avowed intention was to restore South Korea to its former borders, but the pursuing South Koreans had already crossed the thirty-eighth parallel, and there seemed little point in permitting the North Koreans to regroup and come again. The U.N. Assembly tacitly authorized a crossing by MacArthur, whom President Truman ordered northward, provided that there was no intervention in force by the Chinese or Soviets.

The Americans thus raised the stakes in Korea, and in so doing, they quickened the fears of another potential player in this dangerous game. The Chinese communists had publicly warned that they would not sit idly by and watch hostile troops approach the strategic Yalu River boundary between Korea and China. But MacArthur pooh-poohed all predictions of an effective intervention by the Chinese and reportedly boasted that he would "have the boys home by Christmas."

MacArthur erred badly. In November 1950 hordes of Chinese "volunteers" fell upon his rashly overextended lines and hurled the U.N. forces reeling back down the peninsula. The fighting now sank into a frostbitten stalemate on the icy terrain near the thirty-eighth parallel.

An imperious MacArthur, humiliated by this rout, pressed for drastic retaliation. He favored a blockade of the China coast and bombardment of Chinese bases in Manchuria. But Washington policymakers, with anxious eyes on Moscow, refused to enlarge the already costly conflict. The chairman of the Joint Chiefs of Staff declared that a wider clash in Asia would be "the wrong war, at the wrong place, at the wrong time, and with the wrong enemy." Europe, not Asia, was the administration's first concern; and the USSR, not China, loomed as the more sinister foe.

Two-fisted General MacArthur felt that he was being asked to fight with one hand tied behind his back. He sneered at the concept of a "limited war" and insisted that "there is no substitute for victory." When the general began to take issue publicly with presidential policies, Truman had no choice but to remove the insubordinate MacArthur from command (April 11, 1951). MacArthur, a legend in his own mind, returned to an uproarious welcome, whereas Truman was condemned as a "pig," an "imbecile," a "Judas," and an appeaser of "Communist Russia and Communist China." In July 1951 truce discussions began in a rude field tent near the firing line but were almost immediately snagged on the issue of prisoner exchange. Talks dragged on unproductively for nearly two years—while men continued to die.

Truman Takes the Heat

Chronology

1944	Servicemen's Readjustment Act (GI Bill) Bretton Woods economic conference
1945	Spock publishes *The Common Sense Book of Baby and Child Care* Yalta conference United States ends lend-lease to the USSR United Nations established
1945–1946	Nuremberg war crimes trials in Germany
1946	Employment Act creates Council of Economic Advisers Iran crisis
1946–1948	Tokyo war crimes trials
1947	Truman Doctrine Marshall Plan Taft-Hartley Act National Security Act creates Department of Defense, National Security Council (NSC), and Central Intelligence Agency (CIA)
1948	United States officially recognizes Israel
1948	"Voice of America" begins radio broadcasts behind iron curtain Hiss case begins Truman defeats Dewey for presidency
1948–1949	Berlin crisis
1949	NATO established Communists defeat Nationalists in China
1950	American economy begins postwar growth McCarthy red-hunt begins McCarran Internal Security Bill passed by Congress over Truman's veto
1950–1953	Korean War
1951	Truman fires MacArthur Rosenbergs convicted of treason
1952	United States explodes first hydrogen bomb
1957	Postwar peak of U.S. birthrate
1973	U.S. birthrate falls below replacement level

Who Was to Blame for the Cold War?

Whose fault was the Cold War? (And, for that matter, who should get credit for ending it?) For two decades after World War II, American historians generally agreed that the aggressive Soviets were solely responsible. This "orthodox" or "official" appraisal squared with the traditional view of the United States as a virtuous, innocent land with an idealistic foreign policy. This point of view also justified America's Cold War containment policy, which cast the Soviet Union as the aggressor that must be confined by an ever-vigilant United States. America supposedly had only defensive intentions, with no expansionary ambitions of its own.

In the 1960s, a vigorous revisionist interpretation flowered, powerfully influenced by disillusion over U.S. involvement in Vietnam. The revisionists stood the orthodox view on its head. The Soviets, they argued, had only defensive intentions at the end of World War II; it was the Americans who had behaved provocatively by brandishing their new atomic weaponry. Some of these critics pointed an accusing finger at President Truman, alleging that he abandoned Roosevelt's conciliatory approach to the Soviets and adopted a bullying attitude, emboldened by the American atomic monopoly.

More radical revisionists like Gabriel and Joyce Kolko even claimed to have found the roots of Truman's alleged belligerence in long-standing American policies of economic imperialism—policies that eventually resulted in the tragedy of Vietnam (see pp. 953–956). In this view, the Vietnam War followed logically from America's insatiable "need" for overseas markets and raw materials. Vietnam itself may have been economically unimportant, but, so the argument ran, a communist Vietnam represented an intolerable challenge to American hegemony. Ironically, revisionists thus endorsed the so-called domino theory, which official apologists often cited in defense of America's Vietnam policy. According to the domino theory, if the United States declined to fight in Vietnam, other countries would lose their faith in America's will (or their fear of American power), and would tumble one after the other like "dominoes" into the Soviet camp. Revisionists stressed what they saw as the *economic necessity* behind the domino theory: losing in Vietnam, they claimed, would unravel the American economy.

In the 1970s a "postrevisionist" interpretation emerged that is widely agreed upon today. Historians such as John Lewis Gaddis and Melvyn Leffler, pooh-pooh the economic determinism of the revisionists, while frankly acknowledging that the United States did have vital security interests at stake in the post–World War II era. The postrevisionists analyze the ways in which inherited ideas (like isolationism) and the contentious nature of post-WWII domestic politics, as well as miscalculations by American leaders, led a nation in search of security into seeking not simply a sufficiency, but a "preponderance," of power. The American *overreaction* to its security needs, these scholars suggest, exacerbated U.S.-Soviet relations and precipitated the four-decade-long nuclear arms race that formed the centerpiece of the Cold War.

In the case of Vietnam, the postrevisionist historians focus not on economic necessity but on a failure of political intelligence, induced by the stressful conditions of the Cold War, that made the dubious domino theory seem plausible. Misunderstanding Vietnamese intentions, exaggerating Soviet ambitions, and fearing to appear "soft on communism" in the eyes of their domestic political rivals, American leaders plunged into Vietnam, sadly misguided by their own Cold War obsessions.

Most postrevisionists, however, still lay the lion's share of the blame for the Cold War on the Soviet Union. By the same token, they credit the Soviets with ending the Cold War—a view hotly disputed by Ronald Reagan's champions, who claim that it was his anti-Soviet policies in the 1980s that brought the Russians to their knees (see p. 1000). The great unknown, of course, is the precise nature of Soviet thinking in the Cold War years. Were Soviet aims predominantly defensive, or did the Kremlin incessantly plot world conquest? Was there an opportunity for reconciliation with the West following Stalin's death in 1953? Should Mikhail Gorbachev or Ronald Reagan be remembered as the leader who ended the Cold War? With the opening of Soviet archives, scholars are eagerly pursuing answers to such questions.

SUGGESTED READINGS

PRIMARY SOURCE DOCUMENTS

George F. Kennan's "long telegram," *Foreign Relations of the United States, 1946* (vol. 6, 1969, pp. 696–709),* outlined the containment doctrine that would form the foundation of U.S. foreign policy in the Cold War era. Harry S Truman first applied the containment doctrine when he enunciated the Truman Doctrine, *Congressional Record*, 80th Congress, 1st Session, p. 1981* (1947). On the changing postwar family, consult Dr. Benjamin Spock, *Baby and Child Care*￼* (1957).

SECONDARY SOURCES

Lucid overviews of the postwar years can be found in James Patterson, *Grand Expectations* (1996), William H. Chafe, *The Unfinished Journey: America Since World War II* (1986); John Patrick Diggins, *The Proud Decades: America in War and Peace, 1941–1960* (1988); and William O'Neill, *American High: The Years of Confidence, 1945–1960* (1986). Harold G. Vatter gives a valuable account of *The United States Economy in the 1950s* (1963). Edward Denison, in *The Sources of Economic Growth in the United States* (1962), argues that improved education was the key to economic growth. The southern economic boom is charted in two books by James C. Cobb: *The Selling of the South* (1982) and *Industrialization and Southern Society* (1984). The rise of the Sunbelt is dramatically portrayed by Kirkpatrick Sale, *Power Shift* (1975), and Kevin Phillips, *The Emerging Republican Majority* (1970). Suburbia is the subject of Herbert J. Gans, *The Levittowners* (1967); Zane Miller, *Suburb* (1981); Carol O'Connor, *A Sort of Utopia: Scarsdale, 1891–1981* (1983); and Kenneth T. Jackson's sweeping synthesis, *Crabgrass Frontier* (1986). On the baby boom and its implications, consult Richard A. Easterlin, *Birth and Fortune: The Impact of Numbers on Personal Welfare* (1980); Landon Y. Jones, *Great Expectations: America and the Baby Boom Generation* (1980); and Michael X. Delli Carpini, *Stability and Change in American Politics: The Coming of Age of the Generation of the 1960s* (1986). Mark Silk chronicles the role of organized religion in America since the 1940s in *Spiritual Politics: Religion and America Since World War II* (1988). On the origins of the Cold War, see the titles cited in Chapter 38 by John L. Gaddis, Lloyd Gardner, Gar Alperovitz, Martin J. Sherwin, Herbert Feis, and Gabriel Kolko. Consult also

Gaddis's *Strategies of Containment* (1982) and Joyce and Gabriel Kolko's *The Limits of Power: The World and United States Foreign Policy, 1945–1954* (1972), which roundly condemns Washington's actions. For an ambitious revisionist synthesis, see Thomas J. McCormick, *America's Half-Century: U.S. Foreign Policy in the Cold War* (1989). Useful surveys of the diplomatic history of the period, all of them in varying degrees critical of American policy, are Stephen Ambrose, *Rise to Globalism: American Foreign Policy since 1938* (rev. ed., 1983); Walter LaFeber, *America, Russia and the Cold War, 1945–1984* (5th ed., 1985); and Daniel Yergin, *Shattered Peace* (1977). Among the most comprehensive post-revisionist studies is Melvyn P. Leffler, *A Preponderance of Power: National Security, the Truman Administration, and the Cold War* (1992). Broader accounts that include discussion of domestic events are David McCullough, *Truman* (1992) and Alonzo L. Hamby, *Beyond the New Deal: Harry S Truman and American Liberalism* (1973). The implications of the election of 1948 are examined in Samuel Lubell's perceptive *The Future of American Politics* (1952). Various aspects of foreign policy are analyzed in Timothy P. Ireland, *Creating the Entangling Alliance: The Origins of the North Atlantic Treaty Organization* (1981); Gordon Chang, *Friends and Enemies: The United States, China and the Soviet Union* (1990); Michael Schaller, *The American Occupation of Japan: The Origins of the Cold War in Asia* (1985); and Robert M. Blum, *Drawing the Line: The Origins of the American Containment Policy in East Asia* (1982). Korea is discussed in Callum A. MacDonald, *Korea: The War Before Vietnam* (1986); Bruce Cumings, ed., *Child of Conflict: The Korean-American Relationship, 1943–1953* (1983); and Bruce Cumings and Jon Halliday, *Korea: The Unknown War* (1988). On the "red scare" at home, see Richard M. Freeland, *The Truman Doctrine and the Origins of McCarthyism* (1971), as well as David M. Oshinsky, *A Conspiracy So Immense: The World of Joe McCarthy* (1983). Daniel Bell, ed., *The Radical Right* (1963), places McCarthyism in a larger context. See also David W. Reinhard, *The Republican Right Since 1945* (1983). For more on J. Edgar Hoover, see Thomas Gid Powers, *Secrecy and Power: The Life of J. Edgar Hoover* (1987). Examinations of the impact of the Cold War on American culture include Nora Sayre, *Running Time: The Films of the Cold War* (1982); Nancy Schwartz, *The Hollywood Writers' Wars* (1982); Ellen Schrecker, *No Ivory Tower: McCarthyism and the Universities* (1986); and Richard H. Pells, *The Liberal Mind in a Conservative Age* (1985). Valuable personal reflections by policymakers include Truman's own *Year of Decisions* (1955) and *Years of Trial and Hope* (1956); George F. Kennan, *Memoirs, 1925–1950* (1967); Dean Acheson, *Present at the Creation* (1969); and Charles Bohlen, *Witness to History* (1973).

*An asterisk indicates that the document, or an excerpt from it, can be found in Thomas A. Bailey and David M. Kennedy, eds., *The American Spirit: United States History as Seen by Contemporaries*, 9th ed. (Boston: Houghton Mifflin, 1998).

40

The Eisenhower Era
1952–1960

Every warship launched, every rocket fired signifies. . . a theft from those who hunger and are not fed, those who are cold and are not clothed.

DWIGHT D. EISENHOWER, APRIL 16, 1953

The Advent of Eisenhower

Democratic prospects in the presidential election of 1952 were blighted by the military deadlock in Korea, Truman's clash with MacArthur, war-bred inflation, and whiffs of scandal from the White House. Dispirited Democrats, convening in Chicago, nominated a reluctant Adlai E. Stevenson, the witty, eloquent, and idealistic governor of Illinois. Republicans headed off a determined attempt by the isolationist wing of their party to nominate "Mr. Republican," Ohio Senator Robert A. Taft. Instead they enthusiastically chose General Dwight D. Eisenhower on the first ballot. As something of a concession to the hard-line anticommunist Taft supporters, the convention selected as "Ike's" running mate California senator Richard M. Nixon, who had distinguished himself as a relentless red-hunter.

Eisenhower was already the most popular American of his time, as "I Like Ike" buttons everywhere testified. His ruddy face, captivating grin, and glowing personality made him a perfect candidate in the dawning new age of television politics. He had an authentic hero's credentials as wartime supreme commander of the Allied forces in Europe, army chief of staff after the war, and the first supreme commander of NATO from 1950 to 1952. He had also been "civilianized" by a brief term as president of Columbia University, from 1948 to 1950.

Striking a grandfatherly, nonpartisan pose, Eisenhower left the rough campaigning to Nixon, who relished pulling no punches. The vice-presidential candidate lambasted his opponents with charges that they had cultivated corruption, caved in on Korea, and coddled communists. He particularly blasted the intellectual ("egghead") Stevenson as "Adlai the appeaser," with a "Ph.D. from [Secretary of State] Dean Acheson's College of Cowardly Communist Containment."

Nixon himself faltered when reports surfaced of a secretly financed "slush fund" he had tapped while holding a seat in the Senate. Prodded by Republican party officials, Eisenhower seriously considered dropping him from the ticket, but a scared Nixon went on national television with a theatrical appeal filled with self-pity, during which he referred to the family cocker spaniel, Checkers. This heart-tugging "Checkers speech" saved him his place on the ticket.

The maudlin Checkers speech also demonstrated the awesome political potentialities of television—foreshadowed by FDR's mastery of the radio. Nixon had defied Republican party bosses and bent Eisenhower himself to his will by appealing directly to the American people in their living rooms. His performance illustrated the disturbing power of the new, vivid medium, which communicated with far more immediacy and effect than its electronic cousin, the radio, ever could.

Even Eisenhower reluctantly embraced the new technology of the black-and-white television screen. He allowed himself to be filmed in a New York TV studio giving extremely brief "answers" to a nonexistent audience, whose "questions" were taped later, then carefully spliced with Eisenhower's statements to give the illusion of a live discussion. "To think that an old soldier should come to this," Ike grumbled. These so-called "spots" foreshadowed the future of political advertising. They amounted, as one critic observed, to "selling the President like toothpaste." Devoid of substance, they vastly oversimplified complicated economic and social issues. "What about the high cost of living?" one spot asked. "My wife Mamie worries about the same thing," Ike answered. "I tell her it's my job to change that on November fourth."

In future years television made possible a kind of "plebiscitarian" politics, through which lone-wolf politicians could go straight to the voters without the mediating influence of parties or other institutions. The new medium thus stood revealed as a threat to the historic role of political parties, which traditionally had chosen candidates through complex internal bargaining, and had educated and mobilized the electorate. And given television's origins in entertainment and advertising, political messages would be increasingly tuned to the standards of show business and commercialism. Gradually, as television spread to virtually every household in the land, those standards would rule

The Republicans' Choice, 1952 Nominee Eisenhower and his vice-presidential running mate Nixon greet the delegates.

politics with iron sway as ten-second television "sound bites" became the most common form of political communication.

The outcome of the presidential election of 1952 was never really in doubt. Given an extra prod by Eisenhower's last-minute pledge to go personally to Korea to end the war, the voters overwhelmingly declared for "Ike." He garnered 33,963,234 votes to Stevenson's 27,314,992. He cracked the solid South wide open, ringing up 442 electoral votes to 89 for his opponent. "Ike" not only ran far ahead of his ticket but managed to pull enough Republicans into office on his military coattails to ensure GOP control of the new Congress by a paper-thin margin.

True to his campaign pledge, president-elect Eisenhower undertook a flying three-day visit to Korea in December 1952. But even a glamorous "Ike" could not immediately budge the peace negotiations off dead center. Seven long months later, after Eisenhower had threatened to use atomic weapons, an armistice was finally signed but was repeatedly violated in succeeding decades.

The brutal and futile fighting had lasted three years. About 54,000 Americans lay dead, joined by perhaps more than a million Chinese, North

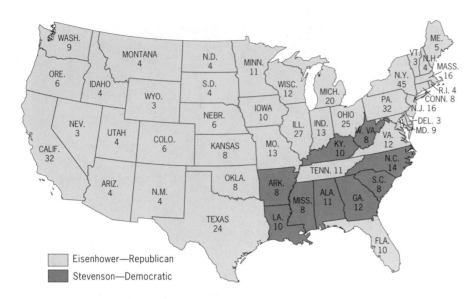

Presidential Election of 1952 (with electoral vote by state) A Democrat quipped that "if the voters liked the Republicans the way they liked Ike, the two-party system would be in bad shape." Fortunately for Democrats, Eisenhower scored a personal, not a party, victory. Republicans won minuscule majorities in Congress, majorities that disappeared in the congressional elections two years later.

Legend:
- Eisenhower—Republican
- Stevenson—Democratic

Koreans, and South Koreans. Tens of billions of American dollars had been poured down the Asian sinkhole. Yet this terrible toll in blood and treasure bought only a return to the conditions of 1950; Korea remained divided at the thirty-eighth parallel. Americans took what little comfort they could from the fact that communism had been "contained" and that the bloodletting had been "limited" to something less than full-scale global war. The shooting had ended, but the Cold War still remained frigidly frozen.

Korean War Scene A grief-stricken American soldier whose buddy has been killed is being comforted, while a medical corpsman fills out casualty tags.

"Ike" Takes Command

In Dwight Eisenhower, the man and the hour apparently met. Americans yearned for a period of calm in which they could pursue without distraction their new visions of consumerist affluence. The nation sorely needed a respite from twenty years of depression and war. Yet the American people unexpectedly found themselves in the early 1950s dug into the front lines of the Cold War abroad and dangerously divided at home over the explosive issues of communist subversion and civil rights. They longed for reassuring leadership. "Ike" seemed ready both to reassure and to lead.

As a military commander, Eisenhower had cultivated a leadership style that self-consciously projected an image of sincerity, fairness, and optimism. He enjoyed remarkable success in harmonizing the efforts of potentially quarrelsome allies. He had been widely perceived during the war as an "unmilitary" general, and in the White House he similarly struck the pose of an "unpolitical" president, serenely above the petty partisan fray. He also shrewdly knew that his greatest "asset" was his enjoyment of the "affection and respect of our citizenry," as he confided to his diary in 1949.

"Ike" thus seemed ideally suited to soothe the anxieties of troubled Americans, much as a distinguished and well-loved grandfather brings stability to his family. He played this role well as he presided over a decade of shaky peace and shining prosperity. Yet critics charged that he unwisely hoarded the "asset" of his immense popularity, rather than spend it for a good cause (especially civil rights), and that he cared more for social harmony than for social justice.

One of the first problems with which Eisenhower had to contend was the swelling popularity and swaggering power of Senator Joseph R. McCarthy, the anticommunist "crusader." McCarthy had crashed into the limelight in February 1950, when he wildly charged in a public speech that Secretary of State Dean Acheson was knowingly employing 205 Communist party members in the State Department. Pressed to reveal the names, McCarthy at first conceded that there were only 57 genuine communists and in the end failed to root out even one. His Republican colleagues nevertheless realized the political usefulness of his kind of attack on the Democratic administration. Even the supposedly fair-minded Senator Robert Taft urged McCarthy, "If one case doesn't work, try another." Ohio's Senator John Bricker reportedly said, "Joe, you're a dirty s.o.b., but there are times when you've got to have an s.o.b. around, and this is one of them."

McCarthy flourished in the seething Cold War atmosphere of suspicion and fear. He was not the first nor even the most effective antired, but he was surely the most ruthless, and he did the most damage to American traditions of fair play and free speech. Elected to the Senate on the basis of a trumped-up war-hero record ("Congress needs a tail-gunner"), McCarthy was just an obscure junior senator until he exploded his bombshell announcement in 1950 of communists in the State Department. For the next four years, "low-blow Joe" proved a master at manipulating the media and exploiting the anxieties of politicians and the public. The careers of countless officials, writers, actors, and others were ruined after Senator McCarthy had "named" them, often unfairly, as communists or communist sympathizers.

As McCarthy's accusations spread ever more widely, his rhetoric grew bolder. Democrats, he charged, "bent to the whispered pleas from the lips of traitors." Incredibly, he even denounced General George Marshall, former army chief of staff and ex–secretary of state, as "part of a conspiracy so immense and an infamy so black as to dwarf any previous venture in the history of man."

Politicians trembled in the face of such onslaughts, especially when opinion polls showed

Senator McCarthy Extinguishes the Torch of Liberty
While preaching patriotism, McCarthy irresponsibly menaced American traditions of civil liberties.

that a majority of the American people approved of McCarthy. Furthermore, his intervention in certain key senatorial elections brought resounding defeat for his enemies. Eisenhower privately loathed McCarthy but publicly tried to stay out of his way, saying, "I will not get in the gutter with that guy." Trying to appease the brash demagogue from Wisconsin, Eisenhower allowed him, in effect, to control personnel policy at the State Department. One baleful result was severe damage to the morale and effectiveness of the professional foreign service. In particular, McCarthyite purges deprived the government of a number of Asian specialists who might have counseled a wiser course in Vietnam in the fateful decade that followed.

McCarthy finally bent the bow too far. The nominal end of the Korean War partly cooled the feverish atmosphere in which he had thrived. When he attacked the United States Army, he at last met his match. The embattled military men fought back in thirty-five days of televised hearings in the spring of 1954. The political power of the new broadcast medium was again demonstrated as up to 20 million Americans at a time watched in fascination while a boorish, surly McCarthy publicly cut his own

In a moment of high drama during the Army-McCarthy hearings, attorney Joseph Welch reproached McCarthy in front of a huge national television audience for threatening to slander a young lawyer on Welch's staff:

"Until this moment, Senator, I think I never really gauged your cruelty or your recklessness. Little did I dream you could be so cruel as to do an injury to that lad. . . . If it were in my power to forgive you for your reckless cruelty, I would do so. I like to think that I am a gentleman, but your forgiveness will have to come from someone other than me. . . . Have you no decency, sir, at long last? Have you left no sense of decency?"

throat by parading his essential meanness and irresponsibility. A few months later the Senate formally condemned him for "conduct unbecoming a member."

Three years later, unwept and unsung, McCarthy died of chronic alcoholism. But "McCarthyism" has passed into the English language as a label for the dangerous forces of unfairness and fear that a democratic society can unleash only at its peril. The senator actually hurt his alleged cause by making Americans more afraid of the supposed communists in their midst than of the real communists in Moscow.

Desegregating the South

America counted some 15 million black citizens in 1950, two-thirds of whom still made their homes in the South. There they lived bound by the iron folkways of a segregated society. A rigid set of antiquated rules known as Jim Crow laws governed all aspects of their existence, from the schoolroom to the restroom. Every day of their lives, southern blacks dealt with a bizarre array of separate social arrangements that kept them insulated from whites, economically inferior, and politically powerless. Later generations, black and white alike, would wonder at how their ancestors could have daily made their way through this anthropological museum of curious and stifling customs.

Blacks everywhere in the South, for example, not only attended segregated schools, but were compelled to use separate public toilets, drinking fountains, restaurants, and waiting rooms. Trains and buses had "whites only" and "colored only" seating. Because Alabama hotels were prohibited from serving blacks, the honeymooning Dr. Martin Luther King, Jr., and his wife, Coretta, spent their wedding night in 1953 in a blacks-only funeral parlor. Only about 20 percent of eligible southern blacks were registered to vote, and fewer than 5 percent in some Deep South states like Mississippi and Alabama. As late as 1960, white southern sensibilities about segregation were so tender that television networks blotted out black speakers at the national political conventions for fear of offending southern stations.

Where the law proved insufficient to enforce this regime, vigilante violence did the job. Six black war veterans, claiming the rights for which they had fought overseas, were murdered in the summer of 1946. A Mississippi mob lynched black fourteen-year-old Emmett Till in 1955 for allegedly leering at a white woman. It is small wonder that a black clergyman declared that "everywhere I go in the South the Negro is forced to choose between his hide and his soul."

In his notable book of 1944, *An American Dilemma*, Swedish scholar Gunnar Myrdal had exposed the contradiction between America's professed belief that all men are created equal and its sordid treatment of black citizens. There had been token progress in race relations since the war—Jack Roosevelt ("Jackie") Robinson, for example, had cracked the racial barrier in big-league baseball when the Brooklyn Dodgers signed him in 1947. But for the most part, the national conscience still slumbered, and blacks still suffered.

Increasingly, however, African-Americans refused to suffer in silence. The war had generated a new militancy and restlessness among many members of the black community. The National Association for the Advancement of Colored People (NAACP) had for years pushed doggedly to dismantle the legal underpinnings of segregation and now enjoyed some success. In 1944 the Supreme Court ruled the "white primary" unconstitutional, thereby undermining the status of the Democratic party in the South as a white person's club. And in 1950, NAACP chief legal counsel Thurgood Marshall (him-

The Face of Segregation   These women in the segregated South of the 1950s were compelled to enter the movie theater through the "Colored Entrance." Once inside, they were restricted to a separate seating section, usually in the rear of the theater.

In a campaign speech of 1946, Mississippi senator Theodore Bilbo (1847–1947) described some of the tactics used to prevent blacks from voting:

"If there is a single man or woman serving [as a registrar] who cannot think up questions enough to disqualify undesirables, then write Bilbo or any good lawyer and there are a hundred good questions which can be furnished, . . . but you know and I know what is the best way to keep the nigger from voting. You do it the night before the election, I don't have to tell you any more than that. Red-blooded men know what I mean."

self later a Supreme Court justice), in the case of *Sweatt* v. *Painter,* wrung from the High Court a ruling that separate professional schools for blacks failed to meet the test of equality.

On a chilly day in December 1955, Rosa Parks, a college-educated black seamstress, made history in Montgomery, Alabama. She boarded a bus, took a seat in the "whites only" section, and refused to give it up. Her arrest for violating the city's Jim Crow statutes sparked a yearlong black boycott of the city buses and served notice throughout the South that blacks would no longer submit meekly to the absurdities and indignities of segregation.

The Montgomery bus boycott also catapulted to prominence a young pastor at Montgomery's Dexter Avenue Baptist Church, the Reverend Martin Luther King, Jr. Barely twenty-seven years old, King seemed an unlikely champion of the downtrodden and disfranchised. Raised in a prosperous black family in

Atlanta and educated partly in the North, he had for most of his life been sheltered from the grossest cruelties of segregation. But his oratorical skill, his passionate devotion to biblical and constitutional conceptions of justice, and his devotion to the nonviolent principles of India's Mohandas Gandhi were destined to thrust him to the forefront of the black revolution that would soon pulse across the South—and the rest of the nation.

Seeds of the Civil Rights Revolution

When President Harry Truman heard about the lynching of black war veterans in 1946, he exclaimed, "My God! I had no idea it was as terrible as that." The horrified Truman responded by commissioning a report entitled "To Secure These Rights." Following the report's recommendations, Truman in 1948 ended segregation in federal civil service and ordered "equality of treatment and opportunity" in the armed forces. The military brass at first protested that "the army is not a sociological laboratory," but manpower shortages in Korea forced the integration of combat units, without the predicted loss of effectiveness. Yet Congress stubbornly resisted passing civil rights legislation, and Truman's successor, Dwight Eisenhower, showed no real signs of interest in the racial issue. Within the government, that left only the judicial branch as an avenue of advancement for civil rights.

Breaking the path for civil rights progress was broad-jawed Chief Justice Earl Warren, former governor of California. Elevated to the supreme bench by Eisenhower, Warren shocked the president and other traditionalists with his active judicial intervention in previously taboo social issues. Publicly snubbed and privately scorned by President Eisenhower, Warren persisted in encouraging the Court to apply his straightforward populist principles. Critics assailed this "judicial activism," and "Impeach Earl Warren" signs blossomed along the nation's highways. But Warren's defenders argued that the Court was rightly stepping up to confront important social issues—especially civil rights for African-Americans—because the Congress had abdicated its responsibilities by refusing to deal with them. When it came to fundamental rights, Warren's allies claimed, "legislation by the judiciary" was better than no legislation at all.

The unanimous decision of the Warren Court in *Brown* v. *Board of Education of Topeka, Kansas,* in May 1954 was epochal. In a forceful opinion, the learned justices ruled that segregation in the public schools was "inherently unequal" and thus unconstitutional. The uncompromising sweep of the decision startled conservatives like an exploding time bomb, for it reversed the Court's earlier declaration of 1896 in *Plessy* v. *Ferguson* (see p. 522) that "separate but equal" facilities were allowable under the Constitution. That doctrine was now dead. Desegregation, the justices insisted, must go ahead with "all deliberate speed."

> *In the desegregation decision of 1954, the Supreme Court quoted approvingly from a lower court:*
>
> "Segregation of white and colored children in public schools has a detrimental effect upon the colored children. The impact is greater when it has the sanction of the law; for the policy of separating the races is usually interpreted as denoting the inferiority of the Negro group. A sense of inferiority affects the motivation of a child to learn. Segregation . . . has a tendency to retard the educational and mental development of Negro children. . . ."

The Border States generally made reasonable efforts to comply with this ruling, but in the Deep South diehards organized "massive resistance" against the Court's annulment of the sacred principle of "separate but equal." More than a hundred southern congressional representatives and senators signed a "Declaration of Constitutional Principles" in 1956, pledging their unyielding resistance to desegregation. Several states diverted public funds to hastily created "private" schools, for there the integration order was more difficult to apply. Throughout the South, white citizens' councils, sometimes with fire and hemp, thwarted attempts to make integration a reality. Ten years after the Court's momentous ruling, fewer than 2 percent of the eligible blacks in the Deep South states were sitting in classrooms with whites. The southern translation of "all deliberate speed" was apparently deliberately slow.

Crisis at Little Rock

President Eisenhower was little inclined toward promoting integration. He shied away from employing his vast popularity and the prestige of his office to educate white Americans about the need for racial justice. His personal attitudes may have helped to restrain him. He had grown up in an all-white town and spent his career in a segregated army. He had advised against integration of the armed forces in 1948 and had criticized Truman's call for a permanent Fair Employment Practices Commission. He complained that the Supreme Court's decision in *Brown* v. *Board of Education* had upset "the customs and convictions of at least two generations of Americans," and he steadfastly refused to issue a public statement endorsing the Court's conclusions. "I do not believe," he explained, "that prejudices, even palpably unjustifiable prejudices, will succumb to compulsion."

But in September 1957, "Ike" was forced to act. Orval Faubus, the governor of Arkansas, mobilized the National Guard to prevent nine black students from enrolling in Little Rock's Central High School. Confronted with a direct challenge to federal authority, Eisenhower sent troops to escort the children to their classes.

In the same year, Congress passed the first Civil Rights Act since Reconstruction days. Eisenhower characteristically reassured a southern senator that

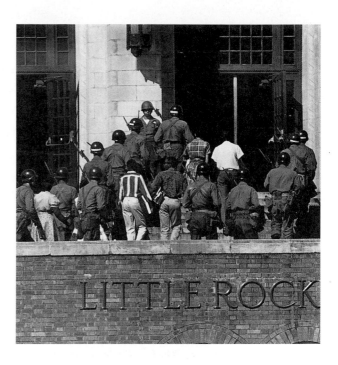

Integration at Little Rock, 1957 While white mobs jeered angrily at the first black students entering Central High School, federal troops, with bayonets fixed, enforced the law.

the legislation represented "the mildest civil rights bill possible." It set up a permanent Civil Rights Commission to investigate violations of civil rights and authorized federal injunctions to protect voting rights.

Blacks meanwhile continued to take the civil rights movement into their own hands. Martin Luther King, Jr., formed the Southern Christian Leadership Conference (SCLC) in 1957. It aimed to mobilize the vast power of the black churches on behalf of black rights. This was an exceptionally shrewd strategy, because the churches were the largest and best-organized black institutions that had been allowed to flourish in a segregated society.

More spontaneous was the "sit-in" movement launched on February 1, 1960, by four black college freshmen in Greensboro, North Carolina. Without a detailed plan or institutional support, they

Martin Luther King, Jr., and His Wife, Coretta, Arrested King and his wife were arrested for the first time in Montgomery, Alabama, in 1955 while organizing a bus boycott.

demanded service at a whites-only Woolworth's lunch counter. Observing that "fellows like you make our race look bad," the black waitress refused to serve them. But they kept their seats and returned the next day with nineteen classmates. The following day, eighty-five students joined in; by the end of the week, a thousand. Like a prairie fire, the sit-in movement burned swiftly across the South, swelling into a wave of wade-ins, lie-ins, and pray-ins to compel equal treatment in restaurants, transportation, employment, housing, and voter registration. In April 1960, southern black students formed the Student Non-Violent Coordinating Committee (SNCC, pronounced "snick") to give more focus and force to these efforts. Young and impassioned, SNCC members would eventually lose patience with the more stately tactics of the SCLC and the even more deliberate legalisms of the NAACP.

Eisenhower Republicanism at Home

The balding, sixty-two-year-old General Eisenhower had entered the White House in 1953 pledging his administration to a philosophy of "dynamic conservatism." "In all those things which deal with people, be liberal, be human," he advised. But when it came to "people's money, or their economy, or their form of government, be conservative." This balanced, middle-of-the-road course harmonized with the depression-daunted and war-weary mood of the times. Some critics called Eisenhower's presidency a case of "the bland leading the bland."

Above all, Eisenhower strove to balance the federal budget and guard the Republic from what he called "creeping socialism." The former supreme allied commander put the brakes on Truman's enormous military buildup, though defense spending still soaked up some 10 percent of the GNP. True to his small-government philosophy, Eisenhower supported the transfer of control over offshore oil fields from the federal government to the states. "Ike" also tried to curb the TVA by encouraging a private power company to build a generating plant to compete with the massive public utility spawned by the New Deal. Speaking of the TVA, Eisenhower reportedly said, "By God, if ever we could do it, before we leave here, I'd like to see us *sell* the whole thing, but I suppose we can't go that far." Eisenhower's secretary

A Popular President   "Ike" exuded grandfatherly graciousness and goodwill.

of health, education, and welfare condemned free distribution of Salk antipolio vaccine as "socialized medicine." Secretary of Agriculture Ezra Taft Benson grappled tenaciously with the soaring costs of farm price supports. Yet prosperity remained beyond the next furrow for most farmers, despite mountains of surplus grain, bought by the government and stored in silo-shaped containers at a cost to taxpayers of nearly $2 million a day. Benson tried to get the government off the farm and to restore "free-market" conditions—but he succeeded only in spending more money than any previous secretary of agriculture.

Eisenhower responded to the Mexican government's worries that illegal Mexican immigration to the United States would undercut the *bracero* program of legally imported farm workers inaugurated during World War II (see p. 853). In a massive roundup of illegal immigrants, dubbed Operation Wetback in reference to the migrants' watery route across the Rio Grande, as many as 1 million Mexicans were apprehended and returned to Mexico in 1954.

In yet another of the rude and arbitrary reversals that long have afflicted the government's relations with Native Americans, Eisenhower also sought to cancel the tribal preservation policies of the "Indian New Deal," in place since 1934 (see p. 807). He proposed to "terminate" the tribes as legal entities and to revert to the assimilationist goals of the Dawes Severalty Act of 1887 (see p. 604). A few tribes, notably the Klamaths of Oregon, were induced to terminate themselves. In return for cash payments, the Klamaths relinquished all claims on their land and agreed to their legal dissolution as a tribe. But most Indians resisted termination, and the policy was abandoned in 1961.

Eisenhower knew that he could not unscramble all the eggs that had been fried by New Dealers and Fair Dealers for twenty long years. He pragmatically accepted and thereby legitimated many New Dealish programs, stitching them permanently into the fabric of American society. As he told his brother: "Should any political party attempt to abolish Social Security, unemployment insurance, and eliminate labor and farm programs, you would not hear of that party again in our political history."

In some ways, Eisenhower even did the New Deal one better. In a public works project that dwarfed anything the New Dealers had ever dreamed of, "Ike" backed the Interstate Highway Act of 1956, a $27 billion plan to build 42,000 miles (67,000 kilometers) of sleek, fast motorways. Laying down these modern, multilane roads created countless construction jobs and speeded the suburbanization of America. The Highway Act offered juicy benefits to the trucking, automobile, oil, and travel industries, while at the same time robbing the railroads, especially passenger trains, of business. The act also exacerbated problems of air quality and energy consumption, and had especially disastrous consequences for cities, whose once-vibrant downtowns withered away while shopping malls flourished in the far-flung suburbs. One critic carped that the most charitable assumption about the

Operation Wetback   Thousands of illegal Mexican immigrants were forcibly repatriated to Mexico in the federal government's 1954 roundup operation, which was promoted in part by the Mexican government. The man in this photograph is being pulled across the border by a Mexican official, while an American spectator tries to pull him back into the United States.

Seldon E. Kirk, President of the Klamath Indian Tribal Council, 1959

Interstate Highway Act was that Congress "didn't have the faintest notion of what they were doing."

Despite his good intentions, Eisenhower managed to balance the budget only three times in his eight years in office, and in 1959 he incurred the biggest peacetime deficit thus far in American history. Yet critics blamed his fiscal timidity for aggravating several business recessions during the decade, especially the sharp downturn of 1957–1958, which left more than 5 million workers jobless. Economic troubles helped to revive the Democrats, who regained control of both houses of Congress in 1954. Unemployment jitters also helped to spark the merger of the AF of L and the CIO in 1955, ending two decades of bitter division in the house of labor.

A New Look in Foreign Policy

Mere containment of communism was condemned in the 1952 Republican platform as "negative, futile, and immoral." Incoming Secretary of State John Foster Dulles—a pious churchgoer whose sanctimonious manner was lampooned by critics as "Dull, Duller, Dulles"—promised not merely to stem the red tide but to "roll back" its gains and "liberate captive peoples." At the same time, the new administration promised to balance the budget by cutting military spending.

How were these two contradictory goals to be reached? Dulles answered with a "policy of boldness" in early 1954. The genial General Eisenhower would relegate the army and the navy to the back seat and build up an air fleet of superbombers (called the Strategic Air Command, or SAC) equipped with city-flattening nuclear bombs. These fearsome weapons would inflict "massive retaliation" on the Soviets or the Chinese if they got out of hand. The advantages of this new policy were thought to be its paralyzing nuclear impact and its cheaper price tag when compared with conventional forces—"more bang for the buck." In 1955, Eisenhower actually threatened nuclear reprisal when Communist China shelled some small islands near the Nationalist Chinese stronghold of Taiwan.

At the same time, Eisenhower sought a thaw in the Cold War through negotiations with the new Soviet leaders who came to power after dictator Joseph Stalin's death in 1953. But the new Soviet premier, Nikita Khrushchev, rudely rejected Ike's heartfelt proposals for peace at the Geneva summit conference in 1955. When Ike called for "open skies" over both the Soviet Union and the United States, to prevent either side from miscalculating the other's military intentions, Khrushchev replied: "This is a very transparent espionage device. . . . You could hardly expect us to take this seriously." Eisenhower went home empty-handed.

In the end, the touted "new look" in foreign policy proved illusory. In 1956 the Hungarians rose up against their Soviet masters and appealed in vain to the United States for aid, while Moscow reasserted its domination with the unmistakable language of force. Embittered Hungarian freedom fighters naturally accused Uncle Sam of "welshing" when the chips were down. The truth was that America's mighty nuclear sledgehammer was too heavy a weapon to wield in such a relatively minor crisis. The rigid futility of the "massive retaliation" doctrine was thus starkly exposed. To his dismay, Eisenhower also discovered that the aerial and atomic hardware necessary for "massive retaliation" was staggeringly expensive. Military costs shot skyward. In 1960, as Eisenhower was about to leave office, he sagely but ironically warned against the dangerous growth of a "military-industrial complex" that his own policies had nurtured.

The Vietnam Nightmare

Europe, thanks to the Marshall Plan and NATO, seemed reasonably secure by the early 1950s, but East Asia was a different can of worms. Nationalist movements had sought for years to throw off the French colonial yoke in Indochina. The Vietnamese leader, goateed Ho Chi Minh, had tried to appeal personally to Woodrow Wilson in Paris as early as 1919 to support self-determination for the peoples of Southeast Asia. Franklin Roosevelt had likewise inspired hope among Asian nationalists.

Cold War events dampened the dreams of anticolonial Asian peoples. Their leaders—including Ho Chi Minh—became increasingly communist while the United States became increasingly anticommunist. By 1954 American taxpayers were financing nearly 80 percent of the costs of a bottomless French colonial war in Indochina. The United States' share amounted to about $1 billion a year.

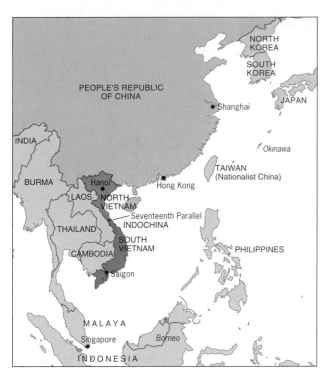

The Far East, 1955–1956

Despite this massive aid, French forces continued to crumble under Viet Minh guerrilla intractibility and insurgency. In March 1954 a key French garrison was trapped hopelessly in the fortress of Dienbienphu at the northwestern corner of Vietnam. The new "policy of boldness" was now put to the test. Secretary Dulles, Vice President Nixon, and the chairman of the Joint Chiefs of Staff favored intervention with American bombers to help bail out the beleaguered French. But Eisenhower, wary about another war in Asia so soon after Korea, and correctly fearing British nonsupport, held back.

Dienbienphu fell, and a multination conference at Geneva roughly halved the two Vietnams at the seventeenth parallel, supposedly temporarily (see map). The victorious Ho Chi Minh in the north consented to this arrangement on the assurance that Vietnam-wide elections would be held within two years. In the south a pro-Western government under Ngo Dinh Diem was soon entrenched at Saigon. The Vietnamese never held the promised elections, primarily because the communists seemed certain to win, and Vietnam remained a dangerously divided country.

Eisenhower promised economic and military aid to the conservative Diem regime, provided that it undertook certain social reforms. Change came at a snail's pace, but American aid continued, as communist guerrillas heated up their campaign against Diem. The Americans had evidently backed a losing horse but could see no easy way to call off their bet. Secretary Dulles, in a vain attempt to prop up his shaky policy in Vietnam, engineered the creation of the eight-member Southeast Asia Treaty Organization (SEATO), including the United States, Britain, and France. Pieced together in late 1954, it was but a pale imitation of NATO and, as events were to prove, a frail crutch on which to lean for the security of South Vietnam.

A False Lull in Europe

The United States had initially backed the French in Indochina in part to win French approval of a plan to rearm West Germany. Despite French fears, the Germans were finally welcomed into the NATO fold in 1955, with an expected contribution of half a million troops. In the same year, the Eastern European countries and the Soviets signed the Warsaw Pact, creating a red military counterweight to the newly bolstered NATO forces in the West.

Despite these hardening military lines, the Cold War seemed to be thawing a bit. Eisenhower earnestly endeavored to cage the nuclear demon by negotiating arms-control agreements with Moscow, and early signs were encouraging. In May 1955 the Soviets rather surprisingly agreed to end the occupation of Austria. A summit conference in July produced little progress on the burning issues, but it bred a conciliatory "spirit of Geneva" that caused a modest blush of optimism to pass over the face of the Western world. Hopes rose further the following year when Soviet Communist party boss Nikita Khrushchev, a burly ex–coal miner, publicly denounced the bloody excesses of Joseph Stalin, the dictator dead since 1953.

Violent events late in 1956 ended the post-Geneva lull. When the liberty-loving Hungarians struck for their freedom, they were ruthlessly overpowered by Soviet tanks. While the Western world looked on in horror, Budapest was turned into a slaughterhouse, and thousands of Hungarian refugees fled their country in panic for the Austrian border. The United States eventually altered its immigration laws to admit thirty thousand Hungarian fugitives.

Egyptian President Gamal Abdel Nasser in Cairo, 1956   Hailed as a hero in the Arab world, Nasser was a thorn in the flesh of American and European policymakers anxious to protect the precious oil resources of the Middle East.

Menaces in the Middle East

Increasing fears of Soviet penetration into the oil-rich Middle East prompted Washington to take audacious action. The government of Iran, supposedly influenced by the Kremlin, began to resist the power of the gigantic Western companies that controlled Iranian petroleum. In response, the American Central Intelligence Agency (CIA) engineered a coup in 1953 that installed the youthful shah of Iran, Mohammed Reza Pahlevi, as a kind of dictator. Though successful in the short run in securing Iranian oil for the West, the American intervention left a bitter legacy of resentment among many Iranians. More than two decades later, they took their revenge on the shah and his American allies (see pp. 985–986).

The Suez crisis proved far messier than the swift stroke in Iran. President Nasser of Egypt, an ardent Arab nationalist, was seeking funds to build an immense dam on the upper Nile for urgently needed irrigation and power. America and Britain tentatively offered financial help, but when Nasser began to flirt openly with the communist camp, Secretary of State Dulles dramatically withdrew the dam offer. Thus slapped in the face, Nasser promptly regained face by nationalizing the Suez Canal, owned chiefly by British and French stockholders.

Nasser's action placed a razor's edge at the jugular vein of Western Europe's oil supply, much of which transited the canal from the Persian Gulf into the Mediterranean Sea for distribution in Europe. Secretary Dulles labored strenuously to ward off armed intervention by the cornered European powers—as well as by the Soviets, who threatened to match any Western invasion by pouring "volunteers" into Egypt and perhaps by launching nuclear attacks on Paris and London. But the United States' apprehensive French and British allies, after deliberately keeping Washington in the dark and coordinating their blow with one from Israel, staged a joint assault on Egypt late in October 1956.

For a breathless week the world teetered on the edge of the abyss. The French and the British, however, had made a fatal miscalculation—that the United States would supply them with oil while their Middle Eastern supplies were disrupted, as an oil-rich Uncle Sam had done in the two world wars. But to their unpleasant surprise, a furious President Eisenhower resolved to let them "boil in their own oil" and refused to release emergency supplies. The oilless allies resentfully withdrew their troops, and for the first time in history, a United Nations police force was sent to maintain order.

The Suez crisis also marked the last time in history that the United States could brandish its "oil weapon." As recently as 1940, the United States had produced two-thirds of the world's oil, while a scant 5 percent of the global supply flowed from the Middle East. But domestic American reserves had been rapidly depleted. In 1948 the United States had become a net oil importer. Its days as an "oil power" clearly were numbered as the economic and strategic importance of the Middle East oil region grew dramatically.

The U.S. president and Congress proclaimed the Eisenhower Doctrine in 1957, pledging U.S. military and economic aid to Middle Eastern nations threatened by communist aggression. The real threat to U.S. interests in the Middle East, however, was not communism but nationalism, as Nasser's wild popularity among the masses of all Arab countries demonstrated. The poor, sandy sheikdoms increasingly resolved to reap for themselves the lion's share of the enormous oil wealth that Western companies pumped out of the scorching Middle Eastern deserts. In a move with portentous implications, Saudi Arabia, Kuwait, Iraq, and Iran joined with Venezuela in 1960 to form the Organization of Petroleum Exporting Countries (OPEC). In the next two decades, OPEC's stranglehold on the Western economies would tighten to a degree that even Nasser could not have imagined.

The Voters Still Like "Ike" in 1956

Blood-spattered Budapest and Suez provided the backdrop for the elections of 1956. Despite a heart attack in 1955 and a major abdominal operation in 1956, Eisenhower still enjoyed the public's confidence and affection. He and Vice President Nixon were unanimously renominated by a jubilant Republican convention in San Francisco. Democrats, for their part, dutifully offered up Adlai Stevenson for a second time. Voters were thus presented with two warmed-over presidential candidates—the first such matchup since 1900.

Democrats charged that the only order the magnetic ex-general had ever given was to mark time. They railed at Republican stand-pattism, at Eisenhower's shaky health (though Stevenson was to die first), and at the dubious moral character of "Tricky Dick" Nixon. In response, the GOP preened itself on being the party of peace, prosperity, and happiness. The biggest Republican asset remained Eisenhower's irrepressible grin—described by one wartime colleague as "worth twenty divisions."

The election was a resounding personal endorsement of Eisenhower. He piled up an enormous majority of 35,590,472 votes to Stevenson's 26,022,752; in the Electoral College the count was 457 to 73. "Any jockey would look good riding Ike," crowed the GOP national chairman. But the general's coattails this time were not so stiff or so broad. He failed to win for his party either house of Congress—the first time since Zachary Taylor's election in 1848 that a winning president had headed such a losing ticket. The country remained heavily Democratic; but Eisenhower remained widely beloved. Voters were especially reluctant to abandon the old war-horse when events abroad threatened to spark off World War III at a push of the button.

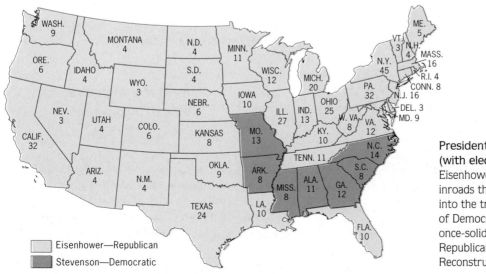

Presidential Election of 1956 (with electoral vote by state) Eisenhower made even deeper inroads than he had in 1952 into the traditional bastion of Democratic strength, the once-solid South. Louisiana went Republican for the first time since Reconstruction days in 1876.

Round Two for "Ike"

In fragile health, Eisenhower began his second term as a part-time president. Critics charged that he had his hands on his golf clubs, fly rod, and shotgun more often than on the levers of power. He seemed to rely more than ever on trusted lieutenants like Secretary of State Dulles and presidential assistant Sherman Adams, the tough-minded ex-governor of New Hampshire who had publicly and repeatedly condemned Democratic corruption.

Adams's chickens came home to roost in 1958, when a House investigation revealed that he had accepted expensive gifts from a Boston industrialist, on whose behalf he had thrice mildly interceded with federal agencies. Adams was forced to leave the White House under a dark cloud of scandal. Secretary Dulles, who had traveled half a million miles by air, died of cancer in 1959. Shorn of his two most trusted aides, "Ike" in his last years did less golfing and more governing.

A key area in which the president bestirred himself was labor legislation. A drastic labor-reform bill in 1959 grew out of recurrent strikes in critical industries and scandalous revelations of gangsterism in unionist high echelons. In particular, fraud and brass-knuckle tactics tainted the Teamsters Union. The millionaire Teamster chief, "Dave" Beck, invoked the Fifth Amendment against self-incrimination 209 times before a Senate investigating committee in 1957 to avoid telling what he had done with $320,000. He was later sentenced to prison for embezzlement. When his union defiantly elected the tough-fisted James R. Hoffa as his successor, the AF of L–CIO expelled the Teamsters. The Senate committee reported that in fifteen years union officials had stolen or misappropriated some $10 million. Hoffa later was jailed for jury tampering, served part of his sentence, and disappeared—evidently the victim of the gangsters whom he had apparently crossed.

Even labor's friends agreed that the house of labor needed a thorough house cleaning. Congress rallied to devise a tough labor reform bill. Teamster boss Hoffa threatened to defeat for reelection congressional representatives who dared to vote for the proposed labor law. Eisenhower responded with a dramatic television appeal, and Congress in 1959 passed the Landrum-Griffin Act. It was designed to bring labor leaders to book for financial shenanigans and to prevent bullying tactics. Seizing the opportune moment, antilaborites also forced into the bill prohibitions against "secondary boycotts" and certain kinds of picketing.

The Helicopter Era, 1957   President Eisenhower was routinely criticized by liberals, as in this Herblock cartoon in the Washington *Post*, for his apparent indifference to many seething social problems of the day. His failure to employ his vast prestige on behalf of civil rights was especially conspicuous.

The Race with the Soviets into Space

Soviet scientists astounded the world on October 4, 1957, by lofting into orbit around the globe a beep-beeping "baby moon" *(Sputnik I),* weighing 184 pounds (83.5 kilograms). A month later they topped their own ace by sending aloft a larger satellite

(Sputnik II), weighing 1,120 pounds (507 kilograms) and carrying a dog.

This amazing scientific breakthrough shattered American self-confidence. The Soviets had long been trying to convince the uncommitted nations that the shortcut to superior industrial production lay through communism and the *Sputnik*s gave credence to their claim. America had seemingly taken a back seat in scientific achievement. Envious "backward" nations laughed at America's discomfiture, all the more so because the Soviets were occupying outer space while American troops were occupying the high school in Little Rock.

Military implications of these human-made satellites proved sobering. If the Soviets could fire heavy objects into outer space, they certainly could reach America with intercontinental ballistic missiles. Old-soldier Eisenhower, adopting a father-knows-best attitude toward the Soviet "gimmick," remarked that it should not cause "one iota" of concern. Others, chiefly Republicans, blamed the Truman administration for having spent more for supporting peanut propagation than for supporting a missile program. Agonizing soul-searching led to the conclusion that while the United States was well advanced on a broad scientific front, including color television, the Soviets had gone all out for rocketry. Experts testified that America's manned bombers were still a powerful deterrent, but heroic efforts were needed if the alleged "missile gap" was not to widen.

"Rocket fever" swept the nation. After humiliating and well-advertised failures (the Soviets concealed theirs), the Americans regained some prestige four months after the initial Soviet space triumph. They managed to put into orbit a grapefruit-sized satellite weighing 2.5 pounds (1.14 kilograms).

The *Sputnik* success led to a critical comparison of the American educational system, which was already under fire as too easygoing, with that of the Soviet Union. A strong move now developed in the United States to replace "frills" with solid subjects —to substitute square roots for square dancing. Congress rejected demands for federal scholarships, but late in 1958 the National Defense and Education Act (NDEA) authorized $887 million in loans to needy college students and in grants for the improvement of teaching the sciences and languages.

The Continuing Cold War

The fantastic race toward nuclear annihilation continued unabated. Humanity-minded scientists urged that nuclear tests be stopped before the atmosphere became so polluted as to produce generations of deformed mutants. The Soviets, after completing an intensive series of exceptionally "dirty" tests, proclaimed a suspension in March 1958 and urged the Western world to follow. Beginning in October 1958, Washington did halt both underground and atmospheric testing. But attempts to regularize such suspensions by proper inspection sank on the reef of mutual mistrust.

Thermonuclear suicide seemed nearer in July 1958, when both Egyptian and communist plottings threatened to engulf Western-oriented Lebanon. After its president had called for aid under the Eisenhower Doctrine, the United States boldly landed several thousand troops and helped restore order without taking a single life.

The burly Khrushchev, seeking new propaganda laurels, was eager to meet with Eisenhower and pave the way for a "summit conference" with Western leaders. Despite grave misgivings as to any tangible results, the president invited him to America in 1959. Arriving in New York, Khrushchev appeared before the U.N. General Assembly and dramatically resurrected the ancient Soviet proposal of complete disarmament. But he offered no practical means of achieving this end.

A result of this tour was a meeting at Camp David, the presidential retreat in Maryland. Khrushchev emerged saying that his ultimatum for the evacuation of Berlin would be extended indefinitely. The relieved world gave prayerful but premature thanks for the "spirit of Camp David."

The Camp David spirit quickly evaporated when the follow-up Paris "summit conference," scheduled for May 1960, turned out to be an incredible fiasco. Both Moscow and Washington had publicly taken a firm stand on the burning Berlin issue, and neither could risk a public backdown. Then, on the eve of the conference, an American U-2 spy plane was shot down deep in the heart of Russia. After bungling bureaucratic denials in Washington, "honest Ike" took the unprecedented step of assuming personal responsibility. Khrushchev stormed

What's So Funny? 1960
Premier Khrushchev gloats over "Ike's" spying discomfiture.

into Paris filling the air with invective, and the conference collapsed before it could get off the ground. The concord of Camp David was replaced with the grapes of wrath.

Cuba's Castroism Spells Communism

Latin Americans bitterly resented Uncle Sam's lavishing of billions of dollars on Europe, while doling out only millions to the poor relations to the south. They also chafed at Washington's continuing habit of intervening in Latin American affairs—as in a CIA-directed coup that ousted a leftist government in Guatemala in 1954. On the other hand, Washington continued to support—even decorate—bloody dictators who claimed to be combating communists.

Most ominous of all was the communist beachhead in Cuba. The ironfisted dictator Fulgencio Batista had encouraged huge investments of American capital, and Washington in turn had given him

some support. When black-bearded Dr. Fidel Castro engineered a revolution early in 1959, he denounced the Yankee imperialists and began to expropriate valuable American properties in pursuing a land-distribution program. Washington, finally losing patience, released Cuba from "imperialistic slavery" by cutting off the heavy U.S. imports of Cuban sugar. Castro retaliated with further wholesale confiscations of Yankee property and in effect made his left-wing dictatorship an economic and military satellite of Moscow. An exodus of anti-Castro Cubans headed for the United States, especially Florida. Nearly 750,000 arrived between 1960 and 1990. Washington broke diplomatic relations with Cuba early in 1961.

Americans talked seriously of invoking the Monroe Doctrine before the Soviets set up a communist base only 90 miles (145 kilometers) from their shores. Khrushchev angrily proclaimed that the Monroe Doctrine was dead and indicated that he would shower missiles upon the United States if it attacked his good friend Castro.

The Cuban revolution, which Castro sought to "export" to his neighbors, brought other significant responses. At San Jose, Costa Rica, in August 1960, the United States induced the Organization of American States to condemn (unenthusiastically) communist infiltration into the Americas. President Eisenhower, whom Castro dubbed "the senile White House golfer," hastily proposed a long-deferred "Marshall Plan" for Latin America. Congress responded to his recommendation with an initial authorization of $500 million. The Latin Americans had Castro to thank for attention that many of them regarded as too little and too late.

Kennedy Challenges Nixon for the Presidency

As Republicans approached the presidential campaign of 1960, Vice President Nixon was their heir apparent. To many, he was a gifted party leader; to others, a ruthless opportunist. The "old" Nixon had been a no-holds-barred campaigner, especially in assailing Democrats and left-wingers. The "new" Nixon was represented as a mature, seasoned statesman. More in the limelight than any earlier vice president, he had shouldered heavy responsibilities and had traveled globally as a "troubleshooter" in various capacities. He had vigorously defended American democracy in a famous "kitchen debate" with Khrushchev in Moscow in 1959. His supporters, flourishing a telling photograph of this finger-pointing episode, claimed that he alone knew how to "stand up to" the Soviets.

Nixon was nominated unanimously on the first ballot in Chicago. His running mate was the patrician Henry Cabot Lodge, Jr., of Massachusetts (grandson of Woodrow Wilson's arch-foe), who had served conspicuously for seven years as the U.S. representative to the United Nations.

By contrast, the Democratic race for the presidential nomination started as a free-for-all. John F. Kennedy—a tall (6 feet; 1.83 meters), youthful, dark-haired, and tooth-flashing millionaire senator from Massachusetts—won impressive victories in the primaries. He then scored a first-ballot triumph in Los Angeles over his closest rival, Senator Lyndon B. Johnson, the Senate majority leader from Texas. A disappointed South was not completely appeased

John F. Kennedy Campaigning for the Presidency, 1960. At right is his wife, Jacqueline Kennedy.

when Johnson accepted second place on the ticket in an eleventh-hour marriage of convenience. Kennedy's challenging acceptance speech called upon the American people for sacrifices to achieve their potential greatness, which he hailed as the New Frontier.

The Presidential Issues of 1960

Bigotry inevitably showed its snarling face. Senator Kennedy was a Roman Catholic, the first to be nominated since Al Smith's ill-starred campaign in 1928. Smear artists revived the ancient charges about the Pope's controlling the White House. Kennedy pointed to his fourteen years of service in Congress, denied that he would be swayed by Rome, and asked if some 40 million Catholic Americans were to be condemned to second-class citizenship from birth.

Kennedy's Catholicism aroused misgivings in the Protestant, Bible Belt South, which was ordinarily Democratic. "I fear Catholicism more than I fear communism," declaimed one Baptist minister in North Carolina. But the religious issue largely canceled itself out. If many southern Democrats stayed away from the polls because of Kennedy's Catholicism, northern Democrats in unusually large numbers supported Kennedy because of the bitter attacks on their Catholic faith.

Kennedy charged that the Soviets, with their nuclear bombs and circling *Sputnik*s, had gained on America in prestige and power. Nixon, forced to

Candidate John F. Kennedy (1917–1963), in a speech to a Houston group of Protestant ministers (September 12, 1960), declared,

"I believe in an America where the separation of church and state is absolute—where no Catholic prelate would tell the President, should he be a Catholic, how to act, and no Protestant minister would tell his parishioners for whom to vote . . . and where no man is denied public office because his religion differs from the President who might appoint him or the people who might elect him."

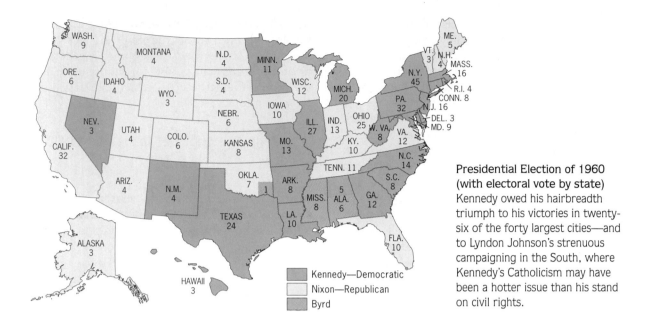

Presidential Election of 1960 (with electoral vote by state) Kennedy owed his hairbreadth triumph to his victories in twenty-six of the forty largest cities—and to Lyndon Johnson's strenuous campaigning in the South, where Kennedy's Catholicism may have been a hotter issue than his stand on civil rights.

Legend:
- Kennedy—Democratic
- Nixon—Republican
- Byrd

defend the dying administration, insisted that the nation's prestige had not slipped, although Kennedy was causing it to do so by his unpatriotic talk.

Television may well have tipped the scales. Nixon agreed to meet Kennedy in four so-called debates. The contestants crossed words in millions of living rooms before audiences estimated at 60 million or more. Nobody "won" the debates. But Kennedy at least held his own and did not suffer by comparison with the more "experienced" Nixon. Many viewers found Kennedy's glamour and vitality far more appealing than Nixon's tired and pallid appearance.

Kennedy squeezed through by the rather comfortable margin of 303 electoral votes to 219,* but with the breathtakingly close popular margin of only 118,574 votes out of over 68 million cast. Like Franklin Roosevelt, Kennedy ran well in the large industrial centers, where he had strong support from workers, Catholics, and African-Americans. (He had solicitously telephoned the pregnant Coretta King, whose husband, Martin Luther King, Jr., was then imprisoned in Georgia for a sit-in.)

Although losing a few seats, the Democrats swept both houses of Congress by wide margins.

---

*Six Democratic electors in Alabama, all eight unpledged Democratic electors in Mississippi, and one Republican elector in Oklahoma voted for Senator Harry F. Byrd.

John Fitzgerald Kennedy—the youngest man to date and the first Catholic to be elected president—was free to set out for his New Frontier, provided that the die-hard conservatives in his party would join the wagon train.

An Old General Fades Away

President Eisenhower, the aging "dynamic" conservative, continued to enjoy extraordinary popularity to the final curtain. Despite Democratic jibes about "eight years of golfing and goofing," of "putting and puttering," Eisenhower was universally admired and respected for his dignity, decency, sincerity, goodwill, and moderation.

Pessimists had predicted that Eisenhower would be a seriously crippled "lame duck" during his second term, owing to the barrier against reelection erected by the Twenty-second Amendment, ratified in 1951. (See the Appendix.) In truth, he displayed more vigor, more political know-how, and more aggressive leadership during his last two years as president than ever before. For an unprecedented six years, from 1955 to 1961, Congress remained in Democratic hands, yet Eisenhower established unusual control over the legislative branch. He wielded the veto 169 times, and only twice was his nay overridden by the required two-thirds vote.

America was fabulously prosperous in the Eisenhower years, despite pockets of poverty and unemployment, recurrent recessions, and perennial farm problems. To the north the vast St. Lawrence waterway project, constructed jointly with Canada and completed in 1959, had turned the cities of the Great Lakes into bustling ocean seaports.

"Old Glory" could now proudly display fifty stars. Alaska attained statehood in 1959, as did Hawaii. Alaska, though gigantic, was thinly populated and noncontiguous, but these objections were overcome in a Democratic Congress that expected Alaska to vote Democratic. Hawaii had ample population (largely of Asian descent), advanced democratic institutions, and more acreage than the mainland states of Rhode Island, Delaware, or Connecticut.

Though a crusading general, Eisenhower as president mounted no moral crusade for civil rights. This was perhaps his greatest failing. Yet he was no bigot, and he had done far more than grin away problems and tread water. As a Republican president, he had further woven the reforms of the Democratic New Deal and Fair Deal into the fabric of national life. As a former general, he had exercised wise restraint in his use of military power and had soberly guided foreign policy away from countless threats to peace. The old soldier left office crestfallen at his failure to end the arms race with the Soviets. Yet he had ended one war and avoided all others. As the decades lengthened, appreciation of him grew.

In his Farewell Address on radio and television, January 17, 1961, President Dwight Eisenhower (1890–1969) warned against a potent new menace:

"This conjunction of an immense military establishment and a large arms industry is new in the American experience . . . . In the councils of government, we must guard against the acquisition of unwarranted influence, whether sought or unsought, by the military-industrial complex."

Changing Economic Patterns

The continuing post–World War II economic boom wrought wondrous changes in American society in the 1950s. Prosperity triggered a fabulous surge in home construction, as a nation of renters became a nation of homeowners. One of every four homes standing in America in 1960 had been built during the 1950s—and 83 percent of those new homes were in suburbia.

More than ever, science and technology drove economic growth. The invention of the transistor in 1948 sparked a revolution in electronics, and especially in computers. The first electronic computers assembled in the 1940s were massive machines with hundreds of miles of wiring and thousands of fickle cathode ray tubes. Transistors and, later, printed circuits on silicon wafers made possible dramatic miniaturization and phenomenal computational speed. Computer giant International Business Machines (IBM) expanded robustly, becoming *the* prototype of the "high tech" corporation in the

An Early Computer, c. 1950 Just a few decades later, technological improvements would bring the computing power of this bulky behemoth to the user's desktop.

Occupational Distribution of Working Women, 1900–1995*

	1900	1920	1940	1960	1980	1995
Total white-collar workers[†]	17.8%	38.8%	44.9%	52.5%	65.6%	71.3%
Clerical workers	4.0	18.7	21.5	28.7	30.5	41.9
Manual workers	27.8	23.8	21.6	18.0	14.8	9.7
Farm workers	18.9	13.5	4.0	1.8	1.0	1.2
Service workers[‡]	35.5	23.9	29.4	21.9	18.1	17.7

*Major categories; percentage of all women workers , age fourteen and older, in each
 category.
[†]Includes clerical, sales, professional, and technical workers, managers and officials.
[‡]Includes domestic servants.
(Sources: *Historical Statistics of the United States* and *Statistical Abstract of the United States,*
relevant years.)

dawning "information age." Eventually, personal computers and even inexpensive pocket calculators contained more computing power than room-size early models. Computers transformed age-old business practices like billing and inventory control and opened genuine new frontiers in areas like airline scheduling, high-speed printing, and telecommunications.

Aerospace industries also grew fantastically in the 1950s, thanks both to Eisenhower's aggressive buildup of the Strategic Air Command, and to a robustly expanding passenger airline business—and to the connections between military and civilian aircraft production. In 1957 the Seattle-based Boeing Company brought out the first large passenger jet, the "707." Its design owed much to the previous development of SAC's long-range strategic bomber, the B-52. Two years later Boeing delivered the first presidential jet, a specially modified 707. "Air Force One" dazzled President Eisenhower with its speed and comfort.

The nature of the work force was also changing. A sort of quiet revolution was marked in 1956, when "white-collar" workers for the first time outnumbered "blue-collar" workers, signaling the passage from an industrial to a postindustrial era. Keeping pace with that fundamental transformation, organized labor withered along with the smokestack industries that had been its sustenance. Union membership as a percentage of the labor force peaked at about 35 percent in 1954, and then went into steady decline. Some observers concluded that the union movement had played out its historic role

of empowering workers and ensuring economic justice, and that unions would eventually disappear altogether in the postindustrial era.

The surge in white-collar employment opened special opportunities for women. When World War II ended, most women, including those who had worked in war plants, returned to highly conventional female roles as wives and mothers—the remarkably prolific mothers of the huge "baby boom" generation. A "cult of domesticity" emerged in popular culture to celebrate those eternal feminine functions. When 1950s television programs like

Women in the Labor Force, 1900–1995
(*Historical Statistics of the United States* and *Statistical Abstract of the United States,* relevant years.)

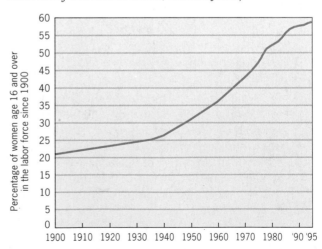

"Ozzie and Harriet"   Throughout the 1950s, the storybook Nelson family triumphed weekly on their television program over the travails of parenting and adolescence. In real life, son Ricky (seated, left) later died in a possibly drug-related plane crash while touring with his rock band.

"Ozzie and Harriet" or "Leave It to Beaver" depicted idyllic suburban families with a working husband, two children, and a wife who did not work outside the home, they did so without irony; much of middle-class America really did live that way. But as the 1950s progressed, another quiet revolution was gaining momentum that was destined to transform women's roles and even the character of the American family.

Of some 40 million new jobs created in the three decades after 1950, more than 30 million were in clerical and service work. Women filled the huge majority of these new positions. They were the principal employment beneficiaries of the postwar era, creating an extensive "pink-collar ghetto" of occupations that were dominated by women.

Exploding employment opportunities for women in the 1950s unleashed a groundswell of

The Booming Service Sector
Services displaced manufacturing as the most dynamic area of the economy in the post–World War II era, and women made up the majority of new workers in this vastly expanded area.

The Godmother   Feminist Betty Friedan (right, shown here with National Organization of Women chairperson Kathryn F. Clarenbach in 1967), gave birth to the modern women's movement with her publication in 1963 of *The Feminine Mystique*, a book that crystallized many of the issues that women had been facing throughout the postwar era.

social and psychological shocks that mounted to tidal-wave proportions in the decades that followed. From one perspective, women's surge into the workplace was nothing new at all, but only a return to the days when the United States was an agricultural nation, and men and women alike toiled on the family farm. But the urban age was not the agricultural age, and women's new dual role as *both* workers *and* homemakers raised urgent questions about family life, and about traditional definitions of gender differences. Feminist Betty Friedan gave focus and fuel to women's feelings in 1963 when she published *The Feminine Mystique,* a runaway best-seller and a classic of feminist protest literature that launched the modern women's movement. Friedan spoke in rousing accents to millions of able, educated women who applauded her indictment of the stifling boredom of suburban housewifery. Many of those women were already working for wages, but they were also struggling against the guilt and frustration of leading an "unfeminine" life as defined by the postwar "cult of domesticity."

Consumer Culture in the Fifties

The 1950s witnessed a huge expansion of the middle class and the blossoming of a consumer culture. Diner's Club introduced the plastic credit card in 1950, and four years later the first McDonald's hamburger stand opened in San Bernardino, California. Also in 1955, Disneyland opened its doors in Anaheim, California. These innovations—easy credit, high-volume "fast-food" production, and new forms of recreation—were harbingers of an emerging new lifestyle of leisure and affluence that was in full flower by the decade's end.

Crucial to the development of that lifestyle was the rapid rise of the new technology of television. Only 6 TV stations were broadcasting in 1946; a decade later, 442 stations were operating. TV sets were rich people's novelties in the 1940s; but 7 million sets were sold in 1951. By 1960 virtually every American home had one, in a stunning display of the speed with which new technologies can pervade and transform modern societies. Attendance at movies sank as the entertainment industry changed its focus from the silver screen to the picture tube. By the mid-1950s, advertisers annually spent $10 billion to hawk their wares on television, while critics fumed that the wildly popular new mass medium was degrading the public's aesthetic, social, moral, political, and educational standards. To the question, "Why is television called a medium?" pundits replied, "Because it's never rare or well done."

Even religion capitalized on the powerful new electronic pulpit. "Televangelists" like the Baptist Billy Graham, the Pentecostal Holiness preacher Oral Roberts, and the Roman Catholic Fulton J. Sheen took to the airwaves to spread the Christian gospel. Television also catalyzed the commercialization of professional sports, as viewing audiences that once numbered in the stadium-capacity thousands could now be counted in the couch-potato millions.

Sports also reflected the shift in population toward the West and South. In 1958 baseball's New York Giants moved to San Francisco and the Brooklyn Dodgers abandoned Flatbush for Los Angeles. Those moves touched off a new westward movement—of sports franchises. Shifting population and spreading affluence led eventually to substantial expansion of the major baseball leagues and the principal football and basketball leagues as well.

Popular music was also dramatically transformed in the fifties. The chief revolutionary was Elvis Presley, a white singer born in 1935 in Tupelo, Mississippi. Fusing black rhythm and blues with white bluegrass and country styles, he created a new musical idiom known forever after as rock and roll. Rock was "crossover" music, carrying its heavy beat and driving rhythms across the cultural divide that separated black and white musical traditions. Listening and dancing to it became a kind of religious rite for the millions of baby boomers coming of age in the 1950s, and Presley—with his fleshy face, pouting lips, and antic, sexually suggestive gyrations—was its high priest. Bloated by fame, fortune, and drugs, he died in 1977 at the age of forty-two.

Traditionalists were repelled by Presley, and they found much more to upset them in the affluent fifties. Movie star Marilyn Monroe, with her ingenuous smile and mandolin-curved hips, helped to popularize—and commercialize—new standards of sensuous sexuality. So did *Playboy* magazine, first published in 1955. As the decade closed, Americans were well on their way to becoming free-spending consumers of mass-produced, standardized products, advertised on the electronic medium of television and often sold for their alleged sexual allure.

Many critics lamented the implications of this new consumerist lifestyle. Harvard sociologist David Riesman portrayed the postwar generation as a pack of conformists in *The Lonely Crowd* (1950), as did William H. Whyte, Jr., in *The Organization Man*. Novelist Sloan Wilson explored a similar theme in *The Man in the Gray Flannel Suit* (1955). Harvard economist John Kenneth Galbraith questioned the relation between private wealth and the public good in a series of books beginning with *The Affluent Society* (1958). The postwar explosion of prosperity, Galbraith claimed, had produced a troublesome combination of private opulence amid public squalor. Americans had televisions in their homes but garbage in their streets. They ate rich food but breathed foul air. Galbraith's call for social spending to match private purchasing proved highly influential in the 1960s. Sociologist Daniel Bell, in *The*

The King   Rock superstar Elvis Presley greets a group of adoring fans in the 1950s.

Coming of Post-Industrial Society (1973) and *The Cultural Contradictions of Capitalism* (1976), found even deeper paradoxes of prosperity. The hedonistic "consumer ethic" of modern capitalism, he argued, might undermine the older "work ethic" and thus destroy capitalism's very productive capacity. Collusion at the highest levels of the "military-industrial complex" was the subject of *The Power Elite* (1956), an influential piece of modern muckraking by radical sociologist C. Wright Mills, who became a hero to "New Left" student activists in the 1960s.

The Life of the Mind in Postwar America

America's affluence in the heady post–World War II decades was matched by a mother lode of literary gems. In fiction writing some of the prewar realists continued to ply their trade, notably Ernest Hemingway in *The Old Man and the Sea* (1952). A Nobel laureate in 1954, Hemingway was dead by his own duck gun in 1961. John Steinbeck, another prewar writer who persisted in graphic portrayals of American society, such as *East of Eden* (1952) and *Travels with Charley* (1962), received the Nobel Prize for literature in 1962, the seventh American to be so honored.

Curiously, World War II did not inspire the same kind of literary outpouring that World War I had. Searing realism, the trademark style of war-writers in the 1920s, characterized the earliest novels that portrayed soldierly life in World War II, such as Norman Mailer's *The Naked and the Dead* (1948) and James Jones's *From Here to Eternity* (1951). But as time passed, realistic writing fell from favor. Authors tended increasingly to write about the war in fantastic and even psychedelic prose. Joseph Heller's *Catch-22* (1961) dealt with the improbable antics and anguish of American airmen in the wartime Mediterranean. A savage satire, it made readers hurt when they laughed. The supercharged imagination of Kurt Vonnegut, Jr., poured forth works of puzzling complexity in sometimes impenetrably inventive prose, including the dark comedy war tale *Slaughterhouse-Five* (1969).

The dilemmas created by the new mobility and affluence of American life were explored by Pennsylvania-born John Updike in books like *Rabbit, Run* (1960) and *Couples* (1968), and by Massachusetts-bred John Cheever in *The Wapshot Chronicle* (1957)

John Steinbeck (1902–1968)   A college drop-out (from Stanford University), Steinbeck wrote naturalistic works about Americans buffeted by forces beyond their control. His most famous work is *The Grapes of Wrath* (1939), a moving tale of the Joad family's migration out of the Oklahoma Dust Bowl to Depression-era California.

and *The Wapshot Scandal* (1964). Louis Auchincloss wrote elegantly about upper-class New Yorkers. Gore Vidal penned a series of intriguing historical novels, as well as several impish and always iconoclastic works, including *Myra Breckinridge* (1968), about a reincarnated transsexual. Together, these writers constituted the rear guard of an older, WASP (White Angle-Saxon Protestant) elite that had long dominated American writing.

Poetry also flowered in the postwar era, though poets were often highly critical, even deeply despairing, about the character of American life. Older poets were still active, including cantankerous Ezra Pound, jailed after the war in a U.S. Army detention center near Pisa, Italy, for alleged collaboration with the Fascists. Connecticut insurance executive Wallace Stevens and New Jersey pediatrician William Carlos Williams continued after 1945 to pursue second careers as prolific poets of world-class stature. But younger poets were coming to the

Death of a Salesman   First performed in 1949, Arthur Miller's play probed the psychic costs of failure in a society that held out the promise of "success" to all. The play especially resonated with audiences in the booming 1950s, and quickly took its place as an American classic. This scene shows the original Broadway cast of Lee J. Cobb and Mildred Dunnock (seated), and Arthur Kennedy (left) and Cameron Mitchell (right), above.

fore during the postwar period. Pacific Northwesterner Theodore Roethke wrote lyrically about the land until his death by drowning in Puget Sound in 1963. Robert Lowell, descended from a long line of patrician New Englanders, sought to apply the wisdom of the Puritan past to the perplexing present in allegorical poems like *For the Union Dead* (1964). Troubled Sylvia Plath crafted the moving verses of *Ariel* (published posthumously in 1966) and a disturbing novel, *The Bell-Jar* (1963), but her career was cut short when she took her own life in 1963. Anne Sexton produced brooding autobiographical poems until her death by apparent suicide in 1974. Another brilliant poet of the period, John Berryman, ended it all in 1972 by leaping from a Minneapolis bridge onto the frozen bank of the Mississippi River. Writing poetry seemed to be a dangerous pursuit in modern America. The life of the poet, it was said, began in sadness and ended in madness.

Playwrights were also active. Tennessee Williams wrote a series of searing dramas about psychological misfits struggling to hold themselves together amid the disintegrating forces of modern life. Noteworthy were *A Streetcar Named Desire* (1947) and *Cat on a Hot Tin Roof* (1955). Arthur Miller brought to the stage searching probes of American values, notably *Death of a Salesman* (1949) and *The Crucible* (1953), which treated the Salem witch trials as a dark parable warning against the dangers of McCarthyism. Lorraine Hansberry offered an affecting portrait of African-American life in *A Raisin in the Sun* (1959). In the 1960s Edward Albee exposed the rapacious underside of middle-class life in *Who's Afraid of Virginia Woolf?* (1962).

Books by black authors also made the best-seller lists, beginning with Richard Wright's chilling portrait of a black Chicago killer in *Native Son* (1940). Ralph Ellison depicted the black individual's quest for personal identity in *Invisible Man* (1952), one of the most haunting novels of the postwar era. James Baldwin won plaudits as a novelist and essayist, particularly for his sensitive reflections on the racial question in *The Fire Next Time* (1963). Black nationalist LeRoi Jones, who changed his name to Imamu Amiri Baraka, crafted powerful plays like *Dutchman* (1964).

The South boasted a literary renaissance, led by veteran Mississippi author William Faulkner, who was a Nobel recipient in 1950. Fellow Mississippians Walker Percy and Eudora Welty grasped the falling torch from the failing Faulkner, who died in 1962. Tennessean Robert Penn Warren immortalized Louisiana politico Huey Long in *All the King's Men* (1946). Flannery O'Connor wrote perceptively of her native Georgia, and Virginian William Styron confronted the harsh history of his home state in a controversial fictional representation of an 1831 slave rebellion, *The Confessions of Nat Turner* (1967).

Especially bountiful was the harvest of books by Jewish novelists. Some critics quipped that a knowledge of Yiddish was becoming necessary to understanding much of the dialogue presented in modern American novels J. D. Salinger painted an unforgettable portrait of a sensitive, upper-class, Anglo-Saxon adolescent in *Catcher in the Rye* (1951), but other Jewish writers found their favorite subject matter in the experience of lower- and middle-class Jewish immigrants. Bernard Malamud rendered a touching portrait of a family of New York Jewish

storekeepers in *The Assistant* (1957). Malamud also explored the mythic qualities of the culture of baseball in *The Natural* (1952). Philip Roth wrote comically about young New Jersey suburbanites in *Goodbye, Columbus* (1959) and penned an uproarious account of a sexually obsessed middle-aged New Yorker in *Portnoy's Complaint* (1969). Chicagoan Saul Bellow contributed masterful sketches of Jewish urban and literary life in landmark books like *The Adventures of Augie March* (1953), and *Herzog* (1962). Bellow became the eighth American Nobel laureate for literature in 1977. Isaac Bashevis Singer emigrated to America from Poland in the 1930s and continued to write in Yiddish. He won the Nobel Prize for literature in 1978. E. L. Doctorow employed Old Testament themes in his fictional account of atomic spies Julius and Ethel Rosenberg, *The Book of Daniel* (1971), and later he imaginatively recast other modern historical materials in books like *Ragtime* (1975), *World's Fair* (1985), and *Billy Bathgate* (1989).

Chronology

1952	Eisenhower defeats Stevenson for presidency Hemingway publishes *The Old Man and the Sea*
1953	CIA-engineered coup installs shah of Iran
1954	French defeated in Vietnam Army-McCarthy hearings *Brown* v. *Board of Education* SEATO formed First McDonald's hamburger stand opens CIA-sponsored coup in Guatemala
1955	Montgomery bus boycott by blacks begins; emergence of Martin Luther King, Jr. Geneva summit meeting Warsaw Pact signed AF of L merges with CIO Tennessee Williams's *Cat on a Hot Tin Roof* first performed
1956	Soviets crush Hungarian revolt Suez crisis Eisenhower defeats Stevenson for presidency Mills publishes *The Power Elite*
1957	Little Rock school desegregation crisis Civil Rights Act passed Southern Christian Leadership Conference (SCLC) formed Eisenhower Doctrine Soviet Union launches *Sputnik* satellites
1958	U.S. troops sent to Lebanon NDEA authorizes loans and grants for science and language education Galbraith publishes *The Affluent Society*
1958–1959	Berlin crisis
1959	Castro leads Cuban revolution Landrum-Griffin Act Alaska and Hawaii attain statehood
1960	Sit-in movement for civil rights begins U-2 incident sabotages Paris summit OPEC formed Kennedy defeats Nixon for presidency

SUGGESTED READINGS

PRIMARY SOURCE DOCUMENTS

Earl Warren's decision in *Brown v. Board of Education of Topeka*, 347 U.S. 492–495* (1954), altered the course of race relations in the United States. It also sparked the opposition of 100 southern congressmen, *Congressional Record*, 84th Congress, 2d Session, pp. 4515–4516* (1956). Eisenhower's Farewell Address* (1961) warned of the dangers of the "military-industrial complex." John Kenneth Galbraith criticized the consumer culture in *The Affluent Society** (1958). Joe McCarthy's vitriol can be found in his *McCarthyism: The Fight for America** (1952).

SECONDARY SOURCES

The era is surveyed readably in several works, including those titles by James Patterson, William H. Chafe, John Patrick Diggins, and William O'Neill, cited in Chapter 39. Eisenhower is the subject of Stephen Ambrose's two-volume biography, *Eisenhower: Soldier, General of the Army, President-Elect, 1890–1952* (1983) and *Eisenhower: The President* (1984). See also Jeff Broadwater, *Eisenhower and the Anti-Communist Crusade* (1992). Eisenhower's own memoirs are rather bland: *Mandate for Change, 1953–1956* (1963) and *Waging Peace, 1956–1961* (1965). Fred I. Greenstein portrays Eisenhower as the master of *The Hidden Hand Presidency* (1982). Robert A. Divine, *Eisenhower and the Cold War* (1981), praises his diplomatic restraint. Various aspects of foreign policy are covered in Douglas Brinkley, *Dean Acheson: The Cold War Years, 1953–71* (1992); Richard Immerman, *The CIA in Guatemala: The Foreign Policy of Intervention* (1982); Walter Isaacson and Evan Thomas, *The Wise Men: Six Friends and the World They Made: Acheson, Bohlen, Harriman, Kennan, Lovett, McCloy* (1986); Richard E. Welch, Jr., *Response to Revolution: The United States and the Cuban Revolution, 1959–1961* (1985); Robert Schulzinger, *The Wise Men of Foreign Affairs: The History of the Council on Foreign Relations* (1984); Henry Kissinger, *Nuclear Weapons and Foreign Policy* (1957); and Herman Kahn's chilling *On Thermonuclear War* (1960). See also Gordon Chang's book cited in Chapter 39. For background and consequences of the Supreme Court's 1954 desegregation decision see Richard Kluger, *Simple Justice: The History of Brown v. Board of Education* (1976); Raymond Wolters, *The Burden of Brown: Thirty Years of School Desegregation* (1984); and Robert A. Margo, *Race and Schooling in the South, 1880–1950* (1990). Especially rich are Taylor Branch, *Parting the Waters: America in the King Years, 1954–1963* (1988), and David J. Garrow, *Bearing the Cross: Martin Luther King, Jr., and the Southern Christian Leadership Conference* (1986). The South before the Civil Rights movement is ably described in John Egerton, *Speak Now Against the Day: The Generation Before the Civil Rights Movement in the South* (1994). For one man's experience of integration, see Jules Tygiel, *Baseball's Great Experiment: Jackie Robinson and His Legacy* (1983). Relevant memoirs and biographies include William O. Douglas, *The Court Years, 1939–1975* (1980); G. Edward White, *Earl Warren* (1982); John Bartlow Martin, *Adlai Stevenson* (2 vols., 1976–1977); and Townsend Hoopes, *The Devil and John Foster Dulles* (1973). On the election of 1960, see Theodore H. White's colorful *The Making of the President, 1960* (1961). For more on cultural developments during the 1950s, see Lary May, ed., *Recasting America: Culture and Politics in the Age of the Cold War* (1989); Elaine May, *Homeward Bound: American Families in the Cold War Era* (1988); Tino Balio, ed., *Hollywood in the Age of Television* (1990); David Halberstam, *The Fifties* (1993); Stephen J. Whitfield, *The Culture of the Cold War* (1991); Tom Engelhardt, *The End of Victory Culture* (1995); and Eugenia Kaledin, *Mothers and More: American Women in the 1950s* (1984). On postwar literature, see Tony Tanner, *City of Words* (1971), and Alfred Kazin, *Bright Book of Life* (1973). On the arts, consult Edward Lucie-Smith, *Late Modern: The Visual Arts Since 1945* (1969). On television, see David Marc, *Demographic Vistas: Television in American Culture* (1984).

---

*An asterisk indicates that the document, or an excerpt from it, can be found in Thomas A. Bailey and David M. Kennedy, eds., *The American Spirit: United States History as Seen by Contemporaries*, 9th ed. (Boston: Houghton Mifflin, 1998).

41

The Stormy Sixties
1960–1968

In the final analysis it is their war. They are the ones who have to win it or lose it . . . the people of Vietnam.

JOHN F. KENNEDY, SEPTEMBER 1963

Kennedy's "New Frontier" Spirit

Complacent and comfortable as the 1950s closed, Americans elected in 1960 a young, vigorous president who pledged "to get the country moving again." Neither the nation nor the new president had any inkling as the new decade opened just how action-packed it would be, both at home and abroad. The 1960s would bring a sexual revolution, a civil rights revolution, the emergence of a "youth culture," a devastating war in Vietnam, and the beginnings, at least, of a feminist revolution. By the end of the stormy sixties, many Americans would yearn nostalgically for the comparative calm of the fifties.

Hatless and topcoatless in the 22 degrees Fahrenheit chill (minus 5 degrees Celsius), John F. Kennedy delivered a stirring inaugural address on January 20, 1961. Tall, elegantly handsome, speaking crisply and with staccato finger jabs at the air,

Kennedy personified the glamour and vitality of the new administration. The youngest president ever elected, he assembled one of the youngest cabinets, including his thirty-five-year-old brother, Robert, as attorney general. "Bobby," the president quipped, would find the experience useful when he began to practice law. The new attorney general set out, among other reforms, to recast the priorities of the FBI. The bureau deployed nearly a thousand agents on "internal security" work but targeted only a dozen against organized crime and gave virtually no attention to civil rights violations. Robert Kennedy's efforts were stoutly resisted by J. Edgar Hoover, who had served as FBI director longer than the new attorney general had been alive. Business whiz Robert S. McNamara left the presidency of the Ford Motor Company to take over the Defense Department. Along with other youthful, talented advisers, these appointees made up an inner circle of "the best and the brightest" men around the president.

From the outset Kennedy inspired high expectations, especially among the young. His challenge

936

President John F. Kennedy and His Wife, Jacqueline Kennedy
The young and vibrant first couple brought beauty, style, and grace to the White House.

of a "New Frontier" quickened patriotic pulses. He brought a warm heart to the Cold War when he proposed the Peace Corps, an army of idealistic and mostly youthful volunteers to bring American skills to underdeveloped countries. He summoned citizens to service with his clarion call to "ask not what your country can do for you: ask what you can do for your country."

Himself Harvard-educated, Kennedy and his Ivy League lieutenants (heavily from Harvard) radiated confidence in their abilities. The president's personal grace and wit won him the deep affection of many of his fellow citizens. A journalist called Kennedy "the most seductive man I've ever met. He exuded a sense of vibrant life and humor that seemed naturally to bubble up out of him." In an unprecedented gesture, he invited white-maned poet Robert Frost to speak at his inaugural ceremonies. The old Yankee versifier shrewdly took stock of the situation. "You're something of Irish

and I suppose something of Harvard," he told Kennedy—and advised him to be more Irish than Harvard.

The New Frontier at Home

Kennedy came into office with fragile Democratic majorities in Congress. Southern Democrats threatened to team up with Republicans and ax New Frontier proposals such as medical assistance for the aged and increased federal aid to education. Kennedy won a first round in his campaign for a more cooperative Congress when he forced an expansion of the all-important House Rules Committee, dominated by conservatives who could have bottled up his entire legislative program. Despite this victory, the New Frontier did not expand swiftly. Key medical and education bills remained stalled in Congress.

Another vexing problem was the economy. Kennedy had campaigned on the theme of revitalizing the economy after the recessions of the Eisenhower years. While his advisers debated the best kind of economic medicine to apply, the president tried to hold the line against crippling inflation. His administration helped negotiate a noninflationary wage agreement in the steel industry in early 1962. The assumption was that the companies, for their part, would keep the lid on prices.

Richard Goodwin, then a young Peace Corps staffer, eloquently summed up the buoyantly optimistic mood of the early 1960s:

"For a moment, it seemed as if the entire country, the whole spinning globe, rested, malleable and receptive, in our beneficent hands."

On the Moon   (left) This moon's-eye view of the earth greeted the first men to land on the lunar surface. (right) Astronaut Edwin ("Buzz") Aldrin poses with a stretched U.S. flag on the windless moon. His companion, Neil Armstrong, said as he stepped from the spacecraft, "That's one small step for man; one giant leap for mankind."

Almost immediately, steel management announced significant price increases, thereby seemingly demonstrating bad faith. The president erupted in wrath, remarking that his father had once said that "all businessmen were sons of bitches." He called the "big steel" men onto the Oval Office carpet and unleashed his Irish temper. Overawed, the steel operators backed down, while displaying S.O.B. buttons, meaning "Sons of Business" or "Save Our Business."

The steel episode provoked fiery attacks by big business on the New Frontier, but Kennedy soon appealed to believers in free enterprise when he announced his support of a general tax-cut bill. He rejected the advice of those who wished greater government spending and instead chose to stimulate the economy by slashing taxes and putting more money directly into private hands. When he announced his policy before a big business group, one observer called it "the most Republican speech since McKinley."

For economic stimulus, as well as for military strategy and scientific prestige, Kennedy also promoted a multibillion-dollar project to land an Amer-ican on the moon. When skeptics objected that the money could best be spent elsewhere, Kennedy "answered" them in a speech at Rice University in Texas: "But why, some say, the moon? . . . And they may well ask, why climb the highest mountain? Why, thirty-five years ago, fly the Atlantic? Why does Rice play Texas?" Twenty-four billion dollars later, in 1969, two American astronauts triumphantly planted human footprints on the moon's dusty surface.

Rumblings in Europe

A few months after settling into the White House, the new president met Soviet Premier Khrushchev at Vienna, in June 1961. Kennedy sought cooperation, but the tough-talking Soviet leader adopted a belligerent attitude, threatening to make a treaty with East Germany and cut off Western access to Berlin. Though visibly shaken, the president refused to be bullied.

The Soviets backed off from their most bellicose threats but suddenly began to construct the Berlin

Wall in August 1961. A barbed-wire and concrete barrier, it was designed to plug the heavy population drain from East Germany to West Germany through the Berlin funnel. But to the free world the "Wall of Shame" looked like a gigantic enclosure around a concentration camp. The Wall stood for almost three decades as an ugly scar symbolizing the post–World War II division of Europe into two hostile camps.

Kennedy meanwhile turned his attention to Western Europe, now miraculously prospering after the tonic of Marshall Plan aid and the growth of the American-encouraged Common Market, the free-trade area later called the European Union. He finally secured passage of the Trade Expansion Act in 1962, authorizing tariff cuts of up to 50 percent to promote trade with Common Market countries. This legislation led to the so-called Kennedy Round of tariff negotiations, concluded in 1967, and to a significant expansion of European-American trade.

But not all of Kennedy's ambitious designs for Europe were realized. American policymakers were dedicated to an economically and militarily united "Atlantic Community," with the United States the dominant partner. But they found their way blocked by towering, stiff-backed Charles de Gaulle, president of France. He was suspicious of American intentions in Europe and on fire to recapture the *gloire* of Napoleonic France. With a haughty *"non,"* he vetoed British application for Common Market membership in 1963, fearing that the British "special relationship" with the United States would make Britain a Trojan horse for deepening American control over European affairs. He likewise dashed cold water on a U.S. proposal to develop a multinational nuclear arm within NATO. De Gaulle deemed the Americans unreliable in a crisis, so he tried to preserve French freedom of action by developing his own small atomic force ("farce," scoffed his critics). Despite the perils of nuclear proliferation or Soviet domination, de Gaulle demanded an independent Europe, free of Yankee influence.

Foreign Flare-ups and "Flexible Response"

Special problems for U.S. foreign policy emerged from the worldwide decolonization of European overseas possessions after World War II. The African

The Berlin Wall, 1961–1989   The wall separating East and West Berlin stood for nearly thirty years as a hated symbol of the division of Europe into democratic and communist camps. Demonstrators celebrating the impending reunification of East and West Germany began to tear it down at last in 1989.

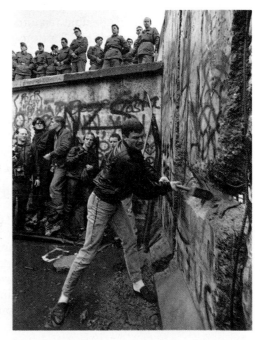

Congo received its independence from Belgium in 1960 and immediately exploded into violence. The United Nations sent in a peacekeeping force, to which Washington contributed much money but no manpower. The United States was picking up the tab for U.N. operations, while the organization itself was becoming dominated by the numerous nascent nations emerging in once-colonial Asia and Africa, who were often critical of U.S. foreign policy.

Sparsely populated Laos, freed of its French colonial overlords in 1954, was festering dangerously by the time Kennedy came into office. The Eisenhower administration had drenched this jungle kingdom with dollars but failed to cleanse the country of an aggressive communist element. A red Laos, many observers feared, would be a river on which the influence of Communist China would flood into all of Southeast Asia.

As the Laotian civil war raged, Kennedy's military advisers seriously considered sending in American troops. But the president found that he had insufficient forces to put out the fire in Asia and still honor his commitments in Europe. Kennedy thus sought a diplomatic escape hatch in the fourteen-power Geneva conference, which imposed a shaky peace on Laos in 1962.

These "brushfire wars" intensified the pressure for a shift away from Secretary Dulles's dubious doctrine of "massive retaliation." Kennedy felt hamstrung by the knowledge that in a crisis he had the Devil's choice between humiliation or nuclear incineration. With Defense Secretary McNamara, he pushed the strategy of "flexible response"—that is, developing an array of military "options" that could be precisely matched to the gravity of the crisis at hand. To this end, Kennedy increased spending on conventional military forces and bolstered the Special Forces (Green Berets). They were an elite antiguerrilla outfit trained to survive on snake meat and to kill with scientific finesse.

Stepping into the Vietnam Quagmire

The doctrine of "flexible response" seemed sane enough, but it contained lethal logic. It potentially lowered the level at which diplomacy would give way to shooting. It also provided a mechanism for a progressive, and possibly endless, stepping-up of

Backbone   The United States supports South Vietnam.

the use of force. Vietnam soon presented grisly proof of these pitfalls.

The corrupt, right-wing Diem government in Saigon, despite a deluge of American dollars, had ruled shakily since the partition of Vietnam in 1954 (see p. 918). Anti-Diem agitation, spearheaded by the local Communist Viet Cong and encouraged by the red regime in the north, noisily threatened to topple the pro-American government from power. In a fateful decision late in 1961, Kennedy ordered a sharp increase in the number of "military advisers" (U.S. troops) in South Vietnam.

American forces had allegedly entered Vietnam to foster political stability—to help protect Diem from the communists long enough to allow him to enact basic social reforms favored by the Americans. But the Kennedy administration eventually despaired of the reactionary Diem and encouraged a successful coup against him in November 1963. Ironically, the United States thus contributed to a long process of political disintegration that its original policy had meant to prevent. Kennedy still told the South Vietnamese that it was "their war," but he had made dangerously deep political commit-

Geneva demarcation line
(seventeenth parallel), July 22, 1954

← Ho Chi Minh Trail

□ Major American bases

Vietnam and Southeast Asia,
1954–1975

ments. By the time of his death, he had ordered more than fifteen thousand American men into the far-off Asian slaughterpen. A graceful pullout was becoming increasingly difficult.

Cuban Confrontations

Although the United States regarded Latin America as its backyard, its southern neighbors feared and resented the powerful Colossus of the North. In 1961 Kennedy extended the hand of friendship with the Alliance for Progress (*Alianza para el Progreso*), hailed as a Marshall Plan for Latin America. A primary goal was to help the Good Neighbors close the gap between the calloused rich and the wretched poor, and thus quiet communist agitation. But results were disappointing; there was little alliance and even less progress. American handouts had little positive impact on Latin America's immense social problems.

President Kennedy also struck below the border with the mailed fist. He had inherited from the Eisenhower administration a CIA-backed scheme to topple Fidel Castro from power by invading Cuba with anticommunist exiles. Trained and armed by Americans and supported by American air power, the invaders would trigger a popular uprising in Cuba and sweep to victory—or so the planners predicted.

On a fateful April 17, 1961, some twelve hundred exiles landed at Cuba's Bay of Pigs. Kennedy had decided from the outset against *direct* intervention, and the ancient aircraft of the anti-Castroites were no match for Castro's air force. In addition, no popular uprising greeted the invaders. With the invasion bogged down at the Bay of Pigs, Kennedy stood fast in his decision to keep hands off, and the bullet-riddled band of anti-Castroites surrendered. Most of the invaders rotted for two years in Cuban jails but were eventually "ransomed" for some $62 million worth of American pharmaceutical drugs and other humanitarian supplies. President Kennedy assumed full responsibility for the failure, remarking that "victory has a hundred fathers, and defeat is an orphan."

The Bay of Pigs blunder, along with continuing American covert efforts to assassinate Castro and overthrow his government, naturally pushed the Cuban leader even further into the Soviet embrace. Wily Chairman Khrushchev lost little time in taking full advantage of his Cuban comrade's position just 90 miles (145 kilometers) off Florida's coast. In October 1962 the aerial photographs of American spy planes revealed that the Soviets were secretly and speedily installing nuclear-tipped missiles in Cuba. The Soviets evidently intended to use these devastating weapons to shield Castro and to blackmail the United States into backing down in Berlin and other trouble spots.

Kennedy and Khrushchev now began a nerve-racking game of "nuclear chicken." The president flatly rejected air force proposals for a "surgical" bombing strike against the missile-launching sites. Instead, on October 22, 1962, he ordered a naval "quarantine" of Cuba and demanded immediate removal of the threatening weaponry. He also served notice on Khrushchev that any attack on the United States from Cuba would be regarded as coming from the Soviet Union and would trigger nuclear retaliation against the Russian heartland.

For an anxious week, Americans waited while Soviet ships approached the patrol line established by the United States navy off the island of Cuba. Seizing or sinking a Soviet vessel on the high seas would unquestionably be regarded by the Kremlin as an act of war. The world teetered breathlessly on the brink of global atomization. Only in 1991 did the full dimensions of this nuclear peril become known, when the Russians revealed that their ground forces in Cuba already had operational nuclear weapons at their disposal and were authorized to launch them if attacked.

In this tense eyeball-to-eyeball confrontation, Khrushchev finally flinched. On October 28 he agreed to a partially face-saving compromise, by which he would pull the missiles out of Cuba. The United States in return agreed to end the quarantine and not invade the island. The American government also quietly signaled that it would remove from Turkey some of its own missiles targeted on the Soviet Union.

Fallout from the Cuban missile crisis was considerable. A disgraced Khrushchev was ultimately hounded out of the Kremlin and became an "unperson." Hard-liners in Moscow, vowing never again to be humiliated in a nuclear face-off, launched an enormous program of military expansion. The Soviet buildup reached a crescendo in the next decade, stimulating, in turn, a vast American effort to "catch up with the Russians." The Democrats did better than expected in the midterm elections of November 1962—allegedly because the Republicans were "Cubanized." Kennedy, apparently sobered by the appalling risks he had just run, pushed harder for a nuclear test-ban treaty with the Soviet Union. After prolonged negotiations in Moscow, a pact prohibiting trial nuclear explosions in the atmosphere was signed in late 1963. Another barometer indicating a thaw in the Cold War was the installation (August 1963) of a Moscow-Washington "hot line," permitting immediate teletype communication in case of crisis.

Most significant was Kennedy's speech at American University, Washington, D.C., in June 1963. The president urged Americans to abandon a view of the Soviet Union as a devil-ridden land filled with fanatics and instead to deal with the world "as it is, not as it might have been had the history of the last eighteen years been different." Kennedy thus tried to lay the foundations for a realistic policy of peaceful coexistence with the Soviet Union. Here were the modest origins of the policy that later came to be known as "détente" (French for "relaxation").

The Struggle for Civil Rights

Kennedy had campaigned with a strong appeal to black voters, but he proceeded gingerly to redeem his promises. Although he had pledged to eliminate racial discrimination in housing "with a stroke of the pen," it took him nearly two years to find the right pen. Civil rights groups meanwhile sent thousands of pens to the White House in an "Ink for Jack" protest against the president's slowness.

Freedom Ride, 1961
Rampaging whites near Anniston, Alabama, burned this bus carrying an interracial group of Freedom Riders on May 14, 1961.

Political concerns stayed the president's hand on civil rights. Elected by a wafer-thin margin, and with shaky control over Congress, Kennedy needed the support of southern legislators to pass his economic and social legislation, especially his medical and educational bills. He believed, perhaps justifiably, that those measures would eventually benefit black Americans at least as much as specific legislation on civil rights. Bold moves for racial justice would have to wait.

But events soon scrambled these careful calculations. Following the wave of sit-ins that surged across the South in 1960, groups of Freedom Riders fanned out to end segregation in facilities serving interstate bus passengers. A white mob torched a Freedom Ride bus near Anniston, Alabama, in May 1961, and Attorney General Robert Kennedy's personal representative was beaten unconscious in another anti–Freedom Ride riot in Montgomery. When southern officials proved unwilling or unable to stem the violence, Washington dispatched federal marshals to protect the Freedom Riders.

Reluctantly but fatefully, the Kennedy administration had now joined hands with the civil rights movement. Because of that partnership, the Kennedys proved ultra-wary about the political associates of Martin Luther King, Jr. Fearful of embarrassing revelations that some of King's advisers had communist affiliations, Robert Kennedy

ordered FBI director J. Edgar Hoover to wiretap King's phone in late 1963. But for the most part, the relationship between King and the Kennedys was a fruitful one. Encouraged by Robert Kennedy, and with financial backing from Kennedy-prodded private foundations, SNCC and other civil rights groups inaugurated a Voter Education Project to register the South's historically disfranchised blacks. Because of his support for civil rights, President Kennedy told a group of black leaders in 1963, "I may lose the next election . . . I don't care."

Integrating southern universities threatened to provoke wholesale slaughter. Some desegregated painlessly, but the University of Mississippi ("Ole Miss") became a volcano. A twenty-nine-year-old air force veteran, James Meredith, encountered violent opposition when he attempted to register in October 1962. In the end President Kennedy was forced to send in four hundred federal marshals and three thousand troops to enroll Meredith in his first class—in colonial American history. He ultimately graduated, with a sheepskin that cost the lives of two men, scores of injuries, and some 4 million taxpayer dollars.

In the spring of 1963, Martin Luther King, Jr., launched a campaign against discrimination in Birmingham, Alabama, the most segregated big city in America. Although they constituted nearly half the city's population, blacks made up fewer than 15 percent of the city's voters. Previous attempts to crack the city's rigid racial barriers had produced more than fifty cross burnings and eighteen bomb attacks since 1957. "Some of the people sitting here will not come back alive from this campaign," King advised his organizers. Events soon confirmed this grim prediction of violence. Watching developments on television screens, a horrified world saw peaceful civil rights marchers repeatedly repelled by police with attack dogs and electric cattle prods. Most fearsome of all were the high-pressure water hoses directed at the civil rights demonstrators. They delivered water with enough force to knock bricks loose from buildings or strip bark from trees at a distance of one hundred feet. Water from the hoses bowled little children down the street like tumbleweed.

Jolted by these vicious confrontations, President Kennedy delivered a memorable televised speech to the nation on June 11, 1963. In contrast to Eisenhower's cool aloofness from the racial question, Kennedy called the situation a "moral issue" and committed his personal and presidential prestige to finding a solution. Drawing on the same spiritual traditions as Martin Luther King, Jr., Kennedy declared that the principle at stake "is as old as the Scriptures and is as clear as the American Constitution." He called for new civil rights legislation to protect black citizens. In August, Martin Luther King, Jr., led 200,000 black and white demonstrators

> *In his civil rights address of June 11, 1963, President John F. Kennedy (1917–1963) said,*
>
> "If an American, because his skin is dark, cannot eat lunch in a restaurant open to the public; if he cannot send his children to the best public school available; if he cannot vote for the public officials who represent him; if, in short, he cannot enjoy the full and free life which all of us want, then who among us would be content to have the color of his skin changed and stand in his place?"

on a peaceful "March on Washington" in support of the proposed legislation. In an electrifying speech from the Lincoln Memorial, King declared: "I have a dream that my four little children will one day live in a nation where they will not be judged by the color of their skin, but by the content of their character."

Still the violence continued. On the very night of Kennedy's stirring television address, a white gunman shot down Medgar Evers, a black Mississippi civil rights worker. In September 1963 an explosion blasted a Baptist church in Birmingham, killing four black girls who had just finished their lesson called "The Love That Forgives." By the time of Kennedy's

Hosing Down Civil Rights Demonstrators Birmingham, Alabama, 1963.

Martin Luther King, Jr., Addresses the March on Washington, August 1963 This was the occasion of King's famous "I Have a Dream" speech, in which he declared, "When the architects of our great republic wrote the magnificent words of the Constitution and the Declaration of Independence, they were signing a promissory note to which every American was to fall heir. This note was a promise that all men, yes, black men as well as white men, would be guaranteed the inalienable rights of life, liberty, and the pursuit of happiness."

death, his civil rights bill was making little headway, and frustrated blacks were growing increasingly impatient.

The Killing of Kennedy

Violence haunted America in the mid-1960s, and it stalked onto center stage on November 22, 1963. While riding in an open limousine in downtown Dallas, Texas, President Kennedy was shot in the brain by a concealed rifleman and died within seconds. As a stunned nation grieved, the tragedy grew still more unbelievable. The alleged assassin, a furtive figure named Lee Harvey Oswald, was himself shot to death in front of the television cameras by a self-appointed avenger, Jack Ruby. So bizarre were the events surrounding the two murders that even an elaborate official investigation conducted by Chief Justice Warren could not quiet all doubts and theories about what had really happened.

Vice President Johnson was promptly sworn in as president on a waiting airplane and flown back to Washington with Kennedy's body. Although he mistrusted "the Harvards," Johnson retained most of the bright Kennedy team. The new president managed a dignified and efficient transition, pledging continuity with his slain predecessor's policies.

For several days, the nation was steeped in sorrow. Not until then did many Americans realize how fully their young, vibrant president and his captivating wife had cast a spell over them. Chopped down in his prime after only slightly more than a thousand days in the White House, Kennedy was acclaimed more for the ideals he had enunciated and the spirit he had kindled than for the concrete goals he had achieved. He had laid one myth to rest forever—that a Catholic could not be trusted with the presidency of the United States.

In later years revelations about Kennedy's womanizing and allegations about his involvement with organized crime figures tarnished his reputation. But despite those accusations, his vigor, charisma, and idealism made him an inspirational figure for the generation of Americans who came of age in the 1960s—including Bill Clinton, who as a boy had briefly met President Kennedy and would himself be elected president in 1992.

The LBJ Brand on the Presidency

The torch had now passed to craggy-faced Lyndon Baines Johnson, a Texan who towered 6 feet, 3 inches (1.91 meters). The new president hailed from the populist hill country of west Texas, whose

President Lyndon Baines Johnson (1908–1973)
Dedicated and hardworking, Johnson saw his presidency
shattered by the trauma of Vietnam. By the end of his term,
he was so unpopular that he could find nonheckling audiences
only on military bases or on navy ships.

people had first sent him to Washington as a twenty-nine-year-old congressman in 1937. Franklin D. Roosevelt was his political "Daddy," Johnson claimed, and he had supported New Deal measures down the line. But when LBJ lost a Senate race in 1941, he learned the sobering lesson that liberal political beliefs did not necessarily win elections in Texas. He trimmed his sails to the right and squeezed himself into a Senate seat in 1948 with a questionable eighty-seven-vote margin—hence the ironic nickname "Landslide Lyndon."

Entrenched in the Senate, Johnson developed into a masterful wheeler-dealer. He became the Democratic majority leader in 1954, wielding power second only to that of Eisenhower in the White House. He could move mountains or checkmate

opponents as the occasion demanded, using what came to be known as the "Johnson treatment"—a flashing display of backslapping, flesh-pressing, and arm-twisting that overbore friend and foe alike. His ego and vanity were legendary. On a visit to the pope, Johnson was presented with a precious fourteenth-century painting from the Vatican art collection; in return, LBJ gave the pope a bust—of LBJ!

As president, Johnson quickly shed the conservative coloration of his Senate years to reveal the latent liberal underneath. "No memorial oration or eulogy," Johnson declared to Congress, "could more eloquently honor President Kennedy's memory than the earliest possible passage of the Civil Rights Bill for which he fought so long." After a lengthy conservative filibuster, Congress at last passed the landmark Civil Rights Act of 1964. The act banned racial discrimination in most private facilities open to the public, including theaters, hospitals, and restaurants. It strengthened the federal government's power to end segregation in schools and other public places. It created a federal Equal Employment Opportunity Commission (EEOC) to eliminate discrimination in hiring. When conservatives tried to derail the legislation by adding a prohibition on *sexual,* as well as racial, discrimination, the tactic backfired. The bill's opponents cynically calculated that liberals would not be able to support a bill that threatened to wipe out laws that singled out women for special protection because of their sex. But the act's Title VII passed with the sexual clause intact. It soon proved to be a powerful instrument of federally enforced gender equality, as well as racial equality. Johnson struck another blow for women and minorities in 1965 when he issued an executive order requiring all federal contractors to take "affirmative action" against discrimination.

Johnson also rammed Kennedy's stalled tax bill through Congress and added proposals of his own for a billion-dollar "War on Poverty." Johnson voiced special concern for Appalachia, where the sickness of the soft-coal industry had left tens of thousands of mountain folk on the human slag heap.

Johnson dubbed his domestic program the "Great Society"—a sweeping set of New Dealish economic and welfare measures aimed at transforming the American way of life. Public support for LBJ's antipoverty war was aroused by Michael Harrington's *The Other America* (1962), which revealed that in affluent America 20 percent of the population—and over 40 percent of the black population—suffered in poverty.

Johnson Battles Goldwater in 1964

Johnson's nomination by the Democrats in 1964 was a foregone conclusion; he was chosen by acclamation in Atlantic City as his birthday present. Thanks to the tall Texan, the Democrats stood foursquare on their most liberal platform since Truman's Fair Deal days. The Republicans, convening in San Francisco's Cow Palace, nominated box-jawed Senator Barry Goldwater of Arizona, a bronzed and bespectacled champion of rock-ribbed conservatism. The American stage was thus set for a historic clash of political principles.

Goldwater's forces had galloped out of the Southwest to ride roughshod over the moderate Republican "eastern establishment." Insisting that the GOP offer "a choice not an echo," Goldwater attacked the federal income tax, the Social Security system, the Tennessee Valley Authority, civil rights legislation, the nuclear test-ban treaty, and, most loudly, the Great Society. His fiercely dedicated followers proclaimed, "In Your Heart You Know He's Right," which prompted the Democratic response, "In Your Guts You Know He's Nuts." Goldwater warmed right-wing hearts when he announced that "extremism in the defense of liberty is no vice. And . . . moderation in the pursuit of justice is no virtue."

Goldwater radiated sincerity and charm, but his aggressive "rightism" repelled millions of his own fellow Republicans. The Arizonan also habitually "shot from the lip," notably when he urged that American field commanders be given discretionary authority to use tactical nuclear weapons. Democrats gleefully exploited the image of Goldwater as a trigger-happy cowboy who would "Barry us" in the debris of World War III.

Johnson cultivated the contrasting image of a resolute statesman by seizing upon the Tonkin Gulf episode early in August 1964. Unbeknownst to the American public or Congress, U.S. Navy ships had been cooperating with South Vietnamese gunboats in provocative raids along the coast of North Vietnam. Two of these American destroyers were allegedly fired upon by the North Vietnamese on August 2 and 4, although exactly what happened still remains unclear. Later investigations strongly suggested that the North Vietnamese fired in self-defense on August 2, and that the "attack" of August 4 never happened. Johnson later reportedly wisecracked, "For all I know, the Navy was shooting at whales out there."

Johnson nevertheless promptly called the attack "unprovoked" and moved swiftly to make political hay out of this episode. He ordered a "limited" retaliatory air raid against the North Vietnamese bases, loudly proclaiming that he sought "no wider war"—thus implying that the truculent

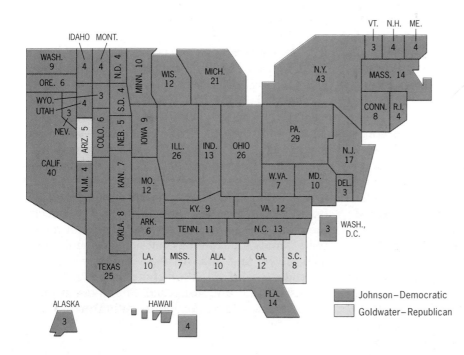

Presidential Election of 1964
States are distorted according to the number of electoral votes indicated on each state. In New Orleans, toward the end of the campaign, a gutsy Johnson displayed his commitment to civil rights when he told a story about an old senator who once said of his Deep South constituents, "I would like to go back down there and make them just one more Democratic speech. . . . The poor old State, they haven't heard a Democratic speech in 30 years. All they hear at election time is Negro, Negro, Negro!" Johnson's open voicing of sentiments like this contributed heavily to his losses in the traditionally Democratic "solid South."

Johnson–Democratic
Goldwater–Republican

Goldwater did. Johnson also used the incident to spur congressional passage of the all-purpose Tonkin Gulf Resolution. With only two dissenting votes in both houses, the lawmakers virtually abdicated their war-declaring powers and handed the president a blank check to use further force in Southeast Asia. The Tonkin Gulf Resolution, Johnson boasted, was "like grandma's nightshirt—it covered everything."

The towering Texan rode to a spectacular victory in November 1964. The voters were herded into Johnson's column by fondness for the Kennedy legacy, faith in Great Society promises, and fear of Goldwater. A stampede of 43,129,566 Johnson votes trampled the Republican ticket with its 27,178,188 supporters. The tally in the Electoral College was 486 to 52. Goldwater carried only his native Arizona and five other states—all of them, significantly, in the racially restless South. This cracking of the once solidly Democratic South afforded the Republicans about the only faint light in an otherwise bleak political picture. Johnson's record-breaking 61 percent of the popular vote swept lopsided Democratic majorities into both houses of Congress.

The Great Society Congress

Johnson's huge victory temporarily smashed the conservative congressional coalition of southern Democrats and northern Republicans. A wide-open legislative road stretched before the Great Society programs, as the president skillfully ringmastered his two-to-one Democratic majorities. Congress poured out a flood of legislation, comparable only to the output of the New Dealers in the Hundred Days Congress of 1933. Johnson, confident that a growing economy gave him ample fiscal and political room for maneuver, delivered at last on long-deferred Democratic promises of social reform.

Escalating the War on Poverty, Congress doubled the appropriation of the Office of Economic Opportunity to $2 billion and granted more than $1 billion to redevelop the gutted hills and hollows of Appalachia. A tireless Johnson also prodded the Congress into creating two new cabinet offices: the Department of Transportation and the Department of Housing and Urban Development (HUD), to which he named the first black cabinet secretary in the nation's history, respected economist Robert C.

Weaver. Other noteworthy laws established the National Endowments for the Arts and the Humanities, designed to lift the level of American cultural life.

Even more impressive were the Big Four legislative achievements that crowned LBJ's Great Society program: aid to education, medical care for the elderly and indigent, immigration reform, and a new voting rights bill.

Johnson neatly avoided the thorny question of separation of church and state by channeling educational aid to students, not schools, thus allowing funds to flow to hard-pressed parochial institutions. (Catholic John F. Kennedy had not dared to touch this prickly issue.) With a keen eye for the dramatic, LBJ signed the education bill in the humble one-room Texas schoolhouse he had attended as a boy.

Medicare for the elderly, accompanied by Medicaid for the poor, became a reality in 1965. Although they were bitter pills for the American Medical Association to swallow, the new programs were welcomed by millions of older Americans who had no health insurance (half of those over the age of sixty-five in 1965) and by the poor who could not afford proper medical treatment. Like the New Deal's Social Security program, Medicare and Medicaid created "entitlements." That is, they conferred rights on certain categories of Americans virtually in perpetuity, without the need for repeated congressional approval. These programs were part of a spreading "rights revolution" that materially improved the lives of millions of Americans—but also eventually undermined the federal government's financial health.

Immigration reform was the third of Johnson's Big Four feats. The Immigration and Nationality Act of 1965 abolished at last the "national origin" quota system that had been in place since 1921 (see p. 748). The act also doubled (to 290,000) the number of immigrants allowed to enter annually, while for the first time setting limits on immigrants from the Western Hemisphere (120,000). The new law further provided for the admission of close relatives of United States citizens, outside those numerical limits. To the surprise of many of the act's architects, more than 100,000 persons per year took advantage of its "family unification" provisions in the decades after 1965, and the immigrant stream swelled beyond expectations. Even more surprising to the act's sponsors, the sources of immigration soon shifted heavily from Europe to Latin America and

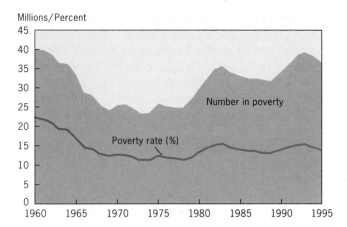

Poverty in the United States, 1960–1995
(U.S. Bureau of the Census, March Current Population Survey)

Asia, dramatically changing the racial and ethnic composition of the American population.

Great Society programs came in for rancorous political attack in later years. Conservatives charged that poverty could not be papered over with greenbacks, and that the billions spent for "social engineering" had simply been flushed down the waste pipe. Yet the poverty rate declined measurably in the ensuing decade. Medicare made especially dramatic reductions in the incidence of poverty among America's elderly. Other antipoverty programs, among them Project Head Start, sharply improved the educational performance of underprivileged youth. Infant mortality rates also fell in minority communities as general health conditions improved. Lyndon Johnson was not fully victorious in the war against poverty, and he doubtless fought some costly and futile campaigns, but he did win several noteworthy battles.

The Black Revolution Explodes

With the last of his Big Four reforms, the Voting Rights Act of 1965, Johnson made heartening headway against one of the most persistent American evils, racial discrimination. In Johnson's native South, the walls of segregation were crumbling, but not fast enough for long-suffering African-Americans. The Civil Rights Act of 1964 gave the federal government more muscle to enforce school-desegregation orders and to prohibit racial discrimination in all kinds of public accommodations and employment. But the problem of voting rights remained. In Mississippi, which had the largest black minority of any state, only about 5 percent of eligible blacks were registered to vote. The lopsided pattern was similar throughout the South. Ballot-denying devices like the poll tax, literacy tests, and barefaced intimidation still barred black people from the political process. Mississippi law required the names of prospective black registrants to be published for two weeks in local newspapers—a device that virtually guaranteed economic reprisals, or worse.

Beginning in 1964, opening up the polling booths became the chief goal of the black movement in the South. The Twenty-fourth Amendment, ratified in January 1964, abolished the poll tax in federal elections. (See the Appendix.) Blacks joined hands with white civil rights workers—many of them student volunteers from the North—in a massive voter-registration drive in Mississippi during the "Freedom Summer" of 1964. Singing "We Shall Overcome," they zealously set out to soothe generations of white anxieties and black fears.

But events soon blighted bright hopes. In late June 1964, one black and two white civil rights workers disappeared in Mississippi. Their badly beaten bodies were later found buried beneath an earthen dam. FBI investigators eventually arrested twenty-one white Mississippians, including the local sheriff, in connection with the killings. But white juries refused to convict whites for these murders. In August an integrated "Mississippi Freedom Democratic party" delegation was denied its seat at the national Democratic convention. Only a handful of black Mississippians had succeeded in registering to vote.

Early in 1965 Martin Luther King, Jr., resumed the voter-registration campaign in Selma, Alabama, where blacks made up 50 percent of the population but only 1 percent of the voters. State troopers with tear gas and whips assaulted King's demonstrators as they marched peacefully to the state capital at Montgomery. A Boston Unitarian minister was killed, and a few days later a white Detroit woman was shotgunned to death by Klansmen on the highway near Selma.

As the nation recoiled in horror before these violent scenes, President Johnson, speaking in soft southern accents, delivered a compelling address on television. What happened in Selma, he insisted, concerned all Americans, "who must overcome the crippling legacy of bigotry and injustice." Then, in a stirring adaptation of the anthem of the civil rights movement, the president concluded: "And we shall overcome." Following words with deeds, Johnson speedily shepherded through Congress the landmark Voting Rights Act of 1965, signed into law on August 6. It outlawed literacy tests and sent federal voter registrars into several southern states.

The passage of the Voting Rights Act, exactly 100 years after the conclusion of the Civil War, climaxed a century of awful abuse and robust resurgence for African-Americans in the South. "Give us the ballot," said Martin Luther King, Jr., "and the South will never be the same again." He was right. The act did not end discrimination and oppression overnight, but it placed an awesome lever for change in blacks' hands. Black southerners now had power and began to wield it without fear of reprisals. White southerners began to court black votes and business as never before. In the following decade, for the first time since emancipation, African-Americans began to migrate *into* the South.

Black Power

The Voting Rights Act of 1965 marked the end of an era in the history of the civil rights movement—the era of nonviolent demonstrations, focused on the South, led by peaceful moderates like Martin Luther King, Jr., and aimed at integrating blacks into American society. As if to symbolize the turn of events, just five days after President Johnson signed the landmark voting law, a bloody riot erupted in Watts, a black ghetto in Los Angeles. Blacks enraged by police brutality burned and looted their own neighborhoods for nearly a week. When the smoke finally cleared over the Los Angeles basin, thirty-one blacks and three whites lay dead, more than a thousand people had been injured, and hundreds of buildings stood charred and gutted. The Watts explosion heralded a new phase of the black struggle—increasingly marked by militant confrontation, focusing on northern and western cities, led by radical and sometimes violent spokespersons, and often aiming not at interracial cooperation but at black separatism.

The pious Christian moderation of Martin Luther King, Jr., came under heavy fire from this second wave of younger black leaders, who pri-

vately mocked the dignified Dr. King as "de Lawd." Deepening division among black leaders was highlighted by the career of Malcolm X. Born Malcolm Little, he was at first inspired by the militant black nationalists in the Nation of Islam. Like the Nation's founder, Elijah Muhammed (born Elijah Poole), Malcolm changed his surname to advertise his lost African identity in white America. A brilliant and charismatic preacher, Malcolm X trumpeted black separatism and inveighed against the "blue-eyed white devils." Eventually, Malcolm distanced himself from Elijah Muhammed's separatist preachings and moved toward mainstream Islam. (By the 1990s, Islam was among America's fastest-growing religions and counted some 2 million African-American converts—or "reverts" as Muslims described it—in its ranks.) Malcolm changed his name yet again, to El Haj Malik El-Shabazz, and began to preach a more conciliatory message. But in early 1965, he was cut down by rival Nation of Islam

Malcolm X   The charismatic black leader was a hypnotizing speaker who could rivet and arouse crowds with his call for black separatism. Yet at the end of his life Malcolm began to temper his separatist creed.

gunmen while speaking to a large crowd in New York City.

With frightening frequency, violence or the threat of violence raised its head in the black community. The Black Panther party openly brandished weapons in the streets of Oakland, California. The following year, Trinidad-born Stokely Carmichael, a leader of the Student Non-Violent Coordinating Committee (SNCC, pronounced "snick"), urged the abandonment of peaceful demonstrations and instead promoted "Black Power."

The very phrase "Black Power" unsettled many whites, and their fears increased when Carmichael was quoted as gloating that Black Power "will smash everything Western civilization has created." Some advocates of Black Power insisted that they simply intended the slogan to describe a broad-front effort to exercise the political and economic rights gained by the civil rights movement, and to speed the integration of American society. But other African-Americans, recollecting previous black nationalist movements like that of Marcus Garvey earlier in the century (see p. 764), breathed a vibrant separatist meaning into the concept of Black Power. They emphasized African-American distinctiveness, promoted "Afro" hairstyles and dress, shed their "white" names for new African identities, and demanded black studies programs in schools and universities.

Ironically, just as the civil rights movement had achieved its greatest legal and political triumphs, more city-shaking riots erupted in the black ghettoes of several American cities. A bloody outburst in Newark, New Jersey, in the summer of 1967, took twenty-five lives. Federal troops restored order in Detroit, Michigan, after forty-three people died in the streets. As in Los Angeles, black rioters torched their own neighborhoods, attacking police officers and even firefighters, who had to battle both flames and mobs howling "Burn, baby, burn."

These riotous outbursts angered many white Americans, who threatened to retaliate with their own "backlash" against ghetto arsonists and killers. Inner-city anarchy baffled many northerners, who had considered racial problems a purely "southern" question. But black concerns had moved north—as had nearly half the nation's black people. In the North the Black Power movement now focused less on civil rights and more on economic demands. Black unemployment, for example, was nearly double that for whites. These oppressive new problems seemed even less likely to be solved peaceably than the struggle for voting rights in the South.

You Don't Understand Boy—You're Supposed to Just Shuffle Along

Despair deepened when the magnetic and moderate voice of Martin Luther King, Jr., was forever silenced by a sniper's bullet in Memphis, Tennessee, on April 4, 1968. A martyr for justice, he had bled and died against the peculiarly American thorn of race. The killing of King cruelly robbed the American people of one of the most inspirational leaders in their history—at a time when they could least afford to lose him. This outrage triggered a nationwide orgy of ghetto-gutting and violence that cost over forty lives.

Rioters noisily made news, but thousands of other blacks quietly made history. Their voter registration in the South shot upward, and by the late 1960s several hundred blacks held elected office in the Old South. Cleveland, Ohio, and Gary, Indiana, elected black mayors. By 1972 nearly half of southern black children sat in integrated classrooms. Actually, more schools in the South were integrated than in the North. About a third of black families had risen economically into the ranks of the middle class—though an equal proportion remained below the "poverty line." King left a shining legacy of racial progress, but he was cut down when the job was far from completed.

The Mechanized War
High technology and modern equipment, such as this helicopter, gave the Americans in Vietnam a huge military advantage. But unaccompanied by a clear political purpose and a national will to win, technological superiority was insufficient to achieve final victory.

Combating Communism in Two Hemispheres

Violence at home eclipsed Johnson's legislative triumphs, while foreign flare-ups threatened his political life. Discontented Dominicans rose in revolt against their military government in April 1965. Johnson speedily announced that the Dominican Republic was the target of a Castrolike coup by "Communist conspirators," and he dispatched American troops, ultimately some 25,000, to protect American lives and restore order. But the evidence of a communist takeover was fragmentary at best. Johnson was widely condemned, at home and in Latin America, for his temporary reversion to the officially abandoned "gunboat diplomacy." Critics charged that the two-fisted Texan was far too eager to back right-wing regimes with rifle-toting troops.

At about the same time, Johnson was floundering deeper into the monsoon mud of Vietnam. Viet Cong guerrillas attacked an American air base at Pleiku, South Vietnam, in February 1965. The president immediately ordered retaliatory bombing raids against military installations in North Vietnam and for the first time ordered attacking U.S. troops to land. By the middle of March 1965, the Americans had "Operation Rolling Thunder" in full swing—regular full-scale bombing attacks against North Viet-

nam. Before 1965 ended, some 184,000 American troops were involved, most of them slogging through the jungles and rice paddies of South Vietnam searching for guerrillas clad in black pajamas.

Johnson had now taken the first fateful steps down a slippery path. He and his advisers believed that a fine-tuned, step-by-step "escalation" of American force would drive the enemy to defeat with a minimum loss of life on both sides. But the president reckoned without due knowledge of the toughness, resiliency, and dedication of the Viet Cong guerrillas in South Vietnam and their North Vietnamese allies. Aerial bombardment actually strengthened the communists' will to resist. The enemy matched every increase in American firepower with more men and more wiliness in the art of guerrilla warfare.

The South Vietnamese themselves were meanwhile becoming spectators in their own war, as the fighting became increasingly Americanized. Corrupt and collapsible governments succeeded each other in Saigon with bewildering rapidity. Yet American officials continued to talk of defending a faithful democratic ally. Washington spokespeople also defended America's action as a test of Uncle Sam's "commitment" and of the reliability of his numerous treaty pledges to resist communist encroachment. If the United States were to cut and run from Vietnam, claimed prowar "hawks," other nations would doubt America's word and crumble under communist pressure (the so-called domino theory), which would ostensibly drive America's first line of defense back to Waikiki Beach, in Hawaii, or even to the coast of California. Persuaded by such panicky thinking, Johnson steadily raised the military stakes in Vietnam. By 1968 he had poured more than half a million troops into Southeast Asia, and the annual bill for the war was exceeding $30 billion. Yet the end was nowhere in sight.

Vietnam Vexations

America could not defeat the enemy in Vietnam, but it seemed to be defeating itself. World opinion grew increasingly hostile; the blasting of an underdeveloped country by a mighty superpower struck many critics as obscene. Several nations expelled American Peace Corps volunteers. Haughty Charles de Gaulle, ever suspicious of American intentions, ordered NATO off French soil in 1966.

Overcommitment in Southeast Asia also tied America's hands elsewhere. Capitalizing on American distractions in Vietnam, the Soviet Union expanded its influence in the Mediterranean area, especially in Egypt. Tiny Israel stunned the Soviet-backed Egyptians in a devastating Six-Day War in June 1967. When the smoke had cleared, Israel occupied new territories in the Sinai Peninsula, the Golan Heights, the Gaza Strip, and the West Bank of the Jordan River, including Jerusalem (see map, p. 999). Although the Israelis eventually withdrew from the Sinai, they refused to relinquish the other areas and even introduced Jewish settlers into the heavily Arab district of the West Bank. The Arab Palestinians already living in the West Bank and their Arab allies elsewhere complained loudly about these Israeli policies, but to no avail. The Middle East was becoming an ever more dangerously packed powder keg that the war-plagued United States was powerless to defuse.

Domestic discontent festered as the Vietnamese entanglement dragged on. Antiwar demonstrations had begun on a small scale with campus "teach-ins" in 1965, and gradually these protests mounted to tidal-wave proportions. As the long arm of the military draft dragged more and more young men off to the Southeast Asian slaughterpen, resistance stiffened. Thousands of draft registrants fled to Canada; others publicly burned their draft cards. Hundreds of thousands of marchers filled the streets of New York, San Francisco, and other cities, chanting "Hell no, we won't go," and "Hey, hey, LBJ, how many kids did you kill today?" Countless citizens felt the pinch of war-spawned inflation. Many Americans also felt pangs of conscience at

The Victors and the Vanquished
An armored Israeli column heading for the Sinai front passes a truckload of Egyptian prisoners during the Six-Day War in June 1967. Israel crushed Egypt and its Syrian and Jordanian allies in this lightning war, but Egypt, allied with Syria, struck back six years later in the Yom Kippur War of October 1973.

the spectacle of their countrymen burning peasant huts and blistering civilians with ghastly napalm.

Opposition in Congress to the Vietnam involvement centered in the influential Senate Committee on Foreign Relations, headed by a former Rhodes scholar, Senator William Fulbright of Arkansas. A constant thorn in the side of the president, he staged a series of widely viewed televised hearings in 1966 and 1967, during which prominent personages aired their views, largely antiwar. Gradually, the public came to feel that it had been deceived about the causes and "winnability" of the war. A yawning "credibility gap" opened between the government and the people. New flocks of antiwar "doves" were hatching daily.

Even within the administration, doubts were deepening about the wisdom of the war in Vietnam. When Defense Secretary McNamara expressed increasing discomfiture at the course of events, he was quietly eased out of the cabinet. (Years later, McNamara wrote that "we were wrong, terribly wrong," about Vietnam.) President Johnson did announce "bombing halts" in early 1966 and early 1967, supposedly to lure the enemy to the peace table. But Washington did not pursue its "peace offensive" with much energy, and the other side did not respond with any encouragement. Both sides used the bombing pauses to funnel more troops into South Vietnam.

By early 1968 the brutal and futile struggle had become the longest and most unpopular foreign war in the nation's history. The government had failed utterly to explain to the people what was supposed to be at stake in Vietnam. Many critics wondered if any objective could be worth the vast price, in blood and treasure, that America was paying. Casualties, killed and wounded, already exceeded 100,000. More bombs had been dropped on Vietnam than on all enemy territory in World War II.

The war was also ripping apart the fabric of American society and even threatening to shred the Constitution. In 1967, President Johnson ordered the CIA, in clear violation of its charter as a *foreign* intelligence agency, to spy on domestic antiwar activists. He also encouraged the FBI to turn its counterintelligence program, code-named "Cointelpro," against the peace movement. "Cointelpro" had been launched by J. Edgar Hoover in the 1950s to infiltrate communist organizations. Now under presidential directive, it sabotaged peace groups by conducting "black bag" break-ins. "Cointelpro" also subverted leading "doves" with false accusations that they were communist sympathizers. These clandestine tactics made the FBI look like a totalitarian state's secret police, rather than a guardian of American democracy.

As the war dragged on, evidence mounted that America had been entrapped in an Asian civil war,

Antiwar Demonstration in California Public opinion gradually but inexorably turned against the war. In 1965, polls showed that only 15 percent of Americans favored withdrawal from Vietnam. But by 1969, 69 percent of those interviewed indicated that they considered the war a "mistake," and by 1970, a majority supported withdrawal of U.S. troops.

fighting against highly motivated rebels who were striving to overthrow an oppressive regime. Yet Johnson clung to his basic strategy of ratcheting up the pressure bit by bit. He stubbornly assured doubting Americans that he could see "the light at the end of the tunnel." But to growing numbers of Americans, it seemed that Johnson was bent on "saving" Vietnam by destroying it.

Vietnam Topples Johnson

Hawkish illusions that the struggle was about to be won were shattered by a blistering communist offensive launched in late January 1968, during Tet, the Vietnamese New Year. At a time when the Viet Cong were supposedly licking their wounds, they suddenly and simultaneously mounted savage attacks on twenty-seven key South Vietnamese cities, including the capital, Saigon. Although eventually beaten off with heavy losses, they demonstrated anew that victory could not be gained by Johnson's strategy of gradual escalation. The Tet offensive ended in a military defeat but a political victory for the Viet Cong. With an increasingly insistent voice, American public opinion demanded a speedy end to the war. Opposition grew so vehement that President Johnson could feel the very foundations of government shaking under his feet. He was also suffering through hells of personal agony over American casualties. He wept as he signed letters of condolence, and slipped off at night to pray with monks at a small Catholic church in Washington.

American military leaders responded to the Tet attacks with a request for 200,000 more troops. The largest single increment yet, this addition would have swollen American troop strength in Vietnam to about the three-quarter-million mark. The size of the request staggered many policymakers. Former Secretary of State Dean Acheson reportedly advised the president that "the Joint Chiefs of Staff don't know what they're talking about." Johnson himself now began to doubt seriously the wisdom of continuing on his raise-the-stakes course.

The president meanwhile was being sharply challenged from within his own party. Eugene McCarthy, a little-known Democratic senator from Minnesota, had emerged as a contender for the 1968 Democratic presidential nomination. The soft-spoken McCarthy, a sometime poet and devout

The Vietnam Quagmire   This soldier, carrying a rocket launcher across a stream in the ironically named "demilitarized zone" (DMZ) that separated North from South Vietnam, was killed in action just days after this photo was taken.

Catholic, gathered a small army of antiwar college students as campaign workers. Going "clean for Gene," with shaven faces and shortened locks, these idealistic recruits of the "Children's Crusade" invaded the key presidential primary state of New Hampshire to ring doorbells. On March 12, 1968, their efforts gave McCarthy an incredible 42 percent of the Democratic votes and twenty of the twenty-four convention delegates. President Johnson was on the same ballot, but only as a write-in candidate. Four days later Senator Robert F. Kennedy of New York, the murdered president's younger brother and by now himself a "dove" on Vietnam, threw his hat into the ring. The charismatic Kennedy, heir to his fallen brother's mantle of leadership, stirred a passionate response among workers, African-Americans, Hispanics, and young people.

These startling events abroad and at home were not lost on LBJ. The country might explode in greater violence if he met the request of the generals for more troops. His own party was dangerously divided on the war issue. He might not even be able to win renomination after his relatively poor showing in New Hampshire. Yet he remained committed to victory in Vietnam, even if the light at the end of the tunnel was vanishing. How could he salvage his blind-alley policy?

Johnson's answer came in a bombshell address on March 31, 1968. He announced on nationwide television that he would finally apply the brakes to

Robert F. Kennedy Campaigning for the Presidency, 1968
Wrapped in the Kennedy family mystique and exuding his own boyish charm, Kennedy excited partisan crowds to wildly adulatory outpourings.

the escalating war. He would freeze American troop levels and gradually shift more responsibility to the South Vietnamese themselves. Aerial bombardment of the enemy would be drastically scaled down. Then, in a dramatic plea to unify a dangerously divided nation, Johnson startled his vast audience by firmly declaring that he would not be a candidate for the presidency in 1968.

Johnson's "abdication" had the effect of preserving the military status quo. He had held the "hawks" in check, while offering himself as a sacrifice to the militant "doves." The United States could thus maintain the maximum *acceptable* level of military activity in Vietnam with one hand, while trying to negotiate a settlement with the other.

North Vietnam responded somewhat encouragingly three days later, when it expressed a willingness to talk about peace. After a month of haggling over the site, the adversaries agreed to meet in Paris.

But progress was glacially slow, as prolonged bickering developed over the very shape of the conference table.

The Presidential Sweepstakes of 1968

Summer in 1968 was one of the hottest political seasons in the nation's history. Johnson's heir apparent for the Democratic nomination was his liberal vice president, Hubert H. Humphrey, a former pharmacist, college professor, mayor, and U.S. senator from Minnesota. Loyally supporting LBJ's Vietnam policies through thick and thin, he received the support of the party apparatus, dominated as it was by the White House. Senators McCarthy and Kennedy meanwhile dueled in several state primaries, with Kennedy's bandwagon gathering ever-increasing speed. But on June 5, 1968, the night of an exciting victory in the California primary, Kennedy was shot to death by a young Arab immigrant resentful of the candidate's pro-Israel views.

Surrounded by bitterness and frustration, the Democrats met in Chicago in late August 1968. Angry antiwar zealots, deprived by an assassin's bullet of their leading candidate, streamed menacingly into Chicago. Mayor Daley responded by arranging for barbed-wire barricades around the convention hall ("Fort Daley"), as well as thousands of police and National Guard reinforcements. Many demonstrators baited the officers in blue by calling them "pigs." Other militants, chanting "Ho, Ho, Ho Chi Minh," shouted obscenities and hurled bags and cans of excrement at the police lines. As people the world over watched on television, the exasperated "peace officers" broke into a "police riot," clubbing and manhandling innocent and guilty alike. Acrid tear gas fumes hung heavy over the city and even drifted up to candidate Humphrey's hotel suite. Hundreds of people were arrested and scores hospitalized, but there were no casualties—except, as cynics said, the Democratic party and its candidate.

Humphrey steamrollered to the nomination on the first ballot. The dovish McCarthyites failed even to secure an antiwar platform plank. Instead, the Humphrey forces, echoing the president, hammered into place their own declaration that armed force would be relentlessly applied until the enemy showed more willingness to negotiate.

Scenting victory as the Democrats divided, the Republicans had jubilantly convened in plush

The Siege of Chicago, 1968
Antiwar demonstrators confront National Guardsmen during the Democratic convention in Chicago in August 1968.

Miami Beach, Florida, early in August 1968. Richard M. Nixon, the former vice president whom John F. Kennedy had narrowly defeated eight years earlier, arose from his political grave to win the nomination. As a "hawk" on Vietnam and a right-leaning middle-of-the-roader on domestic policy, Nixon pleased the Goldwater conservatives and was acceptable to party moderates. He appealed to white Southern voters and to the "law and order" element when he tapped as his vice-presidential running mate Maryland's governor Spiro T. Agnew, noted for his tough stands against dissidents and black militants. The Republican platform called for victory in Vietnam and a strong anticrime policy.

A "spoiler" third-party ticket—the American Independent party—added color and confusion to the campaign. It was headed by a scrappy ex-pugilist, George C. Wallace, former governor of Alabama. In 1963 he had stood in the doorway to prevent two black students from entering the University of Alabama. "Segregation now! Segregation tomorrow! Segregation forever!" he shouted. Wallace jabbed repeatedly at "pointy-headed bureaucrats," and he taunted hecklers as "bums" in need of a bath. Speaking behind a bullet-proof screen, he called for prodding the blacks into their place, with bayonets if necessary. He and his running mate, former air force general Curtis LeMay, also proposed smashing the North Vietnamese to smithereens by "bombing them back to the Stone Age."

Victory for Nixon

Vietnam proved a less crucial issue than expected. Between the positions of the Republicans and the Democrats, there was little choice. Both candidates were committed to carrying on the war until the enemy settled for an "honorable peace," which seemed to mean an "American victory." The millions of "doves" had no place to roost, and many refused to vote at all. Humphrey, scorched by the LBJ brand, went down to defeat as a loyal prisoner of his chief's policies, despite Johnson's last-minute effort to bail him out by announcing a *total* bombing halt.

Nixon, who had lost a cliff-hanger to Kennedy in 1960, won one in 1968. He garnered 301 electoral votes, with 43.4 percent of the popular tally (31,785,480), as compared with 191 electoral votes and 42.7 percent of the popular votes (31,275,166) for Humphrey. Nixon was the first president-elect since 1848 not to bring in on his coattails at least one house of Congress for his party in an initial presidential election. He carried not a single major city, thus attesting to the continuing urban strength of the Democrats, who also won about 95 percent of the black vote. Nixon had received no clear mandate to do anything. He was a minority president who owed his election to divisions over the war and protest against the unfair draft, crime, and rioting.

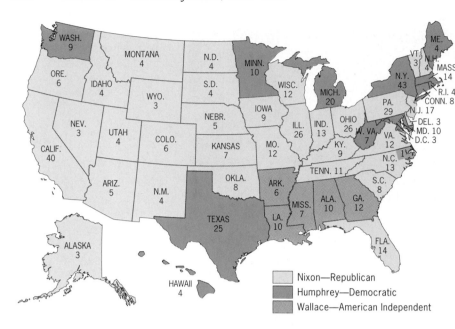

Presidential Election of 1968 (with electoral vote by state) George Wallace won in five states, and he denied a clear majority to either of the two major-party candidates in twenty-five other states. A shift of some fifty thousand votes might well have thrown the election into the House of Representatives, giving Wallace the strategic bargaining position he sought.

Nixon—Republican
Humphrey—Democratic
Wallace—American Independent

Wallace did worse than expected. Yet he won an impressive 9,906,473 popular votes and 46 electoral votes, all from five states of the Deep South, four of which the Republican Goldwater had carried in 1964. Wallace remained a formidable force, for he had amassed the largest third-party popular vote in American history. Wallace had also resoundingly demonstrated the continuing power of "populist" politics, which appealed to voters' fears and resentments rather than to the better angels of their nature. His candidacy foreshadowed a coarsening of American political life that would take deep root in the ensuing decades.

The Obituary of Lyndon Johnson

Talented but tragedy-struck Lyndon Johnson returned to his Texas ranch in January 1969 and died there four years later. His party was defeated, and his "me-too" Hubert Humphrey was repudiated. His popularity remained low in the opinion polls, although it had risen somewhat after his "great renunciation"—ironically, one of his most popular acts.

Yet Johnson's legislative leadership for a time had been remarkable. No president since Lincoln had worked harder or done more for civil rights. None had shown more compassion for the poor, blacks, and the ill educated. LBJ seemed to suffer from an inferiority complex about his own arid cultural background, and he strove furiously to prove that he could be a great "people's president" in the image of his idol, Franklin Roosevelt. His legislative achievements in his first three years in office indeed invited comparison with those of the New Deal.

But by 1966 Johnson was already sinking into the Vietnam quicksands. The Republicans had made gains in Congress, and a white "backlash" had begun to form against the black movement. Great Society programs began to wither on the vine, as soaring war costs sucked tax dollars into the military machine. Johnson had promised both guns and butter but could not keep that promise. Ever-creeping inflation blighted the prospects of prosperity, and the War on Poverty met resistance that was as stubborn as the Viet Cong and eventually went down to defeat. Great want persisted alongside great wealth.

Johnson had crucified himself on the cross of Vietnam. The Southeast Asian quagmire engulfed his noblest intentions. Committed to some degree by his two predecessors, he had chosen to defend the American foothold and enlarge the conflict rather than be run out. He was evidently persuaded by his brightest advisers, both civilian and military, that a "cheap" victory was possible. It would be achieved by massive aerial bombing and large, though limited, troop commitments. His decision not to escalate the fighting further offended the "hawks," and his refusal to back off altogether antagonized the "doves." Like the Calvinists of colonial days, luckless Lyndon Johnson was damned if he did and damned if he did not.

The Cultural Upheaval of the 1960s

The struggles of the 1960s against racism, poverty, and the war in Vietnam had momentous cultural consequences. The decade came to be seen as a watershed dividing two distinct eras in terms of values, morals, and behavior.

Everywhere in 1960s America a newly negative attitude toward all kinds of authority took hold. Disillusioned by the discovery that American society was not free of racism, sexism, imperialism, and oppression, many young people lost their traditional moral rudders. Neither families nor churches nor schools seemed to be able to define values and shape behavior with the certainty of shared purpose that many people believed had once existed. The upheaval even churned the tradition-bound Roman Catholic church, among the world's oldest and most conservative institutions. Clerics abandoned their Roman collars and Latin lingo, folk songs replaced Gregorian chants, and meatless Fridays became ancient history. No matter what the topic, conventional wisdom and inherited ideas came under fire. "Trust no one over thirty" was a popular sneer of rebellious youth.

Skepticism about authority had deep historical roots in American culture, and it had even bloomed in the supposedly complacent and conformist 1950s. "Beat" poets like Allen Ginsberg and icono-

As a tough motorcycle-gang leader, Marlon Brando (b. 1924) in the film The Wild One *(1954) summed up the anarchic impulses of the decade when he was asked, "What are you rebelling against?" His reply: "What d'ya got?"*

clastic novelists like Jack Kerouac had voiced dark disillusion with the materialistic pursuits and "establishment" arrogance of the Eisenhower era. In movies like *Rebel Without a Cause* (1955), the attractive young actor James Dean expressed the restless frustration of many young people.

The disaffection of the young reached crisis proportions in the tumultuous 1960s. One of the first organized protests against established authority broke out at the University of California at Berkeley in 1964, in the so-called Free Speech Movement. One of its leaders, condemning the impersonal bureaucratization of higher education, urged students to "put your bodies against the gears, against the wheels—and make the machine stop until we are free." Fired by seething resentment against the war in Vietnam, many sons and daughters of the middle class turned to mind-bending drugs, tuned in to "acid rock," and dropped out of "straight"

The "Free Speech Movement," Berkeley, California, December 4, 1964 Student leader Mario Savio addresses a crowd at the University of California at Berkeley. The Free Speech Movement marked the first of the large-scale student mobilizations that would rock campuses across the country throughout the rest of the 1960s.

The Counterculture   Flower children get married on the summer solstice in 1960s New Mexico.

society. Others "did their own thing" in communes or "alternative" institutions. Patriotism became a dirty word. Beflowered women in trousers and long-haired men with earrings heralded the rise of a self-conscious "counterculture" blatantly opposed to traditional American ways.

The 1960s also witnessed a "sexual revolution," though its novelty and scale are often exaggerated. Without doubt, the introduction of the birth-control pill in 1960 made unwanted pregnancies much easier to avoid and sexual appetites easier to satisfy. But as early as 1948, Indiana University sexologist Dr. Alfred Kinsey had published sensational revelations

Historian Theodore Roszak (b. 1933) wrote in 1969,

"It would hardly seem an exaggeration to call what we see arising among the young a 'counter culture': meaning, a culture so radically disaffiliated from the mainstream assumptions of our society that it scarcely looks to many as a culture at all, but takes on the alarming appearance of a barbarian intrusion."

about American sexual habits in *Sexual Behavior in the Human Male,* followed five years later by *Sexual Behavior in the Human Female.* Based on thousands of interviews, Kinsey's findings about the incidence of premarital sex and adultery caused a ruckus at the time and have been hotly debated ever since. Most controversial was Kinsey's estimate that 10 percent of American males were homosexuals. Whatever the exact number, by the 1960s gay men and lesbians were increasingly emerging from the closet and demanding sexual tolerance. The Mattachine Society, founded in Los Angeles in 1951, was a pioneering advocate for gay rights. A brutal attack on gay men by off-duty police officers at New York's Stonewall Inn in 1969 powerfully energized gay and lesbian militancy. Widening worries in the 1980s about sexually transmitted diseases like genital herpes and AIDS (acquired immunodeficiency syndrome) finally slowed, but did not reverse, the sexual revolution.

Launched in youthful idealism, many of the cultural "revolutions" of the 1960s sputtered out in violence and cynicism. Students for a Democratic Society (SDS), once at the forefront of the antipoverty and antiwar campaigns, had by decade's end spawned an underground terrorist group called the Weathermen. Peaceful civil rights demonstrations had given way to blockbusting urban riots. What started as apparently innocent experiments with drugs like marijuana and LSD had fried many youthful brains and spawned a loathsome underworld of drug lords and addicted users.

Straitlaced guardians of respectability denounced the self-indulgent romanticism of the "flower children" as the beginning of the end of modern civilization. Sympathetic observers hailed the "greening" of America—the replacement of materialism and imperialism by a new consciousness of human values. But the upheavals of the 1960s could be largely attributed to three *P*s: the youthful population bulge, protest against racism and the Vietnam War, and the apparent permanence of prosperity. As the decade flowed into the 1970s, the flower children grew older and had children of their own, the civil rights movement fell silent, the war ended, and economic stagnation blighted the bloom of prosperity. Young people in the 1970s seemed more concerned with finding a job in the system than with tearing the system down. But if the "counterculture" had not managed fully to replace older values, it had weakened their grip, perhaps permanently.

Chronology

1961 Berlin crisis and construction of the Berlin Wall
Alliance for Progress
Bay of Pigs
Kennedy sends "military advisers" to South Vietnam

1962 Pressure from Kennedy results in a rollback of steel prices
Trade Expansion Act
Laos neutralized
Cuban missile crisis

1963 Anti-Diem coup in South Vietnam
Civil rights march in Washington, D.C.
Kennedy assassinated; Johnson assumes presidency

1964 Twenty-fourth Amendment (abolishing poll tax in federal elections) ratified
"Freedom Summer" voter registration in the South
Tonkin Gulf Resolution

1964 Johnson defeats Goldwater for presidency
War on Poverty begins
Civil Rights Act

1965 Great Society legislation
Voting Rights Act
U.S. troops occupy Dominican Republic

1965-1968 Race riots in U.S. cities
Escalation of the Vietnam War

1967 Six-Day War between Israel and Egypt

1968 Tet offensive in Vietnam
Martin Luther King, Jr., and Robert Kennedy assassinated
Nixon defeats Humphrey and Wallace for presidency

1969 Astronauts land on moon

The Sixties: Constructive or Destructive?

The 1960s were convulsed by controversy, and they have remained controversial ever since. Conflicts raged in that turbulent decade between social classes, races, sexes, and generations. More than three decades later, the shock waves from the 1960s still reverberate through American society. The "Contract with America" that swept conservative Republicans to power in 1994 amounted to nothing less than a wholesale repudiation of the government activism that marked the sixties decade, and a resounding reaffirmation of the "traditional values" that sixties culture supposedly trashed. Liberal Democrats, on the other hand, continue to press affirmative action for women and minorities, protection for the environment, an expanded welfare state, and sexual tolerance—all legacies of the stormy sixties.

Four issues dominate historical discussion of the 1960s: the struggle for civil rights; the Great Society's "War on Poverty"; the Vietnam War and the antiwar movement; and the emergence of the "counterculture."

Although most scholars praise the civil rights achievements of the 1960s, they disagree over the civil rights movement's turn away from nonviolence and its embrace of separatism and Black Power. The Freedom Riders and Martin Luther King, Jr. find much more approval in most history books than do Malcolm X or the Black Panther party. But some scholars, notably William L. Van Deburg in *New Day in Babylon: The Black Power Movement and American Culture, 1965–1975*

(1992), argue that the "flank effect" of radical Black Power advocates like Stokely Carmichael actually enhanced the bargaining position of moderates like Dr. King. Deburg also suggests that the enthusiasm of Black Power advocates for African-American cultural uniqueness reshaped both black self-consciousness and the broader culture as well, as it provided a model for the feminist and multiculturalist movements of the 1970s and later.

Johnson's War on Poverty has found its liberal defenders in scholars like Allen Matusow (*The Unraveling of America,* 1984) and John Schwarz (*America's Hidden Success,* 1988). Schwarz demonstrates, for example, that Medicare and Social Security reforms virtually eliminated poverty among America's elderly. But the Great Society has also provoked strong criticism from writers such as Charles Murray (*Losing Ground,* 1984) and Lawrence Meade (*Beyond Entitlements,* 1986). As those conservative critics see the poverty issue, to use a phrase popular in the 1960s, the Great Society was part of the problem, not part of the solution. In their view, the War on Poverty did not simply fail to eradicate poverty among the so-called underclass; it actually deepened the dependency of the poor on the welfare state and even generated a multigenerational "cycle" of poverty. In this argument, Johnson's Great Society stands indicted of creating, in effect, a permanent welfare class.

For many young people of the 1960s, the antiwar movement protesting America's policy in Vietnam provided their initiation into politics, and their introduction to "movement culture,"

with its sense of community and shared purpose. But scholars disagree over the movement's real effectiveness in checking the war. Writers like John Lewis Gaddis (*Strategies of Containment,* 1982) explain America's eventual withdrawal from Vietnam essentially without reference to the protesters in the streets. Others, like Todd Gitlin (*The Sixties: Years of Hope, Days of Rage,* 1987), insist that mass protest was the force that finally pressed the war to a conclusion.

Debate over the counterculture not only pits liberals against conservatives, but also liberals against radicals. A liberal historian like William O'Neill (*Coming Apart,* 1971) might sympathize with what he considers some of the worthy values pushed by student activists, such as racial justice, nonviolence, and the antiwar movement, but he also claims that much of the sixties "youth culture" degenerated into hedonism, arrogance, and social polarization. In contrast, younger historians such as David Farber, Michael Kazin, and Maurice Isserman argue that cultural radicalism and political radicalism were two sides of the same coin. Many young people in the sixties made little distinction between the personal and the political. As Sara Evans demonstrates in *Personal Politics* (1980), "the personal *was* the political" for many women. She finds the roots of modern feminism in the sexism women activists encountered in the civil rights and antiwar movements.

While critics may argue over the "good" versus the "bad" sixties, there is no denying the degree to which that tumultuous time, for better or worse, shaped the world in which we now live.

SUGGESTED READINGS

PRIMARY SOURCE DOCUMENTS

Norman Mailer paints vivid portraits of the 1968 conventions in *Miami and the Siege of Chicago* (1968) and of the anti-war March on Washington in his *Armies of the*

Night (1968). Martin Luther King, Jr.'s *Letter from Birmingham Jail** (1963) eloquently defends the civil rights movement. The progress of the war in Vietnam is chronicled in *The Pentagon Papers** (1971). Students for a Democratic Society (1962) and Young Americans for Freedom (1960) both issued manifestos* that suggest the political temper of the era. Stewart Alsop penned a notable editorial in *Newsweek** in 1970 that reflects the "establishment's" disgust with the cultural upheavals of the decade.

---

*An asterisk indicates that the document, or an excerpt from it, can be found in Thomas A. Bailey and David M. Kennedy, eds., *The American Spirit: United States History as Seen by Contemporaries,* 9th ed. (Boston: Houghton Mifflin, 1998).

SECONDARY SOURCES

The tumultuous decade of the 1960s is treated in William L. O'Neill, *Coming Apart: An Informal History of America in the 1960s* (1971); in Alan Matusow, *The Unraveling of America* (1984); and in John Morton Blum, *Years of Discord* (1991); as well as in the surveys cited in Chapter 40. On Kennedy see Theodore C. Sorenson, *Kennedy* (1965), and Arthur M. Schlesinger, Jr., *A Thousand Days* (1965), both appreciative accounts by insiders. More critical is Henry Fairlie, *The Kennedy Promise* (1973). Other useful biographies include Arthur M. Schlesinger, Jr., *Robert F. Kennedy and His Times* (1978); Nigel Hamilton, *JFK: Reckless Youth* (1992); and Warren I. Cohen, *Dean Rusk* (1980). Seymour Harris is informative on *Economics of the Kennedy Years* (1964). Michael Beschloss details *The Crisis Years: Kennedy and Khrushchev, 1960–1963* (1991). The Cuban missile crisis is chronicled in Robert F. Kennedy, *Thirteen Days* (1969), and Graham Allison, *Essence of Decision* (1971). On the space program, consult Walter McDougall, *. . . the Heavens and the Earth* (1985), and Clayton Koppes, *JPL* [Jet Propulsion Laboratory] *and the American Space Program* (1982). Kennedy's assassination is scrutinized, not entirely satisfactorily, in *The Official Warren Commission Report* (1964). See also Gerald Posner, *Case Closed* (1993). Gripping reading is William Manchester, *Death of a President* (1967). A splendid short biography is Bruce J. Schulman, *Lyndon B. Johnson and American Liberalism* (1994). Eric Goldman, *The Tragedy of Lyndon Johnson* (1969), is a sympathetic yet critical account of the Johnson presidency. In the same vein, with a psychoanalytic touch, is Doris Kearns, *Lyndon B. Johnson and the American Dream* (1976). Johnson's own memoir, *The Vantage Point* (1971), is marred by excessive self-justification. Equally unbalanced antidotes are Robert Caro, *The Years of Lyndon Johnson: The Path to Power* (1982), and *Means of Ascent* (1990). For a more complex portrait, see Robert Dallek, *Lone Star Rising: Lyndon Johnson and His Times, 1908–1960* (1991). The conditions that called forth the Great Society programs are movingly described in Michael Harrington, *The Other America: Poverty in the United States* (1962). James Patterson summarizes *America's Struggle Against Poverty* (1981). Two superb chronicles of the civil rights movement focusing on Martin Luther King, Jr., are the books by Taylor Branch and David J. Garrow cited in Chapter 40. The racial upheavals of the decade are discussed in Harvard Sitkoff, *The Struggle for Black Equality, 1954–1992* (1993); Clayborne Carson, *In Struggle: SNCC* [Student Non-Violent Coordinating Committee] *and the Black Awakening of the 1960s* (1981); and William H. Chafe, *Civilities and Civil Rights: Greensboro, North Carolina, and the Black Struggle for Freedom* (1980). See also

Stephen B. Oates, *Let the Trumpet Sound: The Life of Martin Luther King, Jr.* (1982); Alex Haley, ed., *The Autobiography of Malcolm X* (1966); and Eldridge Cleaver, *Soul on Ice* (1968). On the New Left, consult two volumes by Todd Gitlin, *The Sixties: Years of Hope, Days of Rage* (1987) and *The Whole World Is Watching: Mass Media in the Making and Unmaking of the New Left* (1980); James Miller, "*Democracy Is in the Streets": From Port Huron to the Sea of Chicago* (1987); Sara Evans, *Personal Politics* (1979); David Harris, *Dreams Die Hard* (1982); and Tom Hayden, *Reunion* (1988). On Vietnam consult Ronald Spector, *The United States Army in Vietnam* (1984), W. H. Brands, *Since Vietnam* (1996), and Stanley Karnow's encyclopedic *Vietnam: A History* (1983). Concise accounts are George Herring, *America's Longest War* (1986) and Marilyn B. Young, *The Vietnam Wars, 1945–1990* (1991). George Q. Flynn looks at *The Draft, 1940–1973* (1993). See also Christian Appy, *Working-Class War* (1993). Neil Sheehan, *A Bright Shining Lie: John Paul Vann and America in Vietnam* (1988), is a gripping account of one unorthodox commander. Jeffrey P. Kimball, ed., *To Reason Why: The Debate About the Causes of U.S. Involvement in the Vietnam War* (1990), contains readings from academic and public-policy figures. Robert S. McNamara, *In Retrospect: The Tragedy and Lessons of Vietnam* (1995), is the sorrowful apology of one of the war's principal architects for the "mistake" of Vietnam. Two works by John Lewis Gaddis shrewdly analyze the Cold War context of the Vietnam conflict: *The Long Peace* (1987) and *The United States and the End of the Cold War* (1992). See also his *Strategies of Containment* (1982). Presidential elections are described in continuing installments of Theodore H. White's *The Making of the President, 1964* (1965) and *The Making of the President, 1968* (1969). The emergence of a "youth culture" in the 1960s is illuminated in three studies by Kenneth Keniston: *The Uncommitted* (1965), *Young Radicals* (1968), and *Youth and Dissent* (1971). Popular books indicating the mood of the 1960s include Theodore Roszak, *The Making of a Counter-Culture* (1969), and Charles Reich, *The Greening of America* (1970). In *American Genesis: A Century of Invention and Technological Enthusiasm* (1989), Thomas Hughes argues that the sixties marked the end of a century-long national love affair with technology. Also intriguing on the 1960s is Morris Dickstein, *The Gates of Eden: American Culture in the Sixties* (1977). A lucid survey of the intellectual history of the postwar era is Richard Pells, *The Liberal Mind in a Conservative Age* (1984). Changes in attitudes toward sex are scrutinized in Daniel Yankelovich, *The New Morality* (1974); Morton Hunt, *Sexual Behavior in the 1970s* (1974); and Paul Robinson, *The Modernization of Sex* (1976).

42

The Stalemated Seventies

1968–1980

---

*In all my years of public life, I have never
obstructed justice. People have got to know
whether or not their President is a crook. Well,
I'm not a crook; I earned everything I've got.*

RICHARD NIXON, 1973

The Economy Stagnates in the 1970s

As the 1960s lurched to a close, the fantastic quarter-century economic boom of the post–World War II era also showed signs of petering out. By increasing their productivity, American workers had doubled their average standard of living in the twenty-five years since the end of World War II. Now, fatefully, productivity gains slowed to the vanishing point. The entire decade of the 1970s did not witness a productivity advance equivalent to even one year's progress in the preceding two decades. At the new rate, it would take five hundred more years to bring about another doubling of the average worker's standard of living. The median income of the average American family stagnated in the two decades after 1970, and failed to decline only because of the addition of working wives' wages to the family income (see chart at right). The rising baby-boom generation now faced the depressing prospect of a living standard that would be lower than that of their parents.

What caused the sudden slump in productivity? Some observers cited the increasing presence in the work force of women and teenagers, who typically had fewer skills than male adult workers and were less likely to take the full-time, long-term jobs where skills might be developed. Other commentators blamed declining investment in new machinery, the heavy costs of compliance with government-imposed safety and health regulations, and the general shift of the American economy from manu-

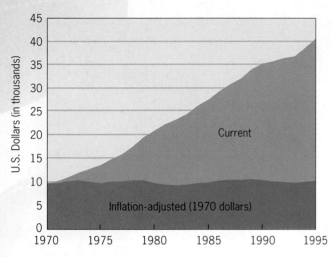

Median Family Income, 1970–1995
During the long post–World War II economic boom (from about 1950 to 1970), family incomes had increased dramatically, but after 1970, "real," or inflation-adjusted, income stagnated. That basic economic fact underlay much of the social and political history of the last third of the century. (Bureau of Labor Statistics Web Site: www.stats. bls.gov/cpihome.htm; accessed 2/13/97, and U.S. Census Bureau Official Statistics Web Site, www. census.gov/hhes/income/histinc/incfamdet.html, accessed 2/13/97.)

facturing to services, where productivity gains were allegedly more difficult to achieve and measure. Yet, in the last analysis, much mystery attends the productivity slowdown, and economists are still wrestling with the puzzle.

The Vietnam War also precipitated painful economic distortions. The disastrous conflict in Southeast Asia drained tax dollars from needed improvements in education, deflected scientific skill and manufacturing capacity from the civilian sector, and touched off a sickening spiral of inflation. Sharply rising oil prices in the 1970s also fed inflation, but its deepest roots lay in government policies of the 1960—especially Lyndon Johnson's insistence on simultaneously fighting the war in Vietnam and funding the Great Society programs at home, all without a tax increase to finance the added expenditures. Both military spending and welfare spending are inherently inflationary (in the absence of offsetting tax collections), because they put dollars in people's hands without adding to the supply of goods that those dollars can buy.

When too many dollars chase too few goods, prices rise—as they did astonishingly in the 1970s. The cost of living more than tripled in the dozen years following Richard Nixon's inauguration, in the longest and steepest inflationary cycle in American history.

Other weaknesses in the nation's economy were also laid bare by the abrupt reversal of America's financial fortunes in the 1970s. The competitive advantage of many major American businesses had been so enormous after World War II that they had

The Nixon Wave During Richard Nixon's presidency, Americans experienced the first serious inflation since the immediate post–World War II years. The inflationary surge grew to tidal-wave proportions by the late 1970s, when the consumer price index rose at annual rates of more than 10 percent.

small incentive to modernize plants and seek more efficient methods of production. The defeated German and Japanese people had meanwhile clawed their way out of the ruins of war and built wholly new factories with the most up-to-date technology and management techniques. By the 1970s their efforts paid handsome rewards, as they came to dominate industries like steel, automobiles, and consumer electronics—fields in which the United States had once been unchallengeable.

For all these reasons, the postwar wave of robust economic growth had clearly crested by the early 1970s. At home and abroad, the "can do" American spirit gave way to an unaccustomed sense of limits. This stifling realization hung over the 1970s like a pall. It frustrated both policymakers and citizens who keenly remembered the growth and optimism of the quarter-century since World War II. The overachieving postwar generation had never met a problem it could not solve. But now a stalemated, unpopular war and a stagnant, unresponsive economy heralded the end of the self-confident postwar era. With it ended the liberal dream, vivid since New Deal days, that an affluent society could spend its way to social justice.

Nixon "Vietnamizes" the War

Inaugurated on January 20, 1969, Richard Nixon urged the American people, torn with dissension over Vietnam and race relations, to "stop shouting at one another." Yet the new president seemed an unlikely conciliator of the clashing forces that appeared to be ripping apart American society. Solitary and suspicious by nature, Nixon could be brittle and testy in the face of opposition. He also harbored bitter resentments against the "liberal establishment" that had cast him into the political darkness for much of the preceding decade. Yet Nixon brought one hugely valuable asset with him to the White House—his broad knowledge and thoughtful expertise in foreign affairs. With calculating shrewdness he applied himself to putting America's foreign-policy house in order.

The first burning need was to quiet the public uproar over Vietnam. President Nixon's announced policy—called "Vietnamization"—was to withdraw the 540,000 U.S. troops in South Vietnam over an extended period. The South Vietnamese—with American money, weapons, training, and advice—

President Richard M. Nixon   Reversing Kennedy's inaugural plea to "bear any burden," Nixon told Congress in February 1970, "America cannot—and will not—conceive all the plans, design all the programs, execute all the decisions and undertake all the defense of the free nations of the world."

could then gradually take over the burden of fighting their own war.

The so-called Nixon Doctrine thus evolved. It proclaimed that the United States would honor its existing defense commitments but that in the future, Asians and others would have to fight their own wars without the support of large bodies of American ground troops.

Nixon sought not to end the war but to win it by other means, without the further spilling of American blood. But even this much involvement was distasteful to the American "doves," many of whom demanded a withdrawal that was prompt, complete, unconditional, and irreversible. Antiwar protesters staged a massive national Vietnam moratorium in October 1969, as nearly 100,000 people jammed the Boston Common and some 50,000 filed by the White House carrying lighted candles.

Undaunted, Nixon launched his own homefront counteroffensive. On November 3, 1969, he delivered a dramatic televised appeal to the great "silent majority," who presumably supported the war. Though ostensibly conciliatory, Nixon's appeal was in fact deeply divisive, as he sought to carve out a political constituency that would back his policies. His intentions soon became clear when he unleashed tough-talking Vice President Agnew to attack the "misleading" news media, as well as the "effete corps of impudent snobs" and the "nattering nabobs of negativism" who demanded quick withdrawal from Vietnam. Nixon himself in 1970 sneered at the student antiwar demonstrators as "bums."

By January 1970 the Vietnam conflict had become the longest in American history and, with 40,000 killed and over 250,000 wounded, the third most costly foreign war in the nation's experience. It had also become grotesquely unpopular, even among troops in the field. Because draft policies largely exempted college students and men with critical civilian skills, the armed forces in Vietnam were largely composed of the least privileged young Americans. Especially in the war's early stages, African-Americans were disproportionately represented in the army and accounted for a disproportionately high share of combat fatalities. Black and white soldiers alike fought not only against the Vietnamese enemy but also against the coiled fear of floundering through booby-trapped swamps and steaming jungles, often unable to distinguish friend from foe among the black-pajama-clad peasants. Drug abuse, mutiny, and sabotage dulled the army's fighting edge. Ugly rumors filtered out of Vietnam that soldiers were "fragging" their own officers—murdering them with fragmentation grenades. Morale was further depleted by the military's decision to fill combat units with individual soldiers as they arrived in Vietnam. By preventing the development of the sort of camaraderie that makes men willing to risk their lives for one another, that practice deprived fighting units of coherence and effectiveness.

Cold War? Not for Some

A marine corps officer expressed the disillusion that beset many American troops in Vietnam:

"For years we disposed of the enemy dead like so much garbage. We stuck cigarettes in the mouths of corpses, put *Playboy* magazines in their hands, cut off their ears to wear around our necks. We incinerated them with napalm, atomized them with B-52 strikes, shoved them out the doors of helicopters above the South China Sea. . . . All we did was count, count bodies. Count dead human beings. . . . That was our fundamental military strategy. Body count. And the count kept going up."

Domestic disgust with the war was further deepened in 1970 by revelations that in 1968 American troops had massacred innocent women and children in the village of My Lai. Increasingly desperate for a quick end to the demoralizing conflict, Nixon widened the war in 1970 by ordering an attack on Vietnam's neighbor, Cambodia.

Cambodianizing the Vietnam War

For several years the North Vietnamese and Viet Cong had been using Cambodia, bordering South Vietnam on the west, as a springboard for troops, weapons, and supplies. Suddenly, on April 29, 1970, without consulting Congress, Nixon ordered American forces, joining with the South Vietnamese, to clean out the enemy sanctuaries in officially neutral Cambodia.

Restless students nationwide responded to the Cambodian invasion with rock throwing, window smashing, and arson. At Kent State University, in Ohio, jumpy members of the National Guard fired into a noisy crowd, killing four and wounding many more; at Jackson State College, in Mississippi, the highway patrol discharged volleys at a student dormitory, killing two black students. The nation fell prey to turmoil as rioters and arsonists convulsed the land.

Nixon withdrew the American troops from Cambodia on June 29, 1970, after only two months. The president's supporters argued that the invasion had captured enemy supplies and given the South Vietnamese eight months to strengthen themselves. But the enemy bases were not eliminated, and Cambodian communists soon overran large areas of the country.

In America the Cambodian invasion deepened the bitterness between "hawks" and "doves," as right-wing groups physically assaulted leftists. Disillusionment with "whitey's war" increased ominously among African-Americans in the armed forces. The Senate (though not the House) overwhelmingly repealed the Gulf of Tonkin blank check that Congress had given Johnson in 1964 and sought ways to restrain Nixon. The youth of America, still aroused, were only slightly mollified when the government reduced draft calls and shortened the period of draftability, on a lottery basis, from eight years to one year. They were similarly pleased, though not pacified, when the Twenty-sixth Amendment, in 1971, lowered the voting age to eighteen.

The War at Home Antiwar students clash with police in Ann Arbor, Michigan, in 1970.

In the spring of 1971, mass rallies and marches once more erupted from coast to coast. Belligerent "doves" attempted to shut down the government in Washington by blocking bridges, streets, and intersections. New combustibles fueled the fires of antiwar discontent in June 1971, when *The New York Times* published a top-secret Pentagon study of America's involvement in the Vietnam War. These Pentagon Papers, "leaked" to the *Times* by former Pentagon official Daniel Ellsberg, laid bare the blunders and deceptions of the Kennedy and Johnson administrations, especially the provoking of the 1964 North Vietnamese attack in the Gulf of Tonkin. As the antiwar firestorm flared ever higher, Nixon grew more daring in his search for an exit from Vietnam.

Nixon's Détente with Beijing (Peking) and Moscow

With bold insight, Nixon concluded that the road out of Vietnam ran through Beijing and Moscow. The two great communist powers, the Soviet Union and China, were clashing bitterly over their rival interpretations of Marxism. Nixon astutely perceived that the Chinese-Soviet tension afforded the United States an opportunity to play off one antagonist against the other—and to enlist the aid of both in pressuring North Vietnam into peace.

Nixon's thinking was reinforced by his national security adviser, Dr. Henry A. Kissinger. Bespectacled and German-accented, Kissinger had reached America as a youth when his parents fled Hitler's anti-Jewish persecutions. A former Harvard professor, in 1969 he had begun meeting secretly on Nixon's behalf with North Vietnamese officials in Paris to negotiate an end to the war in Vietnam. He was meanwhile preparing the president's path to Beijing and Moscow.

Nixon, heretofore an uncompromising anticommunist, announced to a startled nation in July 1971 that he had accepted an invitation to visit China the following year. He made his historic journey in February 1972. Between glass-clinking toasts and walks on the fabled Great Wall of China, he paved the way for improved relations between Washington and Beijing.

Nixon next traveled to Moscow in May 1972 to play his "China card" in a game of high-stakes

Some Chicken, Some Egg, 1975   This cartoon pokes fun at Henry Kissinger as a global statesman. Serving first as President Nixon's national security adviser and then as secretary of state in the Nixon and Ford administrations, the German-born Kissinger brought with him to Washington a sophisticated—some said cynical—view of the world honed during his nearly two decades as a political science professor at Harvard.

Balancing Act   Nixon treads delicately between the two communist superpowers in 1973, holding some of the wheat with which he enticed both into détente.

diplomacy in the Kremlin. The Soviets, hungry for American foodstuffs and alarmed over the possibility of intensified rivalry with an American-backed China, were ready to deal. Nixon's visits ushered in an era of *détente,* or relaxed tension, with the two communist powers. Détente resulted in several significant agreements. One product of eased relations was the great grain deal of 1972—a three-year arrangement by which the food-rich United States agreed to sell the Soviets at least $750 million worth of wheat, corn, and other cereals.

Far more important were steps to stem the dangerously frantic competition in nuclear arms. The first major achievement was an anti–ballistic missile (ABM) treaty, which limited each nation to two clusters of defensive missiles. The second significant pact was an agreement, known as SALT (for Strate-

gic Arms Limitation Talks), to freeze the numbers of long-range nuclear missiles for five years. These accords, both ratified in 1972, constituted a long-overdue first step toward slowing the arms race. Yet even though the ABM treaty forbade elaborate defensive systems, the United States forged ahead with the development of "MIRVs" (Multiple Independently-targeted Reentry Vehicles), designed to overcome any defense by "saturating" it with large numbers of warheads, several to a rocket. Predictably, the Soviets proceeded to "MIRV" their own missiles, and the arms race ratcheted up to a still more perilous plateau, with over sixteen thousand nuclear warheads deployed by both sides by the end of the 1980s.

Nixon's détente diplomacy did, to some extent, de-ice the Cold War. Moreover, by checkmating and co-opting the two great communist powers, the president had cleverly set the stage for America's exit from Vietnam. But the concluding act in that wrenching tragedy still remained to be played.

A New Team on the Supreme Bench

Nixon had lashed out during the campaign at the "permissiveness" and "judicial activism" of the Supreme Court presided over by Chief Justice Earl Warren. Following his appointment in 1953, the jovial Warren had led the Court into a series of decisions that drastically affected sexual freedom, the rights of criminals, the practice of religion, civil rights, and the structure of political representation. The decisions of the Warren Court reflected its deep concern for the individual, no matter how lowly.

In *Griswold* v. *Connecticut* (1965), the Court struck down a state law that prohibited the use of contraceptives, even among married couples. In an opinion that critics repeatedly assailed for its "invention" of rights not specified in the Constitution, the Court proclaimed a "right of privacy" with which the Connecticut statute was in conflict. The concept of a constitutionally guaranteed right of privacy soon provided the intellectual foundation for Court decisions protecting women's abortion rights.

In 1963 the Court held (*Gideon* v. *Wainwright*) that all defendants in serious criminal cases were entitled to legal counsel, even if they were too poor to afford it. More controversial were the rulings in two cases—*Escobedo* (1964) and *Miranda* (1966)—that ensured the right of the accused to remain silent and to enjoy other protections when accused of a crime. In this way safeguards were erected against confessions extorted under the rubber hose and other torture. Critics of these decisions were loud in their condemnation of "crook coddling" and demanded that the courts handcuff criminals, not the "cops."

Freedom of the press was also emphatically endorsed by the Warren Court in the case of *New York Times* v. *Sullivan* (1964). The Court ruled unanimously that public figures could sue for libel only if they could prove that "malice" had motivated their defamers. The decision opened a wide door for freewheeling criticism of the public actions as well as the private lives of politicians and other officials.

Nor did the Court shy away from explosive religious issues. In two stunning decisions, *Engel* v. *Vitale* (1962) and *School District of Abington Township* v. *Schempp* (1963), it voted against required prayers and Bible reading in the public schools.

These rulings were based on the First Amendment, which requires the separation of church and state, but to many religious believers they seemed to put the justices in the same bracket with atheistic communists. Cynics predicted that the "old goats in black coats" would soon be erasing "In God We Trust" from all coins.

Infuriating to many southerners was the determination of the Court, following the school-desegregation decision of 1954, to support black people in civil rights cases. Five southern state legislatures officially nullified the "sociological" Supreme Court decision, but they in turn were overruled by the high tribunal. In general, it held that the states could not deny to blacks the rights that were extended to whites. Conservatives maligned the Warren Court for not interpreting the Constitution but rewriting it, at the expense of states' rights and other constitutional guarantees. It was acting, they charged, too much like a legislature and not enough like a judicial body.

The Warren Court also struck at the overrepresentation in state legislatures of cow-pasture agricultural districts. Adopting the principle of one-man-one-vote, the Court in *Reynolds* v. *Sims* (1964) ruled that the state legislatures, both upper and lower houses, would have to be reapportioned according to the human population, irrespective of cows. States' righters and assorted right-wingers raised anew the battle cry "Impeach Earl Warren." But the legislatures grudgingly went ahead with reapportionment.

From 1954 onward the Court came under relentless criticism, the bitterest since New Deal days. Its foes made numerous but unsuccessful efforts to clip its wings through bills in Congress or through constitutional amendments. But for better or worse, the Court was grappling with stubborn social problems spawned by midcentury tensions, even—or especially—if duly elected legislatures failed to do so.

Fulfilling campaign promises, President Nixon undertook to change the Court's philosophical complexion. Taking advantage of several vacancies, he sought appointees who would strictly interpret the Constitution, cease "meddling" in social and political questions, and not coddle radicals or criminals. The Senate in 1969 speedily confirmed his nomination of white-maned Warren E. Burger of Minnesota to succeed the retiring Earl Warren as chief justice. Before the end of 1971, the Court counted four conservative Nixon appointments out of nine members.

Yet Nixon was to learn the ironic lesson that many presidents have learned about their Supreme Court appointees: once seated on the high bench, the justices are fully free to think and decide according to their own beliefs, not according to the president's expectations. The Burger Court that Nixon shaped proved reluctant to dismantle the "liberal" rulings of the Warren Court; it even produced the most controversial judicial opinion of modern times, the momentous *Roe* v. *Wade* decision in 1973, which legalized abortion (see p. 1004).

Nixon on the Home Front

Surprisingly, Nixon presided over significant expansion of the welfare programs that conservative Republicans routinely denounced. He approved increased appropriations for entitlements like Food Stamps and Medicaid, as well as for the largest federal welfare program, Aid to Families with Dependent Children (AFDC), which especially targeted single mothers of young children. Nixon also implemented a new federal program, Supplemental Security Income (SSI), which gave generous benefits to the indigent aged, blind, and disabled. He signed legislation in 1972 that raised Social Security old-age pensions and provided for automatic increases when the cost of living rose more than 3 percent in any year. Ironically, though designed to protect the elderly against the ravages of inflation, this "indexing" actually helped to fuel the inflationary fires that raged out of control later in the decade. Yet in the short run, Nixon's generous expansion of Great Society programs—along with continuing economic growth—helped reduce the nation's poverty rate to 11 percent in 1973, its lowest level in modern history.

Amid much controversy, Nixon also did the Great Society one better in his attack on racial discrimination. His so-called Philadelphia Plan of 1969 required construction-trade unions working on federal contracts in Philadelphia to establish "goals and timetables" for the hiring of black apprentices. Nixon may have been motivated in part by a desire to weaken the forces of liberalism by driving a wedge between blacks and trade unions. But whatever his reasoning, the president's new policy had

far-reaching implications. Soon extended to all federal contracts, the Philadelphia Plan in effect required thousands of employers to meet hiring quotas or to establish "set-asides" for minority subcontractors.

Nixon's Philadelphia Plan drastically altered the meaning of "affirmative action." Lyndon Johnson had intended affirmative action to protect *individuals* against discrimination. Nixon now transformed and escalated affirmative action into a program that conferred privileges on certain *groups*. The Supreme Court went along with Nixon's approach. In *Griggs* v. *Duke Power Co.* (1971), the black-robed justices prohibited intelligence tests or other devices that had the effect of excluding minorities or women from certain jobs. The Court's ruling strongly suggested that the only sure protection against charges of discrimination was to hire minority workers—or admit minority students—in proportion to their presence in the population.

Together, the actions of Nixon and the Court opened broad employment and educational opportunities for minorities and women. They also opened a Pandora's box of protest. Critics assailed the new style of affirmative action as "reverse discrimination." They objected especially that such a sweeping policy had been created by executive order and judicial decision, not by democratically elected representatives in the legislature. Yet what other remedy was there, defenders asked, to offset centuries of prejudice and opportunity denied?

Among the other major legacies of the Nixon years was the creation in 1970 of the Environmental Protection Agency (EPA), and a companion body, the Occupational Health and Safety Administration (OSHA). Their births climaxed two decades of mounting concern for the environment, beginning with the establishment in Los Angeles of an Air Pollution Control Office in 1950. Author Rachel Carson gave the environmental movement a huge boost in 1962 when she published *Silent Spring*, an enormously effective piece of latterday muckraking that exposed the poisonous effects of pesticides. Legislatively armed by the Clean Air Act of 1970, the Endangered Species Act of 1973, and similar laws, EPA and OSHA stood on the frontline of the battle for ecological sanity. They made notable progress in the ensuing decades on reducing automobile emissions and cleaning up befouled waterways and toxic waste sites. Impressed by the new environmentalist mood, Congress refused after 1972 to pay for any more of the huge irrigation projects that had watered—and ecologically transformed—much of the arid West over the preceding half century.

Worried about creeping inflation (then running at about 5 percent), Nixon overcame his distaste for economic controls and imposed a ninety-day wage and price freeze in 1971. To stimulate the nation's sagging exports, he next stunned the world by taking the United States off the gold standard and devaluing the dollar. These moves effectively ended the "Bretton Woods" system of international currency stabilization that had functioned for more that a quarter of a century after World War II.

Elected as a minority president, with only 43 percent of the vote in 1968, Nixon devised a clever but cynical plan—called the "southern strategy"—to achieve a solid majority in 1972. His Supreme Court nominations constituted an important part of his scheme. The southern strategy emphasized an appeal to white voters by soft-pedaling civil rights

Author Rachel Carson   Some call her the mother of the modern conservation movement because of the impact of her 1962 book, *Silent Spring.*

and openly opposing school busing to achieve racial balance. But as fate would have it, the southern strategy became superfluous as foreign policy dominated the presidential campaign of 1972.

The Nixon Landslide of 1972

Vietnam continued to be the burning issue. Nearly four years had passed since Nixon had promised, as a presidential candidate, to end the war and "win" the peace. Yet in the spring of 1972, the fighting escalated anew to alarming levels when the North Vietnamese, heavily equipped with foreign tanks, burst through the demilitarized zone (DMZ) separating the two Vietnams. Nixon reacted promptly by launching massive bombing attacks on strategic centers in North Vietnam, including Hanoi, the capital. Gambling heavily on foreign forbearance, he also ordered the dropping of contact mines to blockade the principal harbors of North Vietnam. Either Moscow or Beijing or both could have responded explosively, but neither did, thanks to Nixon's shrewd diplomacy. The North Vietnamese offensive finally ground to a halt.

The continuing Vietnam conflict spurred the rise of South Dakota Senator George McGovern to the 1972 Democratic nomination. McGovern's promise to pull the remaining American troops out of Vietnam in ninety days earned him the backing of the large antiwar element in the party. But his appeal to racial minorities, feminists, leftists, and youth alienated the traditional working-class backbone of his party. Moreover, the discovery shortly after the convention that McGovern's running mate, Missouri senator Thomas Eagleton, had undergone psychiatric care forced Eagleton's removal from the ticket and virtually doomed McGovern's candidacy.

Nixon's campaign emphasized that he had wound down the "Democratic war" in Vietnam from some 540,000 troops to about 30,000. His candidacy received an added boost just twelve days before the election when the high-flying Dr. Kissinger announced that "peace is at hand" in Vietnam and that an agreement would be settled in a few days.

Nixon won the election in a landslide. His lopsided victory encompassed every state except Massachusetts and the nonstate District of Columbia. He piled up 520 electoral votes to 17 and a popular majority of 47,169,911 votes to 29,170,383.

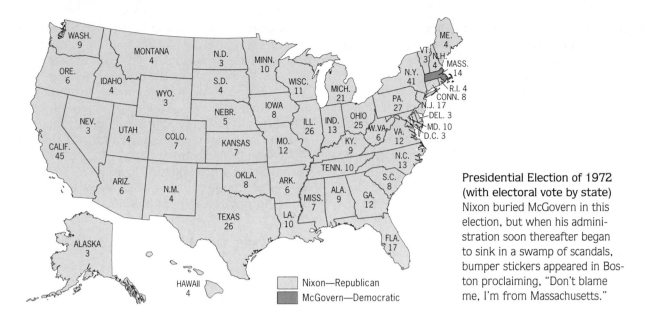

Presidential Election of 1972 (with electoral vote by state) Nixon buried McGovern in this election, but when his administration soon thereafter began to sink in a swamp of scandals, bumper stickers appeared in Boston proclaiming, "Don't blame me, I'm from Massachusetts."

McGovern had counted on a large number of young people's votes, but less than half the 18–21 age group even bothered to register to vote. Nixon's claim that the election gave him an unprecedented mandate for his policies was weakened by Republican election losses in both the House and Senate.

Bombing North Vietnam to the Peace Table

The dove of peace, "at hand" in Vietnam just before the balloting, took flight after the election, when Nixon refused to be stampeded into accepting terms pocked with obvious loopholes. After the fighting on both sides had again escalated, he launched a furious two-week bombing of North Vietnam in an ironhanded effort to force the North Vietnamese back to the conference table. This attack was the heaviest of the war and resulted in substantial losses of America's big B-52 bombers. But this merciless pounding drove the North Vietnamese negotiators to agree to cease-fire arrangements on January 23, 1973, nearly three months after peace was prematurely proclaimed.

Nixon hailed the face-saving cease-fire agreements as "peace with honor," but the boast rang hollow. The United States was to withdraw its remaining 27,000 or so troops and could reclaim some 560 American prisoners of war. The government of South Vietnam would be permitted to continue receiving limited U.S. support but no more U.S. fighting forces. An election was eventually to be held to determine the future of the country. The North Vietnamese were allowed to keep some 145,000 troops in South Vietnam, where they could be used to spearhead a powerful new offensive when the time seemed ripe. Ominously, the North Vietnamese still occupied about 30 percent of South Vietnam. The shaky "peace" was in reality little more than a thinly disguised American retreat.

Watergate Woes

Nixon's electoral triumph was soon sullied by the so-called Watergate scandals. On June 17, 1972, some two months before his renomination, a bungled burglary had occurred in the Democratic headquarters, located in the Watergate apartment-office complex in Washington. Five men were arrested inside the building with electronic "bugging" equipment in their possession. They were working for the Republican Committee for the Re-election of the President—popularly known as CREEP—which had managed to raise tens of millions of dollars, often by secretive, unethical, or unlawful means. CREEP had also engaged in a "dirty tricks" campaign of espionage and sabotage, including faked documents, directed against Democratic candidates in the campaign of 1972.

The Watergate break-in was only the tip of an iceberg in a slimy sea of corruption that made the Grant and Harding scandals look almost respectable. Several prominently placed White House aides and advisers were forced to resign. Many were involved in the criminal obstruction of justice through tangled cover-ups or payments of hush money. By early 1974, twenty-nine people had been indicted, had pleaded guilty, or had been convicted of Watergate-related crimes.

The scandal in Washington also provoked the improper or illegal use of the Federal Bureau of Investigation and the Central Intelligence Agency. Even the Internal Revenue Service was called upon by Nixon's aides to audit or otherwise harass political opponents and others who had fallen into disfavor. A White House "enemies list" turned up that included innocent citizens who were to be hounded or prosecuted in various ways. In the name of national security, Nixon's aides had authorized a burglary of the files of Dr. Daniel Ellsberg's psychiatrist, so great was the determination to destroy the man who had "leaked" the Pentagon Papers. This was the most notorious exploit of the White House "plumbers unit," created to plug up leaks of confidential information.

A select Senate committee, headed by the aging Senator Sam Ervin of North Carolina, conducted a prolonged and widely televised series of hearings in 1973–1974. John Dean III, a former White House lawyer with a remarkable memory, testified glibly and at great length as to the involvement of the top echelons in the White House, including the president, in the cover-up of the Watergate break-in. Dean in effect accused Nixon of the crime of obstructing justice. But the committee then had only the unsupported word of Dean against weighty White House protestations of innocence.

The Great Tape Controversy

A bombshell exploded before Senator Ervin's committee in July 1973 when a former presidential aide reported the presence in the White House of "bugging" equipment, installed under the president's authority. President Nixon's conversations, in person or on the telephone, had been recorded on tape without notifying the other parties that electronic eavesdropping was taking place.

Nixon had emphatically denied prior knowledge of the Watergate burglary or involvement in the cover-up. Now Dean's sensational testimony could be checked against the White House tapes,

John Dean Testifies at the Watergate Hearings   When Dean's testimony was later corroborated by tape recordings of presidential conversations, President Richard Nixon was forced to resign. Behind Dean is his wife, Maureen.

Smoking Pistol Exhibit A
The tape-recorded conversations between President Nixon and his top aide on June 23, 1972, proved mortally damaging to Nixon's claim that he played no role in the Watergate cover-up.

and the Senate committee could better determine who was telling the truth. But for months Nixon flatly refused to produce the taped evidence. He took refuge behind various principles, including separation of powers and executive privilege (confidentiality). But all of them were at least constitutionally dubious, especially when invoked to cover up crime or obstruct justice.

The anxieties of the White House deepened when Vice President Agnew, whom Nixon had lifted from relative obscurity in 1968, was forced to resign in October 1973, having been accused of taking bribes or "kickbacks" from Maryland contractors while governor and also as vice president. President Nixon himself was now in danger of being removed by the impeachment route, so Congress invoked the Twenty-fifth Amendment (see the Appendix) to replace Agnew with a twelve-term congressman from Michigan, Gerald ("Jerry") Ford. His record in public life was politically respectable and his financial affairs proved to be above suspicion at a time when unquestioned honesty was in short supply.

Ten days after Agnew's resignation came the famous "Saturday Night Massacre" (October 20, 1973). Archibald Cox, a Harvard law professor appointed as a "special prosecutor" by Nixon in May, issued a subpoena for relevant tapes and other documents from the White House. A cornered Nixon thereupon ordered the firing of Cox and then accepted the resignations of the attorney general and the deputy attorney general because they refused to fire Cox.

The Secret Bombing of Cambodia and the War Powers Act

As if Watergate were not enough, the constitutionality of Nixon's continued aerial battering of Cambodia came under increasing fire. In July 1973 America was shocked to learn that the U.S. Air Force had already secretly conducted some 3,500 bombing raids against North Vietnamese positions in Cambodia. They had begun in March 1969 and had continued for some fourteen months prior to the open American incursion in May 1970. The most disturbing feature of these sky forays was that while they were going on, American officials, including the president, were avowing that Cambodian neutrality was being respected. Countless Americans began to wonder what kind of representative government they had if the United States was fighting a war they knew nothing about.

Defiance followed secretiveness. After the Vietnam cease-fire in January 1973, Nixon openly carried on his large-scale bombing of communist forces in order to help the rightist Cambodian government. This stretching of presidential war-making powers met furious opposition from the public and from a clear majority in both houses of Congress, which repeatedly tried to stop the bombing by cutting off appropriations. But Nixon's vetoes of such legislation were always sustained by at least one-third-plus-one votes in the House. Finally, with appropriations running short, Nixon agreed to a compromise in June 1973 whereby he would end the Cambodian bombing six weeks later and seek congressional approval of any future action in that bomb-blasted country.

The years of bombing had inflicted grisly wounds on Cambodia. Incessant American air raids had blasted its people, shredded its economy, and revolutionized its politics. The long-suffering Cambodians soon groaned under the sadistic heel of Pol Pot, a murderous tyrant who dispatched as many as two million of his people to their graves. He was forced from power, ironically enough, only by a full-dress Vietnamese invasion in 1978, followed by military occupation that dragged on for a decade.

Congressional opposition to the expansion of presidential war-making powers by Johnson and Nixon led to the War Powers Act in November 1973. Passed over Nixon's veto, it required the president to report to Congress within forty-eight hours after committing troops to a foreign conflict or "substantially" enlarging American combat units in a foreign country. Such a limited authorization would have to end within sixty days unless Congress extended it for thirty more days.

Compelling Nixon to end the bombing of Cambodia in August 1973 was but one manifestation of what came to be called the "New Isolationism." The draft had ended in January 1973, although it was retained on a standby basis. Future members of the armed forces were to be well-paid volunteers—a change that greatly eased tensions among youth. Insistent demands arose in Congress for reducing American armed forces abroad, especially because

The Washington Post *(July 19, 1973) carried this news item:*

"American B-52 bombers dropped about 104,000 tons of explosives on Communist sanctuaries in neutralist Cambodia during a series of raids in 1969 and 1970. . . . The secret bombing was acknowledged by the Pentagon the Monday after a former Air Force major . . . described how he falsified reports on Cambodian air operations and destroyed records on the bombing missions actually flown."

some 300,000 remained in Europe more than a quarter of a century after Hitler's downfall. The argument often heard was that the Western European countries, with more population than the Soviet Union, ought by now to be willing and able to provide for their own defense against the forces of communism. But President Nixon, fearful of a weakened hand in the high-stakes game of power politics, headed off all serious attempts at troop reduction.

The Arab Oil Embargo and the Energy Crisis

Adding to Nixon's problems, the long-rumbling Middle East erupted anew in October 1973, when the rearmed Syrians and Egyptians unleashed surprise attacks on Israel in an attempt to regain the territory they had lost in the Six-Day War of 1967. With the Israelis in desperate retreat, Kissinger, who had become secretary of state in September, hastily flew to Moscow in an effort to restrain the Soviets, who were arming the attackers. Believing that the Kremlin was poised to fly combat troops to the Suez area, Nixon placed America's nuclear forces on alert and ordered a gigantic airlift of nearly $2 billion in war materials to the Israelis. This assistance helped save the day, as the Israelis aggressively turned the tide and had stormed to a stone's throw from Cairo when American diplomacy brought about an uneasy cease-fire.

America's policy of backing Israel against its oil-rich neighbors exacted a heavy penalty. Late in October 1973, the Arab nations suddenly clamped an embargo on oil for the United States and for other countries supporting Israel. Americans had to suffer through a long, cold winter of lowered thermostats and speedometers. Lines of automobiles at service stations lengthened as tempers shortened and a business recession deepened.

The "energy crisis" suddenly energized a number of long-deferred projects. The costly oil pipeline from northern to southern Alaska received congressional sanction in 1974, over the protests of conservationists and environmentalists. Congress enacted a national speed limit of 55 miles per hour in order to save fuel. Proposals multiplied for utilizing energy from the sun or wind, from the earth's molten core (geothermal sources), and even from untapped coal deposits, despite the damaging pollutants that burning coal emitted into the atmosphere. Agitation mounted for the construction of more nuclear power plants, though they posed the ever-present threat of catastrophic accident and though no means had been devised for disposing of their long-lived radioactive wastes.

The five months of the Arab "blackmail" embargo in 1974 clearly signaled the end of an era—the era of cheap and abundant energy. A twenty-year surplus of world oil supplies had masked the fact that since 1948 the United States had been a net importer of oil. American oil production peaked in 1970 and then began an irreversible decline. Blissfully unaware of their dependence on foreign suppliers, Americans, like revelers on a binge, had more than tripled their oil consumption since the end of World War II. The number of automobiles increased 250 percent between 1949 and 1972, and Detroit's engineers gave nary a thought to building more fuel-efficient engines. King Coal was dethroned as an energy source in favor of oil. Homeowners replaced coal bins with oil tanks, and environmentalists persuaded public utilities to fire their electrical generating plants with clean-burning oil instead of air-blackening coal.

By 1974 America was oil addicted and extremely vulnerable to any interruption in supplies. That stark fact colored the diplomatic and economic history of the 1980s and 1990s. The Middle East loomed ever larger on the map of America's strategic interests, until the United States in 1990 at last found itself pulled into a shooting war with Iraq to protect its oil supplies.

The Middle Eastern sheiks, flexing their economic muscles through OPEC (the Organization of Petroleum Exporting Countries), approximately quadrupled their price for crude oil after lifting the embargo in 1974. Huge new oil bills wildly disrupted the U.S. balance of international trade and added further fuel to the already raging fires of inflation. The United States took the lead in forming the International Energy Agency in 1974 as a counterweight to OPEC, and various sectors of the economy, including Detroit's carmakers, began their slow, grudging adjustment to the rudely dawning age of energy dependency. But full reconciliation to that uncomfortable reality was a long time coming.

The Unmaking of a President

Political tribulations added to the nation's cup of woe in 1974. The continuing impeachment inquiry cast damning doubts on Nixon's integrity. Responding at last to the House Judiciary Committee's demand for the Watergate tapes, Nixon agreed in the spring of 1974 to the publication of "relevant" portions of the tapes, declaring that these would vindicate him. But substantial sections of the wanted tapes were missing, and Nixon's frequent obscenities were excised with the phrase "expletive

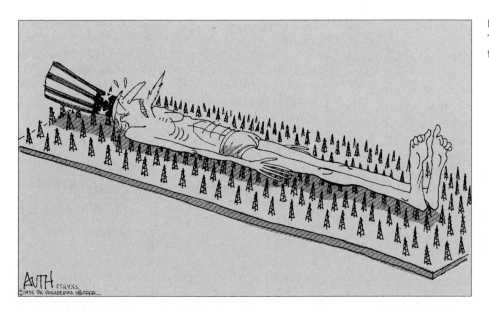

Uncle Sam's Bed of Nails
The oil crises of the 1970s tortured the American economy.

Nixon, the Law-and-Order Man

deleted." Confronted with demands for the rest of the material, Nixon flatly refused. On July 24, 1974, the president suffered a disastrous setback when the Supreme Court unanimously ruled that "executive privilege" gave him no right to withhold from the special prosecutor portions of tapes relevant to criminal activity. Skating on thin ice over hot water, Nixon reluctantly complied.

The House Judiciary Committee pressed ahead with its articles of impeachment. The key vote came late in July 1974, when the committee adopted the first article, which charged obstruction of "the administration of justice," including Watergate-related crimes. Two other articles were later approved by the committee accusing Nixon of having abused the powers of his office and of having shown contempt of Congress by ignoring lawful subpoenas for relevant tapes and other evidence.

Seeking to soften the impact of inevitable disclosure, Nixon voluntarily took a step, on August 5, 1974, that had a devastating effect on what remained of his credibility. He now made public three subpoenaed tapes of conversations with his chief aide on June 23, 1972. One of them had him giving

orders, six days after the Watergate break-in, to use the CIA to hold back an inquiry by the FBI. Now Nixon's own tape-recorded words convicted him of having been an active party to the attempted cover-up, in itself the crime of obstructing justice. More than that, he had solemnly told the American people on television that he had known nothing of the Watergate whitewash until about nine months later.

The public backlash proved to be overwhelming. Republican leaders in Congress concluded that the guilty and unpredictable Nixon was a loose cannon on the deck of the ship of state. They frankly informed the president that his impeachment by the full House and removal by the Senate were foregone conclusions. They made it clear that he would best serve his nation, his party, and himself by resigning with honor, or a semblance of it. If convicted by the Senate, he would lose all his normal retirement benefits; if he resigned he could retain them—more than $150,000 a year—and retire in royal splendor.

Left with no better choice, Nixon choked back his tears and announced his resignation in a dramatic television appearance on August 8, 1974. Few presidents had flown so high, and none had sunk so low. In his Farewell Address, Nixon admitted having made some "judgments" that "were wrong" but insisted that he had always acted "in what I believed at the time to be the best interests of the nation." Unconvinced, countless Americans would change the song "Hail to the Chief" to "Jail to the Chief."

The nation had survived a wrenching constitutional crisis, which proved that the impeachment machinery forged by the Founding Fathers could work when public opinion overwhelmingly demanded that it be implemented. The principles that no person is above the law and that presidents must be held to strict accountability for their acts were strengthened. The United States of America, on the eve of its two-hundredth birthday as a republic, had given an impressive demonstration of self-discipline and self-government to the rest of the world.

The First Unelected President

Gerald Rudolph Ford, the first man to be made president solely by a vote of Congress, entered the besmirched White House, in August 1974, with serious handicaps. He was widely—and unfairly—

suspected of being little more than a dim-witted former college football player. President Johnson had sneered that "Jerry" was so lacking in brainpower that he could not walk and chew gum at the same time. Worse, Ford had been selected, not elected, vice president, following Spiro Agnew's resignation in disgrace. The sour odor of illegitimacy hung about this president without precedent.

Then, out of a clear sky, Ford granted a complete pardon to Nixon for any crimes he may have committed as president, discovered or undiscovered. Democrats were outraged. They wanted iron-toothed justice, even vengeance. They heatedly charged, without persuasive evidence, that Ford was carrying out a "buddy deal" that had been cooked up when Nixon nominated him for the vice presidency. Ford explained that he only wanted to end Nixon's private agony, heal the festering wounds in the body politic, and let the country get on with its business, undistracted by a possibly sensational trial. But lingering suspicions about the circumstances of the pardon cast a dark shadow over Ford's prospects of being elected president in his own right in 1976.

Ford at first sought to enhance the so-called détente with the Soviet Union that Nixon had crafted. In July 1975 President Ford joined leaders from thirty-four other nations in Helsinki, Finland, to sign several sets of historic accords. One group of agreements officially wrote an end to World War II by finally legitimizing the Soviet-dictated boundaries of Poland and other East European countries. In return, the Soviets signed a "third basket" of agreements, guaranteeing more liberal exchanges of people and information between East and West and protecting certain basic "human rights." The Helsinki accords kindled small dissident movements in Eastern Europe and even in the USSR itself, but the Soviets soon poured ice water on these sputtering flames of freedom. Moscow's restrictions on Jewish emigration had already, in December 1974, prompted Congress to add punitive restrictions to a U.S.-Soviet trade bill.

West Europeans, especially the West Germans, cheered the Helsinki conference as a milestone of détente. But in the United States, critics increasingly charged that détente was proving to be a one-way street. American grain and technology flowed across the Atlantic to the USSR, and little of comparable importance flowed back. And Soviet ships and planes continued to haul great quantities of arms and military technicians to procommunist forces around the globe.

How Long Will Nixon Haunt the GOP?   Doubts about Ford's pardon of Nixon clouded his brief presidency.

Despite these difficulties, Ford at first clung stubbornly to détente. But the American public's fury over Moscow's double-dealing so steadily mounted that by the end of his term the president was refusing even to pronounce the word *détente* in public. The thaw in the Cold War was threatening to prove chillingly brief.

Defeat in Vietnam

Early in 1975 the North Vietnamese gave full throttle to their long-expected drive southward. President Ford urged Congress to vote still more weapons for Vietnam, but his plea was in vain, and without the crutch of massive American aid, the South Vietnamese quickly and ingloriously collapsed.

The dam burst so rapidly that the remaining Americans had to be frantically evacuated by helicopter, the last of them on April 29, 1975. Also rescued were about 140,000 South Vietnamese, most of

Passing the Buck A satirical view of where responsibility for the Vietnam debacle should be laid.

them so dangerously identified with the Americans that they feared a bloodbath by the victorious communists. Ford compassionately admitted these people to the United States, where they added further seasoning to the melting pot. Eventually, some 500,000 arrived (see "Makers of America: The Vietnamese," pp. 982–983).

America's longest, most frustrating war thus ended, not with a bang but a whimper. In a technical sense, the Americans had not lost the war; their client nation had. The United States had fought the North Vietnamese to a standstill and had then withdrawn its troops in 1973, leaving the South Vietnamese to fight their own war, with generous shipments of costly American aircraft, tanks, and other munitions. The estimated cost to America was $118 billion in current outlays, together with some 56,000 dead and 300,000 wounded. The people of the United States had in fact provided just about everything, except the will to win—and that could not be injected by outsiders.

Technicalities aside, America had lost more than a war. It had lost face in the eyes of foreigners, lost its own self-esteem, lost confidence in its military prowess—and lost much of the economic muscle that had made possible its global leadership since World War II. Americans reluctantly came to realize that their power as well as their pride had been deeply wounded in Vietnam and that recovery would be slow and painful.

The Bicentennial Campaign and the Carter Victory

America's two-hundredth birthday, in 1976, fell during a presidential election year—a fitting coincidence for a proud democracy. Gerald Ford energetically sought nomination for the presidency in his own right and won the Republican nod at the Kansas City convention.

The Democratic standard-bearer was fifty-one-year-old James Earl Carter, Jr., a dark-horse candidate who galloped out of obscurity during the long primary-elections season. Carter, a peanut farmer from Plains, Georgia, had served as his state's governor from 1971 to 1975. Flashing a toothy smile and insisting on humble "Jimmy" as his first name, this born-again Baptist touched many people with his down-home sincerity. He ran against the memory of Nixon and Watergate as much as he ran against Ford. His most effective campaign pitch was his promise that "I'll never lie to you." Untainted by ties with a corrupt and cynical Washington, he attracted voters as an outsider who would clean the disorderly house of "big government."

Carter squeezed out a narrow victory on election day, with 51 percent of the popular vote. The electoral count stood at 297 to 240. The winner swept every state except Virginia in his native South.

Especially important were the votes of African-Americans, 97 percent of whom cast their ballots for Carter.

Carter also enjoyed hefty Democratic majorities in both houses of Congress. Hopes ran high that the stalemate of the Nixon-Ford years between a Republican White House and a Democratic Capitol Hill would now be ended. At first, Carter enjoyed notable political success. Congress granted his request to create a new cabinet-level Department of Energy. Calling the American tax system "a disgrace to the human race," Carter also proposed tax reform and reduction. Congress eventually obliged him, in part, with an $18 billion tax cut in 1978. The new president's popularity remained exceptionally high during his first few months in office, even when he courted public disfavor by courageously keeping his campaign promise to pardon some ten thousand draft evaders of the Vietnam War era.

But Carter's honeymoon did not last long. An inexperienced outsider, he had campaigned against the Washington "establishment" and never quite made the transition to being an insider himself. He repeatedly rubbed congressional fur the wrong way, especially by failing to consult adequately with the leaders. Critics charged that he isolated himself in a shallow pool of fellow Georgians, whose ignorance of the ways of Washington compounded the problems of their greenhorn chief.

Carter's Humanitarian Diplomacy

As a committed Christian, President Carter displayed from the outset an overriding concern for "human rights" as the guiding principle of his foreign policy. In the African nations of Rhodesia (later Zimbabwe) and South Africa, Carter championed the oppressed black majority, whose cause was also eloquently defended by U.N. Ambassador Andrew Young.

The president's most spectacular foreign-policy achievement came in September 1978 at Camp David, the woodsy presidential retreat in the Maryland highlands. By August 1978 relations between Egypt and Israel had deteriorated so far that another blowup in the misery-drenched Middle East seemed imminent. So grave was the danger that Carter courageously risked humiliating failure by inviting President Anwar Sadat of Egypt and Prime Minister Menachem Begin of Israel to a summit conference at Camp David.

Skillfully serving as go-between, Carter after thirteen days persuaded the two visitors to sign an accord (September 17, 1978) that held considerable promise of peace. Israel agreed in principle to withdraw from territory conquered in the 1967 war, and

Celebrating the Camp David Agreement, September 1978 Anwar Sadat of Egypt, left, and Menachem Begin of Israel, right, join U.S. President Jimmy Carter, center, in confirming the historic accord that brought hopes of peace to the war-torn Middle East.

MAKERS OF AMERICA

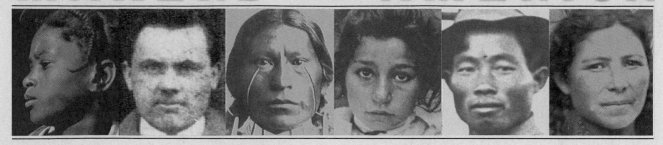

The Vietnamese

At first glance, the towns of Westminster and Fountain Valley, California, seem to resemble other California communities nearby. Tract homes line residential streets; shopping centers flank the busy thoroughfares. But these are no ordinary American suburbs. Instead, they make up "Little Saigons," vibrant outposts of Vietnamese culture in the contemporary United States. Shops offer exotic Asian merchandise; restaurants serve such delicacies as lemon-grass chicken. These neighborhoods, living reminders of America's anguish in Vietnam, are a rarely acknowledged consequence of that sorrowful conflict.

Before South Vietnam fell in 1975, few Vietnamese ventured across the Pacific. Only in 1966 did U.S. immigration authorities even designate "Vietnamese" as a separate category of newcomers, and most early immigrants were the wives and children of U.S. servicemen. But as the communists closed in on Saigon, many Vietnamese, particularly those who had worked closely with American or South Vietnamese authorities, feared for their future. Gathering together as many of their extended-family members as they could assemble, thousands of Vietnamese fled for their lives. In a few hectic days in 1975, some 140,000 Vietnamese escaped before the approaching gunfire, a few dramatically clinging to the bottoms of departing helicopters. From Saigon they were conveyed to military bases in Guam and the Philippines. Another 60,000 less fortunate Vietnamese escaped at the same time over land and sea to Hong Kong and Thailand, where they waited nervously for permission to move on. To accommodate the refugees, the U.S. government set up camps across the nation. Arrivals were crowded into army barracks affording little room and less privacy. These were boot camps not for military service but for assimilation into American society. A rigorous program trained the Vietnamese in English, forbade children from speaking their native language in the classroom, and even immersed them in American slang. Many resented this attempt to mold them, to strip them of their culture.

Their discontent boiled over when authorities prepared to release the refugees from camps and board them with families around the nation. The resettlement officials had decided to find a sponsor for each Vietnamese family—an American family that would provide food, shelter, and assistance for the refugees until they could fend for themselves. But the Vietnamese people cherish their traditional extended families—grandparents, uncles, aunts,

The Last Days of Saigon   Violence often attended the frantic American evacuation from Vietnam in 1975.

and cousins living communally with parents and children. Few American sponsors would accommodate a large extended family; fewer Vietnamese families would willingly separate.

The refugees were dispersed to Iowa, Illinois, Pennsylvania, New York, Washington, and California. But the settlement sites, many of them tucked away in rural districts, offered scant economic opportunities. The immigrants, who had held mainly skilled or white-collar positions in Vietnam, bristled as they were herded into menial labor. As soon as they could, they relocated, hastening to established Vietnamese enclaves around San Francisco, Los Angeles, and Dallas.

Soon a second throng of Vietnamese immigrants pushed into these Little Saigons. Fleeing from the ravages of poverty and from the oppressive communist government, these stragglers had crammed themselves and their few possessions into little boats, hoping to reach Hong Kong or get picked up by ships. Eventually, many of these "boat people" reached the United States. Usually less educated than the first arrivals and receiving far less resettlement aid from the U.S. government, they were, however, more willing to start at the bottom. Today these two groups total more than half a million people. Differing in experience and expectations, the Vietnamese share a new home in a strange land. Their uprooting is an immense, unreckoned consequence of America's longest war.

Boat People   Vietnamese refugees flee to freedom.

Preserving the Past
A Vietnamese-American boy learns classical calligraphy from his grandfather.

Historical Double Take   Many Americans who looked back reverently to Roosevelt's "Rough Rider" diplomacy were outraged at the Panama "giveaway." But the Carter administration, looking to the future, argued persuasively that relinquishing control of the canal would be healthy for U.S.–Latin American relations.

Egypt in return promised to respect Israel's borders. Both parties pledged themselves to sign a formal peace treaty within three months. The president crowned this diplomatic success by resuming full diplomatic relations with China in early 1979, after a nearly thirty-year interruption. Carter also successfully proposed two treaties turning over complete ownership and control of the Panama Canal to the Panamanians by the year 2000.

Despite these dramatic accomplishments, trouble stalked Carter's foreign policy. Overshadowing all international issues was the ominous reheating of the Cold War with the Soviet Union. Détente fell into disrepute as thousands of Cuban troops, assisted by Soviet advisers, appeared in Angola, Ethiopia, and elsewhere in Africa to support revolutionary factions. Arms control negotiations with Moscow stalled in the face of this Soviet military meddling.

Carter Tackles the Ailing Economy

Adding to Carter's mushrooming woes was the failing health of the economy. Prices had been rising feverishly, increasing at a rate of more than 10 percent a year by 1974 ("double-digit" inflation). Crippling oil-price hikes from OPEC in that same year dealt the reeling economy another body blow. A stinging recession brought the inflation rate down temporarily during Gerald Ford's presidency, but virtually from the moment of Carter's inauguration, prices resumed their dizzying ascent, driving the inflation rate well above 13 percent by 1979. The soaring bill for imported oil plunged America's balance of payments deeply into the red (an unprecedented $40 billion in 1978), as Americans paid more for foreign products than they were able to earn from selling their own goods overseas.

The "oil shocks" of the 1970s taught Americans a painful but necessary lesson: that they could never again seriously consider a policy of economic isolation, as they had tried to do in the decades between the two world wars. For most of its history, America's foreign trade had accounted for no more than 10 percent of gross national product (GNP). But the need to pay for huge foreign-oil bills drove that figure steadily upward in the 1970s and thereafter. By the century's end, some 27 percent of GNP depended on foreign trade. In turn, the nation's new economic interdependence meant that the United States could not dominate international trade and finance as easily as it had in the post–World War II decades. Americans, once happily insulated behind their ocean moats, would have to master foreign languages and study foreign cultures if they wanted to prosper in the rapidly globalizing economy that was now taking shape.

Yawning deficits in the federal budget, reaching nearly $60 billion in 1980, further aggravated the U.S. ecomony's inflationary ailments. Americans living on fixed incomes—mostly elderly people or workers without a strong union to go to bat for them—suffered from shrinking real incomes, as their dollars diminished in purchasing power. People with money to lend pushed interest rates ever higher, hoping to protect themselves from being repaid in badly depreciated dollars. The "prime rate" (the rate of interest that banks charge their very best customers) vaulted to an unheard-of 20 percent in early 1980. The high cost of borrowing money shoved small businesses to the wall and strangled the construction industry, which was heavily dependent on loans to finance new housing and other projects.

From the outset, Carter diagnosed America's economic disease as stemming primarily from the nation's costly dependence on foreign oil. Accordingly, one of the first acts of his presidency was a dramatic appeal to embark on an energy crusade that he called "the moral equivalent of war." The president called for legislation to improve energy conservation, especially by curtailing the manufacture of large, gas-guzzling automobiles. But these proposals, in April 1977, ignited a blaze of indifference among the American people. They had already forgotten the long gasoline lines of 1973, when OPEC had first imposed an oil embargo for the United States. Public apathy and congressional hostility smothered President Carter's hopes of quickly initiating an energetic energy program.

Carter's Energy Woes

Events in Iran jolted Americans out of their complacency about energy supplies in 1979. The imperious Mohammed Reza Pahlevi, installed as shah of Iran with help from America's CIA in 1953, had long ruled his oil-rich land with a will of steel. His repressive regime finally provoked a backlash, and the shah was forced into globe-wandering exile in January 1979. Violent revolution was spearheaded in Iran by Muslim fundamentalists who fiercely resented the shah's campaign to Westernize and secularize his country. Denouncing the United States as the "Great Satan" that had abetted the shah's efforts, these extremists engulfed Iran in chaos in the wake of his departure. The crippling upheavals soon spread to Iran's oil fields. As Iranian oil stopped flowing into the stream of world commerce, shortages appeared, and OPEC again seized

The History of the Consumer Price Index, 1967–1995   This graph shows both the annual percentage of inflation and the cumulative shrinkage in the dollar's value since 1967. (By 1995, it took nearly five dollars to buy what one dollar purchased in 1967.) (*Statistical Abstract of the United States, 1996.*)

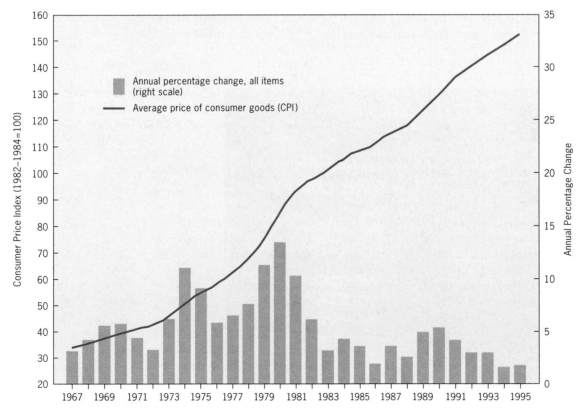

the opportunity to hike petroleum prices. Americans once more found themselves waiting impatiently in long lines at gas stations or buying gasoline only on specified days.

As the oil crisis deepened, President Carter sensed the rising temperature of popular discontent. In July 1979 he retreated to the presidential mountain hideaway at Camp David, where he remained largely out of public view for ten days. Like a royal potentate of old, summoning the wise men of the realm for their counsel in a time of crisis, Carter called in over a hundred leaders from all walks of life to give him their views. Meanwhile, the nation waited anxiously for the results of these extraordinary deliberations.

Carter came down from the mountaintop on July 15, 1979. He revealed his thoughts to the American people in a remarkable television address, which amounted to a kind of old-fashioned "jeremiad." He chided his fellow citizens for falling into a "moral and spiritual crisis" and for being too concerned with "material goods."

While Carter's address stunned and even perplexed the nation, he let drop another shoe a few days later. In a bureaucratic massacre of almost unprecedented proportions, he fired four cabinet secretaries. At the same time, he circled the wagons of his Georgian advisers more tightly about the White House by reorganizing and expanding the power of his personal staff. Critics began to wonder aloud whether Carter, the professed man of the people, was losing touch with the popular mood of the country.

Foreign Affairs and the Iranian Imbroglio

Hopes for a less dangerous world rose slightly in June 1979, when President Carter met with Soviet leader Leonid Brezhnev in Vienna to sign the long-stalled SALT II agreements, limiting the levels of lethal strategic weapons in the Soviet and American arsenals. Yet from the outset, Carter faced an uphill battle in trying to persuade the Senate to approve the SALT II treaty. Conservative critics of the president's defense policies remained deeply suspicious of the Soviet Union, which they regarded as the Wicked Witch of the East. These hard-liners unsheathed their long knives to carve up the SALT II treaty when it came to the Senate for debate in the summer of 1979. Their hand was strengthened when news reports broke that a Soviet "combat brigade" was stationed in Castro's Cuba.

Coping with the Energy Crisis
A highly mobile people accustomed to limitless gasoline supplies, Americans were rudely reminded of their dependency on foreign oil imports during the "oil shocks" of the 1970s.

Political earthquakes in the petroleum-rich Persian Gulf region finally buried all hopes of ratifying the SALT II treaty. The Western world depended heavily on the gulf nations for oil, the black milk from Mother Earth that nourishes all modern industrial economies. Yet this vital lifeline lay dangerously close to the Soviet Union. The prospect that political turmoil in the region might provide an excuse for the Soviet army to march in and seize control of essential oil supplies caused nightmares throughout the Western world.

Nightmare seemed to become reality on November 4, 1979, when a howling mob of rabidly anti-American Muslim militants stormed the United States embassy in Teheran, Iran, and took all of its occupants hostage. The captors then demanded that the American authorities ship back to Iran the exiled shah, who had arrived in the United States two weeks earlier for medical treatment. The shaky Iranian government, barely visible through the smoke of revolution and religious upheaval then rocking the country, refused to intervene against the militants. Ayatollah Ruhollah Khomeini, the white-bearded Muslim holy man who inspired the revolutionaries, even accused the United States of masterminding an attack on the sacred Muslim city of Mecca, in Saudi Arabia.

Two-Way SALT Talks   The grim specter of nuclear holocaust haunted the SALT II talks between Carter and Soviet leader Leonid Brezhnev in Vienna in June 1979.

President Jimmy Carter (b. 1924) addressing the nation on January 4, 1980, about the Soviet invasion of Afghanistan:

"History teaches, perhaps, very few clear lessons. But surely one such lesson learned by the world at great cost is that aggression, unopposed, becomes a contagious disease."

World opinion hotly condemned the diplomatic felony in Iran, while Americans agonized over both the fate of the hostages and the stability of the entire Persian Gulf region. The Soviet army then aroused the West's worst fears on December 27, 1979, when it blitzed into the mountainous nation of Afghanistan, next door to Iran, and appeared to be poised for a thrust at the oil-jugular of the gulf.

President Carter reacted vigorously to these alarming events. He slapped an embargo on the export to the USSR of grain and high-technology machinery and called for a boycott of the upcoming Olympic games in Moscow. He proposed the creation of a "Rapid Deployment Force" to respond to suddenly developing crises in faraway places and requested that young people (including women) be made to register for a possible military draft. The president proclaimed that the United States would "use any means necessary, including force," to protect the Persian Gulf against Soviet incursions. He grimly conceded that he had misjudged the Soviets, and the SALT II treaty became a dead letter in the Senate. Meanwhile, the Soviet army met unexpectedly stiff resistance in Afghanistan and bogged down in a nasty, decade-long guerrilla war that came to be called "Russia's Vietnam." But though the Soviets were stalled in Afghanistan, the crisis in Iran ground on.

The Iranian Hostage Humiliation

The Iranian hostage episode was Carter's—and America's—bed of nails. The captured Americans languished in cruel captivity, while the nightly television news broadcasts in the United States showed

Iranians Denounce President Jimmy Carter, November, 1979   Scenes like this one appeared almost nightly on American television during the 444 days of the Iranian hostage crisis, humiliating Carter and angering American citizens.

humiliating scenes of Iranian mobs burning the American flag and spitting on effigies of Uncle Sam.

Carter at first tried to apply economic sanctions and the pressure of world public opinion against the Iranians, while waiting for the emergence of a stable government with which to negotiate. But the political turmoil in Iran rumbled on endlessly, and the president's frustration grew. Carter at last ordered a daring rescue mission. A highly trained commando team penetrated deep into Iran's sandy interior. Their plan required tick-tock-perfect timing to succeed, and when equipment failures prevented some members of the team from reaching their destination, the mission had to be scrapped. As the commandos withdrew in the dark desert night, two of their aircraft collided, killing eight of the would-be rescuers.

This disastrous failure of the rescue raid proved anguishing for Americans. The episode seemed to underscore the nation's helplessness and even incompetence in the face of a mortifying insult to the national honor. The stalemate with Iran dragged on throughout the rest of Carter's term, providing an embarrassing backdrop to the embattled president's struggle for reelection.

Chronology

1970 Nixon orders invasion of Cambodia	**1973–**
Kent State and Jackson State incidents	**1974** Watergate hearings and investigations
Environmental Protection Agency (EPA) created	
Clean Air Act	**1974** Nixon resigns; Ford assumes presidency
	First OPEC oil-price increase
	International Energy Agency formed
1971 Pentagon Papers published	
Twenty-sixth Amendment passed (voting age lowered to eighteen)	**1975** Helsinki accords
	South Vietnam falls to communists
1972 Nixon visits China and the Soviet Union	**1976** Carter defeats Ford for presidency
ABM and SALT I treaties ratified	
Nixon defeats McGovern for presidency	**1978** Egyptian-Israeli Camp David agreement
1973 Vietnam cease-fire and U.S. withdrawal	**1979** Iranian revolution and oil crisis
Agnew resigns; Ford appointed vice president	SALT II agreements signed (never ratified by Senate)
War Powers Act	Soviet Union invades Afghanistan
Arab-Israeli war and Arab oil embargo	
Endangered Species Act	**1979–**
	1981 Iranian hostage crisis

SUGGESTED READINGS

PRIMARY SOURCE DOCUMENTS

Richard Nixon's vision of the international order is delineated in his *RN: The Memoirs of Richard Nixon** (1978). The articles of impeachment reported against Nixon can be found in *House of Representatives Report No. 93-1305, 93d Congress, 2d Session*, pp. 1–2* (1974). Opposing opinions on the Panama Canal treaty were voiced by Cyrus Vance and Ronald Reagan, *Hearings Before the Committee on Foreign Relations*, United States Senate, 95th Congress, 1st Session, pp. 10–15, 96–103 (1977).

SECONDARY SOURCES

The most comprehensive account of Nixon's early career is Stephen E. Ambrose, *Nixon: The Education of a Politician (1913–1962)* (1987). See also his *Nixon: The Triumph of a Politician, 1962–1972* (1989). Nixon's intriguing personality is examined in Gary Wills, *Nixon Agonistes: The Crisis of the Self-Made Man* (1970). Theodore White continues his chronicle of presidential electioneering in *The Making of the President, 1972* (1973). Consult also Hunter S. Thompson's savagely masterful *Fear and Loathing on the Campaign Trail, 1972* (1973) and Timothy Crouse's insightful study of the political press, *The Boys on the Bus* (1973). A wide-ranging discussion of the homefront is in Kim McQuaid, *The Anxious Years: America in the Vietnam-Watergate Era* (1989). Valuable background on U.S. foreign policy in the Nixon years can be found in David P. Calleo and Benjamin Rowland, *America and the World Political Economy* (1973). On multinational corporations see Richard J. Barnet and Ronald E. Muller, *Global Reach* (1974). On the Paris peace negotiations, see Gareth Porter, *A Peace Denied* (1975). Retrospectives on Vietnam include George C. Herring, *America's Longest War* (1986); William Buckingham, *Operation Ranch Hand: The Air Force and Herbicides in Southeast Asia, 1961–1971* (1982); and William Shawcross's chilling account of U.S. involvement in Cambodia, *Sideshow* (2d ed., 1981). Shawcross is vigorously rebutted in Henry Kissinger's rich memoirs, *White House Years* (1979) and *Years of Upheaval* (1982). A good biography of Nixon's secretary of state is Robert D. Schulzinger, *Henry Kissinger: Doctor of Diplomacy* (1989). The Middle East is the focus of William B.

Quandt, *Decade of Decisions: American Policy Toward the Arab-Israeli Conflict, 1967–1976* (1977), and Wilbur C. Eveland, *Ropes of Sand* (1980). The background to the oil crisis is charted in Michael B. Stoff, *Oil, War and American Security* (1980). Arthur M. Schlesinger, Jr., traces the growth of *The Imperial Presidency* (1973). The Watergate crisis is vividly described in two books by Carl Bernstein and Robert Woodward, *All the President's Men* (1974) and *The Final Days* (1976), and in Stanley I. Kutler, *The Wars of Watergate* (1990). Jonathan Schell, *The Time of Illusion* (1976), assesses the impact of the crisis on the nation's spirit and institutions. Many of the fallen president's former men have written of their involvement in the Watergate affair, including Jeb Stuart Magruder, John Dean, John Erlichman, and H. R. Haldeman. Robert Woodward and Scott Armstrong provide a behind-the-scenes look at key decisions of the Burger Court in *The Brethren: Inside the Supreme Court* (1979). John Robert Greene describes the Nixon and Ford administrations in *The Limits of Power* (1992). "Jerry" Ford, the first appointed president, is analyzed by his former press secretary in J. F. ter Horst, *Gerald Ford and the Future of the Presidency* (1974). For a sharply critical view, see Clark Mollenhoff, *The Man Who Pardoned Nixon* (1976). Consult also Richard Reeves, *A Ford, Not a Lincoln* (1975), and Ford's own *A Time to Heal: The Autobiography of Gerald Ford* (1979). Jimmy Carter wrote his autobiography, *Why Not the Best?* (1975), as did his wife, Rosalynn Carter, *First Lady from Plains* (1984). They should be supplemented by David Kucharsky, *The Man from Plains* (1976), and Betty Glad, *Jimmy Carter: In Search of the Great White House* (1980). Sharply critical are Clark R. Mollenhoff, *The President Who Failed: Carter Out of Control* (1980), and Joseph A. Califano, Jr. (whom Carter fired from the cabinet), *Governing America: An Insider's Report from the White House and the Cabinet* (1981). Other useful memoirs are Carter's own *Keeping Faith* (1982) and National Security Adviser Zbigniew Brzezinski's *Power and Principle* (1983). The debate on Panama spawned two noteworthy books: Walter LaFeber's prowithdrawal *The Panama Canal: The Crisis in Historical Perspective* (1978) and Paul B. Ryan's antiwithdrawal *The Panama Canal Controversy* (1977). On other aspects of Central American policy, see Richard Fagen, *The Nicaraguan Revolution* (1981), and LaFeber's *Inevitable Revolutions: The United States in Central America* (1983). The catastrophe in Iran is described in Michael Ledeen and William Lewis, *Debacle: The American Failure in Iran* (1981); Barry M. Rubin, *Paved with Good Intentions: The American Experience and Iran* (1980); and Pierre Salinger, *America Held Hostage* (1981).

---

*An asterisk indicates that the document, or an excerpt from it, can be found in Thomas A. Bailey and David M. Kennedy, eds., *The American Spirit: United States History as Seen by Contemporaries*, 9th ed. (Boston: Houghton Mifflin, 1998).

43

The Resurgence of Conservatism
1980–1996

It will be my intention to curb the size and influence of the federal establishment and to demand recognition of the distinction between the powers granted to the federal government and those reserved to the states or to the people.

RONALD REAGAN, INAUGURAL, 1981

The Triumph of Conservatism

Bedeviled abroad and becalmed at home, Carter's administration struck many Americans as bungling and befuddled. Carter's inability to control double-digit inflation was especially damaging. Frustrated critics bellyached loudly about the Georgian's alleged mismanagement of the nation's affairs.

Disaffection with Carter's apparent ineptitude ran deep even in his own Democratic party, where an "ABC" (Anybody but Carter) movement gathered steam. The president's fiscal conservatism, as well as his removal of regulatory controls from major indus-

tries (such as the airlines), prompted the charge that he was a Republican wolf camouflaged as a Democratic sheep. The liberal inheritors of the Democratic New Deal tradition grew especially disgruntled. They found their champion in Senator Edward Kennedy of Massachusetts, the last survivor of the assassin-plagued Kennedy brothers. In late 1979 Kennedy declared his intention to contest Carter's renomination. But Kennedy was handicapped from the outset by lingering suspicions about his involvement in a 1969 automobile accident on Chappaquiddick Island, Massachusetts, in which a young woman assistant was drowned when his car plunged off a bridge.

While Kennedy and Carter noisily slugged it out in a series of bruising primary elections, delighted

Republicans decorously proceeded to select their presidential nominee. Ronald Reagan, perennial darling of the right wing, easily outdistanced his rivals and secured the nomination he had sought for over a decade.

The hour of the conservative right seemed at last to have arrived. Census figures confirmed that the average American was older than in the stormy 1960s and much more likely to live in the South or West, the traditional bastions of the "old right." The conservative cause drew added strength from the emergence of a "new right" movement, partly in response to the "countercultural" protests of the 1960s. Spearheading the new right were evangelical Christian groups like the Moral Majority, which was composed of a dedicated minority of believers who enjoyed startling success as political fund-raisers and organizers.

Many new-right activists were far less agitated about economic questions than about cultural concerns—the so-called social issues. They denounced abortion, pornography, homosexuality, feminism, and especially affirmative action. They championed prayer in the schools and tougher penalties for criminals. Together, the old and new right added up to a powerful political combination.

Of all the social issues, those involving race were the most politically explosive. The Supreme

In a speech to the National Association of Evangelicals on March 8, 1983, President Ronald Reagan (b. 1911) defined his stand on school prayer:

"The Declaration of Independence mentions the Supreme Being no less than four times. 'In God We Trust' is engraved on our coinage. The Supreme Court opens its proceedings with a religious invocation. And the Members of Congress open their sessions with a prayer. I just happen to believe the schoolchildren of the United States are entitled to the same privileges as Supreme Court Justices and Congressmen."

Court in *Milliken* v. *Bradley* (1974) blindsided school integrationists when it ruled that desegregation plans could not require students to move across school-district lines. The decision effectively exempted suburban districts from shouldering any part of the burden of desegregating inner-city schools, thereby reinforcing "white flight" from cities to suburbs. By the same token, the decision distilled all the problems of desegregation into the

The Abortion Wars
Pro-choice and pro-life demonstrators brandish their beliefs. By the end of the twentieth century, the debate over abortion had become the most morally charged and divisive issue in American society since the struggle over slavery in the nineteenth century.

A Sad Day for Old Glory
In 1976, America's bicentennial year, anti-busing demonstrators convulsed Boston, the historic "cradle of liberty." White disillusionment with the race-based policies that were a legacy of Lyndon Johnson's "Great Society" programs of the 1960s helped to feed the conservative, anti-government movement that elected Ronald Reagan in 1980.

least prosperous districts, often pitting the poorest, most disadvantaged elements of the white and black communities against one another. Boston and other cities were shaken to their foundations by attempts to implement school-desegregation plans under these painful conditions.

Affirmative action programs also remained highly controversial. White workers who were denied advancement and white students who were refused college admission continued to raise the cry of "reverse discrimination." They charged that their rights had been violated by employers and admissions officers who put more weight on racial or ethnic background than on ability or achievement.

One white Californian, Allan Bakke, made headlines in 1978 when the Supreme Court, by the narrowest of margins (five to four) upheld his claim that his application to medical school had been turned down because of an admissions program that partially favored minority applicants. In a tortured decision, reflecting the troubling moral ambiguities and insoluble political complexities of this issue, the Court ordered the University of California at Davis medical school to admit Bakke, and declared that preference in admissions could not be given to members of any group, minority or majority, on the basis of ethnic or racial identity alone. Yet at the same time, the Court said that racial factors might be taken into account in a school's overall admissions policy. Among the dissenters on the sharply

divided bench was the Court's only black justice, Thurgood Marshall. He warned in an impassioned opinion that the denial of racial preferences might sweep away years of progress by the civil rights movement. But many conservatives cheered the decision as affirming the principle that justice is colorblind.

The Election of Ronald Reagan, 1980

Ronald Reagan was well suited to lead the gathering conservative crusade. Reared in a generation whose values were formed well before the upheavals of the 1960s, he naturally sided with the new right on social issues. In economic and social matters alike, he denounced the activist government and failed "social engineering" of the 1960s. He skillfully mobilized political resentments in a manner reminiscent of his early political hero, Franklin D. Roosevelt. Both Roosevelt and Reagan championed the "common man" against vast impersonal menaces that overshadowed the individual. But where the Democratic Roosevelt had branded big business the foe of the "forgotten man," the Republican Reagan depicted big government as the archvillain. He preached a "populist" political philosophy that condemned federal intervention in local affairs, favoritism for minorities, and the elitism of arrogant bureaucrats. He aimed especially to win over from the Democratic column working-class and lower-middle-class white voters by implying that the Democratic party had become the exclusive tool of its minority constituents.

Though Reagan was no intellectual, he drew on the ideas of a small but influential group of thinkers known as "neoconservatives." Their ranks included Norman Podhoretz, editor of *Commentary* magazine, and Irving Kristol, editor of *The Public Interest.* Reacting against what they saw as the excesses of 1960s liberalism, the neoconservatives championed free-market capitalism liberated from government restraints, and they took tough, harshly anti-Soviet positions in foreign policy. They also questioned liberal welfare programs and affirmative-action policies and called for reassertion of traditional values of individualism and the centrality of the family.

An actor-turned-politician, Reagan enjoyed enormous popularity with his crooked grin and aw-shucks manner. The son of a ne'er-do-well, impoverished Irish-American father with a fondness for the bottle, he had grown up in a small Illinois town. Reagan got his start in life in the depressed 1930s as a sports announcer for an Iowa radio station. Good looks and a way with words landed him acting jobs in Hollywood, where he became a B-grade star in the 1940s. He displayed a flair for politics as president of the Screen Actors Guild in the McCarthy era of the early 1950s, when he helped purge communists and other suspected "reds" from the film industry. In 1954 he became a spokesman for the General Electric Corporation at a salary of some $150,000 per year. In that position he began to abandon his New Dealish political views and increasingly to preach a conservative, antigovernment line. Reagan's huge visibility and growing skill at promoting the conservative cause made him attractive to a group of wealthy California businessmen, who helped launch his political career as governor of California from 1966 to 1974.

Memories of Chappaquiddick and the country's conservative mood killed Kennedy's candidacy. A badly battered Jimmy Carter, his party divided and in disarray, was left to do battle with Ronald Reagan. The Republican candidate proved to be a formidable campaigner. He used his professional acting skills to great advantage in a televised "debate" with the colorless Carter. Reagan attacked the incumbent's fumbling performance in foreign policy and blasted the "big-government" philosophy of the

President Ronald Reagan   The oldest man ever elected to the presidency, Reagan displayed youthful vigor both on the campaign trail and in office.

Democratic party (a philosophy that Carter did not fully embrace). Galloping inflation, sky-high interest rates, and a faltering economy also put the incumbent president on the defensive. Carter countered ineffectively with charges that Reagan was a trigger-happy cold warrior who might push the country into nuclear war.

Carter's spotty record in office was no defense against Reagan's popular appeal. On election day the Republican rang up a spectacular victory, bagging over 51 percent of the popular vote, while 41 percent went to Carter and 7 percent to independent candidate John Anderson. The electoral count stood at 489 for Reagan and 49 for Carter. (Anderson failed to gain a single electoral vote.) Carter managed to win only six states and the District of Columbia, a defeat almost as crushing as George McGovern's loss to Richard Nixon in 1972. He was the first elected president to be unseated by the voters since Herbert Hoover was ejected from office in 1932. Equally startling, the Republicans gained control of the Senate for the first time in twenty-five

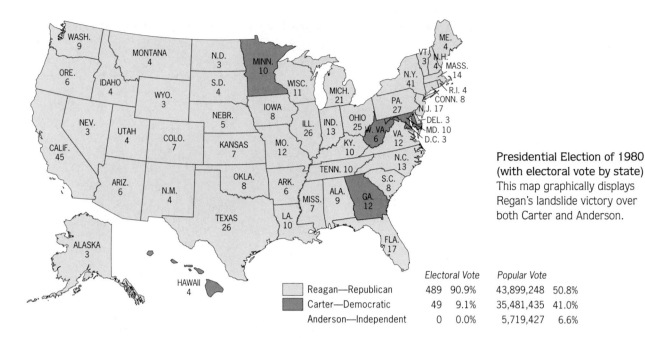

Presidential Election of 1980
(with electoral vote by state)
This map graphically displays
Regan's landslide victory over
both Carter and Anderson.

		Electoral Vote		Popular Vote	
	Reagan—Republican	489	90.9%	43,899,248	50.8%
	Carter—Democratic	49	9.1%	35,481,435	41.0%
	Anderson—Independent	0	0.0%	5,719,427	6.6%

years. Leading Democratic liberals who had been targeted for defeat by well-heeled new-right groups went down like dead timber in the conservative windstorm that swept the country.

Carter showed dignity in defeat, delivering a thoughtful Farewell Address that stressed his efforts to scale down the deadly arms race, to promote human rights, and to protect the environment. In

One of Jimmy Carter's former speechwriters commented in 1979 on Carter's sometimes puzzling personality: The president, he said, displayed

a combination of arrogance, complacency, and—dread thought—insecurity at the core of his mind and soul. . . . He holds explicit, thorough positions on every issue under the sun . . . but he has no large view of the relations between them. . . . He fails to project a vision larger than the problem he is tackling at the moment. . . . [Yet] with his moral virtues and his intellectual skills, he is perhaps as admirable a human being as has ever held the job.

one of his last acts in office, he signed a bill preserving some 100 million acres of Alaskan land for national parks, forests, and wildlife refuges. An unusually intelligent, articulate, and well-meaning president, he had been hampered by his lack of managerial talent and had been badly buffeted by events beyond his control, such as the soaring price of oil, runaway inflation, and the galling insult of the continuing hostage crisis in Iran. If Carter was correct in believing that the country was suffering from a terrible "malaise," he never found the right medicine to cure the disease.

The Reagan Revolution

Reagan's arrival in Washington was triumphal. The Iranians contributed to the festive mood by releasing the hostages on Reagan's Inauguration Day, January 20, 1981, after 444 days of captivity.

Reagan assembled a conservative cabinet of the "best and the rightest." It included a highly controversial Coloradan, James Watt, as secretary of the interior. Watt was a product of the "Sagebrush Rebellion," a fiercely anti-Washington movement that had sprung up to protest federal control over the rich mineral and timber resources in the western states. Environmentalists howled loudly about

Watt's schemes to hobble the Environmental Protection Agency and to permit oil drilling in scenic places. After bitter protests they succeeded in halting Watt's plan to allow oil exploration off the California coastline. Watt blithely rebuffed critics by saying, "I make lots of mistakes because I make lots of decisions." He made one mistake too many in 1983, when he thoughtlessly told an offensive ethnic joke in public and was forced to resign.

The new president, a hale and hearty sixty-nine-year-old, was devoted to fiscal fitness. A major goal of Reagan's political career was to reduce the size of the government by shrinking the federal budget and slashing taxes. He declared, "Government is not the solution to our problem. Government is the problem." Years of New Deal–style tax-and-spend programs, Reagan jested, had created a federal government that reminded him of the definition of a baby as a creature who was all appetite at one end, with no sense of responsibility at the other.

By the early 1980s, this antigovernment message found a receptive audience. In the two decades since 1960, federal spending had risen from about 18 percent of gross national product to nearly 23 percent. At the same time, the composition of the federal budget had been shifting from defense to entitlement programs, including Social Security and Medicare (see chart p. 1042). In 1973 the budget of the Department of Health, Education, and Welfare surpassed that of the Department of Defense. Citizens increasingly balked at paying the bills for further extension of government "benefits." After four decades of advancing New Deal and Great Society programs, a strong countercurrent took hold. Californians staged a "tax revolt" in 1978 (known by its official ballot title of Proposition 13) that slashed property taxes and forced painful cuts in government services. The California "tax quake" jolted other state capitals and even rocked the pillars of Congress in faraway Washington, D.C. Ronald Reagan had ridden this political shock wave to presidential victory in 1980 and now proceeded to rattle the "welfare state" to its very foundations.

With near-religious zeal and remarkable effectiveness, Reagan set out to persuade Congress to legislate his smaller-government policies into law. He proposed a new federal budget that necessitated cuts of some $35 billion, mostly in social programs like food stamps and federally funded job-training centers. Reagan worked naturally in harness with the Republican majority in the Senate, but to get his way in the Democratic House, he undertook some old-fashioned politicking. He enterprisingly wooed a group of mostly southern conservative Democrats

Coming Home   After more than a year in captivity in Iran, these hostages were released on the very day of Ronald Reagan's presidential inauguration.

WELCOME BACK TO FREEDOM

In his inaugural address, Ronald Reagan summoned Americans to "an era of national renewal." He explained,

"It is not my intention to do away with the government. It is rather to make it work—work with us, not over us; to stand by our side, not ride on our back. . . . Can we solve the problems confronting us? The answer is an unequivocal and emphatic yes. To paraphrase Winston Churchill, I did not take the oath I have just taken with the intention of presiding over the dissolution of the world's strongest economy."

The Triumph of the Right, 1980 Republican conservatives scored a double victory in 1980, winning control of both the White House and the Senate. Aided by conservative Democratic "boll weevils," they also dominated the House of Representatives, and a new era of conservatism dawned in the nation's capital.

(dubbed "boll weevils"), who abandoned their own party's leadership to follow the president.

Then on March 30, 1981, a deranged gunman shot the president as he was leaving a Washington hotel. A .22-caliber bullet penetrated beneath Reagan's left arm and collapsed his left lung. With admirable courage and grace, and with impressive physical resilience for a man his age, Reagan recovered rapidly from his violent ordeal. Twelve days after the attack, he walked out of the hospital and returned to work. When he appeared a few days later on national television to address the Congress and the public on his budget, the outpouring of sympathy and support was enormous.

The Battle of the Budget

Swept along on a tide of presidential popularity, Congress swallowed Reagan's budget proposals, approving expenditures of some $695 billion, with a projected deficit of about $38 billion. To hit those financial targets, drastic surgery was required, and Congress plunged its scalpel deeply into Great Society–spawned social programs. Wounded Democrats wondered if the president's intention was to cut the budget or to gut the budget.

Reagan's triumph amazed political observers, especially defeated Democrats. The new president

had descended upon Washington like an avenging angel of conservatism, kicking up a blinding whirlwind of political change. He sought nothing less than the dismantling of the welfare state and the reversal of the political evolution of the preceding half-century. His impressive performance demonstrated the power of the presidency with a skill not seen since Lyndon Johnson's day. Out the window went the textbooks that had concluded, largely on the basis of the stalemated 1970s, that this office had been eclipsed by a powerful, uncontrollable Congress.

Reagan hardly rested to savor the sweetness of his victory. The second part of his economic program called for deep tax cuts, amounting to 25 percent across-the-board reductions over a period of three years. Once again, Reagan displayed his skill as a performer and a persuader in a highly effective television address in July 1981, when he pleaded for congressional passage of the tax-cut bill. Democrats, he quipped, "had never met a tax they didn't hike." Thanks largely to the continued defection of the "boll weevils" from the Democratic camp, the president again had his way. In August 1981 Congress approved a set of far-reaching tax reforms that lowered individual tax rates, virtually eliminated federal estate taxes, and created new tax-free savings plans for small investors. Reagan's "supply-side" economic advisers assured him that the combination of budgetary discipline and tax reduc-

Wallflowers Reagan's budget cuts fell almost exclusively on social programs, whereas military outlays increased substantially.

tion would stimulate new investment, boost productivity, and foster dramatic economic growth.

But at first "supply-side" economics seemed to be a beautiful theory mugged by a gang of brutal facts, as the economy slid into its deepest recession since the 1930s. Unemployment reached nearly 11 percent in 1982, businesses folded, and several bank failures jolted the nation's entire financial system. The automobile industry, once the brightest jewel in America's industrial crown, turned in its dimmest performance in history. Battling against Japanese imports, major automakers reported losses in the hundreds of millions of dollars. Fuming and frustrated Democrats angrily charged that the president's budget cuts slashed especially cruelly at the poor and the handicapped and that his tax cuts favored the well-to-do. They accused Reagan of trying to make those Americans with the frailest shoulders carry the heaviest burden in the fight for fiscal reform. In fact, the anti-inflationary "tight money" policies that precipitated the "Reagan recession" of 1982 had been initiated by the Federal Reserve Board in 1979, on Carter's watch.

Ignoring the yawping pack of Democratic critics, President Reagan and his economic advisers serenely waited for their supply-side economic policies ("Reaganomics") to produce the promised results. The supply-siders seemed to be vindicated when a healthy economic recovery finally got under way in 1983. Yet the economy of the 1980s was not uniformly sound. For the first time in the twentieth century, income gaps widened between the richest and the poorest Americans. The poor got poorer and the very rich grew fabulously richer, while middle-class incomes largely stagnated. Symbolic of the new income stratification was the emergence of "yuppies," or young, urban professionals. Sporting Rolex watches and BMW sports cars, they made a near religion out of conspicuous consumption. Though numbering only about 1.5 million people and being something of a stereotype, yuppies showcased the values of materialism and the pursuit of wealth that came to symbolize the high-rolling 1980s.

Some economists located the sources of the economic upturn neither in the president's budget cuts and tax reforms nor in the go-get-'em avarice of the yuppies. It was massive military expenditures, they argued, that constituted the real foundation of 1980s prosperity. Reagan cascaded nearly 2 trillion budget dollars onto the Pentagon in the 1980s,

asserting the need to close a "window of vulnerability" in the armaments race with the Soviet Union. Ironically, this conservative president thereby plunged the government into a red-ink bath of deficit spending that made the New Deal look downright stingy. Federal budget deficits topped $100 billion in 1982, and the government's books were nearly $200 billion out of balance in every subsequent year of the 1980s. Massive government borrowing to cover those deficits kept interest rates high, and high interest rates in turn elevated the value of the dollar to record altitudes in the international money markets. The soaring dollar was good news for American tourists and buyers of foreign cars, but it dealt crippling blows to American exporters, as the American international trade deficit reached a record $152 billion in 1987. The masters of international commerce and finance for a generation after World War II, Americans suddenly became the world's heaviest borrowers in the global economy of the 1980s (see the graph in the Appendix).

Reagan Renews the Cold War

Hard as nails toward the Soviet Union in his campaign speeches, Reagan saw no reason to soften up after he checked in at the White House. As the Soviets carried on their war in Afghanistan, Reagan continued to condemn the Kremlin. In one of his first presidential news conferences, he claimed that the Soviets were "prepared to commit any crime, to lie, to cheat," in pursuit of their goals of world conquest. In a later speech he characterized the Soviet Union as the "focus of evil in the modern world."

Reagan believed in negotiating with the Soviets —but only from a position of overwhelming strength. Accordingly, his strategy for dealing with Moscow was simple: by enormously expanding U.S. military capabilities, he could threaten the Soviets with a fantastically expensive new round of the arms race. The American economy, theoretically, could better bear this new financial burden than could the creaking Soviet system. Desperate to avoid economic ruin, Kremlin leaders would come to the bargaining table and sing Reagan's tune.

This strategy resembled a riverboat gambler's ploy. It wagered the enormous sum of Reagan's defense budgets on the hope that the other side

Star Wars Fantasies   President Reagan's Strategic Defense Initiative (popularly known as Star Wars) evoked extravagant hopes for an impermeable defensive shield, but its daunting physical and engineering requirements also occasioned much ridicule in the scientific community.

would not call Washington's bluff and initiate a new cycle of arms competition. Reagan played his trump card in this risky game in March 1983, when he announced his intention to pursue a high-technology missile-defense system called the Strategic Defense Initiative (SDI), popularly known as Star Wars. The plan called for orbiting battle stations in space that could fire laser beams or other forms of concentrated energy to vaporize intercontinental missiles on lift-off. Reagan described SDI as offering potential salvation from the nuclear nightmare by throwing an "astrodome" defense shield over American cities. Most scientists considered this an impossible goal. But the deeper logic of SDI lay in its fit with Reagan's overall Soviet strategy. By pitching the arms contest onto a stratospheric plane of high technology and astronomical expense, it would further force the Kremlin's hand.

By emphasizing defense rather than offense, SDI upset four decades of strategic thinking about nuclear weaponry. Many experts remained deeply skeptical about the plan. Those who did not dismiss it as ludicrous feared that Star Wars research might be ruinously costly, ultimately unworkable, and fatally destabilizing to the distasteful but effective "balance of terror" that had kept the nuclear peace since World War II. Scientific and strategic doubts combined to constrain congressional funding for SDI through the remainder of Reagan's term.

Relations with the Soviets further nose-dived in late 1981, when the government of Poland, needled for over a year by a popular movement of working people organized into a massive union called "Solidarity," clamped martial law on the troubled country. Reagan saw the heavy fist of the Kremlin inside this Polish iron glove, and he imposed economic sanctions on Poland and the USSR alike. Notably absent from the mandated measures was a resumption of the grain embargo, which would have pinched the pocketbooks of too many American farmers.

Dealing with the Soviet Union was additionally complicated by the inertia and ill health of the aging oligarchs in the Kremlin, three of whom were swept away by death between late 1982 and early 1985. Relations grew even more tense when the Soviets, in September 1983, blasted from the skies a Korean passenger airliner that had inexplicably violated Soviet airspace. Hundreds of civilians, including many Americans, plummeted to their deaths in the frigid Sea of Okhotsk. By the end of 1983, all arms-control negotiations with the Soviets were broken off. The deepening chill in the Cold War was further felt in 1984, when USSR and Soviet-bloc athletes boycotted the Olympic games in Los Angeles.

Troubles Abroad

The volatile Middle Eastern pot continued to boil ominously. Israel badly strained its bonds of friendship with the United States by continuing to allow new settlements to be established in the occupied territory of the Jordan River's West Bank. Israel further raised the stakes in the Middle East in June 1982 when it invaded neighboring Lebanon, seeking to suppress once and for all the guerrilla bases from which Palestinian fighters harassed beleaguered Israel. The Palestinians were bloodily subdued, but Lebanon, already pulverized by years of episodic civil war, was plunged into armed chaos. President Reagan was obliged to send American troops to Lebanon in 1983 as part of an international peacekeeping force; but their presence did not bring peace. A suicidal bomber crashed an explosives-laden truck into a United States Marine barracks on October 23, 1983, killing more than two hundred marines. President Reagan soon thereafter withdrew the remaining American troops, while miraculously suffering no political damage from this horrifying and humiliating attack. His mystified

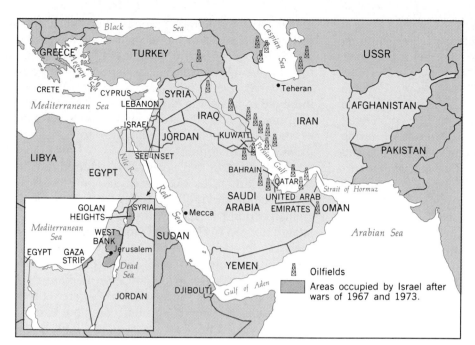

The Middle East   A combination of political instability and precious petroleum resources has made the region from Egypt to Afghanistan an "arc of crisis."

Democratic opponents began to call him a "Teflon president," to whom nothing hurtful could stick.

Central America, in the United States' own backyard, also rumbled menacingly. A leftist revolution had deposed the longtime dictator of Nicaragua in 1979. President Carter had tried to ignore the hotly anti-American rhetoric of the revolutionaries,

known as "Sandinistas," and to establish good diplomatic relations with them. But Reagan took their rhetoric at face value and hurled back at them some hot language of his own. He accused the Sandinistas of turning their country into a forward base for Soviet and Cuban military penetration of all of Central America. Brandishing photographs taken from

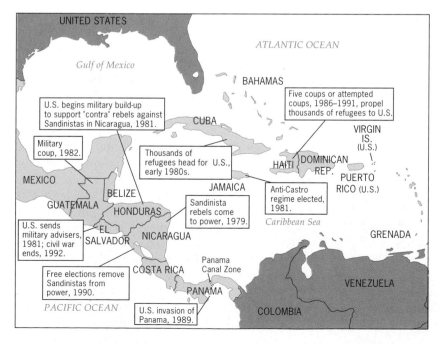

Central America and the Caribbean This region of historical importance to the United States experienced dramatic political upheavals in the 1970s, 1980s, and 1990s.

high-flying spy planes, administration spokespeople claimed that Nicaraguan leftists were shipping weapons to revolutionary forces in tiny El Salvador, torn by violence since a coup in 1979.

Reagan sent military "advisers" to prop up the pro-American government of El Salvador. He also provided covert aid, including the CIA-engineered mining of harbors, to the "contra" rebels opposing the anti-American government of Nicaragua. Reagan also flexed his military muscles elsewhere in the turbulent Caribbean. In a dramatic display of American might, in October 1983 he dispatched a heavy-fire-power invasion force to the island of Grenada, where a military coup had killed the prime minister and brought Marxists to power. Swiftly overrunning the tiny island and ousting the insurgents, American troops vividly demonstrated Reagan's determination to assert the dominance of the United States in the Caribbean, just as Theodore Roosevelt had done.

Round Two for Reagan

A confident Ronald Reagan, bolstered by a buoyant economy at home and by the popularity of his muscular posture abroad, handily won the Republican nomination in 1984 for a second White House term. His opponent was Democrat Walter Mondale, who made history by naming as his vice-presidential running mate Congresswoman Geraldine Ferraro of New York. She was the first woman ever to appear on a major-party presidential ticket. But even this dramatic gesture could not salvage Mondale's candidacy, which was fatally tainted by his service as vice president in the deeply discredited Carter administration. On election day Reagan walked away with 525 electoral votes to Mondale's 13, winning everywhere except in Mondale's home state of Minnesota and the District of Columbia. Reagan also overwhelmed Mondale in the popular vote—52,609,797 to 36,450,613.

Shrinking the federal government and reducing taxes had been the main objectives of Reagan's first term; foreign policy issues dominated the news in his second term. The president soon found himself contending for the world's attention with a charismatic new Soviet leader, Mikhail Gorbachev, installed as chairman of the Soviet Communist party in March 1985. Gorbachev was personable, energetic, imaginative, and committed to radical reforms in the Soviet Union. He announced two

policies with remarkable, even revolutionary, implications. *Glasnost*, or "openness," aimed to ventilate the secretive, repressive stuffiness of Soviet society by introducing free speech and a measure of political liberty. *Perestroika*, or "restructuring," was intended to revive the moribund Soviet economy by adopting many of the free-market practices—such as the profit motive and an end to subsidized prices—of the capitalist West.

Both *glasnost* and *perestroika* required that the Soviet Union shrink the size of its enormous military machine and redirect its energies to the dismal civilian economy. That requirement, in turn, necessitated an end to the Cold War. Gorbachev accordingly made warm overtures to the West, including an announcement in April 1985 that the Soviet Union would cease to deploy intermediate-range nuclear forces (INF) targeted on Western Europe, pending an agreement on their complete elimination. He pushed this goal when he met with Ronald Reagan at their first of four summit meetings, in Geneva in November 1985. A second summit meeting, in Reykjavik, Iceland, in October 1986 broke down in stalemate. But at a third summit, in Washington, D.C., in December 1987, the two leaders at last signed the INF treaty, banning all intermediate-range nuclear missiles from Europe. This was a result long sought by both sides; it marked a victory for American policy, for Gorbachev's reform program, and for the peoples of Europe and indeed all the world, who now had at least one less nuclear weapon system to worry about.

Reagan and Gorbachev capped their new friendship in May 1988 at a final summit in Moscow. There Reagan, who had entered office condemning the "evil empire" of Soviet communism, warmly praised Gorbachev. Reagan, the consummate cold warrior, had been flexible and savvy enough to seize a historic opportunity to join with the Soviet chief to bring the Cold War to a kind of conclusion. For this, history would give both leaders high marks.

Reagan made other decisive moves in foreign policy. His administration provided strong backing in February 1986 for Corazon Aquino's ouster of dictator Ferdinand Marcos in the Philippines. Reagan ordered a lightning air raid against Libya in 1986, in retaliation for alleged Libyan sponsorship of terrorist attacks, including a bomb blast in a West Berlin discotheque that killed a U.S. serviceman. In the summer of 1987, U.S. naval vessels began escorting oil tankers through the Persian Gulf, inflamed by a long, brutal war between Iran and Iraq.

East Meets West
President Reagan greets
Soviet leader Mikhail
Gorbachev at a summit
meeting in Moscow in
May 1988.

The Iran-Contra Imbroglio

Two foreign-policy problems seemed insoluble to Reagan: the continuing captivity of a number of American hostages, seized by Muslim extremist groups in bleeding, battered Lebanon; and the continuing grip on power of the left-wing Sandinista government in Nicaragua. The president repeatedly requested that Congress provide military aid to the contra rebels fighting against the Sandinista regime. Congress repeatedly refused, and the administration grew increasingly frustrated, even obsessed, in its search for a means to help the contras.

Unknown to the American public, some Washington officials saw a possible linkage between the two thorny problems of the Middle Eastern hostages and the Central American Sandinistas. In 1985 American diplomats secretly arranged arms sales to the embattled Iranians in return for Iranian aid in obtaining the release of American hostages held by Middle Eastern terrorists. At least one hostage was eventually set free. Meanwhile, money from the payment for the arms was diverted to the contras. These actions brazenly violated a congressional ban on military aid to the Nicaraguan rebels—not to mention Reagan's repeated vow that he would never negotiate with terrorists.

News of these secret dealings broke in November 1986 and ignited a firestorm of controversy. President Reagan claimed he was innocent of wrongdoing and ignorant about the activities of his subordinates, but a congressional committee condemned the "secrecy, deception, and disdain for the law" displayed by administration officials and

Contra Rebel Troops Head for Battle   These rebels were long-seasoned and battle-scarred veterans of Nicaragua's civil war by the time this photograph was taken in 1987.

On March 4, 1987, President Ronald Reagan somewhat confusingly tried to explain his role (or lack of role) in the arms-for-hostages deal with Iran:

"A few months ago I told the American people I did not trade arms for hostages. My heart and my best intentions still tell me that is true, but the facts and the evidence tell me it is not."

concluded that "if the president did not know what his national security advisers were doing, he should have." Criminal indictments were later brought against several individuals tarred by the Iran-contra scandal, including marine colonel Oliver North; North's boss at the National Security Council, Admiral John Poindexter; and even Secretary of Defense Caspar Weinberger. North and Poindexter were both found guilty of criminal behavior, though all their convictions were eventually reversed on appeal. Weinberger received a presidential pardon before he was formally tried.

The Iran-contra affair cast a dark shadow over the Reagan record in foreign policy, tending to obscure the president's outstanding achievement in establishing a new relationship with the Soviets. Out of the several Iran-contra investigations a picture emerged of Reagan as a lazy, perhaps even senile, president who napped through meetings and paid little or no attention to the details of policy. Reagan's critics pounced on this portrait as proof that the former-movie-star-turned-politician was a mental lightweight who had merely acted his way through the role of the presidency without really understanding the script. But despite these damaging revelations, Reagan remained among the most popular and beloved presidents in modern American history.

Reagan's Economic Legacy

Ronald Reagan had taken office vowing to invigorate the American economy by rolling back government regulations, lowering taxes, and balancing the budget. He did ease many regulatory rules, and he pushed major tax reform bills through Congress in 1981 and 1986. But a balanced budget remained

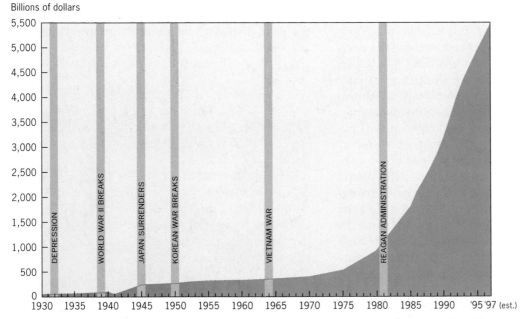

The National Debt, 1930–1997   World War II provided the first major boost to the national debt. But it was the policies of the Reagan and Bush administrations, 1981–1993, that explosively expanded the debt to the $4 trillion level. By the 1990s, 14 percent of federal revenues went to interest payments on the debt. (*Historical Statistics of the United States* and *Statistical Abstract of the United States*, relevant years; 1996 and 1997 figures from *Economic Indicators*, Council of Economic Advisors.)

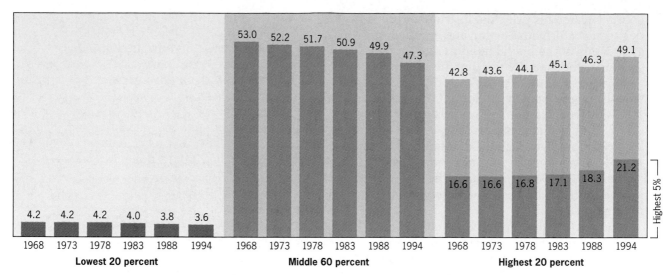

Share of Aggregate Household Income, by Quintile, 1968–1994   [U.S. Census Bureau. Downloaded from (http://www.census.gov/population/www/pop-profile/moninc.html> on November 5, 1996.)]

grotesquely out of reach. Supply-side economic theory had promised that lower taxes would actually *increase* government revenue because they would so stimulate the economy as a whole. But in fact the combination of tax reduction and huge increases in military spending opened a vast "revenue hole" of $200 billion annual deficits. In his eight years in office, President Reagan added nearly $2 trillion to the national debt—more than all of his predecessors combined, including those who had fought protracted global wars (see chart on p. 1002).

The staggering deficits of the Reagan years assuredly constituted a great economic failure. And because so much of the Reagan-era debt was financed by foreign lenders, especially the Japanese, the deficits virtually guaranteed that future generations of Americans would either have to work harder than their parents, lower their standard of living, or both, to pay their foreign creditors when the bills came due. The yawning deficits prompted Congress in 1986 to pass legislation mandating a balanced budget by 1991. Yet even this drastic measure proved pitifully inadequate to the task of closing the gap between the federal government's income and expenditures, and the national debt continued to grow.

But if the deficits represented an economic failure, they also constituted, strangely enough, a kind of political triumph. Among the paramount goals of Reagan's political life was his ambition to slow the growth of government, and especially to block or

even repeal the social programs launched in the era of Lyndon Johnson's Great Society. By making new social spending both practically and politically impossible for the foreseeable future, the deficits served exactly that purpose. They achieved, in short, Reagan's highest political objective: the containment of the welfare state. Ronald Reagan thus ensured the long-term perpetuation of his dearest political values to a degree that few presidents have managed to achieve. For better or worse, the consequences of "Reaganomics" would be large and durable.

Yet another legacy of the 1980s was a sharp reversal of a long-term trend toward more equitable distribution of income, and an increasing squeeze on the middle class. In the early 1990s, median household income (in 1993 dollars) actually declined, from about $33,500 in 1989 to about $31,000 in 1993. Whether that disturbing trend should be attributed to Reagan's policies, or to more deeply running economic currents, remained controversial. (See chart above.)

Culture Wars

Reagan's legacy was also likely to be lasting with respect to the social issues that first helped get him elected president in 1980. If the budget was his chief weapon in the war against the welfare state, the courts became his principal instrument in his battles against affirmative action and abortion, the two great icons of the liberal political culture that Reaganism repudiated. By the time he left office, Reagan had appointed a near-majority of all sitting federal judges. Equally important, he had named three conservative-minded justices to the Supreme Court. They included Sandra Day O'Connor, a brilliant Stanford Law School graduate and public-spirited Arizona judge. When she was sworn in on September 25, 1981, she became the first woman to ascend to the high bench in the Court's nearly two-hundred-year-history.

The Court showed its newly conservative coloration in 1984, when it decreed, in a case involving Memphis firefighters, that union rules about job seniority could outweigh affirmative-action concerns in guiding promotion policies in the city's fire department. In two cases in 1989 (*Ward's Cove Packing* v. *Antonia* and *Martin* v. *Wilks*), the Court made it more difficult to prove that an employer practiced racial discrimination in hiring and made it easier for white males to argue that they were the victims of reverse discrimination by employers who followed affirmative-action practices. Congress passed legislation in 1991 that partially reversed the effects of those decisions.

The contentious issue of abortion also reached the Court in 1989. In the case of *Roe* v. *Wade* in 1973, the Supreme Court had prohibited states from making laws that interfered with a woman's right to an abortion during the early months of pregnancy.* For nearly two decades, that decision had been the bedrock principle on which "pro-choice" advocates built their case for abortion rights. It had also provoked bitter criticism from Roman Catholics and various "right-to-life" groups who wanted a virtually absolute ban on all abortions. In *Webster* v. *Reproductive Health Services,* the Court in July 1989 did not entirely overturn *Roe,* but it seriously compromised *Roe*'s protection of abortion rights. By approving a Missouri law that imposed certain restrictions on abortion, the Court signaled that it was inviting the states to legislate in an area in which *Roe* had previously forbidden them to legislate. The Court renewed that invitation in *Planned Parenthood* v. *Casey* in 1992, when it ruled that states could

---

*In 1995, Norma McCarvey, the pseudonymous "Jane Roe" in the *Roe* v. *Wade* case, declared that she personally no longer supported abortion rights.

> *Speaking to the National Association of Evangelicals, President Ronald Reagan said the following about abortion:*
>
> "More than a decade ago, a Supreme Court decision [*Roe* v. *Wade*, 1973] literally wiped off the books of fifty states statutes protecting the rights of unborn children. Abortion on demand now takes the lives of up to $1\frac{1}{2}$ million unborn children a year. Human life legislation ending this tragedy will some day pass the Congress, and you and I must never rest until it does. Unless and until it can be proven that the unborn child is not a living entity, then its right to life, liberty, and the pursuit of happiness must be protected."

restrict access to abortion as long as they did not place an "undue burden" on the woman. Using this standard, the Court held that Pennsylvania could not compel a wife to notify her husband about an abortion but could require a minor child to notify parents, as well as other restrictions.

Right-to-life advocates were at first delighted by the *Webster* decision. But the Court's ruling also galvanized pro-choice organizations into a new militancy. Bruising, divisive battles loomed as state legislatures across the land confronted abortion. This painful cultural conflict over the unborn was also part of the Reagan era's bequest to the future.

Referendum on Reaganism in 1988

Republicans lost control of the Senate in the off-year elections of November 1986. Hopes rose among Democrats that the "Reagan Revolution" might be showing signs of political vulnerability at last. The newly Democratic majority in the Senate flexed its political muscle in 1987 when it rejected Robert Bork, Reagan's ultraconservative nominee for a Supreme Court vacancy.

Democrats also relished the prospect of making political hay out of both the Iran-contra scandal and the allegedly unethical behavior that tainted an unusually large number of Reagan's "official family." Top administrators of the Environmental Protection Agency resigned in disgrace over a misappropriation of funds. Reagan's secretary of labor stepped down in 1985 to stand trial on charges of fraud and larceny. (He was eventually acquitted.) The president's personal White House aide was convicted of perjury in 1988. The nation's chief law enforcement officer, Attorney General Edwin Meese, came under investigation by a federal special prosecutor on charges of influence-peddling. Reagan's secretary of housing and urban development was also investigated on charges of fraud and favoritism in the awarding of lucrative federal housing grants.

Disquieting signs of economic trouble also seemed to open political opportunities for Democrats. The "twin towers" of deficits—the federal budget deficit and international trade deficit—continued to mount ominously. Falling oil prices blighted the economy of the Southwest, slashing real estate values and undermining hundreds of savings-and-loans (S&L) institutions. The damage to the S&Ls was so massive that a federal rescue operation was eventually estimated to carry a price tag of well over $500 billion. Meanwhile, many American banks found themselves holding near-worthless loans they had unwisely foisted upon Third World countries, especially in Latin America. In 1984 it took federal assistance to save Continental Illinois Bank from a catastrophic failure. More banks and savings institutions were folding than at any time since the Great Depression of the 1930s. A wave of mergers, acquisitions, and leveraged buyouts washed over Wall Street, leaving many brokers and traders megarich and many companies saddled with megadebt. A cold spasm of fear struck the money markets on "Black Monday," October 19, 1987, when the leading stock-market index plunged 508 points—the largest one-day decline in history. This crash, said *Newsweek* magazine, heralded "the final collapse of the money culture . . . , the death knell of the 1980s." But as Mark Twain famously commented about his own obituary, this announcement proved premature.

Hoping to cash in on these ethical and economic anxieties, a pack of Democrats—dubbed the "Seven Dwarfs" by derisive Republicans—chased after their party's 1988 presidential nomination. But the Reaganites proved to have no monopoly on shady behavior. Ironically enough, the handsome and charismatic Democratic front-runner, former Colorado senator Gary Hart, was himself forced to

Bailing Out the Banks   Lax regulation and a booming real-estate market imperiled hundreds of financial institutions in the 1980s, necessitating a massive taxpayer-funded bailout.

drop out of the race in May 1987 after charges of sexual misconduct.

Black candidate Jesse Jackson, a rousing speechmaker who hoped to forge a "rainbow coalition" of minorities and the disadvantaged, campaigned energetically, but the Democratic nomination in the end went to the coolly cerebral governor of Massachusetts, Michael Dukakis. Republicans nominated Reagan's vice president, George Bush, who ran largely on the Reagan record of tax cuts, strong defense policies, toughness on crime, opposition to abortion, and a long-running if hardly robust economic expansion. Dukakis made little headway exploiting the ethical and economic sorespots and came across to television viewers as almost supernaturally devoid of emotion. On election day the voters gave him just 40,797,905 votes to 47,645,225 for Bush. The Electoral College count was 112 to 426.

George Bush and the End of the Cold War

George Herbert Walker Bush was born with a silver spoon in his mouth. His father had served as a U.S. senator from Connecticut, and young George had enjoyed a first-rate education at Yale. After service in World War II, he had amassed a modest fortune of

George Bush (b. 1924), Forty-first President of the United States

Tiananmen Square, Beijing, China, June 1989   Before they were brutally suppressed by Chinese authorities, student demonstrators paraded a homemade Statue of Liberty to signify their passion for democracy.

his own in the oil business in Texas. His deepest commitment, however, was to public service; he left the business world to serve briefly as a congressman and then held various posts in several Republican administrations, including emissary to China, ambassador to the United Nations, director of the Central Intelligence Agency, and vice president. He capped this long political career when he was inaugurated as president in January 1989, promising to work for "a kinder, gentler America."

In the first months of the Bush administration, the communist world commanded the planet's fascinated attention. Everywhere in the communist bloc it seemed, astoundingly, that the season of democracy had arrived.

In China hundreds of thousands of prodemocracy demonstrators thronged through Beijing's Tiananmen Square in the spring of 1989. They proudly flourished a 30-foot-high "Goddess of Democracy," modeled on the Statue of Liberty, as a symbol of their aspirations.

But in June of that year, China's aging and autocratic rulers brutally crushed the prodemocracy movement. Tanks rolled over the crowds, and machine-gunners killed hundreds of protesters. In the following weeks, scores of arrested demonstrators were publicly executed after perfunctory "trials."

World opinion roundly condemned the bloody suppression of the prodemocracy demonstrators.

President Bush joined in the criticism. Yet despite angry demands in Congress for punitive restrictions on trade with China, the president insisted on maintaining normal relations with Beijing.

Stunning changes also shook Eastern Europe. Long oppressed by puppet regimes propped up by Soviet guns, the region was revolutionized in just a few startling months in 1989. The Solidarity movement in Poland led the way when it toppled Poland's communist government in August. With dizzying speed, communist regimes collapsed in Hungary, Czechoslovakia, East Germany, and even hyper-repressive Romania. In December 1989, jubilant Germans danced atop the hated Berlin Wall, symbol of the division of Germany and all of Europe into two armed and hostile camps. The Wall itself soon

The End of the Post–World War II Era, 1989 Jubilant Berliners partied atop the hated Berlin Wall in December 1989, dramatically symbolizing the end of the Cold War division of Germany.

came down, heralding the imminent end of the forty-five-year-long Cold War. Chunks of the Wall's concrete became instant collectors' items—gray souvenirs of a grim episode in Europe's history. With the approval of the victorious Allied powers of World War II, the two Germanies, divided since 1945, were at last reunited in October 1990.

Most startling of all were the changes that rolled over the heartland of world communism, the Soviet Union itself. Mikhail Gorbachev's policies of *glasnost* and *perestroika* had set in motion a groundswell that surged out of his control. Old-guard hardliners, in a last-gasp effort to preserve the tottering communist system, attempted to dislodge Gorbachev with a military coup in August 1991. With the support of Boris Yeltsin, president of the Russian Republic (one of the several republics that composed the Union of Soviet Socialist Republics, or the USSR), Gorbachev foiled the plotters. But his days were numbered. In December 1991 Gorbachev resigned as Soviet president. He had become a leader without a country as the Soviet Union dissolved into its component parts, some fifteen republics loosely confederated in the Commonwealth of Independent States (CIS), with Russia the most powerful state and Yeltsin the dominant leader. To varying degrees, all the new governments in the CIS repudiated communism and embraced democratic reforms and free-market economies.

These developments astonished the "experts" who had long preached that the steely vise-grip of communist rule never could be peacefully broken.

Yet suddenly and almost miraculously, the totalitarian tonnage of communist oppression had been rendered politically weightless. Most spectacularly, the demise of the Soviet Union wrote a definitive finish to the Cold War era. More than four decades of nail-biting tension between two nuclear superpowers, the Soviet Union and the United States, evaporated when the USSR dismantled itself. With the Soviet Union swept into the dustbin of history and communism all but extinct, Bush spoke hopefully of a "new world order" where democracy would reign and diplomacy would supersede weaponry. Some observers even saw in these developments "the end of history" in the sense that democracy, victorious in its two-century-long struggle against foes on the left and right, had no ideological battles left to fight.

Exultant Americans joked that the USSR had become the "USS *were*." But the disintegration of the Soviet Union was no laughing matter. Rankling questions remained. For example, who would honor arms-control agreements with the United States? Which of the successor states of the former Soviet Union would take command of the formidable Soviet nuclear arsenal? (A partial answer was provided in early 1993, when President Bush, in one of his last official acts, signed the START II accord with Russian president Boris Yeltsin, committing both powers to reduce their long-range nuclear arsenals by two-thirds within ten years.)

Throughout the former Soviet empire, waves of nationalistic fervor and long-suppressed ethnic and racial hatreds rolled across the vast land as communism's roots were wrenched out. A particularly nasty conflict erupted in the Russian Caucasus in 1991,

when the Chechnyen minority tried to declare their independence from Russia, prompting President Yeltsin to send in Russian troops. Ethnic warfare flared in other disintegrating communist countries as well, notably in misery-drenched Yugoslavia, racked by vicious "ethnic cleansing" campaigns against various minorities.

The cruel and paradoxical truth stood revealed that the calcified communist regimes of Eastern Europe, whatever their sins, had at least bottled up the ancient ethnic antagonisms that were the region's peculiar curse and that now erupted in all their historical fury. Refugees from the strife-torn regions flooded into Western Europe. The sturdy German economy, the foundation of European prosperity, wobbled under the awesome burden of absorbing a technologically backward, physically decrepit communist East Germany. The stability of

The End of the Cold War Changes the Map of Europe

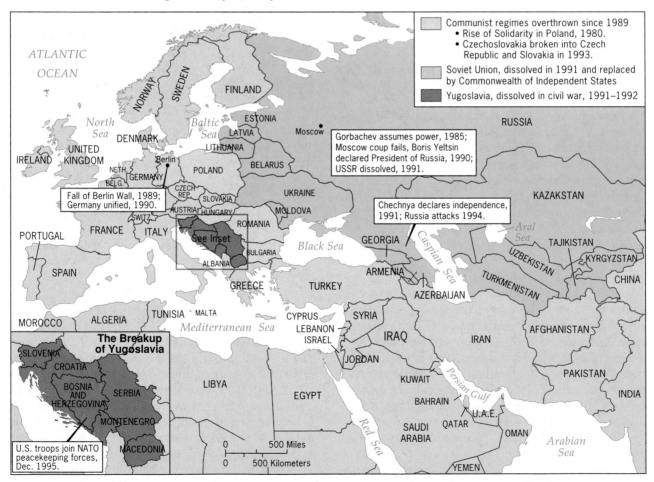

The Agony of Yugoslavia, 1992
These Bosnian refugees from the town of Jajce illustrated the plight of millions of Yugoslavians as their country slid into vicious interethnic battles in the wake of the Cold War's conclusion.

the entire European continent seemed at risk. The Western democracies, which for more than four decades had feared the military *strength* of the Eastern bloc, now ironically saw their well-being threatened by the social and economic *weakness* of the former communist lands.

The end of the Cold War also proved a mixed blessing for the United States. For nearly half a century, the containment of Soviet communism had been the paramount goal of U.S. foreign policy. Indeed the Cold War era had been the only lengthy period in American history when the United States had consistently pursued an internationalist foreign policy. With the Soviet threat now canceled, would the United States revert to its traditional isolationism? What principles would guide American diplomacy now that "anticommunism" had lost its relevance?

The Soviet-American rivalry, with its demands for high levels of military preparedness, had also deeply shaped and even invigorated the U.S. economy. Huge economic sectors such as aerospace were heavily sustained by military contracts. The economic cost of beating swords into plowshares became painfully apparent in 1991 when the Pentagon announced the closing of thirty-four military bases and canceled a $52 billion order for a navy attack plane. More closings and cancellations followed. Communities that had been drenched with Pentagon dollars now nearly dried up, especially in hard-hit southern California, where scores of de-

fense plants shut their doors and unemployment soared. The problems of weaning the U.S. economy from its decades of dependence on defense spending tempered the euphoria of Americans as they welcomed the Cold War's long-awaited finale.

Elsewhere in the world, democracy marched triumphantly forward. The white regime in South Africa took a giant step toward liberating that troubled land from its racist past when in 1990 it freed African leader Nelson Mandela, who had served twenty-seven years in prison for conspiring to overthrow the government. Four years later Mandela was elected South Africa's president. Free elections in Nicaragua in February 1990 removed the leftist Sandinistas from power. Two years later, peace came at last to war-ravaged El Salvador.

The Persian Gulf Crisis

Sadly, the end of the Cold War did not mean the end of all wars. President Bush flexed the United States' still-intimidating military muscle in tiny Panama in December 1989, when he sent airborne troops to capture dictator and drug lord Manuel Noriega.

Still more ominous events in the summer of 1990 severely tested Bush's dream of a democratic and peaceful new world order. On August 2 Saddam Hussein, the brutal and ambitious ruler of Iraq, sent his armies to overrun Kuwait, a tiny, oil-rich desert sheikdom on Iraq's southern frontier.

Oil fueled Saddam's aggression. Financially exhausted by its eight-year war with Iran that had ended in stalemate in 1988, Iraq needed Kuwait's oil to pay its huge war bills. Saddam's larger design was iron-fisted control over the entire Persian Gulf region. With his hand thus firmly clutching the world's economic jugular vein, he dreamed of dictating the terms of oil supplies to the industrial nations, and perhaps of totally extinguishing the Arabs' enemy, Israel.

Ironically, the United States and its allies had helped supply Saddam with the tools of aggression. He was widely known to be a thug and assassin who intimidated his underlings by showing them the bodies of his executed adversaries hanging on meathooks. But in the 1980s, American enmity for Islamic-fundamentalist Iran was intense, and Saddam was at war with Iran. Assuming that "the enemy of my enemy is my friend," American policymakers aided Iraq's war against Iran. In the process they helped build Saddam's military machine into one of the world's largest and most dangerous.

This formidable force, some 100,000 strong, roared into Kuwait on August 2, 1990. Soon Iraq had nearly half a million men in the field, and Saddam announced that he was annexing Kuwait as Iraq's "nineteenth province," disregarding Iraq's formal recognition of Kuwait's independence as recently as 1962.

The swiftness and audacity of the Iraqi invasion of Kuwait was stunning, but the world responded just as swiftly. The U.N. Security Council unanimously condemned the invasion on August 3, 1990, and demanded the immediate and unconditional withdrawal of Iraq's troops. Three days later the Security Council ordered an economic embargo against Iraq, designed to squeeze the aggressor into compliance with international law. After months went by with no sign of Iraqi willingness to withdraw, the Security Council on November 29, 1990, delivered an ultimatum to Saddam: leave Kuwait by January 15, 1991, or U.N. forces would "use all necessary means" to expel Iraq. For perhaps the first time in the post–World War II era, the United Nations seemed to be fulfilling its founders' dreams that it could preserve international order by putting guns where its mouth was.

In a logistical operation of astonishing complexity, meanwhile, the United States spearheaded a massive international military deployment on the sandy Arabian peninsula. As the January 15 deadline approached, some 539,000 U.S. soldiers, sailors, and pilots—many of them women and all of them members of the new, post-Vietnam, all-volunteer American military—had swarmed into the Persian Gulf region. They were joined by nearly 270,000 troops, pilots, and sailors from twenty-eight other countries in the coalition opposed to Iraq. When all diplomatic efforts to resolve the crisis failed, the U.S. Congress voted regretfully on January 12 to approve the use of force. The time bomb of war now ticked off its final few beats.

Fighting "Operation Desert Storm"

On January 16, 1991, the United States and its U.N. allies unleashed a hellish air war against Iraq. For thirty-seven days, warplanes pummeled targets in occupied Kuwait and in Iraq itself. Computerized fighter-bomber cockpits helped pilots fire "smart" bombs that homed in with astonishing accuracy. Air-launched, laser-guided rockets blasted Iraqi tanks and even flew right through the doors of fortified aircraft hangars. The air campaign constituted an awesome display of high-technology, precision-targeting modern warfare. Yet the Iraqis claimed, probably rightly, that civilians were nevertheless killed.

Iraq responded to this pounding by launching several dozen "Scud" short-range ballistic missiles against military and civilian targets in Saudi Arabia and Israel. These missile attacks claimed several lives but did no significant military damage.

Yet if Iraq made but a feeble military response to the air campaign, the allied commander, the beefy and blunt American general Norman ("Stormin' Norman") Schwarzkopf, took nothing for granted. Saddam, who had threatened to wage "the mother of all battles," had the capacity to inflict awful damage. Iraq had stockpiled tons of chemical and biological weapons, including poison gas and the means to spread epidemics of anthrax, and Iraq might use them at any minute.* The Iraqis had dug themselves deeply into their desert fortifications,

---

*Allegations persisted after the war that coalition troops suffering from a mysterious "Gulf War syndrome," including extreme fatigue and skin rashes, had been exposed to Saddam's chemical arsenal when they had detonated certain of his sprawling ammunition depots.

surrounding their positions with oil-filled moats that could be set aflame as attackers approached. Saddam's tactics also included ecological warfare as he released a gigantic oil slick into the Persian Gulf to forestall amphibious assault and ignited hundreds of oil-well fires whose smoky plumes shrouded the ground from aerial view. Faced with these horrifying tactics, Schwarzkopf's strategy was starkly simple: soften the Iraqis with relentless bombing, then suffocate them on the ground with a tidal-wave rush of troops and armor.

On February 23 the dreaded and long-awaited land war began. Dubbed "Operation Desert Storm," it lasted only four days—the "hundred-hour war." With the Iraqi air forces grounded or destroyed, Schwarzkopf had secretly moved a huge force far across the desert to the extreme western end of the Iraqi fortifications. With lightning speed it penetrated deep into Iraq, outflanking the occupying forces in Kuwait and blocking the enemy's ability either to retreat or to reinforce. Allied casualties were amazingly light, whereas much of Iraq's remaining fighting force was quickly destroyed or captured. On February 27 Saddam accepted a cease-fire, and Kuwait was liberated.

Most Americans cheered the war's rapid and enormously successful conclusion. Some, remembering the antiwar movement of the 1960s, had protested against going to war. But the end had come so suddenly and decisively that antiwar sentiment on a large scale never crystallized. And unlike the forlorn veterans of Vietnam who had straggled

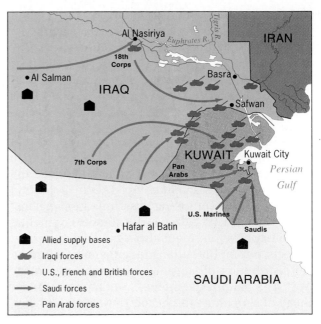

Operation Desert Storm: The Ground War, February 23–27, 1991

back to their embittered and disillusioned homeland, the troops from Operation Desert Storm returned home to enthusiastic heroes' welcomes.

The war had nevertheless failed to dislodge Saddam from power. When the smoke cleared, he had survived to menace the world another day. The perpetually troubled Middle East knew scarcely less trouble after Desert Storm had ceased to thunder,

The Hundred-Hour War
In what some have called a lightning victory, the U.N. allies' fighting men and women reduced Saddam's military machine, the fourth-largest army in the world, to wreckage and rubble.

and the United States, for better or worse, found itself even more deeply ensnared in the region's web of mortal hatreds and intractable conflicts.

Bush on the Home Front

In his inaugural address, George Bush pledged that he would work for a "kinder, gentler America." He redeemed that promise in part when he signed the Americans with Disabilities Act (ADA) in 1990, a landmark law prohibiting discrimination against the 43 million U.S. citizens with physical or mental disabilities. The president also signed a major water projects bill in 1992 that fundamentally reformed the distribution of subsidized federal water in the West. The bill put the interests of the environment ahead of agriculture, especially in California's heavily irrigated Central Valley, and made much more water available to the West's thirsty cities.

The new president continued to aggravate the explosive "social issues" that had so divided Americans throughout the 1980s, especially the nettlesome questions of affirmative action and abortion. In 1990 Bush's Department of Education challenged the legality of college scholarships targeted for racial minorities. Bush repeatedly threatened to veto civil rights legislation that would make it easier for employees to prove discrimination in hiring and promotion practices. (He grudgingly accepted a watered-down civil rights bill in 1991.)

Most provocatively, in 1991 Bush nominated for the Supreme Court the conservative African-American jurist Clarence Thomas. A stern critic of affirmative-action policies, Thomas was slated to fill a seat vacated by the retirement of Thurgood Marshall, the Court's lone black justice and an outspoken champion of civil rights.

Thomas's nomination was loudly opposed by liberal groups, including organized labor, the National Association for the Advancement of Colored People (NAACP), and the National Organization for Women (NOW), which objected to Thomas's presumed opposition to abortion rights—though the nominee studiously refrained from publicly commenting on the landmark abortion case of *Roe* v. *Wade,* claiming, incredibly, that he had never thought about it or discussed it.

Reflecting irreconcilable divisions over affirmative action and abortion, the Senate Judiciary Committee concluded its hearings on the nomination with a divided 7–7 vote and forwarded the matter to the full Senate without a recommendation. Then, just days before the Senate was scheduled to vote in early October 1991, someone leaked to the press that Anita Hill, a law professor at the University of Oklahoma, had submitted an affidavit to the committee alleging that Thomas had sexually harassed her when she had worked in his office some ten years earlier. The public outcry at this allegation forced the Senate Judiciary Committee to reopen its hearings. For days, a prurient American public sat glued to their television sets as Hill graphically detailed her charges of sexual improprieties and Thomas angrily responded. Although Hill passed a lie detector test, thirteen other female colleagues of Thomas testified that they had never witnessed any improper behavior. In the end, by a 52–48 vote, the Senate narrowly confirmed Thomas as the second African-American ever to sit on the supreme bench. Hill's charges had failed to block Thomas's nomination, but many Americans hailed her as a heroine for her role in focusing the nation's attention on issues of sexual harassment. (Oregon's Republican senator Robert Packwood was among the most prominent officials to fall victim to the new sexual etiquette when he was forced to resign from the Senate in 1995 after charges that he had sexually harassed several women.) Thomas maintained that Hill's widely publicized, unproved allegations amounted to "a high-tech lynching for uppity blacks who in any way deign to think for themselves, to do for themselves."

The furor over Clarence Thomas's confirmation suggested that the social issues that had helped produce three Republican presidential victories in the 1980s were losing some of their electoral appeal. Many women, enraged by the all-male judiciary committee's behavior in the Clarence Thomas hearings, grew increasingly critical of the president's uncompromising stand on abortion. A "gender gap" opened between the two political parties, as pro-choice women grew increasingly cool toward the strong anti-abortion stand of the Republicans.

Still more damaging to President Bush's political health, the economy sputtered and stalled almost from the outset of his administration. By 1992 the unemployment rate exceeded 7 percent. It approached 10 percent in the key state of California, ravaged by defense cutbacks. The federal budget deficit continued to mushroom cancerously, top-

Justice Clarence Thomas   Despite vivid allegations of sexual impropriety by law professor Anita Hill, Thomas was confirmed by the Senate in 1991 as the second African-American to serve on the Supreme Court (the other was former NAACP counsel Thurgood Marshall, who retired in 1991).

Professor Anita Hill Testifies Against Supreme Court Nominee Clarence Thomas, October 11, 1991
Her testimony failed to stop his confirmation, but did sensitize the country to issues of sexual harassment.

ping $250 billion in each of Bush's years as president. In a desperate attempt to stop the hemorrhage of red ink, Bush agreed in 1990 to a budget agreement with Congress that included $133 billion in new taxes.

Bush's 1990 tax and budget package added up to a political catastrophe. In his 1988 presidential campaign, Bush had belligerently declared, "Read my lips—no new taxes." Now he had flagrantly broken that campaign promise.

The intractable budgetary crisis and the stagnant economy congealed in a lump of disgust with all political incumbents. Disillusion thickened in 1991 when it was revealed that many members of the House of Representatives had written thousands of bad checks from their accounts in a private House "bank." Although no taxpayers' money was involved, the image of privileged politicians incompetently managing their private business affairs, with no penalty, even while they were grossly mis-

managing the Republic's finances, further soured the voters. A movement to impose limits on the number of terms that elected officials could serve gained strength in many states. Sniffing this prevailing wind, unprecedented numbers of officeholders announced that they would not stand for reelection.

In a further manifestation of robust anti-incumbentism, the Twenty-seventh Amendment to the Constitution was ratified in 1992. It prohibited congressional pay raises from taking effect until an election had seated a new session of Congress. First proposed by James Madison in 1789, the amendment had long languished along the road to ratification. Only eight states had passed it in the 189 years down to 1978. But debate over a congressional pay hike in the 1980s stimulated more than thirty states to approve the amendment between 1983 and 1992. Despite objections that the two-century-long ratification process violated the principle of

READ MY NOSE...

NO NEW TAXES

ROTHCO

KIRK

©1990 THE (TOLEDO) BLADE

Read My Nose   When President Bush reneged on his 1988 campaign promise of "no new taxes," he inflicted mortal political damage on his reelection campaign in 1992.

contemporaneous consideration by the states, the amendment was incorporated into the Constitution on May 18, 1992.

Bill Clinton: The First Baby-Boomer President

The slumbering economy, the widening gender gap, and the rising anti-incumbent spirit spelled opportunity for Democrats, frozen out of the White House for all but four years since 1968. In a bruising round of primary elections, Governor William Jefferson Clinton of Arkansas weathered blistering accusations of womanizing and draft evasion to emerge as his party's standard-bearer. Breaking with the tradition of a "balanced ticket," he selected a fellow fortysomething southern white male Protestant moderate, Senator Albert Gore of Tennessee, as his vice-presidential running mate.

Clinton claimed to be a "new" Democrat, chastened by the party's long exile in the political wilderness. Spurred especially by Walter Mondale's galling defeat at the hands of Ronald Reagan in 1984, Clinton and other centrist Democrats had formed the Democratic Leadership Council to point the party away from its traditional antibusiness, dovish, champion-of-the-underdog orientation and toward progrowth, strong defense, and anticrime policies.

Clinton campaigned especially vigorously on promises to stimulate the economy, reform the welfare system, and overhaul the nation's health-care apparatus, which had grown into a scandalously expensive contraption that failed to provide medical coverage to some 37 million Americans.

Trying to wring one more win out of the social issues that had underwritten two Reagan and one Bush presidential victories, the Republican convention in Houston in August 1992 dwelt stridently on "family values" and, as expected, nominated George Bush and Vice President J. Danforth Quayle for a second term. A tired and apparently dispirited Bush then took to the campaign trail. His listless performances and spaghetti sentences set him sharply apart from his youthful rival, the superenergetic, articulate Clinton. Bush half-heartedly attacked Clinton's character, contrasting the Arkansan's evasion of military service in the Vietnam War with his own heroic record as a navy flier in World War II. The president seemed to campaign more for vindication in the history books than for victory in the election. He tried to take credit for the end of the Cold War and trumpeted his leadership role in the Persian Gulf War.

But fear for the economic problems of the future swayed more voters than pride in the foreign policies of the past. The purchasing power of the average worker's paycheck had actually declined during Bush's presidency. At Clinton's campaign headquarters, a simple sign reminded staffers of his principal campaign theme: "It's the economy, stupid." Reflecting pervasive economic unease and the virulence of the throw-the-bums-out national mood, nearly 20 percent of voters cast their ballots for independent presidential candidate H. Ross Perot, a bantam-weight, jug-eared Texas billionaire who harped incessantly on the problem of the federal deficit and made a boast of the fact that he had never held any public office.

Perot's colorful presence probably accounted for the record turnout on election day, when some 100 million voters—55 percent of those eligible—went to the polls. The final tallies gave Clinton 43,728,275 popular votes and 370 votes in the Electoral College. He was the first baby boomer to ascend to the White House, a distinction reflecting the electoral profile of a population 70 percent of whom had been born after World War II. Bush polled some 38,167,416 popular and 168 electoral votes. Perot won no Electoral College votes but did gather 19,237,247 in the popular count—the strongest showing for an independent or third-party candidate since Theodore Roosevelt ran on the Bull Moose ticket in 1912. Democrats also racked up clear majorities in both houses of Congress, which seated near-record numbers of new members, including thirty-nine African-Americans, nineteen Hispanic-Americans, seven Asian-Americans, one

Presidential Campaign Debate, 1992   George Bush, Ross Perot, and Bill Clinton squared off at the University of Richmond (Virginia) on October 16, 1992. The telegenic Clinton handily dominated the television debates, especially in the "talk-show" format used on this occasion.

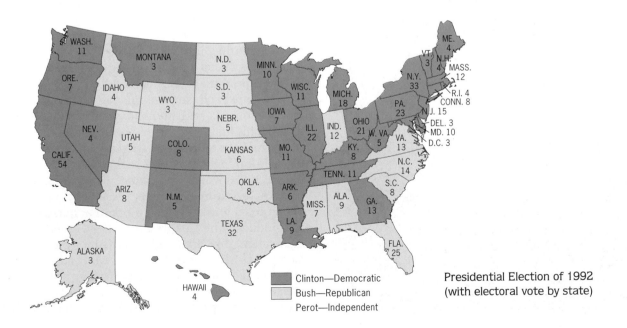

Clinton—Democratic
Bush—Republican
Perot—Independent

Presidential Election of 1992
(with electoral vote by state)

Native American, and forty-eight women. In Illinois Carol Moseley Braun became the first African-American woman elected to the U.S. Senate, where she joined five other women in the largest female contingent ever in the upper chamber.

Women also figured prominently in President Clinton's cabinet, including the first female attorney general, Janet Reno, and former Wisconsin University president Donna Shalala, who became the secretary of health and human services. Vowing to shape a government that "looked like America," Clinton appointed several ethnic and racial minority members to his cabinet contingent, including former San Antonio mayor Henry Cisneros at Housing and Urban Development and an African-American, Ron Brown, as secretary of commerce. Clinton also seized the opportunity in 1993 to nominate Ruth Bader Ginsburg to the Supreme Court, where she joined Sandra Day O'Connor to make a pair of women justices.

A False Start for Reform

Badly overestimating his electoral mandate for liberal reform, the young president made a series of costly blunders upon entering the White House. In one of his first initiatives on taking office, he stirred a hornet's nest of controversy by advocating an end to the ban on gays and lesbians in the armed services. Faced with ferocious opposition, the president finally had to settle for a "don't ask, don't tell" policy that quietly accepted gay and lesbian soldiers and sailors without officially acknowledging their presence in the military.

Even more damaging to Clinton's political standing, and to his hopes for lasting liberal achievement, was the fiasco of his attempt to reform the nation's health-care system. In a dramatic but personally and politically risky innovation, the president appointed his wife, nationally prominent lawyer and child-advocate Hillary Rodham Clinton, as the director of a task force charged with redesigning the medical-service industry. After months of highly publicized hearings and scrappy planning sessions, the task force unveiled its stupefyingly complicated plan in October 1993. Critics immediately blasted the cumbersome, convoluted proposal, which was virtually dead on arrival in Congress, where it was finally buried one year later. As the reform plan's principal architect, the First Lady was doused with a torrent of abuse. She had entered the White House as a full political partner with her husband, sharing the national spotlight as no previous First Lady had done. But midway through his first term she had become a political liability and sidestepped quietly to the shadows.

Clinton had better luck with a deficit-reduction bill in 1993, which combined with a moderately buoyant economy by 1996 to shrink the federal deficit to its lowest level in more than a decade. He also induced the Congress in 1993 to pass a gun-control law, the "Brady Bill," named for presidential aide James Brady, who had been wounded and disabled by gunfire in the assassination attempt on President Ronald Reagan in 1981. In July of 1994, Clinton made further progress against the national

The Ghosts of Presidents Past, 1993   In this fanciful portrait of President Bill Clinton's inauguration, past presidents listen attentively as the new chief executive gives his inaugural address.

plague of firearms when he persuaded Congress to pass a $30 billion anticrime bill, which contained a ban on several types of assault weapons.

With these measures the government struggled to hold the line against an epidemic of violence that rocked American society in the 1990s. A radical Muslim group bombed New York's World Trade Center in 1993, killing six people. A still larger blast destroyed a federal office building in Oklahoma City, Oklahoma, in 1995, taking 169 lives, presumably in retribution for a 1993 stand-off in Waco, Texas, between federal agents and a fundamentalist sect known as the Branch Davidians. That showdown ended in the destruction of the sect's compound and the deaths of many Branch Davidians, including women and children. All these episodes brought to light a lurid and secretive underground of paramilitary private "militias," composed of alienated citizens armed to the teeth and ultrasuspicious of all governments.

Even many law-abiding citizens shared to some degree in the antigovernment attitudes that drove the militia members to murderous extremes. Thanks largely to the disillusioning agony of the Vietnam War and the naked cynicism of Richard Nixon in the Watergate scandal, the confidence in government that had come naturally to the generation that licked the Great Depression and won the Second World War was in short supply by the century's end. Reflecting that pervasive disenchantment with politics and politicians, some twenty-three states had imposed restrictions on elected officials with term-limit laws by the mid-1990s, though the Supreme Court ruled in 1995 that such laws did not apply to federal officeholders.

The Politics of Distrust

Clinton's failed initiatives and widespread antigovernment sentiment offered conservative Republicans a golden opportunity in 1994, and they seized it aggressively. Led by outspoken Georgia representative Newt Gingrich, conservatives offered voters a "Contract with America" that promised an all-out assault on budget deficits and radical reductions in welfare programs. Liberal Democrats countered that the conservative pledge should be called a "Contract *on* America," but their protests were drowned in the right-wing tornado that roared across the land in the 1994 congressional elections. Every incumbent Republican gubernatorial, senatorial, and congressional candidate was reelected. Republicans also picked up eleven new governorships, eight seats in the Senate, and fifty-three seats in the House (where Gingrich became Speaker), giving them control of both chambers of the federal Congress for the first time in forty years.

But if President Clinton had overplayed his mandate for liberal reform in 1993, the congressional Republicans now proceeded to overplay their mandate for conservative retrenchment. The new Republican majority did legislate one long-standing conservative goal when they restricted "unfunded mandates"—federal laws that imposed new obligations on state and local governments without providing new revenues. And in 1996 the new Congress achieved a major conservative victory when it compelled a reluctant Clinton to sign a welfare-reform bill that made deep cuts in welfare grants, and required able-bodied welfare recipients to find employment. The new welfare law also tightly restricted welfare benefits for legal and illegal immigrants alike, reflecting a rising tide of anti-immigrant sentiment as the numbers of newcomers climbed toward an all-time high. Old-line liberal Democrats howled with pain at the president's alleged betrayal of his party's heritage, and some prominent administration members resigned in protest against his decision to sign the welfare bill. But Clinton's acceptance of the welfare reform package was part of his shrewd political strategy of accommodating the electorate's conservative mood by moving to his right.

President Clinton was at first stunned by the magnitude of the Republican congressional victory in 1994. For a time he was reduced to lamely reminding Congress that the president was still relevant to the political and policy-making process. But many Americans gradually came to feel that the Gingrich Republicans were bending their conservative bow too far, especially when the new Speaker advocated provocative ideas like sending the children of welfare families to orphanages. In a tense confrontation between the Democratic president and the Republican Congress, the federal government actually had to shut down for several days at the end of 1995, until a budget package was agreed upon. These outlandishly ideological provocations and outrageously partisan antics bred a backlash that threatened to deny the Republicans the ultimate political prize for which they lusted in 1996: the White House.

As the presidential election approached, Clinton looked like a dead duck, but thanks to a marvelously efficient presidential fund-raising effort, no serious Democratic challenger emerged to contest for the party's nomination. The Republicans meanwhile slugged it out in a noisy round of primaries, and eventually nominated the Senate majority leader, Kansas senator Bob Dole, a wounded veteran of World War II. A skeletal Reform party, in actuality little more than the personal organization of Texas billionaire and 1992 presidential wanna-be H. Ross Perot, obediently nominated its egomaniacal founder. Dole ran a listless, dispirited campaign that amounted to a pathetic last hurrah for his proud World War II generation. Clinton, buoyed by a healthy economy and by his artful trimming to the conservative wind, breezed to an easy victory, with 45,628,667 popular votes to Dole's 37,869,435. Perot ran a sorry third, picking up less than half the number of votes he had managed to win in 1992, and not a single vote in the Electoral College. Dole was victorious in only eleven states; Clinton garnered all the rest, winning 379 electoral votes to Dole's 159.

Problems Abroad

Absorbed with domestic issues, President Clinton at first seemed uncertain and even amateurish in his conduct of foreign policy. He followed his predecessor's lead in dispatching American troops as part of a peacekeeping mission to Somalia, in Africa's eastern horn, and reinforced the U.S. contingent after Somali rebels killed more than a dozen Americans in late 1993. But in March 1994 the president quietly withdrew the American units, without having accomplished any clearly defined goal. To the discomfiture of the British, Clinton also meddled in the achingly stubborn conflict between the Protestant majority and the Catholic minority in Northern Ireland, but to no very evident effect.

A similar lack of clarity and even inconsistency beset American policy in other parts of the globe. Candidate Clinton had denounced George Bush in 1992 for not imposing economic sanctions on China as punishment for Beijing's wretched record of human rights abuses. But President Clinton soon learned what President Bush had long known: that

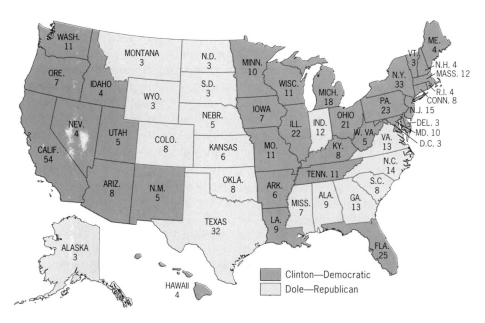

The Presidential Election of 1996 (with electoral vote by state)   The "solid South," once a safe Democratic stronghold, had by century's end largely become Republican territory.

China's economic importance to the United States did not permit Washington the luxury of taking the high road on human rights issues. Clinton soon soft-pedaled his criticism of the Beijing regime and instead began seeking improved trade relations with that rapidly industrializing country and potential market bonanza. In the former Yugoslavia, as vicious ethnic conflict burned through Bosnia, the Washington government dithered until finally deciding to commit American troops to a NATO peacekeeping contingent in late 1995. Comparable indecision afflicted policy toward Haiti, where democratically elected president Jean-Bertrand Aristide had been deposed by a military coup in 1991. Clinton at last committed twenty thousand American troops to return Aristide to the Haitian presidency in 1994, after thousands of desperate Haitian refugees had sought asylum in the United States.

On some foreign matters Clinton displayed conviction and even political courage. He resolutely supported the North American Free Trade Agreement (NAFTA), creating a free-trade zone encompassing Mexico, Canada, and the United States. In so doing he reversed his own stand in the 1992 election campaign and bucked the opposition of many people in his own party, especially labor leaders fearful of losing jobs to low-wage Mexican workers. The NAFTA was signed at last in November 1993, and a year later Chile was invited to join. Chile's membership in the NAFTA was perhaps a stepping-stone toward the possible creation of a Free Trade Area of the Americas that would embrace the entire Western Hemisphere. Clinton took another step in 1994 toward a global free-trade system when he vigorously promoted the creation of the World Trade Organization, the successor to the General Agreement on Tariffs and Trade (GATT), and a cherished goal of free-trade advocates since the end of the Second World War. Clinton also put the government's money where its mouth was when he overrode congressional objections in 1995 and provided $20 billion in temporary aid to the faltering Mexican economy—a bet that paid off quickly, as Mexico began rapidly putting its financial house in order as part of its commitment to the NAFTA process.

Clinton also presided over a historic reconciliation between Israelis and Palestinians in late 1993, when Israeli premier Yitzhak Rabin and Palestinian Liberation Organization leader Yasir Arafat met at the White House and agreed in principle on self-rule for the Palestinians within Israel. But hopes for peace in the perpetually troubled Middle East flickered some two years later when Rabin fell to an assassin's bullet, presumably in retaliation for his peaceful overtures to the Palestinians.

A Sea of Troubles

The end of the Cold War robbed the United States of the basic principles on which it had conducted foreign policy for nearly half a century, and Clinton groped for a diplomatic formula to replace anticommunism as the guiding mechanism in America's foreign affairs. The Cold War's finale also shook a number of skeletons loose from several government closets. Sensational revelations about misconduct in the Central Intelligence Agency and the FBI rattled official Washington when it was disclosed that double-agents had sold secrets to the Soviets during the Cold War years, resulting in the execution of American agents abroad and serious damage to American national security. The political fallout from these lethal shenanigans demonstrated that the ghost of Cold War past continued to cast its frosty shadow over Washington.

The president's own past, meanwhile, refused to go away. Allegations of flagrant womanizing continued to dog him, and even found fictional expression in a runaway 1996 best-seller, *Primary Colors*, whose author, political reporter Joe Klein, cleverly kept his identity a secret for months in a marvel of marketing acuity. More seriously, federal prosecutors pressed ahead with investigations of alleged improprieties in the Clinton's prepresidential involvement with a failed real estate investment known as the Whitewater Land Corporation. Suspicions were especially aroused by the death from apparent suicide in 1993 of White House counsel and close Clinton associate Vincent W. Foster, Jr., who had handled many of the Clintons' legal and financial affairs. Repeated presidential denials of wrongdoing evoked cynical ho-hums from a jaded public.

As Clinton began his second term—the first Democrat since Franklin Roosevelt to be reelected—he once again composed a diversified cabinet, but the heady promises of far-reaching reform with which he had entered the White House four years earlier were no longer heard. Clinton faced Republican majorities in both houses of Congress and a skeptical electorate utterly disenchanted with politics as usual, and with politicians. Curiously, many voters told pollsters in 1996 that they voted for Clinton even though they disbelieved him on many matters and held him in low personal esteem. In a stunning commentary on the demythologizing of the American presidency, many Americans expressed the hope that their children would *not* grow up to be president. If distrust is fatal to the fragile tissue of democracy, these disturbing symptoms pointed to a seriously unhealthy republic.

Chronology

1980	Reagan defeats Carter for presidency
1981	Iran releases American hostages "Reaganomics" spending and tax cuts passed Solidarity movement in Poland O'Connor appointed to Supreme Court (first woman justice)
1981–1991	United States aids antileftist forces in Central America
1982	Recession hits U.S. Economy
1983	Reagan announces SDI plan (Star Wars) U.S. Marines killed in Lebanon U.S. invasion of Grenada
1984	Reagan defeats Mondale for presidency
1985	Gorbachev comes to power in Soviet Union First Reagan-Gorbachev summit meeting, in Geneva
1986	Reagan administration backs Aquino in Philippines Iran-contra scandal revealed Second Reagan-Gorbachev summit meeting, in Reykjavik, Iceland
1987	Senate rejects Supreme Court nomination of Robert Bork U.S. naval escorts begin in Persian Gulf 508-point stock-market plunge Third Reagan-Gorbachev summit meeting, in Washington, D.C.; INF Treaty signed
1988	Fourth Reagan-Gorbachev summit meeting, in Moscow Bush defeats Dukakis for the presidency
1989	Chinese government suppresses prodemocracy demonstrators *Webster* v. *Reproductive Health Services* Eastern Europe throws off communist regimes Berlin Wall torn down
1990	Iraq invades Kuwait East and West Germany reunite Americans with Disabilities Act (ADA)
1991	Persian Gulf War Thomas appointed to Supreme Court Gorbachev resigns as Soviet president Soviet Union dissolves; republics form Commonwealth of Independent States
1992	Twenty-seventh Amendment (prohibiting congressional pay raises from taking effect until an election seats a new session of Congress) *Planned Parenthood* v. *Casey* Clinton defeats Bush and Perot for presidency
1993	NAFTA signed
1994	Republicans win majorities in both houses of Congress
1996	Welfare reform bill becomes law Clinton defeats Dole for presidency

Where Did Modern Conservatism Come From?

Ronald Reagan's election surprised many historians. Reflecting a liberal political outlook that is common among academic scholars, they were long accustomed to understanding American history as an inexorable, almost evolutionary, unfolding of liberal principles, including the quests for economic equality, social justice, and active government. That point of view animated the enormously popular writings of the so-called progressive historians, such as Charles and Mary Beard, earlier in the century (See Chapter 28, Varying Viewpoints: The Populists: Radicals or Reactionaries?). For the Beards, "conservatives" were the rich, privileged elites bent on preserving their wealth and power and determined to keep government impotent, but doomed in the end to give way to the forces of liberal democracy.

Even the "New Left" revisionists of the 1960s, while critical of the celebratory tone of their progressive forebears, were convinced that the deepest currents of American history flowed leftward. But whether they were liberal or revisionist, most scholars writing in the first three post–World War II decades dismissed conservatism as an obsolete political creed. The revisionists were much more interested in decrying liberalism's deficiencies than in analyzing conservatism's strengths. Liberals and revisionists alike abandoned the Beards' image of powerful conservative elites and offered instead a contemptuous portrait of conservatives as fringe wackos—paranoid McCarthyites or racist demagogues who, in the words of the liberal critic Lionel Trilling, trafficked only in "irritable mental gestures which seem to resemble ideas." Such an outlook is conspicuous in books like Daniel Bell, ed., *The Radical Right* (1963), and Richard Hofstadter, *The Paranoid Style in American Politics* (1965).

But what flowed out of the turbulent decade of the 1960s was not a strengthened liberalism, but a revived conservatism. Ronald Reagan's huge political success compelled a thorough reexamination of the tradition of American conservatism, and the sources of its modern resurgence.

Historians including Leo Ribuffo and Alan Brinkley have argued that characters once dismissed as irrational crackpots or colorful irrelevancies—including religious fundamentalists and depression-era figures like Huey Long and Father Charles Coughlin—articulated values deeply rooted and widely shared in American culture. Those conservative spokespersons, whatever their peculiarities, offered a vision of free individuals, minimal government, and autonomous local communities that harkened back to many of the themes of "civic republicanism" in the era of young nationhood.

But modern conservatism, however deep its roots, is also a product of the recent historical past. As scholars like Thomas Sugrue and Thomas Edsall have shown, the economic stagnation that set in after 1970 made many Americans insecure about their futures and receptive to new political doctrines. At the same time, as the commentator Kevin Phillips has stressed, "social issues," with little or no apparent economic content, became increasingly prominent, as movements for sexual liberation, abortion on demand, and women's rights sharply challenged traditional beliefs. Perhaps most importantly, the success of the civil rights movement thrust the perpetually agonizing question of race relations to the very center of American political life. Finally, the failure of government policies in Vietnam, runaway inflation in the 1970s, as well as the disillusioning Watergate episode, cast doubt on the legitimacy, efficacy, and even the morality of "big government."

Many modern conservatives, including the pundit George Will, stress the deep historical roots of American conservatism. In their view, as

Will once put it, it took sixteen years to count the ballots from the 1964 (Goldwater versus Johnson) election, and Goldwater won after all. But that argument is surely overstated. Goldwater ran against the legacy of the New Deal, and was overwhelmingly defeated. Reagan ran against the consequences of the Great Society, and won decisively. Many conservatives, in short, apparently acknowledge the legitimacy of the New Deal and the stake that many middle-class Americans feel they have in its programs of Social Security, home mortgage subsidies, farm price supports, and similar policies. But they reject the philosophy of the Great Society with its more focused attack on urban poverty and its vigorous support for affirmative action. Modern conservatism springs less from a repudiation of government per se and more from a disapproval of the particular priorities and strategies of the Great Society. The different historical fates of the New Deal and the Great Society suggest the key to the rise of modern conservatism.

SUGGESTED READINGS

PRIMARY SOURCE DOCUMENTS

The debate over "Reaganomics" can be followed in Reagan's nationally televised address of July 27, 1981, *Weekly Compilation of Presidential Documents,* Vol. 17, no. 31* and in the critical response of *The New York Times,* August 2, 1981.* See also the comments of Budget Director David Stockman, in William Greider, *The Education of David Stockman and Other Americans* (1982). On arms control see the pastoral letter of the National Council of Catholic Bishops and the reply of Albert Wohlstetter in Charles Kegley and Eugene Wittkopf, eds., *The Nuclear Reader* (1985). On Central American policy, see Reagan's remarkable speech of March 16, 1986.* The inside workings of the Iran-contra scandal can be studied in *The Tower Commission Report* (1987).

SECONDARY SOURCES

Ronald Reagan is portrayed in Lou Cannon, *Reagan* (1982); Laurence Barrett, *Gambling with History* (1984); Fred Greenstein, *The Reagan Presidency* (1983); Michael Schaller, *Reckoning with Reagan* (1992); and Lou Cannon, *President Reagan: The Role of a Lifetime* (1992). Reagan's economic policies are discussed in Paul C. Roberts, *The Supply-Side Revolution* (1984), and are sharply criticized in David A. Stockman, *The Triumph of Politics: Why the Reagan Revolution Failed* (1986). Alter-

nate views on the economy can be found in Lester Thurow, *The Zero-Sum Society* (1981), and Samuel Bowles et al., *Beyond the Wasteland* (1984). The debate over nuclear policy is covered in R. James Woolsey, *Nuclear Arms* (1984); Strobe Talbott, *The Russians and Reagan* (1984); and Charles Kegley and Eugene Wittkopf, eds., *The Nuclear Reader* (1985). The neoconservative movement is best elucidated by the writings of its leaders. See Norman Podhoretz, *Breaking Ranks* (1979), and Irving Kristol, *Reflections of a Neoconservative* (1983). For a critical view, consult Peter Steinfels, *The Neoconservatives* (1979). Issues of special concern to the neoconservatives are treated by Charles Murray, *Losing Ground* (1984), an indictment of federal government social programs. Its conclusions are sharply contested by John E. Schwartz, *America's Hidden Success* (rev. ed., 1988). This debate is put into historical perspective in James T. Patterson, *America's Struggle Against Poverty, 1900–1980* (1981). Two studies of affirmative action are Allan P. Sindler, *Bakke, DeFinis and Minority Admissions* (1978), and J. Harvie Wilkinson, *From Brown to Bakke* (1979). The presidential election of 1980 is chronicled by Jules Witcover and Jack Germond in *Blue Smoke and Mirrors* (1981), and put into historical perspective in Theodore H. White, *America in Search of Itself* (1982). For more on conservatism in the last decades of the twentieth century, see William C. Berman, *America's Right Turn: From Nixon to Bush* (1994). Kevin P. Phillips is also insightful about the implications of the conservative revival in *Post-Conservative America* (1982). Eugene Genovese explores *The Southern Tradition: The Achievement and Limitations of an American Conservatism* (1994). Useful books on the role of religion in modern

---

*An asterisk indicates that the document, or an excerpt from it, can be found in Thomas A. Bailey and David M. Kennedy, eds., *The American Spirit: United States History as Seen by Contemporaries,* 9th ed. (Boston: Houghton Mifflin, 1998).

politics include Robert Booth Fowler, *A New Engagement: Evangelical Political Thought, 1966–1976* (1982); Robert Wuthrow, *The New Christian Right* (1983); and Richard John Neuhaus, *The Naked Public Square: Religion and Democracy in America* (1984). On the Supreme Court see Richard L. Pacelle, Jr., *The Transformation of the Supreme Court's Agenda: From the New Deal to the Reagan Administration* (1991). Critical of Reagan are William Leuchtenburg, *In the Shadow of FDR: From Harry Truman to Ronald Reagan* (1983); Paul D. Erickson, *Reagan Speaks: The Making of an American Myth* (1985); Garry Wills, *Reagan's America: Innocents at Home* (1987); Ronnie Duggar, *On Reagan* (1983); June Mayer and Doyle McManus, *Landslide: The Unmaking of the President, 1984–88* (1988); and Richard Reeves, *The Reagan Detour* (1985). More balanced are two books by John L. Palmer, *The Reagan Record* (co-edited with Isabel V. Sawhill, 1984) and *Perspectives on the Reagan Years* (1986). Among the interesting memoirs by Reagan administration officials, in addition to David Stockman's book, are Martin Anderson's strongly pro-Reagan *Revolution* (1989); Secretary of State Alexander Haig's *Caveat* (1984); press secretary Larry Speakes's *Speaking Out* (1988); Michael Deaver's anecdotal *Behind the Scenes* (1987); Donald R. Regan's tattletale *For the Record* (1988); and speech writer Peggy Noonan's somewhat bemused

What I Saw at the Revolution: A Political Life in the Reagan Era (1990). Important topics in foreign policy are covered in John Ehrman, *The Rise of Neoconservatism: Intellectuals and Foreign Affairs, 1945–1994* (1995); Walter LaFeber, *Inevitable Revolutions* (2d ed., 1984), which discusses Central America; Robert Pastor's more probing study, *Condemned to Repetition: The United States and Nicaragua* (1987); and Bob Woodward, *Veil: The Secret Wars of the CIA* (1987). Theodore Draper details the Iran-contra affair in *A Very Thin Line* (1991). In *The Devil We Knew: Americans and the Cold War* (1993), H.W. Brands attempts to calculate how much it cost the United States to win the Cold War. The legacy of the Reagan era is the subject of Kevin P. Phillips's devastating *The Politics of Rich and Poor: Wealth and the American Electorate in the Reagan Aftermath* (1990), and Barbara Ehrenreich, *The Worst Years of Our Lives: Irreverent Notes from a Decade of Greed* (1990). The Clarence Thomas/Anita Hill hearings of 1991 are discussed in Toni Morrison, ed., *Racing Justice, En-gendering Power* (1992). Bob Woodward, *The Agenda* (1994), and the same author's *The Choice* (1996) provide inside glimpses of politics in the Clinton years. On the precedent-shattering First Lady, see David Brock, *The Seduction of Hillary Rodham* (1996). James B. Stewart, *Blood Sport* (1996), is especially good on Clinton's complex relationship with the media.

44

The American People Face a New Century

As our case is new, so we must think anew and act anew. We must disenthrall ourselves, and then we shall save our country.

ABRAHAM LINCOLN, 1862

The Weight of History

More than two hundred years old as the twentieth century drew to a close, the United States was both an old and a new nation. It boasted one of the longest uninterrupted traditions of democratic government of any country on earth. Indeed, it had pioneered the techniques of mass democracy and was, in that sense, the oldest modern polity. As one of the earliest countries to industrialize, America had also dwelt in the modern economic era longer than most nations.

But the Republic was in many ways still youthful as well. Innovation, entrepreneurship, and risk-taking—all characteristics of youth—were honored national values. The twentieth century was ending as it began, with American society continuing to be rejuvenated by fresh waves of immigrants, full of energy and ambition. The U.S. economy, despite problems, was generating new jobs at a rate of some 2 million per year. American inventions—especially computer and communications technologies—were transforming the face of global society. The whole world seemed to worship the icons of American culture—downing soft drinks and donning blue jeans, watching Hollywood films, listening to rock or country-and-western music, even adopting indigenous American sports like baseball and basketball. In the realm of consumerism, American products appeared to have Coca-Colonized the globe.

The history of American society also seemed to have increased global significance as the third millennium of the Christian era opened. Americans were a pluralistic people who had struggled for centuries to provide opportunity and to achieve tolerance and justice for many different religious, ethnic, and racial groups. Their historical experience could offer valuable lessons to the rapidly internationalizing planetary society that was emerging at the dawn of the twenty-first century.

In politics, economics, and culture, the great social experiment of American democracy was far from completed as the United States faced its future. Much history remained to be made as the country entered its third century of nationhood. But men and women make history only within the framework bequeathed to them by earlier generations. For better or worse, they march forward along time's path bearing the burdens of the past. Knowing when they have come to a truly new turn in the road, when they can lay part of their burden down, and when they cannot, or should not—all this constitutes the sort of wisdom that only historical study can engender.

Economic Revolutions

When the twentieth century opened, United States Steel Corporation was the flagship business of America's booming industrial revolution. U.S. Steel was a typical "heavy industry," cranking out the ingots and girders and sheet metal that built the nation's basic physical infrastructure. A generation later, General Motors, annually producing millions of automobiles, became the characteristic American corporation, signaling the historic shift to a mass consumer economy that began in the 1920s and flowered fully in the 1950s. Following World War II, the rise of International Business Machines (IBM) symbolized yet another momentous transformation, to the fast-paced "information age," when the storing, organizing, and processing of data became an industry in its own right.

The pace of the information age soon accelerated. By century's end, the rapid emergence of Microsoft Corporation and the phenomenal growth of the Internet heralded an explosive communications revolution. Americans now rocketed down the "information superhighway" toward the uncharted terrain of an electronic global village, where traditional geographic, social, and political boundaries could be vaulted with the tap of a keypad.

The communications revolution was full of both promise and peril. In the blink of an eye, ordinary citizens could now gain access to information once available only to privileged elites with vast libraries or expert staffs at their disposal. Businesspeople now instantaneously girdled the planet with transactions of prodigious scope and serpentine complexity. Japanese bankers might sell wheat con-

tracts in Chicago and simultaneously direct the profits to buying oil shipments from the Persian Gulf offered by a broker in Amsterdam.

But the very speed and efficiency of the new communications tools threatened to wipe out entire occupational categories. Postal delivery people, travel agents, store clerks, bank tellers, stock brokers, and all kinds of other workers whose business it was to intermediate between product and client, might find themselves rendered obsolete in the era of the Internet. And as the computer makes possible "classrooms without walls," where students can pursue learning largely on their own, even teachers, whose job is essentially to mediate between students and various bodies of knowledge, might well end up as road-kill on the information superhighway.

Increasingly, scientific research was the engine that drove the economy, and new scientific knowledge posed new social and moral dilemmas. When scientists first unlocked the secrets of molecular genetic structure in the 1950s, the road lay open to breeding new strains of high-yield, pest- and

The University Without Walls Students getting their education from this facility at the Iowa Distance Learning Center need never enter a classroom.

Where in the World is the Teacher?   The computer and communications revolutions threatened to make age-old forms of instruction obsolete as the twentieth century reached its end.

weather-resistant crops; to curing hereditary diseases; and also, unfortunately, to unleashing genetic mutations that might threaten the fragile ecological balance of the wondrous biosphere in which humankind was delicately suspended. As technical mastery of biological and medical techniques advanced, unprecedented ethical questions clamored for resolution. Should the human gene pool itself be "engineered"? What principles should govern the allocation of human organs for lifesaving transplants, or of scarce dialysis machines, or of artificial hearts? Was it wise in the first place to spend money on such costly devices rather than devoting society's resources to improved sanitation, maternal and infant care, and nutritional and health education? Who was the rightful parent of a child born to a "surrogate mother" or conceived by artificial insemination? How, if at all, should society regulate the increasingly lengthy and often painful process of dying? What rules should guide efforts to clone human beings—or should such efforts even be attempted?

Affluence and Inequality

Americans were still an affluent people at the twentieth century's end. Median household income declined somewhat in the early 1990s, but rebounded slightly by the mid-1990s to about $34,000. Yet even those Americans with incomes below the government's official poverty level (defined in 1995 as $15,771 for a family of four) enjoyed a standard of living higher than that of two-thirds of the rest of humankind.

Americans were no longer the world's wealthiest people in the 1990s, as they had been in the quarter-century after World War II. Citizens of several other countries enjoyed higher average per capita incomes, and many nations boasted more equitable distributions of wealth. In an unsettling reversal of long-term trends in American society, during the last two decades of the twentieth century the rich were getting richer and the poor were getting poorer at accelerating rates. The richest 20 percent of Americans in the 1990s raked in nearly half the nation's income, whereas the poorest 20 percent received less than 4 percent of national income. The gap between rich and poor began to widen in the 1980s, and the rift grew wider still in the 1990s. That trend was evident in many industrial societies, but was most pronounced in the United States. Between 1968 and 1994 the share of the nation's income that flowed to the top 20 percent of its households swelled from 40 percent to nearly 47 percent. Even more striking, in the same period the top 5 percent of income receivers saw their share of the national income grow from about 15 percent to more than 20 percent.

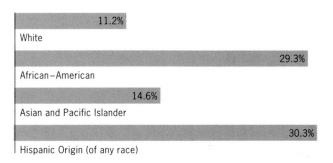

Poverty Rates of Americans by Race and Hispanic Origin, 1995   (U.S. Bureau of the Census, March Current Population Survey)

Two Nations? While decaying neighborhoods and the sad legions of the homeless blighted American urban life in the closing decades of the twentieth century, affluent Americans took refuge in gated communities like this one in the Brentwood section of Los Angeles.

Widening inequality could be measured in other ways as well: chief executives in the 1970s typically earned forty-one times the income of the average worker in their corporations; by the 1990s, they earned 225 times as much. At the same time, some 36 million people, 13.8 percent of all Americans (about 12 percent of whites, 29.3 percent of African-Americans, and just over 30 percent of Hispanics), remained mired in poverty—a depressing indictment of the inequities afflicting an affluent and allegedly egalitarian republic.

What caused the widening income gap? Some critics pointed to the tax and fiscal policies of the Reagan and Bush years, which favored the wealthy and penalized the poor. But deeper-running historical currents probably played a more powerful role, as suggested by the similar experiences of other industrialized societies. Among the most conspicuous causes were intensifying global economic competition; the shrinkage in high-paying manufacturing jobs for semiskilled and unskilled workers; the greater economic rewards commanded by edu-

cated workers in high-tech industries; the decline of unions; the growth of part-time and temporary work; the rising tide of relatively low-skill immigrants; and the increasing tendency of educated men and women to marry one another and both work, creating households with very high incomes.

Who Pays Federal Income Taxes?
(Share of U.S. income tax, by income percentile)

Income group (income base)	1984	1994*
Top 1% (above $195,981)	21.1%	28.7%
Top 5% (above $90,913)	38.0%	47.4%
Top 10% (above $68,737)	50.6%	59.1%
Top 25% (above $42,734)	73.5%	79.5%
Top 50% (above $21,817)	92.6%	95.2%
Bottom 50% (below $21,817)	7.4%	4.8%

*Latest tax year for which analysis available
Source: Tax Foundation, Internal Revenue Service data

The Feminist Revolution

All Americans were caught up in the great economic changes of the late twentieth century, but no group was more profoundly affected than women. When the century opened, women made up about 20 percent of all workers. Over the next five decades, they increased their presence in the labor force at a fairly steady rate, except for a temporary spurt during World War II. Then, beginning in the 1950s, women's entry into the workplace accelerated dramatically.

By the 1990s nearly half of all workers were women, and the majority of working-age women held jobs outside the home. Most astonishing was the upsurge in employment of mothers. In 1950, 90 percent of mothers with children under the age of six did not work for pay. But by the 1990s, a majority of women with children as young as one year old were wage earners. Women now brought home the bacon and then cooked it, too.

Beginning in the 1960s, many all-male strongholds, including Yale, Princeton, West Point, Annapolis, the Air Force Academy, and even, grudgingly and belatedly, southern military academies

Women's World: Something Old, Something New   By the 1990s revolutionary changes in the economy and in social values had opened new career possibilities to women, while not fully relieving them of their traditional duties as mothers and homemakers. Dramatic changes in race relations and the redefinition of gender roles at the end of the twentieth century transformed even tradition-bound institutions like the U.S. Military Academy at West Point, New York, as this gathering of cadets suggests. Women's athletics came into their own in the wake of the feminist revolution. Here the U.S. Women's Basketball Team is on its way to a gold medal in the 1996 Olympic Games.

Percentage of Working Married Women with Children (Husband Present), 1950–1994

Year	Total Percentage	No Children Under 18	Children 6–17 Only	Children Under 6
1950	23.8	30.3	28.3	11.9
1960	30.5	34.7	39.0	18.6
1970	40.8	42.2	49.2	30.3
1980	50.1	46.0	61.7	45.1
1994	60.6	53.2	76.0	61.7

Source: *Statistical Abstract of the United States,* relevant years.

"WELL, IT'S ABOUT TIME"

The Justice Is a Lady, 1981   Herblock hails Sandra Day O'Connor's appointment to the Supreme Court.

like the Citadel and Virginia Military Institute, opened their doors to women. Women are now piloting commercial airliners and orbiting in outer space. They govern states and cities, write Supreme Court decisions, and debate the law of the land in both houses of Congress. In 1996 women cracked another gender barrier when they launched a professional basketball league of their own.

Yet despite these gains, many feminists remained frustrated. Women continued to receive lower wages than men in corresponding jobs, and they tended to concentrate in a few low-prestige, low-paying occupations (the "pink-collar ghetto"). Although they made up more than half the population, women in the 1990s accounted for only 25 percent of lawyers and judges (up from 5 percent in 1970), and 22 percent of physicians (up from 10 percent in 1970). Overt sexual discrimination explained some of this occupational segregation, but most of it seemed attributable to the greater burdens of parenthood on women than on men. Women were far more likely than men to interrupt their careers to bear and raise children, and even to choose less demanding career paths to allow for fulfilling those traditional roles.

As the revolution in women's status rolled on in the 1990s, men's lives changed as well. A men's movement sprang up that sought to redefine male roles in a new age of increasing gender equality. Some employers provided paternity leave as well as maternity leave, in recognition of the shared obligations of the two-worker household. As traditional female responsibilities such as cooking, laundry, and child care spilled over to men, many corporations sponsored highly popular fatherhood seminars and husbands' support groups. Recognizing the new realities of the modern American house-

hold, Congress passed a Family Leave Bill in 1993, mandating job protection for working fathers as well as mothers who needed to take time off work for family-related reasons.

The Fading Family

The nuclear family, once prized as the foundation of society and the nursery of the Republic, suffered heavy blows in modern America. By the 1990s one out of every two marriages ended in divorce. Seven times more children were affected by divorce than at the beginning of the century. Kids who commuted between separated parents were commonplace. The 1950s ideal of a family with two parents, only one of whom worked, was now a virtually useless way to picture the typical American household.

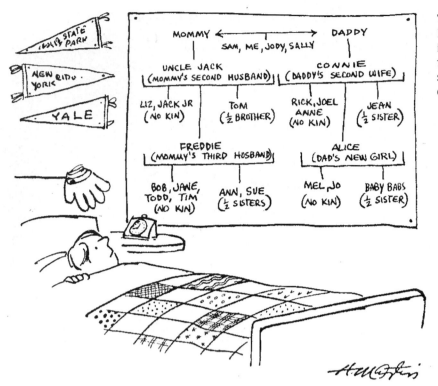

The Modern Family Tree
High divorce rates and the increasing numbers of "blended families" in modern American society could often be confusing.

Traditional families were not only falling apart at an alarming rate but were also increasingly slow to form in the first place. The proportion of adults living alone tripled in the four decades after 1950, and by the 1990s nearly one-third of women aged twenty-five to twenty-nine had never married. In the 1960s, 5 percent of all births were to unmarried women, but three decades later one out of four white babies, one out of three Hispanic babies, and two out of three African-American babies were born to single mothers. Every fourth child in America was growing up in a household that lacked two parents.

In his inaugural address in January 1989, President George Bush (b. 1924) declared,

"My friends, we are not the sum of our possessions; they are not the measure of our lives. In our hearts we know what matters: . . . to be a loyal friend, a loving parent, a citizen who leaves his home, his neighborhood, and his town better than he found it."

The collapse of the traditional family contributed heavily to the pauperization of many women and children, as single parents (usually mothers) struggled to keep their households economically afloat and their families emotionally intact.

Child-rearing, the family's foremost function, was being increasingly assigned to "parent-substitutes" at day-care centers or schools—or to television, the modern age's "electronic babysitter." Estimates were that the average child by age sixteen had watched up to fifteen thousand hours of TV—more time than was spent in the classroom. Parental anxieties multiplied with the advent of the Internet—an electronic cornucopia where youngsters could "surf" through poetry and problem sets as well as pornography.

Born and raised without the family support enjoyed by their forebears, Americans were also increasingly likely to be lonely in their later years. Most elderly people in the 1990s depended on pension plans and government Social Security payments, but not on their loved ones, for their daily bread. The great majority of them drew their last breaths not in their own homes but in hospitals and nursing facilities. From youth to old age, the role of the family was dwindling.

The Aging of America

Old age was more and more likely to be a lengthy experience for Americans, who were living longer than ever before. A person born at the dawn of the century could expect to survive less than fifty years, but a white male born in the 1990s could anticipate a life span of more than seventy-six years. His white female counterpart would probably outlive him by seven years. (The figures were slightly lower for nonwhites, reflecting differences in living standards, especially diet and health care.) The census of 1950 recorded that women for the first time made up a majority of Americans, thanks largely to greater female longevity. Miraculous medical advances lengthened and strengthened lives. Noteworthy were the development of antibiotics after 1940 and Dr. Jonas Salk's discovery in 1953 of a vaccine against a dreaded crippler, polio.

Longer lives spelled more older people. One American in eight was over sixty-five years of age in the 1990s, and projections were that one of every five people would be in the "sunset years" by 2050, as the median age rose toward forty. This aging of the population raised a host of political, social, and economic questions. Elderly people formed a potent electoral bloc that aggressively lobbied for government favors, and achieved real gains for senior citizens. The share of GNP spent on health care for people over sixty-five more than doubled in the three decades after the enactment of Medicare in 1965. This growth in medical payments for the old far outstripped the growth of educational expenditures for the young, with corresponding consequences for the social and economic situation of both populations. As late as the 1960s, nearly a quarter of Americans over the age of sixty-five lived in poverty; three decades later, only about one in ten did. The figures for young people moved in the reverse direction: 15 percent of children were living in poverty in the 1970s, but over 20 percent were in the 1990s.

These triumphs for senior citizens also brought fiscal strains, especially in the Social Security system, established in 1935 to provide income for retired workers. When Social Security began, most workers continued to toil after age sixty-five. By century's end only a small minority did (about 15 percent of men and 8 percent of women), and a majority of the elderly population relied primarily

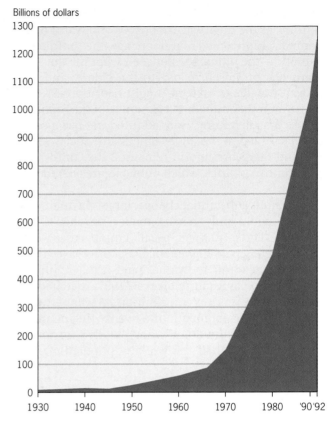

Billions of dollars

Government Expenditures for Social Welfare, 1930–1992
"Social welfare" includes unemployment and old-age insurance, medical insurance, and veterans' benefits. The skyrocketing costs from the mid-1960s onward reflect the increasing size (and political clout) of the elderly population, who were the main beneficiaries of Great Society programs like Medicare. The steep rise after 1970 is also explained by the galloping inflation of the decade of the 1970s.

on Social Security checks for their living expenses. Contrary to popular mythology, Social Security payments to retirees did not simply represent reimbursement for contributions that the elderly had made during their working lives. In fact, the payments of current workers into the Social Security system funded the benefits to the current generation of retirees. By the 1990s, those benefits had risen so high, and the ratio of active workers to retirees had dropped so low, that drastic adjustments were necessary. The problem had intensified in the 1960s, when Medicare was added to the list of benefits to the elderly, and again in the 1970s, when a compassionate Congress dramatically increased retirement payments at a time when productivity growth was stalling. By the beginning of the new century, as the huge wave of post–World War II baby boomers approached retirement age, the "unfunded liability"—the difference between what the government has promised to pay to the elderly and the taxes it expects to take in—might rise above $7 trillion, a sum that threatened to bankrupt the republic unless drastic reforms were adopted. Yet because of the electoral power of older Americans, Social Security and Medicare reform remained the "third rail" of American politics, which public figures dared not touch.

Without substantial change, larger payments to retirees could only mean smaller paychecks for workers. Three-quarters of all employees in the 1990s already paid higher Social Security taxes than income taxes. (An individual paid a maximum of $4,054 in Social Security taxes in 1997, matched by an identical employer contribution.) A war between the generations loomed in the twenty-first century, as payments to the nonworking elderly threatened to soak up fully half the working population's income by about 2040.

Senior Power   Living longer and living healthier, older Americans coalesced into one of America's most politically powerful interest groups as the twentieth century drew to a close.

The New Immigration

Newcomers flooded into modern America. They washed ashore in waves that numbered nearly one million persons per year in the 1980s and 1990s—the heaviest inflow of immigrants in America's experience. In striking contrast to the historic pattern of immigration, Europe contributed far fewer people than did the teeming countries of Asia and Latin America, especially Mexico.

What prompted this new migration to America? The truth is that the newest immigrants came for many of the same reasons as the old. They typically left countries where populations were growing rapidly and where agricultural and industrial revolutions were shaking people loose from old habits of life—conditions almost identical to those in nineteenth-century Europe. And they came to America, as previous immigrants had done, in search of jobs and economic opportunity.

The Southwest, from Texas to California, felt the immigrant impact especially sharply, as Mexican migrants—by far the largest contingent of modern immigrants—concentrated heavily in that region. By the turn of the century Latinos would make up nearly one-third of the population in Texas, Arizona, and California, and almost half in New Mexico—a population shift that amounted to a demographic *reconquista* of the lands lost by Mexico in the war of 1846.

The size and geographic concentration of the Hispanic population in the Southwest had few precedents in the history of American immigration. Most previous groups had been so thinly scattered across the land that they had little choice but to learn English and make their way in the larger American society, however much they might have longed to preserve their native language and customs. But Mexican-Americans might succeed in creating a truly bicultural zone in the booming southwestern states, especially since their mother culture lay just next door and was easily accessible—another factor that differentiated this modern immigrant community from its nineteenth-century European and Asian antecedents.

Some old-stock Americans worried about the capacity of the modern United States to absorb these new immigrants. The Immigration Reform and Control Act of 1986 attempted to choke off illegal entry by penalizing employers of undocumented

In thousands

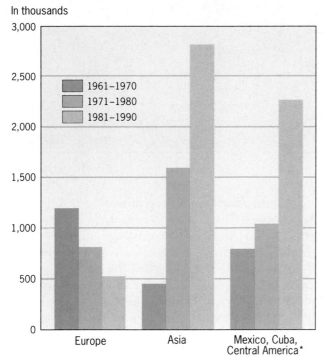

*Mexico represents approximately 73 percent of total.

Recent Legal Immigration by Area of Origin, 1961–1990

and Congress in 1996 tried to restrict access to welfare even for *legal* immigrants.

Yet the fact was that foreign-born people accounted for less than 9 percent of the American population in the 1990s—a far smaller proportion than the historical high point of nearly 15 percent recorded in the census of 1910—and a number that suggested the society's ability to take in newcomers was far from exhausted. Somewhat inconsistently, critics charged both that immigrants robbed citizens of jobs and that they dumped themselves on the welfare rolls at the taxpayers' expense. But studies showed that immigrants took jobs scorned by Americans and that they paid more dollars in taxes (withholding and Social Security taxes, as well as sales taxes) than they claimed for welfare payments. A more urgent worry was that unscrupulous employers might take cruel advantage of alien workers, who often had scant knowledge of their legal rights.

Ethnic Pride

Thanks both to continued immigration and to their own high birthrate, Hispanic-Americans were becoming an increasingly important minority (see "Makers of America: The Latinos," pp. 1034–1035). The United States by the 1990s was home to about 27 million Hispanics. They included some 17 million Chicanos, or Mexican-Americans, mostly in the Southwest, as well as nearly 3 million Puerto Ricans, chiefly in the Northeast, and about 1 million Cubans

aliens and by granting amnesty to many of those already here. Anti-immigrant sentiment flared especially sharply in California in the wake of an economic recession in the early 1990s. California voters approved a ballot initiative that attempted to deny benefits, including education, to illegal immigrants,

Changing Colors   A second-grade bilingual class recites the Pledge of Allegiance (in both Spanish and English) in Austin, Texas. By the end of the twenty-first century, Americans who can trace their ancestry directly to Europe might well be a minority in the United States.

MAKERS OF AMERICA

The Latinos

Today Mexican food is handed through fast-food drive-up windows in all fifty states, Spanish-language broadcasts fill the airwaves, and the Latino community has its own telephone book, the *Spanish Yellow Pages*. Latinos send representatives to Congress and mayors to city hall, record hit songs, paint murals, and teach history. Hispanic-Americans, among the fastest-growing segments of the U.S. population, include Puerto Ricans, frequent voyagers between their native island and northeastern cities; Cubans, many of them refugees from the communist dictatorship of Fidel Castro, concentrated in Miami and southern Florida; and Central Americans, fleeing the ravages of civil war in Nicaragua and El Salvador.

But the most populous group of Latinos derives from Mexico. The first significant numbers of Mexicans began heading for *El Norte* ("the North") around 1910, when the upheavals of the Mexican Revolution stirred and shuffled the Mexican population into more or less constant flux. Their northward passage was briefly interrupted during the Great Depression, when thousands of Mexican nationals were deported. But immigration resumed during World War II, and since then a steady flow of legal immigrants has passed through border checkpoints, joined by countless millions of their undocumented countrymen and countrywomen stealing across the frontier on moonless nights.

For the most part, these Mexicans came to work in the fields, following the ripening crops northward to Canada through the summer and autumn months. In winter many headed back to Mexico, but some

Cuban Refugees Arriving in the United States, 1980 These multi-racial exiles were among the many thousands of Cubans who fled to the United States in the years following Fidel Castro's seizure of power in Cuba in 1959.

Chicana Pride   A Mexican-American girl celebrates her cultural heritage at the Texas Folklife Festival in San Antonio.

Between Two Worlds   Reading newspapers in both English and Spanish.

gathered instead in the cities of the Southwest—El Paso, Los Angeles, Houston, and San Bernardino. There they found regular work, even if lack of skills and racial discrimination often confined them to manual labor. City jobs might pay less than farm labor, but the work was steady and offered the prospect of a stable home. Houses may have been shabby in the barrios, but these Mexican neighborhoods provided a sense of togetherness, a place to raise a family, and the chance to join a mutual-aid society. Such societies, or *Mutualistas*, sponsored baseball leagues, helped the sick and disabled, and defended their members against discrimination.

Mexican immigrants lived so close to the border that their native country acted like a powerful magnet, drawing them back time and time again. Mexicans frequently returned to see relatives or visit the homes of their youth, and relatively few became U.S. citizens. Indeed, in many Mexican-American communities, it was a badge of dishonor to apply for U.S. citizenship.

The Mexican government, likewise influenced by the proximity of the two countries, intervened in the daily lives of its nationals in America, further discouraging them from becoming citizens of their adopted country. As Anglo reformers attempted to Americanize the immigrants in the 1910s and 1920s, the Mexican consulate in Los Angeles launched a Mexicanization program. The consulate sponsored parades on *Cinco de Mayo* ("Fifth of May"), celebrat-

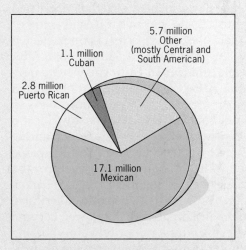

Sources of Latino Population in the United States, 1994

ing Mexico's defeat of a French Army at the Battle of Puebla in 1892, and opened special Spanish-language schools for children. Since World War II, the American-born generation has carried on the fight for political representation, economic opportunity, and cultural preservation.

Fresh arrivals from Mexico and from the other Latin American nations daily swell the Hispanic communities across America. As the United States heads toward the twenty-first century, it is taking on a pronounced Spanish accent.

The Oldest Americans   These Native Americans in Corpus Christi, Texas, protested against the 500th anniversary of Columbus's discovery in 1992.

in Florida (where it was jokingly said that Miami had become the most "Anglo" city in Latin America).

Flexing their political muscles, Latinos elected mayors of Miami, Denver, and San Antonio. After years of struggle, the United Farmworkers Organizing Committee (UFWOC), headed by soft-spoken and charismatic César Chávez, succeeded in improving work conditions for the mostly Chicano "stoop laborers" who followed the cycle of planting and harvesting across the American West. Hispanic influence seemed likely to grow, as suggested by the increasing presence of Spanish-language ballots and television broadcasts. Hispanic-Americans, newly confident and organized, might well become the nation's largest ethnic minority, outnumbering even African-Americans, by the turn of the century. Indeed, predictions were that the Chicano population of America's largest state, California, would equal the "Anglo" population by the year 2000, when there would no longer be a single ethnic majority in the state, only a patchwork of minorities.

Asian-Americans also made great strides. By the 1980s they were America's fastest-growing minority. Their numbers nearly doubled in that decade alone, thanks to heavy immigration, and continued to swell in the 1990s. Once feared and hated as the "yellow peril" and relegated to the most menial and degrading jobs, citizens of Asian ancestry were now counted among the most prosperous and successful of Americans—a "model minority." The typical Asian-American household enjoyed an income nearly 20 percent greater than that of the typical white household. In 1996 the voters of Washington elected the first Asian-American to serve as governor of a mainland American state.

Indians, the original Americans, shared in the general awakening of ethnic and cultural pride. The 1990 census counted some 1.5 million Native Americans, half of whom had left their reservations to live in cities. Meanwhile, unemployment and alcoholism had blighted reservation life. Many tribes tried to take advantage of their special legal status as independent nations by opening bingo halls and gambling casinos for white patrons on reservation lands, but the cycle of discrimination and poverty proved hard to break.

Cities and Suburbs

America's "alabaster cities" of song and story grew more sooty and less safe in the closing years of the century. Crime was the great scourge of urban life. The rate of violent crimes committed in cities reached an all-time high in the drug-infested 1980s ad showed little sign of slackening in the 1990s. Statistically, murder victims in 1995 fell at the rate of one every 24 minutes; a burglary occurred every 12 seconds; three cars were stolen every minute; every 5 minutes a woman was raped. America imprisoned a larger fraction of its citizens than almost any other country in the world. Desperate citizens often set up vigilante patrols to protect their neighborhoods. Frightened urbanites cowered like nightly prisoners in the fortresses of their locked and bolted apartments.

Millions of Americans fled the cities altogether for the supposedly safer suburbs. So swift and massive was the exodus from the old urban neighborhoods that by the mid-1990s it ended the nation's rather brief "urban age," whose dawn had been heralded by the census of 1920, the first to show a majority of city-dwellers.

A majority of Americans now lived in the suburbs, a historic phenomenon that many observers blamed for the spreading fragmentation and isolation of American life. Entire suburban neighborhoods, usually containing economically and racially homogeneous populations, walled themselves off behind elaborate security systems in "gated communities." In these safe but segregated enclaves, the sense of a larger and inclusive national community might prove hard to sustain.

Minority America

Racial and ethnic tensions exacerbated the problems of American cities. These stresses were especially evident in Los Angeles, which, like New York a century earlier, was a magnet for minorities, especially immigrants from Asia and Latin America. When in 1992 a mostly white jury exonerated white Los Angeles police officers who had been videotaped ferociously beating a black suspect, the minority neighborhoods of South Central Los Angeles erupted in rage. Arson and looting laid waste entire city blocks, and scores of people were killed. In a sobering demonstration of the complexity of modern American racial rivalries, many black rioters vented their anger at the white police and the judicial system by attacking Asian shopkeepers, who in turn formed armed patrols to protect their property.

The Los Angeles riots vividly testified to black skepticism about the American system of justice. Just three years later, again in Los Angeles, the gaudy televised spectacle of former football star O. J. Simpson's murder trial fed white disillusionment

Looter Insurance   This Korean-American in Los Angeles totes an automatic weapon to defend a grocery store from rioters protesting the Rodney King trial verdict in April 1992.

Rebuilding the Community   African-Americans help to restore a Korean-owned TV repair shop in the aftermath of the Los Angeles riots of April 1992.

with the state of race relations. After months of testimony that seemed to point to Simpson's guilt, the jury acquitted Simpson, presumably because certain Los Angeles police officers involved in the case had been shown to harbor racist sentiments. In a later civil trial, another jury unanimously found Simpson liable for the "wrongful deaths" of his former wife and another victim. The reaction to the Simpson verdicts revealed the yawning chasm that separated white and black America, as most whites continued to believe Simpson guilty, while majorities of African-Americans told pollsters that the original not-guilty verdict was justified.

American cities have always held an astonishing variety of ethnic and racial groups, but in the late twentieth century, minorities made up a majority of the population of many American cities, as whites fled to the suburbs. More than three-quarters of African-Americans lived in cities by the 1990s, whereas only about one-quarter of whites did. The most desperate black ghettoes, housing a hapless "underclass" in the inner core of the old industrial cities, were especially problematic. Successful blacks who had benefited from the civil rights revolution of the 1950s and 1960s followed whites to the suburbs, leaving a residue in the old ghetto of the poorest poor. Without a middle class to sustain community institutions like schools and small businesses, the inner cities, plagued by unemployment

> *In 1990, the African-American intellectual Shelby Steele declared in his provocative book,* The Content of Our Character:
>
> "What is needed now is a new spirit of pragmatism in racial matters where blacks are seen simply as American citizens who deserve complete fairness and in some cases developmental assistance, but in no case special entitlements based on color. We need deracinated social policies that attack poverty rather than *black* poverty and that instill those values that make for self-reliance."

and drug addiction, seemed bereft of leadership, cohesion, resources, and hope.

The friendless underclass, heavily composed of blacks and other minorities, represented a sorry—and dangerous—social failure that eluded any known remedy. But other segments of the African-American community had clearly prospered in the wake of the civil rights gains of the 1950s and 1960s, though they still had a long hill to climb before reaching full equality. By the 1990s, about 40 percent of blacks were counted in the middle class (defined as enjoying family income greater than

A Difference of Opinion Black and white Americans divided sharply in their reactions to the murder-trial acquittal of former football star O.J. Simpson in 1995.

$25,000 per year). The number of black elected officials had risen above the seven thousand mark, including more than a thousand in the Old South, some two dozen members of Congress, and the mayors of several large cities. Voting tallies demonstrated that successful black politicians were moving beyond isolated racial constituencies and into the political mainstream by appealing to a wide variety of voters. In 1989 Virginians, only 15 percent of whom were black, chose L. Douglas Wilder as the first African-American elected to serve as a state governor. In 1994 voters in Illinois made Carol Mosely-Braun the first African-American woman elected to the United States Senate.

Single women headed over half of black families, almost three times the rate for whites. Many of those African-American women, husbandless and jobless, necessarily depended on welfare to feed their children. As social scientists increasingly emphasized the importance of the home environment for success in school, it became clear that many fatherless, impoverished African-American children seemed consigned to suffer from educational handicaps that were difficult to overcome. Black youths in the 1990s still had about one year less schooling than whites of the same age and were less than half as likely to earn college degrees. Yet Congress, responding to persistent national exasperation with the welfare system, legislated a major overhaul of welfare programs in 1996. The new law restricted access to social services and required able-bodied welfare recipients to find work—where, nobody seemed to know—within two years.

The 1996 welfare reform bill was a bold stroke, but also something of a shot in the dark. Many critics warned that the proposed changes threatened to replace "welfare as we know it" with "welfare as we don't know it." In the state of California, meanwhile, voters in 1996 approved Proposition 209, the "California Civil Rights Initiative," which required an end to all affirmative-action programs in the state. This ringing victory for the foes of affirmative action reflected smoldering resentment against liberal "social engineering" programs and mounting impatience with American society's apparent inability to resolve its racial problems. The action in California, so often a bellwether state, instigated a growing national effort to repeal the affirmative-action programs that had done so much since the 1960s to accelerate the growth of the black middle class and to advance the status of women.

The Life of the Mind

Despite the mind-sapping chatter of the "boob tube," Americans in the late-twentieth century read more, listened to more music, and were better educated than ever before. By the 1990s colleges were awarding nearly a million degrees a year, and one person in four in the twenty-five-to-thirty-four-year-old age group was a college graduate. This expanding mass of educated people lifted the economy to more advanced levels while creating consumers of "high culture." Americans annually made some 300 million visits to museums in the 1990s and patronized about a thousand opera companies and fifteen hundred symphony orchestras—as well as countless popular music groups, including the inventive performers known as Phish, and the long-lived sixties survivors, The Grateful Dead.

What Americans read said much about the state of American society at century's end. Among the most striking development in American letters was the rise of authors from the once-marginal regions and ethnic groups now coming into their own. Reflecting the general population shift westward, the West became the subject of a particularly rich literary outpouring. Larry McMurtry wrote about the small-town West, and lovingly recollected the end of the cattle-drive era in *Lonesome Dove* (1985). Raymond Carver penned understated and powerful stories about working-class life in the Pacific Northwest. Annie Dillard, Ivan Doig, and Jim Harrison recreated the gritty frontier history of that same verdant region. David Guterson penned a moving tale of interracial anxiety and affection in the World War II–era Pacific Northwest in *Snow Falling on Cedars* (1994). Wallace Stegner, the acknowledged dean of western writers, produced several works that far transcended their regional themes, including *Angle of Repose* (1971) and *Crossing to Safety* (1987). Norman MacLean, a former English professor who turned to fiction writing in his retirement, left two unforgettable accounts of his boyhood in Montana: *A River Runs Through It* (1976) and *Young Men and Fire* (1992).

African-American authors and artists also increasingly made their mark. Playwright August Wilson retold the history of black Americans in the twentieth century, with special emphasis on the psychic costs of the northward migration (*Fences,*

(left) Author Toni Morrison
(right) Author Amy Tan

1986; *Joe Turner's Come and Gone,* 1988). In the usually lighthearted medium of the Broadway musical, George Wolfe sensitively explored sobering questions of black identify in *Jelly's Last Jam* (1992), the lifestory of the great New Orleans jazzman "Jelly Roll" Morton. Alice Walker gave fictional voice to the experiences of black women in her hugely popular *The Color Purple* (1982). Toni Morrison wove a bewitching portrait of maternal affection in *Beloved* (1987), and in 1993 became the first African-American woman to win the Nobel Prize for literature. Native-Americans, too, achieved literary recognition. Kiowa author N. Scott Momaday won a Pulitzer Prize for his portrayal of Indian life in *House Made of Dawn* (1968). James Welch wrote movingly about his Blackfoot ancestors in *Fools Crow* (1986).

Asian-American authors also flourished, among them playwright David Hwang and essayist Maxine Hong Kingston, whose *The Woman Warrior* (1976) and *China Men* (1980) imaginatively reconstructed the obscure lives of the earliest Chinese immigrants. Amy Tan's *The Joy Luck Club* (1989) explored the sometimes painful relationship between immigrant Chinese parents and their Asian-American children.

Women writers and women's themes forged to the fictional forefront as the feminist movement advanced. Jane Smiley modeled her touching narrative of a Midwestern farm family on Shakespeare's *King Lear* in *A Thousand Acres* (1991), and followed up with a hilarious spoof on university life in *Moo* (1995). Ann Tyler penned memorable portraits of quirky characters, male as well as female, in *Dinner at the Homesick Restaurant* (1982) and *The Acciden-*

> *In her touching novel,* The Joy Luck Club, *Amy Tan explores the complex dilemmas of growing up as a Chinese-American:*
>
> "'A girl is like a young tree,' [my mother] said. 'You must stand tall and listen to your mother standing next to you. That is the only way to grow strong and straight. But if you bend to listen to other people, you will grow crooked and weak. . . .' Over the years I learned to choose from the best opinions. Chinese people had Chinese opinions. American people had American opinions. And in almost every case, the American version was much better.
>
> It was only later that I discovered there was a serious flaw with the American version. There were too many choices, so it was easy to get confused and pick the wrong thing."

MECHA Mural, by Student Artists Directed by Sergio O'Cadiz, 1974   People have scribbled on walls since time immemorial, but in the 1960s and 1970s, mural painting emerged as a new form of American folk art. Drab buildings and bare fences, often in minority inner-city neighborhoods, were turned into huge canvases. This mural incorporates many Mexican-American and Mexican themes, including the United Farm Workers' bird symbol and a skeleton, a frequent motif in Mexican art.

tal Tourist (1985). E. Annie Proulx won widespread acclaim with her comical yet tender portrayal of a struggling family in *The Shipping News* (1993). The rising interest in feminist and African-American themes revived the popularity of a 1930s writer, Zora Neale Hurston, especially her naturalistic novel *Their Eyes Were Watching God,* first published in 1937.

New York became the art capital of the world after World War II, as well-heeled Americans supported a large number of painters and sculptors. The Ford Foundation also became a major patron of the arts, as did the federal government after the creation of the tax-supported National Endowment for the Arts in 1965. The open and tradition-free American environment seemed especially congenial to the experimental mood of much modern art. Jackson Pollock pioneered abstract expressionism in the 1940s and 1950s, flinging paint on huge flats

stretched on his studio floor. Realistic representation went out the window, as artists like Pollock and Willem de Kooning strove to create "action paintings" that expressed the painter's individuality and made the viewer a creative participant in defining the painting's meaning. Pop artists in the 1960s, notably Andy Warhol, canonized on canvas everyday items of consumer culture, such as soup cans. Robert Rauschenberg made elaborate collages out of objects like cardboard boxes and newspaper clippings. Claes Oldenburg tried to stun viewers into a new visual awareness with unfamiliar versions of familiar objects, such as giant plastic sculptures of pillow-soft telephones. The venerable Georgia O'Keeffe, whose first exhibit was in 1916, continued well into the post–WWII period to produce stunningly immaculate, vividly colored paintings of her beloved Southwest, and moved increasingly into abstract works as her career progressed.

On the stage, playwright David Mamet analyzed the barbarity of American capitalism in plays like *Glengarry Glen Ross* and *American Buffalo,* in which he crafted a kind of poetry from the sludge of American slang. Mamet also made savage sport of feminism and "political correctness" in *Oleanna,* a biting satire about a woman student and her professor. The AIDS epidemic inspired Tony Kushner's sensationally inventive *Angels in America,* a broadranging commentary, alternately hilarious and touching, about the condition of American life at century's end. Film, the most characteristic American art form, continued to flourish, especially as a wave of younger film-makers like George Lucas, Steven Spielberg, Spike Lee, and the Coen brothers, as well as the innovative documentary artist, Ken Burns, made their influence felt.

Architecture also benefited from the building boom of the postwar era. Old master Frank Lloyd Wright produced strikingly original designs, as in the round-walled Guggenheim Museum in New York. Louis Kahn employed stark geometric forms and basic building materials like brick and concrete to make beautiful, simple buildings. Eero Saarinen, the son of a Finnish immigrant, contributed a number of imaginative structures, including two Yale University residential colleges that evoked the atmosphere of an Italian hill town. Chinese-born I. M. Pei designed numerous graceful buildings on several college campuses, as well as the John F. Kennedy Library in Boston. Philip Johnson artfully rendered huge edifices intimate in structures like New York City's Seagram Building, and the New York State Theater at Lincoln Center in Manhattan.

The American Prospect

The American spirit pulsed with vitality as the nation headed into the twenty-first century, but grave problems continued to plague the Republic. Women still fell short of first-class economic citizenship, and American society groped for ways to adapt the traditional family to the new realities of women's work outside the home. A whole generation after the civil rights triumphs of the 1960s, full equality remained an elusive dream for countless Americans of color. The scourge of drug abuse afflicted all sectors of U.S. society but wreaked its cruelest damage in the tortured underclass neighborhoods of the inner city.

Powerful foreign competitors challenged America's premier economic status. The alarming redistribution of wealth and income threatened to turn America into a society of haves and have-nots, mocking the ideals of democracy, and breeding seething resentments along the economic frontier that divided rich from poor.

Environmental worries clouded the country's future. Coal-fired electrical generating plants helped form acid rain and probably contributed to the greenhouse effect, an ominous warming in the planet's temperature. The unsolved problem of radioactive waste disposal hampered the development of nuclear power plants. The planet was being drained of oil, and disastrous accidents like the grounding and subsequent oil spill of the giant tanker *Exxon Valdez* in 1989 in Alaska's pristine

The Federal Budget Dollar and How It Is Spent, by Major Category

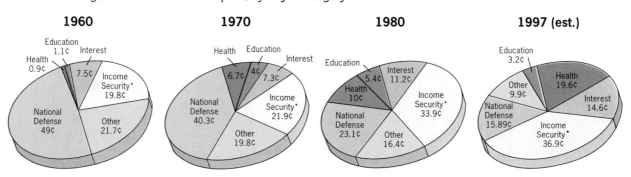

*Includes Social Security payments to the elderly and disabled, unemployment compensation, and welfare. Note the the shifting emphasis in the budget from defense spending to health and income security, and to interest payments on the national debt.

Prince William Sound demonstrated the ecological risks of oil exploration and transportation at sea.

Some Americans, soured on the false satisfactions of wealth and anxious to set the globe on the path to ecological stability, welcomed the prospect of a "no-growth" economy. But enlarging the economic pie had historically been the American way of satisfying the appetites of virtually all people for a richer life. Because of fabulous growth, Americans have until now been spared bitter battles over the distribution of a relatively fixed supply of this world's goods. "No-growth" would change the rules of the political game, with consequences that no one could foresee. And for the great majority of the world's aspiring peoples, who still plowed with oxen and nightly went to bed hungry, "no-growth" seemed a cruel and cynical joke perpetrated by the privileged few who had already grown fat and happy.

America was born as a revolutionary force in a world of conservatism; for much of this century it has stood as a conservative force in a world of revolutionism. It has held aloft the banner of liberal democracy in a world buffeted by revolutions of left and right, including communism, Nazism, and fascism. But much that is revolutionary remains in America's liberal democratic legacy, and its people have pioneered in the revolutions against colonialism, racism, sexism, ignorance, and poverty that have roiled the planet in the twentieth century. As the human family grows at an alarming rate on a shrinking globe, America's revolutionary heritage does not lack for new challenges.

The task of cleansing Spaceship Earth of its abundant pollutants—including nuclear weapons —is one urgent mission confronting the American people in the opening years of the twenty-first century. Another is seeking ways to resolve the ethnic and cultural conflicts that erupted with renewed virulence around the globe in the wake of the Cold War's end. At the same time, new opportunities beckon both in outer space and on inner-city streets, at the artist's easel and in the concert hall, at the inventor's bench and in the scientist's labora-

The Price of Petroleum This bald eagle fell victim to the oil spill from the tanker *Exxon Valdez* in Alaska's Prince William Sound in 1989.

tory, and in the unending quest for social justice, individual fulfillment, and international peace. The challenges facing Americans, at home and abroad, are formidable, but so is the Republic. As the twentieth century approaches its sunset, the people of the United States still aspired to live up to Lincoln's conviction that they and their heritage represented "the last best hope of earth."

SUGGESTED READINGS

PRIMARY SOURCE DOCUMENTS

Up-to-date data on income and poverty can be found at the Census Bureau's web site, http://www.census.gov/hhes/income. The classic book that launched the modern women's movement is Betty Friedan, *The Feminine Mystique** (1963). For the views of a Christian conservative on the abortion issue, see Ralph Reed, "We Stand at a Crossroads," *Newsweek,* May 13, 1996, p. 28.* *Statistical Abstract of the United States* is an annual government publication with a wealth of information on a variety of topics, including immigration, Social Security funding, and the social and economic condition of minorities.

SECONDARY SOURCES

A useful overview of recent history is Paul Boyer, *Promises to Keep: The United States Since World War II* (1995). Growing income inequality is discussed in Barbara Ehrenreich, *Fear of Falling: The Inner Life of the Middle Class* (1989), and in Kevin P. Phillips, *The Politics of Rich and Poor: Wealth and the American Electorate in the Reagan Aftermath* (1990). The evolving social participation of women, and the dilemmas thereby created, are clearly spelled out in Rosalind Rosenberg, *Divided Lives* (1992), and in William H. Chafe, *The Paradox of Change: American Women in the 20th Century* (1991). See also Betty Friedan, *The Second Stage* (1981); Sylvia Ann Hewlett, *A Lesser Life: The Myth of Women's Liberation in America* (1986); Susanne M. Bianchi, *American Women in Transition* (1987); Marion Faux, *Roe vs. Wade* (1988); Jean E. Friedman, et al., eds., *Our American Sisters* (1987); and Susan Faludi's provocative best-seller, *Backlash: The Undeclared War Against American Women* (1991). George Masnick and Mary Jo Bane, *The Nation's Families: 1960–1990* (1980), is rich in statistical information. For a brilliant discussion of the same subject from an economic perspective, see Victor R. Fuchs, *How We Live* (1983), and also his *Women's Quest for Economic Equality* (1988). On the looming problems in the Social Security system, see Peter G. Peterson, *Will America Grow Up Before it Grows Old?* (1996); for a provocative analysis of the leading senior citizens' lobby, the Association of American Retired Persons, consult Charles R. Morris, *The AARP: America's Most Powerful Lobby and the Clash of Generations* (1996). George J. Borjas turns an economist's critical eye on recent immigration in *Friends or Strangers* (1990). America's newest immigrants are the subjects of David M. Reimers, *Still the Golden Door: The Third World Comes to America* (1986). On Mexican-Americans, see Carlos Munoz, Jr., *Youth, Identity, Power: The Chicano Movement* (1989), George J. Sanchez, *Becoming Mexican American* (1989), and Richard Rodriguez's poignant memoir, *Hunger of Memory* (1982). Asian-Americans are discussed in Bill Ong Hing, *Making and Remaking Asian America Through Immigration Policy* (1993), and in Ronald Takaki, *Strangers from a Different Shore* (1989). On blacks see Harvard Sitkoff, *The Struggle for Black Equality, 1954–1992* (rev. ed, 1993), Andrew Hacker, *Two Nations: Black and White, Separate, Hostile, Unequal* (1992), and Gerald David Jaynes and Robin M. Williams, Jr., *A Common Destiny: Blacks and American Society* (1989). Oscar Lewis movingly depicts the problems of Puerto Ricans in *La Vida* (1966). Regarding Native Americans consult Alvin M. Josephy, *Now That the Buffalo Have Gone: A Study of Today's American Indians* (1982). The problems of the cities are examined in Jon C. Teaford, *The Rough Road to Renaissance: Urban Revitalization in America, 1940–1985* (1990), and Larry Bennett, *Fragments of Cities: The New American Downtowns and Neighborhoods* (1990). Suburbs are the subject of Paul G. Lewis's *Shaping Suburbia* (1996). On crime consult James Q. Wilson and Richard J. Hernstein, *Crime and Human Nature* (1986), and Elliott Currie, *Confronting Crime: An American Challenge* (1986). For penetrating analyses of the problems of the inner cities, consult three studies by William J. Wilson, *The Truly Disadvantaged: The Inner City, the Underclass, and Public Policy* (1987); *Poverty, Inequality, and the Future of Social Policy* (1995); and *When Work Disappears* (1996). Welfare reform is the subject of Mary Jo Bane, *Welfare Realities* (1994). Nicholas Lemann, *The Promised Land* (1991), provides a vivid account of the welfare system and the failed promises of Lyndon Johnson's "War on Poverty." The political implications of the debates over race and welfare policies are spelled out in Thomas Byrne Edsall and Mary D. Edsall, *Chain Reaction: The Impact of Race, Rights, and Taxes on American Politics* (1991). The broader cultural controversies of the era are examined in Arthur M. Schlesinger, Jr., *The Disuniting of America* (1992), Robert Hughes, *Culture of Complaint: The Fraying of America* (1993), and Henry Louis Gates, Jr., *Loose Canons: Notes on the Culture Wars* (1993). A sensitive and intriguing study of the values of modern Americans is Robert N. Bellah, *Habits of the Heart: Individualism and Commitment in American Life* (1985). See also Allan Bloom's conservative critique of modern higher education, *The Closing of the American Mind* (1987), and the rejoinder by Lawrence Levine, *The Opening of the American Mind* (1996)

---

*An asterisk indicates that the document, or an excerpt from it, can be found in Thomas A. Bailey and David M. Kennedy, eds., *The American Spirit: United States History as Seen by Contemporaries,* 9th ed. (Boston: Houghton Mifflin, 1998).

APPENDIX

Declaration of Independence

In Congress, July 4, 1776

The Unanimous Declaration of the Thirteen United States of America

[Bracketed material in color has been inserted by the authors. For adoption background see pp. 147–148.]

When, in the course of human events, it becomes necessary for one people to dissolve the political bonds which have connected them with another, and to assume, among the powers of the earth, the separate and equal station to which the laws of nature and of nature's God entitle them, a decent respect to the opinions of mankind requires that they should declare the causes which impel them to the separation.

We hold these truths to be self-evident: That all men are created equal; that they are endowed by their Creator with certain unalienable rights; that among these are life, liberty, and the pursuit of happiness; that, to secure these rights, governments are instituted among men, deriving their just powers from the consent of the governed; that whenever any form of government becomes destructive of these ends, it is the right of the people to alter or to abolish it, and to institute new government, laying its foundation on such principles, and organizing its powers in such form, as to them shall seem most likely to effect their safety and happiness. Prudence, indeed, will dictate that governments long established should not be changed for light and transient causes; and accordingly all experience hath shown that mankind are more disposed to suffer, while evils are sufferable, than to right themselves by abolishing the forms to which they are accustomed. But when a long train of abuses and usurpations, pursuing invariably the same object, evinces a design to reduce them under absolute despotism, it is their right, it is their duty, to throw off such government, and to provide new guards for their future security. Such has been the patient sufferance of these colonies; and such is now the necessity which constrains them to alter their former systems of government. The history of the present King of Great Britain is a history of repeated injuries and usurpations, all having in direct object the establishment of an absolute tyranny over these states. To prove this, let facts be submitted to a candid world.

He has refused his assent to laws, the most wholesome and necessary for the public good. [See royal veto, p. 123.]

He has forbidden his governors to pass laws of immediate and pressing importance, unless suspended in their operation till his assent should be obtained; and, when so suspended, he has utterly neglected to attend to them.

He has refused to pass other laws for the accommodation of large districts of people [by establishing new countries], unless those people would relinquish the right of representation in the legislature, a right inestimable to them, and formidable to tyrants only.

He has called together legislative bodies at places unusual, uncomfortable, and distant from the depository of their public records, for the sole purpose of fatiguing them into compliance with his measures. [e.g., removal of Massachusetts Assembly to Salem, 1774.]

He has dissolved representative houses repeatedly, for opposing, with manly firmness, his invasions on the rights of the people. [e.g., Virginia Assembly, 1765.]

He has refused for a long time, after such dissolutions, to cause others to be elected; whereby the legislative powers, incapable of annihilation, have returned to the people at large for their exercise; the state remaining, in the mean time, exposed to all the dangers of invasions from without and convulsions within.

He has endeavored to prevent the population [populating] of these states; for that purpose obstructing the laws for naturalization of foreigners; refusing to pass others to encourage their migration hither, and raising the conditions of new appropriations of lands. [e.g., Proclamation of 1763, p. 119.]

He has obstructed the administration of justice, by refusing his assent to laws for establishing judiciary powers.

He has made judges dependent on his will alone, for the tenure of their offices, and the amount and payment of their salaries. [See Townshend Acts, p. 129.]

He has erected a multitude of new offices, and sent hither swarms of officers to harass our people and eat out their substance. [See enforcement of Navigation Laws, p. 131.]

He has kept among us, in times of peace, standing armies, without the consent of our legislatures. [See pp. 126, 130.]

He has affected to render the military independent of, and superior to, the civil power.

He has combined with others to subject us to a jurisdiction foreign to our constitution, and unacknowledged by our laws, giving his assent to their acts of pretended legislation:

> For quartering large bodies of armed troops among us [See Boston Massacre, p. 130];
>
> For protecting them, by a mock trial, from punishment for any murders which they should commit on the inhabitants of these states [See 1774 Acts, pp. 133–134];
>
> For cutting off our trade with all parts of the world [See Boston Port Act, p. 133];
>
> For imposing taxes on us without our consent [See Stamp Act, p. 125];
>
> For depriving us, in many cases, of the benefits of trial by jury;
>
> For transporting us beyond seas, to be tried for pretended offenses;
>
> For abolishing the free system of English laws in a neighboring province [Quebec], establishing therein an arbitrary government, and enlarging its boundaries, so as to render it at once an example and fit instrument for introducing the same absolute rule into these colonies [Quebec Act, p. 133];
>
> For taking away our charters, abolishing our most valuable laws, and altering fundamentally the forms of our governments [e.g., in Massachusetts, p. 133];
>
> For suspending our own legislatures, and declaring themselves invested with power to legislate for us in all cases whatsoever [See Stamp Act repeal, p. 127.]

He has abdicated government here, by declaring us out of his protection and waging war against us. [Proclamation, p. 144.]

He has plundered our seas, ravaged our coasts, burned our towns, and destroyed the lives of our people. [e.g., the burning of Falmouth (Portland), p. 144.]

He is at this time transporting large armies of foreign mercenaries [Hessians, pp. 143–144] to complete the works of death, desolation, and tyranny already begun with circumstances of cruelty and perfidy scarcely paralleled in the most barbarous ages, and totally unworthy the head of a civilized nation.

He has constrained our fellow-citizens, taken captive on the high seas [by impress-ment], to bear arms against their country, to become the executioners of their friends and brethren, or to fall themselves by their hands.

He has excited domestic insurrection among us [i.e., among slaves], and has endeav-ored to bring on the inhabitants of our frontiers the merciless Indian savages, whose known rule of warfare is an undistinguished destruction of all ages, sexes, and conditions.

In every stage of these oppressions we have petitioned for redress in the most hum-ble terms; our repeated petitions have been answered only by repeated injury. [e.g., pp. 142–145.] A prince, whose character is thus marked by every act which may define a tyrant, is unfit to be the ruler of a free people.

Nor have we been wanting in our attentions to our British brethren. We have warned them, from time to time, of attempts by their legislature to extend an unwarrantable jurisdiction over us. We have reminded them of the circumstances of our emigration and settlement here. We have appealed to their native justice and magnanimity; and we have conjured them, by the ties of our common kindred, to disavow these usurpations, which would inevitably interrupt our connections and correspondence. They, too, have been deaf to the voice of justice and of consanguinity [blood relationship]. We must, therefore, acquiesce in the necessity which denounces [announces] our separation, and hold them, as we hold the rest of mankind, enemies in war, in peace friends.

We, therefore, the representatives of the United States of America, in General Con-gress assembled, appealing to the Supreme Judge of the world for the rectitude of our intentions, do, in the name and by the authority of the good people of these colonies, solemnly publish and declare, That these United Colonies are, and of right ought to be, FREE AND INDEPENDENT STATES; that they are absolved from all allegiance to the British crown, and that all political connection between them and the state of Great Britain is, and ought to be, totally dissolved; and that, as free and independent states, they have full power to levy war, conclude peace, contract alliances, establish commerce, and do all other acts and things which independent states may of right do. And for the sup-port of this declaration, with a firm reliance on the protection of Divine Providence, we mutually pledge to each other our lives, our fortunes, and our sacred honor.

[Signed by]   JOHN HANCOCK [President]
                                                                                  [and fifty-five others]

Constitution of the United States of America

[Boldface headings and bracketed explanatory matter and marginal comments (both in color) have been inserted for the reader's convenience. Passages that are no longer operative are printed in italic type.]

PREAMBLE

On "We the people," see p. 271n.

We the people of the United States, in order to form a more perfect union, establish justice, insure domestic tranquility, provide for the common defense, promote the general welfare, and secure the blessings of liberty to ourselves and our posterity, do ordain and establish this CONSTITUTION for the United States of America.

Article I. *Legislative Department*

SECTION I. Congress

Legislative power vested in a two-house Congress. All legislative powers herein granted shall be vested in a Congress of the United States, which shall consist of a Senate and a House of Representatives.

SECTION II. House of Representatives

1. The people elect representatives biennially. The House of Representatives shall be composed of members chosen every second year by the people of the several States, and the electors [voters] in each State shall have the qualifications requisite for electors of the most numerous branch of the State Legislature.

2. Who may be representatives. No person shall be a Representative who shall not have attained the age of twenty-five years, and been seven years a citizen of the United States, and who shall not, when elected, be an inhabitant of that State in which he shall be chosen.

See 1787 compromise, p. 179.

See 1787 compromise, p. 180.

3. Representation in the House based on population; census. Representatives and direct taxes[1] shall be apportioned among the several States which may be included within this Union, according to their respective numbers, *which shall be determined by adding to the whole number of free persons, including those bound to service for a term of years* [apprentices and indentured servants], *and excluding Indians not taxed, three-fifths of all other persons* [slaves].[2] The actual enumeration [census] shall be made within three years after the first meeting of the Congress of the United States, and within every subsequent term of ten years, in such manner as they shall by law direct. The number of Representatives shall not exceed one for every thirty thousand, but each State shall have at least one Representative; *and until such enumeration shall be made, the State of New Hampshire shall be entitled to choose three, Massachusetts eight, Rhode Island and Providence Plantations one, Connecticut five, New York six, New Jersey four, Pennsylvania eight, Delaware one, Maryland six, Virginia ten, North Carolina five, South Carolina five, and Georgia three.*

---

[1]Modified in 1913 by the Sixteenth Amendment re income taxes (see p. 707).

[2]The word *slave* appears nowhere in the original, unamended Constitution. The three-fifths rule ceased to be in force when the Thirteenth Amendment was adopted in 1865 (see p. 69 and amendments below).

4. Vacancies in the House are filled by election. When vacancies happen in the representation from any State, the Executive authority [governor] therefore shall issue writs of election [call a special election] to fill such vacancies.

See Chase and Johnson trials, pp. 217, 503; Nixon trial preliminaries, pp. 977–978.

5. The House selects its Speaker; has sole power to vote impeachment charges (i.e., indictments). The House of Representatives shall choose their Speaker and other officers; and shall have the sole power of impeachment.

Section III.   Senate

1. Senators represent the states. The Senate of the United States shall be composed of two Senators from each State, *chosen by the legislature thereof,*[1] for six Years; and each Senator shall have one vote.

2. One-third of senators chosen every two years; vacancies. *Immediately after they shall be assembled in consequence of the first election, they shall be divided as equally as may be into three classes. The seats of the Senators of the first class shall be vacated at the expiration of the second year, of the second class at the expiration of the fourth year, and of the third class at the expiration of the sixth year,* so that one-third may be chosen every second year; *and if vacancies happen by resignation or otherwise, during the recess of the legislature of any State, the Executive* [governor] *thereof may make temporary appointments until the next meeting of the legislature, which shall then fill such vacancies.*[2]

3. Who may be senators. No person shall be a Senator who shall not have attained to the age of thirty years, and been nine years a citizen of the United States, and who shall not, when elected, be an inhabitant of that State for which he shall be chosen.

4. The vice president presides over the Senate. The Vice President of the United States shall be President of the Senate, but shall have no vote, unless they be equally divided [tied].

5. The Senate chooses its other officers. The Senate shall choose their other officers, and also a President *pro tempore,* in the absence of the Vice President, or when he shall exercise the office of the President of the United States.

See Chase and Johnson trials, pp. 217, 504.

6. The Senate has sole power to try impeachments. The Senate shall have the sole power to try all impeachments. When sitting for that purpose, they shall be on oath or affirmation. When the President of the United States is tried, the Chief Justice shall preside[3]: and no person shall be convicted without the concurrence of two-thirds of the members present.

7. Penalties for impeachment conviction. Judgment in cases of impeachment shall not extend further than to removal from office, and disqualification to hold and enjoy any office of honor, trust or profit under the United States: but the party convicted shall nevertheless be liable and subject to indictment, trial, judgment and punishment, according to law.

Section IV.   Election and Meetings of Congress

1. Regulation of elections. The times, places and manner of holding elections for Senators and Representatives shall be prescribed in each State by the legislature thereof; but the Congress may at any time by law make or alter such regulations, except as to the places of choosing Senators.

2. Congress must meet once a year. The Congress shall assemble at least once in every year, and such meeting *shall be on the first Monday in December, unless they shall by law appoint a different day.*[4]

---

[1]Repealed in favor of popular election in 1913 by the Seventeenth Amendment.
[2]Changed in 1913 by the Seventeenth Amendment.
[3]The vice president, as next in line, would be an interested party.
[4]Changed in 1933 to January 3 by the Twentieth Amendment (see p. 816 and below).

SECTION V.   **Organization and Rules of the Houses**

1.   Each house may reject members; quorums. Each house shall be the judge of the elections, returns and qualifications of its own members, and a majority of each shall constitute a quorum to do business; but a smaller number may adjourn from day to day, and may be authorized to compel the attendance of absent members, in such manner, and under such penalties, as each house may provide.

See "Bully" Brooks case, pp. 424–425.

2.   Each house makes its own rules. Each house may determine the rules of its proceedings, punish its members for disorderly behavior, and with the concurrence of two-thirds, expel a member.

3.   Each house must keep and publish a record of its proceedings. Each house shall keep a journal of its proceedings, and from time to time publish the same, excepting such parts as may in their judgment require secrecy; and the yeas and nays of the members of either house on any question shall, at the desire of one-fifth of those present, be entered on the journal.

4.   Both houses must agree on adjournment. Neither house, during the session of Congress, shall, without the consent of the other, adjourn for more than three days, nor to any other place than that in which the two houses shall be sitting.

SECTION VI.   **Privileges of and Prohibitions upon Congressmen**

1.   Congressional salaries; immunities. The Senators and Representatives shall receive a compensation for their services, to be ascertained by law and paid out of the treasury of the United States. They shall in all cases except treason, felony and breach of the peace, be privileged from arrest during their attendance at the session of their respective houses, and in going to and returning from the same; and for any speech or debate in either house, they shall not be questioned in any other place [i.e., they shall be immune from libel suits].

2.   A congressman may not hold any other federal civil office. No Senator or Representative shall, during the time for which he was elected, be appointed to any civil office under the authority of the United States, which shall have been created, or the emoluments whereof shall have been increased, during such time; and no person holding any office under the United States shall be a member of either house during his continuance in office.

SECTION VII.   **Method of Making Laws**

See 1787 compromise, p. 179.

1.   Money bills must originate in the House. All bills for raising revenue shall originate in the House of Representatives; but the Senate may propose or concur with amendments as on other bills.

Nixon, more than any predecessors, "impounded" billions of dollars voted by Congress for specific purposes, because he disapproved of them. The courts generally failed to sustain him, and his impeachment foes regarded wholesale impoundment as a violation of his oath to "faithfully execute" the laws.

2.   The president's veto power; Congress may override. Every bill which shall have passed the House of Representatives and the Senate, shall, before it become a law, be presented to the President of the United States; if he approve he shall sign it, but if not he shall return it with his objections to that house in which it shall have originated, who shall enter the objections at large on their journal, and proceed to reconsider it. If after such reconsideration two-thirds of that house shall agree to pass the bill, it shall be sent, together with the objections, to the other house, by which it shall likewise be reconsidered, and, if approved by two-thirds of that house, it shall become a law. But in all such cases the votes of both houses shall be determined by yeas and nays, and the names of the persons voting for and against the bill shall be entered on the journal of each house respectively. If any bill shall not be returned by the President within ten days (Sundays excepted) after it shall have been presented to him, the same shall be a law, in like manner as if he had signed it, unless the Congress by their adjournment prevent its return, in which case it shall not be a law [this is the so-called pocket veto].

3.   All measures requiring the agreement of both houses go to president for approval. Every order, resolution, or vote to which the concurrence of the Senate and House of Representatives may be necessary (except on a question of adjournment) shall be presented to the President of the United States; and before the same shall take effect, shall be approved by him, or being disapproved by him, shall be repassed by two-thirds of the Senate and House of Representatives, according to the rules and limitations prescribed in the case of a bill.

SECTION VIII. **Powers Granted to Congress**

Congress has certain enumerated powers:

1. It may lay and collect taxes. The Congress shall have power to lay and collect taxes, duties, imposts, and excises, to pay the debts and provide for the common defense and general welfare of the United States; but all duties, imposts and excises shall be uniform throughout the United States;

2. It may borrow money. To borrow money on the credit of the United States;

3. It may regulate foreign and interstate trade. To regulate commerce with foreign nations, and among the several States, and with the Indian tribes;

For 1798 naturalization see p. 204. **4. It may pass naturalization and bankruptcy laws.** To establish an uniform rule of naturalization, and uniform laws on the subject of bankruptcies throughout the United States;

5. It may coin money. To coin money, regulate the value thereof, and of foreign coin, and fix the standard of weights and measures;

6. It may punish counterfeiters. To provide for the punishment of counterfeiting the securities and current coin of the United States;

7. It may establish a postal service. To establish post offices and post roads;

8. It may issue patents and copyrights. To promote the progress of science and useful arts by securing for limited times to authors and inventors the exclusive right to their respective writings and discoveries;

9. It may establish inferior courts. To constitute tribunals inferior to the Supreme Court;

See Judiciary Act of 1789, p. 192. **10. It may punish crimes committed on the high seas.** To define and punish piracies and felonies committed on the high seas [i.e., outside the three-mile limit] and offenses against the law of nations [international law];

11. It may declare war; authorize privateers. To declare war,[1] grant letters of marque and reprisal,[2] and make rules concerning captures on land and water;

12. It may maintain an army. To raise and support armies, but no appropriation of money to that use shall be for a longer term than two years;[3]

13. It may maintain a navy. To provide and maintain a navy;

14. It may regulate the army and navy. To make rules for the government and regulation of the land and naval forces;

15. It may call out the state militia. To provide for calling forth the militia to execute the laws of the Union, suppress insurrections, and repel invasions;

See Whiskey Rebellion, p. 195. **16. It shares with the states control of militia.** To provide for organizing, arming, and disciplining the militia, and for governing such part of them as may be employed in the service of the United States, reserving to the States respectively the appointment of the officers, and the authority of training the militia according to the discipline prescribed by Congress;

---

[1] Note that presidents, though they can provoke war (see the case of Polk, p. 391) or wage it after it is declared, cannot declare it.

[2] Papers issued private citizens in wartime authorizing them to capture enemy ships.

[3] A reflection of fear of standing armies earlier expressed in the Declaration of Independence.

17. It makes laws for the District of Columbia and other federal areas. To exercise exclusive legislation in all cases whatsoever, over such district (not exceeding ten miles square) as may, by cession of particular States, and the acceptance of Congress, become the seat of government of the United States,[1] and to exercise like authority over all places purchased by the consent of the legislature of the State, in which the same shall be, for the erection of forts, magazines, arsenals, dock-yards, and other needful buildings;—and

Congress has certain implied powers:

This is the famous "elastic clause"; See p. 194.

18. It may make laws necessary for carrying out the enumerated powers. To make all laws which shall be necessary and proper for carrying into execution the foregoing powers, and all other powers vested by this Constitution in the government of the United States, or in any departure or officer thereof.

SECTION IX. Powers Denied to the Federal Government

See 1787 slave compromise, p. 180.

1. Congressional control of slave trade postponed until 1808. *The migration or importation of such persons as any of the States now existing shall think proper to admit shall not be prohibited by the Congress prior to the year 1808; but a tax or duty may be imposed on such importation, not exceeding $10 for each person.*

See Lincoln's unlawful suspension, p. 455.

2. The writ of habeas corpus[2] may be suspended only in cases of rebellion or invasion. The privilege of the writ of habeas corpus shall not be suspended, unless when in cases of rebellion or invasion the public safety may require it.

3. Attainders[3] and ex post facto laws[4] forbidden. No bill of attainder or ex post facto law shall be passed.

4. Direct taxes must be apportioned according to population. No capitation [head or poll tax] or other direct, tax shall be laid, unless in proportion to the census or enumeration herein before directed to be taken.[5]

5. Export taxes forbidden. No tax or duty shall be laid on articles exported from any State.

6. Congress must not discriminate among states in regulating commerce. No preference shall be given by any regulation of commerce or revenue to the ports of one State over those of another; nor shall vessels bound to, or from, one State, be obliged to enter, clear, or pay duties in another.

See Lincoln's unlawful infraction, p. 455.

7. Public money may not be spent without congressional appropriation; accounting. No money shall be drawn from the treasury, but in consequence of appropriations made by law; and a regular statement and account of the receipts and expenditures of all public money shall be published from time to time.

8. Titles of nobility prohibited; foreign gifts. No title of nobility shall be granted by the United States; and no person holding office of profit or trust under them, shall, without the consent of Congress, accept of any present, emolument, office, or title, of any kind whatever, from any king, prince, or foreign state.

---

[1]The District of Columbia, ten miles square, was established in 1791 with a cession from Virginia (see p. 193).

[2]A writ of habeas corpus is a document that enables a person under arrest to obtain an immediate examination in court to ascertain whether he or she is being legally held.

[3]A bill of attainder is a special legislative act condemning and punishing an individual without a judicial trial.

[4]An ex post facto law is one that fixes punishments for acts committed before the law was passed.

[5]Modified in 1913 by the Sixteenth Amendment (see p. 707 and amendments below).

Section X.   Powers Denied to the States

Absolute prohibitions on the states:

On contracts see Fletcher *v.* Peck, *p. 249.*

1. The states are forbidden to do certain things. No State shall enter into any treaty, alliance, or confederation; grant letters of marque and reprisal [i.e., authorize privateers]; coin money; emit bills of credit [issue paper money]; make anything but gold and silver coin a [legal] tender in payment of debts; pass any bill of attainder,[1] ex post facto,[1] or law impairing the obligation of contracts, or grant any title of nobility.

Conditional prohibitions on the states:

Cf. Confederation chaos, pp. 172–173.

2. The states may not levy duties without the consent of Congress. No State shall, without the consent of Congress, lay any imposts or duties on imports or exports, except what may be absolutely necessary for executing its inspection laws: and the net produce of all duties and imposts, laid by any State on imports or exports, shall be for the use of the treasury of the United States; and all such laws shall be subject to the revision and control of the Congress.

3. Certain other federal powers are forbidden the states except with the consent of Congress. No State shall, without the consent of Congress, lay any duty of tonnage [i.e., duty on ship tonnage], keep [nonmilitia] troops or ships of war in time of peace, enter into any agreement or compact with another State, or with a foreign power, or engage in war, unless actually invaded, or in such imminent danger as will not admit of delay.

Article II.   *Executive Department*

Section I.   President and Vice President

1. The president is the chief executive; term of office. The executive power shall be vested in a President of the United States of America. He shall hold his office during the term of four years,[2] and, together with the Vice President, chosen for the same term, be elected as follows:

See 1787 compromise, p. 180.

See 1876 Oregon case, p. 519

2. The president is chosen by electors. Each State shall appoint, in such manner as the legislature thereof may direct, a number of electors, equal to the whole number of Senators and Representatives to which the State may be entitled in the Congress; but no Senator or Representative, or person holding an office of trust or profit under the United States, shall be appointed an elector.

See Burr-Jefferson disputed election of 1800, p. 211.

A majority of the electoral votes needed to elect a president. *The electors shall meet in their respective States, and vote by ballot for two persons, of whom one at least shall not be an inhabitant of the same State with themselves. And they shall make a list of all the persons voted for, and of the number of votes for each; which list they shall sign and certify, and transmit sealed to the seat of government of the United States, directed to the President of the Senate. The President of the Senate shall, in the presence of the Senate and House of Representatives, open all the certificates, and the votes shall be counted. The person having the greatest number of votes shall be the President, if such number be a majority of the whole number of electors appointed; and if there be more than one who have such majority, and have an equal number of votes, then the House of Representatives shall immediately choose by ballot one of them for President; and if no person have a majority, then from the five highest on the list the said house shall in like manner choose the President. But in choosing the President the votes shall be taken by States, the representation from each State*

---

[1]For definitions see footnotes 3 and 4 on preceding page.

[2]No reference to reelection; for anti–third term Twenty-second Amendment, see below.

having one vote; a quorum for this purpose shall consist of a member or members from two-thirds of the States, and a majority of all the States shall be necessary to a choice. In every case, after the choice of the President, the person having the greatest number of votes of the electors shall be the Vice President. But if there should remain two or more who have equal votes, the Senate shall choose from them by ballot the Vice President.[1]

See Jefferson as vice president in 1796, p. 201.

3. Congress decides time of meeting of Electoral College. The Congress may determine the time of choosing the electors and the day on which they shall give their votes; which day shall be the same throughout the United States.

To provide for foreign-born people, like Alexander Hamilton, born in the British West Indies.

4. Who may be president. No person except a natural-born citizen, *or a citizen of the United States at the time of the adoption of this Constitution,* shall be eligible to the office of President; neither shall any person be eligible to that office who shall not have attained to the age of thirty-five years, and been fourteen years a resident within the United States [i.e., a legal resident].

Modified by Twentieth and Twenty-fifth Amendments below.

5. Replacements for president. In case of the removal of the President from office or of his death, resignation, or inability to discharge the powers and duties of said office, the same shall devolve on the Vice President, and the Congress may by law provide for the case of removal, death, resignation, or inability, both of the President and Vice President, declaring what officer shall then act as President, and such officer shall act accordingly, until the disability be removed, or a President shall be elected.

6. The president's salary. The President shall, at stated times, receive for his services a compensation, which shall neither be increased or diminished during the period for which he shall have been elected, and he shall not receive within that period any other emolument from the United States, or any of them.

7. The president's oath of office. Before he enter on the execution of his office, he shall take the following oath or affirmation:—"I do solemnly swear (or affirm) that I will faithfully execute the office of the President of the United States, and will to the best of my ability preserve, protect and defend the Constitution of the United States."

Section II.   Powers of the President

See cabinet evolution, p. 191.

1. The president has important military and civil powers. The President shall be commander in chief of the army and navy of the United States, and of the militia of the several States, when called into the actual service of the United States; he may require the opinion, in writing, of the principal officer in each of the executive departments, upon any subject relating to the duties of their respective offices, and he shall have power to grant reprieves and pardons for offenses against the United States, except in cases of impeachment.[2]

For president's removal power, see p. 504.

2. The president may negotiate treaties and nominate federal officials. He shall have power, by and with the advice and consent of the Senate, to make treaties, provided two-thirds of the Senators present concur; and he shall nominate, and by and with the advice and consent of the Senate, shall appoint ambassadors, other public ministers and consuls, judges of the Supreme Court, and all other officers of the United States, whose appointments are not herein otherwise provided for, and which shall be established by law: but the Congress may by law vest the appointment of such inferior officers, as they think proper, in the President alone, in the courts of law, or in the heads of departments.

3. The president may fill vacancies during Senate recess. The President shall have power to fill up all vacancies that may happen during the recess of the Senate, by granting commissions which shall expire at the end of their next session.

---

[1] Repealed in 1804 by the Twelfth Amendment (for text see below).

[2] To prevent the president's pardoning himself or his close associates, as was feared in the case of Richard Nixon. See pp. 977–978.

Section III.   Other Powers and Duties of the President

For president's personal appearances, see p. 708.

Messages; extra sessions; receiving ambassadors; execution of the laws. He shall from time to time give to the Congress information of the state of the Union, and recommend to their consideration such measures as he shall judge necessary and expedient; he may, on extraordinary occasions, convene both houses, or either of them, and in case of disagreement between them, with respect to the time of adjournment, he may adjourn them to such time as he shall think proper; he shall receive ambassadors and other public ministers; he shall take care that the laws be faithfully executed, and shall commission all the officers of the United States.

Section IV.   Impeachment

See Johnson's acquittal, p. 504; also Nixon's near impeachment, pp. 977–978.

Civil officers may be removed by impeachment. The President, Vice President and all civil officers[1] of the United States shall be removed from office on impeachment for, and on conviction of, treason, bribery, and other high crimes and misdemeanors.

Article III.   *Judicial Department*

Section I.   The Federal Courts

See Judiciary Act of 1789, p. 192.

The judicial power belongs to the federal courts. The judicial power of the United States shall be vested in one Supreme Court, and in such inferior courts as the Congress may from time to time ordain and establish. The judges, both of the Supreme and inferior courts, shall hold their offices during good behavior, and shall, at stated times, receive for their services a compensation which shall not be diminished[2] during their continuance in office.

Section II.   Jurisdiction of Federal Courts

1. Kinds of cases that may be heard. The judicial power shall extend to all cases, in law and equity, arising under this Constitution, the laws of the United States, and treaties made, or which shall be made, under their authority;—to all cases affecting ambassadors, other public ministers and consuls;—to all cases of admiralty and maritime jurisdiction;—to controversies to which the United States shall be a party;—to controversies between two or more States;—*between a State and citizens of another State*[3];—between citizens of different States;—between citizens of the same State claiming lands under grants of different States, and between a State, or the citizens thereof, and foreign states, citizens or subjects.

2. Jurisdiction of the Supreme Court. In all cases affecting ambassadors, other public ministers and consuls, and those in which a State shall be a party, the Supreme Court shall have original jurisdiction.[4] In all the other cases before mentioned, the Supreme Court shall have appellate jurisdiction,[5] both as to law and fact, with such exceptions, and under such regulations, as the Congress shall make.

3. Trial for federal crime is by jury. The trial of all crimes, except in cases of impeachment, shall be by jury; and such trial shall be held in the State where the said crimes shall have been committed; but when not committed within any State, the trial shall be at such place or places as the Congress may by law have directed.

---

[1] i.e., all federal executive and judicial officers, but not members of Congress or military personnel.

[2] In 1978, in a case involving federal judges, the Supreme Court ruled that diminution of salaries by inflation was irrelevant.

[3] The Eleventh Amendment (see below) restricts this to suits by a state against citizens of another state.

[4] i.e., such cases must originate in the Supreme Court.

[5] i.e., it hears other cases only when they are appealed to it from a lower federal court or a state court.

SECTION III. Treason

See Burr trial, p. 222.

1. Treason defined. Treason against the United States shall consist only in levying war against them, or in adhering to their enemies, giving them aid and comfort. No person shall be convicted of treason unless on the testimony of two witnesses to the same overt act, or on confession in open court.

2. Congress fixes punishment for treason. The Congress shall have power to declare the punishment of treason, but no attainder of treason shall work corruption of blood, or forfeiture except during the life of the person attained.[1]

Article IV.   *Relations of the States to One Another*

SECTION I.   Credit to Acts, Records, and Court Proceedings

Each state must respect the public acts of the others. Full faith and credit shall be given in each State to the public acts, records, and judicial proceedings of every other State.[2] And the Congress may by general laws prescribe the manner in which such acts, records, and proceedings shall be proved [attested], and the effect thereof.

SECTION II.   Duties of States to States

1. Citizenship in one state is valid in all. The citizens of each State shall be entitled to all privileges and immunities of citizens in the several States.

This stipulation is sometimes openly flouted. In 1978 Governor Jerry Brown of California, acting on humanitarian grounds, refused to surrender to South Dakota an American Indian, Dennis Banks, who was charged with murder in an armed uprising.

Basis of fugitive-slave laws; see pp. 408–410.

2. Fugitives from justice must be surrendered by the state to which they have fled. A person charged in any State with treason, felony, or other crime, who shall flee from justice, and be found in another State, shall on demand of the executive authority [governor] of the State from which he fled, be delivered up, to be removed to the State having jurisdiction of the crime.

3. Slaves and apprentices must be returned. *No person held to service or labor in one State, under the laws thereof, escaping into another, shall, in consequence of any law or regulation therein, be discharged from such service or labor, but shall be delivered up on claim of the party to whom such service or labor may be due.*[3]

SECTION III.   New States and Territories

e.g., Maine (1820); see p. 245.

1. Congress may admit new states. New States may be admitted by the Congress into this Union; but no new State shall be formed or erected within the jurisdiction of any other State; nor any State be formed by the junction of two or more States, or parts of States, without the consent of the legislatures of the States concerned as well as of the Congress.[4]

2. Congress regulates federal territory and property. The Congress shall have power to dispose of and make all needful rules and regulations respecting the territory or other property belonging to the United States; and nothing in this Constitution shall be so construed as to prejudice any claims of the United States, or of any particular State.

SECTION IV.   Protection to the States

See Cleveland and the Pullman strike, p. 631

United States guarantees to states representative government and protection against invasion and rebellion. The United States shall guarantee to every State in this Union a

---

[1]i.e., punishment only for the offender; none for his or her heirs.

[2]e.g., a marriage in one is valid in all.

[3]Invalidated in 1865 by the Thirteenth Amendment (for text see below).

[4]Loyal West Virginia was formed by Lincoln in 1862 from seceded Virginia. This act was of dubious constitutionality and was justified in part by the wartime powers of the president. See pp. 444–445.

republican form of government, and shall protect each of them against invasion; and on application of the legislature, or of the executive [governor] (when the legislature cannot be convened), against domestic violence.

Article V.   *The Process of Amendment*

The Constitution may be amended in four ways. The Congress, whenever two-thirds of both houses shall deem it necessary, shall propose amendments to this Constitution, or, on the application of the legislature of two-thirds of the several States, shall call a convention for proposing amendments, which, in either case, shall be valid to all intents and purposes, as part of this Constitution, when ratified by the legislatures of three-fourths of the several States, or by conventions in three-fourths thereof, as the one or the other mode of ratification may be proposed by the Congress; provided *that no amendments which may be made prior to the year one thousand eight hundred and eight shall in any manner affect the first and fourth clauses in the ninth section of the first article;*[1] and that no State, without its consent, shall be deprived of its equal suffrage in the Senate.

Article VI.   *General Provisions*

This pledge honored by Hamilton, p. 192.

1. The debts of the Confederation are taken over. All debts contracted and engagements entered into, before the adoption of this Constitution, shall be as valid against the United States under this Constitution, as under the Confederation.

2. The Constitution, federal laws, and treaties are the supreme law of the land. This Constitution, and the laws of the United States which shall be made in pursuance thereof; and all treaties made, or which shall be made, under the authority of the United States, shall be the supreme law of the land; and the judges in every State shall be bound thereby, anything in the Constitution or laws of any State to the contrary notwithstanding.

3. Federal and state officers bound by oath to support the Constitution. The Senators and Representatives before mentioned, and the members of the several State legislatures, and all executive and judicial officers, both of the United States and of the several States, shall be bound by oath or affirmation to support this Constitution; but no religious test shall ever be required as a qualification to any office or public trust under the United States.

Article VII.   *Ratification of the Constitution*

See 1787 irregularity, pp. 181–182.

The Constitution effective when ratified by conventions in nine states. The ratification of the conventions of nine States shall be sufficient for the establishment of this Constitution between the States so ratifying the same.

Done in Convention by the unanimous consent of the States present, the seventeenth day of September in the year of our Lord one thousand seven hundred and eighty-seven and of the Independence of the United States of America the twelfth. In witness whereof we have hereunto subscribed our names.

[Signed by]

G° Washington

Presidt and Deputy from Virginia
[and thirty-eight others]

---

[1]This clause, re slave trade and direct taxes, became inoperative in 1808

AMENDMENTS TO THE CONSTITUTION

Amendment I.   *Religious and Political Freedom*

For background of Bill of Rights, see pp. 191–192.

Congress must not interfere with freedom of religion, speech or press, assembly, and petition. Congress shall make no law respecting an establishment of religion,[1] or prohibiting the free exercise thereof; or abridging the freedom of speech, or of the press; or the right of the people peaceably to assemble, and to petition the government for a redress of grievances.

Amendment II.   *Right to Bear Arms*

The people may bear arms. A well-regulated militia being necessary to the security of a free State, the right of the people to keep and bear arms [i.e., for military purposes] shall not be infringed.[2]

Amendment III.   *Quartering of Troops*

See Declaration of Independence and British quartering above.

Soldiers may not be arbitrarily quartered on the people. No soldier shall, in time of peace, be quartered in any house without the consent of the owner, nor in time of war, but in a manner to be prescribed by law.

Amendment IV.   *Searches and Seizures*

A reflection of colonial grievances against the crown.

Unreasonable searches are forbidden. The right of the people to be secure in their persons, houses, papers, and effects, against unreasonable searches and seizures, shall not be violated, and no [search] warrants shall issue but upon probable cause, supported by oath or affirmation, and particularly describing the place to be searched, and the persons or things to be seized.

Amendment V.   *Right to Life, Liberty, and Property*

When witnesses refuse to answer questions in court, they routinely "take the Fifth Amendment."

The individual is guaranteed certain rights when on trial and the right to life, liberty, and property. No person shall be held to answer for a capital, or otherwise infamous crime, unless on a presentment [formal charge] or indictment of a grand jury, except in cases arising in the naval forces, or in the militia, when in actual service in time of war or public danger; nor shall any person be subject for the same offense to be twice put in jeopardy of life or limb; nor shall be compelled in any criminal case to be a witness against himself, nor be deprived of life, liberty, or property, without due process of law; nor shall private property be taken for public use [i.e., by eminent domain] without just compensation.

Amendment VI.   *Protection in Criminal Trials*

See Declaration of Independence above.

An accused person has important rights. In all criminal prosecutions, the accused shall enjoy the right to a speedy and public trial, by an impartial jury of the State and district

---

[1]In 1787 "an establishment of religion" referred to an "established church," or one supported by all taxpayers, whether members or not. But the courts have often acted under this article to keep religion, including prayers, out of the public schools.

[2]The courts, with "militia" in mind, have consistently held that the "right" to bear arms is a limited one.

wherein the crime shall have been committed, which district shall have been previously ascertained by law, and to be informed of the nature and cause of the accusation; to be confronted with the witnesses against him; to have compulsory process [subpoena] for obtaining witnesses in his favor, and to have the assistance of counsel for his defense.

Amendment VII.   *Suits at Common Law*

The rules of common law are recognized. In suits at common law, where the value in controversy shall exceed twenty dollars, the right of trial by jury shall be preserved, and no fact tried by a jury shall be otherwise re-examined in any court of the United States, than according to the rules of the common law.

Amendment VIII.   *Bail and Punishments*

Excessive fines and unusual punishments are forbidden. Excessive bail shall not be required, nor excessive fines imposed, nor cruel and unusual punishment inflicted.

Amendment IX.   *Concerning Rights Not Enumerated*

The Ninth and Tenth Amendments were bulwarks of southern states' rights before the Civil War.

The people retain rights not here enumerated. The enumeration in the Constitution, of certain rights, shall not be construed to deny or disparage others retained by the people.

Amendment X.   *Powers Reserved to the States and to the People*

A concession to states' rights, p. 194.

Powers not delegated to the federal government are reserved to the states and the people. The powers not delegated to the United States by the Constitution, nor prohibited by it to the States, are reserved to the States respectively, or to the people.

Amendment XI.   *Suits Against a State*

The federal courts have no authority in suits by citizens against a state. The judicial power of the United States shall not be construed to extend to any suit in law or equity, commenced or prosecuted against one of the United States by citizens of another State, or by citizens or subjects of any foreign state. [Adopted 1798.]

Amendment XII.   *Election of President and Vice President*

Forestalls repetition of 1800 electoral dispute, pp. 211–212.

See 1876 disputed election. p. 519.

See 1824 election, pp. 259–260.

1. Changes in manner of electing president and vice president; procedure when no presidential candidate receives electoral majority. The electors shall meet in their respective States, and vote by ballot for President and Vice President, one of whom, at least, shall not be an inhabitant of the same state with themselves; they shall name in their ballots the person voted for as President, and in distinct ballots the person voted for as Vice President, and they shall make distinct lists of all persons voted for as President, and of all persons voted for as Vice President, and of the number of votes for each, which lists they shall sign and certify, and transmit sealed to the seat of government of the United States, directed to the President of the Senate;—the President of the Senate shall, in the presence of the Senate and House of Representatives, open all the certificates and the votes shall be counted;—the person having the greatest number of votes for President shall be the President, if such number be a majority of the whole number of electors appointed; and if no person have such majority, then from the persons having the highest numbers not exceeding three on the list of those voted for as President, the House of Representatives shall choose immediately, by ballot, the President. But in choosing the President, the votes shall be taken by States, the representation from each State having one vote; a quorum for this purpose shall consist of a member or members from two-thirds of the States, and a majority of all the States shall be necessary to a choice. And if the House of Representatives shall not choose a President whenever the right of choice shall devolve upon them, before *the fourth day of March*[1] next following, then the Vice President shall act as President, as in the case of the death or other constitutional disability of the President.

2. Procedure when no vice presidential candidate receives electoral majority. The person having the greatest number of votes as Vice President, shall be the Vice President, if such number be a majority of the whole number of electors appointed; and if no person have a majority, then from the two highest numbers on the list the Senate shall choose the Vice President; a quorum for the purpose shall consist of two-thirds of the whole number of Senators, and a majority of the whole number shall be necessary to a choice. But no person constitutionally ineligible to the office of President shall be eligible to that of Vice President of the United States. [Adopted 1804.]

Amendment XIII.   *Slavery Prohibited*

For background see p. 468.

Slavery forbidden. 1. Neither slavery[2] nor involuntary servitude, except as a punishment for crime whereof the party shall have been duly convicted, shall exist within the United States, or any place subject to their jurisdiction.

2. Congress shall have power to enforce this article by appropriate legislation. [Adopted 1865.]

Amendment XIV.   *Civil Rights for Ex-slaves,[3] etc.*

For background see pp. 495–496.

For corporations as "persons," see pp. 550–551.

Abolishes three-fifths rule for slaves, Art. I., Sec. II, para. 3.

1. Ex-slaves made citizens; U.S. citizenship primary. All persons born or naturalized in the United States, and subject to the jurisdiction thereof, are citizens of the United States and of the State wherein they reside. No State shall make or enforce any law which shall abridge the privileges or immunities of citizens of the United States; nor shall any State deprive any person of life, liberty, or property, without due process of law; nor deny to any person within its jurisdiction the equal protection of the laws.

2. When a state denies citizens the vote, its representation shall be reduced. Representatives shall be apportioned among the several States according to their respective numbers, counting the whole number of persons in each State, excluding Indians not taxed. But when the right to vote at any election for the choice of Electors for President and Vice President of the United States, Representatives in Congress, the executive and judicial officers of a State, or the members of the legislature thereof, is denied to any of the male inhabitants of such State, being twenty-one years of age and citizens of the United States, or in any way abridged, except for participation in rebellion, or other crime, the basis of representation therein shall be reduced in the proportion which the number of such make citizens shall bear to the whole number of male citizens twenty-one years of age in such State.[4]

Leading ex-Confederates denied office. See p. 496.

3. Certain persons who have been in rebellion are ineligible for federal and state office. No person shall be a Senator or Representative in Congress, or Elector of President and Vice President, or hold any office, civil or military, under the United States, or under any State, who, having previously taken an oath, as a member of Congress, or as an officer

---

[1]Changed to January 20 by the Twentieth Amendment (for text see below).

[2]The only explicit mention of slavery in the Constitution.

[3]Occasionally an offender is prosecuted under the Thirteenth Amendment for keeping an employee or other person under conditions approximating slavery.

[4]The provisions concerning "male" inhabitants were modified by the Nineteenth Amendment, which enfranchised women. The legal voting age was changed from twenty-one to eighteen by the Twenty-sixth Amendment.

of the United States, or as a member of any State legislature, or as an executive or judicial officer of any State, to support the Constitution of the United States, shall have engaged in insurrection or rebellion against the same, or given aid or comfort to the enemies thereof. But Congress may, by a vote of two-thirds of each house, remove such disability.

The ex-Confederates were thus forced to repudiate their debts and pay pensions to their own veterans, plus taxes for the pensions of Union veterans, their conquerors.

4. Debts incurred in aid of rebellion are void. The validity of the public debt of the United States, authorizing by law, including debts incurred for payment of pensions and bounties for services in suppressing insurrection or rebellion, shall not be questioned. But neither the United States nor any State shall assume or pay any debt or obligation incurred in aid of insurrection or rebellion against the United States, or any claim for the loss or emancipation of any slave; but all such debts, obligations, and claims shall be held illegal and void.

5. Enforcement. The Congress shall have power to enforce, by appropriate legislation, the provisions of this article. [Adopted 1868.]

Amendment XV.   *Suffrage for Blacks*

For background see p. 498.

Black males are made voters. 1. The right of the citizens of the United States to vote shall not be denied or abridged by the United States or by any State on account of race, color, or previous condition of servitude.

2. The Congress shall have power to enforce this article by appropriate legislation. [Adopted 1870.]

Amendment XVI.   *Income Taxes*

For background see pp. 632, 707.

Congress has power to lay and collect income taxes. The Congress shall have power to lay and collect taxes on incomes, from whatever source derived, without apportionment among the several States, and without regard to any census or enumeration. [Adopted 1913.]

Amendment XVII.   *Direct Election of Senators*

Senators shall be elected by popular vote. 1. The Senate of the United States shall be composed of two Senators from each State, elected by the people thereof, for six years; and each Senator shall have one vote. The electors in each State shall have the qualifications requisite for electors of [voters for] the most numerous branch of the State legislatures.

2. When vacancies happen in the representation of any State in the Senate, the executive authority of such State shall issue writs of election to fill such vacancies: Provided, that the Legislature of any State may empower the executive thereof to make temporary appointments until the people fill the vacancies by election as the Legislature may direct.

3. This amendment shall not be so construed as to affect the election or term of any Senator chosen before it becomes valid as part of the Constitution. [Adopted 1913.]

Amendment XVIII.   *National Prohibition*

For background see p. 752.

The sale or manufacture of intoxicating liquors is forbidden. 1. *After one year from the ratification of this article the manufacture, sale, or transportation of intoxicating liquors within, the importation thereof into, or the exportation thereof from the United States and all territory subject to the jurisdiction thereof, for beverage purposes, is hereby prohibited.*

2. *The Congress and the several States shall have concurrent power to enforce this article by appropriate legislation.*

3. *This article shall be inoperative unless it shall have been ratified as an amendment to the Constitution by the legislatures of the several States, as provided by the Constitution,* *within seven years from the date of the submission thereof to the States by the Congress.* [Adopted 1919; repealed 1933 by Twenty-first Amendment.]

Amendment XIX.   *Woman Suffrage*

For background see p. 729.

Women guaranteed the right to vote. 1. The right of citizens of the United States to vote shall not be denied or abridged by the United States or by any State on account of sex.

2. Congress shall have power to enforce this article by appropriate legislation. [Adopted 1920.]

Amendment XX.   *Presidential and Congressional Terms*

Shortens lame duck periods by modifying Art. I, Sec. IV, para. 2.

1. Presidential, vice presidential, and congressional terms of office begin in January. The terms of the President and Vice President shall end at noon on the 20th day of January, and the terms of Senators and Representatives at noon on the 3d day of January, of the years in which such terms would have ended if this article had not been ratified; and the terms of their successors shall then begin.

2. New meeting date for Congress. The Congress shall assemble at least once in every year, and such meeting shall begin at noon on the 3d day of January, unless they shall by law appoint a different day.

3. Emergency presidential and vice presidential succession. If, at the time fixed for the beginning of the term of the President, the President-elect shall have died, the Vice President–elect shall become President. If a President shall not have been chosen before the time fixed for the beginning of his term, or if the President-elect shall have failed to qualify, then the Vice President–elect shall act as President until a President shall have qualified; and the Congress may by law provide for the case wherein neither a President-elect nor a Vice President–elect shall have qualified, declaring who shall then act as President, or the manner in which one who is to act shall be selected, and such persons shall act accordingly until a President or Vice President shall have qualified.

4. The Congress may by law provide for the case of the death of any of the persons from whom the House of Representatives may choose a President whenever the right of choice shall have devolved upon them, and for the case of the death of any of the persons from whom the Senate may choose a Vice President whenever the right of choice shall have devolved upon them.

5. Sections 1 and 2 shall take effect on the 15th day of October following the ratification of this article.

6. This article shall be inoperative unless it shall have been ratified as an amendment to the Constitution by the Legislatures of three-fourths of the several States within seven years from the date of its submission. [Adopted 1933.]

Amendment XXI.   *Prohibition Repealed*

For background see p. 806.

1. Eighteenth Amendment repealed. The eighteenth article of amendment to the Constitution of the United States is hereby repealed.

2. Local laws honored. The transportation or importation into any State, Territory, or Possession of the United States for delivery or use therein of intoxicating liquors, in violation of the laws thereof, is hereby prohibited.

3. This article shall be inoperative unless it shall have been ratified as an amendment to the Constitution by conventions in the several States, as provided in the Constitution, within seven years from the date of the submission thereof to the States by the Congress. [Adopted 1933.]

Amendment XXII.

Sometimes referred to as the anti–Franklin Roosevelt amendment.

Anti–Third Term Amendment

1. Presidential term is limited. No person shall be elected to the office of President more than twice, and no person who has held the office of President, or acted as President, for more than two years of a term to which some other person was elected President shall be elected to the office of President more than once. But this article shall not apply to any person holding the office of President when this article was proposed by the Congress [i.e., Truman], and shall not prevent any person who may be holding the office of President, during the term within which this article becomes operative [i.e., Truman] from holding the office of President or acting as President during the remainder of such term.

2. This article shall be inoperative unless it shall have been ratified as an amendment to the Constitution by the legislatures of three-fourths of the several States within seven years from the date of its submission to the States by the Congress. [Adopted 1951.]

Amendment XXIII.

Designed to give the District of Columbia three electoral votes and to quiet the century-old cry of "No taxation without representation." Yet the District of Columbia still has only one nonvoting member of Congress.

District of Columbia Vote

1. Presidential electors for the District of Columbia. The District, constituting the seat of government of the United States, shall appoint in such manner as the Congress shall direct:

A number of electors of President and Vice President equal to the whole number of Senators and Representatives in Congress to which the District would be entitled if it were a State, but in no event more than the least populous State; they shall be in addition to those appointed by the States, but they shall be considered for the purposes of the election of President and Vice President, to be electors appointed by a State; and they shall meet in the District and perform such duties as provided by the twelfth article of amendment.

2. Enforcement. The Congress shall have the power to enforce this article by appropriate legislation. [Adopted 1961.]

Amendment XXIV.

Designed to end discrimination against poor people, including southern blacks who were often denied the vote through inability to pay poll taxes. See p. 949.

Poll Tax

1. Payment of poll tax or other taxes not to be prerequisite for voting in federal elections. The right of citizens of the United States to vote in any primary or other election for President or Vice President, for electors for President or Vice President, or for Senator or Representative in Congress, shall not be denied or abridged by the United States or any State by reason of failure to pay any poll tax or other tax.

2. Enforcement. The Congress shall have the power to enforce this article by appropriate legislation. [Adopted 1964.]

Amendment XXV.

Gerald Ford was the first "appointed president." See pp. 975, 978.

Presidential Succession and Disability

1. Vice president to become president. In case of the removal of the President from office or of his death or resignation, the Vice President shall become President.[1]

2. Successor to vice president provided. Whenever there is a vacancy in the office of the Vice President, the President shall nominate a Vice President who shall take office upon confirmation by a majority vote of both Houses of Congress.

---

[1]The original Constitution (Art. II, Sec. I, para. 5) was vague on this point, stipulating that "the powers and duties" of the president, but not necessarily the title, should "devolve" on the vice president. President Tyler, the first "accidental president," assumed not only the powers and duties but the title as well.

3. Vice president to serve for disabled president. Whenever the President transmits to the President pro tempore of the Senate and the Speaker of the House of Representatives his written declaration that he is unable to discharge the powers and duties of his office, and until he transmits to them a written declaration to the contrary, such powers and duties shall be discharged by the Vice President as Acting President.

4. Procedure for disqualifying or requalifying president. Whenever the Vice President and a majority of either the principal officers of the executive departments or of such other body as Congress may by law provide, transmit to the President pro tempore of the Senate and the Speaker of the House of Representatives their written declaration that the President is unable to discharge the powers and duties of his office, the Vice President shall immediately assume the powers and duties of the office as Acting President.

Thereafter, when the President transmits to the President pro tempore of the Senate and the Speaker of the House of Representatives his written declaration that no inability exists, he shall resume the powers and duties of his office unless the Vice President and a majority of either the principal officers of the executive department[s] or of such other body as Congress may by law provide, transmit within four days to the President pro tempore of the Senate and the Speaker of the House of Representatives their written declaration that the President is unable to discharge the powers and duties of his office. Thereupon Congress shall decide the issue, assembling within forty-eight hours for that purpose if not in session. If the Congress, within twenty-one days after receipt of the latter written declaration, or, if Congress is not in session, within twenty-one days after Congress is required to assemble, determines by two-thirds vote of both Houses that the President is unable to discharge the powers and duties of his office, the Vice President shall continue to discharge the same as Acting President; otherwise, the President shall resume the powers and duties of his office. [Adopted 1967.]

Amendment XXVI.   *Lowering Voting Age*

A response to the current revolt of youth. See p. 968.

1. Ballot for eighteen-year-olds. The right of citizens of the United States, who are eighteen years of age or older, to vote shall not be denied or abridged by the United States or any state on account of age.

2. Enforcement. The Congress shall have the power to enforce this article by appropriate legislation. [Adopted 1971.]

Amendment XXVII.   *Restricting Congressional Pay Raises*

Reflects anti-incumbent sentiment of early 1990s See p. 1013.

Congress not allowed to increase its current pay. No law varying the compensation for the services of the Senators and Representatives shall take effect, until an election of Representatives shall have intervened. [Adopted 1992.]

*An American Profile:
The United States
and Its People*

Population, Percentage Change, and Racial Composition For the United States, 1790–1990

| Census | Population of United States | Increase over Preceding Census | | Racial Composition, Percent Distribution* | | | |
		Number	Percentage	White	Black	Hispanic	Asian
1790	3,929,214			80.7	19.3	NA	NA
1800	5,308,483	1,379,269	35.1	81.1	18.9	NA	NA
1810	7,239,881	1,931,398	36.4	81.0	19.0	NA	NA
1820	9,638,453	2,398,572	33.1	81.6	18.4	NA	NA
1830	12,866,020	3,227,567	33.5	81.9	18.1	NA	NA
1840	17,069,453	4,203,433	32.7	83.2	16.8	NA	NA
1850	23,191,876	6,122,423	35.9	84.3	15.7	NA	NA
1860	31,433,321	8,251,445	35.6	85.6	14.1	NA	NA
1870	39,818,449	8,375,128	26.6	86.2	13.5	NA	NA
1880	50,155,783	10,337,334	26.0	86.5	13.1	NA	NA
1890	62,947,714	12,791,931	25.5	87.5	11.9	NA	NA
1900	75,994,575	13,046,861	20.7	87.9	11.6	NA	0.3
1910	91,972,266	15,997,691	21.0	88.9	10.7	NA	0.3
1920	105,710,620	13,738,354	14.9	89.7	9.9	NA	0.3
1930	122,775,046	17,064,426	16.1	89.8	9.7	NA	0.4
1940	131,669,275	8,894,229	7.2	89.8	9.8	NA	0.4
1950	150,697,361	19,028,086	14.5	89.5	10.0	NA	0.4
1960†	179,323,175	28,625,814	19.0	88.6	10.5	NA	0.5
1970	203,235,298	23,912,123	13.3	87.6	11.1	NA	0.7
1980	226,504,825	23,269,527	11.4	85.9	11.8	6.4	1.5
1990	249,975,000	22,164,068	9.8	83.9	12.3	9.0	2.9

*Not every racial group included (e.g., no Native Americans). Persons of Hispanic origin may be of any race. Data for 1980, 1990 add up to more than 100% because those who identify themselves as "Hispanic" could still be counted as "White."
†First year for which figures include Alaska and Hawaii.
(Source: Census Bureau, *Historical Statistics of the United States,* updated by relevant *Statistical Abstract of the United States.*)

Population Density and Distribution, 1790–1990

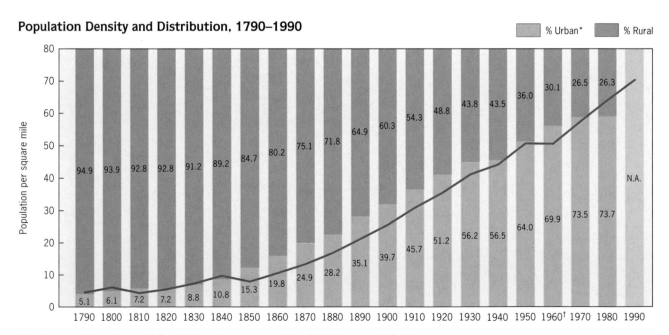

% Urban*   % Rural

*The Bureau of the Census defines "urban" as communities of 2,500 or more inhabitants.
†First year for which figures include Alaska and Hawaii.
(Source: Census Bureau, *Historical Statistics of the United States,* updated by relevant *Statistical Abstract of the United States.*)

Changing Characteristics of the U.S. Population

Birth rates per thousand women ages 15–44

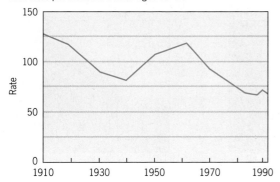

Life expectancy at birth

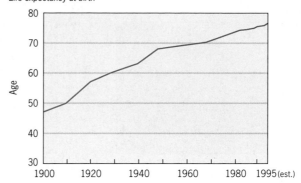

Median age of population (years)

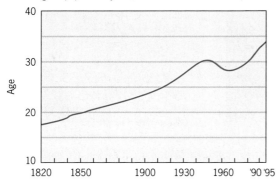

Infant mortality

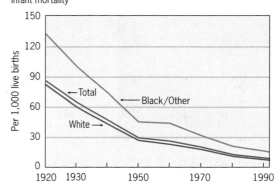

Household size

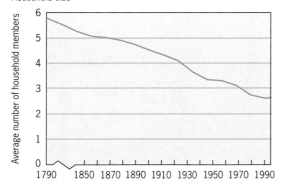

Median age at first marriage

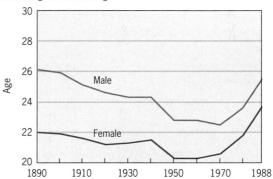

(Sources: *Historical Statistics of the United States* and *Statistical Abstract of the United States,* relevant years.)

Changing Lifestyles in the Twentieth Century

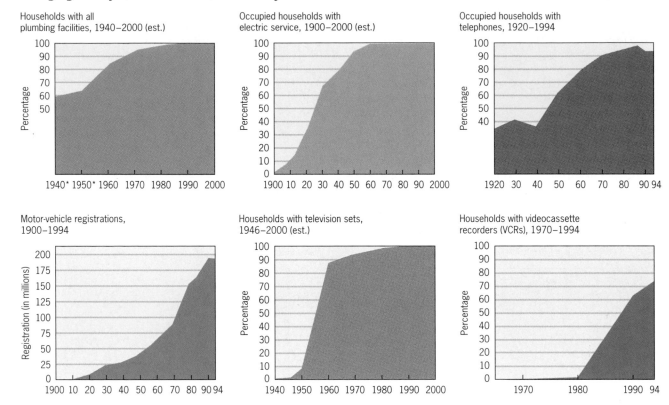

Households with all plumbing facilities, 1940–2000 (est.)

Occupied households with electric service, 1900–2000 (est.)

Occupied households with telephones, 1920–1994

Motor-vehicle registrations, 1900–1994

Households with television sets, 1946–2000 (est.)

Households with videocassette recorders (VCRs), 1970–1994

*Except for 1940 and 1950, figures for "all plumbing facilities" (not detailed in source). For 1940, figure is for flush toilet, inside structure, private use (64.7 percent had flush toilet, and private and/or shared inside structure, and 60.9 percent had installed bath or shower). For 1950, figure designates units with private toilet and bath, and hot running water (flush toilet, private or shared inside structure is 74.3 percent; installed bathtub or shower, 72.9 percent).

(Sources: *Historical Statistics of the United States* and *Statistical Abstract of the United States*, relevant years.)

Characteristics of the U.S. Labor Force

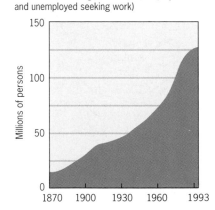

Total labor force (age 16 or over, employed and unemployed seeking work)

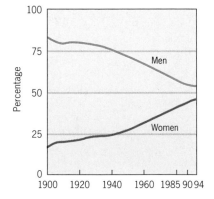

Sex composition of labor force, 1900–1994 (percentage of men and women in civilian labor force)

Top three occupational categories (rank based on total numbers) for workers age 14 and older

*Manual workers = operators, fabricators, and laborers plus precision production, craft, and repair.

†White-collar workers = managerial and professional plus technical, sales, and administrative support.

(Sources: *Historical Statistics of the United States* and *Statistical Abstract of the United States*, relevant years, and Department of Labor, Bureau of Labor Statistics, *Handbook of Labor Statistics*, relevant years.

Leading Economic Sectors (Various Years)

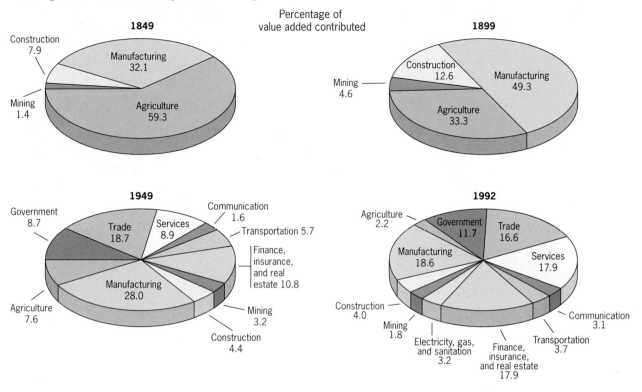

Percentage of value added contributed

1849

Construction 7.9
Mining 1.4
Manufacturing 32.1
Agriculture 59.3

1899

Construction 12.6
Mining 4.6
Manufacturing 49.3
Agriculture 33.3

1949

Government 8.7
Trade 18.7
Services 8.9
Communication 1.6
Transportation 5.7
Finance, insurance, and real estate 10.8
Mining 3.2
Construction 4.4
Manufacturing 28.0
Agriculture 7.6

1992

Agriculture 2.2
Government 11.7
Trade 16.6
Manufacturing 18.6
Services 17.9
Construction 4.0
Mining 1.8
Electricity, gas, and sanitation 3.2
Finance, insurance, and real estate 17.9
Transportation 3.7
Communication 3.1

(Sources: *Historical Statistics of the United States* and *Statistical Abstract of the United States,* relevant years.)

Per Capita Disposable Personal Income in Constant (1987) Dollars, 1940–1994

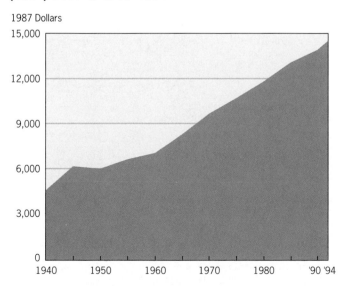

1987 Dollars

15,000
12,000
9,000
6,000
3,000
0

1940   1950   1960   1970   1980   '90 '94

Comparative Tax Burdens (Percentage of Gross Domestic Product Paid as Taxes in Major Industrial Countries, 1994)

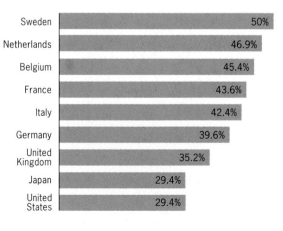

Sweden	50%
Netherlands	46.9%
Belgium	45.4%
France	43.6%
Italy	42.4%
Germany	39.6%
United Kingdom	35.2%
Japan	29.4%
United States	29.4%

(Source for both graphs: *Statistical Abstract of the United States.*)

Value of Imports and Exports by Selected Place of Origin and Destination (Millions of Dollars)

Year	Canada		United Kingdom		Japan	
	Imports from	Exports to	Imports from	Exports to	Imports from	Exports to
1900	39	95	160	534	33	29
1910	95	216	271	506	66	22
1920	612	972	514	1,825	415	378
1930	402	659	210	678	279	165
1940	424	713	155	1,011	158	227
1950	1,960	2,039	335	548	182	418
1960	2,901	3,810	993	1,487	1,149	1,447
1970	11,092	9,079	2,194	2,536	5,875	4,652
1980	41,459	35,395	9,842	12,694	30,714	20,792
1990	91,372	82,697	20,288	23,484	89,655	48,585
1994	128,947	114,255	25,063	26,833	119,149	53,481

The U.S. Balance of Trade, 1900–1994

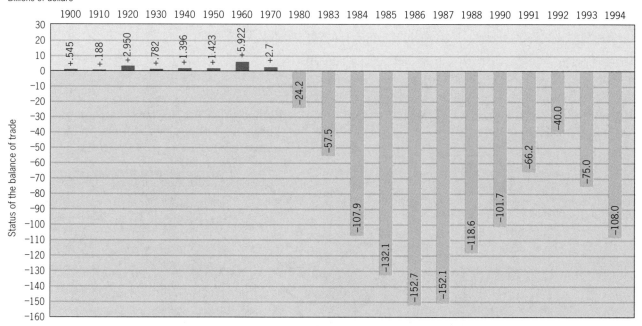

Billions of dollars

(Sources: *Historical Statistics of the United States* and *Statistical Abstract of the United States,* relevant years.)

Tariff Levies on Dutiable Imports, 1821–1994 (Ratio of Duties to Value of Dutiable Imports)

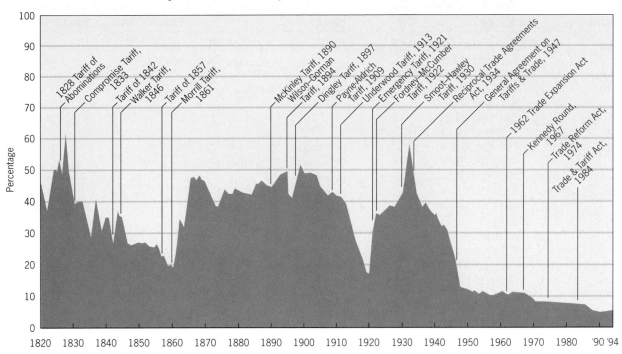

(Sources: *Historical Statistics of the United States* and *Statistical Abstract of the United States,* relevant years.)

Gross Domestic Product in Current and Constant 1995 Dollars*

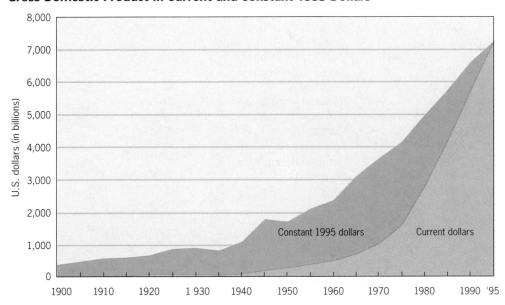

*Gross *national* product before 1960. Gross national product includes income from overseas investment, and excludes profits generated in the United States but accruing to foreign accounts. Gross *domestic* product excludes overseas profits owed to American accounts, but includes the value of all items originating in the United States, regardless of the ultimate destination of the profits. Until recent years, those factors made for negligible differences in the calculation of *national* and *domestic* product, but most economists now prefer the latter methodology.

Presidential Elections*

Election	Candidates	Parties	Popular Vote	Electoral Vote
1789	GEORGE WASHINGTON	No party designation		69
	JOHN ADAMS			34
	MINOR CANDIDATES			35
1792	GEORGE WASHINGTON	No party designation		132
	JOHN ADAMS			77
	GEORGE CLINTON			50
	MINOR CANDIDATES			5
1796	JOHN ADAMS	Federalist		71
	THOMAS JEFFERSON	Democratic-Republican		68
	THOMAS PINCKNEY	Federalist		59
	AARON BURR	Democratic-Republican		30
	MINOR CANDIDATES			48
1800	THOMAS JEFFERSON	Democratic-Republican		73
	AARON BURR	Democratic-Republican		73
	JOHN ADAMS	Federalist		65
	CHARLES C. PINCKNEY	Federalist		64
	JOHN JAY	Federalist		1
1804	THOMAS JEFFERSON	Democratic-Republican		162
	CHARLES C. PINCKNEY	Federalist		14
1808	JAMES MADISON	Democratic-Republican		122
	CHARLES C. PINCKNEY	Federalist		47
	GEORGE CLINTON	Democratic-Republican		6
1812	JAMES MADISON	Democratic-Republican		128
	DEWITT CLINTON	Federalist		89
1816	JAMES MONROE	Democratic-Republican		183
	RUFUS KING	Federalist		34
1820	JAMES MONROE	Democratic-Republican		231
	JOHN Q. ADAMS	Independent Republican		1
1824	JOHN Q. ADAMS (Min.)†	Democratic-Republican	108,740	84
	ANDREW JACKSON	Democratic-Republican	153,544	99
	WILLIAM H. CRAWFORD	Democratic-Republican	46,618	41
	HENRY CLAY	Democratic-Republican	47,136	37
1828	ANDREW JACKSON	Democratic	647,286	178
	JOHN Q. ADAMS	National Republican	508,064	83
1832	ANDREW JACKSON	Democratic	687,502	219
	HENRY CLAY	National Republican	530,189	49
	WILLIAM WIRT	Anti-Masonic	33,108	7
	JOHN FLOYD	National Republican		11
1836	MARTIN VAN BUREN	Democratic	765,483	170
	WILLIAM H. HARRISON	Whig		73
	HUGH L. WHITE	Whig	739,795	26
	DANIEL WEBSTER	Whig		14
	W.P. MANGUM	Whig		11
1840	WILLIAM H. HARRISON	Whig	1,274,624	234
	MARTIN VAN BUREN	Democratic	1,127,781	60
1844	JAMES K. POLK (Min.)†	Democratic	1,338,464	170
	HENRY CLAY	Whig	1,300,097	105
	JAMES G. BIRNEY	Liberty	62,300	

* Candidates receiving less than 1 percent of the popular vote are omitted. Before the Twelfth Amendment (1804), the Electoral College voted for two presidential candidates, and the runner-up became vice president. Basic figures are taken primarily from *Historical Statistics of the United States, Colonial Times to 1970* (1975), pp. 1073–1074, and *Statistical Abstract of the United States,* relevant years.

†"Min." indicates minority president—one receiving less than 50 percent of all popular votes.

Presidential Elections (Continued)

Election	Candidates	Parties	Popular Vote	Electoral Vote
1848	ZACHARY TAYLOR	Whig	1,360,967	163
	LEWIS CASS	Democratic	1,222,342	127
	MARTIN VAN BUREN	Free Soil	291,263	
1852	FRANKLIN PIERCE	Democratic	1,601,117	254
	WINFIELD SCOTT	Whig	1,385,453	42
	JOHN P. HALE	Free Soil	155,825	
1856	JAMES BUCHANAN (Min.)*	Democratic	1,832,955	174
	JOHN C. FRÉMONT	Republican	1,339,932	114
	MILLARD FILLMORE	American	871,731	8
1860	ABRAHAM LINCOLN (Min.)*	Republican	1,865,593	180
	STEPHEN A. DOUGLAS	Democratic	1,382,713	12
	JOHN C. BRECKINRIDGE	Democratic	848,356	72
	JOHN BELL	Constitutional Union	592,906	39
1864	ABRAHAM LINCOLN	Union	2,206,938	212
	GEORGE B. MC CLELLAN	Democratic	1,803,787	21
1868	ULYSSES S. GRANT	Republican	3,013,421	214
	HORATIO SEYMOUR	Democratic	2,706,829	80
1872	ULYSSES S. GRANT	Republican	3,596,745	286
	HORACE GREELEY	Democratic Liberal Republican	2,843,446	66
1876	RUTHERFORD B. HAYES (Min.)*	Republican	4,036,572	185
	SAMUEL J. TILDEN	Democratic	4,284,020	184
1880	JAMES A. GARFIELD (Min.)*	Republican	4,453,295	214
	WINFIELD S. HANCOCK	Democratic	4,414,082	155
	JAMES B. WEAVER	Greenback-Labor	308,578	
1884	GROVER CLEVELAND (Min.)*	Democratic	4,879,507	219
	JAMES G. BLAINE	Republican	4,850,293	182
	BENJAMIN F. BUTLER	Greenback-Labor	175,370	
	JOHN P. ST. JOHN	Prohibition	150,369	
1888	BENJAMIN HARRISON (Min.)*	Republican	5,447,129	233
	GROVER CLEVELAND	Democratic	5,537,857	168
	CLINTON B. FISK	Prohibition	249,506	
	ANSON J. STREETER	Union Labor	146,935	
1892	GROVER CLEVELAND (Min.)*	Democratic	5,555,426	277
	BENJAMIN HARRISON	Republican	5,182,690	145
	JAMES B. WEAVER	People's	1,029,846	22
	JOHN BIDWELL	Prohibition	264,133	
1896	WILLIAM MC KINLEY	Republican	7,102,246	271
	WILLIAM J. BRYAN	Democratic	6,492,559	176
1900	WILLIAM MC KINLEY	Republican	7,218,491	292
	WILLIAM J. BRYAN	Democratic; Populist	6,356,734	155
	JOHN C. WOOLLEY	Prohibition	208,914	
1904	THEODORE ROOSEVELT	Republican	7,628,461	336
	ALTON B. PARKER	Democratic	5,084,223	140
	EUGENE V. DEBS	Socialist	402,283	
	SILAS C. SWALLOW	Prohibition	258,536	
1908	WILLIAM H. TAFT	Republican	7,675,320	321
	WILLIAM J. BRYAN	Democratic	6,412,294	162
	EUGENE V. DEBS	Socialist	420,793	
	EUGENE W. CHAFIN	Prohibition	253,840	

* "Min." indicates minority president—one receiving less than 50 percent of all popular votes.

Presidential Elections (Continued)

Election	Candidates	Parties	Popular Vote	Electoral Vote
1912	WOODROW WILSON (Min.)*	Democratic	6,296,547	435
	THEODORE ROOSEVELT	Progressive	4,118,571	88
	WILLIAM H. TAFT	Republican	3,486,720	8
	EUGENE V. DEBS	Socialist	900,672	
	EUGENE W. CHAFIN	Prohibition	206,275	
1916	WOODROW WILSON (Min.)*	Democratic	9,127,695	277
	CHARLES E. HUGHES	Republican	8,533,507	254
	A. L. BENSON	Socialist	585,113	
	J. F. HANLY	Prohibition	220,506	
1920	WARREN G. HARDING	Republican	16,143,407	404
	JAMES M. COX	Democratic	9,130,328	127
	EUGENE V. DEBS	Socialist	919,799	
	P. P. CHRISTENSEN	Farmer-Labor	265,411	
1924	CALVIN COOLIDGE	Republican	15,718,211	382
	JOHN W. DAVIS	Democratic	8,385,283	136
	ROBERT M. LA FOLLETTE	Progressive	4,831,289	13
1928	HERBERT C. HOOVER	Republican	21,391,993	444
	ALFRED E. SMITH	Democratic	15,016,169	87
1932	FRANKLIN D. ROOSEVELT	Democratic	22,809,638	472
	HERBERT C. HOOVER	Republican	15,758,901	59
	NORMAN THOMAS	Socialist	881,951	
1936	FRANKLIN D. ROOSEVELT	Democratic	27,752,869	523
	ALFRED M. LANDON	Republican	16,674,665	8
	WILLIAM LEMKE	Union	882,479	
1940	FRANKLIN D. ROOSEVELT	Democratic	27,307,819	449
	WENDELL L. WILLKIE	Republican	22,321,018	82
1944	FRANKLIN D. ROOSEVELT	Democratic	25,606,585	432
	THOMAS E. DEWEY	Republican	22,014,745	99
1948	HARRY S TRUMAN (Min.)*	Democratic	24,179,345	303
	THOMAS E. DEWEY	Republican	21,991,291	189
	J. STROM THURMOND	States' Rights Democratic	1,176,125	39
	HENRY A. WALLACE	Progressive	1,157,326	
1952	DWIGHT D. EISENHOWER	Republican	33,936,234	442
	ADLAI E. STEVENSON	Democratic	27,314,992	89
1956	DWIGHT D. EISENHOWER	Republican	35,590,472	457
	ADLAI E. STEVENSON	Democratic	26,022,752	73
1960	JOHN F. KENNEDY (Min.)*†	Democratic	34,226,731	303
	RICHARD M. NIXON	Republican	34,108,157	219
1964	LYNDON B. JOHNSON	Democratic	43,129,566	486
	BARRY M. GOLDWATER	Republican	27,178,188	52
1968	RICHARD M. NIXON (Min.)*	Republican	31,785,480	301
	HUBERT H. HUMPHREY, JR.	Democratic	31,275,166	191
	GEORGE C. WALLACE	American Independent	9,906,473	46
1972	RICHARD M. NIXON	Republican	47,169,911	520
	GEORGE S. MC GOVERN	Democratic	29,170,383	17
1976	JIMMY CARTER	Democratic	40,828,657	297
	GERALD R. FORD	Republican	39,145,520	240

* "Min." indicates minority president—one receiving less than 50 percent of all popular votes.

†Six Democratic electors in Alabama, all eight unpledged Democratic electors in Mississippi, and one Republican elector in Oklahoma voted for Senator Harry F. Byrd.

Presidential Elections (Continued)

Election	Candidates	Parties	Popular Vote	Electoral Vote
1980	RONALD W. REAGAN	Republican	43,899,248	489
	JIMMY CARTER	Democratic	35,481,435	49
	JOHN B. ANDERSON	Independent	5,719,437	0
1984	RONALD W. REAGAN	Republican	52,609,797	525
	WALTER MONDALE	Democratic	36,450,613	13
1988	GEORGE BUSH	Republican	47,946,000	426
	MICHAEL DUKAKIS	Democratic	41,016,000	111
1992	WILLIAM CLINTON	Democratic	43,738,275	370
	GEORGE BUSH	Republican	38,167,416	168
	H. ROSS PEROT	Independent	19,237,247	
1996	WILLIAM CLINTON	Democratic	45,628,667	379
	ROBERT DOLE	Republican	37,869,435	159
	H. ROSS PEROT	Reform	7,874,283	

* "Min." indicates minority president—one receiving less than 50 percent of all popular votes.

Presidents and Vice Presidents

Term	President	Vice President
1789–1793	George Washington	John Adams
1793–1797	George Washington	John Adams
1797–1801	John Adams	Thomas Jefferson
1801–1805	Thomas Jefferson	Aaron Burr
1805–1809	Thomas Jefferson	George Clinton
1809–1813	James Madison	George Clinton (d. 1812)
1813–1817	James Madison	Elbridge Gerry (d. 1814)
1817–1821	James Monroe	Daniel D. Tompkins
1821–1825	James Monroe	Daniel D. Tompkins
1825–1829	John Quincy Adams	John C. Calhoun
1829–1833	Andrew Jackson	John C. Calhoun (resigned 1832)
1833–1837	Andrew Jackson	Martin Van Buren
1837–1841	Martin Van Buren	Richard M. Johnson
1841–1845	William H. Harrison (d. 1841) John Tyler	John Tyler
1845–1849	James K. Polk	George M. Dallas
1849–1853	Zachary Taylor (d. 1850) Millard Fillmore	Millard Fillmore
1853–1857	Franklin Pierce	William R. D. King (d. 1853)
1857–1861	James Buchanan	John C. Breckinridge
1861–1865	Abraham Lincoln	Hannibal Hamlin
1865–1869	Abraham Lincoln (d. 1865) Andrew Johnson	Andrew Johnson
1869–1873	Ulysses S. Grant	Schuyler Colfax
1873–1877	Ulysses S. Grant	Henry Wilson (d. 1875)
1877–1881	Rutherford B. Hayes	William A. Wheeler
1881–1885	James A. Garfield (d. 1881) Chester A. Arthur	Chester A. Arthur

Presidents and Vice Presidents (Continued)

Term	President	Vice President
1885–1889	Grover Cleveland	Thomas A. Hendricks (d. 1885)
1889–1893	Benjamin Harrison	Levi P. Morton
1893–1897	Grover Cleveland	Adlai E. Stevenson
1897–1901	William McKinley	Garret A. Hobart (d. 1899)
1901–1905	William McKinley (d. 1901) Theodore Roosevelt	Theodore Roosevelt
1905–1909	Theodore Roosevelt	Charles W. Fairbanks
1909–1913	William H. Taft	James S. Sherman (d. 1912)
1913–1917	Woodrow Wilson	Thomas R. Marshall
1917–1921	Woodrow Wilson	Thomas R. Marshall
1921–1925	Warren G. Harding (d. 1923) Calvin Coolidge	Calvin Coolidge
1925–1929	Calvin Coolidge	Charles G. Dawes
1929–1933	Herbert Hoover	Charles Curtis
1933–1937	Franklin D. Roosevelt	John N. Garner
1937–1941	Franklin D. Roosevelt	John N. Garner
1941–1945	Franklin D. Roosevelt	Henry A. Wallace
1945–1949	Franklin D. Roosevelt (d. 1945) Harry S Truman	Harry S Truman
1949–1953	Harry S Truman	Alben W. Barkley
1953–1957	Dwight D. Eisenhower	Richard M. Nixon
1957–1961	Dwight D. Eisenhower	Richard M. Nixon
1961–1965	John F. Kennedy (d. 1963) Lyndon B. Johnson	Lyndon B. Johnson
1965–1969	Lyndon B. Johnson	Hubert H. Humphrey, Jr.
1969–1974	Richard M. Nixon	Spiro T. Agnew (resigned 1973); Gerald R. Ford
1974–1977	Gerald R. Ford	Nelson A. Rockefeller
1977–1981	Jimmy Carter	Walter F. Mondale
1981–1985	Ronald Reagan	George Bush
1985–1989	Ronald Reagan	George Bush
1989–1993	George Bush	J. Danforth Quayle III
1993–	William Clinton	Albert Gore, Jr.

Admission of States

(See p. 182 for order in which the original thirteen entered the union.)

Order of Admission	State	Date of Admission	Order of Admission	State	Date of Admission
14	Vermont	Mar. 4, 1791	33	Oregon	Feb. 14, 1859
15	Kentucky	June 1, 1792	34	Kansas	Jan. 29, 1861
16	Tennessee	June 1, 1796	35	W. Virginia	June 20, 1863
17	Ohio	Mar. 1, 1803	36	Nevada	Oct. 31, 1864
18	Louisiana	April 30, 1812	37	Nebraska	Mar. 1, 1867
19	Indiana	Dec. 11, 1816	38	Colorado	Aug. 1, 1876
20	Mississippi	Dec. 10, 1817	39	N. Dakota	Nov. 2, 1889
21	Illinois	Dec. 3, 1818	40	S. Dakota	Nov. 2, 1889
22	Alabama	Dec. 14, 1819	41	Montana	Nov. 8, 1889
23	Maine	Mar. 15, 1820	42	Washington	Nov. 11, 1889
24	Missouri	Aug. 10, 1821	43	Idaho	July 3, 1890
25	Arkansas	June 15, 1836	44	Wyoming	July 10, 1890
26	Michigan	Jan. 26, 1837	45	Utah	Jan. 4, 1896
27	Florida	Mar. 3, 1845	46	Oklahoma	Nov. 16, 1907
28	Texas	Dec. 29, 1845	47	New Mexico	Jan. 6, 1912
29	Iowa	Dec. 28, 1846	48	Arizona	Feb. 14, 1912
30	Wisconsin	May 29, 1848	49	Alaska	Jan. 3, 1959
31	California	Sept. 9, 1850	50	Hawaii	Aug. 21, 1959
32	Minnesota	May 11, 1858			

Estimates of Total Costs and Number of Battle Deaths of Major U.S. Wars*

War	Total Costs** (Millions of Dollars)	Original Costs	Number of Battle Deaths
Vietnam Conflict	352,000	140,600	47,355[†]
Korean Conflict	164,000	54,000	33,629
World War II	664,000	288,000	291,557
World War I	112,000	26,000	53,402
Spanish-American War	6,460	400	385
Civil War { Union only	12,952	3,200	140,414
Civil War { Confederacy (est.)	N.A.	1,000	94,000
Mexican War	147	73	1,733
War of 1812	158	93	2,260
American Revolution	190	100	6,824

* Deaths from disease and other causes are not shown. In earlier wars especially, owing to poor medical and sanitary practices, nonbattle deaths substantially exceeded combat casualties.

** The difference between total costs and original costs is attributable to continuing postwar payments for such items as veterans' benefits, interest on war debts, and so on.

† 1957–1990

(Sources: *Historical Statistics of the United States, Statistical Abstract of the United States,* relevant years, and *The World Almanac and Book of Facts, 1986.*)

INDEX

PHOTOGRAPH CREDITS

Makers of America masthead (left to right) Library of Congress, Chicago Historical Society, Smithsonian Institution, National Anthropological Archives #76-5800, Library of Congress, Western History Department/Denver Public Library, Courtesy of "La Rochester," Mexico City. (Pages 16, 48, 70, 86, 116, 150, 246, 284, 304, 308, 344, 396, 524, 560, 572, 658, 668, 750, 808, 834, 850, 856, 888, 982, 982, 1034.)

Part One
p. 2 © British Museum; p. 3 Library of Congress.

Chapter 1
p. 5 Steve Proehl/The Image Bank; p. 9 Cahokia Mounds Historic Site. Painting by Lloyd K. Townsend. Photo by Art Grossman; p. 10 Courtesy of the John Carter Brown Library at Brown University; p. 11 Lee Boltin/Boltin Picture Library; p. 13 Scala/Art Resource, NY; p. 15 The Bettmann Archive; p. 16 Giraudon/Art Resource, NY; p. 17 Library of Congress; p. 19 (left) Mexican National Tourist Council; p. 19 (right) Library of Congress; p. 20 Bibliothèque Nationale.

Chapter 2
p. 27 Picture Library, National Portrait Gallery, London; p. 29 National Portrait Gallery, Smithsonian Institution/Art Resource, NY; p. 30 The Granger Collection; p. 34 (inset) Library of the Gray Herbarium, Harvard University; p. 34 (top) The Granger Collection; p. 35 Larry Stevens/Nawrocki Stock Photo; p. 38 Peabody Essex Museum, Salem, Mass./Photo by Jeffrey Dykes; p. 39 New York State Museum.

Chapter 3
p. 44 Judith Canty/Stock Boston; p. 47 Mike Mazzaschi/Stock Boston; p. 48 Margo Taussig Pickerton/New England Stock Photo; p. 51 The Granger Collection; p. 53 (left) Massachusetts Historical Society; p. 53 (right) The Granger Collection; p. 55 The British Library; p. 56 Abby Aldrich Rockefeller Folk Art Center Williamsburg, VA; p. 57 The Granger Collection; p. 58 (left) Friends Historical Library at Swarthmore; p. 58 (right) The Historical Society of Pennsylvania; p. 59 The Gilcrease Institute of American History and Art Tulsa, Oklahoma.

Chapter 4
p. 65 Courtesy Imperial Tobacco Ltd; p. 67 Library of Congress; p. 69 Library of Congress; p. 70 (right) Historical Society of Pennsylvania; p. 70 (left) Historical Society of Pennsylvania; p. 71 (left) Historical Society of Pennsylvania; p. 71 (right) Abby Aldrich Rockefeller Folk Art Collection. Photo courtesy of the Colonial Williamsburg Foundation; p. 72 Ayer Collection, Newberry Library; p. 73 (left) The Historic Houses are the Property of the City of Norfolk and are operated by The Chrysler Museum, Norfolk, VA; p. 73 (right) Historic Houses are the Property of the City of Norfolk and are operated by The Chrysler Museum of Art, Norfolk, VA; p. 74 Worcester Art Museum Worcester, MA. Gift of Mr. and Mrs. Albert W. Rice; p. 75 American Antiquarian Society; p. 76 The Granger

Collection; p. 77 The Granger Collection; p. 79 Connecticut Historical Society, Hartford, Connecticut.

Chapter 5
p. 85 New York Public Library; p. 86 John Neubauer; p. 87 (right) The Granger Collection; p. 87 (left) Collection of The New-York Historical Society; p. 90 The Saint Louis Art Museum. Museum Purchase; p. 92 The Granger Collection; p. 94 Picture Library, National Portrait Gallery, London; p. 96 Massachusetts Historical Society; p. 97 The Granger Collection; p. 98 Library Company of Philadelphia.

Chapter 6
p. 106 By permission of Service Hydrographique et Océanographique de la Marine, France; p. 108 National Gallery of Art, Washington, Paul Mellon Collection; p. 110 Yale University Art Gallery, The Mabel Brady Garvan Collection; p. 113 The Granger Collection; p. 116 (left) Cameramann International; p. 116 (right) Museum of American Textile History; p. 117 Joseph Nettis/Stock Boston.

Chapter 7
p. 123 The Print Collection, Lewis Walpole Library, Yale University; p. 124 Gift of Joseph W., William B., and Edward H.R. Revere. Courtesy of The Museum of Fine Arts, Boston; p. 126 American Antiquarian Society; p. 127 The Granger Collection; p. 128 John Carter Brown Library at Brown University Providence, Rhode Island; p. 129 The Granger Collection; p. 130 Library of Congress; p. 131 (left) Deposited by the City of Boston. Courtesy of Museum of Fine Arts, Boston; p. 131 (right) New York State Historical Association, Cooperstown; p. 132 The Granger Collection; p. 135 Photograph courtesy of the Concord Museum, Concord, MA; p. 137 Massachusetts Historical Society, gift of Mrs. John W. Davis, 1835.

Chapter 8
p. 143 The Henry Francis du Pont Winterthur Museum; p. 144 The Granger Collection; p. 146 The Granger Collection; p. 147 The National Portrait Gallery, London; p. 149 Kirby Collection of Historical Paintings, Lafayette College, Easton, PA; p. 150 Collection of Jean M. Browne; p. 151 New York Public Library p. 153 The Metropolitan Museum of Art, Gift of John S. Kennedy, 1897. (97.34); p. 154 First Troop Philadelphia City Calvary Museum; p. 158 New York State Historical Association, Cooperstown; p. 160 Historical Society of Pennsylvania; p. 161 New York Public Library.

Part Two
p. 164 Art Collection of The Boatmen's National Bank of St. Louis; p. 165 Yale University Art Gallery, The Mabel Brady Garvan Collection.

Chapter 9
p. 167 Massachusetts Historical Society. Gift of Maria Banyer Sedgwick, 1884; p. 168 © 1993 National Gallery of Art,

Washington, D.C., Andrew W. Mellon Fund; p. 170 Printed in the Decorative Arts of the China Trade, © 1991 by Carl L. Crossman. Photo courtesy of the author; p. 173 Historical Society of Pennsylvania; p. 178 Independence National Historic Park Collection. Photo by Thomas L. Davis; p. 179 National Portrait Gallery, Smithsonian Institution, Art Resource; p. 185 The Bank of New York.

Chapter 10
p. 190 The Metropolitan Museum of Art. Gift of Edgar William and Bernice Garbisch, 1962; p. 192 The Granger Collection; p. 193 National Portrait Gallery, Smithsonian Institution, Art Resource, New York; p. 196 Henry Francis du Pont Winterthur Museum; p. 197 Boston Public Library; p. 201 Harvard University Art Museums, Bequest of Ward Nicholas Boylston to Harvard College, 1828; p. 202 The Lilly Library, Indiana University, Bloomington; p. 203 Prints Division, the New York Public Library, Astor, Lenox and Tilden Foundations; p. 205 The Bettmann Archive; p. 207 Kirby Collection of Historic Paintings, Lafayette College, Easton, Pennsylvania.

Chapter 11
p. 211 Massachusetts Historical Society; p. 213 (left) The Litchfield Historical Society. Photo © 1993 Robert Houser; p. 213 (right) The Litchfield Historical Society. Photo © Robert Houser; p. 214 Corbis-Bettmann; p. 215 Houghton Library, Harvard University; p. 219 The Granger Collection; p. 221 (right) Missouri Historical Society; p. 221 (left) Collection of The New-York Historical Society; p. 222 (right) American Numismatic Society; p. 222 (left) American Numismatic Society; p. 223 Houghton Library, Harvard University; p. 225 New York Public Library, Prints Division Astor Lenox and Tilden Foundations; p. 225 Peabody & Essex Museum, Salem, Massachusetts/Essex Institute; p. 227 Copyrighted by the White House Historical Association: photograph by The National Geographic Society; p. 228 Field Museum of Natural History, Chicago (neg. A93851c); p. 230 Prints Collection Miriam and Ira D. Wallach Division of Art, Prints and Photographs, New York Public Library, Astor, Lenox and Tilden Foundations.

Chapter 12
p. 235 Anne S.K. Brown Military Collection, Brown University Library; p. 236 (left) The Bettmann Archive; p. 236 (right) Steve Dunwell/The Image Bank; p. 238 Massachusetts Historical Society; p. 240 The Metropolitan Museum of Art, Purchase, Joseph Pulitzer Bequest, 1942; p. 241 Library of Congress; p. 242 White House Historical Association. Gift of Michael Straight. Photograph by The National Geographic Society; p. 243 Maryland Historical Society, Baltimore; p. 244 DAR Museum. Gift of Mrs. Erwin L. Broeke; p. 246 The Granger Collection; p. 247 The Granger Collection; p. 248 The Bettmann Archive; p. 249 The Metropolitan Museum of Art. Gift of I. N. Phelps Stokes, Edward S. Hawes, Alice Mary Hawes, Marion Augusta Hawes, 1937; p. 251 ©1993 National Gallery of Art, Washington, D.C., Andrew W. Mellon Collection.

Chapter 13
p. 257 The Granger Collection; p. 258 The Nelson-Atkins Museum of Art, Kansas City, MO. Purchase: Nelson Trust; p. 259 Historical Society of Pennsylvania; p. 261 The Metropolitan Museum of Art, Gift of I.N. Phelps Stokes, Edward S. Hawes, Alice Mary Hawes, p. 263 The Granger Collection; p. 264 National Portrait Gallery, Smithsonian Institution/Art Resource; p. 265 The Granger Collection; p. 267 Division of Political History, National Museum of American History, Smithsonian Institution; p. 270 Division of Political History, National Museum of American History, Smithsonian Institution.

Chapter 14
p. 276 Tennessee State Library and Archives, Nashville, Photograph by June Dorman; p. 277 The Historical Society of Pennsylvania; p. 278 Boston Public Library; p. 282 (top) The Granger Collection; p. 282 (bot.) Thomas Gilcrease Institute of American History and Art; p. 283 Phyl Picardi/Stock Boston; p. 284 Texas State Library, Archives Division, Austin; p. 285 Courtesy of Bexar County and The Witte Museum, San Antonio, Texas; p. 286 The Granger Collection; p. 288 The Granger Collection; p. 290 National Portrait Gallery, Smithsonian Institution/Art Resource, NY; p. 291 (left) Division of Political History, National Museum of American History, Smithsonian Institution; p. 291 (right) Division of Political History, National Museum of American History, Smithsonian Institution; p. 292 Library of Congress; p. 293 The Art Collection of the Boatman's National Bank of St. Louis.

Chapter 15
p. 298 The Granger Collection; p. 299 The Metropolitan Museum of Art, Morris K. Jesup Fund, 1933 (33.61); p. 301 Collection of the Public Library of Cincinnati and Hamilton County; p. 304 The Granger Collection; p. 305 Museum of the City of New York; p. 306 The Granger Collection; p. 307 Slater Mill Historical Site, Pawtucket, Rhode Island; p. 308 State Historical Society of Wisconsin; p. 309 (top) Cincinnati Historical Society; p. 309 (bot.) Bob Sacha; p. 310 (top) Yale University Art Gallery, Gift of George Hoadley, B.A., 1801; p. 310 (bot.) Corbis-Bettmann; p. 311 Joseph E. Taulman Collection. The Center for American History. The University of Texas at Austin; p. 313 E. F. Fisher; p. 315 The Granger Collection; p. 316 The Saint Louis Art Museum. Bequest of Edgar William and Bernice Chrysler Garbisch; p. 317 McCormick Collection, State Historical Society of Wisconsin; p. 318 Chicago Historical Society; p. 319 Mr. & Mrs. Karolik Collection. Museum of Fine Arts, Boston; p. 322 The Bettmann Archive; p. 323 The Granger Collection; p. 325 Peabody & Essex Museum Salem, Massachusetts. Photograph by Mark Salem.

Chapter 16
p. 330 Boston Athenaeum; p. 331 Collection of The New-York Historical Society; p. 332 Photograph by A.J. Russell. Collection of the Oakland Museum; p. 334 The St. Louis Art Museum. Museum Purchase; p. 336 Mount Holyoke College Art Museum, South Hadley, Massachusetts; p. 337 Houghton Library, Harvard University; p. 338 The Connecticut p. 341 Stock Montage; p. 342 Hancock Shaker Village, Pittsfield, Massachusetts; p. 343 (left) Collection of The New-York Historical Society; p. 343 (right) American Museum of Natural History; p. 345 (right) The Granger Collection; p. 345 (top) Oneida Community Mansion House; p. 345 (bot.) Oneida Community Mansion House; p. 346 The Granger Collection; p. 347 ©1993 National Gallery of Art, Washington. Gift of the Avalon Foundation; p. 349 Concord Free Public Library, gift of Mrs. Arthur Holland; p. 350 Rare Book Division, New York Public Library, Astor, Lenox and Tilden Foundations; p. 351 Culver Pictures, Inc; p. 353 Peabody & Essex Museum, Salem, Mass. Photograph by Mark Sexton.

Part Three
p. 358 New-York Historical Society; p. 359 Cook Collection/The Valentine Museum.

Chapter 17
p. 362 The Granger Collection; p. 367 (both) Photothèque Musée de l'Homme; p. 368 (bot.) The Granger Collection; p. 368 (top) The Chicago Historical Society; p. 369 Missouri Historical Society; p. 370 Kennedy Galleries Inc., New York; p. 372 (left)

Garrison's Liberator; p. 372 (right) Corbis-Bettmann; p. 373 (right) Library of Congress; p. 373 (left) National Portrait Gallery, Smithsonian Institution/Art Resource, NY.

Chapter 18

p. 381 White House Historical Association. Photograph by the National Geographic Society; p. 382 Punch; p. 386 St. Louis Art Museum, Eliza McMillan Purchase Fund; p. 387 The Denver Public Library, Western History Department; p. 388 National Museum of American Art, Washington. D.C./Art Resource, NY; p. 389 Copyrighted by the White House Historical Association. Photograph by The National Geographic Society; p. 391 Bancroft Library, University of California, Berkeley; p. 393 The Manoogian Foundation; p. 396 Culver Pictures, Inc; p. 397 Bancroft Library, University of California, Berkeley.

Chapter 19

p. 401 Collection of The New-York Historical Society; p. 403 California State Library; p. 404 ©1993 National Gallery of Art. Gift of Edgar William and Bernice Chrysler Garbisch; p. 405 The Granger Collection; p. 409 The Brooklyn Museum. Gift of Miss Gwendolyn O.L. Conkling; p. 413 The Chrysler Museum, Norfolk, VA, Norfolk Newspaper's Art Rust. Purchase and gift of Mr. and Mrs. Victor Spark in memory of their son Donald; p. 416 (left) National Portrait Gallery, Smithsonian Institution/ Art Resource, NY.

Chapter 20

p. 421 (left) The Metropolitan Museum of Art. Gift of I. N. Phelps Stokes, Edward S. Hawes, Alice Mary Hawes and Marion Augusta Hawes, 1937; p. 421 (right) The Granger Collection; p. 423 The Kansas Historical Society; p. 424 Chicago Historical Society; p. 426 The Maryland Historical Society; p. 428 Corbis-Bettmann; p. 429 Museum of the City of New York. Gift of the Hon. Irwin Utermyer; p. 430 The Granger Collection; p. 431 Illinois State Historical Society; p. 432 The Metropolitan Museum of Art. Gift of Mr. and Mrs. Carl Stoeckel, 1897. (97.5); p. 434 Library of Congress; p. 438 National Portrait Gallery, Smithsonian Institution. Gift of Joel A. H. Webb and Mrs. Varina Webb Stewart/Art Resource, NY; p. 440 Chicago Historical Society.

Chapter 21

p. 446 The Granger Collection; p. 448 James F. Gibson, Library of Congress/Michael Campbell Photography; p. 449 The Bettmann Archive; p. 450 Collection of The New-York Historical Society; p. 451 Culver Pictures, Inc; p. 453 U.S. Navy; p. 454 Culver Pictures, Inc; p. 456 The Vanity Fair; p. 459 Courtesy of the Decorative & Industrial Arts Department of the Chicago Historical Society.

Chapter 22

p. 462 (bot.) The West Point Museum, United States Military Academy, West Point, New York; p. 462 (top) Library of Congress; p. 463 Frank Leslie's Illustrated Newspaper; p. 464 Division of the Armed Forces History, Smithsonian Institution; p. 467 Library of Congress; p. 468 Massachusetts Commandery Military Order of the Loyal Legion and The U.S. Army Military Historical Institute; p. 470 Broadside printed in Boston by J.E. Farwell & Co., 1863. Massachusetts Historical Society; p. 471 (left) The U.S. Army Military History Society; p. 471 (right) U.S. Army Military Institute; p. 474 (left) The Granger Collection; p. 474 (right) National Archives; p. 476 Daguerreotype courtesy of Tom Farish The Civil War, Master Index copied by Michael Latil © 1987, Time-Life Books, Inc; p. 477 Culver Pictures, Inc; p. 478 Collection of The New-York Historical Society; p. 481 Library of Congress; p. 482 The

Granger Collection; p. 483 (bot.) The Metropolitan Museum of Art, Gift of Mrs. Frank B. Porter, 1922. (22.207); p. 483 (top) Sea Island Company.

Chapter 23

p. 488 Library of Congress; p. 489 The Valentine Museum; p. 491 Massachusetts Commandery Military Order of the Loyal Legion and the U.S. Army Military History Institute; p. 492 (top) National Portrait Gallery, Smithsonian Institution/Art Resource, NY; p. 492 (bot.) The Granger Collection; p. 495 The Valentine Museum; p. 496 Thomas Nast, Harper's Weekly; p. 498 Library of Congress; p. 501 The Granger Collection; p. 502 The Granger Collection; p. 503 Tennessee State Museum Collection. Photo by Jane Dorman; p. 505 The Granger Collection.

Part Four

p. 511 Chicago Historical Society.

Chapter 24

p. 514 The Bettmann Archive; p. 516 Thomas Nast in Harper's Weekly p. 521 The National Archives; p. 523 (left) The Bancroft Library; p. 523 (right) The Bancroft Library; p. 524 Amon Carter Museum, Brininstool Collection, Fort Worth, Texas Acc. #67.727; p. 525 The Bancroft Library; p. 526 The Bettmann Archive; p. 527 Culver Pictures, Inc; p. 528 "The Proper Thing" James A. Wales as printed in Judge November 19, 1881. Harvard College Library; p. 530 The Granger Collection; p. 531 Puck; p. 532 Puck, November 26, 1896; p. 533 Harper's Weekly; p. 534 Division Political History, National Museum of American History, Smithsonian Institution.

Chapter 25

p. 538 © Gilcrease Museum, Tulsa, Oklahoma; p. 539 Union Pacifc Railroad Museum Collection; p. 540 The Granger Collection; p. 541 (left) The Granger Collection; p. 541 (right) UPI/Corbis-Bettmann; p. 543 Library of Congress; p. 544 The Granger Collection; p. 546 Library of Congress; p. 547 Library of Congress; p. 548 The Verdict, January 22, 1900. New York Public Library; Special Collections, The Research Libraries, New York Public Library; p. 549 The Granger Collection; p. 550 (left) The Granger Collection; p. 550 (right) International Museum of Photography at The George Eastman House; p. 552 The Valentine Museum; p. 554 (left) National Archives; p. 554 (right) The Bettmann Archive; p. 555 The Granger Collection; p. 559 National Archives; p. 560 The Granger Collection; p. 561 (top) The Granger Collection; p. 561 (bot.) Corbis-Bettmann; p. 566 Library of Congress.

Chapter 26

p. 567 International Museum of Photography, The George Eastman House; p. 570 Culver Pictures, Inc; p. 571 Brown Brothers; p. 572 (left) Brown Brothers; p. 572 (right) Jacob Riis Collection #160/Museum of the City of New York; p. 575 Jane Addams Memorial Collection, Special Collections, The University Library, The University of Illinois at Chicago; p. 576 (right) Brown Brothers; p. 576 (left) Culver Pictures Inc.; p. 576 General Research Division, The New York Public Library, Prints Division, Astor, Lenox and Tilden Foundations; p. 577 ©Musée Carnavalet/Laurie Platt Winfrey, Inc.; p. 579 Used with permission ©1929, renewed 1957, The Christian Science Publishing Society. All rights reserved; p. 581 (left) Johnston Collection, Library of Congress; p. 581 (right) UPI/Corbis-Bettmann; p. 584 The Chicago Historical Society; p. 586 (left) Amherst College Library; p. 586 (right) The Bettmann Archive; p. 587 Collection of Lee Baxandall; p. 588 The Van Pelt Library/University of Pennsylvania, Special Collections; p. 590

CANADA

Vancouver I.

Seattle
Olympia ★
WASHINGTON
Spokane
Portland
Salem ★
COAST RANGE
Eugene
CASCADE MTS.
Columbia R.
OREGON
Great Falls
Helena
MONTANA
Missouri R.
NORTH DAKOTA
Bismarck ★
Fargo
SOUTH DAKOTA
Pierre ★
IDAHO
Boise ★
Snake R.
ROCKY
WYOMING
BLACK HILLS
Sioux Falls
COAST RANGE
GREAT BASIN
Great Salt Lake
Salt Lake City
MOUNTAINS
Cheyenne ★
NEBRASKA
GREAT
Reno
Carson City ★
Sacramento ★
San Francisco
San Jose
NEVADA
UTAH
Boulder
Denver ★
COLORADO
PLAINS
Platte R.
Omaha
Lincoln ★
SIERRA NEVADA
Fresno
Las Vegas
Arkansas R.
KANSAS
Topeka ★
Wichita
CALIFORNIA
Los Angeles
Santa Fe ★
Albuquerque
Oklahoma City ★
Tulsa
ARIZONA
NEW MEXICO
Amarillo
OKLAHOMA
San Diego
Phoenix ★
Colorado R.
Red R.
PACIFIC OCEAN
Tucson
Lubbock
Ft. Worth
Dallas
GULF OF CALIFORNIA
El Paso
Rio Grande
TEXAS
Austin ★
San Antonio

MEXICO

HAWAII
Niihau Kauai
Oahu
Honolulu ★
Molokai
Lanai Maui
Kaho'olawe
PACIFIC OCEAN
Hawaii
0   100   200 Miles
0   100   200 Kilometers

RUSSIA (EX-USSR)
ARCTIC OCEAN
BROOKS RANGE
Bering Strait
Yukon R.
ALASKA
ALASKA RANGE
Anchorage
CANADA
BERING SEA
Aleutian Islands
GULF OF ALASKA
Juneau ★
0   200   400 Miles
0   200   400 Kilometers